international encyclopedia of

terrorism

international encyclopedia of

terrorism

FITZROY DEARBORN PUBLISHERS
CHICAGO & LONDON

For information, write to:
FITZROY DEARBORN PUBLISHERS
70 East Walton Street
Chicago, IL 60611
U.S.A.

or

FITZROY DEARBORN PUBLISHERS
11 Rathbone Place
London W1P 1DE
England

Cataloguing-in-Publication Data is available from the British Library and Library of Congress

ISBN 1-57958-022-X

First published in the U.K. and U.S. in 1997
Printed by Braun-Brumfield, Inc., Ann Arbor, Michigan

Cover design by Peter Aristedes.

CONTENTS

Introduction to the INTERNATIONAL ENCYCLOPEDIA OF TERRORISM

Terrorism – defined as the indiscriminate use of force to achieve political aims – is one of the major problems facing the world as the twentieth century closes. The problem exists on various levels, but can be reduced to the fact that an individual, acting within a committed terrorist organization, is very difficult to stop when prepared to kill in a random manner.

There have been acts of terror throughout history, but in the late twentieth century a set of events came together that created a new military target: the civilian who had no link to the front line nor, indeed, any conscious link to the war-making capacity of a nation. The key period in which this change came about was during World War II. Partly, the civilian was brought into the equation by the racial policies of the German Nazis, who tried to exterminate whole races. German racial policies were mirrored (although at a less extreme level) by Japanese atrocities in the Far East. In both these cases, however, non-combatants, women, and children were killed for reasons that had little or nothing to do with military necessity.

A further aspect of World War II that brought the innocent civilian directly into the firing line was the aerial bombing of population centers. The arguments for bombing German cities and for such acts as the dropping of the atom bombs on Japan have been much rehearsed. There is no doubt, however, that in many raids the target was the civilian population, that children too small to speak, never mind express a political opinion, would be killed, the intention being to so intimidate the ordinary people that they would no longer support their country's war effort.

This legacy of the targeting of civilians, and of a war whose horror had surpassed all others in history, was then compounded during the two decades after 1945 by a series of nationalist campaigns against the colonial powers. From Malaya to Algeria and from southern Africa to Cyprus, terrorism became inextricably a component of guerrilla campaigns across the developing world. For the future, the most menacing campaign was that fought in the 1940s in Palestine by Jewish terrorists against British rulers and the Palestinian Arabs.

The result of these campaigns was that terrorism became an accepted tactic of the insurgent, and has remained so ever since. Insurgencies throughout the developing world, such as in Sri Lanka during the 1990s, made ample use of terror tactics. Terrorism has also affected the first world: the IRA in Northern Ireland has become one of the world's most successful terrorist groups.

The next wave of terrorism to strike the world came in the late 1960s and 1970s, when Palestinian organizations, trying to overthrow the state of Israel, struck at vulnerable international targets such as airliners. The Palestinian groups became closely associated with various Arab states that supported their aims. The international dimension of terrorism has continued up to the present day, although it has diminished a little since the 1993 Arab-Israeli agreement over the establishment of a Palestinian authority in the Occupied Territories.

At the time that the Palestinian terrorist campaigns were beginning, there was also a wave of revolutionary insurgency using terrorism in many Latin American states, often employing the example of Castro's success in Cuba as a model. These terrorist campaigns were failures, but in many of them the state used a punitive form of counterterror that also led to many innocent deaths.

Palestinian terrorist groups were also closely associated with European organizations that wanted to change their society by using terrorist methods. This kind of terror has had little success in the developed world, but has been attractive to many malcontents, from those wanting to change society root and branch (such as the Unabomber in the U.S.) to those wishing to affect society's attitude to a single issue like abortion.

The final wave of terrorism that has affected the world is one that has developed in the past 20 years. This is terrorism associated with religious fundamentalism in the Islamic world. It originally took its lead from Iran, where the Ayatollah Khomeini established a revolutionary theocracy in 1979, and has grown to be a severe threat over much of the Middle East, partly because fundamentalist terrorists are often prepared to die during a terrorist act – to act as suicide bombers.

Dealing with these kinds of terrorism – terror connected with World War II, post-war campaigns to establish new nation states, Palestinian terror against Israel, social revolutionaries in the developed world and Latin America, and religious fundamentalist terrorism – presents four major problems.

The first is philosophical. There are few states in the world today that have not, in the past 60 years, been involved in activities in which civilians have been targeted in some kind of terror campaign. Many states have engaged directly in terrorist acts; others have sponsored or aided terrorist groups. It is certainly true that many states would prefer now not to have taken steps that they then considered necessary, but this does not alter the fact that terrorizing the more or less innocent civilian has become a staple of modern warfare.

The second problem is practical. Modern democratic society is extremely vulnerable to terrorism. There are immensely destructive weapons readily available to terrorists, including nerve agents. The networks of modern society – communications vehicles such as aircraft or buses, or urban concentrations of population within business districts and schools – are good targets, while modern methods of transport allow terrorists to move vast distances to strike. Terrorists find the freedom of working within a democracy much easier than trying to work within an autocracy. The restrictions available to autocratic governments mean that they can usually cope with terrorism by instigating a counterterrorist campaign that uses terror itself. Democracies can rarely act in such a manner, however, without damaging the foundations of their very being.

The third problem is political. Terrorists are rarely isolated madmen. Instead, they are usually members of a team that firmly believes in the righteousness of a cause – a cause for which the team is prepared to kill. As long as such causes continue to exist, whether they be the rights of the Kurds to self-determination, or the desire for a fundamentalist Islamic government in Algeria, then the possibility of terrorism of some kind will always be present. And in the modern world, there are many such causes.

The fourth problem lies in the apparent success of terrorism. Jewish Irgun terrorists forced many Palestinian Arabs to flee after the massacre at Deir Yassin in 1948, and made a powerful contribution to the establishment of the state of Israel. Hizb'allah terrorist suicide bombers forced Israeli and international troops from Lebanon in the 1980s. "Ethnic cleansing" moved whole populations in the former Yugoslavia in the 1990s.

The 1993 agreement between Israel and the Palestine Liberation Organization seemed to have reduced world terrorist problems somewhat by easing the situation in the Middle East. Then, in 1996, an outbreak of bombings, in particular a spate of attacks against the U.S., catapulted terrorism to the top of the political agenda. In June, a massive truck bomb went off at an American airbase in Dhahran, in Saudi Arabia, killing 19 U.S. servicemen. A month later, at the Atlanta Olympic Games, a person or persons unknown at the time of writing exploded a bomb in Centennial Park, causing carnage at a concert. Meanwhile, in Europe the Basque separatists of ETA were once again active.

The commitment needed to become a terrorist is usually not taken on lightly. If individuals feel that their cause or their grievance has a chance of being carried through or remedied without terrorism, then they will usually seek the easier, and less dangerous, road. Yet there is no doubt that terrorism is a prominent part of the world today, and will continue to present a very considerable threat for the foreseeable future. ■

JOHN PIMLOTT

THE PROBLEMS OF DEFINING TERRORISM

Terrorism is used to describe different things by different people. As a label for acts of violence, it reflects negatively on those who are labeled as terrorists. In this sense, the term *terrorist* is comparable to other insulting terms in the political vocabulary, such as racist, fascist, or imperialist.

Used carelessly, such terms often lose their original meanings and become part of the rhetoric of insults exchanged between political opponents. If one side in a dispute can characterize the enemy in a negative way, and so win public opinion over to their point of view, they will not hesitate to do so. Hence the saying: "One man's terrorist is another man's freedom fighter."

While the use of a word like *terrorism*, as a means of political insult is now widespread practice, it is highly unsatisfactory from both a moral and a legal point of view. Language ought to be a tool for careful thinking, not an instrument of propaganda. It is important to arrive at a clear definition of terrorism. Only then can we be certain of what is meant by the word, and then design laws to punish the terrorists.

THE ORIGIN OF THE TERM

By looking at the uses of the term *terrorism*, and at the acts of violence attributed to individual terrorists, terrorist groups, and terrorist organizations, it should be possible to find a precise definition. It is useful to examine the historical origin of the word *terrorism*, before moving on to a clarification of its modern meaning, and to place acts of terrorism in the broader context of political actions and legal practice.

"The purpose of terrorism is to produce terror," dryly noted Vladimir Lenin, the Russian communist leader responsible for the "Red Terror" of 1917-21. Terrorists produce, or aim to produce, terror – extreme fear – among their opponents. Although the word *terror* is of Latin origin (from *terrere*, to frighten), it entered modern Western vocabularies only in the fourteenth century through the French language. The first English usage was recorded in 1528. The basic mechanism of terror was captured in an ancient Chinese proverb: "Kill one, frighten ten thousand."

SUMMARY

- From its origins as a specific policy in the French Revolution, the concept of terrorism has gradually changed.
- The problems of distinguishing between a terrorist act and criminal act is complicated by the viewpoint of the observer.
- The clearer the definition of terrorism, the easier it is to legislate against it.

TERROR – AN INSTRUMENT OF GOVERNMENT

A clearly political meaning was given to the word during the French Revolution. In 1793, France's revolutionary government found itself threatened by aristocratic emigrants who conspired with foreign rulers to invade the country. At the same time, treason at home in support of this reactionary move was suspected. The French legislative, the National Convention – led by a radical faction, the Jacobins, under Maximilien Robespierre – adopted a policy of terror on August 30, 1793, ordering mass executions of suspected traitors.

The newspaper *Courier de l'Égalité* approved: "It is necessary that the terror caused by the guillotine spreads in all of France and brings to justice all the traitors. There is no other means to inspire this terror that will consolidate the Revolution. The Jacobin club has massively adopted this measure – a universal enthusiasm has manifested itself following this order, which will probably mark one of the greatest periods of our history." Originally conceived as a tool to combat subversion by those who supported the former

Hulton Getty Picture Collection

Lenin, instigator of the "Red Terror" in Russia, addresses a crowd in 1917.

king and the monarchy, the Terror soon began to make victims of those who had originally been supporters of the revolution and the republic established after the downfall of the monarchy. Former allies of the Jacobins perished in the wave of executions. The moderate "Indulgents" under Georges Danton and the extremist left-wing "Hébertists" both fell victim to Robespierre's campaign. Altogether, at least 300,000 people were arrested during the Terror (August 30, 1793–July 27, 1794). Of these, 17,000 were officially executed, but many other people died in prison, often without a trial.

Those who had originally supported the harsh measures proposed by Robespierre against counter-revolutionaries began to fear for their own lives and conspired to overthrow him. They could not accuse him of *terreur* (terror) because they themselves had earlier declared terror to be a legitimate instrument of government. Therefore, they accused Robespierre of *terrorisme* (terrorism), a word that suggested illegal conduct. For this, Robespierre and his associates were guillotined on July 17 and 28, 1794. The political pendulum had finally swung back and now the agents and partisans of the revolutionary tribunals were termed *terrorists* and thrown into prison.

TERROR AS PROPAGANDA BY THE DEED

The term *terrorism* spread fast throughout Europe, into Russia, and even into India. As it spread, the word changed its meaning. By the late nineteenth century, the term *terrorist*, originally used for those who made unjust mass arrests in the name of the state, became more strongly associated with anti-state violence. The violent French and Russian anarchists of the 1880s and 1890s were the main groups responsible for this shift in meaning.

If the guillotine that beheaded enemies of the revolution had been the symbol of state terror at the end of the eighteenth century, the bomb that exploded in the midst of the political elite became the hallmark of nineteenth-century terrorism. The bomb and the assassin's pistol were used for two purposes. The so-called "exemplary deed" directed at government ministers, parliamentarians, and judicial officers was intended to spread terror among state officials. Such violent acts, especially for the Russian terrorists of the period, were also part of a program to bring about political change. The Russian anarchists' goal was to arouse the masses by acts of violence against targets with a high symbolic value, such as police chiefs or members of the royal family.

Terrorist violence used in this way becomes a means of communication. "Propaganda by the deed" was how nineteenth-century revolutionaries, like the German John Most, described the value of terrorism as a form of communication. Both aims of terrorist murder were established in the late nineteenth century. They were later picked up by post-1945 terrorist groups and remain in use today.

Hulton Getty Picture Collection

The guillotine, the main instrument of the Terror of 1793-94, as used by French revolutionaries in Paris.

THE MEANINGS OF TERROR AND TERRORISM

The meaning of the words *terror* and *terrorism* have altered only slightly since the late nineteenth century, but the change is significant. In the 1890 edition of *Webster's International Dictionary*, the word *terror* is defined as "Extreme fear, fear that agitates body and mind, violent dread; fright." As a second meaning Webster's lists "that which excites dread; a cause of extreme fear." Today, *Webster's New Twentieth Century Dictionary* covers essentially the same meanings, listing: "1. intense fear; 2. a person or thing that causes intense fear;" but has the important additions: "3. a period characterized by political executions, as during the French Revolution; 4. a program of terrorism or a party, group, etc. resorting to this."

For *terrorism*, the modern *Webster's* dictionary offers the following: "1. a terrorizing; use of terror and violence to intimidate, subjugate, etc. especially as a political weapon or policy; 2. intimidation and subjugation so produced." There is some dispute among scholars of the precise meaning of adding the suffix -*ism* to the word *terror* to produce the word *terrorism*. The *-ism* suffix is sometimes added to a word to refer to the theoretical level of a political doctrine. Familiar examples of this include the conversion of *liberal* to *liberalism* and *social* to *socialism*. A more practical use of the suffix is where it refers to a manner of acting or an attitude, such as when *fanatic* becomes *fanaticism*. Both meanings have been applied to the word terrorism. While a few experts attribute a doctrinal quality to terrorism, far more define it as a manner of acting or as a method of action.

However, the historical root of the *-ism* suffix in *terrorism* refers to neither of these two possibilities. It originated in the excessive abuse of violence under the Terror of the French Revolution. Because there have been numerous other reigns of terror since the French Revolution, the term *terror* has become increasingly detached from this specific historical period (1793-94). It has become a generic term applied to regimes that rule by a fear caused by unjust mass arrests and arbitrary trials and executions in which the guilt of the individual matters less than the political intimidation of the populace.

THE PSYCHOLOGY OF TERRORISM

The basic purpose of terrorism is to produce terror in a target audience. A civilian population at large may be targeted, or police officers or government officials may be targeted to deter them from carrying out their duties. It is important, therefore, to look at the psychological dimension of terror. However, remarkably little of the literature on terrorism has paid much attention to terror as a state of mind. Only in the more recent literature on hostages has the experience of being terrorized received some attention.

When terrorists are able to organize a series of acts of violence into a campaign of terror, they manage to maximize fear. Repeated acts of violence make the question "Will I be next?" loom large in the minds of target audiences. The suicide-bomber attacks in Israel

Rex Features/Roger Lewis

A Hamas suicide squad, photographed in a secret hideout in the Gaza Strip in 1993.

carried out by the Palestinian Hamas group in 1996 provoked exactly this response among Israelis. When the targeted population is in near-panic and confusion, the desired psychological impact has been reached.

Depending on the setting of terrorist acts, prospective victims may be shocked by numbing fear – as in a hostage situation when the deadline for an ultimatum approaches. Alternatively, those who have witnessed a shooting or bombing may panic and flee at the mere hint of a terrorist attack, to avoid becoming a victim.

NATURAL ANXIETY VERSUS TERRORISM

The fear created by terrorist acts is not the same as the chronic anxiety caused by natural disasters. Natural disasters strike with little warning, and have random effects. A pervasive atmosphere of anxiety can exist in the minds of those who live in the shadow of a volcano, near an earthquake fault, or beside a dam. But such natural terror is likely to be less intense than human-made terror, although both are responses to situations in which survival is in doubt.

More terrifying than natural terror are wartime or criminal acts, such as mass bombings or armed robbery. Here, however, terror is to some extent an unintended by-product of violence. Only when violence is used to intimidate a wider audience than those immediately affected can we speak of terrorism in its pure form.

The victim of a terrorist attack is not necessarily the same thing as the target. The choice of the victim may be almost random. A police officer may be gunned down unaware of the political situation the terrorists are fighting, while a colleague who holds anti-terrorist views is ignored. A government building administering social security payments may be bombed because it is easy to park a truck outside it in the street, even though no law enforcement activity takes place within.

These victims are chosen to reach a wider target audience that identifies in one way or another with the victim. For a single killing to have a widespread effect,

Popperfoto

Rubble in the World Trade Center after the bomb blast of February 27, 1993, which killed five people.

terrorist violence has to be attention-grabbing or in some way extraordinary. This impact can be created in a number of ways. The victim may be a particularly famous or prominent person. The method of attack may involve an unusual form of criminal ingenuity. The location of the attack may be important, or involve a maximum number of observers, such as during the Munich Olympic Games of 1972, or the 1996 Olympic Games in Atlanta. The number of potential victims may be very large, as in the case of the thousands of people affected by the 1993 World Trade Center bombing in New York. Finally, the ruthlessness of the act may be particularly striking, as was the Oklahoma bombing, which killed 15 children.

In classic terrorist assassinations – as opposed to purely criminal ones – there is a distinct difference between the target and victim. The actual victim of the violence is not the real target of this violence.

Individuals, consciously or unconsciously, often identify themselves with people who are prominent in the press or on TV. This identification may be made on the basis of shared opinions, or more superficially because of good looks or an attractive manner. In the popular imagination, these people become symbols. When these symbols are hurt, the people who hold them dear share the hurt. The symbol may be a charismatic leader who embodies the aspirations of the followers, such as the Reverend Martin Luther King, Jr. If the leader is killed, the followers are deprived of their object of identification. They experience a variety of feelings, ranging from grief and powerlessness to outrage and terror.

However, the symbolic victim does not have to be a prominent person. A terrorist attack on a building or religious ceremony, such as the Vietcong assault on the U.S. embassy in Saigon during the 1968 Tet offensive, can have even stronger effects. The identification felt by the larger audience is normally directed toward the victims. This is especially the case if the victims were in an everyday situation, such as riding on a bus. It may prompt members of the audience to think "it could have been me or my child."

Hulton Getty Picture Collection

The aftermath of a bomb attack on Czar Alexander II's personal train near Moscow, December 1879.

However, if the victim is perceived as a guilty person or organization – perhaps a dictator or an army of occupation – the attack is likely to produce feelings of relief among those who have suffered because of the victim. Some people might then identify with the terrorists themselves, seeing them as heroic martyrs who risk their lives to confront an evil force. Terrorism not only produces terror in an opponent, but it can also produce enthusiasm in the opposite camp, as is indicated in the quote from the *Courier de l'Égalité* earlier. This also brings us back to the saying that "one man's terrorist is another man's freedom fighter." Basques whose desire for national autonomy was denied by Spanish dictator Francisco Franco supported nationalist terrorists.

JUDGING THE TERRORISTS

People judge terrorism by making a comparison either with crimes or with warfare. Those who use comparisons with criminal acts regard terrorism as illegal. Police, for example, are authorized by law to arrest and imprison a person, but a terrorist group abducting someone and holding him or her to ransom has no such approval. The effect in both cases, however, is to deprive a person of his or her liberty. Using a comparison with warfare, on the other hand, draws on the famous statement by the Prussian officer, Karl von Clausewitz: "War is a continuation of politics by other means." A political activist who turns to terrorist violence in a struggle against an oppressive regime becomes a "freedom fighter" in a war for liberty.

However, these frameworks used by ordinary people tend to become blurred by politicians and scholars of political violence. All too often people make their choice between the war model and the crime model, not on logical grounds, but based on their own opinions of the ethnic or political dispute. For instance, a person from the same ethnic group as the government may share the view that the terrorists are criminals, while a person from the ethnic group of the terrorists may instinctively think of them as soldiers at war.

Such contrasting psychological standards do not work well in moral and intellectual terms when judging acts of violence. The reactions of the opposing extremes do not make for calm discussion. There is little or no common ground to offer room for negotiation. In a community divided by acts of terror, such as Northern Ireland, the fact remains that acts of violence are aimed at only one section of society.

FOUR VIEWS OF TERRORISM

The objectivity of any discussion of terrorism is limited by the relationship of the participants to terrorist acts. It is possible to distinguish four different groups who take a view of terrorism.

1. *Academics* attempt to take an entirely objective view. Ideally, universities offer an intellectual forum in which scholars can discuss terrorism without either being attacked by terrorists or being suspected of sympathizing with terrorists.

2. *Governments*, in contrast, are frequent victims of terrorist activity. The official view of terrorism presented by press secretaries whose statements are

colored by the knowledge that those they represent may become involved in fighting terrorism.

3. The *public* may change its opinion dramatically in response to a single incident. In open societies, its view is articulated and influenced through the media.

4. The views of the *terrorists and their sympathizers* reflect the beliefs of people who think they live under a repressive government.

Each of these four groups has a valid view.

THE ACADEMIC VIEW

When scholars look at terrorism, the distance they can keep from the conflict should allow them a more objective perspective. Academics should pursue an intellectual, but not a moral, neutrality between terrorists and victims for the purpose of investigation. The academic culture of curiosity, skepticism, and methodical inquiry can lead to a more independent, non-partisan assessment than is usually possible elsewhere.

Scholars from various universities have come close to agreement on a definition of terrorism. In 1984, an analysis was made of more than 100 existing definitions. A new one was drawn up and circulated. The comments and criticisms made on this were used to amend it until 81 percent of scholars approached could partially, or even fully, agree on it.

The resulting academic definition of terrorism was finalized in 1988. "Terrorism is an anxiety-inspiring method of repeated violent action, employed by (semi-) clandestine individual, group, or state actors, for idiosyncratic, criminal, or political reasons, whereby – in contrast to assassination – the direct targets of violence are not the main targets. The immediate human victims of violence are generally chosen randomly (targets of opportunity) or selectively (representative or symbolic targets) from a target population, and serve as message generators. Threat and violence-based communication processes between terrorist (organization), (imperiled) victims, and main targets are used to manipulate the main target (audience(s)), turning it into a target of terror, a target of demands, or a target of attention, depending on whether intimidation, coercion, or propaganda is primarily sought."

Although the definition is rather long and clumsy, the core elements are now generally accepted. Brian Jenkins, one of the pioneers of empirical research on terrorism, noted in 1992 that "a rough consensus on the meaning of terrorism is emerging without any international agreement on the precise definition." However, this consensus is more obvious among academics than among politicians and civil servants.

THE OFFICIAL VIEW

A precise but lengthy definition such as the one developed by scholars is not likely to be used by governments. Government officials tend to be clearer and harsher in their views, being actively engaged in countering terrorist activity – and being victims of it.

The British government was one of the first to attempt to draw up a legal definition that distinguishes a terrorist act from a criminal act. In 1974, the United Kingdom government concluded that: "For the purposes of the legislation, terrorism is the use of violence for political ends, and includes any use of violence for the purpose of putting the public, or any section of the public, in fear." This British definition is extremely broad and could be interpreted to include conventional war as well as limited nuclear strikes.

The 1975 European TREVI definition (named after a fountain in Rome near which European ministers of justice and the interior deliberated on terrorism) has been modeled on the British definition, except that it excludes war: "Terrorism is defined as the use, or the threatened use, by a cohesive group of persons of violence (short of warfare) to effect political aims."

The European Convention to Combat Terrorism (1977) did not use any definition of terrorism. It simply listed a number of crimes that would make those committing them liable to extradition from one country to another. However, this avoidance of the problem was no solution – as various controversies concerning extradition have made clear ever since.

In 1985, the West German Office for the Protection of the Constitution stated: "Terrorism is the enduringly conducted struggle for political goals, which are intended to be achieved by means of assaults on the life and property of other persons, especially by means of severe crimes as detailed in article 129a, section 1 of the penal code (murder, homicide, extortionist kidnapping, arson, setting off a blast by explosives) or by means of other acts of violence, which serve as preparation of such criminal acts."

The United States government has never issued a formal definition, but its government agencies have proposed unofficial definitions. The Central Intelligence Agency (CIA) was one of the first, in 1976, with this definition of international terrorism: "The threat or use of violence for political purposes when (1) such action is intended to influence the attitudes and behavior of a target group wider than its immediate victims, and (2) its ramifications transcend national boundaries (as a result, for example, of the nationality or foreign ties of its perpetrators, its locale, the identity of its institutional or human victims, its declared objectives or the mechanics of its resolution)."

Over the years, the wording of CIA definitions has fluctuated. In 1980, for instance, terrorism was defined as: "The threat or use of violence for political purposes by individuals or groups, whether acting for, or in opposition to, established governmental authority, when such actions are intended to shock or intimidate a large group wider than the immediate victims."

In 1983, the United States Army used this definition of terrorism: "The calculated use of violence or the threat of violence to attain goals political or ideological in nature. This is done through intimidation, coercion, or instilling fear."

Also in 1983, the Federal Bureau of Investigation (FBI) used this wording: "Terrorism is defined as the unlawful use of force or violence against persons or property to intimidate or coerce a government, the civilian population, or any segment thereof, in furtherance of political and social objectives."

However, the most influential American definition has turned out to be the one proposed by the U.S. Department of State in 1984. Terrorism was defined as: "Premeditated, politically motivated violence perpetrated against noncombatant targets by subnational groups or clandestine agents, usually intended to influence an audience."

One element that kept recurring in U.S. government debates on defining terrorism was whether or not attacks on U.S. military personnel could be labeled terrorist. On October 23, 1983, 241 American Marines died in their barracks in Beirut, Lebanon, when a suicide bomber in a truck crashed through the base's security perimeter. Was this terrorism or was the label *terrorism* to be reserved for attacks against noncombatant civilians?

The U.S. Department of State solved this dilemma by interpreting the term noncombatants to "include, in addition to civilians, military personnel who at the time of the incident are unarmed and/or not on duty." It also considers "as acts of terrorism attacks on military installations or on armed military personnel when a state of military hostilities does not exist at the site, such as bombings against U.S. bases in Europe, the Philippines, or elsewhere."

The many U.S. definitions show that the official discourse varies as circumstances change. At the same time, they share a large common ground.

THE PUBLIC VIEW

The image of terrorism in the media is different from those already examined. A survey among 20 editors of news agencies, television and radio stations, and the press, mostly from Western Europe, provided the following responses.

Answers to the question: "What kind of (political) violence does your medium commonly label terrorism?"

Type of Violence	Percentage of editors using label "terrorism"
Hostage-Taking	80%
Assassination	75%
Indiscriminate Bombing	75%
Kidnapping	70%
Hijacking for Coercive Bargaining	70%
Urban Guerrilla Warfare	65%
Sabotage	60%
Torture	45%
Hijacking for Escape	35%

The answers show agreement in labeling some but not other acts of violence as terrorism. While the European Convention for the Suppression of Terrorism assumes that all hijackings are acts of terrorism, editors make a distinction between a hijacking for escape and one for coercive bargaining. In this particular case, the majority of editors appear closer to the experience of the victims than do the drafters of the European Convention.

Hijacking. Imagine the situation in which an aircraft is hijacked and the hijacker asks the pilot to fly to a different country to that of the original flight destination. In this instance, the passengers will probably feel less terrorized than when the hijacker demands the liberation of 700 prisoners by a country that may not even be the home base of the airliner. In the first case, the pilot can, by altering course, escape the threat of violence. In the second case, the attitude or behavior of the pilot and crew does not matter, only the behavior of the government being blackmailed. In the second example, the term terrorist is more appropriate, the random victims cannot affect the outcome by compliance to demands.

Kidnapping. In the same way, a kidnapping can be either a terrorist act or a crime. When, out of personal greed, a kidnapper asks for money in exchange for an abducted millionaire, the situation is clearly criminal. The crime becomes terrorism when political concessions are asked from a government in return for the victim, as was the case with the German industrialist Hans-Martin Schleyer, who was abducted by the Red Army Faction in 1977.

Political murder. A similar distinction can be made when it comes to murders of politicians or civil service workers. Criminal political assassinations kill an opponent whose policies are different from those of the murderer. The aim of the murder is simply to remove a rival from the scene. The assassination of President Abraham Lincoln is an example of this kind of murder. A terrorist political assassination, on the other hand, involves more parties than the killer and victim. There is the perpetrator, who may act alone or as part of a conspiracy. Then there is the victim of the attack. Finally, there is the target audience at whom the terrorist message or demand delivered by the killing is aimed.

There is a difference, in all political terrorism, between the target of violence and the target of terror. The target of violence is the person who is attacked; the target of terror is the larger audience, whom the terrorist hopes to influence. In a terrorist murder, one victim can be easily substituted for another because the effect on the wider audience is what really counts.

Those who study terrorism distinguish between a criminal and a terrorist assassination by labeling the first "individuated" political murder and the second "de-individuated" political murder. In the case of individuated murder, the victim is chosen as an individual, usually one who knows the opponents and the potential threat before being killed. In the case of de-individuated murder, the victim is chosen because of the post he or she holds, and is often unaware of being a target. The attack is completely unexpected.

This unexpectedness is also the deeper reason why terrorism terrorizes. It does so because the victims are caught by surprise; they are generally victimized arbitrarily and without apparent provocation. Suddenly, they and those around them are struck with terror. In this form, terror becomes a state of mind.

Terrorism intentionally produces a state of extreme anxiety among possible targets of attack, who fear becoming a victim of arbitrary violence. Terrorists exploit this emotional reaction to manipulate the wider target audience.

THE TERRORISTS' VIEW

Those involved in terrorism and those who support terrorists have a very different viewpoint from all other observers. While in the late nineteenth century many Russian anarchist and socialist bomb-throwers did not shrink from being labeled terrorists, this is not the case with contemporary terrorists and their sympathizers. They are aware of the stigma of being called terrorists and so try to avoid the label.

During a conference on terrorism organized in Leiden, in the Netherlands in 1989, graffiti was painted by a group calling themselves the "Revolutionary Commando Marinus van de Lubbe." The group was named after a Dutch Communist convicted by the Nazis of a terrorist arson attack on the German parliament in the 1930s, a crime of which he was almost certainly innocent. The Revolutionary Commando sent a letter to the local newspaper expressing solidarity with what they claimed were oppressed people in, among other places, Palestine, Ireland, Central America, and Kurdistan. They wrote: "It is clear that so-called terrorism is the logical and just resistance of the people against state terrorism, capitalism, racism, sexism, and imperialism."

Apologists for terrorism often attempt to counter moral objections by comparing their own violence with real or alleged examples of violence by their opponents. By making such a comparison, terrorists and their supporters try to place their aims and actions on the same moral level as their government enemies.

Terrorist groups also use propaganda to achieve the moral high ground in the public's view. They hope that the public or foreign governments might then put pressure on the government or organization they are fighting. To do this, they attempt to justify both themselves and their actions at the same time as putting blame on their opponents.

In World War II, the German occupation forces labeled all members of resistance groups as "terrorists"; the latter, however, thought of themselves as patriots and freedom fighters. The attempt to justify

Hulton Getty Picture Collection

Yugoslav partisans, labeled terrorists by German forces occupying their country in World War II.

acts whose moral standing is doubtful is part and parcel of the terrorist campaign. The father of modern state terror, Maximilien Robespierre, justified his brutal actions in his February 1794 declaration: "Terror is nothing else than immediate justice, severe, inflexible; it is therefore an outflow of virtue, it is not so much a specific principle as a consequence of the general principle of democracy applied to the most pressing needs of the motherland."

Nearly 100 years later, in 1879, the Russian terrorist underground organization, the People's Will, described terrorism in rather more instrumental terms: "Terrorist activity consists of the destruction of the most harmful persons in the government, the protection of the People's Will from spies, and the punishment of official lawlessness and violence in all the more prominent and important cases where it is manifested. The aim of such activity is to break down the prestige of government, to furnish continuous proof of the possibility of pursuing a contest with the government, to raise in that way the revolutionary spirit in the people and, finally, to form a body suited and accustomed to warfare."

Both of these definitions – by terrorists themselves – emphasize their ultimate aims rather than their tactics. Generally, terrorists try to avoid a discussion of their tactics because this would help label them as criminals; they much prefer a discussion that places their struggle in a framework of a war for political ends. When the language describing terrorism used concentrates on crime, it raises questions of legitimacy very different from when the terminology of war is used to describe terrorism.

TERRORISM AS A WAR CRIME

Which definition of terrorism is correct? Generally, a good definition of a difficult subject is one with which most people can agree. Many people will object to a broad definition – such as "terrorism is violence for political purposes" – for the simple reason that it turns most practitioners of violence into terrorists. In contrast, a lengthy academic definition may be too detailed to be of much practical use. An agreed-upon definition could help governments cooperating to stamp out international terrorism, by establishing a universal standard that would reduce differences between national codes of law. Such a legal definition already exists for other controversial acts, such as war crimes, and there is broad international agreement about what actions should be considered war crimes.

A look at how this agreement developed on what defines a war crime may help set up a model for international collaboration against terrorists.

Included among the acts considered war crimes are attacks on persons taking no active part in hostilities. This also includes members of the armed forces who have surrendered. This protection of the noncombatant stands at the core of international humanitarian law as codified in the Hague Regulations and Geneva Conventions. The rules of war prohibit not only the use of violence against captives but also hostage-taking and most of the other acts committed by terrorists.

Terrorists have, in fact, elevated practices that are considered crimes in war situations to the level of routine tactics. They do not engage in open combat, as do soldiers. Instead, they prefer to strike against the unarmed. Injury to the defenseless is not an accidental side-effect but a deliberate strategy of terrorists.

Categorizing acts of terrorism as war crimes is also appropriate in the sense that terrorists consider themselves as being at war with their opponents. What makes them different from soldiers, however, is that terrorists do not carry their arms openly nor discriminate between armed adversaries and noncombatants. Because terrorists are not fighting by the rules of war, they are, for all practical purposes, war criminals. Like war crimes, acts of terrorism distinguish themselves from conventional warfare, and to some extent from guerrilla warfare, through the disregard of principles of humanity contained in the accepted rules of war.

THE BEST DEFINITION OF TERRORISM

If the international community could agree upon a legal definition of acts of terrorism as *"peacetime equivalents of war crimes,"* a more uniform treatment of terrorists would become possible. A narrow definition of terrorism, placing it on a par with war crimes, excludes some forms of violence and coercion, such as certain types of attacks on the military and destruction of property, which are currently labeled terrorism by some governments. However, this type of narrow and precise definition of terrorism is likely to find broader acceptance than one that includes a wider variety of violent protest.

Lesser forms of political violence, such as vandalizing an opponent's home, are already outlawed by national legislation. Terrorist offenses could be considered international crimes, requiring special treatment. If a definition were accepted that stressed the tactics and not the ends, nobody would be able to confuse terrorists and freedom fighters.

Freedom fighters who adhere to the rules of warfare should be treated like soldiers. Those freedom fighters who target civilians, on the other hand, should be dealt with as war criminals. The same categorization applies to those soldiers acting on behalf of a government. A desirable cause does not excuse acts of violence against unarmed civilians and neutral bystanders.

By placing narrowly defined acts of terrorism in the same category as war crimes, confusion over whether violence is criminal or political will be minimized. Where national authorities are unable or unwilling to deal with such acts, these could be dealt with, as in the case of war crimes, by a special international penal court with power over terrorist offenses as well as other crimes against humanity.

Alex P. Schmid

SEE ALSO: TERROR IN THE FRENCH REVOLUTION 1789-1815; RUSSIAN ANARCHIST TERROR; FRENCH ANARCHIST TERROR; TERROR IN THE RUSSIAN CIVIL WAR; WORLD WAR II RESISTANCE IN YUGOSLAVIA AND TERRORISM; THEORIES OF TERROR IN URBAN INSURRECTIONS; CATEGORIES OF TERROR; ASSASSINATION; SUICIDE BOMBING; THE BLACK SEPTEMBER ORGANIZATION; TERROR IN LEBANON 1980-1987; THE WORLD TRADE CENTER BOMBING; THE OKLAHOMA CITY BOMBING AND THE MILITIAS; BRITISH COUNTERTERROR METHODS AFTER DECOLONIZATION; THE AMERICAN RESPONSE TO TERRORISM; INTERNATIONAL COOPERATION AGAINST TERRORISM; THE MEDIA AND INTERNATIONAL TERRORISM.

FURTHER READING

- Fattah, E. A. *Terrorist Activities and Terrorist Targets: A Tentative Typology.* New York: Pergamon Press, 1981.
- Groth, A. "A Typology of Revolution," in *Revolution and Political Change,* edited by C. E. Welch and M. B. Taintor. Belmont, CA: Duxbury Press, 1972.
- Rubin, A. P. "Terrorism and the Law of War," in *Denver Journal of International Law and Politics* 17, nos. 2-3 (Spring 1983): 219-235.
- United States Department of State. *Patterns of Global Terrorism, 1994.* Washington, DC: Office of the Coordinator for Counterterrorism, April 1995.

THE HISTORICAL BACKGROUND

E. T. Archive

A Serbian terrorist assassinates Austro-Hungarian Archduke Franz Ferdinand at Sarajevo, June 28, 1914.

THE HISTORICAL BACKGROUND: *Introduction*

Terrorism is not a modern invention. It has been a recurring theme in the story of humankind. Terrorism of some kind became a standard course of action in many historical cultures. Where one side believed that the threat of violence might intimidate a foe into submission, it usually did not hesitate to use such threats. The definition of *terrorism* in some of these historical cases is necessarily broad, but in order to set modern terrorism in context, it is necessary to look at how it reflects a broad sweep of human behavior. Terrorism in the ancient world often did not demonstrate all the aspects that go to make up the phenomenon of modern terrorism. Many examples from ancient and medieval history of what, broadly defined, might be termed terrorism, relate more to the use of terror as an instrument of policy.

Historical sources as old as the Bible record many instances of terror being used to achieve an objective. The book of Joshua states that the Israelites "utterly destroyed all that was in the city [Jericho], both man and woman, young and old, and ox, and sheep, and ass, with the edge of the sword." This massacre of a city after it had fallen to an army after a long siege was typical of warfare of this time, and for centuries to come. If a besieged town continued to resist attempts to capture it, the attackers, after successfully overcoming it, would put all its inhabitants to the sword. This slaughter served specifically to frighten neighboring peoples into early submission when their turn came to be under attack.

Another theme that stands out strongly in looking at the history of terrorism up to 1945 is the extent to which terror became easier to use when the group being attacked was something separate – either in terms of race, ideology, or religion. Being able to demonize, or even to dehumanize, their enemies makes it easier for the group using terror to inflict horrors on them. For example, a whole race could be described as "savages" for having customs such as scalping dead or wounded enemies. This label of alleged savagery is then used to justify conduct toward them that is in itself equally savage.

Colonial Europeans used such arguments to justify their brutal suppression of indigenous resistance. Demonization and dehumanization of enemies reached new levels during the Nazis' "Final Solution" – their slaughter of over six million Jews and other allegedly "asocial" groups.

The development of technology in the 2,000 years up to 1945 undoubtedly has made the implementation of terror on a massive scale more achievable. Those perpetrators of terror often hold the general principle that the greater the number of victims, the greater the degree of terror created. As long as individuals had to execute victims personally with sword or gun, then the extent of the slaughter was limited. Of course, the numbers of people a plundering army could kill in a few days was still considerable. In the 1576 "Spanish Fury" at Antwerp, in the Netherlands, during the War of Dutch independence, Spanish troops sacked the captured town, killing 7,000 people in 11 frenzied days.

During World War II, the Nazis became frustrated with the slowness with which the *Einsatzgruppen*, the murder squads slaughtering Jews in the Soviet Union, were accomplishing their murderous task. The development of the gas chambers at extermination camps was a huge leap forward for the heinous process of mass slaughter. Some 2,000 Holocaust victims could be killed in the gas chambers in just 15 minutes using the poison Zyklon-B. Potentially, several tens of thousands of victims could be killed each day. The process of annihilation had reached new levels because of technological advances.

Technological progress has coincided with a general increase in the power of the state. The radicals in the French Revolution may have declared terror "the order of the day," and executed "suspects." But the impact of these examples of state terror were paltry compared with the dreadful results of Nazi control of Europe, or of Stalin's Great Purge in the Soviet Union. The degree of organization and bureaucratization within a state's terror program reached new heights under these reigns of terror, setting the scene for the terrorism we know today. ■

CHAPTER ONE

Terror in History to 1939

The word *terrorism* was coined in the guillotine days of the French Revolution, but the practice is much older. Terrorism stretches back in time to the bloody assassinations of the ancient Greeks and Romans and to barbaric customs such as suspending people over fires for not paying their taxes. Few parts of the world have escaped the brutalities and the climate of fear that terrorism creates. Among many examples, there were religious murder cults in the Middle East, massacres during the American Indian resistance, and Stalin's purges in Russia, when some 20 million people died at his hands to make sure that those still alive were cowed into submission.

TERROR IN HISTORY TO 1939: Introduction

It is easy, in our concern about terrorism today, to lose sight of the historical perspectives on the subject that enable us to piece together a proper analysis of terror, and, therefore, to work out strategies for coping with it. The examples chosen in this chapter demonstrate different aspects of terror over a period of more than 2,000 years. These case-studies also show how terror can come from the state, from those resisting the state, from the excesses of warfare, from small dedicated ideological groups, and from clashes between different societies or views of society.

Examples of terror used by the state range from Imperial Rome to Stalin's purges in the Soviet Union. Both these examples demonstrate how a ruling class can be cowed by terrorist methods and forced to acquiesce in a dictatorship. The most famous introduction of terror by a state was that of the Committee of Public Safety in 1794. Under pressure from a European-wide coalition and having to deal with a series of revolts within France, the revolutionaries decided that they would terrorize their own population into obedience. The results were undeniably successful: the French armies defeated their enemies both on the frontiers and also within France.

This state terror has in turn produced theories that justify use of any means – including terror – to resist tyrants. Such ideas, ("tyrannicide"), were put forward in Ancient Greece and in the later Roman republic, the most famous example being the assassination of Julius Caesar. Some 1,800 years later the Russian anarchist terrorists cited ideas of tyrannicide in their attempts to murder the Czar.

Fear and terror are a necessary part of warfare. The knowledge that you are likely to die if you undertake a particular course of action – whether it be advancing across a fire-swept plain or climbing a scaling ladder to a fortress – is at the very heart of military science. However, to this can be added the aspect of deliberately threatening civilians. An obvious example of terror against civilians was in medieval siege warfare. Here, there were commonly understood rules about how long fortified places could resist before the inhabitants risked massacre. Similarly, the Mongols made it clear to their enemies that they would exact a savage vengeance if there was any resistance at all. During World War I, however, German threats against civilians in the territories they had occupied were more covert, an approach perhaps influenced by German policies toward subject populations in their colonies.

Much modern terrorism is carried out by small groups with a particular ideology or aim that they wish to force upon others. Again, there are examples of this throughout history. During the Middle Ages, the sect known as the Assassins in the Middle East, representing a particular schism within Islam, used selective assassination of enemy leaders as a weapon. The anarchists of the late nineteenth century also used terror for their ends. Such methods were again adopted by various nationalist groups in the early twentieth century, such as the Serbs who assassinated the Archduke Ferdinand in Sarajevo in 1914.

The use of terror policies may have taken most lives, however, in conflicts between different societies, or different views of society. Where two societies clashed, especially where they were at different levels of technological development, then terror was common. A typical example was in North America, where terror was used by both sides in the wars between the European settlers and the Indian tribes. The tide of European colonization across the world during the eighteenth and nineteenth centuries also saw the use of widespread terror. Massacre was used to terrify and subdue whole populations, and in retaliation by those being conquered.

But if different societies used terror against one another, so too did members of the same society who professed different views. These differences could be ideological, as in the Paris Commune, or in the civil war that broke out in the aftermath of the Russian revolution. In both cases, left-wing radicals fought reactionary conservative forces. Perhaps the most awful examples of this kind of terror took place where religious or racial differences were latched onto by the state. The brutal state-inspired Turkish treatment of Christian Armenians during World War I was an episode that prefigured the Nazi Holocaust. ■

TERROR IN ANCIENT GREECE AND THE ROMAN REPUBLIC

There are several famous instances of political assassination, a form of terror, occurring in the classical world. The methods varied according to the circumstances. In Ancient Greece, assassination and tyrannicide were among the methods employed during struggles between rival factions in city states.

GREEK MURDERS

In Ancient Greece, a tyrant was specifically a ruler who had taken power by force, although some had full popular support. Such was the case with the brothers Hipparchus and Hippias, who became rulers of Athens in 527 B.C. on the death of their father, Pisistratus. However, other aristocrats resented their power and looked for a pretext to bring them down. When Hipparchus sexually assaulted the sister of Harmodius, the vengeful brother and his friend Aristogeiton murdered Hipparchus during a festival procession in 510 B.C.

This left Hippias as sole ruler, and so his enemies brought rivalry with a foreign state into play to further their ends. Conflict frequently broke out between the city states of ancient Greece. None was so bitter and protracted as that between Athens and Sparta. Pisistratus had expelled the powerful Alcmaeonidae family from Athens, who now saw their chance to gain control. They bribed the Spartans to send an army against Athens. Hippias surrendered and was exiled in 509 B.C. The significance Athens attached to the overthrow of these tyrants was indicated by the erection of statues to Harmodius and Aristogeiton in city market places, an honor never previously accorded to anyone. Popularity with the common people counted for nothing in aristocratic power struggles.

> **KEY FACTS**
>
> ● Philip II of Macedon, father of Alexander the Great, was assassinated in 336 B.C. Alexander's own involvement has never been ruled out.
>
> ● Two acts of terror altered the course of Roman history: the murder of the last king, Tarquin II, in 509 B.C., and the assassination of Julius Caesar in 44 B.C.

ASSASSINATIONS IN ROME

The republic of Rome was born out of such conflicts between aristocrats. A similar pride was held in the ejection of the Etruscan kings in the sixth century B.C. Yet evidence exists that Rome was on friendly terms with Etruria, a region situated northwest of Rome across the Tiber river, and the kings, such as Tarquin I, had their supporters among Romans. Nevertheless, Tarquin was assassinated by supporters of his successor, Servius Tullius. Servius, in turn, met his death in a coup led by his son-in-law Tarquin II, whose overthrow by aristocrats ushered in the republic in 509 B.C.

The constitution of the Roman Republic was designed to avoid this kind of bloodletting. The city was ruled by two consuls, who were elected annually and could not hold office in successive years. Consuls were elected from the ruling body, the Senate, meaning that power rested with a collective body instead of with an individual. Political assassination was generally viewed as a waste of time since officeholders would be gone in a year.

The Senate at this time comprised a small group of noble families, while a panel of tribunes looked after the interests of the masses. The Senate viewed anyone with popular support as a dangerous threat to their power. Two such individuals were the Gracchi brothers – Tiberius who became tribune in 133 B.C., and Gaius, who held office for two terms from 123-122 B.C. They both instigated programs of land reform to help the poor. Both were seen to be usurping the Senate's

Mary Evans Picture Library

Julius Caesar falls in the Senate House in Rome in 44 B.C., knifed by senators opposing his rule.

power by appealing to the masses and were murdered.

Julius Caesar, however, was assassinated because he did not represent the people. He came to power via military prowess, at a time when Rome governed most of the Mediterranean basin. His victories in war enabled him to join two other politicians, the wealthy Crassus and the soldier Pompey. They formed the Triumvirate, or body of three men. Using the power of patronage, they controlled elections in the republic. After Crassus' death in 53 B.C. civil war broke out between Caesar and Pompey. It ended in Pompey's assassination in Egypt.

When Caesar returned to Rome, he became dictator, an ancient republican office offered to a general in times of national emergency. He defeated Pompey's sons in battle and, in late 45 B.C., was offered life dictatorship. Even his supporters saw this as a threat to the republic. On March 15, 44 B.C., a conspiracy of senators assassinated him. Caesar's appointment as dictator ended the republic. The establishment of Roman rule under an emperor was a direct result of his death.

Paul Szuscikiewicz

SEE ALSO: TERROR IN THE ROMAN EMPIRE; THE ASSASSINS: A TERROR CULT; RUSSIAN ANARCHIST TERROR.

FURTHER READING

- Finley, M. I. *Politics in the Ancient World.* Cambridge and New York: Cambridge University Press, 1983.
- Grant, Michael. *Myths of the Greeks and Romans.* Rev. ed. London: Phoenix, 1994; New York: Meridian, 1995.
- Kraut, Richard, ed. *The Cambridge Companion to Plato.* London and New York: Cambridge University Press, 1995.
- Meier, Christian. *Caesar: A Biography.* London and New York: HarperCollins, 1995.

TERROR IN THE ROMAN EMPIRE

We know that terror was an accepted instrument of government and war in the Roman empire because contemporary writers make clear reference to it. The Roman historian Tacitus says this of his father-in-law Agricola, governor of Roman Britain: "When he had sufficiently terrorized [the British], by showing mercy he displayed the attractions of peace." The Ancient Britons saw the Romans this way too. Tacitus reports chieftain Calgacus encouraging his warriors before the battle of Mons Graupius in A.D. 83 by saying: "When [the Romans] make a desolation, they call it peace."

The Romans waged war to acquire land or quell rebellions. Most of their enemies, particularly in the west, were individual tribes. Many did not have professional armies which the Romans could face in a pitched battle, and there was usually no key city or center whose capture would end the war or put down the insurrection. Fighting could be protracted and unnecessarily tie up much-needed legions, and so the Romans employed terror to settle matters quickly.

WARTIME TERROR TACTICS

Tacitus, writing about a German campaign in A.D. 16, records a Roman general's orders to his troops to be "resolute in killing and taking no prisoners; nothing but the extermination of the race would end the war." Against hostile populations, the pattern was invariable. There was devastation, which involved burning

Woodfin Camp & Associates

Augustus, emperor of Rome from 27 B.C. to A.D. 14.

KEY FACTS

- After a successful siege, the Roman army often slaughtered entire populations, as in Jerusalem in A.D. 70.
- In the bitter civil war after the assassination of Julius Caesar in 44 B.C., 2,130 political rivals died.
- The Roman criminal code was particularly harsh on slaves and the poor. By law, the testimony of slaves was acceptable only under torture.

E. T. Archive

This scene, from Trajan's Column in Rome, commemorates the Dacian campaigns of A.D. 101-106. It depicts the savagery of the fighting and the cruel subjugation of the vanquished Dacians.

villages, destroying or carrying off crops, slaughtering animals, and killing or enslaving the population. This is shown vividly on Trajan's Column in Rome, which carries scenes in relief of campaigning in Dacia (modern Romania) by the Emperor Trajan.

MASS SLAUGHTER IN SIEGES

In the battle zone, non-combatants – people considered unfit to fight – normally moved to a place of comparative safety. But in siege warfare, everyone was a combatant. Stubborn resistance might also lead to the extermination of a tribe. This was the fate of the Salassi, an Alpine people whom the Emperor Augustus ordered to be killed or sold into slavery.

But it was not simply blood-lust on the part of the Romans which fueled this savagery. Those terrorized always had the option of accepting their terms for surrender. These were rarely punitive. Hostages were taken, usually eminent leaders or their families, to ensure continued cooperation. But Rome was savage in dealing with rebellion.

The siege of Jerusalem in A.D. 70 was a result of the Jews rebelling. Their religious beliefs clashed with Roman emperor worship, making it peculiarly difficult for Jews to accept Roman rule. The Romans gave their usual choice to the Jews: terms if they gave in, terror if they refused. By way of encouragement, the Roman general crucified some captives outside the walls of the city, and sent others to offer terms. First, he cut off their hands, to make clear they were genuine prisoners. Rome's determination to extinguish all traces of rebellion explains the effort expended at the siege of

Masada, in A.D. 73, which ended the Jewish War. Many Jewish rebels had retreated to this impregnable hill stronghold. Roman soldiers took months to build a ramp to reach up to the fortress walls. But with defeat – and the fate meted out to the defiant – inevitable, the 1,000 Jews inside committed mass suicide.

The Romans put down the revolt of populations in newly conquered territory with the utmost brutality. In A.D. 60-61, Boudicca of the Iceni tribe in what is now eastern England led her warriors in revolt against 20 years of harsh Roman subjugation. An alleged 70,000 Britons were massacred for being Roman or friendly to Rome. Boudicca was defeated by the Roman garrison.

CRUSHING REVOLTS IN ROME

The authorities treated rebellion in Rome itself with equal harshness. Wealthy Romans administered the empire. They derived their fortunes largely from farms using slave labor. In 73 B.C., as many as 120,000 slaves, led by Spartacus, rose up against their masters and roamed Italy for two years. When Crassus put down the rebellion in 71 B.C., he crucified some 6,000 slaves along the Appian Way, the main road from Rome to southern Italy. The crosses stretched the 100 miles to Capua.

Roman rulers also used terror against movements which they considered might present a threat to the stability of the empire. The fourth-century emperor Diocletian had thousands of Christians hunted down, tortured, and publicly martyred in ever-increasing degrees of gruesomeness.

TORTURE OF ROMANS

Rome used terror as a means of enforcing discipline in the army. The practice of decimation, the selection by lot and putting to death of one-tenth of a body of soldiers who had shown cowardice in the field, was rare under the empire, as was the execution of individuals. But lesser punishments – floggings and mutilations, for example – were available and used.

Terror was also a feature of the Roman criminal code. When Pedanius Secundus, a leading citizen, was murdered by one of his slaves in A.D. 61, the murderer was one of 400 slaves executed for the crime. The other 399 were slaughtered in accordance with a law that require all the slaves in a household to be punished for killing their master.

In Roman law, slaves and the poor could be scourged, sent to the mines, thrown to wild beasts in the arena, or crucified. This was part of a legal code that sought to preserve the interests of the propertied classes by intimidating the poor and the enslaved.

However, terror was most obviously applied in conflicts within the ruling class of the Roman empire. This was nothing new. The general Sulla took power in 82 B.C., when Rome was still a republic, and purged 2,690 enemies, who were hunted down and executed without trial.

During the first century A.D., Roman emperors such as Tiberius, Nero, and Domitian found many victims among the political elite. They used vague accusations of treason to counter the possibility of conspiracies against their rule. The fears of the emperors were genuine. Four of the first 12 were assassinated by conspiracies of senators and officers of the imperial guard. The best protection against such attempts was the existence of an adult successor, provided he was loyal. There was nothing to be gained from assassinating emperors if they had already named as heir someone old enough to step straight into their shoes.

It is notable that dangers of assassination did not seem to come from the external enemies of Rome. Access to the emperor, or to a general, was not easy, but in any case assassination would not benefit them greatly. The fate of Rome was not dependent on one individual. Examples are difficult to find even of successful or attempted assassinations by outsiders of subordinate figures, some of whom were much hated.

Assassination was the Roman empire's closest parallel to modern terrorism. Terror was an instrument of policy that the Romans were willing to adopt when it suited their aims.

Paul Szuscikiewicz

SEE ALSO: TERROR IN ANCIENT GREECE AND THE ROMAN REPUBLIC; JUSTINIAN II'S REIGN OF TERROR; TERROR IN MEDIEVAL WARFARE; MEDIEVAL SIEGE WARFARE AS TERROR.

FURTHER READING

- Bunson, Matthew. *Encyclopedia of the Roman Empire*. New York: Facts on File, 1994.
- Grant, Michael. *The Fall of the Roman Empire*. London: Weidenfeld and Nicolson, 1996.
- Scarre, Chris. *Chronicle of the Roman Emperors: The Reign-by Reign Record of the Rulers of Imperial Rome*. London and New York: Thames & Hudson, 1995.

JUSTINIAN II'S REIGN OF TERROR

During the third century A.D., the Roman empire entered into a lengthy crisis that only ended during the reign of Justinian I (525-565). By this time, the empire was no longer pagan, or centered in Rome, or across thc whole Mediterranean basin. It had become a Christian empire whose ruler lived in Constantinople (modern Istanbul) and reigned over parts of Italy and the eastern Mediterranean. This successor state was known as the Byzantine empire, although its people still called themselves Romans.

Terror was a feature of the political strife among the ruling elite of the Byzantine empire just as in Roman times. For example, Byzantine emperors were just as liable to be victims of conspiracy. The penalties for those guilty of treason, though, could be far more savage.

RECKLESS YOUTH

One emperor who was both victim and perpetrator of terror is Justinian II. He was just 16 years old when he ascended to the throne in 685. One writer described him as "a bold, reckless, callous, and selfish young man, with a firm determination to assert his own individuality and have his own way – he was, in short, of the stuff of which tyrants are made." Yet his intelligence and resourcefulness cannot be underestimated.

Whether it was extravagant building projects, legal reform, or wars of reconquest, Justinian II was always trying to surpass the accomplishments of Justinian I, his great-great-grandfather. In part, he succeeded – but it came at a price. Justinian II was an unpopular sovereign. To pay for his excesses, he burdened his subjects with heavy taxation, which was in fact extortion carried out by ruthless officials. The population became disillusioned. By the year 695, Leontius, a general of repute, had enlisted a group of supporters which included the Patriarch Callinicus, head of the Orthodox Church in Constantinople. They marched on the palace and put Justinian in chains; he was spared execution only because of his father's friendship with Leontius. Instead, Justinian's nose was cut off and his tongue slit, earning him the nickname Rhinotmetus, or "cut-nose." He was paraded around the Hippodrome and exiled to the outer reaches of the empire in the Crimean town of Cherson. This humiliation was too much for him to bear and he swore vengeance.

Determined to seek revenge, Justinian set sail with a group of followers for the kingdom of the Bulgars, then enemy of the Byzantines, hoping to enlist support for a plan to capture Constantinople. As the story goes, a terrible storm threatened to sink Justinian's ship. One of his men implored him to repent his anger and swear to God that he would spare his enemies in return for a safe journey and the restoration of his throne. On the contrary, Justinian declared: "If I spare a single one of them, may I be drowned this instant." The storm subsided. The Bulgar king gave his support, and in 705 he helped Justinian to besiege Constantinople.

Meanwhile, a usurper named Tiberius had removed Leontius from power. While the Bulgar army remained outside the city gates, Justinian slipped inside and recaptured the royal palace. Encouraged by what he had interpreted as a sign of God's will, he became more ruthless than ever. He captured Leontius and Tiberius, paraded them at the Hippodrome, and, placing one foot on each of their necks, watched the chariot races for more than an hour. Then he ordered their decapitation. The patriarch who had crowned them was blinded and exiled.

REIGN OF REVENGE

Thereafter followed a six-year reign of revenge and terror. Justinian put to death most of the empire's best army officers. The terror became so widespread, it

> **KEY FACTS**
>
> - Justinian II's head of finances was a monk who hung people above a slow and smoky fire when they could not pay their taxes.
> - At the assassination of Justinian II, his son and mother took refuge in a church. Both were slaughtered to wipe out the Heraclian dynasty.

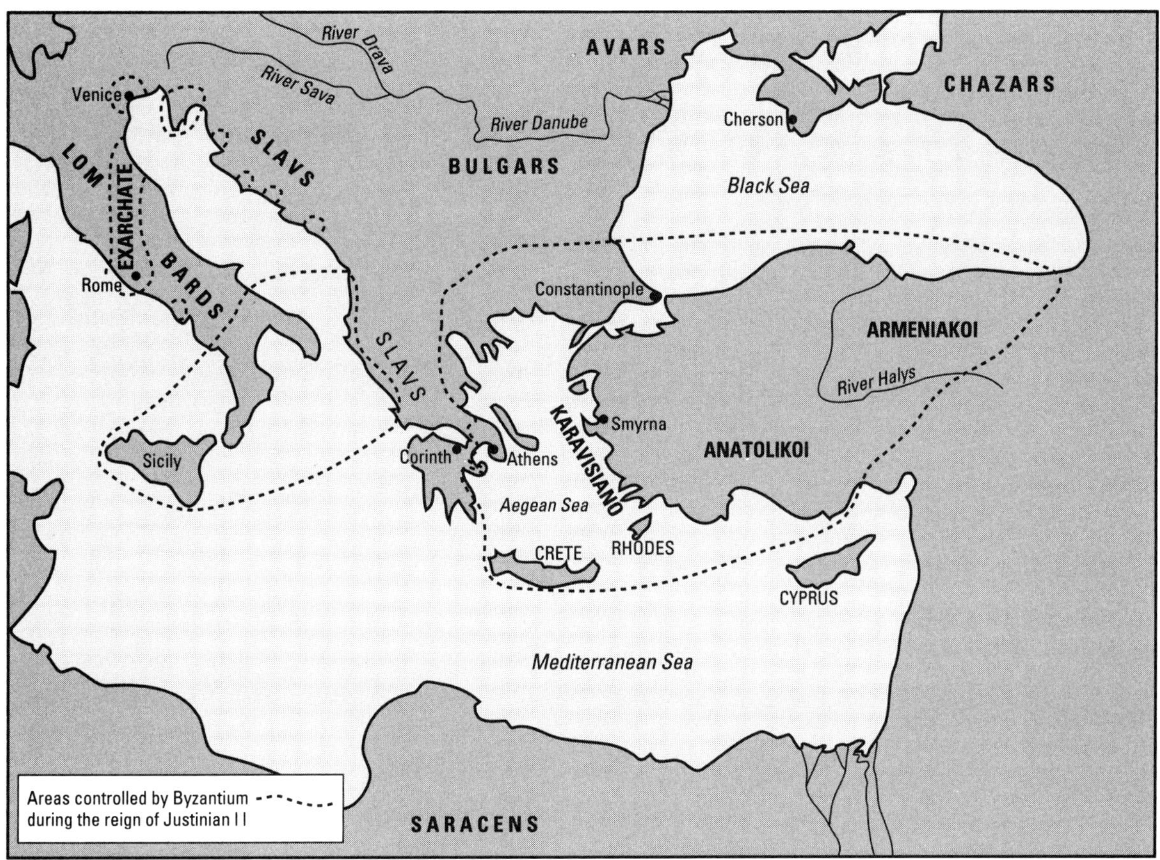

The Byzantine empire at the end of the seventh century A.D.

moved one observer to write of Justinian that "as often as he wiped the drops of rheum from his [cut-nose] rhinotmetus, almost as often did he order another one of those who opposed him to be slain."

His desire for revenge was strongest against the Chersonites, who had insulted him during his exile. Justinian ordered Stephen the Savage to terrorize them with the order: "All are guilty and all must perish." Although the slowness of his attack allowed the majority to flee, Justinian's minister still took his toll. He roasted alive seven principal citizens, drowned 20, and sent 42 in chains to the emperor to meet their doom.

Still Justinian was thirsty for vengeance and sent another expedition to Cherson under the patrician officer Bardanes. This time, however, the Chersonites were prepared for the attack and overpowered the emperor's troops. Justinian's soldiers were threatened with death unless they swore their allegiance to Bardanes, who was crowned as Emperor Philippicus in 711. Philippicus sailed to Constantinople where Justinian II, devoid of allies, was overthrown and executed. For the terrified Byzantine populace, it came not a moment too soon.

Paul Szuscikiewicz

SEE ALSO: TERROR IN THE ROMAN EMPIRE; TERROR IN MEDIEVAL WARFARE; THE ASSASSINS: A TERROR CULT.

FURTHER READING

- Norwich, John Julius. *Byzantium: The Apogee.* London: Penguin, and New York: Knopf, 1991.
- Ostrogorsky, G. *History of the Byzantine State.* Rev. ed. Oxford: Blackwell, 1980.
- Vasiliev, A. A. *History of the Byzantine Empire.* 2 Vols. Oxford: Blackwell, 1952; Madison: University of Wisconsin Press, 1980.

TERROR IN MEDIEVAL WARFARE

"All the common people were put to the sword, and all the priests of the Lord God, with those who served them, were murdered where they stood at the church altars. When they had killed every living soul...the troops burned the whole city, with all the churches and every single building, leaving there nothing but the bare earth." These words, from The History of the Franks, written by Gregory (c. 538-94) bishop of Tours, describe taking the town of Comminges in southwestern France.

The besiegers captured Gundovald, the city's commander, by tricking him into leaving the town. His captors, Count Ullo and Boso, led him to a steep ravine where: "Ullo pushed Gundovald over and, as he fell, the Count shouted: 'There goes your pretender, who pretends that he is the son of one king and the brother of another.' He thrust his lance at Gundovald and tried to transfix him. The rings of Gundovald's [chain-mail suit] withstood the lance and he was not wounded. He picked himself up and tried to scramble to the top of the cliff. Boso threw a rock at him and hit him full in the head. Gundovald fell and as he fell he died. The mob surrounded him and prodded him with their spears. They tied his feet together with a rope and dragged him through the whole army encampment. They pulled out his hair and his beard. Then they left his body unburied on the spot where he had met his death."

KEY FACTS

- Such was the value of ransoming captives that, in 1217 at a battle in Lincoln, England, only one knight died on the winning side and two on the losing side. Around 400 were taken prisoner.
- When captured in 1356, John II of France paid the Black Prince, son of Edward III of England, three million gold coins in ransom.
- A medieval army could never muster more than 100,000 troops, compared with 360,000 during the Roman empire and France's 300,000 in 1710.

These excerpts from a medieval history show how terror was used in warfare to intimidate the defeated. Its use in the early part of the Middle Ages, from the fifth to eleventh centuries, was a continuation of those methods characteristic of warfare since organized human societies first emerged in prehistory. The homes of the defeated were pillaged and prisoners were sold into slavery. Leaders who fell into enemy hands could expect a quick death if they were lucky, and a lingering one by torture if they were not.

RULES OF WARFARE

However, a new attitude toward warfare began to develop during this period, influenced by Christian theology. During the second half of the Middle Ages, from the eleventh to sixteenth centuries, the commanders of armies more often than not accepted the discipline of these new rules and customs. An important idea was that the use of force was permissible only as part of a process of obtaining justice. Armies should help extend peace on earth by refraining from acts of violence on certain days of the week, such as Sunday, and in places like churches, hospices, and markets.

There were also attempts to control the use of weapons. In 1139, the Church's Lateran Council banned the use of the crossbow in wars between Christians; its use was restricted to wars against pagans and infidels. French heretical mercenaries, however, known as Brabançons, who had broken away from the king's control, continued to use it. Indeed, it was a Brabançon captain who accounted for taking the life of the English king Richard I ("the Lionheart") with a crossbow bolt at the siege of Gaillon.

Christian ethics were not the sole influence on this process. The concept of subjecting warfare to rules also developed out of the conditions of medieval warfare. Commanders feared risking their armies in battles, and regarded sieges as difficult, dangerous, and lengthy operations. To maintain an army in the field for more than a few weeks was a major problem. So medieval campaigns tended to be plundering

Mary Evans Picture Library

Edward the "Black Prince" commanded the English in their victory over the French at Poitiers in 1356.

expeditions. Their aim was to force the enemy to sue for peace by ravaging their land. This inevitably resulted in prolonged conflict, as the Hundred Years' War (1337-1453) between England and France illustrates. The king of England, Edward III, believed he had a claim to be king of France, and he asserted it. The war dragged on into the reigns of his grandson and his grandson's three successors. The countryside of France and the southern coast of England suffered badly, and their populations generally lived in a state of terror. In one four-week campaign in the autumn of 1339, Edward III reportedly sacked 2,117 villages and castles in the north of France. Devastation on such a scale was common for many years to come in the campaigns led by Edward the "Black Prince."

Warfare with rules also protected the rulers of medieval society. Knights were more valuable to the enemy alive than dead, since such a prisoner could be ransomed. The chance of a poorer knight or a common soldier making a fortune from ransoming a valuable captive was an important incentive for their going to war. In the battle of Bremule in 1119, out of 900 knights, only three were killed.

However, other groups who took their place on the medieval battlefield did not receive the same protection. Those among the poorer classes who appeared in the ranks of the defeated army were slaughtered. In the battle of Cassel in 1328, at least half of the Flemish city militias were annihilated.

Peasant uprisings habitually resulted in wholesale killing. The later Middle Ages were marked by a long succession of city and peasant rebellions – a notable example being the Peasants' Revolt in England in 1381. In this, peasants from the eastern and southeastern counties of England protested at the new poll tax that had been imposed on them in addition to their traditional duties to their feudal overlords. The peasants received guarantees of reforms, but once they had dispersed back to their homes the local nobility beat some and murdered others. The promises that King Richard II had made were ignored.

The extent to which limits on terror were accepted depended crucially on the social group to which one belonged. In this sense, terror remained a tool used to enforce and maintain the social order of the medieval world, even if attempts were made to restrain it in armed conflict between the ruling elite.

Paul Szuscikiewicz

SEE ALSO: MEDIEVAL SIEGE WARFARE AS TERROR.

FURTHER READING

- Allmand, Christopher. *The Hundred Years War: England and France at War, 1300-c.1450.* Cambridge and New York: Cambridge University Press, 1988.
- Riley-Smith, Jonathan. *The Crusades: A Short History.* London: Athlone Press, and New Haven, CT: Yale University Press, 1990.
- Wedgwood, C. V. *The Thirty Years War.* New York and London: Routledge, 1991.

THE ASSASSINS: A TERROR CULT

The Assassins were a fanatical and murderous Muslim sect active in the Middle East from the eleventh century to the thirteenth century. They were members of the Ismaili branch of Shia Islam, the principal branch of which, the Twelver branch, is the official religion of modern Iran. The Ismailis seized power in Egypt in the tenth century and founded the Fatimid dynasty. At the end of the eleventh century, a schism occurred in the Fatimid leadership. The Ismaili missionaries living in Iran supported Nizar in the ensuing power struggle, and became known as the Nizari Ismailis. When Nizar was defeated, the leader of the Nizari Ismailis in Iran, Hasan-i Sabbah, seized the castle of Alamut in the Alburz mountains south of the Caspian Sea. There he dedicated himself to spreading Ismaili Islam throughout the Middle East and formed a devoted group of terrorists, to help him in his quest. These became known as the Assassins.

SUDDEN DEATH BY THE DAGGER

The Nizaris were generally fairly few in number. As a result, they could not meet their enemies in pitched battle with any hope of success. Instead, they developed an approach to warfare that has made them infamous. The sect would send a single member, or a small group, to kill their enemy's leader, almost always with a dagger. The Nizaris saw themselves as emissaries of god, and carrying "his" message was a divine act. They used the sacredness of their mission to justify the murder of anyone who opposed their attempts to convert people to their form of Islam.

Murdering enemy leaders proved effective in reducing the power and influence of the sect's foes. The Nizaris' rivals were more inclined to sacrifice large numbers of troops in battle rather than run the personal risk of sudden, violent death at the hands of a dagger-wielding fanatic. Apologists for the Nizaris have suggested that their ruthless use of terror was a merciful, economical way to achieve their goals without causing unnecessary bloodshed.

KEY FACTS

- Simply using the threat of assassination was often enough for the Assassins to cow their potential enemies into submission.
- Sabbah was so devout that he even had one of his sons executed after he was accused of drunkenness.
- An Assassin once killed a religious enemy as he knelt at prayer in a mosque – even though the victim's bodyguard was standing behind him.

FIRST TO DIE

The Nizaris claimed their first victim in 1092, when they sent a lone killer to murder Nizam al-Mulk, the Turkish sultan's chief minister. Butahir Arrani disguised himself as a holy man to get close to the minister. As Nizam was carried from his tent in a litter, Butahir plunged a knife into his chest. The murderer had no chance of escape, and the minister's guards killed him instantly. One of Nizam's sons, Fakhri, also died at the hands of a Nizari. Fakhri's killer was disguised as a beggar.

It may have been the seemingly fanatical courage of the Nizaris, together with the fact that a Nizari rarely made any attempt to escape after committing a murder, that gave rise to the belief that they acted under the influence of drugs. The story goes that the Nizaris drugged the member who was about to undertake a mission and carried him into a beautiful garden, leading him to believe that it was paradise. They then drugged the chosen killer again. When he woke up, they told him to go and carry out his mission.

The Nizaris encouraged the killer to believe that he would be allowed back into paradise on his return, and that if he were killed during the execution of his mission, he would reach paradise even more quickly. However, most modern scholars think that stories of drug-taking are probably untrue, suggesting that they were invented to discredit the sect. After all, a drug-befuddled emissary would hardly be an effective killer.

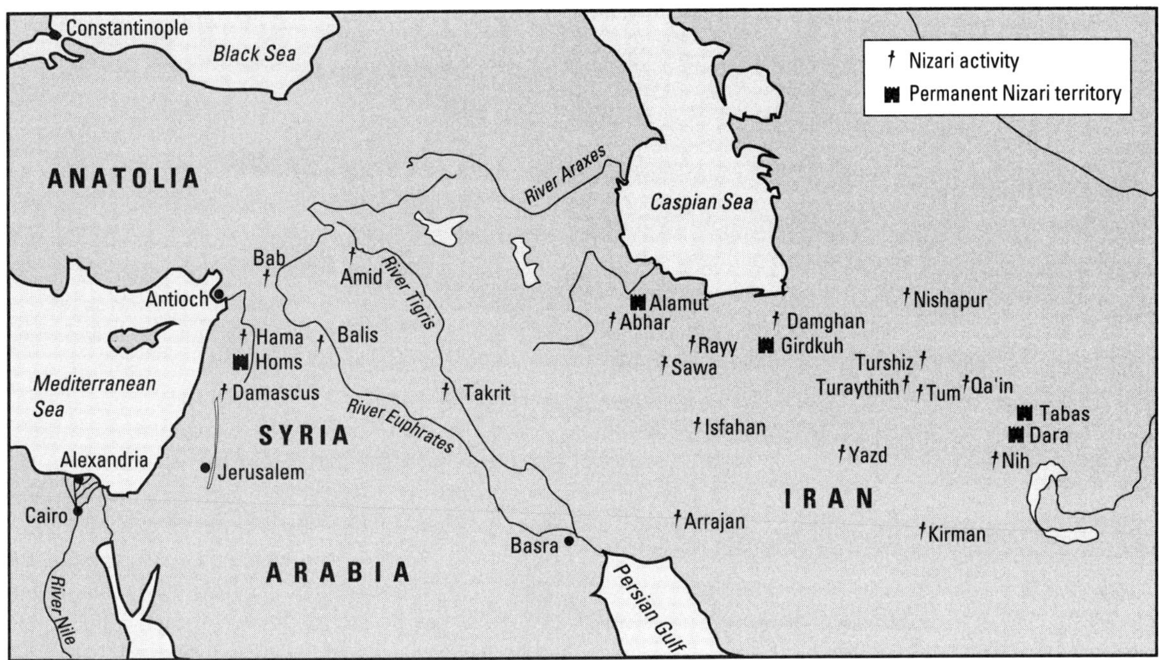

The Muslim sect usually known as the Assassins terrorized the Middle East from the eleventh century to the mid-thirteenth century.

Nevertheless, it was certainly the widespread stories of drug-taking that earned the Nizari Assassins their name. Hashish was allegedly their most widely used narcotic. Thus, the sect became known as *hashishiyya*, *hashishiyyin*, or *hashishin* in Arabic. The Christian Crusaders in Syria picked up these names and carried them back to Europe in the form of *assassin*. The word then became common in many European languages. Its use as a term for political and other murderers survived through the ages. But its Arabic derivation was forgotten until the early nineteenth century.

RELIEF AT THE ASSASSINS' DOWNFALL

The Assassins' contemporaries in the Muslim world regarded the sect with near-universal horror and disgust. This may have been in part because of the Assassins' unusual approach to warfare. But it can be more properly explained in terms of orthodox Muslim abhorrence toward the Assassins' beliefs. At one point, the religious views of the sect involved abandoning strict adherence to Islamic law.

As a result, when the second wave of Mongol conquests reached Iran and Syria in the middle of the thirteenth century, the orthodox Muslim world was delighted with the invaders' determination to wipe out the Assassins. The latter were rumored to have sent a group to assassinate the Great Khan. But they met a more terrible force. Contemporary Muslims felt that the Mongols, despite the general horrors they inflicted, performed a valuable service in obliterating the Assassins. Many had considered the sect a real threat to stability in the Muslim world.

David Morgan

SEE ALSO: MONGOL TERROR; RELIGIOUS EXTREMISM; ASSASSINATION; TERRORISM AND REVOLUTION IN IRAN.

FURTHER READING

- Daftary, Farhad. *The Isma'ilis: Their History and Doctrines.* London and New York: Cambridge University Press, 1992.
- Daftary, Farhad. *The Assassin Legends: Myths of the Isma'ilis.* New York and London: Tauris, 1994.
- Lewis, Bernard. *The Assassins: A Radical Sect in Islam.* London: Zed Books, 1985; New York: Oxford University Press, 1987.

MONGOL TERROR

No conquests in history claimed more civilian lives, nor spread greater terror to a larger part of the world, than those accomplished by the Mongol empire under Genghis Khan. For the Mongols, terror was simply a weapon of war.

Born in the 1160s, Genghis spent until 1206 uniting the various nomadic tribes of Mongolia under his own supreme rule. He then spent the rest of his life directing his armies in a series of military conquests. By the time of his death in 1227, he had achieved astonishing successes in China, Central Asia, and the Middle East. Military expansion continued under the rule of his four sons and a grandson for a further half-century. The Mongol empire reached its greatest extent around the year 1280, when it covered a continuous stretch of territory from Korea to Hungary.

This unparalleled military achievement owed much to organization, strategy, and tactics. Among the various characteristics of the Mongol approach to warfare, the use of terror held a prominent place.

OTHERS DIE BUT NOT THE MONGOLS

Mongol men were hardened soldiers from adolescence. They were not, however, enthusiastic about dying unnecessarily in battle. They were always anxious to avoid Mongol casualties as much as possible, so to ensure that any dying was done by others, the Mongols used terror. When they besieged a city, they made it clear that if surrender was immediate, they would spare its residents, though not necessarily their homes or possessions. But resistance meant no mercy. According to contemporary sources, the Mongols would often put to death the entire population of a city. They killed countless thousands, but usually as quickly as possible, without needless cruelty. The Mongols seem to have regarded such massacres as a military necessity, not as a form of sadistic enjoyment.

The rationale behind such savagery was perfectly clear: it was designed to reduce future Mongol casualties. If a city resisted, and Mongol soldiers were consequently killed, the rest of the army would exterminate the city's residents. Word would quickly spread that it was wise to surrender to the Mongols when summoned to do so. In this way other cities would surrender rather than fight, and Mongol casualties would be avoided.

KEY FACTS

- Genghis Khan aimed at nothing less than conquest of the world.
- If the Mongols killed a city's inhabitants, they generally let craftsmen live. These would then be marched to Mongolia to work for the khan (ruler).
- In 1281, the Mongols launched a naval attack on Japan, but the fleet was destroyed by a storm. In Japanese, this storm was called *kamikaze*, the name later given to Japanese suicide pilots of World War II.

TERROR TACTICS

The policy of giving citizens the choice of surrender or death amounted to state terrorism on a grand scale. Its effect may be gauged by examining the death toll provided by contemporary writers when the Mongols massacred a city. The Persian historian Juzjani gives a typical example. After the Mongol capture of Herat (now in western Afghanistan) in 1221, Juzjani claims, the victors slaughtered a total of 2.4 million people. When Merv fell in the same year, even more people are said to have died.

These figures should not be taken as reliable statistics. Judging by the physical size of the city, it would have been impossible for Herat to have contained more than a tenth of the number of people stated. Also, the Mongols would have found great practical difficulties in killing so many people in one place in a short space of time. The alleged death toll at Herat and Merv alone was almost as high as the number of Jews killed during all the years of the Holocaust – when the Nazis had available to them all the destructive resources of twentieth-century technology.

What the figures do show, however, is the psychological effect of the ferocity of the Mongol campaigns. Those who suffered Mongol attacks could conceive of nothing so appalling: hence the impossible figures.

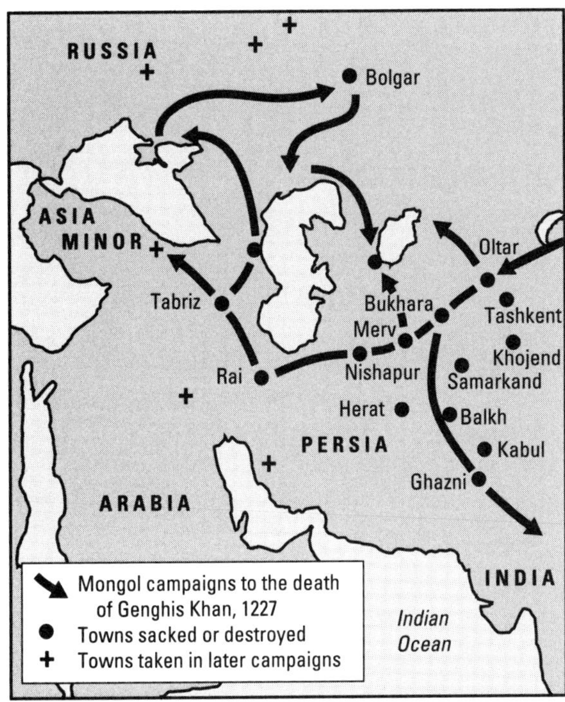

By 1206, Genghis Khan had united the nomadic tribes of Mongolia. He began an 80-year campaign of conquest, continued by his sons and a grandson.

When the Mongols invaded Russia in 1237, they surprised and terrified the entire population by attacking in winter. The invaders' hardy ponies used the frozen rivers as vast, snow-free roads. In a few weeks, the Mongols stormed and captured every Russian city, burning Kiev to the ground. It would be two centuries before the Russians regained their freedom.

CONQUEST OF CHINA

In China, the Mongols were equally skillful at the use of terror. For centuries the nomadic Mongols had raided the Chinese, but Genghis Khan was intent on conquest. In 1211, the Mongols broke through the Great Wall to attack the Chin empire, which covered northern China. The Mongol army succeeded in partially subjugating it. After crushing the Chin armies, Genghis captured Peking in 1215, massacring the population. Like a true nomad, Genghis had only contempt for peasant farmers and measured his wealth in livestock. He ordered his men to exterminate the peasants, both by putting them to the sword and by burning their crops to cause starvation. More than 15 million may have died before Genghis Khan's advisers persuaded him that he would be richer if he kept the peasants alive and taxed them.

Genghis then crushed the Muslim states of central Asia before returning to China. In 1234, the Mongols finished off the Chin and then moved on to destroy the Sung empire in 1279. It was during this campaign that the Mongols made great use of Chinese religious beliefs. After the Mongols captured a city, they did not kill the population at once but instead forced it to march along with the Mongol army. When the Mongols encountered a Chinese force they advanced, driving the captured civilians in front of them. Unwilling to kill possible relatives, the opposing army refused to fight.

MESMERIZED BY FEAR

Anecdotes written at the time of the Mongols demonstrate the effectiveness of their terror policy. According to a Persian chronicler, a Mongol came across a fleeing Persian peasant, stopped to kill him, but found he had left his sword in his tent. He therefore instructed the peasant to wait, rode back to fetch his sword, and returned. The peasant, frozen rigid by terror, was still there when the now armed Mongol came back to kill him.

Whether this story is true or not is not the point. That such tales could be told, and believed, shows the effect Mongol terror had. Clearly terror, from the Mongols' point of view, achieved its end of making conquest easier. For the Mongols, terror was good policy in terms of the military casualties it saved them.

David Morgan

SEE ALSO: THE ASSASSINS: A TERROR CULT; MEDIEVAL SIEGE WARFARE AS TERROR.

FURTHER READING

- Chambers, James. *The Devil's Horsemen.* New York: Atheneum, 1985; London: Cassell, 1988.
- Marshall, Robert. *Storm from the East: From Genghis Khan to Khubilai Khan.* London: Penguin, 1994.
- Morgan, David. *The Mongols.* Cambridge, MA and Oxford: Blackwell, 1990.

MEDIEVAL SIEGE WARFARE AS TERROR

One of the outstanding features of the Middle Ages (from about the year 700 to the sack of Constantinople in 1453) was the extensive use of fortifications as a means of protection. Local rulers had thick-walled castles surrounded by wide moats and impenetrable curtain walls put up wherever they felt their land was vulnerable to attack. Walls encircled cities and towns, too, with gates that were shut tight when danger threatened.

Taking refuge in a fortress had advantages over the battlefield. It fell to the attackers to take all the risks, while the defenders repelled all-comers from a position of safety. Besiegers had to resort to other means of weakening the enemy. Terror became an essential weapon in the attackers' armory if they were to avoid a direct assault or a long and costly siege.

The use of terror by attackers took a variety of forms. At Nicaea, Asia Minor, in 1097, Christian Crusaders catapulted the heads of Turkish corpses into the town. At Antioch in 1098, the Franks beheaded Muslim prisoners in front of the gates. But when Frederick Barbarossa had many prisoners hanged and hacked to death at the siege of Crema, northern Italy, in 1160, the defenders retaliated by killing their captives in full sight of the attackers.

KEY FACTS

- When the First Crusade captured Jerusalem in 1099 after a five-week siege, the Christian troops massacred all the inhabitants to purge the holy city and make it entirely Christian.
- In 1105, English King Henry I burned Bayeux after capturing it. The terror this induced caused several other towns to surrender at once.
- When Edward III of England captured Calais, he demanded that the six most important citizens march out with nooses round their necks ready to be hanged. Having thus terrorized the men, he then let them live to show his mercy.

Attackers also ruthlessly exploited bonds of loyalty between a garrison and a captured lord. King John of England frequently threatened to starve to death lords and their relatives unless castles were surrendered at once. This tactic proved to be useful during his suppression of a widespread baronial revolt in 1215-16 and had been used earlier by his predecessors. In 1174, King Henry II of England imprisoned Robert, Earl of Leicester, without food and threatened to starve him until his retainers surrendered their castles.

THE RIGHT OF STORM

Such terror tactics, designed to encourage surrender in order to save attackers' lives, were not as persuasive as the "right of storm" convention. If the defenders of a fortress refused an initial demand to surrender (known as a summons), and were then defeated and the fortress seized, the attackers had the right to take possession of all the property within the fortress. They could also decide whether to kill or spare the occupants.

The right of storm is mentioned as early as the time of the Old Testament, and examples are quoted in the Book of Deuteronomy. The Romans and other imperial powers of the ancient world, such as Greece and Persia, also carried on the tradition.

The object of invoking this right was to let defenders know exactly what they faced if they chose to refuse the initial invitation to surrender. Besiegers reasoned that they had given their enemies every opportunity to save themselves and, if they were forced to attack, then the defenders would have to take the consequences. From the attackers' point of view, there was an element of justice in this and therefore they had the right to devastate or sack the fortress once it was taken. Sacking usually took the form of indiscriminate destruction and murder.

Mercy was at the victorious commander's discretion. Individual nobles might be moved by piety, chivalry, and the desire for ransom to spare women, members of religious orders, and knights of equal

E. T. Archive

A fresco in Moldovita Monastery, Romania, depicting Turks killing Christians during the Siege of Constantinople in 1453.

rank. Victors showed such mercy at Caen, in northern France, in 1346, during the Hundred Years' War between England and France.

But conquerors usually pillaged and killed ordinary citizens without mercy when the right of storm was invoked. In the sack of Lincoln, England, in 1141, the victors killed far more citizens than during the preceding battle between King Stephen and the forces of Mathilda, his rival for the throne. Another feature of the right of storm was that the victors frequently attacked churches for the wealth to be found within them. Churches were normally immune from attack.

By the right of storm, held to be in operation once the besieger had fired his first cannon, all property was forfeit to the victors. If the besieged fortress was a wealthy one, it was not uncommon for the attackers to frustrate a negotiated peace that might cheat them of booty. For many commanders and common soldiers alike, plunder was the chief motive for waging war.

Sometimes, however, financial gain was not the main reason for sacking captured fortresses. The attackers carefully calculated some acts of terror based on the right of storm. In 1191, the Muslim garrison of Acre, now in modern Israel, surrendered on terms after a siege of nearly three years. King Richard I of England ("the Lionheart") executed about 2,700 of the garrison when their leader Saladin failed to ratify the agreement.

The extent to which the right of storm was implemented varied considerably. In the eleventh and twelfth centuries, death threats to a garrison were common preliminaries to siege. Yet attackers rarely carried them out. The majority of garrisons negotiated acceptable terms according to the convention of the "law of surrender," whereby the defenders agreed to surrender unless relieved after a set number of days.

It was rare for rulers to refuse pleas to surrender. But they often refused mercy when the adversaries were retainers who had broken their oath of loyalty. Richard I insisted on unconditional surrender by the garrison of Nottingham in 1194, who had aligned themselves with his treacherous brother John and plotted against him. Richard hanged several rebel serjeants in front of the city walls to show the severity with which he would treat the defenders if surrender was not rapid.

Under the right of storm, warlords could in theory do what they liked with vanquished defenders of a fortress. In practice, vengeance was often limited by notions of chivalry and the desire to avoid precedents which might later endanger their own lives. Sacks were bloodiest in wars against the infidel, heretics, or rebels, who were not judged to be of equal status.

The terror that the right of storm inspired often had a bearing on the outcome of negotiations. In the wars of the Spanish Netherlands in the seventeenth century, the Dutch general Justinus readily surrendered the town of Breda to the Spanish under Spinola. He was aware of the terrible precedent of the "Spanish Fury" of 1576 when Spanish troops sacked Antwerp, leaving 7,000 dead after 11 days of savage pillaging.

Antony B. Shaw

SEE ALSO: TERROR IN MEDIEVAL WARFARE; MONGOL TERROR.

FURTHER READING

- Bradbury, Jim. *The Medieval Siege*. Rochester, NY: Boydell and Brewer, 1992.
- Seymour, William. *Great Sieges of History*. London and McLean, VA: Brassey's Inc., 1991.
- Watson, Bruce. *Sieges: A Comparative Study*. Westport, CT: Praeger, 1993.

TERROR AND AMERICAN INDIAN RESISTANCE

Contact between settlers and the Indian peoples of North America was dominated by violence. It dated from the earliest days of European settlement in the mid-sixteenth century, when the Spanish came in search of gold. Initial curiosity rapidly gave way to bloody confrontation as the American Indians realized that the newcomers were intent upon exploitation and conquest. Their resistance was hampered by the failure of the different tribes to unite against the settlers. In spite of this, the American Indians did not relinquish their ancestral lands without a long and bitter struggle during which both sides deliberately used terror.

The first clashes between Indians and settlers began when Spanish conquistadors went north from lands already conquered in South and Central America. They were intent on plundering raids in the southeast and southwest of what is now the United States. The violence rooted in that era continued for 350 years, climaxing with the war on the open plains in the late nineteenth century. It ended in 1890 when 150 Sioux died at the hands of the U.S. Seventh Cavalry at Wounded Knee in the South Dakota Badlands.

Throughout the centuries of colonization, acts of cruelty and betrayal by one side triggered retaliatory terror from the other. Tension between the English settlers of Virginia and the local Powhatan Confederacy, for example, erupted in massacres in 1622 and 1644. The two bloodbaths claimed the lives of some 850 men, women, and children among the settlers. The survivors exacted an equally savage retribution in a bitter conflict, not only killing Indians, but also destroying their villages and crops.

> **KEY FACTS**
>
> - European contact at first benefited tribes as they acquired horses, sheep, metal, and other European goods, but terror quickly followed.
> - During the Colonial wars, 1689-1760, the French and British used Indian allies to terrorize civilian populations.
> - By 1875, the U.S. government had forced most Indians to live on reservations.

RECIPROCAL TERROR

Relations between settlers and American Indians in New England also degenerated into a pattern of reciprocal terror. At first, the English fugitives from religious persecution and the Indians had the common goal of making a living from the land. As the settlements became successful, however, and the settlers wanted more land, disputes arose between the two peoples. The tone was set by the vicious Pequot War of 1637. Massachusetts and Connecticut were alarmed by the militancy of the Pequot Indians and resolved to teach the tribe a lesson. A colonial force surprised the Pequots in their village on the Mystic River. In the ensuing slaughter, the New Englanders butchered every Pequot, including women and children, who came within range of their muskets or swords. The savagery of the attack, combined with the deliberate policy of destruction that followed, exterminated the Pequots and shocked the survivors' Indian allies, the Mohegan and Narragansett tribes.

Throughout the American Indian resistance wars the innocent suffered. In 1782, for example, at Gnadenhutten, Ohio, militiamen massacred 90 peaceful Delaware Indian converts to the Moravian faith. The incident was not forgotten. When Indians routed the Pennsylvania militia at Sandusky, Ohio, later that year, they roasted to death captured commander Colonel Crawford in reprisal.

As the frontier moved west in the next century, the familiar pattern of massacre and retaliation continued.

Peter Newark's Western Americana

Sioux dead are buried following a bloody massacre by the U.S. Army at Wounded Knee, December 29, 1890.

In 1864, at Sand Creek, Colorado, state militia killed and mutilated some 150 Cheyenne of both sexes and all ages. Chief Black Kettle survived that massacre, only to die four years later when General Custer's troops killed another 100 Cheyenne on the Washita River in western Oklahoma. Both incidents heralded reigns of terror for frontier settlers as enraged Indian warriors sought revenge.

Warfare with American Indians was brutal and inglorious by "Old World" standards. Through generations of conflict, both sides waged war with a ruthlessness summed up in the following remark by the Civil War veteran General Sheridan: "The only good Indians I ever saw were dead." Captives could face prolonged torture, while Indians and whites alike employed scalping. Combats frequently ended in massacres rather than simple defeats. For example, when the Sioux leader Red Cloud ambushed Captain Fetterman near Fort Phil Kearny in 1866, he killed all 80 men under the captain's command. Over 200 troops were killed along with Custer in his attack on an Indian encampment at Little Big Horn a decade later. The mutilation of the dead outraged the whites.

GUERRILLA WARFARE

Conventional European methods of warfare were ill-suited to frontier conflicts. The American Indians' aptitude for guerrilla warfare often put Europeans at a disadvantage. The Eastern Woodlands Indians used guns with surprising accuracy. And in the west, horses attained from the Spaniards transformed the tribes of the Great Plains into devastating mounted raiders. Because of their preference for evasive tactics, American Indians were difficult to defeat in pitched battle. In addition, the whites relied on cumbersome wagon trains for supplies. Only when commanders discarded these in favor of pack horses were they able to pursue their elusive foes. These techniques permitted destructive campaigns to deny American Indians food and shelter. For example, in 1761, a lightly equipped Anglo-American punitive expedition broke Cherokee resistance by burning 15 tribal villages.

Europeans also knew that an effective tactic was to exploit the enmity already existing between some tribes and encourage them to fight each other. General Crook employed American Indian allies from Oregon to Arizona during his campaigns of the 1860s to 1880s. After Custer's disaster at Little Big Horn, it was the Pawnee and the Crow, sworn enemies of the Sioux, who guided the avenging U.S. Army. And when the Apache leader Geronimo was forced to surrender in 1886, it was enemies among his own people who tracked him down.

Both American Indians and settlers used deliberate acts of terror in an effort to intimidate the opposition and preserve two very different ways of life. Despite centuries of bloody and determined resistance by native peoples in defense of their lands and culture, the superior numbers and industrial resources of the encroaching settlers meant that the conflict could have only one outcome.

Steve Brumwell

SEE ALSO: TERROR IN COLONIAL CONQUESTS.

FURTHER READING

- Utley, Robert M. *The Indian Frontier of the American West, 1846-1890.* Albuquerque: University of New Mexico Press, 1984.
- Waldman, C. *Encyclopedia of Native American Tribes.* New York: Facts on File Publications, 1988.
- Washburn, W. E. "History of Indian-White Relations," in the *Handbook of North American Indians,* Vol. 4. Washington, DC: Smithsonian Institution Press, 1988.

TERROR IN THE FRENCH REVOLUTION 1789-1815

Terror as a tactic to frighten a population into subjugation is forever associated with the period known as the Reign of Terror during the French Revolution. Between February and April 1793, following the execution of the deposed Bourbon king, Louis XVI, the machinery of terror was fashioned into an efficient political instrument by revolutionary leader Maximilien Robespierre. During his rule, countless thousands of French citizens died. The term *terror* thus entered the vocabulary of Western politics.

The Terror, as it became known, is particularly associated with the Reign of Terror conducted by the Committee of Public Safety (the Committee) of the National Convention (the Convention) in 1793-94. But the Terror is also used to describe the whole period of so-called Revolutionary Government from the overthrow of the Bourbon monarch Louis XVI in 1792, to the inauguration of the regime of the Directory (1795-99).

Before 1792, terror was used to describe policies of intimidation and repression of political enemies, if necessary through unlawful acts of violence. But it was largely under the Committee that such policies became official state policy.

The fall from power and execution of Robespierre in July 1794 produced a reaction against state endorsement of terror. Yet many of the repressive and violent policies that had been associated with the height of the Terror continued to be used spasmodically through successive regimes that governed France – the Directory (1795-99), the Consulate (1799-1804), and the First Empire (1804-15). The same period also saw the emergence of what came to be known as the White Terror – violence, reprisals, and assassinations by enemies of the revolutionary regimes.

KEY FACTS

- The term *terror* has become synonymous with the Reign of Terror of 1793-94 under the Committees of Public Safety and General Security.
- In just two months, June and July 1794, the revolutionary courts in Paris sent 1,515 people to the guillotine. Many were innocent of any crime.
- Between 1794 and 1802, royalist murder gangs roamed southern France, spreading terror to those who had been involved in the Revolution. Over 10,000 people are thought to have been killed.
- In the southern French city of Lyon, in June 1794, over 700 people were sentenced to death. The guillotine could not cope, so the victims were marched to a square and mown down by cannon.

THE CONTEXT OF FEAR

The political atmosphere in Paris, and at certain times throughout much of France, during the period from 1789 to 1795 was one of fear: of plots, of famine, and of invasion. The language of revolutionaries, and by their reactionary enemies, was deliberately violent and threatening.

The politicians in Paris had few historical parallels on which they could draw; they had no way of guessing what the future would hold. What they did know was that violence and threats of violence had saved the revolution and impelled it forward at key points. In the summer of 1789, for example, when the king was preparing a coup against the radicals in the parliament (the Estates General), the Paris crowd, as the members of the revolution came to be known, altered the political landscape by their assault on the Bastille prison. After the storming, the crowd massacred the garrison and paraded the governor's head on a pike.

The more radical politicians came increasingly to rely on the support of the politicized Paris crowd, especially after the beginning of the war with Austria and Prussia in 1792. The war introduced violence more directly into the political process. As the professional

MASSACRES A PARIS LES 2, 3, 4, 5 ET 6 SEPTEMBRE 1792

D'après une estampe allemande conservée à la Bibliothèque nationale. — A gauche, le couvent des Carmes où fut égorgé l'archevêque d'Arles qui offrait son sang pour apaiser les meurtriers; à droite, est figurée la prison de l'Abbaye; au fond, le Temple; et, sur une terrasse, Louis XVI et Marie-Antoinette à laquelle un forcené présente la tête de la princesse de Lamballe au bout d'une pique. A cette vue, la reine s'évanouit. — Le 2 septembre, au bruit du tocsin ordonné par Danton, la tuerie commence, elle dure six jours et cinq nuits. On compte 1,368 meurtres (MORTIMER-TERNAUX, *Histoire de la Terreur*, III, p. 548); et, « parmi les morts, deux cent cinquante prêtres, trois évêques ou archevêques, des officiers généraux, des magistrats, un ancien ministre, une princesse du sang, un nègre, des femmes du peuple, des gamins, des forçats, de vieux pauvres. » (TAINE, *La Révolution*, II, p. 307.)

Peter Newark's Historical Pictures

A pro-royalist contemporary print of the September Massacres of 1792 in Paris, in which the people's resentment at generations of repression exploded into murderous riots, which left some 1,300 people dead.

reactionary armies invaded France in 1792, their commander, the duke of Brunswick, issued a manifesto threatening "exemplary and memorable vengeance" against Paris if the king should be harmed. The response of the Paris crowd was to storm the royal palace (massacring its defenders, the king's Swiss Guard) in August 1792, an action that led to the deposition and execution of the king. The next month saw more violence in the "September Massacres," when the inmates of jails were murdered by terrified crowds fearing a reactionary uprising in Paris.

By June 1793, the dominant politicians in Paris were the so-called "Montagnards" – radicals who had benefited from the violence of the people of Paris and for whom compromise was impossible. They found themselves fighting for a war not only against most of their European neighbors, but against enemies within France. Their extreme policies alienated opinion over much of the country, including important cities such as Lyon and Bordeaux, and whole sections of the countryside, especially in the west.

In a situation of internal and external crisis, and under pressure from the revolutionaries, who were worried about rising food prices, the Montagnard politicians declared terror to be the "the order of the day" on September 5, 1793.

THE REIGN OF TERROR

The range of policies implemented under the Reign of Terror included a surveillance of people and opinions, and the expulsion or imprisonment of political enemies, including fellow republicans such as the Girondins, as well as of counterrevolutionaries and royalists. The Montagnards enacted harsh repressive legislation against the rebels, together with laws confiscating the lands and wealth of the nobles and the clergy who had emigrated.

The Terror saw the introduction of policies aimed at securing broad popular support. Notable here was the policy of the Maximum – state price-fixing and other economic measures. The Montagnards also introduced radical educational reforms, abolished slavery, and attempted to create a system of state pensions and support (what would now be called a welfare state), and made plans for land redistribution.

During the time when the Terror was official state policy, France was governed by the Committee, which was set up in April 1793, and consisted of 12 members of the Convention, to which it reported. The members of the Committee never changed when it was at the height of its powers between July 1793 and July 1794. Robespierre was its principal spokesman on policy matters. A number of initiatives, notably the move to establish a new state religion, the Cult of the Supreme Being, were largely his idea. Not all the members shared his political views. Louis de Saint-Just and Bertrand Barère were Robespierre's closest Montagnard allies, but Jean Nicolat Billaud-Varenne and Jean Marie Collot-d'Herbois had strong links with Parisian extremists and were more radical than Robespierre himself.

The Committee controlled every aspect of government but some members were responsible for implementing particular policies. Lazare Carnot and Jean Bon Saint André, for example, were effectively war and navy ministers, respectively.

THE APPARATUS OF DEATH

Although the Committee had wide-ranging powers, it was not in sole control of the Terror in France. State security, political policing, and counterespionage were in the hands of the 12-strong Committee of General Security, which reported to the Committee of Public Safety but acted independently at times. The Paris Revolutionary Tribunal tried counterrevolutionary offenses and was under their joint control.

Key organizers and revolutionary activists in the provinces, the "representatives on mission," were deputies from the Convention sent out to maintain central authority in the country at large. They worked closely with local administrative bodies, political clubs, surveillance committees, and local paramilitary forces. These representatives could also act independently, although they were supposed to work closely with the Committee. Representatives in provinces affected by civil war carried out the most horrific examples of terror. The suppression of revolts in Marseille and Toulon was accompanied by a policy of shooting hundreds of prisoners, under the orders of the Representative Fréron. At Lyon, revolutionaries retook the city and executed over 2,000 "enemies of the people;" while at Nantes, Representative Jean Baptiste Carrier had thousands of prisoners loaded into boats that were scuttled in the Loire river. News of such events, especially of the mass drownings (*noyades*), led the Committee to recall all of the more violent representatives in the spring of 1794.

THE AFTERMATH

The Reign of Terror was marked by mass political mobilization. France's army swelled to over a million out of a total population of 28 million, while membership of political clubs may have exceeded even this.

The repressive effects of the Terror were considerable. The Revolutionary Tribunal executed fewer than 3,000 people in Paris. But deaths in revolutionary jails throughout the country totaled 12,000 out of the 500,000 imprisoned as political suspects at this time.

Deaths were particularly high in the main areas of civil war, notably in the west around the Vendée department, and the Rhône valley, particularly in Lyon. These areas, together with Paris, accounted for 90 percent of known deaths. Recent research suggests that the previously accepted total of 30,000-40,000 deaths throughout the Reign of Terror, spectacularly underestimates the extent of population losses in the Vendée alone. Revolutionary forces implemented policies of razing everything to the ground to reduce counterrevolutionary peasant royalism. Total deaths in the west over the 1790s as a whole, including deaths of revolutionaries caused by the Vendée rebels and deaths from semi-famine conditions in certain years, may well have reached 200,000.

Contrary to a well-established myth, the vast majority of victims of the Terror were not aristocrats. Nobles accounted for only 20 percent of those executed in Paris, only 10 percent of individuals executed by other revolutionary courts, and an even smaller number of those executed in civil war conditions.

TERROR AFTER ROBESPIERRE

The need for terror ceased in 1794, when revolutionary forces had contained civil insurrection within France and victories against the anti-French coalition in Europe had transformed the military situation. Some members of the Committee, including Robespierre, wanted to continue a policy of national regeneration. The Committee members used state terror to establish

Hulton Getty Picture Collection

Maximilien Robespierre: the French Revolution's great "incorruptible" or its most brutal dictator?

a "Republic of Virtue" and also to step up repression, even though threats to the Republic were receding. The Paris Revolutionary Tribunal executed more individuals in June and July 1794 than in all its previous period of existence. Robespierre himself kept a small book in which he would write the name of anyone who opposed him in debate, terrorizing enemies into silence. Eventually, a conspiracy of deputies from both left and right brought about the coup d'état of Thermidor on July 27, 1794, which toppled Robespierre and his allies.

VIGILANTES AND COUNTERTERROR

After the removal of Robespierre's faction, the Convention gradually removed the most striking features of the Reign of Terror. It curbed the wide powers of the Committee and recalled the representatives on mission. It dissolved the popular societies, abolished the Maximum, and freed hundreds of political prisoners.

The Convention was replaced by the Directory in 1795. The regime was no longer provisional and, with the military situation fairly secure, there seemed no need for the emergency measures of the Terror. But the fall of Robespierre unleashed a White Terror – vigilante attacks on and assassination of ex-terrorists by disgruntled victims of the Terror.

White Terror was pronounced in the south of France, where royalist murder gangs such as the Company of Jehu and the Company of the Sun operated. It was also common in the west of France, where rural bandits operated in the Vendée and Brittany, home of royalist peasant rebels called Chouans. After Napoleon came to power in 1799, he set up special courts to break the resistance of the peasant rebels.

NAPOLEON AND ASSASSINATION

Napoleon added one extra string to the bow of state terror pioneered in the French Revolution: state-led assassination of political enemies. The Committee had distanced itself from the popular lynchings enacted by the crowd of Paris during the September Massacres and assassination as state policy. Napoleon, however, may have used this policy in 1804 to kidnap and execute the duc d'Enghien, grandson of France's most active counterrevolutionary, the prince of Condé, and a relative of the exiled king Louis XVIII.

Although historians have not proved Napoleon's personal involvement in the assassination, this act compromised his reputation in Europe. Subsequent commentators, however, have inseparably linked the Terror in the French Revolution not with Napoleon, but with the era of the Committee under Robespierre.

Colin Jones

SEE ALSO: THE PARIS COMMUNE: STATE TERROR; FRENCH ANARCHIST TERROR; THEORIES OF TERROR IN URBAN INSURRECTIONS.

FURTHER READING

- Doyle, W. *The Oxford History of the French Revolution.* New York and Oxford: Oxford University Press, 1989.
- Furet, F., and M. Ozouf, eds. *A Critical Dictionary of the French Revolution.* Cambridge, MA: Belknap Press, 1989.
- Jordan, D. *The Revolutionary Career of Maximilien Robespierre.* New York: Free Press, 1985.
- Schama, Simon. *Citizens: A Chronicle of the French Revolution.* New York: Knopf, and London: Penguin, 1989.

THE PARIS COMMUNE: STATE TERROR

In the late nineteenth century, terror as an instrument of government was a distant memory for the people of France. But in 1871, nearly 80 years after Robespierre's infamous Reign of Terror, violence returned to the streets of Paris.

Like the Terror of 1793-94, the violence that occurred in Paris from March to May 1871 was the result of war. During the Terror, however, the violence was a matter of national emergency. In 1871, the violence occurred because of bitterness at the humiliating defeat in the Franco-Prussian War.

In an attempt to resolve the political and social turmoil into which France fell after the defeat, the government called national elections. Provincial France as a whole voted for the Monarchists, not because they particularly wanted a king but because the Monarchists were the only political group who stood for peace. But Paris voted for Republican factions, and the citizens of the poorer districts believed they could lead a radical national revolution.

KEY FACTS

- In 1871, after the crushing defeat of France by Prussia, the left-wing working classes of Paris rebelled against the new French government.
- The Parisian rebels began systematically terrorizing other sections of society. They executed hundreds of their enemies without formal trial.
- Government troops used terrorism as they recaptured Paris. The soldiers set up execution squads in the Père Lachaise cemetery and in the Luxembourg Gardens. These squads shot at least 25,000 residents of working class areas.
- The radicals of Paris led four revolutions between 1789 and 1871, but, after the crushing of the Commune, there was no further uprising until 1968.

The new parliament, the National Assembly, sat in Versailles, outside Paris, while the government set up its offices in the capital. The head of the government, Adophe Thiers, immediately set about establishing his authority against open armed opposition from the Paris National Guard. He sent army units into the city to seize the rebel weapons and, around Montmartre, soldiers confronted a crowd of national guards and civilians. Shots fired from the crowd hit two generals.

The situation soon became very ugly, and the government withdrew to Versailles. For a week, Paris had no administration at all. Parisian officials held city elections. On March 28, 1871, before a crowd estimated by some at 100,000, the officials proclaimed the Commune of Paris. Civil war began five days later.

CHAOS LEADS TO TERROR

Authority in France disintegrated, and a cycle of violence, terror, and reprisal filled the vacuum. Communication between the various parties collapsed. The government was out of touch with the realities of opinion in Paris; while the population of Paris was ignorant of government attitudes. Neither was there any communication or understanding between the moderate provinces and radical Paris.

Nobody knew who was in control. Thiers had his government, but the Monarchist-dominated Assembly effectively set up another, known as the Committee of Fifteen. Similarly, the army in Versailles had no commander until April. The situation in Paris was even worse. Five political bodies could have claimed to be the city government.

In such chaos, violence ran unchecked. The first stage was a few on-the-spot executions by the army at Versailles. Perhaps two dozen Parisians were shot in April. But the rumor in Paris was that government forces had executed 50, 100, or even as many as 200 people. The damage was done. Pressure for reprisals

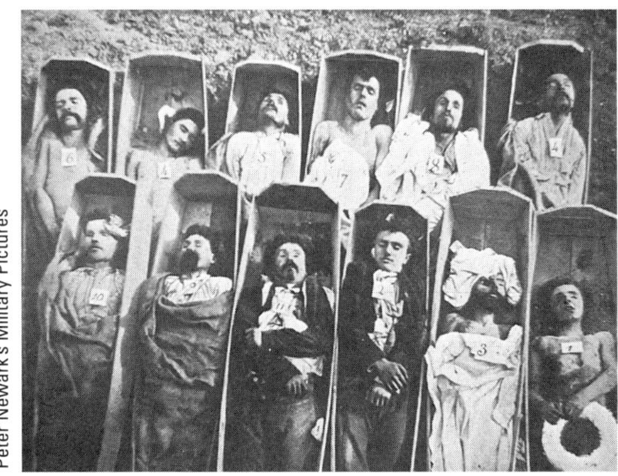

Peter Newark's Military Pictures

Corpses of Communard rebels executed by French troops are displayed to terrorize other resisters.

built up in the Paris press and in the poor eastern districts of the capital.

This led the Council of the Commune to pass a "Law of Hostages," allowing them to seize and execute government figures, although few of the councillors wanted it put into action. There was, however, a small group at the Préfecture of Police who did want to pursue the idea. Their aged hero, Auguste Blanqui, was notorious for conspiring against every French regime since 1815 and was once more in prison. The group was directed by Raoul Rigault, a talented organizer in his early twenties, who set up his own Committee of General Security. In effect, this was a government within a government.

On his own initiative, Rigault ordered the arrest of a number of Republicans, who received no protection from the Monarchist-dominated Assembly. Rigault also arrested various priests and, after trumping up evidence of a plot, the Archbishop of Paris, Georges Darboy. Using the "Law of Hostages" as a pretext, Rigault's Committee tried to obtain from the Versailles government a pledge to stop the summary executions and an exchange of their prisoners for Blanqui.

Secret letters were exchanged between the archbishop in Mazas prison and Thiers in Versailles. They achieved nothing. The negotiators contacted diplomats from other European countries, but none wanted to get involved. Finally, U.S. Ambassador Washburne, who had kept his embassy open, offered his services.

While Washburne was fruitlessly negotiating in Versailles, the Commune's council adopted a procedure for formally determining which of its prisoners were to be designated hostages. On April 26, Rigault had himself nominated as public prosecutor, giving him direct responsibility for this matter. The prisoners' prospects began to look bleak.

Only one formal trial actually took place. Commune officials declared 12 men from Montmartre "hostages," and then adjourned the session. The Commune authorities never reconvened the court because, two days afterward, on Sunday, May 21, 50,000 Versailles troops advanced, virtually unopposed, into western Paris. In the evening the street battles for central and eastern Paris began. The Versailles army committed atrocities on a massive scale almost at once. Among the victims was Raoul Rigault. Washburne, in the meantime, had failed to persuade the government at Versailles even to consider an exchange of Darboy for Blanqui.

The execution of the 12 hostages from Montmartre was carried out by supporters of the Commune (Communards), all of whom had lost relatives in the fighting. There were more than 100 volunteers for the first execution squad. Archbishop Darboy was among the first to be shot.

By May 28, the army had captured the city. The Assembly took control of government, and the brief terror of 1871 ended with the demise of the Commune. The hostage-taking of the Communards had had little effect on events, save to inflame the feeling of the Versailles troops. However, the atrocities committed by the Versailles troops could be said to have been a very efficient use of terror.

Paris had been the driving force behind revolution in 1789-94, in 1830, in 1848–50, and again in 1871. Yet in 1871, the conservative provinces took their revenge and crushed the left-wing capital.

Gregor Dallas

SEE ALSO: TERROR IN THE FRENCH REVOLUTION 1789-1815.

FURTHER READING

- Christiansen, Rupert. *Paris Babylon: The Story of the Paris Commune.* New York: Penguin, 1996.
- Gibson, W. *Paris During the Commune.* London: Whittaker, 1872; New York: Haskell House, 1974.
- Tombs, R. *The War Against Paris, 1871.* Cambridge and New York: Cambridge University Press, 1981.

TERROR IN COLONIAL CONQUESTS

The establishment of European empires over much of the world from the eighteenth century onward involved the widescale use of terror. Fundamentally, this was because the conquerors considered the conquered to be inferior, and were able to justify using terror by pointing to the "barbarous" practices of their victims. This use of terror was evident from the early period of Spanish conquest in the Americas in the sixteenth century. It accelerated, however, during the period after 1850, when European technological superiority became more evident.

During this period, several European powers, including Great Britain, France, Belgium, Portugal, and Germany, secured lands in Asia and Africa, while the Japanese had designs on East Asia. In most cases, colonial rulers thought and behaved as if subject peoples were inferior. In the nineteenth century, many aboriginal peoples in Australia and the Americas were hunted down and killed or forced into reservations simply because they got in the way of European settlers.

"SAVAGE WARS"

Wars by Europeans against Africans or Asians were termed "savage wars"; as compared to the "civilized wars" between Europeans. The terms came into being because many native societies had no concept of either surrender or a distinction between combatants and civilians. Brutality, massacre, and torture were frequent occurrences even before Europeans arrived.

Colonial armies often had access to more modern weapons than their enemies. So colonial conquest inflicted unprecedented violence on many societies in Africa and Asia. Brutal methods were employed, including burning villages and crops, and murdering civilians and prisoners. Terror tactics subdued hostile civilian populations. During the Dutch pacification of Borneo in the 1850s, a Dutch official told the military not to listen to the "voice of humanity"; while a French officer fighting in Madagascar in the late 1890s reported that "the punishment was terrible; we burned all rebel villages and cut off all rebel heads."

In nearly all colonial wars the imperial states recruited local allies whom they did not restrain on the battlefield. The French advancing into Chad in 1898 used terror to force people to become bearers. In East Africa during World War I, all the colonial powers used threats and violence to secure bearers, of whom about 100,000 died. Bearers sometimes included women and children, as in the Ashanti campaigns in Africa during 1873-74 and 1895-96.

Resistance to colonial rule was often put down with great brutality, as during the Indian Mutiny of 1857 and the Morant Bay rebellion in Jamaica in 1865. In many cases, colonial rulers used their military and judicial powers to exact revenge and to demonstrate their coercive power. The many people who died in anti-colonial revolts in Asia and Africa demonstrate the harsh means and tactics used to crush resistance.

Colonial powers responded to resistance to their authority with severe punishments. Africans were dynamited in caves in the 1896-97 Rhodesian risings against British rule. The British also put down the Zulu rising of 1906 in Natal, southern Africa, with great ferocity. In India, British soldiers killed 400 protesters at Amritsar in 1919. The Herero tribes resisting the Germans in South West Africa were driven into the desert to die. In the 1905-06 Maji Maji rising in Tanganyika (part of modern Tanzania) against the

KEY FACTS

- Colonial powers often used terror policies in order to suppress resistance by natives to their conquests and continued exercise of authority.
- Europeans in Tasmania persecuted Aborigines ruthlessly. The natives became extinct less than a century after the first European settlement.
- Some local peoples fought back. The Zulus wiped out a British army of 1,500 men in 1879. The Ethiopians defeated an Italian army at Adowa in 1896 and remained independent until 1936.

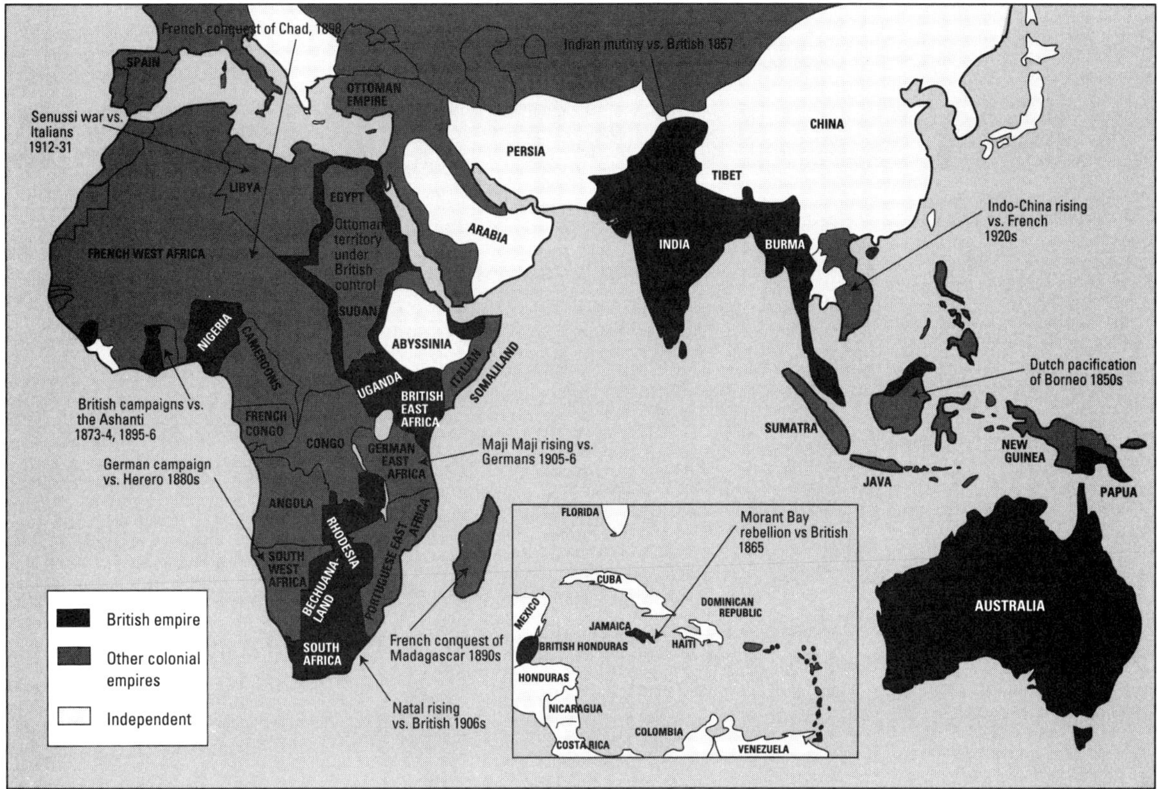

A map of colonial empires in 1898 showing clashes between colonialists and indigenous peoples.

Germans, as many as 100,000 people died. The French killed 60,000-100,000 people during the 1947 revolt in Madagascar. The occasional protests by humanitarians in Europe had little effect; they were too distant, too few, and too late.

TWENTIETH-CENTURY HORROR

Colonial conquest and pacification continued into the twentieth century. Terror policies were extensively used by the authoritarian regimes of Italy and Japan in the 1930s. Both powers used the latest machines and means of war against less technologically advanced peoples. In 1931, the Italians brutally crushed Senussi resistance to their rule in Libya. In the mid-1930s, they attacked Abyssinia (modern Ethiopia) with tanks, aircraft, bombs, and gas. They murdered civilian hostages in an attempt to break Abyssinian resistance.

Japanese attacks on China in 1937 led to mass murder, as in the killing of 100,000 people during the "Rape of Nanking." Similarly brutal methods were used by the Japanese military in many parts of Southeast Asia from 1942 to 1945. With such figures in mind, it is hardly surprising that terrorism in colonial struggles has been so bloody.

Antony B. Shaw

SEE ALSO: THE AMRITSAR MASSACRE; JAPANESE TERROR IN THE FAR EAST; JAPANESE TERRORIZATION OF PRISONERS; TERRORISM IN COLONIAL INDIA 1900-1947.

FURTHER READING

- Olson, James. S. et al., eds. *Historical Dictionary of the British Empire.* Westport, CT: Greenwood Press, 1996.
- Porter, A. N. *European Imperialism.* Basingstoke, Hampshire: Macmillan, 1994.
- Smith, Woodruff D. *European Imperialism in the Nineteenth and Twentieth Centuries.* Chicago: Nelson-Hall, 1982.

RUSSIAN ANARCHIST TERROR

The frequent use of the word *anarchism* does not conceal the fact that it is not a precise term. This imprecision is due to the wide variety of political and social theories included under this heading. In the aftermath of the French Revolution, anarchism became synonymous with chaos, revolutionary terror, and politically motivated murder. By the late nineteenth century, assassination plots were the trademark of several political movements that based their actions on anarchist writings.

NO NEED FOR GOVERNMENT

Anarchism generally describes a principle or theory of life and conduct in which society exists without a government. Harmony is obtained not by submission to law or by obedience to an established authority, but by free agreement between the various groups of society. The key principle is voluntarism – the free association of free individuals. This principle may include voluntary revolutionary activity. This is based on belief in the existence of a dormant, revolutionary popular energy. Anarchists have contended that this energy could be unleashed by propaganda or by terror, the so-called propaganda of action.

The idea of the propaganda of action was particularly common in nineteenth-century Russian anarchism. Unlike in Western Europe, anarchist theories did not take root in Russia until the middle of the century. Their full development is particularly associated with one charismatic figure, Mikhail Bakunin. Like so many Russian anarchists, Bakunin was born of an aristocratic family and served briefly as an officer in the Imperial Guard. In 1835, he resigned his commission, disgusted by the oppressive character of Czarist autocracy.

Under the influence of the writings of the German philosopher G. W. F. Hegel and the French anarchist Pierre J. Proudhon, Bakunin developed his own brand of anarchism. For most of his life Bakunin lived abroad. For his participation in the 1848-49 revolution in Germany, however, Bakunin was handed over to the Russian authorities. In 1855, he was banished to eastern Siberia, from where he escaped to the United States and then to Britain in 1861. He spent the rest of his life in exile, mostly in Switzerland.

FREEING THE ENSLAVED MASSES

Bakunin's revolutionary anarchism was extremely frank and comprehensive in its destructiveness. He rejected all ideal systems, in whatever shape or name, from the idea of God downward, and every form of external authority, be it monarchic or parliamentary. According to Bakunin, each form of authority enslaves a large majority of the people. To free the enslaved majority, he argued, existing society had to be overturned. For this purpose, Bakunin developed a revolutionary system that had to be pursued without scruples of morality, religion, or private feelings.

Although Bakunin spent most of his politically active life outside Russia, his periodic expressions of a belief in a revolt by the oppressed Russian peasants found ready admirers there. Bakunin's most important remaining link with Russia was through Sergei Nechayev. In 1869, after meeting Bakunin in Switzerland a year earlier, Nechayev set up a revolutionary organization in Moscow, the Narodnaya Rasprava (the People's Reckoning). Though suppressed by the government in the same year, parts

KEY FACTS

- The anarchist movement in Russia began with a group of 44 people and never rose above 500, out of a population of nearly 100 million.
- In January 1878, the mass trial of 193 anarchists prompted the movement's first terrorist act, the shooting of the St. Petersburg police chief.
- After the arrests of key activists in 1881 and 1882, the anarchist party fell under the influence of left-wing radicals, including Alexander Ulyanov, brother of the future Bolshevik leader, Lenin.

Hulton Getty Picture Collection

Czar Alexander II is killed by a bomb planted by the terrorist group, the People's Will, on March 1, 1881.

of the organization survived, to be replaced in 1873 by a mass movement known as Back to the People. The movement derived its name from a pamphlet written by Alexander Herzen entitled *Narod* (To the People).

Herzen's pamphlet, an appeal to Russia's youth, made a strong impact in student circles. Its title gave a name to the revolutionary movement which began to develop in 1870s known as the Narodniki (Populists). Their activities were initially confined to propaganda – their main aim was to preach a vague revolutionary message to the rural masses. Despite these propagandist efforts to stir up the peasants against the injustices of the Czarist regime, the masses remained inert. As followers of Bakunin, however, Populists continued to believe that the peasants were instinctive rebels who would rise up once they were told that their strength lay in their vast numbers.

FROM WORDS TO VIOLENCE

Disillusioned with the negligible effect of their radical propaganda on the people, the most determined and political radicals were driven toward terrorism. The shift indicated their increasing isolation from the object of their liberation movement, the rural masses.

In the fall of 1879, this minority took the name of Narodnaya Volya (the People's Will). It was a secret organization which comprised 30 members; it was dedicated to fighting the Czarist regime using systematic terror in the hope of kindling the revolutionary energy of the peasants. On its founding, the executive committee of the organization passed a death sentence on Czar Alexander II. The assassination of the Czar was now the group's prime objective. The People's Will was the first terrorist group in Russian history and a model for later groups. The very existence of this group resulted in terrorist violence becoming a recognized means of opposition.

The People's Will was as secretive as it was elitist. Indeed, the organization's name was a misnomer. The people had become an abstract concept with no equivalent in the real world. It was, however, on behalf of the people that the People's Will assumed the authority to speak. The organization's objective was to assassinate government officials and, ultimately, the Czar himself. This, it was hoped, would help to undermine the regime and break down the mystique surrounding rulers.

ASSASSINATING THE CZAR

The terrorist campaign launched by the People's Will caught the government unprepared. Still, three times the organization failed in its attempts to assassinate the Czar. These failures led to a considerable thinning of the membership of the People's Will.

The police arrested the guiding figures of the group, including A. D. Mikhailov. Sofya Perovskaya now carried on the activities of the dwindling organization. It was Perovskaya who achieved the group's main objective, by organizing the assassination of the Czar. On March 1, 1881, Alexander II fell victim to a terrorist bomb. But the assassination did not produce the desired political results: the peasantry did not rise; moderate urban public opinion was horrified; and the radical cause lost support. Anarchist terrorism, exemplified by the Populists, had run its course.

Thomas G. Otte

SEE ALSO: FRENCH ANARCHIST TERROR; THEORIES OF TERROR IN URBAN INSURRECTIONS.

FURTHER READING

- Avrich, Paul. *Anarchist Portraits*. Princeton, NJ: Princeton University Press, 1988.
- Avrich, Paul. *The Russian Anarchists*. Westport, CT: Greenwood Press, 1980.
- Joll, James. *The Anarchists*. London: Methuen, 1979; Cambridge, MA: Harvard University Press, 1980.

FRENCH ANARCHIST TERROR

Anarchism in the late nineteenth century is popularly associated with terrorist violence by sinister conspirators. Bombs in public places and attempted murders of individuals by anarchists became increasingly widespread in Europe and the United States from the 1880s to the 1900s. These attacks claimed their most prominent victims through the assassinations of politicians or members of royal families, including Canovas del Castillo, prime minister of Spain, in 1892; the Empress Elizabeth of Austria in 1898; King Umberto of Italy in 1900; and President McKinley in 1901.

The practice of terrorism was intended to be propaganda by the deed, but it was only one aspect of anarchism at a particular period. The nature of anarchist theory excluded large-scale political movements geared to fighting in the public arena to conquer state power. There were widespread claims in the press that a Black International of anarchists was orchestrating the violence, but although the tactic had been approved at international anarchist meetings in 1880 and 1881, such decisions did not lead to concerted action by anarchists.

The reality was one of scattered small groups or isolated individuals who shared some measure of common ideology and in some cases shared readership of the same books or periodicals. International contacts between anarchists were made largely on an individual level when activists moved from one country to another, often as exiles.

The question was how to promote the move from capitalism under state authority to an anarchistic form of social organization. This implied either gradual change through teaching and example, or else some form of revolution, or a combination of the two. However, even those who believed in revolution did not necessarily think in terms of armed overthrow by systematic violence. The revolutionary general strike was one example of a non-violent anarchist weapon.

KEY FACTS

- Anarchist terrorism began in France in the early 1880s and was largely abandoned by 1895.
- Léon-Jules Léauthier's stabbing of a Serb diplomat in a Paris café in November 1893 shocked French society. Cafés were widely used as friendly meeting places and the attack did much to lose public support for the anarchists.
- In August 1894, the French authorities put 30 French anarchists on trial in Paris. The public objected to the atmosphere of the show trial, and the jury acquitted 27 of the defendants.

ANARCHIST TERRORISM

The idea of using terrorism as a weapon of propaganda had begun to take root in anarchist circles during the 1870s. The meeting of Russians Sergei Nechayev and Mikhail Bakunin in Geneva in 1869 led to collaborative production of a number of pamphlets expounding the notion of terrorism. The successful assassination of Czar Alexander II in 1881 also played its part in spreading the attraction of acts of violence against persons and/or property seen as symbols of the established social order.

Meanwhile, in Italy, Errico Malatesta, Carlo Cafiero, and others had fomented attempts at insurrection intended to stir the oppressed classes to spontaneous revolt. These actions were abortive and extremely limited in scope. Nevertheless, they contributed to the spread of ideas concerning propaganda by the deed. This term meant, in effect, seeking to carry out exemplary acts of violence against symbolic targets to raise the awareness among the oppressed and to spread fear among the oppressors.

The fact that the perpetrators of terrorist acts were often caught and subjected to execution or long prison sentences created martyrs. At first, this only served to encourage recruitment. Furthermore, the trials of suspected anarchists also provided a pulpit in the courtroom where they could proclaim their views.

Hulton Getty Picture Collection

June 24, 1894: French president Sadi-Carnot is assassinated in Lyon by the anarchist Santo Caserio.

In France, with its revolutionary tradition still alive despite the bloody suppression of the Paris Commune of 1871, anarchist theorists preached propaganda by the deed in the 1880s. Yet there were few significant acts of terrorism in France during that period and some of those that were attributed to anarchists may not have been their work. By the early 1890s, some theorists were becoming increasingly wary of terrorism and favored more patient means of spreading the word. But by then a number of anarchists, inspired at least in part by the writings of revolt, were turning to acts of terrorism.

ASSASSINATION ATTEMPTS

The peak of anarchist outrages in France occurred in 1892-94, with 11 significant bombings and many lesser incidents. The most notorious of the bombings were those committed by Emile Henry, François-Claudius Ravachol (two attempts to blow up judicial officers), and Auguste Vaillant (a bomb hurled down on parliamentarians in the Chamber of Deputies). Sometimes the weapon of attack was the knife or the gun, as when Charles Gallo fired off shots in the Paris stock exchange in 1886, and when Santo Caserio stabbed President Sadi-Carnot to death on June 24, 1894, on a public street.

The motives of the attacker were often complicated by personal desperation or by criminality. Nevertheless, their shared aim was to destabilize bourgeois society, avenging the suffering of the oppressed and that of earlier, martyred terrorists. Their hope was to serve as pointers toward revolution so that the working masses would in turn rise up.

These outrages gave the authorities the pretext they wanted for taking determined action. In the spring of 1894, there were over 100 anarchists in custody in French prisons waiting for trial on some charge or other. Doubts now hung over the value of propaganda by the deed.

Nevertheless, anarchist commentators tended not to condemn the terrorists outright. They had to acknowledge the extent to which terrorism attracted massive publicity. Although terrorist attacks were the object of frenzied denunciations in the mainstream press, anarchism also profited from these acts. This was especially true in avant-garde circles, where anarchism gained a following for a time. Furthermore, there was some unwillingness among the public to endorse wholesale repression of the movement.

After 1894, anarchist terrorism largely ceased in France. Instead, propaganda was carried out through writing, education, and the development of anarcho-syndicates. Increasingly, the anarchists influenced French labor unions through Syndicalism. Syndicalism preached an anarchic society composed of individuals linked into unions by class or trade and freely cooperating without a state apparatus. The Syndicalist movement was behind the strikes of 1909, but was swept away by the patriotic mobilization of 1914. The last expression of anarchism had failed.

Chris Flood

SEE ALSO: RUSSIAN ANARCHIST TERROR; THEORIES OF TERROR IN URBAN INSURRECTIONS.

FURTHER READING

- Avrich, Paul. *Anarchist Portraits.* Princeton, NJ: Princeton University Press, 1988.
- Joll, James. *The Anarchists.* London: Methuen, 1979; Cambridge, MA: Harvard University Press, 1980.
- Sonn, Richard D. *Anarchism.* New York: Twayne, 1992.

TERROR'S USE IN MACEDONIA 1893-1934

In the Balkans, almost 40 percent of the historic region of Macedonia now belongs to the Republic of Macedonia. The rest is shared between Bulgaria and Greece. Between the fourteenth century and early twentieth centuries, Macedonia lay within the Ottoman Turkish empire and was administratively divided into three provinces.

The population, numbered at 2.5 million according to the Turkish census of 1904, was divided by nationality. The largest group comprised Orthodox Christian Slav-speakers. Most of these defined themselves as Bulgarians and spoke a language closely akin to Bulgarian. There were also large numbers of Albanians, Serbs, Greeks, Muslim Slavs, Vlachs, and Turks. The economy was mainly rural.

RIPE FOR REVOLUTION

In the nineteenth century, the Ottoman empire in Europe was disintegrating. Greece, Serbia, Romania, and Bulgaria became independent states. Macedonia remained within the empire, where its population was subject to heavy tax and the arbitrary rule of local administrators. But Turkish rule in the Macedonian provinces was largely confined to the main cities and communication routes. The weakness of Turkish authority in the countryside made possible the emergence of a revolutionary organization – with terrorism at its core.

KEY FACTS

- In 1902, the Ottoman authorities amassed over 300,000 troops in Macedonia in response to the Supremacist revolt. Albanian and Ottoman irregulars supported the authorities, intimidating the local population by raping and murdering villagers.
- A revolutionary organization (later known as IMRO) rose up the next year, 1903, burning haystacks, destroying bridges and telegraph lines, occupying strategic centres, and intimidating village headmen.
- In 1993 the Yugoslav republic of Macedonia declared itself independent, leading to disputes with Greece and Serbia.

"FREEDOM OR DEATH"

The Internal Macedonian Revolutionary Organization (IMRO) was founded in 1893 in Thessaloniki, although it was only so named in 1906. At its start, IMRO committed itself to "freedom or death," and to ridding Macedonian territory of Turkish rule.

Nevertheless, IMRO was divided as to its other goals. Some members wanted to create an autonomous Macedonian state as the focus of a Balkan federation of Christian Slavonic peoples. Others saw the liberation of Macedonia as the forerunner of annexation by Bulgaria. IMRO was followed in 1895 by the establishment of an "external" counterpart, based in Bulgaria and known as the Supremacists. This group supported the aim of Macedonia's inclusion in the Bulgarian state.

Although IMRO claimed its support was strongest among the peasantry, its members came mostly from the intellectual and professional classes. IMRO was based upon a network of cells, grouped within a hierarchy of local and regional committees, and headed by a central committee. Warbands, or *chetas*, usually consisting of 15-20 men, operated largely independently of this framework.

THE MOST EFFECTIVE TERROR TACTICS

The principal tactic of IMRO was to commit spectacular terrorist acts in order to draw the attention of the great powers to the plight of the Macedonians. IMRO also wanted to force reprisals that would attract the peasantry to become members of IMRO.

Internal records, however, show disputes between those who favored a general insurrection and those who recommended terrorist acts. After 1897, members of IMRO engaged in sporadic violence, including the murder of Turkish border guards and Ottoman sympa-

In the late nineteenth century, Macedonia was divided among three provinces of the Ottoman empire in the central Balkans.

thizers. Since membership dues secured very little money, IMRO's *comitadji* or "committee-men" had to raise money through extortion, kidnapping, and protection rackets.

GOVERNMENT RESPONSE

The Ottoman authorities responded to IMRO's activities with mass arrests and the destruction of villages of supposed sympathizers. IMRO was also involved in running battles with members of the Bulgaria-based Supremacists and with pro-Serbian and pro-Greek guerrilla units operating in Macedonia. They were ill-equipped to keep a revolutionary movement going and support among the local population was never particularly strong. In 1903, IMRO could scarcely muster 40,000 activists.

In 1902, the Macedonian Supremacists had launched a revolt in Macedonia, which was rapidly suppressed. Fearful in case its own networks were uncovered in the crackdown, IMRO launched its own uprising in August 1903. This was known as the St. Elijah's Day (Illinden) Uprising, and was followed some days later by the Resurrection Day (Preobrazhenski) Rising in the region of Adrianople, which bordered Macedonia. Neither rebellion gathered much support among the peasantry. By mid-September, the revolt was largely over, although the Ottoman authorities were forced to promise that they would make reforms.

THE DEMISE OF THE ORGANIZATION

After the failure of the Illinden-Preobrazhenski Uprisings, IMRO's influence waned. Macedonia never achieved independence, but was partitioned among neighboring Serbia, Bulgaria, and Greece after the Balkan Wars of 1912-13 and World War I. Between 1918 and 1939, IMRO engaged in terrorist actions to liberate those parts of Macedonia that had been incorporated into Yugoslavia in 1919, and to set up an effective state-within-a-state at Petrich on the Bulgarian-Yugoslav border. IMRO also mounted terror attacks against the Bulgarian government and in 1923 were involved in the assassination of the Bulgarian prime minister. In 1934, a new Bulgarian government, installed in the wake of a military coup, effectively broke up IMRO.

With the collapse of communism in Yugoslavia, IMRO reformed in Macedonia in 1990. But it was now a nationalist political party, not a terrorist organization.

Martyn Rady

SEE ALSO: WORLD WAR II RESISTANCE IN YUGOSLAVIA AND TERRORISM; TERROR IN THE FORMER YUGOSLAVIA.

FURTHER READING

- Jelavich, Charles, and Barbara Jelavich. *The Establishment of the Balkan National States, 1804-1920.* Seattle: University of Washington Press, 1986.
- Perry, Duncan. *The Politics of Terror: The Macedonian Revolutionary Movements, 1893-1903.* Durham, NC: Duke University Press, 1988.
- Pribichevich, Stoyan. *Macedonia: Its People and History.* University Park: Pennsylvania State University Press, 1982.

ASSASSINATION AT SARAJEVO 1914

Few cases of terrorist murder had such momentous consequences as the assassination of Archduke Franz Ferdinand, the heir to the Habsburg throne and future ruler of the multi-ethnic Austro-Hungarian empire. The event triggered a chain reaction among the powers of Europe, resulting in the outbreak of World War I (1914-18). At the war's end, the monarchies of Eastern and Central Europe were swept away; the political map of Europe was redrawn; and the seeds of World War II were sown.

It was hardly surprising that the Archduke Franz Ferdinand should be a target for extremist nationalist groups in the Balkans. The withdrawl of the Ottoman empire from the Balkans in the course of the nineteenth century left a power vacuum which Austria-Hungary and its rival power in the region, Russia, were keen to fill. Austria annexed Bosnia in 1908, causing great resentment among parts of the population who had hoped for some measure of independence from foreign powers. Serbia, the largest most powerful Balkan state and enjoying the backing of Austria's rival, Russia, was also bitterly opposed to the move. Bosnia, then as now, had a large population of Serbs, giving Serbia a reason to lay claim to the land. There was no hope of the Serbian government taking on the fading, but still mighty, Austrian empire. But extreme nationalists began to form secret underground societies whose aim was to destabilize the region using terrorist tactics.

KEY FACTS

- Resentment of Austrian rule in Bosnia was concentrated among the middle classes, the majority population was largely indifferent.
- June 28, 1914, the day of the assassination, was the 525th anniversary of the destruction of the medieval Serb empire at the battle of Kosovo – a highly symbolic date for Serbs.
- Serb support of the terrorists led directly to the Austro-Bulgarian conquest of Serbia in 1915.

THE BLACK HAND

One such group was the conspiratorial organization Ujedinjenje Ili Smrt ("Union or Death"), better known as Crna Ruka or the Black Hand, which had been created in May 1911 by a group of Serbian army officers angered by the cautious stance of Serbian prime minister Nikola Pasic. The Black Hand was a secret society which supported a number of terrorist groups in Macedonia and Bosnia, although it was never clear whether the Black Hand wanted a united Slav state ("Yugoslavia") or simply a Greater Serbia.

By late 1911, the Black Hand was under the energetic leadership of Colonel Dragutin Dimitrijevic, former head of Serb intelligence. He had come to political prominence because of his leading role in the assassination of King Alexander of Serbia in 1903. That murder had ended the pro-Austrian Obrenovic dynasty and brought to power the pro-Russian, Serb nationalist Petar Karadjordjevic. This accounted for Serbian opposition to Austria's taking power in Bosnia-Herzegovina five years afterward.

The Black Hand, under the control of Dimitrijevic, intensified its terrorist connections, concentrating on Austrian targets in Bosnia such as government buildings. Among its contacts in that province were Trifko Grabez, Nedeljko Cabrinovic, and a 19-year-old student called Gavrilo Princip. These three wanted a spectacular outrage that would shake Austria's resolve to keep troublesome Bosnia within its empire. As early as summer 1913, they were conspiring with four other sympathizers, Mehmed Mehmedbasic, Danilo Ilic, Cvetco Popovic, and Vasa Cubrilovic, to plan the assassination of Archduke Franz Ferdinand.

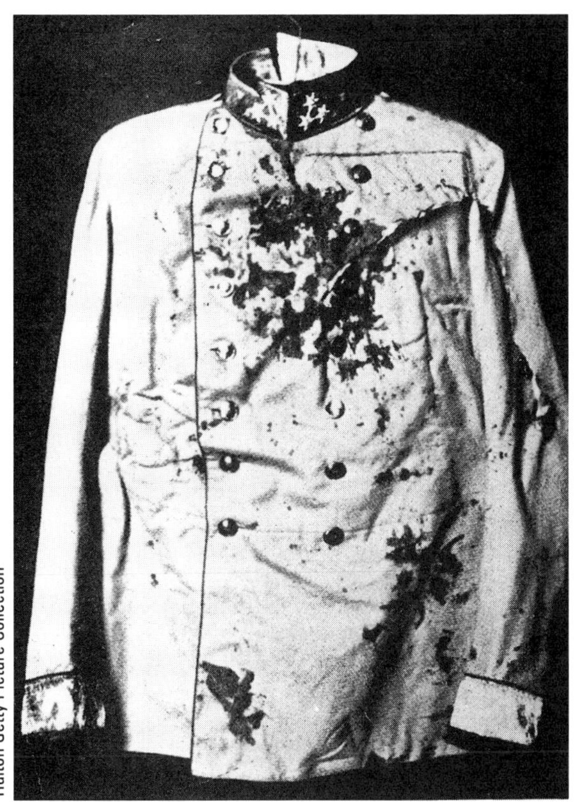

Hulton Getty Picture Collection

The blood-stained coat of Archduke Franz Ferdinand, assassinated by Gavrilo Princip in 1914.

In late spring 1914, Cabrinovic, Grabez, and Princip were brought out of Bosnia to the Serbian capital Belgrade for weapons training by the Black Hand. In May, they were smuggled back into Bosnia by secret service officers under the command of Dimitrijevic. Determined to further the cause of Serb nationalism and encouraged by the support of Dimitrijevic, they and their four co-conspirators went ahead with their plan to kill Franz Ferdinand.

PISTOL SHOTS

The archduke had repeatedly been advised against making a long-planned visit to Sarajevo, the capital of Bosnia-Herzegovina, because of the explosive situation in the province, but he insisted on going. He finally decided to make the visit on June 28, 1914. For Serbia and the Serbs living in Bosnia, this date marked a day of national mourning to commemorate the crushing defeat of the medieval Serb empire by the Turks at the battle of Kosovo in 1389. For the heir to the throne of Bosnia's oppressors to parade in its streets on that very day was regarded as provocative.

Habsburg intelligence had been carefully monitoring the situation in Bosnia and had little doubt that the archduke was in danger from Serb nationalists. Despite repeated warnings not to go, Franz Ferdinand rejected all advice and went to Sarajevo with his wife Sophie, duchess of Hohenburg.

The plan was to drive through the streets to an official reception given by the mayor at the town hall. Possibly by way of protest, the Bosnians did not make the security arrangements that were usual for visiting royalty. No soldiers lined the route, and no extra police were put on duty, even though the procession of the archducal couple through the town would attract a large crowd of onlookers.

Hidden in the crowd, and positioned at different places along the route, were the seven conspirators. Their first attempt on the archduke's life was a grenade attack on his open car. Eyewitnesses claim the archduke picked up the bomb and hurled it behind him, where it exploded, injuring the occupants of the following car.

Incredibly, the procession was not halted. Instead, the route was changed, but the driver of the first vehicle continued to drive along the original route, until his mistake was pointed out and he slowed down to change direction. Gavrilo Princip saw his chance. He broke through the thin line of police officers posted in front of the crowd, pulled out a Browning automatic pistol, and shot the archduke and his wife at point-blank range. The duchess died instantly, and Franz Ferdinand expired ten minutes later, at 11:30 A.M.

AUSTRIA RETALIATES

The Austrian authorities quickly rounded up and arrested all of the conspirators. Their link with Serbia was soon established but their association with Dimitrijevic and other high-ranking officials in the Serbian government only emerged after 1918. At the time, the Austrian government only had strong suspicions that Serbia was involved. Such suspicions were strengthened when Serbia failed to launch an immediate inquiry into the role played by the Black Hand organization in the assassination plot.

Austria was more or less forced into making an appropriate response to the outrage, for it was a direct challenge to its authority in Bosnia. To do nothing might encourage Serbia to annex Bosnia itself. This in

Hulton Getty Picture Collection

Franz Ferdinand, moments from death, rides with scant security through troubled Sarejevo.

turn might precipitate a wave of independence movements in other parts of the creaking empire, and hasten its disintegration.

Ironically, although Franz Ferdinand was unpopular at court in the Austrian capital Vienna, he had been a moderating influence for peace within the government. Hence, his death was an event of considerable importance. After this, nothing shielded the aging Emperor Franz Joseph and foreign minister Count Leopold Berchtold from the demands of the more warlike members of the government and the army. The latter's chief of staff, Field Marshal Franz Freiherr Conrad von Hötzendorf, in particular, had long demanded a military action against the increasingly hostile and pro-Russian Serbian state.

HURTLING TOWARD WAR

Any punitive action against Serbia, however, would involve great risks. If Russia, the self-appointed protector of the Serbs, opposed such action, Austria-Hungary either had to back down or risk all-out war with Serbia and Russia. As a result, Austria sought the support of her ally Germany, and duly obtained firm backing for a swift military retaliation against Serbia.

On July 23, the Habsburg government presented Belgrade with a 48-hour ultimatum, including what they knew to be unacceptable conditions. Failing acceptance, the Austro-Hungarian ambassador to Serbia was instructed to sever diplomatic relations with Belgrade.

Serbia retaliated by mobilizing its troops on July 25, and events escalated at an alarming rate. On July 28, Austria-Hungary declared war on Serbia, and the next day its navy began to bombard Belgrade. Two days afterward, Russia mobilized 1.2 million troops. Germany, fearing an imminent Russian attack on its ally Austria, demanded the immediate cessation of Russia's mobilization preparations. This demand, together with the Austrian bombardment of Belgrade, convinced the Russians that the two powers had intended war from the start.

On August 1, Germany declared war on Russia. France, committed by a treaty of alliance to come to Russia's aid, placed its army on a war footing but did not declare war on Germany. On August 3, however, the German government declared war on France, and marched into Belgium. As Belgian neutrality was guaranteed by Britain in a treaty dating back to 1839, Britain joined the war on the side of France and Russia, and declared war on Germany on August 4.

All the great powers of Europe were now at war. World War I had begun, just five weeks after a terrorist attack intended to make Austria-Hungary consider pulling out of Bosnia.

Thomas G. Otte

SEE ALSO: TERROR'S USE IN MACEDONIA 1893-1934; TERROR IN WORLD WAR I.

FURTHER READING

- Gilbert, Martin. *The First World War: A Complete History.* London: Routledge, and New York: Henry Holt, 1994.
- Joll, James. *Origins of the First World War.* London and New York: Longman, 1992.
- Joyce, C. Patrick. *Sarajevo Shots: Studies in the Immediate Origin of World War I.* Brooklyn, NY: Revisionist Press, 1978.
- Williamson, Samuel R., Jr. *Austria-Hungary and the Origins of the First World War.* London: Macmillan, and New York: St. Martin's Press, 1991.

TERROR IN WORLD WAR I

The horrors of World War I were not confined to the battlefields. The armies of the Central Powers – Germany and Austria-Hungary – both used terror tactics against civilians.

An important part of the strategy of the German army, which invaded Belgium and France in 1914, was a set of policies known as *Schrecklichkeit* ("dreadfulness" or "frightfulness".) German forces had already used such an approach in colonial warfare. In German South West Africa between 1904 and 1906, for example, the Germans used particularly callous methods to crush the revolts of the Herero and Hottentot peoples who lived in the colony. Thousands of men, women, and children were murdered. They were shot, hanged, or forced out into the desert to die of starvation. The final death toll – amounting, in the case of the Herero people, to 80-85 percent of the population – amounted to genocide.

The greatest fear of the German forces during the invasion of France was of the *francs-tireurs* (sharpshooters), partisans (guerrillas) who operated in the rear of the invading army. During the invasion of France in 1871, some 25 percent of German forces were employed in guarding such rear areas. From the start of World War I, the Germans pursued a policy of brutal reprisals against civilians in Belgium and France in response to partisan activity. If there were German casualties, civilians were rounded up and shot, often in far greater numbers than the German soldiers killed. This policy was intended to act as a deterrent to civilians, warning them not to resist the German occupation or undertake resistance activities.

KEY FACTS

- At the start of World War I, the German advance into Belgium and France in the autumn of 1914 was marked by the adoption of a terror policy of *Schrecklichkeit* (dreadfulness).
- In March 1917, the Germans withdrew to a more defensible position, the Siegfried Stellung, known to the Allies as the Hindenburg Line. The German army evacuated 125,000 French inhabitants to camps in German-held territory. The Germans destroyed bridges, roads, railroads, and buildings. They chopped down fruit trees, polluted wells, and laid ingenious booby traps.
- Turkey used deliberate terror in World War I, directed against its ethnic minorities to prevent their taking advantage of war chaos to rise up.

METHODS OF BRUTALITY

Hostage-taking was another method used to keep the local populations in line. Both male and female civilian hostages, usually the most prominent citizens, were taken by the German forces as a matter of course. The Germans did not have any scruples about executing such hostages in retaliation for partisan activity. Even priests, who were regarded by the Germans as ringleaders of partisan activity, were taken. Six are known to have been executed in the Belgian town of Warsage.

The threat to kill the hostages was sometimes enough to subdue local populations, but often their capture was only a pretext to remove leaders who might organize resistance. In Belgium, around 150 hostages were killed at Aerschot, and 612, including a baby, at Dinant. When the town of Tamines was sacked, over 380 civilians were shot outside the church.

CRUSHING RESISTANCE

Belgian resistance to the advance of the German army undoubtedly led to a hardening of attitudes within the German military. Worse, the Belgian army's destruction of key points, such as bridges, in an attempt to delay the enemy advance was interpreted by the Germans – made nervous by memories of the 1870-71 war – as the work of partisans. Incidents in which parties of Germans accidentally shot at each other (what would now be called "friendly fire" incidents) were also regarded as the work of partisans. While there was some partisan activity in Belgium, it was

Peter Newark's Military Pictures

The passenger liner Lusitania *is sunk by a German submarine on May 7, 1915, with the loss of 1,400 lives.*

nowhere near the scale the Germans believed. Life for civilians in German-occupied France and Belgium was hard. The Belgian birth rate declined and the death rate rose sharply. The German army dragged hundreds of thousands of civilians from their homes to be used as forced labor in Germany's mines and factories. About 120,000 Belgians and 100,000 French workers were deported to Germany during the occupation.

OUTRAGE AT ATROCITIES

German terror tactics may have subdued the terrified citizens in occupied territories, but they were counterproductive in the effect they had on the civilian population of Germany's enemies, particularly Britain. Stories of atrocities against women and children, brought back by returning soldiers, were a gift to recruiting sergeants.

The initial rush of volunteers had begun to dry up as tales of horror in the trenches filtered back home. Clever propaganda posters showing "the Hun" impaling babies on bayonets brought outraged citizens flocking to join up. Furthermore, any qualms the civilian populations of the Entente Powers – France, Britain, Russia – might have had about the legalities of declaring war were swept away and replaced by a conviction that they were fighting a just war against unspeakable evil. Meanwhile, the Germans excelled in their capacity for outrage when they burned the Belgian medieval university town of Louvain on August 26, 1914. On the previous night, nervous German troops had opened fire, probably as a response to an unexpected noise in the dark, but the Germans claimed Belgian snipers had been at work. The complete destruction of the town, and especially the famous library with its irreplaceable collections, greatly shocked the world.

Similar actions were carried out in France. The village of Nomeny, in the north-eastern province of Lorraine, for example, was destroyed by the Germans on August 20, 1914. Fifty civilians died in the inferno.

The Germans justified their policy of *Schrecklichkeit* on the grounds that Belgium, as a neutral power, had broken international law by their resistance. The Germans saw the hand of the Belgian government and local authorities in the organization of what they termed "illegal resistance." The commander of the German Third Army, General von Hausen, justified the destruction of Dinant by claiming that it was the fault of the Belgian authorities, because they had "approved this perfidious street fighting contrary to international law."

The German military's view of the illegality of Belgian resistance was plainly hypocritical. By invading Belgium, Germany knew that it was breaking an international treaty that it had signed in 1839 along with Britain, Russia, France, and Austria. This treaty declared that Belgium was an "independent and perpetually neutral state." But, because Germany's plans for the invasion of France, made in the decade preceding 1914, depended on its troops' being able to go through Belgium, such legal niceties as Belgian neutrality had been brushed aside in favor of the strategic considerations.

Another German strategy that might be construed as the use of terror tactics against civilians was the move toward unrestricted submarine warfare. In the early part of the war, submarines were instructed to attack only enemy shipping, and to give a warning beforehand so that the ship's personnel could be evacuated first. Soon, however, the order was given that any shipping entering enemy waters was at risk. The sinking of the passenger liner *Lusitania* in May 1915, with the loss of 1,400 lives, was a tragic consequence of this policy.

EASTERN FRONT TERROR

The pattern of German behavior in France and Belgium during World War I was also repeated on the Eastern Front. Here, Germany, together with its Central Power ally, the Austro-Hungarian empire, fought against France's ally Russia.

Early in August 1914, the Germans indiscriminately shelled the town of Kalisz in Prussian Poland in retaliation for shots fired at German troops by suspected partisans. During the following year, the Central Powers captured much of Poland from the Russians, and the Germans stripped Poland of factory machinery and raw materials.

The Austro-Hungarian forces also had a similar, if less dramatic, policy of economic asset stripping. These forces also retaliated savagely against any Poles and Ukrainians accused of collaborating with the enemy when the Russians successfully advanced into eastern Galicia. Such use of terror, however, was not the sole prerogative of the Central Powers: the Russians also carried out acts of terror during their retreat from Poland during 1914.

THE AUSTRIANS IN SERBIA

The Austrians carried out a form of *Schrecklichkeit* during their abortive invasion of Serbia in 1914. The Serbs proved to be a tough and resourceful enemy, and Austro-Hungarian failures on the battlefield resulted in the punishment of Serb civilians. Many became the victims of reprisals, such as the mass execution of Serb women at Macva in August 1914. According to a *Report on Atrocities Committed by the Austro-Hungarian Army*, there were many examples of the rape, torture, and murder of females.

In Serbia and elsewhere, Austrian troops committed atrocities against enemy civilians, possibly out of sheer frustration. The Austro-Hungarian empire went into the war against Serbia believing that it would win an easy victory. The reality was a war of attrition that drained its resources and hastened its downfall.

The Central Powers' use of terror in World War I prefigured the behavior of the Nazi German occupying armies. German counterinsurgency in World War II, particularly in Poland and the Soviet Union, fitted into a pattern of response that stretched back beyond the conflict of 1914-18 to the conflict with *franc-tireurs* in the Franco-Prussian War of 1870-71.

W. B. Brabiner

SEE ALSO: TERROR IN COLONIAL CONQUESTS; TERROR IN THE GERMAN OCCUPATION OF THE EAST; GERMAN TERROR IN FRANCE AND ITALY; TERROR IN THE FORMER YUGOSLAVIA.

FURTHER READING

- Cull, N. J. *Selling War: The British Propaganda Campaign against American Neutrality in World War I.* New York: Oxford University Press, 1995.
- Gilbert, Martin. *Atlas of World War I.* 2nd ed. London: Routledge, 1994; New York: Oxford University Press, 1995.
- Gilbert, Martin. *The First World War: A Complete History.* London: Routledge, and New York: Henry Holt, 1994.
- Marshall, S. L. A. *The American Heritage History of World War I.* Boston: Houghton Mifflin, 1987.

TERROR IN IRELAND 1916-1923

When World War I broke out in 1914, Ireland was a largely Catholic nation (albeit with an important Protestant majority in the northern province of Ulster) and an unwilling part of the British empire. The case for independence was overwhelmingly popular within Ireland, while even the Parliament at Westminster seemed to have accepted the justice of the Irish Nationalist cause by agreeing to a Home Rule Bill. The bill, however, never took effect – its provisions were suspended as soon as war broke out.

THE EASTER RISING

The issue may have been shelved in Britain, but not in Ireland. Despairing of a political solution, nationalists in Ireland, the Irish Volunteers, rebelled on Easter Monday, April 24, 1916. After taking key buildings in the capital Dublin, they declared an Irish Republic, with Commandant Padraig Pearse as president. The British sent in troops, fought pitched battles all over the city center, and sent gunboats up the River Liffey to shell rebel strongholds. It was all over in a week.

The Easter Rising was doomed by bad luck, lack of popular support, and the failure of the efforts of rebel retired British diplomat Sir Roger Casement to secure German aid. Pearse was executed on May 12, with six others including one James Connolly, who had to be wheeled from his hospital bed to meet the firing squad. Casement was tried for high treason and hanged in London. The British executed 16 rebels for an insurrection that caused 794 civilian and 521 military casualties. The British had responded with excessive brutality, making the rebels into martyrs, the Easter Rising into a legend, and further alienating the Irish.

> **KEY FACTS**
>
> - When Irish nationalists rose up in the Easter Rising in 1916, the British were outraged at rebellion while the United Kingdom was in the throes of World War I. Their sense of indignation fueled the force with which they put down the rebellion.
> - The 1921 treaty leaving Ulster under British control did not satisfy hard-line members of the IRA. In April 1922, opposers to the treaty seized the Four Courts, a large building in the Irish capital, Dublin, and barricaded themselves in. The Irish government had to drive them out.

BIRTH OF THE IRISH REPUBLICAN ARMY

After the failure of the Easter Rising, some nationalists realized that a new strategy was needed. A new type of resistance began to take shape. The Irish Volunteers were reorganized into the Irish Republican Army (IRA) and prepared for a guerrilla war.

The nationalists also formed a political party named Sinn Féin (Ourselves Alone), which ran candidates in elections to the British House of Commons in 1918. They won all the Irish seats except those in the northern province of Ulster. The Protestant majority there supported the Ulster Unionist Party, which insisted that Ulster be excluded from any deals on Home Rule.

While the Sinn Féin Members of Parliament (MPs) argued their case publicly, the IRA practiced terrorist methods designed to frustrate the British authorities and to make the policing of Ireland much more difficult and costly. There were rural guerrilla attacks on troops and police, and serious rioting in the cities, incited by secret IRA brigades. Terrorist activity was coordinated by Michael Collins, a former civil servant turned gifted, ruthless guerrilla fighter.

Unlike Pearse and the Irish Volunteers of 1916, Collins enjoyed mass popular support. The nationalists were confident enough in 1919 to form an unofficial Irish parliament, which included the 25 Sinn Féin MPs who had refused to take their seats in the House of

Peter Newark's Historical Pictures

The civil war in Ireland in April 1922: the two sides clashed in the Battle for the Four Courts in Dublin.

Commons. Their president was Eamon de Valera, a Sinn Féin MP jailed in 1918, when British forces rounded up 500 Sinn Féin supporters after IRA attacks.

BLACK AND TANS

The British responded to IRA attacks with counterterror, most notably with the arrival in Ireland, on March 26, 1920, of 800 jobless disbanded soldiers, known as the Black and Tans from the color of their uniform. The Black and Tans' use of violence against the ordinary Irish people was excessive. This and other methods of suppression were met by a Sinn Féin arson campaign. On the fourth anniversary of the Easter Rising 120 police stations and 22 tax offices were burnt.

Acts of terror on both sides reached fever pitch during 1920. The IRA routinely murdered police and troops, and bombed public buildings such as Cork City town hall on October 9. The British fought city rioters with the utmost ferocity and threw hundreds into jail. Many of the prisoners went on hunger strikes. Some, like Cork mayor Tomas MacSwiney, died in prison and became instant martyrs. By December, the British had 43,000 troops in Ireland and had declared martial law.

Matters were getting out of hand when a political initiative put forward by British prime minister David Lloyd George a year earlier resulted in the Government of Ireland Act of 1920. This offered limited self-government to the loyalists in the North and nationalists in the rest of Ireland. The Ulster Protestants accepted London's offer. In the rest of Ireland, nationalists dedicated to an all-Ireland republic fought on.

The British became bogged down in a guerrilla war with the IRA and so, in December 1921, Lloyd George offered a treaty that created an Irish Free State, excluding six of the eight Ulster counties. A majority of nationalists accepted this offer. But nationalists who wanted nothing less than a united free Ireland, including Eamon de Valera, refused to sign. He resigned as president, and became a leader of the rebels. Michael Collins became head of government. The differences between government and nationalist supporters erupted into civil war in 1922.

Running battles were fought to control whole towns and cities. Government property and personnel became legitimate targets for IRA bombs and bullets, one of which killed Michael Collins on August 22. In 1923 de Valera gave up the struggle and formed a new political party, but the IRA went underground.

The legacies of the IRA's early struggles – the role of martyrs, symbols, spies, money, and smuggled arms; the blend of politics, terror, and propaganda; the appeal to legitimacy, the military techniques and tactics – have become hallmarks of modern terrorism worldwide.

John Bowyer Bell

SEE ALSO: IRA: ORIGINS AND TERROR TO 1976; NATIONALIST TERROR IN NORTHERN IRELAND 1976-1996; COUNTERTERROR IN THE BRITISH EMPIRE BEFORE 1945.

FURTHER READING

- Bell, John Bowyer. *The Gun in Politics: An Analysis of Irish Violence.* New Brunswick, NJ: Transaction Publishers, 1991.
- Foster, Roy F. *Modern Ireland, 1600-1972.* London and New York: Penguin, 1989.
- Ward, Alan J. *The Easter Rising.* Arlington Heights, IL: Harlan Davidson, 1980.

THE AMRITSAR MASSACRE

By 1919, British rule in India had lasted nearly 200 years. It was first founded on trade through the East India Company in the early eighteenth century. The colonial administration, which became known as the Raj, was at its height in the late nineteenth century. Its success was due to the effective combination of organization – a few hundred civil servants ran a country of 300 million people – and military control. Indian rebellion against British rule was put down with ruthless ferocity. The Indian Mutiny of 1857, which began when Sikh soldiers refused to bite ammunition that had been oiled in pig fat, was just one example.

One of the most brutal suppressions of a public demonstration came when Britain's imperial power was beginning to wane. By the early twentieth century, there were increasing calls for independence in India. One famous leader was Mohandas Gandhi, known as the Mahatma, or wise man. During World War I, Britain had seemed to favor constitutional reforms. In 1918-19, however, the British delayed the promised reforms and introduced instead the draconian Rowlatt Act. Far from loosening the bonds of colonial rule, this measure extended into peacetime security regulations introduced during the war. The Act caused widespread discontent throughout the whole of India. In the state of Punjab, Gandhi organized a strike for March 30, 1919, and a second on April 6, 1919. This action fanned the belief among British officials that an outbreak of rebellion in the region was imminent. As a result, several known agitators were arrested in the Sikh holy city of Amritsar.

KEY FACTS

- Three days before the Amritsar massacre, General Dyer had flogged any Indian who refused to crawl at a point in the road where someone had attacked a white woman.
- At the enquiry into the massacre, Dyer stated that he would have used the machine guns on his armored cars if he could have done so, and that his intention was to cause terror. "I thought I would be doing a jolly lot of good," he said.
- The majority of the British community living in the Punjab initially hailed Dyer as the "savior of India." They believed that he had averted another Indian rebellion.

TERROR IN AMRITSAR

News of the arrests caused a mob of 30,000 Indians to run riot in the city on April 10. They destroyed the railway station and rampaged through the European quarter, killing three people. The civil police sent for British army reinforcements from the garrison at Lahore, which were placed under the command of Brigadier-General R. H. Dyer on April 11, 1919. After a series of arrests by the civil police, there was peace throughout the city on April 12.

But Dyer marched the British and Indian troops around the town's outer wall in a show of strength. He issued a proclamation that banned all movement in and out of the city by the local inhabitants and imposed an 8 p.m. curfew. The proclamation also forbade public meetings, stating that "any processions or gathering of four men will be looked upon as an unlawful assembly and dispersed by force if necessary." Despite the declaration, various acts of sabotage occurred during the next day, April 13. These actions convinced Dyer that revolutionaries were plotting a full-scale insurrection.

News then reached the general that an unauthorized mass meeting was to take place at 4:30 p.m. that day in the Jallianwalla Bagh. The latter was a large enclosed piece of wasteland near the Sikh Golden Temple. Dyer hurriedly led 90 Gurkha and Indian Baluchi troops supported by two armored cars to disperse the illegal meeting. However, without giving any prior warning to the crowd to disperse or face the consequences, Dyer ordered his troops to open fire. As the crowd of 20,000 unarmed men, women and

Topham Picture Library

Brigadier-General Dyer ordered his troops to open fire on unarmed demonstrators, killing 380 people.

children ran about in panic, the troops continued firing, discharging over 1,650 rounds of ammunition. Within ten minutes, 380 people were dead and 1,200 wounded, according to official estimates. Dyer only withdrew his forces when their ammunition was nearly exhausted. The dead and wounded were left where they fell.

THE REPERCUSSIONS

The Amritsar incident was a deliberate act of terror, calculated to frighten people involved in other disturbances taking place throughout Punjab. It had the desired effect. The riots very quickly subsided and the British managed to restore order in the state. Dyer's actions at Amritsar were endorsed by Punjab's lieutenant governor, Sir Michael O'Dwyer.

However, as news of the shooting and the number of casualties spread in Britain and India, it provoked outrage in the press and led to a debate in the British parliament. A committee of enquiry was appointed to investigate the incident. Controversy regarding Dyer's actions focused on his intentions and the background against which his actions took place. He clearly believed that by issuing his proclamation, martial law was in effect and therefore he was justified in using whatever force he thought necessary to restore order. The committee did not agree. It concluded that Dyer was not suppressing a rebellion, but was merely dispersing an unlawful assembly.

Dyer was censured for acting "out of a mistaken concept of his duty" by not giving advance warning of firing and continuing after the crowd had begun to disperse. He was relieved of his command and sent back to Britain in disgrace, despite continued strong public support and efforts made by O'Dwyer to clear both their names.

Amritsar was a turning point for Anglo-Indian relations. The political damage done to the Raj by the massacre was incalculable. The Amritsar incident alienated Indian public opinion, and poisoned relations with nationalist leaders, who were now united in their belief that Britain was indifferent to their political aspirations. The moral basis of British rule was undermined. The Jallianwalla Bagh became a memorial and a rallying call for resistance to British rule. Indeed, in March 1940, the Jallianwalla Bagh claimed its last casualty when O'Dwyer was assassinated in London by Udam Singh in an act of direct revenge for the massacre.

Tim Moreman

SEE ALSO: TERROR IN COLONIAL CONQUESTS; TERRORISM IN COLONIAL INDIA 1900-1947.

FURTHER READING

- Fein, Helen. *Imperial Crime and Punishment at Jallianwalla Bagh and British Judgment.* Honolulu: University of Hawaii Press, 1977.
- Sarkar, Sumit. *Modern India,1885-1947.* London: Macmillan, and New York: St. Martin's Press, 1989.
- Shepherd, C. *Crisis of Empire: British Reactions to Amritsar.* Cambridge, MA: Harvard University Press, 1992.
- Wolpert, Stanley. *A New History of India.* 5th ed. New York: Oxford University Press, 1997.

TERROR IN THE RUSSIAN CIVIL WAR

On August 31, 1918, the Bolshevik prime minister of Soviet Russia, Vladimir Lenin, was shot and gravely wounded in a terrorist assassination attempt at a Moscow factory. Combined with the killing, on the same day, of the head of the Soviet secret police in Petrograd (St. Petersburg) this gave the new regime a sense of extreme vulnerability, both to external and internal enemies.

SOCIALIST FATHERLAND IN DANGER

On September 5, 1918, the Bolshevik government made a declaration of Red Terror – consciously imitating the Jacobin Terror in revolutionary France. The Bolsheviks took hostages and sent enemies to concentration camps. They punished conspiracy against Soviet rule by anti-Bolshevik former Czarist officers, or Whites, with immediate death. In Petrograd (St. Petersburg) alone, they executed 900 hostages. Many victims were senior officials of the imperial government. The focus was not on individual guilt but on class membership, and the aim was to terrorize. Such terrorism was a central feature of the Russian Civil War (1917-21), although the Red Terror decree only gave a formal basis to existing practices.

In the autumn of 1918, the Bolsheviks faced a perilous situation. They had negotiated Russia's way out of World War I, but German and Austrian armies were still deep in Russia. Also, the peace had alienated both Russia's former external allies and the Socialist Revolutionaries. The consequences included the uprising of the Czechoslovak Legion and the emergence of an anti-Bolshevik front east of Moscow. A Socialist Revolutionary uprising took place in Moscow, while north of Moscow the Socialist Revolutionary terrorist Boris Savinkov organized a revolt. For this reason, in late July 1918, the Bolsheviks passed a decree declaring the "Socialist Fatherland in Danger" and calling for "mass terror" against the bourgeoisie. The July 1918 execution of the Czar and his family, ordered by Moscow, was part of this campaign.

KEY FACTS

- The Bolsheviks used terror throughout 1917-21, to destroy opponents and control their own people. The Red Terror employed concentration camps, hostage-taking, and execution without trial.
- Trotsky embraced terrorism to the extent of writing a pamphlet towards the end of 1919, called *Terrorism and Communism.*

RED TERROR

The Red Terror was not simply counterterror in an emergency. Its roots lay in the class hatred of Bolshevik activists. The pre-revolutionary Bolsheviks, unlike the Socialist Revolutionaries, had rejected terrorist attacks against individual representatives of the czarist regime. But after the revolution, these same Bolsheviks had no doubts about their right to defend the new regime by any means possible. So, in 1918, the Bolshevik leaders, particularly Lenin and Commissar for War Leon Trotsky, turned to terrorism. This was a correct move in terms of Marxist theories of class conflict. The Marxists rejected the idea, held by orthodox lawyers, that all legal systems should be impartial.

For the party's mass of new recruits, the Red Terror was based less on ideas than on centuries of oppression. For Soviet leaders and ordinary party members, terror was an effective tool for creating order in the turmoil that followed the Bolshevik coup of October 1917.

It is significant that the organization that carried out the Bolshevik terror was created early in the regime's history – in December 1917. This organization was the Extraordinary Commission for the Struggle with Counterrevolution and Sabotage (Cheka). Its leader was the fanatical Pole, Feliks Dzerzhinskii. The Revolutionary Tribunal, based on the French Revolutionary example, was also important. It was introduced in November 1917 to hand out instant justice.

Peter Newark's Military Pictures

Bolshevik Commissar for War Leon Trotsky (left) was an unflinching proponent of terror.

By late 1918, large White armies were advancing from southern Russia and Siberia on Moscow. The Bolsheviks had created an army to defend the state against these counterrevolutionaries, but they felt they could not trust it. The Red Terror, therefore, changed its point of focus to the army's front lines. Here it imposed discipline both among the peasant conscripts and among the ex-Czarist officer staffs. Its methods included deploying detachments behind the front line to prevent desertion, making hostages of commanders' families, and employing firing squads.

But the Bolsheviks applied Red Terror even more ruthlessly to their enemies. In 1918-19, they attempted to wipe out the Cossacks in southeastern Russia. And right up to the fall of the last White base area, in 1920 in the Crimea, they often tortured or shot captured officers.

A further, hidden side of Red Terror was directed at the population within Soviet-controlled Russia. The Mensheviks (a rival Marxist faction) and the Socialist Revolutionaries still had some influence among the urban working class and the peasantry. Even without this influence, workers and peasants were dissatisfied with Bolshevik rule. The collapse of the economy meant that the Bolsheviks could secure food only through brute force – by mass arrests and hostage-taking. The Cheka and other paramilitary bodies kept order through terror. The struggle intensified when frontline fighting ended late in 1920. The Cheka brutally crushed rural disorder and urban unrest at Petrograd (St. Petersburg) and Kronstadt.

WHITE TERROR

The use of terror was not confined to the Bolsheviks. The Socialist Revolutionaries carried out acts of individual terrorism, most notably attempts to kill Lenin. The Whites were merciless with captured Communists, and Red propaganda made much of White Terror. The Whites also used punitive detachments against the peasantry. But White Terror was much less systematic than its Red counterpart, under which an estimated 50,000 to 200,000 people were executed.

The Bolsheviks use of terror proved essential to the survival of their minority regime. In this way, the Red Terror may have changed history by consolidating the Bolshevik grip on power. But the price was high. Terrorism isolated the Bolsheviks from world socialism and set back the prospects of revolution elsewhere.

Evan Mawdsley

SEE ALSO: TERROR IN THE FRENCH REVOLUTION 1789-1915; THE PARIS COMMUNE: STATE TERROR; RUSSIAN ANARCHIST TERROR; TERROR IN THE FINNISH CIVIL WAR; STALIN'S GREAT TERROR.

FURTHER READING

- Brovkin, V. N. *Behind the Front Lines of the Civil War: Political Parties and Social Movement in Russia, 1918-1922.* Princeton, NJ: Princeton University Press, 1994.
- Chamberlain, William H. *The Russian Revolution, Volume II: 1918-1921: From the Civil War to the Consolidation of Power.* Princeton, NJ: Princeton University Press, 1987.
- Leggett, George. *The Cheka: Lenin's Political Police.* Oxford: Clarendon Press, and New York: Oxford University Press, 1986.
- Mawdsley, Evan. *The Russian Civil War.* Boston: Unwin Hyman, 1989.

TERROR IN THE FINNISH CIVIL WAR

Amid the chaos of the Russian Revolution, on January 4, 1918, Finland received its independence from the Bolshevik leader Vladimir Lenin. It was barely two months since he had taken power, and Lenin had too many pressing problems associated with establishing Bolshevik authority throughout the vast Russian empire to worry about Finnish separatism.

The Bolsheviks were confident that the Finnish socialists would soon take power in the revolutionary atmosphere of the newly independent Finland. There were shortages, strikes, and food riots. Parliamentary government had largely broken down and, on January 28, 1918, left-wing Red Guards, the workers' militia, seized power in the capital, Helsinki. Civil war broke out between the Reds and the government forces.

Unlike much of the revolutionary unrest in Europe following World War I, the Finnish conflict was a full-scale civil war fought on several fronts. The experienced ex-Czarist officer General Mannerheim led the Finnish Government's forces, known as the White Guards, to ultimate victory against the poorly trained and led Finnish Red forces. The small number of ex-Czarist Russian army troops remaining in Finland who did fight for the Red Guards against the Finnish White Guards were ill-disciplined and had poor morale. In encounters between Red and White troops, these forces tended to be more of a liability than an asset.

KEY FACTS

- The Finnish Civil War, fought between the anti-Bolshevik White Guards and Finnish socialists, or Red Guards, lasted just four months, between January 28 and May 18, 1918.
- Though short, the civil war was very bloody. Out of a population of just 3 million, the war accounted for the deaths of close to 30,000 people, or nearly one percent of the population.
- Nearly 12,000 Red prisoners died in White captivity. The Red Terror killed almost 1,700 Whites.

RED GUARDS TERRORISM

Before the Finnish civil war, the Red Guards had gained a wide reputation for brutality, particularly during the general strike of November 1917. Undoubtedly some used the opportunity for looting and revenge that this unrest presented. The socialist leadership could not control some elements of the Red Guards, and once civil war broke out in Finland the problem became worse. It is clear that during the four-month civil war, the Reds murdered 1,649 people. These killings came in two waves. There were 703 deaths from the war's start until the end of February, 1918, during the establishment of the new independent regime. Killings dropped to 205 in March 1918, but in April in the confusion of the Red defeat, 697 people were killed.

Surprisingly, the obvious targets of class-conflict – the rich, the clergy, and opposition political leaders – went largely unscathed, although the Red Guards executed 184 captured White troops. Aside from this, the Reds treated their prisoners reasonably well. The worst single exception was the Reds, massacre of 30 White troops in Viipuri prison just before the city fell. Overall, the Red Terror was irrational, purposeless, and tragic. It was not authorized by the socialist leaders. It caused internal dissent, undermined the workers' morale, and let the Whites present the Reds, both at home and abroad, as barbaric.

THE WHITE TERROR

On the other hand, the Whites also frequently shot Red prisoners taken in battle. Although Mannerheim had instructed that "in no circumstances may prisoners be shot out of hand," his orders were sometimes ignored. This was particularly the case after the fall of the

Hulton Getty Picture Collection

Field Marshal Carl Gustav Mannerheim led the White Guards, the Finnish government's forces.

strategic inland city of Tampere. Here, around 200 people who could be identified as Russians were summarily executed, as were 150 Finns. A Swedish observer wrote that "the sight was unimaginably repulsive: a heap of bleeding bodies on the ground." This case of mass murder could not even be justified as an spontaneous act of soldiers seeking vengeance. There had been no Red Terror in Tampere during the period when the town was under their control, nor had any of the White prisoners held by the Reds in the city during the siege been harmed.

When the town of Viipuri fell to the Whites, similar incidents occurred. Again, all Russians found were killed, including a number of bourgeois White sympathizers and the unfortunate odd Pole and Ukrainian. Their monument at Viipuri cemetery reads: "We waited for you as liberators and you brought us death." But the worst single atrocity committed by the White Guards was the mass killing of 50 workers by machine-gun fire in a ditch after the end of hostilities.

THE SCALE OF THE WHITE TERROR

The number of deaths caused by White Guards' terrorist activity totalled 2,400 by the end of April 1918. But, in the following five weeks, from April 28 to June 1, the figure almost doubled to 4,745. In the peak period of May 5-11 there was an average of 200 killings a day. In total there were at least 8,380 illegal murders of captured Reds, including 58 males under the age of 16 and 364 women. After the defeat of the Reds, the White government set up special courts to provide legal retribution and to halt the unauthorized killing. These special courts convicted 67,000 people of terrorist crimes and passed 555 death sentences, of which 265 were carried out.

The most tragic aspect to the White Terror was that it was largely avoidable. The Finnish military authorities had made little provision for the 80,000 prisoners in their custody. The country was suffering from a famine and feeding Red prisoners was not high on the Whites' priorities. Consequently, 11,783 prisoners died in captivity of malnutrition and disease.

Some 23,000 Finnish Reds died on the battlefield, in prisoner-of-war camps, and by summary execution. Many thousands more were imprisoned. Yet the majority of the Finnish population supported the White Terror. The only possible justifications for the appalling brutality of the Finnish civil war were that it helped ensure continued Finnish independence and led to the establishment of a strong democracy.

M. Christopher Mann

SEE ALSO: TERROR IN THE RUSSIAN CIVIL WAR.

FURTHER READING

- Alapuro, R. *State and Revolution in Finland.* Berkeley: University of California Press, 1988.
- Hamalainen, Pekka K. *In Time of Storm: Revolution, Civil War, and the Ethnographic Issue in Finland.* Albany, NY: SUNY Press, 1979.
- Nordstrom, Byron J. *Dictionary of Scandinavian History.* Westport, CT: Greenwood Press, 1986.

THE ARMENIAN MASSACRES

Modern Armenia, situated in Asia Minor east of the Black Sea, is a former member state of the Soviet Union. For centuries, however, it was divided between two empires – the Ottoman empire (modern Turkey) in the west and, in the east, first Persia (modern Iran) until 1828, then Russia.

Generally, the eastern regimes tolerated their Christian Armenian subjects. But the Muslim Ottoman Empire harbored an ongoing ill-feeling toward Armenia which, after 1870, developed into outright persecution. Religious differences were only marginally responsible for this situation. A stronger reason was that the position of all minorities was deteriorating within the weakening Turkish empire as the central power grew suspicious of culturally independent peoples within its sphere.

Within Turkish Armenia itself, Turkish administration amounted to little more than tax-gathering. The Armenians shared much of their land with the Kurds, a nomadic people who still occupy land in Turkey and in what is now northern Iraq. When the Kurds became violent toward the Armenians, the Turkish authorities did not intervene. Indeed, the Turkish authorities actively encouraged the Kurds in acts of atrocity.

By 1890, the Kurds were well organized into military regiments. The Turkish authorities were actively encouraging them to harass the Armenians and to commit acts of violence and murder. Turkish government policy meant that Armenians, particularly those in rural areas, were outside the protection of the law.

An eyewitness account of the situation in 1895 vividly describes the brutal injustices practiced by the Ottoman authorities against their subject people. The evidence of armed extortion, torture, rape, and murder against Armenians because of their religion and nationality is a shocking example of a government employing terrorist tactics to displace an unwanted population. There was a deliberate policy to reduce the number of Armenian people, either by driving them out of their homeland or by killing them.

Many Armenians were fortunate enough to evade persecution and reach the frontier with Russian Armenia, but hundreds of thousands fell victim to what amounted to organized state terrorism. In the autumn of 1895 alone, as many as 200,000 Armenians were massacred, not just in their homeland, but at many locations throughout the Ottoman empire.

KEY FACTS

- In 1894, Turkish troops and Kurds slaughtered thousands of Armenians for not paying their taxes.
- In 1896, when Armenian rebels seized the Ottoman Bank, more than 50,000 Armenians were killed by state-coordinated mobs of Muslim Turks.
- In 1915, the Turkish government deported about 1,750,000 Armenians. Hundreds of thousands died of starvation or exhaustion in the desert, or were executed by Turkish troops.

THE ARMENIAN REACTION

Acts of state terror provoked a spiral of individual terrorist acts by Armenians as they sought to defend themselves. They murdered government officials and staged spectacular attacks, such as seizing the Imperial Ottoman Bank in Istanbul in August 1896.

In April 1909, the reigning Ottoman sultan was overthrown by the Young Turks, a revolutionary movement that was supported by the army. With the downfall of the despotic Sultan Abdul Hamid II, ethnic minorities were briefly left in peace. However, a key policy of the Young Turks was the creation of a homogeneous state, with a uniform language and culture. Since the Ottoman Empire was multi-ethnic, and the Turks were the ruling nationality, such a policy posed a serious threat to non-Turkish cultures.

Meanwhile, the Ottoman Armenians were making some headway with the new regime and in February 1914 scored some minor diplomatic successes. When Turkey entered World War I in October of that year, there was no immediate hostility toward the

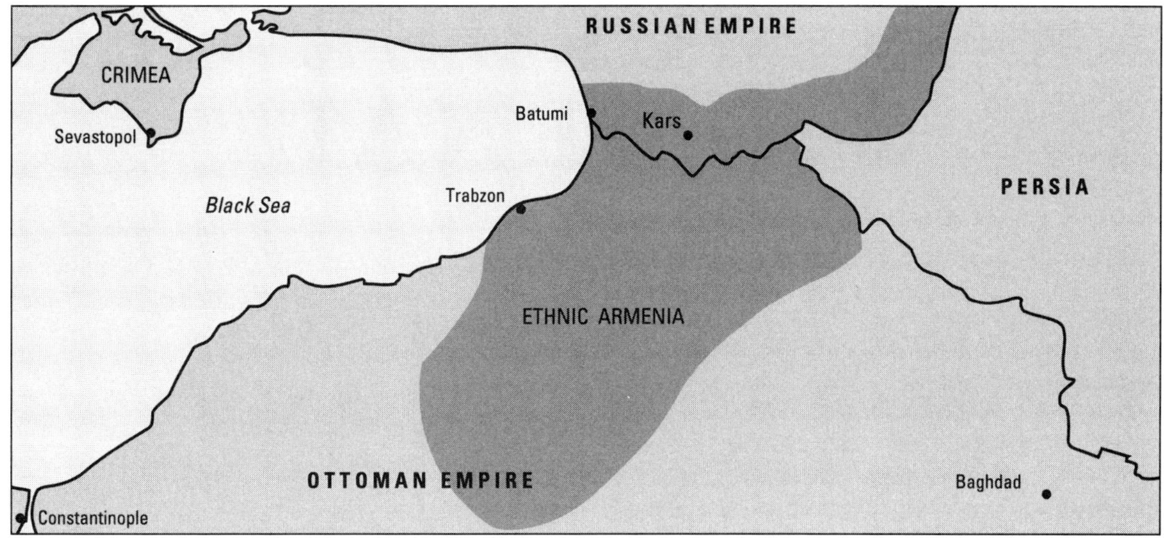

The areas of the 1915 Ottoman and Russian empires populated by ethnic Armenians.

Armenians, even though the Turks could claim they were a security risk because half of Armenia was under enemy Russian control.

By March 1915, the situation had changed. The Young Turks regime began to persecute Armenians. The government defended its actions by citing the disloyalty of a number of Armenians, who had joined volunteer regiments in enemy Russian territory, across the border.

But anti-Armenian measures went far beyond any possible punishment for disloyalty, since most Turkish Armenians remained loyal to their empire. It is more likely that the Young Turks used disloyalty as a pretext to clear out the Armenians. Completely different culturally, Armenians stood in the way of pan-Turkism, an ideology that sought uniformity of language, culture, and religion right across the Turkish empire.

SYSTEMIZED GENOCIDE

The Young Turks now implemented a policy of massive depopulation by genocide, not only in Armenia itself, but of Armenians living all over the empire. They shot Armenians in their homes, or force-marched them hundreds of miles over rough terrain until they died from exhaustion. They penned up many more thousands in open-air concentration camps, where the prisoners eventually died of exhaustion. At one place, Deir-en-Zor, the Young Turks herded thousands of Armenians into caves, which were then sealed. Government guards stopped those people driven over the border into neighboring countries from accepting food and drink offered by charities from neutral nations. The Turkish explanation for this mass displacement was that the Armenians were being relocated away from the war zone for their own safety. But the explanation was a cover-up. Government telegrams in the Ottoman archive suggest that there was a coordinated plan of extermination. By August 1916, a total of 1.5 million Armenians were reported dead, and more than a million had been deported. This decimation of Armenians at the hands of a fading imperial power constituted one of the most atrocious acts of state terrorism in the twentieth century.

Robert P. Anderson

SEE ALSO: THE HOLOCAUST; SADDAM HUSSEIN'S TERROR IN KURDISTAN.

FURTHER READING

- Hovannisian, Richard G., ed. *The Armenian Genocide: History, Politics, Ethics.* London: Macmillan, and New York: St. Martin's Press, 1992.
- Somakian, M. J. *Empires in Conflict: Armenia and the Great Powers, 1895-1920.* London and New York: Taurus, 1995.
- Walker, C. *Armenia: The Survival of a Nation.* 2nd ed. London: Routledge, and New York: St. Martin's Press, 1990.

THE MURDER OF RATHENAU

Hulton Getty Picture Collection

German foreign minister, Walther Rathenau, in 1922, shortly before his murder.

The murder of Walther Rathenau on June 24, 1922 was an act of extreme right-wing terrorism. The assassination had a traumatic effect on the development of democracy in Germany after the country's defeat in World War I, four years earlier.

Rathenau was a businessman who had been in charge of distributing raw materials in World War I. His efforts to increase the efficiency of the German war economy helped Germany sustain the conflict for four years until 1918. After hostilities ended with the signing of the armistice in November of the same year, Rathenau joined the liberal German Democratic Party. He quickly became a prominent politician and gained ministerial office. But he made many enemies among right-wing factions because of his left-wing, social-reforming principles and because he was Jewish.

Rathenau was no less patriotic than his nationalist opponents. In 1921, he resigned his ministerial post in protest against the division of Upper Silesia, which gave territory to Poland, although he accepted the post of foreign minister shortly afterward.

Rathenau came in for abuse from anti-communist and anti-Semitic right-wing nationalists. He incensed his enemies more by signing the Treaty of Rapallo with the Soviet Union in May 1922. The treaty restored diplomatic relations and both countries dropped war reparations claims. Right-wing pamphlets called for his assassination. He was accused of complicity in a Jewish conspiracy against Germany, and of selling out the country's interests as foreign minister.

Such propaganda persuaded three students, Erwin Kern, Hermann Fischer, and Ernst Techow, to murder Rathenau. After serving in the Navy during World War I, they had joined a right-wing paramilitary group then the conspiratorial nationalist group "Organization C." On June 24, 1922, as Rathenau's car left his villa in a Berlin suburb, the assassins pulled their car alongside. Kern fired nine shots and Fischer threw a grenade, killing Rathenau almost instantly. The murderers then fled to the Baltic coast but missed the boat to Sweden. They were caught in a shoot-out in which Kern was killed, Fischer shot himself, and Techow was arrested.

Rathenau's assassination created an enormous sensation and exposed internal unrest in Germany. It was regarded as a rejection of the new constitutional order by growing nationalist factions.

Thomas G. Otte

SEE ALSO: ASSASSINATION AT SARAJEVO 1914; THE HOLOCAUST.

FURTHER READING

- Felix, David. *Walther Rathenau and the Weimar Republic: The Politics of Reparations.* Baltimore, MD: Johns Hopkins University Press, 1971.
- Peukert, Detler J. *Weimar Republic.* London: Penguin, and New York: Hill & Wang, 1993.

STALIN'S GREAT TERROR

In 1956, the rulers of the Soviet Union made their first public admission of the existence of a police terror apparatus. They blamed Joseph Stalin, who had died in 1953 after nearly 25 years as absolute ruler. He was not the first to use government terror. Labor camps had appeared after the October Revolution of 1917, when the Bolsheviks came to power under Vladimir Lenin. He used class enemies as forced labor.

In 1922, Stalin became secretary of the Communist party, as the Bolsheviks were now known. When Lenin died in 1924, Stalin became the dominant figure among Bolshevik leaders, and from 1928 was in effect dictator.

Stalin's reign of terror began as an offshoot of an economic policy, his first five-year plan. Designed to make the Soviet Union a modern industrialized economy, the five-year plan requisitioned all land for state use and nationalized all industries. Mass resistance from the peasantry, especially the upper class land-owning "kulaks," led to famine. Thousands of kulaks disappeared into remote labor camps or died under a hail of bullets from Stalin's death squads.

The same techniques were used in industry, when inefficient, ill-disciplined workers failed to meet targets. Failures were blamed on saboteurs or "wreckers." They too were sent to work-camps. Forced labor became a basic part of the Soviet economy, and fear of arrest, torture, and execution by Stalin's police, a way of life.

Stalin made the show trial a hallmark of his terror system. Highly placed dissident officials and groups of lowly workers were arrested and put on public trial. The evidence was rigged and a guilty verdict certain.

Hulton Getty Picture Collection

Joseph Stalin, who ruled the Soviet Union as effective dictator from 1928 to 1953, unleashed a reign of terror that left millions dead.

Stalin made sure the trials were high profile to stifle opposition and encourage people to work harder.

Stalin first used show trials to do with economic issues. In May 1928, for example, he condemned engineers at the Shakhty mines for failure to meet productivity targets. But Stalin next extended the reign of terror to the Communist party itself, with a series of brutal purges. While purges were not new, previously they had only involved expulsion from the party. The innovation of the 1930s was to criminalize the victims, who could now be sent to one of the many harsh labor camps or even be executed.

KEY FACTS

- Some 25 million farming households were forced to collectivize, dissenters were shot, and famines resulted. About 10 million peasants perished.
- In 1989, a Soviet historian estimated that more than 20 million died as a result of the labor camps, execution, forced collectivization, and famine.

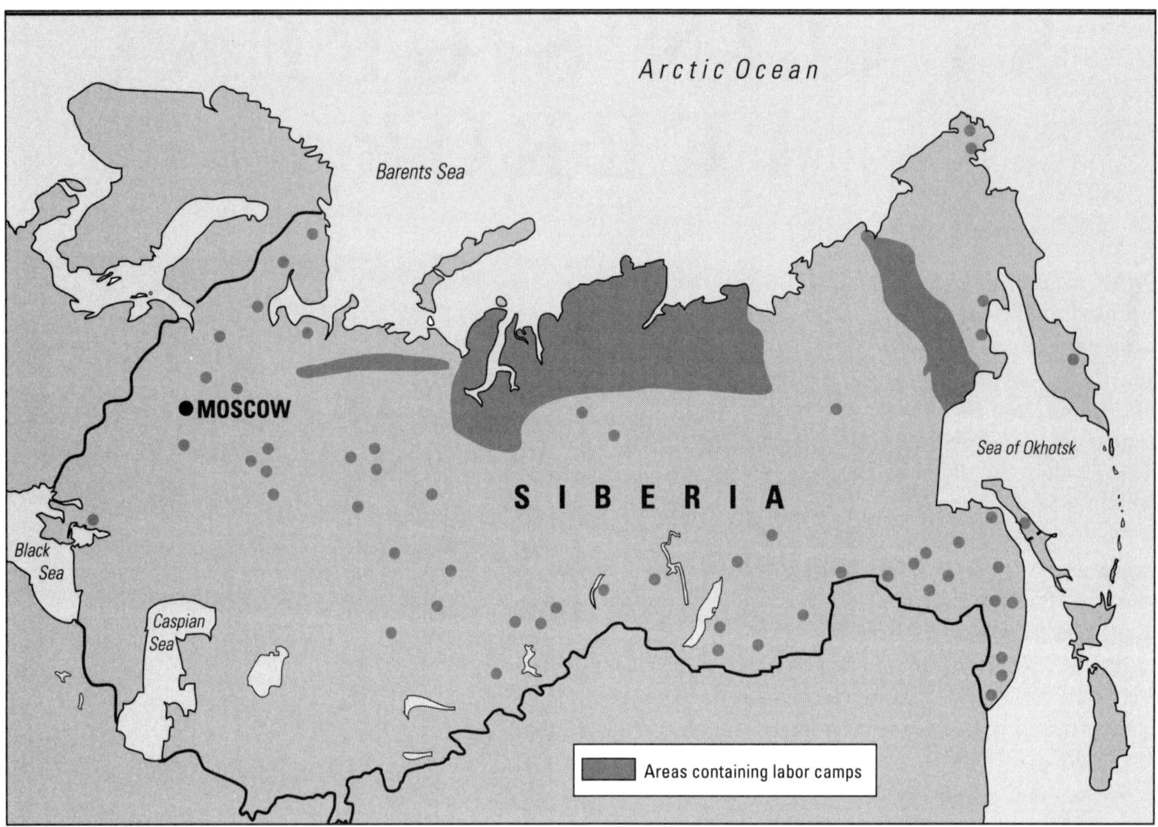

Soviet labor camps were mainly located in the harsh wilderness of Siberia.

State prosecutors conducted show trials at which they forced the accused to "confess" to crimes of disloyalty. Some even asked for death to purify the communist system. By 1938, party membership had fallen from 3,555,000 to 1,920,000. Purged members filled the camps. and terror was used against any threats. Even its perpetrators were not safe. Yagoda and Yezhov, the commissars responsible for the terror, became its victims in 1936-38. In 1937-38, nine-tenths of the army's generals disappeared, seriously weakening the Soviet military.

The number of purge victims is unclear since Soviet government secrecy, together with the many forced labor institutions, prevent accuracy. It is impossible, then, to be sure that the figure of seven million executions, recently quoted in Russian publications, is correct.

More than 18 million people were probably inmates of the camps between 1934 and 1952. By 1952, they included enemies, returning Soviet prisoners of war, dissident nationalists from newly acquired territories, and those suspected of collaborating with the Nazis.

By the time of Stalin's death in 1953, few Soviet citizens did not know of a "kulak" or a "wrecker" and what had happened to them. Many detainees were released after 1956, but often never came to terms with the psychological effects of their confinement.

Peter Morris

SEE ALSO: TERROR IN THE RUSSIAN CIVIL WAR; RESISTANCE IN THE EAST AND TERRORISM.

FURTHER READING

- Conquest, Robert. *The Great Terror: A Reassessment.* London: Hutchinson, and New York: Oxford University Press, 1990.
- Mandelstam, N. Nadezhda. *Hope Against Hope: A Memoir.* New York: Atheneum, 1987; London: Collins-Harvill, 1989.
- Tucker, Robert C. *Stalin in Power.* New York: Norton, 1990.

CHAPTER TWO

Terror During World War II

As if the horrors of the battlefield were not enough, much terrorism occurs on the sidelines of war. World War II saw examples of the worst atrocities of all time. Many acts of violence were sanctioned by governments, others were the work of frenzied individuals. The war was characterized by a degree of savagery in Axis occupation policy never before witnessed. Even the norms of warfare were barbarized by the bitter, often ideologically inspired, fighting. The line between combatants and civilians blurred as few could escape the effects of all-out slaughter and torture.

TERROR DURING WORLD WAR II: Introduction

In 1939, Nazi Germany's aggressive foreign policy eventually forced the Allies to make a stand over the German invasion of Poland. In this way World War II in Europe began, fought between the Allies – Britain, France, the Soviet Union (from June 1941) and the United States (from December 1941) and the European Axis – Germany, Italy and their satellites. The war fought by Japan, the other Axis power, with China, from 1933, escalated by 1940-41 to a conflict in the Pacific ocean with the western Allies, and not with the Soviet Union until 1945. World War II became the greatest conflict in history. The societies and economies of the combatant nations were mobilized to a greater extent than ever before. The conflict was also portrayed as a total battle between the forces of democracy and the evil of right-wing, racist extremism. Consequently, this conflict witnessed the emergence of total war. Given the scale of effort being directed toward prosecuting the war, the stakes involved in the conflict rose correspondingly. Consequently, the war could only be settled by a total victory of one side over the other. Hence, the notion of the total surrender of the enemy was implemented. There were three contributory developments that influenced this emergence of total war: the savagery of Axis occupation policies, the barbarization of the norms of warfare, and the particular odiousness of the racist policies of the Nazis, and their genocide of the Jews and the Slavs in Eastern Europe.

During the war there was an unprecedented savagery in Axis occupation policies. Throughout history, military forces had used terror to facilitate their conquests and to subdue resistance to their authority. Equally, terror had been used to help with the economic exploitation of conquered territories, as in the colonial conquests of the late nineteenth and early twentieth centuries. However, in the age of total war, these methods were greatly intensified and systematized. The Axis deliberately plundered occupied economies on a hitherto unknown scale. Moreover, the Axis crushed Resistance acts with the utmost savagery and the deliberate use of terror. The Axis adopted the policy of brutal reprisals against innocent hostages, usually notable community figures, in response to Resistance activity. The key principle to this policy was asymmetry: the reprisal was always many times – often ten or one hundred times – worse than the original Resistance act that had inspired it.

Another key development in World War II was the barbarization of warfare. This was both related to, and influenced in turn, the savage occupation policies and the emergence of total war. All the Axis powers, as well as the Soviets, mistreated prisoners of war. Moreover, in the brutal partisan conflicts occurring behind the front, many innocent civilians were killed.

The savagery of Axis occupation policies, and the barbarization of warfare were also two components in the process toward the emergence of total war. One aspect of this process was the debate over aerial warfare. In 1939 there was an aversion, particularly by the Allies, to adopting indiscriminate terror bombing of civilian areas to break the morale of the enemy. Yet the Germans initiated terror bombing, and by 1944 the British in particular were prepared to resort to these methods as the most effective way of prosecuting the war. The ultimate example of this process was America's decision to drop the atomic bomb on Japan in August 1945. During World War II, therefore, there emerged one of the preconditions of the later phenomenon of modern terrorism; that there was no such things as innocent civilians, that all members of an enemy society were legitimate targets. This development, when coupled with the nationalism erupting in the Imperial colonies in the aftermath of the war, led to the campaigns of decolonization of the 1950s.

After victory in 1945, the Allies tried the Axis leaders as war criminals. This was an attempt to impose justice on those who had callously used terror for their own ends. The issues were complicated, however: the dropping of the atomic bomb, for instance, was the ultimate in terror bombing. Such ambiguities again haunt the quest for justice underway in the war crimes trials being held in 1996 regarding the conflicts in Rwanda and the former Yugoslavia. ■

TERROR IN THE GERMAN OCCUPATION OF THE EAST

One of the major instruments of terror in the Third Reich was the German army. Critical historians base this damning assertion not on its front-line combat role, but rather on its sinister activities in the rear areas. One myth, created after 1945, was that the German army had been engaged in a "normal war" against enemy soldiers; any brutal action behind the front was a direct response to partisans (civilian forces organized to drive out occupying troops) who had taken the first step in abandoning the accepted rules of warfare. The brutal treatment of civilian populations in the rear areas cannot, however, be separated from Nazi racial policy. The army was the instrument by which the Nazi regime spread ideologically motivated murder and terror all over Europe.

Terrorist policies were particularly evident in the vast areas of the Soviet Union, which remained under military occupation during 1941-44. Popular views of the conflict attribute the mass killings, especially of the Jews, to Nazi special agencies such as the party's paramilitary arm (the SS) and the Security Service (SD). However, the army was deeply implicated in this systematic and deliberate policy of extermination. Plans to conduct a genocidal war against the Soviets had been drawn up by the German High Command several months before the attack on the Soviet Union in June 1941. Military planners intended to pursue a "hunger-strategy" that would condemn millions of Russians to death through starvation.

To implement its plans, the army introduced new martial laws. They encouraged German soldiers to abandon rules of warfare regarding captured enemy troops and the rights of civilians. Such cruel terror policies were an essential aspect of the initial successful advance of the German army into Russia. Such policies were not, as apologists argue, a forced response to the later problems of military stalemate or the increased Soviet partisan menace in the rear areas.

KEY FACTS

- As a reprisal for the murder of Reinhard Heydrich, the Nazi protector of Bohemia-Moravia, the Czech village of Lidice was destroyed. The men were shot, the women imprisoned in concentration camps, and the children sent to be brought up in German families. In all, 1,300 civilians were killed.
- Following the Commissar Order, the German army executed on the spot some 60,000 Russian soldiers after they were captured.

DEATH IN NAZI CAPTIVITY

As many as 3.3 million of the 5.7 million Soviet Red Army prisoners of war who had surrendered to the German armed forces died in captivity. To accord with the Nazi Commissar Order, all Soviet political officers and Jews were singled out immediately for liquidation. Hundreds of thousands of other Red Army prisoners died after deliberate mistreatment, particularly of starvation, exposure to cold, exhaustion, and beatings.

Official plans for the economic exploitation of the occupied territories in the east did not just encourage terrorization of the entire civilian population. Systematic terror was even included in the army's mandate. The army was ordered to live off the land, which necessitated the plunder of the already impoverished local inhabitants. The army's commands were also to remove by force vast quantities of food and raw materials, as well as slave-labor, for shipment back to the Reich. Russian peasants responded initially to these seizures with grim resignation rather than active resistance. Yet, despite the absence of any concerted opposition, the German army, under the guise of the necessity of war, took the severest measures against anyone who withheld their total cooperation.

Novosti

A Red Army partisan hanged by the Germans as a deterrent to other guerrilla activity.

The army also took an active part in implementing the Holocaust. Army units not only assisted the SS and the Security Service (SD) in rounding up Soviet Jews for transportation to the extermination camps, but often undertook large-scale summary executions of Soviet Jews behind the front line. This was terror motivated by ideology rather than by any clear military purpose, even though the pretense was made that the Jews helped the Soviets.

Terror by the German army was most graphically illustrated in the area where racially motivated extermination of the Jewish population blurred with perceived threats to rear-area security. New martial laws let the army execute individuals merely suspected of lending assistance to "bandits," and also allowed for "collective reprisal measures." Numerous villages were razed to the ground, with the inhabitants expelled or murdered, and hostage-taking and execution occurred on a horrific scale. Army commanders recommended the shooting of all suspicious persons, including women, children, and the elderly. Tens of thousands of villages were destroyed and hardly a single Russian family in the occupied area remained untouched by some act of savagery. The number of civilians eradicated is thought to have exceeded 1.4 million. By contrast, German losses in anti-partisan actions were usually small, and sometimes as low as six percent of those of the "enemy."

PROVOCATION BY THE PARTISANS

A main objective of the Soviet partisans was to provoke the German forces into reprisal actions. Terror against Russians in the German-appointed local administration eroded any tendency on the part of the population to coexist with the occupiers. The Russian civilians found themselves beaten between the hammer of the German army and the anvil of the partisan movement. They usually sided with whomever was strongest at a given time. A small number of German officers realized that indiscriminate terror was counter-productive since it drove the locals into the hands of the partisans. Yet, despite these reservations, the level of violence continued to escalate. The impulse for terror was increasingly based on ideology rather than military pragmatism.

The barbarous acts committed by the army were much more than a simple litany of crimes that developed ad hoc in an attempt to pacify the rear areas. The war of terror fought by the German army should be regarded as an integral component of the Nazis' racially determined extermination policies.

Theo J. Schulte

SEE ALSO: GERMAN TERROR IN FRANCE AND ITALY; TERROR AND THE NAZI BARBARIZATION OF WARFARE.

FURTHER READING

- Bartov, Omer. *Hitler's Army: Soldiers, Nazis, and War in the Third Reich.* New York: Oxford University Press, 1991.
- Hirschfeld, G., ed. *The Policies of Genocide: Jews and Soviet Prisoners of War in Nazi Germany.* Boston: Allen & Unwin, 1986.
- Schulte, Theo J. *The German Army and Nazi Policies in Occupied Russia.* Oxford and New York: Berg, 1989.

ROMANIAN TERROR IN TRANSNISTRIA

The experience of Romania in World War II demonstrates how devastating the use of terror tactics can be when applied even for a short period. But it also shows that other methods can be more effective in pacifying a conquered population.

During the 1930s, pro- and anti-German factions battled to control Romania. The fascist, anti-Semitic Iron Guard movement advocated terrorism to overthrow the state and assassinated two prime ministers. In September 1940, the Iron Guard and General Ion Antonescu jointly came to power in Romania in a German-sponsored coalition. Their government continued to have Nazi support after the German occupation of Romania from October 7, 1940. The four months in which the Iron Guard shared government were marked by the murder of hundreds of political opponents and Jews. The Iron Guard's reign of terror ended in their failed January 1941 attempt to seize sole power. The ensuing riots and massacres were so damaging to Romania's internal stability that Hitler let Antonescu suppress his one-time Fascist allies.

THE DOOM OF THE JEWS

From 1942, Antonescu eased Romania's policy toward the Jews, and those living in central Romania were the biggest Jewish community in Axis Europe to survive the war largely intact. Despite the relative good fortune of these Jews, Romania was still responsible for the second-largest number of Jewish deaths in Axis Europe. The eastern provinces of Bukovina and Bessarabia (now in modern Moldova, a former member state of the Soviet Union, situated on Romania's eastern border) fell under the control of the Soviet Union following the latter's invasion of June 28, 1940. At the outbreak of war between the Soviet Union and Germany in June 1941, German and Romanian forces reclaimed these provinces. The Romanians now treated the Jews of Bessarabia and Bukovina as enemy aliens, whereas previously the Jews had lived relatively safety as Romanian nationals. The Romanian army and Germany's Einsatzgruppe D, one of the four groups ordered to destroy Soviet Jews, conducted mass killings as they advanced through the province. At least 13,000 Jews were killed within three months.

Later in 1941, the remaining Bessarabian and Bukovinan Jews were driven into Transnistria, a province in Soviet Ukraine, just over Romania's south-eastern border. Transnistria's vast territory, covering 15,600 square miles between the Dniester and Bug rivers, was now occupied by Romanian troops. Here, some 17,000 Jews died from starvation and fatigue on the long march east and another 67,000 later perished in makeshift concentration camps, largely from typhus. Only 52,000 Jews survived this attempted genocide. General Antonescu repatriated them in 1943.

Transnistria bore the brunt of Romanian revenge after the Romanian Fourth Army suffered huge casualties against Soviet forces in the fight for Odessa, Transnistria's capital, on October 16, 1941. Romanian troops immediately began to take hostages and hang suspected collaborators and spies from streetlights. Six days later, a bomb destroyed the Romanian headquarters in Odessa, killing the general commanding the garrison and 51 of his staff. Although probably preset by the retreating Red Army, the Romanians blamed local partisans for the bomb. The Romanian army, again assisted by the Germans of Einsatzgruppe D, responded by massacring up to 19,000 Odessan

KEY FACTS

- Romanian troops arrested 3,500 local Jews on July 29, 1941. The day before, a Romanian soldier of the 14th Infantry Division reported that he had seen a Jew in the town of Iasi signalling to Soviet aircraft. They executed most Jews in the first of several mass killings that took place over the following months.
- From 1942, Romanian ruler General Antonescu relaxed the policy of persecuting Jews – but not before his troops had killed over 100,000 of them.

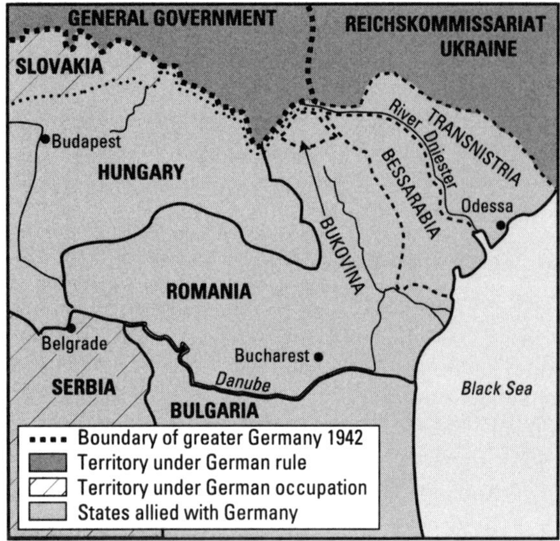

Wartime Romania: most victims of atrocities were Jews from the provinces of Bessarabia and Bukovina or the occupied Ukrainian territory of Transnistria.

civilians, mostly Jews. The remaining Transnistrian Jews were herded into concentration camps where tens of thousands died over the savage winter of 1941-42. It is impossible to establish accurate figures for Jewish deaths attributable to the Romanians. They undoubtedly totalled at least 110,000, and possibly twice that number.

ANTI-PARTISAN POLICY

Transnistria had a wartime population of 2.25 million, of which 80 percent were Ukrainians. In 1942-43, the Romanian garrison there averaged 100,000 troops. The Romanians set reprisal ratios of 200 communists to be executed for every officer killed by partisans, and 100 for every soldier. But after late 1941, however, the Romanians did not implement such terror tactics. Some 90 percent of executions in Transnistria were in the first few weeks of the occupation.

The Red Army had left behind groups of activists in Odessa to serve as partisans under the direct orders of Stalin himself. From late 1941, the Romanians introduced the efficient Special Intelligence Service to counter them. This agency had frequent success against partisans in Odessa using intelligence, infiltrators, and informants. But the Service could not eliminate those partisans using the 125 miles of uncharted catacombs beneath the city. The Romanians tried blocking many of the 160 known entrances, and a number of partisans were starved to death. According to Soviet reports, the Romanians also tried to saturate the catacombs with tear gas, and later used poison gas, but this failed because the complex was too large. Even so, the catacomb partisans were reduced to a low of about 35 people in late 1942. Although their numbers grew into hundreds by 1944, they had little impact beyond providing an example of legendary endurance. The few small Soviet partisan bands in the interior of Transnistria had equally little success.

Romanian security policy in 1942-43 was very effective in keeping Transnistria passive without resorting to the ruthless terrorist measures used elsewhere with less success by the more powerful Germans. Indeed, refugees tried to flee from German to Romanian jurisdiction. Romanian policies in Transnistria resulted in the best food, health, and education provisions in Axis-occupied eastern Europe. The Romanians allowed religious and cultural revivals, released Transnistrian prisoners of war, and amnestied many local communists.

Such leniency eased Transnistrian hostility toward Romanian occupation after the initial terror of 1941. The moderation also undermined Soviet attempts to recruit partisans. Even when the withdrawing Romanians looted Transnistria in March 1944, the local partisans could not mobilize civilian support.

Despite his relative restraint in subjugating civilians in occupied Transnistria, Antonescu, his interior minister, and his governor of Transnistria, were all executed for war crimes on June 1, 1946.

Bertrande Roberts

SEE ALSO: TERROR IN THE GERMAN OCCUPATION OF THE EAST; RESISTANCE IN THE EAST AND TERRORISM; TERROR AND THE WAFFEN SS.

FURTHER READING

- Axworthy, Mark, Cornel Scafes, and Cristian Craciunoiu. *Third Axis, Fourth Ally.* London: Arms and Armour, and New York: Sterling, 1995.
- Butnaru, I. C. *The Silent Holocaust: Romania and its Jews.* New York: Greenwood Press, 1992.
- Schulte, Theo J. *The German Army and Nazi Policies in Occupied Russia.* Oxford and New York: Berg, 1989.

GERMAN TERROR IN FRANCE AND ITALY

By the fall of 1941, much of Europe was under German occupation. Hitler's *Blitzkrieg* ("lightning war") policy had paid off and his armies had thundered over the continent, pushing all before them. Just as swift, however, was the need to make the newly occupied territories secure and to eliminate the resistance that would inevitably follow from the conquered civilian populations.

The German authorities had had nearly a decade of practice in suppressing opposition. A quarter of a million of their own people had been sent to concentration camps after Hitler had come to power. It was unlikely that foreign nationals would be treated any better. Nazi occupation policies in France from 1940 and Italy from 1943 were extremely harsh. Deliberate and systematic methods of terror were used to deter civilians from resisting Nazi authority and to crush this resistance as soon as it arose.

FRANCE, 1940-44

After France capitulated in 1940, Germany established its own military administration in the north and west of the country. In the south, a substitute French government was installed in the spa town of Vichy. This regime was compelled to collaborate with the Germans. The head of state was the aged World War I hero Marshal Pétain, but the effective ruler was Pierre Laval, who had twice briefly served as prime minister in the 1930s and as foreign minister in 1934–36.

German occupation policy was to maintain a stable and peaceful France, so that the country's economic resources could be exploited fully to support the German war machine. But both the German regime and its puppet Vichy government rigorously pursued a policy of subduing the civilian population by terror. Attacks on German installations and personnel were met with summary reprisals in the form of random executions and hostage-taking.

In addition, as early as October 1940, German racial ideology had also become a reason for persecuting French civilians. The Germans in northern France and the Vichy government progressively enacted anti-Semitic legislation. Laval's regime even blamed the Jews for the fall of France. In August 1942, the Germans and the Vichy government had begun to round up and deport Jews from both the occupied and unoccupied regions. One third of France's Jewish population ended up in German concentration camps, where most subsequently perished.

The German invasion of the Soviet Union on June 22, 1941, transformed Nazi occupation policy in France. It led to the recruitment of a French volunteer regiment for service in the East and the drafting of French civilians for forced labor in German factories. This was because the increasing German losses on the Eastern Front during 1942 meant more German nationals were conscripted to fight, leaving a shortage of workers at home. Unsurprisingly, this sparked off a wave of protests.

The French Resistance, by now a nationwide network of regional cells, capitalized on the situation and organized strikes, as in the province of Haute Savoie in early November 1942. The resistance also carried out attacks on German personnel. The Germans responded by strengthening the presence of

KEY FACTS

- On June 10, 1944, in response to Resistance support for the D-Day invasion of Normandy, the SS Nazi militia murdered 642 civilians in the village of Oradour-sur-Glane.
- In March 1944, in the Ardeatine caves outside Rome, 335 Italian prisoners were executed as a reprisal for the killing of 32 SS officers.

Popperfoto

Police indicate finger marks on a wall left by manacled prisoners of the Gestapo.

the Nazi party militia (SS) and the Security Service in the occupied north under the command of Brigadier Karl Oberg.

VICHY OCCUPIED

On November 11, 1942, German forces occupied Vichy France, as a direct response to the Allied landings in French North Africa (Operation Torch). Although now under direct occupation by the Germans, the Vichy authorities attempted to resist increased German control of French internal security by reducing the need for German intervention. To do this, the Vichy government needed to combat the resistance, so in January 1943, it set up its own paramilitary force, known as the Milice.

The Milice quickly gained a reputation for brutality. The force was hated and feared more for this than for its obvious collaboration with the Germans, because it was terrorizing its own people. The German occupiers also replied to intensified resistance with brutality. German troops shot civilian hostages in retaliation for resistance attacks. At the same time, captured partisans were routinely tortured and killed.

By the spring of 1944, it was clear that German terror tactics were having little effect in curbing the activities of the French Resistance. The campaign was partly misdirected because of the Nazi obsession with the Jews, who were seized as hostages or executed whether they were active in the resistance or not. Prior to the D-Day invasion of Normandy (June 6, 1944), partisans attacked French communications in order to assist the Allies in isolating the region. After D-Day, the resistance sabotaged movements of German reinforcements and supplies to the front. Inevitably, the Germans responded with ferocious reprisals.

With Allied troops now on French soil, the clashes between the Milice and the resistance in the south became more bitter and savage. And during July 1944, when the resistance encouraged a general uprising in the southwest, the German security forces mounted a final, coordinated, anti-partisan operation.

However, the progress of the Allied advance from Normandy and, from August, from the south of France, forced the Germans to abandon the interior of the country rapidly. The final act of the German occupation was the forcible removal of the Vichy government to Germany in September 1944.

ITALY, 1943-45

Mussolini's fascist Italy had entered World War II in summer 1940 as Germany's ally in order to benefit from German successes in the war. But military disasters in North Africa and on the Eastern Front meant that by 1943 the war was unpopular in all sections of Italian society. In September, after the Allied invasion of Sicily, Mussolini was deposed and a new government under Marshal Badoglio signed an armistice with the Allies.

The Germans had been expecting this development and immediately occupied Italy. German forces took Rome after a brief fight, occupied Italy as far south as Naples, and disarmed the Italian military. German troops executed several thousand Italian officers who had ordered their troops to resist. Meanwhile, Allied forces landed on the southern Italian mainland and began fighting their way north.

German occupation policy was to reestablish a fascist republic – the Italian Social Republic – at Salo on Lake Garda in northern Italy. The republic was led by Mussolini, who had been sprung from prison by German commandos in early September. The German military strategy in Italy was mainly defensive, aiming to slow down the progress north of the Allies and inflict heavy casualties.

The Germans raised, trained, and equipped a small new Italian National Republican Army loyal to Mussolini, while the Italians themselves raised their own National Republican Guard for internal security operations. At the same time, Hitler annexed the South Tirol in northern Italy, which had a large ethnic German population. General Karl Wolff was appointed head of internal security and anti-partisan operations there, crushing opposition with hand-picked men from the SS.

Along with the occupying forces came Hitler's racial policy. For the first time in modern Italy, Jews were at risk. Although they were a small minority, Italian Jews were loyal, even to the fascists. But after the Nazi occupation, widespread anti-Semitic riots broke out in September 1943. Jews from the northern Italian cities were rounded up and deported, first to the Fossoli di Carpi concentration camp in the South Tirol and later to a host of similar camps throughout northern Italy, where thousands perished.

ANTI-COMMUNIST OPERATIONS

The strongest opposition to Nazi rule in Italy came from communists, who were concentrated in the urbanized north. During the spring of 1944, the resistance from communist partisans intensified, especially in the Italian Alps. Germany's response was to strengthen its security forces. However, German troops were in short supply, for they were now having to defend German occupied territories on the Eastern and Western Fronts from imminent invasion.

Instead, an array of anti-communist Cossacks, Turks, and sympathizers from the Baltic States (Estonia, Latvia, and Lithuania) arrived for occupation duties. General Wolff increasingly relied on Mussolini's forces to fight the communist partisans. The security forces routinely murdered hostages in retaliation for partisan attacks. One act of reprisal followed a bomb attack that killed 33 German police officers. Italian priests, Jews, women, and two 14-year-old boys were arrested and shot in Rome by the Gestapo.

The formation of a united front among the various guerrilla groups in mid-1944 prompted Mussolini to reform the infamous fascist Blackshirt militia, known as the Armata Milizia, to fight the partisans. The Blackshirts' response to the resistance's assassinations, bombings, and ambushes was a deliberate campaign of terror. They destroyed many towns and villages, deported thousands of people to concentration camps, and carried out summary mass executions of the male population.

Yet even this orchestrated terror failed to suppress partisan activity. As the Allies advanced on northern Italy during the fall of 1944, resistance activity intensified. The partisans escalated their activities from sabotage, bombings, and individual assassinations to more ambitious, larger-scale military operations designed to wipe out Axis forces and liberate entire Italian communities from fascist control.

Despite constant, vigorous, and murderous Axis anti-partisan sweeps, large swathes of northern Italy were under partisan control by spring 1945. In April, the partisans launched a general insurrection that liberated Genoa, Milan, and Turin. They now threatened to sever German communications as Axis forces attempted a general withdrawal through the Alpine passes and Germany beyond. This action helped force the German command to a separate surrender of the Axis forces in Italy to the Allies on May 2, 1945, six days before Germany's formal capitulation.

Russell A. Hart

SEE ALSO: TERROR IN WORLD WAR I; TERROR IN THE GERMAN OCCUPATION OF THE EAST; GERMAN TERROR IN NORWAY; TERROR'S USE BY THE FRENCH RESISTANCE; WWII RESISTANCE IN YUGOSLAVIA AND TERRORISM; TERROR AND THE WAFFEN SS.

FURTHER READING

- Gordon, B. *Collaborationism in France During the Second World War.* Ithaca, NY: Cornell University Press, 1980.
- Puzzo, D. *The Partisans and the War in Italy.* New York: P. Lang, 1992.
- Zuccotti, S. *The Italians and the Holocaust: Persecution, Rescue, and Survival.* London: Halbon, and New York: Basic Books, 1987.

GERMAN TERROR IN NORWAY

The Germans invaded Norway on April 9, 1940. In a brilliant yet costly two-month campaign, the German armed forces (Wehrmacht) decisively beat the unprepared Norwegian forces and their equally disorganized British and French allies. King Haakon VII and his government fled to London, and the Germans were left in control of a dazed population. The invaders were eagerly welcomed by Vidkun Quisling, whose name remains synonymous with the word *traitor*. He headed the previously unimportant Nazi-style Nasjonal Samling (National Union) and proclaimed himself head of government.

QUISLING AND COLLABORATION

It suited the Germans to have such a willing collaborator as Quisling. They needed a stable base in Norway from which to mount attacks upon Britain. In addition, the country was rich in mineral resources, especially coal, which were vital to the German war economy.

There was also the ideological factor. As Norwegian historian Olav Riste wrote, the Norwegians had the "dubious honor of being regarded [by the Nazis] as a kindred folk – a wayward Nordic tribe that should be led into the Greater German Reich through persuasion." When Nazi attempts at persuasion failed, Reichskommissar Josef Terboven, chief German official in Norway, resorted to more traditional Nazi terror methods.

KEY FACTS

- The Germans operated a brutal reprisal policy to deter resistance acts. In late 1942, in Trondheim, west-central Norway, the Nazis executed ten prominent civilians as "atonement" for sabotage.
- After British agents attacked German facilities near Bergen, in southern Norway, on January 25, 1943, the Nazis arrested 200 Norwegian civilians and deported them to concentration camps.

In the first year of German occupation, there was little resistance in Norway. However, Quisling soon alienated the Norwegian people by attempting to intimidate a society unused to political violence. He believed that the active demonstration of his Nasjonal Samling party's power would stimulate fear and respect. A campaign of street violence by party workers was organized and, in the schools, teachers and school administrators were beaten up.

The Norwegian people staged large-scale protests in Oslo in December 1940. Quisling's attempt at the Nazification of the Norwegian education system was also deeply resented by the people. The German navy complained that such actions were destabilizing the country and threatening the security of their bases. But Reichskommissar Terboven could not allow the authority of the Nasjonal Samling to be flouted. He decided to stage a demonstration of German power.

GERMAN REPRESSION

In September 1941, Terboven observed that: "I have without success placed myself at the beck and call of the Norwegians. I will now force them to their knees." Thus, when the Norwegian Federation of Trade Unions declared a strike in Oslo on September 8, 1941, Terboven saw his chance and declared a state of emergency. The Nazi party's paramilitary force, the Schutz Staffeln (SS), and the Nazi secret police, (Gestapo), rounded up 300 resistance workers and trade unionists, two of whom were executed.

The rounding up and execution of Norwegians was the first use of systematic terror by the Germans in Norway and it served as a warning to the population that Terboven was willing to use terror. One of his officials, Dr. Alfred Huhnhäser, noted that if Terboven had in the beginning been inclined to treat the Norwegians well in order to win them over, as was Hitler's wish, then he changed his mind "from the time of the state of emergency and began a reign of terror."

Terboven decided to help Quisling with the Nazification of education by arresting 1,300 male

Mary Evans Picture Collection

"The truth about the Swastika" – this caption, in a Norwegian resistance propaganda photograph depicting Germans rounding up suspects, emphasizes the repressive terror of the Nazi occupation.

teachers, of whom 500 were sent as forced labor to the extremely harsh conditions of the Arctic. And when the Norwegian police refused to round up laborers for Quisling's 1943 Work Effort, Terboven had the police leader Gunnar Eilifsen executed and 1,300 officers deported to a concentration camp in Poland.

THE CONSEQUENCES OF RESISTANCE

The German response to resistance, either by British agents or the Norwegian resistance, was even more brutal. In April 1942, British agents killed two Gestapo men at Tælevåg, near Bergen. The Nazis obliterated the village, interned every inhabitant, shot 18 hostages, and deported all the males to the Sachsenhausen concentration camp, where 76 of them died. Such a brutal reprisal had the desired effect on the Norwegian people. It caused great local resentment against the resistance and led the Norwegian government-in-exile to demand of their British ally "No more Tælevåg!"

On October 5, 1942, British agents, aided by the local Norwegian resistance, attacked the iron ore mines at Fosdalen. In retaliation, the Germans executed 35 local villagers without trial. When the Norwegian police chief Karl Marthinsen was killed on February 8, 1945, 30 hostages were shot in reprisal.

The public reaction forced the resistance to stop killing Nasjonal Samling members. But one month later, the resistance warned that continued use of terror would lead to an escalation of defiance. By this time, the Germans knew the war was lost and retribution imminent. They executed no more hostages.

PERSECUTING NORWEGIAN JEWS

Quisling was a fervent anti-Semite, and the Nasjonal Samling actively aided the Nazis' round-up of Norwegian Jews late in 1942. The Norwegian resistance managed to spirit 925 to Sweden, but 759 were deported, most of them to the Auschwitz death camp, where only 25 survived.

Compared with the extreme brutality of German rule in Eastern Europe, the suffering in Norway was not extensive, largely because of the high status of Norway in Nazi racial theories. But although both Terboven and Quisling were prepared to use ruthless measures when necessary, the use of terror to intimidate the population was a failure. It merely united the Norwegians against him. The German repression met with some success, however, causing temporary suspensions of resistance activity.

M. Christopher Mann

SEE ALSO: TERROR IN WORLD WAR I; TERROR IN THE GERMAN OCCUPATION OF THE EAST; GERMAN TERROR IN FRANCE AND ITALY; TERROR'S USE BY THE FRENCH RESISTANCE; THE HOLOCAUST.

FURTHER READING

- Hayes, Paul M. *Quisling: The Career and Political Ideas of Vidkun Quisling, 1887-1945.* Newton Abbot, Devon: David and Charles, 1971; Bloomington: Indiana University Press, 1972.
- Petrow, Richard. *The Bitter Years: The Invasion and Occupation of Denmark and Norway, April 1940-May 1945.* London: Hodder and Stoughton, 1975; New York: Morrow, 1979.
- Vigness, Paul C. *The German Occupation of Norway.* New York: Vantage, 1970.

RESISTANCE IN THE EAST AND TERRORISM

On June 22, 1941, Nazi Germany invaded the Soviet Union in a war designed to eliminate the "Jewish Bolshevik enemy," and Soviet Communism. Hitler aimed to subjugate the "sub-human" Slavs, which included most western Soviet citizens, and to win vast territories as new settlements for Germany. At first, German troops were welcomed in many areas as liberators from communist rule, but they soon met increasing popular resistance as the brutality of Nazi occupation policies became apparent. But German terror was only half of an increasingly dreadful picture. Soviet terror quickly formed the other. For example, at the outbreak of war, Soviet dictator Joseph Stalin ordered the immediate execution of political prisoners and suspected spies.

Next, the Soviet secret police, the NKVD, and the regional committees of the Soviet Communist Party received orders to set up a resistance network in areas occupied by the Germans. On July 3, 1941, in his first wartime broadcast, Stalin announced that a "people's war" involving a vast partisan movement would be waged against the Germans with the the aim of producing "intolerable conditions for the invaders."

The partisan movement, which unleashed a savage internal war in German-occupied Soviet territory, grew slowly. No preparation had been made for partisan warfare in the Soviet Union before 1941. The first partisan groups consisted mainly of NKVD sabotage groups plus Red Army soldiers cut off in the rear by the advancing Germans. Weapons were extremely scarce and this severely hampered any expansion. The main activities were sporadic raids on German headquarters or small German garrisons.

KEY FACTS

- During the 1941-45 Soviet-German conflict, Stalin established large numbers of partisan detachments to carry on a brutal terror struggle against Nazism behind enemy lines.
- The Nazis also used terror tactics to defeat the Soviet partisans. In a March 1942, operation in the Crimea, on the Black Sea, the Germans killed not only 153 partisans, but also 1,800 innocent peasants, to warn others not to aid the partisans.

A large-scale partisan movement only appeared in late 1942. After this, the partisans were regularly reinforced by Red Army troops who parachuted behind German lines. Neither the German army in its anti-partisan operations nor the Soviet partisans paid any heed to the accepted laws governing war conduct, and neither showed any concern for the local population. Both sides used widespread terror against peaceful populations in a savage struggle that cost more than 1 million lives.

The communist partisans gathered intelligence, infiltrated German military staffs as interpreters or clerks, organized sabotage, and assassinated German officers. Soviet terrorist actions were often calculated provocations designed to stimulate ferocious German reprisals, making coexistence between the population and the German occupiers virtually impossible. In one Soviet village, for instance, the Germans shot over 300 local Russians in revenge after partisans killed three German officers. Similarly, in March 1942, the Germans discovered that villagers near Bobruisk, White Russia, to the east of Poland, were aiding the partisans. The Nazis launched a terror reprisal, burning down villages and killing 3,500 peasants to warn others not to cooperate with the partisans.

Soviet partisans, however, also used terror against their own population. The partisans assassinated collaborators or attacked their families. Partisans also attacked German camps holding captured Soviet soldiers, presumably to discourage surrender at the front or to swell the ranks of partisan units with escaped prisoners. The partisans also terrorized Russians who worked for the German administration as mayors or policemen. In areas under their control, partisans put up Red Flags, symbols of communist sympathies, which they attached to hidden mines. The mines blew up any anti-Soviet sympathizers attempting to remove the flags.

Novosti

Soviet Partisans in Vitebsk, White Russia (east of Poland), take an oath of allegiance to the struggle of the Great Patriotic War against Nazism.

While the partisans brought a degree of Soviet rule back to the occupied areas, for the local population they simply replaced Nazi terror with their own Red terror.

Partisans also used terror within their own ranks. The death penalty was the basis of discipline within partisan units, and executions were used deliberately as a means of intimidation and coercion.

TAKING THE PARTISAN WAR ABROAD

Up to 1944, Soviet partisans had also carried on within the Soviet Union a bitter war of extermination against anti-Soviet organizations and nationalist political groups such as those in the Ukraine. In 1944, after the advancing Red Army had liberated all Soviet territory, the partisan movement changed. Stalin ordered the partisans to advance across the Soviet frontier to begin a "revolutionary struggle" in Soviet-occupied eastern Europe, which would introduce a Stalinist political system. The partisans infiltrated behind German lines and advanced ahead of the Red Army into Poland. These communist bands both provoked German reprisals against the local population and also killed members of the anti-Soviet Polish resistance.

With the Red Army closing on Czechoslovakia in the spring of 1944, the partisans decided to "assist" the Czechoslovaks by sending ten Soviet-trained partisan groups into Slovakia. In reality, these partisans were preparing the way for Soviet domination of Slovakia. During the last months of the war, the partisan struggle against German occupation of Slovakia became a bitter struggle between communist and anti-communist elements. The Soviet partisans deliberately used terror tactics to destroy their non-communist opponents.

The Soviet struggle against German occupation cost more than 1 million lives and was characterized by universal use of terror.

John Erickson

SEE ALSO: TERROR IN THE GERMAN OCCUPATION OF THE EAST; WWII RESISTANCE IN YUGOSLAVIA AND TERRORISM; TERROR AND THE NAZI BARBARIZATION OF WARFARE; TERROR AND THE SOVIET BARBARIZATION OF WARFARE.

FURTHER READING

- Dallin, Alexander. *German Rule in Russia, 1941-1945.* London: Macmillan, and Boulder, C.O.: Westview Press, 1981.
- Linz, S. J. ed. *The Impact of World War II on the Soviet Union.* Totowa, NJ: Rowman and Allanheld, 1985.
- Lukas, R. C. *Forgotten Holocaust: The Poles Under German Occupation, 1939-1944.* 2nd ed. New York: Hippocrene Books, 1997.

TERROR'S USE BY THE FRENCH RESISTANCE

The Resistance in France consisted of a network of groups acting against the German occupation of 1940-44. Resistance activity was not substantial or widespread at first but, as the Allies slowly gained military dominance over the Germans in 1943-44, the Resistance became invaluable to preparations for the invasion of Europe.

Resistance fighters were routinely called terrorists by the Germans, but only some of their activities fit that description in any way. Espionage and helping shot-down airmen return to Allied territory were important Resistance activities, but those engaged in them usually tried to avoid violent incidents that might lead to detection. However, other resisters carried out sabotage, assassination, and other "terrorist" attacks on the Germans and their French collaborators.

VICHY AND THE FREE FRENCH

After defeating France in May–June 1940, the Germans did not overrun the whole country but chose instead to divide it into two zones. The Germans occupied the northern one and left the southern part to be controlled by a French puppet government based in the town of Vichy. The Vichy government was led by Marshal Philippe Pétain, one of France's heroes of World War I. Pétain's government was regarded by most French people, in 1940 at least, as the legitimate government of France. The Germans occupied the whole of France from November 1942, when the Allies liberated the French colonies in North Africa. After this, with the Allies clearly winning the war, Resistance activities increased and Pétain's position declined.

Some Frenchmen denied Vichy's authority from the start. Charles de Gaulle, the most junior general in the French army (Pétain was the most senior), escaped to Britain, announced the existence of "Free France," and, with a few followers, urged all French people to fight on. Pétain condemned de Gaulle as a traitor but de Gaulle was supported by the British and, from mid-1943, by the Americans, although he had many disagreements with both. By the time of the Allied invasion in 1944, de Gaulle and the Free French had become the major focus of the French Resistance.

KEY FACTS

- The Resistance was a loose network of groups determined to fight the German occupation of northern France and the collaborators at Vichy.
- The Resistance used terror tactics, particularly assassination, against the German occupation forces and their Vichy collaborators. They also used terror against rival resistance groups and to discipline members of their own organization.

THE ROLE OF THE COMMUNISTS

The French Communist Party had been banned by the French government early in the war. However, from June 1940 until the Nazis invaded the Soviet Union a year later (while the Nazi–Soviet Pact of 1939 was still operative) the communists were tolerated by the Germans and, obedient to Moscow, they did not resist the German occupation. Like communists elsewhere, however, the French communists' history of clandestine political operations and their influence in labor unions gave them a leading role in the Resistance when the party line turned against the Nazis after the June 1941 German invasion of the Soviet Union. The main communist organizations involved in the Resistance were the National Front and its military wing, the Francs-Tireurs et Partisans. From late 1943, the communists, too, reluctantly accepted de Gaulle's authority as leader of the French forces in exile.

Various British organizations were involved in helping develop the Resistance. MI6 (the British spy

Hulton Getty Picture Collection

French Resistance members capture a wounded German soldier near Montneyan in September 1944.

service) and MI9 (the department responsible for escape lines) did important work, but in terms of "terrorist" activity the most significant department was the Special Operations Executive (SOE), whose role was to stir up armed rebellion against the Germans. In 1944, the British sent special forces' teams, consisting mainly of Special Air Service personnel, to France to lead and direct local uprisings. As British contact with the Resistance was already well established when the United States entered the war (and because the U.S. Government's political relations with de Gaulle were very poor), the American role in assisting the French Resistance was less substantial than Britain's. However, the U.S. Office of Strategic Services (OSS), the forerunner of the modern CIA, joined the SOE and other British agencies in their activities.

Resistance in France began with small, separate groups of like-minded people starting to work against the Germans. These groups had a vast range of personal and political motives, and enormously varied backgrounds, training, and aptitude for resistance work. By 1944, these ineffective and disparate groups had joined a single organization with substantial training, access to large quantities of arms and explosives, and the capability of carrying out a wide range of tasks in response to orders from Allied commanders.

Arms and explosives came, apart from small amounts purloined from the Germans, from the Allies. In the course of the war, Britain and the U.S. sent 500,000 weapons to the Resistance. SOE transported 700 agents in and out of France and distributed thousands of copies of pamphlets on guerrilla warfare and bomb-making to provide further training. Orders were received by secret radio operators and coded messages were included in British BBC broadcasts.

The work of unifying the various separate groups in France was led by Jean Moulin, a former civil servant dismissed by the Germans for refusing to carry out punitive measures they had ordered. By the time the Allies invaded France in June 1944, all important Resistance groups were part of a formal military structure known as the French Forces of the Interior.

ASSASSINATION AND SABOTAGE

Assassination was a favorite Resistance tactic. One example is the August 1941 murder on the Paris subway of a German naval official, Alphonse Moser, by communist Resistance member Pierre Félix Georges. Another example is the October 1941 killing of Colonel Holtz, the German town commandant at Nantes.

Most victims of assassination were Germans, but some 5,000 were French collaborators. A notable example occurred in December 1942, when Bonnier de la Chapelle, a supporter of de Gaulle, assassinated Admiral Jean Darlan, deputy to President Pétain, in Algiers. The Resistance also carried out reprisals against sections of its own organization, executing many Francs-Tireurs as "bandits." Resistance members justified their behavior on the grounds that this was a fight for survival against a brutal occupying power.

Resistance members considered themselves "freedom fighters," but the Germans looked upon them as "terrorists" unprotected by the laws of war. The Nazis responded to Resistance terror with terror of their own. Assassinations resulted in a gruesome spiral of reprisal and counter-reprisal. Within a few days of the Holtz killing, for example, the Germans had taken some 600 hostages and shot over 100.

Sabotage was an even more important Resistance role, bringing a steady drain of German casualties. These actions were very effective – on the night of June 5-6, 1944, as Allied forces approached the Normandy beaches, Resistance groups cut railroad tracks in 950 places throughout France. This was in addition to many other sabotage tasks and direct attacks on German forces at the same time. The June 1944 murder by SS troops of 642 villagers from Oradour-sur-Glane was the most notorious German atrocity carried out as revenge for resistance attacks.

Besides the German secret police and security organizations, those engaged in the brutal struggle against the Resistance included various Vichy police forces and other collaborationist groups, notably the 45,000-strong paramilitary Milice Française.

As well as carrying out sabotage and other small-scale operations, Resistance leaders hoped to organize insurrections to liberate large areas of the country in conjunction with the invading Allied armies. In 1943, therefore, resistance groups collaborated to organize a secret army known as the Maquis. Maquis uprisings took place in several rural areas, particularly in southern France, in the weeks following the Allied landings in Normandy. Although they certainly hampered the Germans, the lightly equipped Maquis were no match for the German army in a stand-up fight.

THE RESULTS OF RESISTANCE

It is hard to judge how effective were Resistance activities. The Resistance became most effective and gained most recruits after the Germans had lost the war. The Resistance alone could not have defeated the Germans but the Allied efforts to develop it, and the German ones to defeat it, suggest that it was effective.

After the war, some 300,000 French people received official veterans' status, and another 170,000 were recognized as Resistance volunteers. About 100,000 had lost their lives in Resistance-related activities. Some two million people, or around 10 percent of the adult population participated in some manner in resisting the German occupation, but at lesser risk.

Steve Weiss

SEE ALSO: GERMAN TERROR IN FRANCE AND ITALY; GERMAN TERROR IN NORWAY; RESISTANCE IN THE EAST AND TERRORISM; WWII RESISTANCE IN YUGOSLAVIA AND TERRORISM; TERROR AND THE WAFFEN SS; WORLD WAR II WAR CRIMES TRIALS.

FURTHER READING

- Funk, Arthur. *Hidden Ally.* New York: Greenwood Press, 1992.
- Kedward, H. Roderick. *In Search of the Maquis.* Oxford: Clarendon Press, and New York: Oxford University Press, 1993.
- Morris, Allan. *Collaboration and Resistance Reviewed.* New York: St. Martin's Press, 1992.
- Novick, Peter. *The Resistance Versus Vichy.* London: Chatto and Windus, and New York: Columbia University Press, 1968.

WWII RESISTANCE IN YUGOSLAVIA AND TERRORISM

The fighting on Yugoslav territory during World War II was partly a war of liberation against the Axis powers (Germany, Italy, and Bulgaria), partly a civil war, and partly a revolution. This complex conflict involved three main groups among the Yugoslavs, a number of smaller groups, and the Axis occupation forces. The use of terror to cow opponents was, at some stage, used by almost all the participants.

Yugoslavia was the name given to a union of Balkan lands – Serbia, Bosnia-Herzegovina, Croatia, Slovenia, Montenegro, and Macedonia – set up in 1918 after World War I when the Austro-Hungarian Empire was broken up. It was never a truly united country, due to the many different cultures, religions, and languages of the member countries. There were always political conflicts over territories within Yugoslavia. The central clash was between Serbs, who saw the whole territory as theirs, and others, especially Croats, who sought their own states.

When war broke out in 1939, therefore, and the country faced German invasion, all manner of separatist groups saw their chance to break free from the union. At first, Hitler guaranteed Yugoslavia's borders but only when the government signed a pro-Axis pact. When a popular uprising finally deposed the government in protest over this alliance, Germany invaded on April 6, 1941. After a ten-day campaign of occupation, Yugoslavia was dismembered. Parts were given to Germany's allies Italy and Bulgaria, while some areas came under direct Nazi occupation.

A Serbian Protectorate was also created under German domination. This was run by General Milan Nedic, who assisted in the Nazi extermination of Jews and others in the region. An independent state of Croatia was established, which incorporated Croatia, and most of Bosnia-Herzegovina, but not the coastal region of Dalmatia. Croatia itself was divided between German and Italian zones of influence.

KEY FACTS

- After Yugoslavia was conquered by the German armed forces in 1941, a multifaceted resistance war and civil war broke out.
- Tito's communist partisans and Mihailovic's royalist Chetniks both fought one another as well as the Axis occupation forces. The latter were supported by the Ustasha, the Croatian fascist regime established by the Nazis, which carried out a brutal campaign of terror against Serbs.

RESISTANCE ACTIVITIES

The three main Yugoslav military-political movements were the communist-led partisans, the Serb royalist Chetniks and the Croatian nationalist Ustasha movement. In addition, there were various other militia-style forces in different parts of the country engaged in resistance activities against the Germans, as well as Albanian and Macedonian nationalist movements. This complex set of conflicts within a war resulted in the death of around one million Yugoslavs. The majority of these are thought to have been killed by other Yugoslavs in a brutal conflict in which terror was the order of the day.

Initial resistance to the German occupation, in the form of spontaneous revolts, first occurred in Serbia and Montenegro. Serbian attacks were led primarily by the Chetniks, who were groups of former royal army officers operating from the mountains in central Serbia following the flight of the royal government to Britain. Their leader, Colonel Draza Mihailovic, was later appointed Minister of Defense by this royal government-in-exile. Communist partisans in Montenegro, encouraged by the strength of local feeling, also began attacking German occupation forces – in spite of

Novosti

A band of Tito's communist partisans sheltering in woods in an attempt to avoid the German forces that were making a sweep of the area.

orders from the leader of the partisans in the Serbian capital Belgrade, Josip Broz, better known as Tito, who believed the time was not right.

REPRISAL KILLINGS

The reaction of the occupation forces to resistance activity was fierce. In Montenegro, the Italians drafted reserves from Albania and used Albanian auxiliary troops to terrorize communities. As a result, most resistance fighters returned home to protect their families. In Serbia, the Germans ordered that 100 Yugoslavs would be executed for every German killed in resistance attacks. This attempt to suppress rebellion by highly disproportionate reprisal killings occurred partly because the Germans were short of manpower for occupation duties in the Balkans. Only four relatively weak divisions were stationed on Yugoslav territory during the war. These were supplemented by a further two divisions for specific anti-partisan offensives.

During the first months of the war in Yugoslavia, the Chetnik leader Mihailovic made contact with partisan chief Tito, although each faction continued to act independently. From September to November 1941, meetings took place to organize a common resistance front. However, the negotiations fizzled out by the end of 1941. The Chetnik leader decided to adopt a waiting policy until he could join an Allied invasion of Yugoslavia; Tito, in contrast, ordered his partisans to undertake a series of uprisings. The positions adopted by these leaders reflected their different objectives. Mihailovic limited Chetnik resistance because he feared that Nazi reprisals would destroy the social structure of the old, royalist Yugoslavia. But Tito maximized his partisan offensives because he wanted to destroy the old order and replace it with a communist republic.

Whatever their political agenda, the partisans gained popular support for three reasons. First, they were prepared to fight the occupying forces. Second, they were a genuinely multi-ethnic group – Tito was a Croat, but the majority of partisans were Serbs. Third, they stood whole-heartedly for a new regime that seemed to offer hope for the future – something the Chetniks, associated with the discredited monarchy, could not do. The strength of this idealism was one reason the Allies ultimately supported the partisans.

The partisan campaign of resistance by terror deliberately provoked German reprisal killings. This was a complete change of plan from earlier in 1941, when Tito had tried to halt communist resistance activity in Montenegro and Slovenia. Tito had a threefold aim: to resist the Axis powers, to conduct a revolution and seize power, and to install a communist regime.

As the only resistance movement whose membership came from many national groups, the partisans could establish a regional government wherever they were based. However, they were not always successful in maintaining control. By the winter of 1941, the partisans were forced to retreat from the republic they had established around the town of Uzice in southern Serbia. They were finally able to establish themselves in western Bosnia during 1942.

The partisans were able to consolidate their position in western Bosnia because their active campaign of resistance attracted strong support from the inhabitants of that area and in the adjacent Dalmatian hinterland. In particular, this support was strong because local Serbs, who made up three-quarters of the total partisan strength at this time, were anxious to join a movement which offered resistance to the Ustasha-ruled Croatian state. If the savage German reprisal campaign had been good for partisan recruitment in southern Serbia, the Ustasha's campaign of terror against the Serbs performed the same function in Croatia and Bosnia.

CROATIAN NATIONALISM

The Ustasha movement, once an illegal Croatian terrorist group led by Ante Pavelic, had been based in Italy and now was installed in power in Croatia following the Axis conquest. Initially the Ustasha was popular in parts of Croatia, but its attraction faded in many places as its rule took effect. The Ustasha government began a program to kill one-third of the Orthodox Serb population, to expell another third, and to convert the final third to Roman Catholicism. The attempt to implement this program included the use of massacre and mutilation as instruments of terror. Slitting throats, gouging eyes, castrating and skinning people alive were methods used, especially in the areas on either side of the border between Croatia and western Bosnia. Concentration camps were also established at this time. The main camp, Jasenovac, doubled as a death camp where tens of thousands of Serbs, Jews, anti-fascist Croats, and others perished. The reactions of the Serbian population to this Ustasha terror campaign were an important factor in the growth of the partisan movement.

As an ultimate Allied victory became likely, the main focus of the war in Yugoslavia was more on the defeat of opposing internal factions. The partisans sought to defeat both the Ustasha and the Chetniks while, after 1941, the main focus of Chetnik activity was to prevent a communist takeover when the Germans left. Chetniks were also involved in the massacre of thousands of Slav Muslims in Bosnia – an act that prefigured the "ethnic cleansing" of the war in the 1990s. Chetniks collaborated first with the Italians, until the latter surrendered in September 1943, and then with the Germans. Partisan contact with the Nazis was limited to one failed attempt to agree to a truce in 1943 to allow the partisans to concentrate on the Chetniks.

The terror was to continue after the war. The communists killed tens of thousands of people who had collaborated or had fought with the Ustasha, the Chetniks, the Albanian nationalists, or the militia forces. Those executed included several thousand Yugoslavs repatriated by British forces in Austria. There is no doubt that the horrors of World War II and its aftermath left bitter memories that would resurface when Yugoslavia broke up 50 years later.

James Gow

SEE ALSO: TERROR IN GERMAN OCCUPATION OF THE EAST; RESISTANCE IN THE EAST AND TERRORISM; TERROR'S USE BY THE FRENCH RESISTANCE.

FURTHER READING

- Djilas, Milovan. *Wartime.* London: Secker and Warburg, 1977; New York, Harcourt Brace, 1980.
- Lindsay, F. *Beacons in the Night.* Stanford. CA: Stanford University Press, 1993.
- Vucinich, W. S. *Contemporary Yugoslavia.* Berkeley: University of California Press, 1969.

THE HOLOCAUST

Between 1933 and 1945, the Nazi regime in Germany implemented policies of increasing persecution against the Jewish people. The maltreatment began with legal restrictions, arrests, and beatings. The Nazis' vicious mistreatment of Jews escalated until the regime, in 1941-42, commenced the deliberate, systematic murder of six and a half million people. Most of the Nazis' victims were Jews, although other "asocials" – Gypsies, homosexuals, the handicapped and mentally ill, and Soviet prisoners – were also included. Historians term this genocide, or the deliberate attempt to destroy a racial group, the Holocaust. The Nazis referred to it as the "Final Solution" to the Jewish Question. Although anti-Semitism, or hatred and persecution of Jews, had occurred for centuries in Europe, the sheer scale and utter brutality of the Holocaust was unique. Throughout history, humans have probably never sunk any lower in terms of organized, large-scale barbarism and savagery.

Nazi anti-Semitism was based on Nazi leader Adolf Hitler's personal loathing of Jews. Key Nazi beliefs were social darwinism, racialism and anti-Semitism, and German military expansion. In the Nazi interpretation of social darwinism, life was a bitter struggle for survival among the world's races. The Nazis ranked these races according to racial "superiority," with the Aryans (Germans and Nordic peoples) at the top.

After the Nazis' 1933 seizure of power in Germany, they passed laws that both forced the Jews out of public life and turned them into second-class citizens. Nazi paramilitary groups also subjected the Jews to increasing violence. Nazi prewar persecution peaked in the brutal Nazi *Kristalnacht* (Crystal night) pogrom, or attack on Jews, of November 9-10, 1938. During the pogrom, 30,000 Jews were arrested, and Nazi attackers looted 7,000 Jewish businesses and killed 91 Jews.

World War II broke out in September 1939, after the German invasion of Poland and the declarations of war by France and Great Britain. Nazi persecution then spread to include all Jews in German-occupied Europe. From mid-1941, Nazi cruelties against Jews further intensified. The German invasion of the Soviet Union on June 22, 1941, had the purpose of racial annihilation. The Nazis entrusted four task forces, or *Einsatzgruppen*, with the execution of Soviet Jews and Bolshevik officials. From mid-1941 until late 1942, these forces, aided by German and Axis (German-allied) army units, killed 1 million Jews and communists in Axis-occupied Soviet territory. Throughout the East, the Schutz Staffeln (SS), the Nazis' elite paramilitary force, shot and killed groups of Jews, after forcing them to dig ditches and kneel in front of them.

In late 1941, the Nazis began planning to deport all Europe's Jews by rail to six extermination camps set up, or to be set up, in Poland, including Auschwitz. While there were appallingly brutal concentration camps in Germany, such as Bergen-Belsen and Dachau, these did not have large gas chambers and did not exist primarily to slaughter thousands of Jews, as did the extermination camps. This extermination plan was finalized at the January 20, 1942, Wannsee Conference. The SS, under the direction of Adolf Eichmann, their expert on Jewish affairs, took control of the Holocaust.

KEY FACTS

- During the Holocaust, in their extermination camps, the Nazis killed 6 million Jews, and at least 500,000 Gypsies, homosexuals, mentally and physically handicapped people, and Soviet prisoners.
- The Nazis murdered millions of Jews in the gas chambers constructed at their death camps, in which 2,000 people could be killed every 15 minutes. Their corpses were burned in vast crematoria.

ORGANIZED TERROR AND DEHUMANIZATION

The Holocaust was made even more terrible by the amount of organization and regimentation involved. Nazi officials organized train timetables and monitored figures for deaths as if these were routine industrial matters, rather than the murder of millions of human beings. One tool employed in the task of killing Jews was the Nazis' deliberate use of terror.

The Nazis used systematic terror during their extermination of Europe's Jews for three main purposes: first, to dehumanize the Jews in the eyes of the Germans and their allies who were charged with carry-

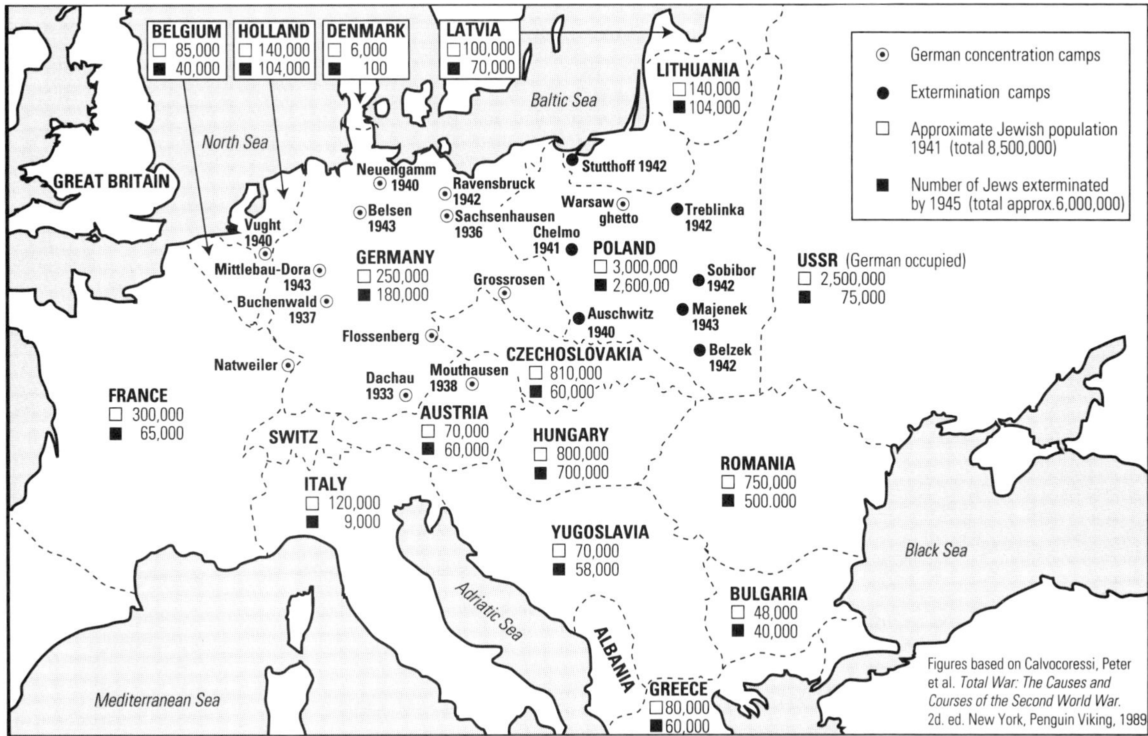

Nazi concentration and extermination camps, and the Jewish population before and after the Holocaust.

ing out the Holocaust; second, to morally corrupt those carrying out the Final Solution; third, to demoralize the victims of the Holocaust to the extent that they would meekly accept the terrible punishment being inflicted on them.

For the Nazis, dehumanizing the Jews was an important factor in achieving the mass slaughter of Europe's Jews. While many of those carrying out the Holocaust were sadistic and brutal Nazis, others were ordinary German policemen. A few of the camp guards found the task of killing Jews psychologically devastating. By 1942, some *Einsatzgruppen* personnel could not carry on killing at the required rate. As a result, some of the Holocaust's appalling brutality sought to make the victims seem like animals rather than human beings in the eyes of their persecutors. Deliberate starvation turned the Holocaust's victims into walking skeletons. With shaven heads and identical uniforms, the thousands of camp prisoners became indistinguishable from one another. This helped ease the death camp guards' work. After the war, a reporter asked a Nazi death camp commandant, "If you were going to kill [the Jews] anyway, what was the point of the humiliation, why the cruelty?" The commandant replied, "To condition those who actually had to carry out the policies, to make it possible for them to do what they did."

The Nazis also used terror in the Holocaust to corrupt those carrying out the process. Camp authorities encouraged guards to inflict sadistic and casual violence on Jews, as this contributed to the guards' moral degeneration. At Chelmno death camp, Poland, the guards placed bottles on inmates' heads and amused themselves with target practice. At one Polish slave labor camp, the commandant fired randomly at the inmates. Particularly bestial camp officials earned deservedly monstrous nicknames. For example, Dr. Josef Mengele, who carried out heinous medical experiments on Jews, was known by the inmates as "the Angel of Death." In this way, camp guards became anesthetized to the horrors inflicted on the Jews.

Potential Jewish resistance also needed to be minimized. The first step toward this occurred even before the Jews reached the death camps. After 1940, the Nazis forcibly moved Polish Jews into ghettos in

Popperfoto

Jewish deportees are rounded up by Nazi police in the Warsaw Ghetto, Poland, after the 1943 uprising.

large cities such as Warsaw and Lodz, and compelled them to subsist on starvation rations. Jewish ghetto leaders were then forced to cooperate with the Nazis under threat of far worse reprisals. Jewish administrators allowed the deportation of groups of Jews because the Nazis had threatened to deport the entire ghetto if the right number was not handed over by the ghetto leaders. As a result, the Jewish authorities were unable to resist the destruction of their own race. The threat of massive and brutal reprisals was a powerful instrument in the hands of the utterly ruthless Nazis.

JOURNEY INTO HELL

The SS police used classic terror tactics during the rounding up process. Round ups of Jews were carried out at dawn, and without warning. The deportees were often given only a couple of minutes to collect their belongings. The SS used random violence and excessive noise. All this was designed to confuse, disorient, and frighten the victims into meek acceptance of their fate. Resisters were shot dead as a warning to others.

Each day, the Nazis sent deported Jews by rail to the death camps in Poland. These journeys, sometimes lasting three to four days, were a nightmarish experience. The SS forced hundreds of Jews to stand tightly packed in horrendously overcrowded cattle cars. The deportees had no food, virtually no water, and no sanitary facilities. By the time the trains reached the death camps, around one in five people had died from exhaustion, cold, hunger, and dehydration. Many had died where they stood, since there was no room for their bodies to fall to the ground. Consequently, even the physically and psychologically strongest Jews reached the camps greatly weakened. These potential resisters were now far less likely to put up a fight against the terrible treatment awaiting them. On arrival, the weakest survivors, especially the young, old, and infirm, were sent to their deaths in the gas chambers.

The Germans feared mass escapes by death camp inmates because the camps were not heavily guarded: the Germans could not spare many soldiers from the front line. To minimize the threat of escape, the Nazis deliberately kept the Jewish camp inmates weak, hungry, and terrorized. Starvation also made economic sense. The destruction of the Jews was not meant to be an economic burden on Germany. The few inmates caught trying to escape were given terrible public punishments that served as warnings to others. At Maidanek, for example, those attempting to escape were beaten to death in front of the camp's inmates.

Even the Jews sent to work at the labor camps attached to the death camps, such as Birkenau at Auschwitz, were fed only enough to keep them working, but not enough to enable them to actively resist their tormentors. Being selected for slave labor only postponed the inevitable because of the workers' pitiful food rations. The Nazis decided that 500 French Jews from a group deported to Auschwitz on March 27, 1942, were fit to labor at Birkenau. Five months later, only 21 remained – the rest had died from exhaustion or had been gassed after becoming too weak to work.

The labor camp population exploded as the German war economy struggled to produce the armaments needed to make up for the huge losses suffered by the Nazis on the Eastern front. The Nazis continued to deport thousands of relatively fit Jews to replace those who had been literally worked to death.

MINIMIZING RESISTANCE

Pockets of Jewish resistance did occur, but were ruthlessly crushed by the Nazis. A train-load of deportees arriving at Sobibor death camp on April 30, 1943, attacked the guards with planks ripped from the sides of the wagon trucks. The SS killed the whole trainload with grenades. In January 1943, the 60,000 Jews remaining in the Warsaw Ghetto refused to be deported and took up arms. In 28 days of fighting, SS troops brutally crushed the revolt. 20,000 Jews were killed, with less than 100 German casualties. The surviving Jews were sent to the death camps. In August 1943, at Treblinka death camp, Jewish slave laborers disposing of corpses discovered that the Nazis planned to shoot them next. Some 700 Jews tried to escape. The Nazis machine-gunned to death all but 150 of them.

Given that many Jews suspected what was going on in the camps, it may to some seem surprising that large-scale, organized Jewish resistance was rare. But this lack of resistance was due to the crippling effects of the Nazis' bestial treatment and their cruel deceptions. The Nazis alleged that the deportations were resettlements to more pleasant farms in the East. In the Warsaw Ghetto in July 1942, thousands of hungry Jews accepted the German offer of bread and jam if they volunteered for deportation. For many it was to be their last meal.

The Nazis also used threats of execution or deportation to the camps against people aiding Jews. While some Poles were anti-Semitic, a few were sympathetic to the Jews' plight. To prevent these Poles from aiding the Jews, the Germans in Przemsyl, in eastern Poland, announced, on June 27, 1942, that anyone impeding "the deportation of the Jews will be shot." In Belzec camp in 1942, 1,500 Poles were gassed for aiding Jews.

THE NAZIS' LEGACY

The systematic murder of 6 million Jews has important resonances both in the Middle East and worldwide. In the late 1940s, displaced Jews felt that the Holocaust justified their use of terrorism to carve out a homeland in the Middle East, an action that has yet to be resolved peacefully with their neighbors. In worldwide terms, the Nazis' use of terror created a climate in which terrorism later flourished. They helped establish both the methods of terror used, and the principle that innocent people are legitimate victims of terror.

Stephen A. Hart

SEE ALSO: TERROR IN THE GERMAN OCCUPATION OF THE EAST; ROMANIAN TERROR IN TRANSNISTRIA; TERROR AND THE NAZI BARBARIZATION OF WARFARE; WORLD WAR II WAR CRIMES TRIALS; TERRORISM IN PALESTINE IN 1947.

FURTHER READING

- Browning, Christopher. *Ordinary Men.* New York: Harper Perennial, 1993.
- Dawidowicz, Lucy. *The War Against the Jews, 1933-1945.* London and New York: Holt, Rinehart and Winston, 1975.
- Hilberg, Raul. *The Destruction of the European Jews.* rev. ed. 3 Vols. London: Weidenfeld and Nicolson, and New York: Holmes and Meier, 1985.
- Yahil, Leni. *The Holocaust: The Fate of European Jewry, 1932-1945.* New York: Oxford University Press, 1990.

JAPANESE TERROR IN THE FAR EAST

At the beginning of World War II in Europe in 1939, much of the Japanese army was based in China, engaged in a campaign of conquest. German victories in Europe opened up possibilities for the takeover of a number of European-held and poorly protected colonies in Southeast Asia and the Pacific. By mid-1942, much of the western Pacific, including most of what is now Indonesia, Malaysia, Singapore, the Philippines, Hong Kong, Thailand, and Burma had fallen to the Japanese. In addition, Japan had ruled Korea since 1910.

As a result, by 1942, the Japanese armed forces were in control of vast areas of the Far East and had to deal with a range of subject populations. Japanese behavior towards these subjects often involved acts of terrorism, which left millions dead. At the same time, the actions of the Japanese occupiers bequeathed a legacy of terror that was important in the nationalist and communist uprisings that convulsed much of the region after 1945.

THE SUBJUGATION OF CHINA

In 1931, the Japanese had entered into a conflict with China that had escalated into full-scale war in 1937. In spite of large areas of the country falling to the invaders, the Chinese Kuomintang government of Chiang Kai-shek refused to capitulate and eventually moved its capital far inland to Chungking. By 1941, the Japanese army was heavily committed in China (with 35 of its 51 divisions stationed there), but was unable to claim a decisive victory. Resistance, from Mao Zedong's communists, among others, led to savage Japanese reprisals. Beatings, arrests, rapes, and killings became commonplace, as the Japanese sought to punish the Chinese for their resistance.

During the initial Japanese conquests in the coastal area, there had been many examples of terror being used to weaken Chinese resistance. The most notorious of these was the 1937 Rape of Nanking. After the capture of the city, Japanese troops went on an orgy of rape, murder, pillage, and destruction in which 200,000 Chinese perished and much of the city was destroyed.

KEY FACTS

- On some islands the problem of food shortages was temporarily "solved" by the mass execution of civilians by their Japanese occupiers.
- The Japanese killed many forced laborers who were unable to continue working because of sickness, disease, or malnutrition.
- The Japanese spared no one in their brutal reign of terror: Red Cross hospitals, orphanages, and churches were all attacked.

SOUTHEAST ASIA AND THE PACIFIC

The takeover of the former European colonies in 1941 and 1942 was principally seen as an opportunity to remedy Japan's chronic shortage of raw materials such as oil, rubber, and tin. But there was also a strong strain of idealism: many Japanese saw it as their destiny to purify and to cleanse Southeast Asia of alien and corrupting Western influences. They intended to liberate Asians from Western exploitation.

During the initial conquest, then, the Japanese forces enjoyed a certain amount of good will, and many Asians were happy to accept them as liberators. In many industries, and in companies selling cash crops such as rubber, the Japanese were able to offer a real increase in status to junior managers who had always been restricted in their opportunities by whites. This was particularly true in Java, but in the Philippines as well, some people worked happily with the Japanese.

However, good will collapsed under twin forces. First, many Japanese soldiers and sailors saw themselves as part of the purest race in the world. As in the case of the Nazis, with whom the Japanese had formed the Axis pact on September 27, 1940, this sense of racial superiority led many Japanese to feel

Hulton Getty Picture Collection

Japanese soldiers in China in 1937, prepare to execute – by beheading – two Chinese civilians.

that other racial groups were almost sub-human. This feeling justified the brutal treatment of other Asians. Second, Japanese forces given occupation duties were under great strain. They were required to extract raw materials as rapidly as possible using forced labor, but found themselves under pressure from guerrilla forces and, as the war dragged on, from Allied blockades.

The extensive raw material extraction meant that the people of the occupied territories were generally deprived of their economic base and left with few resources on which to survive. The problem was exacerbated by severe Japanese import restrictions. The people of the occupied territories soon fell victim to starvation and disease.

Racist acts of violence by the Japanese were common among the many atrocities carried out against civilians in Japanese-occupied territories. Torture, humiliation, and summary execution of suspects were day-to-day realities. In February 1942, Japanese soldiers occupying Singapore killed 5,000 ethnic Chinese residents over a two-week period. Tens of thousands of Asian women were forced to become "comfort women," or prostitutes, for the Japanese military; and Japanese military doctors conducted grotesque medical experiments on live patients, including vivisection and mutilation. At times, some prisoners were even used as live targets for firing squads or for bayonet practice by Japanese soldiers.

TERROR IN DEFEAT

In the latter stages of the war, atrocities increased as isolated Japanese garrisons ran low on provisions. On Andaman Island, off the east coast of India, "useless" civilians were deported to nearby uninhabited islands redundant and left to starve to death. Similarly, Japanese occupation forces came close to exterminating the entire Sulak people, who inhabited a number of islands off north Borneo.

Atrocities also occurred when Japanese troops were forced to withdraw from occupied territories. Japanese troops often engaged in the massacre of civilians and implemented systematic destruction of settlements, utilities, and infrastructure. The worst of these incidents occurred on the eve of the liberation of Manila, in the Philippines, in February 1945, when Japanese soldiers murdered 91,000 Filipinos.

The mortality rates were enormous among Asian civilians in the territories occupied by the Japanese. An estimated 10 million Chinese died in the war with Japan and at least 3 million civilians died during the Japanese occupation of Java.

Russell A. Hart

SEE ALSO: TERROR IN THE GERMAN OCCUPATION OF THE EAST; GERMAN TERROR IN FRANCE AND ITALY; TERROR AND THE NAZI BARBARIZATION OF WARFARE; JAPANESE TERRORIZATION OF PRISONERS; WORLD WAR II WAR CRIMES TRIALS; THE DEBATE OVER THE ATOM BOMB.

FURTHER READING

- Dower, John. *War Without Mercy: Race and Power in the Pacific War.* London: Faber, and New York: Pantheon, 1986.
- Piccigallo, Philip. *The Japanese on Trial: Allied War Crimes Operations in the East, 1945-1951.* Austin: University of Texas Press, 1979.
- Spector, Ronald H. *Eagle Against the Sun: The American War with Japan.* New York: Free Press, 1984; London: Viking, 1985.

JAPANESE TERRORIZATION OF PRISONERS

The Japanese armed forces of World War II were extraordinarily effective. Initially, they inflicted a series of defeats on armies that were numerically superior but unable to resist the ability and confidence of the often poorly equipped Japanese units. During the campaign in Malaya, for example, 90,000 British Commonwealth troops surrendered to just 30,000 invaders. The relative morale of the two forces is perhaps best expressed in the contrasting nicknames the troops had for their respective commanders: to his soldiers, the Japanese commander Tomoyuki Yamashita was "the Tiger." The British troops called General Arthur Percival "the Rabbit."

However, Japanese success in combat was linked to a disregard for prisoners and defeated enemies that led to widespread abuses and the use of terror against prisoners of war. There were three main reasons why the Japanese treatment of prisoners of war often plumbed the depths of human behavior, and they were mirror images of the attributes that made Japanese combat forces so formidable.

The first reason was the nature of the warrior code, *Bushido*, which governed the Japanese attitude to war. Every Japanese soldier had it instilled into him that he was a warrior whose duty it was to fight and that warriors do not surrender. The Japanese Field Service Instructions included the instruction: "Never permit yourself to be humiliated by being taken prisoner alive. Do not leave behind a name sullied by dishonor – kill yourself first." This helped create a body of fighting men who were dominant in combat, but it also meant that they had little or no respect for enemies who did surrender. There was thus little or no attempt to mitigate the harsh circumstances in which many prisoners found themselves when captured.

Second, and linked to this warrior ethos, was a very definite feeling of hostility to white prisoners. Many Japanese demonized Westerners as hostile, materialistic, selfish, decadent, and weak. Even today, some Japanese still refer to the 1868 American diplomatic contacts as "the coming of the barbarians." The chance to inflict some kind of revenge on the West for forcing Japan to open its doors to the outside world in the late 19th century helped motivate fighting men. All this led to treatment of prisoners that was not in accord with the 1929 Geneva Convention. In fact, although a signatory to this convention – which set out rules governing the treatment of prisoners of war and of conquered civilians – Japan had never actually ratified the treaty.

The third reason prisoners suffered was that the Japanese army, as a warrior force, had a logistics problem. Supply and organization off the battlefield was its great weakness. As a result, Allied prisoners of war had a poor diet, but so did their captors. The logistics problem was also the reason that the Japanese used Allied prisoners as slave labor.

KEY FACTS

- Between July 1941 and May 1942, Japanese armed forces took control of French Indochina (modern Vietnam, Laos, and Cambodia), Malaya, the Philippines, Borneo, New Guinea, Singapore, Java, and Burma.
- Reports of Japanese atrocities reached the West in early 1944 via liberated prisoners of war.

THE BATAAN DEATH MARCH

The most notorious example of Japanese maltreatment of prisoners of war was the Bataan "death march." Allied resistance on the Philippines ended when about 70,000 soldiers defending the Bataan peninsula surrendered in 1942. They were ordered to undertake a 65-mile trek to detention camps, a trek that claimed the lives of nearly 10,000 prisoners,

Hulton Getty Picture Collection

U.S. troops dig up the remains of prisoners of war who had been burnt alive by their Japanese captors.

mostly Filipinos. Weakened by combat, malnutrition, and disease, the troops were forced to march under constant threat of beatings and clubbings, and without adequate shelter, food, or medicine. Often, prisoners who fell were bayoneted or buried alive. There was little or no attempt to care for the injured, and many of the survivors believed that their captors were happy about the large number of fatalities.

This treatment of recently surrendered enemy troops was not confined to the land war. At sea, from spring 1943, Japanese submarines killed survivors of torpedoed enemy ships. On January 28, 1944, for example, the Japanese battened down the hatches on a sinking U.S. ship, condemning 1,800 men to drown.

TREATMENT IN CAMPS

Even when prisoners were in camps, their guards were not inclined to treat them with respect and were prepared to use terror tactics to cow their charges and make discipline easier. There were many recorded instances of brutal treatment of Allied prisoners, who were decapitated, bayoneted, or incarcerated in cages and exposed to the unremitting tropical sun.

Terror was used as a deterrent to escape, but the worst punishments were inflicted on those escaped prisoners whom the Japanese managed to recapture. Recaptured prisoners were beheaded, or put to the agonies of torture, such as being forced to drink gasoline and then shot in the stomach with incendiary bullets so that they exploded in flames.

However, these brutal punishments accounted for far fewer fatalities than malnutrition, disease, and exhaustion. Most prisoners of war were required to carry out tasks of arduous labor while being kept on a wretched diet. For example, the Japanese believed a railroad was critical for getting supplies to their forces in the north of Burma. Consequently, in 1942, thousands of Allied prisoners were sent to build the Burma–Siam railroad. Allied prisoners and Asian slave laborers worked 14–20 hours a day, seven days a week, with a daily ration of one cup of rice. In all, 16,000 Allies and at least 42,000 Asians died.

Such treatment meant that mortality rates among Allied prisoners in the Pacific theater – 27 percent – were much greater than in Europe, which amounted to only 4 percent. Of the 20,000 American prisoners of war taken after the fall of the Philippines in January 1942, for example, only 8,000 survived the war. But it is important to emphasize that although terror was certainly a significant element in the treatment of Allied prisoners of war, the vast majority of deaths were caused by starvation and inadequate shelter.

Russell A. Hart

SEE ALSO: TERROR AND THE NAZI BARBARIZATION OF WARFARE; JAPANESE TERROR IN THE FAR EAST; WORLD WAR II WAR CRIMES TRIALS.

FURTHER READING

- Dower, John. *War Without Mercy: Race and Power in the Pacific War.* London: Faber, and New York: Pantheon, 1986.
- Russell, Lord. *The Knights of Bushido: The Shocking History of Japanese War Atrocities.* London: Cassell, and New York: Dutton, 1958.
- Spector, Ronald H. *Eagle Against the Sun: The American War with Japan.* New York: The Free Press, 1984; London: Viking, 1985.

TERROR AND THE NAZI BARBARIZATION OF WARFARE

Both the German armed forces (Wehrmacht) and the Waffen SS (fighting units of the Nazi party's paramilitary organization, the Schutz Staffel) fought on the Eastern Front between 1941 and 1945. They did not confine their use of terror to controlling the population of conquered territories and intimidating enemy forces. The Germans also employed terror tactics among their own soldiers to maintain discipline and discourage faintheartedness at the front.

Commanding officers were willing to clamp down with the utmost severity on any signs of weakness in the ranks and slackness in combat. According to recent estimates, German officers executed at least 20,000 of their own soldiers. The officers imposed such terror partly to force the soldiers to endure the exceptional harshness of the fighting conditions and partly to put Hitler's master plan into practice on the Eastern Front.

Hitler based all his expansionist plans on his ideology of racial mastery. His drive into the Soviet Union was not merely to conquer territory but also to wipe out populations. Punishing any lack of enthusiasm among the German rank and file helped goad soldiers into suppressing the Soviet population. Then Germany could secure territories gained in battle. Terror also encouraged soldiers to follow the policy of the Nazi regime – systematically to destroy what Hitler considered the "racially inferior" Slavs and Jews, and also other political groups under German control.

The fighting ability of the German armed forces during World War II was impressive. The Germans achieved astonishing early victories, and they still proved tenacious defenders during the final phase of the war, when they were retreating on all fronts in the face of the Allies' overwhelming strength.

The discipline of the German troops was the result of many factors, not just the brutality and terror that controlled them. The soldiers had a strong sense of loyalty to their colleagues, an ideological conviction, a fear of the enemy (especially the Red Army), and a powerful belief in Hitler as the invincible leader of the Third Reich, the new German empire. This combination of hope and fear bound the army together.

KEY FACTS

- The SS killed about 700,000 Soviet civilians in the first year of the Soviet-German conflict.
- From mid-August to mid-October 1941, the Germans murdered 18,000 Soviet prisoners of war in Sachsenhausen concentration camp alone. The average was 300 deaths a day.
- An estimated 3.3 million Russian prisoners of war died at the hands of the Nazis.

CRUELTY TO SOVIET CITIZENS

The ruthless disciplinary system brutalized the troops, but did not regulate how the army treated conquered populations. Officers knowingly overlooked criminal actions against civilians in occupied countries. The Soviets had not signed the Geneva Convention, which governed the rules of warfare. So German officers rarely checked acts of cruelty against Red Army prisoners. Letting the soldiers pass on harsh treatment served the goals of the Third Reich. Its policy had always been that the German army could not fight the Soviet Union according to the conventional rules of war. Eradication was the ultimate objective. Hitler needed troops with the humanity beaten out of them if

Novosti

Nazi forces carried out summary executions of suspected Soviet partisans as a common terror tactic.

they were to implement his racial policies successfully.

It was not just professional soldiers who carried out acts of extreme cruelty against a defenseless population. Conscript soldiers were equally zealous. This willingness to commit atrocities had its roots in the skillful propaganda the Nazi regime employed to control the attitude of its fighting forces. Years of Nazi indoctrination in school motivated the Hitler Youth. Army training continued to encourage the troops to regard the Soviets as subhuman and worthy only of total eradication. And officers constantly repeated images depicting the Soviet people as agents of the devil to soldiers under their command.

The German army invaded the Soviet Union on June 22, 1941. Its commanders received orders drafted by the High Command of the Land Forces and approved by the Supreme Command of the Armed Forces and Hitler himself. It was now a soldier's duty to execute on sight all Red Army commissars – Communist party officials attached to military units. Soldiers were also to collaborate closely with the *Einsatzgruppen*, or task forces, the death squads composed of men from the SS and the *Sicherheitsdienst* (the Nazi security service). This meant treating as partisans all political and racial enemies of Nazism – Jews, Communist party members, and other "inferior races." The German troops were to kill them or hand them over to the SS.

The German High Command's orders did not indicate that conquered populations were to be treated decently. Any legal protection was abandoned as far as Soviet civilians were concerned. No one punished criminal actions against civilians unless they interfered with combat discipline. The "criminal orders," as they have come to be known, had devastating and often fatal consequences for millions of Soviet citizens.

During their occupation, the Nazis laid to waste vast tracts of Soviet territory and burned thousands of villages to the ground. They murdered the inhabitants or transported them to concentration camps where the majority died. The German army commandeered food wherever it went. It so exploited the economy of the occupied territories that famine became common and epidemics rampaged. This brutality grew out of the Nazi desire to conquer *Lebensraum* (living space) in the East for ethnic Germans subsequently to colonize.

CIVILIANS RETALIATE

The slaughter of a country's civilian population after the defeat of its armed forces in battle was nothing new. But the concept of conquered civilians organizing themselves into paramilitary units to resist the occupying forces was relatively recent. The French fought in this way during the Franco-Prussian War of 1870-71, and so did some of Europe's beleaguered citizenry in World War I. The conquering German armies in both these wars had to contend with civilian partisans attacking their rear, as well as with armed forces on the battle front. It was the same when Hitler's armed forces poured into the Soviet Union in 1941.

The scale of partisan resistance roughly matched the level of brutality the German armed forces showed civilians as they pushed deep into Soviet territory. Accordingly, the scale of German reprisals rose to exceed resistance attacks, murders, and assassinations. Both soldiers and generals of the German army were now terrified. The Nazi regime's brutality and its portrayal of the enemy as subhuman had already terrorized the soldiers. But the generals were fearful of having to deal with partisans supported by the enemy population. German generals were thus determined to stamp out Soviet guerrilla warfare by using the deterrents of massive retaliation and collective punishment.

While German terror against the Soviet population led to fierce resistance, German commanders used this partisan activity to justify even harsher reprisals. The war behind the lines in the East soon became a vicious spiral of massacres. The SS suspected any civilians in authority and killed factory managers or farm foremen on the slightest pretext. If the SS suspected a village of aiding the partisans, they took hostages for questioning and torture. On January 22, 1943, near Slonim, in White Russia, east of Poland, the Germans launched a reprisal action after a partisan attack. In addition to killing 1,676 partisans, the Germans murdered 1,510 civilians as alleged sympathizers. Often entire villages and their inhabitants were destroyed in such reprisals. But the secret police and security services could not achieve such devastation alone.

Since the war, historians have found enough evidence to disprove German claims that the armed forces were confined solely to combat. The German army was deeply involved in terrorist and criminal acts against the Soviet population. Documents discovered in the former Soviet Union, along with detailed research in German archives, provide conclusive evidence. The army commanders were willing to collaborate with the SS in bringing about Hitler's Final Solution – the Nazis' murder of 6 million European Jews. But ordinary soldiers also participated directly in mass executions. They assisted the SS in placing large numbers of Jews in ghettos and concentration camps, as well as in deporting them to death camps.

The participation of regular troops in such atrocities was usually passed off as being part of legitimate actions against partisans. But these operations often involved the mass murder of civilians. Many combat units and individual soldiers also acted on their own initiative. They either passively observed or actively took part in executions. This evidence demonstrates that large numbers of soldiers were directly implicated in actions previously blamed only on the Gestapo (Nazi secret police) and the SS death squads.

To conclude, Hitler used the regular German armed forces as a deliberate instrument of terror on the Eastern Front. The army was an essential tool in the implementation of Nazi policies. German troops were terrorized by a brutal disciplinary system and images of the enemy. They, in turn, terrorized the enemy population and massacred prisoners of war.

Bertrande Roberts

SEE ALSO: TERROR IN THE GERMAN OCCUPATION OF THE EAST; RESISTANCE IN THE EAST AND TERRORISM; THE HOLOCAUST; TERROR AND THE WAFFEN SS; WORLD WAR II WAR CRIMES TRIALS.

FURTHER READING

- Bartov, Omer. *Hitler's Army: Soldiers, Nazis, and War in the Third Reich.* New York: Oxford University Press, 1991.
- Hirschfeld, G., ed. *The Policies of Genocide: Jews and Soviet Prisoners of War in Nazi Germany.* Boston: Allen & Unwin, 1986.
- Klee, E., W. Dressen, and V. Riess, eds. *"The Good Old Days": The Holocaust as Seen by Its Perpetrators and Bystanders.* New York: The Free Press, 1991.

TERROR AND THE SOVIET BARBARIZATION OF WARFARE

The 1941-45 Soviet-German war was waged with unparalleled savagery. Both sides, but particularly the Germans, massacred civilians, and shot, tortured, and starved prisoners of war. Both sides disregarded the Geneva Convention, which set humane conditions for the treatment of battle casualties, prisoners of war, and civilians in the war zone. The Soviets were not signatories to the Convention, so neither side felt obliged to apply its constraints to their treatment of enemy soldiers or civilians.

The German army in the Soviet Union pursued its own reign of terror at the front and in occupied territory. The Red Army experienced not only the brutal fighting but also the terror imposed upon it by Soviet dictator Joseph Stalin and his secret police, the NKVD. Stalin used terror on a massive scale to force Soviet soldiers and civilians to resist the Germans.

After suffering huge losses in the summer of 1941, the Red Army faced the "discipline of the revolver" on Stalin's orders. Fearing his soldiers would desert, Stalin instructed his secret police to shoot "cowards." The NKVD executed both generals and frontline soldiers for failing to halt the German advance. The secret police also branded as traitors Soviet soldiers taken prisoner. Soldiers attempting to desert faced NKVD machine-gunners deployed as "holding units" behind them. When Soviet soldiers escaped German capture and reached Soviet lines, the NKVD secret police interrogated them as "traitors and spies," and sent most to forced labor camps, the infamous Gulag.

KEY FACTS

- Soviet propaganda – through radio, movies, the press, and Party agitators – instilled hatred for the Germans with slogans like "Let us kill. If you have killed one German, kill another."
- During the battle of Stalingrad in 1942-43, 13,500 Red Army soldiers were shot for disobeying orders or allegedly displaying cowardice.

THE PROPAGANDA CAMPAIGN

Two particular factors stimulated the brutal behavior of the Red Army soldier, besides the influences of patriotism and fear of German conquest. The first was the suffering inflicted on Soviet soldiers by the Soviet regime's use of systematic terror. Beatings, imprisonment, and execution were common punishments for even the most minor infraction of army rules. The second stimulus came from Joseph Stalin's summons, in his broadcasts of July 3 and November 6 and 7, 1941, to wage an all-out war of extermination against the Germans. Stalin knew that Hitler's war against him aimed at annihilation, and that the Germans would pitch the bulk of their military might against him.

To meet this threat, a torrent of propaganda rained down on both Soviet soldiers and civilians. Killing Germans was declared a patriotic duty and a sacred obligation to deliver Mother Russia from the invader. Coupled with knowledge of the many atrocities committed by the Germans, this propaganda aroused the Soviet soldier's desire for revenge on the invader.

During the further German advances of mid-1942, Stalin intensified the use of terror, creating Red Army penal battalions. More than 400,000 Soviet soldiers convicted of offenses were forced to fight in these units. These punishment units undertook the most hazardous assignments, some little better than suicide missions. Few armies used penal troops on this scale.

TRH Pictures

Thousands of captured German soldiers are herded through the streets during a Soviet victory parade before being sent to brutal prisoner of war camps.

In 1943, supervision of the Red Army was taken over by SMERSH. This organization's title was an acronym of the Russian phrase meaning "death to spies," and accurately described its role. Stalin no longer kept the Red Army in line by terror, as both morale and the supply of weapons had improved after the January 1943 Soviet victory at Stalingrad. But SMERSH watched the troops closely to root out "spies." SMERSH abandoned regular military procedures, executing vast numbers of "unreliables" without trial.

After 1943, the Red Army advanced westward. The Germans had moved vast columns of Soviet prisoners west in 1941, many to be killed or to die from neglect. Now the Red Army sent thousands of German prisoners east, many to die in captivity. For both sides, the Eastern Front remained a nightmarish place.

Discipline in Red Army frontline units remained strong. But units assembled from Soviet soldiers liberated from German prisoner-of-war camps, gave them a weapon, and sent them to the front. These troops left behind a trail of rape, murder, and looting, which forced Soviet officers to take drastic action to restore military discipline.

In 1945, collaborators were hanged, while "passive traitors," including forced laborers and prisoners of war, were sent to the Gulag. The barbarization of the battlefield finally engulfed both the conquerors and the conquered.

John Erickson

SEE ALSO: TERROR IN THE GERMAN OCCUPATION OF THE EAST; RESISTANCE IN THE EAST AND TERRORISM; TERROR AND THE NAZI BARBARIZATION OF WARFARE.

FURTHER READING

- Glantz, D. M. *When Titans Clashed: How the Red Army Stopped Hitler.* Lawrence: University of Kansas Press, 1995.
- Linz, S. J., ed. *The Impact of World War II on the Soviet Union.* Totowa, NJ: Rowman and Allanheld, 1985.
- Ziemke, Earl F. *Stalingrad to Berlin: The German Defeat in the East.* Washington, DC: Center of Military History, U.S. Army, 1968.

TERROR AND THE WAFFEN SS

The Waffen SS was the armed fighting branch of the general Schutz Staffel (SS) – the elite paramilitary organization of the Nazi party. The Waffen SS was deployed alongside the German armed forces (Wehrmacht) as they advanced across Europe during 1939-41. But the Waffen SS was also used both to maintain internal security within the Nazi empire and to carry out the Nazis' genocidal racial policies.

Unlike Wehrmacht troops, who were a mixture of professional soldiers and conscripts, Waffen SS troops were mostly volunteers. And while the ordinary German soldier fought for Hitler and the Fatherland, many Waffen SS men were Nazi fanatics dedicated to the aims of the Nazi party, and, in particular, the eradication of "inferior races." For many Waffen SS soldiers, their struggle was as much ideological as it was military. Consequently, their foe was the entire enemy population. The beliefs and training of SS men blurred the distinctions between combatant and civilian traditionally accepted in international law. This was crucial in the desperate conflict of annihilation to be fought out on the eastern front. Hitler had used terror to subjugate the German population and to eliminate opposition. The Waffen SS merely extended this policy into the frontline.

The Nazis' belief that the so-called Aryan people – Caucasians of non-Jewish descent – were engaged in a racial struggle for survival allowed Nazi propagandists to portray non-Aryan civilians as racial enemies. As the vanguard of an Aryan empire, the Waffen SS viewed itself as an organization above international law. Hence, the Waffen SS was quite ready to use terror as an instrument of policy to achieve its ends.

KEY FACTS

- The ideological motivation of the Waffen SS led to contempt for prisoner's rights and a blurring of the distinction between civilians and combatants.
- During the May 1940 German invasion of western Europe, Waffen SS soldiers murdered 85 British prisoners in a barn at Wormhout, near Dunkirk, in northern France.
- An infamous Waffen SS atrocity in western Europe was the murder of 83 American prisoners at Malmédy, Belgium, in December 1944.

THE FIRST SS ATROCITIES

The first use of the SS as the Nazis' spearhead force, and the first recorded SS atrocity, occurred during the 1939 Polish campaign. On September 19, an SS private summarily executed 50 Jews. In a strange turn of events, in the light of later developments, the private was actually tried and convicted by a courtmartial, although he was immediately pardoned and never served a day in prison.

After the fall of Poland, forces closely associated with the Waffen SS, the Totenkopf ("Death's Head") concentration camp guard regiments and the Police Division cleansed Poland of "undesirables." These included Jews, communists, gypsies, homosexuals, and intellectuals. Thereafter, SS training units maintained the internal security of the General Government, as the Polish state was now known. In April 1943, for example, some of the 60,000 Jews of the Warsaw Ghetto took up armed resistance to avoid deportation to the Nazis' death camps. SS trainees suppressed the revolt, in which 20,000 Jews perished, while the remainder were sent to the death camps.

The first recorded Waffen SS atrocity against Western Allied troops occurred in 1940. During the German offensive in France, British troops repulsed the attacks of the newly raised SS Totenkopf Division at La Bassée Canal, near Bailleul, close to the Belgian border. This reverse was perceived as a slur on the combat reputation of this elite Nazi force. In retaliation, junior officer Lieutenant Fritz Knochlein killed 100 prisoners from Britain's Royal Norfolk Regiment at Le Paradis farm. Knochlein was neither punished nor was his career adversely affected by the massacre; he even went on to win the Knight's Cross later in the war.

TRH Pictures/U.S. Army

The bodies of captured American soldiers shot by the Waffen SS at Malmédy in December 1944 are left to be covered by snow.

During 1940-41, the Waffen SS expanded to five divisions of 20,000 men each, including the raising of the Wiking division. This consisted of western Europeans who were expressly recruited for the Nazi "Crusade against Bolshevism" following Operation Barbarossa, Hitler's invasion of the Soviet Union, on June 22, 1941. Hitler believed that his new German empire, which he expected would last 1,000 years, needed *Lebensraum* (living space) to survive. To achieve this living space, Germany conducted a genocidal war of annihilation (*Vernichtungskrieg*) in the east to destroy communism, subjugate the allegedly racially inferior Slavic peoples, and eliminate eastern Europe's Jews. The Waffen SS was intended to spearhead this struggle, and thus the bulk of Waffen SS atrocities occurred on the Eastern Front.

The Waffen SS provided about one quarter of the personnel for the infamous *Einsatzgruppen*, or task forces, which carried out special operations (*Sonderbehandlung*) in occupied Soviet territory. During these operations, 500,000 Soviet citizens were exterminated in 1941 alone. At the same time, three SS brigades and Order Police units, under the direct command of Reichsführer SS Heinrich Himmler, ruthlessly imposed Nazi authority over German-occupied Soviet territories. The shooting of prisoners and civilian hostages as well as the complete destruction of towns and villages became commonplace. Barely two weeks into Barbarossa, the Wiking division of the Waffen SS set the tone for subsequent behavior by murdering 600 Jews from Galicia, in southern Poland. As the struggle on the Eastern Front became more desperate and bitter, the scale of atrocities increased. During a spring 1942 German reprisal against partisan attacks, the 1st SS Division, named Leibstandarte, executed 4,000 Soviet prisoners of war.

THE WAFFEN SS ON MANY FRONTS

At the front, Waffen SS units suffered appalling casualties during the bitter fighting of 1941-42. As German prospects of immediate victory dimmed, Hitler ordered the expansion of the Waffen SS and withdrew its formations for rebuilding. In spring 1943, the three senior SS formations, Leibstandarte, Das Reich, and Totenkopf, returned to the Eastern Front grouped in a new SS Corps commanded by General Paul Hausser. The new SS Corps acted as an elite mobile force being rushed from one crisis to another. During Field Marshal Erich von Manstein's spring 1943 counteroffensive, the SS Corps recaptured the city of Kharkov in the Ukraine in an aggressive drive. But during their brief occupation of the city, SS troops murdered an estimated 20,000 Soviet prisoners and civilians.

Waffen SS formations also became locked in a vicious cycle of atrocity and reprisal with Yugoslav partisans in the Balkans. Here, the SS relied heavily on ethnic German (*Volksdeutsch*) and volunteer formations raised from Croatia, Albania, Bosnia, Hungary, and Romania to destroy the partisans. The mix of ethnic and religious hatred fueled this brutality. When Hitler's allies, the Italians, surrendered to the Allies in September 1943, Hitler sent German troops into northern Italy and also unleashed the Waffen SS on them. The SS Leibstandarte Division destroyed the town of Boves and executed most of its inhabitants as part of the general subjugation of the population. The following summer, in 1944, the new 16th SS Division, known as Reichsführer SS, killed 3,000 Italian civilians after British forces defeated the division on the Arno River.

After the Allied invasion of France on June 6, 1944, (D-Day), the Waffen SS used terror tactics as reprisals for military setbacks or resistance attacks. The 12th SS Panzer Division Hitlerjugend, consisting largely of determined 18-year-old Hitler Youth members, was deployed to spearhead the German effort to push the Allies back into the sea on June 7. When the Canadian 3rd Division managed to repulse them, the young Nazi fanatics murdered 64 Canadian prisoners. Thereafter, the two divisions fought a vicious struggle in which no quarter was given by either side.

The invasion also intensified French resistance activity. When the resistance killed one of the SS Das Reich Division's senior commanders on June 10, the division conducted a "cleansing operation," in which 642 people, virtually the entire population of Oradour-sur-Glane, in southwest France, were burned or shot to death, mostly in the village church.

One highly publicized SS combat atrocity occurred during the December 1944 German counteroffensive in the Belgian Ardennes area (the so-called Battle of the Bulge). The spearhead battlegroup of the SS division Leibstandarte, commanded by Joachim Peiper, massacred 83 American prisoners of war near Malmédy.

THE ANNIHILATION OF WARSAW

Some of the worst atrocities committed by the Waffen SS occurred during the Warsaw Uprising of August-September 1944. With most of its troops fighting the Red Army, the Germans employed two unsavory SS brigades, Dirlewanger and Kaminski, named after their infamous commanders. Dirlewanger was a discredited commander, convicted of sex crimes, who had salvaged his career thanks to his close friendship with SS recruitment chief Gottlob Berger. Berger allowed Dirlewanger to raise a penal unit from convicted poachers, political prisoners, and courtmartialled soldiers. The unit was infamous for its lack of discipline. Kaminski was a pro-Nazi White Russian who raised his own private army. When the Soviets recaptured White Russia in 1944, Kaminski retreated westward and the Waffen SS absorbed his so-called army, forming the SS Kaminski Brigade. In Warsaw, these two formations were so undisciplined and their behavior so barbaric that they appalled even hardened Nazis; the two brigades were subsequently withdrawn. Kaminski died soon after in mysterious circumstances, but Dirlewanger received the coveted Knight's Cross medal for his pacification of Warsaw.

Hitler finally ordered Waffen SS forces to fire on their own countrymen. As the Wehrmacht was pushed back on all fronts in early 1945, SS flying courts summarily executed thousands of German soldiers and civilians for alleged negligence or cowardice.

During the series of trials of war criminals begun at Nuremberg in 1946, the International Military Tribunal indicted the Waffen SS as a criminal organization. It stood accused of the mass murder of Jews and of atrocities committed against prisoners and enemy civilians. The Allies convicted several hundred Waffen SS personnel and many were executed, including Fritz Knochlein for the Le Paradis massacre. Joachim Peiper and 42 other Leibstandarte personnel were condemned to death for the Malmédy massacre, but these sentences were commuted to prison terms. Peiper served only ten years for his crimes, while General Kurt Meyer, whose death sentence for the murder of Canadians in Normandy was also commuted, served only eight years in prison.

Nazi apologists have campaigned vigorously ever since to rehabilitate the Waffen SS. They disassociate the frontline, regular Waffen SS formations from atrocities committed by general SS security and police forces in occupied territory. They also claim that Waffen SS troops were just fighting soldiers like members of the Wehrmacht. But the Waffen SS, like the regular German army, was deeply implicated in the Nazi atrocities that occurred during the war.

Russell A. Hart

SEE ALSO: TERROR IN THE GERMAN OCCUPATION OF THE EAST; WWII RESISTANCE IN YUGOSLAVIA AND TERRORISM; TERROR AND THE NAZI BARBARIZATION OF WARFARE; WORLD WAR II WAR CRIMES TRIALS.

FURTHER READING

- Reitlinger, G. *The SS: Alibi of a Nation, 1922-1945.* London: Arms and Armour Press, and Englewood Cliffs, NJ: Prentice Hall, 1981.
- Schulte, Theo J. *The German Army and Nazi Policies in Occupied Russia.* Oxford and New York: Berg, 1989.
- Stein, George H. *The Waffen SS: Hitler's Elite Guard at War, 1939-1945.* Ithaca, NY: Cornell University Press, 1966.

WORLD WAR II WAR CRIMES TRIALS

At the end of World War II, the victorious Allies were determined to punish the Axis powers for their aggression and use of terror as part of state policy. This resulted in the Nuremberg and Tokyo war crimes trials before the United Nations (U.N.) International War Crimes Tribunal. The tribunal leveled four indictments against Axis defendants: conspiracy to commit aggressive war; crimes against peace; war crimes; and crimes against humanity.

The tribunal had strong legal precedents for indictments of war crimes based on contraventions of the 1907 Hague and 1929 Geneva Conventions (which established rules for wartime treatment of prisoners, the sick, and the wounded). But few precedents existed for the indictments of unlawful aggressive war, which were the cornerstone of the proceedings. The Allied attempt to find precedent for this charge in the provisions of the 1928 Briand–Kellogg Pact, in which the signatories agreed to seek peaceful solutions to international disputes, was not compelling.

THE NUREMBERG TRIALS

The problems of securing convictions on such novel charges were most evident in the Nuremberg trials, where only a single defendant was condemned to death solely on the grounds of conspiring to conduct aggressive war; a further three defendants were acquitted. The emphasis on charges of aggressive war made the tribunal's task of prosecution more complex and ensured that the trials placed less emphasis on crimes against humanity, such as the Holocaust.

> **KEY FACTS**
>
> - Of 22 German military and political leaders indicted at Nuremberg, 12 were hanged, 7 were jailed from 10 years to life, and 3 were acquitted.
> - The tribunal rejected the commonly offered major defense that only the state, not the individual, could be found guilty of war crimes.

Moreover, the tribunals had to wrestle with the problems inherent in victor's justice – the fact that those who had won the war were doing the prosecuting – in particular, the difficulty of corroborating evidence. For example, the Soviet Union blamed the Nazis for the Katyn massacres of Polish soldiers that had in fact been committed by the Soviets in 1940. Another thorny legal issue was whether to prosecute as war crimes the Germans' unrestricted use of submarine warfare and area bombing of civilian population centers, methods which were subsequently adopted by the Allies themselves. Indictments for such "crimes" were noticeably absent at Nuremberg.

THE TOKYO TRIBUNAL

As at Nuremberg, the United States and Great Britain took the lead in prosecuting Japanese war criminals. In January 1946, the International Military Tribunal for the Far East indicted 28 alleged war criminals on 55 counts of crimes against humanity committed between January 1, 1928, and September 2, 1945. The trial took place in Tokyo from June 3, 1946, until November 1948.

Of those initially indicted by the Tokyo tribunal, three died during the trial and 16 were condemned to life imprisonment, largely for waging a war of aggression. Two received shorter prison sentences and seven were condemned to death by hanging for crimes against humanity. Of those sentenced to death, the most infamous were Colonel Itagaki, General Iswane Matsui, Tomoyuki Yamashita, and Hideki Tojo.

The tribunal found Itagaki, minister of war in 1938, guilty of ordering, authorizing, and permitting those in charge of prisoner of war camps and civilian labor camps to violate the laws of war by maltreating prisoners. It found General Matsui responsible for the Rape of

TRH Pictures/ US National Archives

Hideki Tojo makes his deposition against prosecutors at the war crimes trials in Tokyo, January 1948.

Nanking. His troops had massacred 200,000 Chinese civilians and raped thousands of women from December 1937 to February 1938. Tomoyuki Yamashita was found guilty of the Rape of Manila, even though he was nowhere near Manila at the time. The Allies needed a scapegoat, and it has been suggested that he was killed in revenge for his defeat of the British forces in Singapore. The tribunal found that Hideki Tojo, head of the Japanese cabinet from 1941, bore primary responsibility for waging a war of aggression. He was held criminally liable for the mistreatment of prisoners in the Bataan Death March and in the construction of the Burma–Siam railroad in 1942. Most participants claimed military necessity. This defense was undermined by the Hague Convention's judgment that the rules of war took specific account of military necessity.

The Allies had intended the tribunal to be a permanent element of the new U.N. Organization to investigate and adjudicate breaches of international law and the laws of war. But the deepening of the Cold War and the rehabilitation of West Germany and Japan as democratic states saw the lapse of the tribunal. In the 1990s, the international community resurrected the notion of a permanent U.N. International War Crimes Tribunal, in the light of atrocities in Rwanda and Bosnia. Whether there will be a permanent tribunal may depend on the success of the war crimes trials in The Hague concerning atrocities in former Yugoslavia.

Russell A. Hart

SEE ALSO: TERROR IN THE GERMAN OCCUPATION OF THE EAST; GERMAN TERROR IN FRANCE AND ITALY; GERMAN TERROR IN NORWAY; THE HOLOCAUST; JAPANESE TERROR IN THE FAR EAST; JAPANESE TERRORIZATION OF PRISONERS; TERROR AND THE NAZI BARBARIZATION OF WARFARE; TERROR AND THE WAFFEN SS.

FURTHER READING

- Piccigallo, P. *The Japanese on Trial: Allied War Crimes Operations in the East, 1945-1951.* Austin: University of Texas Press, 1979.
- Smith, B. F. *The Road to Nuremberg.* London: Deutsch, and New York: Basic Books, 1981.
- Taylor, Telford. *The Anatomy of the Nuremberg Trials.* New York: Knopf, 1992; London: Bloomsbury, 1993.

THE DEBATE OVER AERIAL BOMBING

Since the beginnings of aerial warfare early in the twentieth century, military commanders have been fascinated by the possibility that air attacks could cripple an enemy's economy or terrorize its people. But these ambitions have always led to a debate over the morality of bombing civilians. Attempts were made before World War I to agree to legal restrictions on the use of air power against civilians, but these failed.

World War I saw the first major use of air power against civilian society in the form of bombing now normally described as "strategic." From 1915, German bomber aircraft and Zeppelin airships mounted a few raids on Britain. They were supposedly aiming at targets with obvious military value, such as London's armament factories, but soon found it hard to pinpoint any target smaller than the city as a whole. Nevertheless, they continued bombing, hoping to destroy the intended targets and to damage British civilian morale. The raids did create short-term panic, but the terror was too localized to have a major impact: 1,117 civilians were killed during 643 raids over Britain.

SUMMARY

- In World War II, the German air force initiated the development of indiscriminate attacks on civilian targets – "terror" bombing.
- For most of the war, the British RAF carried out indiscriminate "area bombing" attacks on German cities. In 1944-45, American forces similarly devastated Japan's cities. Allied leaders accepted that area bombing would cause major civilian casualties. Critics questioned the morality of the strategy.
- The most notorious events, before the atom bomb attacks, were the fire bombing of Dresden and the attacks on Tokyo early in 1945.

In 1918, the British formed an independent air force, the Royal Air Force (RAF), to defend their cities and to retaliate against Germany, but the war ended before the new RAF had launched more than a handful of raids. The French also conducted a number of raids on Germany.

By the end of World War I, military commanders had only limited experience in using bombers as instruments of terror. Civilian populations, too, had had only a small taste of being on the receiving end of such bombing, and the effects of larger and more sustained assaults could not really be predicted.

BOMBING TO TERRORIZE THE ENEMY

Between the two world wars, the RAF was a new armed service competing with the army and navy for limited defense funds. The RAF made a strong case to Britain's political leaders that it should have an independent role, separate from any land and sea battles, in their plans in any future war. The proposal was to use a strategic bombing offensive to cripple an enemy state. Concentrated attacks on the enemy economy and infrastructure would destroy such targets as factories, rail yards, and oil installations.

The enemy population was not a specific target, but it would be intimidated by the bombing and dismayed by the shortages and the disruption of essential services. Strategic bombing would thus lead to an atmosphere of crisis and collapse. In support of this policy, Lord Trenchard, the RAF's chief of staff from 1919-29, said (without substantial evidence) that the overall psychological effect of such bombing would be 20 times greater than the physical destruction caused.

Trenchard had commanded the Royal Flying Corps during World War I. Two other leaders of air services in World War I also contributed to the development of theories of air power. Brigadier Billy Mitchell had commanded the small U.S. Army air forces during

World War I. In the 1920s, as assistant chief of the Army Air Service, Mitchell strongly argued that the U.S. should establish an independent air force like the RAF. He also believed in the power of aerial bombing and staged a number of unrealistic tests in 1921-23 in which, to "prove" his point, various dilapidated warships were bombed and sunk. Mitchell resigned after quarrels with his superiors, but his ideas remained influential in U.S. aviation circles. However, America's air force (officially named the U.S. Army Air Force – USAAF – during World War II) remained weak until after America entered World War II in 1941.

The other important advocate of bombing was the Italian Giulio Douhet, commander of Italy's first military aviation unit in 1912-15. After World War I, he commanded Italy's Army Aviation Service and wrote extensively on the role and potential of air power. His influential book, *The Command of the Air* (1921), predicted how massed bomber fleets would devastate cities and terrorize populations in a future war, making bombers the decisive factor in determining an outcome.

When Hitler's Germany rearmed during the 1930s, one of the first and most important steps taken was the creation of a powerful air force, the Luftwaffe. In fact, the Luftwaffe concentrated its development of tactics and aircraft on assisting the German army on the battlefield, with strategic bombing of cities seen only as a subsidiary. Despite this, fears of whether British cities and their populations could stand up to enemy bombardment came to dominate British policy-making. Predictions made before 1938 expected up to 750,000 casualties for London during the first three weeks of an air attack. These fears were reinforced by images of German terror bombing in Spain during the Spanish Civil War (especially the bombing of Guernica in 1937), by Italian attacks on Abyssinia (modern Ethiopia) in 1935-36, and by Japanese sorties over China throughout the 1930s.

In this pre-radar era, there was a belief that "the bomber would always get through," whatever fighter defenses were in position. The British response was to build a bomber force as a deterrent against air attack.

LEGAL LIMITATION ON BOMBING

International law concerning bombing remained unchanged in the interwar period. A Hague Conference during 1922-23, considering limitations on aerial warfare, prohibited bombing "for the purpose of terrorizing the civilian population," and stated that bombing was legitimate only when directed at military installations. Legitimate targets also included factories engaged in war production and military communication systems, but these were not to be attacked if it would involve the incidental bombing of adjacent civilian areas. However, the rules were never adopted by any state, mainly because countries were reluctant to accept restrictions that would limit their own war strategies. At the outbreak of World War II, in September 1939, U.S. President Franklin D. Roosevelt appealed to Britain, France, and Germany to refrain from all but strictly military bombing. All three powers accepted the appeal, but also stated that they would ignore this obligation if their opponents reneged on it.

GERMANY BREACHES THE LIMITATION

The first bombing outside a strictly military context was undertaken by Germany on Warsaw after Hitler invaded Poland on September 1, 1939. Raids on the city were planned for the first days of the war, but were cancelled due to bad weather. They actually began on September 24, 1939, when the city was within the zone of fighting on the ground. According to the Germans, being in the battle zone made Warsaw a legitimate target, and military installations were targeted.

The first major German bombing raid of the war in the West came on May 14, 1940. Rotterdam, the major oil terminal and refinery in the Netherlands, was close to the front line and the attack was nominally aimed at military targets. However, the center of the city was destroyed and 980 civilians were killed, although contemporary reports put the death toll at up to 30,000. Germany used the terror imagery of the raid in propaganda aimed at other countries that it was about to invade, in an attempt to weaken resistance.

The British government judged the attack indiscriminate and a breach of the limitations on air attacks agreed to at the start of the war. On May 15, 1940, the RAF was therefore authorized to attack military and industrial targets throughout Germany, on the basis that its navigation and bomb-aiming were sufficiently precise to hit them without causing major civilian casualties. The limited attacks on German shipping carried out in the earlier months of the war had shown that daylight attacks cost the bombers unacceptably high casualties. Consequently, although the RAF's Bomber Command was now free to implement its pre-war strategy of mass attacks on Germany, for now such attacks would have to be carried out by night.

"THE BLITZ" TERRORIZES BRITAIN

Bombing on a large scale was first carried out by Germany against Britain. During the summer of 1940, the Luftwaffe attacked Britain's air defense network as the first stage of Hitler's invasion plan, Operation Sea Lion. On August 24, German aircraft bombed London, triggering in retaliation a British raid on specific targets in Berlin the following night. From this point, Germany persisted in attacks on British cities with the urban population sanctioned as a target. As the German raids were increasingly flown at night to avoid British fighters, they became entirely indiscriminate. The resultant terror bombing campaign was commonly known as "the Blitz" (from *Blitzkrieg* – "lightning war") and lasted until May 1941. During this period of area bombing, the British government estimated that 3,000 civilians were killed a week and 350,000 houses were destroyed. Much of this damage was inflicted during the last two weeks of November 1940, including the notorious bombing of Coventry on the night of November 14, followed by raids on Birmingham, Glasgow, Sheffield, Liverpool, and Southampton. On some nights, more than 400 bombers were sent over to drop hundreds of tons of bombs and incendiaries on British cities, particularly on the ports.

Despite this escalation of hostilities into "total war," this was a much lower level of destruction than had been projected, and it was soon apparent that the civilian population was far more resilient in living with bombing than had been expected. Once people had survived the initial shock, and a system of air raid precautions was functioning smoothly, it was possible to continue with daily life despite severe disruptions.

AREA BOMBING: THE BRITISH RESPONSE

This German campaign can be contrasted with the British Bomber Command's operations during the same period. British aircraft were given very specific industrial targets, but they were forbidden to bomb general urban areas, unlike their German counterparts. Significant results were claimed, but in August 1941, an official investigation, the Butt Report, came up with very different conclusions. Photographs taken from the bombers showed that, on moonlit nights, only a third of bombs fell within five miles of the target. On moonless nights results were far worse. German production remained virtually unaffected.

However, as an invasion of German-occupied Europe remained only a distant possibility, bombing appeared to be the single means of attacking Germany. Bombing attacks were also politically necessary to demonstrate to the Soviet Union (attacked by Germany in June 1941) that Britain was still very much in the war. Britain had, therefore, committed much of her war effort, up to one-third according to some estimates, to the production of heavy bombers.

Hulton Getty Picture Collection

Britain's Air Chief Marshal Arthur "Bomber" Harris studies a map of possible targets in Germany.

A new bombing policy accordingly came into effect from February 14, 1942. This stated that attacks "should now be focused on the morale of the enemy civil population and, in particular, of the industrial workers." The new targets were to be residential areas, since they were larger and easier to hit and more flammable than factory sites. Stress was placed on "de-housing" the workers and depressing and terrorizing them to the point where it affected German war production. Killing civilians was supposedly not a deliberate aim of this policy, but it was accepted as an unavoidable consequence. Whether such attacks were morally justified was not an issue for the British

Hulton Getty Picture Collection

The ruins of Hamburg after the Allied bombing raid of July 27-28, 1943; 40,000 Germans died, either as a result of the bombs or from the ensuing firestorm.

leaders; the only concern was for the campaign's effectiveness. German propaganda, however, described the raids as "terror attacks" and cited these as examples of their enemies' "barbarism."

This "area bombing" strategy was vigorously put into effect by Air Chief Marshal Arthur "Bomber" Harris, who led the RAF Bomber Command from late February 1942 until the end of the war. One of the most devastating raids was on Hamburg on the night of July 27–28, 1943. Bombs dropped by 787 aircraft combined with the hot, dry conditions to create a single huge fire which sucked in surrounding oxygen, suffocating large numbers of people. More than 40,000 died, 900,000 lost their homes, and Hamburg lost two months of war production. However, the constantly improving German defenses meant Bomber Command always sustained heavy losses. By the winter of 1943-44, radar developments and other innovations had made bombers as vulnerable by night as by day. For example, on the night of March 30-31, 1944, 95 British bombers were lost during a raid on Nuremberg, while only 69 Germans were killed.

AMERICAN OPERATIONS

By the time the United States joined the war on December 7, 1941, after the Japanese attacked Pearl Harbor, a massive aircraft building program had begun to create a powerful air force. The leaders of the USAAF believed in daylight precision bombing of military and industrial targets, with the bombers protecting themselves from enemy fighters by their own defensive machine guns. It took some time to build up this force and it was not until the summer of 1943 that the USAAF was able to operate in strength.

The first important tests of its bombing strategy were attacks made on factories at Schweinfurt in central Germany, which made most of Germany's ball-bearings. In theory these were crucial to the German war effort since ball-bearings formed part of every important machine. Although the bombers inflicted significant damage on the factories, the attacks failed because of the horrendous losses that the bomber forces sustained.

Hulton Getty Picture Collection

The ruins of Dresden after the Allies' controversial attack of February 13-14, 1945.

The USAAF found an effective answer to these losses in the P-51D Mustang fighter. It could escort bombers all the way to Germany from bases in eastern England. Through the spring of 1944, these aircraft destroyed the Luftwaffe's fighters, and by the summer, Allied bombers could operate freely during daylight.

Throughout this period and until the end of the war, the USAAF maintained its policy of precision attacks on targets with clear military value. The reality, however, was that weather conditions and the shortcomings of the available equipment meant that many raids were no more accurately targeted than those of the RAF and were "area attacks" in all but name.

Both the British and American bomber forces reduced their attacks on targets in Germany during the summer of 1944 to support the Allied invasion of France, which began on June 6, 1944. Their main targets were roads and railroads, which they attacked as precisely as possible in an effort to avoid French civilian casualties.

THE FINAL STAGES

Germany's Luftwaffe was unable to mount any important strategic bombing raids after 1941, but German scientists did develop two new terror weapons that were used to attack civilian targets. These were the jet-engined V1 cruise missile and the rocket-powered V2 ballistic missile. Neither type was accurate enough to hit any military target; for the Germans they were seen as retaliation for the equally indiscriminate Allied air attacks. Over 9,000 V1s were launched against Britain from France and Belgium. Roughly 5,000 reached their targets (the V1 flew slowly enough to be intercepted by Allied fighter aircraft or anti-aircraft fire). The supersonic V2 could not be intercepted. Over 1,000 were fired at targets in Britain, and others at Allied forces in

France and Belgium after these countries had been liberated in 1944.

From September 1944, both the Allied bomber forces resumed major attacks on Germany. Air Marshal Harris maintained his policy of area bombing, while the American leaders, and some senior British officers, argued for attacks to be focused on specific sectors of the German war effort. The Americans accordingly concentrated on precision attacks on Germany's oil industry to dramatic effect.

By the winter of 1944-45, some politicians and religious leaders were beginning to question the morality of continuing with the all-out bombing of Germany. These doubts came to a head with a series of raids carried out by both British and American bombers against Dresden on February 13-15, 1945. At least 30,000 civilian deaths resulted, although figures of more than 100,000 have been claimed. Dresden was said to have had little military value and was certainly crowded with helpless refugees fleeing the advance of the Soviet forces from the east. By this stage, the German war effort was in shambles and doubts about the bombing campaign became secondary as Germany itself was overrun by Allied armies.

STRATEGIC BOMBING AGAINST JAPAN

In the Pacific war, Allied strategic bombing was conducted solely by American forces. They attacked Japan from bases in China and later from the Marianas Islands in the Pacific Ocean south of Japan. They captured the Marianas bases from the Japanese in the summer of 1944, but for months the air attacks on Japan were ineffective.

From March 1945, American forces carried out low-level area bombing raids over Japanese cities. Since many buildings were built of flammable materials, the effect was devastating. In a raid on Tokyo on March 9-10, 1945, at least 87,000 Japanese were killed, more than the death toll after the atomic bomb was dropped on Hiroshima in August 1945. By the end of the war, 66 Japanese cities were more than 40 percent destroyed.

As in Europe, the tactics used were those judged to cause the most damage to the enemy war effort, without regard to the civilian casualties they might involve.

THE EFFECTS OF BOMBING

Strategic bombing in World War II evolved from an initial policy of bombing only military targets in a vicious spiral toward indiscriminate and terror bombing. When they held the upper hand in the early war years, the Axis powers made little effort to avoid civilian casualties and hoped for a terror effect. Having originally attempted more discriminate bombing, the Allies eventually followed a similar policy.

Terror became an aspect of both British and American bombing policy, though rarely the dominant one. The overriding objective was to wreck enemy war efforts. This was achieved to a lesser extent against Germany and to a greater extent against Japan. Both bombing campaigns contributed significantly to the defeat of these states. The bombing policies followed were authorized by British Prime Minister Winston Churchill and U.S. President Franklin D. Roosevelt, the popular leaders of the world's two largest democracies, during the crisis of a total war. The massive scale on which the assault was mounted led to at least a million civilian deaths. This in turn meant the moral basis of the campaign became increasingly dubious until final victory was assured, although not as far as ordinary people were concerned.

By the end of the war, the Allied leaders were well aware of concern about morality. At the post-war war crimes trials of Axis leaders, the Allies did not charge anyone with organizing indiscriminate air attacks, to stop them from citing Allied actions in their defense. Second thoughts about the bombing campaign also had other effects. Of all the campaign medals awarded to British forces for outstanding duty, no medal was ever struck for Bomber Command's veterans.

Stephen Prince

SEE ALSO: THE DEBATE OVER THE ATOM BOMB; TERROR IN THE KOREAN WAR; TERROR IN THE VIETNAM WAR; COUNTERTERROR IN THE BRITISH EMPIRE BEFORE 1945.

FURTHER READING

- Boog, Horst, ed. *The Conduct of the Air War in the Second World War.* Oxford and New York: Berg, 1991.
- Howard, Michael, George J. Andreopoulos, and Mark R. Shulman. *The Laws of War.* London and New Haven, CT: Yale University Press, 1994.
- Schaffer, Ronald. *Wings of Judgment.* Oxford and New York: Oxford University Press, 1988.
- *The United States Strategic Bombing Survey.* Washington: National Archives, 1991.

THE DEBATE OVER THE ATOM BOMB

On August 6, 1945, the world discovered the terrors of the atomic age. Acting on the orders of U.S. President Harry S. Truman, the United States Army Air Force (USAAF) dropped an atomic bomb on the Japanese city of Hiroshima. This uranium fission weapon – nicknamed "Little Boy" – inflicted instant devastation on the city, causing 70-80,000 deaths. On August 9, a second atomic weapon (a plutonium fission device, nicknamed "Fat Man") was detonated over Nagasaki, a shipbuilding center on the island of Kyushu. Although less effective than the first weapon in terms of material and personal damage, some 35-40,000 people were killed. Six days later, Japanese Emperor Hirohito announced that his government had accepted the Potsdam Declaration, an ultimatum issued by the Allied powers on July 26, 1945, which called for Japan's unconditional surrender. Japan's war in Asia and the Pacific had ended.

THE JAPANESE WARRIOR CODE

The Pacific War had illustrated to the Allied powers the tenacity of the Japanese fighting soldier. From the earliest combat engagements in the war, it had been made readily apparent that the "warrior-code" ethic ingrained within the Japanese military prohibited any consideration of surrender. By the middle of 1945, Japanese resistance still remained firm in the face of the overwhelming offensive power of the Allies, particularly the forces of the United States. American aerial bombers based on the tiny islands of Saipan and Tinian in the Pacific Ocean had already inflicted devastating saturation attacks against economic, military, and civilian targets in an attempt to induce Japan to surrender. Many of Japan's leading cities were in ruins. A single raid on Tokyo during the night of March 9-10, 1945, burned out 40 percent of the Japanese capital and killed an estimated 87,000 civilians.

KEY FACTS

- In early August 1945, America dropped two atomic bombs on the Japanese cities of Hiroshima and Nagasaki.
- The prospect of continued fanatical resistance to an Allied invasion of the Japanese mainland persuaded the Americans to use the ultimate terror weapon, the atom bomb, to compel Japan to accept unconditional surrender.
- These two bombs clearly demonstrated the awesome destructive power of the atomic bomb.

NO SURRENDER

In addition to these highly destructive raids against urban areas, Japanese merchant shipping had been reduced to a mere 12 percent of its pre-war strength by continuous U.S. air and naval attacks. For a country dependent on sea communications, the American blockade effectively strangled the Japanese economy. By 1945, Japan's munitions output had fallen to less than half its wartime peak. The Japanese population also suffered through lack of food. The daily rations fell below 1,500 calories per person, about half of today's recommended daily intake for an adult male.

On the surface, Japan appeared to be on the verge of collapse. Yet Japanese policy continued to be one of resistance. As late as April 1945, the Japanese defense of Okinawa island, situated south of Japan's "Home Islands," produced some of the bloodiest fighting of the war, resulting in considerable U.S. casualties.

Despite the destruction being inflicted upon the Home Islands, the Japanese policy of "no surrender" continued because of the complex nature of Japan's political system. The political world was dominated by a military high command that would not permit surrender, even when faced with certain annihilation.

As long as Japan had soldiers to fight and inflict injury on the enemy, the Japanese armed forces did not consider themselves defeated. Furthermore, the military exerted a substantial influence over the Japanese emperor. He, in turn, commanded the loyal

TRH Pictures

The charred remains of a young boy, about half a mile from the center of the atomic explosion at Nagasaki, Japan, on August 9, 1945.

support of his subjects, who regarded the emperor as a divine being.

For the Allies, unable to bomb the Japanese into submission, the alternative seemed to be to mount a seaborne invasion of the Japanese mainland. Given that the Japanese forces would probably fight to the last person, such an operation promised to be bloody. Allied staffs estimated that a million Allied servicemen would die in such an invasion plus a far greater number of Japanese military personnel and civilians.

Unknown to most Allied planners, however, there was another possibility. Since late 1941, at a vast cost of $2 billion, an international group of scientists led by U.S. nuclear physicist J. Robert Oppenheimer had worked toward creating an atomic explosion. The destructive power and force of an atomic weapon would be unparalleled in the history of warfare. The prototype atomic bomb, a plutonium weapon, produced the effects of an explosion of 20,000 tons of TNT when successfully detonated on July 16, 1945. A terrible weapon was waiting in the wings if the leaders of the Allied powers had the courage to use it. But there had to be overwhelming reasons to visit such devastation on what would be a mainly civilian target.

STRATEGIC AIR POWER DOCTRINE

Bombing Japanese civilians to frighten them into submission was not a new strategy, but it was not a successful one either. For General Curtis LeMay, commander of XXI Bomber Command, America's bomber force in the Pacific, the previous application of terror bombing against highly populated areas, in combination with attacks against Japanese war production, had not provided the anticipated psychological dislocation of Japanese morale. General LeMay could not understand how a civilian population could take such punishment and not surrender. He was a disciple of the Italian Giulio Douhet, who claimed that populations would eventually rise up in the face of repeated aerial attacks and force their governments to demand peace. Using the atom bomb did not conflict with such ideas but instead represented a further stage in their development.

THE DECISION TO DROP THE BOMB

Various agencies within the Japanese government were putting out tentative diplomatic feelers, which implied a willingness to surrender. But these feelers were not on a scale that the Allies believed should be taken seriously. Equally quickly disregarded were suggestions made by some of the atom-bomb scientists that a demonstration atomic explosion should be arranged to show the Japanese what awaited them if they continued to fight rather than surrender.

Instead, President Truman and his advisers, with the agreement of the British who had contributed their own atomic research to the bomb project, decided that it was essential to drop the bomb in order to achieve the final defeat of Japan with the fewest possible casualties. American strategists hoped to convince the Japanese that the United States now held the power to bring about the total destruction of the Japanese nation. Faced with this possibility, the Japanese government would surely surrender unconditionally, as the Potsdam Declaration demanded.

"A BOILING BLACK MASS"

The first atom bombs were accordingly dropped on Hiroshima on August 6 and over Nagasaki on August 9, 1945. Colonel Paul Tibbets, commander of the B-29 bomber "Enola Gay," which dropped the Hiroshima bomb, starkly recalled the visual effect of the first atomic bomb: "I couldn't see any city down there, but what I saw was a tremendous area covered by – the only way I could describe it is – a boiling black mass." For the Japanese civilians on the ground, Hiroshima brought terror that could not have been surpassed if "the sun had crashed and exploded." The scene was one of utter devastation: "Yellow fireballs were splashing down...people's clothes had been blown off and their bodies burned by the heat rays." One solitary bomber had successfully reduced an entire Japanese city to rubble. The terror impact on the surviving civilian population was enormous.

DID THE ATOM BOMB WIN THE WAR?

At the same time, on August 8, 1945, the Soviet Union declared war on Japan and the next day the Red Army attacked Japanese forces in the occupied Chinese province of Manchuria (now Dongbei). The Japanese army in Manchuria collapsed almost immediately under the Soviet attack, illustrating to Japan's military leaders the hopelessness of their position.

The initial reactions by Japanese military leaders to the first atomic bomb were indifferent, even dismissive – probably because they failed to appreciate the full horror of what had happened since it was so far beyond their experience. However, after the dropping of the second bomb, and the Soviet entry into the conflict, only a small minority within the Japanese hierarchy was prepared to fight on, but they were overruled by the emperor. It is not clear whether the atom bombs or the Soviet attacks were the decisive factors in finally causing Japan's surrender.

The dropping of atomic bombs on Hiroshima and Nagasaki was a necessary evil as far as the Allies were concerned. The terror it produced and the slaughter it inflicted on the Japanese civilian population were offset by the Allied lives saved. Along with concern about casualties from the fighting, the Allied leaders and populations were already angered by the ample evidence of barbaric Japanese treatment of prisoners of war, many of whom were still in Japanese hands, and they feared what would happen to them if the war were prolonged.

With two opposing sides, one committed to a policy of no surrender and the other to total victory, enormous destruction was inevitable. The atomic bomb's capacity for utter devastation made it the ultimate weapon in a conflict that had entered the rarely explored realms of "total war." This blurring between civilian and military targets, which had been a dominant feature of the aerial war, not only over Japan but also over Europe, would now become an even greater feature in future military thinking.

Christopher J. Baxter
Andrew Douglas Stewart

SEE ALSO: JAPANESE TERROR IN THE FAR EAST; JAPANESE TERRORIZATION OF PRISONERS; WORLD WAR II WAR CRIMES TRIALS; THE DEBATE OVER AERIAL BOMBING; NUCLEAR TERRORISM.

FURTHER READING

- Costello, John. *The Pacific War.* New York: Quill,1982; London: Pan, 1985.
- Feis, H. *The Atomic Bomb and the End of World War II.* Princeton, NJ: Princeton University Press, 1966.
- Spector, Ronald. *Eagle Against the Sun: The American War with Japan.* New York: The Free Press, 1984; London: Viking, 1985.

THE BACKGROUND TO MODERN TERRORIST CAMPAIGNS

Popperfoto

George Grivas returns to Athens on March 19, 1959, after leading the EOKA campaign in Cyprus.

THE BACKGROUND TO MODERN TERRORIST CAMPAIGNS: *Introduction*

The terrible experiences of World War II set the scene for modern terrorism in two major ways. First, during this bitterly-fought conflict the notion emerged that civilians could be legitimate targets of violence and terror. Second, the war also set the scene in the way that it opened up much of Asia for nationalist and often communist, revolution. The example of revolution in Asia, particularly the example of China, then became very important for the rest of the world, as the old colonial empires of the Europeans crumbled and what became known as the developing world came into being.

In the 1950s and 1960s, there were many nationalist struggles to rid countries of their despised European regimes. The French, for example, faced bloody anti-colonial conflict in Algeria and Indochina, while the British faced the Mau Mau revolt in Kenya and communist insurrection in Malaya. Other European nations also faced such revolts: the Dutch fought a war in what is now Indonesia, for example.

These wars of national liberation threw up a variety of theories and justifications for the use of what we would describe as terror tactics within the context of a more general armed struggle. Terrorism, therefore, was usually one method used in a wider insurgency movement. Some of the theories justifying terror tactics came from the nineteenth century, and were part of the more general revolutionary theories, often connected to Marxism. Such theories did influence to some degree the behavior and strategies used by insurgent movements during the struggles of decolonization.

As these anti-colonial campaigns progressed, however, contemporary theorists added to the mixture, showing how the use of violence could be justified and how it could be used most effectively. Some of the leaders of these anti-colonial struggles produced theories based on their experiences. Now, therefore, practice was feeding back into the theory of terrorism. This two-way dynamic between terrorist theory and its practice would remain a prominent feature of the modern phenomenon of terrorism.

The struggles of decolonization also influenced later terrorism in the sense that they provided the ground for ideas, strategies, tactics, and weapons to be tested. The terrorist campaigns that sprung up in the 1960s and 1970s, many of which are still claiming lives today, learned a great deal from these earlier anti-colonial struggles. In many ways these later terrorist campaigns were both more sophisticated and more deadly due to the knowledge and expertise on terror tactics inherited from the era of decolonization. ■

Theories of Insurgency and Terrorism

When a bomb explodes and hundreds die, people start asking why some groups turn to terrorism and how it has become so widespread that it affects everyone's lives. Behind most terrorist groups there is a political influence and often a figure of inspiration, whether a thinker such as Karl Marx or a man of action like Che Guevara. Some terrorists want sweeping change on the scale of the French Revolution, while others such as the colonists in the American Revolution wage wars against a colonial power. Sometimes the government terrorizes its own people, as in many South American countries.

THEORIES OF INSURGENCY AND TERRORISM: Introduction

The first modern political theorist was the Italian Niccolò Machiavelli. In his book *The Prince*, he wrote: "Since some men love as they please but fear when the prince pleases, a wise prince should rely on that which he controls, not on what he cannot control." The twentieth century has seen the systematic use of secret police to control societies by instilling fear in their citizens, as the Shah did in Iran. Governments have also used methods in their relations with foreign states that they would find unacceptable or unconstitutional at home. Bulgaria's secret service assisted a Turkish right-winger in his attempt to assassinate Pope John Paul II in 1981. State terrorism is used by governments to achieve their own national objectives – for instance, Iraq's savage treatment of its Kurdish minority.

Terrorism can be defined as the selective or indicriminate use of violence in order to bring about political change by inducing fear. Terrorism is one of the methods frequently used by the would-be revolutionary. This form is called agitational terror. A form called enforcement terror is adopted by governments prepared to use any means to protect themselves from their political opponents. These two examples show that terrorism can be described and even classified.

The term *terror* was first used to indicate a general state of fear deliberately created for political purposes during the French Revolution (1789-94). It particularly referred to the Reign of Terror of 1793-94. Governments like to apply the term to any violent methods used by a political opposition. In all societies, there is a close relationship between government and opposition. The nature of government helps determine the nature of opposition. Where there are no elections, and freedom of speech is limited, opposition groups sometimes resort to violence. However, violence is also used by minorities who feel excluded by society.

Terrorism is not an option chosen by large groups, but rather a strategy adopted by small groups, meeting secretly to organize violent acts. An *insurgency* occurs when an opposition movement combines violence with a political strategy to defeat and replace a government. Terrorism is, however, inextricably linked with insurgencies. There are at least six different goals of insurgent movements: reform, secession, revolution, restoration, reaction, or maintenance of the status quo. Most terrorists are rebels and an understanding of why they use terror requires knowledge of insurgent strategies.

Insurgent strategy can range from political assassination to all-out revolutionary civil war. Terrorism may be used as part of any of these strategies. Being a tool of small groups, terrorism presents governments with a dilemma. It may be possible to defeat a terrorist group if the government is prepared to accept the cost in money and lives, but it usually proves very difficult to eliminate the movement altogether. Terrorist goals can often only be satisfied by a range of concessions the government had previously refused to make.

Three categories of terrorism can be identified: revolutionary, sub-revolutionary, and repressive terrorism. The second and third categories relate to the opposition and government respectively. The first is more complex and embraces both sides. It is difficult to draw a boundary between these categories – the same conflict may have features of more than one category.

Several writers have constructed theories of insurgency involving one or more of these forms of action. Many of these theories are part of a fascist or communist strategy for comprehensive social change using violence. Some theories are part of a program of less far-reaching changes, such as a war of national liberation. Others are from the viewpoint of the government forces whose duty it is to put a stop to insurgency.

Since World War II, a body of writing has developed on the subject, examining insurgency from the "legitimate" government's point of view. The term *low-intensity conflict* has been applied to terrorism, but it is more generally described as counterinsurgency. However, it is often very difficult to make hard and fast distinctions between an insurgency that includes terrorism and one that does not. ■

THEORIES OF TERROR IN URBAN INSURRECTIONS

Revolutionary terrorism has been defined as the use of "systematic tactics of terrorist violence with the objective of bringing about political revolution." This form of terrorism has four major characteristics. First, it is carried out by groups, rather than individuals, which have clearly defined leaderships. Second, it is driven by a clear ideology and intends to create new institutional structures. Third, the movement has a definite strategy involving the planned use of violence against victims who have been selected for their symbolic value for a wider audience. Fourth, the purpose of this violence is to change permanently people's attitudes and behavior.

REVOLUTION

The modern notion of revolution originated at the end of the eighteenth century. Thirteen of the British colonies of North America successfully waged a war of national liberation against the government in London. The independence of the United States was finally secured by the Treaty of Paris in 1783. The French Revolution, which began in 1789, dominated radical political thinking for over 100 years. Both revolutions challenged the notion of a divinely appointed monarch as the head of a hierarchical society. But where the Americans simply transferred political authority from London, ultimately, to Washington, DC, the French tried to transform the social order completely.

A new revolutionary era began in which constitutional republics became the goals for radical political movements. It also set the stage for the nineteenth century as an age of nationalism. Combining the political state and the people's nation into a single entity soon became the ideal of the Serbs, the Greeks, the Poles, the Hungarians, and the Irish, among others.

Revolution was seen by many as the best way to achieve this objective. However, the differences between the American and French revolutions took on great significance. America's revolution had been carefully controlled by its leaders. The French experience involved mass urban insurrections in Paris, such as the storming of the Bastille fortress on July 14, 1789, and the Tuileries palace on August 17, 1792.

For radical revolutionaries of the nineteenth century, the aim was mass urban insurrection. All modern insurgent movements seeking a revolutionary change have been influenced by the popular idea of urban insurrection.

KEY FACTS

- The first use of terror as a deliberate political tool occurred during the French Revolution.
- Ideas of revolution developed in different ways during the nineteenth century by radical political theorists like Karl Marx and Mikhail Bakunin.
- Radical theorists differed in the degree to which they planned to use violence to cause and consolidate a revolution.
- Terrorist methods are sometimes used by established governments against their opponents at home or abroad.

URBAN INSURRECTIONS

Theorists working since the French Revolution have identified three distinct elements of urban insurrections. First, there is a state of dual power as the government changes. At this stage, the opposition has gained sufficient strength to make a bid for power but the government has not yet been forced to give it up. Second, the government is already shaken by economic crisis and industrial strikes make its position impossible. Third, the opposition is temporarily united behind a leadership that has widespread popular support.

Hulton Getty Picture Collection

Karl Marx believed that governments would use violence to prevent the workers from organizing a socialist economy. He felt therefore that terror was a necessary part of a revolutionary strategy.

Terror is a standard tactic in urban insurrection. The assassination of political opponents may mark the start of an insurrection and bombings may be an integral part of its strategy. Further, the government may use terror in an attempt to suppress insurrection. Most of the great social revolutions have been characterized by the use of terror in their later stages. At this point, terror can enforce the authority of the new government to carry through its program of reform. Occasionally, as in Iran after 1979, terror has been used to establish a more traditional regime.

MARX, ENGELS, TROTSKY, AND LENIN

The first important theorist of mass insurrection was Karl Marx. The objective of Marx and his associate Friedrich Engels was to create a mass movement capable of directing revolution to social ends. Other important contributors to the Marxist theory of insurrection have been Vladimir Lenin and Leon Trotsky.

INSURRECTION BRINGS CHANGE

Early examples of insurrection seem to suggest that enthusiasm is the main ingredient necessary for their success. In 1830, an operatic performance in Brussels triggered a mass insurrection for Belgian independence. In 1848, the revolt that overthrew King Louis-Philippe in France apparently also broke out spontaneously. In the same year, some 50 insurrections in the Italian states brought about varying degrees of constitutional government and the proclamation of a Roman Republic.

Such dramatic events caused great excitement throughout Europe. They also gave rise to some well-justified fears among those in power. Government ministers remembered the savagery of the French Revolution, even if now they confronted insurrectionists who avoided widespread terrorism.

NEW SOCIAL ORDERS FROM TERROR

The Terror is the name given to the period in 1793-94 during the French Revolution when the most extreme faction among the revolutionaries, the Jacobins, were in power. The Jacobins deliberately used state power in an attempt to create a new social order. The Terror was used in particular to reduce the authority of local government in France. The revolutionary zealots sent from Paris to purge provincial society of aristocrats also created a more centralized state. Terror was seen as a method of eliminating the regime's opponents. The Jacobins tried to intimidate political neutrals and potential opponents through terror so that they would wholeheartedly support the new government.

The Terror's most spectacular feature was the execution of aristocrats. The nobles were not indicted for any crimes, not even conspiracy against the state (although that was alleged in some cases). Instead, they were charged simply because they had been born into the aristocracy. Those executed, and the many more who fled abroad, were merely incidental victims of a process that was really aimed at other revolutionaries. Opposition to aristocracy, and zeal in rooting it out, became the test of loyalty to a regime based on shaky popular support.

The Terror of the French Revolution, however, came at the end and not at the beginning of a great social revolution. Scholars have described a combination of factors causing the development of terror out of traditional violence like rioting. Such factors include civilian militarism – the desire of some civilians for a government with military overtones; the tendency of extremist governments to value loyalty over competence in their personnel; an acute economic crisis complicated by antagonism between rich and poor; and religious hysteria.

Overturning the old order in the 1917 Russian Revolution, as in the French Revolution and in a number of other great revolutions, was actually a slow process. The immediate aftermath of the urban uprising in each case was a period of provisional government marked by martial law, revolutionary tribunals, and the establishment of a secret police. In each case, the new government was supposed to be more representative than its predecessor.

But each provisional regime turned to terror when its leaders became aware that the old social order was stronger than they thought. Above all, these regimes resorted to terror when they found themselves faced with a combination of internal opposition and external attack or foreign threat. In the case of the Russian Revolution, terror began after the attempted assassination of Lenin in August 1918. In the case of the French Revolution, this change can be dated to the assassination of Jean Paul Marat, one of the radical leaders, in July 1793.

Historians writing 100 years after the French Revolution identified a sequence of events that indicated the point at which terror was likely to occur in a revolution. First, the new regime concentrates on taking control of public administration. Second, the new rulers attack their political enemies. Initially, they target individual opponents, then they conduct a wholesale purge to terrorize potential opponents. Persecution is then relaxed, perhaps accompanied by the execution of the terror's most extreme leaders. Finally, the new regime adopts a form of government strongly resembling that of the old order.

Hulton Getty Picture Collection

Louis Auguste Blanqui, the nineteenth-century French revolutionary agitator and theorist, believed that a successful revolutionary insurrection would occur spontaneously.

COMMUNISM AND TERRORISM

Karl Marx and Friedrich Engels, writing 70 years after the French Revolution, were utterly convinced that large-scale social transformation could only be achieved by revolution. However, generally they ridiculed those who believed in terror as a means to start one. In Western Europe, Marx thought, revolution would be the product of the gradual development of class awareness among the urban working class (the proletariat). In other parts of the world, particularly in Russia, Marx was more tolerant of those who used terror against tyranny. In praising the assassins of Czar Alexander II in 1881 for their heroism, Marx stated that their action was historically inevitable in the backward political society in which they lived.

Marx therefore rejected the notion of spontaneity, associated with Louis Auguste Blanqui, the French revolutionary theorist and agitator. Blanqui had been involved with many revolutionary movements in France during the nineteenth century. His study and experience of the 1848 insurrection in Paris helped him form the idea that revolutionary uprisings could occur spontaneously in the right political conditions.

Hulton Getty Picture Collection

Mikhail Bakunin, Russian anarchist and opponent of Marx, regarded individual terrorist acts as a crucial element in a revolutionary strategy.

Marx argued instead for revolution as the end-product of patient organization by workers' movements.

PARIS UPRISING OF 1871

An example of an unprising in Marx's own time were the events in France following its defeat in the war with Prussia in 1871. In Paris, working-class radicals won an election to the city government after the old regime had fallen but before a new one was properly organized. Members of this Paris government rejected the authority of a more conservative regime based in Versailles. They began to organize the city themselves. The conservatives could hardly tolerate the independence of the national capital. The army at Versailles shot some radicals, the radicals in Paris arrested some conservatives, and a civil war broke out. Although the Versailles army savagely repressed the Paris Commune, Marx hailed it as evidence that a mass political movement could achieve a revolution.

In his writings, Marx focused on the way in which government acts encouraged demand for change. State repression after the defeat of any attempt at radical reform was a step towards a revolutionary situation. In France, nine years after the Paris Commune's fall, the workers organized a revolutionary political party.

Following the failure of the Commune, Engels wrote: "Does this mean that in future street fighting will no longer play any role? Certainly not! It only means that conditions since 1848 have become far more unfavorable for civilian fighters and far more favorable for the military. Accordingly, it will...have to be undertaken with greater forces."

Engels' most important contribution to the theory of insurgency, however, was probably inadvertent. In rebutting others, he emphasized the need to destroy the state's tendency to repress its citizens. This could only be done, he argued, through what Marx had described as a period of economic and political control by the workers – "the dictatorship of the proletariat." Marx himself had believed that once this phase had ended, the state would wither away.

When Vladimir Lenin found himself at the head of the revolutionary government in Russia, he did believe that the control of the state by the workers was essential to create a communist society. Furthermore, Lenin was also convinced that the media, the political process, and education all had to work for the transformation of a capitalist society into a socialist one. But Lenin dismissed Marx's hopes of an end to repression as impractical in the circumstances facing the Russian socialist republic in 1918. In short, for Lenin, the expression "dictatorship of the proletariat," never carefully defined by Marx, required a repressive state apparatus wielded by a working-class party.

THE ANARCHISTS AND TERRORISM

Meanwhile, the anarchists had drawn very different conclusions from the failure of the Paris Commune. They now rejected both the legitimacy of any government, even a working-class one, and the idea of revolutionary insurrection. Anarchists turned to terrorist methods such as political assassination. Since they did not seek to replace one government by another, but merely to destroy the existing order, they did not require leadership or organization. Hence, many of their actions seem to have been the work either of individuals or of very small conspiratorial groups.

Directed terror was employed in Russia between 1878 and 1881 by the People's Will (Narodnaya Volya) group to destroy the czarist regime. It was justified by

Hulton Getty Picture Collection

Vladimir Ilyich Lenin, leader of the October 1917 Russian Revolution, turned to terrorist measures after the attempt on his life in August 1918.

Nikolai Morozov, one of their leading theorists, as costing fewer lives and therefore being ethically more acceptable: "All that the terroristic struggle really needs is a small number of people and large material means." Terrorism's advantage, Morozov continued, was that assassination often hit the intended target. During insurrections, however, the fighting was liable to kill workers and destroy their homes.

Although anarchists killed a small number of prominent political figures, including Presidents Sadi Carnot of France in 1894, and William McKinley of the United States in 1901, their movement seldom achieved much impact outside of Spain and soon dwindled.

Meanwhile, the main trend in socialism was to try to make use of the potentially vast power of the votes of the workers. In France and Germany, most socialists cooperated with capitalist governments to gain social reforms. By the end of the century, socialist ministers were being appointed. In Italy in 1907, the first general strike took place. This event successfully demonstrated the power of the organized workers to bring the economic system to a standstill. One theorist, the French social philosopher Georges Sorel, argued that it would be possible to overthrow the state and to replace it by a workers' government solely by the means of a general strike by the working class.

In Russia, this route was closed off by the government's policy of repression after the assassination of Czar Alexander II. Lenin followed Marx's teaching: He did not see terrorism as having a role in the promotion of revolution. In 1902, Lenin attacked the Socialist Revolutionaries, (another Russian radical political group), for their enthusiasm for terrorist methods. Lenin argued that their use of terrorism was the result of their close political connections with the peasants.

However, as a Russian, he saw terror as having a role in carrying out the revolution once open resistance had begun. As he wrote in 1906, "The party must regard the fighting guerrilla operations of the squads affiliated to or associated with it as being, in principle, permissible and advisable in the present period." But Lenin was specific about the objective of all such guerrilla operations, which was "to destroy the government, police, and military machinery." Furthermore, Lenin maintained that terrorism should always be under the control of the party to prevent effort from being dissipated uselessly.

Lenin's main contribution to the theory of successful insurrection was that it should be led by a relatively small and disciplined party in the name of the working class. The main purpose of the party was to prepare for urban insurrection. In the towns, where the working class was concentrated, the party could exercise the greatest influence on events. But the preparation of an urban insurrection under the eyes of a watchful secret police was not easy. Lenin solved this problem by basing his organization, the Bolsheviks, outside Russia and communicating with his followers through a secret newspaper. This was probably the only way in which the revolution could have been staged.

TROTSKY AND THE RED GUARD

With the outbreak of World War I, Lenin emphasized the importance of two tasks: the subversion of the armed forces, and the preparation of a revolutionary military force, the Red Guard. The latter, he argued,

Hulton Getty Picture Collection

Leon Trotsky (foreground), the founder of the Red Army, used terrorist measures to enforce discipline in the ranks.

could be set up under the cover of being an ex-servicemen's organization. The Red Guard could come out into the open only when the government was already on the point of collapse. Yet it was vital that the Red Guard be ready, which presented a problem of both training and supply. Lenin wrote that the insurgents "must arm themselves as best they can....Under no circumstances should they wait for help from other sources...they must procure everything themselves."

TROTSKY'S RUSSIAN REVOLUTION

Despite Lenin's enthusiasm for insurrection, in 1917 it was Leon Trotsky who directed the Bolshevik's seizure of power in Petrograd (now St. Petersburg). The term Bolshevik, meaning majority, dated from a split in the Russian Social Democratic Labor Party in 1903. Trotsky, as people's commissar for war from 1918 to 1925, consolidated the Russian Revolution.

Trotsky thought that only a global revolution could assure the Russian Revolution's success. Trotsky's original contribution to the theory of insurgency was the notion of dual power, the first element required by an urban insurrection. Trotsky aruged that dual power was the key to understanding not only the Russian Revolution of 1917, but to any successful socialist revolution. Dual power referred to the situation in March-November 1917 when there were two centers of power in Russia.

One source of authority was the weak provisional government in Petrograd, which had yet to seek popular endorsement through elections. The other source was the Workers' and Peasants' Soviets, or councils, which had been set up in Petrograd and all over the country. The Bolsheviks, therefore, had made their slogan "All power to the Soviets!" This strategy not only gave the Soviets legitimacy but ensured that the main strength of the alternative government would be provided by the armed workers of the Red Guard.

Trotsky argued pointedly that in taking power and enacting land reform, the Bolsheviks were in fact only legalizing what was already going on in the countryside. Both the czar's regime and the provisional government had been unable to resist the illegal land seizures by the peasants. Trotsky derived from this idea his argument that mass mobilization was the only possible route to a workers' government. Anything less, including the use of terrorist methods, would be unacceptable, since at best it could only lead to a military counter-coup.

Trotsky rejected terrorism in setting the stage for revolution. However, the assumption that the Bolsheviks were the true representatives of the working class led Trotsky to support the use of state terror against those who opposed the revolution: "A victorious war, generally speaking, destroys only an insignificant part of the conquered army, intimidating the remainder and breaking their will. The revolution works in the same way: it kills individuals, and intimidates thousands. In this sense, the Red Terror is not distinguishable from the armed insurrection, the direct continuation of which it represents."

In 1919, the new Soviet Government established the Third International, or Comintern, to promote worldwide revolution. In 1928, Mikhail Tukhachevsky, a former czarist officer turned leading Bolshevik general, wrote about insurrection in the Comintern manual. He took a Leninist line, but went to a lot of trouble to argue that the use of terrorist methods also had a proper part to play. The forces of the government could be disorientated by picking off the leaders and killing them as quickly as possible. The essence of the insurrectionist strategy, too, was surprise. The action had to be carefully planned. The insurgents must not rely on an initial single, physical signal, in case failures of communication put the whole plan at risk.

In the 1920s, there were a number of unsuccessful attempts to carry out insurrections in other major cities in Europe and Asia. But there has been no clear example of a communist government coming to power by insurrection. Romania in 1989, however, is one example of a communist government being overthrown by popular unrest.

After World War II, the traditional Marxist process of slowly building popular support through mass organization demanded too much patience from some revolutionary socialists. Terrorism allied with Marxist ideology was adopted by such groups as the Italian Red Brigades (Brigate Rossi) and the Baader-Meinhof Gang in West Germany.

1968 PARIS STUDENT UPRISING

Both groups advocated the use of armed struggle to overthrow the capitalist state and bring about a socialist revolution. But armed insurrection remained an ideal for many on the Left. In *les évenements* ("the events") of 1968 in Paris, radical students tried to link hands with workers in order to overthrow capitalism and establish in its place a form of socialism.

In some ways closer to anarchism than to Marxism, the French student movement rejected concepts of leadership and political organization. Instead they preferred spontaneously uprising groups, which could neither be penetrated nor co-opted by the regime.

The French government, led by Charles de Gaulle, was not unduly alarmed, and rightly so as it turned out. The workers did not take the students seriously, either. In the end, everyone went back to work, and de Gaulle only lost power in the following year when he resigned after a referendum did not go the way he wanted. There was no revolution in France in 1968.

REVOLUTION IN TEHRAN

Successful urban insurrections, however, did occur in other parts of the world. In 1979, mass demonstrations in the streets precipitated the fall of Mohammad Reza Pahlavi, the shah of Iran. In the weeks that followed, Islamic fundamentalists used demonstrating crowds to bring to power in Iran a clerical regime led by Ayatollah Ruhollah Khomeini.

The Iranian Revolution was significant in the history of insurgency for two reasons. First, a religious belief, Islam, that made no distinction between the sacred and the secular dominated the insurgency.

Second, the objective of the insurgents was not merely to topple the shah. They were also united in a desire to remove the foreign influences that the shah had promoted. The shah had sought to make Iran a modern nation-state. Not only did he bring in bitterly resented foreign capital and multinational corporations, but he also imported the liberal ideas dominant in Western political thought since the French Revolution.

The hostility of the insurgents focused above all on the United States, whose government had helped

Hulton Getty Picture Collection

Mass demonstration in Tehran in favor of Ayatollah Ruhollah Khomeini during the Iranian revolution of 1979. Under the Khomeini regime religous terrorism became an deliberate instrument of Iranian foreign policy.

restore the shah to his throne following an uprising in 1953. Soon after the success of the revolution, armed revolutionary guards broke into the United States' Embassy in Tehran. The guards seized the diplomatic personnel and held them hostage for 444 days.

Terrorism has served as an element of revolutionary urban insurrections since the nineteenth century. Terrorist acts served as a signal for action, and terrorist methods were used in the aftermath of a successful insurrection to intimidate any likely oppostion. But terrorism has always been far less significant than political organization and ideological motivation, as theorists of urban insurrection have come to realize.

Peter Calvert

SEE ALSO: TERROR IN THE FRENCH REVOLUTION 1789-1815; THE PARIS COMMUNE: STATE TERROR; FRENCH ANARCHIST TERROR; RUSSIAN ANARCHIST TERROR; NATIONALIST TERRORISM; REVOLUTIONARY TERRORISM; DOMESTIC VERSUS INTERNATIONAL TERRORISM; URBAN VERSUS RURAL TERRORISM; TERRORISM AND REVOLUTION IN IRAN; RED BRIGADES.

FURTHER READING

- Hutton, P. H. *The Cult of the Revolutionary Tradition: The Blanquists in French Politics, 1864-1893.* Berkeley: University of California Press, 1981.
- Mayer, T. F. *Analytical Marxism.* Thousand Oaks, CA: Sage Publications, 1994.
- Melograni, P. *Lenin and the Myth of World Evolution: Ideology and Reasons of State.* Atlantic Highlands, NJ: Humanities Press International, 1989.
- O'Neill, B. E., W. R. Heaton, and D. J. Alberts. *Insurgency in the Modern World.* Boulder, CO: Westview Press, 1980.
- Wright, R. *Sacred Rage: The Crusade of Modern Islam.* New York: Simon & Schuster, 1985; London: Deutsch, 1986.

NATIONAL LIBERATION WARS AND TERROR

The American Revolution, though scarcely a revolution in the sense of a complete transformation of society, was one of the first modern wars of national liberation. At its beginning, one of the principal patriots, Benjamin Franklin, put the main requirement for the insurgents succinctly: "Depend upon it, we must hang together, for if we do not, assuredly we shall all hang separately."

The Declaration of Independence, the manifesto of the American Revolution, was designed to serve two purposes. First, it claimed legitimacy for the new government by asserting the right of citizens to "alter or to abolish" the form of government under which they lived. Second, the intent of the Declaration was to persuade other powers that America's cause was just. This would be done by making it clear that the insurrectionists were responsible people driven to rebellion by the unjust treatment suffered at the hands of the British government of King George III. The author of the Declaration was Thomas Jefferson.

As with more recent revolutions, overseas support was forthcoming. The main support came from the French government of King Louis XVI, but supposedly neutral powers supplied aid tacitly. The fact that Jefferson had placed the rebels' case in a broad philosophical context that could be recognized by educated Europeans was, therefore, of key importance. Almost all later insurgent movements have issued a manifesto to the world, setting out their aims and appealing for support and understanding.

KEY FACTS

- British collectors of the stamp tax in the American colonies in the 1760s were tarred and feathered in acts of terror to scare them into leaving the taxes uncollected.
- The Cypriot nationalist George Grivas wrote extensively in his memoirs about the decision-making process required of the leader of a national liberation struggle.

COLONIAL RESISTANCE

The Americans created the idea of a citizen militia army. Where a militia could be set up before the colonial power could stop it, insurrection became possible, as demonstrated much later in Vietnam and

Hulton Getty Picture Collection

Thomas Jefferson, author of the Declaration of Independence, which has been a model for later proclamations justifying rebellion against foreign rule.

Hulton Getty Picture Collection

French philosopher Jean-Paul Sartre (left) had a great influence on the Parisian students who took to the streets in 1968. He also helped popularize the work of Frantz Fanon, the theorist of colonial resistance.

Indonesia. These two countries had been French and Dutch colonies respectively before World War II, when they were occupied by Japan. After Japan surrendered, it took the colonial powers some time to reestablish control, since both territories were situated far away. This distance was also a disadvantage for the insurgents, since they were unable to strike at the heart of the colonial state, but were themselves open to constant attack. The nearer the colony was to its ruling state, the more effective terrorist acts became.

SECESSIONIST MOVEMENTS

Secessionist movements, groups whose territory is located within a state, have made full use of their ability to strike at the center of power. This has been done for its own sake and for its value as "revolutionary theater." Movements of this type are often able to appropriate generally recognized symbols of national identity to their own causes. This ability was displayed by the Basque nationalist movement, Fatherland and Liberty (ETA), in Spain. ETA drew on a distinctive language, region, and set of cultural traditions, including the ancient tradition of Basque autonomy, to consolidate support for violence against the dictatorship of General Francisco Franco. It gained strength from the trials of some of its supporters in 1970. There was even admiration for ETA when it assassinated the Spanish prime minister Admiral Carrero Blanco in 1973. The murder was carried out in the most spectacular manner, by planting a mine in the road which blew the admiral and his car over a five-story building into the courtyard of the building he had just left.

Rohan Gunaratna

Tamil Tigers. Their campaign against the Sinhalese majority on the island of Sri Lanka has been prolonged and violent.

However, with the restoration of democracy after Franco's death in 1975, the tacit French support on which the Basques had relied was reduced. Moreover, the Spanish government's decision to grant the Basques a degree of autonomy removed much of the justification for the movement. ETA split in 1977, the majority choosing to pursue the electoral road to autonomy.

One of the most distinctive features of nationalist movements that has emerged is the fact that they operate on two levels. On the surface, there is a legal organization, which can raise funds and publicize the cause. Underneath, there is an illegal organization, made up of individuals whose identity as members is not a matter of public record (though it is often known to security forces). Thus Sinn Fein, a legal political party in Northern Ireland, has been closely linked with the illegal Provisional Irish Republican Army.

Algeria's war of independence from France began in 1954 and resulted in Algerian independence in 1962. Here the sense of Islamic identity and the linguistic difference from their French rulers were important in generating resistance to the harsh regime of the French settlers. It was in this context that Frantz Fanon developed his belief in the cleansing quality of violence.

VIOLENCE – A CLEANSING FORCE

Born in Martinique and educated in the French West Indies, Frantz Fanon trained as a psychologist. He argued that violence could and should be used to free black-skinned peoples of the sense of inferiority instilled by centuries of slavery. Otherwise, true independence would not be attained, since citizens continued to carry around inside themselves the marks of their colonial status. Of killing, Fanon observed that "at the level of individuals, violence is a cleansing force. It frees the native from his inferiority complex and from his despair and inaction; it makes him fearless and restores his self-respect. Even if the armed struggle has been symbolic and the nation is demobilized through a rapid movement of decolonization, the people have time to see that the liberation has been the business of each and all and that the leader has no special merit."

In his introduction to Fanon's work, the French philosopher Jean-Paul Sartre commended it to his countrymen. They will not like it, he said, but they must read it. For colonialism had not only bred violence in the colonized, it had also damaged the European psyche irreparably. Sartre argued that all Europeans, especially in "that super-European monstrosity, North America," had implicitly supported the inherently oppressive colonial system. "We in Europe too are being decolonized; that is to say...the settler which is in every one of us is being rooted out."

Fanon's argument in some respects carries to an extreme conclusion the idea of placing a positive emphasis on a person's African origins. This was first termed *négritude* in 1939 in a poem by Aimé Césaire, who also came from Martinique. The concept was elaborated after World War II by Léopold S. Senghor, a former deputy in the French National Assembly who became president of Senegal.

However, Senegal, like the majority of French territories in Africa, gained independence without an armed struggle. Yet, Fanon's predictions that even a merely symbolic struggle would create a shared experience of liberation have not been fulfilled. Many African countries seem trapped in a cycle of military coups and unstable civilian regimes. This political turmoil has only worsened the economic difficulties they face. On the other hand, the radical wing of the Black Power movement in the 1960s confirmed the predictions of

Associated Press

The corpse of Indian prime minister Rajiv Gandhi (foreground) lies in the street after he was assassinated by Tamil Tigers in May 1991.

Fanon and Sartre of the potential impact of African nationalism on American society.

Ethnic and linguistic differences were crucial to the majority of the successful guerrilla movements of the 1980s. Soviet intervention in Afghanistan in 1979 resulted in a long-running guerrilla campaign against the occupying forces. In time, the campaign was to wear down the structure of the Soviet state and help precipitate its collapse. Ethnic nationalism continues to fuel civil war, even within the Russian Federation. The campaign against the Chechen insurgents begun in 1995 discredited President Boris Yeltsin's government. During the 1996 presidential election, Yeltsin reached a truce with the Chechens to reduce the risk of the war becoming a major campaign issue. However, even during the Cold War era (1946-87), guerrilla action did not necessarily involve either of the superpowers.

SECRECY AND COMMITMENT

The Tamil Tigers of Sri Lanka came into existence after attacks by members of the Sinhalese majority on the Tamil quarter of Colombo in 1983. The Tigers' aim is the creation of a Tamil homeland on Sri Lanka. They received Indian support, official and unofficial, and established control of the island's Jaffna Peninsula. The movement is marked by great secrecy. Members carry cyanide capsules to ensure they are not taken alive. Spectacular terrorist acts carried out by the Tigers include the assassinations by suicide bombers of the Indian prime minister, Rajiv Gandhi, President Premadasa of Sri Lanka, and his would-be successor.

The other successful movement of the 1980s was the Shining Path in Peru. Its founder, Abimael Guzmán, was a philosophy professor well acquainted with the theories of insurrection. Like the Tamil Tigers, the group was characterized by two features: extreme secrecy and a key role played by women. The early movement conducted small-scale, low-risk terrorist acts designed to attract maximum publicity to the cause. The very secretive nature of the organization meant, however, that it has had relatively little impact outside Peru.

Peter Calvert

SEE ALSO: TERRORISM IN FRENCH ALGERIA; TERROR AGAINST THE FRENCH IN INDOCHINA; TERRORISM IN PERU; TAMIL TIGER TERROR IN SRI LANKA; TERROR IN AFGHANISTAN; BASQUE NATIONALIST TERROR: ETA; NATIONALIST TERROR IN NORTHERN IRELAND 1976-1996.

FURTHER READING

- Brown, Richard Maxwell. "Violence and the American Revolution,"in *Essays on the American Revolution*, edited by Stephen G. Kurtz and James H. Hutson. New York: Norton, 1973.
- O'Neill, B. E., W. R. Heaton, and D. J. Alberts. *Insurgency in the Modern World.* Boulder, CO: Westview Press, 1980.
- Palmer, David Scott. *The Shining Path of Peru.* 2nd ed. London: Hurst, 1992; New York: St. Martin's Press, 1994.

GUERRILLAS AND TERROR

Incidents of violence can be used, not to defeat an opponent, but merely to call attention to a cause and dramatize its importance. Political movements that lack the strength to overthrow the established order, or which are denied the right to protest peacefully, may adopt terrorist strategies. While revolutionaries use political assassinations as a signal for a larger insurgency or revolt, terrorist assassinations can also be independent of any strategic revolutionary plan.

Resistance can take the form of a campaign of intimidation of the regime's supporters. It can also take the form of absenteeism, sabotage, crop destruction, or land occupations, which in themselves do not amount to a campaign of violence.

A systematic and prolonged campaign of terrorism with the aim of defeating a foreign enemy (or one seen to be supported by foreigners), is called partisan or guerrilla warfare.

GUERRILLA WARFARE

Guerrilla warfare is first described during the fifth century B.C., when the Chinese general Sun Tzu, wrote about tactics to be used in support of conventional war in *The Art of War*. However, he neglected to give the phenomenon a name.

Until recent times, irregular war was hard to distinguish from ordinary warfare. The Prussian soldier and military theorist Karl von Clausewitz wrote *On War* in the nineteenth century. This book drew on his experiences as a soldier in campaigns against the French emperor Napoleon Bonaparte. Clausewitz observed the value of bands of armed civilians making hit-and-run raids on supply lines or communications centers in order to make the enemy divert forces from the main army. *On War* had a powerful influence on military theory throughout the nineteenth century.

Although guerrilla warfare is often thought of as being alien to the European tradition, the term *guerrilla* originated in Spain. The Spanish word *guerrilla*, strictly speaking, means "little war"; the word for a guerrilla (the person participating in a little war) is *guerrillero* or *guerrillera*. The term was coined in the Spanish War of Independence following Napoleon's invasion of Spain in 1808.

Like those first Spanish guerrillas, today's guerrillas often fight outside the rules of war, sometimes without uniform, and use surprise as a main weapon. Governments and security forces usually treat guerrillas as terrorists or bandits and employ terror tactics against them.

Since 1808, guerrilla warfare has been used in a wide variety of situations. Nineteenth-century references to it, however, were sparse. Most writers seem to have regarded the rural guerrilla as the Marxists did, as a useful addition to urban insurrection, pinning down troops and making the real revolutionaries' task easier.

WARS OF INDEPENDENCE

The Spanish War of Independence (1808-1814) was a partisan war – a war of resistance against foreign occupiers by armed civilians organized on military lines. The Spanish army had largely been defeated by the French, who had captured the capital, Madrid. Some Spanish continued to resist, but not in the traditional way as an organized army. Spain's allies, the British and Portuguese armies under the Duke of Wellington, supported the Spanish partisans. Wellington started out from Portugal and advanced into Spain, supported by the *guerrilla* (little war) of the Spanish partisans, defeating the French in a series of decisive battles.

The success of the guerrillas was directly related to the efforts of Spanish nationalistic political leaders to

SUMMARY

- In the twentieth century, Mao Zedong and others developed theories of how to use terror in a revolutionary guerrilla war.
- Ernesto "Che" Guevara wrote his theories of guerrilla warfare after his role as Fidel Castro's second-in-command in the Cuban revolution.

organize resistance. The Spanish peasants hated the French, and eagerly joined the nationalists' fighting force. Spain was powerless without the Portuguese and British, but Wellington could not have won without the diversions carried out by the Spanish guerrillas. As a modern historian has written: "It was this continuous resistance, feeble as it often was, which broke Napoleon's doctrine of maximum concentration in the attempt to solve contradictory demands of operation and occupation in the hostile countryside."

The guerrilla element in the Spanish War of Independence converted the enemy's strength into weakness. It wore down the French and it destroyed what should have been their advantage, their superior numbers. When the French tried to concentrate their troops for battle, they found the vulnerability of their supply lines increased as their dependence on them increased. A large army assembled in one place could not live off the country for any prolonged period.

The guerrillas used terrorism to force Spaniards into joining the war against the invader. When they reoccupied areas evacuated by the French, they would punish anyone who had collaborated with the occupying forces. It was much less likely that the victims of terror would cooperate with the next French search for supplies.

The guerrillas' national pride and militaristic organization became part of Spanish progressive political movements. As historian Raymond Carr says in his *Spain, 1808-1939*, the war "gave liberalism its program and its technique of revolution. It defines Spanish patriotism and endows it with an enduring myth. It saddled liberalism with the problems of generals in politics and the mystique of the guerrilla."

TERROR IN THE SPANISH EMPIRE

Three broad geographic areas once part of the Spanish empire have undergone periods of insurgency in modern times. The cultural links between them and Spain are clear. However, it may not be that guerrilla warfare was exported from Spain. It may have been that conditions in the colonies were similar and so the same methods evolved independently.

First, there were the Central and South American countries that became independent in the nineteenth century. Guerrilla warfare in fact went on in various South American countries throughout the nineteenth century. It was responsible to a considerable extent for the ultimate defeat in 1824 of the Spaniards in Peru. Spanish rule had enjoyed considerable support in Peru, but this was eroded by the irregular forces. Guerrilla warfare toppled regimes in many countries, as in Guatemala in 1871. Used to resist foreign intervention, it was very successful in wearing down the French occupation of Mexico in 1862-67.

Cuba represents the second area of sub-revolutionary terrorism in the Spanish colonial empire. It had not gained its independence at the same time as the mainland states. Cuba's wars of independence began in earnest in 1868, but the first phase, the so-called Ten Years' War (1868-78), was unsuccessful. The struggle was resumed in February 1895, when a small invasion force led by the writer and patriot José Martí landed in Cuba. Martí fell into the hands of the Spanish authorities and was put to death. But his movement survived because his efforts inspired two experienced military leaders who had both fought in the Ten Years' War.

Máximo Gómez and Antonio Maceo recruited their forces from the blacks and poor whites of the rural areas. They also received arms shipments from the United States, which the Spanish fleet was unable to intercept. To prevent this traffic, the Spanish commander herded the civilian population into *campos de reconcentración*, or concentration camps. Such camps were also used in 1900-1902 in a similar way by the British in their war with the Boers of South Africa. Both there and in Cuba the death rate of camp prisoners from disease was high. Reports of the conditions in Cuba were a major factor in causing the U.S. to intervene, and led to the Spanish-American War in 1898. (It should be noted that a concentration camp was a place in which the civilian population was concentrated. Only since 1944 has the term become a euphemism for extermination camp.)

The third area affected by the Spanish experience is that of the Philippines in Southeast Asia. Defeated in the Spanish-American War, Spain ceded possession of the Philippines to the United States. However, many Filipinos who wanted nothing less than independence waged an unsuccessful guerrilla war against the American authorities between 1899 and 1902.

THE POLITICAL GUERRILLA

Guerrilla warfare has been used extensively in the twentieth century. This tradition began with T. E. Lawrence, better known as Lawrence of Arabia. He was the first Western military thinker to regard partisan or guerrilla warfare as a strategy in itself.

Lawrence's theory of guerrilla warfare, as set out in his book *The Seven Pillars of Wisdom*, emphasizes two points. First, Lawrence argued that guerrilla forces must avoid engaging the enemy. Guerrillas must be capable of protecting themselves against enemy attacks, but they must not attempt battlefield assaults. Nor did Lawrence consider a guerrilla band to have the potential to be converted into a conventional army. Lawrence instead regarded the Arab guerrillas as a political force. Their existence in itself denied legitimacy to Turkish rule over the Arabian states.

Second, he argued that the best way for guerrillas to attack the enemy was to destroy its supplies and lines of communication. He believed that to destroy the enemy's military infrastructure was to destroy the enemy itself.

Lawrence's small forces, drifting around "like a gas," were entirely at home in the Arabian territory since they could disappear into the civilian population. Lawrence's theory, in fact, described the kind of desert warfare traditional in Arabia. In the first decades of the twentieth century, open areas could be treated as a military asset. The Turks had few aircraft and limited capabilities to transport troops, so forces could hide in the desert and strike at bases and communications with the full advantage of surprise.

It is worth pointing out that if guerrillas wish to blend into a civilian population, they must have a civilian population to disappear into. In South Vietnam during the Vietnam War, all men of fighting age served in the military. This left the old, women, and children as the only people who could sink into the background. Consequently, Vietnamese insurgents frequently used children to carry out bombing attacks.

Hulton Getty Picture Collection

Lawrence of Arabia allowed his Arab guerrillas to massacre Turkish soldiers.

MAO'S GUERRILLA WAR MODEL

During the interwar period Mao Zedong developed a new model for guerrilla warfare, creating a political framework for military strategy. Mao profited from native Chinese experience, and his extensive knowledge of Chinese history and writing since Sun Tzu. The heroes whom he followed were specifically those Chinese who had fought against foreigners.

The theory was developed in Mao's tract *Guerrilla Warfare*, in 1937, and is based on a three-stage model. The first stage is the organization, consolidation, and preservation of base areas. Training programs and village meetings are used to create a network of sympathizers in the countryside around the base area, who eventually form the basis for a militia as well as the party organization. In Peru, the Shining Path closely followed the teaching of Mao Zedong. Their organizational groundwork in the highlands of Peru was well laid before the armed struggle started in 1980.

The second stage of guerrilla war involves the expansion of the base areas. The military campaign features acts of sabotage and the killing of those either collaborating with the enemy or opposed to the guerrillas' politics. Attacks aim at capturing medical supplies and military equipment from outlying police posts and weak groups of troops in the field. For Mao, the expansion of the base areas takes place by recruiting large numbers of defensive militia rather than full-time guerrillas. The militia, being part-time soldiers, can be based in their own homes, which could be behind enemy lines or in the main combat zone. People who collaborate with the enemy in places where there are militia forces can be assassinated, thus eliminating important enemy organizers. Killing collaborators hampers the enemy's efforts to supply its own troops and to gather intelligence about guerrilla operations. Mao referred to this as the "oilspot technique."

The third stage of guerrilla warfare is the destruction of the enemy. This is achieved by turning guerrilla forces into a conventional army capable of defeating the government in pitched battles. The needed retraining of the guerrillas in this phase can be conducted while guerrilla leaders negotiate with the government. Mao emphasized that negotiations would be for purely military purposes, to wear down the opponent's morale, and to allow the guerrillas time to regroup and resupply.

MAO'S ASSUMPTIONS OF GUERRILLA WAR

Mao's work is based on three basic assumptions. The first is the doctrine of strength and weakness. If, for example, the enemy outnumbers the guerrillas, it means their forces require a lot of supplies. The guerrillas should therefore turn the strength of numbers into a weakness by attacking the enemy's supply lines.

The second assumption is the relationship between time, space, and will. Guerrillas should be willing to surrender areas in their control if it will gain time to spread propaganda among the people.

The third, and most dubious, preconception is that guerrillas will have full intelligence and the government will have none. This belief assumes that the guerrillas will succeed in denying all information about themselves to the government. It also assumes that the insurgents, through their network of sympathizers, will discover the strategic and tactical state of the government. This may have been possible when Mao was writing in 1937, but advances in technology since then have strengthened the government's resources. Major powers now have earth satellites, infrared detectors, guided missiles, and smart bombs. Psychological warfare and torture methods have also been developed as ways of gaining information.

The chance of a guerrilla movement being able to deny all knowledge of its activities to the government is now much less likely than it was in Mao's time. Thus, anyone following his advice will be in trouble, unless they remember that the main purpose of guerrilla warfare is not to defeat the enemy's army, but to turn the people into a revolutionary force. This is the difference between Mao and other theorists, with the possible exception of Lawrence, who regarded Arab participation in the fight against the Turks as being essential to fueling Arab nationalism.

Hulton Getty Picture Collection

Mao Zedong, creator of the People's Republic of China and its ruler from 1949 until his death in 1976.

MAO'S SIMPLE RULES OF INSURGENCY

Although there is little practical detail in Mao's thought, there are the Three Rules and the Eight Remarks. The Three Rules were general points, while the Eight Remarks were specific ones, relating to how insurgents should conduct themselves. The central aspect of Mao's thought was the close relationship it encouraged between the guerrilla and the people: "It is only undisciplined troops who make the people their enemies and who, like the fish out of its native element, cannot live." Elsewhere he says that the guerrilla moves among the people and is sustained by them like the fish in water.

Hence Mao's forces had to be supported by an organization of agents and informants living legal lives but keeping them provided with food, ammunition, and information about government forces. For this purpose, Mao and his guerrillas had the added advantage of being able to make use of the existing structure of the Triad secret societies, which had emerged as early as the seventeenth century as a reaction to the Manchurian conquest of China. Their nationalist origins made them a natural ally in the Chinese struggle against the Japanese invaders during World War II. This resistance gained Mao many supporters.

In 1949, after four more years of warfare against the Chinese nationalist government, Mao's troops finally entered Beijing, and the Chinese communists took power. It is doubtful, however, if they could have done so by guerrilla warfare had the corrupt nationalist government not already been weakened by a generation of war against the Japanese.

GUERRILLAS IN WORLD WAR II

The Chinese were not the only people to use guerrilla tactics in World War II. In the mobile phases of the war, countries collapsed very quickly. This left a great deal of their social structures intact, with many people opposed to the new occupiers and ready to take up arms against them. However, terrorism in occupied Europe brought massive retaliation from the German secret police. In Warsaw, the Polish capital, both the 1943 Jewish Warsaw Ghetto revolt and the 1944 Home Army uprising were ruthlessly crushed.

However, it was possible to keep guerrilla forces on the edge of the main theaters of conflict to perform an important role in holding down regular troops. The British and American governments encouraged the activities of partisan forces in this way in both Europe and Asia. The Red Army supported similar bands operating behind the German lines on the Eastern Front. One important practitioner was Orde Wingate, who became best-known for his leadership of the Chindits, a behind-the-lines force fighting the Japanese in Burma in 1943 and 1944. Wingate's forces used hit-and-run raids to disrupt Japanese supply lines.

SOUTHEAST ASIA, 1945-60

There are four major postwar examples of insurgency in southeast Asia. After the United States granted the Philippines independence in 1946, a nationalist guerrilla movement began fighting the new, American-backed government. In Indonesia, nationalists waged a war of independence against the Dutch from 1945 to 1948. The Vietnamese fought for their independence from France from 1945 to 1954, and in Malaya, a communist insurgency against the British produced the Malayan Emergency, from 1948 to 1960.

In each case, Western powers had supported guerrilla insurgencies against the Japanese during World War II. By 1945, a great many local inhabitants had been issued guns by the Allies, trained in military techniques, and had four years' experience in fighting the Japanese. The communists, natural opponents of fascism and militarism, had readily joined these resistance movements. But when the war ended, the communists saw no justification in handing back their weapons and submitting to rule by colonial regimes that they opposed just as much as they opposed Japanese militarists.

Malaya supplies one example of how this process worked in practice. In World War II, the Allies had supported the Malayan People's Anti-Japanese Army under the leadership of Chin Peng. In 1945, this force, already well armed and trained, renamed itself the Malayan Races Liberation Army (MRLA). In 1948, it commenced a 12-year campaign to drive the British out of Malaya, in succession to the campaign against the Japanese. The MRLA used surprise tactics to strike at economic targets such as rubber plantations and mines. They ambushed military and police patrols, and used explosives to blow up roads and railroad lines. In 1951, the British High Commissioner, Sir Henry Gurney, was assassinated in the mistaken belief that he was a senior military commander rather than a politician.

Guerrillas do not always resist the temptation to strike too soon or in the wrong place to avoid alerting the government to the urgency and the necessity of combating the insurgency. In this way, Gurney's death forced the British to turn their weakness into strength by developing a systematic anti-guerrilla campaign strategy called the Briggs Plan.

The Malayan guerrillas' selective assassination of key figures in outlying villages was initially successful in making villagers cooperate. However, this terror was countered by the creation of the New Villages, the grouping together of villagers behind fortified stockades defended by militia forces. The mobility of the guerrillas was restricted by a rigorous food rationing system and strict limits on the transportation of food. In addition, the Commonwealth forces enjoyed two great advantages. First, the British had command of sea and air. Second, they had the support of the Malay majority (most terrorists were ethnic Chinese) that came to power when Malaya was granted its independence in 1957.

MAO'S INFLUENCE ON HO CHI MINH

The French in Vietnam were not so fortunate. With the Japanese collapse, the communists under Ho Chi Minh declared Vietnam independent and established a national government. France had the problem of reconquering land from a group who, at least in theory, had been allied with them against the Japanese.

Ho had been a founding member of the French Communist Party in 1920 and of the Indochinese Communist Party in 1930. In 1941, he had a leading role in establishing the League for the Independence of Vietnam. This group, better known as the Vietminh, was formed to fight the Japanese. Ho and the Vietminh received American assistance during the war.

Ho's objective was a Vietnam free of the French colonial system, an aim that enabled him to present his movement in terms that won it broad-based nationalist support. Ho was able to illustrate his arguments with examples of cruelties practiced against the Vietnamese by the colonial settlers. Even now, his descriptions have not lost their capacity to shock.

Ho and his chief military theorist, Vo Nguyen Giap, made intensive use of guerrilla tactics to make the position of the French government impossible. In 1954, after advice from Mao and backed by Chinese supplies, the Vietminh successfully entrapped General de Castries and a large French army at Dien Bien Phu. After this defeat, the French government hastily abandoned Vietnam along with Laos and Cambodia, the other two provinces of French Indochina.

Ho had spent much of World War II in China, which gave him the great advantage of close links with the Chinese communist leadership after it came to power in 1949. It is clear from Ho's work that he shared another aspect of Mao's thought that is often misunderstood: the use of negotiations as a military tactic. Mao is quite clear that nothing less than victory is acceptable to his cause. Negotiations, therefore, are only one further strategy in seeking to achieve that ultimate objective.

Events during the second phase of the Vietnam War provide an example of this strategy. The United States had supported the French in their struggle with the Vietminh. The U.S. continued to support the state of South Vietnam, established on the division of Vietnam after the French withdrawal. Conflict continued with North Vietnamese-backed Vietcong guerrillas fighting against the South Vietnamese government.

In the mid-1960s, the U.S became entangled in a second major campaign in Vietnam. The Americans drew on massive air power and other weaponry, and by the end of 1967 claimed the war was almost won. Then, in January 1968, the Vietnamese launched the Tet offensive. This was a propaganda success but a military failure, and terror featured in the campaign. In accordance with Mao's ideas, the Vietcong shot any prisoner who was identified with the South Vietnamese government. The Vietnamese were no doubt sincere in their desire to negotiate after Tet ended. They also reorganized the Vietcong in South Vietnam (who had lost heavily during Tet) under cover of the negotiations.

Hulton Getty Picture Collection

Ho Chi Minh prepares for a mission against the French in 1945, shortly after the end of World War II.

FIDEL CASTRO AND CHE GUEVARA

The idea that guerrilla warfare can be used to overthrow a non-colonial government was produced by Fidel Castro and Che Guevara in Cuba. This idea owes more to the native Cuban tradition of insurgency than it does to any foreign theoretical model.

Fidel Castro Ruz had been active in radical politics before attempting unsuccessfully to overthrow the government of General Fulgencio Batista in 1953.

Hulton Getty Picture Collection

The Vietminh's military theorist Vo Nguyen Giap (right foreground).

Castro seized the military barracks in Cuba's second city, Santiago. Several days later, he fell into the hands of a military patrol in the nearby mountains. He was tried and sentenced to 15 years' imprisonment, but was soon released. He took refuge in Mexico, from where he set sail for Cuba in late 1956 to launch another coup attempt. On landing, he and his companions were ambushed by Cuban forces. The 15 survivors took refuge in the mountains of the Sierra Maestra where, largely by trial and error, they formed the nucleus of a guerrilla force. The ultimate success of the Cuban Revolution created a myth of the intrepid guerrilla, which Castro himself certainly did nothing to restrain.

Those wanting to learn about Cuban methods found them in the writings of Castro's second-in-command, Che Guevara. Ernesto Guevara de la Serna was an Argentine by birth ("Che" is a common nickname for Argentines in Latin America). Guevara had studied medicine before traveling into exile in Mexico, where he met Cubans planning to return to their homeland. In combat he became a leader, directing the crucial battle of Santa Clara in 1958. This proved to be the decisive psychological stroke in the campaign against Batista.

Soon after victory, Guevara wrote his account of the campaign and a handbook for the guerrilla fighter, *Guerrilla Warfare*. Both stress the practical approach he brought to the subject, but the latter work also enunciated three principles which had greater theoretical appeal. The first was that popular forces could win a war against the army. Second, Guevara argued that it was not necessary to wait until all conditions for revolution existed, since the insurrection itself would create them. Last, he suggested that in underdeveloped Latin America, the countryside was the key area.

This was a heady message for his admirers. It was not necessary, they believed, to create a party or even a trained army. All that was needed was a group of guerrillas. This was the theory of the *foco* (focus). The idea of a small group of guerrillas as the starting point for social revolution, *Foquismo*, was elevated to a theory by a French-born professor at the university of Havana, Régis Debray. The *Foquismo* theory had a profound

Hulton Getty Picture Collection

The guerrilla leader Che Guevara, second-in-command to Cuban revolutionary Fidel Castro.

influence on insurgents in Latin America and the rest of the Third World well into the 1970s.

Much of what Guevara wrote was very down-to-earth. As one historian commented, *Guerrilla Warfare* is "a strange mixture of traditional precepts, an elementary exposé of the principles of military training...nostalgic descriptions of life in the open air among men, and the kind of enthusiasm engendered by ex-servicemen looking back."

The book's practical approach disguised the fact that its basic theory was unsound. It was true that in Cuba the party had hardly existed before the guerrillas started their campaign. Before 1959, many Cubans had not realized that they were fighting for any political party, far less a communist one. At this stage even Castro was not a Marxist-Leninist, despite his claim to the contrary in December 1961. This claim reflected a desire to obtain Soviet support after the U.S.-backed Bay of Pigs invasion in 1961 had tried to depose him.

NO CUBAN GUERRILLA VICTORY

A more serious shortcoming of the theory was that the Cuban revolution was not a victory for guerrilla warfare, for the guerrillas' contribution was minimal. What eventually defeated Batista was the mass withdrawal of support by workers in the cities. This proved fatal to the regime when coupled with its inability to control the plantation workers. Moreover, the Cuban situation had no real parallel in Latin America. Even in the 1960s, many Latin Americans did not live in the countryside waiting to be mobilized by Guevara's guerrillas. Instead, it was only by the conquest of the cities that power could be achieved.

Guevara also believed that revolution would not be possible until all other methods of changing the social system had failed. He even thought that in democratic societies where a route to power by peaceful means lay open, neither guerrilla war nor terrorist action could ultimately be successful.

Guevara served in Castro's government, but later left Cuba in an attempt to spread revolution to other South American countries. He was eventually killed by government troops in Bolivia. It is hard to say whether his theories of guerrilla warfare failed in Bolivia because of deficiencies in the theory or in its implementation. Evidence suggests that almost every mistake that could have been made was made.

CHE'S MISTAKES

On the strategic level, the decision to pick Bolivia was a mistake. The decision took no account of the rigors of the climate and the mountains. The peasants in Bolivia had benefited from a political revolution in 1952 and did not wish to risk the gains made then. Besides, they were suspicious of white-skinned bearded people, who reminded them too strongly of the Conquistadors, the sixteenth-century Spanish invaders who had taken their lands in the first place. The guerrillas wisely made no attempt to use terrorist acts to bully the peasants into supporting them. Even if the *foco* had been successful, Bolivia offered too weak a base from which to create revolutions in the rest of South America, as Guevara had hoped.

On the tactical level, errors were legion. Guevara's Cubans had learned Quechua, so that they could talk to the Bolivians in their own language. However, they picked Ñancuahuazu in the southeast of the country as the site for their operations, where the peasants spoke Guaraní. They attacked a government force before they were ready to defend themselves. They took countless photographs of each other, which, with much of their supplies and vital evidence that linked them to Cuba, fell into the hands of government forces.

Even the most trivial mistakes turned out to be fatal. "Tania la guerrillera," apparently both a KGB and an East German agent in her spare time, was killed because she wore a white shirt in the middle of the green jungle, presenting an easy target to her pursuers.

SANDINISTAS VERSUS CONTRAS

The death of Guevara and the destruction of his *foco* did not immediately end guerrilla warfare in Latin America, but by the beginning of the 1970s, government responses had reduced the surviving groups to insignificant levels. The one major exception, the Sandinista movement in Nicaragua, attained power in 1979 as a result of quite exceptional circumstances. The group's success was due to the fact that the Nicaraguan president Anastasio Somoza had concentrated so much power and wealth in his own hands that he had totally alienated all the major groups that might otherwise have helped him.

The Sandinistas were divided initially into three factions. One, the insurrectionist faction, favored the Marxist-Leninist viewpoint, emphasizing the support of organized labor. The second, the Prolonged Popular War (Guerra Popular Prolongada, GPP) followed a Maoist line. This faction relied on a guerrilla campaign in the countryside. It was the third faction, the Terceristas, led by Daniel Ortega Saavedra, who won out. The Terceristas favored an alliance with non-Marxist opponents of the regime that would ensure broad support for strikes in the cities and guerrilla warfare in the countryside.

Helped by the fact that the corrupt Somoza regime had grafted the aid money for the victims of the Managua earthquake of 1972, the Terceristas were able to form a coalition. This included on the one hand the insurrectionary Sandinistas and on the other the church and the Conservative party. The coalition fought their way into what was left of the capital in a two-pronged military campaign that enjoyed support from both socialist Cuba and democratic Costa Rica. In this campaign, terrorism played little or no part.

The Sandinista government of Nicaragua was in turn challenged by an insurgent movement called the Nicaraguan Democratic Force (FDN), but usually known by the Sandinista nickname of Contras (for counterrevolutionaries). The Contras were set up by the Central Intelligence Agency (CIA) under National Security Decision Directive 17, signed by President Ronald Reagan in 1981. Though primarily a guerrilla force, the Contras sought to drive Nicaragua into bankruptcy by attacking economic targets such as coffee mills and warehouses. The force was also implicated in the attempted assassination of the rival insurgent leader Edén Pastora ("Commander Zero"). It was not successful and its activities were wound down in the mid-1980s, after the U.S. Congress refused to go on providing the funds after the Iran-Contra connection was exposed.

MARIGHELLA'S URBAN GUERRILLA

An attempt was made to transfer rural guerrilla principles to the city to create a form of insurgency called urban guerrilla warfare. Carlos Marighella was a Brazilian politician who had served in the Federal Congress as a deputy. Later, he had been editor of the Brazilian communist party journal *Problemas* and visited the People's Republic of China in 1953-54. After Brazil's military coup in 1964, Marighella and others became opposed to the party's strategy of collaboration. In August 1967, they traveled to Cuba against party instructions to attend the conference of the Latin American Solidarity Organization (OLAS) in defiance of the party line. Subsequently, Marighella wrote to Castro to declare that he had chosen the path of guerrilla warfare. Marighella stated that he believed this to be the only course that would unite the different revolutionary groups in Brazil.

In practice, however, Marighella meant something very different from the Cuban model. In his *Minimanual of the Urban Guerrilla*, he argued that in a vast country like Brazil, actions in the large cities would have a much more striking effect those carried out in the countryside. He published his manifesto on September 25, 1968, in a leading newspaper. His aim was to create a crisis that would force the regime to adopt a military response. This in turn, he explained, would lead to a mass uprising, through which "power would pass to the armed people." His approach follows the Marxist strategy known as "the intensification of contradictions." This assumes that revolutionary fervor will be intensified by political repression.

The problem of urban guerrilla warfare is threefold. First of all, urban guerrillas generally lack a safe base to which they can retreat. In principle, every house is safe since the occupants can control entry and exit. Yet

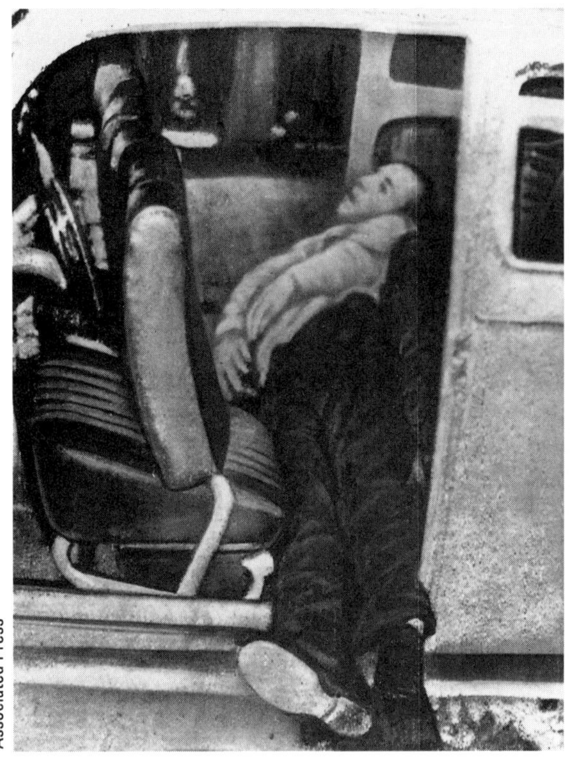
Associated Press

Security forces shot the terrorist Carlos Marighella in São Paolo, Brazil, on November 6, 1969.

at the same time, every house is dangerous, since the occupants are isolated from their comrades in other houses. There is no front line. Second, the urban guerrilla is wholly dependent on terrorist methods, which generate an all-pervading sense of insecurity that the government may manipulate to turn public opinion against the insurgents. Third, the urban terrorist has to rely on absolute secrecy. On the other hand, if secrecy fails, as it did under the repressive regime in Brazil, no organization member is safe. If complete secrecy is maintained, an urban guerrilla movement is almost entirely inhibited from recruiting from its natural sources of support.

Police killed Carlos Marighella, urban terrorism's chief figure, in an ambush in 1969. Urban terrorism in Latin America proved to be a considerable nuisance to governments, but at no time did it threaten to overthrow any of them. Its theory was only sketchily formed. Equally, urban terrorism created a powerful reaction in favor of repression. In Argentina, for example, many citizens were afraid that the urban guerrillas would start a civil war, and so welcomed the army's takeover in 1976.

TERRORISTS, GUERRILLAS, POLITICIANS

Some insurgents practice guerrilla warfare and terrorism without reference to any theoretical framework, and certainly not a Marxist one. One example of this type was George Grivas in Cyprus in 1955-59. Grivas shunned any association with the communists. In his view, communist theory had nothing to do with any war of national liberation.

Grivas is a rare example of a successful guerrilla leader who used terror tactics. But he kept a low political profile after Cyprus gained its independence in 1959. It is hard to think of any major terrorist who has become a successful politician. Those who have took little or no part in terrorist acts. Mao, probably the most successful guerrilla leader of all time, emphasized his talents as a military and ideological thinker. Terrorism may be a fundamental element of guerrilla warfare, but it is apparently not a respectable one.

Peter Calvert

SEE ALSO: NATIONALIST TERRORISM; REVOLUTIONARY TERRORISM; DOMESTIC VERSUS INTERNATIONAL TERRORISM; URBAN VERSUS RURAL TERRORISM; TERRORISM IN NICARAGUA; TERRORISM IN PERU; TERROR IN THE PHILIPPINES; TERROR IN THE VIETNAM WAR; NICARAGUAN GOVERNMENT'S RESPONSES TO TERRORISM.

FURTHER READING

- Daniels, Robert Vincent. *Year of the Heroic Guerrilla: World Revolution and Counterrevolution in 1968.* Cambridge, MA and London: Harvard University Press, 1996.
- Guevara, Ernesto. *Guerrilla Warfare.* London: Cassell, 1969; Lincoln: University of Nebraska Press, 1985.
- Kohl, John, and James Litt, eds. *Urban Guerrilla Warfare in Latin America.* Cambridge, MA and London: MIT Press, 1975.
- Marighella, Carlos. *Manual of the Urban Guerrilla.* Chapel Hill, NC: Documentary Publications, 1985.
- Moreno, José Antonio. *Che Guevara on Guerrilla Warfare,* London and New York: Cambridge University Press, 1970.

THEORIES OF STATE TERROR

Terror can be used as a repressive force by a government against its own citizens. Some commentators, such as Noam Chomsky, take the view that national authorities commit most terrorist acts. The aim is to undermine society and subject it to totalitarian rule. The Soviet Union experienced just such state terror on a grand scale during the 1930s. First, in 1930-32, the security police arrested and executed or sent to labor camps large numbers of peasant farmers. Then, in 1936-40, the police arrested millions of members of the Communist Party and their families and subjected them to the same fate as the peasants. These purges crushed any organized opposition to Stalin's personal control of the party, and therefore of the state. Before the 1930s communists discussed and voted on alternative policies. Afterwards, there was only dictatorial rule by Stalin and his inner circle.

Some of the most striking examples of repressive terrorism have occurred in Latin America. During the 1920s, the revolutionary government of Mexico arrested and executed Catholic priests throughout the country. During the 1930s, any priest captured by the authorities in the Mexican state of Tabasco was shot. These policies aimed at wiping out religious institutions, which provided an alternative political power base for conservatives opposed to the revolution.

Repressive terrorism on the part of conservatives dominated Latin American politics during the later 1970s. The excuse for repression during the late 1960s and early 1970s was provided by urban terrorism in Argentina and Uruguay, and the success of leftists in elections in Bolivia, Peru, and Chile. The threat of nationalization of businesses, land reforms, and other social changes provoked a new wave of coups that were followed by repressive military governments.

KEY FACTS

- Conservative regimes in Latin America in the 1970s employed U.S. military instructors who spread the doctrine that any means of repression was justified to halt the spread of communism.
- It is widely believed that the actual number of people "disappeared" by the Argentine military regime during the Dirty War was more than 15,000.

THE DIRTY WAR

There was, however, a substantial difference between the ideas of the new 1970s Latin American military governments and those of the traditional style of rule by generals. The new military regimes did not even pay lip service to the idea that military rule was a temporary expedient. These new regimes believed that the purpose of military rule was to stay in power as long as necessary to obtain a range of objectives. Their aim was not just to put right inconvenient election results or to reverse a military coup. Rather it was to eradicate the entire basis for left-wing power. This set of ideas was known as the national security ideology. The term refers to the belief that national security was threatened by the spread of revolutionary ideas that ran contrary to the values of western Christian civilization.

When the military seized power in Argentina in 1976, it began the Process of National Reorganization (usually known simply as the Process). This drive was to penetrate the whole of Argentine society, beginning in the schools and universities. Teachers were purged, books burned, political channels closed down, and artists proscribed and driven into exile. A wholesale counterterrror was unleashed on all those thought to be left-wing sympathizers.

Estimates of the number of people who perished in what became known as the "Dirty War" (*la guerra sucia*) fluctuated at the time. However, the figure is now known to be at least 15,000 and almost certainly much more. Many of "the Disappeared," who were rounded up, tortured, and never seen again, were not left-wingers. Friends and relations of subversives were seized merely on suspicion and were also killed. Some children were murdered on the argument that, since

Popperfoto

Workers exhume bodies from unmarked graves in a suburb of Buenos Aires, the Argentine capital, in 1983. The government that succeeded the military regime investigated the disappearance of thousands of people during the military's "Dirty War."

their brothers and sisters were suspects, they in turn would grow up into subversives. The babies of some of "the Disappeared" were taken away from their mothers at birth to be brought up by military families. Other Latin American states whose regimes acted in a similar way at this time included Bolivia, Brazil, Chile, El Salvador, and Guatemala. Amnesty International also has cases from many other countries.

Moreover, these military regimes claimed that any means were justified in countering this left-wing threat. Many Argentine officers who seized power from a democratic government in 1976 believed that World War III had already begun. As General Leopoldo Galtieri, the Argentine president from 1981 to 1983, said: "The First World War was one of armies against armies, the Second World War was one of weapons against weapons, the Third World War is one of ideology against ideology."

RIGHTS AND REPRESSION

The question that now seems most important is why is repressive terrorism used at all. As Frantz Fanon, the French West Indian writer on colonial liberation struggles, recognized, the sustained use of violence, brutality, and torture causes severe psychological damage to the torturer.

The postwar wave of insurgent movements gave rise to extensive literature on counterinsurgency that will influence insurgents of the future. Most counterinsurgency writers stress the importance of civilian control of military operations. They also emphasize the necessity of good intelligence, effective command, appropriate tactics, and the use of advanced technology where available. Ironically, many of these points are equally applicable to the insurgents.

There is a special problem that governments face which insurgents do not. Public support for counterinsurgency is more important to a government than it is to insurgents. Democratic states engaged in counter-insurgency operations have found themselves particularly vulnerable to charges of human rights violations. On the other hand, such states may be equally vulnerable to the gradual withdrawal of public confidence when facing an apparently endless insurgency campaign.

Peter Calvert

SEE ALSO: STALIN'S GREAT TERROR; URBAN VERSUS RURAL TERRORISM; TERRORISM IN ARGENTINA; TERRORISM IN GUATEMALA; TERRORISM IN PERU; RESPONSES TO TERRORISM IN LATIN AMERICA.

FURTHER READING

- Ames, B. *Rhetoric and Reality in a Militarized Regime: Brazil since 1964.* Beverly Hills, CA: Sage Professional, 1973.
- Lopez, George A. "Terrorism in Latin America," in *The Politics of Terrorism*, 3d ed., edited by Michael Stohl. New York: Marcel Dekker, Inc., 1988.
- Tucker, Robert C. *Stalin in Power: The Revolution from Above, 1928-1941.* New York: Norton, 1992.

CHAPTER FOUR

Campaigns of Decolonization

Few causes make people feel so desperate as the quest to rule themselves in their own country. The 1900s have seen many nationalists who felt passionate enough to turn to terrorism in their desire to be rid of a colonial power. Quite often, the violence has worked and the country has gained its independence, but only after ferocious battles of terrorism and counterterrorism. Africa had a particularly bitter struggle against its various European rulers, but there were vicious campaigns in India, southeast Asia, and parts of Europe, too.

CAMPAIGNS OF DECOLONIZATION: Introduction

In the aftermath of World War II, a series of bitter wars erupted across the globe. Most were fought between indigenous nationalists and the European colonial powers that had conquered large parts of the world in the nineteenth century. The nationalists strove to rid their countries of European rule. These wars saw the widespread use of terror by both sides. The experiences of these colonies during World War II was the catalyst that triggered these wars of decolonization. In some conflicts, as in Malaya and Indochina, the colonial powers had previously armed the guerrilla terrorists to fight the Japanese who were occupying the two countries during World War II. While many of these conflicts had common features, each had their own distinctive characteristics.

In one exceptional case, however, that of India, terror had been used by nationalists long before World War II. Many Indian soldiers had served with the British army in World War I. The experiences of these indian soldiers dispelled the myth that the European powers were invincible and superior. This realization gave same Indians the strength to challenge British colonial rule. In the 1920s and 1930s, some Indian nationalists, wishing to oust the British colonialists and rule themselves, were prepared to use terror to achieve their aims. Eventually, the burden of governing a huge country like India, when most of the people there wanted independence and the army might mutiny, was too much for Britain to bear.

In other European colonies, it took the events of World War II to make indigenous peoples see that the European empires were shaky. The latter's weakness persuaded many nationalists to make a bid for independence. These nationalists were prepared to use terror since they believed that victory would justify any means they used to attain their end.

The colonial experience itself had also put pressure on some societies. In Kenya, for example, problems of land ownership among the Kikuyu fostered the explosive social conditions that led to Mau Mau terrorism. However, the racism of the white troops maintaining order led to reprisals that fueled the spiral of atrocities.

The most brutal terrorism occurred in countries where the colonial power was determined not to withdraw. Resistance to the nationalists' onslaught was stronger in possessions that had been heavily settled by people from the colonial power. In Algeria, for example, the existence of the *colons*, a large population of white settlers, made a simple French withdrawal impossible. The war in Algeria saw widespread terror used by both sides, and culminated in a bombing campaign by right-wing extremists determined to prevent French withdrawal.

The decolonization struggles were lengthy and vicious. France took eight years to crush the nationalists in Algeria, by which time France was close to civil war. The struggle in Zimbabwe, then called Rhodesia, was prolonged because the country had become an independent state run by white settlers. In Zimbabwe, terrorists led their campaign against a white government that considered itself indigenous, rather than against a foreign European power.

In many decolonization campaigns, the nationalists did not direct terrorism solely at Europeans. Rather, the nationalists also targeted people of the same race as themselves who they suspected of collaborating with the colonial regime. In Malaya and in Portugal's African colonies, the campaigns were rural, targeted at planters and white settlers living in isolated areas.

In Namibia, the terrorism was both urban and rural-based. Although Namibia was not ruled by a European power, South Africa was governing the country as a League of Nations mandate. South Africa defied UN instructions to leave Namibia, leading to a vicious guerrilla war.

The success differed in the various campaigns of decolonization. In Cyprus, terrorism had much impact, but was less influential in Malaya. But all the colonies achieved their independence eventually.

The price of victory, however, was often the sewing of seeds of future conflict, as was the case in 1980s Algeria. Above all, the terrorists that emerged in the 1970s learned much about the practice of terrorism from these struggles. ■

TERRORISM IN FRENCH ALGERIA

The Algerian war of independence, fought by Algerian nationalists of the National Liberation Front (FLN) against the French authorities between 1954 and 1962, saw terrorism employed on a variety of levels. Indeed, it may well be accurate to say that this conflict was dominated by sheer terrorism to a greater degree than any other modern war.

The first major signs of trouble occurred just after World War II. The French had always encouraged their citizens to settle in Algeria. By 1945, ten percent of the population of Algeria were of European descent – the so-called *colons*. The *colons* had a privileged position and would not give it up without a struggle. However, Muslim nationalism, divided into fundamentalist and liberal wings, was also a powerful force.

World War II victory parades in May 1945 brought violence. In the town of Sétif, an Arab crowd overwhelmed and killed 20 French police officers. They went on to kill 103 Europeans, brutalizing their victims. Men's genitals were hacked off and sewn into their mouths; women were raped and their breasts were cut off. Order was swiftly restored. Security forces killed thousands of Muslims while *colons* lynched others. But such acts could not deflect Muslim nationalism.

In the early 1950s, anti-colonial campaigns were taking place worldwide. The French were embroiled in a losing war in Indochina that ended with the spectacular defeat on May 1954 at Dien Bien Phu. In North Africa, there was nationalist discontent in two of Algeria's neighbors, Morocco and Tunisia (also ruled by France), while in Egypt, the strident nationalist Colonel Gamal Abdel Nasser was proclaiming a new start for the Arab world. In this context, the creation of the FLN in Algeria in October was probably inevitable.

The FLN nationalists planned a series of raids on army installations for November 1, 1954, but these had little effect on French forces who had been expecting an uprising. In order to maintain its control in rural areas, the FLN began using terror on a wide scale. They routinely cut off the lips and nose of anyone suspected of minor crimes and slit the throats of those believed to be collaborating with the French.

KEY FACTS

- In 1961-62, the Secret Army Organization (OAS), made up of army deserters, mercenaries, students, and schoolchildren, went on a spree of anti-Muslim attacks in Algeria. They murdered about 1,200 Muslims, French soldiers, and civilians.
- As independence neared, most European settlers left Algeria – of 900,000 settlers in Algeria in 1954, only 30,000 remained by the summer of 1962.

SPIRALING VIOLENCE

In April 1955, the nationalists provoked an uprising in the town of Philippeville. Rioters killed and mutilated Europeans, including children. French troops responded by slaughtering Muslims, and a spiral of terror and counterterror began. The nationalist leadership considered the Philippeville massacre a success. In 1956, they decided to launch a terror campaign in Algiers.

The bombing in Algiers was run by Ben M'Hidi and controlled by Saadi Yacef, who used a team of women operatives to plant bombs. Then, in December 1956, FLN terrorists assassinated a well-known conservative politician, Amédée Froger. The discovery of a bomb at the cemetery where his funeral was to take place infuriated Europeans, who rioted against Muslims.

The nationalists were confident early in 1957. With the enforced withdrawal of French and British troops from Egypt after the invasion of the Suez Canal Zone in October, international events seemed to be going their way. Moreover, the United Nations had agreed to debate the situation in Algeria. Ben M'Hidi called a general strike by Muslims in Algiers in January 1957 to show their strength and serious intent.

The French, however, now had their 10th Colonial Parachute Division, under General Jacques Massu, in Algiers. Using the muscle of the paratroopers, the French broke the strike and destroyed the nationalist

Hulton Getty Picture Collection

Female Algerian rebels undergo weapons training in a camp in Tunisia in the late 1950s.

network in the casbah, the crowded old quarter of Algiers. The French needed good intelligence to achieve this. A major means of gaining it was through terror and torture, particularly by using electrical equipment and half drowning suspects. Once captives talked, their torturers often threw them from helicopters into the sea. The French captured Ben M'Hidi in February and then announced that he had hanged himself. Whether or not their claim was true, it further cowed the nationalists. By October 1957, there was little terrorist activity in Algiers. The ruthless French methods had secured a key victory.

The French military victory within Algiers was soon mirrored by successful campaigns elsewhere in Algeria. Extensive frontier defenses cut nationalist infiltration from Tunisia and Morocco, while attacks on rural guerrillas showed impressive results.

The Algerian conflict was a source of anxiety in France. Politicians agonized about the morality of the war, especially over the tactics used against the terrorists in the battle of Algiers in 1957. For their part, the Algerian nationalists were often divided, but they knew how to influence world opinion.

The French politicians soon had another problem. In 1958, the Europeans in Algeria feared that politicians in Paris were seriously considering Algerian independence. The constitution of the Fourth Republic was overthrown, bringing an end to short and unstable governments. In its place, war hero Charles de Gaulle was installed as president with sweeping powers.

DE GAULLE AND ALGERIAN INDEPENDENCE

De Gaulle was seen as a strong leader who would prosecute the war against the nationalists with vigor. But within two years it was clear that his vision of the future did not include Algeria as a French province. He believed that France's world role lay in leading a loose federation of former colonies, and that old-style

Hulton Getty Picture Collection

French paratroopers, carrying submachine guns, challenge Islamic demonstrators in Algiers in 1960.

imperialism was finished in the modern world. He announced Algeria's right to self-determination in September 1959. The Algerian *colons* attempted a coup in January 1960. French commander-in-chief General Challe's lukewarm response to putting down this insurrection lost him the confidence of the president. De Gaulle recalled him from his post in Algiers.

De Gaulle's policy was unpopular with others besides the Europeans in Algeria. It also angered many soldiers who had given their all in the fight against the nationalists. Four generals – Challe, Salan, Jouhaud, and Zeller – attempted another coup in April 1961. When it failed, the opponents of de Gaulle's policy were left with few options. Some of them chose terrorism. The Secret Army Organization (OAS) took up arms, planting bombs in Algiers and in France, killing Muslims, and attempting to assassinate de Gaulle.

A timetable for independence was agreed at Evian, eastern France, in March 1962, and a cease-fire was proclaimed. Independence was, for many Algerians, merely the start of terror, however. The nationalists had been split into many factions during the long war. There were two major divisions: first between those who had stayed in Algeria (the internals) and those who had gone abroad (the externals); and second between the political and the army leaderships. Old scores could be settled in the aftermath of victory, often disguised as punishment for traitorous behavior. There was an immediate and savage backlash against those who had helped the French. Individuals were tortured and killed. In many cases their families also suffered, as did whole villages. The lingering unease afflicting the country led to the Islamic fundamentalist uprising in the 1990s, which was in many ways a continuation of this earlier struggle.

Ashley Brown

SEE ALSO: TERROR AGAINST THE FRENCH IN INDOCHINA; ISLAMIC FUNDAMENTALISM AND TERRORISM IN ALGERIA; THE FRENCH RESPONSE TO TERRORISM.

FURTHER READING

- Crenshaw, Martha. *Revolutionary Terrorism: The FLN in Algeria, 1954-62.* Stanford, CA: Hoover Institution Press, 1978.
- Horne, Alistair. *Savage War of Peace: Algeria, 1954-1962.* Rev. ed. London: Papermac, 1996.
- Lacouture, Jean. *De Gaulle: The Ruler, 1945-1970.* New York: Norton, 1992; London: Harvill, 1993.

TERRORISM IN CYPRUS

On April 1, 1955, pamphlets proclaimed the existence of the National Organization of Cypriot Fighters, usually known by the acronym EOKA. The pamphlets were written by a Greek Cypriot nationalist, George Grivas, a retired colonel in the Greek army. Along with many Greek Cypriots, Grivas wanted *enosis*, or union with Greece, for Cyprus. He formed EOKA with the aim of bringing about the end of British rule of the island so that such a union would be possible. He was prepared to use terrorism to get his way.

Greek Cypriots made up about four-fifths of the population of Cyprus, and Turkish Cypriots accounted for most of the remainder. This Turkish minority, whose relations with the Greek Cypriots were shaky, was alarmed by the calls for union with Greece. Britain, which had administered the island since 1878, refused to give up control because it wanted to retain Cyprus as a strategic asset in the Mediterranean. The British also wanted to protect the Turkish Cypriots from the wave of Greek Cypriot nationalism.

In 1954, Greece had tried and failed to persuade the UN to take up the case for Cyprus's self-determination. The Greek Cypriots responded by demonstrating in the Cypriot capital, Nicosia, in December. Then, on April 1, 1955, the same day it issued its pamphlets, EOKA began its terrorist campaign. Using explosives stolen from the British army and weapons smuggled from Greece, EOKA bombed British government offices in Cyprus and murdered British subjects and Cypriots. Attacks often took place in broad daylight, killing women, children, and members of the clergy.

Principal towns in Cyprus, and the locations of major EOKA terrorist attacks.

KEY FACTS

- In its terrorist campaign from 1954 to 1958, EOKA exploded 1,782 bombs, causing damage in the millions of dollars.
- The EOKA campaign cost the lives of at least 104 soldiers, 50 police, 238 civilians, and 90 EOKA operatives.
- Colonel George Grivas, the EOKA leader, used the *nom de guerre* Dighenis during the Cyprus campaign. On his return to Greece afterward, Grivas was rewarded for his efforts with promotion to lieutenant general.

EOKA'S CAMPAIGN OF VIOLENCE

On May 24, Empire Day, EOKA tried to kill the governor of Cyprus, Sir Robert Armitage, by bombing a movie house he was attending. The explosives, stuffed into a soft drink bottle, blew up, wrecking several rows of seats, but not until after Sir Robert had left.

By November, the situation was so serious that the British declared a state of emergency on Cyprus. Firm retaliatory measures were taken against the Greek Cypriot community, such as levying collective fines on villages, imposing curfews, and introducing the death penalty. The armed forces imposed a blockade to prevent further arms shipments. Remarkably, though, sympathizers could still get weapons to the island in the mail, which was not searched.

On November 26, the day the emergency was declared, EOKA terrorists hurled a grenade into the ballroom of the Ledra Palace Hotel in Nicosia, where a

Popperfoto

Colonel George Grivas (third from right), also known as Dighenis, with a band of EOKA gunmen.

large party of Scottish people were celebrating St. Andrew's Day. Four British were wounded, including the wife of the British police commissioner.

No fewer than 21 terrorist shootings and bombings took place in Nicosia from November 1955 to March 1956. On March 3, 1956, 68 air passengers – serving soldiers and their families – had a narrow escape when terrorists planted a timebomb on a Hermes aircraft. The bomb destroyed the plane before the passengers were aboard, the flight having been delayed.

Also in March 1956, the British authorities deported Archbishop Makarios III, the political head of the Greek Cypriot movement for union with Greece. Makarios refused to condemn EOKA's use of violence, and the authorities suspected him of having close links with the terrorists. However, his exile to the Seychelles Islands, in the Indian Ocean, was a cue for rioting among the Greek Cypriots, with much of the violence directed against Turkish Cypriots. A third major incident in March 1956 was an attempt on the life of the new governor of the island, Sir John Harding. On the 22nd, an EOKA terrorist placed a bomb in the governor's bed. He set the device to go off in the early morning at a temperature of 67 degrees Fahrenheit. However, it failed to go off, since the bomber had not taken into account the drop in nighttime temperature and the habit of many people, Sir John apparently among them, of sleeping with the windows open.

EOKA divided its military campaign into rural and urban theaters. EOKA's fighting force was small – a few hundred activists against a British garrison of 25,000. Mountain groups of five to fifteen men engaged in guerrilla warfare in the Troodos mountains, ambushing military patrols and raiding remote police posts.

Popperfoto

Greek Cypriot Nikos Sampson (right) at the Nicosia courthouse on 25 April, 1957, where he was accused in connection with murders of Britons in Nicosia.

Meanwhile, five-man groups carried out urban terrorist attacks, including street shootings, arson attacks, and bombings. For example, in April 1956, terrorists killed a senior policeman visiting his wife and newborn son at a maternity clinic. On June 16, EOKA bombed a restaurant, mistakenly killing the U.S. vice consul.

During so-called Black November, in 1956, there were 416 terrorist incidents in which more than 35 people died. Even British civilians who had been living in Cyprus for many years were not safe. That month, terrorists killed a certain Dr. Bevan in the sick bay of the Amiandos Mining Company. As the doctor examined a patient, the latter's "escort" shot him dead.

By now, though, the British army had curtailed EOKA's mountain activities, and Greek Cypriots loyal to the authorities had infiltrated the organization. Being a British agent was a risky business, since EOKA dealt ruthlessly with anyone considered a traitor. The usual penalty was death, often at the hands of shotgun squads of village sympathizers. As a result, Grivas was forced temporarily to suspend terrorist activities.

The terror was far from over, however. In the first ten days of April 1957, EOKA exploded 50 bombs, and on May 4, terrorists assassinated two British soldiers. Then, on November 26, 1957, EOKA destroyed a Royal Air Force Canberra bomber on the ground at Akrotiri airbase. Ten months later, the organization attempted to assassinate Major-General D. A. Kendrew, military commander of the Cyprus district. Other less spectacular but no less appalling attacks also took place. In October 1958, EOKA murdered the wife of a British serviceman while she was shopping in Varosha. This incident so outraged army personnel that in the following round-up, hundreds of Cypriots were badly beaten and two died, although one British soldier also died.

PARTITION OR DEATH

Much of the violence after 1957 was intercommunal, and the situation approached civil war. However, a political solution was in sight. The Greek Cypriots, at the start of the campaign, would settle for nothing less than union with Greece. As has been mentioned, this was unacceptable to Turkish Cypriots, and to Turkey. When Britain released Archbishop Makarios from detention in the Seychelles in March 1957, Turkey interpreted it as a step toward *enosis* and called for Cyprus to be partitioned into Greek and Turkish zones under the slogan "Partition or Death." Eventually, though, all parties eased their demands and agreed to independence for Cyprus without either union with Greece or partition. EOKA halted operations on December 31, 1958, and Makarios became president of the republic of Cyprus on December 14, 1959.

Chris Marshall

SEE ALSO: TERRORISM IN FRENCH ALGERIA; TERRORISM IN COLONIAL INDIA 1900-1947; TERROR AGAINST THE FRENCH IN INDOCHINA; TERRORISM IN MALAYA; TERRORISM IN KENYA; NATIONALIST TERRORISM; BRITISH COUNTERTERROR IN THE ERA OF DECOLONIZATION.

FURTHER READING

- Dewar, Michael. *Brush Fire Wars: Minor Campaigns of the British Army since 1945.* London: Hale, and New York: St. Martin's Press, 1984.
- Foley, Charles, and W. I. Scobie. *The Struggle for Cyprus.* Stanford, CA: Hoover Institution Press, 1975.
- Markides, K. *The Rise and Fall of the Cyprus Republic.* New Haven, CT: Yale University Press, 1977.

TERRORISM IN GREECE

Before World War II most members of the Greek Communist Party (KKE) had been exiled or imprisoned by the Metaxas dictatorship. However, from the 1941 German invasion of Greece until 1949, the KKE used terrorism in attempts first to control the resistance to German occupation and then forcibly to seize power.

During the 1941-44 German occupation of Greece, the KKE developed a guerrilla front organization, the People's National Army of Liberation (ELAS). The KKE used ELAS to control the population and destroy other resistance movements, while avoiding direct fighting with the Germans. The KKE launched another attempt to take power in 1946. Its armed wing, now renamed the Democratic Army (DA), fought a terrorist campaign against the Greek state until 1949.

THE PATH OF TERRORISM

The KKE first employed terrorism during 1942-44 to subdue the countryside and secure local support for ELAS. This terrorism involved executions, imprisonment, and torture under the pretext of punishing collaboration with the German forces. In 1944, ELAS undertook widespread terrorism in the Peloponnese, in southern Greece. However, these KKE/ELAS atrocities merely drove many locals to join German-armed security battalions to combat ELAS, thus creating a state of virtual civil war.

From mid-1944, with liberation approaching, the KKE launched a terrorist campaign in occupied Athens to eliminate the non-communist resistance. The party also tried to subvert the power of the police so that it would be able to occupy Athens as soon as the Germans left. The Athens police had managed, despite the occupation, not to collaborate with the Germans, and was an organized, disciplined, armed force that the communists could not infiltrate.

The KKE terrorist organizations in the Athens area were the Organization for the Protection of the People's Struggle (OPLA), the People's National Guard (EP), and the Guardforce. In late 1944, these three organizations eliminated many political opponents. OPLA maintained its grip on large parts of Athens after the German withdrawal. When the KKE attempted to take power in December 1944, OPLA conducted a purge in which at least 5,000 people perished.

However, the defeat of the KKE/ELAS in Athens in early January 1945 forced ELAS to retreat to central Greece. As ELAS retreated, it took several thousand hostages with it, many of whom died during forced marches. The hostages became bargaining chips for the KKE in the subsequent peace negotiations.

Despite the January 1945 Varkiza agreement, which ended the fighting, communist terrorism continued. Until March 1946 this terrorism was aimed mainly at countering retaliation by anti-communist armed groups. In the Peloponnese, for example, right-wing groups attacked ELAS bands.

UNDERGROUND FORCE

During 1945, the KKE created Aftoamyna (Self-defense), an underground communist network of small cells. Its task was to organize intelligence collection against the Greek government, to harass the state with terrorism, and to provide the KKE with an escape and recruitment network. Aftoamyna terrorism took the form of kidnapping, assassinations, bombing of urban centers, and the destruction of communications.

After the resumption of full-scale civil war in March 1946, there were increased numbers of communist terrorist attacks on prominent community figures, such as mayors, teachers, and local administrators. In

KEY FACTS

- At their peak, the communists had 25,000 fighters in the field and 50,000 active supporters.
- Troops attacked a major communist base on Mount Grammos in 1948-49, and killed 9,000 terrorists. After this action rural terrorism declined dramatically across Greece.

Associated Press

Some of the 50 civilians and 40 troops killed by 600 ELAS terrrorists near Mount Paikon, Macedonia.

this way Aftoamyna imposed a climate of fear that helped the KKE to control the rural population. In many areas Aftoamyna destroyed the structures of traditional Greek society by the intensive use of terror.

FOREIGN ASSISTANCE

After 1947, the Greek army was able to deal with communist forces by using American aid. The major communist weakness was their reliance on aid from the communist regimes of Yugoslavia, Bulgaria, and Albania. This support made many Greeks suspicious of the KKE's motives, and it led to a disaster when the regimes withdrew support in 1948-9 for reasons connected with relations within the communist bloc.

In the Peloponnese, Aftoamyna proved very resistant. However, in late 1948, the Greek army isolated the area from the mainland and destroyed Aftoamyna by arresting 4,300 suspects in one night.

The police had dismantled the Aftoamyna apparatus in Athens in 1946-47. The remaining Aftoamyna cells were captured during 1950-53. About 8,000 terrorists escaped to Albania, and the army caught any that tried to return to Greece near the border. Many captured terrorists informed on the few remaining cells.

Ashley Brown

SEE ALSO: WWII RESISTANCE IN YUGOSLAVIA AND TERRORISM; GUERRILLAS AND TERROR.

FURTHER READING

- Averoff-Tossizza, E. *By Fire and Axe: The Communist Party and the Civil War in Greece, 1944-49.* New Rochelle, NY: Caratzas Brothers, 1978.
- O'Ballance, Edgar. *The Greek Civil War, 1944-1949.* London: Faber, and New York: Praeger, 1966.
- Stavrakis, Peter J. *Moscow and Greek Communism, 1944-1949.* Ithaca, NY: Cornell University Press, 1989.

TERROR IN COLONIAL INDIA 1900-1947

The use of political violence was a distinctive feature of politics in Bengal in British colonial India during the first half of the twentieth century. The intermittent terrorist campaign in Bengal, northeast India, which periodically spilled over into other provinces, posed a serious threat to the British regime, known as the Raj.

In the early 1900s, the local British administration in Bengal was challenged by the growth of a politically motivated extremist revolutionary movement. Its objective was the establishment of Indian self-government, or *swaraj*. Brothers Barin and Aurobindo Ghose were the two principal advocates of violence. They filled newspaper columns with calls for revolutionary action and distributed pamphlets that glorified revolution as a religious duty.

THE RISE OF SECRET SOCIETIES

The propaganda aroused an enthusiastic response from the more prosperous and intellectual sections of the population. Terrorist activity gathered strength after the partition of Bengal in 1907, which was unpopular with the educationally and politically westernized Hindu elite, or *bhadlarok*. Terrorist secret societies, or *samitis*, were founded. These societies were composed of young, idealistic *bhadlarok* students, eager to redress their perceived grievances by force of arms. The two main groups were the Jugantar and Anushilan *samitis*.

Both of these groups resorted to terrorist tactics such as beatings and killings, together with armed robberies known as *dacoities*. The objective was to publicize the existence of the *samitis* and their aims and to collect funds to buy arms and ammunition. Terror was achieved by inflicting casualties on British police, civil officials, and Indian staff in the government. The societies encouraged mass riots, such as those that occurred throughout 1908 and early 1909. The riots were intended to gain public support and lead to nationwide armed rebellion against British rule.

Indian revolutionary groups were even active in north London, U.K. In 1908, for example, the Free India Society acquired a Russian handbook on bomb manufacturing that had been translated for them by a Russian student. The handbook was then sent to India.

KEY FACTS

- From 1905 to 1915, Indian nationalism was expressed through violence and boycotts of British goods.
- In 1942, violent riots and protests spread across India as nationalist leaders were arrested by the British authorities.
- Terrorism continued after India was granted independence. Pacifist nationalist leader Mohandas Gandhi was assassinated in 1948 and thousands killed in sectarian violence.

BRITISH COUNTERTERRORISM

The initial British response to Bengali terrorism was hesitant, but the amateurish nature of the terror campaign meant that the police were able to seize the leaders of the *samitis* with ease.

Later British action was more decisive. In 1907-08, the British authorities imposed strict censorship of the local press, banned secret societies, and extended the activities of the secret police. The government also authorized imprisonment without trial for certain political offenses. The measures were needed because it was proving difficult to convict terrorists since witnesses and juries were often intimidated. During these security operations by the British security forces, 205 people were convicted.

A brief lull in terrorist activities occurred after the leaders of the *samitis* were arrested in 1908 and 1909. However, on December 23, 1912, *samitis* members tried to assassinate British Viceroy Lord Hardinge in the capital Delhi. Although the attempt failed, it encouraged further attacks on officials and more *dacoities* as public support for the nationalists gradually increased.

Hulton Getty Picture Collection

The bodies of several policemen who died when terrorists burned down their station and threw them into the fire at Chauri Chaura in 1921.

British opinion was divided on how best to counter this round of terrorism in Bengal. Governor Lord Carmichael favored a conciliatory approach that would secure *bhadlarok* support against the violence. But the Raj took a far firmer line: it pursued a policy of vigorous repression. By 1914, the terrorist violence in Bengal was regarded by the British authorities as "a well-developed criminal conspiracy aimed at the destruction of British rule."

THE GOVERNMENT TAKES A HARSH LINE

During World War I, the British administration took even stronger measures to maintain law and order. However, this did not stop a renewed outbreak of terrorism in Bengal during 1915-16. In addition, evidence was uncovered that Indian terrorists were attempting to secure German support.

Improved police intelligence was highly effective and, by 1917, the terrorist campaign had almost completely broken down. The introduction of preventive arrest meant that all of the main terrorists were in prison. Those still at large were so demoralized and disorganized that their activity ceased almost entirely.

PEACEFUL NONCOOPERATION

One outcome of the unrest and terrorism was a promise from the British authorities to set in place constitutional reforms. But instead, the British government extended the emergency repression powers into peacetime. As a result, Bengali opposition to the Raj grew widespread in India.

Opposition to British rule immediately after World War I came mainly from the moderate noncooperation movement. The call for independence was led by the Indian National Congress (Congress), a legal political

Hulton Getty Picture Collection

Sir John Anderson, a counterinsurgency expert, was appointed Governor of Bengal in 1932.

party. This was inspired by the Indian lawyer Mohandas Gandhi and was committed to nonviolent protest and civil disobedience. As most leaders of the *samitis* were still in prison, terrorist activity in Bengal was suspended. In the meantime, this allowed the effectiveness of Gandhi's strategy to be tested, while the shattered *samitis* recovered their strength.

But the rate of progress of this policy of noncooperation was far too slow for an Indian population impatient for change. So when the detainees were released by a royal pardon in 1920, new terrorist groups modeled on the *samitis* of the prewar period sprang up. There were riots in Madras, Bombay, and Chauri Chaura, where 22 police officers were burnt and killed in February, 1921. Exactly a year later, the Congress suspended the noncooperation campaign.

A second terrorist campaign in Bengal began. Jugantar gangs carried out a series of assassinations and *dacoities* in the name of the Congress, demonstrating that radical factions within the party remained firmly committed to violence. At the same time, under the leadership of the 26-year-old socialist Subhas Chandra Bose, the Bengal branch of Congress was influenced by supporters of political violence.

In 1924, there were further attacks on European administrators and police officers. In response, the authorities introduced new emergency legislation in October 1925. The laws allowed them to arrest suspected terrorists and to try them before special tribunals without right of appeal. The prompt arrest of all prominent terrorist leaders achieved immediate results. Over 180 suspects were imprisoned by 1927, quashing the movement before it became widespread.

Order was quickly restored once again and, at the end of 1927, the imperial authorities released all detainees. During their time in prison, however, Jugantar and Anushilan terrorists had discussed new methods of terrorism. More importantly, a logical justification for the use of force had been developed. These ideas were based on those which had been used by the Irish Republican Army (IRA) in Ireland.

Terrorism in Bengal resumed dramatically on April 18, 1930, when 100 terrorists, calling themselves the Indian Republican Army, raided the Police and Auxiliary Force armories in Chittagong, today in Bangladesh. They killed several soldiers, seized 60 rifles and 22 revolvers, and destroyed the telephone exchange, telegraph office, and rail lines. The terrorists then attacked the local European club, but it was empty and they were unable to massacre its members. The size and military organization of the raid, along with the discipline and training of the raiders, shook the British community. On April 22, a brief engagement occurred between troops and the gang in the Jalalabad hills, after which the terrorists returned to forms of violence familiar from the *samitis* activities.

Terrorist activity mounted steadily during the early 1930s. Actions included the assassination of several British and Indian police, and government officials and staff. Female terrorists took an active part in the campaign for the first time and were involved in several attacks, including the attempted assassination of Governor Sir Stanley Jackson in February 1932.

EMERGENCY LEGISLATION

The existing penal code and emergency provisions proved to be insufficient as the violence spread and became more organized. In response, the government introduced a number of new laws. The colonial police were given sweeping powers to stop and search all suspects, impose dawn-to-dusk curfews, and intercept mail. In areas of unrest, district magistrates could confiscate personal property, regulate travel and the movement of goods, and restrict access to certain areas. Heavy fines were imposed on anyone who flouted these new regulations. At the same time, police punishment squads were deployed in villages to prevent the spread of disorder.

Anyone with the slightest suspicion of links to terrorists was rounded up and taken into custody. The authorities hoped that these measures would curtail terrorist activity, but they only produced further political difficulties as the Indian public resented the restrictions put on daily life. In addition, the detention camps became a focus of anti-government feeling and a breeding ground for discontent.

Despite these sweeping measures, fear of insurrection was rife in the British community in Bengal. In 1932, military intelligence officers and seven battalions of regular troops were deployed as backup to the civilian police. Perhaps of greater significance was the appointment of Sir John Anderson as the new governor of Bengal. He was a civil servant with extensive experience of counterinsurgency tactics in Ireland, and his appointment restored police morale.

It was Anderson who recognized that a political solution, hand in hand with repressive measures, was the only way forward. He told the local legislative council: "It is not enough to meet force by force or to answer lawlessness by asserting the majesty and power of the law. An atmosphere must be created in which the seeds of disorder will not germinate."

THE DEFEAT OF INSURGENCY

Following several defeats by government forces in the Jalalabad hills, terrorist groups were forced to revert to isolated robberies and assassinations. In addition, improved police intelligence on terrorist activity and better targeting of searches gradually produced results for the authorities. All known or suspected revolutionaries were detained or watched and all sources of new recruitment were blocked.

Terrorist actions declined by 90 percent during 1932-34. By 1936, the imperial authorities declared the insurgency defeated. The cost was estimated at millions of pounds, and the credibility of the British government had been seriously challenged.

The 1930-36 terrorist campaign made it clear to the Indian revolutionaries in Bengal that isolated acts of violence, while seizing the headlines, would not dislodge the Raj. When the terrorist detainees were released from captivity in 1937-38, both the Jugantar and Anushilan groups disbanded. Terrorism in Bengal never again assumed the same dimensions.

During World War II, the Indian National Congress and the noncooperation movements posed a far more serious threat to the Raj than terrorism, which was conspicuous by its absence. In 1942, Congress began the Quit India movement, which absorbed the few remaining Bengali terrorists into the general resistance to British rule. The movement disrupted rail communications and made the United Provinces, Bihar, Bengal, and elsewhere virtually ungovernable.

At the height of the Quit India movement, the British position in India was endangered seriously enough for the British government to deploy 57 infantry battalions to maintain a semblance of order. This was despite the Japanese threat in neighboring Burma, where manpower was most urgently needed.

Terrorist activity against the Raj finally ended when independence was granted to India by the British government in August 1947. But the struggle to achieve independence left the new state with a legacy of political violence in Bengal. Terrorism between the Hindu and Muslim communities cost tens of thousands of lives in the following decade.

Tim Moreman

SEE ALSO: TERROR IN COLONIAL CONQUESTS; THE AMRITSAR MASSACRE; TERRORISM IN MALAYA; TERRORISM IN KENYA.

FURTHER READING

- Broomfield, J. H. *Elite Conflict in a Plural Society: Twentieth-Century Bengal.* Berkeley: University of California Press, 1968.
- Brown, Judith M. *Gandhi: Prisoner of Hope.* London and New Haven: Yale University Press, 1991.
- Pandey, B. N. *The Break-Up of British India.* London: Macmillan, and New York: St. Martin's Press, 1969.
- Parekh, B. "Gandhi's Theory of Non-Violence," in *Terrorism, Ideology, and Revolution*, edited by Noel O'Sullivan. Boulder, CO: Westview Press, and Brighton, Sussex: Wheatsheaf Books, 1986.

TERROR AGAINST THE FRENCH IN INDOCHINA

Indochina is the former name of the region containing the three modern states of Vietnam, Cambodia, and Laos. During the 1940s and 1950s, communists in the area that is now Vietnam fought a long war against the region's French colonial regime. Terror was an important part of the communists' strategy in this war. They used it to extend their control over the local population. Terrorism also kept the French security forces fully occupied while the communists prepared for a decisive military victory. The strategy paid off, and victory came in 1954, when the Vietnamese communists defeated the French at Dien Bien Phu.

Vietnam had been under French rule since the late nineteenth century. But when Germany defeated France in 1940 the Japanese seized control. The takeover was a blow to France's prestige in Southeast Asia and gave Vietnamese nationalist activists a chance to make their mark. The Chinese and the U.S.-armed nationalist groups in north Vietnam acted as guerrillas against the Japanese. One leader, Ho Chi Minh, set up an efficient guerrilla network, with Vo Nguyen Giap as military commander. By mid-1945, there were more than 1,000 fighters under Giap's command. This force was called the Vietminh and had its stronghold in the mountainous Viet Bac provinces.

When the Japanese surrendered in September 1945, the guerrillas in northern Vietnam were able to come out into the open. Nationalist Chinese troops moved down to occupy the northern capital, Hanoi, and the guerrillas set up a provisional government. They also extended their influence into all aspects of village life. More than 80 percent of Vietnamese lived in villages, and the Vietminh set up committees, together with other nationalist groups, run by what was ostensibly a multiparty League for National Salvation.

In the south of Vietnam, French administration was reestablished with British help, after a short struggle with the nationalists. There were negotiations between the Vietminh and the French. But Vietminh operations continued. Under the strain of such activities, the talks eventually broke down, and the French made a successful assault that took them into Hanoi.

KEY FACTS

- The Vietminh created a climate of fear to force the people of the countryside into submission.
- They executed villagers, left their mutilated bodies for all to see, and burned their houses.
- To intimidate the populace, the Vietminh blew up Saigon's pyrotechnics factory in April 1946, killing its 40 Vietnamese workers.

TAKING OVER THE COUNTRYSIDE

Although the French controlled the cities, the Vietminh had established themselves thoroughly in the countryside and were almost impossible to root out. To gain control of the villages, the Vietminh not only appealed to inhabitants' sense of nationalism but also spread terror. The Vietminh murdered many village elders and officials of the French administration. In this way the Vietminh broke down the already weak links between the villages and the French administration in the cities.

The Vietminh severely punished villages that failed to cooperate fully – they killed village elders and randomly selected peasants for torture and death. Occasionally the terrorists burned down entire villages. Through this terror, the Vietminh compelled each village in their power to provide five people to prepare for operations against the French, while another 12 were to be ready for armed action.

Within a relatively short period, the Vietminh had made much of the countryside a hostile area for the French. At the lowest level was a peasant militia. Although poorly armed, it is estimated that by the early

Tonkin and Cochinchina in what is now Vietnam bore the brunt of terrorism in the 1940s and 1950s.

1950s there may have been up to 75,000 Vietnamese organized into what Giap called his "Regional Forces." These troops were capable of setting booby traps, taking pot shots at French forces at night in fortified buildings called blockhouses, or planting a bomb in a restaurant in Hanoi or Saigon.

The French struggled to combat the Vietminh rural takeover partly because their forces were not committed to the kind of "hearts and minds" operations that would have won back villagers' allegiance.

The French failed to offer a clear vision to the Vietnamese of what to expect if the Vietminh were defeated and were unwilling to allow other nationalist groups to present themselves as a credible alternative. The leaders of such groups were, in any case, the target of a successful Vietminh assassination campaign, which effectively neutralized all other nationalist opposition.

In Cochinchina, the Vietminh were organized by Nguyen Binh. He undertook a terror campaign around Saigon that extended to bombs in factories and French enterprises in the city. When the French established a national Vietnamese government of Cochinchina in Saigon in 1949, Binh immediately reacted. He sent terrorists into Saigon, to undertake assassinations and bombings, while the Vietminh radio issued lists of "traitors" to be eliminated. The French security police managed to block this offensive, but were forced to adopt terror methods. They used informers and ruthless interrogation to strike terrorists. They also left the mutilated bodies of Vietminh activists in the streets to serve as a warning to other members.

The French had some success in more regular warfare against the Vietminh, inflicting heavy casualties on the nationalists in the Red River Delta in 1951. However, the French authorities could not offer security to the terrorized rural population in the delta. The only sections of Vietnamese society that could resist Vietminh incursion were certain religious sects (one, for example, worshiped both Karl Marx and Victor Hugo as saints). These sects were strong enough to be impervious to Vietminh terror tactics.

Vietminh control of the countryside was so effective that the French forces were spread very thinly. By 1953, they maintained only a vestige of power, while the communists created a large, well-equipped military force. The French's increasing failure to control the countryside led them to take on regular Vietminh forces at Dien Bien Phu, an attack which ended with a crushing French defeat. Thus, terror played a critical part in the downfall of a colonial regime.

Ashley Brown

SEE ALSO: NATIONAL LIBERATION WARS AND TERROR; TERRORISM IN FRENCH ALGERIA; TERROR IN THE VIETNAM WAR.

FURTHER READING

- Andrade, D. *Ashes to Ashes: The Phoenix Program and the Vietnam War.* Lexington, MA: Lexington Books, 1990.
- Fall, Bernard. *Street Without Joy: Indochina at War 1946-54.* Harrisburg, PA: Stackpole, 1961.
- Maclear, Michael. *The Ten Thousand Day War.* London: Methuen, and New York: St. Martin's Press, 1981.

TERRORISM IN MALAYA

In response to a rising wave of terrorism by guerrillas of the Malayan Communist Party (MCP), the British colonial government in Malaya declared a state of emergency in June 1948. It lasted until 1960. Emergency regulations allowed for detention, deportation, and even death for insurgency-related offenses.

The communist guerrillas, organzied after the Japanese invasion of 1941, were drawn largely from Malaya's Chinese community. The British encouraged the MCP during the war, sending in arms, supplies, and advisors until it fielded some 7,000 guerrillas. Led by the tactician Chin Peng, the MCP scored some successes over the invaders.

SETTING UP A TERRORIST WING

After the war, however, the MCP aimed to overthrow the colonial government and set up a communist regime in Malaya. The organization infiltrated labor unions and attempted a Soviet-style revolution through strikes and protests, some violent. In 1948, it accepted that the tactic had failed and launched an armed revolt.

The MCP's military wing was originally called the Malayan People's Anti-British Army. It was renamed the Malayan Races' Liberation Army (MRLA) in 1949 in order to appeal to the non-Chinese majority populace.

In May 1948, Chin Peng mobilized eight regiments using weapons saved from the war. Guerrillas ambushed civilian and military buses, trains, and trucks. They murdered government supporters and informers, abducted businessmen, and extorted bribes. On June 29, terrorists shot up Jerantut township, 20 miles from Kuala Krau, burned down the police station and took Chinese and Malay prisoners.

In the meantime, communist cells on British-owned rubber plantations and in tin mines orchestrated strikes and takeovers. On July 12, communist terrorists attacked the police post at Batu Arang, Malaya's only coal mine, overwhelming the occupants and cutting the telephone wires. The terrorists managed to sabotage machinery before colonial police reinforcements could get to the mine. In response to the agitation and violence, the government banned the MCP.

Although there was substantial support for the insurgency among the Chinese community in Malaya, there was nothing like the general popular uprising that had been predicted by the communist leadership. This disappointment, coupled with the strong response of the colonial police and army, forced the MRLA into the jungle, where they established bases near weapons stashes. The bases were often located near Chinese settlements so that the MRLA could obtain supplies and information from a network of supporters known as Min Yuen.

KEY FACTS

- The insurgency resulted in the deaths of 11,000 people, of whom 2,500 were civilians.
- In 1948, about 3,000 full-time and 7,000 part-time communist MRLA guerrillas began making terror attacks against targets throughout Malaya.
- The number of terrorist incidents per month was about 200 in 1948. It dropped to 100 a month in 1949, while the MRLA regrouped.

NEW TERRORIST ATTACKS

Malaya was comparatively calm during the guerrilla reorganization, but by the end of 1949, the terrorists were back in business. The terrorists mostly attacked village police posts, but towns and farming estates were also raided. Attacks were often large-scale. On September 11, a force of 300 communist terrorists raided the town of Kuala Krau, killing four police officers, two British railway engineers, and two Malayan women. The following month, 200 terrorists struck at an isolated rubber plantation in Pahang, setting fire to several buildings.

By early 1950, the MRLA communists had built an organization capable of protracted warfare. They had a hierarchy of military-type units that ranged from terror and sabotage sections in populated areas to village

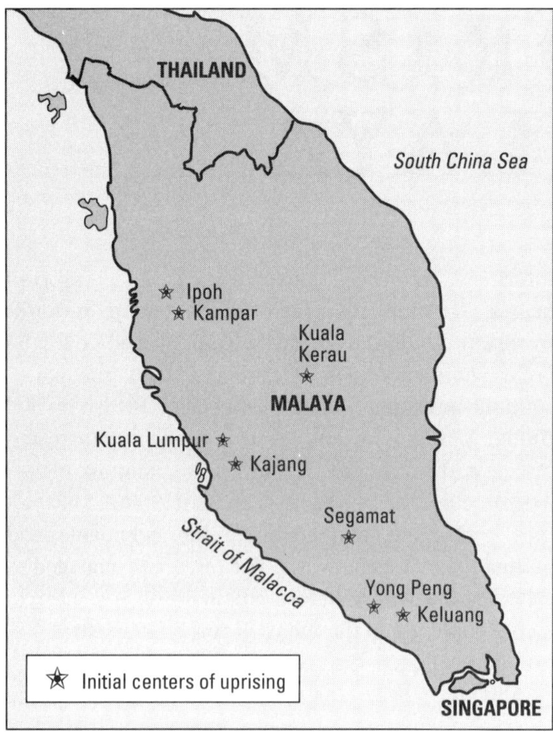

Malaya, scene of a 12-year insurgency campaign.

guerrilla units, up to regular units. Food supplies and intelligence were provided by the political organization and the Min Yuen, so military camps in the jungle had to be within a few hours' walking distance of populated areas. Communication between the settlements and the jungle camps was a weak link.

The guerrillas increased their activity until incidents were occurring at the rate of 400 a month – twice their 1948 rate. The terrorists singled out the British planters and their families for particular attention. One family had to withstand no less than 25 terrorist attacks on their plantation in a two-week period in 1951, including three in one night.

The terrorists also took to machine-gunning the "New Villages," set up by Lieutenant General Sir Harold Briggs, the British director of operations in Malaya. Briggs's plan was to separate the MRLA from its supporters in the community, so he resettled the Chinese into newly constructed villages away from the old settlements. Here, housing and sanitary conditions were far superior than in the old shanties and many Chinese welcomed the change. Briggs also imposed strict allocations of rice. There was little left over to pass to the MRLA, so the terrorists were forced into the open to find food. At the same time, the British army, including the Special Air Service, was getting used to finding and dealing with the terrorists.

By late 1951, the terrorists had been forced to come up with a new strategy. They split their large military units into smaller groups and withdrew deeper into the jungle to rest and retrain.

AMBUSH AND ASSASSINATION

Nonetheless, terrorist incidents continued to take place. In fact, on October 6, 1951, the terrorists pulled off their most notorious operation of the campaign – the assassination of the British high commissioner, Sir Henry Gurney. The terrorists ambushed Sir Henry on the road to Fraser's Hill, a rest station where British officers and officials could get away from the heat and humidity of the Malayan plains. The road was steep and winding for the last 20 miles to the station and was bordered by thick jungle and, in some places, high cliffs. The heavily armed terrorist force chose a 200-yard section of this part of the road as their killing zone and settled down to wait.

At about lunchtime, some 27 hours after the ambush was set, Sir Henry's motorcade came in sight. When it left the capital, Kuala Lumpur, the convoy had consisted of an armored car, a radio vehicle, an unarmored Landrover, and the high commissioner's Rolls-Royce. Unfortunately, the radio truck had broken down en route and the armored car had stopped to help, leaving the limousine only lightly guarded.

As the convoy reached the ambush site, the terrorists opened fire, making short work of the escort before turning their attention to the official car. Trapped in the vehicle in a hail of gunfire, Sir Henry opened the door, possibly to try to make cover. He was killed instantly. Only the arrival of the armored car, machine guns blazing, saved his wife and his private secretary from the same fate. The high commissioner's assassination stunned Malaya.

Soon, the terrorists again struck in spectacular fashion. On October 8, the mail train from Johore to Kuala Lumpur struck a terrorist mine near Johore Bharu. The explosion derailed the train, killing the driver and wounding two railwaymen and three passengers. That same autumn, the terrorists chalked up their first British female fatality, ambushing a British tin miner's wife on the Taiping to Selama road.

TRH Pictures

Derailing trains was a tactic of the terror campaign of the Malayan Races' Liberation Army (MRLA).

Some attacks were particularly brutal. On November 25, with her parents away in Kuala Lumpur, a plantation owner's daughter was out for a ride in the family Landrover with the estate cook. Terrorists sprang an ambush, shooting the girl through the head. She was only two years old.

Although the insurgency continued for a further nine years, the end of 1951 marked a turning point. Until then the terrorists had been effective. Now, with the guerrillas starved of food and support from the population and suffering high numbers of casualties, the government went on the attack. Using a combination of conventional military force and psychological warfare, including leaflet drops and broadcasting propaganda from aircraft, the British closed in. Many guerrillas turned their backs on communism and accepted British bribes to turn in their fellow terrorists. Malaya was granted independence from Britain on August 31, 1957, and it was only the tenacity of the few remaining hardline guerrillas that kept the emergency in place until 1960.

Chris Marshall

SEE ALSO: TERRORISM IN FRENCH ALGERIA; TERRORISM IN CYPRUS; TERROR AGAINST THE FRENCH IN INDOCHINA; TERROR IN NAMIBIA; TERROR CAMPAIGNS IN PORTUGUESE AFRICA.

FURTHER READING

- Clutterbuck, Richard. *The Long, Long War: Counterinsurgency in Malaya and Vietnam*. New York: Praeger, 1966.
- Dewar, Michael. *Brush Fire Wars: Minor Campaigns of the British Army since 1945*. London: Hale, and New York: St. Martin's Press, 1984.
- Stubbs, Richard. *Hearts and Minds in Guerrilla Warfare: The Malayan Emergency 1948-1960*. New York: Oxford University Press, 1989.

TERRORISM IN KENYA

The Mau Mau was a secret society that led a terrorist campaign against colonial rule in the British African colony of Kenya. Like many secret societies in Africa, the Mau Mau was based on a single tribe and evoked supernatural powers.

It is unclear how ancient the Mau Mau was or what its name actually meant. However, by the late 1940s, the society had a political message. It taught that the white farmers who had grown prosperous through raising cash crops had built their success on the backs of the Kikuyu tribesmen. Many unemployed men, able to see the wealth of the whites, joined the movement.

MAGICAL OATHS

The main increase in Mau Mau numbers came in 1949, as the society carried out an aggressive recruitment campaign. Kikuyu were persuaded, or forced, to take an oath, or *thenge*, in a ceremony that often included ritual self-scarring with knives. The recruits swore to carry out Mau Mau instructions on pain of death at the hands of supernatural beasts. The violent deaths of a few recruits served to convince any uncertain tribesmen.

The rising number of initiation ceremonies led the Kenyan colonial government to ban the Mau Mau in 1950. However, by 1952, the society had organized a guerrilla army and begun a campaign of violence. The aim was to overthrow the colonial regime and replace it with Kikuyu supremacy over neighboring tribes.

The forests and mountains north of Nairobi were home to around 12,000 Mau Mau guerrillas, mostly armed with traditional spears and clubs. About 30,000 tribesmen in villages formed the "passive wing," which sent supplies to the guerrillas. Most of the other Kikuyu were bound by magical oath to support the movement. In Nairobi, a central committee gathered information, coordinated activity, and issued orders to the guerrillas. The command structure was loose and relied on obedience to the oath for its efficiency.

During 1951 and 1952, the Mau Mau carried out attacks on isolated white-owned farms and murdered several Kikuyu who opposed the movement. These attacks became so frequent that the government declared a state of emergency in October 1952. At first the authorities could do little because of the lack of troops and poor intelligence work. In January 1953, the Ruck family (husband, wife, and six-year-old son) were hacked to death, an act which outraged the settlers.

In response, the colonial regime imprisoned the leaders of the Kenya African Union, the legal political party representing the Kikuyu. It also increased the British military strength in Kenya, called up native home defense forces, and strengthened the police. In 1953, a conventional military campaign against the Mau Mau began but achieved little. The Mau Mau, which now numbered up to 15,000 fighters, proved an elusive enemy and suffered few losses. Mau Mau guerrilla attacks on villages continued, and the bodies of victims were often mutilated in ritual fashion.

In early 1954, the new British commander, Sir George Erskine, introduced counterinsurgency tactics used in Malaya. He set up propaganda and psychological warfare staffs, improved intelligence gathering, and ensured cooperation between the military and police.

The first major mission under this new initiative was Operation Anvil in April 1954. The Kikuyu population of Nairobi, some 30,000 people, were rounded up and interrogated. Hooded informants were used to identify Mau Mau activists, who were placed in detention camps. Operation Anvil effectively broke the central committee and ended coordinated activity between the different groups of Mau Mau guerrillas.

KEY FACTS

- The sudden intensification of Mau Mau violence in October 1952 caused the British to declare a state of emergency.
- In four years, the Mau Mau suffered 11,500 casualties. The security forces lost 63 Europeans, 3 Asians, and 524 Africans. Some 8,000 indigenous Kenyans were killed in the terror campaigns.

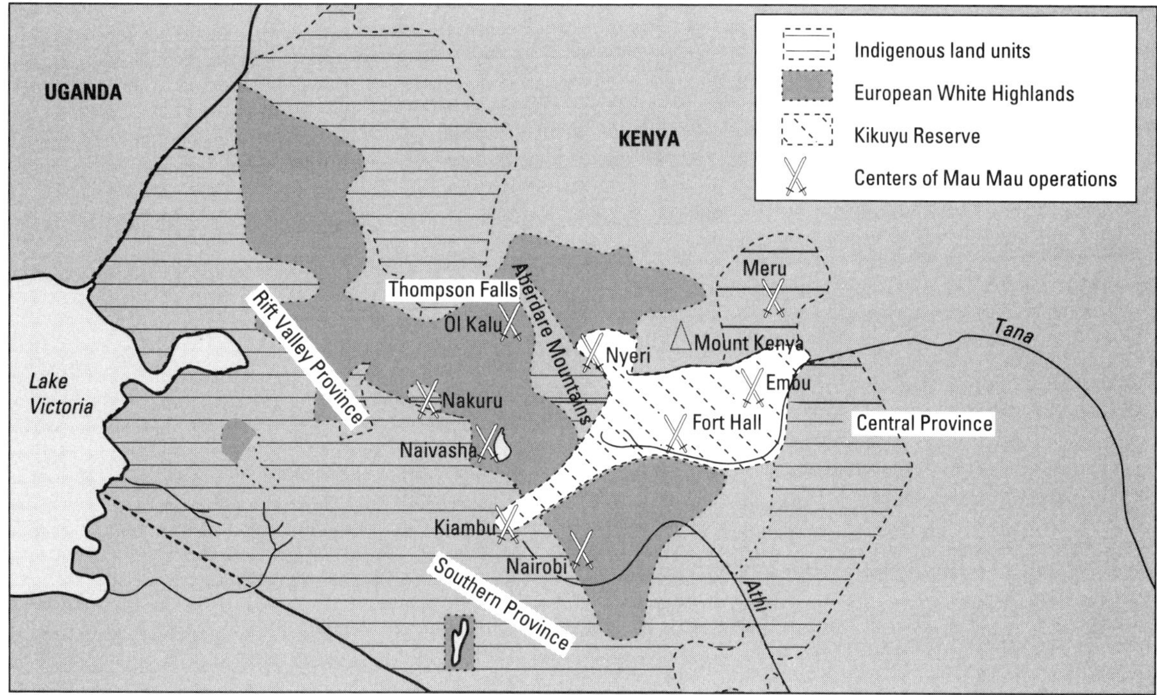

Kikuyu reservations and areas of Mau Mau activity.

Meanwhile, the British declared the denser forests of Kenya to be war zones in which the security forces could shoot on sight, and they often did. The Kikuyu villages were searched for Mau Mau supporters and surrounded by stockades. These measures seriously reduced the Mau Mau's ability to continue its terrorist campaign. Another effective tool was the introduction of cleansing oaths to counter the Mau Mau oath of obedience. Once the British hired witch doctors to cleanse large numbers of Kikuyu in this way, the Mau Mau lost its base of unwilling support.

CLEARING THE FORESTS

In 1955, British military raids forced the guerrillas to split into small groups and flee the forest, making them easier to eliminate. Attempts were made to negotiate surrenders. Captured Mau Mau leader, General China, persuaded guerrillas to surrender and 1,200 members of the passive wing were arrested. There were allegations of torture brought against the security forces. A total of 430 detainees were shot "trying to escape," and over 1,000 executions had been carried out by 1956.

The Mau Mau was also faced with "counter gangs," made up of native soldiers and cleansed Mau Mau fighters who posed as Mau Mau to locate guerrillas. They successfully made contact with the guerrillas that the large-scale sweeps missed. These tactics had effectively destroyed the Mau Mau by November 1956.

Kenya gained its independence in 1963 under Jomo Kenyatta, who had been arrested as a leading member of the Kenya African Union during the crisis. Kenyatta, a Kikuyu, rapidly established his tribe in power, though without the radical land policies of the Mau Mau.

John Finlayson

SEE ALSO: TERRORISM IN CYPRUS; TERRORISM IN MALAYA; BRITISH COUNTERTERROR IN THE ERA OF DECOLONIZATION.

FURTHER READING

- Barnett, D. *Karari Njama: Mau Mau from Within.* London: MacGibbon and Kee, 1966; New York: Monthly Review Press, 1970.
- Edgerton, Robert B. *Mau Mau: An African Crucible.* London: Tauris, 1990; New York: Ballantine, 1991.
- Majdalani, F. *State of Emergency: The Full Story of Mau Mau.* Boston: Houghton Mifflin, 1963; London: Transworld, 1964.

TERROR IN ZIMBABWE (RHODESIA)

On November 11, 1965, the British colony of Rhodesia (now Zimbabwe) declared itself independent. Prime Minister Ian Smith declared that "never in a thousand years" would he accept black majority rule, although only five percent of Rhodesia's population was white. As a result, African nationalists set up two terrorist groups to oppose white rule. The Zimbabwe People's Revolutionary Army (ZIPRA), based in Zambia, drew strength from the small but powerful Ndebele community. The Zimbabwe African National Liberation Army (ZANLA), based in Mozambique, was based on the larger Shona tribe.

Differences between the two forces soon became apparent, although their targets were initially similar. China armed and influenced ZANLA. The Soviet Union armed and trained ZIPRA. Both groups launched guerrilla attacks on white-owned farms and police bases between 1966 and 1969, but were all but annihilated by the Rhodesian security forces.

After peace talks failed in 1971, ZANLA hit white targets again. They attacked a farm on December 21, 1972, wounding a three-year-old girl. The Rhodesians countered by launching Operation Hurricane and, by September 1975, claimed 651 guerrillas deaths at a cost of 73 fatalities among their own troops. In June 1975, when neighboring Mozambique became independent, ZANLA gained safe bases from which to attack eastern Rhodesia. By 1978, an estimated 4,645 ZANLA and 953 ZIPRA recruits were active in Rhodesia.

Whites were not the only targets of ZANLA. The terrorists also wished to control the Shona population and began a campaign to intimidate villagers. For example, on August 13, 1973, in the Kandeya area, a headman was shot dead in front of his assembled villagers. The terrorists also committed other atrocities including bayonetting, stabbing, or beating villagers to death, shooting parents in front of their children, blowing up country buses, hacking off fingers and lips, severing feet, and inflicting burns.

KEY FACTS

- During 1965-79, 1,300 members of the security forces and 9,000 civilians died in the terror campaigns. However, the estimated death toll of guerrillas was far higher – about 10,000.
- One of the worst ZANLA terrorist incidents was the massacre of 27 tea-plantation workers in the Honde Valley on December 20, 1976.

USING TORTURE TO ENFORCE SUPPORT

ZANLA lectured people on nationalist aims at compulsory rallies called *pungwes*, reinforcing speeches with calculated terror. They tortured or killed suspected pro-government black Africans. In the Mt. Darwin District in 1973, for example, terrorists beat two wives of an alleged informer and shot his third wife. Terrorists shot another headman, killed his cattle – the wealth of the village – and burnt down every hut. On April 18, 1974, in the Madziwa area, terrorists entered a beerhall. They had a "death list" of those sentenced to die for helping the security forces. Two men answered when their names were called out. Their hands were tied and they were beaten to death before the crowd of 150 people.

The terrorists also attacked rival nationalists, passing strangers, and even people using skin-lightening cosmetics. The police registered 2,751 such killings by 1979. Most people executed at *pungwes* were denounced by *mujibas*, local youths who helped the guerrillas. Many *mujibas* abused their authority by raping, stealing, or killing. The terrorists also killed missionaries and teachers and abducted thousands of pupils for guerrilla training. At night the terrorists forced people to demolish bridges, dig up roads, and cut telephone and electricity lines. Through terror, ZANLA came to dominate the countryside.

From their bases, ZANLA guerrillas regularly raided the 6,000 economically crucial white-owned farms that covered nearly half the country. The terrorists ambushed white farming families, attacked their homes,

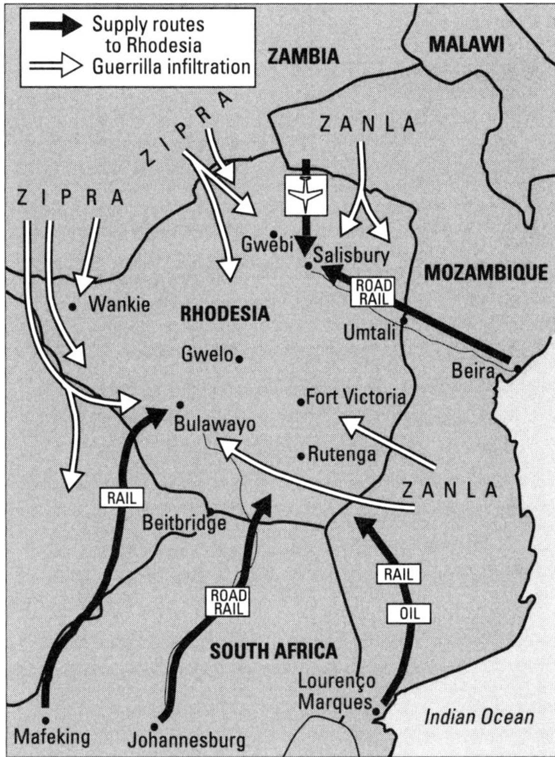

The terrorist group ZIPRA was based in Zambia; ZANLA operated from Mozambique.

burned their barns, and stole their cattle. They intimidated or killed black farm workers and burned down their huts. As a result, people abandoned hundreds of the most exposed white farms.

The guerrillas ambushed roads and railroads, and mortared Umtali city, but police intelligence made urban terrorism rare. One exception was a bomb that killed 11 black Africans in the capital, Salisbury. The most serious blow to white morale occurred when ZIPRA SAM-7 missiles downed two airliners in September 1978 and February 1979. In the first crash, terrorists shot ten women and children who survived.

HARSH GOVERNMENT COUNTERMEASURES

In May 1973, the Rhodesian security forces declared a no-go zone 190 miles inside the northeastern border and laid widespread minefields. From late 1973, they forcibly removed to protected villages people living in the areas most affected by terrorism in order to deny the guerrillas food, intelligence, and recruits.

In June 1974, the Rhodesians introduced fire forces. A fire force consisted of several helicopters, each carrying four people who would be dropped around a guerrilla sighting. Backed up by helicopter gunships, they would close in on the guerrillas and destroy them.

Rhodesian special forces also resorted to unconventional countermeasures. One unit, the Selous Scouts, instigated clashes between ZANLA and ZIPRA. The Grey's Scouts, a mounted unit, bred killer dogs to hunt down terrorists. Rhodesia's Central Intelligence Organization assassinated nationalist leaders in exile. Rhodesia's Special Air Service laid mines in neighboring countries. By 1976, the conflict was too expensive for any side to maintain. South Africa put pressure on the Rhodesian regime to come to a political settlement, and countries helping the guerrillas began to insist on a compromise.

A conference in Geneva between groups broke down in January 1977. War continued. More guerrillas entered Rhodesia from neighboring states, forcing white farmers to build security fences around their homes and to armor their vehicles. The whites also formed local self-defense militias. But the cost of these measures was immense and prime minister Smith conceded majority rule to moderate Africans in Rhodesia. Neither ZANLA nor ZIPRA leaders accepted this deal and continued their attacks.

In 1979, Britain sponsored a cease-fire, and elections followed in 1980. The new constitution included majority rule and safeguards for the white minority. Most of the black population voted along tribal lines. As the Shona was the largest tribe, ZANLA leader Robert Mugabe became president of Zimbabwe.

Bertrande Roberts

SEE ALSO: TERRORISM IN NAMIBIA; TERROR CAMPAIGNS IN PORTUGUESE AFRICA.

FURTHER READING

- Charlton, Michael. *The Last Colony in Africa.* Oxford and Cambridge, MA: Blackwell, 1990.
- Cilliers, J. K. *Counterinsurgency in Rhodesia.* London and Dover, NH: Croom Helm, 1985.
- Godwin, Peter, and Ian Hancock. *"Rhodesians Never Die."* Oxford and New York: Oxford University Press, 1993.

TERROR IN NAMIBIA

During World War I, South Africa conquered the neighboring German colony of South West Africa on behalf of the Allies. At the war's end, the League of Nations granted South Africa a mandate to govern the territory. In 1946, the League's successor, the United Nations, recommended that South Africa prepare the region for independence.

The South African government in Pretoria, however, continued to govern it as a part of their own country and introduced *apartheid* – the system of legal racial discrimination. This attitude antagonized many and, in October 1966, the United Nations' General Assembly recommended that the mandate be revoked. In June 1968, the assembly renamed the territory Namibia, instructing South Africa to grant independence. Finally, in July 1971, the International Court of Justice declared South Africa's presence there illegal.

Pretoria's control was also challenged by Namibian nationalist movements, most notably the South West Africa People's Organization (SWAPO), founded in April 1960 and drawing most of its members from the Ovambo tribe. The South African authorities soon took repressive measures against SWAPO. Many members fled to Tanzania to organize the People's Liberation Army of Namibia, which led an insurgency combining guerrilla warfare, terrorism, and political activity.

In late 1965, the first trained insurgents set up camps in Ovamboland. These activists attacked security forces and pro-government blacks, and sabotaged installations. In 1966, SWAPO also carried out a number of terrorist attacks on white civilians. In response, Pretoria arrested and convicted 37 Namibians for supporting terrorism. From the first clash with South African forces on August 26, 1966 until 1975, the insurgents made little progress militarily. But their political activities gradually made progress, as SWAPO exploited disquiet over *apartheid.*

SWAPO's prospects improved after 1975 when the Portuguese withdrew from Angola. Independent Angola allowed SWAPO to use that country as a base. By now SWAPO was gaining greater international recognition, including a declaration of support from the United Nations in December 1976. SWAPO gained more recruits, got better weapons from the Soviet Union, and received better training by Cuban and Eastern Bloc personnel in Angola. From 1975, SWAPO tried to extend its campaign beyond Ovamboland.

While SWAPO used traditional guerrilla techniques, they also sometimes resorted to terrorist attacks. According to South African reports, on December 20, 1976, terrorists shot dead a white farmer's wife and her 12-year-old son near Grootfontein, northern Namibia. Moreover, on New Year's Eve, 1976, in Oshandi, Ovamboland in northern Namibia, ten terrorists fired at shoppers, killing two civilians.

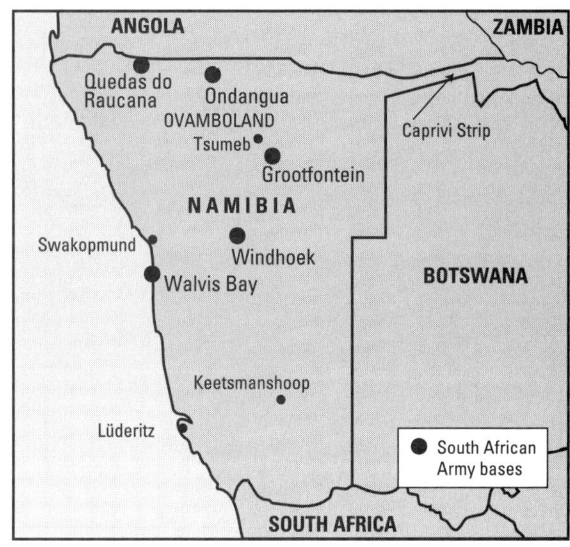

South African army bases in Namibia and the Ovamboland region where SWAPO was active.

KEY FACTS

- In 1966, SWAPO's military strength numbered about 1,000, rising to 10,000 by 1978.
- During the fighting, SWAPO lost 10,000 troops, compared to 700 losses for the security forces.
- In 1980, the Pretoria regime reported 1,175 incidents of what it termed "terrorism" in Namibia.

Associated Press

South African troops in the Caprivi Strip view the corpses of suspected SWAPO guerrillas in August 1978, following a counterinsurgency mission.

South African troops responded with counterinsurgency operations, attacking SWAPO bases in southern Angola. These missions were effective, with SWAPO allegedly suffering ten times as many dead as the security forces. Pretoria also sought to undermine the guerrillas by promising Namibia eventual independence. The insurgents also failed to extend their influence beyond Ovamboland, since ethnic groups other than the Ovambo did not see SWAPO as liberators.

In early 1988, SWAPO again resorted to terrorism as part of their insurgency campaign. On February 19, 1988, the insurgents exploded a bomb in a bank at Oshakati, in Ovamboland, killing 21 civilians.

In 1988, the Soviet Union and the United States sponsored a settlement linking a South African withdrawal from Namibia to a Cuban and Eastern Bloc withdrawal from Angola. In the November 1989 elections, SWAPO's political wing won the most votes, albeit not an absolute majority, and in March 1990 SWAPO formed the first government of the new independent state of Namibia.

Henry Longstreet

SEE ALSO: TERROR IN COLONIAL CONQUESTS; TERRORISM IN KENYA; TERROR IN ZIMBABWE (RHODESIA); TERROR CAMPAIGNS IN PORTUGUESE AFRICA; STATE-SPONSORED TERRORISM.

FURTHER READING

- Beckett, Ian, and John Pimlott, eds. *Armed Forces and Modern Counterinsurgency.* London: Croom Helm, and New York: St. Martin's Press, 1985.
- Herbstein, Denis, and John A. Everson. *The Devils Are Among Us: The War for Namibia.* Atlantic Highlands, NJ. and London: Zed Books, 1989.
- Leys, Colin. *Namibia's Liberation Struggle: The Two Edged Sword.* Athens, OH: Ohio University Press, and London: J. Curry, 1995.

TERROR CAMPAIGNS IN PORTUGUESE AFRICA

Portugal was the first European colonial power to arrive in Africa and, with Spain, the last to withdraw. Portuguese navigators reached each of the three principal colonies of Angola, Portuguese Guinea (now Guinea-Bissau), and Mozambique by the end of the fifteenth century.

The Portuguese claimed that, uniquely, their imperialism was based not upon racial discrimination but upon educating the local people to take their place in Portuguese society. In 1951, they named the three colonies overseas provinces of Portugal but, in reality, the policy was exploitative. Back in 1878, the Portuguese had replaced slavery with a contract labor system. They forced local farmers to grow cash crops for the government rather than food crops for themselves. As an added insult, education was not commonly made available.

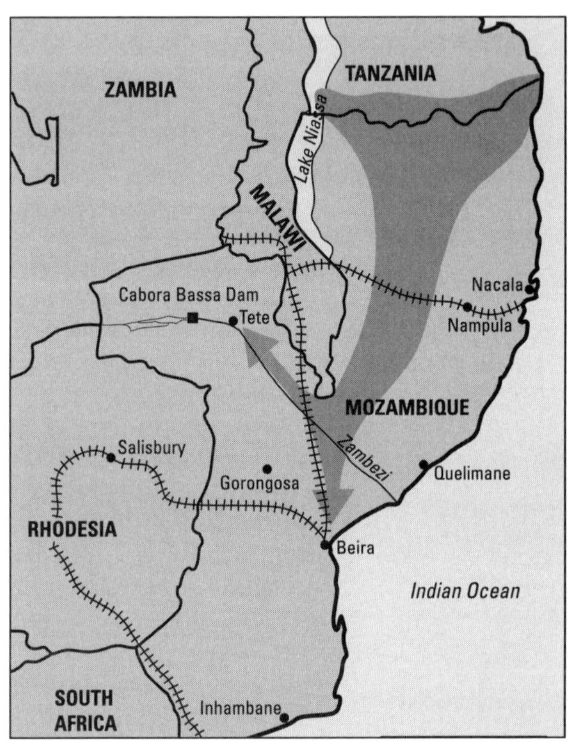

Spurred on by the example of Angolan nationalists, the Mozambique Liberation Front (FRELIMO) advanced from 1964-75.

ANGOLAN MILITANTS ATTACK PLANTATIONS

Initially, nationalist groups were content to pursue economic or social objectives, but by the late 1950s, meager social progress and the collapse of Belgian authority in the Congo gave rise to a growing militancy. The trigger for violence came in 1961 in Angola. Militants attacked Portuguese cotton plantations in protest over laws forcing farmers to grow cash crops.

KEY FACTS

- The liberation movements in the Portuguese African colonies were divided up along tribal lines.
- Five weeks of atrocities started the revolt in Angola in 1961 – 267 civilians, mainly Europeans, were killed. A further 72 were listed as missing.
- Random violence was rare. In general, terrorism toward civilians took the form of outbursts against tribes allied with the Portuguese.

Meanwhile, an opponent of the then dictator of Portugal, António Salazar, hijacked a Portuguese liner and tried to bring it to Luanda, the Angolan capital. The world press hurried to Angola. On February 4, 1961, three bands of armed Angolans attacked Luanda prison and two police barracks, possibly for the benefit of the press. The militants tried to free African prisoners detained for minor offenses. Security forces beat off the attackers, but there were many deaths.

Topham Picturepoint

By 1971, the Angolan FNLA had up to 8,000 troops, ready to fight a guerrilla war for independence.

The next day, at the funeral of the seven policemen killed, shooting broke out. In all, 36 Africans and eight members of the security forces died.

FULL-SCALE REVOLTS IN ANGOLA

A month later, on March 15, terrorists armed with machetes and cutlasses hacked to death 300 farmers, shopkeepers, and their families in the northern cotton plantations. They attacked Portuguese farms, houses, crops, and government property. Refugees shuttled out by aircraft described how the terrorists had butchered the Portuguese without regard to age or sex.

The division was not as simple as native Angolans against the Portuguese. There was much rivalry between nationalist Angolan groups, based on tribal differences. Many refugees reported how the local African population had fought side by side with the Portuguese against the terrorists.

On April 13, 1961, terrorist violence went from bad to worse. Several thousand rebels launched an attack on Ucua village, 100 miles north of Luanda, killing 13 Portuguese. A reporter described how the terrorists were armed with cutlasses inscribed with UPA – standing for the Union of Angolan Peoples – and how they attacked "as if demon-possessed, dancing and singing and shouting."

UPA (later the National Front for the Liberation of Angola, or FNLA) leader Holden Roberto said that the Angolan uprising was "an expression of desperation against Portuguese terrorism over the past 500 years." But he added, "We are deeply sorry that women and children have been killed." Holden Roberto stated that the attacks were the work of laborers rebelling against the Portuguese forced labor system. He admitted that some of his members had taken part but insisted they had done so against orders. The revolt caught the Portuguese army by surprise, but it easily suppressed the rebels. Airpower was used ferociously, killing an estimated 50,000 Africans by September.

The uprising prompted the Portuguese to make concessions. They abolished compulsory cash crop cultivation. They replaced the desire to "civilize" the natives with a declaration that all local people in overseas provinces were equal to Europeans as

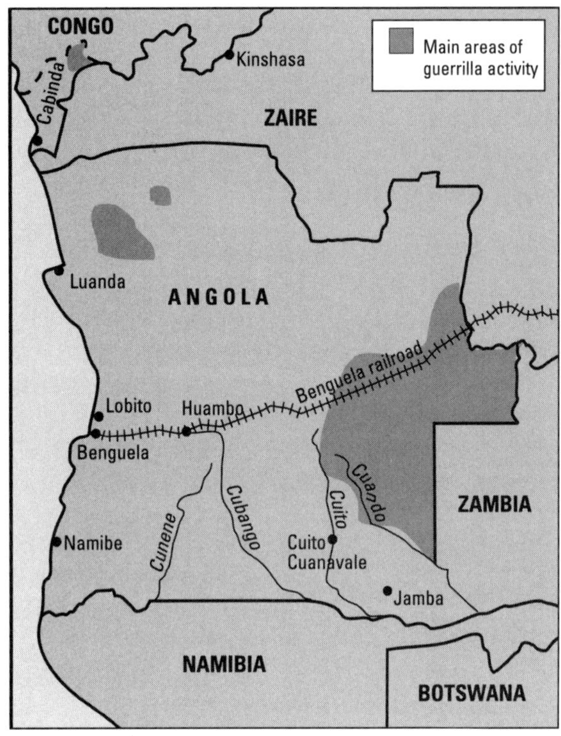

Angola, showing the main areas of guerrilla activity.

Portuguese citizens. But insurgency still spread to Portuguese Guinea in 1963 and to Mozambique in 1964.

GUINEA STRUGGLES TO BREAK FREE

The main insurgent group in Portuguese Guinea was the African Party for Independence for Guinea and Cape Verde (PAIGC). The group's targets were primarily the Portuguese military. On January 25, 1963, the terrorists attacked Portuguese barracks in the southeast of the country. They killed 20 army troops. On March 10, PAIGC units killed eight Portuguese troops and, on May 22, they shot down two aircraft. One pilot died in the crash; the terrorists captured the other.

The Portuguese answer to the insurgents was to put more and more troops on the ground. From 1,000 troops in 1961, government forces grew to 30,000 by 1967. The Portuguese intensified counterinsurgency effort centered on concentrating local populations in defended villages. When General Antonio de Spínola took over the military command in Guinea in 1968, he initiated a coordinated "hearts and minds" strategy to win over the local people. Adopting the slogan "Better Guinea," Spínola based his program on the villages and used the army to build 15,000 houses, 164 schools, 40 hospitals, 163 fire stations, and 86 water points.

MOZAMBIQUE STEPS UP ITS CAMPAIGN

As in Guinea, the Mozambique Liberation Front (FRELIMO) started off in 1964 with military targets, such as a rocket attack on the Cabora Bassa dam in Mozambique. But during late 1973 and early 1974, FRELIMO terrorists shifted emphasis, mounting more than 40 operations against civilian targets. Violent acts included mortar attacks on villages, hostage-taking, and the downing of a private aircraft, killing six. According to the Portuguese, FRELIMO killed more than 300 civilians during 1973, wounded a further 554, and kidnapped 1,768 more. The Portuguese increased troop numbers from 16,000 in 1964 to more than 60,000 in 1974. They took a more active stand against the insurgents after 1968. In 1973, the army was accused of a massacre in which more than 400 African civilians were said to have died. This claim was denied, but some deaths almost certainly occurred.

In the face of an increasingly unpopular campaign at home and in Africa, the Portuguese granted independence to Portuguese Guinea (as Guinea-Bissau) in September 1974, to Mozambique in June 1975, and to Angola in November 1975. In military terms, neither the terrorists nor the authorities had won or lost. It was a military coup in Portugal that destroyed the country's "historic mission" in Africa.

Ian F. W. Beckett

SEE ALSO: TERROR AGAINST THE FRENCH IN INDOCHINA; TERRORISM IN KENYA; TERRORISM IN ZIMBABWE (RHODESIA).

FURTHER READING

- Beckett, Ian and John Pimlott, eds. *Armed Forces and Modern Counter-Insurgency.* London: Croom Helm, and New York: St. Martin's Press, 1985.
- Bruce, Neil. *The Last Empire.* Newton Abbot, Devon and North Pomfret, VT: David and Charles, 1975.
- Henriksen, Thomas H. *Revolution and Counter-Revolution: Mozambique's War of Independence. 1964-1974,* Westport, CT: Greenwood Press, 1983.
- Porch, Douglas. *The Portuguese Armed Forces and the Revolution.* London: Croom Helm, and Stanford, CA: Hoover Institute Press, 1977.

THE GENERAL BACKGROUND TO MODERN TERRORISM

Popperfoto

March 1948: a small Arab boy looks through the bullet-holed window of a bus attacked by Jewish terrorists.

THE GENERAL BACKGROUND TO MODERN TERRORISM: *Introduction*

There are many reasons why individuals or political groups turn to terrorism. Equally, there are many methods that terrorists may use to attack targets or to organize their groups. In order to understand terrorism, it is important to be able to recognize these different aspects - which may, of course, run into each other in various ways. For example, a nationalist may also be a social revolutionary or a religious extremist, as in the case of Hizb'allah in Lebanon.

The most important types of terrorists are those that are fighting for a cause that strikes a chord in many hearts. Thus, nationalists or religious fundamentalists may find themselves representing a cause that has mass appeal and to which it is easy to enlist recruits. But equally, terrorists that represent a desire for social change, be it of a general revolutionary nature, or a single issue such as a desire to end abortion, may find that they have a ready-made constituency of like-minded supporters. And although terrorists are usually thought of as being left-wing and revolutionary in intent, there have been many examples of terrorists acting from a right-wing position. Sometimes such terrorists aim to destabilize a state, but more frequently – as in Latin America – they act as hit squads against left-wing revolutionaries and terrorists.

The methods that terrorists use are often defined, to a large extent, by how they are set up and how they identify the audience that they wish to impress or to persuade. One key factor is whether terrorists are sponsored by a state: if they are, this defines and limits their actions, but also gives them access to large amounts of weapons, ready cash and transport to wherever they will be operating. Another key factor is whether they are operating in a rural or an urban environment, for these offer quite different challenges and opportunities. Then there is the target audience – do the terrorists want to make a splash on the international stage, or is this pointless, with only a domestic audience worth influencing?

Many terrorist groups have found it effective to use certain organizational methods, such as independent cells each with a handful of activists. Equally, there are only a certain number of ways of raising funds. And there are also only a limited range of techniques that terrorists can use to gain public attention.

The favourite terrorist technique has always been bombing. It enables the activist to plant a device and then get away before the bomb does its deadly work. There are growing fears that terrorists may use weapons more deadly than a bomb packed with conventional explosive - either some kind of chemical or nuclear device. Either of these could be fired using a rocket or mortar, two means of delivery favored by terrorists.

However, bombs left to explode in a city centre do not necessarily gain the terrorist the exposure that other techniques can. Hijacking an aircraft, something that became a common occurrence in the late 1960s and early 1970s, automatically gave terrorists the ear of the world's media. Hostage-taking, too, sets off a running story that can stay as a headline for weeks. Last, assassination of key political figures also guarantees extensive media coverage. Some terrorists are so committed to their cause that they are prepared to die as suicide bombers. Such attacks can also have wide effects, and are undeniably effective.

The final aspect to terrorism considered as a phenomenon of the modern world is the mind both of the terrorist and of the victim. It is hard to find abnormal psychological traits that link all terrorists – many of them are level-headed operatives who believe that terrorism is the best way to achieve their goals. Nevertheless, the stress of operating in an enclosed world, often lacking contacts outside the terrorist cell, does tend to impose a certain pattern of behavior. Studying these patterns can give those combating terrorism a vital edge in the struggle.

Victims tend to behave in certain patterns too, mainly because they are shocked and bewildered by the train of events in which they have been unwittingly trapped. They are not the real targets of the terrorist - they are often merely the route by which the terrorist intends to influence the real target. The fate of the innocent victims of terror attack is often deeply shocking, and they or their families may never recover from it. ■

CHAPTER FIVE

Types of Terrorism

Terrorism has become such an inescapable fact of life that it now falls into clear categories. Some terrorists are committed to a single cause such as anti-abortion, but far right political views or religious zeal motivates others. Terrorism crosses borders, too, with groups carrying out acts of violence on people and property in countries other than their own. Governments are known to sponsor some terrorists, although many groups operate alone. Terrorists organize themselves differently, depending on whether their base is urban or rural, just as the presence of terrorist violence affects citydwellers and countryfolk in dissimilar ways.

CATEGORIES OF TERROR

Many analysts have attempted to classify terrorism. There are four common types or categories into which terrorism and terrorists can be divided: first, by ideological type; second, by the nature of the terrorist's goals; third, by the setting of terrorist violence – by the nature of their targets, and the terrain over which they operate; and last, by the historical origins of terrorist groups.

IDEOLOGY OF TERRORISM

Ideology, the body of ideas that a political group adopts, is a basic method of categorizing terrorists. However, ideology can prove highly misleading as an analytical tool. For example, the early 1970s Red Army Faction terrorist group in Germany could be categorized as Marxist in ideology. They used the language of class analysis, arguing that society is divided by its economic system into classes, a key element of Marxism. However, the Red Army Faction did not attempt to organize the workers into a mass political movement, which Karl Marx would have regarded as the main point of being a Marxist. It is, therefore, not particularly useful to categorize the Red Army Faction as Marxist in anything except rhetoric.

KEY FACTS

- The linguistic theorist Noam Chomsky, writing with Edward S. Herman, identified two categories of terrorism – *wholesale* by fascist regimes and *retail* by insurgents.
- The first attempts to identify terrorism by type were made by Thomas P. Thornton in 1964. He distinguished between enforcement terror and agitational terror.
- The example of the Irish nationalist Michael Collins illustrates the difficulty intrying to categorize terrorism. He fought against the British in Ireland, then fought for the Irish Free State against his former terrorist comrades.

However, the Red Army Faction was clearly a revolutionary political movement, since it aimed to overthrow the existing social order and replace it with something else. But this kind of thinking is not the sole property of left-wingers. The Militia movement in the United States has a revolutionary intent. It objects to the secular tradition of American politics, in which a person's religious and moral views are a matter for their own conscience, and not for government legislation. The Militias, in that respect, are alien intruders on the American political landscape.

Categorizing by ideology is also a complicated task. An ideology can be a political one, such as Marxism-Leninism, or a religious one, such as the fundamentalist Christianity that motivates members of the Militias. Religious dogma is highly political. Apart from such well-known cases as Islamic Jihad in the Middle East, Catholic Irish nationalists established the breakaway Provisional Irish Republican Army (IRA) after a Marxist-influenced leadership took control of the original movement's governing Army Council.

The tangles caused by attempts to categorize terrorism by ideology reach their most extreme form in dealing with the Middle East. Two strands have always coexisted, often uneasily, in Arab nationalism. There have been secular Arab nationalists, such as Gamal Abdel Nasser of Egypt or Hafez Assad of Syria, for whom Arab identity is defined by geography and language. There have also been religious Arab nationalists, such as the Muslim Brotherhood founded in 1928, at one time including the PLO's Yassir Arafat among its members, who regard Islam a vital part of Arab culture. Secular nationalists with Marxist politics from the Popular Front for the Liberation of Palestine planted the bomb in Jerusalem on February 20, 1969, which killed two supermarket shoppers. A devout Muslim convinced that he would awaken in paradise carried out the suicide bombing of the U.S. Marine Corps barracks in Beirut in October 1983. Yet all these terrorists shared a common ideology opposing Western influence in the Middle East.

Hulton Getty Picture Collection

The French Jacobin leader Robespierre operates a guillotine in an anti-revolutionary caricature. The Reign of Terror in France in 1793-94 falls into the goal-oriented category of repressive terror.

Despite the complexities of terrorist ideologies, however, ideology does play a role in distinguishing types of terrorism. Some accommodation may be possible with a nationalist terrorist group such as the Basques of ETA (Fatherland and Liberty). The Spanish regime's granting of greater autonomy to the Basque provincial administration appeased all but the most hardline nationalists. A left-wing revolutionary group aiming to overthrow capitalism will be less likely to find common ground with a government.

GOALS OF TERRORISTS

The goals of a terrorist to an extent overlap with the ideologies he or she may follow. The ideology of a revolutionary terrorist specifically includes the overthrow of the established order. The nationalist terrorist will be working to achieve self-determination for his national group or region. A revolutionary nationalist terrorist, such as a member of Colombia's M-19 movement, will be working to achieve both of these specific aims.

The advantage of categorizing by goals allows a distinction between terror sponsored or conducted by a state and terror against a state. The Reign of Terror during the French Revolution in 1793-94 was the means the Committee of Public Safety used to destroy any possible alternative to the revolutionary regime. It had a repressive effect on the political life of France. Likewise, death squads in El Salvador or Argentina terrorized civil rights groups and labor organizations.

Categorizing terrorism by goals helps identify regimes that are terrorizing their citizens. The links between governments and death squads in Latin America are not always clear. But vigilantes who kill a regime's opponents arouse suspicion that they have been operating with official sanction.

There are drawbacks to categorizing by goals. Both the leftists of the Red Brigades and neo-Nazi racists seek to overthrow the state, a revolutionary aim. But they sit uneasily together in the same bracket, since the Red Brigades profess a rationalist ideology while the neo-Nazis draw inspiration from Nordic myths. The measures needed to deal with groups with such divergent ideologies requires different emphases, since their supporters are very different people.

TARGETS FOR TERRORIST VIOLENCE

Terrorists can also be categorized in terms of the setting in which they operate. The term setting, in the context of terrorism, refers to the types of victims terrorists target and the terrain in which they operate. Grouping terrorists by what they choose as their targets has been examined since the 1970s. Two types of targets emerged: attacks on carefully selected targets, and indiscriminate acts against random targets. An example of the first would be a kidnapping such as that of the CIA's Beirut station chief, William Buckley, in Lebanon in 1984. In this case, a vital member of the U.S. espionage establishment was seized by anti-Western Islamic fundamentalists. He was no doubt interrogated to gather intelligence information concerning networks of American agents active in Lebanon, and then killed to disrupt American intelligence efforts in the Middle East.

An example of the second type of terrorist targeting would be the Bologna, Italy, railroad station bombing in 1980, believed to be the work of neo-fascists. The bomb devastated the station, disrupting rail traffic, and causing more than 325 casualties. It created a climate of fear among Italians, and encouraged law-abiding citizens to press for more action to be taken in defense of social order. But the people who were its victims included a cross-section of the Italian people, and for all the terrorists knew, some could have sympathized with their ideology or goals.

It was thought, at one time, that leftist groups were more likely to be selective, while right-wing ones would be indiscriminate. However, research revealed that a terrorist group's politics made little difference in target selection.

Linked to categorizing by target is categorizing by the terrain in which terrorists operate. For example, Brazil's National Liberation Action group led by Carlos Marighela operated in an exclusively urban environment, while Peru's Shining Path guerrillas apply terror tactics in the countryside. This method of categorization could be extended to include whether a terrorist organization operates exclusively within its own country, like the Zapatistas in Mexico, or attacks targets internationally, as did the Japanese Red Army.

HISTORICAL ORIGINS OF TERRORISM

A final method of categorizing terrorism has been by the historical origins of the group. There is some overlap between this method and the attempt to categorize by ideology. Revolutionaries such as the Red Army Faction or the Weathermen emerged during the 1960s' student unrest.

Categorization by origin may prove useful in analysing terrorism in post-colonial struggles. The Tamil Tigers, Sikh nationalist terrorism, and terrorists in Kashmir each have their origin in post-colonial political boundaries cutting across ethnic groups. They have more in common with the Moro terrorists of the Philippines than the Moros have with their allies in the social revolutionary New Peoples' Army.

No system of categorization has proven ideal for makers of anti-terrorist policy. Those combating terrorism are devising increasingly complex methods of classification. In these models, terrorist groups are categorized by combinations of numerous variables. Hence, counterterrorist officials have classified the American Militia movement as a Religious-Indigenous-Nongovernment-Anarchist group. However, one problem may be that classification categories are conceived by people who are trying to put a stop to terrorism, rather than by those actually carrying out terrorism. Hence, while categorizing terrorist groups is an essential part of the fight against terrorism, it is difficult for such categorization to be definitive.

Michael Brewer

SEE ALSO: THE PROBLEMS OF DEFINING TERRORISM; TERROR IN THE FRENCH REVOLUTION 1789-1815; TYPES OF TERRORISM; BOMBING OPERATIONS; HIJACKING AND KIDNAPPING; ASSASSINATION; THE MINDSET OF THE TERRORIST; SUICIDE BOMBING; ARAB NATIONALISM AND THE RISE OF FATAH; TERROR IN LEBANON 1980-1987; TERRORISM IN BRAZIL; TERRORISM IN PERU; TERROR IN THE PHILIPPINES; TAMIL TIGER TERROR IN SRI LANKA; SIKH NATIONALIST TERRORISM IN INDIA; TERROR BY THE HOLY WARRIORS OF KASHMIR; STUDENT TERROR: THE WEATHERMEN; OKLAHOMA CITY BOMBING AND THE MILITIAS; RED ARMY FACTION: THE BAADER-MEINHOF GANG; RED BRIGADES; JAPANESE TERRORISM; BASQUE NATIONALIST TERROR: ETA; IRA: ORIGINS AND TERROR TO 1976; NATIONALIST TERROR IN NORTHERN IRELAND 1976-1996; ARGENTINE GOVERNMENT'S RESPONSES TO TERRORISM; BRAZILIAN GOVERNMENT'S RESPONSES TO TERRORISM; SALVADORAN GOVERNMENT'S RESPONSES TO TERRORISM.

FURTHER READING

- Flemming, Peter A., Michael Stohl, and Alex P. Schmid. "The Theoretical Utility of Typologies of Terrorism: Lessons and Opportunities," in *The Politics of Terrorism*, 3d ed., edited by Michael Stohl. New York: Marcel Dekker, Inc.,1988.
- Laqueur, Walter. *The Terrorism Reader*. New York: New American Library, 1978; London: Wildwood House, 1979.
- Livingstone, Marius H. *International Terrorism in the Contemporary World*. Westport, CT: Greenwood Press, 1978.
- Wardlaw, Grant. *Political Terrorism: Theory, Tactics, and Counter-Measures*. 2d ed. Cambridge and New York: Cambridge University Press, 1989.

NATIONALIST TERRORISM

Historically, nationalism is a relatively recent phenomenon, but a powerful one. Some historians argue that nationalism caused the two world wars. It has certainly created some of the most prominent terrorist movements.

The nations of modern Europe took shape during the fourteenth century. States then began to organize themselves along national lines. The English King Edward I (reigned 1272-1307), for example, ruled over a people who spoke a single language, shared the same religion, and had a common legal system. Uniting nations, however, was a slow process. At the same time, Catholic Spain was divided into three separate kingdoms, plus the Muslim enclave of Granada, and only became a united nation in 1512. The Austrian statesman Prince Metternich could legitimately describe Italy as "a geographical expression" in 1849, since it was still divided into seven separate states.

Nationalism only became a powerful political force during the nineteenth century. At this time, certain peoples, who lived in multinational states, identified themselves as a community entitled to choose their own leaders and make their own laws. Between 1820 and 1863, nationalist rebellions occurred in Greece, Poland, and Hungary. Also in the nineteenth century, nationalist political movements emerged in Britain (Irish and Scottish nationalists), Germany (Poles), and Austria (Hungarians, Poles, Italians, Czechs, and Slovaks), among other countries. This enthusiasm for the nation-state then spread to the European colonial empires in the third world in the twentieth century.

KEY FACTS

- Nationalist terrorism is often employed by people with a common identity to help achieve independence from a ruling power.
- Terrorist attacks are often dramatic. Two Sikh attacks on Indians took place on the same day, June 23, 1985. A bomb blew up an Air India flight over the Irish Sea killing 329 passengers and crew, and a bomb planted on an Air India plane at Tokyo's Narita airport killed two baggage handlers.

NATIONAL IDENTITY

The nation-state is the physical and political territory of a people who share a culture and live within a defined area. Nation-states are a product of the desire of a people to be self-determined – that is, able to determine their own form of government. Religion, language, economics, ethnicity, and geography are all factors that create a national identity. When a people comes to believe that its rulers are of a different nationality, the pressure for self-determination may propel the people into using any means necessary – including terrorism – to achieve this goal.

TERRORISM FOR POLITICAL CHANGE

Groups that use terrorism to nationalist ends aim to overturn the ruling elite by intimidating, scaring, or panicking the general public. The Provisional Irish Republican Army (IRA), for example, uses terror both in Ireland and Britain. It largely restricts its targets in Ireland to the security services, whom its members see as an army of occupation. The terrorists attack malls and business districts in Britain, however, to influence the people against the government's policy of keeping Northern Ireland a part of the United Kingdom.

Very few individuals are needed to conduct a nationalist terrorist campaign. The important motivator is the depth of their resentment of the ruling power. But the terrorists must achieve a great appeal within the nation they seek to represent in order to have any hope of success. The Algerian nationalists who fought the French in the 1950s numbered fewer than 400 activists in 1954. Thanks to the exploits of prominent nationalists like Ramdane Abane, who became a national hero, their numbers expanded to an army of some 20,000 based in Tunisia in 1956.

The Algerian war was one of national liberation as a colony sought independence from an imperial power.

Reuters

Palestinian religious and nationalist militants demonstrate against Israeli attacks on bases in southern Lebanon, May 1995.

In the aftermath of such wars of independence, nationalists can again turn to terrorism to accomplish their goals. For example, the Sikhs in India have a distinct religion from the Hindu majority. From this, a sense of a distinct national identity emerged among some Sikhs after India gained its independence from Britain in 1947. Sikh extremists turned to terrorism during the 1980s in an attempt to achieve independence.

Political movements of minorities often generate an extremist faction that turns to terror when constitutional politics is perceived to be a dead end. Terrorist groups committed to achieving independence from larger states have emerged in Europe during the postwar era. Basque nationalists in Spain, Corsicans and Bretons in France, and South Tyrolians in Italy have used bombing campaigns to influence the political process. None has yet succeeded in attaining self-determination, but terrorism is seen as the only defense of the nationalists against cultural oblivion.

Terror is also used by nationalist groups to oppose foreign influences in their countries. Many Latin American terrorist campaigns in the 1960s and 1970s were directed against the United States. While Castro's Communists in Cuba and the Sandinistas in Nicaragua used revolutionary rhetoric, they also identified themselves with anti-American nationalism.

NATIONALISM IN THE MIDDLE EAST

The Middle East has witnessed much nationalist-rooted terrorist activity. Zionism emerged in Europe during the nineteenth century at the same time as other minorities within the multinational empires, such as Habsburg Austria, asserted a right to national self-determination. Menachem Begin, the leader of the Israeli Likud party who was prime minister of Israel during 1977-83, was involved in terrorism. His followers participated in the bombing and shooting of British

Masked members of the Provisional IRA patrol the Falls Road area of Belfast during a Sinn Fein march in August 1979. Many Irish see its members as heroes of a national liberation struggle.

soldiers during the late 1940s. Begin's actions helped establish the independent state of Israel in 1948.

Nationalist terrorism was also used by the Palestine Liberation Organization (PLO) against Israel. The PLO organized itself along the lines of a government-in-exile. It had its own army, a system of political representation in the Palestine National Council, and a means of taxing Palestinians. These traditional instruments of state power proved indispensable to giving the PLO the moral authority of a state after signing the Declaration of Principles with Israel in 1993.

Nationalist terrorists direct their actions against the authority that stands in the way of their aspirations. Although government offices, miltary bases, officials, and soldiers are important targets, terrorism differs from guerrilla war in that it is the civilian population rather than the military which is the main target.. The Tamil Tigers, a Sri Lankan group, targeted public utilities, civilians, and government officials. Diplomats are also victims when the government they represent is seen to be opposed to self-determination. For example, because the British monarch, as Canada's head of state, had an interest in Canada's unity, in 1970 Quebec nationalists separatists kidnapped British trade commissioner James Cross.

INNOCENT VICTIMS

Besides attacking individuals directly connected with authority, nationalist terrorists also target businesspeople and even tourists. In Angola, the Front for the Liberation of the Enclave of Cabinda has attacked representatives of foreign corporations that deal with the national government. The United Liberation Front of Assam operates in India mainly by kidnapping and extortion. As long as peoples continue to seek self-determination, the danger remains that they will turn to terrorism to attain their goals.

Noemi Gal-Or

SEE ALSO: NATIONAL LIBERATION WARS AND TERROR; TERRORISM IN FRENCH ALGERIA; TERRORISM IN CYPRUS; TERROR AGAINST THE FRENCH IN INDOCHINA; TERRORISM IN MALAYA; TERROR CAMPAIGNS IN PORTUGUESE AFRICA; DOMESTIC VERSUS INTERNATIONAL TERROR; HIJACKING AND KIDNAPPING; ASSASSINATION; THE ORIGINS OF ARAB-JEWISH TERRORISM; ARAB NATIONALISM AND THE RISE OF FATAH; THE BIRTH OF THE PLO AND THE 1967 WAR; TERRORISM IN NICARAGUA; NATIONALIST TERRORISM IN POST-COLONIAL ASIA AND AFRICA; NATIONALIST TERRORISTS.

FURTHER READING

- Gilbert, Paul. *Terrorism, Security and Nationality.* New York: Routledge, 1994.
- Harris, Nigel. *National Liberation.* London: Penguin, 1992; Reno: University of Nevada Press, 1993.
- Moxon-Browne, Edward. *European Terrorism.* Aldershot, Hampshire: Dartmouth, 1993; New York: G. K. Hall, 1994.
- O'Brien, Conor Cruise. *Passion and Cunning: Essays of Nationalism, Terrorism and Revolution.* London: Weidenfeld and Nicolson, 1988; New York: Simon and Schuster, 1989.

REVOLUTIONARY TERRORISM

Terrorists seeking to overthrow a constitutional government as part of a program of social transformation can be called revolutionary terrorists. Left-wing political movements are the obvious ones to use revolutionary terrorism, but revolutionary politics are not restricted to the Left. The Nazi party in 1930s Germany was as much a revolutionary party as were the Communists.

Revolutionary terrorism has its roots in a political ideology, from the Marxist-Leninist thinking of the Left, to the fascists found on the Right. Both ideologies emerged in the first decades of the twentieth century. Each was influenced by the revolutionary socialists of the late nineteenth century, who are often numbered among the first revolutionary terrorists.

A COMMON WEAPON

Despite the differences in motivation and intention, terrorism is the common weapon for all these groups, based on the principle that actions speak louder than words. Revolutionary terrorism employs a vast arsenal of violence ranging from discriminate terrorism, such as political assassination, to the use of lethal indiscriminate tactics. Planting bombs in airplanes and market places, and introducing poison into food, the water supply, or the air are examples of methods designed to injure the general population.

Terrorist actions in themselves are revolutionary. They disrupt the social order, for an instant transforming it from an orderly group of people into a chaotic mass of individuals, each striving to escape the panic that surrounds a bomb blast or gunshot.

KEY FACTS

- Marxist revolutionaries do not believe in indiscriminate violence. Frederich Engels wrote that they should behave like soldiers and only kill those fighting against them.
- Revolutionary terrorists (such as the Red Brigades in Italy) use violence against constitutional democracies because they believe it is the only way to expose these regimes' repressive nature.

THE CHARACTER OF THE REVOLUTIONARY

Social hardships like unemployment and related poverty and racial or sexual discrimination cause people to join left-wing revolutionary political movements. The social system itself breeds revolution. The accident of birth can condemn an individual to an inferior education and a lifetime of poor housing and inadequate medical care. Those who benefit from the system live in good neighborhoods, have plenty to eat, and the money to enjoy a fulfilling social life. The revolutionary believes this system can be changed to eliminate or at least reduce the level of injustice. Left-wing revolutionary movements emphasize how new social forms can be created. People will have more influence over social conditions in the post-revolutionary world. The promise of this future motivates the revolutionary terrorist. The system itself is worth destroying by any means necessary.

The ability to see the system as an impersonal force victimizing working people aids the intention of the revolutionary terrorist to commit violent acts. A police officer becomes an individual who opposes any possibility of improving housing for thousands. A building full of government workers becomes a center for administering injustice. Police and government officials condemn themselves by assisting the system.

Right-wing revolutionaries find their motivation from another source. They often feel threatened by the left-wing view that working people all have the same political interests, regardless of nationality. In other cases, they fear the direction of social changes that give equal opportunities to women or people of a different race. A political system seen to support this kind of social agenda becomes a threat. As with the left-wing revolutionary, the people carrying out or aiming at these social changes acquire the characteristics of an impersonal, even non-human, force.

Hulton Getty Picture Collection

French writer Regis Debray faces trial in 1967 for aiding revolutionary guerrilla groups in Bolivia.

THE OPTION OF TERRORISM

Social revolutionaries have turned to terrorism in many countries. It is frequently a response to specific circumstances, and normally carried out by small groups of conspirators. But an individual's actions against some perceived injustice can be construed as revolutionary terrorism. A prime example of an individual terrorist is Theodore Kaczynski, thought to be the so-called Unabomber. Kaczynski waged a private mail-bomb campaign in his fight against the U.S. establishment.

Nationalist terrorism has a clear purpose, but the aims of revolutionary terrorism are often also present within a movement for national liberation. Radical social change may coexist in the same political movement as the struggle for national self-determination. For example, the Palestinian Liberation Organization (PLO) sought to establish a Palestinian state on land occupied by Israel. But the PLO has many factions, each with its own vision for a post-independence Palestine. These agenda range from the Marxism-Leninism of the Democratic Front for the Liberation of Palestine and the Popular Front for the Liberation of Palestine, to the traditionalist, religiously inspired members of Hamas and the Palestinian Islamic Jihad.

When revolutionary ideology is the only excuse for terrorism, and terrorism is the sole strategy employed in the armed struggle, the terrorist campaign usually fails. Thus, Nazi terrorism during the Germany's Weimar republic of the late 1920s and early 1930s was able to undermine the constitution specifically because it was coupled with legal political activism. By contrast, the German Red Army Faction in the 1970s used terrorism exclusively in its struggle against the German Federal Republic and failed.

Revolutionary terrorism does not seek to preserve the status quo. The aim is to change the rules of the political game. Left-wingers such as the Red Army Faction used terror to reveal the repressive character of the state they opposed, because the state's position was that civil liberties must be restricted in order to catch the terrorists. In general, gun battles between police and revolutionaries reveal the violence inherent in the system, and law enforcement agencies certainly make mistakes, imprisoning innocent political activists who may be opposed to the state but who do not use terrorism against it.

The Red Army Faction's logic for adopting a terrorist strategy to achieve political change shows how terrorism has appealed to many other revolutionaries. Membership of a political movement opposed to the status quo is a choice made by people angry with the system. Those whose personalities require them to act may find constitutional approaches too limiting. Someone opposed to the established order can fight it more dramatically using a bomb or a gun than by attending political rallies or selling a party journal. The burning government building or the shot police officer is a far more dramatic route for a revolutionary.

REVOLUTIONARY TERROR BY THE RIGHT

Fascist terrorist acts have a slightly different objective. Like the Red Army Faction in Germany, they seek to create a sense of alarm on the part of those in power. But what they wish to achieve is a general crisis that will require an increase in repression.

In August 1980, terrorists blew up a bomb in the Bologna railroad station, killing 75 people. This event occurred at a time of Red Brigade activity. In the same way that investigators at first believed the Oklahoma City bombing in 1995 to be the work of Middle Eastern terrorists, so the Bologna bombing was initially blamed on the Red Brigades. The inability of investigators to link Bologna with the Red Brigades led them to a group of Neo-Fascists called the Armed Revolutionary Nuclei, who had set the bomb. The Bologna bombing was part of a right-wing strategy of

Rex Features

The body of a Red Brigade terrorist lies in a Roman street in February 1986. Security forces killed him during an attempt to assassinate Antonio da Empoli, an aide to the Italian prime minister.

terror to force the authorities to suspend civil liberties, or encourage generals to stage a coup to restore order. In either case, a dictatorial regime would result, which was the Neo-Fascists' aim.

Similarly, the Nazis in Germany engaged in street battles with Communists. The Nazis had a party militia, called the Stormtroopers or Brownshirts. They played on the fears of middle-class people with a small stake in the system, such as their own home or a family business. These people were concerned about damage to their property. The sense of anarchy that emerged whenever a political rally degenerated into a brawl helped make Hitler's message of a leader who would restore order to Germany more appealing. They overlooked other parts of Hitler's platform – his denunciation of the Weimar constitution and of elected parliaments – which should have been things they wished to safeguard.

THE REVOLUTIONARY STATE

Terror is also a strategy for governments committed to social revolutionary programs. Two of the best-known examples of state terror occurred in the aftermath of major revolutions.

In France during 1793, the Jacobin faction faced domestic opposition to their economic program. The Jacobins responded by sending their political enemies to the guillotine while they took over local government by imposing greater control from Paris, the capital. In 1928, the communist regime in the Soviet Union began a program of economic modernization. Part of the program required grain requisitioning to provide the industrial workers with cheap bread, and to force the collectivization of peasant landholdings. Farmers and their families were left to starve to death in the streets of their villages. The police arrested those who protested – and many who didn't – and sent them to forced labor camps. The police shot anyone who took a leading role in organizing protests.

In both these cases, terror was a weapon used against opponents of the revolutionary order. However, at the same time it helped the revolutionaries to accomplish their goals. Local government in France remained centralized until the 1980s, in spite of the collapse of the Jacobin government nearly two centuries before in 1794. Collective farms replaced small peasant farms in the Soviet Union from the 1930s until the 1990s. Society in both these cases had been wholly reshaped by terrorism.

Noemi Gal-Or

SEE ALSO: TERROR IN THE FRENCH REVOLUTION 1793-1815; RUSSIAN ANARCHIST TERROR; FRENCH ANARCHIST TERROR; THEORIES OF TERROR IN URBAN INSURRECTIONS; FAR-RIGHT EXTREMISM; RELIGIOUS EXTREMISM; THE BEGINNING OF INTERNATIONAL TERRORISM; THE POPULAR FRONT FOR THE LIBERATION OF PALESTINE; TERRORISM IN LATIN AMERICA; BLACK PANTHERS AND TERROR; STUDENT TERROR: THE WEATHERMEN; URBAN TERROR: THE SYMBIONESE LIBERATION ARMY; THE OKLAHOMA CITY BOMBING AND THE MILITIAS; RED ARMY FACTION: THE BAADER-MEINHOF GANG; ACTION DIRECTE; FRENCH RIGHT-WING TERRORISM; RED BRIGADES; MODERN GREEK TERRORISM; JAPANESE TERRORISM; TERROR IN CAMBODIA.

FURTHER READING

- Ellis, John. *From the Barrel of a Gun: A History of Revolutionary and Counter Insurgency Warfare.* London: Greenhill, and Mechanicsburg, PA: Stackpole, 1995.
- Rubenstein, R. E. *Alchemist of Revolution: Terrorism in the Modern World.* London: Tauris, and New York: Basic Books, 1987.
- Rubin, Barry, ed. *The Politics of Terrorism.* Washington, DC: Foreign Policy Institute, and London: University Press of America, 1989.

FAR-RIGHT EXTREMISM

In several parts of the world, including Europe, acts of terrorism increasingly come from the extreme right. The forces of racism and militant nationalism have adopted slogans such as "ethnic cleansing" and "race war." This resembles the situation between the world wars, when fascism was a major force.

Since the late 1980s, nationalist movements and rebellious youth cultures have turned to notions of "people, blood, and soil." These ideas emphasize the race or nationality of people, and how they are linked to historic territories. Such ideas are often associated with right-wing and fascist ideologies. The trend is being expressed through electoral support for radical right-wing parties, through the growth of neo-Nazi organizations, and through youth cultures that despise foreigners. At the same time religious militancy and millenarian movements, which believe the world will soon end, are growing. Some of their beliefs fit well with far-right politics and violence.

There are five common explanations for this shift in youth ideology. First, the collapse of Soviet domination in the late 1980s meant that communism was no longer a credible model for radical change. Second, modern youth rebels want to go against their parents, who were influenced by the leftist youth rebellion movements during the 1960s and 1970s. Third, in times of social and economic crisis, young people may look for security by being part of a group, and characteristics of race and nationality are easy to define. Fourth, increasing immigration has raised racial tension. Fifth, loss of confidence in established political parties has given far-right groups a chance to present themselves as a fresh alternative to a corrupt old guard.

KEY FACTS

- Many of the beliefs of far-right groups are based on racial or national superiority over others.
- Adverse economic conditions have led to hostility to racial minorities and immigrants.
- Adolf Hitler, the Nazi dictator of Germany from 1933 to 1945, is an inspirational figure for many far-right terrorist groups.

EXTREMIST IDEOLOGY

The far right can be difficult to define. What is considered rightist changes from country to country and over time. Many groups and individuals who carry out acts of violence for far-right or racist motives may turn out to have no connections with political organizations.

However, the basic elements of right-wing extremism can be sketched out. There is usually the idea that certain groups of people are inferior or superior as an innate principle. This is combined with an acceptance of violence as a legitimate form of action.

There are other issues and values often promoted by groups described as extreme right-wingers. Authoritarianism, the belief that human society needs a strong leader, is common, as is a hatred of communism or socialism. Militant nationalism can involve racism or anti-Semitism and intolerance toward minorities. The most extreme groups, such as the Nazis and modern Italian neo-fascists, see violence as a creative, cleansing force. Some groups like the Militias create "Golden Age myths," beliefs that there was a time when conditions were perfect for that group. "Golden Age myths" are often important components in the millenarian belief systems, which hold that some gigantic disaster will occur soon to transform the world. Right-wing millenarianists like the American Christian Identity movement usually believe that they will survive this event and emerge to rule the world.

Some modern reactionary groups deliberately link themselves to the past history of the extreme right – to the German Nazi Party and Italian Fascist Party, for example. Other groups deny that they have any connection with this past. Some movements considered as "extreme right" may also promote certain issues that are more often associated with the left, such as socialism or environmentalism.

Rex Features

A Turkish guest-worker's home in Germany, bombed in 1992 by Germans resentful of jobs going to foreigners.

It is not possible to define the essence of right-wing extremism in terms of a core issue. Nor is it true to say that violence and terrorism follow automatically from right-wing extremism. Violent right-wing groups tend to be those who think their opponents are dangerous. They also believe their opponents are less than human. Such is the case in France, where extreme followers of the National Front party attack French Algerians.

FAR-RIGHT GROUPINGS

The types of far-right terrorist groups can be classified by the principles around which they are organized and by their relations with minority and authority enemies. The discussion below is based on a typology originally developed by Ehud Sprinzak

Revolutionary terrorism of the far right is historically represented by Italian fascism and German Nazism. These movements aimed to overthrow the established political regime and take over the state apparatus. Although they used illegal methods to cause unrest, their eventual take-over of power happened in relatively legal ways.

Present-day racial revolutionaries have refined the old anti-Semitic idea of a Jewish world conspiracy. They believe in the Zionist Occupation Government (ZOG), said to be a worldwide network of Jews who have gained control of the political establishment. The revolutionaries think these Jews can be overthrown only through a total race war. The war would be against Jews, foreign intruders, and "racial traitors" in the white race.

Reactive terrorism, in contrast, is carried out by those wishing to maintain an established system. They may fear that their privileges are threatened, or are struggling to restore lost political power. Such terrorism has come from Jewish settlers in Israeli-occupied territories. Israeli prime minister Yitzhak Rabin was assassinated in 1995 to undermine the Palestinians peace process. And the Italian masonic organization P2 is thought to be behind the killing of Roberto Calvi,

Popperfoto

German neo-Nazis give the fascist salute at a rally on August 17, 1991, to celebrate the fourth anniversary of the death of Rudolf Hess, Hitler's deputy.

the Vatican's chief banker found hanging from a bridge in London in 1986. He may have been about to expose high-level corruption, so upsetting the status quo.

Those who have lost power may attack the new regime, as in the case of the fascist Ustasha movement in the 1950s in Croatia (then part of Yugoslavia) in southern Europe. The Ustasha ruled Croatia until 1945, but were ousted by the communists. The Ustasha then ran a terrorist campaign against the new regime.

Vigilante terrorism is a variant of reactive terrorism. Initially, such terrorists do not feel they oppose the government or the law. They believe that the authorities have failed in their task of keeping order. Vigilante terrorists use stronger means than the authorities themselves. Prime examples are Latin American death squads, often consisting of off-duty police and military officers, striking against left-wing revolutionaries.

Millenarian terrorism is the hallmark of groups that believe a new age will come out of a disaster, as already mentioned. Most such groups wait for the cataclysm to happen, but a few use violence to try to bring it about. A bizarre variant on this theme are neo-Nazis who have taken up Odinism, the pre-Christian pagan religion of Germany. They believe the gods and demons will gather for a final battle, called Ragnarok. Humans will fight alongside gods and be destroyed, except for one couple who will repopulate the Earth.

Skinheads and similar youth subcultures are often alienated from the mainstream community. Their violence and the texts of their music and fanzines are directed against immigrants, Jews, communists, and homosexuals. Such gangs have carried out much of the racist violence in Europe that has caused public concern in recent years. In Britain, the group Combat 18 (the numbers correspond to A and H in the alphabet, Adolf Hitler's initials) is responsible for many racial attacks. Skinheads in Germany have bombed houses of foreign guest-workers, refugees from former Yugoslavia, and Eastern Europeans.

However, some individuals and groups may adopt more radical ideological notions and ultimately turn into revolutionary terrorists. These subcultures constitute important pools of recruitment for more organized neo-Nazi and racial revolutionary groups.

Tore Bjorgo

SEE ALSO: THE BIRTH OF JEWISH TERRORISM; JEWISH TERROR IN THE WEST BANK; JEWISH TERRORISM IN THE 1990s; KU KLUX KLAN TERROR; FRENCH RIGHT-WING TERRORISM.

FURTHER READING

- Heitmeyer, W. "Hostility and Violence against Foreigners in Germany," in *Racist Violence in Europe,* edited by Tore Bjorgo and R. Witte. London: Macmillan, and New York: St. Martin's Press, 1993.
- Hoffman, Bruce. *Right-Wing Terrorism in West Germany.* Santa Monica, CA: Rand Corporation, 1986.
- Sprinzak, Ehud. "Right-Wing Terrorism in a Comparative Perspective: The Case of Split Delegitimization," in *Terror from the Extreme Right,* edited by Tore Bjorgo. London and Portland, OR: Frank Cass, 1995.

SINGLE-ISSUE GROUP TERRORISM

The activists in single-issue groups have chosen to focus on a specific concern that they believe demands immediate attention. It is a concern for "the one issue" above all else that separates them from revolutionary groups with wider aims. Most single-issue groups have their origins in the democratic process. They turn to violent tactics only when they believe that the issues they promote become too urgent for the slow progress of traditional campaigning. Activists' main goals are publicity or changes in the law. Focusing on the one cause, the groups usually ignore the wider effect of their efforts, believing their violent acts are justified because they are morally superior to those who hold a different view.

What constitutes a single-issue group? During his early phase, the Unabomber appeared to be a single-issue terrorist – a violent environmental activist who targeted technocrats and businessmen. However, the publication of his manifesto in 1995 highlighted the Unabomber's aim to overthrow modern society itself. Animal rights activists, on the other hand, pursue an identifiable single issue, as do anti-abortion groups. Single-issue groups are not prevented from being part of larger campaigns – the anti-abortionists can be set within a wider Christian movement pressing for improved public morals, for example, and the animal rights people within a larger movement concerned with environmental issues.

KEY FACTS

- Earth First! monkey wrenchers refer to industrialists and developers as "concreteheads."
- In April 1994, a British ALF leader who had escaped from police custody the previous year was recaptured – by a police dog.
- According to National Abortion Federation figures, 161 bombings and arsons took place against abortion clinics between 1977 and 1992.

ANTI-ABORTION TERRORISM

The violent anti-abortion groups are the undemocratic face of a movement for law reform. Frustrated by an inability to overturn the Supreme Court's 1973 decision that laws forbidding abortion are an unconstitutional infringement of a citizen's rights, anti-abortionists have formed a number of groups to campaign against abortion providers. Defensive Action, Operation Rescue, the American Family Association, Lambs of Christ, and similar organizations have demonstrated outside clinics, even establishing blockades to prevent people going in or leaving.

Some anti-abortionists have turned to firebombing clinics and murdering medical staff. The Reverend Paul Hill, director of Defensive Action, was charged with the murders of Dr. John Britton and James Barratt, who were shot outside a clinic in Pensacola, Florida. In December 1994, John Salvi went on a shooting spree at clinics in Massachusetts and Virginia, killing two people.

EARTH FIRST!

Earth First! is the foremost militant environmentalist group in America and is another prime example of a single-issue activist organization. It was founded in 1980, with the rallying cry of "No compromise in defense of Mother Earth." The group seeks to save as much of the American wilderness as possible from modern society. Earth First! began by staging a series of theatrical publicity stunts. The campaign escalated into one of fully fledged industrial sabotage, or "monkey wrenching." The sabotage included arson, disabling logging equipment, and strewing metal spikes onto rural roads to make them impassable to

Hulton Getty Picture Collection

John Salvi during his arraignment for opening fire on an abortion clinic in Norfolk, Virginia.

tree-felling machinery. As a part of their campaign against the cutting down of forests, Earth First! supporters also hammered spikes into trees so that they would be useless for felling as lumber.

Besides the forestry industry, Earth First! monkey wrenchers also targeted the nuclear power industry in their environmental campaign. The group severed power lines and caused domestic blackouts. Members have also been accused of sabotaging a ski lift and an atomic-weapons factory.

ANIMAL LIBERATION FRONT

On the extreme fringe of the animal rights movement is the Animal Liberation Front (ALF). In Britain, the ALF has not hesitated to use terrorism against those who, in its opinion, maltreat animals. In January 1981, the homes of several Oxford University scientists were attacked by ALF activists. The activists daubed slogans on walls, and damaged a garage and cars. In March 1984, the group issued a warning that it had contaminated bottles of shampoo in stores in London, Leeds, and Southampton, claiming the manufacturers tested the product on animals. Bottles spiked with bleach were discovered in Leeds and Southampton.

On October 24, 1984, a group of ALF activists attacked a dog kennel in southern England, assaulting three people. Simultaneously, other ALF supporters attacked buildings at two research laboratories with sledgehammers. A fourth group visited the home of a laboratory research director, who was beaten with an iron bar. In December 1987, the ALF targeted the fur trade, firebombing stores selling furs in Manchester, Liverpool, and Cardiff.

America also has a group called the Animal Liberation Front. It is one of the U.S.'s most publicized illegal activist organizations. In April 1985, 16 members of the group raided the Riverside Life Sciences Building of the University of California, taking hundreds of animals. ALF spokespeople claimed that the institution caused the animals to suffer in isolation and sight-deprivation experiments. Sabotage makes research more expensive, so the movement hopes its actions will encourage animal friendly methods – the attack at Riverside caused hundreds of thousands of dollars' worth of damage. The U.S. version of the Animal Liberation Front has a policy of avoiding injuries to people.

In terms of a group being able to realize its goals, though, the shift from democratic campaigning to direct violent action may prove counterproductive. Single-issue groups that move outside the democratic process automatically lose the moral high ground, and with it may go any public support they have.

Toby Dodge

SEE ALSO: NUCLEAR TERRORISM; THE MINDSET OF THE TERRORIST; ANTI-ABORTION ACTIVISTS' TERROR CAMPAIGN.

FURTHER READING

- Finsen, L., and S. Finsen. *The Animal Rights Movement in America: From Compassion to Respect.* New York: Twayne Publishers,1994.
- Lee, M. F. "Violence and the Environment: The Case of Earth First," in *Terrorism and Political Violence* 7, No. 3 (Autumn 1995): 109-127.
- National Abortion Federation. *Incidents of Violence & Disruption Against Abortion Providers.* Washington, DC: National Abortion Federation, 1993.

DOMESTIC VERSUS INTERNATIONAL TERRORISM

Some terrorist groups are exclusively concerned with affecting politics within a single state. Such groups include pro-life (anti-abortion) terrorists, some animal rights activists, and the individuals who planted the bomb in Oklahoma City in 1995. However, most terrorism has some kind of international tinge. It is the international aspect that makes cooperation between states essential in combating terrorist activity, and which makes terrorism so difficult to root out.

Since 1945, there have been three aspects of the relations between states that have fostered the internationalization of terrorism. The first is the collapse of European colonial empires. Many states have aided the campaigns of terrorists seeking to end colonial dominance. In the 1950s, for example, Morocco and Tunisia helped Algerian National Liberation Front terrorists against the French. The second aspect is the Cold War. Both the West and communist states aided groups that they described as freedom fighters but which their opponents described as terrorists. The final aspect in international relations that made terrorism an international activity is the situation of Israel, a state created within an Arab bloc. Many of these Arab states have, at some point, assisted terrorist groups.

Within this general climate, there are a number of levels at which terrorists operate internationally. The first level of international terrorism is one in which some of one country's population actively help terrorists from another country. The examples of the Basques of ETA, operating in Spain, and the Provisional IRA, operating in Northern Ireland, are instructive. Although there was no state aid to either group in neighboring France or the Irish Republic respectively, there was certainly a sizable group of sympathizers who were prepared to give help, or at least turn a blind eye, to would-be terrorists.

In the case of ETA, there was a large expatriate Basque community in southern France, and many French people were inclined to be sympathetic to ETA while the dictator General Franco ruled Spain. In the Republic of Ireland, the wish of the IRA to unite the whole of Ireland struck a chord in many hearts. Events such as "Bloody Sunday" in 1972, when British paratroopers killed 13 Catholic demonstrators, reinforced such feelings of nationalism.

KEY FACTS

- In 1944, Jewish terrorists of the Stern Gang assassinated British minister Lord Moyne in Egypt, carrying out an operation outside Palestine in order to sway world opinion to their cause.
- In 1985, Middle Eastern groups carried out 75 terrorist attacks in Western Europe, killing 65 people. Twenty of these attacks were aimed at Western people or property, rather than at Arab and Palestinian or Israeli and Jewish targets.

SYMPATHY IN ANOTHER COUNTRY

Support and help from elements within states takes many forms. At one level, there is covert protection. At another, there is fundraising, lobbying of government, and enthusiastic propagandizing. The Provisional IRA provides a good example of popularity abroad. In the Republic of Ireland and especially in the U.S., large groups of people are prepared to do much to help the Provisional IRA, and have raised millions of dollars that sustain terrorist activity. The attempt to mobilize U.S. public opinion and to gain support from within the U.S. government achieved great success in 1995, when Sinn Fein president Gerry Adams was invited to the White House.

Another good example of this kind of international help from sympathetic communities has occurred in the case of the Tamil Tigers, fighting for a Tamil state

Hulton Getty Picture Collection

Spanish repression, including death sentences on these Basque separatists at Burgos in 1970, encouraged French sympathies for the Basque cause.

within what is now Sri Lanka. They have an effective fundraising organization within Tamil communities worldwide that gives them the resources to buy whatever weapons and equipment they feel they need. For a long period they were also able to smuggle such arms into Sri Lanka with the active help of the Tamil population of southern India, even though there was no help given them by the Indian authorities.

When a nation state, rather than individuals within that state, aids a terror group, then potentially there is a great benefit to the terrorists. In many struggles since 1945 which have involved terrorism, such aid has been available across borders. The communist Chinese gave aid to the Vietminh nationalists in Vietnam in the 1950s. In the 1980s, the South Africans helped guerrillas in neighboring Mozambique to destabilize the government there.

State aid to terrorists is not only confined to obvious movement across a border. In the modern world, aid from state governments is often sent to terrorists from long distances. For example, in Central America during the 1980s, the U.S. government aided the Contras in their fight against the Sandinista regime by secretly funneling weapons and money to them. During the Cold War, states in the Soviet Eastern Bloc also aided terrorists if they considered communism's interests best served by such terror groups. Since the fall of communist regimes in Europe in 1989, information has emerged detailing many links between Eastern bloc countries and terrorists. The communist East German regime, for example, gave support to the Baader-Meinhof terrorists operating in West Germany.

STATE SPONSORSHIP

The most notorious examples of state sponsoring of terrorism have come from the Middle East. Since the 1960s, both Syria and Colonel Muammar al-Qaddafi's Libya have provided arms, funding, and training for a variety of guerrillas and terrorists. The fighters were mainly Palestinian, or linked to Palestinian organizations, but Qaddafi, for example, also sent large quantities of arms and explosives to the Provisional IRA in Northern Ireland. Even after air strikes against Libya in the 1980s and the alignment of Syria with Western powers during the Gulf War of 1990-91, it is still suspected that Libya and Syria have many terrorist connections. The planting of a bomb on Pan Am Flight 103, which exploded over Lockerbie, Scotland, in 1988, has been generally laid at the door of agents working with Libyan backing. But many commentators believe that Syrian terrorists, not the Libyans, were involved.

In the 1980s, Syria and Libya were joined by Iran in sponsoring terrorism. Under the fundamentalist regime of Ayatollah Khomeini, Iran funded many organizations involved in terrorist activities, such as the Palestinian Hizb'allah group based in Lebanon.

Many states have concluded that sponsoring terrorism is a successful way of achieving foreign policy objectives. States where foreign policy involves an ideological struggle are most likely to lean toward sponsoring international terrorism. Examples are found in the Cold War struggle between countries espousing capitalist and communist ideologies or in the Middle East, where religion and nationalism are intertwined.

Given that so much modern terrorism has an international dimension, it is not surprising that terrorist acts themselves often take on an international form. Terrorists may direct their violence against people or property having only a loose connection with the main aims of the terrorist group. The intention is to gain worldwide publicity that is considered an end in itself. The terrorists may also plot actions to make the whole international community feel unsafe while the group's objectives remain unfulfilled. There is the additional attraction that targets in countries not directly involved in a terrorist campaign may be easy to attack.

Reuters

This memorial at Arlington, Virginia, honors the 270 victims of the Lockerbie Pan Am Flight 103 bombing in 1988. Libyan or Syrian terrorists are thought to have been behind the explosion over Scotland.

In this context, Palestinian groups or their supporters have carried out the most notorious acts of international terrorism. The Palestinians' view of the late 1960s was that there was an American-Zionist plot to stop them from attaining a Palestinian homeland. Palestinian groups then considered that any attacks on property belonging to America or its allies were justified. They also wanted publicity for their cause. From

Popperfoto

In October 1985, Arab terrorists hijacked the Italian cruise liner Achille Lauro *in the Mediterranean Sea.*

1968, there were attacks on Israeli targets in Europe, which evolved into a wave of airline hijackings by Palestinian groups such as Black September and the Popular Front for the Liberation of Palestine (PFLP).

The most spectacular single hijacking incident was in 1970, when the PFLP blew up three airliners it had had flown to Dawson's Field in Jordan. But the attack that made the most impact was in 1972, when Black September terrorists took Israeli athletes hostage at the Munich Olympic Games. The event ended tragically when the hostages were killed in a furious gun battle between terrorists and security forces.

Since the mid-1970s, such international acts have been rarer, partly because of better security by national and international police forces. But they still occur. One example was the hijacking of the cruise ship *Achille Lauro* in 1985 by Palestinians. One justification terrorists use for attacks on innocent victims is the belief that there is an international conspiracy to prevent the achievement of Palestinian aims. This leads naturally to treating the leading Western power, the U.S., as an enemy. On the *Achille Lauro*, the terrorists killed Leon Klinghoffer, a disabled U.S. citizen. Americans have also been singled out in other attacks.

Similarly, European terrorists sympathetic to the Palestinians have often targeted U.S. officials. In 1981 in Italy, the Red Brigades kidnapped U.S. general James Dozier. Before then, the Red Brigades had been a purely Italian problem. In the Middle East, distrust of the U.S. received a boost in the 1980s after the Islamic revolution in Iran. Militant fundamentalists described America as the "Great Satan." The most notable terrorist act expressing this hatred was the bomb planted by Islamic militants in the World Trade Center in 1993.

Effectively, then, terrorism in the modern world has been pushed into an international position because certain states use it and encourage it, and individual terrorists feel justified in attacking foreign states that they consider to be ideologically hostile to them.

Noemi Gal-Or

SEE ALSO: TERRORISM IN FRENCH ALGERIA; TERROR AGAINST THE FRENCH IN INDOCHINA; SINGLE-ISSUE GROUP TERRORISM; BOMBING OPERATIONS; HIJACKING AND KIDNAPPING; COLLABORATION BETWEEN TERRORISTS; THE BEGINNING OF INTERNATIONAL TERRORISM; THE BLACK SEPTEMBER ORGANIZATION; TERRORISM AND REVOLUTION IN IRAN; HIZB'ALLAH; TERRORISM IN NICARAGUA; TAMIL TIGER TERROR IN SRI LANKA; THE OKLAHOMA CITY BOMBING AND THE MILITIAS; RED ARMY FACTION: THE BAADER-MEINHOF GANG; RED BRIGADES; BASQUE NATIONALIST TERROR: ETA; IRA: ORIGINS AND TERROR TO 1976; NATIONALIST TERROR IN NORTHERN IRELAND 1976-1996; STATE-SPONSORED TERRORISM.

FURTHER READING

- Chomsky, Noam. *Pirates and Emperors: International Terrorism in the Real World.* New York: Black Rose Books, 1991.
- Guelke, Adrian. *The Age of Terrorism and the International Political System.* New York: St. Martin's Press, 1995.
- Heitmeyer, W. "Hostility and Violence against Foreigners in Germany," in *Racist Violence in Europe,* edited by Tore Bjorgo and R. Witte. London: Tauris, and New York: St. Martin's Press, 1993.

STATE VERSUS NON-STATE TERRORISM

The term *terrorism* has been used to describe violent political acts carried out by informal, illegal, and basically private groups. In recent years a number of analysts have criticized this approach. They argue that acts carried out by governments, or security forces, should also be included.

Some claim that governments have all too often used terrorism, employing the same fear-inducing methods as illegal, revolutionary groups. In reality, both government and non-government violence has intimidated and terrorized civilian populations.

It is not always easy to distinguish between state and non-state terrorism since the strategies and tactics may be identical. But terrorism carried out in the service of a government is classed as state terrorism. Sometimes the government carries out the actions itself; sometimes it uses agents to do its dirty work.

WHAT IS STATE TERRORISM?

Most analysts distinguish between three types of state terrorist activity. The first, state terror, is the use of terrorism by a government turning against its own citizens to enforce its rule. The second is usually termed state-sponsored terrorism, in which the government controls a terrorist group abroad. Finally, state-supported terrorism occurs when a government provides funds or supplies to an independent terrorist group. Both of the latter forms of state terrorism are usually directed against foreign governments or critics abroad.

State terror by the authorities is a means of oppression and intimidation. The government may direct it against the whole population or just particular groups. Often laws are passed that legalize torture, beatings, and killing by police or the army under certain conditions. Alternatively, terror practices may be carried out in violation of the legal code. The state may justify these illegal acts as necessary for the defense of law and order or for the survival of the regime. Those who act illegally in this way are rarely punished.

State terror can suppress resistance and subdue populations. Dictators or governments that cannot be charged by judicial investigators use it. Stalin's purges or Saddam Hussein's gas attacks on Iraqi Kurds are typical of such acts. In Central and South America, right-wing regimes that do not wish to be directly connected to state terror have formed unofficial death squads to strike at their opponents. Members of the police or armed forces often staff the squads.

STATE SPONSORSHIP AND SUPPORT

Whereas repressive state terror is designed to maintain a country's internal status quo, state-sponsored and state-supported terrorism are intended to destabilize a hostile foreign government. The support of guerrilla insurgents in Mozambique and Angola by the South African government in the 1980s is a classic example.

State-sponsored terrorism occurs when a government plans, directs, and controls terrorist operations in another country. The activities may be carried out by individuals or by government officials. State-supported terrorism has less involvement, providing a

KEY FACTS

- In an example of state-supported terrorism in 1991, Gulbuddin Hekmatyar became the most powerful guerrilla in Afghanistan because of Pakistani government funding.
- During 1975-79 the Cambodian government employed state terror, killing a million of its own citizens to stay in power.
- The Iranian government has sponsored uprisings in Bahrain, Iraq, and Lebanon.

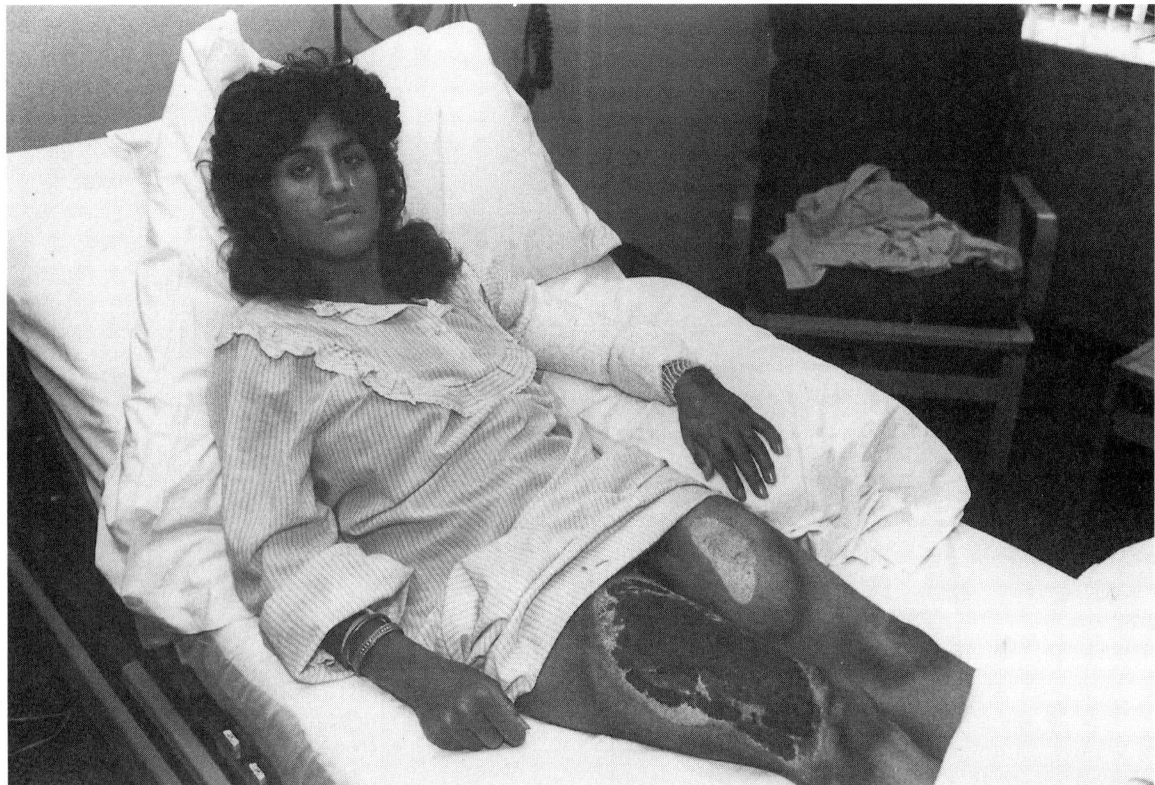

Hulton Getty Picture Collection

revolutionary group with transport, training sites, money, propaganda, and diplomatic protection.

Iran is a notorious example of a state practicing all three forms. It has a record of terrorizing members of ethnic and religious minorities within Iran, and has assassinated exiled members of the opposition. Iran has also provided funds, weapons, training, and protection to terrorists from Islamic organizations. It has a special relationship with the Lebanese group Hizb'allah, which it gives nearly $5 million a year.

Although associated with authoritarian regimes, terror has also been supported by democracies. The U.S. has participated in running countries in Central America, supporting right-wing regimes in Nicaragua and El Salvador. In Guatemala in 1954, the U.S. supported a regime that massacred 100,000 peasants.

States have the advantage over terrorist groups, in terms of means at their disposal. But the non-state terrorist can at least make some claim to be at war with the enemy, whereas the state hides behind the terrorist smokescreen, blurring the boundaries between peace and war.

Noemi Gal-Or

A Kurdish victim of a 1988 Iraqi gassing. Saddam Hussein instigated the attacks on his own people.

SEE ALSO: STALIN'S GREAT TERROR; THEORIES OF STATE TERROR; TERRORISM AND REVOLUTION IN IRAN; HIZB'ALLAH; TERROR BY THE HOLY WARRIORS OF KASHMIR; THE ISRAELI RESPONSE TO TERRORISM; STATE SPONSORSHIP OF TERRORISM; SADDAM HUSSEIN'S TERROR IN KURDISTAN; TERROR IN CAMBODIA.

FURTHER READING

- Agger, I. and S. B. Jensen. *Trauma and Healing Under State Terrorism.* London and Atlantic Highlands, NJ: Zed Books, 1996.
- Bushnell, P. T., ed. *State Organized Terror: The Case of Violent Internal Repression.* Boulder, CO: Westview Press, 1991.
- Murphy, J. F. *State Support for International Terrorism.* Boulder, CO: Westview Press, and London: Mansell, 1989.

URBAN VERSUS RURAL TERRORISM

Terrorism in the countryside is totally unlike terrorism in urban areas, and this divide is important in understanding modern terrorism. The same groups may operate in both areas but use different methods. The key differences arise from the physical environments in city and country. In a city, there are usually crowds and security forces are rarely far away. Urban terrorists must move secretly, strike quickly, and then hide again. If properly handled, a single dramatic act by an urban terrorist group in a major city can attract headlines worldwide.

In the countryside, there is more space and freedom for the terrorists or guerrillas to operate. Rural groups are more able to control large areas. They can openly take over a village, murder a headman or government representative in front of the villagers, propose a political program, and promise to return – a promise the population knows they probably will keep.

RURAL THEORIES

Another distinction between urban and rural terrorism derives from their histories. Terrorists and guerrillas operating in rural areas in the two decades after 1945 owed a great debt to the ideas of Mao Zedong. He devised a plan for rural guerrilla warfare after his successful campaign for communism in China. He argued that safe base areas should be established from which a more conventional military campaign could be launched. Later, in the 1960s, the success of the Cuban revolutionaries meant that the theories of Che Guevara took precedence. Guevara followed Mao in advocating that insurgents establish bases, but believed the group could form a *foco*, or ideological focus, which would inspire a widespread revolutionary uprising.

> **KEY FACTS**
>
> - In rural areas, small squads conduct a slow war of attrition on isolated security forces units.
> - Urban campaigns focus on mass action and single acts of violence. Their aim is to win over their own community, maintain social pressure on their nation, and manipulate world opinion.
> - Rural terror involves tactical planning; urban organizations are more managerial and financial.

URBAN STRUGGLES FOR VICTORY

By contrast, urban terrorism has never had a strong theoretical base. Sometimes urban terror has been added to a campaign of rural terrorism, as in Vietnam during the 1950s and 1960s, or has been used simply because enemy targets are concentrated in urban areas, as in Cyprus during the 1950s.

There were some attempts to create theories of urban action against the state in the 1960s, notably by the Brazilian Carlos Marighella. However, all these theorists have failed to solve a central problem: how to progress from small-scale action to takeover of the state. Mao's theories showed how rural guerrillas could develop into large conventional forces that could confront the government army, and Guevara's theories combined guerrilla forces with civilian revolution. However, urban guerrillas have never known how to translate the first stages of their action – bombs or assassinations – into a final victory.

SEEKING A GOVERNMENT RESPONSE

Unable to achieve military victory, urban terrorist action has three underlying aims. First, it may show up the weakness of the state to the population. Second, it may cause the government to retaliate and so alienate the population. Third, the terrorist attacks may impose so high a price that the government may decide to concede to terrorist demands.

This latter aim has not been achieved in modern times. Urban guerrillas have rarely been able to present more than a short-term threat. The Irish Republican Army (IRA), for example, has not been able to impose an unacceptable cost on the British government to drive them out of Northern Ireland. Perhaps the largest urban terrorist operation in

Hulton Getty Picture Collection

The London department store Harrods was bombed in 1993 by the Provisional Irish Republican Army.

modern times was that of the Algerian nationalists who set up an urban terrorist network in Algiers in 1957, but they were rounded up in a matter of months.

These differences between rural and urban tactics affect operating methods and structures. Rural guerrillas tend to have a military structure, which can deploy large units. When government or enemy forces attack, the rural guerrillas aim to resist by ambushes, delaying tactics, and booby traps. If the forces involved are too large, they retreat and regroup elsewhere.

URBAN ADVANTAGES

Urban terrorists, on the other hand, rarely assemble in large military groups. Typically, they will be organized in cells of four or so activists, only one of whom will have other contacts within the organization. They may do little or nothing for long periods of time; and even when they do get the opportunity to act, this action may involve nothing more than taking a package from one place to another. Confrontation with government forces is usually avoided at all costs.

Virtually the only occasion when urban terrorists are prepared to confront government forces is during mass crowd action, when the overwhelming military force available to the government is almost useless. When the government does make use of such force, there is the possibility of adverse publicity. For example, on "Bloody Sunday," January 30, 1972, British paratroopers killed 13 Catholic protesters during a mass demonstration in Northern Ireland. Worldwide condemnation followed, and the army lost the respect of the Catholic population.

Urban terrorists benefit from the fact that they are operating in a vulnerable environment. A firebomb in a store or a hand grenade in a crowded street can have a great impact on a society. Few single actions by rural guerrillas will ever have the same effect.

The final comparison between rural and urban terrorists lies in their vulnerability to security forces. In general, the two forms of terrorism are met in different ways. Classically, rural counterinsurgency begins by guarding potential targets, then cutting the guerrillas off from the rural population, and only later progresses to fighting the guerrillas themselves. In Mao's terms, the fish cannot be caught until the sea in which they are swimming is hostile to them.

To protect every vulnerable point of a modern city from urban terrorists would impose terrible constraints on the population as a whole, which might prove to be unacceptable politically. Consequently, the general method of combating urban terrorists is to penetrate their networks and groups of possible sympathizers, using informers and undercover police. This is usually a long-term process. Arrests and discoveries of caches of arms punctuate prolonged periods of painstaking detective work – mirroring the urban group's careful planning before a terrorist act.

Heinz Tittmar

SEE ALSO: TERROR'S USE BY THE FRENCH RESISTANCE; THEORIES OF TERROR IN URBAN INSURRECTIONS; GUERRILLAS AND TERROR; TERRORISM IN FRENCH ALGERIA; TERRORISM IN CYPRUS; TERRORISM IN KENYA; TERRORISM IN ZIMBABWE (RHODESIA); TERRORISM IN BRAZIL; TERROR IN AFGHANISTAN.

FURTHER READING

- Black, I. and B. Morris. *Israel's Secret Wars: A History of Israel's Intelligence Services.* London: Futura, and New York: Grove Weidenfeld, 1992.
- Spencer, M. *Foundations of Modern Sociology.* 7th ed. Scarborough, Ont.: Prentice-Hall, 1996.
- Toolis, Kevin. *Journeys Within the IRA's Soul.* London: Picador, and New York: St. Martin's Press, 1996.

RELIGIOUS EXTREMISM

"I have no regrets. I acted alone and on orders from God," was the explanation offered by Yigal Amir, the young Jewish extremist who assassinated Israeli prime minister Yitzhak Rabin in November 1995. His words were not the rantings of a madman, but expressed the views of a religious zealot and terrorist. His violent act was not only calculated to achieve a political end – to destroy the Arab-Israeli peace process – but was also motivated by the desire to fulfil, in his own mind, a divine command. If terrorism is in essence the use of violence, or the threat of it, for political purposes, then Rabin's assassination was undoubtedly a terrorist act. But it was one with a distinct, profoundly significant, religious background.

This mix of political and religious motivations is found in many extremist groups that emerge from mostly peaceful, mainstream religious movements. The divinely inspired explanation offered by Amir could as easily have come from the lips of other religious terrorists. The Islamic Hamas terrorists, responsible for the wave of suicide bombings that convulsed Israel in the 1990s, could have spoken Amir's lines. So could the Muslim Algerian terrorists who, in 1995, bombed commuter trains, tourist spots, schools, and markets in France. The Japanese followers of the Aum Shinri-kyu sect who allegedly perpetrated the March 1995 gas attack on the Tokyo subway were similarly motivated.

KEY FACTS

- In 1968, none of the 11 identifiable active terrorist groups were religious. Today, there are about 50 known groups, and about a quarter of them are religious in motivation.
- Religious terrorists want sweeping change and are prepared to inflict a high death toll to achieve it.
- Since 1982, Shiite Muslim terrorists have committed eight percent of terrorist acts, but are responsible for 30 percent of deaths.

In all these cases, the perpetrators were driven by the belief that their acts were not only fulfilling God's will, but were also hastening the redemption of mankind. The aims of religious terrorists go beyond the fundamental political, social, or territorial changes that most non-religious terrorists seek. Religious terrorists often pursue a quirky combination of mystical, transcendental, and divinely inspired objectives. In most cases, they are vehemently anti-government on religious, racial, and political grounds.

TRADITIONS OF DIVINE INSPIRATION

Religion has increasingly become a rallying point for terrorism in the post–Cold War era because communist ideologies have been discredited by the collapse of the Soviet Union, and the promises of well-being prophesied by capitalist states have not been fulfilled.

But the link between religion and terrorism is not new. More than 2,000 years ago, the first acts of what is now termed "terrorism" were perpetrated by religious fanatics. Some of the words that describe terrorists and their actions come from the Jewish, Hindi, and Muslim terrorist groups active long ago.

The word *zealot*, for example, now meaning a fanatic, comes from the name of a Jewish sect which opposed the Roman empire's conquest of what is now Israel. The Zealots waged a ruthless campaign of assassination. A Zealot would emerge from the anonymity of a crowded market and draw out the *sica* (dagger) concealed beneath his robes. In full view, he would slit the throat of a Roman legionnaire or Jewish citizen judged guilty of betrayal or religious heresy.

The Zealots' public acts of violence – like those of terrorists today – were designed to have repercussions far beyond killing the victim of the attack. Murders were supposed to send a powerful message to a wider "target audience" – in this case, the Romans and the members of the Jewish community who collaborated with the invaders.

Similarly, the word *thug*, now meaning a rough or brutal hoodlum, comes from a religious cult that

Rex Features

A Palestinian suicide bomber blew up five other people with him on a bus in Tel Aviv, Israel, in 1995.

terrorized India until its suppression in the mid-nineteenth century. On holy days throughout the year, members would lie in wait for innocent travelers and ritualistically strangle them as sacrifices to Kali, the Hindu goddess of terror and destruction. According to some accounts, the Thugs killed a million people during their 1,200-year existence, an average of more than 800 victims a year. Such an assassination rate is rarely achieved by the Thugs' modern counterparts, even with their advantage of more lethal weaponry. The word *assassin* itself literally means "hashish-eater" – a reference to the ritual drug-taking of an eleventh-century Muslim sect before they went on their divinely inspired murder missions.

RELIGIOUS TO SECULAR AND BACK

Religion and terrorism share a long history. But for most of the twentieth century, ethnic, nationalist, or ideological issues have motivated terrorist groups. The end of the divine right of monarchs to rule, Marxist ideology, and movements such as anarchism completed terrorism's shift to the secular. Now the pendulum of terrorism is swinging back toward religion.

While religious terrorism has been growing steadily in recent years, fewer than 15 of the known terrorist groups active worldwide today have a predominantly religious motivation. Many contemporary terrorist groups also have a religious background – such as the Catholic-dominated Provisional IRA and the Protestant paramilitary groups in Northern Ireland – but it is the nationalist or separatist aspects of these groups that predominate.

Motives are different for the religious terrorist. Violence is an inspired duty carried out in response to some specific theological belief. So this extremism has a god-driven aspect absent from secular terrorism. Religious and secular terrorists also differ in the "audience" toward which their acts are directed. Secular terrorists attempt to appeal to sympathizers, members of the communities that they claim to defend, or the aggrieved people they say they speak for. But some religious terrorists are engaged in what they regard as a "total war." This sanctions almost limitless depths of violence, and anyone who is not a member of the terrorists' religion may be seen as a legitimate target.

Popperfoto

Shoko Asahara, leader of Japan's Aum Shinri-kyu sect, alleged to have unleashed gas on Tokyo's subway.

Religious terrorists usually want the greatest benefits for members of their faith only. They are not interested in the greater good. Secular terrorists see violence primarily as a means to an end. But religious extremists, because of the divine element of their motivation, often view violence as an end in itself. Clerical authorities – be they ayatollahs or mullahs, priests or rabbis, pastors or reverends – may interpret sacred texts so that religion justifies violence.

Religious and secular terrorists can have very different perceptions of themselves and their acts. Whereas secular terrorists may regard violence as a way of improving an existing system, religious terrorists often see themselves as outside a system not worth preserving. They seek vast changes. This sense of alienation lets religious extremists contemplate far more destructive violence against far more people than do secular terrorists. Religious extremists also view people outside their community as inferior. They describe them in deliberately dehumanizing and denigrating terms, calling them names such as nonbelievers, dogs, children of Satan, and mud people.

Contrary to popular belief, terrorism motivated by religion is not restricted to Islamic groups in the Middle East. The Tokyo subway gas attack, the Oklahoma City bombing, and the assassination of Yitzak Rabin all demonstrate this fact. Just since 1985 there has been a string of international attempts at mass slaughter. An unnamed group of 14 white supremacists plotted to dump cyanide into reservoirs in Washington, DC, and Chicago, Illinois. The Rajneesh cult, followers of an Indian mystic living in a rural Oregon religious commune, contaminated the salad bars of restaurants with salmonella bacteria to influence the outcome of local elections. In Israel, the Lifta Gang, a group of Jewish fanatics, plotted to blow up Jerusalem's Dome of the Rock, Islam's third holiest shrine. They hoped to provoke a massive "holy war" that would obliterate the Muslim world.

Extremist religious groups can represent a different and potentially far more deadly threat than traditional terrorists. These groups are unpredictable. No one is sure why many fringe movements or hitherto peaceful religious sects suddenly turn to violence and embark on lethal campaigns of indiscriminate terrorism. Traditional policies designed to counter terrorism, such as political concessions, financial rewards, and amnesties, are wasted on religious zealots. Instead, new approaches are needed to bridge the chasm between these extremist religious organizations and mainstream society.

Bruce Hoffman

SEE ALSO: THE ASSASSINS: A TERROR CULT; TERRORISTS' USE OF CHEMICAL WEAPONS; TERRORISM AND REVOLUTION IN IRAN; HIZB'ALLAH; HAMAS; THE WORLD TRADE CENTER BOMBING; ANTI-ABORTION ACTIVISTS' TERROR CAMPAIGN; THE OKLAHOMA CITY BOMBING AND THE MILITIAS.

FURTHER READING

- Brackett, D. W. *Holy Terror: Armageddon in Tokyo.* New York: Weather Hill, 1996.
- Hoffman, Bruce. "Holy Terror: The Implications of Terrorism Motivated by a Religious Imperative," in *Studies in Conflict and Terrorism,* Vol.18, No.4 (Winter 1995): 271-84.
- Rapoport, D. C. "Fear and Trembling: Terrorism in Three Religious Traditions," in *American Political Science Review,* Vol. 78, No. 3 (Sept. 1984): 668-72.
- Wright, Robin B. *Sacred Rage: The Wrath of Militant Islam.* London: Deutsch, and New York: Simon and Schuster, 1986.

CHAPTER SIX

Terrorist Techniques and Methods

Today's terrorists have the full battery of modern weaponry at their disposal, from surface-to-air missiles to chemicals, as well as more traditional bombs and mortars. There's even the horrific specter of a nuclear weapon getting into the hands of terrorists. But first, any terrorist group needs some kind of structure so that their campaigns run efficiently – just like a legal political party. They have to plan whether they are going to plant bombs, carry out hijackings and kidnappings, or assassinate a prominent figure, or whether to use a combination of methods. Whatever tactics they use, they need to raise funds to finance their operations.

TERROR GROUP ORGANIZATION

There are three critical issues to consider in a discussion of the organization of terrorismand terrorist groups. The first is the different ways in which rural and urban terrorists construct and organize their movements; the second is the role of leadership and control; and, finally, the relationship between such movements and more or less legitimate political groups.

Rural terrorism is almost always associated with guerrilla warfare, in which terror is part of a larger campaign. The single most influential advocate of terror was Mao Zedong. He stated that the ultimate military aim of the guerrilla army was to create a force capable of operating in open battle, and that this force should be built up in a safe base area while enemy forces were kept occupied by small guerrilla groups. The key to this organization was the establishment of core units within villages. The Vietminh in Vietnam in the 1940s, for example, applied Mao's theories. In areas where the Vietminh had some influence, each village was expected to provide a "self-defense" core unit of 12 guerrillas, in addition to a further five who could be used on operations outside the village's immediate area. These core units gave the Vietminh a strong base and made it difficult to root out their organization, even when French forces moved into an area with force.

KEY FACTS

- Rural and urban terrorists adopt different structures. Urban terrorists generally use a cellular structure; rural terrorists build up large structured groups out of small assault groups.
- The Provisional IRA reorganized itself into cells in the late 1970s to evade British security services.
- Many terrorist groups have a close but informal relationship with a political group, which acts as their mouthpiece and provides helpers and recruits.

Although this Maoist model has been most important in rural terrorism, in South America, Che Guevara's *foco* theory was very influential. The *foco* was a group of guerrillas who would establish themselves locally and then grow to take on the forces of the state. Various unsuccessful attempts were made to establish such groups in Latin America during the 1960s and 1970s.

Urban terrorism demands different structures. It requires great secrecy, and the terrorists often move in an environment physically dominated by their opponents. The problem for the leadership is how to maintain control and pass on orders without leaving the organization open to being broken up by a few arrests or even a single informer. The answer to this is a cellular structure, in which each cell, consisting of maybe four individuals, contains only one member who has any contact with others in the organization. Whereas rural terrorists are engaged in propaganda and broadening the organization's base as well as in guerrilla warfare, urban terrorists who launch attacks are usually isolated from other aspects of a campaign.

A typical example of cellular organization was that of the Algerian urban terrorists of the National Liberation Front (FLN) who carried out a bombing campaign in Algiers during the late 1950s. The French authorities eventually broke the campaign by using massive force and by constructing a huge organization chart on which they gradually filled in, and eliminated, names in all the cells. To extract detailed information, they routinely tortured suspects.

In Northern Ireland, the Provisional IRA was set up using an essentially rural structure inherited from earlier in the century. British security services had penetrated the terrorist group by the mid-1970s. In response, the IRA established a cell network and drastically reduced the number of activists. Today, it is estimated that there are just a few dozen IRA terrorists active at any one time.

Another terrorist organization that set up a successful cellular network was the Italian Red Brigades. It

Italian Red Brigades Organization

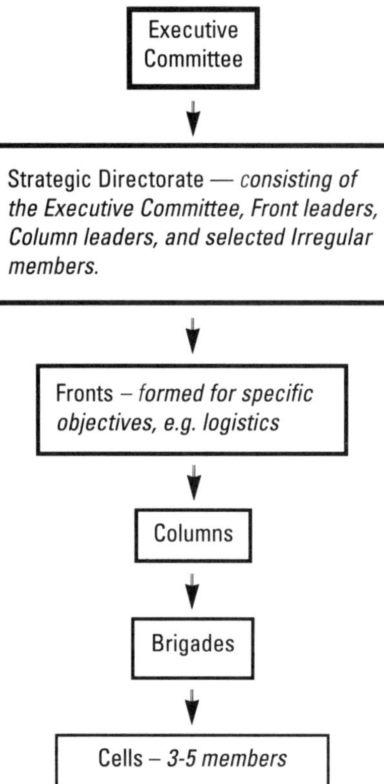

Like many terrorist groups, the Red Brigades had a clear hierarchical structure. Brigades and cells consist of regular members (illegal activists) and irregulars (activists involved in legal activities).

was only late in the group's operational life that the Italian government was able to get near its leadership.

The problem with this cellular organization is that leaders are not able to communicate very quickly with operatives. Good communication is crucial, partly because terrorist groups are often based on charismatic leaders. For example, Menachem Begin commanded the Jewish terrorist group Irgun like an older brother guiding the younger members of his family. George Grivas ran the Cypriot EOKA group like a Greek patriarch, and George Habash dominated the Popular Front for the Liberation of Palestine by strength of character and mastery of ideology.

But in a more general sense, the central leadership must be able to allot certain tasks (operational direction, intelligence, and acquiring, storing, and deploying arms, for example) and maintain contact with the direct operatives. This is normally done through a network of individuals who are sympathetic to the cause, but who are not full-time terrorists. Like the cell members, they have little contact with other members of the formal organization and are given occasional tasks – delivering a package here, making a telephone call there. They are, however, the sinews that bind the organization together. Without them the active cells could quickly become isolated.

These sympathetic individuals are often members of some kind of political organization. Some groups – such as the Italian Red Brigades – did not have a legitimate mouthpiece so they publish their own manifestos. The Provisional IRA, however, has an informal relationship with Sinn Féin, a legal political party.

The Palestine Liberation Organization (PLO) is often described as terrorist. Its leadership regularly denies knowledge of terrorist activities. However, it is now widely accepted in political and academic circles that Yasser Arafat, head of the PLO and of its major component, the party Fatah, set up Black September as a terrorist unit in the early 1970s to retain the allegiance of disaffected activists. Again, PLO involvement was strenuously denied, but there was a tight, if informal, relationship.

John Bowyer Bell

SEE ALSO: TERRORISM IN FRENCH ALGERIA; TERRORISM IN CYPRUS; TERROR AGAINST THE FRENCH IN INDOCHINA; COLLABORATION BETWEEN TERRORISTS; THE BLACK SEPTEMBER ORGANIZATION; RED BRIGADES; NATIONALIST TERROR IN NORTHERN IRELAND 1976-1996.

FURTHER READING

- Becker, J. *Hitler's Children: The Story of the Baader-Meinhof Terrorist Gang.* London: Panther, 1978.
- Bell, John Bowyer. *The Secret Army: The IRA 1916-1996.* 3rd ed. New Brunswick, NJ: Transaction Publishers, 1997.
- Collin, R. O., and G. L. Freedman. *Winter of Fire: The Abduction of General Dozier and the Downfall of the Red Brigades.* New York: Dutton, 1990.
- Livingstone, N. C. and D. Halevy. *Inside the PLO.* London: Hale, and New York: Morrow, 1990.

BOMBING OPERATIONS

Most terrorist groups find that bombs are convenient and effective weapons. Bombs can be used in small but lethal booby traps or in massive, headline-grabbing acts. Repeated attacks can traumatize a society, eventually producing precisely the sort of disruption the terrorists want.

Most terrorist groups have few active members and operate by means of still smaller cells. Bombs enable terrorists to be economical in their use of limited numbers and still kill many of their enemies. In addition, a bomb exploded by a small cell of terrorists can gain worldwide publicity while offering the terrorists a fair chance of escaping unharmed; even in suicide attacks only one terrorist is sacrificed.

Governments and other victims routinely describe bomb attacks as "cowardly," but such name-calling is unlikely to stop terrorists from planting bombs. Terrorists usually see themselves as engaged in a war. Successful war strategies are about achieving political ends by violent means with minimal losses on one's own side. Bombs work well for terrorists for exactly these reasons.

WHAT TERRORISTS USE TO MAKE BOMBS

Bombs are composed of three elements: explosives, detonators, and fuses. Most terrorists have two problems: first, getting hold of the relevant materials, and second, developing the knowledge to assemble these into reliable and effective weapons.

Governments that carry out terrorist-type attacks generally do not share these difficulties and can prepare sophisticated devices such as the booby-trapped cellular phone used by Israel to kill a Hamas bombmaker in January 1996. Other terrorist groups receive training and supplies of explosives and related items from foreign governments. Libya, for example, maintains training camps for a number of Middle East terrorist groups and has made large shipments of arms and explosives to the Irish Republican Army (IRA). During the 1980s, the U.S. did the same for the Mujahidin fighting the Soviets in Afghanistan.

In addition to clandestine shipments and purchases, terrorists can obtain explosives by thefts or armed raids on their military opponents or from civilian users, such as quarries. Armies use explosives so powerful that bombs can be small and easily hidden or carried, but still greatly effective. Plastic explosives used by terrorists, including the exceptionally powerful Semtex type, are often stuffed into confined spaces or molded to resemble an innocent object.

However, when powerful explosives are not available, terrorists have used common materials. Gasoline, fertilizers, and weed-killers have been combined to make bombs. The truck bomb that exploded in April 1995 in front of the Alfred P. Murrah federal building in Oklahoma City, killing 168, contained a mixture of gasoline and ammonium nitrate.

Having obtained or made the explosive, the terrorist provides it with a detonator and a fuse or timing device to ensure that the bomb explodes, and does so where and when intended. Military explosives, designed to be stored and handled safely in difficult conditions, need a correctly placed, powerful detonator. Home-made compounds must be stable enough not to explode prematurely (possibly killing the bomber) but sufficiently explosive to cause damage.

Simple fuses and timing devices are often used by terrorists, such as the burning cord used at Oklahoma

KEY FACTS

- On July 22, 1946, a bomb placed by the Zionist guerrillas Irgun in Jerusalem's King David Hotel killed 91 people. The hotel was being used as headquarters for the British authorities.
- A right-wing Italian terrorist group killed 75 and wounded 186 in a bomb attack on a station in Bologna, Italy, in 1980.
- On June 23, 1985, 329 people died when a bomb attributed to Sikh extremists exploded on an Air India flight from Toronto while over the Atlantic.

TRH Pictures

An American killed by a suicide truck bomb attack on the U.S. embassy in Beirut, Lebanon, on April 18, 1983. At least 40, including the bomber, were killed.

City; but they can also be sophisticated. The timer bomb placed in the Grand Hotel in Brighton, England, by the IRA in 1984, claimed a number of victims and nearly succeeded in killing Prime Minister Margaret Thatcher. The items to make such devices can be as cheap and readily available as the batteries that are often used to provide the power.

This encyclopedia has no intention of providing anyone with instructions on how to make explosives or timing devices. But terrorists easily manage to find the information they need, in addition to whatever training they may receive from their organization and its sympathizers.

Skilled bombmakers are rare in most terrorist organizations. They have invariably had to learn from experience, and many have been killed by their own mistakes. Within a terrorist organization, a distinction is often made between the bombmaker, who never goes near a target and whose skills are carefully preserved, and the other operatives who risk arrest and premature detonations while planting the devices.

TYPES OF TERRORIST BOMBS

Letter and package bombs are probably the smallest terrorist devices used. They seldom fully achieve the terrorists' aims, however. Even if they actually reach their destination, their victims are as likely to be office staff as the prominent individuals targeted. Those likely to receive such items quickly learn to take effective precautions. Research scientists have been targets for letter-bomb attacks by animal rights activists in a number of countries, and the Unabomber also used this method.

Various types of suspect packages, booby traps, and incendiary devices have been used by almost every terrorist group. They have been carried by hand and left in a phone booth or garbage can, or introduced as luggage or freight on aircraft or buses. In one incident in October 1994, a Hamas suicide bomber blew up a bus in Tel Aviv killing 21 people and wounding 45. Just one of many notorious aircraft bombings was the downing of PanAm Flight 103 on December 21, 1988, over Lockerbie, Scotland. Police investigating the wreckage revealed that a bomb in a luggage rack had caused the explosion. It killed all 259 people aboard and 11 on the ground.

Car and truck bombs are used by most terrorists. Some of these bombs have been huge and have caused great destruction. In February 1993, a large car-bomb

Central Press Photos

British politician Airey Neave died when his car was bombed by an Irish group in 1979. The terrorists gained extra publicity because the bomb placed in the car exploded outside the British parliament.

exploded in a parking garage below the World Trade Center in New York. Six were killed, and 1,000 injured. In an incident in 1991, a massive IRA truck bomb exploded in London's financial district, killing three. The loss of life, however, was surprisingly small considering the widespread damage to the area, totaling more than $1 billion. Bombs can also be placed in houses or vehicles used by specific targets. Pakistan's General Zia and Mozambique's Samora Machel are only two of the national leaders assassinated in this way, both being killed when their aircraft blew up. Sometimes terrorists place the bomb to intercept a victim – for instance, under a street or in a culvert – and then explode the device when the relevant vehicle passes over it.

TRANSPORT OF BOMBS

Letter and package bombs reach their targets with the unwitting assistance of the postal service, and terrorists are seldom concerned if a postal worker is injured. Even more cynical are the terrorists who trick friends into carrying their bombs. In 1986, Nezar Hindawi, a Jordanian associated with the hard-line Palestinian Abu Nidal Organization, persuaded his pregnant girlfriend to carry a package onto an airliner at London's Heathrow Airport. Both were arrested before the bomb could explode.

Suspect packages and car bombs are placed by terrorists who then escape, or they are detonated by suicide bombers. Suicide bombers drive their vehicles through protective barriers to carry a bomb nearer its target. This method was used in Islamic Jihad's bombing of two barracks in Beirut that killed 241 U.S. Marines and 58 French soldiers in October 1983.

TARGETS

By definition, terrorist attacks are designed to produce terror or, in other words, to defeat the enemy, not by the killing or destruction they cause, but by the threat of killing and destruction yet to be carried out. Some bomb attacks, especially the attempts to assassinate prominent individuals, are very precisely targeted. Others seek to cause clear economic or military damage to the terrorists' enemies. But many terrorists are ruthless and indiscriminate.

Assassinations of national leaders are difficult for terrorists to achieve because of heightened security, but they still occur. Zia and Machel have been mentioned. Others include Spanish prime minister Carrero Blanco, killed by a bomb in his car by the Basque separatist group ETA in 1973, and Lebanese president-elect Bashir Gemayel, blown up in his office in Beirut in 1982. Such assassinations are in fact one of the oldest forms of terrorism. Czar Alexander II of Russia was killed by a bomb in 1881, and the British still celebrate Guy Fawkes Day (November 5), the anniversary of a thwarted attempt to blow up their king and parliament in 1605.

Terrorist groups often claim to attack military targets, but their definition of the term *military* is a broad one. Soldiers carrying out security work are often hit by land mines. Even more common are terrorist attempts against those off duty, such as the attack on the U.S. and French troops in Beirut in 1983. Soldiers engaged in ceremonial functions are also targeted. In 1982, the IRA attacked a military band playing in a London park and a Household Cavalry detachment on ceremonial duties. Pubs frequented by off-duty British soldiers have also been IRA targets on a number of occasions. The terrorists claim that any civilians injured or killed are legitimate targets because their presence was in indirect support of the military. The IRA has also attacked civilian contractors who carry out work on police stations.

For the committed terrorist, the end clearly justifies the means, but terrorists occasionally react to public opinion. In December 1983, an IRA bomb killed six and wounded 94 people doing their Christmas shopping at London's most famous store, Harrods. The IRA leadership responded to worldwide condemnation by declaring that the bombers had acted without permission.

Many bomb attacks make no concession to such considerations, working instead on the belief that the higher profile the target and the more casualties inflicted, the more publicity and terror caused. Crowds offer terrorists anonymity when placing a bomb and are easy targets when it goes off. On July 27, 1996, during the Olympic Games, one woman was killed and 111 people were injured by a bomb at Atlanta's Centennial Olympic Park. The device used was a pipe bomb, an explosive-filled length of pipe that burst into shrapnel on detonation.

DOES BOMBING WORK?

Terrorist bombings have occasionally influenced wider events in the way that the terrorists planned. There is no doubt, for example, that the American and French forces left Beirut far more quickly after the massive bombings of October 1983 than they otherwise would have done. Bombings have also been effective as part of a longer struggle, as in the case of the successful campaign for independence waged by the Algerian National Liberation Army against France in the 1950s.

In other cases, the verdict has not been so clear-cut, but even if a terrorist group never achieves its ultimate aim, bombings most certainly hurt their targets. Governments often claim that they never give in to terrorist threats and hence never allow the terrorists to "win." However, the British government has for years tried to silence Sinn Fein, the political wing of the IRA. Most recently, the group was barred from talks on the future of Northern Ireland in July 1996. Yet the talks would not have taken place without the impetus of the IRA's bombing campaign.

Even when bombing has an effect, it may not be the one the terrorists desire. Hamas' suicide bombing campaign in Israel in 1993-96 put in jeopardy the developing peace between the Palestine Liberation Organization (PLO) and the Israelis, as Hamas undoubtedly wished. But it may also have helped to bring about the election of a new Israeli government, which has more hard-line views than those of its predecessors.

Terrorists view events from an entirely different perspective from that of the societies they try to change. They do not necessarily judge their actions by the same standards of success and failure used by politicians. Asking if terrorist bombings are effective may not be a useful question. Terrorists are ultimately distinguished by the violence with which they are prepared to support their views, and bombs are among the methods used. Whether they work or not, we can expect bombings to continue as long as there are terrorists – or until the terrorists find something worse.

Donald Sommerville

SEE ALSO: SUICIDE BOMBING; TERRORISM IN THE 1948-1949 ARAB-ISRAELI WAR; HAMAS; TAMIL TIGER TERROR IN SRI LANKA; SIKH NATIONALIST TERRORISM IN INDIA; TERROR BY THE HOLY WARRIORS OF KASHMIR; THE WORLD TRADE CENTER BOMBING; BASQUE NATIONALIST TERROR: ETA; NATIONALIST TERROR IN NORTHERN IRELAND 1976-1996; TERRORISM IN THE CITY OF LONDON.

FURTHER READING

- Bell, John Bowyer. *The Irish Troubles: A Generation of Political Violence, 1967-1992.* New York: St. Martin's Press, 1993.
- Emerson, Steven, and Brian Duffy. *The Fall of Pan Am 103: Inside the Lockerbie Investigation.* New York: Putnam, and London: Futura, 1990.
- Hammel, Eric. *The Root: The Marines in Beirut, August 1982-February 1984.* San Diego: Harcourt, Brace, Jovanovich, 1985.

HIJACKING AND KIDNAPPING

Hijacking and kidnapping have been important components of the terrorist's arsenal since the start of modern international terrorism in the late 1960s. The international nature of these terrorist methods is closely associated with worldwide advances in communications, which terrorists have exploited to publicize their causes, and with technologies that have provided them with new modes of mobility and anonymity. The frequency of hijacking and kidnapping has increased with the advent of state sponsorship of terrorism.

However, hijacking and kidnapping or hostage-taking are not new inventions. They have been used frequently throughout history as effective means to achieve strategic or tactical objectives. Political kidnapping was well known in antiquity. Roman emperors took hostages from tribes subject to Rome as a guarantee of good behavior. The emperors brought the hostages to Rome and assimilated them into the wealthiest, most educated families. If the hostages returned to their provinces, such friendships would encourage them to spread the pro-Roman word.

Also in antiquity, the Roman general Julius Caesar (102-44 B.C.) was captured by pirates who then held him for ransom. The practice of holding prisoners for ransom has continued from ancient to modern times. It is especially commonplace in the various cultures of the Middle East, where it has long been customary to abduct and conceal hostages and then to trade them for political purposes, or to kill them to exact revenge.

Similarly, long before the invention of the first aircraft, hijacking of ships was common throughout history. In 1789, Barbary pirates captured 11 American ships and 98 sailors. They were taken to North Africa and held for ransom. U.S. president George Washington was forced to negotiate and eventually handed over money and arms to secure the release of the seized ships and sailors.

Since the late 1960s, terrorists have refined the techniques of hijacking aircraft or ships and have come to rely on this activity as a source of funds and publicity. Extensive campaigns of kidnapping have also been launched to achieve an array of strategic and tactical aims. These goals have included pressuring governments into implementing policy changes and releasing other terrorists held in jail. Other objectives involved raising the terrorists' cause from obscurity through publicity and obtaining substantial sums of money to be used to fund further political goals.

Hijacking and kidnapping incidents have tended to fluctuate in scale and frequency because of changes in the terrorists' own objectives and in response to improved countermeasures by targeted states.

SUMMARY

- Kidnapping and holding people as hostages is an activity that has been used by criminals and terrorists for centuries.
- The number of hijackings declined after 1985 as security measures improved.
- Many countries now have specialist hostage-rescue teams to deal with hijackings and kidnappings if negotiations break down.
- Probably the foremost objective of hijackings and kidnappings is to enable terrorists to manipulate the news media and spread their message.

SEIZURE AND DETENTION

Hijacking, kidnapping, and hostage-taking share a number of common elements. First, they all involve the seizure and detention of a single person or a group of individuals such as diplomats, government officials, tourists, or businesspeople. The victims may be held in either a known siege site – such as an embassy, a private house, or public building; a passenger airliner, train, or ship – or in a concealed place that is known only to the terrorists.

In a siege situation, the terrorists and their victims are besieged in a location that is known to and

Popperfoto

A British SAS man enters a window of the Iranian embassy in London, ending a six-day siege in 1980.

controlled by the authorities. This is a serious disadvantage to the terrorists, because their mobility is severely restricted and they are unable to escape. They are vulnerable to hostage-rescue operations launched by the authorities.

The 1980 Iranian embassy episode in London illustrates the vulnerability of the terrorist in a siege situation. After six days of unsuccessful negotiation, 12 Special Air Service (SAS) commandos blew their way into the embassy. They killed five of the six militants holding the building and rescued the 19 hostages.

In a kidnapping, the perpetrators hold hostages at a location unknown to the authorities. These incidents usually last longer because they provide the terrorists with anonymity, security, and mobility, while rendering the security forces almost powerless to intervene.

Latin American terrorist groups have long favored this technique. The left-wing Tupamaros in Uruguay held British ambassador Sir Geoffrey Jackson hostage for nine months in 1971, then released him in return for the freedom of 106 prisoners and for a large sum of money in ransom.

Muslim terrorist groups have also frequently used kidnapping. Notable examples are the Hizb'allah (Party of God) in Lebanon – which held a total of over 130 foreigners hostage in secret locations between 1982 and 1991 – and the Iranian militants who seized the U.S. embassy in Tehran in 1979, holding 52 American diplomats hostage for 444 days.

The continuous mobility of the terrorists in some hijackings has been as effective as having a hideout. During the 17-day hijacking of TWA flight 847 in June 1985, the Lebanese hijackers – who denied belonging to any organized group – forced the flight to make several trips between Beirut and Algiers. After finally halting in Beirut, they removed 39 passengers from the plane and hid them in different places in the city. The hijackers eventually released the passengers in return for the freedom of 766 prisoners held in Israel.

THE THREAT TO KILL

The second shared element of hijacking and kidnapping is that both involve the threat to kill, to injure, or to continue the detention of a hostage in order to compel a third party to perform or abstain from specific acts.

In the bargaining process between a hostage-taker and a third party, the hostage-taker has two options to achieve concessions if the first threat is not successful. Either the level of the threat may be raised to force submission or inducements may be offered to reward compliance. The credibility of threats depends on the willingness of the terrorists to kill some of their hostages after a deadline has passed to raise the cost of noncompliance. Noncompliance is often punished by the sequential killing of additional hostages.

A prime example was the 1985 hijacking of an EgyptAir Boeing 737 by three members of the radical Palestinian Abu Nidal Organization. While the Maltese authorities refused to refuel the aircraft during the first 12 hours of the hijacking, the terrorists methodically shot five passengers – two Israelis and three Americans. Similarly, when the hijackers of TWA flight 847 needed to put pressure on the U.S. and Israeli authorities to comply with their demands, they severely beat U.S. Navy diver Robert Stetham before they killed him and dumped his body on the tarmac. The TWA flight hijackers also offered inducements, releasing hostages in batches in response to concessions and to show good faith.

Events have shown that terrorists are usually not interested in killing most or all of their captives in major incidents. Such action would probably be counterproductive. This is especially the case in siege situations because it is in the terrorists' own interest to keep hostages alive as an insurance against armed assault and their own possible deaths.

Many terrorists feel that their best insurance against potential hostage-rescue operations is to seize highly prominent officials or businesspeople. This increases the publicity for their cause as well as the bargaining value of the hostage.

In one of the most famous hostage-taking incidents of the 1970s, the terrorist known as "Carlos the Jackal" and five members of the Popular Front for the Liberation of Palestine (PFLP) raided a meeting of the Organization of Petroleum Exporting Countries (OPEC) in Vienna, Austria, in December 1975. After a one-day standoff, the terrorists were granted free passage to Algeria where they released the 11 Arab oil ministers in exchange for a $25 million ransom.

HOSTAGE MURDER

However, hostage-taking incidents have on occasion ended in the murder of the hostage when the authorities failed to comply with the terrorists' demands. In practice this seems to be most often the case with the abduction of a single prominent captive. Under such high-profile pressure, many governments feel unable to give in to demands and attempt to maintain a policy of not negotiating with terrorists.

Among the most notorious cases were the kidnap and murder of prominent West German businessman Hanns-Martin Schleyer by the Baader-Meinhof gang (also known as the Red Army Faction, or RAF) in late 1977 and the kidnap and murder of former Italian prime minister Aldo Moro by the Red Brigades in the spring of 1978.

The terrorists' decision to use the techniques of hijacking and kidnapping is usually influenced by their particular strategic and tactical objectives at any given time. Their choice of tactics is also influenced by the reactions of the targeted states and the employment of effective countermeasures, such as improved X-ray machines at airports, or the states' willingness to use hostage-rescue teams. Often the decision to switch between hijacking and kidnapping is inspired by successful acts by other groups, assisted by the media's intense coverage of major terrorist events.

HIJACKING HEYDAY

Since 1968-69, an array of different terrorist groups have targeted civil airline passengers and their crews for hijacking. The trend began with a spate of more than 120 hijackings by Cuban criminals and refugees in 1969-70, diverting the aircraft between the U.S. and Cuba. The practice was reduced by the U.S.-Cuba Hijack Pact of 1973, which extradited hijackers to their country of origin and severely punished them.

Various Palestinian terrorist groups quickly emulated this tactic. By hijacking an El Al airliner to Algeria in August 1969, the Fatah organization was the first to employ the headline-grabbing tactic of holding airline passengers hostage in an attempt to exchange them for the release of imprisoned Palestinians. After two months of negotiations, Israel yielded and released 16 imprisoned terrorists in exchange for the the passengers being held hostage.

This success led to more than a dozen hijackings by Palestinian terrorists between 1968 and 1972. The most spectacular of these was the PFLP's simultaneous seizures of five airliners on September 6-9, 1970. For four days, PFLP terrorists kept more than 300 passengers in three of the airliners at Dawson's Field in the Jordanian desert. The hostages were released only after the British, Swiss, and West German governments agreed to free seven Palestinian terrorists from prison. These concessions did not, however, get the airliners back intact. Before television cameras, the terrorists blew up all three aircraft at Dawson's Field.

In May 1972, a Sabena Boeing 707 airliner at Lod airport in Tel Aviv was hijacked by four Palestinian members of the Black September terrorist group. The Israeli authorities pretended to be willing to grant the hijackers' demands for the release of 317 Palestinians being held in Israel. But the elite Israeli counterterrorist unit, Sayaret Matkal, managed to board the plane. They killed or arrested the terrorists and rescued the 89 passengers. This was the first time a hostage-rescue unit had managed to storm a hijacked airliner successfully.

Governments were alarmed by the wave of 286 hijackings worldwide between 1969-72 and began to take significant steps to improve airline security. In 1973, it became obligatory for all U.S. airports to process every passenger through metal detectors. The

Hulton Getty Picture Collection

The body of Italian politician Aldo Moro is found in Rome, May 1978, after his kidnappers shot him.

effectiveness of this procedure was rapidly demonstrated the following year when 25 potential hijackings were averted and more than 2,400 firearms were confiscated at various airports in the United States. The spate of hijackings also led to the 1970 Hague Convention, which required contracting states either to extradite apprehended hijackers to their country of origin or to prosecute them.

However, this convention and other legislation did not provide a complete barrier against aircraft hijackings or attacks, especially because some states remained non-signatories and provided safe havens to which the terrorists could direct hijacked aircraft. Equally, while improved airport and airline security measures deterred some attacks, as shown by the reduction of annual incidents from 80 to 30 between 1973 to 1981, terrorists could simply switch to less protected airports. They also supplemented hijacking with other methods, such as hostage-taking and seizing embassies or other public locations. At the 1972 Munich Olympic Games, the Palestinian Black September group seized and killed Israeli athletes, and in December 1972 the Israeli embassy in Bangkok was seized and held for 19 hours. A series of hijackings then followed to gain the release of imprisoned terrorists held in Israel and West European countries, in revenge for successful hostage-rescue missions and once again to publicize the terrorists' causes.

THE DECLINE OF HIJACKING

The PFLP was responsible for two of the most dramatic hijackings during the 1970s. In 1976, six PFLP members hijacked an Air France airliner and diverted it to Uganda's Entebbe airport. There they demanded the release of 53 terrorists, most of whom were held in Israel. The hijacking was foiled by the dramatic hostage-rescue operation by Israeli units in which 100 passengers were rescued, although three were killed along with one Israeli commando, Jonathan Netanyahu, brother of Israeli politician and later prime minister, Benjamin Netanyahu. The second spectacular incident was the hijacking of a Lufthansa plane in

1977, by the PFLP in conjunction with four West German Baader-Meinhof terrorists. The hijackers diverted the plane to Mogadishu, Somalia. They demanded the release of imprisoned Baader-Meinhof terrorists and killed the airline captain. Using "flash-bang" grenades – which stun people into temporary insensibility with a mixture of noise and light – 28 West German GSG-9 commandos stormed the plane and rescued the remaining 91 passengers and crew, while killing the hijackers.

While scores of hijackings of airliners occurred in the mid- to late 1970s, these were mainly perpetrated by splinter groups of the Palestine Liberation Organization (PLO). The PLO itself tried to distance itself from terrorism in foreign countries and concentrated on attacks against Israeli targets. Airliners were not the only targets for hijacking. The PFLP was involved in a joint operation with the Japanese Red Army to hijack a ferry in Singapore in 1974.

The decrease in the number of incidents toward the end of the 1970s was due mainly to internal Palestinian feuds. These were brought forcibly to world attention in November 1974 with the hijacking at Dubai of a British Airways jet, later flown to Tunis. The four terrorists called themselves followers of Abou Mahmoud, a Palestinian executed two months earlier by the PLO leadership. The terrorists demanded the release of extremist Palestinians held by Egypt and the Netherlands. These men were released, and the hijackers surrendered on a promise of asylum. Despite this promise, Tunisian authorities arrested the terrorists and sent them to the PLO for trial and imprisonment.

HIJACKING TRENDS

Since 1982, the average number of hijackings has reduced to fewer than 20 per year. Terrorists have switched to other methods, such as bombing, shooting, and kidnapping.

However, a few major Palestinian hijackings have occurred in this period. In two cases, unsuccessful military rescue operations resulted in massive casualties. In the autumn of 1985 three Abu Nidal terrorists hijacked an EgyptAir plane. The event ended in disaster, with the deaths of more than 60 passengers after Egyptian commandos made a failed rescue attempt. Similarly, Abu Nidal's 1986 hijacking of a New York-bound PanAm Boeing 747 ended in tragedy at Pakistan's Karachi airport when the terrorists began firing with Kalashnikov AK-47 assault rifles at the passengers. In all there were 21 deaths and more than 100 people wounded.

STORMING SHIPS AND AIRCRAFT

In 1985, four members of the Palestine Liberation Front (PLF) hijacked the cruise ship *Achille Lauro*. During the hijack, they killed an American wheelchair-bound passenger before receiving free passage out of Egypt on board an airliner. In a dramatic interception of the EgyptAir jet carrying the hijackers, U.S. fighter jets forced it to land in Sicily. Italy, however, failed to detain all the members of the terrorist group for political reasons. The resulting confrontation between Italian and U.S. authorities constituted a major setback in dealing with terrorists through international legal cooperation. While the four hijackers were eventually tried, convicted, and imprisoned in Italy, the Italian government collapsed as a result of its lenient action toward the other members of the terrorist group.

During the 1980s, there were two spectacular hijackings by the Muslim terrorist group Hizb'allah, who took elaborate precautions against any hostage-rescue attempts. Mention has already been made of the 1985 TWA flight 847 hijacking. During this flight the Hizb'allah hijackers flew back and forth between Beirut and Algiers to avoid a commando assault. They used statements to the international mass media to strengthen their bargaining positions. After the release of prisoners held in Israel, the hostages were released but the hijackers went free via Algeria.

In their next hijacking, of Kuwait Airlines flight 422 in 1988, Hizb'allah showed that they had learned from earlier mistakes. The type of aircraft chosen, a 747 jumbo jet, made rescue attempts hard because of its internal layout. One hijacker was reportedly capable of flying the aircraft. The terrorists took the precaution of wiring the doors with explosives and maintaining tight control over the passengers. They also made shrewd use of the media to gain publicity and by indicating their willingness to die for their cause.

The selection of Algeria, a consistent supporter of the PLO and Palestinian causes, as the final destination indicated careful planning. When Algeria granted them free passage back to Lebanon, the ineffectiveness of international agreements to suppress hijackings was revealed. Despite these apparent successes, however, the hijackers failed to achieve their principal objective, which was gaining the release of imprisoned members held in Kuwait.

The trends of hijackings in the 1980s differed greatly from those of the 1970s. The hijackings of the early 1970s were occasionally carried out by a few armed terrorists. These prompted the development of tighter aviation security procedures, international agreements, and the establishment of hostage-rescue units which were successfully deployed in the Mogadishu and Entebbe incidents.

In the mid-1980s, however, hijackers became increasingly operationally sophisticated as well as more willing to kill their hostages. This led to several failed rescue attempts resulting in many deaths. At the same time, terrorists increasingly switched to sabotaging and bombing airliners as the continuously improved aviation security measures made hijacking more difficult. In the 1990s, the majority of hijackings have been carried out by individuals seeking asylum in the West from the former Soviet Union and other countries with repressive regimes.

HOSTAGE-TAKING

The wave of Palestinian hijackings during the early 1970s was complemented by the takeover of several embassies around the world by the Black September organization. In 1972, four terrorists seized the Israeli embassy in Thailand and made a demand for the release of 36 comrades imprisoned in Israel, which was refused. This was followed by Black September's seizure of the Saudi Arabian embassy in Khartoum, Sudan, when they demanded the release of imprisoned comrades in Israel and of members of the Baader-Meinhof gang in West Germany. This incident revealed the emergence of extensive cooperation and solidarity between terrorist organizations. This proved to be especially true of links between Palestinian groups, Baader-Meinhof, and the Japanese Red Army.

But the most famous hostage-taking incident of all was staged by the Black September group. It occurred at the 1972 Olympic Games in Munich. Eight terrorists managed to seize 11 Israeli athletes at the Olympic village. The terrorists demanded the release of more than 200 of their comrades held in Israeli prisons. While Israel refused to grant the demands, West German police attempted a rescue by force. It ended in tragedy when the hostages were killed in a fire fight, which also cost the lives of a policeman and four of the terrorists.

The Munich incident prompted extensive improvement in the training of existing hostage–rescue teams

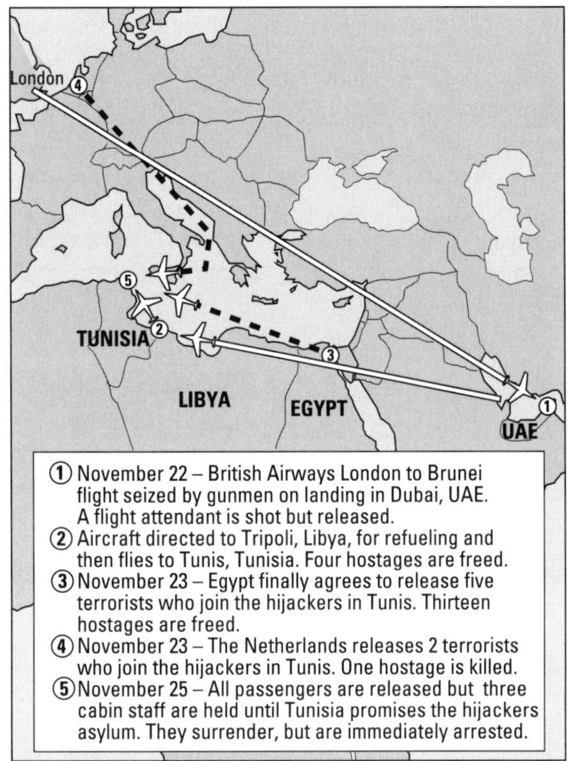

A Palestinian group calling itself the Martyr Abou Mahmoud Squad carried out the 1974 Dubai hijack.

in those countries that had them, and to the establishment of similar elite units in several other countries. At the same time, the publicity surrounding the Munich incident, coupled with the increase in the number of joint operations between terrorist groups, led to a wave of further siege situations. In many cases, the terrorists hoped to strike before hostage–rescue teams improved their tactics.

In 1974, the Democratic Front for the Liberation of Palestine (DFLP) infiltrated the Israeli town of Ma'alot and seized a school with more than 90 teenage students. The terrorists demanded the release of 20 Palestinian comrades held in Israel. They threatened to blow up the building with wired charges unless their demands were met. The incident ended in tragedy when Israeli elite units stormed the building, but failed to kill one of the terrorists outright. Although wounded, he turned his guns and grenades toward the teenagers. Before Israeli commandos killed him, the terrorist had slain 21 teenagers and wounded 65 others.

Hulton Getty Picture Collection

American hostages arrive at Frankfurt in 1981 after being released from their 444-day ordeal in Iran.

There were also a number of hostage-taking incidents in Europe. For example, in 1974, the Japanese Red Army seized the French embassy in The Hague, Netherlands. In 1975, the Baader-Meinhof gang took the West German embassy in Sweden, demanding the release of their jailed leaders. Apart from free passage out of the country in some instances, these hostage-taking incidents generally failed to achieve their objectives. However, South Moluccan terrorists did achieve their aim of obtaining publicity for their problems in Indonesia when they seized the Indonesian embassy and a train in Holland in 1975, and then a second train and a school six months later.

EMBASSY CRISES

Between 1971 and 1980, there were more than 50 terrorist embassy seizures. In 1979 alone, terrorists occupied no less than 26 embassies worldwide. However, events showed that the terrorists had only a 50 percent chance of avoiding capture or death because more countries had formed elite hostage-rescue units and showed a willingness to use them.

However, the elite U.S. Delta Force was unsuccessful in its attempt to rescue the 52 American diplomats held in Tehran after 400 Iranian students stormed the U.S. embassy on November 4, 1979. The students demanded the extradition of the shah of Iran, then in exile and receiving medical treatment in New York. The Iranian government sanctioned the embassy siege, grossly violating international laws of diplomacy. The Iranians used the hostage crisis to inflict maximum embarrassment on the United States and President Jimmy Carter. Carter made the release of the American hostages a central issue in his unsuccessful campaign for re-election. The Iranians were keen to humiliate Carter after he gave sanctuary to the shah. The hostages were not released until after he handed over office to Ronald Reagan in 1981.

This incident marked a watershed since it revealed the West's vulnerability, and it led to a rapid increase in state-sponsored terrorism. Hizb'allah, actively encouraged by Iran, later exploited this weakness through the kidnappings of Westerners in Lebanon during the 1980s. Embassy sieges, on the other hand, declined during the 1980s.

Other spectacular terrorist incidents occurred in the developing world, including the taking of 300 hostages in the Palace of Justice in Colombia in 1985. As in the case of hijackings, the overall incidence of siege-hostage situations declined as security improved and hostage-rescue operations increased in number, raising the risk of capture and death for the terrorists.

Instead, most terrorist groups relied more and more on kidnappings and bombings as more effective and less risky means to achieve their objectives. And an added advantage was that there was less danger of capture and interrogation by the authorities. This became particularly important with the increase of state sponsorship of terrorism as the states involved wished to conceal their part in the terrorist activities.

KIDNAPPING

The kidnapping and holding of individuals at secret locations has often been used by a variety of Middle Eastern and Latin American terrorist groups. They frequently demand money, changes in government policy, and the release of prisoners in return for the safe release of kidnap victims.

Latin American terrorists particularly have resorted to politically motivated kidnappings of foreign businessmen and diplomats. Colombia's kidnapping rates, which ran at an annual 600 cases in both 1988 and 1989, clearly demonstrate the popularity of the tactic. The Armed Forces of National Resistance (FARN) abducted multinational executives in El Salvador between 1978 and 1980. And mention has already been made of the Sir Geoffrey Jackson case, which took place in Uruguay in 1972 during the first wave of Latin American kidnappings.

Kidnapping is popular because it is a relatively low-risk and high-yield method. Between 1971 and 1975 in Latin America, kidnappers managed to extort more than $80 million in ransom. In most cases of kidnappings, the terrorists have an 80 percent chance of escaping capture or death. At the same time, the hostages themselves are relatively safe since only four percent of all kidnap victims are killed by terrorists. Ransom is paid in over 50 percent of all kidnappings.

Governments face two problems in responding to kidnapping: first, it is difficult to locate hostages; second, most governments have publicly declared policies of no concessions to terrorists. However, refusal to accede to terrorist demands has resulted in instances in which the terrorists have killed their hostages: the murder of business leader Hanns-Martin Schleyer by the German Red Army Faction in 1977 is one example.

By kidnapping a number of individuals at the same time, terrorists have continued to raise the pressure on the authorities by sequentially killing hostages, as hijackers also have done.

Hizb'allah used this strategy in Lebanon. Hizb'allah's kidnappings of more than 100 foreigners were a prolonged and effective campaign. Although the terrorists killed only a handful of these hostages, they managed to exact huge ransom payments and the release of prisoners, and induced a number of Western governments to modify or change their policies in various ways. One of the most dramatic changes of government policy was the U.S.-Iranian arms-for-hostages deal in the mid-1980s. Although it had previously refused to trade in arms with Iran, the U.S. secretly now did so in order to secure the release of hostages held in Lebanon. When this deal was exposed, it caused one of the most serious crises of the Reagan administration during its two terms in office.

Magnus Ranstorp

SEE ALSO: TERROR IN ANCIENT GREECE AND THE ROMAN REPUBLIC; HOSTAGE NEGOTIATIONS; MIDDLE EASTERN TERRORISM 1948-1969; MIDDLE EASTERN TERRORISM 1970-1987; MIDDLE EASTERN TERRORISM 1988-1996; TERRORISM AND REVOLUTION IN IRAN; HIZB'ALLAH; TERRORISM IN LATIN AMERICA; RED ARMY FACTION: THE BAADER-MEINHOF GANG; RED BRIGADES; JAPANESE TERRORISM.

FURTHER READING

- Arey, J. *The Sky Pirates.* New York: Scribners, 1972; London: Allen, 1973.
- Aston, C. *A Contempory Crisis: Political Hostage-taking and the Experience of Western Europe.* Westport, CT: Greenwood Press, 1982; London: Institute for Study of Conflict, 1984.
- McClintock, M. C. "Skyjacking: Its Domestic, Civil, and Criminal Ramifications," in *Journal of Air Law and Commerce* (Winter 1973).
- Middendorff, W. *New Developments in the Taking of Hostages and Kidnapping.* Washington, DC: National Criminal Justice Reference Service, 1975.

ASSASSINATION

Assassination is the murder of a prominent person for political reasons. It is illegal but not always irrational – the act is usually carefully planned and long premeditated. There have been many famous victims od assassination in recent history – the Kennedys and Martin Luther King, and the Gandhis in India among others. Targets of unsuccessful assassination attempts include Ronald Reagan, Margaret Thatcher, Benito Mussolini, Adolf Hitler, and Pope John Paul II. But assassination is by no means a recent development. Several Roman statesmen, notably Julius Caesar in 44 B.C., met sudden death at the hands of opponents. Emperors Caligula, Nero, Domitian, and Elagabalus were all victims of assassination. Even the word *assassin* has ancient origins, deriving from an eleventh-century Islamic sect that specialized in political murder.

The typical assassination may seem to be an isolated, arbitrary act of violence. But this is rarely the case. Assassination can be part of a wider terrorist campaign or one tactic of a guerrilla war. It may be a stunt that a group tries once and then abandons, or it may be used regularly.

Most assassinations are part of a conspiracy. However, there are examples of lone assassins – Israeli prime minister Yitzhak Rabin was killed on November 4, 1995, by Yigal Amir, a lone gunman discontented with the Israeli-Palestinian peace process.

Whatever the motive and background to a murder, it is easy to define a killing as an assassination if both the perpetrator and the victim are engaged in politics. It is less clear-cut if the act is part of a broader pattern of violence such as war. Some ideological murders are carried out on a vast scale, for example, those of the Holocaust in World War II or Pol Pot's killing fields in Cambodia. Many experts prefer to treat these mass killings as genocide, while reserving the term *assassination* for the violent death of specific individuals.

KEY FACTS

- Rumors of conspiracy still surround the assassination of U.S. president John F. Kennedy in 1963. He was shot dead in his motorcade in Dealey Plaza, Dallas, by Lee Harvey Oswald, himself later shot dead as he was taken out of a police station.
- In 1968, civil rights leader Martin Luther King's assassination by James Earl Ray in Memphis, Tennessee, led to widespread rioting.
- In 1984, Indian prime minister Indira Gandhi was assassinated; her son Rajiv took over the premiership but was himself killed by a bomb in 1991.

THE ENVIRONMENT OF POLITICAL MURDER

Some societies are plagued by acts of political murder. There can be many reasons for this – the government may be tyrannical, or have been put in place by foreign invaders, or the society may be divided on ethnic, religious, or political lines.

In Western society, assassination is generally not the first choice of groups intent on political violence. Western groups that do turn to assassination almost always lack the means to wage a more conventional terrorist campaign or guerrilla war. Cultures with traditions of religious fanaticism, however, opt for assassination more readily. The Palestinians have made extensive use of political murder, as have the Tamil Tigers in Sri Lanka.

Assassinations are easiest to carry out in societies where the government authority is weak, as in Sri Lanka today and Russia during the period 1917-23. Brutal authoritarian states – such as Stalin's Soviet Union or Mao's China – have such powerful state security forces that political killers tend to be those secretly sponsored by the state against internal opposition.

THE PURPOSE OF KILLING

Assassins are usually proponents of a political theory that gives legitimacy to their actions. The few who target prominent figures for personal reasons may be compelled to do so because of psychological disorders. In 1981, in his assassination attempt on U.S. president Ronald Reagan, John Hinckley appeared to have been influenced by the film *Taxi Driver*. He was acquitted and committed to a mental institution.

Killers often believe that a single murder will change the future. They may believe that one spectac-

Popperfoto

Secret service agents arrest John Hinckley. He fired six shots, wounding President Reagan, who was leaving the Hilton hotel in Washington D.C. in 1981.

ular event will help publicize their political ideas and make the authorities more aware of them. More directly, they may hope that eliminating a major figure will be enough to topple a government or rival cause.

The sudden killing of a powerful individual will undoubtedly have a significant political impact, whatever the original motive. For example, the assassinations of American presidents have had dramatic repercussions, although they were not all politically motivated. They were generally the acts of weak individuals who believed that they would gain personal prestige by killing an important person. The widespread political fallout was incidental.

Famous politicians are most often singled out for assassination. But other targets include state officials, such as judges or police officers. If the state itself practices assassination, terrorists themselves may become targets. Assassins may choose the victim because of his or her political actions and beliefs or because he or she holds a particular office of state or somehow symbolizes the rival cause. Earl Louis Mountbatten was chosen as an assassination victim by the Provisional Irish Republican Army (IRA) in 1979 for symbolic reasons. He had little power, but as a member of the royal family and a retired senior naval officer he epitomized the British establishment.

Although most assassins working to preserve the status quo are authorized or encouraged by the government, some illegal groups kill to defend the existing order. In Northern Ireland, Protestant paramilitaries have targeted Catholic political leaders who oppose their desire to maintain union with Great Britain. Such paramilitary defenders of a status quo are more likely to kill vulnerable targets than powerful, usually protected, individuals.

Each assassination has not only a victim but also a target audience. The audience is the wider public, which the assassin wishes to influence, either by striking fear or by gaining support. The attack may intimidate or horrify an audience. Equally, an assassination may reassure or reward it. The more important the target, the greater the audience, and the wider the impact. Even if the attempt fails, it may serve to highlight a grievance.

The victim may be not only a symbol, as was Mountbatten, but also irreplaceable. In 1944, a group of German army officers attempted to assassinate Adolf Hitler in what became known as the July Bomb Plot. If they had succeeded, it is likely Germany would have surrendered sooner than it did.

In any effective assassination, the greater the symbolic value of the target, the greater the impact. Some targets are high-profile leaders while others have a key, if invisible, role – for example, the head of counterintelligence or a propaganda chief. A long campaign will target all of these. Rebels with limited capabilities or a greater sense of urgency will choose more prominent targets.

ACCESS TO THE VICTIM

Assassins have used the full range of weapons: explosive devices, pistols, knives, firing squads, and even poison. The reasons behind a murder do not often have any impact on the method of assassination chosen. Usually, the assassin chooses the method that is most likely to achieve success. The crucial, and often trickiest, part has always been gaining access to the victim. In the fifteenth century, John the Bold, duke of Burgundy, was lured to a bridge ostensibly to discuss peace negotiations with the king of France. There, he was stabbed to death by assassins.

If the chosen weapon is a revolver or knife, the killers have to determine how to get close enough to touch the target. To poison, the assassins need access only to the victim's food. To plant a time-bomb, they need to know the victim's intended route or location.

In 1984, the IRA terrorists knew British prime minister Margaret Thatcher's schedule during the Conservative party conference in Brighton in October. The terrorist group was able to plant a bomb in her hotel weeks before her arrival. An electronic timer detonated the device when the prime minister was present in the hotel. She had just emerged from the bathroom of her hotel suite when the bomb went off. Although she was shaken, she escaped physically unscathed. But other politicians and members of their families were seriously injured, and five people died.

More successful was the attack on the Spanish premier Carrero Blanco in December 1973. Basque separatists (ETA) planted a massive mine under a road along which it was known that Blanco would travel. The mine was detonated as the car passed over it, killing Blanco and his entire entourage.

Another requirement for most assassins is a reliable escape route. The team who planted the Brighton bomb had made their getaway weeks before the explosion took place, while the Basque terrorist squad who killed Blanco set off the mine from a distance and fled the area.

However, those who kill at close range have more difficulty in escaping the security team surrounding a target. The squad of al-Jihad Islamic fundamentalists who machine-gunned Egypt's President Anwar Sadat in 1981 were immediately attacked by loyal army units. The few who survived were later sentenced to death.

A few assassins have no escape route at all. Palestinian groups, for example, have made use of suicide bombers. Driving vehicles packed with explosives to a target and then detonating the bomb, these religious fanatics know that their death is certain. But so too is that of their victims.

AUTHORIZED ASSASSINS

Assassination may be used as a tactic in conventional war. Modern wars are generally fought between massive organized forces, but sometimes a key individual presents a target. In April 1943, with World War II at its height, the Americans shot down the aircraft carrying Japanese naval commander-in-chief Admiral Yamamoto, having discovered its flight plans. Earlier in the same conflict, the Germans bombed Buckingham Palace and the House of Commons, hoping to kill important members of the British royalty or government. Such assassinations and attempts are generally reckoned to be legitimate acts of war – murder carried out under government orders.

More conventional assassinations are also authorized by governments. Many nations have used assassination because it is sometimes convenient, often cheap, and easily denied. Most often this tactic is used by totalitarian governments against internal dissidents. It is a convenient way to quell dissent at home and to terrorize opponents into silence. For example, Mussolini had his greatest domestic critic, Giacomo Matteoti, murdered in June 1924. The interests of national security can be invoked to legitimize assassination by the government.

THE IMPACT OF ASSASSINATION

Assessing the impact of an assassination is tricky. Governments tend to deny that the assassination achieved anything at all (unless they sanctioned or engineered it). In contrast, the assassins usually suggest that they have gained far more advantage from the deed than they actually have. The killing of President Sadat of Egypt, for instance, did little to harden that country's attitude to Israel, which was the goal of the assassins.

At the very least, an assassin wants to draw attention to a grievance. Far more preferable is to force a change in the political situation. The degree of change anticipated gives some indication of how realistic the assassins are. The German conspirators of July 1944 expected too much when they thought the death of Hitler would lead to a negotiated peace with the Allies rather than unconditional surrender. However, the Basque terrorists who killed Spanish premier Blanco were correct in thinking that the assassination would make the government believe ETA a formidable force.

Another obstacle to judging the impact of a successful assassination is that it is, of course, impossible to know what would have happened without the attack. Some political analysts believe that major historical trends are unlikely to be shifted by a single murder. For instance, they argue that Egyptian policy would have differed little had President Sadat lived from the course the government took without him. Others believe that the contribution of individual leaders to the political landscape of their times is so fundamental that their removal alters history.

But whatever the impact of assassinations on mainstream politics, such killings can have profound effects on the organizations that carry them out. In March 1978, the Italian left-wing Red Brigades murdered Aldo Moro, one of the most important politicians in Italy. The terrorist group believed that the Italian government had been corrupted by what they called the State of Imperialist Multinationals (SIM), a sinister group of large companies based in America. Despite the death of Moro, the government did not

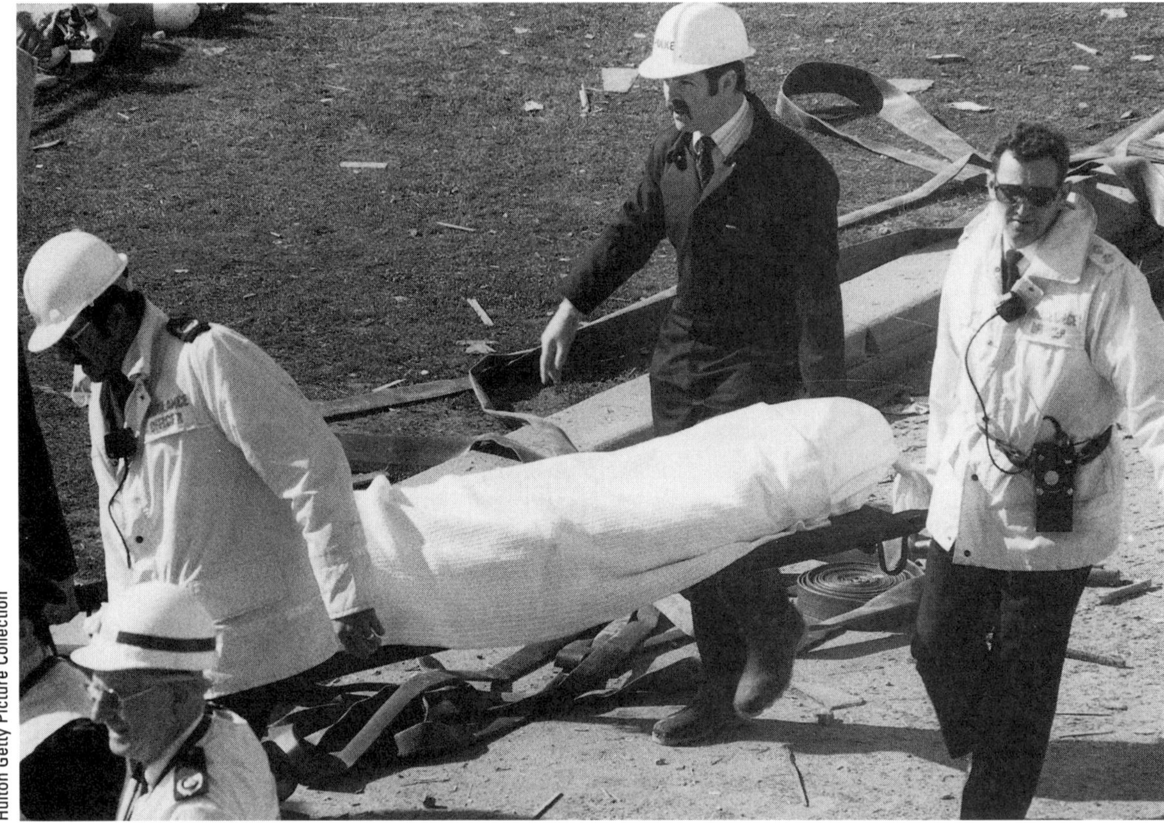

Hulton Getty Picture Collection

In 1984, the Provisional IRA bombed a hotel in Brighton, England, in an unsuccessful attempt to assassinate British premier Margaret Thatcher. There were, however, several other victims.

collapse because there was no such thing as the SIM group. The operation allowed the security forces to gain invaluable intelligence about the terrorists. Many of the Red Brigades' volunteers were swiftly arrested and the organization was weakened. Although the attack on Moro was effective as a murder and had an immediate destabilizing impact on Italy, it was ultimately unsuccessful because it marked the beginning of the end of the terrorist group.

Despite the general distaste of the public, assassination has long been an acceptable revolutionary method. It appears to offer a low-cost means of changing public opinion. It has been so attractive that even established states have used authorized assassins. Active most often during times of turmoil in divided societies and uncertain governments, the assassin finds it difficult to act against leaders of authoritarian states. Events may not always change as anticipated, but assassination remains a terrible but compelling way to alter history.

John Bowyer Bell

SEE ALSO: THE ASSASSINS: A TERROR CULT; ASSASSINATION AT SARAJEVO 1914; BOMBING OPERATIONS; SUICIDE BOMBING; TAMIL TIGER TERROR IN SRI LANKA.

FURTHER READING

- Bell, John Bowyer. *Assassin. The Theory and Practice of Political Murder.* New York: St. Martin's Press, 1979.
- Clarke, J. W. *American Assassins: The Darker Side of Politics.* 2nd ed. Princeton, NJ: Princeton University Press, 1990.
- Ford, F. L. *Political Murder, From Tyrannicide to Terrorism.* Cambridge, MA: Harvard University Press, 1985.

ROCKETS, MORTARS, AND MISSILES

By a combination of theft, improvisation, and knowing the right people, terrorists can lay their hands on destructive but sophisticated mortars, rockets, and surface-to-air missiles, or SAMs.

Mortars are muzzle-loading weapons used to fire shells at low-velocity and at short range. The mortars terrorists use fall into two categories. First, there are conventional, factory-made mortars, which can be fired at some distance from the target, granting the terrorists a good chance of escaping. They can also do significant damage, even against fortified targets. Terrorists have managed to get hold of mortars by robbing armories or through arms shipments from sympathetic states, and they are not afraid to use them. The Islamic fundamentalist group Hizb'allah has regularly used mortars to bombard villages in northern Israel from just over the border in southern Lebanon.

The second category of mortars favored by terrorists is the homemade type. This is the preferred weapon of the Irish Republican Army (IRA). Homemade mortars are easy to make. The IRA, for example, used tubes mounted on trucks to bombard police and army posts in Northern Ireland. They have also used portable homemade mortars. From the terrorists' point of view, the drawback of such crude devices is their lack of accuracy and unpredictability. Many bombs fall wide of the target, and accidents are common. But when the bomb is on target, the damage can be high. On the morning of February 7, 1991, the IRA mortared the British prime minister's London house at No. 10 Downing Street. The projectile missed the house and landed in the garden. The damage was slight, but it was a close call that shook the nation.

KEY FACTS

- Terrorists believed to be Muslim extremists mortared Maganoy in the Philippines in May 1995, killing three people during a referendum on the first three years of President Fidel Ramos's rule.
- On January 13, 1975, the international terrorist Carlos the Jackal and associates from the Popular Front for the Liberation of Palestine opened fire on an El Al airliner with RPG-7 grenade launchers at Orly airport, Paris, France. They missed the target but hit a Yugoslav aircraft and a building.

FROM SIMPLE TO SOPHISTICATED

Terrorists also use various types of rockets. There are comparatively simple, unguided, rocket-propelled grenade launchers, such as the Soviet-made RPG-7. Terrorist organizations, such as the IRA, Palestinian groups, and Zimbabwean nationalist guerrillas, have had the RPG-7 in their armories. The weapon is basically an anti-tank rocket, but terrorists have found other uses for it. In September 1991 in Germany, terrorists fired an RPG-7 at the armored limousine of U.S. General Frederick Kroesen while the car was stopped at a traffic light. Although the projectile found its mark, it caused only superficial injuries.

The second category of rockets used by terrorists includes the sophisticated guided anti-tank missiles, such as the American M72.750 LAW (light anti-tank weapon). This highly portable weapons weighs a mere seven pounds, yet its projectile can penetrate one and a half inches of armor. More powerful weapons include the wireguided Russian Spigot and NATO's MILAN anti-tank missiles. MILAN's missile weighs 25 pounds and the launching and guidance system weighs a further 37 pounds. The extra weight makes it less portable than the M72. But MILAN fits in the trunk of a car and is very accurate at distances between 250 and 2,000 yards. However, throughout the missile's flight, the operator must keep the target in view in the crosshairs of the launcher's sight to be sure of a hit.

TRH Pictures

The IRA has used homemade mortars such as this captured weapon in attacks in Northern Ireland.

The third type of rocket that terrorists use are the "Katyushas." These are Russian-made weapons whose multi-barreled launchers are usually vehicle-mounted. In the 1990s, Hizb'allah have made great use of Katyushas, along with mortars, to bombard northern Israel. While the Russian army carries its Katyushas on specially-built trucks, Hizb'allah mounts its rockets onto pickup trucks. The terrorists can launch a salvo from close to the Israeli-Lebanese border, then dash for cover before the Israeli security forces locate them.

Some terrorist organizations have acquired handheld guided surface-to-air missiles, or SAMs. SAMs can be carried and operated by one person, making them suitable for terrorist acts. But SAMs are expensive and require extensive training to be operated successfully. This means that terrorist groups require state sponsorship both to obtain the SAMs and to operate them effectively. That terrorists had surface-to-air missiles first became clear on September 5, 1973, when Italian police in Rome arrested five members of the Palestinian Black September organization. The Arabs were armed with two Soviet-made SAM-7s and were occupying an apartment beneath the flight path into Rome airport. Their intention was to shoot down an aircraft belonging to El Al the Israeli airline. Since then, terrorists have successfully used SAMs. In 1978, guerrillas in Zimbabwe (then Rhodesia) shot down a civil airliner, killing 48 people. The next year, the terrorists downed another airliner, killing 59.

SAMs are also used by terrorists to deny free use of the skies to government forces. During the war in Afghanistan in the 1980s, Mujahedin used U.S. Stinger missiles with great success to shoot down Soviet helicopter gunships. This made it increasingly difficult for the Soviets to prosecute the war. These attacks both hampered Soviet re-supply to remote bases from the air and also limited the Russians' ability to provide close air support to soldiers on the ground. It has been argued that the Mujahedin Stinger campaign accelerated the Soviet decision to withdraw from Afghanistan, which was reached in 1988.

In Northern Ireland, the opposite may be the case. Some experts maintain that the IRA's failure to deploy SAMs was a factor in the group's inability to force the British government to look for a solution to the conflict. In some border areas, the casualties caused by IRA bomb attacks on army vehicles forced the British to re-supply isolated bases from the air. But the IRA has been unable to impede the army because it cannot shoot down the British helicopters.

Nadine J. Gurr

SEE ALSO: TERROR IN ZIMBABWE (RHODESIA); THE BLACK SEPTEMBER ORGANIZATION; CARLOS THE JACKAL; HIZB'ALLAH; TERROR IN THE PHILIPPINES; NATIONALIST TERROR IN NORTHERN IRELAND 1976-1996.

FURTHER READING

- Clutterbuck, Richard. *Terrorism in an Unstable World.* London and New York: Routledge, 1994.
- Gander, Terry. *Guerrilla Warfare Weapons: The Modern Underground Fighters' Armory.* New York: Stirling, 1990.

TERRORISTS' USE OF CHEMICAL WEAPONS

On March 20, 1995, several small gas dispensers were smuggled onto three subway trains in Tokyo, the Japanese capital. The dispensers released a nerve gas called Sarin, which killed 12 people, including two U.S. citizens. The attack was carried out by the Aum Shrinri-kyu sect, a religious cult led by Shoko Asahara. Although the attack was the first successful use of chemical weapons by terrorists, the death toll would have been much higher if Asahara's chemists had made the concoction stronger.

In its purest form, Sarin is colorless and odorless. But the low-quality Sarin used in Tokyo smelled of rotting vegetables. Nevertheless, over 5,500 people were injured, many seriously. Nerve gases such as Sarin attack the central and peripheral nervous system. Symptoms are progressive and include breathing difficulties, sweating, vomiting, cramps, involuntary bowel movements, fainting, and confusion, usually leading to coma and death.

The significance of the Tokyo incident was that it showed how easily terrorists could deploy chemical and biological weapons in an open society. When police finally broke into the sect's headquarters, they found over 500 drums of phosphorus trichloride, an essential ingredient in Sarin. It became clear that Asahara's doomsday cult had the facilities to produce other nerve agents, including Tabun, Soman, and the highly dangerous chemical known by the symbol VX.

The use, or threatened use, of chemical and biological weapons is one of the most frightening forms of terrorism. The advantages to the terrorist are that nerve agents are cheap and easy to obtain, no training is required in their use, and production of the crude agents is straightforward. Terrorists can steal chemical and biological weapons from laboratories or manufacturing plants. They may even use commercially available insecticides such as parathion.

KEY FACTS

- About 1,800 pounds of Sarin can inflict heavy casualties over a square mile. A quarter ounce of anthrax spores can do the same job. Anthrax is a disease harnessed as a biological weapon.
- In 1995, a U.S. court found two people guilty of possessing ricin in breach of the Chemical and Biological Weapons Anti-Terrorism Act. Ricin is a poison derived from beans of the castor-oil plant.

TARGETS OF CHEMICAL ATTACKS

Mounting a direct attack on a military or civilian target, as in Tokyo, is the most straightforward way in which terrorists can use chemical or biological agents. It is also a way for a government to launch a low-cost terror campaign as an alternative to conventional war. In the 1980s, President Saddam Hussein of Iraq used chemical weapons against the Kurds of northern Iraq. In one infamous incident, in March 1988, Iraqi aircraft bombed the town of Halabja with chemical weapons, killing more than 6,000 Kurdish civilians in two days.

Terrorists might choose slightly more indirect methods of turning chemical and biological agents to their advantage. By bombing a chemical plant, for example, a terrorist organization could cause toxic material to leak into a city's water supply or into the atmosphere. The accident at Bhopal in India in 1984, in which thousands died when gas leaked from a factory, showed the potential for disaster if a terrorist attack on a chemical plant should ever take place.

Besides the Aum Shrinri-kyu sect, a number of terrorist groups have been linked to chemical and biological weapons. In 1978, a group of Palestinians injected Jaffa oranges with cyanide to damage Israeli citrus fruit exports. In the same year, the British police

Popperfoto/Reuters

Japanese troops clean a Tokyo subway car contaminated by the nerve agent Sarin on March 20, 1995.

uncovered a plot to detonate cans of dioxin all over Cyprus unless the Cypriot government paid out a $15 million ransom. Dioxin is the toxic by-product of pesticide production and an ingredient of Agent Orange, a defoliant used by the U.S. in Vietnam. In 1984, police in Paris found a culture of the bacterium that forms botulin in a safe house of the German Baader-Meinhof gang. Botulin is the toxin that causes botulism, an often fatal disease of the nervous system. In 1991, the German authorities foiled a neo-Nazi plot to pump hydrogen cyanide into a synagogue.

There have been other examples, but chemical and biological terrorism is still relatively rare. One reason is that terrorists prefer the immediate, dramatic effect produced by a hijacking or a bombing. Chemical weapons can also be dangerous to handle. An attack generally requires vast amounts of chemicals to have any significant effect. Chemical weapons are hard to control and might cause massive loss of life and lingering illness – possibly a counterproductive result on the terrorists. Still, events in Tokyo show that some groups regard chemical warfare as a justifiable tactic.

Nadine J. Gurr

SEE ALSO: RELIGIOUS EXTREMISM; NUCLEAR TERRORISM; SADDAM HUSSEIN'S TERROR IN KURDISTAN.

FURTHER READING

- Douglass, J. E., and N. C. Livingstone. *America the Vulnerable: The Threat of Chemical and Biological Weapons.* Lexington, MA: Lexington Books, 1987.
- Spiers, Edward M. *Chemical and Biological Weapons.* London: Macmillan, and New York: St. Martin's Press, 1994.
- Spiers, Edward M. *Chemical Weaponry.* London: Macmillan, and New York: St. Martin's Press, 1989.

NUCLEAR TERRORISM

The threat of nuclear terrorism covers a broad spectrum, from low-level threats or hoaxes involving radioactive material, through attacks on reactors, to a terrorist nuclear bomb. The most likely of all scenarios is sabotage or a siege-and-hostage situation at a nuclear facility, staged in all likelihood by an antinuclear group. In most cases, these terrorist tactics aim to highlight failures in security and safety at facilities. Another scenario would be an attack on the missiles used to carry nuclear warheads. In the past, antinuclear protesters have concentrated on trespassing at military sites, but there have also been a few attacks on factories that make nuclear missiles. However, where the objective is to embarrass the government or to gain leverage for a terrorist group, other types of nuclear terrorism are becoming increasingly likely. Acquiring fissile material (an essential ingredient for making a nuclear bomb) is becoming easier and thus a more attractive proposition for terrorists.

GROWTH IN NUCLEAR TRAFFICKING

That fissile material is now easier to access, is largely thanks to the collapse of the former Soviet Union and the growth in nuclear trafficking that has stemmed from it. Even though Russian nuclear weapons are under tight military supervision, there is a huge quantity of nuclear material dispersed throughout Russia is far less secure, and which is, therefore, difficult to keep track of. In addition, poor security at nuclear sites – often situated in secret cities not on the map due to the sensitive research carried out there, and at research institutes heightens the danger. Much of the theft is by "insiders" – staff who have access to nuclear material.

There is much debate about the extent of this secretive market. Some say that the traffic is almost exclusively in non-weapons-grade material, and that it is a situation artificially created by journalists and the security services. But there is evidence that at least some weapons-grade material is being trafficked.

On November 29, 1993, Lieutenant-Colonel Tikhomirov of the Russian navy, and Alyak Beranov, deputy administrator of the Polyarnyy submarine base, entered a naval fuel store through a hole in the perimeter fence and stole three fuel rods of uranium 235, intending to sell it for $50,000. The fuel was kept in Beranov's garage for seven months, until Tikhomirov got drunk and boasted of the theft to fellow officers. Both were arrested.

In 1994, German police intercepted four separate radioactive shipments, three of which were of plutonium 239 – an essential component in nuclear weapons. The shipments probably came from Russia.

Most of the smuggling so far has been by amateurs trying to make quick money. Increasingly, though, it appears that entrepreneurs are treating smuggling as an extension of their legitimate activities. In 1994, German police discovered a vial containing a fifth of an ounce of plutonium 239 in the garage of businessman Adolf Jaekle. Its origins are still unknown.

BUYERS OF NUCLEAR MATERIAL

The main buyers of nuclear material are almost certainly those states eager to take a shortcut towards nuclear programs of their own. Some people doubt whether there really is a demand for stolen or illegally bought nuclear material. However, in view of the expense and time needed to develop a nuclear capability legally, it seems unlikely that states would miss out on such an opportunity. Whether this will equate with an increased likelihood of state-sponsored nuclear

KEY FACTS

- Many states have tried to acquire nuclear weapons by various means since World War II.
- Mafia involvement in nuclear trafficking is unclear: the latter has few incentives and is high risk compared to the Mafia's other, safer activities.
- In March 1993, Japanese police seized nuclear information from the doomsday cult Aum Shinri-kyu, which staged the Tokyo subway gas attack in 1995.

TRH Pictures

Members of the U.S. Nuclear Emergency Search Team (NEST) remove radioactive debris from a Russian satellite that fell over Canada in 1978.

terrorism has yet to be seen. It makes sense to suggest that, having obtained such material, a state would exploit the situation. As yet, there is little evidence that independent terrorists are capable of buying nuclear material. But if the flow of nuclear goods out of Russia continues, it probably will happen eventually.

The amount of fissile material required to build a bomb, and the difficulty of doing so, is also a matter of debate. The International Atomic Energy Agency assumes that 18 pounds of weapons-grade plutonium is enough for a bomb, but other sources put the figure at much less. However, the sort of efficiency required with a small amount requires computer-modeling and components testing. Without these techniques, it is still possible to make a device, but it would require more material. Still, if a terrorist group is contemplating buying a nuclear device, it would be unwise to suppose that it cannot acquire enough fissile material. The technical knowledge needed depends on the weapon desired: an advanced plutonium device requires precision engineering, specialists, and the facilities for testing; but the design for a crude "gun-barrel" uranium bomb has been in the public domain for many years. But whether nuclear terrorism is made more likely because of this is far from clear.

HIGH-LEVEL NUCLEAR TERRORISM

One problem with high-level acts of nuclear terrorism is credibility. Terrorists have to prove to governments that they can carry out the acts they threaten. But both sides know that low-level threats can give almost as much leverage. For example, shortly after the World Trade Center bomb in February 1993, the FBI investigated allegations that Iranian terrorists were planning to release radioactive material in Manhattan. A successful attack would have been an ecological and human disaster. New York would have become a no-go zone, even without the use of a nuclear bomb. The FBI was also worried that the availability of fissile material from the former Soviet Union would result, not in a nuclear bomb, but in a nuclear-rich conventional explosion.

However, it is less likely that terrorists will opt for nuclear weapons. A disadvantage in using high-level nonconventional weapons such as nuclear, biological, or chemical ones, is that the effects are unpredictable and continue over a long period. This could bring the group involved bad publicity long after the event. The devastation caused by fertilizer bombs at the World Trade Center and at Oklahoma suggests that, for most groups, conventional weaponry is still the primary option. Furthermore, conventional weapons are cheaper, easier to access, harder for the authorities to detect and, given most terrorists' unfamiliarity with nonconventional weapons, probably safer to use. All of these factors militate very strongly against high-level nuclear terrorism, and to a lesser extent against any terrorist use of other weapons of mass destruction. However, the availability of fissile material has meant that the authorities have to take all threats seriously, giving the terrorist much leverage.

MOTIVATIONS FOR NUCLEAR TERRORISM

Terrorists have never used nuclear weapons for mass murder, one important reason being that they have yet to reach their killing potential using conventional weapons, and so do not need to be innovative. But terrorism is becoming increasingly lethal. In the 1980s, terrorist incidents rose by a third compared with the 1970s, but there was a twofold increase in fatalities.

One possible motivation for nuclear terrorism is if a group decides it has nothing to lose. If the group feels that it is in decline, dissolving into factions, or being usurped by another group, it might launch an act of nuclear terrorism to justify and call attention to its existence. Ideology erodes the moral constraints against terrorism, causing a gulf between "them" and "us." If an act, no matter how terrible, furthers the cause, then, by definition, it must be good.

Religious terrorists seem more likely to resort to nuclear weapons than other terrorist groups. Religion is a legitimizing force that can inspire total loyalty and commitment. Morally, it can justify, and even require, indiscriminate violence. A religious group may want to remove sections of society unconstrained by the political, practical, or moral factors that limit others' actions. But other groups may also feel less constrained if it is a matter of carrying out a nuclear hoax or seizing a nuclear weapon rather detonating it.

Democratic governments are limited in their ability to deal with the problem of nuclear terrorism, but they have to take preventive measures. Soft targets, such as reactors or convoys carrying nuclear material, have been hardened against attacks. Some nations have emergency response plans, including, in the U.S., a highly skilled Nuclear Emergency Search Team (NEST), which gives technical and scientific support to the FBI. The team deals with all potential nuclear emergencies, and is equipped to search and recover lost or stolen materials and to deactivate any homemade devices.

However, since no target can ever be completely secure, the best means of countering nuclear terrorism lies with effective intelligence. Intelligence also has a role in promoting nonproliferation by ensuring compliance with agreements such as the Non Proliferation Treaty, between major nuclear powers.

The biggest problem with antinuclear terrorist policies in former Eastern-bloc states is a shortage of money, but the West is not able to make up this shortfall. Any such policy, therefore, must apply resources and influence wherever it is needed most. It is a far from ideal solution to this escalating problem.

Gavin Cameron

SEE ALSO: THE DEBATE OVER THE ATOM BOMB; THE WORLD TRADE CENTER BOMBING; THE OKLAHOMA CITY BOMBING AND THE MILITIAS.

FURTHER READING

- Allison, G. *Avoiding Nuclear Anarchy.* Cambridge, MA: MIT Press, 1995.
- Leventhal, P. and Y. Alexander, eds. *Nuclear Terrorism: Defining the Threat.* Washington, DC: Pergamon-Brassey's, 1986.
- Leventhal, P. and Y. Alexander, eds. *Preventing Nuclear Terrorism.* Lexington, MA: Lexington Books, 1987.
- Norton, A. R. and M. H. Greenberg, eds. *Studies in Nuclear Terrorism.* Boston: G. K. Hall, 1979.

TERRORIST FUNDRAISING

Every armed struggle and terror campaign, especially urban campaigns, needs money – to pay volunteers, to support families of activists taken prisoner, to buy guns and other weapons, to buy safe houses, to pay for international travel, and to fund propaganda. There are a number of methods that terrorist groups use to raise money – and if they are successful, vast amounts may be at their disposal.

At the beginning of campaigns, terrorists may raise income by legal means, such as contributions from supporters and fundraising at rallies. Until 1971, for example, the Provisional IRA in Northern Ireland existed on the charity of sympathizers and modest contributions. The few salaries given were tiny and bills were seldom paid on time. Volunteers spent much of their time looking not so much for more money as for any money. Even so, it was rare for the IRA to resort to illegal means during this very early period.

A few terrorist groups make enough money from their groups of supporters without having to resort to other methods. The Palestinians, with a relatively high level of education, prospered economically throughout the Middle East in the years after the 1948 Arab-Israeli War that established the state of Israel, and have invested wisely in the West. Legal Palestinian organizations can collect official grants and contributions from Palestinians worldwide, much of which may filter down to terrorist organizations. Similarly, the Tamil Tigers in Sri Lanka command large financial reserves, freely given by the prosperous Tamil community throughout the world. Another valuable source of income for terrorists is money from a sympathetic state. It is estimated, for example, that Colonel Qaddafi of Libya gave $30 million to the Palestinian group Black September in the 1970s.

But although payments from sympathizers or sympathetic states are important sources of terrorist funding, they have their drawbacks. Paymasters usually demand some say in the activities of their clients, while funds may be cut off by a change of government or a change in public perceptions. Sooner or later, most organizations wish to control their own cash.

KEY FACTS

- The German Baader-Meinhof terrorist group raised $185,000 from a two-month spate of six bank robberies in 1972.
- After "Carlos the Jackal," leader of international terrorism in 1970s Europe, kidnapped the Organization of Petroleum Exporting Countries (OPEC) oil ministers in Vienna in 1975, the Libyan head of state Colonel Qaddafi gave him $1.5 million.

THE POWER OF THE GUN

Each movement undertakes the kind of crime that appeals to its membership. Rural insurgents seize foreigners and resort to banditry, or they hold up cars and take money from the passengers. Urban terrorists rely more on theft, fraud, and extortion.

Terrorist groups usually rationalize their illegal fundraising, explaining away extortion as "revolutionary taxes." In the 1970s, the military cells of the People's Revolutionary Army of Argentina (ERP) concentrated on bank robberies and kidnapping for ransom, crimes they euphemistically described as "expropriation." The group built up a central fund of $30 million from these activities. Ulrike Meinhof of the Baader-Meinhof Gang also justified bank robbery: "No one claims that bank robbery of itself changes anything. It is logistically correct, since otherwise the financial problem could not be solved at all. It is tactically correct, because it is a proletarian action. It is strategically correct because it serves the financing of the guerrilla."

Many terrorist organizations have dealt in drugs to gain money for operations. Latin American rebels such as Peru's Shining Path and some Palestinian factions – operating in regions rich in the crops needed for drugs such as cocaine and marijuana – are known for drug dealing. The terrorists explain, in ideological terms, their production, refinement, packaging, and shipment

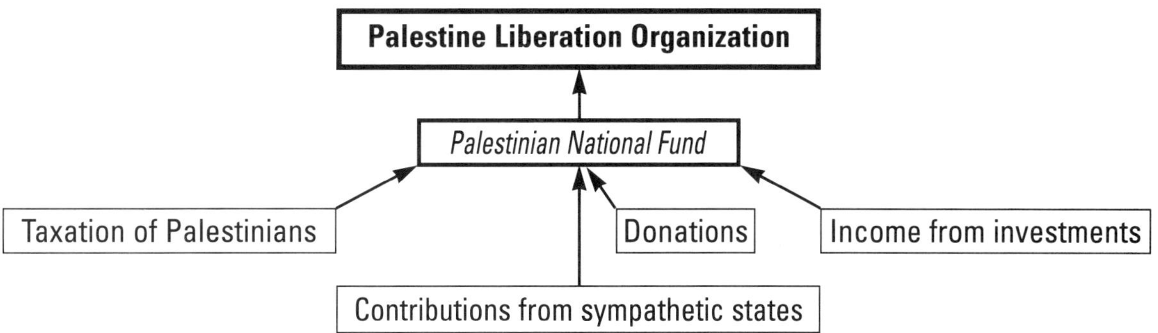

The PLO gathers funds from a variety of sources, and some of this money finds its way to terrorists.

of drugs as a way of corrupting the enemy state, normally the market for their goods.

There is, of course, a danger that involvement in criminal activities involving large amounts of money may in some way corrupt a movement. Criticism of the Baader-Meinhof terror group in West Germany often focused on the lavish life-style that huge amounts of money gained from successful bank robberies gave its leaders. Indeed, one of its most important leaders, Gudrun Ensslin, was arrested while out shopping.

Other methods of using armed force to extort money include kidnapping and hijacking. These have the advantage that they are political acts as well as being effective for fundraising. Huge sums have been raised by kidnapping. In 1975, the Argentinian terrorist group the Montoneros claimed to have exchanged the lives of businessmen Jorge and Juan Born for $60 million in cash and $1.2 million in food and clothing for the poor. Hijacking too has raised enormous amounts. However, terrorists may well find that their need to find a safe haven means that they have to share the money with others. In 1972, the Lufthansa airline paid $5 million for the release of passengers from a hijacking carried out by the Popular Liberation Front of Palestine. However, the government of Yemen, in which the hijackers had landed the plane, demanded $1 million as their share of the booty.

In the long run, a movement may even set up its own "black economy," or illegal trading where no tax passes to the government. In Northern Ireland, both loyalist paramilitaries, such as the Ulster Defence Volunteers and the Ulster Freedom Fighters, and the Provisional IRA have "taxed" private enterprise and directly controlled commerce and manufacture. The fact that these illegal practices bleed the state legitimizes them in the terrorists' eyes. Smuggling, fraudulent welfare claims, pirate video cassettes, and tax-free liquor became common in Northern Ireland.

Once they get their hands on money, terrorist groups may then wish to invest it. Again, there may be a "virtuous circle" in which well-placed sympathizers advise on investments and help find ways to "launder" the money, or channel it into legal ventures to conceal its illegal origins. For its fifth revolt in India, the United Liberation Front of Assam collected hundreds of millions of dollars in local currency by "taxing" tea plantations, companies, and individuals. It spent money on arms and any money left over was legitimately invested in Calcutta. The insurrection continued until 1991 and only ended when the Indian government responded by clamping down on fund sources.

John Bowyer Bell

SEE ALSO: HIJACKING AND KIDNAPPING; COLLABORATION BETWEEN TERRORISTS; THE BLACK SEPTEMBER ORGANIZATION, THE POPULAR FRONT FOR THE LIBERATION OF PALESTINE; RED ARMY FACTION: THE BAADER-MEINHOF GANG; NATIONALIST TERROR IN NORTHERN IRELAND 1976-1996.

FURTHER READING

- Adams, James. *The Financing of Terror.* New York: Simon and Schuster, 1980.
- Bell, John Bowyer. *The Secret Army: The IRA, 1916-1996.* 3rd ed. New Brunswick, NJ: Transaction Publishers, 1997.
- Dobson, Christopher and Ronald Payne. *The Terrorists: Their Weapons, Leaders, and Tactics.* Rev. Ed. New York: Facts on File, 1982.

COLLABORATION BETWEEN TERRORISTS

During the 1940s and 1950s, the opportunities for collaboration between terrorist groups were limited. At this time, terrorism was mainly carried out by nationalist guerrillas in colonial wars. Nationalist terrorists were concerned with gaining independence for their own countries and tended not to have links with organizations fighting similar campaigns elsewhere. In the late 1960s, though, new types of terrorist groups began to emerge, and by the 1970s there was wide-scale collaboration between terrorists. It took many forms: moral support or help with propaganda; help in training or getting weapons; provision of safe havens or giving shelter; and, at the most extreme level, joint operations by terrorist groups.

The new terrorist groups that came to the fore in the late 1960s were of two main types. In western Europe and in Japan, social revolutionary terrorists appeared. In these places, young people were dissatisfied with traditional institutions and expressed this feeling in mass demonstrations in 1968. When these demonstrations failed to transform society, hard-line activists created small terrorist groups. The Red Army in Japan, the Red Army Faction in Germany, the Red Brigades in Italy, and Action Directe in France all aimed to destroy the fabric of Western society by violent means. In the Middle East, meanwhile, Palestinians were looking for ways to destroy Israel, whose territories they claimed as their own. In the late 1960s, Palestinian groups took their struggle beyond the Middle East, hijacking aircraft and attacking Israeli targets abroad to attract attention to their cause.

KEY FACTS

- In July 1976, a group of terrorists from the Popular Front for the Liberation of Palestine and the German Red Army Faction hijacked a plane from Paris to Tel Aviv with 246 passengers aboard.
- Libyan leader Colonel Qaddafi was suspected of instigating Black September's 1973 attack on the Saudi Arabian embassy in Khartoum, in which three diplomats were held hostage and later killed.
- At a conference of "anti-NATO" terrorist groups in Lisbon in June 1984, the Red Army Faction, Action Directe, and Belgian and Italian comrades formed the "Political-Military Front."

JOINT ATTACKS

The European/Japanese social revolutionaries and the Palestinian radicals had common enemies. Both hated Israel, the U.S., and capitalist society in general. Links were soon forged between European/Japanese organizations and the Palestinian groups and their supporters. It is widely believed that various Arab regimes used diplomatic bags to move terrorist money, information, and weapons around the world. In addition, training camps were established in South Yemen, where terrorists mingled to learn how to operate more effectively. Support was also forthcoming from communist regimes, such as East Germany.

During the 1970s, a number of terrorist attacks took place that could be described as joint operations. In March 1971, the Popular Front for the Liberation of Palestine (PFLP), run by George Habash, allied with French left-wing terrorists to blow up oil tanks in Rotterdam in the Netherlands. Habash's group went on to collaborate on several occasions with non-Palestinian organizations.

In November 1971, a new terrorist group shot and killed Jordanian prime minister Wasfi Tal. Called Black September, this mysterious group appeared to have no known base or leadership. But, in later years, it emerged that Black September was merely a front. The funds and recruits for individual missions came from Yasser Arafat's militant Fatah organization. In April

Hulton Getty Picture Collection

Israeli defense minister Moshe Dayan visits Tel Aviv's Lod airport after the massacre carried out by the Japanese Red Army, working with Palestinians.

1972, Black September sent the "Easter commando" into Israel to carry out attacks during the pilgrimage season. Led by Evelyne Barges, a Frenchwoman who had taken part in the PFLP operation in Rotterdam, the mixed nationality team arrived with toiletries impregnated with incendiary chemicals. But Israeli security forces were alert and arrested all the terrorists.

In May 1972, the PFLP called a meeting for Black September and other allies in an attempt to organize on an international scale. Three weeks later, the PFLP sent the Japanese Red Army on a kamikaze mission. Three Japanese terrorists opened fire in the lounge at Tel Aviv's Lod airport, killing 26 people and wounding 76. The event, which shocked the world, came to be known as the Lod massacre.

In September 1972, Black September gunmen massacred Israeli athletes at the Munich Olympics, but after 1973 the group took a less active part in terrorism. The network of contacts was established, however. The Popular Front (PFLP) and European terrorists carried on their campaign. Ilyich Ramírez Sánchez, known as "Carlos the Jackal," was a central figure, responsible for many acts of terrorism from late 1973 to late 1975. In the most spectacular event, Carlos led a gang of German Red Army Faction and Palestinians in a raid on the Organization of Petroleum Exporting Countries headquarters in Vienna in 1975. The terrorists held 11 oil ministers hostage.

In the 1980s, mutual support was still prevalent. In a coordinated action on July 9, 1986, the German Red Army Faction killed a top business director in Strasslach, near Munich, while the French Action Directe bombed the anti-terrorist base in Paris. Improved international security networks, however, were easing the situation for Western governments. The crisis came in 1977, when PFLP and Red Army Faction terrorists hijacked a Lufthansa airliner. German and British anti-terrorist troops combined to storm the aircraft. Thereafter, the threat ebbed. There is still collaboration among groups, notably those attempting to destroy Israel, such as the PFLP, Hizb'allah, and Hamas; there is also a network of Islamic fundamentalists. However, with the Soviet communist bloc's collapse and the decline in social revolutionary fervor in the West, terrorist links have become less important.

John Bowyer Bell

SEE ALSO: THE BLACK SEPTEMBER ORGANIZATION; CARLOS THE JACKAL; ENTEBBE; RED ARMY FACTION: THE BAADER-MEINHOF GANG; JAPANESE TERRORISM.

FURTHER READING

- Cline, R. S. and Y. Alexander. *Terrorism: The Soviet Connection.* New York and London: Crane Russak, 1986.
- Ra'anan, U., R. L. Pfaltzgraff Jr., R. H. Shultz, E. Halperin and I. Lukes. *Hydra of Carnage: International Linkages of Terrorism – The Witnesses Speak.* Lexington, MA: Lexington Books, D. C. Heath, 1986.
- Sterling, Claire. *The Terror Network: The Secret War of International Terrorism.* New York: Holt, Rinehart, and Winston, and London: Weidenfeld and Nicolson, 1981.

CHAPTER SEVEN

The Psychology of Terrorism

What is it like to be a terrorist and why should anyone want to be one? It is easy to dismiss terrorists as mad fanatics, but in fact they need to be level headed to cope with long periods of meticulous planning in between bouts of violent activity. It is fascinating to gain some insight into the mindset of terrorists, especially those so completely convinced of their cause to act as suicide bombers. And what about those unfortunate enough to be victims of terrorism? Being bombed or held hostage by terrorists is the stuff of nightmares, but the legacy of dread after the ordeal can be even worse.

THE MINDSET OF THE TERRORIST

Blanket psychological explanations of terrorism are difficult to construct, because there are many varieties of terrorism and because all terrorist campaigns are different. The mindset of someone who acts alone to change the nature of society, such as the Unabomber in the U.S., is very different from a religiously inspired suicide bomber who is part of a nationalist movement in the Middle East. However, there are certain aspects of the terrorist mindset that can be examined. These include: the reasons for joining a terrorist movement; the relationship between individuals within a terrorist movement; the strength of terrorists' beliefs; how the developing psychology of a terrorist group affects the way terrorists operate; and how terrorists justify their acts.

These aspects are all important for the security forces who have to deal with terrorists. They try to build up a psychological profile so they can act against groups such as the left-wing Weathermen of the 1960s; they also try to predict where a group is likely to strike next and decide the best way of negotiating with hijackers who are demanding money and the release of imprisoned members of the group.

THE TERRORIST PERSONALITY

Psychological profiles of terrorists are often completely different from popular perceptions or media portrayals. When news of an outrage breaks, there is a tendency to describe the terrorist as being mentally unbalanced, having broken the rules of "normal" behavior. In fact, the terrorist does follow rules – but not necessarily those followed by most of the population. And although the acts are violent, such extreme violence is common in other contexts – in warfare or self-defense, for example.

The starting point for the psychologist, then, is that the terrorist will usually have a relatively normal psychological profile. There is no common personality that is unique to those who commit acts of political violence; the violence occurs because people have chosen that path for a variety of reasons. The overwhelming majority of terrorists are not mentally ill, abnormal, psychopathic, or even especially predisposed to violence. An individual may be predisposed to terrorism, but it is unlikely that a terrorist group would knowingly choose an unstable individual. Such a person would be a loose cannon – a security threat that could endanger the whole group.

In any case, most terrorism involves long periods of inaction interspersed with short bouts of activity. The terrorist needs to be able to be patient during the long and dull planning stages of preparation for an attack. It is doubtful whether such inactivity would appeal to, or satisfy the needs of, a psychopathic personality.

A common reaction from politicians when a terrorist bomb has been planted is to label the bombers as "cowards." But this label does not aid our understanding any more than does assuming they are all abnormal. Terrorists are committed individuals, prepared to carry out often horrific acts, accepting that such deeds may have severe consequences for them personally. They perform violent actions because they believe in their cause. Terrorists may be unpleasant and they may be scared, but they are rarely cowards. If they were, it is unlikely that they would have become terrorists in the first place.

The reasons a person joins a terrorist group often define how effective they will be as terrorists, and how they will operate. It is difficult to make sweeping generalizations because people become terrorists for

SUMMARY

- Social revolutionary terrorists use Lenin as an icon – as leader of a minority group, he manipulated a favorable situation to reach power in 1917.
- "Ethnic cleansing" of Muslims by Serbs is an example of nationalism leading to terror.
- Terrorist groups may make it difficult for members to leave by making them commit some crime as a kind of initiation.

very different reasons. However, for many it seems to involve a desire to belong to an organization or to be part of a movement.

NATIONALISM AS A MOTIVATION

Nationalism is perhaps the strongest motivation to take up terrorism. The appeal of being part of a national group fighting for a homeland is very strong. Indeed, many of the most notorious terrorist acts of modern times have been part of nationalist struggles.

For example, the Tamil Tigers in Sri Lanka have proved impossible to control because of the powerful attraction of Tamil nationalism within the Tamil community – not only in Sri Lanka itself, but in southern India and worldwide as well. The appeal of nationalism in the human psyche is rooted in a deep emotional need to bond to a group. It can lead to acts of great self-sacrifice, and to acts that have horrible consequences for those who get in the way.

Popperfoto

The massacre of Palestinians at Sabra and Chatila in 1982 drove many to terrorism for revenge.

The importance of nationalism is reinforced if it is linked to political or social repression or lack of opportunity. Thus, Palestinian terrorist groups have a ready-made pool of recruits in the refugee camps of Lebanon or the crowded tenements of Gaza. Many young Palestinians growing up in poverty know that their families were forced off their land in 1948, and may even have seen the Israelis launch air raids against refugee camps, or fail to prevent the massacre of Palestinians at the Sabra and Chatila camps in 1982. If someone is convinced that Israel will never permit the existence of a Palestinian state, joining a terrorist group becomes a chance to achieve more status and to strike a blow against the "oppressors." Acts of terrorism do not seem mad or irrational to a young Palestinian. The idea that Western-style democracy could persuade Israel to create a Palestinian homeland or stop the influx of Jewish settlers onto the west bank of the Jordan River may seem far more irrational.

Nationalism as a motive is often reinforced by religion. In Sri Lanka, Hindu Tamils fight against the majority Buddhist Sinhalese; in Northern Ireland, the IRA represents a Catholic nationalism fighting against Protestant loyalists; and in Bosnia, Catholic Croats, Muslim Bosnians, and Orthodox Serbs are the three competing parties.

However, religion may also outweigh nationalism as a motive. The most important examples of this are found in the Middle East. The mix of religion, particularly fundamentalist Islam, with nationalism has led to extravagant terrorist acts. Here, the idealism and intensity that characterize nationalism are mixed with the certainties of faith. This results in patterns of terrorism such as suicide bombings, where the bombers are convinced they will rest in paradise and so are prepared to detonate a bomb, for example, while sitting on a crowded bus in Tel Aviv.

A SENSE OF BELONGING

The certainties of nationalism and religion are not the motivation for all terrorists. Some become terrorists because of their commitment to a political cause or from a desire to revolutionize their society. The cause may be animal rights or a pro-life campaign; it may also be a desire to create a communist society.

It is in groups on the fringe of mainstream society that individuals who have problems adjusting to

TRH Pictures

Rioters form part of the support network for the IRA, stirring up conflict, as here at Bogside, a Catholic area of Londonderry, in the 1970s.

society, or who have an overwhelming need to belong, may find sanctuary. In psychological terms, individuals who are alienated from society or who feel worthless may find purpose and a positive identity within a terrorist group. Such people can abandon their individ ual responsibilities and embrace the collective identity of the group. Of course, not all terrorists are motivated simply by a need to belong; but there is a tendency within such groups to attract negative individuals. Nationalist or religious terrorist groups may also attract such individuals.

THE IMPORTANCE OF A GROUP NETWORK

It is important to remember that there are many different layers to terrorist organizations. Only a minority of members plant bombs or take hostages. The majority are involved in setting up the network that enables such acts to be committed. They may be fundraisers, sympathizers providing safe houses, observers providing information, technicians making bombs, or politicians who direct terrorist activity or act as spokespeople. This network sustains the active terrorist who plants the bomb. The different members may have varying motives, and the strength of their commitment may be greater or lesser. Nevertheless, the network is crucial to bolstering morale.

It is useful, in this sense, to compare social revolutionary terrorists, such as the Baader-Meinhof gang (also known as the Red Army Faction) in West Germany, with nationalist terrorists such as the IRA in Northern Ireland. The Baader-Meinhof gang appeared to pose a major threat to West German democracy in the mid-1970s, primarily because its support seemed to be spread throughout German society, especially among young people and at professional levels. This was because there was a strong intellectual and political tide of opinion that Germany's liberal democracy was a failure. Many of the laws passed to limit the activities of the gang were actually aimed at curbing access of the captured terrorists to lawyers: the suicides of three of the gang's leaders in custody in 1977 were partly blamed on lawyers smuggling in guns. But the group lost power rapidly after the suicides. Neither the remaining terrorists nor their sympathizers were sufficiently motivated to sustain the campaign, partly because the broad and diffuse social background that had once seemed so threatening weakened the cohesiveness of the group.

The IRA, by contrast, has managed to sustain a campaign for more than 25 years, because the commitment of its active terrorists is aided by a background of support, both in Northern Ireland and in the Irish Republic, that hardly wavers. There is a widespread social and religious identity in the IRA and its supporters, as well as an intellectual and political common ground. Under these circumstances, the identity and prestige that the terrorist achieves through IRA membership is reinforced at every turn.

JUSTIFICATION OF VIOLENT ACTS

For most terrorists, membership of a group may be the main motive, but usually there is a progression through the ranks before a person can become a full-fledged terrorist. The decision to use violence, though, is not a sudden one. Eventually, the choice will be to participate in violence or to leave the group. This is a difficult choice for an individual who has become emotionally dependent on the group. A powerful need to belong and intellectual agreement with the aims of the group often leads to acceptance of violence.

The first step for an individual is to forget that others are being killed through some small action in which the individual has taken part. Once this step has been taken toward accepting violence, the individual may experience a sense of purpose and control over his or her life, and over the lives of others. Feelings of futility, for example from having been raised in the poverty of a refugee camp or from a disturbed adolescence, may be replaced by the feeling that he or she is an important person whom the authorities must respect.

Once in this position, other emotions such as excitement and stress become important. Some individuals, such as the international terrorist "Carlos the Jackal," are effectively "guns for hire" whose motives are emotional and financial not political. Aggression is another important motivation. In some terrorist groups, such as the Quebec Liberation Front, active in Canada during the 1970s, the aggressive instincts of certain individuals seem to have taken over as motivating factors for the group as a whole. However, it is important to recognize that these emotional factors become important only after the individual has become a member of the group.

Rex Features

The international terrorist "Carlos the Jackal" enjoys a night out with his girlfriend in 1994.

PSYCHOLOGICAL IMPACT OF THE GROUP

A terrorist group offers members a counterculture, with its own norms and values into which it indoctrinates new recruits. The group tends to demand complete obedience and isolation from society. It strives for uniformity and cohesion, building the group on the political homogeneity of like-minded individuals, whose lives, goals, and futures are identified with the group. Often there are few alternatives to membership, and the main fear of group members is that they will be abandoned.

KEEPING THE GROUP TOGETHER

But this very cohesion and obedience of the group can cause its own problems. The first is that authorities trying to break up terrorist groups can offer the individual a positive route of escape. Once an alternative is shown to the attraction of belonging to a terrorist group, the terrorist may lose all loyalty.

A second problem is that groups tend to be self-perpetuating. The group and its survival become paramount; its aims become less so. Ultimately, violence may become an end in itself. Ironically, the achievement of political aims may actually be unpopular, because their achievement will result in the destruction of the group. The tendency is to reject any "compromise," and for the group to become ever more purist, and to use more absolutist rhetoric.

A third problem is that terrorist groups tend to become very authoritarian, even when their political aims ostensibly may be libertarian, and they clamp down hard on dissent. When members wish to leave, there can be furious internal feuds. If the individuals who leave set up similar but rival organizations, they may compete furiously and violently with the established group, claiming a greater degree of ideological purity for themselves.

The final problem is the way terrorists justify the horror that they inflict on others, especially on those who seem innocent. The sense of exclusiveness explains much of this. The group filters all news of external events that reaches its members, putting an interpretation on such events that emphasizes the evils of the enemy.

Terror group leaders tend to dehumanize any victims, accusing them of crimes and outrages. Alternatively targets are portrayed as being a structure or organization, not individual human beings with personal lives. Every effort is also made to associate the victims of the attack in some way with the enemies the terrorists are fighting.

Even when it is clear that one terrorist must carry out an attack, the cohesion of the group takes away the sense of personal responsibility. Membership of the group may heighten a terrorist's self-worth, but when it comes to deadly action, the terrorist becomes a foot soldier in a much wider movement.

In assessing the mindset of the terrorist, then, two factors stand out. The first is that terrorists usually have a very strong motivation, and the strength of this motivation is the principle key to why they are prepared to kill and maim. The second is that terrorists usually operate in close-knit groups that reinforce this motivation and encourage certain tendencies, particularly ones that enable individual terrorists to escape the intense guilt that they might otherwise feel for the consequences of their actions.

FUTURE HEROES?

The group reinforces belief in the cause by reminding the individual of how previous individuals have risen from being minor terrorists and bandits to great national icons or heroes.

It has become almost a truism of politics in the Third World, for example, that those imprisoned as criminals or accused of terrorism by colonial or other ruling powers have gone on to be regarded as fathers of their country: the most recent examples being Nelson Mandela in South Africa and Yasser Arafat in the Middle East. In the same way, there is no doubt that the success of Fidel Castro and Che Guevara in 1950s Cuba had an enormous effect on Latin America as a whole. For terrorists, a successful insurgency helps them to feel part of an historical process that will eventually condone the violent action.

Gavin Cameron

SEE ALSO: CATEGORIES OF TERROR; HOSTAGE NEGOTIATIONS; SUICIDE BOMBING; CARLOS THE JACKAL; TERROR IN LEBANON 1980-1987; TAMIL TIGER TERROR IN SRI LANKA; RED ARMY FACTION: THE BAADER-MEINHOF GANG; IRA: ORIGINS AND TERROR TO 1976; NATIONALIST TERROR IN NORTHERN IRELAND, 1976-1996; TERROR BY QUEBEC SEPARATISTS.

FURTHER READING

- McKnight, G. *The Terrorist Mind.* Indianapolis, IN: Bobbs-Merrill, and London: Michael Joseph, 1974.
- Taylor, M. and E. Quayle. *Terrorist Lives.* Washington, DC: Macmillan, 1994.
- Taylor, M. *The Fanatics.* London and Washington, DC: Brassey's, 1991.

VICTIMS OF TERRORISM

The ultimate target of terrorist activity is a large institution, such as a government or large corporation. The terrorist organization is trying to weaken this entity, either through direct strikes and intimidation or by shifting public opinion on a national or international basis. In the study of terrorism, the focus is generally on the terrorists themselves, their tactics, and the processes required by their opponents to arrest and prosecute them. Little attention is paid to the human victims of this violent process.

There are two types of victims of terrorist activity: selected targets, who are generally high-profile individuals, and random targets, who happen to be in the wrong place at the wrong time. Some people, including politicians, those holding high ranks in the military, and senior business figures, may be aware that they are at risk of terrorist attack or kidnapping; other people may simply be caught by chance, as is the case of victims of skyjacking or of terrorist bombs. But for both kinds of victims, the experience is a horrible ordeal, as the accounts of former hostages and others who have experienced terrorist attacks have shown.

Terrorists often choose as targets for assassination or kidnapping, well-known figures such as diplomats and other government officials, high-ranking military officers, or senior businesspeople. An attack on a prominent personality invariably attracts a great deal of media attention for the terrorists. If successful, this type of attack can also serve to intimidate the terrorists' enemies – whoever they are. Well-known figures often have substantial personal security, and by outwitting or overpowering their safety measures, the terrorist organization can show its tactical intelligence and strength. By targeting a supposedly well-protected person, the terrorist organization is able to demonstrate the vulnerability of the enemy.

Terrorists carefully plan their attacks on high-profile targets and carry them out with military precision, often putting their human targets under surveillance for long periods. The assault itself may take place somewhere the victim is most comfortable: in his or her home, club, office, or car. Although familiar surroundings may provide victims with a sense of security, they are often easier marks because such places are readily identifiable. And when places are secluded, they are easier to watch without detection.

KEY FACTS

- An individual who has been taken hostage or injured or killed in a bombing is the victim of terrorist activity, but may not be the principal target.
- When terrorists target public places, such as airports, shopping centers, and large offices, they can cause a great deal of material damage at the same time as endangering many innocent lives.
- The families and friends of victims of terrorist activity can be considered secondary victims, because they may also suffer emotionally and sometimes financially.

HIGH-PROFILE VICTIMS

Government officials and military personnel are often considered the most valuable trophies for terrorists. Governments immediately respond to the kidnapping of an official, which suggests a willingness to bargain. There are many examples of this kind of terrorist activity, including the kidnapping of former Italian prime minister Aldo Moro. The capture of Organization of Petroleum Exporting Countries (OPEC) foreign ministers in Vienna in December 1975 by Carlos the Jackal and Palestinian terrorists was a major coup.

Terrorist groups have also considered members of the business community to be legitimate targets. This form of terrorist action was particularly prevalent in the 1970s. In Latin America, the Tupamaros in Uruguay viewed Western businesspeople as representatives of capitalism, social injustice, and exploitation of the poor. Similarly in Europe, left-wing socialist groups such as the Red Army Faction in Germany and Action Directe in France kidnapped high-ranking executives.

The kidnap and murder in Rome of Aldo Moro, former Italian prime minister, shocked the world in 1978.

The ransoms paid to gain the freedom of kidnapped businesspeople can fund a terrorist organization's other activities. In the 1970s, the Montoneros in Argentina were able to collect as much as $60 million for the release of two industrialists, the Born brothers.

Many organizations, both professional and governmental, have tried to limit the opportunities for terrorist groups. They have adopted rigorous security measures, including securing offices and personal residences, and using armored vehicles and security guards. They have also established survival training programs for employees and their families who are potential targets, particularly for those who travel abroad. This training can increase their chances of survival if they are taken hostage.

People can also be selected as targets for terrorist activity because of their affiliation with a particular national, religious, or political group, rather than because of any individual notoriety. Victims selected for hostage-taking do not necessarily have any intrinsic value as individuals. They are simply a form of leverage – bargaining chips – with authorities.

An example of this kind of targeting is the kidnapping of foreign nationals in Lebanon in the 1980s. With the exception of Terry Waite, the British Anglican Church Envoy who had gone to Lebanon on a high-profile mission to negotiate for the release of other hostages, Hizb'allah and Islamic Jihad targeted their victims simply on the basis of their nationality. For example, Jean-Paul Kaufman and Michel Seurat, the two French citizens captured, were relief workers. The American Thomas Sutherland, kidnapped in 1985, was a professor. Terry Anderson, also American, was a reporter for CNN; he was captured in 1985 and spent more than seven years in captivity. Other hostages held in Lebanon were Irish, Greek, German, and Dutch.

The Palestinian Black September was able to capture world attention by taking Israeli athletes hostage at the 1972 Olympic Games in Munich. None of the athletes were well known as individuals – the terrorists targeted them simply because of their nationality. After 15 hours of grueling negotiations, the nine athletes died in a shootout (two died during the terrorists' assault on the athletes' housing area).

RANDOM ATTACKS

Terrorist groups can also choose their hostages randomly. Rather than targeting individuals, they target a place or a circumstance and select hostages from the pool of people who happen to be there. Terrorist groups often choose crowded public places in which there will be victims of both sexes and all ages, nationalities, races, and social strata. Large numbers of hostages guarantee safe passages for terrorists, and a range of nationalities gives a larger number of host governments to negotiate with.

The victims in situations like these tend to feel that they are totally innocent and not related in any way to the cause of the terrorist attack. However, George Habash, head of the radical Popular Front for the Liberation of Palestine (PFLP), declared that: "There are no innocent victims. All share the responsibility for society's wrongs. No one is innocent."

In the event of such a group hostage-taking, the pool of victims are confused and panicked, while the terrorists, who have generally meticulously planned

Popperfoto

U.S. Marines carrying out the body of a victim after terrorists bombed a Marine base in Beirut, Lebanon, in 1983. The blast killed 241 American servicemen.

their attack, are more organized, which allows them to consolidate their control. Because the hostages are in all likelihood strangers to each other, their group dynamics will not threaten the terrorists.

SKYJACKING

Middle Eastern terrorists often turned to hijacking in the 1970s and 1980s, taking hostages on American, French, Greek, German, and other airlines. This kind of attack came to be known as skyjacking. According to the terrorist groups, the air carriers were targets because they were flying to Israel. Because of the threat of skyjacking, El Al, the Israeli national carrier, imposed tight security measures to defend itself against skyjacking and other forms of terrorist activity. It remains one of the safest airlines in this regard.

On a hijacked plane, as in any other public place, an individual passenger is the victim but not the target. For innocent people taken hostage, this increases the shock. They often cannot understand why they have been caught up in the violence and the terror.

During this period of hijacking and skyjacking, Middle Eastern terrorists ranked Israeli passengers as the most desirable, with American officials and members of the U.S. military ranking second and third. Non-Israeli Jewish passengers were also singled out: for example, after hijacking the Italian ship *Achille Lauro* in October 1985, the Palestinian Liberation Front (PLF) murdered Leon Klinghoffer, a wheelchair-using elderly Jewish American.

Leftist European and Latin American terrorist groups have often selected American victims because of the significant role of the U.S. in world affairs, the likelihood of media coverage, and because of their perceptions of the American government as an evil world force. Terrorists may single out other nationals depending on the political climate. At various times, French, German, Italian, Spanish, and Turkish nationals have been singled out during hostage situations.

Women and children, when they are taken hostage, may be treated with greater leniency than other victims, often being released immediately. However, there are exceptions. In the skyjacking of a TWA flight in June 1985, Shiite Muslim terrorists initially mistreated the women and children on board, although they released them after a few days. In November 1985, Palestinian terrorists of the Abu Nidal Organization hijacked an EgyptAir flight from Athens to Cairo. On board they identified three American and two Israeli women. They shot and killed all five.

In general, though, few hostages are killed. They often endure verbal and physical abuse, torture, beatings, starvation, and sleep deprivation, however. Their physical survival is threatened daily. All victims of hostage-taking experience emotional and psychological traumas of the highest degree. They go through extreme feelings of fear, anxiety, disbelief, guilt, shock, and denial. After their release, many ex-hostages suffer post-traumatic stress syndrome, experiencing withdrawal, isolation, fear, and nightmares.

MASS ATTACKS

Many of the highest-profile terrorist actions of the late twentieth century have been attacks on public places. Examples include the bombing of the World Trade Center in New York City in 1992, the Oklahoma City bombing in April 1995, the chemical attack on the Tokyo subway in 1995, the IRA bomb in the town center of Manchester, England, in 1996, and the bombing in Atlanta, Georgia, during the 1996 Olympics. Sometimes such attacks have a high death toll, as in the Oklahoma City bombing. At other times, the terrorists issue an advance warning in order to minimize the deaths and injuries while still demonstrating their ability to cause large-scale destruction.

An attack on a public place guarantees immediate media coverage; in this way, a terrorist group can be assured of achieving publicity if nothing else. These attacks also put the government on the defensive. A successful assault on a public place shows that the authorities have failed in their responsibility to protect the citizenry. Therefore, the terrorists hope they will force the government to negotiate.

The terrorists involved carefully select the sites they attack, and part of the places' attraction is the combination of human and non-human targets. Frequent targets include airplanes and airports, trains, buses, stations or terminals, shopping centers, marketplaces, and large public buildings such as military barracks or government institutions. Terrorists may also choose to target hotels, restaurants, or bars that are frequented by foreigners, in an attempt to include people of several nationalities among the victims. The human victims, who may suffer injury or death in such attacks, are randomly selected, and their individual identities rarely have any significance to the terrorists.

SECONDARY VICTIMS

Family members and close friends of victims of terrorist attack also experience trauma. If the victim was targeted because of an affiliation with the government, the military, or a large business corporation, there is often a great deal of support for the family. This help comes in the form of counseling, financial support, information, and contacts. For example, the U.S. government provided support to the families of the 52 American hostages held in Iran from October 1979 until January 1981. In the 1970s, many corporations whose executives were kidnapped in Latin America paid high ransom to obtain release of their employees.

The families of victims who do not have that sort of professional affiliation rarely receive much support, either from the private or the public sector. Even the information they receive from the authorities may be limited. This was the experience of the families of the American hostages held in Lebanon. They complained about the limited assistance from the Reagan administration, saying that they were left in the dark. Many also suffered financial difficulties, particularly when the hostage was the family's primary wage earner.

R. Reuben Miller

SEE ALSO: BOMBING OPERATIONS; HIJACKING AND KIDNAPPING; ASSASSINATION; THE WORLD TRADE CENTER BOMBING; THE OKLAHOMA CITY BOMBING AND THE MILITIAS.

FURTHER READING

- Carlson, K. *One American Must Die*. New York: Congdon & Weed, 1986.
- Jacobsen, D. and G. Astor. *Hostage: My Nightmare in Beirut*. New York: Donald I. Fine, 1991.
- Ochberg, F. M. and D. A. Soskis, eds., *Victims of Terrorism*. Boulder, CO: Westview Press, 1982.
- Kleinman, Stuart B. "A Terrorist Hijacking: Victim's Experiences Initially and Nine Years Later," in *Journal of Traumatic Stress*, Vol. 2, No. 1, (Jan. 1989): 49–58.

HOSTAGE NEGOTIATIONS

At the heart of almost all dealings with hostage takers is an impossible equation. The desire to secure the freedom of the hostages must be balanced against reluctance to concede to the terrorists' demands. Even if the demands are met, hostages may still be killed. Worse, surrender to demands may simply encourage the terrorists to strike again.

In practice, the response of most authorities falls between giving in to demands and refusing to talk. Negotiations lower tensions and help gain an understanding of the terrorists. In 1975, the British police commissioner Sir Robert Mark remarked on siege situations that: "Human life is of little importance when balanced against the principle that violence must not be allowed to succeed." But in reality, however, negotiators are sensitive to loss of life among hostages.

DEMANDS OF HOSTAGE TAKERS

Hostage taking has several advantages for the terrorist. It forces governments to negotiate with groups they refuse to recognize. Taking important hostages also gives the impression that the terrorists are a powerful force. In the 1970s, the Organization of Petroleum Exporting Countries (OPEC) enjoyed great power and prestige. Hence, when the terrorist "Carlos the Jackal," in reality Ilich Navas, took 11 OPEC ministers hostage in Austria in 1975, his prestige soared.

Hostage taking is less likely to alienate public support than are other terrorist acts like bombing since its main aim is not to harm its victims. If victims are hurt, the authorities may be partly blamed for not making greater efforts to negotiate a settlement.

Ransoming hostages can be a way for terrorists to raise funds. Japanese Red Army terrorists demanded and were granted a $6 million ransom after hijacking a Japanese Airlines plane in 1976. However, the main object of terrorists is to instill terror, and hostage taking can be very effective. In in the 1980s, during a spate of abductions in Lebanon fear spread widely among Westerners in the Middle East. Normal business activity became almost impossible.

KEY FACTS

- In 1974, in return for Patty Hearst's release, her father gave $2 million in free food to the poor.
- In London in 1980, gunmen killed two hostages in the Iranian embassy. The Special Air Service (SAS) stormed the building, saving the other 19.
- American Terry Anderson was held hostage in the Middle East for 2,455 days, from 1985 to 1991.

THE TECHNIQUES OF NEGOTIATION

Experience has shown that negotiating with hostage takers is a complicated task. The first step is to understand the psychology of the terrorists. Hostage takers' demands and their attitude about their survival and that of the hostages varies greatly. But negotiators find some common ground in different hostage situations.

The first problem is that terrorists may act apparently irrationally. For example, they may be willing to sacrifice their lives. So negotiators need to be aware that a promise of safety is not always a bargaining chip.

Even if shrouded in a ski mask, the hostage taker is an exhibitionist and one prepared to kill. Negotiators must respect, and even appear to give in to this characteristic, while they work on a psychological profile and examine alternative strategies.

During sieges, the authorities have some advantages, chiefly being able to supply or withhold various services. In 1984, British police cornered four Irish Republican Army (IRA) terrorists in a London flat, where the gunmen held hostage an elderly couple. The police withheld food for a week, then supplied some to gain better treatment of the hostages. Later, when the gunmen turned violent, police cut off electricity and other supplies. Eventually the terrorists released the hostages unharmed and surrendered.

Other pressures were used in the 1993 siege of the Branch Davidian religious cult at Waco. Eventually, the FBI played loud music and shined strong lights to deny

TRH Pictures/Associated Press

Palestinian terrorists, during their 1985 seizure of the cruise ship Achille Lauro, *executed the disabled American hostage Leon Klinghoffer.*

sleep to the cult members. Here, the pressure failed and the siege ended in heavy loss of life.

Negotiators need both to persuade hostage takers that their demands are being taken seriously, and to drag out negotiations. The longer the negotiations, the better the chance of hostage survival since a lengthy relationship between the terrorists and their hostages makes the captors less prepared to kill their captives.

Although their safety is of prime importance, hostages are rarely involved in negotiations. This assures that the hostage takers get the center stage, and helps avoid complications if the hostages act out of fear or desperation, or even side with their captors.

Negotiators also need to know what deal is politically acceptable to their own authorities. There is greater willingness to concede to armed criminals who take hostages, since they can be pursued by normal legal processes. Terrorists, however, have safe havens and, hence, giving them money increases their ability to undertake further attacks. In 1973, when Carlos took Jewish emigrants hostage in Austria the authorities gave in to all demands. This ensured the hostages' release, but also encouraged Carlos to take hostage the OPEC ministers in Austria in 1975.

The history of hostage taking suggests that a firm response is best in the long run. But there is always a likelihood of compromise since there are few votes in body bags draped in the national flag.

John Collis

SEE ALSO: HIJACKING AND KIDNAPPING; TERRORIST FUNDRAISING; THE MINDSET OF THE TERRORIST; JAPANESE TERRORISM.

FURTHER READING

- Antokol, Norman. *No One a Neutral: Political Hostage-Taking in the Modern World.* Medina, OH: Alpha, 1996.
- Howard, Lawrence, ed. *Terrorism: Roots, Impact, Response.* London and New York: Praeger, 1992.
- Livingston, Marius H., ed. *International Terrorism in the Contemporary World.* Westport, CT: Greenwood Press, 1978.

SUICIDE BOMBING

The sheer terror induced by suicide bombers was first experienced in modern times on Allied warships in the Pacific during World War II. It was clear that one aircraft crashing into a ship did more damage than a squadron of bombers. In October 1944, when Takijiro Onishi took command of the outdated Japanese air force in Manila, he made the deliberate crashing of aircraft an official tactic. The advantages of suicide or "kamikaze" attacks was plain: inexperienced pilots could carry out the raids, a kamikaze plane was hard to combat since it had to be destroyed to be stopped, and such heroism would boost Japanese morale and inspire terror in the enemy.

The pilots were assured of national honor. Onishi told them, "You are already gods." There was no shortage of volunteers. Between April 6 and June 22, 1945, 1,465 aircraft were spent in ten kamikaze raids. Before his mission, one pilot wrote: "Please congratulate me, I have been given a splendid opportunity to die."

HIZB'ALLAH AND RELIGIOUS TERROR

Suicide bombings have again emerged as a tactic, particularly by Islamic terror groups in the Middle East. Although there were sporadic Palestinian suicide bomb attacks during the 1970s, the tactic developed specifically in response to Israel's invasion of Lebanon in 1982. A Muslim terrorist group, Hizb'allah, formed a religiously motivated guerrilla army and began using suicide bombings against the Israelis. Iran's spiritual leader, Ayatollah Khomeini, greatly influenced Hizb'allah's ideology. As a leader of the Shiites, one of the two major branches of Islam, he reinterpreted the Shia cult of martyrdom. Islam bans suicide, but death in holy struggle assures the faithful a place in heaven. Muslim cleric Sheikh Fadlallah claimed: "There is no difference between dying with a gun in your hand and exploding yourself."

At the same time, a group called Islamic Jihad began to stage suicide bombings. In November 1983, an Islamic Jihad operative drove a truck full of explosives into the Israeli Border Guard headquarters in Tyre, waving and smiling as he passed a United Nations checkpoint. The bomber negotiated three concrete barriers and machine-gun fire to get his truck to the target. That he accomplished his goal shows the determination of suicide bombers to complete their missions. By the time the truck reached the headquarters, the driver was dead, but the vehicle continued on its course, knocking down the main gate. Troops blew up the truck before it reached the main building, but the damage was severe and 28 Israelis died. Also killed in the blast were 32 Palestinian and Shiite prisoners. Islamic Jihad knew these people were being held prisoner in the base but decided to martyr them.

In Beirut in 1983, suicide bombs at the U.S. embassy, U.S. Marine Headquarters, and French army headquarters caused huge loss of life and cataclysmic political effects. Young men exploding themselves sent shock waves through Lebanon. The multinational peacekeeping troops began to pull out. Israeli forces vacated most of Lebanon's southern territory after two years' occupation. Suicide bombing declined in Lebanon after 1985, but its effectiveness had been noted.

KEY FACTS

- On October 23, 1983, suicide bombs struck bases of the U.S. and French marines in Beirut, Lebanon, killing 241 Americans and 58 French troops.
- It is estimated that 30 percent of Palestinians support the suicide bombers.
- The Tamil Tigers of Sri Lanka have used suicide bombs, both in vehicles and on motorcycles. Tamil Tigers carry cyanide capsules with which to commit suicide if captured. The group venerates its martyrs.

HAMAS TERROR

From the early 1990s, the Palestinian Islamic fundamentalist group Hamas employed its own brand of martyrdom. Hamas rejected the peace accord between Israel and the PLO reached in September 1993. Under

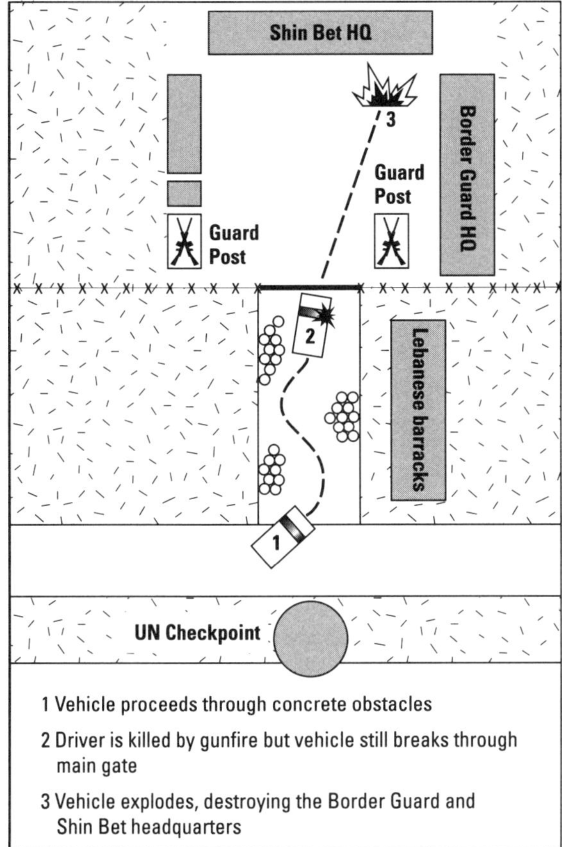

The suicide attack on the Border Guard headquarters at Tyre, November 4, 1983, which killed 28 Israelis.

the accord, a Palestinian National Authority was granted limited self-government in Gaza and the West Bank, previously defined as integral parts of Israel. In the weeks after Hamas rejected the accord, they staged suicide bombings. Bombs exploded in the Gaza Strip, including one on a bus carrying Israeli troops. In 1994, two bombs killed 13 Israelis in Jerusalem, and a crowded bus exploded in Tel Aviv, killing 21. A Hamas bomber killed himself and injured 13 Israelis in a Christmas Day attack in Jerusalem. Two Muslim suicide bombers killed 32 people in Jerusalem and Tel Aviv on March 3 and 4, 1996.

The suicide bombers of Hizb'allah and Hamas have much in common. They are motivated by a heady mix of nationalism, Islam, rhetoric, and poverty. Lebanese and Palestinian militants have suffered physically and economically under Israeli occupation. They are often from the poorest sections of society, with few opportunities. Extreme Islamists exploit this sense of despair by recruiting them to their cause.

Bombers are usually in their mid-to-late teens. They are regarded by the community as old enough to be responsible for their actions, but too young to have wives and children. According to Hizb'allah, the volunteers are "married to death" and know their families will be supported by the terrorist organizations.

Hamas claims that suicide bombers repeatedly volunteer to be allowed to go to their death. Years of prayer in Hamas mosques lead young men to believe that, as martyrs in the struggle for an Islamic Palestine, they will go to heaven and receive posthumous adulation. One volunteer, a 15-year-old from Gaza City, claimed that, in heaven, "I would enjoy a special place near Allah (God), along with the prophets and saints. This vision so excited me that I could hardly bear the wait for my face-to-face encounter with Allah." Belief in heavenly reward, the ideology of revolutionary Islam, and conviction in the need for a Palestinian state sends young Muslims to their death.

The Israeli government has acknowledged that it has yet to find a way to combat such zealots. When technology confronts radical theology, not much can be done to deter individuals set on destruction.

Toby Dodge

SEE ALSO: BOMBING OPERATIONS; THE MINDSET OF THE TERRORIST; TERROR IN LEBANON 1980-1987; THE ORIGINS OF PALESTINIAN ISLAMIC JIHAD; THE PALESTINIAN INTIFADA; PALESTINIAN ISLAMIC FUNDAMENTALISM; TERROR IN LEBANON 1987-1996; THE 1996 SAUDI TRUCK BOMB IN DHAHRAN; HIZB'ALLAH; HAMAS; ISLAMIC FUNDAMENTALIST TERRORISM IN EGYPT; TAMIL TIGER TERROR IN SRI LANKA.

FURTHER READING

- Abraham, A. J. *The Warriors of God: Jihad and the Fundamentalists of Islam.* Bristol, IN: Wyndham Hall Press, 1989.
- Krammer, Martin. "Sacrifice and Fratricide in Shiite Lebanon," in *Terrorism and Political Violence* 3, no. 3 (November 1991).
- Reich, Walter. *Origins of Terrorism: Psychologies, Ideologies, Theologies, States of Mind.* Cambridge and New York: Cambridge University Press, 1990.

TERRORIST GROUPS AND CAMPAIGNS

Hulton Getty Picture Collection

The aftermath of a Jewish terrorist attack on an English troop train in Palestine, April 24, 1947.

TERRORIST GROUPS AND CAMPAIGNS: *Introduction*

There are few countries around the world that have been immune to terrorism in the twentieth century. Although the Middle East has been rarely out of the headlines due to the seemingly intractable Arab-Israeli problem, terrorism has spread across the globe. The underlying themes, particularly since the end of World War II, have been the growing frequency of terrorist attacks and their "internationalization." No longer is terrorism simply an internal matter between ethnic or ideological rivals within a single country, or a struggle between a colonial power and a subject people fighting for independence. Today, it is likely to be played out on the international stage. Terrorist incidents involving citizens from another country are now more prevalent that ever before. This is especially true with regard to the Middle East, where foreign citizens, often from the U.S. and Western Europe, have been targeted by the terrorists. They believe their cause will be strengthened by striking at those countries which they perceive as being closely involved with their opponents. Spectacular terrorist acts against powerful countries usually help the groups to publicize their cause.

Terrorist groups in the modern world usually have one of two aims. Either they desire the overthrow of the existing government, or else they are ardent nationalists dedicated to the establishment of their own nation-state. The urban and rural terrorists of Latin America, for example, have carried out acts of violence to oust right-wing military dictatorships. The Tamil Tigers of Sri Lanka are using terror as part of a wider guerrilla war that is aiming to create an independent homeland. In the Middle East, the Jewish community used violence to help create and then maintain the state of Israel. Arabs have resorted to terrorism to bring about the downfall of Israel and the creation of a Palestinian state. Because of its strategic situation, particularly in relation to the flow of oil, the Middle East has also experienced considerable intervention by the world's leading powers. The terrorists believe that this involvement can be used to justify their attacks against targets overseas.

Certainly, the vast majority of hijackings of passenger jets and ships have targeted foreign nationals, and the wave of hostage-taking in Lebanon in the 1980s was directed against citizens of countries the terrorists viewed as supporting Israel.

One of the most recent developments in terrorism has been the growth of radical religious groups whose members are willing to die for their cause. Chief among these are fundamentalist Muslims, who are not only dedicated to the downfall of Israel but also to the creation of strict Muslim regimes throughout the Middle East and beyond. Consequently, they have targeted Israel and its backers, and other, more moderate, Muslim states in the region.

Terrorist groups have specific aims and wage campaigns of violence that vary in their intensity depending on the wider political situation. The most significant feature of modern terrorists is that they take a global view. Potentially, they are willing to strike at targets worldwide. Today terrorism is no longer someone else's problem. ■

CHAPTER EIGHT

Middle Eastern Terrorism 1920-1947

The widespread mistrust between the Arab and Jewish communities in Palestine gradually degenerated into outright violence and terror in the late 1920s. This intensified as Jewish refugees fled to Palestine from Europe in the aftermath of Hitler's rise to power in Germany. Despite British efforts to prevent the intercommunal violence from escalating, the number of murders and assassinations continued to rise. Unable to halt the terrorists, the British began to train and arm Jewish security forces, turning their backs on the Arabs.

THE ORIGINS OF ARAB-JEWISH TERRORISM

The origins of Arab-Jewish terrorism can be traced back to World War I. This conflict marked the demise of the Ottoman empire. The decision of the Ottomans to oppose Britain, France, and Russia in their conflict with Germany sealed the fate of this once great empire. At its peak the Ottoman empire ruled North Africa, southeast Europe, the Middle East, and Anatolia (Turkey). By 1914, only some territory in the Middle East and Anatolia remained. The Ottomans had traditionally benefited from British backing in order to block Russian expansion against the empire, but Britain ended its longstanding support when the Ottoman empire sided with Germany in 1914. The following year, Britain, France, and Russia decided on future partition for the empire, arranging through the Constantinople Agreements that Russia would receive the Straits region around Istanbul after the war.

In May 1916, the British and French divided the Middle East provinces of the Ottoman empire in the Sykes–Picot Agreement. The agreement stipulated that after the war Britain would have the area making up present-day Jordan, along with Mesopotamia (present-day Iraq), minus the northern region around Mosul. France would obtain Syria and Lebanon, plus Mosul. Palestine would be an international zone, but with British ports at Haifa and Acre.

Britain also made promises – or was at least perceived to have made promises – to both Arabs and Jews in order to gain their support against Germany, Austria, and the Ottoman empire. The promises concerned the future of the Arabs and the Jews in the postwar Middle East. However, after the war, it became clear that it was impossible for Britain to grant the expectations of one people without alienating the other. The stage was set for an era of strife – marked by periodic wars and continual terrorist campaigns – that has lasted with little interruption into the 1990s.

KEY FACTS

- The Zionist movement originated in the nineteenth century. The movement takes its name from Zion, the hill in ancient Jerusalem on which King David built his palace.
- It is not necessary to be Jewish to support the aims of Zionism. Whereas Judaism is a religion, Zionism is a political movement.
- In an incident in Hebron in August 1929, Arabs killed and dismembered 23 Jews with daggers and axes in an upstairs room of an inn.

EUROPE CARVES UP THE MIDDLE EAST

When World War I ended in 1918, the division of the Middle East between Britain and France took place. France took control of Syria and Lebanon, and Britain secured Trans-Jordan (present-day Jordan) and Mesopotamia. However, because British troops occupied Palestine at the end of the war, Britain was able to include the whole of Palestine in the British-controlled part of the Middle East. The borders of post-1918 British-controlled Palestine were similar to present-day Israel with the West Bank and Gaza Strip.

The period of British and French rule in the region lasted until after World War II. Britain and France ruled through a mandate – a type of license to rule – granted by the League of Nations. The plan was that the mandated territories would eventually become independent. In essence, though, the mandated territories were run in the same way as old-style colonies.

THE ZIONIST MOVEMENT

A major problem confronting the British in Palestine after World War I was that two groups of people claimed the right to live in the territory – the Arabs and

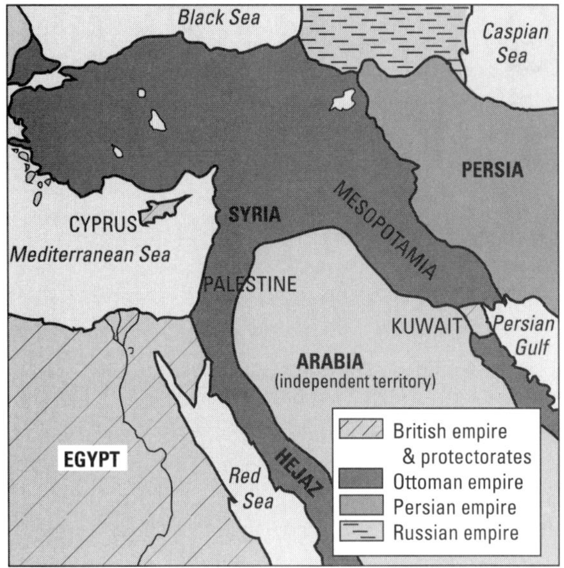

A map showing the division of the Middle East in 1914.

the Jews. The Arabs made up the majority of the population, but a Jewish organization had emerged that called for the return of Jews to their historic home. This organization was the Zionist movement. Since the destruction of the Jewish kingdoms in Palestine by the Romans in the first two centuries after Christ, no Jewish state had existed. After their defeat by the Romans, the Jews were forced to leave Palestine and became scattered throughout Europe and the Middle East. Now, in the wake of World War I, the Zionist movement was promoting the creation of a Jewish state in Palestine.

Even before World War I, Palestinian Arabs were concerned about Jewish immigration into Palestine. Then, during the war, Britain issued the infamous Balfour Declaration. The Balfour Declaration came on November 2, 1917, in the form of a short letter from British foreign secretary Arthur Balfour to Lord Rothschild, a leading British Zionist. The letter was published in *The Times* of London seven days later.

The Balfour Declaration outlined how Britain would view with favor the establishment of a national home for the Jewish people in Palestine. While Britain made provisions for the rights of the Arabs of Palestine in the same document, its wording was ambiguous. Britain hoped that through the Balfour Declaration it could secure Zionist support for the war effort against Germany – it was felt that a pro-Zionist declaration would help bring in Jewish support in the United States and Russia.

However, besides the Balfour Declaration concerning a Jewish homeland in Palestine, Britain also made wartime commitments to the Arabs. During 1915-16, British diplomats made private promises to King Hussein of the Hejaz (the area around the holy cities of Mecca and Medina). In July and November 1918, Britain made public declarations of these promises of independence to the Arabs then under Ottoman rule. These promises, if not at direct variance with the Balfour Declaration, were certainly difficult to reconcile with the promise of a Jewish national homeland in Palestine. As a result, both Arabs and Jews felt that they had a claim on this small wedge of land by the Mediterranean Sea.

THE LEGACY OF WORLD WAR I

The political decisions made during World War I formed the basis for the modern Middle East. In helping the Zionist cause in Palestine, the British laid the foundations for conflict in the Middle East, since Zionists sought to settle Jews in Palestine while the Arabs resisted their presence. Both Arabs and Zionists used every means available, including terrorism, to achieve their political goals. The result was a spiral of violence and counter-violence, in which victims of terrorism sought revenge through retaliation.

The mandates also, however, affected the other Arab states in the Middle East. The Arabs believed they had been promised independence in return for their cooperation with the Allies during World War I, and the mandate system created much bitterness. The Arabs of Syria, Lebanon, and Iraq felt that they had exchanged the colonial yoke of the Ottomans for that of western Europe. Deep-seated resentments were building up, which have since expressed themselves in violence.

JEWISH IMMIGRATION

In the 1920s, terrorism in Palestine was instigated by Arabs who aimed to halt Jewish settlement of the territory. The terrorism took the form of communal violence, rioting, and attacks on Jews. These attacks were increasingly countered by Jewish reprisals. Arabs believed that any growth in the Jewish population would be at the Arabs' expense and would result in their being dispossessed of their lands. Zionist claims that there was enough land in Palestine for both

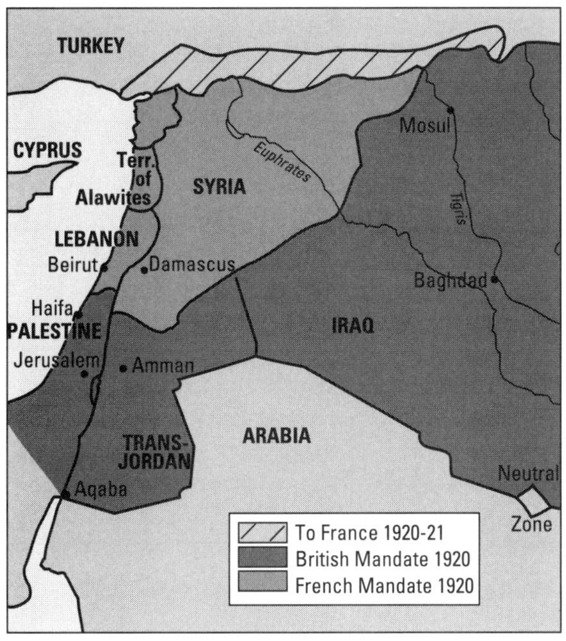

A map of the Middle East, showing British and French mandated territories in 1920.

Arab peasants and Jewish settlers did not convince the Arabs. At the end of World War I, Palestine had some 700,000 inhabitants, of whom 80 percent were Muslim (the vast majority of Palestinian Arabs were Muslims), 10 percent were Jewish, and 10 percent were Christian Arabs. By 1947, the size of the population and its makeup had changed drastically. There were 2 million inhabitants, of which one-third were Jewish.

The increased Jewish proportion was principally the result of immigration: of the 404,000 Jews in Palestine in 1936, some 280,000 were recent immigrants. The migration of European Jews into Palestine was the key political issue of the years between the two world wars. The situation was not helped by the fact that the majority of Jewish immigrants came from a disturbed and poor eastern Europe, where violent anti-Semitism had been institutionalized since the late nineteenth century, making these Jews strongly pro-Zionist. The Arabs resisted the influx of Jews, ultimately through armed action and terror, and the Jewish settlers responded in kind.

The landholding situation in Palestine further fueled discontent. Zionists bought land from absentee Arab landholders, and the Arab peasants who lived on the land in Palestine paid taxes to these landlords. Normally, when land in Palestine was sold, it was the right to tax the peasants that was being bought, rather than physical possession of the land. The Zionists had a different view, because their aim was to populate the land with Jewish settlers. While the Zionists were legally in the right, the resentment of displaced Arab peasants raised opposition to any peaceful solution.

TERRORISM IN PALESTINE

In March 1920, an Arab attack on Jewish settlements in northern Palestine left one of the defenders dead. This death marked the beginning of a period of Arab-Jewish violence and terror that would last until the establishment of Israel in 1948. In April 1920, communal rioting erupted in Jerusalem, with Arabs attacking the Jewish quarter. Nine people died in the violence, and 244 were wounded. More disturbances followed in May 1921. However, the Arab violence was not premeditated. It was more a reaction to months of brooding and fear caused by Jewish immigration to Palestine. Nevertheless, attack and counterattack spread, leaving 47 Jews and 48 Arabs dead.

In response to the tensions between Arabs and Jews, many turned to extremist leaders who saw little future in peaceful dialogue. On the Palestinian side, Haj Amin al-Husseini emerged as a leader. He had been sentenced to 15 years' imprisonment for his role in the 1920 Arab-Jewish violence, but had been pardoned by the British in August of that year and was appointed Grand Mufti (religious judge) of Jerusalem in May 1921. This prestigious post combined legal and administrative functions, and during British rule in Palestine it became an office of power.

For the Jews, Vladimir Jabotinsky represented a hardline strand in Zionism. Jabotinsky also received a 15-year jail sentence for his part in the 1920 riots, being released under an amnesty in 1921. He went on to found the Revisionist branch of Zionism that rejected any compromise that would endanger the foundation of a Jewish state encompassing the whole of Palestine. The Revisionists opposed, for example, the British decision to separate Trans-Jordan from Palestine, believing that the territory should be part of a greater Jewish state. The stage was set for confrontation. Moderate Arab and Zionist leaders had to contend with those willing to use terror. As Jabotinsky chillingly observed: "The Arabs loved their country as much as the Jews did. Instinctively they understood Zionist

Hulton Getty Picture Collection

The Grand Mufti of Jerusalem, Haj Amin al-Husseini, aimed to make Palestine an independent Arab state.

aspirations very well, and their decision to resist them was only natural. There was no misunderstanding between Jew and Arab, but a natural conflict."

THE WAILING WALL DISTURBANCES

Conflict erupted again in 1929 with a dispute over the Wailing Wall in Jerusalem. The wall was sacred to Jews and also to Muslims. In 1928, a seemingly trivial episode over a screen erected to divide Jewish men and women praying at the wall was exacerbated by tactless handling of the matter by the British authorities. The situation in Jerusalem was volatile and all that was needed was an incident.

In August 1929, a Jewish boy kicked a ball into the garden of an Arab. In a subsequent brawl, the Jewish youth was stabbed to death, and the Zionists seized the opportunity to hold a demonstration at the Wailing Wall. In reply, Arab villagers came into Jerusalem armed with clubs, knives, and firearms. The police were unable to disarm the Arabs, principally because there were insufficient numbers of reliable non-Arab officers. Only 300 British police officers could be mustered because of force reductions, and the authorities refused to arm the Jews. The ensuing violence in Jerusalem spread across Palestine.

Several days of violence in Palestine left 133 Jews dead and 339 wounded. In suppressing the Arab attacks, the police and British soldiers killed 110 Arabs and wounded 232. The Wailing Wall violence left lasting marks on Jews and Arabs in Palestine and reduced the likelihood of a peaceful settlement of the differences between them. The ideas of those like Jabotinsky, who had been on the fringe, became more acceptable. Zionism was no longer committed to the peaceful achievement of a Jewish state. Violence had become a legitimate route to attaining that goal.

Matthew Hughes

SEE ALSO: TERROR IN THE ROMAN EMPIRE; THE ARMENIAN MASSACRES; MIDDLE EASTERN TERRORISM 1948-1969; MIDDLE EASTERN TERRORISM 1970-1987; MIDDLE EASTERN TERRORISM 1988-1996; HIZB'ALLAH; HAMAS.

FURTHER READING

- Bell, John Bowyer. *Terror out of Zion: Irgun, Lehi, and the Palestine Underground, 1929-1949.* New York: St. Martin's Press, 1977.
- Mansfield, Peter. *The Arab World: A Comprehensive History.* 3rd ed. New York and London: Penguin, 1992.
- Yapp, Malcolm E. *The Near East since the First World War.* 2nd ed. London and New York: Longman, 1996.

ARMED TERRRORIST BANDS IN PALESTINE

The slaughter of Jews by Arab mobs in 1929 in the Wailing Wall incident and ensuing disturbances profoundly altered Zionists' attitude toward how they could achieve their objective. This objective was to establish a Jewish homeland in Palestine, which was currently governed by Britain through a League of Nations mandate (a license to rule). The hardline Zionist Vladimir Jabotinsky had advocated armed preparedness, and his views now seemed vindicated. Even more moderate Zionist leaders like David Ben-Gurion realized that confrontation with the Arabs in Palestine was almost inevitable. In fact, another bloody round of terrorism and reprisal was just around the corner.

THE ARAB REBELLION

On January 30, 1933, Adolf Hitler became German chancellor, and anti-Semitism in Germany assumed an open and official tone. Persecution of Jews increased, and naturally many Jews looked for a way out. Palestine was one destination for Jewish migrants. Whereas 4,075 Jews entered Palestine in 1931, in 1933 the figure was 30,327. This total rose to 42,359 in 1934, and to a record in 61,854 the following year. In protest against Jewish immigration the Arabs began a general strike on April 15, 1936. Then, on May 7, Arab leaders demanded an end to Jewish immigration and Jewish land purchases, and requested the establishment of an Arab majority government.

In April 1936, ominous atrocities occurred. Two Jews were murdered on a bus held up by Arab robbers. The next night, two Arabs sleeping in a hut near the scene of the hold-up were found dead, having reportedly been killed in an act of Jewish revenge. Anti-Muslim rioting following the death of the two Jews was the worst since 1929. The trouble quickly spread, with armed Arab bands attacking Jewish farms, burning and looting houses, killing settlers, and destroying orchards. Within a month, 21 Jews were dead. In their attempts to keep order, British troops killed more than 140 Arabs, themselves losing 33 soldiers between May and October 1936.

The violence spread across Palestine, and atrocities multiplied. A crowd at a movie theater was raked by bullets, and Jewish staff and patients in a hospital were butchered en masse. Jewish children were killed, and the murderers were never found. Arab attacks grew on fellow Arabs who worked for Jews or who collaborated with the British authorities. Increasingly, the Arab attacks were as much against the British mandate authorities as against Jewish settlers.

The Arab rebellion continued until 1939 in an unending cycle of terror and counterterror that ultimately cost the lives of 3,232 Arabs, 329 Jews, and

KEY FACTS

- In 1931, Izz al-Din al-Qassem, an Islamic cleric, set up a terrorist group in Palestine to attack Jewish settlements and liberate the territory from British rule. He was killed in 1935. The terrorist organization Hamas named its military wing the Izz al-Din al-Qassem brigades in his honor.
- In 1938, Irgun considered bringing 40,000 Jewish partisans from Poland to Palestine to stage an anti-British campaign. World War II intervened before the plan was realized.
- On February 27, 1939, Zionist terrorists set off bombs all over Palestine, killing 38 Arabs.

Hulton Getty Picture Collection

Arab fighters in Palestine around the time of the Arab rebellion of 1936-39.

135 Britons. Arabs working for Jews remained favorite targets for Arab terrorists, and in June 1938, seven were murdered. Among the dead were several women. Violence and counterviolence spiraled. With increasing frequency, terrorists planted bombs in order to maximize destruction. Jewish bombers targeted innocent Arabs, while Arab attacks cut off isolated Jewish settlements.

ARAB REBELLION IN THE COUNTRYSIDE

There were about 10,000 Arab villagers involved in the rebellion. Of this number, about 3,000 formed a hard core of fighters who attacked government property, Jewish settlements, and Arab collaborators. The Arab rebellion had no central leadership and was primarily a spontaneous rural movement. When the grand mufti of Jerusalem, Hajj Amin al-Husseini, tried to direct the revolt from his safe haven in Damascus, Syria (he had narrowly escaped arrest by the British), he discovered that the real power was in the hands of local commanders. There were three main areas of disturbance: Galilee in the north; the region south and west of Jerusalem; and the central region of Tulkarm, Jenin, Nablus, and Ramallah.

Meanwhile, the Jews created armed groups of their own. In 1937, David Raziel founded Irgun Zvai Leumi (Hebrew for National Military Organization). Also known as ETZEL, Irgun was an illegal Jewish right-wing movement made up of Revisionist Zionists. The Revisionists, led by Vladimir Jabotinsky, were a hardline group that called for the use of force to establish a Jewish state on both sides of the River Jordan. Irgun launched preemptive operations against the Arabs and committed terrorist acts against the British. A future Israeli prime minister, Menachem Begin, led Irgun from 1943 until its disbandment in 1948.

HAGANAH

The main Jewish armed force in Palestine, though, was Haganah (Hebrew for "defense"). Haganah had been created secretly in 1920. Whereas Irgun was a terrorist organization, Haganah at first concentrated on defending Jewish settlements. Haganah was careful to avoid terrorism, its members being restrained and disciplined in their actions. After the 1929 incidents that cost the lives of 133 Jews, the rate of Haganah recruit-

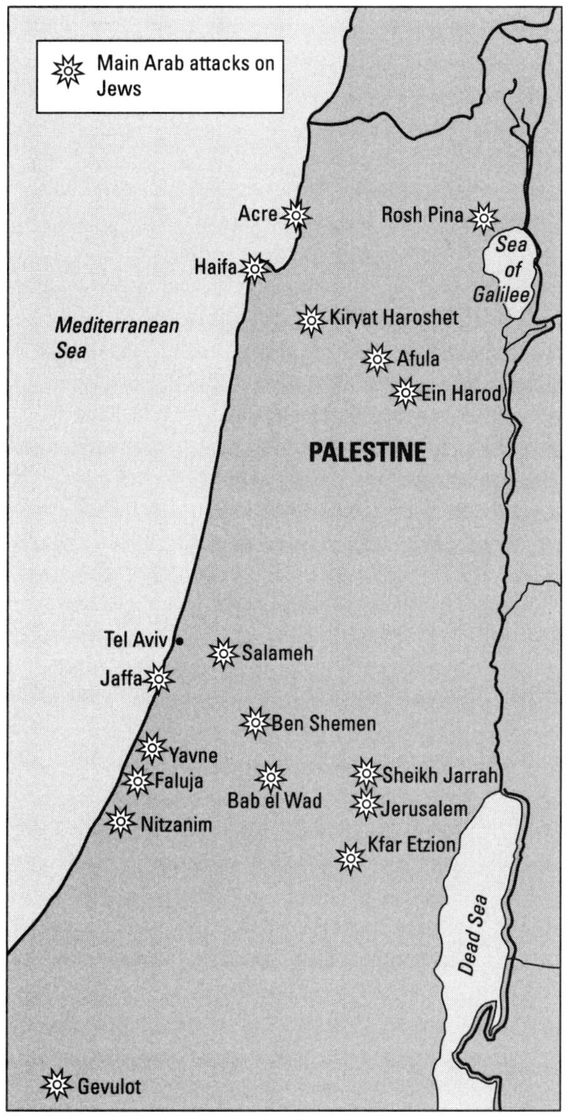

A map showing principal Arab terrorist attacks on Jewish targets during Britain's control of Palestine.

ment and training increased. By the time the Arab rebellion started in 1936, Haganah had about 10,000 members. In 1937, in response to Arab terror attacks on Jewish settlements, elements of Haganah switched from their defensive role and went on the attack.

The traditional Jewish policy of self-restraint (called Havlaga) became strained after the 1929 Wailing Wall disturbances. By 1937 it was becoming untenable. A small section of Haganah called Fosh (from the Hebrew initials for "field troops") was used to counter the Arab rebellion. Encouraged by Haganah high command, Fosh adopted a policy of counterattack that was described in Hebrew as Yetziah minn ha'gader, meaning "going beyond the hedge." The development of a policy of aggressive defense led to the formation of Fosh patrols known as Plugot Sadeh, who tracked down Arab guerrilla fighters in their hideouts. The British knew what was going on, but did little to stop Fosh's activities. In 1941, the elite Fosh element in Haganah developed into the Palmach, Haganah's assault companies that would perform well in the war with the Arabs in 1948-49.

Fosh's actions were given particular prominence through the intervention of Orde Wingate, a young British army intelligence officer. His proficiency as an Arabic-speaker resulted in his being transferred to the British Fifth Division garrisoned in Palestine. Although a Christian, Wingate embraced Zionism with a fervor that perplexed even Jewish Zionists in Palestine, and he became a close friend of future Israeli president Chaim Weizmann. Wingate's views were similar to those of the extremist Vladimir Jabotinsky, and he hoped that in the event of partition between Arab and Jewish territories in Palestine – a solution that was being considered – he could be transferred to the Jewish army.

Wingate's dream of leading a Jewish army to victory never materialized, but in 1938 he helped the future Jewish army by establishing Special Night Squads (SNS) from Fosh personnel. Wingate had observed that the successes of the Arab terrorists during the revolt resulted from the fact that they operated at night. The daytime sweeps by British troops met with little success, despite the numbers of soldiers deployed. Wingate therefore worked out a scheme for regular night operations in Galilee, in northern Palestine, which aimed both to defend the oil pipeline to Haifa and track down Arab bands. Although some British soldiers would take part, Wingate envisaged that Jewish volunteers would form the bulk of his Special Night Squads.

SNS FOUNDATIONS OF THE ISRAELI ARMY

At first, the British high command was strongly against the proposal, because it directly contradicted their policy of doing everything possible to avoid Arab-Jewish conflict. Eventually, however, the British general in charge in Palestine, Archibald Wavell,

Hulton Getty Picture Collection

Women members of the Jewish Haganah in training at a settlement in Palestine in 1938.

agreed to the SNS operations, and Wingate established his headquarters in the eastern end of the Vale of Esdraelon in Galilee. Operating from the Jewish settlement of Ein Harod, Wingate took his largely Fosh force out for the first time on June 3, 1938. The night squads operated continuously until December 1938, with sporadic patrols taking place in the summer of 1939.

SNS operations were on a small scale, and Wingate's force never numbered more than 200. The significance of their actions was largely psychological, because the policy of self-restraint had resulted in a lack of confidence among Jews in their ability to fight back. Wingate, as an outsider, showed through his operations that with training Jewish soldiers could be a match for Arabs. This was an important achievement, and Israelis today credit Wingate with being one of the founders of the Israeli army. The military training that the British gave the Jews in the late 1930s stiffened Jewish resistance. Ironically, it was these toughened troops who turned on the British in the 1940s.

It would be a mistake, however, to believe that the relatively restrained members of the SNS were the only armed Jews with significance for the future. Jewish terrorist groups still existed, and many Jews favored indiscriminate retaliation. In June 1938, the British sentenced to death two youths belonging to Vladimir Jabotinsky's hardline Revisionist party for shooting at Arabs on a bus. Despite pleas for clemency, one, Slomo Ben Josef, was executed. Irgun retaliated in July 1938 by exploding land mines in the Arab fruit market at Haifa. Seventy-four were killed and 129 wounded. The most brutal single terrorist act in Palestine up to 1938, this was a grim warning of events to come.

Matthew Hughes

SEE ALSO: THE ORIGINS OF ARAB-JEWISH TERRORISM; THE BIRTH OF JEWISH TERRORISM; TERRORISM IN PALESTINE IN 1947; TERRORISM IN THE 1948-1949 ARAB-ISRAELI WAR.

FURTHER READING

- Bell, John Bowyer. *Terror out of Zion: Irgun, Lehi, and the Palestine Underground, 1929-1949.* New York: St. Martin's Press, 1977.
- Mattar, Philip. *The Mufti of Jerusalem: Al-Hajj Amin al-Husayni and the Palestinian National Movement.* Rev. ed. New York: Columbia University Press, 1992.
- Slater, Leonard. *The Pledge.* New York: Simon and Schuster, 1970.

THE BIRTH OF JEWISH TERRORISM

In the period from the Balfour Declaration of 1917 to the Arab rebellion that began in 1936, the Jewish community in Palestine felt that the British were helping to defend its position. However, this impression changed in the late 1930s. The most important reason was the British decision to limit Jewish immigration into Palestine and restrict Jewish land purchase there as a way of calming Arab fears. This decision coincided with news of the Nazi campaign against the Jews in Europe. To many Jews, Nazi persecution demonstrated the futility of attempting to assimilate into European Christian society. A Jewish state now seemed necessary for survival. Many Jewish youths looked to extremist groups like Irgun (a Zionist terrorist organization), which were prepared to take on the British and force them out of Palestine as the first step in a war to establish a Jewish state.

As Zionists learned of the Nazi atrocities in the parts of Europe that Germany had occupied, they became outraged at the refusal of Britain to reconsider its postion on Jewish immigration into Palestine. Opinions hardened when the prominent Palestinian Arab politician Haj Amin al-Husseini, grand mufti of Jerusalem, went to Berlin and offered Hitler the Arabs' support in helping to bring about the downfall of what he termed the English-Jewish coalition.

KEY FACTS

- In May 1942, the American Zionist Conference at the Biltmore Hotel, New York, adopted a resolution that called for a Jewish homeland in Palestine. This now became the official policy of the large American Jewish community.
- The Stern Gang's assassination of Lord Moyne in Cairo in November 1944 was the first modern international terrorist incident specifically designed to attract world publicity.
- Yitzhak Shamir, Israeli prime minister in the 1980s, was a prominent Stern Gang leader.
- The Zionist terror groups acquired weapons through raiding British armories and smuggling arms from abroad, usually hidden in machinery.

THE *PATRIA* TRAGEDY

In their desperate need to escape the Nazis, thousands of European Jews inevitably tried to migrate to Palestine. Boatloads of wretched and sick Jews were intercepted between Europe and Palestine by the British navy and prevented from landing. In November 1940, the Palestinian Zioinists decided to take action to try to help these unfortunate refugees. That month, the *Milos* and the *Pacific* reached Haifa with a total of 1,771 illegal immigrants on board. The British high commissioner in Palestine refused them permission to land, and they were transferred to the French liner *Patria*, which was to take them to the island of Mauritius in the Indian Ocean. Days later, on November 24, another immigrant ship, the *Atlantic*, with 1,783 refugees on board, was escorted into Haifa harbor by the British navy.

The following day, as the British began the process of transferring the refugees from the *Atlantic* to the *Patria*, Palestinian Jewish commandos blew up the French liner. Within 15 minutes the *Patria* had sunk, drowning more than 250 Jewish refugees and a dozen police officers. Although the authorities at first blamed Irgun for the *Patria* tragedy, it became clear after investigation that Haganah had been responsible. Haganah was the the Palestinian Jewish militia, recognized and legalized by the British. The aim of the operation had been to halt the deportation of the refugees by blowing up the *Patria*'s engines, but a miscalculation resulted in the bomb blowing a hole in the side of the ship instead. Because of the scale of the

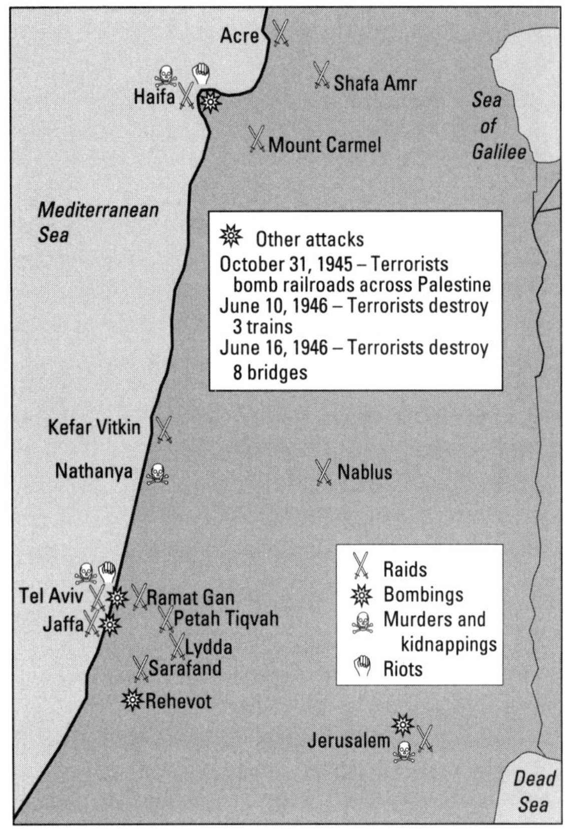

Locations of major Zionist terrorist operations in Palestine, 1944-47.

tragedy, the British accepted the survivors of the *Patria* into Palestine, but the refugees already on board the *Atlantic* were still taken on to Mauritius.

THE EMERGENCE OF THE STERN GANG

Despite their differences, the mainstream Zionists in Palestine and the British fought alongside each other against the Nazis in World War II. Even Irgun was generally restrained in its anti-British activities for most of the war. However, certain elements within Irgun rejected this cooperative approach, and in 1940 these split with the main organization. The splinter group became known as the Stern Gang, after its leader Abraham Stern, formerly one Irgun's most senior commanders. The Stern Gang was also called Lehi from the Hebrew Lohame Herut Yisra'el (Fighters for the Freedom of Israel). The group was fanatically anti-British and repeatedly attacked British army personnel in Palestine. Stern's hatred was even directed at moderate Jews. In January 1942, his operatives murdered two officials of the Jewish labor organization, the Histadrut. Stern was killed in his apartment by a British police officer in 1942, and many members of the group were arrested during World War II. But the Stern Gang survived, and by the fall of 1944 had murdered some 15 people.

ASSASSINATION OF LORD MOYNE

Among the Stern Gang's victims was Lord Moyne, British minister-resident in the Middle East, who was murdered, along with his driver, in Cairo, on November 6, 1944. Moyne's assassination showed the reach of the Stern Gang, and this ability to strike targets far from Palestine proved to be a characteristic of later Middle Eastern terrorism.

After Moyne's death, the Jewish Agency (the official body representing Jewish interests in Palestine) allowed Haganah to help the British round up almost 300 extremists, whom the British then deported. The deportees included not only Stern Gang sympathizers, but also supporters of Irgun, which had called off its wartime truce with the British in January 1944. However, many Jews in Palestine did not agree with the official Zionist condemnation of the extremists. Many Jews sympathized with the extremists and refused to cooperate with the British and Haganah in their search for Irgun and Stern activists.

WIDE-SCALE JEWISH TERROR BEGINS

The end of the war in Europe, in May 1945, released a wave of Jewish terrorism and resistance that had remained largely latent during the war. By July 1945, attacks on British targets were commonplace. With the defeat of Hitler, all the Jewish resistance groups could join in a common cause, and three months later, all Zionist organizations launched a simultaneous campaign against the British. While Haganah concentrated on aiding illegal immigration and attacking British lines of communication, extremist groups such as Irgun and the Stern Gang mined roads, derailed trains, destroyed British warplanes on the ground, and attacked patrol vessels. Terrorists also attacked British police and military personnel. On December 27, 1945, Irgun killed nine British servicemen.

There was wide support in the United States for Zionism. The British Labor government elected in 1945 protested that this support was an attempt to halt

Jewish immigration to the United States. At a conference held on June 12, 1946, the British foreign secretary, Ernest Bevin, rejected the American recommendation that 100,000 Jews should be allowed into Palestine immediately. Bevin claimed that Britain could not afford the hundreds of millions of dollars required to finance their transfer, and that another British infantry division would have to be sent to the region to help keep the peace. In response to Bevin's refusal to increase immigration, four days later Haganah struck in Palestine, blowing up eight bridges and damaging the Haifa railway workshops.

BRITISH COUNTERTERRORISM

In June 1946, Jewish terrorists kidnapped five British officers. The British retaliated by sealing the Jewish Agency buildings and arresting Jewish activists, before taking the dramatic step of ordering the arrest of moderate Jewish Agency leaders. Positions were hardening. Britain was desperately trying to halt Jewish migration to Palestine, while simultaneously having to contend with attacks on military personnel. British courts handed down death sentences on terrorists. But such severe penalties did little to halt the violence as Zionists sought to channel to Palestine the Jews leaving the European concentration camps, and thus make Britain's position untenable.

Then, on July 22, 1946, Irgun struck dramatically by carrying out Operation Chick against the King David Hotel in Jerusalem. The hotel housed British troops and a headquarters unit and was the social center of the British administration in Palestine. The terrorists packed explosives into seven milk churns, and posing as Arab tradesmen drove the bombs to the hotel. They succeeded in placing the churns in the basement, but had to shoot their way out after being discovered by British soldiers. The British now knew something was wrong, but they did not find the churns, and the warnings telephoned by Irgun were not correctly passed on. At 12:37 P.M., the bombs went off, killing 91 and wounding 45. The death toll included Arabs, Jews, and British servicemen. The British responded with the policy of non-fraternization (having nothing to do with the local population), which was similar to that imposed on British forces that had occupied Germany at the end of World War II.

The British continued their struggle to combat terrorism. Arms searches were carried out, and Jews caught with weapons were arrested and imprisoned. Under emergency laws, the British army could arrest people without confering with the police, and could itself try cases that normally would go to a civil court. The British also established a special counterterrorist unit, but it was later accused of killing a young terrorist in suspicious circumstances.

Despite all British efforts to contain it, terrorism flourished. In April 1946, Stern Gang terrorists murdered seven British paratroopers. British troops reacted by wrecking a Jewish village and seriously maltreating a number of Jewish villagers. Such reprisals eroded the little remaining Jewish support the British enjoyed.

Morale was sinking fast in the face of continued terrorist attacks that the British forces felt powerless to prevent. On December 27, 1946, a 16-year-old terrorist – too young to hang – was sentenced to 18 strokes of the cane, in addition to 18 years' in jail, and the punishment was carried out. Two days later, Irgun seized a British major and three sergeants and gave them 18 strokes each in retaliation.

By the end of 1946, Irgun and the Stern Gang had killed 373 people, of whom some 300 were civilians. The British government now decided that its continued presence in Palestine was impossible. Confronting a grave financial crisis, at home and with no military answer to Jewish attacks, in February 1947, Britain referred the Palestine question to the recently formed United Nations. The Jewish terrorists had won their first round.

Matthew Hughes

SEE ALSO: NATIONALIST TERRORISM; BOMBING OPERATIONS; ASSASSINATION; THE ORIGINS OF ARAB-JEWISH TERRORISM; ARMED TERRORIST BANDS IN PALESTINE; TERRORISM IN PALESTINE IN 1947.

FURTHER READING

- Bell, John Bowyer. *Terror out of Zion: Irgun, Lehi, and the Palestine Underground, 1929-1949.* New York: St. Martin's Press, 1977.
- Clarke, Thurston. *By Blood and Fire: The Attack on the King David Hotel.* New York: Putnam, and London: Hutchinson, 1981.
- Silver, Eric. *Begin: The Haunted Prophet.* New York: Random House, 1984.

TERRORISM IN PALESTINE IN 1947

At the start of 1947, Jewish anti-British violence in Palestine reached new heights. The situation was so bad that the British evacuated 2,000 personnel and enclosed their major administrative buildings in a stockade that became known as Bevingrad, after the British foreign secretary of the time. In February, the British government asked the newly formed United Nations to find a solution to the Jewish-Arab problem.

While the United Nations considered the deadlock in the Middle East, the terrorism continued. In March, the Irgun kidnapped a British judge and a civilian in Tel Aviv in retaliation for the death sentence passed on a Jewish terrorist who had been involved in the killing of a policeman. The same month, 20 British soldiers died in an attack on the officers' club in Jerusalem. Britain imposed martial law, though only briefly.

On May 4, the Irgun carried out one of its most daring operations to date, when it broke into Acre jail, where four alleged terrorists had been hanged three weeks earlier. The terrorists, many of whom wore stolen British army uniforms, succeeded in releasing 251 prisoners, many of whom were Arabs. The raid was carried out in daylight, the terrorists blasting their way in using charges placed against the prison walls.

Later that month, on the 15th, the United Nations appointed a Special Committee on Palestine (known as UNSCOP) . The same day , two British bomb squad officers were killed as they were dismantling a mine on a railroad.

KEY FACTS

- In April 1947, two terrorists – Meir Feinstein of Irgun and Moshe Barazani of the Stern Gang – blew themselves up in jail with a grenade, just hours before they were due to be hanged.
- A number of Jewish terrorist attacks on Arabs took place at the end of 1947. A Jewish bomb at Jerusalem's Damascus gate killed 15 Arabs; Irgun terrorists killed a further 17 Arabs when they rolled an oil drum packed with explosives into a crowd waiting for a bus.
- Arab terrorism was less organized than Jewish terrorism and concentrated on attacking isolated Jewish communities. The Arabs tortured and mutilated Jews who fell into their hands.

THE *EXODUS* FIASCO

While the Special Committee members were in Palestine in July 1947, the Zionist refugee ship *Exodus 1947* arrived off the coast. After three Jews were killed in a skirmish with the British navy, the ship was towed into Haifa harbor, where the British ordered the 4,500 Jews on board back to Europe, providing a ship for the journey. The refugees refused to move peacefully to the second vessel, and British soldiers had to use rifle butts, tear gas, and water cannon during the transfer. This fiasco, witnessed by some of the Special Committee members, convinced many people that the British mandate in Palestine had to end.

The British public was also in favor of withdrawing British troops from Palestine, and opinion hardened still further when news reached Britain of the grisly murder of two soldiers in late July. The British authorities in Palestine had sentenced to death three Irgun terrorists. The Zionist group retaliated by taking two army sergeants hostage in an attempt to force the British to reconsider their decision. The two were kept in a tiny cell buried beneath a diamond factory. In their dark prison, they had to breathe air from oxygen cylinders to stay alive. When the convicted terrorists were hanged in Acre on July 29, the Irgun removed the soldiers and executed them. Their bodies were found on July 31, booby-trapped and hanging from trees. The

Popperfoto

The Exodus *in Haifa in July 1947. The damage was caused in the British navy's struggle to board it at sea.*

impact in Britain was immense and influenced the British government decision to send the *Exodus* refugees back to Europe.

THE UNITED NATIONS PARTITION PLAN

In August 1947, the Special Committee put forward its proposals. It recommended the partition of Palestine into an Arab state with a population of 725,000 Arabs and 10,000 Jews, and a Jewish state that would contain 498,000 Jews and 407,000 Arabs. The proposed Jewish state was about half the size of the eventual state of Israel. The city and environs of Jerusalem, with 105,000 Arabs and 100,000 Jews, was to be an international zone. The Special Committee's partition proposal was agreed to by a United Nations vote on November 29, 1947, and it was decided that the British mandate would end in May 1948.

Fierce fighting broke out almost immediately between Jews and Arabs in Palestine. Britain refused to take any action, leaving the two sides to fight it out. Between November 1947 and May 1948 a civil war between Jews and Arabs took place. Knowing the British were going meant the strategy for both Jews and Arabs was one of calculated attack and atrocity to gain land. Among Jewish fighting forces, the Haganah, the Irgun, and the Stern Gang operated with a common aim – the creation of a Jewish state in Palestine.

Matthew Hughes

SEE ALSO: ARMED TERRORIST BANDS IN PALESTINE; THE BIRTH OF JEWISH TERRORISM; TERRORISM IN THE 1948-1949 ARAB-ISRAELI WAR.

FURTHER READING

- Bell, John Bowyer. *Terror out of Zion: Irgun, Lehi, and the Palestine Underground, 1929-1949.* New York: St. Martin's Press, 1977.
- Silver, Eric. *Begin: The Haunted Prophet.* New York: Random House, 1984.
- Slater, Leonard. *The Pledge.* New York: Simon and Schuster, 1970.

CHAPTER NINE

Middle Eastern Terrorism 1948-1969

The founding of the state of Israel in 1948 was followed by a war with neighboring Arab states and the forced expulsion of many Palestinians. Many others lived in little more than ghettos, and clamor grew for an independent Palestinian homeland and the destruction of Israel. Terrorism by both Arab and Jew became more common and less random. Sustained terror campaigns were initiated by the newly founded Palestine Liberation Organization. These activities intensified following the Arabs' military defeat in the Six-Day War of 1967.

TERRORISM IN THE 1948-1949 ARAB-ISRAELI WAR

The year 1948 opened in chaos and conflict. Arabs and Jews were fighting a bitter civil war, carrying out many acts of terrorism. The United Nations General Assembly's resolution of November 29, 1947, had approved the partition of Palestine into Jewish and Arab regions, with Jerusalem designated as an international city. In May, with the declaration of the state of Israel, the civil war in Palestine merged seamlessly into the first Arab-Israeli war.

THE OPPOSING FORCES

Although all the main parties in Palestine in the first half of the twentieth century – Ottoman Turks, Arabs, Jews, and the British – had used violence, the Jews proved the most proficient and successful in employing it to attain their military and political objectives. There were Jewish terrorists of Irgun and the Stern Gang, a large defensive force called Haganah, and effective, well-trained Haganah units, the Palmach, which were capable of carrying out conventional military operations.

Arab forces were less well organized. Recalling Arab guerrilla action against the British and Jews in the 1930s during the Arab rebellion, two main Arab guerrilla forces began disjointed operations against the Jewish forces during late 1947 and early 1948. One was the Arab Army of Liberation, headed by Fawzi al-Kawukji, a veteran of the Turkish army of World War I. This force was raised and trained mainly in Syria. The second important Arab guerrilla force was the Jeish al-Mukadis, or Arab Army of Salvation, commanded by Abd al-Kader al-Husseini, a relative of Haj Amin al-Husseini, the grand mufti of Jerusalem. Its volunteers served directly under the orders of the mufti.

These two forces, soon to be supported by elements of the armies of Egypt, Jordan, Syria, Iraq, and Lebanon, numbered up to 15,000 men, depending on the time and the circumstances. There were also two principal Palestinian Arab terrorist organizations: the al-Futuwwah (or, Young Chivalry), which had formed in the 1930s and was originally under the leadership of the grand mufti of Jerusalem, and the independent al-Najjadah (or, the Helpers).

From January to May 1948, Palestine gradually fragmented into hostile Jewish and Arab enclaves. The key area at this stage of the war was the road to Jerusalem, a city of enormous symbolic value. The Jewish community there was isolated, and Arab fighters were determined to prevent support getting through to the Jews. Convoys were ambushed, and prisoners were tortured and mutilated. Since divided Jerusalem contained one-sixth of the Jewish population of Palestine, Haganah desperately fought to lift the Arab siege of the city that had been imposed at the beginning of 1948.

Meanwhile, throughout Palestine, terrorism and sniper attacks escalated into street fighting and more organized guerrilla warfare. The British army withdrew from successive areas according to a prearranged timetable, in order to complete its evacuation by May 15, when the mandate (the British license to rule) ran out. During this period, the two Jewish

KEY FACTS

- In early 1948, the Stern Gang bombed Arab committee offices in Haifa, claiming they were used to plan military operations. At least 34 Arabs died in the attack.
- In February 1948, 52 people were killed in a single incident when Arab terrorists exploded a bomb in Jerusalem.
- By the end of the 1948-49 war, of about 1.3 million Arab inhabitants of the former Palestine, more than 700,000 had been displaced or had fled.

Hulton Getty Picture Collection

Haganah fighters capture Castel on the Jaffna Road, during fierce fighting with Arab guerrillas, 1948.

terrorist groups, Irgun and the Stern Gang, demonstrated the same ruthless effectiveness that they had shown in their struggle against the British.

DEIR YASSIN

Kfar Sha'ul is today an outer suburb of Jerusalem. In 1948, it was an Arab, not a Jewish, community named Deir Yassin, and its 400 Arab inhabitants were mainly stonemasons working in a nearby quarry. They were not politically active. The village had a peaceable reputation and its inhabitants had even collaborated with the Jews in keeping out Arab militants. Only a few night-watchmen, with old Mauser rifles and even older Turkish muskets, protected Deir Yassin.

At 4:30 A.M. on April 10, 1948, a 138-strong force of Irgun and Stern Gang terrorists attacked the sleeping village. By noon, 254 of the inhabitants had been killed, including many women and children. In this operation, as in the bombing of the King David Hotel in 1946, Haganah and the official Jewish leadership knew what the terrorists were doing. A unit of the Palmach even supplied covering fire with mortars. Accounts by a Palmach eyewitness and investigations by Jacques de Reynier, head of the International Red Cross delegation in Palestine, and a British officer, Assistant Inspector-General Richard Catling, disclosed many cases of looting, rape, mutilation, and shooting of hostages. Atrocities like Deir Yassin built up a cruel momentum – four days later, Arabs killed 77 Jewish medical personnel. "Remember Deir Yassin" was to become a rallying call for Arabs opposed to Israel.

Just as they had after the King David Hotel explosion, official Zionist leaders publicly denounced the Irgun "dissidents," as they called the terrorists. Zionist leader David Ben-Gurion sent a message of apology to King Abdullah of Trans-Jordan, and the chief rabbi of Jerusalem condemned the killers. However, the official Zionist leadership immediately made a formal alliance with Irgun. While keeping its own military structure, Irgun now fell under overall Haganah command.

Twelve days after Deir Yassin, the two forces attacked the Arab quarters of Haifa, shortly after the British had withdrawn.

By the end of the British mandate on May 15, the terrorist units of Irgun (between 3,000 and 5,000 fighters) and the Stern Gang (200–300 people) had been effectively absorbed into the regular Zionist forces. The new Israeli "army" now numbered 30,000 fully mobilized regulars, about 32,000 second-line troops on regional defense duties, 15,000 Jewish settlement police organized in British mandate times, and a home guard of 32,000. This force was far better trained and motivated than the Arab armies. As the war developed and spread, many observers realized the truth of the words of General J.C. D'Arcy, commander of British forces in Palestine in 1946; not only could the Haganah hold Palestine against local Arabs, but "they could hold it against the entire Arab world."

OPERATION NACHSON

Deir Yassin and 20 other villages inside, or flanking, the corridor linking Jerusalem with mainly Jewish Tel Aviv were originally marked for destruction and evacuation in Operation Nachson, which was part of the Jewish leadership's Plan D. The goals of Plan D were to gain control of the partition plan's Jewish area, and of Jewish settlements inside and outside the partiton boundaries, and then to defend them against all enemy forces. After Deir Yassin, most Arab residents fled their homes. Israeli historian Arie Yitzhaqu described the tactics used to encourage the Arab exodus: "Haganah and Palmach troops carried out dozens of operations of this kind, the method adopted being to raid an enemy village and blow up as many houses as possible in it. In the course of these operations many old people, women, and children were killed wherever there was resistance. In this connection I can mention several operations of this kind carried out [by] the Palmach irregulars who were trained to be concerned 'for the purity of Hebrew arms.'"

A WHISPERING CAMPAIGN

Yigal Allon, Israel's leading military commander in the 1948-49 war, recalled tactics used to "cleanse" Galilee of Arabs, before troops from Syria or Lebanon could come to their aid: "I gathered all of the Jewish *mukhtars* who had contact with Arabs in different villages and asked them to whisper in the ears of some Arabs that a great Jewish reinforcement had arrived in

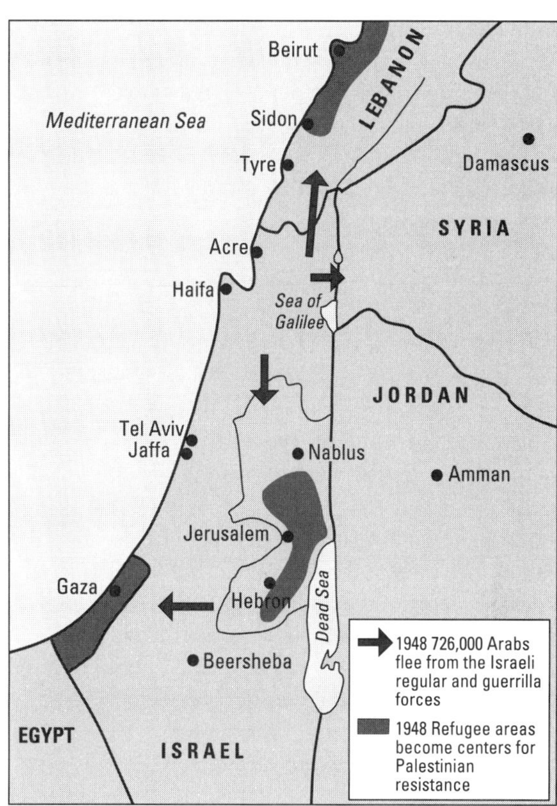

A map showing the expulsions of Palestinian Arabs in the 1948-49 Arab-Israeli war.

Galilee and that it was going to burn all the villages. ...And the rumor spread....The flight numbered myriads. The tactic reached its goal completely."

A Palestinian witness was George Habash, a Greek Orthodox Christian Arab from Lydda (Lod). As a 22-year-old, he and his family, like the rest of the Arabs in Lydda, were given a few hours' notice to leave by the loudspeaker vans of Haganah. "We suffered a profound shock," he said, "seeing people driven out by force. The scenes at the time were indescribable – people were shot in the streets....Arab young people as a whole were deeply stirred." Habash went to Beirut, where he enrolled at the American University of Beirut to study medicine. He later founded the Popular Front for the Liberation of Palestine, which led a ruthless terror campaign against Israel.

Well before the end of the summer of 1948, as many as 400,000 Palestinian refugees, according to records of American and UN diplomats, had left towns such as

Jaffa and Haifa, where Arabs had once been a majority. The journalist and future president of Ireland, Erskine Childers, and other independent researchers investigated early Zionist claims – widely believed in the West – that Arab leaders inside and outside Palestine exhorted their people to flee. No record was found of such broadcasts or exhortation. On the contrary, there were many admonitions to remain and defend Palestinian homes and farms and industrial property.

FOUNDATION OF THE STATE OF ISRAEL

On May 14, 1948, David Ben-Gurion declared the independence of the Jewish state, which was to be called the State of Israel. The Arab world was as determined to destroy the newborn Jewish state by violence as the Jews were that their state should survive. All-out war began, as Jewish and regular Arab forces from Syria, Lebanon, and Egypt battled it out. Trans-Jordan's small regular army, the Arab Legion, commanded by a British general, Sir John Glubb, reinforced the siege of Jerusalem. The Legion captured the Old, or Arab, City of East Jerusalem in late May.

By the end of 1948, Jewish forces were largely triumphant in Palestine. The new Israeli state controlled approximately 30 percent more territory than had been allotted by the UN, while Jerusalem was divided between the military forces of Israel and Trans-Jordan. When the final armistice agreements ended the war in early 1949, Israel occupied 77 percent of Palestine, compared with the 57 percent allotted to it under the partition plan. Israelis had taken entire cities and towns, and hundreds of villages. They took over the farms, factories, livestock, houses, furniture, carpets, clothes, and works of art of the Palestinian Arabs. About half the total businesses, shops, and citrus plantations were in Israeli hands.

But the Arabs were not willing to take such treatment without response. When Jewish troops moved in to drive out Arab villagers, sporadic violence broke out. Several young Arabs took to terrorism, kidnapping and torturing Jews more or less at random. The war, its prelude, and its aftermath engendered thousands of acts of individual terrorism.

One terrorist act that shocked the West was the killing of UN mediator Count Folke Bernadotte by Jewish terrorists. Count Bernadotte was a member of the Swedish royal family who had worked in humanitarian ventures such as prisoner exchanges in World War II. Like most Europeans who had witnessed the Nazi Holocaust, he came to Palestine predisposed to favor the Jewish cause. Arriving in Jerusalem, he was bewildered to see Stern Gang banners with slogans hostile to the UN and himself. After arranging the ceasefire of June 11, 1948, he attempted to consolidate in a subsequent armistice some political arrangements for peace, based on modifications to the partition plan.

THE STERN GANG AND COUNT BERNADOTTE

After the July 9 collapse of the first truce, Bernadotte became concerned with the tragic plight of the Arab refugees. Although warned of mounting Jewish hostility, he insisted on touring the dangerous area of Jerusalem on September 17, after submitting a report containing his peace proposals to the UN. It was part way through this visit that men wearing Israeli army uniforms shot Bernadotte and his French deputy, Colonel Serotat, at point-blank range. The killers later identified themselves as members of Hazit ha-Moledet (the Homeland Front), a part of the Stern Gang.

After two months of international pressure, the Israeli authorities arrested Stern's leaders, Nathan Yellin-Mor and Matitiahu Schmulevitz, both Polish-Jewish immigrants. Yellin-Mor, who was later to change his views and write on behalf of Palestinian rights, denounced Bernadotte in court as an enemy of Israel. The defendants were given prison sentences of eight and five years. Later, the court revoked the sentences and released them, since they proclaimed their desire to become "law-abiding citizens."

John Cooley

SEE ALSO: NATIONALIST TERRORISM; ASSASSINATION; MIDDLE EASTERN TERRORISM 1920-1947; ARAB NATIONALISM AND THE RISE OF FATAH; THE BIRTH OF THE PLO AND THE 1967 WAR; THE BEGINNING OF INTERNATIONAL TERRORISM; MIDDLE EASTERN TERRORISM 1970-1987.

FURTHER READING

- Ilan, Amitzur. *Bernadotte in Palestine.* New York: St. Martin's Press, 1989.
- Morris, Benny. *The Birth of the Palestinian Refugee Problem, 1947-1949.* Cambridge and New York: Cambridge University Press, 1987.
- Silver, Eric. *Begin: The Haunted Prophet.* New York: Random House, 1984.

ARAB NATIONALISM AND THE RISE OF FATAH

Arab historians term the defeat in the 1948-49 war "the Disaster." Terrorism and violence erupted in the Arab states and societies that had taken part. There was no Palestinian state and that Palestinian territory still in Arab hands was divided. The West Bank was under Trans-Jordanian rule, while the Gaza Strip was under Egyptian control.

A major reason for the Arabs' defeat had been the confusion in Arab aims. The Palestinians had had no effective political organization in 1948; even if one had existed, it would have been opposed by King Abdullah of Trans-Jordan, who claimed that Palestine was part of his kingdom. Palestine's other major neighbors, Syria and Egypt, also had their own agendas that did not necessarily coincide with those of the Palestinians.

The Arab world in the 1950s was in ferment, with nationalists, modernizers, and fundamentalists working with (and often against) each other. From this, a Palestinian resistance movement arose among small groups of Palestinian refugees, mainly students and university-educated people. By 1970, the resistance movement was a central force in the Middle East and was undertaking its own terrorist campaigns. How this came about is in large measure the story of the movement for Palestinian nationalism, of its leading figure, Yasser Arafat, and of the Fatah organization.

KEY FACTS

- On October 13, 1953, terrorists operating from Jordan killed a woman and two children at Tirat Yehuda, Israel. The Israelis responded by attacking the Jordanian village of Qibya, killing 66 Arabs.
- Eleven Israelis were killed in an Arab machine-gun attack on a bus at Beersheba, Israel, on March 17, 1954. Israel retaliated, killing nine villagers in Nahhalin.
- In July 1958, the pro-Nasser Iraqi army deposed and executed King Feisal of Iraq, the crown prince, and the prime minister.

THE MURDER OF KING ABDULLAH

The first major act by Palestinians after the 1948-49 war was a terrorist attack. By 1951, the kingdom of Trans-Jordan was involved in secret peace talks with Israel. King Abdullah met with Golda Meir, a senior member of the Israeli leadership, seeking a permanent peace. On July 19, 1951, the king inaugurated the Royal Jordanian Air Force at a ceremonial parade in Amman. The next day, at the entrance to the Great Mosque in Trans-Jordanian-held East Jerusalem, a Palestinian terrorist shot and killed Abdullah, setting back by generations the chances of permanent peace between Trans-Jordan and Israel – just as the killer intended.

The most important development in the Arab world from the Palestinian point of view was the overthrow of the Egyptian monarchy in 1952 by General Mohammed Naguib, Lieutenant-Colonel Gamal Abdel Nasser, and a group of like-minded nationalist and reformist army officers. Naguib in turn was replaced by Nasser in 1954. From this time until the 1967 war, the Palestinian resistance was closely linked with Egypt, which still occupied the Gaza Strip where half a million Palestinian refugees lived in crowded camps.

Although the coup was carried out by reformists, the most important organization within Egypt for the Palestinians at this stage was the Muslim Brotherhood, set up in 1928. The Brotherhood believed in government by religion (theocracy) and formed open and

Popperfoto

Gamal Abdel Nasser, prime minister (1954-56) then president (1956-70) of Egypt.

clandestine chapters in Arab nations and former Palestinian territory in the early 1950s. Its aim was to create an Islamic state, first in Egypt, then elsewhere, including Palestine. Brotherhood members tried unsuccessfully to assassinate President Nasser in 1954 (they disagreed with his more secular philosophy), and many members fled to Saudi Arabia.

In the 1950s, young Egyptians and other Arabs were recruited by the Muslim Brotherhood to carry out terrorism against British troops in the Suez Canal Zone in Egypt. The Muslim Brotherhood and the conservative Islamic elements in Egypt and Saudi Arabia nurtured Palestinian aspirations: in 1953, the Brotherhood formed an Islamic Council for the Palestine Question, and Brotherhood spokesmen urged that the anti-British armed struggle in the Canal Zone be extended to Israel.

Some Palestinians were already taking action, and, from his different viewpoint, President Nasser was also beginning operations. Nasser later told *The New York Times* correspondent Kennett Love that he had withheld *fedayeen* (Palestinian fighters) raids on Israel until August 25, 1955. That was the day he also decided to buy arms from Czechoslovakia, in the Soviet bloc, the U.S. and Britain, having refused to sell Egypt weapons. In fact, from late 1954, Nasser had sponsored what one Arab military historian called "organized, attritive [*sic*] and relentless *fedayeen* raids into Israel from the Gaza Strip and from Jordan."

TERROR AND COUNTERTERROR

In reprisal against these terrorist attacks, the Israelis made a major attack on an Egyptian army base in Gaza in February 1955, and hit other bases at Khan Yunis on September 1, 1955, and at Sabha on November 2. Between February 1955 and the Suez War of October 1956, the Israelis carried out 15 major reprisal raids, not only against Arab army camps and police posts, but also against border villages. The largest such attack was against the West Bank village of Qalqiliya on October 10, 1956.

Israeli counterterror activity (as distinct from full-scale military operations) also began in Gaza before the 1956 Suez War. Two Egyptian intelligence officers supervising *fedayeen* activities, Salah Mustafa and Mustafa Hafez, were assassinated by Israeli counter-terrorist action, the second by a package bomb.

In April 1955, an important *fedayeen* commando unit was set up under the supervision of the Egyptian army in Gaza. It included about 700 men, some of them Palestinians. Many had fought against the British in the Canal Zone. Palestinians in this unit (which included Khalil al-Wazir, one of the founders of Fatah) later formed the initial complement of Fatah's military wing.

YASSER ARAFAT

Yasser Arafat was born in Jerusalem in 1929 to upper-middle-class Palestinian parents. His father died when Arafat was young. By the age of 15, Arafat was running guns for the Arab irregulars formed to fight the Israeli army and the Zionist terrorist bands. In late 1947, he apparently served in the Arab Army of Salvation. When they realized that the 1948-49 war was lost, Arafat and his family fled to Gaza, where they experienced the grim life of refugees. Cairo, Egypt, was the easiest Arab capital to reach from Gaza, so Arafat enrolled at the university there in 1951. He joined the Muslim Brotherhood, and, in 1954, when President Nasser deported the Brotherhood's leadership, Arafat left for Beirut, Lebanon, and later Kuwait, where he worked

Hulton Getty Picture Collection.

Jordan's King Hussein (right) with King Faisal of Iraq in Amman, Jordan, in 1956.

for an engineering and contracting firm. He was allowed to return to Cairo in 1955, where he enrolled in an Egyptian army commando training course.

Just before the 1956 Suez War, Arafat visited friends in Gaza, who helped him to create a new Palestinian nationalist organization, Fatah. He and his friends laid the logistical and financial groundwork by enlisting bankers, contractors, and other wealthy Palestinians. Gaza became the breeding ground for the new group, and by 1959, the first fully operational cells had taken root there and also in Kuwait. The name *Fatah* is a reverse Arabic acronym for Harakat al-Tahrir al-Watani al-Falistini or Palestine National Liberation Movement. The word *fatah* itself means "conquest."

Fatah adopted the conservative Islamic values coupled with respect for Western technology that characterized the Muslim Brotherhood, Fatah's major source of inspiration in the 1950s. In the 1960s, practical support for Fatah in logistics and organization, as well as the influence of different views, came from the more radical left-wing Arab nationalist groups. These groups included Algeria's National Liberation Front (FLN), victorious in the war for independence from France in 1962, and Syria's Ba'ath Party, which seized power in Damascus in 1963.

Arafat became friendly with Muhammad Khidder, one of the Algerian revolution's toughest organizers and the FLN treasurer. The two set up fund-raising, recruiting, and training for Fatah in Algeria after 1962. Selected Palestinians trained at the Algerian military academy. One of Arafat's associates who developed strong links with the Algerians was Khalil al-Wazir.

Arafat needed a secure base near Israel. After the Suez War of 1956, however, Nasser was no longer in any position to help, and in fact repeatedly warned other Arab leaders that the Arab world was not ready to fight Israel. He stated also that he would not be dragged into war by Palestinian guerrilla or terrorist action "before we are ready to choose the time and place of the battle." Neither Jordan nor Lebanon would help. Both were imprisoning Palestinians known for affinities with Arafat and Fatah.

SYRIA AND BA'ATHISM

Fatah now turned to Syria and the new government there. On March 8, 1963, a group of Syrian officers who belonged to the secretive Ba'ath (Arab Socialist Resurrection) party had seized power in Damascus. The Ba'ath party had an ideology that mixed Arab nationalism, Marxism, and nineteenth-century Germanic Romanticism, conceived largely by Michael Aflaq, a Damascus schoolteacher. One of its main principles was the "liberation of Palestine."

Arafat and his "brains' trust," especially Khalil al-Wazir (who later took the *nom de guerre* Abu Jihad) and Salah Khalaf (Abu Iyad), reckoned correctly that their concept of a revolutionary war to regain Palestine suited Ba'athist ideology and propaganda. Arafat accordingly found support from two Syrian officers, Colonel Abd al-Karim al-Jundi, head of military intelligence, and Colonel Ahmed Sweidani, the chief of staff. By the summer of 1963, Arafat shifted the Fatah's base of operations to Syria.

Arafat's men began to mount covert missions into Israel, and in 1964, the Fatah leaders met to discuss a starting date for guerrilla operations. A minority of Fatah's ruling revolutionary council, then numbering about 20, insisted that conditions were still too unfavorable. Further meetings reached no decision.

Apart from Fatah, there was an important radical branch of Palestinian nationalism. After refugee George Habash reached Beirut in the early 1950s to study medicine, he and other Arab intellectuals, including Hanni al-Hindi, a Syrian, and Ahmed al-Khatib, a Kuwaiti, formed a discussion group called The Firm Tie. This merged with the Arab Nationalist movement (ANM), founded in Jordan in 1953 by another medical graduate, Wadi Haddad. The prestige Habash and others had among radical young Palestinians led to the formation of one the first secret terrorist organizations, the Phalange of the Redeemers.

By the late 1950s, Habash had finished medical school in Beirut and opened a clinic, treating the poor for free. Gradually, he abandoned medicine for politics. The roots of what Habash and his sympathizers call "the internationalization of the Palestinian resistance," and what the rest of the world came to know as international terrorism, began to grow out of ANM cells. Graduates formed the cells in Aden (then capital of British-ruled South Arabia; after 1967 it became the capital of South Yemen), in Kuwait, and in what was then the pre-Qaddafi kingdom of Libya.

In Jordan, the ANM developed more medical clinics for the poor, and started schools to supplement those established by the government and the United Nations to fight widespread illiteracy. Everywhere, ANM cells preached against Israel and Western "imperialism." ANM members also took part in Nasser-controlled *fedayeen* operations in Gaza in the mid-1950s.

The ANM believed that Arab unity was necessary if the Palestinians were to regain their homeland and supported countries it thought might bring the Arabs together. During the 1956 Suez War, the ANM cooperated with Egypt. Its founders viewed Syria's Ba'athists, who were supporting Fatah, as partners in Arab nationalism. "From 1956 to 1964," Habash asserted, "we worked for Arab unity, in order to bring about a state encircling Israel."

John Cooley

SEE ALSO: TERROR IN FRENCH ALGERIA; NATIONALIST TERRORISM; ASSASSINATION; COLLABORATION BETWEEN TERRORISTS; TERRORISM IN THE 1948-1949 ARAB-ISRAELI WAR; THE BIRTH OF THE PLO AND THE 1967 WAR; THE BEGINNING OF INTERNATIONAL TERRORISM; MIDDLE EASTERN TERRORISM 1970-1987; MIDDLE EASTERN TERRORISM 1988-1996; RADICAL MUSLIM TERRORISM; ISRAELI RESPONSES TO TERRORISM.

FURTHER READING

- Abu Iyad. *My Home, My Land: A Narrative of the Palestinian Struggle.* New York: Times Books, 1981.
- Cobban, Helena. *The Palestinian Liberation Organization: People, Power, and Politics.* Cambridge and New York: Cambridge University Press, 1984.
- Ovendale, Ritchie. *The Origins of the Arab-Israeli Wars.* 2d ed. London and New York: Longman, 1992.

THE BIRTH OF THE PLO AND THE 1967 WAR

During the early 1960s, Palestinian raids against Israel continued and were met with Israeli retaliation. Three events had huge significance for the future of terrorism, however: these were the foundation of the Palestine Liberation Organization (PLO); its subsequent takeover by Yasser Arafat's Fatah, the organization's dominant group; and the defeat of the Arab states in the 1967 war with Israel.

The PLO was founded almost as an afterthought during a conference hosted by Egypt's President Gamal Abdel Nasser in January 1964 to discuss Israel's plan to divert water from the Jordan River. Israel's new national water system was based on a pipe carrying water from the Jordan in Galilee to the Negev Desert, to permit new agricultural settlement there. In the end, the conference took no direct action at all on the water question. Instead, it decided on the creation of the PLO as the Arab League's official Palestinian entity. Its declared purpose was to give the Palestinians direct responsibility for their own liberation and future.

The intention in founding the PLO was to draw together the terrorist and political groups that had emerged in the dispossessed Palestinian refugee communities. The PLO's first leader was a verbose Palestinian lawyer, Ahmed Shuqairy. He proved to be an asset to Israeli publicists and Western journalists, who would repeatedly quote his words (which he denied ever saying) about "throwing Israel into the sea." Israeli spokesmen used such statements to argue that the PLO, which developed a vast network of banks, trade unions, student associations, and other organizations for social and charity work, was in reality only a "terrorist" organization.

The PLO's founding conference convened in East Jerusalem, then still governed by Jordan, in May 1964. The 422 participants endorsed two documents: a constitution and the Palestinian National Covenant or Charter, issued on May 28. Several of the clauses committed the PLO to the destruction of Israel. This commitment would remain in force until April 1996.

SUMMARY

- The Palestine Liberation Organization (PLO) was set up in 1964 after a meeting of Arab states to discuss Israeli plans to divert the Jordan River.
- The PLO and its armed force, the Palestine Liberation Army (PLA), were largely ineffective from 1964 to 1969.
- In 1967, the armies of Jordan, Syria, and Egypt suffered a catastrophic defeat by Israel. In the wake of the 1967 war, the PLO became dominated by Yasser Arafat's Fatah group which was committed to armed confrontation with Israel.

PLO DISPUTES WITH JORDAN

Internal controversy within the PLO and friction with its Arab creators arose almost at once. On July 2, 1964, Shuqairy released a statement in the Jordanian capital, Amman, claiming that the whole territory of the Hashemite Kingdom of Jordan (formerly Trans-Jordan), including the part east of the Jordan River, was part of Palestine. This seriously offended the PLO's Jordanian hosts. It was one cause of King Hussein's determination to keep PLO chapters formed in the West Bank disarmed, despite their constant demand for weapons.

In addition, many Arabs, especially in Egypt, were skeptical that the PLO had a useful role to play. In their view, the PLO had not been created to further the Palestinian cause, but mainly to lift the burden of confronting Israel from the shoulders of the Arab regimes, in particular that of President Nasser in Egypt. Nor did groups such as Arafat's Fatah take the new organization at all seriously.

The PLO leadership also established a fighting force, the Palestine Liberation Army (PLA), for operations against Israel in time of war. It was intended to give the PLO a regular military force. This Palestinian army evolved as an independent force, with its own budget, cadres, training, and sources of supply. Almost from its start, the army's leadership contested the PLO's control. In the Lebanese civil war after 1975, for example, the army's Hittin Brigade, based in Syria, fought the PLO in Lebanon.

Hulton Getty Picture Collection

Yasser Arafat, right, one of the founders of Fatah and chairman of the PLO from 1969, talks with PLO spokesman Kamal Nasser.

RECRUITMENT TO THE PALESTINIAN ARMY

Because of concern that the Palestinian army might threaten its host governments, only Egypt and Iraq permitted recruitment of small Palestinian units under the host's military command. A unified Arab command was supposed to supervise the army, although its main headquarters was set up in Damascus, Syria, and would remain there until Arafat ordered it moved to Beirut in 1976. King Hussein allowed no formal army presence in Jordan and only symbolic PLO offices. In addition to severe restrictions on its weapons, the PLO was not allowed to tax or to recruit Palestinian refugees. Lebanon did not permit the Palestinian army on its territory, though it did allow Palestinians living in Lebanon to join. However, once a Lebanese Palestinian had joined the PLA, he was no longer allowed to return to Lebanon, even to visit his family.

The Palestinian army had four separate brigades, attached to the host armies, and recruited first from Palestinians, including professional officers already serving with the Egyptian, Syrian, and Iraqi armies. One brigade was recruited directly from the Gaza Palestinians. This was the only Palestinian unit to play a military role in the 1967 war, fighting a desperate and sometimes suicidal holding action against the Israeli army on June 5 and 6, 1967. Some survivors formed guerrilla and terrorist cells to resist Israeli occupation.

Since the Soviet Union was unwilling to supply arms to the PLO or its army directly, Shuqairy and the Fatah leaders (although Fatah and the army were in some respects rivals) together turned to China. Arafat, Shuqairy, and others travelled to Beijing in 1965. The Chinese offered arms and financing, complementing what was already trickling in from a few Arab governments, especially Algeria. By 1966, Chinese equipment was arriving, including rifles, grenade launchers, mortars, some aging field guns and rocket launchers, and some old M-48 tanks and armored cars. Training before the 1967 war went on in Gaza, Syria, China, and North Vietnam. By June 1966, there were 4,000-6,000 recruits training in Syria and 8,000-9,000 in Gaza.

TERROR FROM "THE STORM"

Meanwhile, a majority of Fatah's ruling revolutionary council, with their Syrian mentors' approval, voted to start independent armed action on January 1, 1965, despite a dire lack of funds, training, arms, and leadership. The Algerians, Arafat argued, had begun their revolution on the eve of All Saints' Day, 1954, under the same conditions and, by 1962, had succeeded in wresting independence from France. Fatah dissenters insisted that military operations begin under a cover name, so that in case of failure, Fatah could then continue secret operations without being compromised.

Thus using the name al-Asifa (the Storm or Tempest), Fatah's military wing launched the first operation on New Year's Eve, 1964, against Israel's national water system near al-Himma, on the Jordanian border where Jordan River water flowed into the Israeli pipeline. This first "official" attack was a military failure, but served as a warning to Arab governments that Fatah had begun operations that the Arab governments had not dared to undertake.

Predictably, both Jordan and Lebanon (but not, at this stage, Fatah's host, Syria) increased their efforts to prevent Palestinians from using their countries as bases for operations against Israel. Jordan especially had suffered too many destructive Israeli reprisal raids for previous cross-border movements to want any more. One of the two *fedayeen* carrying out the New Year's Eve raid – the first was killed by the Israelis – was captured by a Jordanian army patrol as he returned across the river. On King Hussein's orders, Jordanian Prime Minister Wasfi Tal's government began a merciless manhunt for *fedayeen*. Ten days after the first operation, a Jordanian soldier killed another al-Asifa guerrilla, Ahmed Musa.

From January 1965 until the war of June 1967, Fatah issued 73 military communiqués on sabotage raids conducted by al-Asifa. Some were directed personally by Arafat, who began making clandestine trips, sometimes disguised as a woman or a peasant, into Israel, including some to Jerusalem. Most of these operations started from Syria; a few, without King Hussein's authorization, were from Jordan.

ISRAELI RETALIATION

In retaliation, on November 13, 1966, Israel struck hard, not at Syria, but at the remote West Bank Jordanian hamlet of Samua, ten miles south of Hebron and four miles north of the Israeli border in the Negev Desert. Jordanian army reinforcements who were rushed in against the Israeli incursion ran into an Israeli ambush; 21 Jordanian soldiers were killed and 37 wounded.

Hussein remained adamant in his opinion that the Samua raid, the most destructive of a series of Israeli reprisals that had begun at the West Bank town of Qibya in 1953, was inevitable. He regarded the raid as the direct result of the refusal of the PLO command to function under the operational control of the Unified Arab Command. This body was largely dominated by Egypt, but other Arab countries, including Jordan, were represented.

The Samua raid might have halted clandestine PLO operations from Jordan, but Fatah continued its incursions from Syria. Israeli Chief of Staff General Yitzhak Rabin and other senior officials threatened that Israeli forces might enter Syria to "teach a lesson" to the Ba'athist regime in Damascus, which was protecting the terrorists. Arab unity, tenuous at best, was further damaged by a vicious argument between Jordan and the rest of the Arab states. There were increasing Arab threats against Israel especially by the PLO's Shuqairy and to a lesser extent by Nasser's Egypt.

Incidents multiplied on the Syrian-Israeli border, especially on and around Lake Tiberias (the Sea of Galilee). In a serious aerial clash in April 1967, six Syrian MiG fighters were shot down by the Israeli air force. In mid-May, Israeli Prime Minister Levi Eshkol issued a "serious warning" to Syria either to curb Fatah or to face the consequences.

THE BUILD UP TO THE 1967 WAR

On May 15, Egyptian President Nasser, influenced by Arab and Soviet intelligence reports of Israeli build-ups and partial mobilization, began his precipitate moves into war, which went counter to his earlier judgments. He ordered a maximum alert of the Egyptian armed forces and instructed the UN forces stationed in Sinai and Gaza to withdraw, which they did on May 19. Nasser next closed the Straits of Tiran, running between Sinai and Saudi Arabia and controlling Israel's Red Sea lifeline to Eilat.

Although reluctant to become embroiled in another Arab-Israel war, King Hussein of Jordan was under great pressure from the 50-60 percent of East Jordan's population that was Palestinian, and because Jordan had endured the worst of the Israeli reprisals since the 1950s. On May 30, Hussein visited Nasser in Cairo to sign a mutual defense pact with Egypt and Iraq, committing Jordan to defending the Arab cause if another signatory was attacked. This step convinced Israeli defense minister Moshe Dayan that Israel should go to war.

On the night of June 3-4, the Israeli cabinet issued orders to attack Egypt and Jordan early on June 5, 1967. The Israeli government believed Israel's national existence was endangered and that war was the only way to end *fedayeen* attacks. The Israelis struck on June 5, wiping out much of the Egyptian, Syrian, and Jordanian air forces on the ground and moving deep into Gaza and Sinai. The Arab world was unprepared militarily, economically, morally, and philosophically for the punishing lightning war that followed.

The Palestinian army played only a small role in the war, tightly controlled by the Syrian high command. Al-Asifa combat units operated separately and claimed a

Hulton Getty Picture Collection

Warplanes lie wrecked on an Egyptian airfield bombed by the Israelis in a raid at the beginning of the 1967 war. The Israelis destroyed three-fifths of the Egyptian air force in preemptive strikes.

few successes against Israeli positions near the Syrian frontier. Some Palestinians fought the Israelis in al-Qunaytirah (Kuneitra), a Syrian city of more than 70,000 people at the western edge of the Golan Heights, but the Syrians failed to give the Palestinians the arms they needed to fight effectively. In Jordan, a small Egyptian army *fedayeen* unit slipped between the Israeli forces and penetrated Israel almost to Tel Aviv's Lod airport. Israeli units detected and destroyed them. In Gaza, some 15,000 army "regulars" and a mixed group of PLO guerrillas fought stubbornly, but Israeli armor and infantry quickly overwhelmed them.

By June 11, when the final cease-fire took effect, Israeli armies had taken the Gaza Strip and Egypt's Sinai, Syria's Golan Heights and, most crucially for King Hussein and the Palestinians, the Jordanian West Bank and East Jerusalem. The walled city was formally annexed by Israel and subsequently proclaimed Israel's eternal capital. Although terrorist violence had earlier done much to bring about the war, neither guerrilla nor terrorist action played any significant role in the war's conduct.

At the war's end, Arafat had still not emerged as Fatah's clear leader. The organization had a collective leadership, and journalists found very few Palestinian insiders willing to be interviewed about the postwar disarray or any future plans.

President Nasser's June 9 admission of defeat, and his declined offer to resign, cast gloom among the Palestinian leaders. They were forced to acknowledge

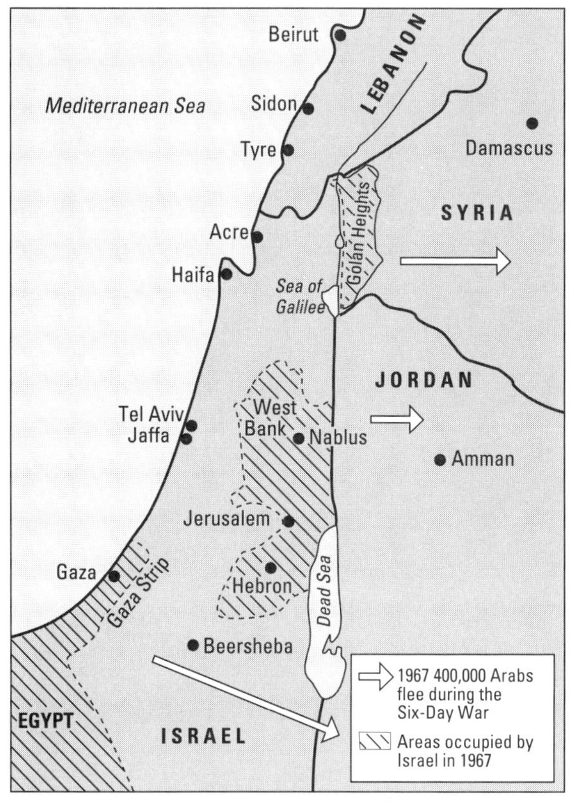

A map showing the exodus of Palestinian Arabs in the Six-Day War of 1967.

that their dependence on Nasser and the Arab governments had gained them nothing. At the end of June 1967, Arafat, Khalil al-Wazir, and about 20 other Palestinians held a meeting. Arafat was for resuming armed action as soon as possible. Most of the others present disagreed.

THE PLO ORGANIZES WITHIN ISRAEL

While Arafat's group resolved to resume operations, Arafat himself, accompanied by a deputy, Abu Ali Shaheen, slipped in disguise into the occupied West Bank and established a clandestine headquarters at Qabatiya, near Jenin. Here they recruited followers, stored arms, and tried to create a network of safe houses and sympathizers. But most of the comfortable, middle-class Palestinians living in cities such as Nablus, Ramallah, and Jerusalem, let alone the small but wealthy patrician class of non-refugees in Gaza, had no stomach for clandestine revolutionary work.

What was more, during the war the Israeli army had captured Jordan's army intelligence files on the PLO and *fedayeen* sympathizers in the West Bank, together with detailed biographical sketches and many photographs. By October 1967, Israeli security had knocked out the Fatah networks. Reprisals and interrogations were harsh. Amnesty International and other human rights groups documented many cases of torture and beatings by Israeli forces.

THE BATTLE OF KARAMA

In March 1968, Arafat scored a significant propaganda victory. The Palestinians were regularly firing Katyusha rockets into Israel from Jordan, and the Israelis decided to retaliate with an attack on Karama, a settlement housing about 35,000 of the refugees from Arab-Israeli conflicts since 1948.

Early on March 21, 1968, Israeli paratroopers landed behind *fedayeen* lines in the Ghor hills behind Karama, and three brigades of tanks and infantry crossed the Jordan. They encountered a small unit of the Popular Front for the Liberation of Palestine and, to their surprise, the Jordanian army. Both the Jordanian army and the *fedayeen* were prepared. Jordanian army artillery halted the Israeli armor, while in the banana groves near the river, a section of 18 *fedayeen* destroyed several Israeli tanks, at the cost of all but one member of the Palestinian unit. Arafat's personal guard was later named "Force 17" to commemorate the event.

General Amar Khammash, the Jordanian commander-in-chief, could do nothing to rescue guerrillas trapped in bunkers and shelters in Karama. Many were killed by the Israelis in hand-to-hand fighting. However, the Jordanians stood their ground and repulsed the Israeli armored thrust. After destroying most of Karama, the Israelis withdrew in the late afternoon, taking about 100 prisoners.

Karama (which means "dignity" in Arabic) gave Palestinian forces credibility. On March 23, for example, King Hussein reversed his earlier coolness toward the *fedayeen*: "The time may come…when we will all be *fedayeen*," he said. The battle became a symbol of Arab steadfastness for the Palestinian resistance. Thousands of recruits streamed to Jordan to join guerrilla organizations. The prestige of Karama enhanced Arafat's position within Fatah, and Fatah's role within the PLO. Fatah's leadership announced on April 16, 1968, that Arafat would henceforth be "its

TRH Pictures

General Mordechai Gur, center, and officers of the Israeli 55th Parachute Brigade discuss the progress of the battle for Jerusalem in 1967.

official spokesman and its representative for all official questions of organization, finance, and information." At a full meeting of the Palestinian National Council, in Cairo in July 1968, Arafat and his companions secured the cooperation of some of the smaller *fedayeen* groups and organized the Palestine Armed Struggle Command. At Palestinian National Councils in February and June 1969, Arafat secured control of the main PLO bureaucracy and established a PLO-Fatah military command.

In February 1969, Arafat became the PLO chairman. His executive committee would provide the core of the PLO for a generation to come. It included Muhammad Najjar of Fatah; Farouk Khaddoumi of Fatah; Khaled al-Hassan of Fatah; and Ibrahim al-Bourji of Saiqa (the Thunderbolt), an official Syrian *fedayeen* organization. Another key member was treasurer Abdul Majid Shoman. The PLO was now an effective organization, ready to control its own strategy.

John Cooley

SEE ALSO: NATIONALIST TERRORISM; ARAB NATIONALISM AND THE RISE OF FATAH; MIDDLE EASTERN TERRORISM 1970-1987; MIDDLE EASTERN TERRORISM 1988-1996.

FURTHER READING

- Cobban, Helena. *The Palestinian Liberation Organization: People, Power, and Politics.* Cambridge and New York: Cambridge University Press, 1984.
- Mishal, Shaul. *The PLO Under Arafat: Between Gun and Olive Branch.* New Haven, CT: Yale University Press, 1986.
- Ovendale, Ritchie. *The Origins of the Arab-Israeli Wars.* 2d ed. London and New York: Longman, 1992.

THE BEGINNING OF INTERNATIONAL TERRORISM

The 1967 war revealed to Palestinian nationalists the failure of their strategy of reliance on the Arab states to achieve their ends. In the wake of the war, Palestinian activists began to organize themselves more efficiently, but the debate continued over the most effective methods that the Palestinian activists could use. Small-scale cross-border raiding, which had been the main tactic in the 1950s and early 1960s, had had little effect. However, it was not Fatah that initiated the move to international terrorism; instead it came from groups descendant from the Arab nationalists, the Arab Nationalist Movement (ANM).

THE FIRST TERRORIST CELLS

In 1963-64, the ANM formed secret terrorist cells, at first with the Land, an illegal group of Arabs in Israel. The ANM carried out reconnaissance and sabotage, but it mostly planted "sleeper" agents, who had organizational and intelligence roles in Israel alone. As early as September 1964, the ANM resolved that Palestine could be freed only through armed struggle, and only with the help of worldwide revolutionary groups. The ANM divided into national leaderships in the various Arab states and an international leadership based in Beirut, the capital of Lebanon. Before the 1967 war, the international leadership included George Habash, Wadi Haddad, Hanni al-Hindi, and Muhsin Ibrahim, who later led the Syrian-backed Saiqa organization. However, as Habash was a Christian, he could not attract the Muslim following of Yasser Arafat.

> **KEY FACTS**
>
> - The PFLP formed as a result of a merger between the ANM and groups including the Organization of Youth for Revenge, the Heroes of the Return, and the Palestine Liberation Front.
> - On July 18, 1969, George Habash's PFLP firebombed Jewish-owned stores in London.
> - On September 9, 1969, three adult Palestinians and three members of the "Lion Cubs," a PFLP youth group, hurled grenades at Israeli embassies in the Netherlands and West Germany and at the El Al office in Belgium.

THE AFTERMATH OF THE 1967 WAR

The Arab defeat by Israel in the 1967 war created a ferment in Palestinian thought. There were meetings between the various Palestinian groups. Habash said that the war "brought a full revolution in our thought. We decided to adopt the Vietnamese model: a strong political party, complete mobilization of the people, the principle of not depending on any regime or government. We were preparing for 20 or more years of war against Israel and its backers." This was the inspiration for the 1967 formation of the Popular Front for the Liberation of Palestine (PFLP).

Habash became the leader of the PFLP. The group's members believed in international revolution and a change in the world order leading to the establishment of a Palestinian state. This led to PFLP involvement in the internal politics of various Arab states. And it meant that its directors also looked at international methods for striking at Israel. At a PFLP meeting in December 1967, Wadi Haddad, the operational commander, urged the group to abandon smuggling men and weapons across the Jordan. The Israeli army, he said, had to be hit in a "qualitative, not a quantitative way...We have to hit the Israelis at the weak points. I mean spectacular, one-off operations." This would focus world attention on the Palestinian problem and hurt the Israelis.

Haddad proposed the hijacking an Israeli airliner. This annoyed Habash, who preferred to emphasize leftist politics over terrorism, to convince somewhat hesitant supporters such as the Soviet Union, who were long on verbal support but short on material aid for the resistance movement. But because Habash had been imprisoned by Syria before the 1967 war and Haddad had him freed, Habash was indebted to Haddad and had to defer to him on the terrorism issue.

THE FIRST PFLP HIJACKINGS

As a result, on July 22, 1968, Haddad's three-man team hijacked a plane belonging to El Al, the Israeli national airline, and forced it to land in Algiers. The terrorists believed that General Ariel Sharon, who had commanded Israeli armored forces in Sinai in 1967, was aboard the flight, and that the pilot carried a diplomatic pouch. Neither was true.

In Algiers, the Algerian government handled the negotiations with the PFLP. The terrorists rapidly released all the hostages with the exception of 12 Israeli passengers and crew. On July 25, the PFLP announced that it had acted to "remind the world" that many Palestinians, imprisoned and tortured in Israel, deserved to be freed. It was not until August 31 that the Algerian government finally freed the plane, securing the release of the hostages in exchange for the release of some Palestinian prisoners, as well as the freedom of the hostage-takers themselves.

Besides striking at Israel and making headlines around the world, the PFLP was trying to make a point to Arafat and Fatah: cross-border guerrilla attacks, costly in casualties and ineffective, did not pay, whereas hijacking did. After this first hijacking, the PFLP and other Palestinian groups continued to carry out "external operations," as they termed these acts of international terrorism. On December 26, 1968, two PFLP men at Athens airport shot up another El Al aircraft, killing a retired Israeli naval officer aboard, wounding two people, and badly damaging the plane. An Athens court imprisoned the attackers for 15 years.

Israel declared Lebanon responsible, because the two attackers had spent time in refugee camps in Lebanon and had taken off for Athens from Beirut airport. In retaliation, Israeli special forces, flown in by helicopter, attacked Beirut airport on December 28. Without causing casualties, they burned 13 airliners belonging to or on loan to Lebanon's Middle East Airlines and Trans-Mediterranean Airways.

On February 18, 1969, a PFLP team and an El Al security guard exchanged fire outside an El Al plane at Zurich airport, killing the pilot and one terrorist and

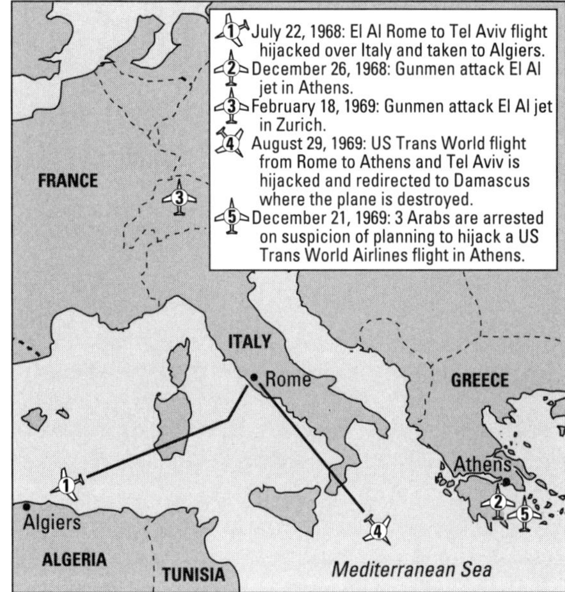

Major acts of international terrorism carried out in 1968-69 by the PFLP and associated terrorists.

wounding the copilot. Two days later, the PFLP bombed a Jerusalem supermarket, killing two Israelis and injuring more than 20. A woman later was jailed for life, both for this attack and for causing a bomb blast in the cafeteria of Jerusalem's Hebrew University.

On March 4, 1970, Habash announced that attacks on Israeli civilian targets would go on "if the Israelis continue to practice atrocities against us." He called the airport assaults "answers to acts of savagery by the Israelis against Arabs in the occupied territories." On August 29, 1969, Leila Khaled, a refugee girl from Haifa who had joined the ANM at 16 and had guerrilla training with the PFLP, led the hijacking of a TWA airliner. She forced it to land at Damascus in Syria. The Syrians held two Israeli passengers for 45 days. One was a professor at the Hebrew University, and the PFLP believed that the other had tortured *fedayeen* prisoners during interrogations. Pressure from governments and the International Airline Pilots' Federation secured their release. The hijackers were detained by the Syrians for 44 days, partly because of an old quarrel between the ANM and the Ba'ath.

The tactics of international terrorism certainly gained worldwide publicity, and were copied by other groups. In October 1969, in a copycat operation, five

Hulton Getty Picture Collection

A burned-out airliner at Beirut airport after the attack by Israeli forces on December 28, 1968.

Palestinians of the Popular Struggle Front (PSF), a small group under the PLO umbrella and headed by Bahgat Abu Gharbiya, a Palestinian linked to Egyptian intelligence, exploded a grenade in the El Al office in Athens. A Greek child was killed and another wounded. The PSF apologized and sent money to the victims' families, but this action won over no Greek hearts and minds to the Palestinian cause.

Two months later, Arab terrorists chose Athens as the starting point for another terrorist operation. This time, Greek police arrested three Arabs as they tried to board a TWA airliner at Athens on December 21, 1969. The three were carrying guns, grenades, and a declaration that the aircraft was being seized on behalf of the Popular Front (PFLP).

Two years after the shattering defeat of 1967, Palestinians had found, in international terrorism, a way of striking out that gave them world headlines. It also, however, led to a great crisis. King Hussein, fearful of the consequences, was struggling to stop Jordan becoming an uncontrolled terrorist base, a situation that led directly to a showdown with the Palestinians in September 1970.

John Cooley

SEE ALSO: DOMESTIC VERSUS INTERNATIONAL TERRORISM; HIJACKING; ARAB NATIONALISM AND THE RISE OF FATAH; THE BIRTH OF THE PLO AND THE 1967 WAR; MIDDLE EASTERN TERRORISM 1970-1987; ARAB STATES AND TERRORISM IN THE 1990S; PALESTINIAN TERRORIST GROUPS AFTER 1988; THE ISRAELI RESPONSE TO TERRORISM.

FURTHER READING

- Cobban, Helena. *The Palestinian Liberation Organization: People, Power, and Politics.* Cambridge and New York: Cambridge University Press, 1984.
- Khaled, Leila. *My People Shall Live: The Autobiography of a Revolutionary.* London: Hodder and Stoughton, 1973.
- Mishal, Shaul. *The PLO Under Arafat: Between Gun and Olive Branch.* New Haven, CT: Yale University Press, 1986.

CHAPTER TEN

Middle Eastern Terrorism 1970-1987

Between 1970 and the late 1980s, Middle Eastern terrorism spread throughout the world. Arab terrorists, sometimes supported by their Western counterparts, carried out bombings, assassinations, and hijackings to highlight their cause and strike back against states believed to be supporting Israel. The terrorists themselves splintered into several distinct groups, the more radical of which clamored for the creation of fundamentalist Muslim regimes throughout the region as well as the destruction of Israel.

MIDDLE EASTERN TERRORISM 1970-1987: Introduction

Between the early 1970s and late 1980s, the face of Middle Eastern terrorism and the international response to such incidents changed beyond all recognition. No longer was terrorism confined to this region, nor were Arabs and Israelis the sole targets of the various terrorist groups. Kidnappings, assassinations, and bombings continued in the Middle East, but they were overshadowed increasingly by terrorist acts played out on the international stage. The terrorists' list of "legitimate" targets now included citizens or installations of countries believed to be involved in the politics of the Middle East. States in the West were targeted if terrorists believed that they were indifferent to the plight of the Palestininans or backed the Israelis with economic aid and weapons.

The defining moment of this new strategy was the highly publicized hijacking of three passenger jets to Jordan by the Popular Front for the Liberation of Palestine in September 1970. The aircraft were blown up and the hostages released once certain Western European countries had freed Palestininans held in their jails. This "victory" suggested that the Arab cause would be best served by acts of terror rather than by attempts to achieve a diplomatic or military solution to the Palestinian question. Certainly, Israel's decisive victories over Arab forces in 1967 and 1973 indicated that the Jewish state could not be destroyed by force of arms.

The spate of international terrorist incidents in the early 1970s caught Western governments off guard and ill-prepared to deal with such attacks. This was confirmed at the Munich Olympics held in West Germany in 1972. During a botched rescue attempt by the police, several of the Israeli atheletes held hostage were killed. The consequences of this fiasco did, however, force most Western governments to create special antiterrorist units. This development soon bore fruit. In 1976, Israeli paratroopers flew to Entebbe, Uganda, to free hostages. A year later, West German special forces ended an airliner hijacking in Mogadishu, Somalia. Antiterrorist operations remained extremely hazardous nevertheless.

The escalation of Middle Eastern violence was paralleled by a growth of left-wing terrorist groups, usually consisting of dissatisfied middle class students in Europe and the Far East. Believing that the citizens of their own states were being oppressed by their governments, they found common cause with the Palestinians, whose aspirations they supported. A degree of cooperation developed between the Western terrorists and their Middle Eastern counterparts, although this was often exaggerated. Western terrorists received training in the Middle East and occasionally carried out joint operations. Entebbe was a joint action between members of West Germany's Red Army Faction and the Palestine Liberation Organization (PLO). However, many Palestinians found the Western groups amateurish, lacking commitment, and with little deep understanding of their cause.

The 1970s also saw the rise of terrorist leaders who gained a high profile from either the scale or the audacity of their activities. Chief among these were "Carlos the Jackal" (Ilich Ramirez Sánchez), a playboy terrorist of Latin American origin, and Abu Nidal, leader of a Palestinian splinter group. "Carlos" was responsible for taking a number of leading oil ministers hostage in Vienna, Austria, in December 1975.

Palestinian terrorism in the 1970s and 1980s was also characterized by the growth of various splinter groups, often more radical than the PLO. The failed attempt to a create a Palestinian regime in Jordan in September 1970 prompted the growth of dedicated terror groups that rejected all links with the Israelis and moderate Arab states. Many were concerned with more than the creation of a Palestininan state and the crushing of Israel.

These radical Muslims also vowed to create fundamentalist regimes throughout the Arab nations of the Middle East. These groups were often backed by Iran and were virulently anti-Western, although they also carried out attacks on their less radical Arab brethren. Their members were willing to be martyred to the cause, as was indicated by the suicide-bombing of the U.S. Marine and French barracks in Beirut, Lebanon, in October 1993. ■

THE BLACK SEPTEMBER ORGANIZATION

King Hussein's expulsion of the Palestine Liberation Organization (PLO) from Jordan in September 1970 led directly to the creation of one of the Middle East's most effective terrorist groups – the Black September Organization. The events of September 1970 grew out of two events. First, in late 1967, Israel clamped down on the Palestinian guerrillas who had been operating inside the West Bank since the end of the 1967 war. The guerrillas involved fled to Jordan, from where they raided the West Bank, attracting Israeli reprisals against their hosts. Second, certain elements in the PLO believed that the use of Jordan as a launchpad for liberating western Palestine could only occur with the overthrow of the king. The Popular Front for the Liberation of Palestine (PFLP) declared on its founding that "the road to Jerusalem goes through Amman [the capital of Jordan]."

ISRAELI REPRISALS

The Israelis responded to attacks by Jordanian-based Palestinians by bombarding the border area. In March 1968, the Palestinians attracted much greater retribution when they mined the road linking Tel Aviv with the Negev Desert. The mine detonated beneath a schoolbus, killing two children and injuring 27 more. With the Israeli public clamoring for revenge, an Israeli army formation crossed into Jordan and attacked the village of Karameh, which housed much of Fatah's organization. Although they suffered heavy casualties, the Palestinians, supported by the Jordanian army, repelled the attackers, and Fatah claimed a victory. However, Israel was also hitting Jordanian civilian targets in retaliation for Palestinian attacks, including the East Ghor Canal irrigation project. Although not seeking to undermine Jordan, Israel was sending King Hussein a clear message to take action against the Palestinian terrorists.

SUMMARY

- In September 1970, the Palestine Liberation Organization was evicted from Jordan by King Hussein's armed forces.
- One of the Palestinian responses was the formation of a new terrorist group: the Black September Organization.
- Black September carried out an attack on the 1972 Olympics in which 11 Israeli athletes died.

HUSSEIN IN DANGER

Hussein's rule was already in great danger. In parts of the country, the Palestinian terrorist groups were in control, and many Palestinians, in particular radical groups such as the PFLP, believed that the king should be deposed. In November 1968, a round of clashes and demonstrations led to Hussein getting tough with the Palestinians. The army surrounded two refugee camps near Amman and shelled them for three days.

Hussein's control over his kingdom continued to diminish, however. Then, in February 1970, he decided to clamp down on the Palestinians once again, issuing a list of restrictions that included a ban on firearms and demonstrations. Clashes took place between the Palestinians and the king's forces that left 300 dead. The king turned to conciliation, withdrawing his restrictions. This further encouraged the leftist Palestinian leaders, who believed Hussein's throne was ripe for the taking.

Riots in Amman in April 1970, were instigated by the PFLP to abort the proposed visit of Joseph Sisco, U.S. Under Secretary of State for the Middle East. Some 10,000 people were brought out on the streets, shops and homes were ransacked, and foreigners were taken hostage. On June 9, after clashes between Palestinians and the army in Amman and nearby Zarqa,

Popperfoto

Palestinian guerrillas crouch around a hole blasted in a kitchen wall at the height of fighting in Amman, in early September 1970.

Hussein narrowly escaped death when Palestinians opened fire on his motorcade near Amman. The king again tried conciliation, declaring, "We are all *fedayeen*," replacing his cousin Sharif Zaid bin Shakr as commander of the 3rd Armored Division, and assembling a "pro-Palestinian" government. On July 10, Hussein made a peace pact with the Palestinians.

The tide was about to turn against the Palestinians, however. Israel and the U.S. were both becoming increasingly concerned at the deteriorating situation in Jordan and the threat to Hussein's throne. Then, on July 23, 1970, President Gamal Abdel Nasser of Egypt accepted an American proposal for a cease-fire between his country and Israel. The Palestinians were furious: an agreement between an Arab country and the archenemy Israel was intolerable to them. The Palestinians accused Nasser of treachery and demonstrated against Hussein, believing that Jordan was also moving toward peace with Israel.

DAWSON'S FIELD

In Amman, under pressure from his army to act, Hussein warned the Palestinians to stop challenging his authority. Clashes followed, as did another assassination attempt on September 1. George Habash's PFLP then threw oil on the fire by seizing three aircraft on September 6. The terrorists hijacked one to Cairo, Egypt, and destroyed it; two were flown to to Dawson's Field, an abandoned airfield outside of Amman. Three days later, the PFLP hijacked a fourth aircraft, which was also taken to Dawson's Field. The terrorists held more than 300 people hostage at the airfield and demanded the release of *fedayeen* from

European and Israeli jails. On September 12, the terrorists blew up the three planes at Dawson's Field and released all the passengers apart from 54 Israelis and American Jews. They in turn were released in exchange for the imprisoned Palestinian terrorists.

BLACK SEPTEMBER

The hijackings and the subsequent destruction of the airliners made the Palestinian cause headline news all over the world. But the PFLP operations also gave Hussein the opportunity to turn his tanks on the *fedayeen*. On September 17, he sent in the army to crush the PLO bases in Palestinian refugee camps and killed several thousand fighters. The king then expelled the PLO from Jordan – a process completed by July 1971. These events led Palestinians to call September 1970 "Black September."

After its expulsion from Jordan, the PLO moved its operational base to Lebanon. The whole episode had been a defeat for the policy of PLO Chairman Yasser Arafat, who had been negotiating behind the scenes and trying to cooperate with Arab states. Now negotiation did not seem to make sense, even to many of his own Fatah party. The Arab neighbors of Israel, vulnerable to counterattack, were unwilling to countenance raids from their territory. So elements within Fatah decided to move against softer, international targets.

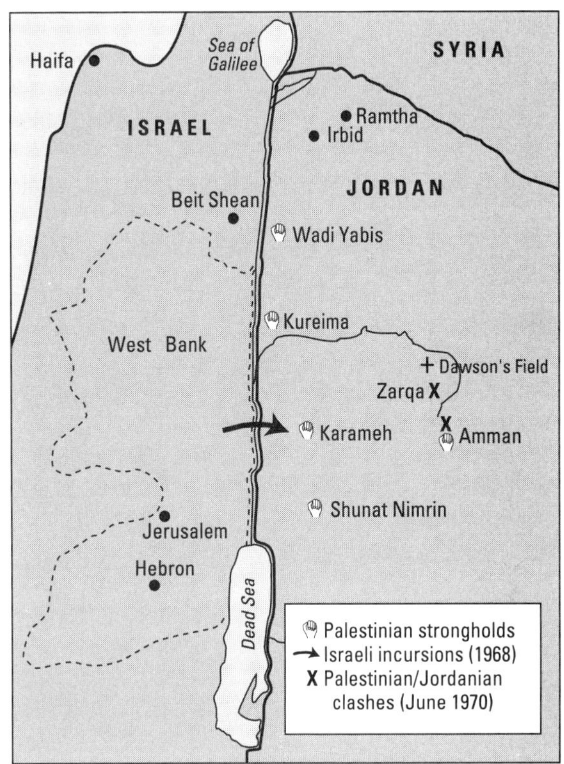

Palestinian strongholds and Israeli incursions leading up to the expulsion of the PLO from Jordan (September 1970 – July 1971).

THE BLACK SEPTEMBER ORGANIZATION

The result of this new direction was the formation of the Black September Organization. It was an offshoot of Fatah, or more precisely, a terror cell within Fatah, formed by those who saw military action rather than diplomacy as the appropriate tactic after the devastation in Jordan that gave the group its name. The Black September Organization's key figures were Abu Iyad, a deputy of Arafat's, and Ali Hassan Salameh.

Black September's first terrorist act was the murder of the Jordanian prime minister, Wasfi al-Tal, in Cairo in November 1971. The killing had the immediate result of boosting the number of volunteers ready to take a militant line against Arab regimes. Black September's next act was a failed assassination attempt on the Jordanian ambassador in London, in December 1971.

Black September was not simply a terror group committed to the belief that armed struggle was the only way to liberate Palestine. The notion that it was just a convenient front for Arafat's military option is also questionable. Taking the struggle into Europe, for which Black September became notorious, was a desperate tactic more in keeping with those whose recklessness had triggered the debacle in Jordan. In truth, Black September was a loose terror group led by Fatah men who wanted to give vent to their frustrations. The group was not a formal part of Fatah nor was it subject to its leadership; however, its ability to use Fatah structures, and the fact that its leaders were part of the Fatah organization, made it difficult for Fatah to disown Black September.

THE ROAD TO THE MUNICH OLYMPICS

In May 1972, Ali Hassan Salameh, Black September's head of European operations, organized the hijacking of a Belgian Sabena aircraft, and forced it to land at Tel Aviv. However, the four terrorists were taken completely by surprise when Israeli commandos of the Sayaret Matkal unit, disguised as white-coated airport technicians, stormed the plane. The commandos killed two terrorists and captured the other two, but also killed one passenger and wounded five more in the process. This was the first instance of a hijacked plane being stormed by an elite counterterrorist unit.

It is the massacre at the 1972 Olympics in Munich, West Germany, for which Black September is most notorious. Abu Iyad, at the time chief of security and intelligence services for both Fatah and the PLO, is the man most commonly linked to this incident. His closeness to Arafat ensured that the PLO chairman is still widely seen at fault. Abu Iyad was obliged by his position to assume executive responsibility for this and other Black September operations and he defended the organization's actions privately as well as publicly. Abu Iyad was involved in the planning of the kidnappings. It seems likely that Arafat gave the go-ahead, but kept a careful distance in order to ensure that the buck would stop with the PLO's security chief.

Hulton Getty Picture Collection

Abu Daoud, a commander of the Palestinian militia in Jordan, became a prominent member of the Black September Organization.

TERROR IN THE VILLAGE

At 4 A.M. on September 5, 1972, two security guards patrolling the Olympic village spotted eight track-suited men climbing over a secruity fence. The guards, however, took the intruders to be athletes returning after a night out. They were in fact Black September terrorists, armed with grenades and Kalashnikov assault rifles, on a mission to take the Israeli Olympic team hostage.

The terrorists moved into Building 31, where the Israeli team was staying. After a violent struggle, in which weightlifter Joseph Romano and wrestling coach Moshe Weinberg were killed, nine athletes and officials were taken hostage. The remainder of the Israeli team managed to escape through windows or out the rear door. Shortly afterward, Building 31 was surrounded by armed police and negotiations began.

The Israeli government refused to comply with the terrorists' demands for the release of prisoners and did not wish the West Germans to continue negotiations. However, West Germany saw its hosting of the Olympics as proof that it was accepted back in the community of nations after the Nazi atrocities of World War II. The kidnapping of Jewish hostages on German soil was thus a disaster for the West Germans.

German security forces devised a plan to free the hostages. They ruled out an assault on Building 31 as it would almost certainly end in the death of the hostages. Consequently, the German forces appeared to accept the terrorists' demand for a plane to fly them and their hostages to Tunisia. The Germans' plan was to mount an attack on the terrorists before they boarded the plane.

SLAUGHTER ON THE TARMAC

At 10 p.m., the terrorists and their bound and blindfolded hostages were taken by bus to a helicopter pad. Three helicopters took off for Fürstenfeldbruck airport, two carrying terrorists and hostages, the other carrying German negotiators. The helicopters landed 165 yards from the escape plane. Two terrorists walked over to inspect the aircraft while another two dismounted with the pilots. As the first two returned from the plane, a Bavarian state police marksman began shooting and three terrorists were killed. The other terrorists immediately opened fire on the hostages and on the control tower where the police had hidden, killing one marksman.

There was then stalemate for a short time, but just after midnight, one of the terrorists leapt from a helicopter and flung a grenade back into it, setting it ablaze. He and another terrorist were then shot dead. The remaining three were captured by security forces in armored cars. All nine hostages were dead.

However, the operation was a failure for Fatah: another "Black September." The terrorists' demand that 200 PLO prisoners be released in exchange for the hostages had failed and the world was horrified. Furthermore, the Bavarian police had been shown to be inadequately trained to deal with terrorists, which led many countries to create special counterterrorist units. In addition, Israel set up "Wrath of God" hit squads to track down Black September members.

FINAL ACTS OF TERROR

The next Black September operation was to send mail bombs, one of which killed an Israeli consul. After this, there was the hijacking, on October 29, 1972, of a Lufthansa aircraft, which secured the release of the three surviving terrorists from Munich. Although the result of this operation was a propaganda coup, Israeli retaliation into Lebanon and Syria meant that the governments of these countries put great pressure on PLO groups to stop Black September actions.

In February 1973, the Israelis shot down an off-course Libyan airliner, killing 106 people. President Muammar al-Qaddafi of Libya then helped Black September set up another strike. Eight Black September terrorists took over the Saudi Arabian embassy in Khartoum, Sudan, on March 1. They demanded the release of of all Palestinian prisoners, as well as Sirhan Sirhan, the Palestinian who killed Robert Kennedy, and Kozo Okamoto, the surviving member of the 1972 Lod massacre terrorists.

The terrorists also demanded the release of prisoners belonging to the West German Baader-Meinhof terrorist gang. U.S. President Richard Nixon refused point-blank to negotiate, and the terrorists mercilessly machine-gunned to death the U.S. ambassador, the U.S. chargé d'affaires, and a Belgian diplomat in the embassy compound.

By now, the Fatah leadership, including Abu Iyad, agreed that Black September's conduct had gotten out of hand. Israeli reprisals were also in full swing. In April, Israeli troops killed 17 Palestinians in Beirut, including three leading Black September members. Fatah was also distancing itself rapidly from Black September. In September 1973, Black September seized the Saudi embassy in Paris in an unsuccessful attempt to secure the release of Abu Daoud, the former Palestinian militia commander now imprisoned in Jordan. Arafat unequivocally condemned the attack.

In the last recorded Black September mission, in September 1973, Italian police arrested five terrorists armed with Soviet SAM-7 ground-to-air rockets. They had taken a house on the flight path to Rome and were planning to shoot down an Israeli El Al airliner.

The 1973 Arab-Israeli war opened up a new chapter in Middle East negotiations. The Arabs now had the "oil weapon," which put them in a strong bargaining position. Yasser Arafat wanted Fatah to be accepted as a part of Middle East negotiations, and so he formally renounced terrorism. He achieved a major aim when he was allowed to address the General Assembly of the United Nations in November 1974. However, he had also alienated some former supporters, such as Abu Nidal. The Black September Organization, though, was no longer in operation.

Neil Partrick

SEE ALSO: HIJACKING AND KIDNAPPING; ROCKETS, MORTARS, AND MISSILES; COLLABORATION BETWEEN TERRORISTS; ARAB NATIONALISM AND THE RISE OF FATAH; THE BIRTH OF THE PLO AND THE 1967 WAR; THE POPULAR FRONT FOR THE LIBERATION OF PALESTINE; ABU NIDAL; ISRAELI RAIDS ON THE PLO; LIBYAN SPONSORSHIP OF TERRORISM; RED ARMY FACTION: THE BAADER-MEINHOF GANG; JAPANESE TERRORISM.

FURTHER READING

- Cobban, Helena. *The Palestinian Liberation Organization: People, Power, and Politics.* Cambridge and New York: Cambridge University Press, 1984.
- Livingstone, Neil, and David Halevy. *Inside the PLO: Covert Units, Secret Funds, and the War Against Israel and the United States.* New York: Morrow, and London: Hale, 1990.
- Groussard, Serge. *The Blood of Israel: The Massacre of the Israeli Athletes, the Olympics, 1972.* New York: Morrow, 1975.
- Mishal, Shaul. *The PLO Under Arafat: Between Gun and Olive Branch.* New Haven, CT: Yale University Press, 1986.

THE POPULAR FRONT FOR THE LIBERATION OF PALESTINE

The Popular Front for the Liberation of Palestine (PFLP), formed in 1967, pioneered the hijacking of aircraft as a means of generating publicity. Two groups that split from the PFLP, the Popular Democratic Front for the Liberation of Palestine (PDFLP) and the PFLP-General Command (PFLP-GC), also perpetrated terrorist acts. Led by George Habash and Wadi Haddad, the PFLP were the main left-wing force within the Palestine Liberation Organization.

The PFLP's role was critical in the events leading up to "Black September," which led to Palestinian armed forces being removed from Jordan by July 1971. First, the PFLP clashed with Jordanian forces through a spate of hijackings, clearly intending to depose King Hussein. Second, the PFLP precipitated the fighting because of events at Dawson's Field. In just one day, PFLP terrorists seized three aircraft: a Pan-Am airliner was taken to Cairo, while TWA and Swissair planes were flown to Dawson's Field in northern Jordan. Three days later, the PFLP also hijacked a British BOAC plane to Dawson's Field. The British and U.S. aircraft, without their passengers, were blown up on September 12. These acts expressed disapproval of Anglo-American policy toward Palestinians, but the hijackings did little for the Palestinian cause. The action prompted King Hussein to rid Jordan of Palestinian terrorist groups. Hussein sent his troops in, and thousands of Palestinians died.

KEY FACTS

- The PFLP is a self-proclaimed Marxist organization with around 1,000 members operating in Lebanon, Israel and the West Bank and Gaza Strip, the remaining Middle East, and Europe.
- Between 1968 and 1987, the PFLP carried out about 38 bombings, 10 hijackings, 11 armed attacks, 9 hostage situations, and 3 assassinations.

George Habash, a Marxist, did not condone the hijackings, but felt powerless to stop Wadi Haddad, the mastermind behind the events. Hijackings were not, tactically at least, deemed appropriate to the "strategy of armed struggle" sanctified in the PLO's 1968 National Charter. However, as a Marxist organization, the PFLP had much in common with other Marxist groups worldwide to whom it offered training and funds. As a result, the PFLP was soon closely linked to international terrorism. Also, there were splits within the PFLP that make it difficult to analyze who ordered what terrorist attack. It is noteworthy that the terrorist "Carlos the Jackal" began his career in a PFLP-linked cell.

THE EUROPEAN CAMPAIGN

In March 1971, the PFLP, led by its chief of European operations, Mohammed Boudia, launched its first attacks in Europe, blowing up oil tanks belonging to Gulf Oil in Rotterdam in the Netherlands. In February 1972, the PFLP hijacked a Lufthansa airliner, demanding and obtaining a ransom of $5 million from the West German government. From 1972 to 1973, Wadi Haddad's men cooperated with Black September (a terrorist group made up of militant Fatah members) in an escalation of terror.

Habash had little faith that terrorism would further the Palestinian cause. At the Third Congress of the PFLP in March 1972, he persuaded the majority of delegates to reject "operations outside Palestine." But Wadi Haddad refused to accept the decision and in May used PFLP allies from the Japanese Red Army (a Japanese left-wing terrorist group with international ties) for what he termed the "Deir Yassin operation." Twenty-five Israelis were killed and 78 wounded, after three Red Army terrorists posing as tourists slipped past Israeli officials in the Lod airport lounge before opening fire with submachine guns. After the killing spree, two of the terrorists shot themselves dead, but the third was captured.

Hulton Getty Picture Collection

The hijacked British BOAC aircraft blown up by the PFLP at Dawson's Field, Jordan, in September 1970.

During the mid-1970s, the PFLP was involved in two hijackings that showed the West's commitment to counter-terror. On June 27, 1976, two Haddad operatives and a West German "couple" (in reality two members of the terrorist Baader-Meinhof Gang) hijacked an Air France jet at Athens Airport, took it to Benghazi in Libya to be refueled, and then to Entebbe in Uganda, where they held the passengers and crew hostage.

Israel's anti-terror strategy gained world respect when Mossad flew in, killed Haddad's men and their accomplices, and saved the passengers. Then, in October 1977, another PFLP-Baader-Meinhof team hijacked a Lufthansa plane to Mogadishu in Somalia, where West German paramilitaries successfully stormed the aircraft.

REJECTION FRONT

The PFLP was in the forefront of the so-called Rejection Front that united it with Arab states opposed to Arafat's attempts to engineer a settlement with Israel. By September 1976, the PFLP had taken its rejectionism outside the PLO by breaking away from the executive committee, and George Habash was widely regarded as a leading proponent of a secular, revolutionary Palestine.

By the late 1970s, PFLP international terrorism had died down. The leadership was now based in Syria – where the Assad regime wanted to minimize trouble with Israel. In 1988, the PFLP accepted the Fatah position of not engaging in terrorism outside Gaza and the West Bank.

Neil Partrick

SEE ALSO: HIJACKING AND KIDNAPPING; COLLABORATION BETWEEN TERRORISTS; THE BLACK SEPTEMBER ORGANIZATION; THE PLO AND THE ARAB STATES; ENTEBBE; RED ARMY FACTION: THE BAADER-MEINHOF GANG; JAPANESE TERRORISM; INTERNATIONAL COLLABORATION AGAINST TERRORISM.

FURTHER READING

- Cobban, Helena. *The Palestinian Liberation Organization: People, Power, and Politics.* Cambridge and New York: Cambridge University Press, 1984.
- Ovendale, Ritchie. *The Middle East Since 1914.* London: Longman, 1992.
- Sobel, Lester A., ed. *Palestinian Impasse: Arab Guerrillas and International Terror.* New York: Facts on File, 1977.

CARLOS THE JACKAL

The terrorist who was to gain international notoriety as "Carlos the Jackal" was born Illich Ramírez Sánchez in Venezuela in 1949. His middleclass father was a communist who sent his teenage son to a terrorist training camp in Cuba to learn the basics of handling weapons and explosives.

Carlos refined his terrorist theories at Patrice Lumumba University in Moscow, an institution set up by the then Soviet Union to give third-world students a communist education. Carlos gained a reputation as a playboy and was expelled for not taking his studies seriously. However, there have been suggestions that he was recruited as a Soviet secret agent in Moscow, although this is unlikely as the Soviets disapproved of the international terrorism into which Carlos leapt.

In the early 1970s, there was a general feeling in European student circles that the West, shamed by its association with the Vietnam War and by its Nazi or colonialist past, was on the brink of a revolution. It was believed that the revolution was likely to be linked with the realization of the aspirations of third-world peoples such as the Palestinians. The Popular Front for the Liberation of Palestine (PFLP) had by now made contact with European terrorists in France, West Germany, Belgium, and Holland, and was already embarking on raids with them.

Carlos became linked with the PFLP and European terrorists. When Israeli agents blew up Mohammed Boudia, the most prominent PFLP organizer in Europe, on June 28, 1973, Carlos took his place. One of the first operations led by Carlos was the December 1973 attempt to kill Jewish businessman Edward Sieff, one of the heads of the Marks and Spencer chain of stores in Britain. According to Carlos, Sieff "was the most important Zionist in Britain." Carlos shot the business man in the head with a high-powered pistol. Remarkably, though, Sieff was not killed in the attack, the bullet ricocheting off his teeth and lodging in his neck. A year later, Carlos is believed to have directed a bombing campaign against three pro-Israeli newspapers in Paris.

Carlos's next major action was a direct attack on an El Al airliner at Orly airport in Paris, on January 13, 1975. The airline had proved especially difficult to target after the hijacking incidents in the late 1960s – security was strenuous. Carlos's plan did not require access to the aircraft as a passenger. Instead he and his collaborators smuggled a Soviet RPG-7 anti-tank rocket launcher into the airport complex and opened fire from long range. The rockets missed their intended target, but hit a Yugoslavian aircraft and an airport building.

KEY FACTS

- Illich Ramírez Sánchez was named after Vladimir Illyich Ulyanov – better known as Lenin.
- Carlos's first act of terrorism was to place a bomb aboard a Swissair plane flying from Zurich to Tel Aviv in 1970; all 200 passengers were killed.
- A machine-gun massacre in 1972 at Israel's Lod airport, organized by Carlos, killed 28, injured 76, and earned the terrorist the name "the Jackal" after Frederick Forsyth's novel, *The Day of the Jackal.*

INTERNATIONAL TERRORISM IN THE 1970s

The most important of Carlos's raids also took place in the 1970s. A key factor in international relations following the 1973 Arab-Israeli war was the decision by Arab oil-producing states to place an embargo on oil exports in 1975, and then to double the price of oil. This severely affected Western economies and made many Palestinians realize that the Arabs had a weapon that gave them enormous leverage. However, the main Arab oil-producing states, particularly Saudi Arabia, had little sympathy with the revolutionary philosophy of the Palestinian terrorists. By 1975, the Organization of Petroleum Exporting Countries (OPEC) was actually discussing how to bring oil prices down to avoid further damage to the world economy.

On December 21, 1975, six terrorists burst into a meeting of 11 OPEC ministers in Vienna. The terrorists killed three people, wounded seven others, and took 81 hostage, including the 11 OPEC ministers and many Austrian nationals. They demanded that an aircraft be put at their disposal, threatening to kill their Saudi and Iranian hostages unless the demand was met. The terrorists were provided with a DC-9. They then freed 41 Austrian hostages and flew to Algiers with the rest.

It is widely believed that Carlos was in charge of this operation, and that the terrorists were part of the PFLP Special Operations Group. One of the hostages, the Venezuelan minister for mines, thought that Carlos had been present. Algerian police later said that the group consisted of two West Germans, two Palestinians, one Lebanese, and one Venezuelan.

The hostages were freed on December 23 in Algiers; the terrorists turned themselves over to the Algerian authorities and were granted asylum on December 29. However, the next day they were flown to another destination, generally assumed to be Libya. It was later alleged that Libyan leader Colonel Muammar al-Qaddafi had given $1 million to finance the Vienna operation. It is also believed that a massive ransom – some $50 million – was paid to gain the hostages' release.

The operation has the classic ingredients of international terrorist acts of the period: a multinational gang; authorities unable to resist the initial demands; and virulent feeling against conservative Arab states. The communiqué of the "Arm of the Arab Revolution," the group that claimed responsibility for the assault, said the raid was aimed at "the alliance between American imperialism and the capitulating reactionary forces in the Arab homeland." Saudi oil minister, Sheikh Yamani, later said that he himself would have been killed but for the intervention of the Algerians.

CARLOS VANISHES

As a result, Carlos became notorious worldwide and was often assumed to be the organizer of international terrorist operations, such as the Air France hijacking in Athens in June 1976 that culminated in the Entebbe raid. It was shortly after this event that Carlos dropped out of sight. He is thought to have gone to work for Syria. When two of his agents were arrested in 1982 by French police, Carlos threatened a terror campaign. From 1983 to January 1984, the Organization for the Armed Arab Struggle, led and funded by Carlos, carried out the threat, bombing railroad facilities in France and French cultural centers in Berlin and Tripoli.

In 1985, the agents arrested in 1982 were released. Soon after, Carlos married one of them, Magdalena Kopp, and moved to Damascus in Syria. However, the French security services kept on his tail and finally tracked him down in Sudan in 1994, where they arrested him. Carlos was later tried and sentenced to prison in Paris.

Ashley Brown

Hulton Getty Picture Collection

Finely honed skills with any caliber weapon and a cool disregard for life made "Carlos the Jackal" one of the world's most wanted terrorists in the 1970s and 1980s.

SEE ALSO: REVOLUTIONARY TERRORISM; DOMESTIC VERSUS INTERNATIONAL TERRORISM; HIJACKING AND KIDNAPPING; ROCKETS, MORTARS, AND MISSILES; COLLABORATION BETWEEN TERRORISTS; VICTIMS OF TERRORISM; THE POPULAR FRONT FOR THE LIBERATION OF PALESTINE; ENTEBBE; DOMESTIC TERRORISM IN THE ARAB WORLD; LIBYAN SPONSORSHIP OF TERRORISM; RED ARMY FACTION: THE BAADER-MEINHOF GANG; JAPANESE TERRORISM.

FURTHER READING

- Dobson, Christopher, and Ronald Payne. *The Carlos Complex: A Study in Terror.* New York: Putnam, and London: Hodder and Stoughton, 1977.
- Dobson, Christopher, and Ronald Payne. *The Terrorists: Their Weapons, Leaders, and Tactics.* Rev. ed. New York: Facts on File, 1982.

KIRYAT SHMONA AND MA'ALOT

After the conclusion of the October 1973 Arab-Israeli war, U.S. Secretary of State Henry Kissinger began diplomatic efforts to establish a durable peace in the Middle East. Fatah, which was the leading Palestinian faction, wanted to ensure that the Palestinian Liberation Organization (PLO) would be party to any settlement. At the same time, other, often tiny, Palestinian groups were intent on undermining the peace negotiations and were prepared to carry out terror attacks on Israeli soil in order to do so.

While major groups such as the Popular Front for the Liberation of Palestine (PFLP) avoided terrorist attacks within Israel, because of the risk of Israeli retaliation against their Arab hosts, some of the smaller groups had no such qualms. In 1974, groups opposed to a negotiated peace carried out two devastating and highly charged terrorist operations in Israel.

KIRYAT SHMONA

The first attack was carried out by the Popular Front for the Liberation of Palestine – General Command (PFLP-GC), which under Ahmad Jibril had split from the PFLP in 1968. On April 11, 1974, the PFLP-GC staged a hostage-taking in the northern Israeli border town of Kiryat Shmona. Three members of the group raided a four-story apartment building, bursting into apartments and shooting the occupants. Israeli forces cornered the terrorists, who were finally killed when the explosives they were carrying blew up. The explosives may have been hit by Israeli gunfire, although some sources state that the terrorists detonated the bombs themselves. Altogether, 18 Israelis, including eight children and five women, died in the attack, and a further 16 were wounded.

A PFLP-GC spokesman described the operation as an example of "revolutionary violence within Israel that aimed at blocking an Arab-Israeli peace settlement." For the PLO, which was then seeking recognition as the legitimate representative of the Palestinian people in the peace talks, the attack was an embarrassment. Since the PFLP-GC was a member of the Palestine National Council (the Palestinian parliament in exile), the PLO was obliged to recognize the action at Kiryat Shmona as official. Two months later, in an attempt to control a tiny but, by virtue of its methods, influential group, the PLO gave the PFLP-GC a seat on its executive committee.

THE MA'ALOT MASSACRE

When the Popular Democratic Front for the Liberation of Palestine (PDFLP) – took 90 Israeli schoolchildren hostage in Ma'alot in the northern Galilee on May 15, 1974, the PLO was once again obliged to give official recognition to an outrage that undermined its political initiatives. The PDFLP, led by Nayef Hawatmeh, was a resolutely left-wing group that believed in international revolution. It had left the PFLP in 1969.

The PDFLP was willing to use terror against Israel, and it was in this light that a three-man team took the Israeli schoolchildren hostage in Ma'alot, a village five miles from the border with Lebanon. The terrorists demanded the release of 26 prisoners, one for each year of Israel's existence. When the terrorists refused to extend a deadline they had set, Israeli soldiers stormed the school. The ensuing firefight resulted in carnage: 16 children died at once, five were mortally wounded, and a further 65 were hit by bullets.

KEY FACTS

- The outrages at Kiryat Shmona and Ma'alot were a factor in the subsequent increase in U.S. arms supplies to Israel.
- Besides taking schoolchildren hostage at Ma'alot in May 1974, the terrorists also raided an apartment in the town, killing three Israelis.
- In October and November 1975, PDFLP terrorists attacked Israeli settlements in the Golan Heights. The terrorists carried hatchets, reportedly to cut off their victims' heads to prove they had accomplished their mission.

Hulton Getty Picture Collection

The scene at Ma'alot, northern Israel, after Israeli troops stormed the school where 90 children were held hostage in May 1974.

Hawatmeh claimed that the raid had been specifically directed against U.S. Secretary of State Henry Kissinger's peace mission.

The PDFLP and the Israelis clashed again, on September 4, when an Israeli patrol thwarted a Palestinian terror squad at the village of Fasuta, three miles south of the Lebanese border. The terrorists, it seems, aimed to take hostages in order to bargain for the release of Hilarion Capucci, the Greek Catholic archbishop of East Jerusalem, who had been convicted of arms smuggling by the Israelis. On November 19, PDFLP terrorists struck against Israel again, raiding an apartment block in Beit Shean, in the north, killing four before being shot themselves.

Such terrorist activity triggered vigorous Israeli retaliation, especially raids into Lebanon, where most of the terrorists were based. By 1975, the pressure of Israeli retaliation had pushed Lebanon into civil war and into its own cycle of terrorism.

Neil Partrick

SEE ALSO: THE POPULAR FRONT FOR THE LIBERATION OF PALESTINE; THE LEBANESE CIVIL WAR; ISRAELI RAIDS ON THE PLO.

FURTHER READING

- Cobban, Helena. *The Palestinian Liberation Organization: People, Power and Politics.* Cambridge and New York: Cambridge University Press, 1984.
- Kissinger, Henry. *White House Years.* Boston: Little Brown, and London: Weidenfeld and Nicolson, 1979.
- Rubin, Barry. *Revolution Until Victory? The Politics and History of the PLO.* Cambridge, MA: Harvard University Press, 1994.

ABU NIDAL

Sabri al-Banna joined Yasser Arafat's Fatah (Palestine National Liberation Movement) in the 1960s, adopting the name Abu Nidal – a name that was to become synonymous with inter-Palestinian terrorism. He became a major figure among those who rejected any compromise with Israel. He collaborated with a number of Arab regimes and assassinated major Palestine Liberation Organization (PLO) figures.

Abu Nidal was appointed to Fatah's Revolutionary Council as early as 1969. A year later he became the Fatah representative to Baghdad. In this capacity, he demanded a hard line from leading Fatah figures, including Arafat's close confidant Salah Khalaf (*nom de guerre* Abu Iyad) during and after the PLO's expulsion from Jordan in September 1970. Abu Nidal was in favor of the terror campaign carried out by the Black September Organization in the early 1970s and disagreed loudly when Fatah began reining in the terrorists. It is possible that Abu Nidal directed attempts to free Abu Daoud, an assassin whom Fatah seemingly betrayed to the Jordanians in 1973.

In 1974, Abu Nidal broke with Fatah completely over the latter's willingness to talk to Israel and was given Iraqi support to establish his own group, Fatah: The Revolutionary Council. Abu Nidal also planned to kill Arafat aide Abu Mazen, for which the PLO sentenced him to death. Abu Nidal's stance reflected a genuine fear among some Fatah activists about the new, seemingly non-revolutionary direction of Fatah. However, what made Abu Nidal unique was his wish to escalate tactics to the point of killing Palestinian moderates. By 1975, Fatah men were having gunfights with Abu Nidal's operatives on the streets of Beirut, Istanbul, Karachi, and Paris. The Abu Nidal terror squads went under various names, such as Black June or the Arab Revolutionary Brigades, and from 1974 carried out attacks designed to stop talks between Palestinian moderates and Israel.

Arab interfactional terrorism reached a peak in 1978. In January of that year, Abu Nidal's men assassinated Sa'id Hammami, PLO general delegate to London. Hammami had been Arafat's unofficial channel of political concessions to Israel, running ahead of official PLO and Fatah policy. Hammami was gunned down in the first of a series of attacks on Fatah moderates in June that included strikes on PLO representatives Ali Yassin in Kuwait, and Izzadin al-Qalaq in Paris. Arafat's Fatah responded by bombing the Iraqi embassy in Beirut in July and storming the Abu Nidal office in Libya. And Fatah did not stop there: a bomb was placed outside the Iraqi embassy in Brussels, and the group even tried to assassinate the Iraqi ambassador to London.

KEY FACTS

- In 1977, three members of Abu Nidal's Black June group were hanged in public in Damascus, Syria, for attacking a hotel and taking hostages.
- From February 1985 to June 1987, Abu Nidal joined with fellow Fatah rebel Abu Musa in a joint terrorist command to stop Yasser Arafat and Jordan's King Hussein from reaching an agreement with Israel.

AN ISRAELI AGENT?

Given the chaos that Abu Nidal's activities have caused in Palestinian ranks, it is hardly surprising that he has been accused of being an Israeli agent. Indeed, author Patrick Seale reports that Abu Nidal conceded that his organization was littered with Israeli agents. It is also true that Israel – especially during the late 1970s and early 1980s when it was intervening in Lebanon – may have had some interest in weakening the forces of Palestinian compromise. Even so, the Israeli-agent theory is far-fetched.

On June 3, 1982, Abu Nidal attempted to assassinate the Israeli ambassador to London, Shlomo Argov. The Israelis used this as a pretext to invade Lebanon in "Operation Peace for Galilee." Abu Nidal was by now working for Syria, although why Syria should want to provoke Israel is unclear. Between June 6 and August 13, Israel destroyed Syria's entire air defense system in Lebanon and shot down 92 Syrian warplanes.

On April 10, 1983, Dr. Issam Sartawi, Arafat's close confidant and chief messenger for political compromise initiatives, was killed in Portugal by Abu Nidal on

Sabri al-Banna, alias Abu Nidal, pictured in 1982. Abu Nidal was once described as the "outstanding practitioner of pure unbridled terrorism."

Syrian president Assad's orders. Abu Nidal's self-styled "People's Army," a conventional rather than terrorist force, then helped chase the PLO out of Lebanon.

At this point, however, Abu Nidal began transferring operations to Libya, perhaps because he preferred terrorism to more conventional military operations. He conducted a number of operations under a variety of guises. He struck at Egyptian targets for Libyan leader Colonel Muammar al-Qaddafi under the alias of the Organization of Egyptian Revolutionaries or the Revolutionary Nasserist League.

In December 1985, Abu Nidal targeted Vienna and Rome airports. As Israeli tourists (and others) waited in line at El Al ticket counters, Abu Nidal terrorists tossed grenades among the passengers and opened fire on them with submachine guns. Fourteen people were killed and more than 100 wounded. It was no accident that the capitals of two countries at the forefront of European efforts to bring the PLO into any peace settlement should be chosen as the venues. Libya was believed to have been behind both operations.

Events on April 17, 1986, seemed to confirm further Syria's continued use of Abu Nidal as a weapon against possible peace moves. Nizar Hindawi, a Jordanian-Palestinian, used Abu Nidal's Syrian air force intelligence links to plan an attack on an El Al airliner at Heathrow Airport, London. He planted the bomb in a suitcase carried by his naïve, pregnant, Irish girlfriend. Fortunately, the bomb was detected in time.

It is not clear if approval came right from the top in Damascus – but the publicity surrounding the case certainly helped to give Assad a pariah status he did not want. The Syrian leader moved quickly to monitor the activities of Abu Nidal, whose organization then wasted no time in terminating its presence in Syria and making the Libyan desert its sole headquarters.

Abu Nidal has been active at a lower level since then. In 1990, the anti-Iraqi speaker of the Egyptian parliament was assassinated, it is widely believed, by Abu Nidal's men. In January 1991, Abu Nidal operatives posing as bodyguards killed PLO second-in-command Abu Iyad, with whom Abu Nidal had disagreed over the Black September Organization in the early 1970s.

Neil Partrick

SEE ALSO: ASSASSINATION; ARAB NATIONALISM AND THE RISE OF FATAH; THE BLACK SEPTEMBER ORGANIZATION; THE LEBANESE CIVIL WAR; TERROR IN LEBANON 1980-1987; LIBYAN SPONSORSHIP OF TERRORISM.

FURTHER READING

- Melman, Y. *The Master Terrorist: The True Story Behind Abu Nidal.* New York: Adama Books, 1986; London: Sidgwick and Jackson, 1987.
- Seale, Patrick. *Abu Nidal: A Gun for Hire.* New York: Random House, 1992; London: Arrow, 1993.
- Sobel, Lester A., ed. *Palestinian Impasse: Arab Guerrillas and International Terror.* New York: Facts on File, 1977.

THE PLO AND THE ARAB STATES

The relationship between the Palestine Liberation Organization (PLO) and the Arab states had a tremendous influence on terrorist incidents in the Middle East during the 1970s and 1980s. In theory, the long-term goal of all Arab states was to "liberate Palestine from Zionist imperialism." The declaration of this goal was originally made at the 1964 summit of the Arab League, an international organization of Arab states. But the actions of individual Arab governments frequently seemed to make it harder to achieve a liberated Palestine.

THE PLO AND TERRORIST GROUPS

The PLO itself developed enormously during the 1970s and 1980s. Under the leadership of Yasser Arafat, and with his Fatah faction dominating decision-making bodies, it took on all the trappings of a government in exile. Many guerrilla and terrorist organizations took part in the formalities of running the PLO. There were eight main groups:

Fatah normally sought a compromise peace.

The *Popular Front for the Liberation of Palestine* (PFLP) was dominated by Marxist leaders who also sought to unify the Arab states.

The *Democratic Front for the Liberation of Palestine* was a Marxist splinter group that broke away from the PFLP in 1969.

Saiqa (Arabic for Thunderbolt) was a Syrian-supported guerrilla force.

> **KEY FACTS**
>
> - In 1970, two-thirds of the Hashemite kingdom of Jordan's population were Palestinian refugees.
> - In October 1974, the Arab states recognized the PLO as the sole representative of the Palestinian people.
> - The massacre of 27 Palestinian refugees living in Lebanon by Christian Lebanese triggered the 1975-77 Lebanese civil war.

The Iraqi government created the *Arab Liberation Front* in 1969 to represent its views in the PLO.

The *Popular Front for the Liberation of Palestine – General Command* (PFLP-GC), the *Palestine Liberation Front*, and the *Popular Struggle Front* are smaller groups within the PLO. All three have followed the twists and turns of Arab politics – sometimes putting them in opposition to, or in the case of the PFLP-GC, in direct confrontation with, the PLO.

All of these groups are set up in the tradition of secular Arab nationalism. Islam and Muslim clerics had far less influence, unlike today, over Arab nationalism during the 1950s and 1960s, the era when these groups were established.

The most important decision-making body in the PLO during the 1970s and 1980s was the Palestine National Council (PNC), which met irregularly. On it sat representatives of the various guerrilla and terrorist groups, and other organizations the PLO has set up. The PNC elects the 15 members of the PLO's executive committee. Fatah could have used its political strength in the PNC to exclude other groups from the executive committee. But the creation of the 40-member PLO central council in 1973, which meets every three months, ensured that minority views had a hearing.

INFLUENCES ON PLO STRATEGY

There were four major elements in the PLO's attitude to terrorism during the 1970s and 1980s. First, the organization sought international respect and so was willing to negotiate and compromise. Second, the PLO needed to keep a loyal following among the Arabs living in the occupied territories of the West Bank and Gaza Strip. Third, it had to deal with the attitude of the Israeli government towards a Middle East peace settlement. Fourth, it had to cooperate with the host states for its military bases and political administration.

Arafat gave priority to gaining diplomatic recognition for the PLO from the international community. At various times during the 1970s and 1980s, he pursued a policy of restraining PLO members seeking violent

Nayef Hawatmeh, a Marxist Palestinian leader, was a founder member of the Popular Front for the Liberation of Palestine in 1968. The next year he left the Popular Front and founded the Democratic Front for the Liberation of Palestine.

confrontations with Israel. These included the period 1969-70 when U.S. Secretary of State William Rogers sponsored a Middle East peace plan; the period from November 1973 to 1975, when negotiations took place between various parties in the aftermath of the 1973 Arab-Israeli war; and the period directly after the 1982 expulsion of the PLO from Lebanon.

In all three of these periods, however, groups inside the PLO, who adopted the name *rejectionist*, defied Arafat and Fatah. In particular, some of the PFLP and Abu Nidal's Fatah: the Revolutionary Council tried to smash attempts at compromise in the period from 1973 to 1975. Indeed, Arafat's appearances as a world statesman prepared to compromise may actually have provoked these rejectionists to terrorist acts.

Fatah, the most moderate group in the PLO, did not altogether reject terrorism either, and certainly encouraged it during 1974-75. Fatah directed its strategy of violence against specifically Israeli targets in Israel and the occupied territories rather than attacking people and property around the globe. Terrorist attacks could take the shape of anything from a random grenade attack in Tel Aviv, to a bombardment of Galilee by Katyusha rockets, to the taking of civilian hostages.. Fatah worked within the PNC to bring the rest of the PLO membership around to their viewpoint, and the number of PLO terrorist acts taking place outside Israel declined during the 1980s.

THE PLO AND PALESTINIANS

The demand in the West Bank and Gaza Strip (the occupied territories) for an end to Israeli occupation encouraged a commitment to political compromise on the part of the PLO leadership. The seventh meeting of the PNC in April 1972 had instructed the PLO executive committee to concentrate their efforts on setting up a "national united front." This was in response to an initiative by King Hussein of Jordan, who suggested that the West Bank and Gaza Strip become part of a federated Jordanian-Palestinian state.

By August 1973, the Palestinian National Front (PNF) had been formed – in part the result of the PLO's decision, but as much out of the efforts of activists belonging to the Palestinian Communist Organization. The PLO had to decide whether to gain the support of those Palestinians in the occupied territories who supported the PNF's strategy of political mobilization to liberate territory occupied by Israel in 1967, or else to side with those who wanted armed confrontation.

ISRAELI RESPONSES TO TERRORISM

Another critical factor for the PLO's use of terrorism was the Israeli attitude. Israeli retaliation for Arab terrorist attacks varied according to the seriousness of the acts. There was no doubt that the right-wing Likud party, which came to power in Israel in 1977, was more willing to take military action. A more aggressive Israeli strategy, one associated with Ariel Sharon, resulted in the invasions of Lebanon in 1978 and, on a larger scale, in 1982. In particular, Palestinians were convinced that Israeli forces conspired with Christian Lebanese Phalangist militia in organizing the massacres of Palestinians at the Sabra and Chatila refugee camps in 1982. Such incidents were used by

Rex Features

Egyptian president Anwar Sadat addresses the Israeli parliament, the Knesset, in Jerusalem in November 1977. On this occasion he made his historic offer to recognize the state of Israel and negotiate a permanent peace settlement.

some Palestinians to justify their own retaliation. The artillery and aerial bombardment of Palestinian refugee camps in Lebanon only served to compound such attitudes.

THE PLO AND THEIR HOSTS

The history of Middle Eastern terrorism between 1970 and 1987 can, to a large exent, be told in terms of the relationship between the PLO and the Arab states. In 1970, the PLO was based in Jordan. From here, since 1969, the PFLP had carried out its campaign of hijacking that culminated in September 1970 with the incident at Dawson's Field, when three jet liners were blown up. Many within the Palestinian organizations, and especially the PFLP, believed it was necessary to overthrow Jordan's King Hussein to establish a safe base for terrorists and guerrillas. However, Hussein was a tough political operator, and he confronted the PLO 11 days after Dawson's Field. The well-trained Jordanian army eventually expelled the Palestinian fighters from Jordan, although the fighting went on until July 1971. Fatah radicals formed the terrorist Black September Organization, which organized many incidents during the early 1970s in reaction to the expulsion from Jordan.

The Palestinians now found themselves without any direct support from the other Arab states. Any Arab state that allowed the PLO to establish a large military force in its territory might experience what occurred in Jordan during the summer of 1970. If an Arab state offered itself as a terrorist base, then it could also expect Israeli retaliation.

The PLO moved its headquarters to Lebanon. The government here was too weak to keep Palestinian fighters out of the many refugee camps founded after the 1948-49 Arab-Israeli war and reinforced by more refugees after the 1967 war. The rest of the organization simply followed in the footsteps of the fighters who had been expelled from Jordan.

THE AFTERMATH OF THE 1973 WAR

The Arab armies of Egypt and Syria fought well in the October 1973 Arab-Israeli war, although Israel won the conflict. In its aftermath, the possibility of a negotiated Middle East peace settlement looked its best since 1967. In this context, Fatah decided to abandon terrorism outside the immediate area of Israel, in the hope that the PLO would be invited to any general negotiated peace settlement. But Arafat's willingness to compromise was not matched by other members of the PLO, who formed a rejection front.

Rejectionist groups such as the PFLP carried on with terrorism and also attacked conservative Arab targets. Abu Nidal's Fatah: The Revolutionary Council was even more extreme in its rejectionism, and attacked the PLO itself. The rejectionists relied heavily on support from Syria, Iraq, and Libya. Without this aid, rejectionist terrorists could never have had the impact they did. Syria, Iraq, and Libya were determined not to recognize Israel and encouraged the terrorists as proxies for their wider aims in the Middle East. Terrorist acts were timed to ensure maximum impact on any peace talks that took place.

Rex Features

A pro-Khomeini demonstration in Tehran during the Iranian revolution of 1978-79. Khomeini offered Muslim groups in the Middle East a powerful alternative to secular nationalism: fundamentalism.

The risk any Arab state took if it chose to act as the PLO's host was illustrated by events in Lebanon during the 1970s and 1980s. Palestinian raids from Lebanese bases into Israel attracted Israeli retaliation. The violence destabilized Lebanon, where tension between different religious groups heightened into a civil war in 1975, in which terrorism, including car-bombs, assassination, and hostage-taking, was prevalent. Faction fighting was followed by an Israeli invasion that forced the PLO to move its headquarters to Tunis in 1983.

During the civil war, an event the PLO considered a far greater disaster than the war itself took place when President Jimmy Carter brokered a peace agreement between President Anwar Sadat of Egypt and Israel's Prime Minister Menachim Begin in 1978. With Fatah's sponsor, Egypt, no longer at war with Israel, Camp David gave Syria and Iraq more control over the anti-Israeli coalition. Both countries were much closer to radical Palestinian terrorists than to Fatah.

The final political development that influenced terrorism lay in the success of the Ayatollah Khomeini in Iran (a non-Arab Muslim country) in 1979. His fundamentalist regime offered Muslims in Arab countries a strategy very different from the secular-nationalist path the PLO favored. Not only was it different, it was also successful. Suicide-bombing attacks by Hizb'allah fundamentalists in Lebanon effectively forced Western peacekeepers to leave Beirut in 1984.

Neil Partrick

SEE ALSO: ARAB NATIONALISM AND THE RISE OF FATAH; THE BLACK SEPTEMBER ORGANIZATION; THE POPULAR FRONT FOR THE LIBERATION OF PALESTINE; THE LEBANESE CIVIL WAR; PALESTINIAN ISLAMIC JIHAD; THE PALESTINIAN INTIFADA; IRAQI SPONSORSHIP OF TERRORISM; IRANIAN SPONSORSHIP OF TERRORISM; HIZB'ALLAH.

FURTHER READING

- Becker, Jillian. *The PLO: The Rise and Fall of the Palestine Liberation Organization.* New York: St Martin's Press, and London: Weidenfeld and Nicolson, 1984.
- Cobban, Helena. "The PLO and the Intifada," in *The Middle East Journal* 44, No. 2 (1990): 207-33.
- Gilmour, David. *Lebanon, the Fractured Country.* New York: St Martin's Press, and London: Sphere, 1984.

THE LEBANESE CIVIL WAR

Lebanon is a state containing many religious groups. Until the mid-1970s, there was a practical consensus about how the government of the country should be managed, so that no one group became too powerful. In 1975, however, this system of powersharing broke down under the impact of Israeli raids and the presence of Palestinian guerrilla groups. The result was a horrific civil war. The old Lebanese state was destroyed, and this set the scene for a further round of terrorism in the 1980s.

The Maronite Christians were the dominant religious/political group, representing about 25 percent of the Lebanese population. A major element of the Maronite community was the extreme right-wing Phalangist Party. The conservative Sunni Muslims were the dominant Muslim group, even though they had only about 20 percent of the population, compared with the Shiite Muslims' 30 percent. The latter had traditionally had little political influence, but this was soon to change. In the mountains was an Islamic sect, the Druze, who had great political influence, although they made up just seven percent of the population. Smaller groups included the Greek Orthodox and Armenian Christians.

Palestinian refugees entered this mix in the 1940s, and after the Palestine Liberation Organization (PLO) was expelled from Jordan in 1970-71 it set up its headquarters in Lebanon, from where the movement struck at Israel. While PLO terror continued, Israel felt free to launch preemptive strikes in Lebanon. Israel targeted Palestinians both in southern Lebanon and in the Lebanese capital, Beirut. Besides attracting Israeli attacks, the Palestinian presence also politicized the previously dormant Shiite Muslims. They began to protest about their exploitation by the wealthy Maronite Christians and in 1973 set up the "Movement of the Dispossessed."

KEY FACTS

- On June 29, 1975, Palestinian terrorists kidnapped U.S. Army Colonel Ernest R. Morgan in Beirut. He was released unharmed on July 12.
- In June 1978, Phalangist assassins murdered fellow-Maronite Tony Franjieh, who was seen as a rival to Bashir Gemayel in the race for the Lebanese presidency.

WAR FOR FISHING

The Lebanese Maronite Christian leaders were prepared to protect their interests with force, however. The beginning of the civil war in 1975 is usually seen as a dispute over fishing rights in the coastal town of Sidon. Before long the local Muslim mayor had been fatally wounded defending Muslim fishermen, and the situation escalated. The main conflict was between the Christian Maronites, in particular the Phalangists, and the left-wing Lebanese National Movement, which united the Druze-led Progressive Socialist Party, smaller communist groups, and the Shiite Movement of the Dispossessed. Both sides had private militias.

In April 1975, a key event took place when Palestinian gunmen shot the bodyguard of Phalangist leader Pierre Gemayel. The Christians retaliated by massacring 27 Palestinians and injuring 19 men on a bus in the Beirut suburb of Ein al-Rumaneh. Druze leader Walid Jumblatt declared that he would no longer accept the presence of Phalangists in the cabinet, effectively tearing up the old constitutional arrangements. Some Palestinians teamed up with the Lebanese Sunni Muslim Mourabitoun militia in Beirut and took the lead in fighting the Phalangists.

In January 1976, Christian Maronite militias besieged Palestinian refugee camps in Karantina and Tel al-Za'atar. PLO leader Yasser Arafat had no choice but to affirm his commitment to war on the side of the Lebanese National Movement. It was probably inevitable that the PLO would ally itself politically with fellow Muslims in Lebanon. The Maronites, for whom the maintenance of the status quo was everything, regarded the Palestinians as a destabilizing force.

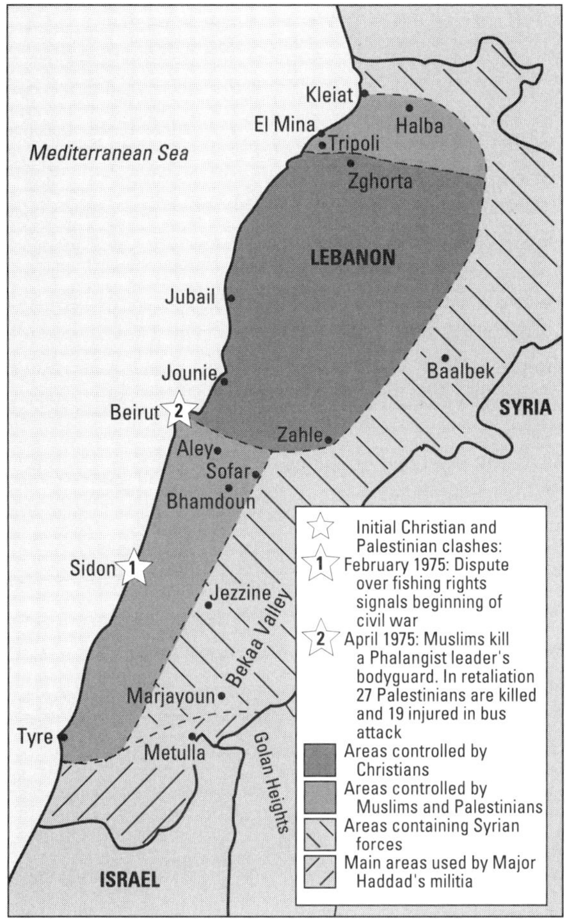

Civil war in the Lebanon 1975-77, showing the areas controlled by the various protagonists.

Arafat's PLO was drawn into what became a mire of bloodletting and terror. PLO forces pushed north toward Beirut from their bases in the south of the country. On January 20, the PLO and Lebanese National Movement forces conducted a bloody raid on the tiny Christian coastal town of Damour, massacring much of the population. Control of the country was slipping from the Maronites' grasp.

In order to prevent a complete Palestinian victory, which might provoke Israeli intervention in Lebanon, President Assad of Syria moved against the Palestinians. His troops encountered stiff resistance, but managed to rescue the Maronite forces from destruction. While the Palestinians were occupied with the Syrians, the Maronites took the opportunity to destroy two Palestinian refugee camps on Christian territory: Jisr al-Pasha and Tel al-Za'atar. The latter held out for 53 days against the Phalangists, who massacred most of the inhabitants when the camp finally fell on August 12.

In October 1976, the Arab states agreed that a predominantly Syrian peacekeeping force should remain in Lebanon. By then, order had all but collapsed in Beirut, and a large number of small, armed groups caused mayhem throughout the country. In March 1977, for example, Druze leader Kamal Jumblatt, father of Walid, was assassinated. Druze slaughtered the Christian inhabitants of a nearby village in revenge. The villagers were almost certainly innocent. All existing evidence points to Syrian involvement in Kamal Jumblatt's killing.

While Lebanon was submerging into terror, PLO groups continued raids into Israel. On March 11, 1978, Fatah terrorists took a busload of Israelis hostage. Thirty-five hostages were killed and 82 were wounded before the terrorists themselves were killed in a shoot-out in Tel Aviv. Now Israel had a perfect reason for entering Lebanon.

On March 14-15, some 20,000 Israeli troops crossed into Lebanon. They pounded Palestinian bases and communities as far north as Tyre. Operation Litani, as the punitive raid was code-named, lasted seven days. During this period, the Israelis created "Free Lebanon," a strip of south Lebanon that served as an Israeli "security zone," controlled by a Christian Lebanese militia under Major Saad Haddad.

Neil Partrick

SEE ALSO: ARAB NATIONALISM AND THE RISE OF FATAH; THE BIRTH OF THE PLO AND THE 1967 WAR; THE BLACK SEPTEMBER ORGANIZATION; ISRAELI RAIDS ON THE PLO; TERROR IN LEBANON 1980-1987.

FURTHER READING

- Brynen, Rex. *Sanctuary and Survival: The PLO in Lebanon*. Boulder, CO: Westview Press, and London: Pinter, 1990.
- Deeb, Marius. *The Lebanese Civil War*. New York: Praeger, 1980.
- Shehadi, Nadim, and Dana Haffar Mills, eds. *Lebanon: A History of Conflict and Consensus*. London: Centre for Lebanese Studies, 1992.

ENTEBBE

The Entebbe raid was a stunning example of a successful counterterrorist operation, in which surprise, international cooperation, and excellent preparation confounded international terror.

Air France flight 139 was hijacked on its way from Tel Aviv to Paris on June 27, 1976. The hijackers got on the aircraft at Athens, where it was making a scheduled stop. They forced the pilot to fly his craft, with its 246 passengers and 12 crew, first to Benghazi in Libya and then to Entebbe in Uganda.

COOPERATION BETWEEN TERRORISTS

The hijackers themselves were a mixed group. Two, who had posed as a couple at Athens airport, were from the West German Baader-Meinhof Group, while others were Palestinians from the Popular Front for the Liberation of Palestine (PFLP). The Arabs belonged to the special operations arm of the PFLP, which was run by hardline terrorist Wadi Haddad, and it is very likely that "Carlos the Jackal," who had PFLP connections, was involved in planning the operation. The terrorists demanded the release of 53 terrorists held in prisons worldwide.

The hijacking presented the international community with a big problem. A particular cause for concern was the involvement of the Ugandan president, Idi Amin Dada, who supported the terrorists' demands. For a nation state to provide blatant assistance to hijackers was a worrying precedent – even if Amin was recognized as an unstable personality – not least because the terrorists now had the support of conventional forces against any rescue attempts.

KEY FACTS

- Thirty-five Ugandan soldiers and 13 terrorists were killed during the Entebbe operation; some 60 Ugandan soldiers escaped from the building.
- From the first shot, the battle at Entebbe lasted less than an hour.
- The Israelis destroyed 11 Ugandan fighter aircraft on the ground so that they could not intercept the Israeli force as it flew home.

The Israelis were determined not to give in to the terrorists' demands and immediately began planning a way to release the hostages. The problem was that if a rescue attempt led to hostages being killed, Israel would attract much criticism. However, this difficulty evaporated when the terrorists freed the non-Israeli hostages. The Israelis now felt free to act without the possibility of pressure from other governments fearing for the lives of their own nationals. On June 30, a large group of released hostages arrived at Orly airport, and the Israelis began planning in earnest to rescue the 103 remaining captives.

PLANNING AND PREPARATIONS

The first stage of the planning was gathering intelligence. Israeli undercover agents interviewed the hostages arriving at Orly about the number of terrorists, their weapons, and Ugandan army involvement. The agents also asked about the terminal building where the hostages were held.

An Israeli company had built some of the installations at Entebbe, and so the blueprints were studied for any help they could offer. Friendly agencies worldwide supplied information on Uganda's armed forces. In fact, some Israeli units had, in the past, helped train Ugandans. A key element in the rescue attempt was to be cooperation from the Kenyan government. The flight from Sharm el-Sheikh at the southern tip of the Sinai peninsula to Uganda was 3,000 miles, and Kenyan refueling facilities would be invaluable.

Meanwhile, crack soldiers from Israeli parachute units and the Golani Brigade were practicing rapid assault techniques. In order to get a small unit quickly into the older of the two terminal buildings where the hostages were being held, a black Mercedes, similar to Idi Amin's personal vehicle, was to be used as a way of confusing Ugandan troops.

The Israeli assault force consisted of troops and medical backup in four Hercules transport aircraft, accompanied by a Boeing 707 to act as a communications center above Entebbe. A second Boeing 707 with more medical teams flew direct to Nairobi in Kenya. The force took off in the early afternoon of July 3 and flew low to avoid radar detection. The first Hercules

Hulton Getty Picture Collection

aircraft landed at Entebbe at 11:01 P.M. Soldiers spilled out of the back of the plane, placing beacons on the ground to aid the following aircraft. The assault squads drove directly to the old terminal building, and were only challenged when they were just 50 yards from it.

The Israelis shot two Ugandan sentries, and although the first door they tried was blocked, the second opened. Forcing their way in, the Israelis had surprise on their side, and the terrorists were unable to offer effective resistance; those who tried to resist were gunned down. Within three minutes of the first Israeli plane's landing, the old terminal building was in Israeli hands. Minutes later, all four Hercules aircraft were on the ground, and the new terminal and control tower were under attack.

The hostages were hustled into a Hercules and the planes took off at 11.52 P.M., flying on to Nairobi to refuel. Only one hostage was missing – she was later murdered on Amin's orders. The only Israeli soldier to die in the raid was Lieutenant-Colonel Jonathan Netanyahu, the operation commander. Originally code-named Operation Thunderball, the Entebbe raid was later renamed Operation Jonathan in his honor.

Ashley Brown

The rescued hostages were flown from Uganda back to Israel in transport planes to be greeted by their shaken relatives.

SEE ALSO: DOMESTIC VERSUS INTERNATIONAL TERRORISM; STATE VERSUS NON-STATE TERRORISM; HIJACKING AND KIDNAPPING; COLLABORATION BETWEEN TERRORISTS; THE POPULAR FRONT FOR THE LIBERATION OF PALESTINE; CARLOS THE JACKAL; RED ARMY FACTION: THE BAADER-MEINHOF GANG; THE ISRAELI RESPONSE TO TERRORISM; TERROR IN IDI AMIN'S UGANDA.

FURTHER READING

- Becker, Jillian. *Hitler's Children: The Story of the Baader-Meinhof Terrorist Gang.* 3rd ed. London: Pickwick, 1989.
- Gal-Or, Noemi. "Perceptions on Israel: Anti-Terrorism Policy," in *Ramsor,* No. 6 (November 1985): 50-53.
- Stevenson, William. *Ninety Minutes at Entebbe.* New York: Bantam Books, 1976; Melbourne: Transworld, 1977.

ISRAELI RAIDS ON THE PLO

The Israeli reaction to terrorism directed at its citizens by Palestinians has been debated since the early 1970s. The Israelis were firm that unless the Palestinians disavowed violence, then retaliation against Palestinian terrorists would occur. If Israel failed to retaliate, the argument went, it would encourage further terrorists attacks.

The key question is whether Israeli retaliation itself constituted terrorism. The Israelis argued that there were a limited number of ways they could retaliate against terrorists. The basic method was to bombard terrorist bases with artillery, or bomb them from the air. However, the terrorists were often based in refugee camps or under cover among the civilian population. Therefore raids aimed at terrorist bases were, in effect, attacks on Palestinian refugee camps or newly built villages, and most of the casualties were civilians. The effectiveness of Israeli retaliation was demonstrated when the Palestinians temporarily moved their base of operations from Lebanon to southern Syria. Israeli retribution against both Syrian and Palestinian communities prompted Syria to block the terrorists' access to Israel through Syrian territory.

INCURSIONS INTO LEBANON

The question of the Israeli treatment of civilians also arises with regard to Operation Litani and Operation Peace for Galilee – the Israeli incursions into Lebanon of 1978 and 1982 respectively. In 1978, Israeli Defense Forces (IDF) chief of staff Rafael Eitan said the intention was "to annihilate the terrorists and their infrastructure," but it is estimated that some 2,000 civilians died in the process.

In 1982, the invading Israeli forces drove through to the Lebanese capital, Beirut, and proceeded to lay

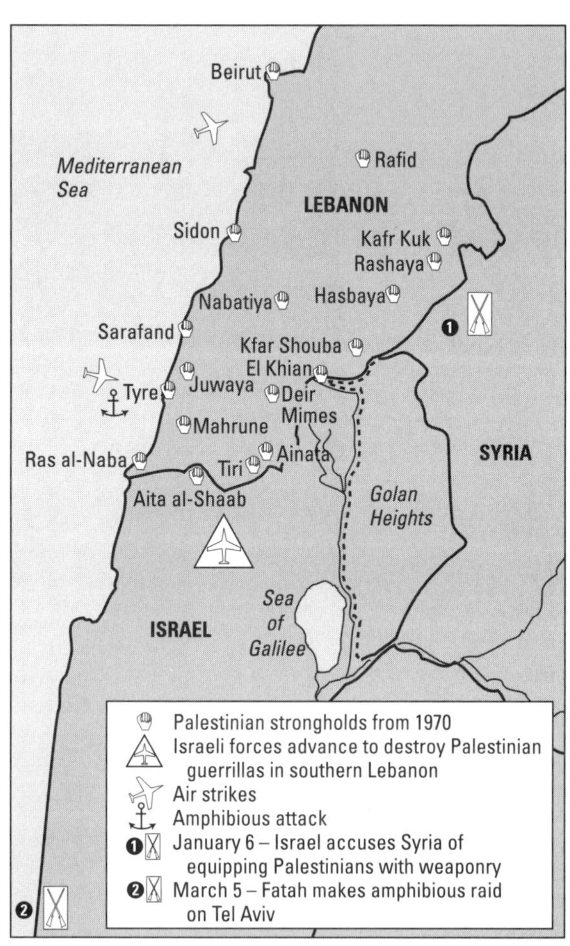

Palestinian strongholds and Israeli raids in Lebanon, 1975.

KEY FACTS

- Israeli intelligence expert Major-General Aharon Yariv was given virtually unlimited powers to destroy Palestinian terrorist cells in Europe. At his disposal were the Israeli foreign intelligence service Mossad, Sayaret Matkal elite counterterrorist troops, the diplomatic corps, and civilian specialists.
- Within a year of the killing of 11 Israeli athletes at the 1972 Olympics, Mossad killed 12 Palestinians directly or indirectly involved with the massacre.

Hulton Getty Picture Collection

An Israeli soldier carries a Kaytusha rocket launcher that belonged to Fatah. It was captured in a raid on Palestinian terrorists in Lebanon.

siege to and bombard West Beirut, where the PLO were trapped. The artillery, naval, and aerial pounding lasted from June 13 to August 12, almost without interruption. Supplies of food and water were cut off to the district, and there were outbreaks of typhoid and cholera. On September 15, with the PLO finally having been evacuated, Israeli forces entered West Beirut. As they did so, Lebanese Christian militiamen massacred hundreds of Palestinians, including women and children, in the refugee camps of Sabra and Chatila on the outskirts of the city. The Israeli forces were not directly involved in this massacre, but they did not prevent the militiamen from going about their bloody business. It is hard to escape the conclusion that Israeli governments and forces were not concerned about Palestinian civilian casualties and accepted that inflicting punishment on the Palestinian community as a whole was a legitimate response to terrorist acts.

Besides using conventional military action to avenge Palestinian terrorist attacks, the Israelis also sent hit squads to kill terrorists and leaders of the Palestinian groups. The most concentrated attempt to do this was in the early 1970s, during the heyday of Black September. In Beirut in 1973, Israeli agents killed Kamal Nasser – *fedayeen* (Palestinian guerrilla) leader in Jordan – along with two Black September leaders, Kamal Adwan and Abu Yousef.

WRATH OF GOD

So-called "Wrath of God" teams were also hunting down Palestinan terrorists in Europe. In December 1972, Israeli agents shot Wael Zwaiter, a Fatah representative in Rome. That same month, a squad killed Mahmoud Hamshari, PLO representative in Paris, using a bomb linked to his telephone. Then, in July 1973, a squad killed an innocent Moroccan waiter in Norway, believing him to be Ali Hassan Salameh, one of the men Israel held responsible for the 1972 Munich Olympics operation. After this, Wrath of God ended its operations in Europe, but hit squads kept up their activities in the Middle East and were particularly active in Lebanon in the late 1970s. They finally caught up with Salameh in Beirut who was killed when a car bomb exploded in January 1979.

Israeli retaliation continued in the 1980s. On October 1, 1985, in response to a Palestinian terrorist attack, the Israelis bombed the PLO headquarters in Tunis, Tunisia, killing 71 people, but missing their main target, PLO leader Yasser Arafat.

Neil Partrick

SEE ALSO: THE BIRTH OF THE PLO AND THE 1967 WAR; THE BLACK SEPTEMBER ORGANIZATION; THE PLO AND THE ARAB STATES; THE LEBANESE CIVIL WAR; TERROR IN LEBANON 1980-1987; FORCE 17 AND THE TUNIS RAID.

FURTHER READING

- Alon, Hanan. *Countering Terrorism in Israel.* Santa Monica, CA: Rand Corporation, 1980.
- Gabriel, Richard A. *Operation Peace for Galilee.* New York: Hill and Wang, 1984.
- Kapeliouk, Amnon. *Sabra and Chatila: Inquiry into a Massacre.* Belmont, MA: Association of Arab-American University Graduates, 1984.

JEWISH TERROR IN THE WEST BANK

Between 1970 and 1987, extremist Jewish organizations made terrorist attacks on Palestinians in the West Bank and Gaza – areas known internationally as the occupied territories.

The Israeli government itself used violence against any signs of Palestinian opposition to the presence of Israeli forces or settlements in the occupied territories. In Gaza, formerly an active center of resistance, General Ariel Sharon arrested or killed more than 1,000 guerrillas in 1971. His repressive policies generated resentment and anger that were the seeds of future problems. Summary executions accompanied the more standard features of the occupation, which included house demolitions and the destruction of fruit orchards – a mainstay of Palestinian livelihoods.

PALESTINE FINDS A VOICE

The Palestine Liberation Organization (PLO) had to work hard, however, to gain mass public support among Palestinians, particularly in the West Bank. The Palestinian Communist Organization (PCO), which aligned itself closely with the Soviet Union's Middle Eastern policies, was the most successful organization in the occupied territories during the early 1970s. The PCO openly called for the partition of Palestine between Jews and Arabs.

KEY FACTS

- After 1967, the Israeli National Religious Party adopted a policy of settling the occupied territories of the West Bank as part of a "Greater Israel."
- Following PLO leader Yasser Arafat's appearance at the United Nations in November 1974, there was an upsurge in Palestinian nationalist feeling on the West Bank.
- The Likud government elected in Israel in 1977 gave great encouragement to Jewish settlement on the West Bank. Prime Minister Menachem Begin called the West Bank "Judea and Samaria."

The Israeli government wanted the appearance of normal political life in the occupied territories, and on April 12, 1976, allowed municipal elections to take place in the West Bank. At this time Syria and its Lebanese allies were attacking the PLO militarily in Lebanon. The Israelis hoped to further embarrass the PLO by holding elections that would demonstrate how weak PLO support was in the occupied territories. They expected voters to continue supporting those candidates who believed the West Bank belonged to Jordan. The plan backfired. In 1973, the PLO joined with the PCO to organize the Palestinian National Front as a political movement in the occupied territories. The front's candidates won a majority on almost all local councils in the West Bank. The Israelis would afterward find it impossible to argue that the people of the West Bank would rather be part of Jordan than be granted Palestinian self-rule, if given a choice.

After the Camp David accords of 1978, which secured peace between Egypt and Israel, the leaders, or mayors, of the West Bank local councils formed a National Guidance Committee (NGC) to oppose the accords. The occupied territories' leadership was now dominated by members of a non-PLO, non-terrorist group based only in the West Bank and Gaza Strip – the communists of the PCO. The NGC was made up of mayors, businessmen, journalists, and representatives of voluntary organizations and labor unions, and students. It gave an organized platform to the Palestinian nationalists of the occupied territories.

THE GROWTH OF ISRAELI SETTLEMENTS

The NGC could hardly have chosen a worse moment to challenge the Israeli authorities. Camp David gave Israel's right-wing Likud government the security to allow the numbers of Israeli settlements on the West Bank to increase. Also, in a highly charged symbolic act, Israel passed a "Basic Law" in June 1980, officially annexing the eastern half of Jerusalem. East Jerusalem, along with the West Bank of the Jordan River, had remained in Arab hands after the end of the

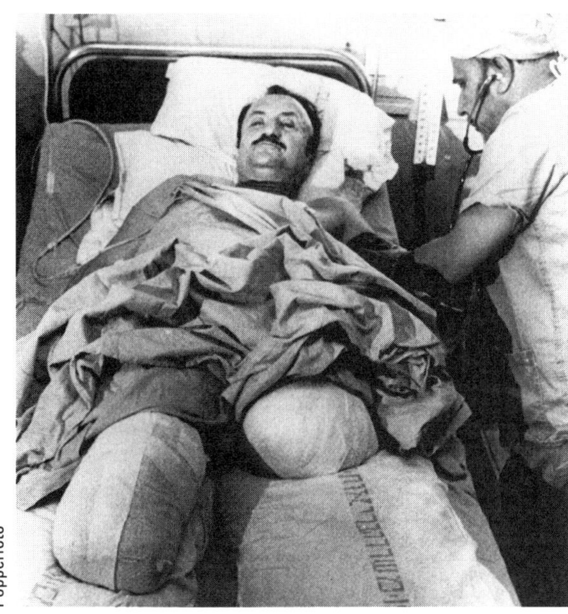

Popperfoto

Bassam Shaka', the mayor of Nablus, in a hospital after losing both his legs to a terrorist bomb. Jewish Underground terrorists planted the bomb in his car.

1948-49 Arab-Israeli war, but after the 1967 war this whole area was occupied by Israeli forces. The growing numbers of Israeli settlements on the West Bank sparked protests in April 1980. The NGC provided a focal point of political opposition, making clashes with the settlers and pressure from the Israeli authorities inevitable. In May, an Israeli officer shot a Palestinian. The PLO killed six settlers in retaliation.

ISRAEL STEPS UP THE PRESSURE

The Israeli government responded to these killings by blowing up houses near where the attacks took place. It also stepped up the pressure on the occupied territories' leadership, deporting the mayors of Hebron and Halhoul, flying them by helicopter to Lebanon.

However, these measures did not go far enough for an increasingly militant settler movement, organized under the leadership of Gush Emunim (Block of the Faithful). Gush Emunim used its lobbying power to direct the settlement policy of the Likud government. Jewish settlers' influence in government, however, did not eliminate their fear of the NGC's power to organize political protests. Jewish terrorism was renewed in the shape of the so-called Jewish Underground.

In June 1980, the Jewish Underground staged a series of bombings, seriously injuring prominent Palestinians: Mayor Bassam Shaka' of Nablus had to have his legs amputated; the mayor of Ramallah, Karim Khalaf, had his foot blown off; and the mayor of El Bireh, Ibrahim Tawil, narrowly escaped serious injury when a booby-trapped device attached to his garage door exploded in the face of an Israeli bomb-disposal expert. In a historic ruling in 1985, an Israeli court convicted three Israeli settlers of murder and found 12 other defendants guilty of violent crimes in cases arising from the attacks on West Bank mayors.

Beginning in the fall of 1981, the Begin government attempted to create a new political force on the West Bank in the shape of the Village Leagues. Anti-nationalist Palestinians were rewarded with government jobs if they worked alongside the Israeli army in breaking up anti-settlement demonstrations. The Village Leagues attracted little support, and the Israeli reaction to this failure was more repressive terror. In March and April 1982, 30 Palestinians died when Israeli soldiers opened fire on demonstrations. In the wake of these incidents, and before the 1982 Israeli invasion of the Lebanon, the Israeli government dissolved the NGC and dismissed the elected mayors. Israeli appointees choices now ruled the West Bank towns. With no high-profile targets for settler anger, the wave of Jewish Underground terror ceased.

Neil Partrick

SEE ALSO: THE ORIGINS OF ARAB-JEWISH TERRORISM; THE BIRTH OF JEWISH TERRORISM; THE BIRTH OF THE PLO AND THE 1967 WAR; THE PLO AND THE ARAB STATES; JEWISH TERRORISM IN THE 1990s; THE ISRAELI RESPONSE TO TERRORISM.

FURTHER READING

- Hadawi, Sami. *Bitter Harvest: A Modern History of Palestine.* 4th ed. New York: Olive Branch Press, 1991.
- Mishal, S. *The PLO Under Arafat : Between Gun and Olive Branch.* New Haven, CT: Yale University Press, 1986.
- Ovendale, Ritchie. *The Origins of the Arab-Israeli Wars.* 2d ed. London and New York: Longman, 1992.
- Perlmutter, Amos. *Israel: The Partitioned State.* New York: Scribner, 1985.

TERROR IN LEBANON 1980-1987

The fighting that took place in Lebanon during the period 1980-87 included a whole series of terrorist acts. Indeed, terror was an integral part of the tactics used by all sides as the country collapsed into a number of armed camps, in a gloomy moral twilight where sworn enemies could meet to plan assassinations, and avowed opponents – such as the U.S. and fundamentalist Iran – could collude in arms trafficking.

The situation in Lebanon had been relatively quiet since the 1975-78 civil war, although there were terrorist incidents. In January 1979, for example, the Israelis detonated a bomb that killed Ali Hassan Salameh, head of Yasser Arafat's bodyguard Force 17 and the man thought responsible for planning the terrorist attack on Israeli athletes at the 1972 Munich Olympics. This bomb also killed six innocent passers-by.

In 1981, there were heavy exchanges of fire between Palestinians and Israelis. Arafat's forces rained down rockets on northern Israeli towns, while Israeli warplanes and artillery pounded Palestinian camps. After letting off steam, and with little hope of matching the Israeli carnage being wrought in Lebanon, the Palestine Liberation Organization (PLO) chairman soon put a stop to the rocket attacks. Arafat agreed to a cease-fire, despite formidable Palestinian resistance. The PLO leader was fearful that Israel just

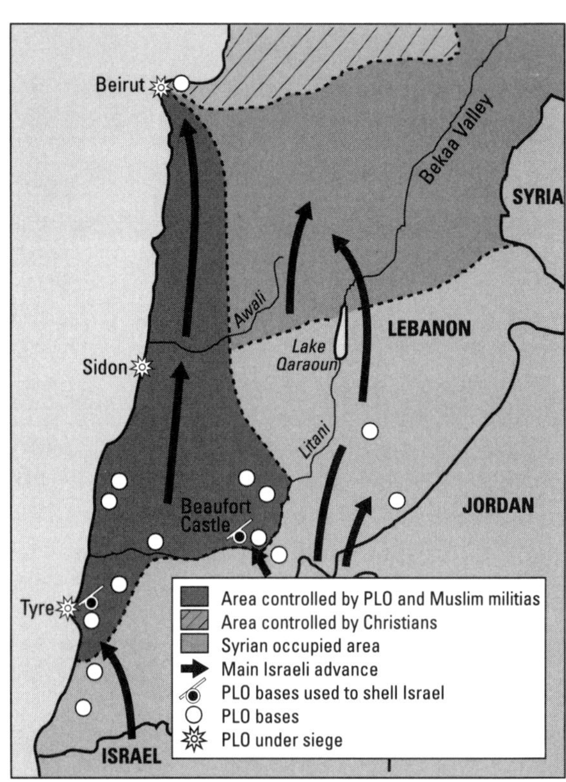

"Operation Peace for Galilee," the Israeli invasion of Lebanon, June 1982. Israel's avowed object was to set up a demilitarized zone to protect its northern border.

KEY FACTS

- On June 6, 1982, Israel invaded Lebanon in "Operation Peace for Galilee."
- The Israeli invasion opened the way for a further round of terrorist activity in Lebanon, including hostage-taking and suicide-bombing.
- The radical Islamic group Hizb'allah emerged as a leading exponent of terrorist violence.

wanted another pretext for what he judged since April 1979 to have been Prime Minister Menachem Begin's wish to send troops into Lebanon to drive out the PLO. Meanwhile, Syrian-controlled terrorists were trying to break the cease-fire, while from the Israeli side, once Begin was re-elected in August 1981, the likelihood of intervention in Lebanon increased, especially once "the hawk" Ariel Sharon became defense minister.

Popperfoto

The corpses of Palestinians lie in the streets of the Sabra refugee camp, victims of the September 1982 massacre in which hundreds were murdered.

OPERATION PEACE FOR GALILEE

On June 6, 1982, Israeli forces did indeed drive into Lebanon in "Operation Peace for Galilee." Although the government announced that it only wished to establish a demilitarized zone to prevent rocket attacks on northern Israel, it seems unlikely that Begin did not know of Sharon's intention to go all the way to Beirut. If Operation Litani, the limited incursion of 1978, had been insufficient, then taking control of Lebanon four years later would seem logical. Destruction of the PLO and knocking out Syria before establishing a proxy Christian regime in Beirut were the undoubted objectives.

The attempted assassination of Shlomo Argov, Israeli ambassador to London, on June 3, probably was not the final straw, as some have argued. Israel knew that agent provocateur Abu Nidal and archenemy of the PLO, had orchestrated the attack – to which Israeli Chief of Staff Rafael Eitan, spoiling for a fight, disdainfully responded, "Abu Nidal, Abu Shmidal … We have to destroy the PLO."

Fighting alongside Bashir Gemayel's Phalangist militias, Israel overran the country in six days. Having pushed most of Syria's troops north after destroying its air force in the Bekaa Valley, Israel now closed in for the kill, holding Muslim West Beirut in a siege, starved of food, fuel, and water. Indiscriminate Israeli aerial bombardment – civilians accounted for an estimated 90 percent of all casualties – continued until August 12. At this point, the Reagan administration called for a cease-fire. The U.S. played a much-publicized part in brokering the cease-fire and securing the evacuation of PLO and Syrian soldiers from Beirut by September 1, 1982.

REFUGEE CAMP MASSACRES

Bashir Gemayel, closely connected to Israel, was elected Lebanese president by the Chamber of Deputies, and Syria signaled its military weakness by signing a cease-fire with Israel on September 11, 1982. However, whatever plans the Israelis may have had now began to unravel. The first problem was that its ally

Popperfoto

Yasser Arafat en route to Tunisia, having been expelled from Lebanon in 1982.

Gemayel was killed by a bomb on September 14 – most likely planted by Syrian agents. The second problem was the international outcry when Israeli troops allowed Phalangist militia to enter the Palestinian refugee camps of Sabra and Chatila in West Beirut, where they massacred hundreds of Palestinian refugees while Sharon's men looked on. The Phalange had been the Israelis' military allies and supposed political puppets. However, their action so besmirched the Israelis and their Lebanon policy that in many ways the beginning of the Israeli withdrawal can be traced to this incident. It also signaled the point at which U.S. troops – dressed up as international forces in the U.S.-dominated Multi-National Force (MNF) – moved into Lebanon.

The Israelis remained in Beirut, withdrawing to the south of the city and then toward the frontier only in 1983. Not until 1985 did they finally withdraw from Lebanon, and even then they left a zone of southern Lebanon dominated by the South Lebanon Army, a Christian force that they controlled. The U.S. component of the MNF remained until February 1984, and the last European contingent of French troops left in 1986.

The main loser in this fight was the PLO. Under attack from an alliance of the Syrians, dissident PLO elements, and Christian militias, Yasser Arafat was forced into the northern Lebanese town of Tripoli, and finally had to evacuate his headquarters from that city in 1983. The PLO headquarters moved to Tunis, in Tunisia – far from the frontiers of Israel.

For the rest of the 1980s, there was constant fighting in Lebanon. The main protagonists were the Christian militias (who were themselves split, principally in a feud between Phalangist Lebanese Forces and the Zghorta Liberation Army); the Syrians and the Israelis, who both had ambitions to mold Lebanon into a client state; the Shiite Amal militia, originally the armed wing of the "Movement of the Dispossessed"; the Palestinians, who had begun infiltrating back into Lebanon after the evacuation of 1982-83 and who were allied with a Sunni muslim militia, the Mourabitoun; and the Islamic fundamentalist group, Hizb'allah.

THE PARTY OF GOD

Hizb'allah (literally "Party of God") had emerged in Lebanon in 1982. Its origins lay in Iran, and there were confirmed reports that Iranian Revolutionary Guards were operating in Lebanon in the early 1980s. Although the inspiration for Hizb'allah came from Tehran, it was assisted by Syria and led by Lebanese Shiite clerics.

There were two tactics that made Hizb'allah so effective and so notorious. The first was the use of suicide bombers, young men who were prepared to drive a car or truck loaded with explosives into an enemy headquarters and blow themselves to pieces in pursuit of their cause. The Israeli headquarters in Tyre was struck twice by suicide bombers: in November 1983 and November 1984. The members of the MNF were also targets. A suicide bomb attack against the U.S. embassy in Beirut in April 1983 killed 16 Americans. The most effective of such attacks took place on October 23, 1983. A suicide bomber broke through the security at the U.S. Marine barracks near Beirut airport; the resultant blast killed 241 Marines. The same day, another bomber drove into the barracks of the French contingent and killed 58 soldiers.

These terror attacks helped intensify the pace of the U.S. and Israeli withdrawal from Lebanon. However, the emergence of Hizb'allah was of grave concern to other states too. In March 1985, a massive car bomb exploded outside the Beirut headquarters of Hizb'allah. It killed 80 people but failed to injure its target: Hizb'allah's spiritual leader, Sheikh Mohammed Hussein Fadlallah. There was much debate over who planted this bomb. The most common explanation was that the CIA and Saudi Arabia had funded a Maronite Christian group to assassinate Fadlallah.

HIJACKING AND HOSTAGES

Lebanese Shiite militants staged an international airplane hijacking in revenge against the CIA car bomb. On June 14, 1985, TWA Flight 847 was taken over, and an American serviceman among the passengers was killed. However, Hizb'allah did not undertake further hijackings, and settled down as a guerrilla resistance group fighting the Israeli presence in the "security zone," having assisted in their removal from the rest of the country.

The second tactic used by Hizb'allah was the taking of hostages – particularly high-profile western hostages. Hostage-taking had been part of the civil war of the mid-1970s – the first U.S. hostage to be taken was Colonel Ernest Morgan in June 1975. In the early 1980s, however, hostage-taking increased greatly. In 1985, it is estimated that Hizb'allah took 19 hostages, including four Americans; in 1986, the figure was 15, followed by 10 in 1987. Two Americans, CIA station chief William Buckley and Marine Lieutenant-Colonel William Higgins were taken hostage and subsequently killed by their Hizb'allah captors.

Negotiations between U.S. officials and the Iranians over sales of arms to Iran generated a great deal of publicity. Hizb'allah took advantage of this widespread interest to further its cause in 1987, by taking hostage British envoy Terry Waite, who was negotiating for the release of other hostages. However, hostage-taking proved to be a short-lived tactic. By the end of 1991, the last western hostages had been released. However, Hizb'allah had made its mark.

THE LATER STAGES OF THE WAR

The phase of the war in Lebanon during the later 1980s was marked by infighting between radical Muslim groups, as well as by terror against all religious groups. For example, when Israel moved out of the Chouf mountains in 1983, Muslim forces moved in. As a result, tens of thousands of Christian villagers had to leave their homes and become refugees. Amal, the militia deriving from the Shia "Movement for the Dispossessed," had become the major indigenous Lebanese armed force by 1984. Over a two-year period from mid-1985, the Amal militia attempted to capture the Palestinian refugee camps in Beirut, in what is known as the "War of the Camps." The clandestine re-entry of some Fatah fighters into Lebanon made the Palestinian refugee community a target for attacks by Shia Muslims. Brutal fratricide ensued as Amal militiamen besieged Palestinian camps using rocket launchers and artillery to try to batter the defenders into submission. The Palestinians held out and the siege ended in January 1988.

Having engaged in a confrontation with the Palestinians, Amal next became engaged in a war with Hizb'allah. There had been disputes between the two groups over the hijacking of the TWA Flight 847 in June 1984, and large-scale fighting broke out in April 1988, initially in southern Lebanon. The conflict soon spread to Beirut, however, where indiscriminate shelling of opposition-controlled areas led to hundreds of deaths. The result of this fighting was that Amal suffered a heavy defeat, and had to be rescued by Syrian intervention. This was the end of major fighting, although there were still many small-scale terrorist acts in a country that had been effectively pulled apart by war.

Neil Partrick

SEE ALSO: THE BLACK SEPTEMBER ORGANIZATION; ABU NIDAL; THE LEBANESE CIVIL WAR; ISRAELI RAIDS ON THE PLO; JEWISH TERROR IN THE WEST BANK; IRANIAN SPONSORSHIP OF TERRORISM; HIZB'ALLAH.

FURTHER READING

- Brynen, Rex. *Sanctuary and Survival: The PLO in Lebanon.* Boulder, CO: Westview Press, and London: Pinter, 1990.
- Kramer, Martin. *Hezbollah's Vision of the West.* Washington, DC: Institute for Near East Policy, 1989.
- Shehadi, Nadim, and Dana Haffar Mills, ed. *Lebanon: A History of Conflict and Consensus.* London: Centre for Lebanese Studies, 1992.
- Sahliyeh, Emilie, ed. *Religious Resurgence and Politics in the Contemporary World.* Albany: State University of New York Press, 1990.

FORCE 17 AND THE TUNIS RAID

During 1985, terrorist attacks by the Palestine Liberation Organization's (PLO) Force 17 provoked the Israeli bombing of Tunis. After the Israeli invasion of Lebanon in June 1982, PLO chairman Yasser Arafat escaped Beirut by sea. He set up his new headquarters in Tunisia, in North Africa. Though most of the PLO's guerrilla fighters remained in northern Lebanon or Syria, PLO intelligence and security services went to Tunis with Arafat.

The 1982 Israeli invasion of Lebanon had been intended to wipe out the PLO. Its objective remained incomplete, even though the Israelis drove the Palestinian leadership out of Beirut, and Israel remained hostile and suspicious toward the PLO. Israeli agents were ever ready to strike, especially when they had the chance of killing any PLO members suspected of terrorism.

ARAFAT'S SECURITY AGENCIES

In Tunis, Arafat had two units to enforce discipline on the organization: Force 17 and Hawari. Force 17 was named after the 17 Fatah guerrillas who died fighting the Israelis at the battle of Karama in 1968. The unit, which was set up in the early 1970s and commanded by Abu Jihad (Khalil al-Wazir), was Arafat's personal guard as Fatah leader. Force 17 also punished Palestinian dissidents. In the mid-1980s, though, Fatah began to use Force 17 as a terrorist arm. Force 17 was seen as a prime target by Israeli intelligence.

KEY FACTS

- Feuds between Fatah loyalists and Syrian-backed dissidents accounted for some Force 17 deaths. Two commanders were assassinated, in August 1987 and May 1989.
- One of the Force 17 terrorists who murdered three Israeli citizens on a yacht in Cyprus was an Englishman, Ian Davison. He was recruited by the PLO while he was traveling around the world.

Hawari was named after its commander and, like Force 17, turned to terrorism in 1985. Initially, Hawari used terrorism to strike at Arab enemies of the PLO – particularly Syria. In April 1985, Hawari terrorists placed a bomb in the Rome office of the Syrian state airline and another in a Syrian diplomat's car. The group was also involved in more general international terror. In April 1986, in spite of the official PLO policy of avoiding civilian targets outside Israel and the occupied territories of the West Bank and Gaza, Hawari terrorists placed a bomb on board a TWA airliner. Hawari himself died in 1991 in a car accident and the group became much less active.

PLO AND FORCE 17 TERRORISM

In April 1985, the PLO launched the first of a series of seaborne raids against Israel. A force of 28 commandos belonging to a PLO organization called "Western Sector" put to sea aboard a freighter called the *Atavirus*. The Israelis intercepted and sank the vessel, killed 20 PLO men, and captured the rest. The next operation took place the following month, carried out by members of Force 17. The Israelis captured their boat too. In September, Force 17 tried again, this time sailing from Larnaca in Cyprus. Once again, the Israelis intercepted the vessel, kidnapping Force 17's deputy commander, Faisal Abu Sharah. It was at this point that Force 17 turned to terrorism.

Two weeks after the September 1985 kidnapping, Force 17 exacted revenge and killed three Israeli civilians on a yacht in Cyprus. The PLO claimed that the victims were agents of Mossad (Israeli foreign intelligence service). Israeli premier Yitzhak Rabin had already issued a thinly disguised warning that the increase in attacks on settlers in the occupied territories would be met with swift reprisals. Rabin took the incident in Cyprus to be an unacceptable act of terrorism and, in response, Israeli jets bombed the PLO's headquarters in Tunis on October 1, 1985. Fifty-six Palestinians and 15 Tunisians were killed. Arafat, the obvious target, narrowly escaped.

Popperfoto

The PLO headquarters at Borj Cedia, south of Tunis, after the Israeli raid of October 1, 1985.

The international community found it difficult to stomach the Israeli attack. Israel's argument was that it had no other means of retaliating when its citizens were the victims of terrorist attack. In support of the Israelis, U.S. President Ronald Reagan declared that the Tunis strike was justified and that the Israelis "had hit the right target."

Force 17 now began a series of terrorist raids into Israel. Under the direction of Abu Jihad, terrorists bombed a bus in Jerusalem in February 1986, injuring six people. They threw explosives into the El Al offices in Tel Aviv in September and stabbed a student to death in Jerusalem in November. In June 1987, they bombed a beach near Haifa and wounded a woman and child. Their most noteworthy act was the killing of two Israeli security agents in November 1987 – their throats were slashed.

The start of the Intifada, the populist Palestinian uprising in the West Bank and Gaza in December 1987, opened a new chapter in the story of terrorism in the Middle East. It was widely blamed on Abu Jihad by Israeli intelligence. He was, therefore, doubly a marked man. The Israelis eventually got to him in April 1988, when a Mossad hit squad assassinated him at his home in Tunis. Force 17, however, continued to be an important part of Fatah.

Neil Partrick

SEE ALSO: ISRAELI RAIDS ON THE PLO; TERROR IN LEBANON 1980-1987; THE HIJACKING OF THE *ACHILLE LAURO*.

FURTHER READING

- Brynen, Rex. *Sanctuary and Survival: The PLO in Lebanon.* Boulder, CO: Westview Press, and London: Pinter, 1990.
- Cobban, Helena. "The PLO in the Mid-1980s," in *International Journal* 38, No. 1: 15-26.
- Freedman, Robert O, ed. *The Middle East after the Israeli Invasion of Lebanon.* Syracuse, NY: Syracuse University Press, 1986.

THE HIJACKING OF THE *ACHILLE LAURO*

On October 1, 1985, Israeli aircraft attacked the headquarters of the Palestine Liberation Organization (PLO) in Tunis, Tunisia, killing 50 people, mostly PLO men. One week later, an Italian cruise liner, the *Achille Lauro* – en route from Genoa, Italy, to Ashdod, the main Mediterranean port in southern Israel – was captured by four young terrorist members (the oldest was just 20) of the Palestine Liberation Front (PLF). The hijacking was interpreted internationally as an act of revenge, particularly since the PLF was associated with the PLO and Mohammad Abul Abbas, leader of the PLF and instigator of the operation, had a seat on the PLO executive committee.

THE PLAN DISCOVERED

The original intention of the PLF terrorists was not to hijack the *Achille Lauro* on its journey, but rather to wait until the liner reached Ashdod and to take Israelis hostage there. However, a member of the crew discovered the four men cleaning their weapons in their cabin. Forced into action, the terrorists seized control of the ship.

The liner was at that time sailing along the Egyptian coast, and the majority of passengers were away visiting the Pyramids. However, there were still 427 passengers and 80 crew members on board. The terrorists demanded the release of 50 Palestinian prisoners in Israel, and threatened to kill the hostages if their demands were not met.

In previous hijackings of aircraft, Middle Eastern terrorists had often specifically targeted and killed U.S. or Israeli officers or state officials. On the *Achille Lauro*, however, the terrorists went further. When Israel refused to agree to the PLF's demands, the terrorists shot and killed a 69-year-old wheelchair-bound American Jew from New Jersey, Leon Klinghoffer, and dumped his body overboard.

The hijacking ended when Abul Abbas managed to negotiate an agreement with the Egyptian government. The Egyptians offered both the hijackers and Abul Abbas free passage in exchange for releasing the ship and the hostages. There was a further twist to the story, however. U.S. warplanes intercepted the aircraft flying the terrorists out of Egypt and forced it to fly to a NATO airbase in Sicily. Here, the Italian authorities took charge of the situation. The Italians, however, were hesitant about the best way to proceed, and began by releasing Abul Abbas, who was carrying an Iraqi diplomatic passport. The four terrorists, however, were tried and convicted for murder and conspiracy, and received sentences ranging from 15 to 30 years. Abul Abbas was convicted only *in absentia*.

There were mutual recriminations over the affair. The U.S. was condemned by some for violating international law and for effectively hijacking an aircraft; the Italians were criticized for letting Abul Abbas slip through their fingers. There was a suspicion that the Italians had released him mainly because they feared reprisal terrorist raids if they did not let him go. Perhaps the most important result of the affair lay in its effects on the PLO. The peculiar horror of the murder of an elderly man in a wheelchair just because he was Jewish led to worldwide condemnation of the PLO.

KEY FACTS

- The Palestinian Liberation Front, responsible for the hijacking of the *Achille Lauro*, was the result of schisms in older Palestinian organizations. It was closely associated with the PLO – the PLF was based near the PLO headquarters in Tunis, Tunisia.
- The Cairo Declaration which followed the *Achille Lauro* crisis was an important step toward the inclusion of the PLO in the Middle East peace process.

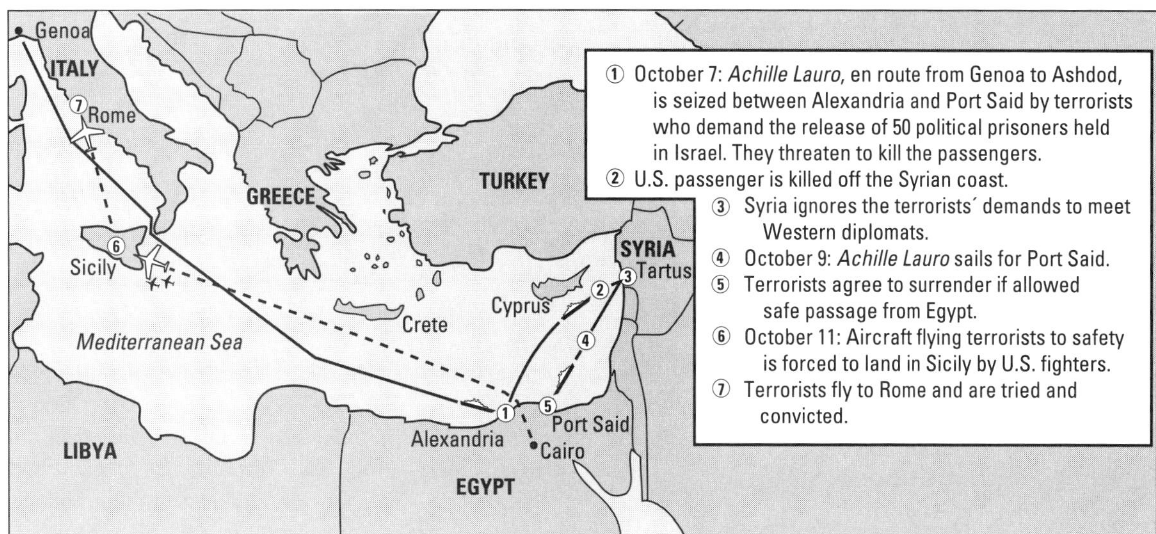

The route followed by the Achille Lauro *after its hijacking by members of the PLF on October 7, 1985.*

ARAFAT RENOUNCES TERRORISM

Arafat's solution to the PLO's isolation was to revert to diplomacy. Encouraged by Egyptian President Hosni Mubarak, Arafat made the Cairo Declaration of November 1985, in which he officially condemned "all outside operations other than in Israel and the occupied territories and all forms of terrorism." In line with United Nations Security Council Resolution 3236, the PLO chairman also proclaimed the right of the Palestinian people to resist foreign occupation. The declaration simultaneously drew on UN resolutions that legitimized force in certain circumstances and affirmed support for a peaceful political process by citing the UN Charter on the "inadmissibility of settling disputes by force."

Arafat seemed to be on safe ground by differentiating between terrorism and armed resistance. The difficulty, as always, came in condemning attacks on "the innocent and defenseless wherever they may be," while legitimizing the right of self-defense, which presumably included the right of Palestinians to threaten the safety of Israeli settlers. However, without spelling it out, the Arafat statement clearly drew a distinction between actions in territories occupied by Israel in 1967 and actions against civilians "outside." The problem, of course, was that "outside" meant outside Palestine and this suggested that such events as the Ma'alot massacre in northern Israel in 1974 were not included in Arafat's condemnation of terrorism.

The Cairo Declaration was a clear attempt by Arafat to distance himself from those members of the PLO who rejected any hint of compromise with Israel and the international community. Such hardliners bitterly criticized Arafat, claiming that the Cairo Declaration was merely a stunt designed to please the U.S. Nevertheless, the declaration was an important step toward peace in the Middle East.

Neil Partrick

SEE ALSO: KIRYAT SHMONA AND MA'ALOT; THE PLO AND THE ARAB STATES; ISRAELI RAIDS ON THE PLO.

FURTHER READING

- Hart, Alan. *Arafat: A Political Biography.* Rev. ed. London: Sidgwick and Jackson, 1994.
- Livingstone, Neil, and David Halevy. *Insidc the PLO: Covert Units, Secret Funds, and the War Against Israel and the United States.* New York: Morrow, and London: Hale, 1990.
- Rubin, Barry. *From War to Peace: Arab-Israeli Relations,1973-1993.* Brighton: Sussex Academic Press, and New York: New York University Press, 1994.
- Rubin, Barry. *Revolution Until Victory? The Politics and History of the PLO.* Cambridge, MA: Harvard University Press, 1994.

THE ORIGINS OF PALESTINIAN ISLAMIC JIHAD

Between 1980 and 1987, following the Islamic revolution of 1978-79 in Iran, the Muslim faith became a far more significant element in the Palestinians struggle for a nation-state. Iranian arms and money contributed to the growth of Islamic politics throughout the Middle East. The assassination of President Anwar al-Sadat of Egypt, in October 1981, was the most striking single example of the new Muslim fundamentalism. Sadat was killed for having recognized the state of Israel, and for having signed a peace agreement with it. Members of the Egyptian Islamic Jihad carried out the assassination. They would soon have imitators all over the Arab world, and they played a crucial role among Palestinians.

THE BROTHERHOOD AND THE JIHAD

Islamic Jihad had its roots in the Muslim Brotherhood, a fundamentalist movement founded in Egypt in 1928. At one stage, the movement numbered 500,000 active members, and influenced Palestinians such as Yasser Arafat during the 1950s. President Gamal Abdel Nasser banned it after its members tried to assassinate him in 1954. The ban remained in place until after Nasser's death in 1970. Nasser's successor, Sadat, restored legality to radical Muslim groups in an attempt to counter the influence of left-wing political parties.

KEY FACTS

- The Muslim Brotherhood's hostility to Israel dates back to the Arab-Israeli war of 1948-49. Brotherhood members were prominent in the fighting around Gaza.
- Hamas drew from the Muslim Brotherhood for its leaders. These included the former Gaza Muslim Brotherhood leader, Sheikh Ahmed Yassin, Dr. Abdel Aziz Rantisi, and Dr. Mahmoud Zahhar.

The Muslim Brotherhood traditionally maintained a strong base around Gaza, where it had retained a presence since spreading there in the 1930s from its Egyptian base. From 1979 onward, the brotherhood began to present a strong challenge to the secular nationalists in student elections held in universities across the occupied territories (the West Bank and the Gaza Strip). It formed electoral alliances where convenient – on occasion with Fatah against the powerful communists – and made a formidable showing in professional bodies such as the Engineers Association, which elected a majority of Muslim Brotherhood supporters in 1981. However, electoral pacts soon gave way to campus clashes between supporters of the Brotherhood and Fatah, primarily, between late 1981 and 1985. The focus was the Islamic University in Gaza, founded by the Brotherhood in 1978; An-Najah University in Nablus; and, to a lesser extent, Hebron and Birzeit universities.

THE GROWTH OF ISLAMIC RADICALISM

The existence of the radical Egyptian Muslims – the Egyptian Islamic Jihad – encouraged a Palestinian equivalent. In the early 1980s, small, more radical groups of fundamentalists began to emerge in Palestine from within those influenced by the Brotherhood. Although they professed dissatisfaction with the Brotherhood's refusal to embrace violence, there was often more in common between them and the Brotherhood than they were prepared to admit, and there was a considerable common membership.

In 1980, these radical Palestinian Muslim Brothers founded the Palestinian Islamic Jihad. The latter group argued that the Muslim Brotherhood's policy of tying the liberation of Palestine to the transformation of the whole Arab world was pointless because Palestine should play the primary role in any Arab liberation struggle. Young fundamentalist leaders such as Fathi

Popperfoto

Security police rush to the aid of President Anwar Sadat of Egypt, fatally wounded in a hail of bullets at the October 6th parade in Cairo, Egypt, 1981.

Shiqaqi and Jihad's spiritual leader, Abdel Aziz Odeh, believed they could challenge the secular (non-religious) nationalism of the Muslim Brotherhood, especially since the PLO's armed struggle was showing no concrete results. The fundamentalists took advantage of the fact that the PLO leaders seemed more concerned with gaining international diplomatic recognition than achieving their official objective of liberating Palestine.

DIVIDE AND RULE

At first, Israel was prepared to encourage the Islamic fundamentalists, allowing them to build their institutional base – and even surreptitiously funding Muslim Brotherhood mosques – in order to divide and rule. Supporting Muslim fundamentalist groups seemed a way of reducing PLO support, especially in Gaza, and at this stage there was no apparent armed fundamentalist threat. While the PLO factions tried to gain control of whatever civil structures the Israelis allowed in the occupied territories, the Islamic Jihad consolidated their own power base. The fundamentalists gathered increasing support in student unions, professional associations, and mosques.

The members of Islamic Jihad had split from the Muslim Brotherhood over the national question, believing that a Palestinian Islamic state could be created without an Islamic revolution in the rest of the Arab world. Support for Islamic Jihad's armed actions would eventually weaken support for the Brotherhood's non-militant line in some of the professional unions. However, the Brotherhood encouraged students to organize under the electoral umbrella of the Islamic Bloc. The Brotherhood also conducted pioneering social, cultural, and educational work under the authority of the Islamic Center in Gaza – headed by its founder, the Gaza Muslim Brotherhood leader, Sheikh Ahmed Yassin.

Islam was becoming a potent political challenge to the PLO's dominance of the Palestinian national cause, although as yet it lacked any prominent leadership. From 1984 onward, however, radical fundamentalists, calling themselves Islamic Jihad, began a series of

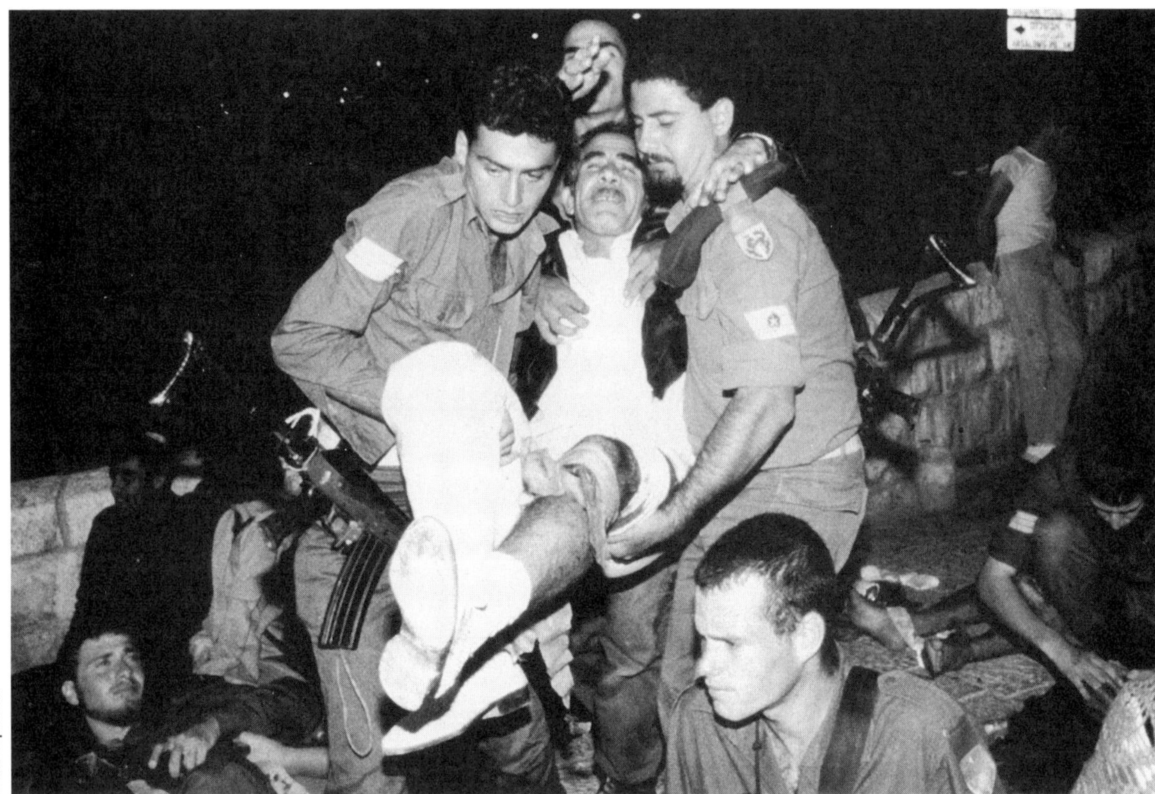

Frank Spooner

A wounded victim is helped to an ambulance after the Islamic Jihad attack at the "Gate of the Moors" in Jerusalem in October 1986.

small attacks on Israeli settlers in the Gaza Strip. They constituted a self-styled armed "Islamic vanguard."

THE GATE OF THE MOORS

On October 16, 1986, 68 army recruits were injured and one soldier's father was killed when two Palestinians threw hand grenades at an army inauguration ceremony at the Western Wall in Jerusalem's Old City. The Islamic Jihad claimed responsibility, as did several Fatah groups, for the "Gate of the Moors" attack. However, despite these claims, the incident was most certainly the work of Islamic Jihad.

The Muslim fundamentalists had arrived as a significant force with a proven ability to organize armed resistance in the occupied territories, where Israel, since 1968, had prevented the PLO from operating as terrorists. In Lebanon, where Israel had sought to destroy the PLO outright during the 1982 invasion, Muslim funadmentalists had already become the primary anti-Israeli guerrilla force. They would soon become the single biggest problem for Israeli forces.

Neil Partrick

SEE ALSO: RELIGIOUS EXTREMISM; ARAB NATIONALISM AND THE RISE OF FATAH; THE PALESTINIAN INTIFADA; ROOTS OF FUNDAMENTALIST TERRORISM; HAMAS.

FURTHER READING

- Abu Amr, Ziad. *Islamic Fundamentalism in the West Bank and Gaza: Muslim Brotherhood and Islamic Jihad.* Bloomington: Indiana University Press, 1994.
- Benvenisti, Meron. *Intimate Enemies: Jews and Arabs in a Shared Land.* Berkeley: University of California Press, 1995.
- Halabi, Rafik. *The West Bank Story: An Israeli Arab's View of Both Sides of a Tangled Conflict.* New York: Harcourt Brace, 1982.

CHAPTER ELEVEN

Middle Eastern Terrorism 1988-1996

Against a background of growing popular unrest among young Palestinians in the Israeli occupied territories, Middle Eastern terrorist organizations have continued to attack both Israel and its international supporters. These terrorist groups have been sponsored by various Arab states, notably Iran, Iraq, and Syria. The continued rise of Islamic fundamentalist terrorist activity has seen these groups hit Israeli, Western, and moderate Arab targets in their campaign to destroy the Jewish state and spread their message across the Middle East.

ARAB STATES AND TERRORISM IN THE 1990s

The symbol of Middle Eastern terrorism changed in the early 1990s from a Palestinian *fedayeen* (fighter) clad in a *keffiyah* (head scarf) brandishing a Kalashnikov assault rifle, to an Islamic militant hurrying to martyrdom with a suicide bomb strapped to his body. Out went the generation of leftist/nationalist, usually secular, terrorists; in came a new generation of religious extremists. Two events symbolized the changing face of Middle Eastern terrorism in the 1990s. In August 1994, Sudan handed over to France the international terrorist "Carlos the Jackal" (Illich Ramírez Sánchez). In March 1996, over 20 world leaders met at a "Summit of the Peacemakers" in Egypt to condemn Islamic extremist terrorism.

The changing face of terrorism also reflected the changing nature of Middle Eastern politics. In 1987, the region was still in the grip of the Cold War and there was no end in sight to the Arab-Israeli conflict. By 1996, the Cold War was over and the U.S. reigned supreme in the region. The Arab-Israeli peace process had made allies out of former enemies. Mainstream Palestinian leaders were working with Israeli, Jordanian, and Egyptian leaders to build a new Middle East under American auspices. Although they were opposed by a number of secular Palestinian groups, these latter had lost most of their influence. The main opposition came from religious fundamentalists, Jews in Israel and Muslims across the region.

KEY FACTS

- During the 1990s, religious motivations, rather than political or nationalist ones, became the dominating inspiration for terrorism in the region.
- Both Jews and Muslims employed terrorism to oppose the "peace process" developing between Israel and her former enemies in the Palestine Liberation Organization.
- Iran, Iraq, Libya, and Sudan all sponsored or carried out terrorist activities outside their home countries in the 1990s.
- With the end of anti-Soviet operations in Afghanistan in 1989, many Muslim fighters joined terror groups in Middle East countries.

STATE SPONSORSHIP OF TERROR

Of course, not everything changed. Libya, Iraq, and Syria continued to sponsor a variety of Palestinian and other groups in order to further their individual foreign policy agendas. Iranian-sponsored groups such as the Lebanese Hizb'allah were well established features on the regional scene.

Nonetheless, the early 1990s saw the culmination of a number of trends in regional and international politics that thrust terrorism into a new era. The old causes that had inspired terrorism since the 1960s now seemed irrelevant. Leftist and nationalist appeals with a track record of repeated disappointments could no longer mobilize young men in the Middle East to take up arms. In the 1990s, the only alternative to the region's governments, most of which were repressive, undemocratic, and economically incompetent, appeared to be Islam in its many guises. The U.S. and the European allies of Israel and of secular and conservative Arab regimes became responsible for the crisis of Arab societies in the eyes of Islamic Arab nationalists. At the same time, the Soviet withdrawal from Afghanistan left thousands of dedicated, and militarily expert, fundamentalist guerrillas at a loose end. Many of these men returned home and lent their expertise to the Islamic nationalist groups.

In this new era, men such as Carlos were an embarrassment to their sponsors. His breed of terrorist would no longer make history in the Middle East.

Rex Features

A member of the Islamic militant group Hamas lies shot dead after throwing grenades into a crowded Jerusalem street on October 9, 1994.

Instead, in the spring of 1996, a handful of fundamentalist suicide bombers striking at Israel almost brought the Middle East peace process to a halt.

THE PALESTINIAN QUESTION

These general changes of the period 1987-96 wrought fundamental transformations in the Palestinian-Israeli conflict. In 1987, a mass civil uprising – the Intifada – broke out in the occupied territories (the West Bank and the Gaza Strip) and this became the main focus of Palestinian-Israeli confrontation. The traditional pattern of armed terrorist attacks by Palestinian groups and Israeli retaliations continued in parallel with the Intifada. However, as the mainstream Palestine Liberation Organization (PLO) moved towards acceptance of a two-state solution, terrorist violence fell. During the 1991 Gulf War a number of Palestinian groups lined up with Iraq and threatened attacks on Israel, but most operations were thwarted.

As peace talks between Israel and the Palestinians began at the 1991 Madrid Conference, the pattern of terrorism shifted dramtically. After the 1993 conclusion of the Oslo peace accord between the PLO and the Israeli government, the mainstream Palestinian leadership and the governing Israeli Labor party cooperated in the struggle against extremists seeking to derail the peace process. With most of the Palestinian nationalist groups committed to the talks or winding down operations, Palestinian Islamic fundamentalists emerged as the main terrorist threat.

The new regional alignment, in which PLO chairman Yasser Arafat stood alongside Israeli leaders, was exemplified on March 13, 1996, when Palestinian and Israeli leaders attended the international summit conference in Egypt called in response to bombings in Israel by Hamas and Palestinian Islamic Jihad. The threat from militant Muslim groups was paralleled, however, by an unprecedented threat from extremist Jewish groups. The danger from this side was highlighted in 1995, when Israeli Prime Minister Yitzhak Rabin was assassinated by a Jewish fundamentalist opposed to the peace process.

Andrew Rathmell

SEE ALSO: CARLOS THE JACKAL; THE ORIGINS OF PALESTINIAN ISLAMIC JIHAD; THE PALESTINIAN INTIFADA; PALESTINIAN TERRORIST GROUPS AFTER 1988; PALESTINIAN ISLAMIC FUNDAMENTALISM; HAMAS; THE ISRAELI RESPONSE TO TERRORISM; THE CHANGING FACE OF TERRORISM.

FURTHER READING

- Dekmejian, R. Hrair. *Islam in Revolution, Fundamentalism in the Arab World.* 2nd ed. Syracuse, NY: Syracuse University Press, 1995.
- Rubin, Barry. *From War to Peace: Arab-Israeli Relations 1973-1993.* Brighton: Sussex Academic Press, and New York: New York University Press, 1994.
- Rubin, Barry. *Revolution with Victory? The Politics and History of the PLO.* Cambridge, MA: Harvard University Press, 1994.

THE PALESTINIAN INTIFADA

The mass civil unrest in the occupied territories of the West Bank and the Gaza Strip, known as the Intifada (an Arab word literally meaning "shaking off"), broke out in December 1987. An Israeli truck driver in the Gaza Strip crashed into a car carrying Palestinian workers. Harsh Israeli repression of the rioting that followed sparked off widespread mass protests which spread rapidly to the West Bank. The uprising undermined Israeli control. Tactics of the protesters ranged from non-cooperation, such as nonpayment of taxes and strikes, to demonstrations, riots, and attacks on Israeli soldiers and settlers. On the whole the protesters were armed with stones and similar implements but, as the struggle went on, they increasingly used weapons such as Molotov cocktails, explosives, and firearms.

THE FIGHT FOR LIBERATION

The Intifada was characteristically fought and led by Palestinian youths who, having grown up since 1967 under Israeli occupation, were frustrated at the failure of the established Palestinian groups to liberate their lands. The uprising was in many ways directed as much against the traditional Palestinian leaders as it was against the Israelis who were confiscating land and permanently settling in the occupied territories. The movement was only informally organized, though a Unified National Leadership of the Uprising did emerge. This body coordinated strike calls and issued statements after discussion between the various nationalist factions.

KEY FACTS

- Although most of the Intifada's activities are regarded as acts of civil violence, rather than terrorism, the presence of the Intifada has heightened Palestinian-Israeli tension, resulting in a number of terrorist incidents during 1990-91.
- By 1991, more Palestinians were being killed by Palestinian activists than by Israeli forces.

In 1988, 11 Israelis and more than 360 Palestinians were killed in clashes. In 1989, 432 Palestinians were killed, 304 by the Israeli Defense Forces (IDF) and Israeli settlers in the occupied territories, and the remainder by other Palestinians. Thirteen Israeli soldiers and civilians died. In 1990, 140 Palestinians were killed by the IDF and settlers, compared to ten Israelis. Casualties fell as a result of a lower profile adopted by the IDF early in the year, but tensions mounted after Saddam Hussein's invasion of Kuwait in August, 1990. On October 8, Israeli Border Guards killed 17 Palestinians in a running battle on the Haram al-Sharif (Temple Mount) in the Old City of Jerusalem. In 1991, mass violence fell as a result of tight Israeli security measures imposed during the Gulf War and the opening of Palestinian-Israeli peace talks. Nevertheless, 101 Palestinians were killed by Israeli troops or settlers, and Palestinians killed 12 Israelis.

TERRORISM IN THE INTIFADA

The majority of the casualties sustained during the Intifada did not arise from terrorism as such. Most of the incidents come under the heading of civil violence. Even in cases where specific armed attacks were carried out against people or property, the diffuse nature of authority in the uprising's leadership made it hard to attribute responsibility for some attacks. Many of them were carried out by individuals only loosely, if at all, linked to organizations.

However, there is no doubt that terror was an integral part of the Intifada. Stabbing, for example, became common. In three separate incidents in March, May, and September 1989, Palestinians stabbed to death five Israelis and injured five others. In July, a young Palestinian forced an Israeli bus off the road along the Jerusalem-Tel Aviv highway, killing 16 passengers. In the following years, many stabbing attacks took place, some carried out by individuals and others claimed by groups.

In October 1990, protesters stabbed to death three Israelis in Jerusalem and injured another three in Tel Aviv in December. On May 18, 1991, Palestinian Islamic

Jihad claimed a knife attack wounding three Israelis. In 1990 and 1991, organized and armed groups carried out a growing number of attacks, and bombings occurred with increasing regularity. Between May and July 1990, three pipe bombs exploded in different Israeli cities, killing two people and injuring 33, including foreign tourists.

In 1991, numerous small bombs and arson attacks signaled Palestinian support for Iraq and Saddam Hussein in his war against the American-led coalition. In September, a bomb at a market in Beersheba injured several people. Firearms were also used: in October, gunmen opened fire on an Israeli bus in the West Bank, killing two Israeli settlers and wounding six. Both the Popular Front for the Liberation of Palestine (PFLP) and the Palestinian Islamic Jihad claimed responsibility. In 1992, the use of guns and explosives by radical groups increased as popular unrest waned. At least 24 Israelis were killed in 1992, while 158 Palestinians were killed by Israeli forces.

Rex Features

West Bank Palestinian youths stone Israeli security forces in February 1988, during the first full year of the Intifada uprising.

THE EFFECTS OF THE UPRISING

The Intifada irrevocably changed the nature of the Palestinian-Israeli conflict. For the Palestinians, the uprising took the initiative out of the hands of the Palestine Liberation Organization (PLO) leadership in exile abroad and brought to the fore the interests of the Palestinians living in the occupied territories. Many of the "insiders" were amenable to compromise – willing to settle for a two-state solution, in which a Palestinian state was set up alongside Israel, rather than fight for the dream of an Arab state in the whole of Palestine. The PLO leadership was forced to pay less attention to the interests of the Palestinian refugees in Lebanon, who insisted on no compromise with Israel. (Israeli intelligence, however, believed that a key PLO leader, Abu Jihad, had organized the initial outbreak of Intifada violence.)

On the Israeli front, years of policing the Intifada eroded public morale and international support. The IDF and Israeli public came to realize that they could not maintain their hold over the occupied territories, except by engaging in the sort of repressive internal security policing that they found distasteful and dangerous. As the economic, military, social, and moral cost of repressing the Palestinians escalated, so the sentiment grew in Israel that, at the least, Gaza and some of the West Bank towns should be handed over to the Palestinians. At the same time, international opinion turned against the Israelis. Repeated television pictures of IDF troops beating Palestinian youngsters eroded international, and especially American, respect for Israel and contributed to a climate in which U.S. policy-makers could, if only tentatively, propose reducing American support for Israel. The combination of these factors meant that some at least in the Israeli political establishment and public were more willing to agree to a compromise solution.

Although these factors were important in the emergence of a negotiated solution to the conflict, their importance should not be exaggerated. By 1991, the Intifada was weakening through sheer exhaustion. Three years of hardship caused by a combination of Israeli repression, strikes, and economic problems had hit morale in the occupied territories. The Israeli forces also began to adopt a less aggressive stance, helping to reduce civil unrest. However, increasingly radical Palestinian youths had started to organize

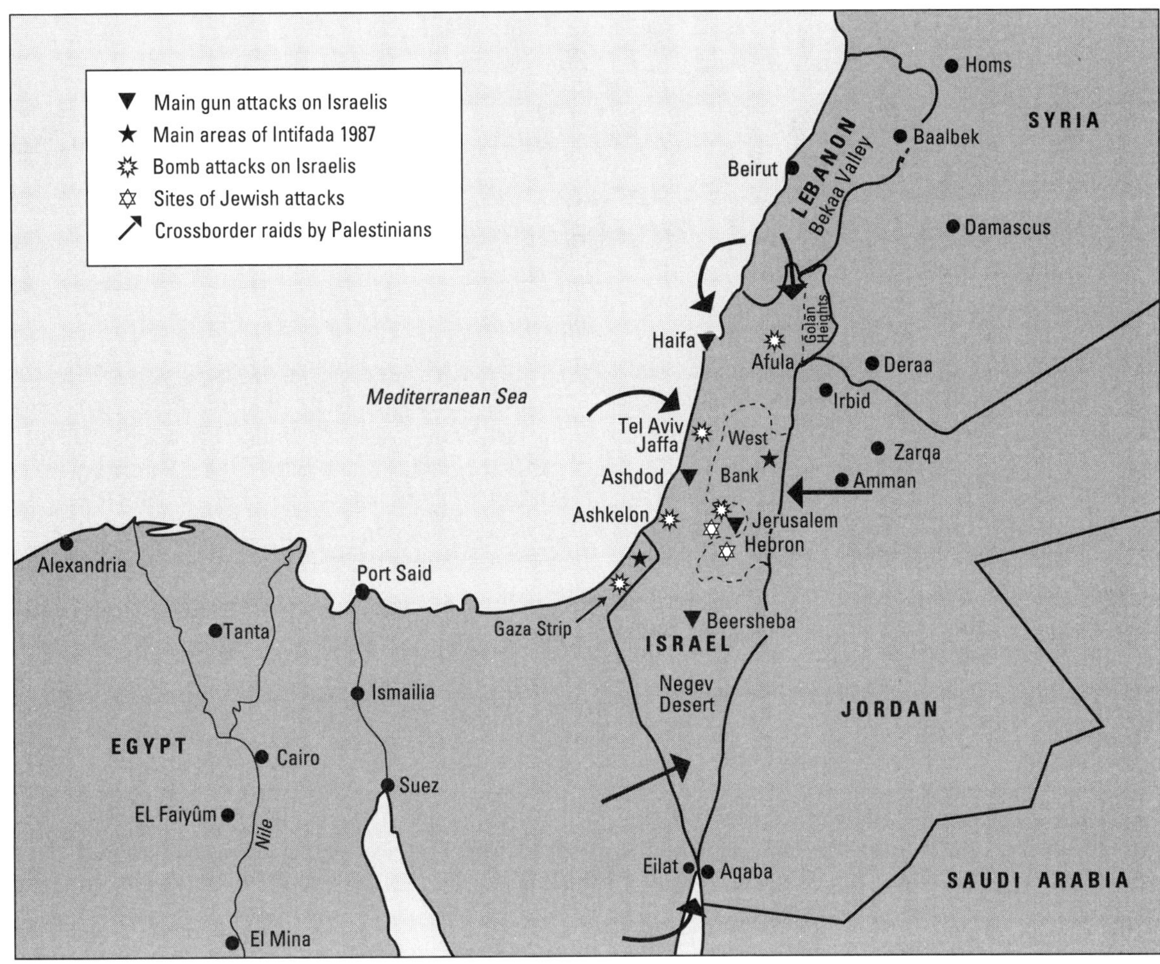

Main areas of the Intifada and terrorist activity during the period 1987-96.

themselves on paramilitary lines and carry out attacks on Israelis. Meanwhile, Israeli intelligence had created a class of Palestinian collaborators who served to break up Palestinian unity. In 1990, the number of alleged Palestinian collaborators killed by Palestinian activists (165) outnumbered those killed in clashes with the IDF and settlers (140). By 1992, the number of Palestinians killed by their fellows had risen to almost 200, greater than the number killed by Israel (158). The Intifada had not only changed the nature of Palestinian-Israeli politics, but, partly through its use of terror, had also brought the possibility of compromise closer.

Andrew Rathmell

SEE ALSO: THE PLO AND THE ARAB STATES; JEWISH TERROR IN THE WEST BANK; THE ORIGINS OF PALESTINIAN ISLAMIC JIHAD; ARAB STATES AND TERRORISM IN THE 1990s; PALESTINIAN TERRORIST GROUPS AFTER 1988; PALESTINIAN ISLAMIC FUNDAMENTALISM.

FURTHER READING

- Freedman, Robert O. *The Intifada: Its Impact on Israel, the Arab World, and the Superpowers.* Miami: Florida International University Press, 1991.
- Hunter, Robert F. *The Palestinian Uprising: A War by Other Means.* Berkeley: University of California Press, and London: Tauris, 1991.
- Khaled, al Hassan. "The PLO and the Intifada," in *American-Arab Affairs* 31 (Winter 1989-90): 42-48.

PALESTINIAN TERRORIST GROUPS AFTER 1988

Long-established forms of Palestinian nationalist terrorism continued in parallel with the Intifada, the mass civil uprising in the occupied territories of the West Bank and Gaza Strip, which began in 1987. The nationalist groups and splinter factions that had committed terrorist acts in the late 1960s were still active. Despite the loss of their base in southern Lebanon after the 1982 Israeli invasion of that country, Palestinians continued to mount attacks against Israel, against Israeli targets abroad, and against other countries. The changing nature of the Palestinian-Israeli conflict also led to changes on this battlefront.

In November 1988, the chairman of the Palestine Liberation Organization (PLO), Yasser Arafat, acceded to U.S. requests, renouncing terrorism and recognizing Israel's right to exist. But there was ambiguity over the extent of the PLO's commitment to talks. It was not clear whether it had renounced attacks on Israeli soldiers and settlers in Israel and the occupied territories, or just on Israelis in Israel itself. In addition, Arafat had control only over his own faction, Fatah. Other Palestinian factions, both inside and outside the PLO, persisted with attacks, sometimes motivated by the foreign policy of their sponsoring states.

KEY FACTS

- Between 1988 and 1994, Palestinian terrorist groups launched more than 50 raids into Israeli territory from bases in Lebanon, Syria, and Jordan.
- During the Gulf War of 1991, the Iraqi dictator Saddam Hussein threatened to use Palestinian terrorist groups to attack countries supporting the international coalition.
- The Israelis and the PLO met in secret talks in Norway in January 1993, establishing principles for the peace agreement signed later that year.

The main Palestinian nationalist groups involved in terrorist attacks during this period included the Popular Front for the Liberation of Palestine (PFLP), the Democratic Front for the Liberation of Palestine (DFLP), the Palestine Liberation Front (PLF), the Popular Front for the Liberation of Palestine – General Command (PFLP-GC) and Saiqa (both Syrian-sponsored groups), the Abu Nidal Organization (ANO), and the Abu Musa group.

RAIDS AGAINST ISRAEL

Some of these nationalist groups had networks and cells within the occupied territories of the West Bank and the Gaza Strip, but generally they found it hard to maintain armed cadres in the face of Israeli surveillance. Since the mainstream PLO groups had been expelled from Lebanon, their ability to mount operations from neighboring countries had been restricted. Nonetheless, many Fatah fighters infiltrated back into southern Lebanon, where they established bases in the Palestinian refugee camps there. Attacks across the Israeli border were launched from these camps, though on a far smaller scale than in the 1970s. In addition, a number of groups based in Damascus, Syria, such as the PFLP-GC, PFLP, and DFLP, operated with considerable freedom from Syrian-controlled areas of Lebanon. Some Palestinian groups operated from Jordan, although the Jordanian authorities sought to prevent cross-border raids.

Aside from Syria, various regional governments sponsored Palestinian militia groups and at times encouraged them to mount terrorist attacks. Iraq, Iran, and Libya were the prime state sponsors of Palestinian terrorist operations against Israel and related targets.

The classic tactic in the Palestinian campaign against Israel was the cross-border raid. In 1987, three major operations were attempted. In April, a group of Fatah fighters crossed from Lebanon, but three were

Hulton Getty Picture Collection

Machine-guns aloft, vigilantes of Fatah Hawks, surrounded by masked comrades, dominate a crowd during a rally for PLO chairman Yasser Arafat in November 1994.

killed in a firefight, along with two Israeli soldiers. In July, three infiltrators from Lebanon were apprehended, two of them from Saiqa. In December, three terrorists from the Abu Abbas faction of the PLF entered Israel from Jordan but were captured. In 1988, two Palestinian gunmen crossed from Lebanon into northern Israel and attacked a civilian truck, wounding the driver. In 1989, a dozen cross-border raids were attempted by Palestinian factions, though none succeeded in killing Israelis.

In 1990, the PLF attempted a seaborne raid on the Tel Aviv beachfront. Four terrorists were killed and 12 were captured by the Israelis. A further dozen or so cross-border raids were attempted from Lebanon, but none of them were successful.

In 1991, there were about 20 cross-border raids by Palestinians from Lebanon, Jordan, and Egypt. Most were intercepted by the Israeli Defense Forces (IDF). In April, a cross-border raid from Jordan left an Israeli farmer dead and three others injured.

In September, Fatah fighters landed by boat in southern Lebanon and kidnapped officers from the United Nations Interim Force in Lebanon (UNIFIL) after failing to penetrate the border. In the ensuing gun-battle involving the IDF, its Lebanese allies, and the terrorists, one UNIFIL officer was killed and five were wounded. In November, the IDF killed four Palestinian fighters in the Negev desert.

In 1992, there were seven attempted border raids, carried out by Fatah, the DFLP, and Palestinian Islamic Jihad. A seaborne raid near Eilat in May left one Israeli dead. In 1993, there was only one successful infiltration attempt. On December 29, a team from the Abu Musa group, a rebel faction of Fatah opposed to Arafat, entered northern Israel, but the three men were killed by Israeli forces. In 1994, when compromise was in the air, the only raid was in March by four DFLP fighters, who were intercepted by the Israelis.

Palestinian nationalist groups also carried out attacks through their cells based in the occupied territories. In March 1988, three Palestinians, reportedly members of Force 17, the internal security unit of Fatah, hijacked a bus near Beersheba and killed three civilians. In August, the PLO claimed a grenade attack in Haifa that injured 25. In July 1991, the PFLP and the DFLP claimed responsibility for Gaza shootings that wounded Israeli drivers.

THE EFFECTS OF COMPROMISE

After the September 13, 1993, signing of the Declaration of Principles between the PLO and Israel, factions loyal to Arafat were ordered to cease their armed operations. Renegade members of the Fatah Hawks, a vigilante group in the occupied territories, were nonetheless behind the unauthorized murders of an Israeli settler in October and two more settlers in December. PLO member groups that rejected the peace deal, notably the PFLP and DFLP, also continued their attacks.

Another long-established Palestinian method was to attack Israeli targets in third countries. Such attacks were, however, much less prevalent than they had been in previous years. In May 1988, the ANO was probably responsible for an attempt to bomb the Israeli embassy in Cyprus. In October 1989, a Belgian Jewish leader was killed. This attack has also been linked to Abu Nidal.

Fatah's deputy military commander, Abu Jihad, believed to be responsible for the Intifada and for the killing of Palestinian collaborators, was himself killed by Israeli intelligence agents in April 1988.

Terrorism directed against officials of Palestinian nationalist groups has been carried out both by rival Palestinian factions, often sponsored by Arab states, and by Israel. Few of these attacks are claimed, and it is rarely possible to discern the links among the Arab intelligence services, the radical Palestinian factions, and the Israeli intelligence services to identify the perpetrator. In 1988, four PLO officials were killed by a car-bomb in Cyprus, and a ship chartered to carry Palestinian refugees to Israel was bombed, also in Cyprus. Both attacks may have been carried out by Israeli agents.

Abu Jihad (the code name of Khalil al-Wazir) was deputy military commander of Fatah and director of Force 17. On April 16, 1988, Israeli commandos in collaboration with a team from Mossad (Israel's foreign intelligence bureau) shot Abu Jihad along with three aides at his house in Tunis. Israel believed Abu Jihad was controlling the Intifada and coordinating the killing of Palestinian collaborators – a serious threat to Israel's intelligence capabilities in the occupied territories. Mossad located Abu Jihad's residence and carried out surveillance tasks. Israeli gunboats, backed by aircraft, then carried a commando team to a position off the Tunisian coast. The commandos met the Mossad team, then entered Abu Jihad's house and shot him. The raid aroused worldwide condemnation, but Israel justified it as a strike on a military target.

On January 14, 1991, Abu Iyad (Salah Khalaf), the PLO's intelligence chief, was shot dead. He was killed along with PLO security chief Abu Hol (Hayel Abdel Hamid) and another aide, Muhammad Fakr Omari, by a Palestinian bodyguard, Hamza Abu Zeid. In a trial held by the PLO, which condemned the assassin to death, Abu Zeid reportedly confessed to working for ANO. Abu Iyad had masterminded splits within the ANO in 1989, which led to the execution of ANO 150 members, and had also attacked its bases in southern Lebanon. In retaliation, Abu Nidal placed Abu Zeid in the household of Abu Hol with orders to kill Abu Iyad. It has been suggested that Iraqi President Saddam Hussein encouraged the murder, as he objected to Abu Iyad's desire that the PLO distance itself from Baghdad in the prelude to the 1991 Gulf War.

Andrew Rathmell

SEE ALSO: THE POPULAR FRONT FOR THE LIBERATION OF PALESTINE; THE PLO AND THE ARAB STATES; ISRAELI RAIDS ON THE PLO; THE ORIGINS OF PALESTINIAN ISLAMIC JIHAD; THE PALESTINIAN INTIFADA; PALESTINIAN ISLAMIC FUNDAMENTALISM; JEWISH TERRORISM IN THE 1990s; IRAQI SPONSORSHIP OF TERRORISM; IRANIAN SPONSORSHIP OF TERRORISM.

FURTHER READING

- Hunter, Robert. F. *The Palestinian Uprising: A War by Other Means.* Berkeley: University of California Press, and London: Tauris, 1991.
- Inbari, Pinhas. *The Palestinians between Terrorism and Statehood.* Brighton: Sussex Academic Press, 1996.
- Lederman, Jim. *Battlelines: The American Media and the Intifada.* Boulder, CO: Westview, 1993.
- Rubin, Barry. *From War to Peace: Arab-Israeli Relations, 1973-1993.* Brighton: Sussex Academic Press, and New York: New York University Press, 1994.
- Rubin, Barry. *Revolution until Victory? The Politics and History of the PLO.* Cambridge, MA: Harvard University Press, 1994.
- Salem, Elie Adib. *Violence and Diplomacy in Lebanon.* New York: St. Martin's Press, 1995.

PALESTINIAN ISLAMIC FUNDAMENTALISM

Between 1988 and 1996, the leading forces in the Palestinian movement were two Muslim fundamentalist movements, Hamas (the Islamic Resistance Movement) and Palestinian Islamic Jihad. They had pushed aside the traditional main advocates of armed struggle, those nationalist Palestinian groups linked to the Palestine Liberation Organization (PLO). Hamas and Palestinian Islamic Jihad have emerged as hard-line opponents of Israel and its Western and Arab allies. They also see themselves in competition with the secular PLO for control of the Palestinian people.

Hamas emerged in 1987 out of the ranks of the Muslim Brotherhood. When the Intifada (civil unrest in the occupied territories) broke out, Sheikh Ahmed Yassin, founder of the Gaza Islamic Center, and a number of other brotherhood leaders in Gaza, called for resistance to Israel. Their first leaflet was issued on December 14, 1987, but they did not identify themselves as Hamas until January 1988. The Hamas charter, issued on August 18, 1988, insists that Palestine is in the trust of the Muslim world and that "it is not right to give it up nor any part of it." Hamas calls for the uprooting of Israel and the establishment of an Islamic state in its place. It characterizes peace initiatives as a waste of time and an absurdity, and calls for all Muslims to engage in *jihad*, or holy war.

SUMMARY

- The fundamentalist Hamas and Islamic Jihad came to prominence during the uprising known as the Intifada.
- Hamas, the more important of the two groups, opposes Yasser Arafat's Palestinian Authority.
- Hamas suicide bombings have stunted the PLO-Israeli peace process and caused hundreds of deaths.

Hamas's popularity grew during the late 1980s and early 1990s because it was able to provide schools, medical centers, and social welfare activities that were otherwise lacking in the occupied territories.

Hamas also both benefited from, and promoted a return to, traditional Islamic values that appealed to many of the disoriented Palestinian youth. At the same time, its uncompromising stance towards Israel attracted many Palestinians who did not agree with the compromise approach of PLO chairman Yasser Arafat and who wanted to continue the fight against Israel. With its daring military operations and use of suicide bombers, Hamas appeared to many to be the main defender of Palestinian rights during a period when many Palestinians perceived the peace process as being weighted against them.

RECRUITING IN GAZA

The overpopulated and poverty-stricken Gaza Strip became Hamas's main base and recruiting ground. However, the movement also gained a following in the West Bank and among Palestinians in Jordan and Lebanon. Hamas enjoyed support from Syria and Iran, although it remained unclear exactly how much help was given. The movement certainly had offices in both countries and the governments in both Damascus and Tehran gave it verbal backing. Much of Hamas's funding came from supporters in the West and in other Muslim countries, notably Saudi Arabia. No evidence supporting American and Israeli claims of Syrian and Iranian funding has yet emerged. As a movement advocating a return to Islamic social values, Hamas could call on sympathy among Muslims worldwide opposed to the secular attitude of the PLO.

Ironically, in its early days, Hamas was also supported by the Israeli authorities. At first, it emphasized its social activities over its military aims, and the Israelis viewed it as a useful counter to the PLO. But

Rex Features

Some of the 400 Palestinian fundamentalist leaders that Israel deported to south Lebanon in December 1992 pray in the open air. They were punished for the murder of an Israeli soldier by militant Muslim terrorists. Most were later allowed to return.

this strategy of divide and rule backfired. By the early 1990s Hamas, with perhaps 40 percent of the popular support in Gaza, had become Israel's deadliest enemy.

PALESTINIAN ISLAMIC JIHAD

Palestinian Islamic Jihad emerged in the late 1970s in the Gaza Strip, founded by two Palestinian refugees influenced by the Muslim Brotherhood, Fathi al-Shaqaqi and Abd al-Aziz al-Auda. Palestinian Islamic Jihad is committed to the establishment of an Islamic state in Palestine, the destruction of Israel, and is opposed to Western influence in the Middle East. It is unclear whether Islamic Jihad is a single organization or a loose affiliation of small groups. It does not see itself as an alternative to the PLO, but criticizes the unwillingness of the PLO to continue the armed struggle against Israel. The group seems to command little popular support, and the PLO and Israel both claim that it is reliant on Iran.

Islamic Jihad terrorists were responsible for a number of knife attacks during the Intifada, and have since mounted a variety of assaults and suicide attacks on Israeli targets. In February 1990, Islamic Jihad terrorists ambushed an Israeli tour bus in Egypt. They killed nine Israelis and wounded 17 other people. The group has also carried out raids into Israel, and threatened U.S. targets.

As the PLO-Israeli peace process advanced, Hamas and Islamic Jihad became more violent. Hamas concentrated at first on operations against Israeli military forces. In early December 1992, it ambushed soldiers in Hebron and Gaza, killing four. In mid-December, an off-duty border guard was kidnapped just outside Tel Aviv and killed. In retaliation, Israel deported some 400 fundamentalist leaders to Lebanon, but they were not allowed into the country and were forced to set up camp on border hillsides. Half the deportees were allowed to return in September 1993, and most of those remaining were returned in December 1993.

Rex Features

Hamas founder Sheikh Ahmed Yassin was sentenced in 1989 to fifteen years' imprisonment for stockpiling automatic weapons and plotting the murder of 300 people.

At the same time as the last deportees returned, Hamas and Islamic Jihad intensified their operations in an attempt to derail the peace process. The two groups were responsible for the majority of Israeli casualties in the year – some 65 dead and 390 injured. Between September and December, Hamas claimed 13 attacks, several of them suicide bombings. On October 4, 1993, a Hamas bomber rammed his explosive-laden car into an Israeli bus, injuring 30 people.

During 1994, Hamas killed more than 50 Israelis and wounded over 150. Thirteen soldiers and settlers were killed in individual knife, axe, and shooting attacks. On April 6, 1994, Hamas took revenge for the Hebron massacre with a car-bomb in Afula that killed seven Israelis. Another bomb in Hadera also killed seven people. Israel responded by sealing off the occupied territories of the West Bank and the Gaza Strip in order to hurt the Palestinian population economically and to prevent bombers from entering Israel proper.

In October, Hamas kidnapped an Israeli Defense Forces (IDF) soldier and demanded the release of Hamas founder Sheikh Ahmed Yassin, who had been jailed in 1989, as well as 200 activists. In a botched rescue mission by IDF commandos on October 15, three kidnappers were killed, along with the hostage and an IDF officer. On the 9th October, Hamas opened fire indiscriminately on the streets of Jerusalem, killing two people and wounding 14. On 19th October, a Hamas suicide bomber blew himself up with 22 passengers in a Tel Aviv bus, wounding at least 48 other people. On December 25, Hamas bombed an IDF bus in Jerusalem, wounding 13 people.

HITTING ISLAMIC JIHAD

On November 2, 1994, Israeli agents killed an Islamic Jihad leader, Hani Abed, in Gaza with a car-bomb. Islamic Jihad retaliated with a suicide bicycle-bomber who killed three IDF officers near the settlement of Netzarim in the Gaza Strip. Earlier in the year, in April, Islamic Jihad had shot dead two Israelis at a bus stop in Ashdod. In response to the Hamas and Islamic Jihad attacks, Israel demanded that Arafat's Palestinian Authority crack down on Hamas and Islamic Jihad activists in the area controlled by Arafat.

Arafat was happy to take on Islamic Jihad since he regarded them as Iranian-backed extremists with no popular base. He recognized, however, that Hamas had wide support. During 1994, he tried to reach an accommodation with Hamas's political wing while reining in the group's terrorist activities. Arafat's main concern was to avoid a Palestinian civil war, but his crackdowns nearly caused a surge of violence. In November 1994, the authority's forces killed 16 demonstrators while dispersing a fundamentalist rally in Gaza.

On January 22, 1995, two Islamic Jihad suicide bombers killed 20 Israeli soldiers and a civilian at Beit Lid, injuring 68 others. In April, six Palestinians were killed in an explosion in a Gaza City apartment complex. The dead included top Hamas military man Kamal Kahil, who was wanted in Israel for a series of bombings and by the Palestinian authorities for the murder of 16 collaborators. A week later, fundamentalist suicide bombers killed eight Israelis in two attacks in the Gaza Strip. In response, Arafat arrested around 200 suspects. Hamas, however, went on with its campaign. On July 24, 1995, a suicide bomber killed six Israelis on a Tel Aviv bus. In a similar attack on August 21, six more Israelis died.

Hulton Getty Picture Collection

Hamas suicide bomber Aymen Radhi blew himself up and injured 13 people at a Jerusalem bus stop on Christmas Day, 1994.

Meanwhile, Arafat demanded that Israel speed up the redeployment of its troops as agreed earlier. On September 24, 1995, Israel and the PLO signed an interim agreement at the Egyptian resort of Taba. The agreement extended the Palestinian Authority's rule in the occupied West Bank, effectively giving it control of over some 1.3 million people. The agreement led to the Israeli army withdrawing from six West Bank towns and over 440 villages, although it remained in Hebron to protect 415 Jewish settlers living in the middle of the town. The Taba agreement paved the way for the Palestinian elections held on January 20, 1996. In these elections, Arafat was elected president of the authority and Fatah supporters won a majority of seats in the 88-member legislative council.

This electoral victory gave Arafat more authority in his dealings with Hamas. The fact that 75 percent of the Palestinian population had voted despite Hamas's call to boycott the poll enabled Arafat to negotiate from a position of strength. However, splits within Hamas had begun to emerge between the Hamas leadership, who were prepared to open a dialogue with Arafat, and the hardcore members of the movement who were strongly opposed to any such peace negotiations. These splits within Hamas and the continued activities of Islamic Jihad undermined Arafat's authority and soon provoked a crisis in the peace process.

On October 26, 1995, Fathi Shaqaqi, Islamic Jihad's founder, was shot dead in Malta by suspected Mossad agents. He had been in transit between Libya and Damascus. Two IDF medics were killed in an ambush in the West Bank by the hitherto unknown group Mujahedin al-Islami. However, the combined Israeli-Palestinian Authority offensive against Hamas and Islamic Jihad appeared to bear fruit during late 1995. The Palestinian authorities rounded up hundreds of fundamentalist activists and pressed the Gulf states to end their financial support for militant Palestinian Islamic groups. Israel, with Palestinian intelligence help, rounded up Hamas military cells in the West Bank. Meanwhile, Arafat began to engage in a dialogue with Hamas's political leadership. A cease-fire was enforced from mid-1995 until early 1996 and the Palestinian Authority arranged an amnesty for some Hamas activists in Palestinian jails.

On January 5, 1996, Yahya Ayyash, Hamas's top bomb-maker involved in many of the suicide bombings, was killed by a booby-trapped cellular phone. Israel did little to hide the fact that Shin Bet, the Israeli security service, was behind the operation. Revenge attacks predictably followed. On February 25, Hamas claimed two suicide-bomb attacks. One in Jerusalem ripped apart a bus, killing 25 and injuring 55 people. An hour later, a second suicide-bomb in Ashkelon injured some 35 Israelis. Hamas claimed that the bombs were in retaliation for the 1994 Hebron massacre as well as for the assassination of Ayyash.

In the wake of the bombings, Israel imposed a clampdown on the Palestinian areas, and the U.S. and Israel called on Arafat to dismantle Hamas. Arafat condemned the attacks as terrorism and launched his police forces against Hamas's military wing, the Izz al-Din al-Qassam Brigades. The Palestinian Authority arrested more than 470 suspected militants.

HAMAS HALTS THE PEACE PROCESS

On March 3 and 4, 1996, a second wave of suicide-bombings struck at the heart of Israeli society, again carried out by militants in Hamas and Islamic Jihad.

Rex Features

A 22-pound Hamas bomb, packed with nails, killed 23 passengers riding this bus as it drove through the center of Jerusalem on February 25, 1996.

The bombings killed 32 people in Jerusalem and Tel Aviv. The Tel Aviv bomb exploded in the heart of the town's Dizengoff shopping area during the Jewish festival of Purim. Thirteen people died, and about 125 were wounded. A caller to Israeli Radio stated that "today's attack is a reply after the government of the so-called Prime Minister and Defense Minister Shimon Peres declared war on Hamas. Let him know that if he does not negotiate with Hamas and if he tries to destroy it there will be even bloodier attacks."

These devastating attacks halted the peace process and led to a major crisis. Israeli troops entered authority-controlled areas and imposed an internal closure on the Palestinian areas, which meant that the IDF controlled all movement between villages and towns in Gaza and the West Bank. All adult males were rounded up and questioned in several towns. Israeli President Ezer Weizman justified these collective punishment measures, saying, "if we cannot find the needle" of Hamas then "we must burn the haystack" of the Palestinian people. Israeli troops also detained over 250 suspects and destroyed the homes of the families of suicide bombers.

The Israeli government began to implement a plan to separate Israel once and for all from Palestinian areas. Israeli troops and police began to set up a mile-wide buffer zone separating the West Bank from Israel. Part of this zone was to be fenced off, and the rest controlled by patrols and surveillance devices.

ARAFAT ENDS DIALOGUE WITH HAMAS

Since the Hamas militants had successfully quashed any opportunity for peace dialogue between Arafat and the Hamas moderates, Arafat had no choice but to join in Israel's declared "war" on Hamas. On March 3, the Palestinian Authority banned six Palestinian militias, including Hamas's Izz al-Din al-Qassam Brigades and Palestinian Islamic Jihad's Qassam militia. He declared that he would "cooperate fully with Israel to wipe out terrorism." On March 6, PLO official Mahmud Abbas also declared "there is now no

Rex Features

Hamas terrorists wielding weapons swear an oath on the Koran during a secret ceremony.

dialogue with either Hamas's political or military wings." Several days later, after being briefed by the CIA, Arafat told a Palestinian rally that he believed the recent suicide operations had been ordered by Iran. This statement reflected his new determination to treat Hamas as a foreign-inspired enemy.

In well-publicized operations, Palestinian police raided mosques, Islamic centers, and universities, and detained hundreds of suspects. The Izz al-Din al-Qassam militia responded by promising more violence. On March 9, it issued a statement, saying, "Qassam has decided to resume its martyrdom attacks against the Zionists." It warned that the Palestinian Authority's actions "will completely destroy any understanding or future agreement" between Hamas and the PLO. These statements showed that the political leaders had lost control of their military counterparts. Hamas political leader Mahmoud al-Zahar told a Gaza press conference that "we are demanding a stop to the military actions against Israeli targets," but added, "we have no organizational relation to the military wing." His calls accordingly had no effect.

Andrew Rathmell

SEE ALSO: THE PLO AND THE ARAB STATES; THE ORIGINS OF PALESTINIAN ISLAMIC JIHAD; THE PALESTINIAN INTIFADA; PALESTINIAN TERRORIST GROUPS AFTER 1988; PALESTINIAN ISLAMIC FUNDAMENTALISM.

FURTHER READING

- Abu-Amr, Ziad. *Islamic Fundamentalism in the West Bank and Gaza: Muslim Brotherhood and Islamic Jihad.* Bloomington: Indiana University Press, 1994.
- Dekmejian, R. Hrair. *Islam in Revolution: Fundamentalism in the Arab World.* 2nd ed. Syracuse, NY: Syracuse University Press, 1995.
- Sivan, Emmanuel, and Menachem Friedman. *Religious Radicalism and Politics in the Middle East.* Albany: State University of New York Press, 1990.

JEWISH TERRORISM IN THE 1990s

Jewish terrorism since the 1980s has been the most radical expression of religious and nationalist fervor in Israel. Some of the terrorists are the direct offspring of right-wing political movements, others simply form groups for terrorist purposes. Still others have carried out violent acts independently.

The extremist wing of the Zionist movement has been prepared to use terrorism to achieve its goals since Zionism was created in the last quarter of the nineteenth century. Zionist terrorists fought fanatically during the Arab-Israeli war of 1948-49. In the 1970s, a number of radical groups attacked Palestinian moderates. In the late 1980s, hard-line Israeli settlers in the occupied territories of the West Bank and Gaza Strip were responsible for a great deal of violence, generally against Palestinian civilians. In addition, organized groups of radicals emerged. As the Israeli-Palestinian peace process accelerated in the early 1990s, these radicals escalated their attacks on Palestinians and also turned their guns on fellow Jews.

Jewish terrorism is almost exclusively domestic. Apart from isolated attempts during the 1970s and 1980s to target representatives and members of the Arab and Palestinian communities in the U.S., Jewish terrorism has mainly been perpetrated within Israel and the occupied territories of the West Bank and the Gaza Strip. Among the most dramatic attempts are the assault on the Palestinian heads of the Committee for National Direction in 1980, the shooting of Emil Greenzweig at a Peace Now rally in 1982, the attack on the praying worshippers at the Tomb of the Patriarch in 1994, and the assassination of Israeli Prime Minister Yitzhak Rabin in 1995. Other attacks have consisted of "routine" vengeance and retribution; planned harassment of and attacks on individuals; the sabotaging of property; and "quick-on-the-trigger" vigilante reactions in the daily interaction between Israeli settlers and Palestinians inhabitants in the occupied territories.

Terrorist tactics have not been consistent, and have been employed both by members of the large movements and by individual terrorists carrying out isolated attacks.

KEY FACTS

- In 1991, the Kach Party fire-bombed the American Cultural Center in Jerusalem.
- Kach Party member Dr. Baruch Goldstein opened fire on Palestinian Arabs in a mosque in Hebron, killing 29 and wounding more than 200 Palestinian Arabs in February 1994.
- In 1995, right-wing Zionist Yigal Amir shot Prime Minister Yitzhak Rabin at a peace rally.

MOTIVATION OF JEWISH TERRORISTS

The motivation of all the Jewish terrorists is to be found in both Jewish history and religious faith. The trauma of the Holocaust perhaps explains the intransigence of Jewish terrorists regarding compromise in the Palestinian-Israeli conflict. The history of exile and statelessness, tied to the experience of genocide have resulted in the lesson that might is right, and that terrorism may help guarantee Jewish survival.

The ideological base of the terrorists in the 1980s lay in the "rejectionist" wing in Israeli politics, hostile to any peace settlement with the Palestinians and the Palestine Liberation Organization (PLO). Gush Emunim (Bloc of the Faithful), the largest ideological movement promoting Jewish settlement in the occupied territories, serves as the moral and legitimating anchor to a number of other organizations working to revive the biblical Kingdom of Israel.

Having interpreted the 1967 conquest of the old city of Jerusalem and the recapture of the Wailing Wall as divinely inspired, and as the signal for accelerating the

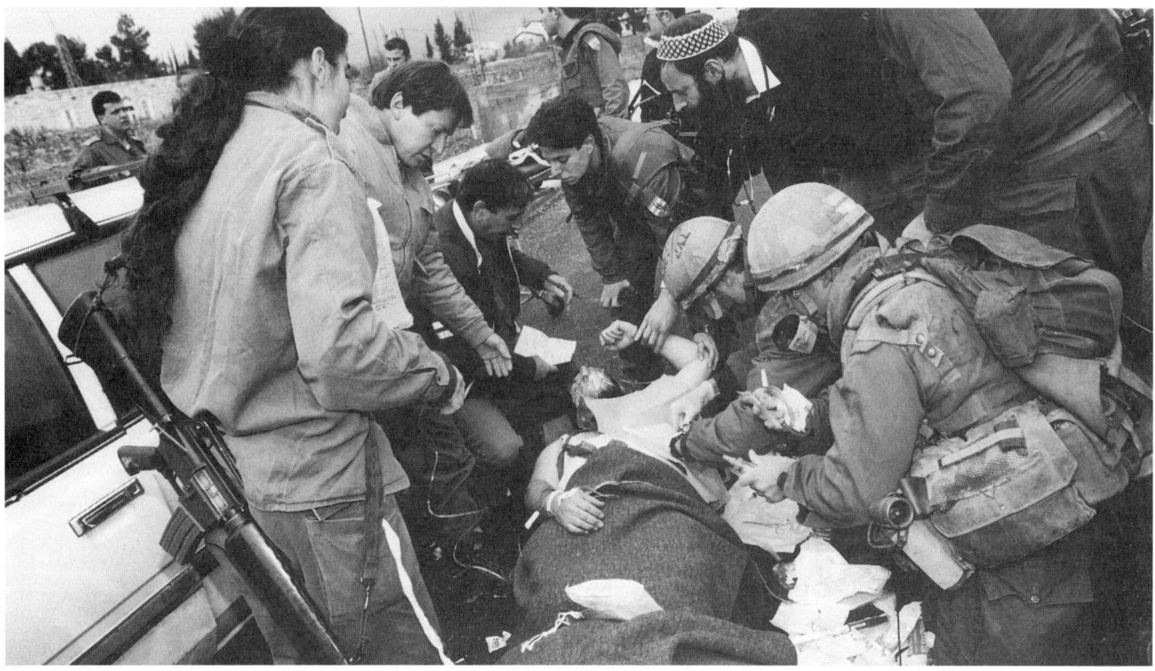

Rex Features

national and religious redemption of Israel, such ideologues were first organized within the main Israeli National Religious Party (*Mafdal*) and the secular Movement for the Greater Land of Israel. The "elite" of the Jewish terrorists, the so-called "Jewish Underground," emerged from this core.

TERROR TACTICS AND AIMS

Foreign terrorism by Zionist extremists has been limited by their reluctance to draw media attention to their cause. World opinion regards Zionist ambitions to be satisfied by the existence of an Israeli state. Claims to the occupied territories easily can be characterized as plain greed in the propaganda war between Israel and the PLO. As a result, the targets of Zionist terror have largely been domestic. Here, elements of the Israeli political establishment are sympathetic to the goals of Zionist terrorists, although not to their means. The terrorists can therefore believe they are assisting the government to redirect its policies.

Indeed, accusations of double standards have been leveled at Israeli government treatment of Jewish attacks on Palestinians in view of the lenient sentencing applied to convicted Jewish terrorists. For instance, in December 1990, the Israeli courts released after only six years in prison, three members of the Jewish Underground who had killed three Arabs and

Dr. Baruch Goldstein (bearded, right) assists in an emergency only days before unleashing his own terrorist assault in a mosque in Hebron, in February 1994.

injured 30 others. At the same time, a Palestinian was sentenced to 16 life terms for killing 16 people in an attack on an Israeli bus. Such apparent double standards caused serious problems during the Intifada, when Jewish settlers were seemingly allowed by the Israeli Defense Forces (IDF) to go on violent rampages in Palestinian towns. Worse, the IDF and Shin Bet, the Israeli security service, were unprepared for the upsurge of radical Jewish violence that upset the peace process in 1994 and 1995.

The most prevalent form of violence by radical settlers was attacks on Palestinian property and individuals in the occupied territories. On numerous occasions in the late 1980s and early 1990s, armed settlers "retaliated" for Palestinian terrorist attacks by smashing Palestinian-owned cars and store windows. On other occasions, settlers shot Palestinians, sometimes allegedly in response to stone-throwing incidents. In 1993, rioting settlers killed one Palestinian and injured 18 others in the West Bank.

A leading Israeli radical activist was Rabbi Moshe Levinger. He was sentenced in January 1991 to four

Rabbi Meir Kahane, the influential leader of the Zionist anti-Arab Kach movement, was shot dead by a fundamentalist Muslim in New York in 1990.

months in prison for assault against a Palestinian family living in Hebron. The sentence was subsequently reduced.

THE SICARII AND KACH

A further group that emerged during this period was the Sicarii (daggermen), who named themselves after an extremist Jewish group from the time of Christ. In April 1989, they placed a bomb near Jaffa Gate in Jerusalem that killed two Palestinians and wounded two others. In December, they claimed responsibility for burning the car and apartment of a professor at Hebrew University. In 1990, the Sicarii threatened four members of the Knesset, the Israeli parliament, who had backed a Palestinian peace demonstration. They also planted a dummy grenade under the car of the wife of the then deputy prime minister, Shimon Peres.

A more influential group was the Kach movement, led until 1990 by Rabbi Meir Kahane. Kach was virulently anti-Arab. Kahane was murdered in New York in 1990, and Kach subsequently issued death threats against moderate Israeli and Palestinian leaders alike. In 1991, Kach activists were probably behind the fire-bombing of the American Cultural Center in Jerusalem. Kahane's son, Binyamin, was arrested in Madrid in October 1991, after he threatened to blow up the Madrid Peace Conference.

In 1992, Kach activists assaulted Palestinian leader Faisal Husseini in a Jerusalem courtroom. In November, they were probably behind a grenade attack on a market in Jerusalem. In 1993, Kach stepped up its attacks in response to the signing in September of the peace accord in Washington between Yitzhak Rabin and PLO chairman Yasser Arafat. On October 24, it set off two bombs near the French embassy in Tel Aviv in retaliation for Arafat's visit to Paris. On November 8, a Kach settler shot and injured two Palestinians in the West Bank.

On February 25, 1994, an American-born Jewish settler perpetrated the bloodiest single terrorist act yet carried out by Jewish extremists. Baruch Goldstein, an extreme adherent of Kach living in the Qiryat Arba settlement near Hebron, entered the Ibrahimi Mosque/Tomb of the Patriarchs in Hebron and opened fire on Palestinian worshipers. He killed 29 people and wounded more than 200 before he was beaten to death. In the wake of the attack, the PLO suspended the peace process and riots broke out across the occupied territories. Twenty-seven Palestinians were killed as the IDF imposed a curfew on Palestinians, though not on the extreme Zionist settlers in and around Hebron. Peace talks were only resumed when 160 European observers were deployed in the town.

PROBLEMS WITH IDF SECURITY

In the Israeli enquiry that followed the mosque massacre the IDF was severely criticised for its lax security measures and its tolerance of Zionist radicals. The site was a notorious flashpoint, since it was holy to both Jews and Muslims and there was constant tension between settlers and Palestinians at the site, despite the presence of an IDF guard. At the enquiry, it emerged that IDF soldiers had orders not to fire on Israelis, even if they were attacking Palestinians.

After the Hebron massacre, the Israeli security services paid closer attention to extremist Zionist groups. Kach and Kahane Chai (Kahane Lives) were banned in Israel when they supported Goldstein's actions. The groups' leaders were arrested after calling

Hulton Getty Picture Collection

for attacks on Palestinians and the Israeli government. In September, 11 Jewish extremists were charged with planning terrorist attacks on Palestinians. The main focus of the Israeli security services, however, remained radical Palestinian groups.

The lack of attention paid to Israel's extremists came home to roost on November 4, 1995, when a right-wing Zionist extremist, Yigal Amir, shot Prime Minister Rabin dead at a peace rally. It emerged subsequently that Amir had not acted alone and a number of other extremists were also arrested. Most shocking to Israel was evidence that there was widespread support for Amir among radical settlers in the occupied territories. Many right-wing Zionists regarded the peace process as a surrender to the Arabs, and death threats were made against other senior government officials.

Andrew Rathmell

SEE ALSO: THE BIRTH OF JEWISH TERRORISM; ARAB NATIONALISM AND THE RISE OF FATAH; JEWISH TERROR IN THE WEST BANK; THE ISRAELI RESPONSE TO TERRORISM.

President Bill Clinton welcomes the historic handshake between Yitzhak Rabin and Yasser Arafat after they signed a peace accord in Washington, DC, in September, 1993. Rabin's willingness to negotiate with Palestinians led to his assassination by a Zionist terrorist in November 1995.

FURTHER READING

- Cohen-Almagor, Raphael. *The Boundaries of Liberty and Tolerance: The Struggle Against Kahanism in Israel.* Gainesville: University Press of Florida, 1994.
- Friedman, Robert I. *The False Prophet – Rabbi Meir Kahane: From FBI Informant to Knesset Member.* New York: Lawrence Hill Books, and London: Faber and Faber, 1990.
- Sivan, Emmanuel, and Menachem Friedman. *Religious Radicalism and Politics in the Middle East.* Albany: State University of New York Press, 1990.
- Sprinzak, Ehud. *The Ascendance of Israel's Radical Right.* New York: Oxford University Press, 1991.

TERROR IN LEBANON 1987-1996

The absence of a strong central government in modern Lebanon and chronic political instability have allowed terrorist groups to find a haven there. Some have fought on Lebanese soil while others have used it as a base for directing international operations. Since the late 1980s, turmoil in Lebanon has remained almost as bad as it was in the early years of the decade.

Lebanon continued to be the site of numerous terrorist incidents and home to both domestic and foreign terrorist groups. The Lebanese people suffered greatly from these attacks, most of which were the result of struggles between Lebanese political factions aided by foreign intelligence services. The terrorist attacks occurred against a background of fierce fighting between rival militias. In 1989, the rival Muslim Amal and Hizb'allah groups battled with each other, as did Christian units of the Lebanese army and the Muslim Lebanese Forces. In 1989 and 1990, the Christian Lebanese army forces under General Michel Aoun fought the Syrian army and its militia allies, and reopened hostilities against the Lebanese Forces. Fighting did not end until October 1990.

In the course of these military struggles, all sides made use of indiscriminate terrorist attacks and assassinations. In 1987, 50 bombing attacks killed 48 people and injured 218. In May 1989, a car-bomb in West Beirut killed 22 people, including moderate Sunni leader Sheikh Hassan Khalid. In November, the Lebanese president, Rene Moawad, was assassinated in a bombing.

SUMMARY

- From the late 1980s to the early 1990s, Lebanon remained one of the centers of world terrorism.
- Many Lebanese terrorist groups are controlled or tolerated by the Syrian government.
- A major conflict exists between the Israelis and the Hizb'allah movement that controls much of southern Lebanon.

THE IMPACT OF THE GULF CRISIS

In 1991, terrorist attacks escalated in protest at the Gulf Crisis. French-owned banks in Lebanon were bombed, and later in the year, eight people died after a car-bomb attempt on the life of the defense minister. Protests at the start of the Israeli-Palestine Liberation Organization (PLO) Madrid peace talks in Spain may have inspired a rocket attack on the U.S. embassy in October and a car-bomb in central Beirut on December 30 that killed some 30 people and injured 120. A bomb at the American University of Beirut on November 8 destroyed the main administration building. It was not claimed, but the Lebanese government blamed Israeli agents for the attack. Other sources cited Hizb'allah. Either group may have been interested in disrupting the process of Lebanese national reconciliation.

During 1992, ten people were killed in Lebanon by assorted car-bombs, shootings, and rocket attacks. In 1993, a variety of groups carried out or planned attacks on a number of targets. In June, two bombs were found near the Danish embassy in Beirut. During the same month, activists of the Sunni Islamic Grouping attempted to bomb a bus carrying Christian delegates to a religious conference in northern Lebanon. Two of the activists were killed and a third injured when their bomb went off prematurely. In December, the Beirut headquarters of the Phalange party (which mainly represents the Maronite Christian portion of the Lebanese population) was blown up. In 1994, two bombings of Christian targets took place. The worst was a bomb blast at the Maronite church in Zuk in February. Eleven people died and 59 were wounded.

The government accused the Muslim Lebanese Forces of planning the attacks and put its leader, Samir Geaga, on trial.

Hostage-taking had become a central part of the Lebanese political scene during the civil war (1975-76). Thousands of Lebanese civilians were taken hostage by the country's militias. Many were tortured, many killed, and many remain unaccounted for. This tactic first began to affect foreigners in the mid-1980s, when Shiite groups began to take foreign hostages in order to apply pressure on Western governments. In the late 1980s, the Iranian-backed Hizb'allah and a variety of associated groups continued to take Western hostages.

At the beginning of 1987, 14 foreigners were held hostage in Lebanon, most by radical Shiite groups. A South Korean diplomat, Do Chae-Sung, was released by the Fighting Revolutionary Cells in October, as was a French journalist, Jean-Louis Normandin, held by the Revolutionary Justice Organization. Press rumors suggested that they had been released as a result of deals made between their governments and the terrorist groups or governments involved.

KIDNAPPING IN LEBANON 1987-88

On January 13, 1987, French journalist Roger Auque was kidnapped but was released on November 27, possibly as a result of a deal struck with the French government. Terry Waite, an envoy of England's archbishop of Canterbury, who had been negotiating the release of other hostages, was kidnapped on January 20, 1987. It later emerged that he had been used as a front man by Colonel Oliver North, the U.S. Marine Corps officer serving with the National Security Council, who was seeking to strike a deal with Iran to release American hostages. This had compromised Waite's position and led his kidnappers to believe he was working with the Americans.

On January 24, 1987, four professors at Beirut University College (BUC) were taken by Islamic Jihad for the Liberation of Palestine. They were three Americans, Robert Polhill, Allan Steen, and Jesse Turner, and one Indian resident in the U.S., Mithileshwar Singh. American journalist Charles Glass was taken hostage on June 17 by a group calling itself the Organization for the Defense of the Free People. He escaped in August in unclear circumstances. Since he was kidnapped in a Syrian-controlled area and had been granted free passage by their officials, it is possible that the Syrian authorities facilitated his "escape."

In addition to the above, two West Germans, Rudolf Cordes and Alfred Schmidt, were kidnapped in January 1987 by a group calling itself the Organization of the Oppressed on Earth. Schmidt was released in September. They were taken by the brother of Muhammad Hamadei, a Hizb'allah terrorist imprisoned in Germany for participation in the hijacking of a TWA flight in 1985, during which the hijackers had murdered a U.S. Navy diver. The aim of kidnapping German nationals was to force the release of Hamadei from jail in West Germany.

In 1988, eight foreigners were kidnapped in Lebanon, generally in attempts to force the release of terrorists in jail in other Arab states or in the West. In January, Hizb'allah-linked groups also took hostage Ralph Schray, a businessman with dual nationality in West Germany and Lebanon. Two Swedish journalists were taken in February, but were released the same day as they had been mistaken for Germans. Also in February, the Organization of the Oppressed on Earth kidnapped U.S. Marine Lieutenant-Colonel William Higgins. He was attached to the U.N. Truce Supervisory Organization, the body responsible for monitoring the cease-fire along the Lebanese-Israeli border. His kidnappers announced that he would be tried as a spy.

FRENCH HOSTAGES RELEASED

During 1988, a number of hostages were also released. Three Frenchmen, diplomats Michel Carton and Marcel Fontaine, and journalist Jean-Paul Kauffman, were freed on May 4. They had been held since early 1985. Their releases were reportedly linked to a French agreement to restore links with Iran and to repay a loan made by the shah. German hostages Ralph Schray and Rudolf Cordes were released in March and September, reportedly after intervention by Syria and Iran. BUC professor Mithileshwar Singh was freed in October in what his kidnappers called a gesture of goodwill toward the U.S.

In July 1989, Hizb'allah released a videotape of Lieutenant-Colonel Higgins's body, claiming that he had been hanged in retaliation for Israel's seizure of Hizb'allah leader Sheikh Obeid from his home in Lebanon. Analysis subsequently revealed that Higgins had died some time earlier and that the abduction of Obeid had been used as an excuse to dispose of the body. In addition, a Briton, two German relief workers, and two Swiss Red Cross members were seized during the same year.

Rex Features

U.S. Marine William Higgins was taken hostage by Hizb'allah in 1988, and was later murdered.

During 1990, Syria tightened its grip on Lebanon, crushing the rebellion led by Christian army commander General Aoun in October. This enabled the Lebanese government, backed by Syria, to extend its control over much of the country, and a number of hostages were set free. Robert Polhill and Frank Reed, the latter an American teacher kidnapped in 1986 by the Arab Revolutionary Cells, were released in April. Two Swiss Red Cross officials, kidnapped in October 1989, were released in August. Brian Keenan, an Irish teacher at the American University of Beirut who had been taken in 1986, was released in August 1990.

The pace of hostage releases accelerated in 1991. On August 8, English journalist John McCarthy was released with a letter from his captors to the United Nations. A UN-sponsored round of negotiations followed involving Iran, Syria, Hizb'allah, and Israel. Six American and three British hostages were then released. The United States received the remains of Lieutenant-Colonel Higgins and of William Buckley, the CIA station chief in Beirut who had been abducted in 1984. Israel received information confirming the death of two of its soldiers missing in Lebanon. In return, Israel and the South Lebanon Army (SLA), an Israeli-backed militia in southern Lebanon, released large numbers of Lebanese held in SLA jails. Additionally, in what it claimed to be an unrelated move, the U.S. released $178 million in Iranian assets that it had sequestrated.

HOSTAGES AS BARGAINING CHIPS

The two German relief workers kidnapped in May 1989 remained in captivity, however. They continued to be held as bargaining chips for the release of Muhammad Hamadei. In April 1991, Muhammad's brother, Abbas, was sentenced in Germany to 13 years' imprisonment for the kidnappings. Their elder brother, Abdel Hadi, Hizb'allah's security chief, is believed to have masterminded the abductions. The two Germans were released in June 1992. The Freedom Movement, which the U.S. government suspected was a front for Hizb'allah, claimed it had released them because of the ongoing efforts to "resolve the issue" of the Hamadei brothers. In August 1993, Germany paroled and deported Abbas Hamadei. He returned to Lebanon.

By mid-1992, the hostage chapter had been closed in Lebanon, with all the foreign hostages having been released. However, the U.S. government in particular remained determined to punish the terrorists who had humiliated it in the 1980s. Two men whom the U.S. authorities had been especially eager to get their hands on were Imad Mugniyeh and Hassan Ezzedine, both Hizb'allah officials who had been involved in attacks on U.S. nationals in the 1980s. Mugniyeh, leader of Islamic Jihad in Lebanon, was responsible for many of the kidnappings of Westerners and has been accused of organizing the suicide-bomb attacks that killed over 500 Americans, French, and Israelis in Lebanon in the early 1980s. He was named in a U.S. indictment stemming from the 1985 hijacking of a TWA airliner. Now a resident in Iran, he visits Lebanon regularly. In April 1995, the FBI attempted to seize him when his plane landed in Jeddah, Saudi Arabia, but the Saudi authorities refused permission.

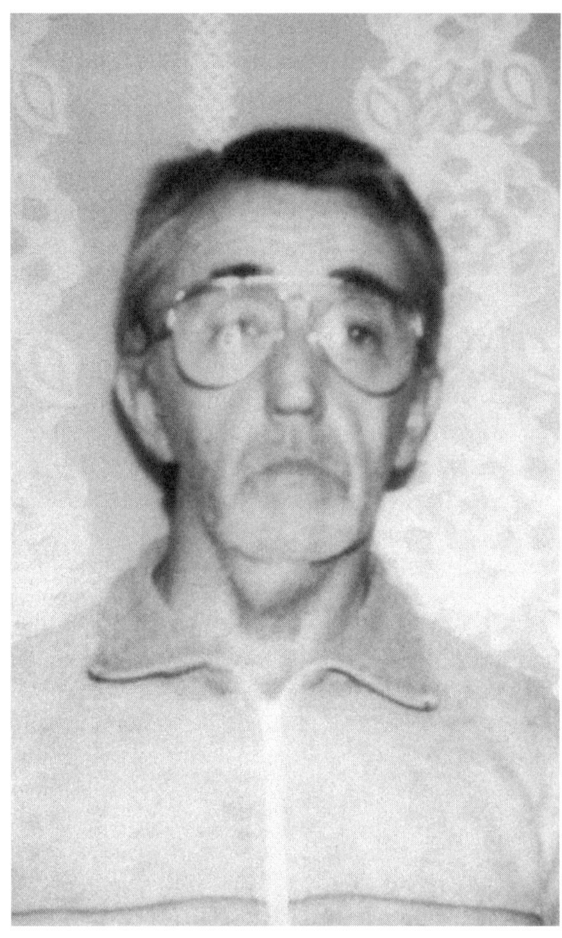

CIA Beirut station chief William Buckley had been taken hostage in Beirut in 1984; it was not until his body was recovered in 1991 that his fate was known.

Ezzedine is a close associate of Mugniyeh, and was also indicted for the 1985 TWA hijacking. He has also been linked to the 1989 hijacking of a Kuwaiti airliner. He is based in Lebanon, where he works with Hizb'allah's security apparatus. In 1994, U.S. agents attempted to kidnap him from Beirut but failed. These covert efforts were, however, very much on the margins of events in the early 1990s, as Hizb'allah's main concern remained the armed struggle against Israel. A low-level guerrilla war raged in southern Lebanon between Hizb'allah's military wing, Islamic Resistance, the Israeli Defense Forces (IDF), and the SLA. Hizb'allah received backing in the form of arms, training, and funds from Syria and Iran. Syria was keen to maintain pressure on Israel in the peace talks. Iran remained ideologically committed to the fight against Israel and to Islamic revolution.

Nonetheless, Iranian support for Hizb'allah became less overt after the moderate government of President Hashemi Rafsanjani came to power in 1989. The contingent of Iranian Revolutionary Guards sent to the Bekaa Valley in Lebanon to train Hizb'allah was reduced. In 1992, the Lebanese army, with Syrian backing, took over the Sheikh Abdallah barracks in Baalbek, which had been the home of the Iranian Revolutionary Guards. In addition, splits emerged within the Hizb'allah leadership, reflecting divisions in Tehran. By the mid-1990s, Hizb'allah's political leaders argued that the movement should concentrate on taking a political role inside Lebanon, where it won eight of 128 seats in the 1992 parliamentary elections. Islamic Resistance leaders, however, demanded a continuation of the armed struggle.

WAR IN SOUTHERN LEBANON

The conflict between Hizb'allah on the one hand and Israel and the SLA on the other took the form of a guerrilla struggle rather than a terrorist campaign, even though Israel officially labeled Hizb'allah attacks as terrorist incidents. Skirmishes continue to this day. The Israeli "Security Zone" in southern Lebanon consists of fortified hilltop encampments occupied by SLA militiamen backed by Israeli tanks, artillery, and aircraft. These positions are frequently attacked by Hizb'allah fighters armed with mortars, rockets, and machine guns, and by direct assaults. Hizb'allah fighters also ambush Israeli patrols, plant roadside bombs in the Security Zone, and fire rockets at civilian targets in northern Israel.

Israel has responded to these attacks by targeting guerrilla camps with air strikes and shelling, and by trying to intimidate the local population. In July 1993, after a spate of successful Hizb'allah raids, the IDF carried out a week-long bombardment of southern Lebanon designed to force the civilian population to flee. This had the intended effect of reducing local support for Hizb'allah and also forced the U.S. to intervene and persuade Syria to reduce Hizb'allah's freedom of action. In April 1996, the IDF launched Operation Grapes of Wrath. For 16 days, Israeli forces attacked Hizb'allah mortar sites and other targets, using aircraft, artillery, and gunboats. More than 160 were killed, mostly Lebanese civilians. The IDF has

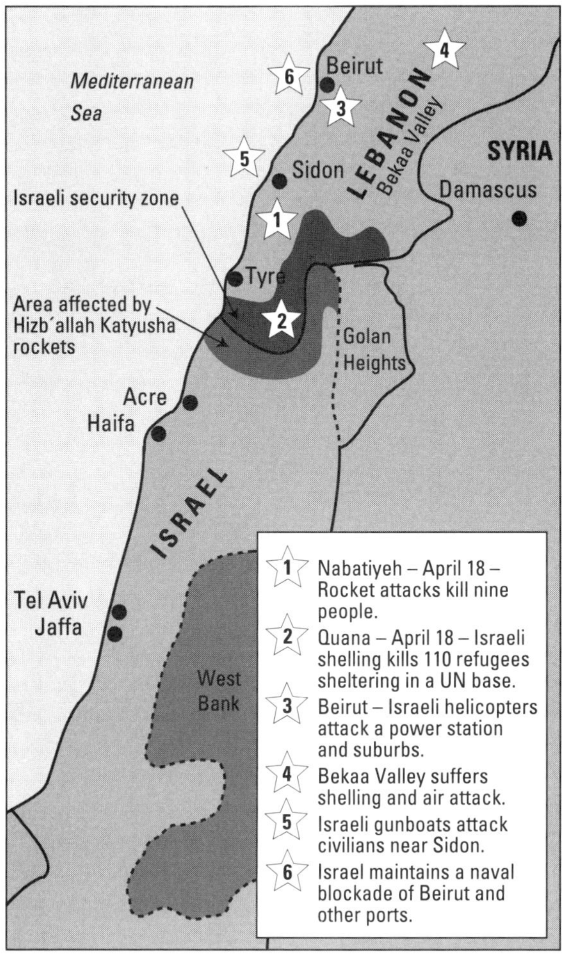

Israel's 1996 Operation Grapes of Wrath targeted Hizb'allah terrorists and their bases in Lebanon.

also responded by targeting individual Hizb'allah leaders. In July 1989, Israeli commandos kidnapped Sheikh Obeid from his home in Lebanon. In February 1992, the IDF used helicopter gunships to assassinate Hizb'allah secretary general, Sheikh Abbas Mousawi, also killing his wife and six-year-old child.

Hizb'allah and its allies have also struck at Israeli targets abroad. In March 1992, Hizb'allah set off a car-bomb outside the Israeli embassy in Buenos Aires, Argentina, the city with the largest Jewish community in South America. Twenty-nine people died and 240 were wounded. Hizb'allah publicized its responsibility by releasing a videotape taken of the embassy prior to the attack and claimed the attack was in response to the killing of Mousawi. The same month, a pro-Iranian fundamentalist group in Turkey exploded a bomb under the car of an Israeli embassy security officer. In July 1994, two bombs in London, England, may have been planted by Hizb'allah. The first bomb devastated the Israeli chancery and injured 14 people. The second car-bomb damaged the home of a Jewish fund-raising organization and wounded five passers-by.

In addition to Hizb'allah, other anti-Israeli groups have used southern Lebanon as a base from which to hit Israel. Many of the fighters in these groups were children of the Palestinians who had fled northern Palestine during the 1948-49 war. The Palestinian groups involved have included the Democratic Front for the Liberation of Palestine, the Popular Front for the Liberation of Palestine (PFLP), the PFLP–General Command, the Abu Nidal Organization, and the Abu Musa group. Other groups, such as Amal, are indigenous Lebanese movements who objected to Israeli occupation of Lebanese soil and to the oppressive tactics used by the IDF and its SLA allies.

SYRIAN-SPONSORED TERRORISTS

Although Lebanon in the late 1980s and early 1990s was much less of a haven for international terrorists than it had been in the 1970s, a variety of such groups maintained bases in the country. Usually these were established with the approval, or even the active support, of the Syrians. It could hardly be otherwise since Syrian troops occupied most of the country, their presence ratified by the "Treaty of Brotherhood and Cooperation" signed in May 1991. The groups included the Armenian Secret Army for the Liberation of Armenia (ASALA), Turkey's Revolutionary Left (Dev Sol), the Japanese Red Army, and the Marxist-Leninist nationalist Kurdish Workers' Party.

ASALA, set up in 1975 to punish Turkey for the country's genocidal attacks on Armenians during World War I, has been quiet since the mid-1980s due to internal schisms. Nonetheless, it is believed to maintain a presence in Lebanon and has close ties to various radical Palestinian groups.

Dev Sol, a Marxist group opposed to U.S. influence in the Middle East, was quiet in the mid-1980s but re-emerged in the latter part of the decade. Most of its attacks have been against Turkish officials, but it resumed operations against other targets in 1991. It claimed responsibility for the murder of two American contractors and a British businessman, as well as for

Hulton Getty Picture Collection

Palestinian fighters stand on guard at a refugee camp in southern Lebanon in November 1994.

more than 30 bombings of Western facilities in Turkey. In 1993, Dev Sol killed several Turkish officials. In September 1994, it claimed to have carried out the assassination of former Turkish justice minister Mehmet Topac. A police offensive against the group, which has included killing several members and arresting dozens of others, has weakened it, however. Since 1992, the group has split along factional lines. Although mainly based in Turkey, Dev Sol is believed to have other bases in Syrian-controlled areas of Lebanon.

The Japanese Red Army, a terrorist group with a vague ideology, has reduced its operations since the 1970s, but it was behind rocket attacks on a number of U.S. embassies in the 1980s. Much of what remains of the organization is based in the Bekaa Valley, and it probably receives help from the PFLP and Syria.

In the 1990s, Lebanon remains one of the centers of world terrorism, with arms, explosives, and seasoned campaigners on hand to ply their deadly trade.

Andrew Rathmell

SEE ALSO: TERROR GROUP ORGANIZATION; BOMBING OPERATIONS; HIJACKING AND KIDNAPPING; VICTIMS OF TERRORISM; HOSTAGE NEGOTIATIONS; THE PLO AND THE ARAB STATES; THE LEBANESE CIVIL WAR; TERROR IN LEBANON 1980-1987; THE ORIGINS OF PALESTINIAN ISLAMIC JIHAD; IRANIAN SPONSORSHIP OF TERRORISM; HIZB'ALLAH; JAPANESE TERRORISM; THE ISRAELI RESPONSE TO TERRORISM; THE AMERICAN RESPONSE TO TERRORISM.

FURTHER READING

- Brynen, Rex. *Sanctuary and Survival: The PLO in Lebanon.* Boulder, CO: Westview Press, and London: Pinter, 1990.
- Kramer, Martin. *Hezbollah's Vision of the West.* Washington, DC: Institute for Near East Policy, Policy Papers No. 16, 1989.
- Phares, Walid. *Lebanese Christian Nationalism: The Rise and Fall of an Ethnic Resistance.* Boulder, CO: Lynne Rienner Publishers, 1995.
- Shehadi, Nadim, and Dana Haffar Mills. *Lebanon: A History of Conflict and Consensus.* London: Centre for Lebanese Studies, 1992.

KURDISH NATIONALIST TERRORISM

The Kurds are a Middle Eastern Muslim people who have never had their own state. Over 15 million Kurds live in scattered communities in eastern Turkey, northern Iraq, and northwestern Iran, with small groups in Syria and the former Soviet Union. A Kurdish state was promised in the Treaty of Sèvres between the Ottoman Turks and the victorious Allied powers shortly after World War I. However, this treaty was never ratified, and in 1923, the newly created Turkish republic signed a treaty with the League of Nations which made no mention of an independent Kurdistan.

REBELLION AGAINST TURKEY

Since the 1923 treaty, the Kurds have rebelled against the governments of Turkey (1925) and Iraq (1943-46 and 1961-75). The Kurds have engaged in guerrilla warfare and terrorism against both of these countries – as well as Iran – almost continuously since 1975. The most prominent guerrilla/terrorist group active in Turkey is the Kurdish Workers' Party (PKK) – a Marxist-Leninist organization set up in the late 1970s with its headquarters located at different times in Syria or Lebanon. The PKK's main aim is to establish a Kurdish state in southeastern Turkey.

KEY FACTS

- The Kurdish Workers' Party (PKK) was founded on November 27, 1978, by leftist students as a Marxist-Leninist group with the aim of establishing an independent Kurdish state.
- In the period 1984-89, the PKK killed about 1,500 Turkish villagers.
- In the 1990s, the PKK has switched from attacking civilians to striking Turkish military, police, and government installations.

With a strength of up to 5,000 fighters and thousands of sympathizers in Turkey and abroad, the PKK initially concentrated on striking military and government officials and civilians inside Turkey. Over the past decade, however, it has launched attacks on Turkish targets abroad and Turkey's NATO allies.

From 1978-80, the PKK concentrated on killing Turkish landlords and obtaining funds from robberies, extortion, and narcotics, but moves against it by the Turks in 1980, which led to the arrested of over 2,000 alleged PKK members, forced the group's leadership to move abroad, initially to Syria.

The most striking PKK operation of recent times was the takeover of several villages in Turkey in 1984, although the PKK abandoned its gains as soon as the Turkish army moved against it. This and other operations had little long-term effect, and the movement began an even more brutal campaign against Turkish villages. In the summer of 1987, the PKK murdered more than 60 villagers in Mardin province, an atrocity that lost the group much support and forced it to resort to other methods such as kidnapping.

In 1991, the PKK kidnapped but subsequently released a number of Westerners in Turkey. Then, in 1993, it launched a major offensive against the Turkish tourist industry and government. Beginning in May, the PKK bombed hotels, restaurants, and other tourist sites on the Turkish Mediterranean coast. In June, PKK activists attacked Turkish facilities in Europe. In November, the PKK fire-bombed Turkish targets in Europe, killing one person in Germany.

BANNING THE PKK

In response to these attacks, European governments took action. France and Germany banned the PKK. French police arrested 20 suspects and German police raided PKK offices. The PKK then escalated its campaign in Turkey in 1994. Three attacks in Istanbul

Rex Features

Some of the PKK's 5,000 guerrilla fighters take part in a parade in northern Iraq.

killed two foreign tourists in May. In June, the PKK bombed Turkish coastal resorts, killing a British woman and injuring more than ten tourists. In August, two Finnish tourists were seized but released three weeks later. Confrontations with European governments escalated. In October, British police arrested Faysal Dunlayici, a senior PKK official.

The PKK's military bases are located in Turkey and in northern Iraq. Since the 1991 Gulf War and the creation of a UN-protected zone for Kurds in northern Iraq, the Turks have launched several armed incursions into Iraq with the purpose of destroying the PKK's infrastructure. In March 1994, after the PKK had killed 18 soldiers in an ambush in Turkey, 35,000 Turkish troops moved into northern Iraq and attacked about 20 alleged PKK camps. Two further incursions followed in 1995, and Turkey threatened to create a self-protection zone in northern Iraq in September 1996, after fighting broke out between Kurdish nationalist factions.

Syria has allowed the PKK to maintain training bases in the Bekaa Valley in Lebanon, despite repeated protests from Turkey. The PKK's leader, Abdullah Ocalan, reportedly resides in Syria and the small Kurdish community there supports the movement. Syrian aid has been given in retaliation for a Turkish irrigation project, which threatens Syria's water supplies.

Andrew Rathmell

SEE ALSO: ARAB STATES AND TERRORISM IN THE 1990s; IRAQI SPONSORSHIP OF TERRORISM.

FURTHER READING

- Bulloch, John, and Harvey Morris. *No Friends but the Mountains: The Tragic History of the Kurds.* New York: Oxford University Press, and London: Viking, 1992.
- Chaliand, Gerard. *A People Without a Country: The Kurds and Kurdistan.* London: Zed Press, and New York: Olive Branch Press, 1993.
- Fuller, Graham E. "The Fate of the Kurds," in *International Affairs* 72, No. 2 (Spring 1993).

DOMESTIC TERRORISM IN THE ARAB WORLD

Many Arab states were plagued with terrorism during the late 1980s and 1990s. Often terrorism and political violence accompanied much wider internal disorders, such as political or ethnic unrest, and was frequently also linked to Islamic fundamentalist groups.

JORDAN: ABU NIDAL AND RADICAL ISLAM

Jordan had long been a target of terrorism by rival Arab states and assorted Palestinian groups. In 1987, two bombs went off in Amman. They were claimed by Black September, at this time no more than a cover name for the Abu Nidal Organization.

Terrorism reerupted in Jordan in 1991 at the time of the Gulf Crisis. An Islamic extremist group calling itself the Prophet Muhammad's Army emerged, made up of militants who had defected from the Muslim Brotherhood. The group admitted responsibility for the murder of a Jordanian intelligence officer, for two car bombings, and for planning attacks on Western embassies. Eight members of the group were convicted and sentenced to death, though the sentences were later commuted to prison terms. Other groups were probably behind a number of attacks on business and diplomatic targets belonging to countries involved in the coalition against Iraq.

In 1992, two Jordanians were convicted of membership of a group calling itself Vanguard of the Islamic Youth. The group had reportedly been funded by Iran, via the Popular Front for the Liberation of Palestine – General Command. It had planned to attack Western embassies in Amman and launch cross-border raids into the West Bank. In November, the two defendants were sentenced to 20 years' hard labor, although King Hussein of Jordan gave them amnesty a few days later. In 1993, Jordanian security forces discovered a plot to assassinate King Hussein by members of the banned opposition Islamic Liberation Party. In November, three gunmen allied to the Egyptian group al-Gamaa al-Islamiyya were killed when they tried to attack a Jordanian army post near the West Bank.

In January 1994, suspected members of the Prophet Muhammad's Army carried out more attacks in Jordan, bombing cinemas in Amman and Zarqa. The police made 25 arrests and claimed some of those detained were former *mujahideen* who had fought in Afghanistan. Those arrested were charged with a plot to overthrow the government. Eleven received death sentences and seven were sentenced to hard labor. Also in 1994, the authorities arrested 30 others suspected of terrorism, including 15 members of the Abu Nidal Organization.

KEY FACTS

- In the 1990s, terrorism in various Arab countries often accompanied either general calls for reform or fundamentalist activity.
- It is alleged that much of this domestic terrorism has been sponsored by Iran.
- Jordan, Yemen, Saudi Arabia, and Bahrain have been particularly troubled by terrorism.

YEMEN: UNITY AND CIVIL WAR

The People's Democratic Republic of Yemen (PDRY) was known during the 1970s and early 1980s as a radical, pro-Soviet state that gave haven to a variety of Palestinian and left-wing guerrilla groups. By 1987, the

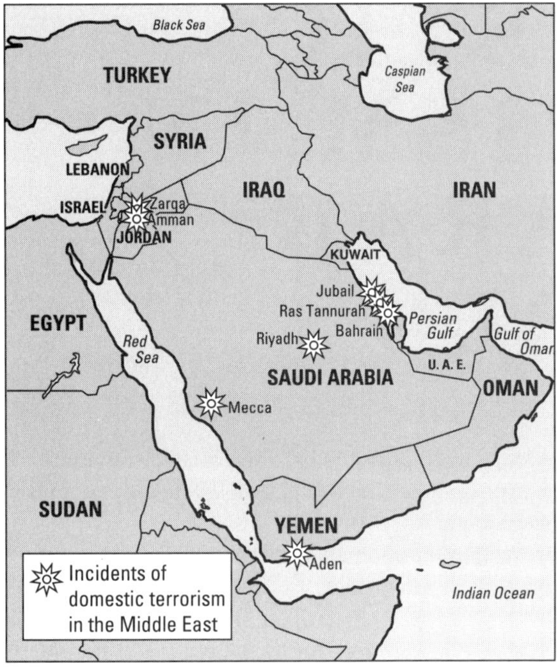

Home-grown terrorism by Islamic fundamentalists against conservative regimes in the Middle East increased between 1988 and 1996.

PDRY had begun to cut back this support. Nonetheless, in 1988, a leading Armenian terrorist was discovered traveling on a Yemeni diplomatic passport.

On May 22, 1990, the PDRY united with North Yemen to form the Republic of Yemen. The new republic made it clear to the outside word that it was determined to cut all ties with terrorist groups. Despite this, foreign governments complained that Yemen still harbored Palestinian nationalist and radical Muslim terrorists. Government control over large parts of Yemen remained weak, and some Yemeni tribes and Islamic leaders still support fundamentalist terrorists.

Yemen itself became the scene of terrorist incidents during and after the Gulf War. In January 1991, the American, Turkish, and Japanese embassies there were attacked. In October, the German and American embassies, along with government buildings, were attacked by unknown groups. In the fall of 1992, bombs went off near the U.S. and German embassies. An explosion in a parking lot in Aden in December killed one civilian while another bomb went off at an hotel. In 1993, a bomb exploded outside the British embassy and a rocket was fired at the American embassy. In 1994, members of the Yemen Islamic Jihad organization were imprisoned for their part in these bombings. At the same time, tensions between the leaders of the former North Yemen and the PDRY were escalating and were accompanied by a number of terrorist incidents. Southern leaders, belonging to the Yemen Socialist Party (YSP), claimed that militias attached to the north's tribal/fundamentalist party, Islah, were behind a series of assaults on YSP officials. Some 150 YSP officials were assassinated between 1990 and 1994, according to YSP leaders.

In 1994, the tensions erupted into civil war. After bitter fighting, the YSP was routed and the country was united under President Ali Abdullah Saleh. The defeated southern leaders, given refuge in Saudi Arabia, threatened to use guerrilla warfare and terrorism to continue the struggle. But by mid-1996, they had only launched a propaganda and diplomatic campaign.

ATTACKS ON SAUDI ARABIA

During the 1980s, the kingdom of Saudi Arabia experienced a number of Iranian-sponsored attacks by indigenous Shiites and Iranian agents. The attacks came as part of the struggle for influence in the Muslim world between Iran and Saudi Arabia. Saudi Arabia's Shiite population, concentrated in the oil-rich Eastern Province, has long felt itself a victim of discrimination. Successive Saudi rulers, adhering to the strict Wahhabi form of Sunni Islam, have regarded Shiites as religiously misguided. Development spending and employment prospects in the Eastern Province have traditionally been lower than in the rest of the country.

In 1987, a number of fires and explosions in the kingdom's oil-fields were attributed by the government to accidents. They may, however, have been the result of sabotage. In 1988, incidents multiplied as a result of rising Iranian-Saudi tensions which had led to riots during 1987's *hajj*, or pilgrimage to Mecca.

In March and April, oil installations at Jubail and Ras Tannurah in the Eastern Province were bombed. Three suspects were arrested in August after a gun battle in which a policeman was killed. The three, along with an accomplice, were charged with sabotage, terrorism, and being Iranian agents. They were convicted and executed.

However, the bulk of anti-Saudi activity, some 22 incidents, happened abroad. A number of attacks were claimed by the Hizb'allah of the Hijaz, a group possibly made up of Saudi Shiites. They murdered a Saudi diplomat in Turkey in October 1988, ostensibly in revenge for the execution of the convicted Shiites. A group calling itself Soldiers of the Right attempted to kill a Saudi diplomat in Karachi, Pakistan, in December. Other attacks were carried out against three Saudi teachers in Nigeria and against offices of the national airline, Saudia.

Tensions remained high in 1989. During the *hajj*, two bombs were set off in Mecca by pro-Iranian pilgrims, killing one person. The Saudi authorities arrested 16 Kuwaiti Shiites, accused them of working for Iran, and beheaded them. Iranian and Hizb'allah leaders promised retaliation. On October 14, a Saudia office in Lahore, Pakistan, was blown up. Two days later a Saudi diplomat in Ankara, Turkey, was injured when his car exploded. On November 1, a Saudi diplomat in Beirut was assassinated by Islamic Jihad. On February 1, 1990, three Saudi diplomats were assassinated in Bangkok, Thailand, shortly after another diplomat had been injured in a bombing in Ankara.

In late 1990 and in 1991, Saudi concerns shifted to possible Iraqi terrorism. Iraq threatened retaliation against the Saudis and other members of the Gulf War coalition assembled against it, but tough security measures forestalled serious incidents. The Saudi government expelled Iraqi diplomats, closed its borders with Jordan and Yemen, and worked closely with its allies in restraining potential terrorists. Only a few incidents took place. For instance, on February 3, 1991, two U.S. airmen and a Saudi guard were injured when a military bus in Jeddah was attacked. Four Palestinians were arrested for the attack.

After the Gulf War, Saudi Arabia sought to improve relations with Iran and to buy off its domestic Shia opponents. Relations with Iran improved in the mid-1990s, and a deal was struck with exiled Shiite groups in 1993 that allowed their leaders to return home.

INTERNAL THREATS IN SAUDI ARABIA

In 1995, however, the focus turned to domestic terrorist threats sponsored by radical Sunni groups. Since the 1991 Gulf War, the Saudi royal family had come under attack from conservative religious scholars and intellectuals, who complained of their excessive reliance on the West, and their alleged corruption and economic mismanagement. These conservatives were suppressed and their supporters jailed or forced into exile. The foremost spokesman was Dr. Muhammad al-Masari, who set up headquarters in London, England, in 1994. His Committee for the Defense of Legitimate Rights (CDLR) carried out a massive and successful propaganda campaign against the royal family which embarrassed the kingdom. The CDLR and its sympathizers avoided violence but warned that government repression might provoke terrorism.

They were proved right in November 1995, when a van-bomb went off outside a U.S.-manned training center for the Saudi National Guard. Four Americans and a Filipino were killed and 60 people injured. Three unknown groups claimed responsibility, but neither the Saudi police nor the FBI made much headway in identifying the perpetrators.

TERRORISM IN BAHRAIN

During the 1980s, Bahrain was plagued by radical Shiite opposition activities, sometimes supported by Iran. A number of groups carried out terrorist attacks and sought to stir up popular discontent. In 1987, the pro-Iranian Shiite opposition group, the Islamic Front for the Liberation of Bahrain (IFLB), attempted to recruit among the country's Shiite population but had little success. In December, a Shiite was arrested and charged with planting a bomb at an oil installation. As the Iran-Iraq War of 1980-88 wound down, Iranian support for these groups in Bahrain was gradually withdrawn and tight security put an end to violence.

In late 1994, however, unrest erupted as a mass civil rights campaign met tough government repression. Opposition leaders, both Sunni and Shiite, sought to present a petition to the emir calling for a restoration of the parliament, which had been dissolved in 1975, and for greater tolerance of opposition groups. The petitioners were supported by many of Bahrain's Shiite youth from poor areas who were suffering from unemployment as the economy stagnated. The government refused to listen, instead treating the protesters as Iranian-inspired subversives. A series of clashes broke out between demonstrators and security forces, accompanied by several incidents of arson and the deaths of a dozen policemen and protesters.

By the spring of 1995, the government had arrested the opposition leaders and deported others. These, led by the IFLB and the Bahrain Freedom Movement (BFM), set up their headquarters in foreign capitals of Tehran, Damascus, and London. Several of the opposition leaders, notably Shiite cleric Sheikh Abdul Amir al-Jamri, were released in the summer of 1995, but by

Rex Features

A member of the Thai emergency services attends the scene of the assassination of three Saudi diplomats in Bangkok on February 1, 1990.

the end of the year they were again leading protests. They claimed the government had reneged on a deal to release detainees, but the government denied this.

In the spring of 1996, clashes escalated and the Bahrain Defense Force threatened to impose martial law. The opposition leaders, along with over 2,000 suspects, were arrested. Human rights groups protested, but Bahrain's foreign allies in the Arab world and the West backed its repression.

BOMBING BANKS AND HOTELS

As tensions mounted, unidentified groups set off a number of bombs in prestige hotels and outside banks in the country. A bomb placed by a bank automated teller machine in March 1996 killed one person. Arson at a restaurant in the same month killed seven Bangladeshi workers.

The government alleged that Iran was sponsoring the unrest and terrorism but failed to produce enough convincing evidence. The BFM condemned the violence but warned that, in the face of continuing repression, it was unable to control the more radical opposition elements.

Andrew Rathmell

SEE ALSO: THE ORIGINS OF ARAB-JEWISH TERRORISM; ABU NIDAL; THE PLO AND THE ARAB STATES; THE ORIGINS OF PALESTINIAN ISLAMIC JIHAD; ARAB STATES AND TERRORISM IN THE 1990s; PALESTINIAN ISLAMIC FUNDAMENTALISM; IRANIAN SPONSORSHIP OF TERRORISM.

FURTHER READING

- Al-Rasheed, Malawi, and Loulouwa Al-Rasheed. "The Politics of Encapsulation: Saudi Policy Towards Tribal and Religious Opposition," in *Middle Eastern Studies* 32, No. 1 (January 1996): 96-119.
- Dekmejian, R. Hrair. "The Rise of Political Islamism in Saudi Arabia," in *The Middle East Journal* 48, No. 4 (Autumn 1994): 627-644.
- Melman, Yossi. *The Master Terrorist: The True Story Behind Abu Nidal.* New York: Adama Books, 1986; London: Sidgwick and Jackson, 1987.

LIBYAN SPONSORSHIP OF TERRORISM

Libyan leader Colonel Muammar al-Qaddafi has supported terrorists fighting for anti-imperialist and Arab nationalist causes since he seized power in 1973. However, the American air strike against Libya and Qaddafi personally in 1986, in response to alleged Libyan support for the bombing of a Berlin disco frequented by U.S. servicemen, forced him to act more cautiously. Qaddafi was careful after 1986 to ensure he secretly operated through others who could be blamed instead.

Qaddafi was also more careful to support groups that could give him value for money – that is, those that could genuinely hurt his enemies, rather than just repeat anti-imperialist slogans. At the same time, he was eager to take revenge on the U.S., and on Britain, which had provided bases for the American bombers.

Libyan support for terrorism was multi-faceted. The country gave funds, for instance, to Saiqa – a Syrian-backed Palestinian splinter group – and to Palestinian Islamic Jihad. Some $1 million was paid to the Popular Front for the Liberation of Palestine–General Command (PFLP-GC) in 1990 alone. The Communist Party of the Philippines' New People's Army received more than $7 million between 1987 and 1991. Libya's Anti-Imperialism Center provided a coordinating point for aid to revolutionaries. Established in 1982, it held conferences of radical groups and acted as a recruiting agency for potential terrorists and guerrillas. Groups from as far afield as Colombia, Chile, Costa Rica, Peru, Haiti, the Philippines, as well as those from the Middle East and Europe received training, funds, and arms from the Anti-Imperialism Center. Training camps included al-Qalah, occupied by the Abu Nidal Organization (ANO); Seven April and Bin Ghashir camps, for Africans and Latin Americans; and the Ras al-Hilal camp, for Palestinian fighters.

SUMMARY

- Under Colonel Muammar al-Qaddafi, Libya has aided and directed many terrorist groups.
- Aid includes money, provision of weapons, and training.
- Two Libyans have been accused of carrying out the bombing of Pan Am Flight 103 – the Lockerbie bombing – on December 21, 1988.

Palestinian groups often receive payments directly into third-country bank accounts; Libyan diplomats and Anti-Imperialism Centers often dispense funds; and sometimes couriers are used to hand out money. Libya has a number of front organizations through which it aids radical groups. Since 1986, it has been careful to make less use of Libyan People's Bureaus (embassies), since these have been closely monitored by host governments.

ATTACKS AGAINST THE WEST

The state airline, Libyan Arab Airlines (LAA), has frequently been used to assist terrorists. For instance, in 1986, a LAA flight from Cyprus smuggled aboard six terrorists who had just raided a British base. Other front companies have smuggled arms and explosives across borders or provided intelligence services. Such companies, according to the U.S. government, have included Exo-Commerce, Sarra, and Neutron International. The Islamic Call Society, a Libyan religious philanthropic foundation, has also been used to recruit and fund radicals, notably in Benin, Africa.

Libyan support for terrorism in the late 1980s was of three kinds: sponsorship of operations against hostile states – notably the U.S., Britain, and France; support for radical Palestinian groups, who operated both on Libya's behalf and according to their own agenda; and attacks on Libyan exiles and political dissidents abroad.

Hulton Getty Picture Collection/Reuters

Libyan leader Colonel Muammar al-Qaddafi. During the late 1980s, he waged war on Western imperialism by sponsoring the use of terrorism against U.S., British, and French targets.

In 1987, Libya sponsored a series of attacks on French targets, in retaliation for France's military support for the Chad government. With French help, Chad defeated a rebel insurgency backed by Libya, which wanted control of resource-rich northern Chad. A Libyan-backed Palestinian group, the Popular Struggle Front, bombed a cafe in the former French territory of Djibouti on the Red Sea, killing eleven people, five of them French citizens. In October, the Armenian Secret Army, a group with ties to Libya, killed two French gendarmes in Beirut, Lebanon. In November 1987, the ANO, operating on Libya's behalf, hijacked the yacht *Silco* in the Mediterranean. Five French and Belgian passengers were taken hostage. They were not all finally released until 1991.

Direct attacks on American targets were less frequent. The U.S. government, however, linked the organization Egypt's Revolution to Libya. This group tried to kill three U.S. diplomats in Egypt. Also, in October 1987, a bomb went off at the offices of an American charity, World Vision, in Chad.

Libya's retaliation against Britain was more extensive. In April 1987, two Libyan-supported terrorists shot at a British soldier near Limassol in Cyprus, wounding him and a companion. In October, the French authorities seized a freighter, the *Eksund II*, carrying 150 tons of arms and explosives from Libya to the Provisional Irish Republican Army (IRA). The shipment turned out to be the fifth such consignment.

LIBYAN ATTACKS ON DISSIDENTS

Libyan agents also carried out three attacks on dissidents. In January 1987, a dissident was murdered in Athens. In May, an agent failed in an attempt to kill a dissident in Vienna. In June, two agents of Libya's Revolutionary Committees killed a senior official of the opposition National Salvation Front for Libya.

In 1988, Libya engaged in a public policy of moderation. It did not attack any dissidents, and even invited exiles to return. The U.S. government, however, linked a number of attacks on American targets to Libya, arguing that a wide variety of terrorist groups had received Libyan aid to mark the second anniversary of the U.S. reprisal attack on Tripoli, Libya. On April 14, the Japanese Red Army (a left-wing anarchist terrorist group) bombed a club in Naples, killing five people including a U.S. servicewoman. On the same day, the Colombian terrorist group M-19 bombed a U.S. Information Service (USIS) building. The following day, a U.S. Air Force post in Spain was bombed. On April 16, the Peruvian Tupac Amaru Revolutionary Movement (MRTA) bombed two USIS centers. On April 19, terrorists in Costa Rica bombed an American cultural center. In addition, Senegal arrested two Libyan agents smuggling arms aboard a flight to Benin. They were believed to have been planning to hit Western targets. Subsequently, Benin expelled the head of the Libyan People's Bureau.

LIBYA AND ABU NIDAL

An important aspect of Libya's support for terrorism during 1988 was its evolving relationship with the Abu Nidal Organization. Libya had given aid to the ANO since the 1970s, and since the ANO transferred its main base to Libya in 1987, the relationship had flourished. Most ANO members were based in Libya; they trained in the al-Qalah camp south of Tripoli; and they were

Rex Features

The Greek cruise ship City of Poros, *hijacked in July 1988 by Abu Nidal Organization terrorists.*

provided with weapons and Libyan passports. Abu Nidal (the code name of Sabri al-Banna) himself lived in Tripoli.

However, the Libyan government did not call all the shots. The ANO was experienced enough as an organization to retain its independence. Therefore, several of its operations could not be directly linked to Libya. A case in point was the July 11, 1988, hijacking of a Greek cruise ship, *City of Poros*. Terrorists fired and threw grenades at passengers as the ship approached port in Athens. Nine Europeans were killed and 100 wounded. Earlier, a bomb had exploded prematurely in a parked car at the pier, killing the two occupants. The ANO did not claim responsibility; only subsequent investigations implicated the group and identified Libyan weapons used in the raid.

In 1989, Qaddafi responded to international criticism by reining in Libyan-sponsored groups. As part of his diplomatic activity to end his country's isolation, he called on Palestinian groups to attack only Israeli targets. Nonetheless, the ANO remained in Libya, while the MRTA again attempted to bomb the USIS Center in Peru to mark the third anniversary of the U.S. air attack on Libya. In 1990, Libyan-backed groups carried out further attacks. The Palestine Liberation Front team that carried out a seaborne raid on Tel Aviv, Israel, had been trained at Libya's Sidi Bilal port and received extensive support for the raid. The mother ship for the raiders, the *Tiny Star*, was owned by a Libyan front company.

Costa Rica accused Libya of training all 15 members of the Santamaria Patriotic Organization, which planned grenade attacks on U.S. facilities in the country. Ethiopia expelled two Libyan diplomats for alleged involvement in the March 30 bombing of the Addis Ababa Hilton.

THE LOCKERBIE AND NIGER BOMBINGS

The most notorious cases of alleged Libyan sponsorship of terrorism were the destruction of Pan Am Flight 103 over Lockerbie, Scotland, on December 21, 1988, and of UTA Flight 772 over Niger on September 19, 1989. Two hundred and seventy people were killed in the Pan Am attack and 171 in the UTA bombing. On October 30, 1991, a French magistrate issued arrest warrants for four Libyan officials accused of masterminding the UTA attack. On November 14, Scottish and American courts issued indictments against two Libyans for their role in the Pan Am attack.

The UTA flight had been flying from Brazzaville, Congo, to Paris via Ndjamena, Chad. The French arrest warrant charged that three Congolese had been recruited by Libya to place a suitcase bomb on the aircraft. One of the Congolese is in jail in Congo and another in Zaire. The French magistrate accused Abdallah Sanussi (a brother-in-law of Qaddafi and deputy commander of Libyan intelligence), Ibrahim Nayli (Libyan intelligence representative in Athens), Abd al-Azragh (first secretary in the Libyan "embassy" in Brazzaville), and Abbas Musbah (a Libyan intelligence officer in Brazzaville) of organizing the plot. In addition, the magistrate issued international lookout notices for Musa Kusa, the deputy foreign minister, and another suspect.

The Scottish indictment accused Abd al-Basit al-Megrahi, a senior intelligence officer, and Lamen Fhimah, a former manager of the LAA office in Malta, of planning the Pan Am bombing. The U.S. has claimed that the operation was planned at the highest levels of the Libyan government. Washington has accused Said Rashid, a leading organizer of Libya's subversive operations and a confidante of Qaddafi, of orchestrating the attack. The Scottish-American case against Libya consists of evidence linking the accused to the attack and argues that the Libyan government was responsible since the accused had senior positions in Libya's intelligence services.

EVIDENCE OF LIBYAN INVOLVEMENT

The indictment charged that Megrahi and Fhimah deposited the suitcase bomb on Air Malta Flight 180 from Valetta, Malta, to Frankfurt, Germany, where it was routed to New York via London on PA 103. The bomb timer, marked MST-13 and manufactured by Swiss electronics firm Meister et Bollier, was one of a batch delivered to the Libyan External Security Organization (ESO) in 1985. The Senegalese authorities found similar timers when they arrested two Libyan terrorists in 1988. The U.S. government claims that the accused acted with the direct backing of senior Libyan officials. Megrahi is a long-serving associate of the ESO. In 1987, he became director of the Center for Strategic Studies, an ESO research unit that worked on covert arms procurement and on building ties with Latin American radicals.

The alleged, but unindicted, mastermind was Said Rashid, Megrahi's cousin. Rashid is a senior ESO officer and member of Libya's Revolutionary Committees Bureau. In 1980, he was briefly jailed in France for his role in the murder of a Libyan dissident in Italy. In the same year, he led a team to Togo to assassinate the Chadian president, Hissen Habré. In the early 1980s, Rashid planned attacks on U.S. targets, including planning an attempt to smuggle a cigarette-carton bomb onto a Pan Am flight from Istanbul. In the mid-1980s, according to the State Department, Rashid planned a series of attacks on U.S. targets. He was responsible for buying the MST-13 timers.

LIBYAN DENIALS OF RESPONSIBILITY

Libya, however, denied its responsibility for the bombings and refused to hand over the suspects. Qaddafi launched a diplomatic counteroffensive, accusing Britain and the U.S. of engaging in a political campaign against him. At the same time, he promised to end support for terrorist groups such as the Provisional IRA. According to Libya, a Libyan judge investigated the case and placed the two suspects in detention. A Libyan offer to discuss the matter with Scottish or American judges was turned down.

In response to the Libyan attitude, the UN Security Council adopted Resolution 731 on January 21, 1992, which demanded that Libya hand over the Lockerbie suspects, acknowledge responsibility for the attack, and cooperate fully with the French investigation. Libya asked the International Court of Justice to declare the resolution illegal but was turned down. On March 31, the UN Security Council passed Resolution 748, imposing mandatory economic sanctions on Libya. All civilian air links were cut and arms supplies banned. In response, angry mobs attacked Western embassies in Tripoli.

Libya offered to hand over the suspects to an Arab state, but the UN renewed sanctions in 1993, despite protests in the Arab world. Britain and the U.S. demanded that Libya hand over the suspects by October 1. Qaddafi refused, attempting various ploys to derail the deadline. When no progress was made, the American, French, and British UN delegations submitted a draft Security Council resolution imposing harsher sanctions on Libya. On November 11, Resolution 883 was adopted. It froze Libyan assets abroad, banned sales of certain oil and gas equipment, and closed down Libyan Arab Airlines' offices abroad.

Rex Features

The wreckage of the cockpit section of the Pan Am airliner blown up over Lockerbie, Scotland, allegedly by Libyan terrorists, in December 1988.

In 1994, Qaddafi declared his willingness to hand over the suspects to the International Court or to a Muslim court in Britain or the U.S. However, Britain and the U.S. demanded that the suspects be tried in Scotland. The UN, which reviews the sanctions every 120 days, has continued to renew the sanctions but European nations have resisted American pressure to intensify the embargo.

DOUBT OVER RESPONSIBILITY

Although the British and American governments remain firm in their campaign to force Libya to hand over the Lockerbie suspects, a variety of critics have countered the Scottish and American charges. One theory is that the PA 103 attack was the work of the PFLP-GC, sponsored by Iran in retaliation for the destruction of an Iran Air flight, shot down in error by the U.S. Navy cruiser *Vincennes* over the Gulf in 1987. Critics of the U.S. charges against Libya point out that PFLP-GC operatives were arrested in Germany with bombs clearly designed to destroy aircraft.

The most prominent of those convicted was an experienced PFLP-GC bomb-maker jailed in 1991 for bombing American troop trains. Critics also argue that the investigation initially pointed the finger at Syria and Iran, but that during the Gulf Crisis of 1990-91, it became politically more convenient to blame Libya, since the West needed Syria and Iran to cooperate in the war against Iraq. Critics of the official line include relatives of the Lockerbie victims, a former senior U.S. intelligence official, and a large number of journalists. The Scottish and American courts have, however, stuck by their accusations; and there can be no doubt that Qaddafi has been a major sponsor of terrorism.

Andrew Rathmell

SEE ALSO: ABU NIDAL; THE PLO AND THE ARAB STATES; THE ORIGINS OF PALESTINIAN ISLAMIC JIHAD; NATIONALIST TERROR IN NORTHERN IRELAND 1976-1996; THE FRENCH RESPONSE TO TERRORISM; THE AMERICAN RESPONSE TO TERRORISM; STATE-SPONSORED TERRORISM; INTERNATIONAL COOPERATION AGAINST TERRORISM.

FURTHER READING

- Chasey, William C. *Pan Am 103: The Lockerbie Cover-Up.* New York: Bridger House, 1995.
- Davis, Brian L. *Qaddafi, Terrorism and the Origins of the U.S. Attack on Libya.* New York: Praeger, 1990.
- Simons, Geoff. *Libya: The Struggle for Survival.* 2nd ed. New York: St. Martin's Press, 1996.

IRAQI SPONSORSHIP OF TERRORISM

Since President Saddam Hussein gained power in a bloody coup in 1979, Iraq's military and security forces have been ruthless in their use of terrorism against their opponents, both at home and abroad, to maintain their leader's grip on power. Under Saddam, Iraq has become a repressive and highly militarized state that has ruled through fear and the fostering of a cult of "strong" leadership. Domestic opponents, invariably rivals for power or members of separatist groups, have been murdered routinely or tortured on a massive scale. Many in opposition to Saddam have simply "disappeared." These home-grown rebel groups were violently suppressed at the end of the war with Iran during the late 1980s. They also suffered in the aftermath of the mass uprisings of Kurds in northern Iraq and of Shiite Muslims in southern Iraq after Saddam's defeat in the Gulf War of 1991.

Iraq had sought to clean up its international image in the late 1980s, as it strove to forge closer ties with the United States and the moderate Arab Gulf states. Many countries saw Saddam as a potentially effective block to the regional ambitions of fundamentalist Iran. They were seemingly willing to turn a blind eye to his sponsorship of terrorism. Indeed, many had supplied Iraq with weapons during Saddam's war against Iran in the 1980s.

KEY FACTS

- In spite of being removed from the U.S.'s official list of state sponsors of terrorism in 1982, Iraq has continued to support and direct terrorists.
- Iraqi-sponsored terrorists attacked U.S. targets during the Gulf War, aid workers in Kurdistan in 1988, and Iraqi dissidents during 1991.
- Iraq supports a guerrilla movement that uses terrorism against the Iranian government.

In 1982, Iraq was removed from the U.S. State Department's official list of countries engaged in or sponsoring terrorism, shortly before Saddam expelled the Abu Nidal Organization (ANO) in 1983. In 1987, however, Iraq probably still gave sanctuary to radical Palestinian groups, such as the Abu Abbas faction of the Palestine Liberation Front and the Arab Liberation Front. Of particular concern to the West was the presence in Baghdad, the Iraqi capital, of Abu Ibrahim, the noted bomb-maker and former leader of the defunct May 15 Organization. This was an obscure splinter group of the Popular Front for the Liberation of Palestine Special Operations Group. It was named after the anniversary of the first declaration of war, in 1948, by the Arab states against the new state of Israel.

Of equal concern to the West was the potentially volatile relationship between Iraq and Turkey. In December 1989, Turkey claimed that Kurdish Workers' Party terrorists, who had been responsible for the massacre of villagers in southeastern Turkey, were based in northern Iraq. In response, Iraq claimed that it was working with Turkey to improve security in their remote border regions.

TERRORISM WITHIN IRAQ

During 1989, Iraq itself was the theater of terrorism in the form of several bombing attacks on foreigners. One, at the New British Club, which injured 20 people, was claimed by the United Organization of the Halabja Martyrs. This radical Kurdish group sought revenge for the 1988 Iraqi massacre of Kurdish civilians through the use of chemical weapons in the town of Halabja. Another bomb in December killed several passers-by.

During the Gulf Crisis of 1990-91, Iraq took hundreds of foreign residents hostage. This policy was openly ordered by Saddam and hostages were displayed on television for propaganda purposes. Many of the hostages were held at strategic sites,

Rex Features

The Iraqi dictator Saddam Hussein ordered the taking hostage of hundreds of foreign nationals living in Iraq during the Gulf Crisis of 1990-91.

including air bases, armaments plants, and research facilities, in an attempt to deter the coalition forces from bombing them. The hostage-taking was condemned by the UN in Resolution 664 and, by December 1990, Iraq had released almost all the imprisoned Western nationals. Over 600 Kuwaitis, however, remained in captivity and their fate is still unknown. It is assumed that many have been killed, but Kuwait demands that the hostages, or their bodies, be returned. Iraq denies holding, or having held, any Kuwaitis against their will.

Iraq also made numerous threats to sponsor terrorism against countries supporting the international coalition during the Gulf Crisis. A number of Palestinian radical groups warned that they would attack enemy targets and the ANO reportedly moved personnel back to Iraq. However, the expected wave of Iraqi-sponsored terrorism did not materialize. This was largely because of tough security measures taken by governments worldwide. Many states interned suspected Iraqi agents and expelled its diplomats. Syria, a state with close ties to many radical groups, was prevailed upon to restrain Palestinian radicals, and American threats of action persuaded Libya to control its agents.

Nonetheless, there were some 200 terrorist incidents related to the Gulf Crisis, the majority carried out by domestic groups with no direct Iraqi involvement. Most involved attacks on businesses in states supporting the coalition. Iraq was directly linked to the attempted bombing of a U.S. cultural center in Manila, in the Philippines, on January 19, 1991. One Iraqi national was killed when the bomb went off prematurely and the Philippines government expelled the Iraqi diplomat who it believed had planned the operation. Iraqis were also behind an attempted bombing of the U.S. ambassador's residence in Indonesia.

TERRORISM AFTER THE GULF WAR

After the Gulf War of 1991, Iraq began to rebuild its intelligence networks but had also to concentrate on matters closer to home. Throughout 1992, Iraqi agents were responsible for dozens of attacks on Kurdish and UN targets in the UN-protected Kurdish safe haven in northern Iraq. In November, bombs exploded under UN trucks in the town of Arbil. In December, 14 relief trucks were blown up by booby-traps after they had passed through an Iraqi checkpoint. UN and aid agency offices, vehicles, and personnel were repeatedly attacked with bombs and gunfire.

Attacks on aid workers continued in 1993. In March, a Belgian aid worker was shot dead. In December, an office of the Handicapped International charity was bombed, killing one worker and injuring six. In addition to these operations, Iraqi agents mounted more ambitious foreign attacks. Two attempts were made to bomb the Kuwait Airways office in Beirut, Lebanon, and one to bomb the Kuwaiti embassy there.

ATTACKS ON WESTERN TARGETS

The most dramatic Iraqi terrorist operation was an unsuccessful plot in Kuwait to assassinate former U.S. President George Bush in April 1993. Fourteen suspects – 11 Iraqis and three Kuwaitis – were arrested in June by the local authorities. They were charged with preparing a car-bomb to kill Bush and with planning a series of other bombings in Kuwait. Several

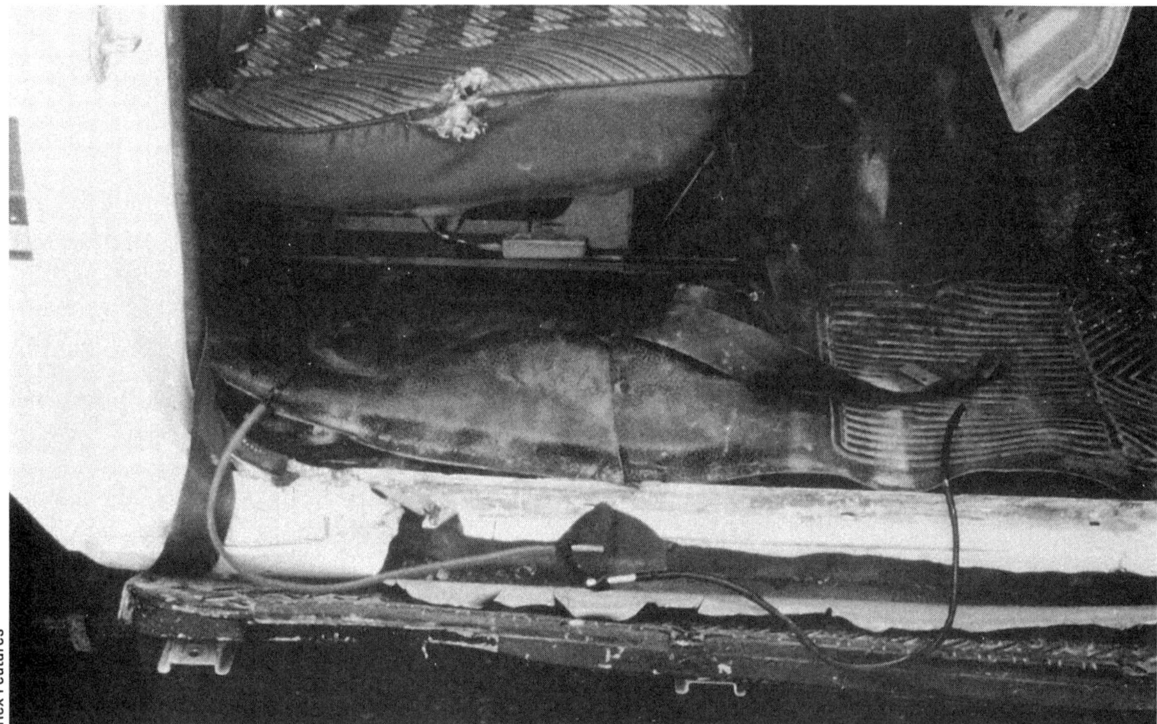

Rex Features

In April 1993, an Iraqi terrorist plot to assassinate former U.S. President George Bush in Kuwait was foiled and the car-bomb (seen here) was destroyed.

defendants turned out to be Iraqi intelligence officers. They had smuggled two vehicles into Kuwait, one of which was loaded with 180 pounds of explosives, as well as bombs, grenades, and handguns. Forensic experts identified the detonation devices and wiring of the car-bomb as having a distinctive Iraqi "signature." In retaliation, U.S. forces fired cruise missiles at the headquarters of Iraqi intelligence in June 1993. The defendants were convicted in June 1994; six received death sentences, seven were given prison terms, and one was acquitted.

In 1994, Iraq continued its attacks on aid workers and journalists in northern Iraq. At least 16 incidents were reported. It emerged that Iraq was willing to reward anyone who killed a foreign worker or correspondent. In March, two Swedish journalists were injured when a bomb went off under their car. In April, a German journalist and her bodyguard were shot dead in an ambush in Kurdistan. In May, two vehicles belonging to the British charity Oxfam were fired on.

Another form of Iraqi terrorism has been its pursuit of dissidents abroad. In 1988, Iraqi intelligence assassinated three dissidents in England, Norway, and Sudan. A favorite technique has been to use poison, notably thallium. Several Iraqi opposition activists have turned up in Western hospitals in recent years suffering the effects of poisoning and some have died. Iraqi agents also shot dead an Iraqi nuclear scientist in Amman who was on the verge of defecting to Jordan in December 1992. In April 1994, a leading Iraqi opposition figure was murdered in Beirut. The Lebanese government claimed that it had evidence of Iraqi involvement, expelled two diplomats, and then broke diplomatic relations with Baghdad.

SUPPORTING TERRORISM AGAINST IRAN

Iraq has also been a long-time supporter of the Mujahedin-e Khalq Organization (MKO) in Iran. This leftist-Islamic group fought against the shah before and during the Iranian revolution of 1979, but has been in opposition to the fundamentalist regime since then. Banned in Iran, MKO has become the mainstay of an opposition coalition, the National Council of Resistance, based in Paris. The movement fields a conventional force, the National Liberation Army

Frank Spooner Pictures

Soldiers of the Mujahedin-e Khalq's conventional National Liberation Army take part in a live-fire exercise in Iraq.

(NLA). This is based in Iraq and is supplied with equipment, personnel, and training by the Iraqi army. During the Iran-Iraq War of 1980-88, the NLA operated closely with the Iraqi military. On several occasions, it sent forces on raids inside Iran, and Iranian forces have frequently attacked NLA bases in Iraq.

The Mujahedin-e Khalq also has a network of activists inside Iran which have engaged in terrorism. The strength of the movement inside Iran is uncertain: hundreds of MKO supporters have been executed and many more tortured and jailed. In June 1994, the Iranians accused MKO of planting a bomb in Mashhad that killed 25 people and injured 70.

In October 1994, border clashes between the NLA and Iranian troops escalated, and Iran fired Scud long-range missiles at the NLA's main base at Ashraf in Iraq. The MKO responded with a bomb planted in Tehran, the Iranian capital, which killed two. Two days later, Iranian jets raided the Ashraf base. These clashes represented a slight flare-up in the low-intensity war between Iran and Iranian dissidents, which continues to involve assassinations, bombings, and armed raids on both sides.

Andrew Rathmell

SEE ALSO: BOMBING OPERATIONS; HIJACKING AND KIDNAPPING; ASSASSINATION; COLLABORATION BETWEEN TERRORISTS; HOSTAGE NEGOTIATIONS; ABU NIDAL; KURDISH NATIONALIST TERRORISM; TERRORISM AND REVOLUTION IN IRAN; STATE-SPONSORED TERRORISM.

FURTHER READING

- Dekmejian, R. Hrair. *Islam in Revolution: Fundamentalism in the Arab World.* 2nd ed. Syracuse, NY: Syracuse University Press, 1995.
- Miller, Judith, and Laurie Mylruie. *Saddam Hussein and the Crisis in the Gulf.* New York: Times Books, 1990.
- Sciolino, Elaine. *The Outlaw State: Saddam Hussein's Quest for Power and the Gulf Crisis.* New York: Wiley, 1991.

THE 1996 SAUDI TRUCK BOMB IN DHAHRAN

On June 25, 1996, a massive truck bomb devastated a U.S. Air Force housing compound in Khobar, near Dhahran airbase in Saudi Arabia. The bomb, a fuel truck packed with explosives, killed 19 U.S. servicemen and injured nearly 400 other people, mostly Americans. The bombing took place just seven months after a car-bomb killed five Americans at a training office for the Saudi National Guard in Riyadh. Four men confessed to the Riyadh incident and were publicly beheaded in May 1996.

The blasts aroused a storm of anger in the United States. Shortly after the attack, President Bill Clinton spoke at the summit of the seven industrialized nations in Lyons, France. He vowed to make the fight against terrorism a top priority. He launched an urgent review of security at U.S. military installations worldwide, while an 80-strong FBI team was sent to Saudi Arabia.

Although Clinton accused Iran, and called on leaders of industrialized nations to isolate "rogue" states, it was widely assumed that the perpetrators hailed from a Saudi Islamic fundamentalist opposition group. The Riyadh bombers had confessed on television to opposing the presence of U.S. troops in Saudi Arabia. Although there were rumours that the men had been tortured, and FBI investigators were not allowed to interrogate them, few observers doubted the integrity of their confessions.

KEY FACTS

- 20,000 U.S. troops were based in Saudi Arabia after 1991 – a presence that created tension among fundamentalist opponents of the Saudi government.
- The Saudi truck bomb was the biggest attack on U.S. servicemen in the Middle East since the bombing of a marine barracks in Beirut in 1983.
- The blast was created by 5 tons of explosives and left a crater 35 feet deep and 45 feet wide.

The only group that claimed the Khobar bombing was the League of the Martyr Abdullah al-Huzaifi. The group demanded the removal of foreign troops from Saudi Arabia and warned that more attacks would follow. The group takes its name from a Saudi dissident who was executed after being convicted of throwing acid in the face of a secret policeman.

PROTECTORS OR OCCUPIERS?

One purpose of both bombings was to highlight the growing American military presence in the kingdom. Only since the Gulf Crisis of 1990-91 have U.S. forces been based in the country. Although nominally only present as advisers and technicians, up to 20,000 U.S. troops were based in Saudi Arabia after 1991. Their presence has become an increasing source of concern to hard-line Saudi fundamentalists, who regard the U.S. troops as unwanted intruders.

The targeting of U.S. forces is, however, only the symbolic tip of the iceberg for Saudi Arabia's dissidents. The Saudi royal family has always sought to legitimize its rule by relying heavily on a combination of force and religion. This has brought it into opposition over the years with more conservative members of the *ulema*, the Islamic clergy. For instance, the introduction of television into the kingdom proved very difficult when the *ulema* opposed television as a morally corrupting force.

The Gulf War of 1991 sparked the most recent round of conflict between the regime and its conservative critics. Although King Fahd justified the presence of foreign troops in the country on Islamic grounds, many members of the *ulema* regarded the king's reliance on infidels as sacrilegious.

After Iraq's defeat, religious leaders presented a series of petitions to the regime in which they demanded political and religious reforms, including the removal of foreign troops, the establishment of a consultative assembly, curbs on corruption, and a stricter application of

Rex Features

The U.S. Air Force housing compound in Khobar lies in ruins after the Saudi truck bomb attack in 1996, which killed 19.

Islamic law. King Fahd responded in part to the demands by establishing a *majlis al-shura* (consultative council) which began work in 1993. The council was, however, seen as a powerless assembly by the dissidents. They complained that Fahd would not acknowledge their other grievances. In response, the Saudi rulers arrested many people, including two outspoken young clerics, Shcikhs al-Awdah and al-Hawali.

Several dissidents escaped abroad. Dr. Muhammad al-Masari, a physicist, moved to London in 1994, where he acted as the spokesman for an umbrella fundamentalist movement, the Committee for the Defense of Legitimate Rights (CDLR). He carried out an active propaganda campaign against the house of Saud.

As Masari has consistently warned since 1994, if the Saudi government continues to repress dissent and refuses to allow more power sharing, then radical dissidents will emerge who see force as the solution. The Riyadh and Khobar bombings demonstrate that this has happened. There are some 20,000 Saudi veterans who fought with the *mujahideen* in Afghanistan. If the government does not accommodate the radical Muslims, then Saudi Arabia may face further terrorist violence.

Ashley Brown

SEE ALSO: BOMBING OPERATIONS; ARAB STATES AND TERRORISM IN THE 1990s; PALESTINIAN ISLAMIC FUNDAMENTALISM; THE AMERICAN RESPONSE TO TERRORISM.

FURTHER READING

- Dekmejian, R. Hrair. *Islam in Revolution: Fundamentalism in the Arab World.* 2nd ed. Syracuse, NY: Syracuse University Press, 1995.
- Dekmejian, R. Hrair. "The Rise of Political Islamism in Saudi Arabia," in *The Middle East Journal* 48, No. 4 (Autumn 1994): 627-44.
- Al-Rasheed, Madawi, and Loulouwa Al-Rasheed. "The Politics of Encapsulation: Saudi Policy Towards Tribal and Religious Opposition," in *Middle Eastern Studies* 32, No. 1 (January 1996): 96-119.

CHAPTER TWELVE

Radical Muslim Terrorism

The radical Muslim revolutionaries who overthrew the shah of Iran in 1979 gave birth to a wave of religious-based terrorism that aims to establish fundamentalist regimes in the Middle East. Targets of these zealots have included Israeli nationals, citizens of Western powers backing the Jewish state, and more moderate Arab nations. Fired by their religious fervor, the terrorists are willing to martyr themselves for their beliefs, and suicide bombers have become a disturbing feature of the terrorist attacks launched by the fundamentalists.

ROOTS OF FUNDAMENTALIST TERRORISM

During the twentieth century, both the Shia and the Sunni branches of Islam have spawned fundamentalist movements that have sought to reestablish Muslim cultural and political autonomy in the Arab states of the Middle East and Africa. These aggressive, defiant movements have sought to throw off the yoke of Western influence, and they share the goal of establishing Shari'a – the religious law derived from the Koran – as the uncontested law of the land. From the late 1980s, in particular, terrorism increasingly has been used as an important method of achieving these goals.

THE RISE OF FUNDAMENTALIST TERROR

The great appeal of fundamentalist Islam in the late twentieth century lies in the fact that secular political parties have failed to give Muslims a dominant position, even in the Middle East. The great symbol of this failure has been the continued existence of the state of Israel. The fundamentalist message is simple but powerful: Muslims are downtrodden because they have allowed foreign ideologies such as capitalism and Marxism to displace the cultural values, philosophy, and way of life that had once served as the foundation of a great civilization; Islam will be able to develop its own modern civilization only by rejecting Western laws and customs and returning society completely to the Shari'a. For fundamentalists, "Islam is the solution" to the social, economic, and moral crises of the day.

There was nothing inevitable about the rise of terrorism in connection with fundamentalism. Fundamentalists have made, and continue to make, their mark on Muslim societies by establishing schools, medical clinics, orphanages, and other social service institutions. Many organizations such as the Muslim Brotherhood in Egypt, for example, have been non-violent for long periods of their history.

However, in the 1980s, three events occurred that radicalized the Muslim world and facilitated a shift towards terrorism. First, there was the 1978-79 revolution in Iran, which established a Muslim Shiite state under the Ayatollah Khomeini. Its example provoked a wave of Shiite militancy throughout the Middle East, and Iran was able to provide vital support to terrorists. More important, however, were the difficulties that the Iranian revolution caused the West. Episodes such as the taking hostage of members of the U.S. Embassy staff in Tehran and the fact that the U.S. had to negotiate a solution gave the Shiite revolution credibility among Muslims of all persuasions.

Second, there was the war in Lebanon, where Iranian-inspired Shiite terrorists, especially from Hizb'allah, again had great success against Western and Israeli forces.

Finally, there was the war in Afghanistan, where Soviet communism was defeated by the *mujahideen* – Islamic warriors who were consciously fighting against Western civilization and who were recruited from throughout the Muslim world. After the

KEY FACTS

- Tension between Islam and Christianity has existed in the Middle East since the Crusades, when religious-inspired terror was employed by both sides.
- Islam is divided into two major branches: Sunnism and Shiism. Sunni believers today account for the vast majority of the Muslim community. There is a long history of bloody antagonism between the two sects.
- The fundamentalist revival of the 1980s and 1990s has its roots in the Shiite movement al-Dawa ("The call of Islam"), founded in the Shiite holy city of Hajaf in the 1960s.

Hulton Getty Picture Collection

The Shiite religious leader Sheikh Mohamed Hussein Fadlallah was an important inspiration for Hizb'allah, the Lebanese fundamentalist terrorist group.

mujahideen success in Afghanistan, these militant warriors provided a core of experienced, committed fighters throughout the Middle East.

Economic crisis and social unrest have played an important role. The *mujahideen* were recruited from the thousands of disaffected young men who, while often highly educated, could not find employment in the stagnant economies of the Middle East and North Africa. In Algeria and Egypt, they were known as the "young men who hold up the walls." In the slums of Gaza in Israeli-occupied Palestine, or the shanty-towns outside war-torn Beirut, there are even younger boys who have helped to form the suicide squads of Hamas in Palestine, and Hizb'allah in Lebanon.

ISLAMIC JUSTIFICATION OF TERRORISM

There is a strong political element in Islam. The basic duty of the Muslim is submission (Arabic: *islam*) to the will of God (*Allah*) through internal struggle (*jihad*) with sin. In itself, this is not unlike the preaching of other religions. Islam, however, does not recognize the compartmentalization of society into public and private realms; nor has it undergone a reformation leading to the legal or constitutional separation between religion and state. Muslims are called upon to bring the behavior of the wider world into conformity with the religious teachings and moral precepts of the Holy Koran (the word of God dictated to the Prophet Muhammad) and the Sunna (the teachings and practices of the Prophet).

At a very basic level, the use of force by the Muslim community is believed to be sanctioned by Allah as a necessary response to the existence of evil in the world. Contemporary fundamentalists have retrieved interpretations of *jihad* formulated during the medieval period. Medieval Muslim jurists divided the world into two spheres, *dar al-Islam* (the realm where Islamic law applied) and *dar al-harb* (all other lands). *Jihad*, properly speaking, is war waged against non-Muslim countries. Sunni fundamentalists have adopted this notion to justify terrorist campaigns in Israel, Europe, and the United States. Modern Muslim theorists have attempted to justify the use of terrorism

Rex Features

Iranians hold aloft an effigy of "Uncle Sam" during anti-U.S. demonstrations in Tehran, 1979.

against competing Muslim sects. Sayyid Qutb, a literary critic and member of the Egyptian Muslim Brotherhood, provided a rationale for eliminating "compromising" Muslim leaders. Imprisoned by President Nasser on charges of sedition, Qutb consulted the Hanbali school of jurisprudence to find a precedent for attacking fellow Muslims.

In an influential treatise *Milestones*, Qutb argued that the Arab world had descended into a state of *jahiliyya*, or pre-Islamic ignorance, characterized by the presence of false Muslims who were undermining the faith from within. Nasser was one such character, Qutb implied, and therefore deserved to die. Qutb's writings gave justification to a generation of Sunni Muslim radicals who believe it their duty to withdraw from society, and to mount terrorist campaigns against infidel Muslims and their Western supporters. Sheikh Omar Abdel Rahman, the blind Muslim preacher convicted of conspiracy to blow up the World Trade Center, is an ideological disciple of Qutb.

The final, and perhaps most powerful, theological justification for fundamentalist terrorism comes from Shiite theorists, especially the Ayatollah Khomeini. This Shiite justification is that Islam is confronted by an apocalyptic crisis, threatening the very survival of the Muslim community, and Shiite believers are obliged to bear arms in self-defense. What added to the power of this argument for many of his followers was the belief that Khomeini was the final Shiite leader who would reverse the misfortunes of history, and lead the true believers to a decisive victory. Perhaps most unusual was the argument that the apocalyptic crisis could justify a suspension of normal Islamic law. In the last year of his life, Khomeini made the extraordinary pronouncement that, in order to preserve Islam, he might suspend the Shari'a and subordinate it to his own political judgments.

This dramatization of the power of their enemies makes fundamentalists difficult to understand, or to deal with, for Western governments operating in a very different moral universe. How can there ever be any real dialogue between Iranian politicians and a U.S. that they categorize as "the Great Satan"? Such fundamentalists sincerely believe that inhuman violence may be necessary to stem the "evil" tide of Western civilization and its "illnesses."

R. Scott Appleby

SEE ALSO: RELIGIOUS EXTREMISM; THE MINDSET OF THE TERRORIST; SUICIDE BOMBING; TERROR IN LEBANON 1980-1987; TERRORISM AND REVOLUTION IN IRAN; IRANIAN SPONSORSHIP OF TERRORISM; HIZB'ALLAH; HAMAS; ISLAMIC FUNDAMENTALIST TERRORISM IN EGYPT.

FURTHER READING

- Hashmi, Sohail H."Interpreting the Islamic Ethics of War and Peace" in *The Ethics of War and Peace: Religious and Secular Perspectives*, edited by Terry Nardin. Princeton, NJ: Princeton University Press, 1996.
- Marty, Martin E., and R. Scott Appleby, eds. *Fundamentalisms and the State: Remaking Polities, Economies, and Militance.* Chicago: University of Chicago Press, 1993.
- Sivan, Emmanuel. *Radical Islam: Medieval Theology and Modern Politics.* London and New Haven: Yale University Press, 1987.

TERRORISM AND REVOLUTION IN IRAN

In Iran, the use of terrorism in the name of religion has a long pedigree. In the eleventh century, the Assassins used terror to gain converts for the Ismaili sect of Islam, "assassinating" the leaders of rival sects. In the twentieth century, terrorism has arisen from the clash between radical Shiite Islam (the majority of the Iranian population are Shiite believers) and secular trends adopted from the West. Also, there has been a powerful strand of leftist militancy which has produced waves of political assassinations.

The tension between Islam and the secular state reached a bloody climax in the the 1978–79 Islamic revolution, which brought to power the fundamentalist regime of the Ayatollah Khomeini. Terrorism not only paved the way for the revolution but also proved crucial to the consolidation of the regime in its early years. Under Khomeini, religious-inspired terrorism gained the sanction of the state, playing an unprecedented role in both the suppression of internal dissent and the execution of foreign policy. There has been no shortage of people who have been willing to kill and to die to further the cause of both Islam and the Islamic Republic. The relationship between terrorism and religion is complex, and Khomeini himself seems to have been deeply aware of this. But it is the ability of the regime to reconcile the criminal and the spiritual that has made fundamentalist terrorism particularly difficult for the West to understand.

SUMMARY

- In the twentieth century, terrorism has been used as a weapon in the struggle between Islamic fundamentalists and pro-Western modernizers.
- Terrorism, particularly from leftist groups such as the People's Fighters, undermined the regime of the pro-Western Shah Mohammed Reza Pahlavi and helped pave the way for the Islamic revolution.
- Under the leadership of the Ayatollah Khomeini, the new Islamic Republic used terrorism to consolidate the revolution – most notably in the U.S. hostage crisis of 1979-80.
- The Islamic Republic itself came under attack from terrorist groups, particularly in the early 1980s.

ANTI-WESTERN TERROR

Under the westernizing Pahlavi dynasty of rulers (who bore the traditional title of *shah*), which ruled Iran from 1925 until the fall of Shah Mohammed Reza Pahlavi in 1978, clerical opposition groups used terrorism as a political weapon. Self-Sacrificers of Islam, formed in 1945, was the most efficient of these groups. It demanded the strict application of the Shari'a (Islamic law) and wanted to ban anything that smacked of Western influence, including Western clothes, tobacco, gambling, even movies. Anti-Western feelings directed the group's choice of targets.

In 1948, it assassinated Ahmad Kasravi, a leading secularist lawyer and historian. In 1951, it assassinated a pro-British prime minister, General Ali Razmara. In 1955, after another assassination attempt, four of the group's leaders were executed and the group disbanded. The Self-Sacrificers was briefly revived during the 1978-79 revolution, and may have been responsible for the murder of one of the shah's nephews in Paris in 1979.

The tension between clerical and secular forces increased in the 1960s. In what is known as the White Revolution, the shah pushed Iran still further towards the West and away from Islam, displaying little sensitivity to his country's traditions as he did so. The country's power structures shifted decisively away from the clerical classes and towards secular government. The clerics lost control of education. Traditional laws were liberalized, particularly with regard to the

Rex Features

Ayatollah Ruhollah Musavi Khomeini, supreme ruler of Iran between 1979 and 1989, brought terrorism into both domestic and foreign policy.

position of women. Crucially, close links were developed with the United States, which required social and economic reforms as a precondition of military aid.

While the White Revolution was generally supported by the Iranian people, the clerical authorities opposed it vehemently. The clerics accused the shah of shamelessly abandoning Iran's core Islamic values for Western values that were inappropriate for the Iranian people. They pointed, too, to the corruption and greed that were endemic in the royal family.

THE AYATOLLAH KHOMEINI

On June 5, 1963, the shah's Imperial Guards attacked Iran's largest theological college in Qom. The intention was to arrest the Ayatollah Khomeini (*ayatollah* is a Shiite religious title meaning "sign of God"), who was the leader of a circle of radical clerics based at the college, and was coordinating the anti-government opposition throughout the country. During the assault, pro-Khomeini riots broke out. Students were thrown off the college roof; others were drowned in a nearby lake. The insurgency spread quickly to Tehran, where in one incident, rioters murdered three unveiled women. The government responded brutally: the security forces killed more than 300 people.

Khomeini himself was deported from Iran a year later and was to spend the next fourteen years in exile, mostly in the Shiite holy city of Najaf in neighboring Iraq. He was nevertheless able to develop his campaign against the shah's government, building up a network of followers in Iran and providing guidance and encouragement through a series of tape recordings that were smuggled into the country.

LEFTIST TERRORISM IN THE 1970s

Despite Khomeini's deportation, opposition to the shah's regime grew. Throughout the 1970s, terrorism proliferated, and was largely perpetrated by leftist groups. Two of the most effective and long-lasting terrorist campaigns were launched by the People's Fighters and Popular Self-Sacrificers.

The People's Fighters was formed secretly in 1965 by radical Shiite graduates of Tehran University, many of whom had been politicized in the 1963 riots. As the group developed, its beliefs became a curious blend of Marxism and Islam: true Muslims must struggle for a classless society and against both Western capitalism and conservative clericalism. The People's Fighters began terrorist actions in August 1971, at the time of celebrations to mark 2,500 years of the monarchy. On August 13, 1972, the People's Fighters murdered Tehran's police chief, General Taheri, responsible for torturing many of its members during the repression after the Qom uprising. On June 2, 1973, the group murdered two U.S. Air Force colonels in Tehran. Then, in August 1976, as the U.S. and Iran announced a $10 billion arms deal, they killed three U.S. technicians who were associated with the military aid program.

The Popular Self-Sacrificers was formed in 1970 by a group of leftist students. The group was inspired by the revolutionary movement of Fidel Castro in Cuba and by Che Guevera's doctrine of "propaganda by the deed," whereby guerrilla acts were deliberately used to provoke government repression and push the country towards a revolutionary crisis. In February 1971,

Rex Features

Militant Shiite students brandish a vandalized photograph of the shah during demonstrations outside the U.S. embassy in Tehran, November 1979.

activists attacked a police station at Siakal, near the Caspian Sea, in an bid to start a guerrilla war against the Iranian government. What became known as the "Siakal Incident" galvanized the Iranian opposition: hundreds of young people, mainly middle-class, joined the group. Many of the leaders of the Popular Self-Sacrificers subsequently received guerrilla training in the Palestine Liberation Organization (PLO) camps in the Lebanon and South Yemen.

In 1975, the People's Fighters split and its Marxist wing joined the Popular Self-Sacrificers. As well as sharing ideological sympathies, their methods were similar. Both robbed banks to finance their struggles. Each killed informers, targeted certain members of the government for assassination, particularly officials of the shah's secret police (Savak), and attacked the property of foreign governments active in Iran. The battle between the terrorists and the shah's government became increasingly brutal throughout the 1970s. The spiralling cycle of terror and counterterror, demonstration and repression, created a situation of near-anarchy which Khomeini was able to exploit.

REVOLUTION

Terrorism played a crucial role in destabilizing the regime, but the shah's ineptitude and Khomeini's patient nurturing of support for his campaign against the shah also contributed. From the mid-1970s, U.S. President Jimmy Carter put increasing pressure on the shah to liberalize his regime, particularly in the light of Iran's appalling human-rights record. The liberalization measures, simply allowed the disaffected to express their opposition more forcefully. Unable to cope, the shah made matters worse by promising reforms and then using his forces to quell the rising opposition. In 1978, the mysterious murder of one of Khomeini's sons led to riots in which angry crowds took to the streets of Qom, wrecking anything they considered Western. A number of protesters were killed, and most of the country went into a 40-day mourning period.

On September 4, 1978, some 100,000 people again took to the streets. Three days later, after another mass demonstration, the shah placed Tehran under martial law. Undeterred, the next day people protested in Jaleh Square. This time the shah's Imperial Guard opened fire. Within minutes, 500 protesters lay dead. The massacre, known as "Black Friday," is as significant for the Islamic revolution as the storming of the Bastille in 1789 is for the French Revolution.

Support for Khomeini continued to grow, and in 1978, the shah persuaded Iraq to deport Khomeini. He went to Paris, as France had somewhat controversially agreed to grant Khomeini refuge. This was another tactical blunder by the shah. France provided Khomeini with a more effective communications base from which to spread his message. Khomeini conducted the revolution by fax and telex.

On November 5, the shah imposed martial law throughout the country, but order was deteriorating rapidly. On January 13, 1979, the beleaguered shah appointed the opposition leader, Shahpour Bakhtiar, as prime minister, in a final attempt act of reconciliation. Bakhtiar, however, would only accept his appointment on condition that the shah leave the country. Three days later, the shah fled. Bakhtiar and his provisional government were helpless. On January 31, Khomeini flew to Tehran, and on February 11, he proclaimed the Islamic Republic.

THE TAKING OF THE U.S. EMBASSY

Terrorism helped to create the right conditions for revolution. After the revolution, however, it took center stage. Khomeini, who had previously managed to keep himself from the taint of terrorist activity, was forced to dirty his hands for the sake of political expedience. The occupation of the American embassy in Tehran can be seen as the turning-point in the changing role of terrorism. The crisis showed that ultimately Khomeini was willing to exploit terrorism for political ends – in both a domestic and international context.

In October 1979, the Carter Administration admitted the deposed shah to the U.S. for medical treatment. This move helped to fuel already widespread anti-American feelings. On November 4, 1979, around 400 militant Islamic students stormed the U.S. embassy in Tehran, taking 49 American citizens hostage. The students burnt the American flag and hung a banner from the embassy roof which proclaimed: "Khomeini struggles, Carter trembles."

The occupation was clearly as much a surprise to the revolutionary government as it was to the U.S. Khomeini, however, was quick to exploit the situation. In an angry public speech in support of the students, he confirmed the students' threat to kill all the hostages if the U.S. made any attempt to attack the embassy. "This is not a struggle between the United States and Iran," Khomeini announced. "It is a struggle between Iran and blasphemy."

The hostage crisis offered Khomeini the perfect opportunity both to undermine the more moderate factions in the Iranian government who favored a more conciliatory attitude towards the U.S., and to discredit the U.S. itself.

THE DELTA FORCE DISASTER

Initially, despite Khomeini's bluster, there were signs that the hostage crisis might be resolved peacefully. On November 20, 1979, Khomeini requested that the students release four women and six blacks who were among the hostages. The students complied. From then on, however, the U.S. and Iranian governments found themselves increasingly at loggerheads. The Iranian students wanted the shah extradited from the U.S. so that he could stand trial. At the same time, hard-liners within the revolutionary government refused to negotiate the release of the hostages. President Jimmy Carter ordered all Iranian assets in the U.S. frozen. But the American public clamored for more decisive action, and on April 24, 1980, the 1st Special Forces Operational Detachment moved in.

Delta Force, as it was known, was set up in 1977, under Captain Charlie Beckwith. Delta Force specialized in counterinsurgency and its personnel were trained to deal with hostage situations. However, in this instance, Delta Force would have to operate in unfriendly territory, and against problems of difficult terrain and poor intelligence. Despite the complexity of the plan, Operation Eagle Claw went ahead, and on April 24, 118 men of Delta Force were flown in to Desert One, a code-named area 200 miles south of Tehran. This first part of the operation went smoothly

Popperfoto

The scene through the main gate at the U.S. embassy in Tehran, October 1979. Khomeini exploited the embassy crisis as a way of consolidating his regime during its precarious early months.

enough: Iranian radars failed to detect the low-flying aircraft. Delta Force secured the area and waited for the helicopters that were to take them to a safe hiding place near Tehran before sunrise. At this point, things started to go terribly wrong.

The helicopters were over an hour late, and only six of the eight expected appeared because of problems caused by sandstorms. When another helicopter developed problems, Beckwith decided to abort the mission. As the troop-carriers prepared for take-off, one of the airborne helicopters got caught up in gusts of wind and smashed into one of the carriers with a huge explosion, killing eight men and sending missiles high into the Iranian sky.

Khomeini used the event to prove both American treachery and the continued existence of traitors within Iran itself. The armed forces were purged, and more than 100 officers were executed. The moderates in the government who had favored a more conciliatory attitude towards the U.S. were progressively neutralized as a political force.

The hostage crisis remained unresolved until January 1981, after the end of the Carter Administration and after the shah's death. The hostages had spent 444 days in captivity.

THE IRANIAN TERROR

The period following the revolution was extremely precarious for the new republic. There were not only counterrevolutionary threats from the monarchists and the army, but also the rival revolutionary claims of leftist groups such as the People's Fighters. Moreover, Khomeini aimed at the complete transformation of Iran and was prepared to use terror to achieve it.

In the immediate aftermath of the revolution, there were wholesale executions of the opposition – both of

Popperfoto

Islamic Revolutionary Guards gather around the debris of the U.S. helicopters downed during the failed Operation Eagle Claw, and the charred bodies of two American members of Delta Force.

monarchists and leftists. Between February 1979 and January 1980, more than 582 people were executed; in the following 18 months, another 904 were killed. It has been calculated that more than 10,000 people were executed between 1979 and 1983.

The institutionalization of terrorism that took place under the Islamic Republic, and the important role terrorism played in the revolution, were nowhere clearer than in the formation of the Islamic Revolutionary Guards Corps (IRGC). In the anarchy of the revolutionary period, lay followers of Khomeini had looted the police and army armories and had set themselves up as *pasdors* or revolutionary guards. There was, however, little coordination behind their activity, which was little better than street thuggery. In May 1979, Khomeini used this powerful but chaotic force to form a state paramilitary organization, the IRGC. The IRGC's existence was even enshrined in the new Constitution: Article 150 charges the IRGC with "defending the Revolution and safeguarding its achievements." Terrorist activity by the IRGC thus played a crucial role in the consolidation of Khomeini's revolution. The IRGC coordinated the activity of the street mobs in the waves of state terror that followed the revolution and in the crushing of counter coups, such as that of the People's Fighters in June 1981.

TERRORISM AGAINST THE REPUBLIC

The government of the Islamic Republic itself quickly became a target for terrorism. Almost immediately after the revolution, a little-known group named Forghan successfully assassinated Iran's army chief of staff, the chairman of the revolutionary council, and several major religious figures, as well as attacking foreign business interests and other supporters of the regime. The true composition of this group was never clarified, and it ultimately disappeared.

In 1981, the People's Fighters attempted to seize power in alliance with communists and Kurdish socialists. After a series of street battles with the IRGC, in which hundreds of people were killed, the leader of the People's Fighters, Massoud Rajavi, was forced to flee the country. Many of his supporters were arrested, tried, and executed. Defeated in open battle, the People's Fighters resorted to terrorism. On June 28 of the same year, a bomb exploded at the headquarters of the government party, killing more than 70 people. Among the victims were the chief justice of the supreme court (a personal friend of Ayatollah Khomeini), four members of the cabinet, seven assistant cabinet ministers, and countless senior members of the party.

This devastating attack led to a brutal period of terror and counterterror, with the People's Fighters engaging in significant numbers of political assassinations throughout the country, targeting members of the government and religious leaders in sympathy with it. On August 30, a bomb killed the newly appointed president, Mohammed Ali Rajai; further bombs killed the new prime minister, the head of police, and the prosecutor-general. The People's Fighters also conducted suicide attacks, in which its members would approach a religious leaders and officials and detonate bombs concealed beneath their clothes. Hundreds of officials were murdered. Indeed, it is thought that 1,000-2,000 government and religious supporters of Khomeini were killed during this period.

The new republic was now at its most vulnerable, and counterterror was ruthlessly employed to preserve the revolution. The Khomeini government executed thousands of supposed opponents of the republic. Demonstrations were broken up and participants – boys as young as 12 among them – shot. The secret headquarters of the People's Fighters was discovered in Tehran, and several of its leaders killed.

By 1981, the leader of the People's Fighters, Masud Rajavi, had fled Iran, and the group ceased to be a significant force in Iranian politics. The group is currently operating from exile in Iraq, and although it is highly active in mobilizing support against the Iranian government, its impact has been quite limited.

KHOMEINI'S AMBIVALENCE TO TERRORISM

The hostage crisis reveals the profound ambivalence of the Ayatollah Khomeini's attitude towards terrorism. Although he could claim that he did not order the occupation of the embassy and could point to the early freeing of the women and black hostages as evidence of his mercy, at the same time he exploited the hostage-taking as a means of furthering the interests of the Islamic Republic. As Khomeini's career progressed and the Islamic Republic became ever more deeply embroiled in terrorism, both at home and abroad, this contradiction deepened.

Initially, Khomeini was publicly scrupulous in his condemnation of terrorism. Traditional Shiite teaching allowed only for defensive war, since *Jihad*, or Holy War, is strictly a Sunni concept. In his handbook on Islamic law, *Treatise on the Clarification of Problematic Issues*, Khomeini endorses this view, justifying defensive war on the grounds of the somewhat vague Koranic injunction "to enjoin the good and prohibit the bad." There is no doubt that his condemnation of terrorism was unreserved in a statement of April 1988: hijacking, hostage-taking and bombing of civilians were "against Islam and against common sense."

However, later in the same year, Khomeini reversed his position. He issued an edict in which he stated that acts of violence that went against Koranic teachings might be justifiable for reasons of state. The issuing of the *fatwa* against Salman Rushdie, the British Muslim author of the novel *The Satanic Verses*, sentencing him to death, was an open confirmation of this policy on terrorism. Khomeini died in June 1989, with the Islamic regime firmly entrenched.

Robert P. Anderson

SEE ALSO: THEORIES OF STATE TERROR; REVOLUTIONARY TERRORISM; RELIGIOUS EXTREMISM; HOSTAGE NEGOTIATION; ROOTS OF FUNDAMENTALIST TERRORISM; IRANIAN SPONSORSHIP OF TERRORISM.

FURTHER READING

- Al-Khalil, Samir. *Republic of Fear*. Berkeley: University of California Press, and London: Hutchinson, 1991.
- Menashri, David. *Iran: A Decade of War and Revolution*. New York: Holmes and Meier, 1990.
- Perdue, William D. *Terrorism and the State: A Critique of Domination through Fear*. New York: Praeger, 1989.

IRANIAN SPONSORSHIP OF TERRORISM

Iran has been a leading supporter of international terrorism since the 1980s. The new regime, led by Ayatollah Ruhollah Khomeini, was eager to export its fundamentalist Islamic revolution and backed radical groups throughout the Middle East, especially in Kuwait, Saudi Arabia, and Bahrain. Iran supported Shiites in Iraq who became useful allies in the Iran-Iraq War. Iran also helped found Hizb'allah in Lebanon.

When Khomeini died in 1989, Hashemi Rafsanjani became president and scaled down Iran's revolutionary aims. Although relations improved with the Arab Gulf states, Iran continued to back anti-Iraqi Shiite groups, fund Hizb'allah, and attack dissidents abroad. By 1990, Iran's ties with Sudan, a major terrorist base, were a cause for concern. Tension mounted in the mid-1990s, when Iran was accused by Egypt of supporting terrorists there and accused by Israel and the U.S. of sponsoring Hamas and Palestinian Islamic Jihad.

TERRORISM IN THE GULF STATES

Iran's support for terrorism against the Arab Gulf states was closely linked to its support for Shiite opposition in these countries. The most important were the Organization of the Islamic Revolution in the Arabian Peninsula, the Islamic Front for the Liberation of Bahrain, the Islamic Call Party, and the Supreme Council for the Islamic Revolution in Iraq.

In January 1987, Kuwaiti Shiite terrorists bombed Kuwaiti oil installations. Also that year, Iran trained a Bahraini engineer to sabotage Bahrain's oil refinery but he was detected before he could carry out the task. Further attacks occurred in April and May in response to Kuwait's decision to ask the U.S. to escort its oil tankers under the American flag. In July, two Kuwaiti Shiites blew themselves up while trying to bomb an Air France office. In the following months, bombs were set off at a Pan Am office, an American insurance company, and the Kuwait Ministry of the Interior. In June 1987, 16 Kuwaiti Shiites (four in absentia) were tried for bombing Kuwaiti oil-fields in 1986 and 1987. Fourteen were convicted and 6 sentenced to death.

A long-running source of antagonism was the fate of 17 members of the Islamic Call Party jailed in Kuwait for the bombings of the U.S. and French embassies in 1983. Numerous terrorist acts were committed in an attempt to force Kuwait to release them. The most dramatic was the hijacking in April 1987 of Kuwait Airways Flight 422. The operation was directed by Hizb'allah official Imad Mughniyah. Two Kuwaitis were killed during the hijacking, but Kuwait refused to release the prisoners. Iran was suspected of aiding the hijackers when the plane landed in Iran, perhaps by allowing extra hijackers and weapons aboard. The terrorists escaped after the 16-day hijacking.

KEY FACTS

- In the 1980s, at the height of Israeli operations in Lebanon, Iran provided Hizb'allah with $60-80 million a year to fund their activities.
- When he placed the *fatwa* (death sentence) on Salman Rushdie, Ayatollah Khomeini offered $1 million to any assassin, or $3 million if the assassin were Iranian. In 1991, after Khomeini's death, a private Iranian foundation doubled the offer.
- In 1990, Iranian agents employed to hunt down dissidents abroad killed four Iranian exiles in Sweden, Switzerland, France, and Pakistan.

TERRORISM AGAINST SAUDI ARABIA

During 1988, Iran shifted its attention to Saudi Arabia. After the death of 257 Iranian pilgrims who were making the *hajj* (the pilgrimage to Mecca that each Muslim should make during his or her lifetime) during a riot in Mecca in 1987, Iranian leaders called for the

Rex Features

Hashemi Rafsanjani arriving at an Islamic conference in Dakar, Senegal, in December 1991. He became President of Iran in August 1989.

overthrow of the Saudi ruling family. A number of operations followed, many directed against offices of Saudi Arabia's national airline, Saudia. Two Saudi diplomats were assassinated in Turkey and Pakistan.

The Saudi-Iranian confrontation escalated in 1989. During a *hajj* two bombs went off, killing one person and wounding 20 more. The Saudi authorities executed 16 Kuwaiti Shiites who admitted to having been trained in Iran for the operation. Iranian and Hizb'allah leaders called for revenge. On October 14, a Saudia office in Lahore, Pakistan, was bombed. On October 16, a Saudi military attaché in Ankara was injured by a bomb. On November 1, a Saudi diplomat in Beirut was assassinated by Islamic Jihad and, on November 24, a Saudi official in Pakistan was killed.

THE SATANIC VERSES

Also in 1989, Ayatollah Khomeini issued a *fatwa*, or death sentence, against Salman Rushdie, the British Muslim author of the novel, *The Satanic Verses*. Khomeini regarded the book as sacrilegious and condemned its author as a blasphemer. Khomeini's *fatwa* made it a sacred duty for Muslims to kill Rushdie, who immediately went into hiding with British police protection. Protests against the book spread worldwide and led to attacks on British Council offices and riots in Pakistan and India. In 1990, following Khomeini's death, Iran reiterated its support for the death sentence on Rushdie.

The feud with Saudi Arabia also continued, with the assassination of three Saudi diplomats. In December, Iran intensified its efforts to improve ties with radical Palestinian groups by holding a "World Conference on Palestine." Representatives from Hizb'allah, the Popular Front for the Liberation of Palestine – General Command, Hamas, the Palestinian Islamic Jihad, and Saiqa, among others, attended. Iran declared its

Popperfoto

support for radical Palestinians opposed to peace with Israel, and reportedly supplied some with funding and arms. A similar conference was held in October 1991, to oppose the Madrid peace process. On October 30, Iran's new spiritual leader, Ayatollah Ali Khamenei, declared: "Those who take part in this treason [the peace process] will suffer the wrath of nations."

TERRORISM IN THE 1990s

During 1991, Iran continued its other terrorist activities. Unidentified assailants, widely believed to be Iranian agents, killed a Japanese translator of Rushdie's works and injured an Italian translator. In addition, Turkish Islamic Jihad, a group closely linked to Iran, bombed the car of an Iraqi diplomat in Ankara, the capital of Turkey, in March. Also in Turkey, car-bombs killed a U.S. Air Force sergeant and injured an Egyptian diplomat in October.

In February 1989, some 10,000 Muslims marched on the British Deputy High Commission in Bombay, India, to condemn Indian-born author Salman Rushdie. Ten people were killed and at least 40 injured when police opened fire on rioters.

In 1992, the British government deported three Iranian officials whom it accused of plotting the murder of Salman Rushdie. Turkish Islamic Jihad made further attacks, bombing an Israeli diplomat and a synagogue in Istanbul – in response to Israel's killing of Hizb'allah leader Musawi in Lebanon.

In 1993, after repeated calls by Iran for the sentence on Rushdie to be carried out, the Norwegian publisher of *The Satanic Verses* was attacked and injured in Oslo. In 1995 and 1996, the European Union (EU) held talks with Iranian officials to try and secure an Iranian pledge not to carry out the *fatwa* in Europe. Although Rafsanjani said the government would not carry it out, Iran could not satisfy the EU and talks broke down.

LINKS WITH SUDAN

Also ruled by a fundamentalist Islamic government, Sudan has allowed many extremist groups to establish training camps on its territory and has become a haven for Islamic and other anti-Western extremists. Groups with bases in Sudan include Hamas, Hizb'allah, the Abu Nidal Organization, Palestinian Islamic Jihad, and Al Gamaat, an Egyptian Islamic movement.

Sudan's role in aiding Islamic fundamentalists has caused increasing concern in recent years. Sudan's National Islamic Front (NIF) has welcomed Islamic fundamentalists from across the region. The government forged close ties with Iran in the early 1990s. Iran's ambassador in Khartoum, Sudan's capital, Majid Kamal, had played a key role in founding Hizb'allah while ambassador to Lebanon in the early 1980s. Sudan makes no secret of its support for fundamentalist Islamic groups, declaring legitimate their struggles against Israel and the West. When Hamas bombed an Israeli bus in 1994, NIF leader Hasan Turabi called the attack "an honorable act."

ATTACKING DISSIDENTS ABROAD

Most Iranian leaders appear to support the policy of attacking Iranian dissidents abroad. In 1987, seven dissidents were murdered in Europe, including one who had been Rafsanjani's chief pilot. In July, Iranian agents used rocket launchers to fire at the houses of dissidents in Karachi and Quetta, in Pakistan. In 1988, Iranian agents tried to kidnap a dissident in Turkey and set fire to a dissident's video store in West Germany. Attacks escalated in 1989. Five dissidents were assassinated, three in Austria, one in Cyprus, and one in the United Arab Emirates. In 1990, more dissidents were killed and France released five pro-Iranian Lebanese terrorists who had been jailed in 1982 for killing a policeman during an attempt on the life of former Iranian prime minister Shahpur Bakhtiar. Reports indicated that the men had been freed in exchange for the release of French hostages in Lebanon.

On August 6, 1991, Iranian agents murdered Shahpur Bakhtiar and an aide in Paris. French investigators arrested three Iranians. France laid the blame squarely on Iran and issued an international arrest warrant for Hussein Sheikhattar, a senior official in the Iranian telecommunications ministry. Relatives of President Rafsanjani and the late Ayatollah Khomeini were among those arrested. Sentences were handed down by a French court in 1994. One defendant received life, one got 10 years, and one was acquitted.

Iranian intelligence agents were behind the September 1992 murder in Berlin of the chief of the opposition Kurdish Democratic Party of Iran (KDPI) and three of his aides. Two Iranians were also arrested in Paris in 1992, and Switzerland requested they be extradited to stand trial for the killing of Mujahideen-e Khalq Organization (MKO) leader Kazem Rajavi in 1990. France expelled them to Iran instead.

In 1993, Iranian agents were probably behind the assassinations of four members of the MKO – one in Italy, one in Pakistan, and two in Turkey. In January 1994, one KDPI official was shot dead in Turkey and another wounded by a letter bomb in Stockholm, Sweden. In March, a KDPI leader was killed in northern Iraq, while in May, two members of the MKO were assassinated near Baghdad, Iraq. There were also strong suspicions of Iranian involvement in the assassination of dissidents in Copenhagen, Denmark, and Bucharest, Romania.

Andrew Rathmell

SEE ALSO: RELIGIOUS EXTREMISM; THE ORIGINS OF PALESTINIAN ISLAMIC JIHAD; ARAB STATES AND TERRORISM IN THE 1990s; PALESTINIAN ISLAMIC FUNDAMENTALISM; TERROR IN LEBANON IN THE 1990s; ROOTS OF FUNDAMENTALIST TERRORISM; TERRORISM AND REVOLUTION IN IRAN; HIZB'ALLAH; HAMAS; ISLAMIC FUNDAMENTALIST TERRORISM IN EGYPT.

FURTHER READING

- Appignanesi, Lisa, and Sara Maitland, eds. *The Rushdie File.* London: Institute of Contempory Arts, 1989; Syracuse, NY: Syracuse University Press, 1990.
- Emadi, Hafizullah. "The Radicalization of the Shiite Movement in Afghanistan," in *Middle East Studies* 31, No. 1, (January 1995): 1-12.
- Menashri, David, ed. *The Iranian Revolution and the Muslim World.* Boulder, CO: Westview Press, 1990.
- Rezun, Miron, ed. *Iran at the Crossroads: Global Relations in a Turbulent Decade.* Boulder, CO: Westview Press, 1990.

HIZB'ALLAH

Hizb'allah (or Party of God) is an extremist political–religious movement based in Lebanon. The movement was created and sponsored by Iran in July 1982, initially as a form of resistance to the Israeli presence in southern Lebanon.

Hizb'allah's followers are Shiite Muslims who took their lead from Ayatollah Khomeini, then Iran's leader. They are strongly anti-Western and anti-Israeli, and unswervingly dedicated to the creation of an Iranian-style Islamic Republic in Lebanon, and the removal of all non-Islamic influences in the area. To this end, Hizb'allah's militia has carried out a number of successful terrorist acts, including over 90 hostage-takings in Lebanon, in other parts of the Middle East, and in Europe and South America.

The scope and nature of Hizb'allah's terrorist campaign reflects its close dependence on Iranian support, both at an ideological and financial level. Examples of its terrorist acts include the abduction of Western hostages in 1982, and suicide attacks on the U.S. Marine and French military barracks in Beirut.

Hizb'allah was established under the spiritual leadership of Sheikh Muhammad Hussein Fadlallah, a Shiite cleric. The movement joined forces with smaller Shiite political parties, such as the Hussein Suicide Squad, Dawah, the Lebanese branch of Iraq-based al-Dawah al-Islamia, and with dissatisfied members of the older Islamic Amal. Iranian officials actively supervised and assisted the movement. The formation of Hizb'allah was crucially assisted by the arrival of Iranian Revolutionary Guards (Pasdaran) in Baalbek in the northern Bekaa Valley of Lebanon. This 1200-strong Pasdaran contingent not only fought against the Israelis and the Southern Lebanon Army (SLA) based in southern Lebanon, but also provided Hizb'allah's fighters with a combination of ideological indoctrination, vast financial support and military training, and equipment. The Iranian presence was a key factor in Hizb'allah's transformation from a loose network into a well-organized and highly disciplined movement with a sophisticated guerrilla force.

KEY FACTS

- Hizb'allah was the brainchild of Ali Akbar Mohtashemi, the Iranian ambassador to Syria.
- Iran donates vast amounts of money to Hizb'allah, which, among other things, funds the movement's health and education services.
- Hizb'allah used American hostages as bargaining tools in exchange for U.S. weapons.

THE STRUCTURE OF HIZB'ALLAH

Hizb'allah is run by a consultative council (*shura*) of 12 clerics led by a secretary-general, with specialized committees dealing with ideological, military, political, judicial, informational, and social affairs. In turn, the consultative *shura* and these committees are replicated in each of Hizb'allah's three main regional and operational areas in Lebanon: the Bekaa Valley, Beirut, and southern Lebanon. All Hizb'allah activity is regulated by decisions taken by the main consultative council, which issues general directives to the regions. The regions, in turn, are left to implement decisions on the operational level. Major decisions are made collectively by the consultative council and approved by Iran.

Within the military committee of Hizb'allah's main consultative council there also exists a separate body, the so-called Special Security Apparatus (SSA), which is responsible for intelligence and security matters. The SSA is itself divided into three sub-groups: the central security apparatus, the preventative security apparatus, and an overseas security apparatus. The preventative security apparatus is responsible for the personal protection of its most senior clerics. The central security apparatus is the clandestine unit responsible for most of the hostage-taking of Westerners as well as the car-bomb and suicide attacks of the early 1980s. The overseas security apparatus was activated when the organization pursued terrorist operations abroad, often in close operational coordination with Iran.

The overall decision to take a hostage is made by the consultative council in liaison with Iranian officials. The instructions are then passed down to the commanders of the SSA. In the execution of the abductions, the SSA maintains a close liaison with Iran's embassies in Beirut and Damascus, which provide intelligence on

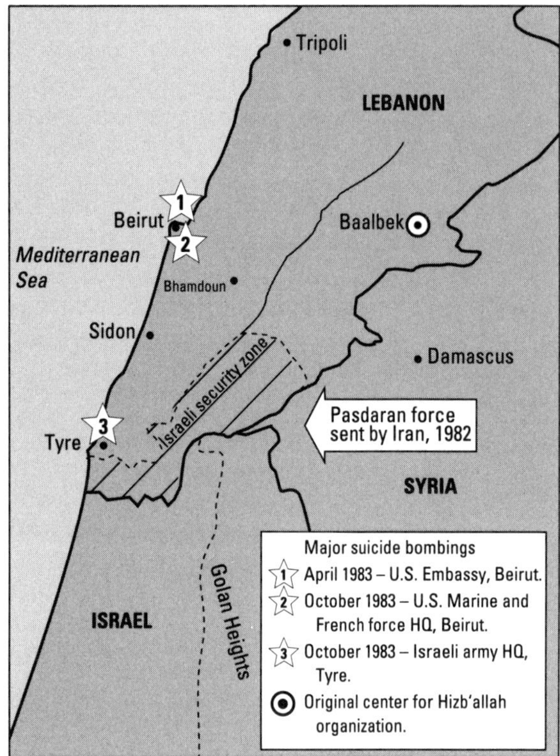

Sites of the major Hizb'allah suicide car-bomb attacks in the Lebanon during 1983.

targets, and with the Pasdaran contingent, which supplies weaponry and training. To maintain security, the core SSA group responsible for Western hostage-taking is composed of a dozen men from various Hizb'allah clans. In major terrorist operations, the SSA receives support from Hizb'allah's military wing, the Islamic Resistance, which is composed of over 5,000 well-trained and well-armed fighters.

HIZB'ALLAH'S GOALS

Hizb'allah's world view, published in a 1985 manifesto, states that all Western influence is detrimental to following the true path of Islam. In its eyes, the West, and particularly the U.S., are the foremost corrupting influence on the Islamic world today: thus the U.S. is known as 'the Great Satan." In the same way, the state of Israel is regarded as the product of Western imperialism and Western arrogance. Hizb'allah believes that the West installed Israel in the region in order to continue dominating it and exploiting its resources. Thus, Israel represents the source of all evil and violence in the region and is seen as an outpost of the U.S. in the heart of the Islamic Middle East. In Hizb'allah's eyes, Israel must therefore be eradicated. Hizb'allah sees itself as the vanguard of oppressed and dispossessed Muslims. The movement's ideological hostility towards its enemies has been translated into a series of central goals which explain the nature and scope of its use of terrorism.

The first goal is the establishment of an exclusively Shiite Islamic state in Lebanon, with Iran as its model. This was the driving force behind Hizb'allah's hostage-taking and suicide bombings during the 1980s.

The second goal of Hizb'allah is the complete destruction of the state of Israel and the establishment of Islamic rule over Jerusalem and Palestine – this is deemed a religious obligation. As such, the movement carries out attacks on the Israeli army occupying part of southern Lebanon, launches rocket attacks at the civilian population in northern Israel, and carries out attacks on Israeli targets abroad: most recently the bombing of the Israeli embassy in Buenos Aires in 1992 that killed 29, and the 1994 destruction of a Jewish cultural center in which nearly 100 people died.

The third goal, linked to the destruction of Israel, is Hizb'allah's implacable opposition to the Middle East peace process, which it tries to sabotage through terrorism. The movement aligns itself with Palestinian Islamic movements such as Hamas and Islamic Jihad, in their struggle against Israel "from within." The uncompromising spirit of Hizb'allah's ideology is clearly reflected in the organization's emblem: a raised arm bearing a rifle against the background of the globe, with the slogan "The Party of God Is Sure to Triumph" (the Koranic verse from which Hizb'allah adopted its name) on top, and the motto "The Islamic Revolution in Lebanon" at the bottom.

THE TIMETABLE OF TERROR

In June 1982, Israel began its occupation of southern Lebanon. One month later, Hizb'allah began its terrorist attacks against both the Western and Israeli presence in its country. Hizb'allah's initial acts of hostage-taking were carried out partly to prevent U.S. involvement in the Gulf War of 1980-88 on the Iraqi side. The movement also took hostages to use as bargaining tools to obtain supplies of U.S.-made weapons for its "sponsor," Iran. Only one U.S. hostage, David Dodge, was taken between July 1982 and

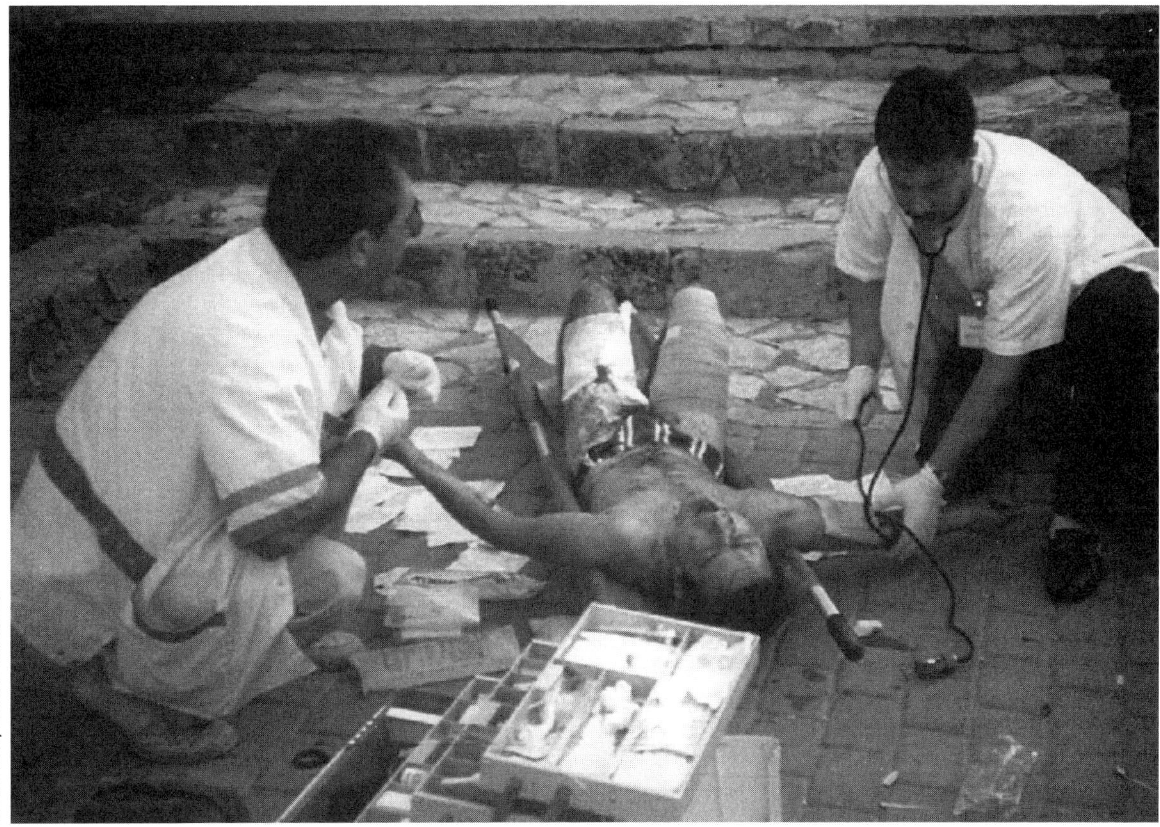

Hulton Getty Picture Collection

One of eight people injured by a salvo of Katyusha rockets fired into western Galilee on June 23, 1995.

February 1984. Instead, the movement focused its activities on suicide car-bomb attacks against Western targets aimed at eliminating them in Lebanon. In April 1983, a suicide car-bomb attack on the U.S. Embassy in Beirut killed 49 and injured 120. In October the same year, Hizb'allah carried out suicide car-bomb attacks on the U.S. Marine and French forces headquarters in Beirut, killing over 300 servicemen, and on the Israeli Army headquarters in Tyre, killing over 50 soldiers.

In February 1984, Hizb'allah increased its hostage-taking activities. Five Americans and one Frenchman were taken hostage by Hizb'allah. This terrorist act was a direct response to the arrest and trial of Hizb'allah members in Kuwait, who had been responsible for perpetrating a string of bombing attacks against the American and French embassies in late 1983. Subsequently, throughout the 1980s, the movement used these hostages as a bargaining tool in its efforts to gain the release of its members held in Kuwait.

Hizb'allah continued to take Westerners hostage between March and June 1985, although its motives varied. For example, the kidnapping of Terry Anderson was a response to the failed assassination attempt on Sheikh Fadlallah in Beirut. In another instance, five Frenchmen were abducted, both in response to France's arms shipments to Iraq (with whom Iran had been at war since 1980), and also in an attempt to gain the release of a convicted Iranian terrorist imprisoned in France. Finally, Hizb'allah hijacked an American airliner TWA-847 in an effort to gain the release of 766 Shiites held by Israel. As a result of this terrorist act, the prisoners were released.

The hostage-taking continued during early 1986. Seven French citizens were abducted in response to several outstanding disputes between Iran and France, ranging from the French policy of supplying arms to Iraq to the repayment of a loan to Iran. Hizb'allah also initiated a bombing campaign in Paris in March 1986, timed to coincide with the French national elections. Hizb'allah also kidnapped two British citizens in response to their country's tacit participation in the American bombing raid on Libya in April 1986.

In November 1986, a Beirut-based magazine revealed that U.S. President Ronald Reagan had secretly supplied arms to Iran in exchange for American hostages. The Irangate affair, as it came to be known, shocked the world. For Hizb'allah, the tactic of taking American hostages had proved successful in damaging U.S.-Iranian relationships.

Hizb'allah's activities continued through 1987, bolstered by continuing military aid from Iran. When U.S. authorities asked for the extradition of a leading Hizb'allah SSA operative arrested in Germany, Hizb'allah responded by taking hostage four American teachers and two Germans in Beirut. Additionally, in January 1987, Terry Waite, the British envoy to the archbishop of Canterbury, was taken hostage by Hizb'allah. Ironically, Waite was on a humanitarian mission to gain the release of other hostages. At this point, however, Syria intervened. Previously, Syria had found Hizb'allah to be a useful instrument of pressure against both Israel and the SLA. However, Syria was now anxious to prevent Hizb'allah from gaining political monopoly among other Shiite groups. For example, Syria encouraged the Islamic Amal group to attack Hizb'allah fighters in southern Beirut.

However, Hizb'allah performed well and continued to carry out acts of terrorism. In February 1988, Lieutenant-Colonel William Higgins, an American UN officer, was abducted by Hizb'allah to put pressure on Israel to release 400 Shiite prisoners. He was later killed. At the same time, the movement hijacked Kuwaiti airliner KU-422 and again demanded the release of its imprisoned members held in Kuwait.

HIZB'ALLAH IN THE 1990s

The death of Iran's Ayatollah Khomeini in 1989, and the conclusion of the Taif Accord, which brought peace to Lebanon after 15 years of civil war, were the crucial factors which ended the spate of hostage-taking. Hizb'allah's involvement in hostage-taking finally drew to a close in late 1991, with a three-way swap brokered under UN auspices, which involved the return of 450 Lebanese and Palestinians detained by the Israelis. They were exchanged for seven dead or captured Israeli servicemen and the remaining Western hostages. Hizb'allah then switched from terrorist acts against Western targets and began escalating its guerrilla confrontation against Israeli forces in southern Lebanon.

Hizb'allah's activities in the 1980s had been funded by vast financial aid from Iran (the organization could depend on receiving between $60 million and $80 million annually from Iranian sources), which Hizb'allah used to expand its influence over the Shiite community. When the movement participated in the 1992 Lebanese national election, it won eight of the 27 seats reserved for Shiites. Although, in the mid-1990s, Hizb'allah has focused mainly on increasing its guerrilla struggle against Israel's occupation of southern Lebanon, the organization continues to rely on terrorism as a means to exact retribution against its enemies abroad. When Israel assassinated the secretary-general of Hizb'allah, Sheikh Abbas al-Musawi, in a helicopter attack in 1992, the movement responded a month later with the car-bomb attack on Israel's embassy in Buenos Aires, killing 29 and wounding over 100.

Hizb'allah continues with its uncompromising stand against Israel's right to exist. In 1991, secretary-general Sheikh Abbas Musavi had declared that while Israel remains in Lebanon, the movement would not lay down its arms. In 1993, the killing of two Israeli soldiers led to massive retaliation by Israel, which left 130 people dead and 300,000 homeless.

Hizb'allah now gives its ideological and moral support to the radical Palestinian Islamic movements, Hamas and Islamic Jihad, in their terrorist campaign against Israel.

Magnus Ranstorp

SEE ALSO: HIJACKING AND KIDNAPPING; HOSTAGE NEGOTIATIONS; SUICIDE BOMBING; THE LEBANESE CIVIL WAR; TERROR IN LEBANON 1980-1987; PALESTINIAN ISLAMIC FUNDAMENTALISM; TERROR IN LEBANON 1987-1996; IRANIAN SPONSORSHIP OF TERRORISM; HAMAS.

FURTHER READING

- Harris, William, W. *Faces of Lebanon: Sects, Wars and Global Extensions.* Princeton, NJ: Markus Wiener Publishers, 1997.
- Ranstorp, Magnus. *Hizb'allah in Lebanon.* New York: St. Martin's Press, 1997.
- Salem, Elie Adib. *Violence and Diplomacy in Lebanon.* London: Tauris, and New York: St. Martin's Press, 1995.
- Winslow, Charles. *Lebanon: War and Politics in a Fragmented Society.* London and New York: Routledge, 1996.

HAMAS

Along with Palestinian Islamic Jihad (PIJ), Hamas is one of the two main Palestinian Islamic terrorist organizations based in the West Bank and Gaza Strip. They are both fiercely anti-Western and committed to destroying Israel and to establishing a Palestinian Islamic state. Since 1987, both Hamas and PIJ have gradually escalated their use of terrorism, especially against Israel, moving from kidnappings and murders of Arab collaborators and Israeli soldiers to the initiation of a series of 13 suicide attacks against Israeli soldiers and civilians. In these attacks, a total of 136 people were killed between April 1994 and March 1996. Since both Hamas and PIJ oppose Israel's existence, they reject any Arab political settlement with Israel and view holy war as the only means to achieve their religious and political objectives. While both organizations advocate terrorism against Israel, Hamas terrorism is part of a mass movement involving political, social, educational, and cultural activities.

THE FOUNDATION OF HAMAS

Hamas is an acronym in Arabic for the Islamic Resistance Movement and the word literally means courage or zeal. Hamas officially came into existence in December 1987. However, the ideas underlying Hamas evolved in the occupied territories of Gaza and the West Bank during the 1970s and 1980s under the influence of the Muslim Brotherhood, which was founded in Egypt in the late 1920s. The group was first registered as a non-profit organization in 1978, under the name of "al-Mujama," by Sheikh Ahmad Yassin, and was primarily engaged in activities geared towards persuading people to become observant Muslims. Hamas was financed principally by Islamic supporters worldwide as part of the Islamic religious tax, or *zakat*. Most Hamas funds were spent on charity and on running hospitals and mosques. Hamas also participated in trade unions and chambers of commerce. It assumed its present militant form after the outbreak of the Palestinian uprising, or Intifada, in 1987.

KEY FACTS

- In 1994 alone, Hamas killed 55 and wounded more than 150 Israelis.
- After the arrest in Gaza of 350 Hamas sympathizers in 1994 by the Palestinian Authority police, opinion polls put support for Hamas at 40 percent.
- On February 25, 1996, a Hamas suicide bomber killed 23 and wounded 49 on a Jerusalem bus. The bomb was packed with nails and other sharp objects to maximize the number of casualties.

THE AIMS OF HAMAS

Hamas considers itself to be the Palestinian branch of the Muslim Brotherhood that seeks the destruction of Israel in holy war, or *jihad* in order to establish Palestine as an Islamic state. It views Palestine as a religious trust, or *waqf*, that should remain under Muslim control for eternity. As stated in the Hamas charter in 1988, its short-term objective is to reverse Israel's occupation of the West Bank, Gaza, and East Jerusalem. In the long term, Hamas aims to establish an Islamic state over the whole area of Palestine "from the Mediterranean Sea to the Jordan River." The charter also disavows the right of any Arab government to determine the fate of the Palestinians.

The Hamas charter rejected the concessional style of the Palestine Liberation Organization (PLO) as a reflection of the devious influences of "western missionaries, orientalists, and colonialists." Hamas has adopted *jihad*, which it considers to be the personal religious duty of every Muslim, as the sole means to achieve this goal. While regarding war against Israel as its top priority, Hamas also aims to reintegrate society at the grassroots level through an Islamic network of mosques and social groups and institutions.

THE ORGANIZATION OF HAMAS

The organizational structure of Hamas has changed with the arrest of some of its top leaders. Sheikh Ahmad Yassin, the spiritual leader, was responsible for most of the organization's activities. His arrest in May 1989 elevated the role of the leadership residing outside the occupied territories, especially in Jordan, Syria, and the U.S. From his prison cell, Sheikh Yassin

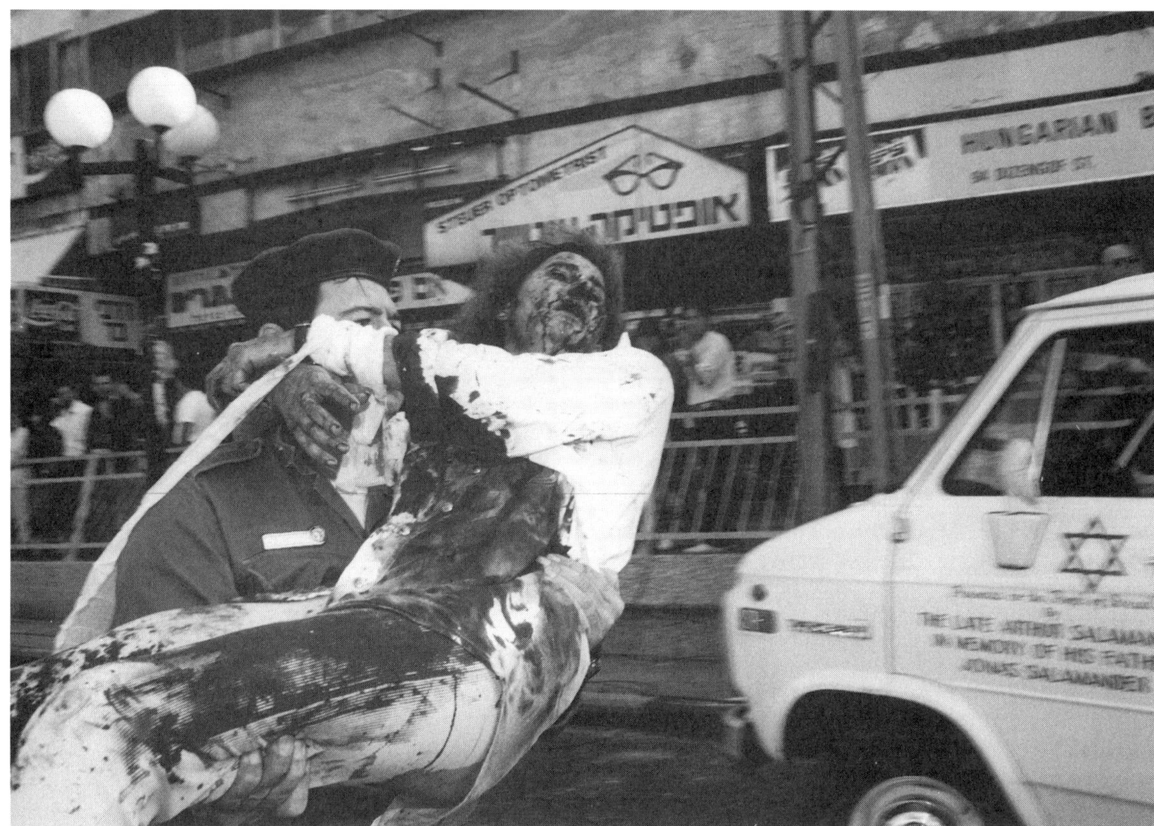

Rex Features

An Israeli serviceman carries away one of the survivors of the Hamas suicide bombing of a bus in Tel Aviv on October 19, 1994. The explosion killed 22 and injured at least 48 more.

is still in control of some aspects of Hamas activity and his release is one of Hamas's current demands. The Hamas leadership consists of senior religious clerics, partly from within the occupied territories but mostly from outside, within the framework of a supreme consultative council.

Within the territories, four separate regional commands exist, three in the West Bank and one in Gaza. Each regional command is led by a commander appointed by and responsible to the supreme consultative council. Subject to the commander is a committee that coordinates activities in each region. Although general instructions are communicated from the exiled leadership, attacks against Jewish settlers and Israeli soldiers do not require explicit approval. However, terrorist attacks on Jewish civilians inside Israel must be sanctioned by the supreme consultative council.

THE AL-QASSEM BRIGADES

Terrorist attacks are the responsibility of Hamas' military wing, the Izz al-Din al-Qassem brigades, formed in 1991 and named after a charismatic cleric killed resisting the British in 1935. These brigades have control over all military and terrorist activity, as well as intelligence and surveillance, recruitment, and training of new members. Once recruited, selected activists undergo extensive training in urban warfare as well as ideological and religious instructions in training camps located in Gaza. The al-Qassem brigades include a commander and executive council appointed by the supreme consultative council. A network of small, separate cells, composed of two or three members, with limited hierarchical communication and no communication between cells, ensures operational secrecy. The total number of al-Qassem members is unknown, but Israel estimates that between 15 and 25 hardcore operatives are deployed in Gaza, and 25 to 30 operatives are working in the West Bank.

Rex Features

On March 4, 1996, a Hamas suicide bomber detonated a bomb in a busy shopping center in Tel Aviv, Israel, killing 12 and wounding 157. At the same time, in Gaza, more than 10,000 Palestinians had taken to the streets to protest against Hamas suicide bombers.

The primary target for Hamas terror is the Israeli population, both in the occupied territories and inside Israel. No non-Jewish individuals or institutions have yet been targeted by Hamas, apart from its secondary target group. This secondary group consists of those members of the Palestinian Muslim community who, in the view of Hamas, display behavior inconsistent with Islamic law. Such people are termed collaborators and are subject to interrogation and sometimes to execution, by the al-Qassem brigades. Indirectly, the PLO is also a target. Hamas aims to undermine PLO authority in maintaining regional security under the terms of the 1993 Israeli-Palestinian peace agreement.

Hamas terrorism has two tactical objectives. The first is to hold the Jewish people hostage through fear, thereby creating Israeli domestic opposition to the occupation and gaining concessions. The second is to provoke Israeli retaliation to stir up Palestinian unrest that can then be mobilized by Hamas.

KNIFE ATTACKS

Hamas' terrorism has evolved in three identifiable stages since the outbreak of the Intifada. Initially, the resistance was limited to stone throwing, demonstrations, strikes, and civil disobedience. The first stage of terrorism included assassination of the so-called Palestinian collaborators, either because of their dealings with the Israelis or for their more moderate ideological positions. In this first stage, Hamas also began to carry out attacks against Israeli soldiers, the first incident occurring in mid-1989 with the kidnapping and killing of two Israeli soldiers. This was followed by knife attacks against Israeli soldiers and civilians, the most serious being the stabbing to death of three factory workers by two Hamas members in Jaffa on December 14, 1990.

Drive-by shootings, firebombings, and stabbings increased rapidly. From the outbreak of the Intifada in 1987 until the end of 1992, Hamas killed over 20 Israeli soldiers and settlers in attacks and assassinated around 100 Palestinians for suspected collaboration.

At the same time, Hamas became more entrenched through the expansion of its social service network. It also capitalized on the PLO's ill-fated support of Iraq's invasion of Kuwait in August 1990. Hamas managed to secure the transfer of funds from the rich Gulf states, funds which were previously donated to the PLO.

ESCALATION OF VIOLENCE

The second stage of Hamas terrorist acts was characterized by an increase in the number of clashes between Hamas and the mainstream secular Palestinian movement, Fatah, as well as an escalation of violence against Israelis. A key event was the kidnapping and execution of an Israeli border policeman in December 1992, after the earlier Hamas shooting of five Israeli soldiers in Gaza. The condition for the police sergeant's release was the release of Sheikh Yassin, the founder of Hamas. During an unsuccessful rescue attempt by Israeli security forces, the policeman was murdered by Hamas.

As a response to this terrorist attack, the Israeli government deported 415 suspected Hamas and Islamic Jihad supporters to southern Lebanon as part of a strategy to curb attacks on soldiers and civilians. This action failed to suppress Hamas terrorism, however. Rather the violence escalated, marking the emergence of the al-Qassem brigades in 1992. Propaganda, in the form of distributed leaflets and sermons, encouraged attacks on Israelis, calling for a "revolution of knives."

SUICIDE BOMBINGS

In September 1993, the Israeli-Palestinian peace agreement was signed. Hamas, who refused even to recognize Israel, started working against the PLO. In order to increase its effectiveness, Hamas entered into an alliance with Iran to sabotage the peace process. In exchange for an increase in attacks on Israeli targets, Iran promised to supply Hamas with $30 million a year. This led to the emergence in April 1994 of the al-Qassem suicide martyrs, who took their inspiration from the pro-Iranian Hizb'allah movement in Lebanon.

Suicide attacks distinguish the third stage of Hamas terrorism. In response to the February 1994 Hebron massacre, in which a Jewish extremist gunned down Palestinian worshippers in a mosque, killing 29 and wounding 150 others, a Hamas suicide bomber attacked a commuter bus in the town of Afula. Eight Israelis were killed and 50 were wounded. Another two suicide bombers attacked an Israeli bus traveling between Afula and Tel Aviv, killing five and injuring another 30 passengers. In October 1994, an al-Qassem suicide bomber boarded and blew up a bus in central Tel Aviv. He killed 22 civilians and wounded 48 others.

STOP-START HOSTILITIES

These attacks led to mass arrests of Hamas members and activists by Israel. In mid-1995, the U.S. arrested Musa Abu Marzuk, Sheikh Yassin's replacement leader since 1989. At the same time, Israeli demands that the Palestinian Authority clamp down on the al-Qassem brigades, pressured Hamas's political wing into accepting a dialogue with the PLO and a temporary halt in the use of terror against Israel.

The dialogue broke down in January 1996, when the Israelis assassinated key al-Qassem leader and explosives expert Yahiye Ayyash. Within a week, five suicide attacks in Jerusalem and Tel Aviv killed 59 people. By this point, Hamas terrorists had killed over 200 Israelis in the three years after the signing of the peace agreement in September 1993.

Magnus Ranstorp

SEE ALSO: SUICIDE BOMBING; THE ORIGINS OF ARAB-JEWISH TERRORISM; THE PLO AND THE ARAB STATES; JEWISH TERROR IN THE WEST BANK; THE ORIGINS OF PALESTINIAN ISLAMIC JIHAD; ARAB STATES AND TERRORISM IN THE 1990s; THE PALESTINIAN INTIFADA; PALESTINIAN TERRORIST GROUPS AFTER 1988; ROOTS OF FUNDAMENTALIST TERRORISM; IRANIAN SPONSORSHIP OF TERRORISM; HIZB'ALLAH.

FURTHER READING

- Abu Amr, Zigad. *Islamic Fundamentalism in the West Bank and Gaza: Muslim Brotherhood and Islamic Jihad.* Bloomington: Indiana University Press, 1994.
- Benvenisti, Meron. *Intimate Enemies: Jews and Arabs in a Shared Land.* Berkeley: University of California Press, 1995.
- Wooten, James P. *The Organization, Goals, and Tactics of a Militant Palestinian Organization.* Washington, DC: Congressional Research Service, Library of Congress, 1993.

ISLAMIC FUNDAMENTALIST TERRORISM IN EGYPT

The assassination of Egyptian President Anwar Sadat in 1981, and the bloody spate of terrorist attacks on tourists in Egypt during the 1990s, have dramatically focused the world's attention on what has been a long and murderous struggle between Egypt's secular government and Islamic fundamentalist groups. Both the major terrorist groups active in Egypt today – the Islamic Group (al-Gamaa al-Islamiyya) and Jihad ("Holy War") – are descended ideologically from the Muslim Brotherhood (Ikhwan al Muslimin), the mainstream Islamic organization founded in the 1920s.

Both the Muslim Brotherhood and its more radical offspring have employed terrorism as part of wider campaigns to root out Western secular influences and return Egyptian state and society to Islamic values. In particular, terrorism has been deemed necessary in the face of the Egyptian regime's step-by-step normalization of relations with Israel.

SUMMARY

- In Egypt, conflict between the secular state and Islamic fundamentalist groups has a long history, dating back to the period of British rule.
- There are two main terrorist groups active in Egypt today, the Islamic Group and Jihad. While they offer a strong contrast in terms of structure and tactics, there is evidence of collaboration.
- For the Islamic Group, tourism has been a major target in the 1990s; tourism is vital to the Egyptian economy.
- Jihad has concentrated on infiltrating the state machinery (e.g., the police and army) and has carried out dramatic assassinations of government figures.

THE RISE OF ISLAMIC TERRORISM

The Muslim Brotherhood was established by a primary school teacher, Hasan al-Banna, in 1928. At this time, Egypt was a British protectorate, and the movement aimed at protecting young men from corrupting Western influences and educating them in Islamic values. Banna argued that Islam offered an ideology capable of regulating every detail of the political, economic, social, and cultural life of believers. The Muslim Brotherhood grew rapidly. By 1940, it had a national network of more than 500 branches, each with its own mosque, school, and club. By 1946, there were 5,000 branches.

In its efforts to implant Islamic values and to punish those who threatened them, the Muslim Brotherhood was prepared to resort occasionally to terrorism. In 1942, Banna had formed a secret network of "spiritual messengers" who were trained in the "art of killing." The organization's leading intellectual, Sayyid Qutb, developed a theory that the killing of traitors against Islam was not only sanctioned by Allah but required.

After a period of intense civil unrest in 1946-48, the government banned the Muslim Brotherhood in December 1948. In the same month, members of the Brotherhood assassinated the Egyptian premier, Mahmud Fahmi Nokrashi. In February 1949, Banna was himself assassinated by Egyptian secret agents. The Brotherhood also inspired the October 1954 assassination attempt against the modernizing and secularizing premier Gamal Abdel Nasser. Subsequently, the organization was banned once more.

Rex Features

The Egyptian embassy in Islamabad, Pakistan, after a car bomb exploded on November 19, 1995, killing 17, including two diplomats. Both Jihad and the Muslim Group claimed responsibility for the blast.

The Muslim Brotherhood, legalized under Nasser's successor, Anwar Sadat, and now Egypt's leading opposition party, maintains at least the appearance of distance from illegal organizations such as the Islamic Group. Whether or not the Muslim Brotherhood is simply a respectable front for the activities of more radical groups (as the government likes to claim), its history and ideology provide an important context for understanding fundamentalist terrorism in the 1980s and 1990s. Qutb's theories, for example, can be shown to have had an important influence on the Islamic Group and Jihad.

ISLAMIC TERRORISM IN THE 1980s AND 1990s

From the assassination of Sadat in 1981 until the present, Islamic terrorism in Egypt has escalated. Popular support for the militants in this period has been in large part due to Egypt's rising economic crisis, with unemployment running at up to 20 percent. In October 1992, a severe earthquake struck Cairo, killing some 500 people in the city's crowded slums. Islamic groups took advantage of the situation to distribute aid to the afflicted, easily out-performing the government's inefficient aid agencies. The fundamentalists' response to the earthquake demonstrates one of their core tactics – to win support with a broad-based social welfare effort.

Both the Islamic Group and Jihad seek revolutionary change through terrorism. The Islamic Group differs from Jihad in that it has a broad-based underground network of followers, primarily strong at universities in Cairo and Asyut, as well as in smaller villages in Upper Egypt and in the deprived suburbs of Cairo. In contrast, Jihad has a more extreme doctrine and is composed of small, organized cells.

The Islamic Group also differs in that it seeks to destabilize the Egyptian regime by striking at tourist targets and other "corrupt" secular and Western institutions, such as banks and cultural centers. An important part of its strategy is the returning of Egyptian society to strict Islamic practice through the running of a vast array of cultural and social services. In contrast, Jihad seeks to battle the Egyptian regime directly, through its infiltration of the military and the police and by assassinating senior officials. Despite differences in strategy and tactics, both organizations seriously challenge the existing Egyptian regime through terrorism and claim to offer a remedy to the country's social, economic, and political problems.

THE ISLAMIC GROUP

The Islamic Group emerged initially in 1971, tacitly encouraged by President Sadat, who provided funding, training, and arms to a number of Islamic groups at universities and factories, in order to counterbalance the growth of the Egyptian left. While Sadat encouraged the growth of the Islamic Group and tried to project a public image as the "believing" president, Islamic fundamentalists were aware that he had also been a member of the tribunals that had previously persecuted the Muslim Brotherhood.

Sadat's proclaimed victory in the 1973 Arab-Israeli war, coupled with his efforts to mollify the fundamentalists through the release of many imprisoned militants, failed to appease the Islamic Group. The first signs of a challenge to the Egyptian regime came with an assassination attempt on Sadat in April 1974.

Egypt's deepening economic crisis and the signing of the Egypt-Israeli peace treaty in 1979 led to protest demonstrations by the Islamic Group and mass arrests of its members by the authorities. In the same year, the blind spiritual leader of the Islamic Group, Sheikh Omar Abdel Rahman, issued a religious verdict condemning President Sadat as an infidel, thereby making him a legitimate target for assassination.

Throughout the 1980s, the Islamic Group carried out only small-scale terrorist attacks (although it did applaud the killing of Sadat in 1981). Instead, the movement concentrated on social welfare work at grassroots level, expanding their support from universities and slum areas to the professional classes and labor unions. The breadth of support – currently standing at 50,000 active members and 200,000 supporters – has made the Islamic Group extremely difficult for the authorities to suppress, especially because of its decentralized structure.

A NEW MILITANCY

The challenge from Islamic fundamentalist terrorism intensified in the late 1980s. In 1987, Islamic fundamentalists carried out three attacks in Egypt, and in 1989 explosive devices were found in American and British cultural centers in Cairo. In October 1990, the Islamic Group claimed the assassination of Dr. Rif'at al Mahgoub, speaker of the People's Assembly (the Egyptian parliament). In March 1991, Sheikh Abdel Rahman (who had spent most of his time in exile in Pakistan, Saudi Arabia, Sudan, and the United States) urged his followers to stage a coup in Egypt and called for the assassination of President Hosni Mubarek.

This new militancy was not only a response to an increasingly repressive campaign by the Egyptian regime against Islamic Group members, but also due to the return of hundreds of militants from Afghanistan, where they had gone to join the struggle of the *mujahideen* against Soviet occupation.

TOURISTS BECOME A TARGET

In mid-1992, the Islamic Group launched a new campaign that was to bring the movement, and Egyptian fundamentalist terrorism in general, to the forefront of Western media attention. The target of the new campaign was the Egyptian tourist industry, and its object was both to counter tourism's importation of "corrupt" Western influences and, by undermining an industry crucial to Egypt's fragile economy, to destabilize and finally overthrow the secular Mubarek regime.

In faxes to news agencies in Cairo, the Islamic Group issued warnings to foreigners, in which they were told "to leave the country in order to preserve their lives." Such threats were swiftly realized: in the fall of 1992, there were extensive terrorist attacks against tourist buses, Nile cruises, and foreign targets in Cairo. The most serious of these attacks included the shooting of a tourist bus at Daryut on October 21, killing one British tourist and wounding two others; the shooting of a bus carrying Egyptian Christians on November 2 near al-Miny, injuring ten; and the November 12 attack on a tourist bus, wounding five Germans and an Egyptian.

Since then, attacks against tourist targets have occurred with almost monotonous, but deadly, frequency. In 1994, for example, five foreign tourists were killed. In February and March, seven foreign banks in Cairo were bombed, and eight tourists were injured in a series of shooting attacks on trains in Assiut province. In August, the Islamic Group attacked a tourist bus in Upper Egypt, killing a Spaniard. In September, the group attacked the Red Sea tourist resort of Hurghada, killing a German and two

Hulton Getty Picture Collection/Reuters

A security guard stands in front of a tourist bus machine-gunned in Cairo by Islamic fundamentalists. Seventeen tourists, most of whom were Greeks died in the attack and 15 others were wounded.

Egyptians. In October, militants fired at a minibus in Upper Egypt, killing a British tourist.

The bloodiest attack in the Islamic Group's four-year campaign against tourists took place outside the Europa hotel in Cairo, in April 1996. Some 200 Greek tourists were about to board buses for a tour of the Christian sites, when three men, using Russian-made automatic rifles and shouting "God is greatest," raked the front of the hotel with bullets. The attack lasted just minutes: bleeding bodies littered the ground in front of the hotel and in the lobby, and were slumped across the reception desk. Eighteen people, including 14 elderly women, died in the attack and 15 were wounded. In a statement released to journalists, the Islamic Group claimed that it had intended to massacre a party of Israeli tourists to avenge Israel's campaign against Hizb'allah fundamentalism in Lebanon. The Greek Orthodox Christians were killed by mistake, it said. If true, the statement reveals the ominous degree to which Islamic militants cooperate throughout the Middle East.

So far, 44 foreigners have been killed in terrorist attacks. The attacks have succeeded in their aim of crippling the tourist industry. In 1993, for example – the year after the campaign began – revenue from tourism fell by a around half. It has been estimated that, in total, the Islamic Group's campaign has been responsible for over $1.5 billion in lost revenue to the Egyptian economy.

INTERNATIONAL TERRORISM

For the most part, the Islamic Group has concentrated on striking at economic targets at home. More recently, however, the organization has broadened its strategy to include international targets. In February 1995, Islamic fundamentalist terrorists bombed the World Trade Center building in New York. The blast killed six people and injured over 1,000 more. The incident led to the arrest, conviction, and sentencing of the exiled leader of the Islamic Group, Sheikh Omar Abdel Rahman, who was the prayer leader of the New Jersey mosque where two of the suspects were

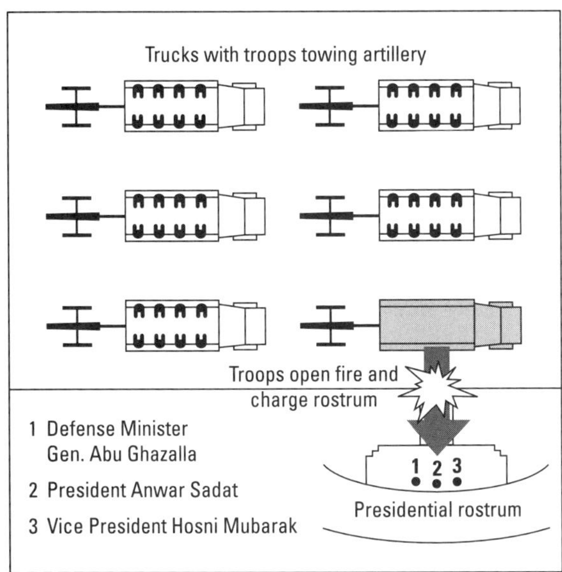

Diagram showing the assassination of President Anwar Sadat by Jihad in 1981.

members. Together with a number of his followers, Sheikh Abdel Rahman was sentenced to life imprisonment in the United States. It would appear that the Islamic Group was also involved in the Jihad bombing of the Egyptian embassy in Islamabad, Pakistan, in November 1995.

Egypt has become increasingly concerned about foreign support for the Islamic fundamentalists and has pointed the finger at Iran and Sudan. On June 26, 1995, an attempt was made to assassinate President Mubarek as he arrived for a Organization of African Unity summit in Addis Ababa, Ethiopia. Egypt blamed Sudan, which it said had sponsored the attack. Egypt subsequently demanded that Sudan extradite three suspects and, in March 1996, the UN Security Council threatened diplomatic sanctions if Sudan did not hand them over.

JIHAD AND THE ASSASSINATION OF SADAT

Jihad forms a strong contrast with the Islamic Group in terms of both structure and doctrine. While the Islamic Group is broad-based and relatively loosely organized, Jihad is tightly compartmentalized and relatively small in size, and has a more extreme and violent religious doctrine. Founded in 1978, Jihad was led by Muhammad Abdul Salam Faraj, an Islamic ideologue, and Abbud Abdul Latif Zumur, who was in charge of the organization's operational wing. In the following year, President Sadat signed the Camp David Peace Accord between Egypt and Israel, and the two Jihad leaders, in an effort to bring about the collapse of secular government in Egypt and an end to the peace accord, devised a plan that would lead to the president's assassination.

The assassination finally took place on October 6, 1981, during a military parade in Cairo held to mark the anniversary celebrations of the October 1973 war. A recent crackdown on religious extremism – including the arrest of around 1,500 Muslims and Coptic Christians – may well have contributed to the timing of the attack. Four men in Egyptian army uniform – all members of Jihad – broke rank from the procession and, armed with automatic assault-rifles and hand grenades, attacked the reviewing stand where President Sadat and his guests were assembled. The president's security guards seemed helpless. Sadat was struck almost immediately and collapsed in a pool of blood. Seven other people were killed and nearly 40 injured, including three U.S. military officers.

Jihad had already nominated Sheikh Abdel Rahman as temporary leader to replace Sadat, but the Islamic revolution that was to bring him to power failed to materialize. Apart from a small uprising in Asyut in Upper Egypt, the Egyptian authorities quickly crushed the insurrection, arresting 3,000 Jihad members. Four of the terrorists who took part in the assassination were executed, and many others received life sentences. While Sheikh Abdel Rahman was acquitted for his crimes, he was continually rearrested and tortured in jail.

INFILTRATION OF THE STATE MACHINERY

Since the assassination of Sadat, Jihad, with its strength much reduced, has concentrated on infiltrating the Egyptian armed forces and police services. Through the establishment of cells within the armed forces, Jihad were responsible for a series of attacks against officials in mid-1980s, most notably against two former interior ministers in 1986. Jihad's strategy was to infiltrate the Mubarek regime's power base – the military – thereby sabotaging the regime's ability to control events as well as to invoke sympathy and support for the militant cause within the army's ranks. Although Jihad perpetrated spectacular isolated attacks towards the end of the 1980s, the organization was significantly weakened by the mass arrests of its members following several disturbances. As with the Islamic Group, the return of the "Afghan" veterans led to a rejuvenation of Jihad and an escalation in its terrorist activities targeting senior government, military, and police officials. Having assassinated the speaker of the Egyptian People's Assembly in 1991, Jihad also succeeded in killing Dr. Farag Foda, a renowned Egyptian anti-extremist writer, in 1992.

The following year, three soldiers with Jihad connections were put on trial on terrorism charges, the first army personnel to be tried after Sadat's assassination. There were two other foiled serious Jihad assassination attempts in 1993. On August 18, Vanguards of Conquest (a group closely associated with Jihad) claimed a bomb that almost killed Interior Minister Hassan Muhammad el-Alfy. Four other people were killed and 21 injured. On November 25, Prime Minister Atef Sedki narrowly escaped death when Jihad detonated a car-bomb on his route. One person was killed in the attack and 18 wounded.

In a departure from its previous modus operandi, Jihad carried out a suicide car-bombing of the Egyptian embassy in Islamabad, Pakistan, which killed 17 and injured 59. While Jihad receives funding and logistical training in Iran, its ability to launch any sustained terrorist campaign is fairly limited, especially as it lacks a mass following to replace those arrested by Egyptian authorities.

GOVERNMENT RESPONSE TO TERRORISM

As Islamic fundamentalist violence has escalated, the Egyptian regime has struck back robustly. The police have used mass arrests, a shoot-to-kill policy, and torture to break the opposition. For example, in March 1993, 49 militants were put on trial. At around the same time, security forces attacked a mosque in Aswan, killing 14 suspects. Other shootouts have left numbers of militants and policemen dead. Counter-terrorist measures have had a degree of success; during 1994, the security forces put the insurgents on the defensive, forcing them to confine their activities to the area around Assuit in Upper Egypt.

In addition to cracking down on the radical Islamic fundamentalists, the Mubarak government has also taken action against the Muslim Brotherhood, which the government claims is simply the legal front for the terrorist groups. In November 1995, on the eve of the parliamentary elections, 54 leaders of the Muslim Brotherhood were jailed by the military police. The convictions aroused an outcry from human rights activists, who condemned the charges as trumped up.

Egypt has also pressed other countries to crack down on Islamic militants and fundraisers. Yemen, for example, was persuaded to deport a number of alleged Egyptian subversives in 1995. Qatar was likewise prevailed upon to cease granting asylum to Islamic radicals. Part of the problem for host countries has been that legitimate Muslim charitable activity is often very hard to distinguish from aid to armed groups. Muslims are duty-bound to give charitable donations to social causes but, since groups such as the Islamic Group usually have welfare branches, it is extremely hard to distinguish between aid that goes to alleviate suffering and money that finances terrorism.

While both the Islamic Group and Jihad have common ideological roots and enemies, though they differ in size as well as in targeting, there is often a degree of cooperation in their use of terrorism. However, Jihad is more vulnerable to repression by the Egyptian authorities than its broad-based counterpart, which is capable of complementing its violence with realistic alternatives to secular values. Both groups are unlikely to achieve their goal of establishing an Islamic state through violence. However, they continue to prove themselves capable of carrying out sporadic and dramatic acts of terrorism.

Magnus Ranstorp

SEE ALSO: RELIGIOUS EXTREMISM; ARAB STATES AND TERRORISM IN THE 1990s; DOMESTIC TERRORISM IN THE ARAB WORLD; ROOTS OF FUNDAMENTALIST TERRORISM.

FURTHER READING

- "Cassandra." "The Impending Crisis in Egypt," in *The Middle East Journal* 49, no. 1 (Winter 1995): 9-27.
- Dekmejian, R. Hrair. *Islam in Revolution: Fundamentalism in the Arab World.* 2nd ed. Syracuse, NY: Syracuse University Press, 1995.
- Fandy, Mamoun. "Egypt's Islamic Group: Regional Revenge?" in *Middle East Journal* 48, no. 4, (Autumn 1994): 607-26.
- Jansen, Johannes J. G. *The Neglected Duty: The Creed of Sadat's Assassins and Islamic Resurgence in the Middle East.* New York: Macmillan, 1986.

ISLAMIC FUNDAMENTALISM AND TERRORISM IN ALGERIA

By granting independence to Algeria in 1962, the French President Charles de Gaulle brought an end to a war that had cost at least a million lives. Thirty years later, a second Algerian war is raging, but this time it is not a war of independence against a colonial power, but rather an internal civil war rooted in religion and ideology, and in which terrorism plays a major part. Since 1992, over 40,000 Algerians have been killed in this war.

THE ORIGINS OF THE TROUBLES

Since 1962, Algeria has been controlled by National Liberation Front (FLN), which had successfully fought France in Algeria's war of independence. Until the 1980s, the regime, far from being democratic, ruled through a combination of repression and military force. By the late 1980s, however, there was mounting civil unrest as the country's economy deteriorated. In September 1988, strikes in protest at corruption and shortages of food and housing became widespread. By October, demonstrations by strikers and students had turned into full-scale riots. The government declared a state of siege and sent the army onto the streets. Before law and order were restored, hundreds of Algerians had been killed and thousands imprisoned. The country was shocked by the severity of the reprisals by the armed forces dealing with the rioters, and Algerians of all classes demanded change. The Algerian President Chadli Bendjedid appealed to the nation through television broadcasts and promised reforms that, for the first time, would make the government accountable to parliament.

The result of the riots of 1988 was a new constitution, which brought about a greater democratization of public life, and the promise of the first multiparty elections since independence. By March 1989, more than 20 new political parties had been formed, including the first overtly Islamic party – the fundamentalist Islamic Salvation Front (FIS). Within this new atmosphere of political liberalization, independent Algeria's first pluralist municipal elections were scheduled, and the country went to the polls on June 12, 1990. The result was a massive victory for the FIS, which won 32 of the 48 regional departments. Significantly, the FIS won all of the key cities: Algiers, Oran, Constantine, Blida, and Jijel. It was a massive repudiation of the FLN and the record of its 28 years of monopoly rule.

The leaders of the FIS called for parliamentary elections, since they claimed the ruling party no longer represented the view of the majority. Intent on seeing through his program of reforms, President Chadli scheduled the elections for June 1991. In the meantime, the FIS took over local government in the regions they had won. Amid this political and social upheaval, the economy worsened. It was not clear whether the Islamic fundamentalists now in power regionally would be any more capable than their predecessors of resolving the staggering economic crisis which faced the nation.

SUMMARY

- Since 1992, the Algerian state has been at war against thousands of armed Islamic militants.
- The terrorists recruit large numbers from Algeria's marginalized and disaffected youth – more than 60 percent of Algerians are under 25.
- It is thought that other governments in the Middle East, such as Iran, have been providing financial and military aid to the extremists.

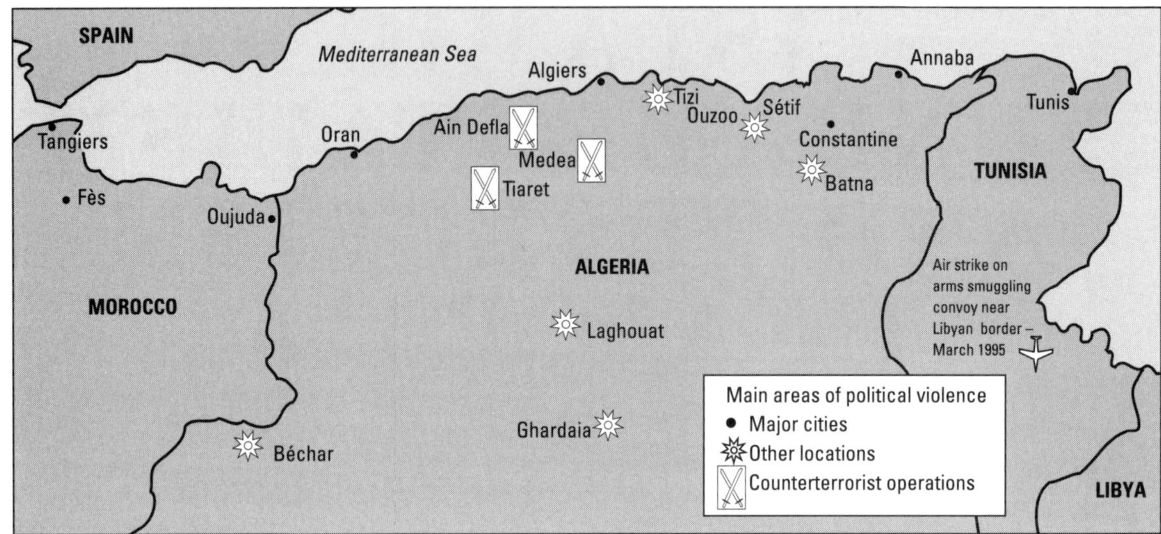

Map showing acts of terrorism and counterterrorism in Algeria since 1992.

By mid-1991, the FIS-run municipal governments were losing popularity. In April, the residents of three towns in southern Algeria occupied town halls in protest at FIS policies, and polls showed that the party's support was shrinking. Fearing defeat in the forthcoming election, the FIS leaders decided to opt instead for confrontation with the authorities. On May 25, they called a general strike. Fundamentalists demanded the establishment of an Islamic state and began to demonstrate. The demonstrations became steadily more violent and, on June 5, the government again declared a state of siege. President Benjedid dismissed the government, called off the elections, and put the troops back onto the streets.

MOUNTING VIOLENCE

Over the next three weeks, there were a number of bloody clashes between demonstrators and security forces, and tens of people were killed. Although the FIS called off the general strike, the disturbances continued. When police tried to remove Islamic signs on FIS-controlled town halls and replace them with symbols of the Algerian republic, large-scale violence once again broke out. Gunfire was heard throughout Algiers, and many died in gun battles across the country. By this time, the FIS leaders – Ali Belhadj and Abbassi Madani – were openly calling on their supporters to engage in a *jihad,* or holy war, against the government. Again, the response of the army was swift and severe, and, on June 30, they arrested hundreds of militants, including Belhadj and Madani.

Eventually the rioting stopped, and, in September 1991, the state of siege was lifted. It was clear that attempts to build a consensus between the government and the fundamentalists had failed. Nevertheless, as it had promised, the government set the date for the first round of legislative elections for December 26, 1991. A second round was to be held on January 16, 1992, in those areas where no candidate had received an overall majority. As before, the results of the first round were a huge shock for the government. The FIS won 188 of the 430 electoral districts, while the FLN won only 15. It was clear that it would take a significant reversal of the trend to prevent the FIS from winning a substantial majority in the second round.

THE ISLAMIC EXTREMIST MANIFESTO

The FIS had entered the election with a manifesto that promised the imposition of the Shari'a, the holy law of Islam. Under the Shari'a, Algeria would have the Koran as its constitution. Women would be required to give up their jobs and to wear headscarves at all times. Mixed classes in schools and universities would be banned, as would physical education for girls. Alcohol would also be prohibited. In economic policy, the financial system would be based on Islamic markets and banks. Since the Koran forbids moneylending, interest-bearing loans would not exist. Partnerships with overseas companies would be allowed only when there was no alternative. Multiparty democracy would also be rejected once the FIS achieved power.

It was this last point that worried the party's opponents the most. Faced with the prospect of being removed from office, members of the FLN questioned whether to permit the second round of elections to take place. President Chadli was committed to the process of political liberalization and was therefore determined to see the elections completed. However, the prime minister, Sid Ahmed Ghozali, and several cabinet ministers were unconvinced, citing the FIS manifesto as proof that a fundamentalist victory, with promises of the Shari'a, would set Algeria back hundreds of years.

A MILITARY COUP

During the two weeks following the December 26 elections, Sid Ahmed Ghozali, backed by army leaders, urged the president to delay the second round. When he refused to comply, a military-led coup d'état dissolved parliament and forced Chadli's resignation. An emergency body instituted a High Council of State (HCS) as a collective presidency. Mohamed Boudiaf was named as head of the five-man council, which immediately declared the first round of the elections void, and cancelled the second round.

Despite protests that the HCS's seizure of power was illegal, the new government refused to back down. Almost immediately, violence returned to the streets of Algeria. Across the country, tens of people were killed and hundreds wounded in battles between fundamentalists and security forces. Many of the dead were police and soldiers. In Algiers, a bomb exploded outside the national police headquarters, and in one gun attack in the city, six policemen were killed. Although no one claimed responsibility for the attacks, leading members of the FIS were arrested.

Meanwhile, the Council of State tightened the rules governing political parties. It declared that no party could be based exclusively on religion, and it outlawed the use of mosques for political purposes. The aim of these amendments was clear – to ban the FIS and bring an end to the violence. However, the fundamentalists ignored the rulings and, despite intimidation from army tanks and forces, continued to rally support at mass-meetings in mosques.

In February 1992, Islamic extremists carried out their first attack on a military target when they raided a naval base in Algiers. On February 9, the government declared a 12-month state of emergency and occupied the FIS headquarters. In a savage army and police crackdown, thousands of FIS activists and supporters were arrested and deported to desert camps. At the outbreak of the violence, the FIS had appealed for restraint. However, after the arrest of their leaders, the party made its first explicit calls for supporters to take up arms against the authorities. With the FIS now officially advocating violence, the government immediately banned the party.

ORGANIZED GUERRILLAS

Once outlawed, the FIS transformed itself and created an armed wing, the Islamic Salvation Army (AIS). The FIS also attempted to unite the several armed Islamic bands that had formed since the start of 1992. One of these bands was the Armed Islamic Group (GIA).

The new extremist force quickly started recruiting among the marginalized and unemployed youth of Algeria's cities. Many AIS members were former soldiers who had fought alongside the *mujahideen* Islamic revolutionaries in Afghanistan. The AIS was organized into tight-knit cells, each containing a small number of guerrillas in order to prevent infiltration by the security forces. These cells were linked through a network of 8,000 mosques under fundamentalist control. Overall leadership of the movement was exercised by the *majlis ash-shura* (consultative council), which contained 20 members. The Algerian government estimated that around 1,100 terrorists were in operation at this time, although Western diplomats put the number between 10,000 and 15,000.

There were probably hundreds of thousands of sympathizers in support of the extremists. The rise of Islamic fundamentalism in Algeria was closely connected with the failure of the government to provide the basic requirements for the population. The support which the movement had acquired among the country's youth was primarily a result of the appalling economic situation in Algeria. Fundamentalism appealed also to traditionalists among the peasantry and urban poor, as well as to small traders and craftsmen who sought an economic recovery.

Furthermore, the support of Western governments for brutal, dictatorial regimes, such as the Shah's government in Iran before the Islamic revolution in 1978-79, undermined faith in secular government. This, in turn, gave rise to Islamic opposition. It was becoming increasingly clear that although they may not

Hulton Getty Picture Collection

Algeria's President Zeroual waves to supporters during the November 1995 electoral campaign.

support the violent methods employed by the extremists, the people of Algeria would not act to defend the existing political order.

Throughout the spring and summer of 1992, the violence escalated from small hit-and-run attacks into lengthy gun battles, sometimes lasting several days. Government buildings were also repeatedly bombed. Attacks spread throughout the country, with guerrillas robbing banks, airline offices, and businesses to bankroll their efforts. As the situation deteriorated into chaos, the extremists took their campaign to a new level. On June 29, Mohamed Boudiaf, the head of the Council of State, was making a routine visit to Annaba, in the east of the country. When he began to speak, a bomb exploded near the podium where he stood. Within seconds a grenade was thrown under his chair and, in the confusion that followed, a gunman killed Boudiaf with two bursts of automatic gunfire.

In August 1992, a powerful bomb planted by fundamentalists ripped through the packed airport terminal in Algiers, killing nine and injuring 128. The force of the blast was so powerful that one body was embedded in the terminal ceiling. Other bombs in the capital caused minor injuries. The government responded by expressing its determination to eradicate the Islamic extremists. It introduced new antiterrorist laws and offered the fundamentalists a partial amnesty. Under the amnesty, members of subversive or terrorist groups had two months to surrender and had to promise not to take part in any banned activities. Those who had not killed would not be prosecuted. Those who had killed would face 15 to 20 years' jail instead of life imprisonment.

The violence continued, however. In February 1993, the government extended the state of emergency, and, in March, militants assassinated a number of prominent politicians and officials, and wounded many others. In one attack on barracks south of Algiers, 18 soldiers were shot dead by gunmen who may have had accomplices within the military. In response, 23 extremists were hunted down and killed by the security forces.

In August 1993, the former prime minister, Kasdi Merbach, was killed in a gun attack on his car. His son, brother, driver, and bodyguard also died in the attack. During the summer of 1993, intellectuals and professionals began to be targeted. Many journalists, writers, teachers, and doctors were killed, including the country's chief pediatrician, Djilali Ben Kenchir, who was shot as he arrived for work at his Algiers hospital.

FOREIGN TARGETS

By the fall of 1993, more than 1,500 people had been killed. Many died at the hands of the GIA, which had surpassed all other Islamic groups in the savagery of its violence, even turning against leaders of rival armed groups. In October, the GIA changed the direction of its campaign. It promised to kill foreigners still in Algeria at the end of November. Governments around the world advised their nationals to leave the country, and a number of them, including Russia and Canada, evacuated their diplomatic staff. By the end of December, the GIA had killed 23 foreigners. Among the dead were French citizens living in Algeria, Spanish and British tourists, and workers from Croatia, Bosnia, and Russia. Throughout 1994, the GIA continued to murder foreigners, particularly priests, monks, and nuns.

The escalating violence was wearing down the Algerian government, now led by President Liamine Zeroual. In September 1994, they tried to start talks with the fundamentalists. Despite the release from prison of Islamic leaders, however, the talks soon broke down and the violence resumed.

Hulton Getty Picture Collection/Reuters

December 1994: French forces storm the plane that GIA terrorists had taken from Algiers to Marseilles.

On December 1994, the GIA hijacked an Air France airplane at Algiers. The hijackers demanded the release of several of its "brothers" who had been arrested in France. The plane was flown to Marseilles, France. After three days of terror, elite French commandos stormed the plane and killed the extremists. In Algeria, four French priests were murdered in reprisal.

In 1995, presidential elections finally took place and, despite intimidation from the armed Islamic groups, voters largely endorsed the rule of President Zeroual. Throughout 1995 and 1996, Islamic extremists continued their attacks in both Algeria and France, including a bomb attack on the Paris subway. By mid-1996, the number of those killed as a result of fundamentalism in Algeria had reached tens of thousands.

Despite the violence, the government is restructuring the economy in line with the strict requirements of its main creditors, in particular those of the International Monetary Fund. That the regime will have to speak to the fundamentalists is now universally recognized. For their part, the extremists have confirmed that they will respect a pluralist political system in future elections. Yet handing over power to a democratically elected FIS will not solve Algeria's problems. As in Iran and Sudan, such a move may well lead Algeria deeper into violence and repression.

Trevor Barker

SEE ALSO: TERRORISM IN FRENCH ALGERIA; REVOLUTIONARY TERRORISM; RELIGIOUS EXTREMISM; ROOTS OF FUNDAMENTALIST TERRORISM; TERRORISM AND REVOLUTION IN IRAN; ISLAMIC FUNDAMENTALIST TERRORISM IN EGYPT.

FURTHER READING

- Chapin Metz, Helen, ed. *Algeria: A Country Study.* 5th ed. Washington, DC: Federal Research Division, Library of Congress, 1994.
- Malley, Robert. *The Call from Algeria: Third Worldism, Revolution and the Turn to Islam.* Berkeley: University of California Press, 1996.
- Mortimer, Robert. "Islamists, Soldiers, and Democrats: The Second Algerian War," in *The Middle East Journal* 50, No. 1 (Winter 1996): 18-39.
- Whitley, Andrew. *Human Rights Abuses in Algeria: No One Is Spared.* New York: Human Rights Watch, 1994.

CHAPTER THIRTEEN

Terrorism in Latin America

The political history of Latin America since World War II has been characterized by bloody coups, popular revolutions, military dictatorships, and chronic economic instability. State terror has been practiced by the authorities to cow the impoverished masses and various left-wing movements have conducted terrorist campaigns. In the past, both the former Soviet Union and the United States provided funds and weapons to their clients, either to prop up a friendly regime or bring about the downfall of a hostile government.

TERRORISM IN LATIN AMERICA: Introduction

Democracy and the rule of law have been in little evidence in Latin America for much of the last 200 years. Many of today's states in the region only gained their independence from their colonial overlords, primarily Spain and Portugal, in the nineteenth century. The wars of liberation were frequently protracted and bloody, and were marked by atrocities on all sides. Violence and terrorism became firmly rooted in the political life of most states and continue today.

In almost all of these countries, chronically poor peasants were ruled by tiny, self-serving elites, who amassed vast wealth and used fear and violence to maintain their grip on power. In El Salvador, for example, just 14 families owned the coffee plantations that generated over 95 percent of the country's export earnings in the 1930s. Both the military and the state security forces were usually given the freedom to act with unrestrained barbarity to preserve the status quo.

The great mass of the population, uneducated, landless, and lacking access to basic amenities, was seen by the politically active left-wing intelligensia as being ripe for revolution. Inspired by Fidel Castro's overthrow of the U.S.-backed military dictatorship of Fulgenico Batista in Cuba during the late 1950s, many felt that other right-wing regimes could be toppled. All that was required was a vigorous guerrilla group that could win over the rural and urban poor.

Terrorism was an integral part of the activities of many revolutionary groups. Assassination was a widely used tactic to gain a broad base of support. Prime targets were representatives of a regime's authority – local landowners, police officers, election officials, and small-time bureaucrats, for example. With the exception of the Tupamaros in Uruguay, guerrilla and terrorist groups in Latin America have had their bases in rural areas. There they built training camps, recruited, and worked to gain the support of the peasants.

Only when they had secured the countryside did revolutionary groups move into towns in force, although sporadic terror campaigns were waged in urban areas. Targets included banks, a source of revenue; seemingly important foreign nationals, particularly those from countries seen to be supporting the existing regime; or high-profile targets, such as government offices. A country's economic infrastructure, including oil storage facilities, power stations, railroads, and bridges, was also given high priority as targets by the terrorists.

The key to successful revolutionary activity was to avoid direct confrontation with a regime's forces unless on favorable terms. Isolated bases or small patrols were often the targets of terror attacks, but large government forces engaged in anti-guerrilla sweeps were avoided if at all possible. However, attacks on well-guarded prestige targets were carried out as a means of publicizing a revolutionary group's agenda. The Sandinista revolutionaries in Nigaragua were able to seize the National Palace in August 1978, forcing the dictator Anastasio Somoza to release key political prisoners. Somoza and his security forces faced acute embarrassment, while the Sandanista cause won considerable international media coverage.

Although most states in Latin America have faced terrorist campaigns by revolutionary organizations, few have been overthrown by them. The various military regimes have proved remarkably resilient, not least because of the support they have received from outside sponsors. Some have defeated their opponents, while others have succumbed not to the bomb and bullet, but to popular protest or coups by their political peers.

Military and financial aid from the U.S. has enabled many right-wing Latin American regimes to stay in power and defeat, or at least control, terrorist groups. The U.S. have viewed the region as a key sphere of influence since the early nineteenth century. President James Monroe issued the Monroe Doctrine in 1823, claiming the Western hemisphere as an exclusively American zone of influence. Terrorists, therefore, have had to face governments that for years could call on the support – weapons, training, and personnel – of one of the world's great military powers. ■

TERRORISM IN ARGENTINA

Terrorism in Argentina for many years revolved around the charismatic personality and political legacy of the dictator Juan Domingo Perón. For the mass of the Argentine population, the period of Perón's long rule – which lasted from 1946 until his exile by the miltary junta in 1955 – represented a golden age in Argentina's history. The popular veneration of "Peronism" extended to the president's glamorous wife Maria Eva Duarte Perón ("Evita"), whose early death at the age of 33 had been met with extravagant mourning. Perón's exile consequently created a political vacuum that a succession of weak military governments, dogged by constant economic crises, was unable to fill. This situation left Argentina vulnerable to terrorist campaigns, both from the Peronist and the Trotskyist left.

"Peronism," however, was politically ambivalent, capable of being claimed by both left- and right-wing groups. On the one hand, Perón owed his presidency to the support of the labor unions and the promise of land reform. On the other hand, his intense nationalism and autocratic style appealed to the extreme right, and by the time of his overthrow by the junta, he was rapidly moving toward more conservative policies. Opposing claimants to the Peronist mantle eventually resorted to violence after Perón's brief return to power in the early 1970s, culminating in the brutal "dirty war" in which thousands of Argentine citizens were murdered, imprisoned, and tortured.

SUMMARY

- The charismatic figures of President Juan Domingo Perón and his second wife "Evita," and their political legacy, "Peronism," dominated Argentina long after the collapse of the first Perón regime in 1955.
- The collapse of the Perón regime created a political vacuum in Argentina that the two main terrorist groups – the People's Revolutionary Army (ERP) and the Montoneros – were able to exploit.
- From the mid-1970s, the military junta followed the Argentine Anti-Communist Alliance (AAA) in waging a massive death squad campaign against leftist terrorists. It is estimated that between 20,000 and 30,000 people disappeared in the "dirty war."

TERRORISM AND THE REBIRTH OF PERONISM

During the 1960s, a long deflationary period gradually eroded standards of living throughout the country. In May 1969, there was a spontaneous uprising in the industrial city of Córdoba. It was led by students and auto workers in protest against the austerity program introduced under the military regime of General Juan Carlos Onganía. The uprising, which came to be known as the Cordobazo, led to a massive nationwide revival in Peronist and Trotskyist militancy among the young and, in particular, to a belief in the effectiveness of revolutionary violence. In this climate, a number of terrorist groups emerged, the most important of which were the Montoneros and the People's Revolutionary Army (ERP).

The Montoneros were a leftist guerrilla group that aimed to promote the populist and nationalistic policies of Perón through socialist revolution. The organization was formed in 1968 by Fernando Abal Medina, Carlos Gustavo Ramus, and Mario Eduardo Firmenich, all of whom were former members of the Catholic Youth movement. These men had been radicalized by contact with the progressive ideas of the Second Vatican Council and its offshoot, Liberation Theology. The Montoneros quickly built up a large membership (numbering roughly 10,000 people in the early 1970s), and established contacts with other insurgents in Latin America, including the M-19 group in Colombia. The group suffered, however, from cumbersome organization and only two members ever received any serious military training.

The much smaller ERP emerged from the Workers' Revolutionary Party (PRT), a Trotskyist party which

Hulton Getty Picture Collection

Argentine President Juan Domingo Perón with his third wife and vice-president "Isabelita."

had been founded in 1965. At the 1968 conference of the PRT, a faction called El Combatiente, led by Luis Pujals and Roberto Santucho, split and formed the ERP under the leadership of Enrique Gorriarán Merlo.

THE FIRST TERRORIST ATTACKS

In the wake of the Cordobazo, it was the ERP who undertook most of the early attacks against the state, carrying out a wave of bombings and arson attacks in 1970. The group also staged successful kidnappings, using the ransoms to finance further activity. However, at the same time, the ERP suffered important casualties and losses: their leader, Gorriarán, was arrested in 1970 (although he escaped from jail in 1972), and founder member Luis Pujals was arrested in 1971 and killed in custody. A popular revolt against the government at Mendoza in April 1972 was followed by a series of assassinations of senior army officers and businessmen. The victims included the managing director of the Fiat car company in Argentina.

The Montoneros, however, were not idle, and their first strike, on May 29, 1970, was spectacular: the kidnapping of General Pedro Eugenio Aramburu. Aramburu's "crime," according to the Montoneros, was that as president between 1955 and 1958 he had rejected compromise and done his utmost to eradicate Peronism from Argentine politics. The Montoneros issued a series of communiqués claiming responsibility and offering to exchange their victim for the return of Evita's corpse, which Aramburu had been responsible for spiriting out of the country. On July 16, Aramburu's body was found buried, precipitating the fall of the Onganía government and its replacement by that of General Roberto Levingston. Meanwhile, on July 1, a group of Montoneros temporarily occupied the town of La Calera, 10 miles from Córdoba. Two were killed and others were arrested.

By the end of 1970, there were only 20 members of the movement left, and the Montoneros' tactics changed accordingly. Direct confrontations with the army or police were replaced by smaller-scale actions designed to serve as "armed propaganda." Over the next three years, a series of bombs exploded at symbolic targets associated with wealth and privilege, but without killing any members of the army or the police. Buildings belonging to foreign companies were set on fire. One kidnapping, that of Vicenzo Russo, production manager of Standard Electric Argentina, brought in a ransom of $1 million. However, the movement also suffered significant casualties, including the death in July 1971 of one of their most able commanders, José Sabino Navarro.

PERON RETURNS

Escalating terrorism and runaway inflation convinced the crumbling military government of General Alejandro Agustín Lanusse that some kind of reconciliation with the Peronist forces was necessary. In January 1972, the government recognized the legality of the Peronist political movement, the Justicialist

Party (PJ). Though Perón was barred from running again, the way was now open for a Peronist party to contest the elections, which the PJ duly won. The new president, Héctor Cámpora, loyal to Perón, quickly called for new elections. This time, the 77-year-old Perón himself was allowed to run and won.

Faced with political power, the profound contradictions of the Peronist movement erupted. On the right, there were the traditional militants who still followed the extreme nationalism of the 1940s and who continued to dominate the labor unions. On the left, there were the liberationist student groups, from whose ranks the backbone of the Montoneros was formed. At a mass rally of about 500,000 supporters on the day of Perón's triumphant arrival at Ezeiza airport on June 20, 1973, the underlying tension between the factions flared. Right-wing Peronists fired on left-wing Peronists; 13 people died and more than 100 were wounded in the ensuing fighting. In retaliation, the Montoneros assassinated José Rucci, secretary-general of the General Confederation of Workers (CGT), and the foremost Peronist in Argentina. Relations between the two factions continued to deteriorate over the year that followed. On February 12, 1974, several Montoneros were arrested in connection with a plot to assassinate Perón and his third wife, María Estela Martínez (popularly known as Isabelita). Perón's government began to implement a purge against the left wing of the party and, on May 1, 1974, publicly broke with the Montoneros, accusing them of being "treacherous and mercenary."

SLIDE INTO CHAOS

With Perón's death in 1974, the country gradually fell into disarray. His widow, Isabelita, who now became president, was an incompetent leader. She relied excessively on the advice of Perón's former secretary, José López Rega, who was also minister of social welfare. López Rega controlled the right-wing Argentine Anti-Communist Alliance (AAA), which provided death squads for the elimination of terrorists. Among the victims were a number of key Peronist figures, as well as opposition figures such as the Marxist Silvio Frondizi. Foreigners were also targeted, notably the Chilean General Carlos Prats, who had been commander-in-chief of the armed forces under President Salvador Allende.

Although the Montoneros ceased revolutionary activity while Perón was in office, the ERP continued its activities even after his return – the ERP planned to force Perón to adopt a left-wing position. In 1973, a series of kidnappings of foreign businessmen brought the ERP millions of dollars in ransom money. Military targets were also attacked, including the Army Medical HQ in Buenos Aires (September 6, 1973), the 10th Armored Cavalry garrison at Azul (January 20, 1974), an arms factory in Córdoba and the Paratroop HQ in Catamarca (August 11, 1974). These actions resulted in heavy losses, the alienation of public opinion, and increasingly effective government action backed up by emergency powers. Sixteen guerrillas, who had been captured in the action at Catamarca, were summarily shot by the army. In retaliation, ERP commandos assassinated ten army officers, suspending the campaign only when they accidentally killed a child.

In late 1974, the ERP switched its attention to Tucumán, Argentina's smallest province, where left-wing support was traditionally strong. The group tried, in the tradition of other Latin American revolutionaries such as Fidel Castro and Che Guevara, to set up rural guerrilla bases there. But Tucumán did not prove to be as easy to infiltrate as they had hoped. At first, the ERP achieved some modest success because the police were unable to mount a concerted action against them. However, once the army stepped in, ERP losses climbed and their forces were pinned down.

Meanwhile, the Montoneros went underground again. Once reorganized, they mounted a series of spectacular incidents, including hostage-taking, which reflected both their large numbers and improved organizational capacity. The most successful hostage-taking was that of businessmen Juan and Jorge Born, from one of Argentina's leading corporations, Bunge y Born, on September 19, 1974. This action provided the movement with a colossal ransom of $60 million, to date the highest ever paid to kidnappers in Latin America. They also assassinated Federal Police Chief Alberto Villar at Tigre, in November 1974, because of his close links with the AAA. After this high-profile strike, the government declared a temporary state of emergency, which rapidly became permanent.

In a series of well-planned operations in 1975, the Montoneros not only continued their campaign of assassinating key figures who were linked to the AAA, but they also struck a series of blows at the armed forces. Some of these clandestine operations involved skills of a high order. In one audacious attack on the navy, the Montoneros managed to plant explosives that

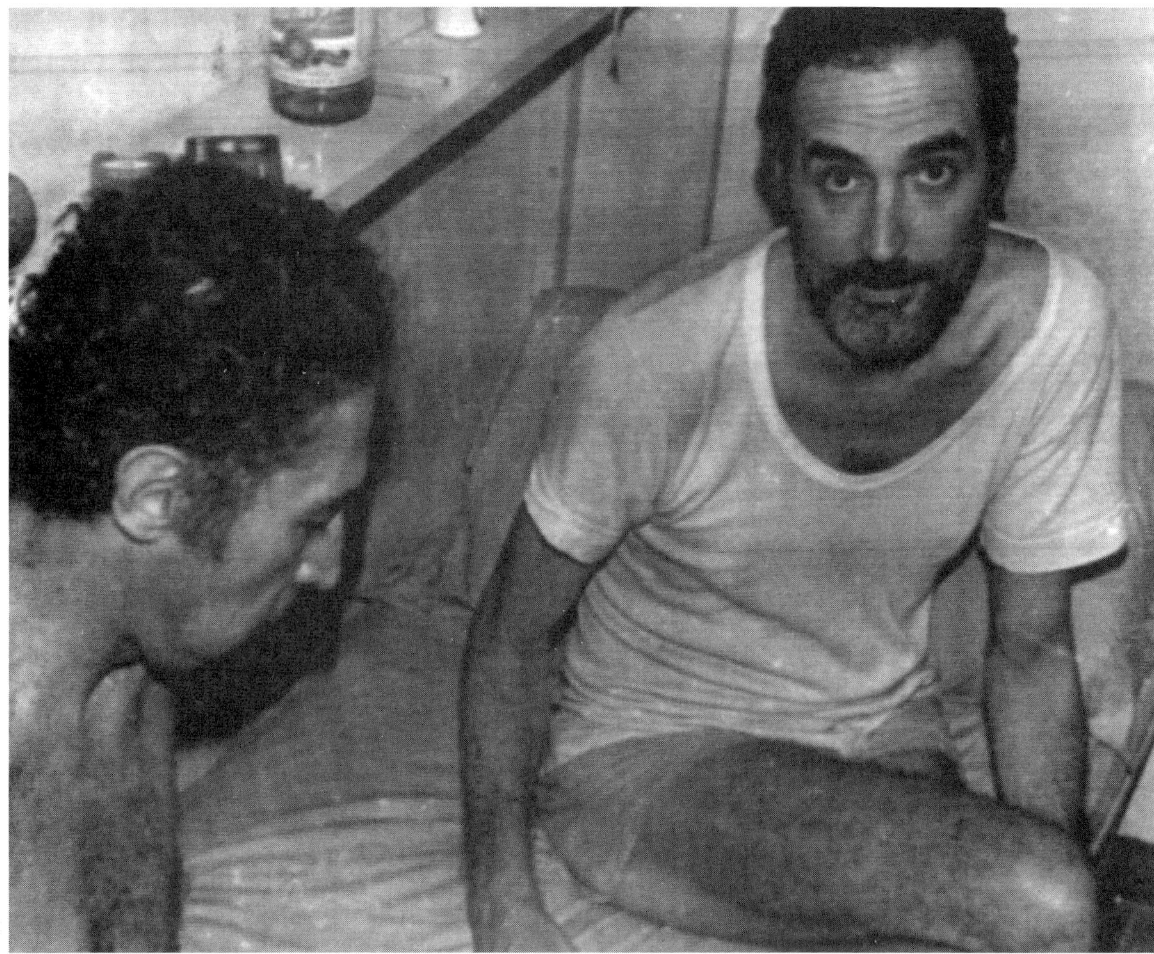
Popperfoto

Businessmen Jorge and Juan Born, from one of the largest private companies in Latin America, were held hostage by the Montoneros in 1973-74.

disabled its new missile-carrying frigate, the *Santísima Trinidad.* However, many of the Montoneros' strikes against the army and police brought about unintended casualties. Innocents, including the wives and children of the assassination targets, were also killed and injured.

THE "DIRTY WAR"

Public opinion was increasingly alienated by the violence on all sides. Atrocities, committed either by terrorists or in retaliation by the authorities, were occurring daily, and the economy was spiraling uncontrollably downward. In March 1976, in a well-planned military coup led by the commander-in-chief of the army, General Jorge Videla, Isabelita Perón was deposed. The military junta immediately set about rooting out all traces of subversion in what they euphemistically termed "the Process of National Reorganization." In this "dirty war," the junta unleashed a state terror campaign against the left, including not only the guerrilla groups, but also politicians, students, and intellectuals. AAA death squads arrested tens of thousands of Argentines, who were tortured to death in prisons and whose bodies were disposed of in the sea or in unmarked graves.

The campaign was highly effective. On July 19, 1976, most of the leadership of the ERP was captured or shot by military intelligence agents in a raid on a safe house in Buenos Aires. Roberto Santucho, one of the founders of the group, was killed. The loss of Santucho seriously damaged the ERP.

The government's campaign against the Montoneros was brutally effective, and within two years the movement was virtually obliterated. There were more than 300 Montonero operations in 1976, claiming the lives of hundreds of business people and members of the security forces. There were also some high-profile near misses: the president was almost killed by a bomb placed in a military barracks, exploding only a few minutes after he had left.

However, of the 600 Montonero operations the movement claimed took place in 1977, only four involved key targets. By August 1978, the Montoneros had lost more than 4,000 members. Nonetheless, they staged a number of successful actions during the World Cup soccer tournament, which was held in Argentina that year, in a bid for international press coverage. The Montoneros were very careful to avoid civilian casualties, and as a result it was easy for the Argentine authorities to suppress news of the terrorist attacks. No Montonero incidents are recorded later than 1979.

The Montoneros leader, Mario Firmenich, escaped and lived in exile in Brazil until he was extradited in 1985 and brought back to stand trial. He was sentenced to 30 years' imprisonment for a 1974 kidnapping. In 1987, José López Rega, the former leader of the AAA, which directed the government terror during the Isabelita Perón period, was also extradited following his detection at Miami airport. Firmenich was later pardoned on December 19, 1990, by President Carlos Menem, along with the members of the military junta who had been sentenced to jail terms for their part in the "dirty war."

THE END OF THE ERP

The ERP was similarly devastated. Its leader, Gorriarán, managed to escape, and attempted unsuccessfully to rebuild the ERP abroad, first in Italy and then in Spain. At the beginning of 1979, Gorriarán joined the Sandinista revolution in Nicaragua, which was fighting to overthrow the dictatorship of General Anastasio Somoza Debayle.

When the revolutionaries were victorious in July 1979, Gorrarián was assigned to the Ministry of the Interior with instructions to root out all enemies of the regime. In this capacity, he was responsible for organizing the assassination of Somoza's henchman, Major Pablo Emilio Salazar, in Tegicigalpa, Honduras. However, it was the assassination of General Somoza himself that really grabbed the headlines. His car was ambushed in the streets of Asunción, Paraguay, on September 17, 1980, blown open with a bazooka, and riddled with machine-gun bullets. The former dictator was killed instantly.

After the restoration of democratic government in Argentina in 1983, Gorriarán returned in secret and tried to build a new insurgent organization, the Everyone for the Fatherland Movement (MTP), based on former members of the ERP. He believed a new military intervention was inevitable. Junior officers did rebel in an Easter uprising in 1987, but were not supported by the senior ranks and democracy survived.

By 1989, however, the government of Raúl Alfonsín was crumbling, due partly to its inability to control Argentina's worsening economy. Discontent among the military was also growing because of low wages and anger about the trials of military figures involved in the "dirty war." Taking advantage of the unrest, Gorriarán launched a terrorist offensive. On January 23, 50 guerrillas under his command led an attack on the La Tablada barracks of the 3rd Infantry Regiment. The revolt was suppressed, leaving 11 soldiers and 34 insurgents dead, but once again its leader escaped.

The incident shifted attention away from the threat to democracy presented by rebellious elements in the army itself, and Alfonsín moved to appease the military. The creation, on January 25, of a National Security Council restored much of the power and some of the prestige to the army.

The attack of January 23 proved to be the final one of its kind, and in October 1995, Gorriarán himself was arrested, tried, and imprisoned.

Peter Calvert

SEE ALSO: REVOLUTIONARY TERRORISM; TERRORISM IN CHILE; TERRORISM IN NICARAGUA; ARGENTINE GOVERNMENT'S RESPONSES TO TERRORISM.

FURTHER READING

- Gillespie, Richard. *Soldiers of Perón: Argentina's Montoneros.* London: Clarendon Press, and New York: Oxford University Press, 1982.
- Hodges, Donald Clark. *Argentina, 1943-1987: The National Revolution and Resistance.* Albuquerque: University of New Mexico Press, 1988.
- Moyano, María José. *Argentina's Lost Patrol: Armed Struggle, 1969-1979.* New Haven, CT: Yale University Press, 1995.

TERRORISM IN BRAZIL

Armed bands of political activists in Brazil turned to terrorism as their only means to overturn the state in the late 1960s and early 1970s. However, so divided were these small groups that their impact was short-lived. Nevertheless, their very existence and their activities, particularly those of the Popular Revolutionary Vanguard (VPR) and the Action for National Liberation (ALN), were instrumental in bringing about the Fifth Institutional Act of 1968. The act helped consolidate the military regime into a far more authoritarian and repressive form, capable of unrestrained acts of counterinsurgency.

In the early 1960s, the terrorists' initial strategy was to establish rural guerrilla groups, under the influence of the Cuban revolution and following the teaching of Che Guevara and Régis Debray. One of the first guerrilla groups was the Maoist Communist Party of Brazil (PCdoB), which established itself in the state of Pará in the early 1960s. The Nationalist Revolutionary Movement (MNR) was formed in 1967 by supporters of the left-wing governor of Rio Grande do Sul, Leonel Brizola. However, its attempt to set up a guerrilla group in the Sierra do Caparáo, on the border between Minas Gerais and Espírito Santo, failed when the force was captured by a battalion of the First Army, and its members dispersed. Some of the survivors, calling themselves the Revolutionary Movement of the 26th (MR-26) after the Cuban movement of the same name, tried again to set up a group in the mountains above Angra dos Reis, about 60 miles south of Rio de Janeiro. They managed to liberate some of their former military colleagues from prison, but when their base area was swamped with troops, they wisely withdrew rather than risk open confrontation.

KEY FACTS

- The Popular Revolutionary Vanguard (VPR) and the Action for National Liberation (ALN) were the most notable guerrilla groups in Brazil's brief history of terrorism.
- The vigilance and tough authority of the Brazilian military made survival, let alone growth, virtually impossible for most guerrilla groups.
- ALN's abduction of Swiss ambassador Giovanni Bucher in 1970 secured the freedom of 70 jailed colleagues – at the time, a record number of prison releases in return for a diplomat's safety.

FIRST ORGANIZED TERROR GROUPS

Among the Cuban-oriented student groups founded in the later 1960s, two were of particular significance. The VPR was formed in 1967 in São Paulo, under the leadership of Carlos Lamarca. It originated from a split within the student movement Workers' Politics (POLOP), and began operations by bombing the U.S. Consulate in São Paulo in March 1968. This was the first of a series of terrorist attacks, though some, such as the bombing of the Sears Roebuck building in São Paulo to coincide with the visit of U.S. Secretary of Defense Robert McNamara to Brazil, were the work of the MNR and other groups.

In January 1969, the VPR launched a suicide attack on the headquarters of the Fourth Infantry Regiment, in order both to make political capital and capture weapons. During the two months that followed, the police captured 30 VPR members and the group was virtually crushed. In December 1970, the VPR kidnapped the Swiss ambassador and secured the release of 70 prisoners. But it suffered serious losses in the months that followed: in August 1971, Lamarca was arrested leading a group of rural guerrillas on the border of São Paulo and Paraná states. He escaped, but was tracked down and shot on September 18, 1971, in Bahía, and the VPR disintegrated.

TERROR STRUGGLES TO SURVIVE

In July 1969, POLOP members from Minas Gerais and Rio de Janeiro, who had been operating separately since 1967 under the name of the National Liberation Commando (COLINA), linked up with a splinter group

Frank Spooner Pictures

Well-armed and vigilant, Brazilian miners of the 1970s were prepared to fend off both rebel groups and government forces.

from VPR. Together they formed a rival organization and called themselves the Armed Revolutionary Vanguard-Palmares (VAR-Palmares), after a seventeenth-century slave republic which had existed briefly in the north of Brazil. VAR-Palmares achieved some success in 1969 with a series of bank raids. However, with the continuation of intense police and military activity in 1970, many of its members were arrested, and the group was destroyed on October 17, 1970, when 24 members of its São Paulo cell were arrested and imprisoned.

A fifth group emerged from splits in the Moscow-oriented Brazilian Communist Party (PCB). The October 8 Revolutionary Movement (MR-8) took its name from the presumed date of the death of Che Guevara (actually the 9th) at Valle Grande in Bolivia in 1969. But it failed to find a satisfactory site for a rural insurgency. When its base near Niteroi was raided by police in April 1969, following a car crash in which weapons were found, MR-8 abandoned its rural strategy and later linked up with the ALN. In as large a country as Brazil, it seems paradoxical that the rural strategy should have been so unsuccessful. However, a suitable base area where there was the necessary rural support simply did not exist. In the northeast, there were neither high mountains nor extensive forests to conceal the presence of a growing guerrilla group. The centers of political power, too, lay in the big cities.

A LEADING FORCE EMERGES

The best-known insurgent group of this period was Action for National Liberation (ALN), founded by PCB dissidents and centered on São Paulo. The PCB leadership had failed to anticipate the military coup of 1964, and with the arrest of many of its principal members the party had begun to disintegrate. The ALN's leader was Carlos Marighella, who had been a member of the

Frank Spooner Pictures

Urban and rural poverty encouraged many Brazilian peasants to support insurgent groups.

PCB since the 1920s, and had served in the Federal Congress as a deputy from his native state of Bahía until 1947, when the PCB was banned. After the military coup of 1964, Marighella formed the "Bahía Group," arguing for an insurrectionary strategy. He was expelled from the PCB in December 1967, after returning from a conference of the Latin American Solidarity Organization (OLAS) in Cuba. OLAS was opposed to the PCB line. Subsequently, Marighella wrote to Fidel Castro to declare that he had chosen the path of guerrilla warfare, which he believed was the only course that would unite the different revolutionary groups in Brazil. However, in practice, Marighella meant something very different from the Cuban model. His main significance was his attempt, in his *Minimanual of the Urban Guerrilla*, to transfer the strategy of the rural guerrilla to the urban context, and thus the ALN was created as an urban guerrilla movement. His argument was that in a vast country like Brazil, actions in the large cities would have much more impact than they would in the countryside. The ALN opened its campaign in 1968 with a series of bank robberies, which were designed both to give the members practice in operating in the urban environment and to build up a war chest.

Marighella emphasized the importance of surprise as a tactic of guerrilla warfare. In June 1968, the armed forces were targeted for the first time when, in a surprise attack, arms were captured from the guard at a military hospital.

Marighella's confidence in his methods was demonstrated by a leading newspaper of the day, the *Jornal do Brasil*. On September 25, 1968, the journal published a manifesto declaring the ALN's aims to create a crisis in the regime that would force it to adopt a military response. This, he explained, would lead to a mass uprising against the regime, through which "power would pass to the armed people."

Hulton Getty Picture Collection

Swiss ambassador to Brazil Giovanni Bucher was kidnapped by the ALN in December 1970 to force the release of 70 ALN and MR-8 prisoners.

This and similar statements finally convinced the police and armed forces that they were not dealing with a crime syndicate, but with organized insurgency. As Marighella had calculated, the government reacted, assuming dictatorial powers under the Fifth Institutional Act, in December. However, the terrorist attacks tended to alienate public opinion and to strengthen support for the military government, which began a massive search-and-destroy operation that resulted in arrests that included many ALN members.

Some were released as a by-product of the kidnapping of the U.S. ambassador to Brazil, Charles Burke Elbrick, by a joint operation of the ALN and MR-8 on September 3, 1969. The ambassador was released unharmed after three days when the government of General Ernesto Geisel agreed to release 15 political prisoners and fly them to Cuba. The government was widely criticized for this concession, but once the ambassador's safety had been assured, the government stepped up the search for the kidnappers. At the same time the death penalty was re-introduced by decree. In the immediate aftermath of this event Marighella was killed by police in São Paulo on November 4, 1969. His successor as leader of the ALN, Joaquim Camara Ferreira, was arrested in January 1970 with an old comrade of Marighella, Mario Alves. The ALN tried to secure their release by kidnapping the Japanese consul-general in São Paulo, Nobuo Okuchi. However, the government disclaimed all knowledge of the ALN members' whereabouts and both died in prison.

ALN'S FINAL SUCCESS

On June 11, 1970, as the West German ambassador to Brazil was being driven home from the embassy in Rio de Janiero, his car was sprayed with bullets, killing one police guard and wounding two others. Unharmed, the ambassador was released a week later on June 17, in exchange for the freedom of 40 prisoners. The detainees told a news conference in Algiers that they had been tortured during their imprisonment and had been threatened with execution.

Despite a further government campaign to root out subversion by mass arrests, incarceration, and torture, the ALN was able, in December 1970, to carry out its final act – the kidnapping of the Swiss ambassador, Giovanni Bucher. To protect its diplomatic credibility, the government agreed to release 70 political prisoners, including members of MR-8 and the ALN. However, intensified police activity and the increased use of violence by the security forces soon dismantled the ALN. By the close of 1971, the problem of urban terrorism in Brazil was virtually at an end.

Peter Calvert

SEE ALSO: HIJACKING AND KIDNAPPING; TERRORISM IN ARGENTINA; TERRORISM IN CHILE; TERRORISM IN PERU; BRAZILIAN GOVERNMENT'S RESPONSES TO TERRORISM.

FURTHER READING

- Alves, Maria Helen Moreira. *State and Opposition in Military Brazil.* Austin: University of Texas Press, 1985.
- Alves, Maria Helen Moreira. *A Grain of Mustard Seed: The Awakening of the Brazilian Revolution.* New York: Doubleday Anchor Press, 1973.
- Petras, James. "The Anatomy of State Terror: Chile, El Salvador, and Brazil," in *Science and Society* 51, No. 3 (1987).

TERRORISM IN CHILE

The Movement of the Revolutionary Left (MIR) waged a revolutionary terrorist struggle in Chile from 1965 until 1989. The MIR initially advocated revolution to overthrow the longest-standing democracy in Latin America in order to establish a Marxist regime. In 1970, when Chile elected as president Dr. Salvador Allende Gossens, a Marxist, the MIR took it upon themselves to implement his policies by force. This prompted a military coup led by General Augusto Pinochet Ugarte, who struck a blow against the left from which the MIR never recovered.

CHILE'S LEFT-WING TRADITION

A vigorous political rivalry between right, moderate, and leftist groups had existed in Chile since 1931. A left-wing coalition, which included the Chilean communists, the socialist party, and the Radicals (a liberal movement) won the presidency in 1938. Allende, supported by a socialist-communist alliance, almost won the presidency in the 1952 and 1958 elections. He also ran in 1964. Finally, his perseverance was rewarded in 1970, when he became the world's first democratically elected Marxist leader.

In 1965, however, a more militant left-wing force was formed. Miguel Enríquez and other students at the University of Concepción in southern Chile founded the MIR. Initially a clandestine organization, the MIR opposed the constitutional stances of even the most left-wing of the country's official radical parties, and took its inspiration and received backing from Castro's regime in Cuba.

KEY FACTS

- By 1972, peasants aided by militias set up by the Movement for the Revolutionary Left (MIR) had seized nearly 75 percent of Chile's cultivated land.
- On September 7, 1986, 21 Manuel Rodríguez Patriotic Front terrorists, armed with grenades and machine guns, ambushed Chilean leader General Pinochet in his car. Five guards were killed and 11 were wounded. Pinochet escaped with a cut hand.
- The MIR has been careful to avoid harming civilians in its terrorist attacks. In June 1988, the MIR bombed four banks in Chile's capital, Santiago, causing serious material damage but no injuries.

FIRST ACTS OF TERRORISM

The MIR revolutionaries began by recruiting radical students. Under the leadership of Enríquez, the MIR transformed itself into a left-wing pressure group prepared to use violence, assassination, and terrorism for political ends in 1967. Enríquez and Andrés Pascal Allende, the nephew of Salvador Allende, won control of the MIR central executive committee. They were responsible for the early MIR low-level operations, such as robbing banks and businesses and illegally seizing building sites. However, the civil police were able to contain them with little difficulty.

By 1970, the MIR had made enough of an impression on Chile to be included in talks with Salvador Allende, the new president. The MIR refused to join his Popular Unity party, preferring to remain outside the government. Instead, they adopted a stance of "critical support" toward Allende's administration. The MIR's aim was to shift Allende away from his congressional alliance with the moderate Christian Democrats. The MIR regarded the alliance as "class collaborationism," and wanted Allende to bring about revolutionary social change by means of more direct action.

What the MIR meant by direct action was seen most clearly in rural areas, where its power base was built on open support for the armed seizure of land. This had begun spontaneously in the province of Cautín, where native Mapuche Indians sought to recover lands that had been taken from them in the nineteenth century. The movement spread rapidly into the Central Valley. Farm workers felt betrayed by successive Chilean governments and were encouraged by the MIR to take matters into their own hands. Many people within the government approved of this action.

Hulton Getty Picture Collection

Despite the protection of armed guards, Chile's President Allende was killed on September 11, 1973, when the armed forces staged a coup.

Some of the farms taken over were used as MIR power bases and training camps. By the end of 1971, enclaves had been established in which MIR commissars held political and military control. The MIR awarded peasant squatters legal titles to plots within these enclaves, in which the MIR was effectively acting as an alternative power to the state.

OPPOSITION FROM THE CIA

Under Allende's predecessor, President Frei, the Christian Democrats had been pursuing a policy of "Chileanization" – bringing foreign industry under state control via shared ownership. Allende went a stage further and introduced a policy of nationalization. His government snatched ownership from multinational corporations, such as the American communications giant ITT, thereby provoking U.S. anger.

The U.S. had been aware of the political swing to the left in Chile long before Allende came to power, and had sent in the CIA to prevent his election. The CIA campaign took the form of spreading anti-Marxist propaganda and inciting violence to provoke a coup. In 1970, however, popular support for Allende was too great for CIA subversion to have much effect. After his election, the CIA continued to work toward destabilizing his government by providing opposition factions such as the ultra-right terrorist group Fatherland and Liberty, with money and arms.

FATHERLAND AND LIBERTY

Fatherland and Liberty was active during the presidency of Allende. Based in Santiago, the group was set up to combat the armed threat presented by MIR terrorists. Fatherland and Liberty generally indulged in low-level sabotage and arson attacks. However, in 1973, the group attempted to asssassinate army leader and cabinet minister General Carlos Prats González. Allende's government responded quickly and little more was heard of Fatherland and Liberty.

Popperfoto

Terrified civilians are caught in the crossfire between Pinochet's troops and resistance fighters in Santiago on June 29, 1975.

Thus opposition in Chile during Allende's term of office existed on two fronts. On the one hand, the U.S. and big businesses reacted because they felt Allende was going too far in his reforms. On the other, the MIR mobilized because he was not going far enough. Opposition to the government began with articles published in the MIR's newspaper *Punto Final*, but soon resulted in armed confrontation. Landowners set up vigilante groups to protect their property from peasants intent on seizing land. Rural shoot-outs between vigilantes and peasants were commonplace and often resulted in loss of life.

MILITARY COUP

The civil unrest destabilized a government already under pressure. Its reforms were proving disastrous for the economy. By 1972, inflation was running at 350 percent and the country was riven with strikes. This eventually prompted the armed forces to intervene.

The military had already helped Allende foil a coup by MIR and communist paramilitary units on June 29, 1973. But fear that the MIR was organizing a revolt among the junior ranks of the navy in the northern city of Valparaíso triggered a military coup on September 11. Allende died in an air force bomb attack on the presidential palace as he resisted calls for his resignation. Members of his government were arrested.

Within weeks, Chile became a police state under the new military junta headed by General Pinochet. Thousands of known or suspected rebel sympathizers were murdered or detained and tortured. Security forces brutally administered physical abuse, such as rape, the application of electrodes to heads and genitals, and merciless beatings.

The MIR was blamed by Pinochet's military regime for the country's plight and became the prime target for reprisals. In keeping with its guerrilla origins, the

MIR beat a hasty retreat to its bases in the countryside after strategic attacks on patrolling soldiers in the capital. Its leader, Carlos Altamirano, escaped but second-in-command Bautista von Schauwen and senior member José Gregorio Liendo were arrested. Schauwen was detained but Liendo, known as "Comandante Pepe," was executed on October 3.

MIR activists launched brief attacks both on the National Stadium in Santiago and on military barracks in the northern city of Valparaíso, where the mass torture and murder of detainees was taking place. They also joined parties of the deposed government coalition in signing a declaration in Rome, in December 1973, pledging resistance to Pinochet's regime, but made it clear three months later that this could only be done effectively by terrorist means.

However, this was easier said than done. Although the MIR linked up with guerrilla groups in neighboring Argentina to organize crossborder sorties, the remote mountainous terrain covering much of Chile meant that terrorist attacks in rural areas had little impact. Those who tried to organize urban terrorism were easily located and killed. In the next few months, most of the MIR leadership was killed, including founder member Miguel Enríquez, who was shot dead in a gun battle with troops in Santiago on October 5, 1974. In October 1975, MIR leader Pascal Allende was wounded but escaped capture. The doctor who treated him, however, was savagely tortured.

Having been allowed to operate legally during most of Allende's government, the MIR fatally underestimated the reaction of the armed forces following the military takeover. The MIR was not equipped as a secret organization and had no strategy to resist Pinochet's ruthless counterinsurgency campaign.

TORTURE, PRISON, AND DEATH

Pinochet's reversal of Allende's social reforms was made possible only by brutal repression. This led to economic depression and near-starvation for millions of peasants. The National Directorate of Intelligence, set up to counter resistance in June 1974, ruthlessly tortured suspected terrorists. Pinochet's brutality drew worldwide condemnation. When he tried to present a more acceptable face, he was frustrated by military politics and by the MIR's resumption of armed struggle.

In 1980, a number of MIR terrorists began a series of attacks on banks and police stations. In July 1980, MIR killers machine-gunned to death Lieutenant-General Roger Vergara, head of the Army Intelligence School. Assassinations of government officials followed, including the military governor of Santiago, in August 1983. The MIR also embarked on a campaign of bombings aimed at causing maximum economic damage rather than human casualties. In a two-week period in October and November 1983, the MIR bombed four businesses with strong U.S. connections, but caused little in the way of human injuries.

A NEW TERRORIST GROUP

In 1983, the Manuel Rodríguez Patriotic Front (FPMR), an offshoot of the Communist Party, began operations as an urban guerrilla group. Between 1983 and 1985, the FPMR carried out bombing campaigns in Chile's eight largest cities. The FPMR's main targets were power stations, but terrorists also attacked the U.S.-Chilean Cultural Institute in Valparaíso and planted a car-bomb outside the U.S. embassy in July 1985.

In 1986, FPMR terrorists ambushed Pinochet's motorcade on a bridge in the Maipó Valley. Five bodyguards were killed, but Pinochet was saved by the quick thinking of his driver, who reversed his bullet-proof Mercedes out of trouble. Though a great many suspects were arrested and brutally tortured, relatively few FPMR members were successfully identified.

The sudden end of Pinochet's regime came with a referendum in October 1988. Much to his surprise, the people refused to vote for an extension of his term of office. The referendum also signaled the end of terrorist operations in Chile. The country returned to civilian rule under Christian Democrat Patricio Aylwin in 1989.

Peter Calvert

SEE ALSO: TERRORISM IN ARGENTINA; TERRORISM IN BRAZIL; CHILEAN GOVERNMENT'S RESPONSES TO TERRORISM.

FURTHER READING

- Arriagada, Genaro. *The Politics of Power.* Boulder, CO: Westview, 1991.
- Constable, Pamela, and Arturo Valenzuela. *A Nation of Enemies: Chile Under Pinochet.* London and New York: Norton, 1991.
- Spooner, Mary Helen. *Soldiers in a Narrow Land: The Pinochet Regime in Chile.* Berkeley: University of California Press, 1994.

TERRORISM IN COLOMBIA

The history of political violence in Colombia has been the bloodiest and most enduring throughout the whole of Latin America. The assassination in 1948 of Liberal politician Jorge Eliécer Gaitán in the capital city, Bogotá, heralded the start of the period known as "The Violence." Between that year and 1962, an estimated 200,000 people were killed in the civil unrest, while inefficient government, poverty, and injustice caused extreme hardship among Colombia's citizens. The Violence was in reality tantamount to a civil war. The fighting was so intense that, in the first ten years, some 80,000 peasants died. In the province of Tolima, in the center of the country, 16,000 peasants were killed and 40,000 rural properties were abandoned.

In the mid-1960s, left-wing guerrilla groups began to form in response to corruption in the political parties. Guerrillas first used terrorism to promote revolution, and later to finance their struggle against the government and its ruthless security forces. Since the cocaine industry came to dominate the economy, drug-related violence has raised the levels of terrorism to new proportions in Colombia.

DECADES OF TERRORISM

The first guerrilla group – also the largest – was set up in 1964. The Revolutionary Armed Forces of Colombia (FARC) started out as a handful of peasant farmer families, and has developed into a rural army comprising more than 7,000 active combatants divided into 60 "Fronts" or assault groups. Other guerrilla groups with a more radical ideology soon emerged. Also founded in 1964, the National Liberation Army (ELN) sprang up as a revolutionary movement intending to "seize power for the people." In 1967, the Popular Liberation Army (EPL) emerged as a result of Chinese influence in revolutionary circles in Colombia. Finally, the April 19 Movement (M-19) emerged in 1973, following the fraudulent elections that brought the right-wing Misael Pastrana Borrero to power.

Despite the diverse ideologies of these groups, they have all used the same terrorist tactics to finance their armed struggle, including attacks and bank robberies. The groups have all perpetrated kidnappings, targeting ranchers, landowners, and employees of wealthy companies. Within their regions of operation, guerrillas have collected protection taxes from individuals or companies. The most recent and most profitable guerrilla activity is the protection of Colombia's extensive coca and poppy plantations, and involvement in the illegal drug trade. Among other drug-related activities, guerrillas have ambushed and killed members of the army and the police; sabotaged bridges, roads, oil pipelines, and hydroelectric installations; and killed supposed guerrilla "deserters" and "informers."

KEY FACTS

- 1990 was a record year for kidnappings in Colombia. A total of 1,280 people were held against their will, with an average of three or four kidnappings a day.
- Between 1988 and 1990, assassins hired by the Medellín cartel killed 290 police.
- In a series of attacks that took place between late August and mid-September 1996, the FARC assassinated a total of 50 soldiers.

THE FARC

The FARC has the reputation for being the best-trained and most effective guerrilla organization in Latin America. During its formative years, hounded by U.S.-backed counterinsurgency operations, the group was never able to consolidate support in any area. During the early 1970s, the FARC began financing itself by kidnapping foreigners and wealthy Colombians and by extorting large sums from international companies. The FARC is also notorious for terrorizing and killing peasants who do not cooperate with it.

In January 1975, the FARC kidnapped the Dutch consul in the city of Cali in western Colombia and did not release him until October 1976. In February 1977,

Rex Features

A terrorist bombing in Medellín on June 10, 1995, killed 28 people and wounded another 205.

terrorists kidnapped a U.S. Peace Corps volunteer and demanded $250,000 for his release. He was freed three years later upon payment of the ransom. In February 1985, FARC terrorists made eight bomb attacks on U.S. industries in Medellín, in the west of Colombia.

The FARC's struggle continued into the 1990s. On August 30, 1996, 500 FARC guerrillas killed 27 soldiers in a military base in the south of Colombia and kidnapped 67 others. A week later, 19 soldiers were killed in another FARC ambush.

THE APRIL 19 MOVEMENT

Three months after its formation in 1973, M-19 stole the spurs and sword of Simón Bolívar from a Bogotá museum. Bolívar had fought for independence from Spain in the nineteenth century, and the theft of his famous sword symbolized a call for armed struggle. In 1976, M-19 kidnapped union leader José Raquel Mercado. On the night of December 26, 1978, M-19 managed to steal 4,000 weapons from a military arsenal by digging a tunnel several hundred yards long.

One of the group's most dramatic actions took place on April 1980, when M-19 guerrillas occupied the embassy of the Dominican Republic in Bogotá for 40 days. Of the 57 people kidnapped, 15 were ambassadors. Although it was never officially confirmed, it is believed that Colombian President Turbay Ayala paid $1 million for the release of the diplomats and granted the kidnappers safe conduct to Cuba.

During the presidency of Ayala (1979-82), M-19 carried out two mortar attacks on the presidential palace in Bogotá in an effort to force the government to sign a peace accord. On two occasions, M-19 managed to interrupt television programs to broadcast its own political propaganda. Following these actions, the group suffered a series of setbacks which reduced its military capacity and precipitated its near-complete collapse in 1990.

Toward the end of April 1983, M-19's leader, Jaime Bateman Cayón, was killed in an air crash in neighboring Panama. Nearly two years later, in November 1985, the disastrous occupation of the Palace of Justice in the heart of the Colombian capital nearly finished off M-19. During the 28-hour duration of the occupation, the army responded with tanks and heavy machine-guns, ignoring a telephoned appeal for a cease-fire

Rex Features

The late Pablo Escobar was one of the kingpins of the Medellín cartel that ruled Colombia's cocaine trade.

issued by the president of the Supreme Court, Reyes Echandía. More than 100 people were killed, including 11 supreme court judges.

Following this atrocity, M-19's only significant action was the attack on the city of Cali by more than 300 guerrillas in March 1986. The attack lasted three days, and in an open confrontation with the Colombian army, an estimated 100 people were killed, including 60 guerrillas.

ECO-TERRORISM OF THE ELN

The ELN took its inspiration from the Cuban revolution in 1959. After the FARC, it is the second largest and most active terrorist group in Colombia. One of its most notable characteristics has been the presence of Catholic priests in its ranks. This phenomenon first occurred in 1966, with the integration into the ELN of priest and sociologist Camilo Torres Restrepo. He died two months later in combat with the army, and his tragic fate captured the imagination of the nation, elevating Restrepo into a figure of mythic proportions and a potent symbol of the struggle. The ELN's marriage of Marxism and Christianity continued in the person of Father Manuel Pérez Martínez, a Spanish priest and the ELN's supreme commander.

The ELN differs from other Colombian guerrilla groups in the way it has systematically purged its own ranks. Between 1965 and 1969, the ELN executed at least 57 of its own members. In Bogotá in 1971, the ELN assassinated Jaime Arenas, a former ELN member who had published a book condemning the execution of organization members.

Under the command of Manuel Pérez, the ELN has centered its terrorist activities on the sabotage of national and foreign oil company pipelines. According to a Colombian newspaper, the ELN made 141 attacks on a vital pipeline from the heart of Colombia to a port on the Atlantic coast between 1987 and 1991. Financial losses sustained during these four years were valued at about $634 million.

Although the intensity of these attacks has diminished in recent years, constant sabotage has obliged Colombian and international oil companies to pay a "war tax" to the Colombian army so it can train specialized personnel to patrol and protect the extensive pipelines. In March 1996, British Petroleum agreed to pay $60 million for the training and maintenance of an elite private army to repel ELN attacks.

Terrorist attacks on oil pipelines resulted in large-scale ecological destruction. For example, when the ELN dynamited a pipeline on June 4, 1990, the crude oil contaminated a large part of the Catatumbo River, affecting about 12,000 peasant farmers. These terrorist attacks ruined some 7,500 acres of fertile land.

EPL GUERRILLAS

The EPL, smallest all the active guerrilla groups, burst onto the political scene in 1965. The movement was on the verge of extinction toward the late 1960s, after two military operations against the ELN during 1968 and 1969 resulted in the death of key EPL leaders. This led to dissent over strategy among the remnants of the group. The reconstitution of the EPL began in 1980. Ten years later, the group secured the sum of $3 million in the region of Córdoba in the northeast of Colombia alone, through extorting money from wealthy landowners. Uniquely among guerrilla groups, the EPL raises funds through cattle rustling and smuggling, and also finances itself through kidnappings and pipeline attacks.

Kidnappings represent a lucrative source of guerrilla funding for groups besides the EPL. Incidents increased rapidly during the late 1980s and early 1990s, and the money acquired from hundreds of kidnappings became the principal source of funding for terrorist activity in Colombia. Although it is difficult to compile reliable statistics, a report by Amnesty International indicated that between 1989 and 1991, guerrilla organizations abducted more than 1,700 people, securing an income of about $35 million. Although the frequency of kidnappings remains high today – about 800 took place in 1995 – this method of terrorist financing has begun to give way to an even more profitable source: the drug trafficking industry.

THE TERRORISM OF DRUGS

As a framework for indiscriminate terrorism, the wars waged by the drug barons have put all other Colombia guerrilla activities to shame. The cultivation of coca leaves, which are used to produce cocaine, took off in Colombia in the 1970s. A number of entrepreneurs in Medellín, Colombia's second-largest city, formed a group or "cartel" to establish a massive coca industry. Using land owned by peasants or their landlords, the cartel set up coca leaf-processing plants in the jungles, along with tiny airstrips to allow the transportation of vast quantities of the rendered coca paste. The drug infrastructure extended to harbors on Caribbean islands and on Gulf of Mexico coast, and then on to distributors in the U.S. and, increasingly in Europe. The leaders of the Medellín cartel included Pablo Escobar Gaviria, Gonzalo Rodríguez Gacha, Carlos Lehrer Rivas, and members of the Ochoa family.

The street value of cocaine fluctuates wildly – depending on the amount on the market – but in a "good year," a drug baron may enjoy a return of 12,000 percent on his investment. The incentive to take part in any part of the drug industry is immeasurably great, and has accounted for thousands of kidnappings, murders, and other terrorist acts in Colombia.

The Medellín drug barons bought the support of other Colombian terrorist groups when the need arose. For example, it was they who orchestrated M-19's attack on the Bogota Palace of Justice in 1985. The cartel intended to disrupt a court debate on the 1979 extradition treaty with the United States. Had the treaty been ratified (it was in fact annulled two years later), it would have constituted a serious blow to the Colombian drug-traffickers.

The increase in terrorism saw the creation of the sinister "Office" in Medellín, in which drug barons recruited young assassins and paid them nearly $1,000 for every police agent killed. Their campaigns also featured bombings. On November 27, 1989, drug-traffickers killed 130 people when they blew up a Colombian airliner on a flight between Bogotá and Medellín – supposedly in order to kill a handful of police informants on board. Two weeks later, a car-bomb at the state security agency headquarters in Bogotá killed 86 people and injured another 100. Terrorist campaigns continued with bombings on indiscriminate targets.

Prominent political figures were also the target of numerous attacks attributed to the Medellín cartel. In 1984, the minister of justice was assassinated by two hired gunmen. The Liberal party's presidential candidate, Luis Carlos Galán, was assassinated in 1989. Within a year, two more presidential candidates lost their lives as a result of terrorist actions.

Security forces captured Carlos Lehrer in 1985. They then killed Gonzalo Rodríguez in 1991 and Pablo Escobar in 1994, and the decapitated Medellín cartel virtually vanished. However, the Colombian government continues to fight the narcotics terrorists. The trafficking infrastructure, now a fully international network, is well established, and Latin America offers a limitless supply of ambitious entrepreneurs willing to reap astronomical profits from a bloody industry.

Jorge Ramírez

SEE ALSO: GUERRILLAS AND TERROR; REVOLUTIONARY TERRORISM; URBAN VERSUS RURAL TERRORISM; HIJACKING AND KIDNAPPING; ASSASSINATION; COLOMBIAN GOVERNMENT'S RESPONSES TO TERRORISM.

FURTHER READING

- Giraldo, Javier. *Colombia: The Genocidal Democracy.* Monroe, ME: Common Courage Press, 1996.
- Lara, Patricia. *The M-19: Sow the Wind and Reap the Whirlwind.* 4th ed. Washington, DC: The Foreign Broadcast Information Service, 1983.
- Mendez, Juan E. *Political Murder and Reform in Colombia: The Violence Continues.* New York: Americas Watch, 1992.

TERRORISM IN EL SALVADOR

The recent history of El Salvador has been marked by a series of democratically elected republican governments being repeatedly obstructed and overthrown by the armed forces. The result was a bitterly-fought, lengthy civil war that began in 1979 and lasted into the 1990s. The struggle became polarized on one side by right-wing military death squads and on the other by the terrorist tactics of the Marxist guerrillas, while the beleaguered Christian Democrat Party (PDC) tried to maintain support for the political center.

THE SEEDS OF REBELLION

During the first half of the twentieth century, the small group of wealthy landowners who ruled El Salvador repeatedly used extreme violence to suppress those opposed to its rule. Revolutionary inspiration in El Salvador has long come from the 1932 peasant revolt led by Farabundo Martí. El Salvador's then ruler, General Maximiliano Hernández Martínez, quashed the uprising, killing more than 20,000 peasants, including Martí, in the process. Then in 1944, students went on strike and were joined by laborers and professionals alike. Hernández overreacted. His police killed indiscriminately and incurred U.S. anger by murdering an American citizen. Hernández was forced into exile.

From the 1940s onward, El Salvador oscillated between democratic governments attempting to implement reforms and military coups cutting short their terms of office. Military leaders ran the economy for their own benefit and for that of the elite landowners. By 1970, however, the political climate in El Salvador was starting to change.

KEY FACTS

- El Salvador was notorious for its great discrepancies of wealth. In the 1970s, 14 families were estimated to own 90 percent of the land.
- During the civil war in El Salvador, between 30,000 and 50,000 people were killed.
- In a single raid on an air force base in Ilopango, El Salvador, in 1982, Farabundo Martí National Liberation Front (FMLN) rebels destroyed 70 percent of El Salvador's military aircraft.

TERRORIST OPPOSITION

In April 1970, radical members of the Salvadoran Communist Party (PCS) broke away to form the Popular Liberation Forces (FPL). The group was committed to armed struggle and was led by a former PCS secretary-general, Salvador Cayetano Carpio.

In March 1972, a coalition of left-wing parties, led by the PDC, won a majority in the general election. However, right-wing army leaders staged a coup to prevent the coalition from forming a government. In response to the coup, the FPL declared a campaign of violence against the military regime. In 1976, the FPL succeeded in assassinating a number of leading Salvadoran political figures. Among its victims were a former president, the foreign minister, and senior military personnel.

In the meantime, dissident PCD members formed a rival militant group called the People's Revolutionary Army (ERP). Led by the poet Roque Dalton García, the ERP was organized into small bands of revolutionary guerrillas. The ERP conducted a policy of kidnapping and murdering mayors and government officials, and terrorizing peasants who collaborated with the government. In December 1974, the ERP bombed eight cities, causing substantial damage but no casualties. In April 1975, members of his own organization accused Dalton of being a collaborator and executed him. After this, in reaction to the group's increasing brutality, many ERP members left to form another guerrilla band, the Armed Forces of National Resistance (FARN).

A UNITED GUERRILLA FORCE

In 1979, a second military coup led to full-scale civil war in El Salvador. Amid the violence, a united guerrilla force emerged under Cayetano's leadership. It was made up of the FPL, the ERP, and three smaller groups. In October

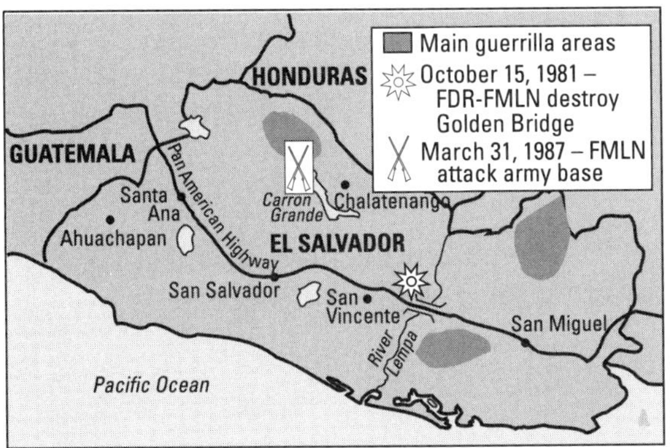

A map of El Salvador, showing the main FMLN strongholds, and two of the group's terrorist acts.

1980, the united force took the name of the Farabundo Martí National Liberation Front (FMLN). At the same time, the FMLN's political wing, the Democratic Revolutionary Front (FDR), publicized the group's aims. By the end of the year, the FMLN was in control of most of Chalatenango in the north and Morazán in the east.

In January 1981, the FMLN began a "final offensive" to gain a decisive victory against the military government. In March, guerrillas launched attacks on cities to disrupt the general elections. The guerrillas targeted the city of Usulután, which contained a small army garrison of 300-400 troops. Hundreds of people took part in a week-long occupation of the city. Violence destabilized the eastern part of the country, preventing the elections from taking place in four areas. Although the expected nationwide uprising did not occur, the armed forces sustained heavy casualties and failed to inflict similar losses on the rebels.

FMLN OCCUPATION

Over the next four years, the rebels controlled much of the countryside, including Chalatenango and much of Morazán, where they operated a radio station, *Venceremos* (We Shall Conquer). In June 1982, FMLN rebels ambushed several hundred troops in a canyon in Morazán. The rebels killed 80 soldiers, captured 43, and seized weapons and ammunition. The FMLN shot down and captured a helicopter carrying the under secretary of defense. Rebels also regularly destroyed bridges on El Salvador's principal road. But, although the FMLN inflicted serious casualties and economic damage, it was unable to break army control of key strongpoints.

In March 1985, the FMLN again launched city offensives to disrupt elections. This time they failed and PDC leader José Napoleón Duarte became president. He began talks in 1986 with the extremists, in spite of hostile criticism from the armed forces who were increasingly confident of destroying the terrorists. The military had closed down one of the three main FMLN fronts, and launched major attacks on the guerrilla strongholds of Chalatenango and Morazán. However, in March 1987, an attack on an army base in Chalatenango killed at least 42, demonstrating that the FMLN's capacity to strike had not been reduced.

After the election of right-wing candidate Alfredo Cristiani as president, the FMLN launched a new offensive in November 1989. The government declared a state of siege and imposed a news blackout. Death squads were deployed to wipe out the terrorists. More than 1,200 people were killed in 12 days of violence.

However, the FMLN remained a powerful threat. In mid-November 1990, guerrillas attacked military installations across the country. In one incident, they even managed to shoot down an air force jet with a Soviet-made SAM-7 surface-to-air missile. In a week of fighting, 90 people were killed and some 300 wounded.

This was the last great FMLN offensive. In January 1991, the government resumed talks with the terrorists. On May 20, the UN sent a team of observers to monitor human rights violations in El Salvador, and on November 16, the FMLN declared a cease-fire. On New Year's Eve, 1991, the UN obtained all-party agreement on a program that led to a definitive peace on October 1, 1992.

Peter Calvert

SEE ALSO: TERRORISM IN GUATEMALA; TERRORISM IN MEXICO; TERRORISM IN NICARAGUA; SALVADORAN GOVERNMENT'S RESPONSES TO TERRORISM.

FURTHER READING

- Fish, Joe, and Cristina Sganga. *El Salvador: Testament of Terror.* London: Zed Books, and New York: Olive Branch Press, 1988.
- Menzel, Sewall H. *Bullets versus Ballots: Political Violence and Revolutionary War in El Salvador.* New Brunswick, NJ: Transaction Publishers, 1994.
- Shenk, Janet. *El Salvador: The Face of Revolution.* 2nd ed. London: Pluto, and Boston: South End Press, 1982.

TERRORISM IN GUATEMALA

Guerrilla insurgency and its terrorist associations in Guatemala lasted for 35 years – longer than in any other Latin American country. From the outbreak of insurgent activity in 1960, a series of groups were involved. Unlike the case in other Latin American countries, the effect of the government's sustained and ruthless counterinsurgency strategy in Guatemala was strikingly unsuccessful.

SEEDS OF CONFLICT

The Spanish conquest of what is now Guatemala was followed by the creation of large estates. The native Indian Maya population was either forced to work on these estates or was driven up into the high ground where the soil was less fertile. In the century following independence from Spain in 1838, the military dictatorships that ruled Guatemala made sure that wealth and power remained firmly in the hands of the ruling elite.

However, in 1944, a popular revolt toppled the military regime. Demonstrations in the streets led to the removal of the military dictator, Jorge Ubico, and the first elections in Guatemala's history. Until 1954, in a period known as the "Ten Years of Spring," a series of moderate reforms took place under the elected governments. The first was headed by a civilian, Juan José Arévalo, and the second was led by a soldier, Colonel Jacobo Arbenz. In 1945, the left-wing Arévalo began a program of long-overdue social reforms. Arbenz succeeded him in 1951 and continued the program, including the expropriation of land owned by U.S.-based companies, such as the vast areas of uncultivated land owned by the United Fruit Company. In 1954, however, the program came to an abrupt end as a result of U.S. intervention.

The CIA, with support from the United Fruit Company, sponsored a force of exiles led by Colonel Carlos Castillo Armas to enter Guatemala. By a combination of threats and bribery, Castillo Armas overthrew Arbenz and became president. In 1954, Colonel Ydígoras Fuentes killed Castillo Armas and succeeded him as president after a rigged election.

Inspired by Fidel Castro's successful revolution in Cuba in 1959, army colonel Rafael Sessan Pereira staged a military coup against Ydígoras. It was a hasty maneuver with little popular support, and it failed. But it was Guatemala's first serious attempt to overthrow a government from within, and it sowed the seeds of future unrest that would last nearly 36 years.

KEY FACTS

- Insurgency in Guatemala lasted longer than anywhere else in Latin America – from 1960 to 1996. In all, the conflict claimed 100,000 lives.
- In 1968, Rebel Armed Forces (FAR) terrorists killed U.S. ambassador Gordon Mein in a failed kidnap attempt. This was the first time a U.S. ambassador was murdered in the line of duty.
- The toll of civilians was high. Few of the 6,000-10,000 Guatemalans who died in the years 1966-68 were members of any terrorist organization.

FIRST GUATEMALAN GUERRILLAS

Two junior officers, Lieutenant Marco Antonio Yon Sosa and Ensign Luis Turcios Lima, who had supported Pereira, linked up with the communist Guatemalan Workers' Party (PGT). Their aim was to restore democracy and human rights, and put an end to the hardships suffered by the peasant majority. Following the failure of Pereira's attempted coup, Yon Sosa and Turcios embarked on a campaign of hit-and-run terrorist action, rather than attempting direct confrontation.

By 1962, they had enough support to begin terrorist operations from their hideout in the eastern mountains of Zacapa. Fifty activists attacked two army posts and robbed an office of the United Fruit Company on February 6. On February 26, they captured two radio stations in the capital, Guatemala City. Ydígoras responded by imposing martial law on the capital. Captured terrorists were either imprisoned and tortured, or executed.

Guerrilla insurgencies took place in most of Guatemala's provinces between 1960 and 1996.

The remaining activists regrouped under the umbrella title Rebel Armed Forces (FAR) in December 1962, led by Turcios, at first in conjunction with Yon Sosa, and later on his own. A student, César Montes, introduced communist recruits from the PGT.

In 1964, Yon Sosa left to form the Revolutionary November 13 Movement (MR-13), named after the date of the 1960 failed coup. In line with Mao's theories, much of the movement's work consisted of "armed propaganda," whereby guerrillas explained their aims to illiterate peasants. In 1965, MR-13 came to prominence by killing U.S. military attaché Colonel Harold Hauser.

Although both the FAR and MR-13 differed in ideology, they functioned in broadly the same way. Neither was backed by foreign influences nor received any outside help. Both factions stole most of their weapons from the army; the rest they bought abroad with funds generated by bank raids. Both movements followed the revolutionary strategies of Che Guevara, hero of the 1959 Cuban revolution. Each group centered on a few hundred dedicated activists based in the countryside, well away from major cities.

In 1966, Guatemalan military officials allowed a relatively free election and the civilian candidate, Julio César Méndez Montenegro, was victorious. His win brought the offer of a truce and amnesty for the terrorists, but the offer was opposed by the military. Colonel Carlos Arana Osorio mobilized his ruthless death squads in a savage counterinsurgency campaign against all terrorist groups.

On March 5, police captured the entire leadership of the PGT, including Secretary General Víctor Manuel Gutiérrez. The terrorists responded by kidnapping the presidential press secretary after a gun battle in Guatemala City, and another key government figure. In exchange for the hostages, the terrorists demanded the release of 28 political prisoners who had disappeared several months before. When the terrorists discovered that the prisoners had been shot on capture, they freed the two officials in exchange for a student activist.

RAISING THE STAKES WITH TERRORISM

The PGT and the FAR vowed to fight on, but they faced a renewed onslaught from the government's armed forces and its death squads. The 300-strong FAR suffered significant losses, and its support in the countryside dwindled. To consolidate guerrilla strength, MR–13 joined the FAR. Yon Sosa became leader after Turcios died in a car crash in October 1966. Then, in January 1968, the FAR broke with the PGT, which was becoming hesitant about carrying on the struggle by increasingly violent means.

The newly combined FAR shifted their tactics from harassment of government troops and agencies in rural areas toward urban guerrilla warfare in Guatemala City. This raised the stakes significantly in terms of terrorist activity. The most notorious act was the shooting dead of U.S. ambassador Gordon Mein in a kidnap attempt in 1967. It was the first abduction of its kind in Latin America, and prompted a wave of similar attacks on diplomats and leading figures in business and industry. In February 1970, for instance, the FAR kidnapped foreign minister Fuentes Mohr and U.S. labor attaché Sean Holly in separate incidents, exchanging them for captured terrorists. Relations with the West became strained, however, when the West German ambassador was shot on April 5.

Hulton Getty Picture Collection

The wreckage of a train sabotaged in 1962 by Guatemalan terrorists fighting for land reforms against the government of General Ydígoras.

Remnants of the MR-13 continued to wage its rural campaign but support among the native Indian population was dwindling. The campaign was seen as more of a power struggle than a means to force through improved living conditions for the peasants. In 1970, Guatemalan generals learned of Yon Sosa's whereabouts in Mexico and hired Mexican soldiers to kill him and other guerrillas. His group, based in El Quiché in the north, barely survived. After six years, terrorists throughout Guatemala were at a low ebb. They had neither moved the government nor mobilized nationwide popular support.

PEASANTS REVOLT

All this changed when military commander General Arana became president in 1970, beginning 22 years of military rule. The constitution remained in place and regular elections were held, but only military candidates and their colleagues stood any realistic chance of success. The plight of the majority of the population worsened as exploitation of resources by governments eager for foreign capital ate up vast tracts of land. The discovery of oil and of mining potential in the north of the country caused the government to declare a development zone, where foreign corporations gained extensive concessions. As a result, less and less land was available to the rapidly growing native population. Thousands were forced to seek work on the lowland plantations, where they suffered harsh treatment and abuses, including exposure to aerial crop-spraying. Many flocked to the cities, where they lived in appalling shantytowns with few or no basic amenities.

The peasants had no champion in government to halt this depopulation of the highlands. In order to defend their livelihoods, they formed movements which linked up to create the national Peasant Unity Committee (CUC). By the late 1970s, the CUC was the largest peasant organization in the highlands and on Guatemala's south coast. Elsewhere, farm workers and peasants without land aired their grievances. The Organization of the People in Arms (ORPA) originated in 1971 among peasants working on the plantations in Quetzaltenango and San Marcos on the Pacific coast. By 1973, it had grown into a significant movement, centered on the heavily populated cities of Sololá and Chimaltenango. The Guerrilla Army of the Poor (EGP) started up in El Quiché in the western highlands in January 1972. Its members were veterans of the 1960s campaigns and established a strategic base in Ixcán.

The EGP waited until it had built up sufficient local support before carrying out terrorist activities. Its first attack was the assassination of much-hated landowner Luis Arenas Barrera, who used forced Indian labor on his San Luis Ixcán plantation and used debtors on his La Perla plantation. Here, on June 7, 1975, a terrorist group shot him dead in front of his workers on payday. The act brought an immediate, massive response from government forces. The army established a permanent presence in the region, attacking peasant cooperatives and intimidating the people into submission.

The more wretched the peasants became, the more they began to support the terrorists. An earthquake in February 1976 claimed 12,000 lives and devastated the houses of tens of thousands more. Desperate peasants joined the FAR in droves, despite the government's programs of reconstruction. Terrorist operations were resumed in Chimaltenango and El Petén, then Guatemala's largest and most northerly province. At the same time, the PGT, which was well-established on the west coast plantations, split. A splinter group, the National Leadership Nucleus (NLN), was formed and began small-scale operations in 1978.

VIOLENT GOVERNMENT RESPONSE

The crisis escalated after April 29, 1978, when more than 300 peasants gathered at the village of Panzós in Alta Verapaz, protesting the loss of their lands to local landlords. More than 100 died when troops from the garrison at Zacapa opened fire. This massacre proved to be only the first move in a campaign of gratuitous violence waged by the army under the leadership of new president Romeo Lucas García.

The atrocities brought new recruits by the thousands to both ORPA and the EGP. Even so, peasants attempted to use non-violent means to air their grievances, only to be met by a ferocious government response. In 1980, for instance, 39 peasants peacefully occupied the Spanish embassy in Guatemala City to draw attention to their cause. All but one of the protestors were killed when troops stormed the building and set it on fire, despite the frantic protests of the ambassador. Spain broke off diplomatic relations with Guatemala and withdrew its mission in protest.

Terrorism now seemed the only way for the peasant movements to gain any headway with the increasingly brutal military regime. Throughout 1981, activists launched a series of bombing attacks on police, government, and business targets in Guatemala City. These raids were backed up by concentrated guerrilla action, such as attacks in October on the provincial capitals Mazatenango and Sololá – with a brief occupation of the latter – while a 500-strong band mounted an attack on an army garrison in December.

THE "ARIAS PLAN"

The Guatemalan National Revolutionary Unity (URNG) brought together the main peasant groups in January 1982, with the declared aim of creating a popular army capable of forcing the military regime to make a deal. All of Guatemala was embroiled in an all-out guerrilla war when a civilian government took office in 1986. Then, on October 25, the URNG signaled its willingness to enter into talks. On October 2, 1987, following a peace plan devised by Costa Rican president Oscar Arias (the "Arias Plan"), talks finally began.

Attacks on government forces continued in rural areas where terrorists were still active. Even a formal agreement in 1990 between the URNG, the government sponsored National Reconciliation Commission, and opposition parties failed to end the conflict. President Jorge Serrano Elias was ousted in a military coup on June 1, 1993. It was not until March 1996, after UN mediation, that the combined terrorist groups and the government finally declared a cease-fire.

Peter Calvert

SEE ALSO: GUERRILLAS AND TERROR; REVOLUTIONARY TERRORISM; URBAN VERSUS RURAL TERRORISM; TERRORISM IN EL SALVADOR; TERRORISM IN NICARAGUA; GUATEMALAN GOVERNMENT'S RESPONSES TO TERRORISM.

FURTHER READING

- Huggins, Martha Kinsley, ed. *Vigilantism and the State in Modern Latin America*. New York: Praeger, 1991.
- Levenson-Estrada, Deborah. *Trade Unionists Against Terror: Guatemala City, 1954-1985*. Chapel Hill: University of North Carolina Press, 1994.
- McClintock, Michael. *State Terror and Popular Resistance*. Atlantic Highlands, NJ and London: Zed Books, 1987.
- Uekert, Brenda K. *Rivers of Blood: A Comparative Study of Government Massacres*. Westport, CT: Praeger, 1995.

TERRORISM IN MEXICO

On New Year's Day, 1994, Mexico joined the North American Free Trade Area (NAFTA). However, the celebrations of Carlos Salinas de Gortari, the Mexican president, were rudely interrupted. He was informed that the previously unknown Zapatista National Liberation Army had seized control of three towns in the southern Mexican state of Chiapas: Ocosingo, Altamirano, and Las Margaritas.

The Zapatistas were southern rural native Mexicans seeking land reform. They also attacked a fourth town, the historic tourist site of San Cristóbal de Las Casas. Here, the insurgents ransacked and set fire to the Palace of Justice before retreating into the mountains. They also took hostage the former state governor, General Absalon Castellanos Domínguez, at his cattle ranch, bundling him into a truck with two of his cows.

In their manifesto, "Today we say enough," the Zapatistas made clear the reason. They claimed that the regional bosses, of whom Domínguez was the most hated, had stolen their land from them. "We possess nothing, absolutely nothing," the manifesto stated, "no home, no land, no work, no education."

Within a week, the guerrillas had extended their control to the towns of San Miguel and Guadalupe Tepayac. The country was put on nationwide alert and a fifth of Mexico's army was deployed to Chiapas. More than 145 people were killed, some executed on the spot. On January 10, the president reshuffled his cabinet, dismissing Secretary of the Interior José Patrocinio González Garrido, who had been governor of Chiapas. Two days later, President Salinas accepted the urgent advice of the bishop of San Cristóbal de Las Casas, Monseñor Samuel Ruiz, and called a truce. The president appointed as negotiator Manuel Camacho Solos, the secretary of external relations, who had been passed over for the presidential nomination in 1993. During the next few weeks, while the truce held, negotiations for a peaceful settlement continued.

KEY FACTS

- Chiapas, the state where the Zapatista insurgency was based, was the poorest in Mexico. In 1994, when the revolt began, its literacy rates were the lowest in the country, a third of households had no electricity, and 40 percent no running water.
- The Zapatistas took their name from Emiliano Zapata (1879-1919), a revolutionary whose slogan was "Land, liberty, and death to the landowners."

THE CAUSES OF THE INSURGENCY

The movement chose the name "Zapatista" in honor of celebrated Mexican revolutionary Emiliano Zapata for two reasons. First, it told the population of the need for a revolution. Second, it revealed the hypocrisy of the ruling Revolutionary Institutional Party's persistent attempts to associate itself with Zapata.

Chiapas was the poorest state in Mexico and the rebels wanted investment, land reform, and the opportunity to choose their own political leaders. Corruption, injustice, and poverty were rife throughout Mexico, but Chiapas suffered from particularly appalling social conditions. It was also the region with the longest and most persistent record of accusations of violations of human rights. The most common charge was against those landowners who hired gunmen to drive the native Mexicans off their traditional lands, in conjunction with the army and the police. Even the former governor, General Domínguez, agreed on his release on February 16, 1994, that social injustice was at the root of the rebellion.

Spearheading the insurgency was a charismatic, ski-masked leader, Rafael Sebastián Guillén Vicente, who was known by his codename, "Subcomandante Marcos." In contrast to his impoverished and poorly educated followers, Marcos was a university teacher and son of a well-to-do furniture dealer. Although the Zapatista movement demanded traditional human rights for the native Indian population, Marcos made use of portable computers and the Internet to bypass the government blocks on communications. During

In early 1994, the Zapatista National Liberation Army seized control of much of Chiapas.

the summer of 1994, while the government was preoccupied with its presidential election campaign, there was stalemate between insurgents and the army. Parts of Chiapas deteriorated into near anarchy.

ESCALATION OF VIOLENCE

In September 1994, 20,000 Tojolabal Indians, organized by the independent Union of Agricultural Workers (CIOAC), declared themselves autonomous. Shortly afterward, on October 10, Marcos temporarily broke off contact with the government negotiator. Violence escalated as peasants armed themselves against the attacks of paramilitary forces organized by ranchers. One group of angry peasants kidnapped the interim governor, Javier López Moreno, holding him hostage for several hours. On the eve of his inauguration on December 8, governor-elect Robledo offered to resign if the guerrillas laid down their arms. They did not do so. On October 19, the guerrillas, who by this time controlled about one-fifth of the state, demonstrated their ability to slip through the army cordon. They erected roadblocks, proclaimed "liberated areas" where government forces were not allowed to enter, and occupied the town of Simojovel and 37 other municipalities. The government had advance warning of this move and, on October 21, attempted to take advantage of the situation to devalue the peso, the unit of currency, while placing the blame on the guerrillas.

Within 24 hours, while fresh troops and tanks moved into place around the guerrilla bases, the devaluation had revealed the flaw in the Mexican economy – its dependence on short-term loans. As capital flooded out of the country, the government lost control of the financial situation. The peso fell to unprecedented depths, precipitating a crisis of confidence.

By contrast, the rebels appeared to gain legitimacy. In the circumstances the new president, Ernesto Zedillo Ponce de León, prudently decided to start fresh negotiations with the rebels. Dialogue was resumed by the new government and continued during the early weeks of 1995. But sporadic attacks on the insurgents continued at the same time. It was not always clear whether the army was following government orders or acting on its own initiative. A government peace offer on March 1 was quickly rejected by the insurgents. However, six further rounds of negotiations finally led to an agreement on September 11, 1995, after the Zapatistas had agreed to participate in dialogue.

Peter Calvert

SEE ALSO: GUERRILLAS AND TERROR; REVOLUTIONARY TERRORISM; URBAN VERSUS RURAL TERRORISM.

FURTHER READING

- Chevigny, Paul. *Edge of a Knife: Police Violence in the Americas.* New York: New Press, 1995.
- Cooper, Marc, *Zapatistas: Spreading Hope for Grassroots Change, Starting in Chiapas, Mexico.* Westfield, NJ: Open Magazine, 1994.
- Johns, Christa Jacqueline. *The Origins of Violence in Mexican Society.* Westport, CT: Praeger, 1995.
- Randall, Laura, ed. *Changing Structure of Mexico: Political, Social, and Economic Prospects.* New York: M. E. Sharpe, 1996.

TERRORISM IN NICARAGUA

In Nicaragua, terror tactics were used by both sides during the fighting that led to the overthrow of the Somoza regime and the installation of a Sandinista government in 1979. Carlos Fonseca Amador organized the Sandinistas as a guerrilla movement in 1961. He took inspiration from the left-wing Cuban revolutionary model of Fidel Castro and Che Guevara. The group's title, the Sandinista National Liberation Front (FSLN), indicated its anti-U.S. stance by paying homage to General Augusto Sandino, the guerrilla hero of resistance against the U.S. in the 1920s and 1930s. However, after the withdrawal of U.S. forces in 1933, National Guard commander Anastasio Somoza García ordered the murder of Sandino and took power in 1936.

Somoza ruled Nicaragua until 1956 and was succeeded by the elder of his two sons, Luis Somoza. Fonseca planned to follow Sandino's example and set up a rural guerrilla movement in the northern hills. However, with poor organization and inadequate secrecy, the campaign was quashed and many guerrillas, including Fonseca, were arrested.

In 1967, Somoza's younger son, Anastasio Somoza Debayle, took over as president. His power was based on the National Guard, which he kept as his private army. In 1973, he amended the Nicaraguan constitution so he could rule indefinitely.

KEY FACTS

- During their rule over Nicaragua, the Somozas accumulated more than $500 million. They owned 20 percent of Nicaragua's farming land and more than 150 businesses, not to mention bank accounts and other assets held in the U.S. and Europe.
- Over 50,000 people are believed to have died in the 18 months of fighting leading up to the overthrow of the Somoza regime in 1979.
- In June 1986, the Reagan administration supplied a $100 million package of aid to the anti-Sandinista guerrilla rebels – the Contras (FDN).

Meanwhile, the Sandinistas had reorganized in the cities, but their success appeared short-lived. In 1969, the Sandinista leadership was identified. Five of the seven members of the group, including its leader Julio César Buitrago, were killed in a shoot-out in downtown Managua, the capital of Nicaragua. Shortly afterward, Fonseca was arrested and imprisoned in Costa Rica. He was freed the following year, when Sandinista guerrillas hijacked a Costa Rican aircraft.

SHATTERED BY AN EARTHQUAKE

On December 23, 1972, an earthquake devastated Managua. Although aid poured in from around the world, it became clear that no one would receive any money except the Somozas and their followers. The National Guard openly looted ruined buildings. The Sandinistas gained support, especially after staging a few money-making outrageous acts. In one such raid on December 27, 1974, a 13-strong Sandinista commando unit, armed with M1 carbines, hunting rifles, and grenades, burst in on a party held by the U.S. ambassador in Managua. They seized the embassy, taking as hostages government ministers, the city mayor, two ambassadors, and leading businessmen. The siege lasted 60 hours until the government gave in. It released political prisoners, including senior Sandinista Daniel Ortega Saavedra, increased wages for industrial and rural workers, and paid a massive $2 million ransom.

The government's reaction was swift and brutal. More than 400 people were murdered in the reprisals that followed. Horror at these state killings served to unite the conventional political parties, most of which, like the Sandinistas, were illegal. But the Sandinistas were divided as to how to respond and, after Fonseca's death in December 1975, they split into three factions. The smallest, Prolonged Popular War (GPP), favored a Maoist strategy of rural-based guerrilla activity. The second group took a Leninist line and opted for mass insurrection led by a small band of urban-based militants. Daniel Ortega led the third faction, which

Popperfoto

President Daniel Ortega defied calls for talks with the Contras (FDN) in a 1985 press conference.

became known as the Terceristas. He argued for immediate insurrection, but in alliance with other disenchanted elements. With the support of the majority of the combatants, Ortega launched a national offensive against the government on October 13, 1977.

OPPOSITION JOINS FORCES

Legal opposition to the government, including elements of the Catholic Church, had long supported the Sandinistas, but the core of this opposition was the historic Conservative party. The remains of Nicaragua's traditional two-party system had been retained by the Somozas for appearances, but the Chamorros, the leading Conservative party family, had never accepted their Somoza rivals.

The signal for insurrection came in January 1978, when a gunman killed Pedro Joaquín Chamorro, editor of *La Prensa* newspaper. Chamorro had been increasingly critical of the regime. His murder, believed to be the work of the National Guard, cemented unity among opposition groups. A general strike was called. Attacks were launched simultaneously from the north by the Sandinistas and from the south by a democratic opposition front sponsored by Costa Rica and Panama.

In another spectacular event, senior Sandinista Edén Pastora, known as "Commander Zero," led 25 insurgents in Operation Pigsty. They attacked Managua's National Palace and held top politicians among their 100 hostages. The regime was forced to hand over $500,000 ransom and release scores of political prisoners. Once again, the Sandinistas escaped.

By mid-September, Nicaragua was facing full-scale civil war. The National Guard fought viciously to retain its power and privileges (rewards for service included appointments as governor of a department, which was a license to collect local taxes). Outside the National Guard, the Somozas lacked support. They had appropriated much of Nicaragua's wealth and had left little for anyone outside their circle. The National Guard's terrorist tactics alienated what little support they had.

U.S. ALARM

President Jimmy Carter viewed this chain of events with concern. His administration had tried to distance itself from the Somozas, but his instructions had not been followed. By the time U.S. diplomats tried to engineer a transfer of power to a compromise candidate, it was too late. The Sandinistas were expecting such a move. They had already joined the other opposition forces in proclaiming a new provisional government from Costa Rican soil. When Somoza fled Nicaragua on July 17, 1979, members of the Sandinista-dominated Junta of National Reconstruction and its Provisional Governing Council flew in to take charge on July 20.

During the next two years, the provisional government embarked on a series of reforms, including a literacy campaign, the provision of free medical care, and the abolition of the death penalty. However, President Ronald Reagan feared the insurrection in neighboring El Salvador was part of a worldwide communist conspiracy. The Reagan administration thought the conspiracy was supported by the Soviet Union through Cuba's capital, Havana, and Managua.

FORMATION OF THE CONTRAS

In November 1981, President Reagan authorized the formation of a clandestine force to launch a counterrevolutionary guerrilla campaign in Nicaragua from bases in Honduras. Although the title chosen by the CIA was the Nicaraguan Democratic Force (FDN), the force became known as the Contras (an abbreviation of the Spanish word for counterrevolutionaries).

By 1981, American financial backing and military training for the Contras were under way. Attacks on Nicaraguan economic targets began in March 1982. Most military activity involved small-scale raids into northern Nicaragua, causing considerable loss of life and economic damage. These raids, however, resulted in the local population uniting behind the Nicaraguan army and establishing their own militias in support.

By 1983, covert U.S. aid had reached $20 million a year and some 150 CIA operatives were believed to be in the area. On January 3, 1984, forces coordinated by a U.S. warship attacked oil facilities at Nicaragua's Puerto Sandino. On February 25, the Contras made similar attacks on the Atlantic port of El Bluff and the Pacific harbor of Corinto. They laid mines, damaging four freighters, one of Soviet registration. On April 5, the U.S. vetoed a United Nations resolution condemning the mining. Meanwhile, at a press conference, President Reagan claimed the Nicaraguan Provisional Government was "exporting revolution" and stated: "We are going to try and inconvenience the government of Nicaragua until they quit that kind of action."

The failure of the Contras stemmed partly from personnel. They were mostly former members of the National Guard of Somoza, chosen more for their anticommunism than their competence. Despite extensive training, they were unable to gain the trust of the local populace. Contra incursions into Nicaragua left a trail of murder, rape, torture, and robbery. In addition, after an Argentine hit squad killed Somoza in Paraguay in 1980, the Contras lacked leadership. Consequently, the CIA sponsored a second opposition force in the south.

ANOTHER CONTRA FORCE

Called the Democratic Revolutionary Alliance (ARDE), the movement was established in Costa Rica, Nicaragua's southern neighbor, by Contras who rejected association with the Somoza dictatorship. One such member was the disaffected ex-Sandinista Edén Pastora, who became its leader. Pastora, who enjoyed the popular appeal that the FDN Contras lacked, began operations in September 1982. By April 1983, ARDE were making incursions into southern Nicaragua. In September 1983, ARDE sent out light aircraft to make a rocket attack on Managua airport.

Because of U.S. aid, the usual balance of insurgency and counterinsurgency was reversed in that the insurgents had the superior weaponry. Air attacks and naval commando raids devastated economic targets, particularly oil facilities, and gasoline rationing was introduced in October 1983. But despite their aerial and naval superiority, the Contras needed a decisive victory on land. Between August 1983 and January 1984, ARDE and FDN Contra forces launched a series of offensives involving 10,000 troops, but the Nicaraguan army, bolstered by local militias, had increased in number to 50,000. Neither the FDN in the north nor ARDE in the south were able to hold territory for long, although with U.S. support, they could continue to operate with losses indefinitely. The U.S. concluded that since the Contras appeared unable to defeat the Sandinistas, they would pursue a war of attrition.

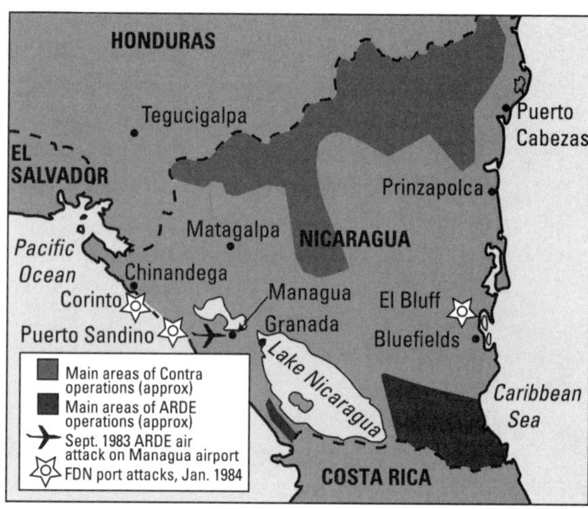

The Democratic Revolutionary Alliance (ARDE) was based in the south; the Contras (FDN) in the north.

ELECTION OF ORTEGA

In May 1984, Pastora was seriously injured by a bomb. The blast destroyed his headquarters and killed four people, including a visiting U.S. journalist. In June, the U.S. Congress voted to cut off aid. In November, a free election was held and Daniel Ortega, representing the united Sandinista party, was elected president.

Ortega's election did not end the terror. An unidentified terrorist threw a grenade onto a crowded dance floor in September 1985, killing seven and wounding 35. Hostility continued between the U.S. and the Sandinista regime. Ortega rejected calls for negotiations with the Contras at the UN General Assembly. Since the coffee harvest had been completed with no casualties, he felt the Contras now posed little threat. But the Contras' very existence encouraged hardline elements within the Sandinista regime. Personal liberties in Nicaragua were curtailed, and Nicaraguan troops took the war across the border. An incursion into Honduras in March 1986 gave Ortega's opponents an opportunity.

Popperfoto

The bearded Edén Pastora led some 5,000 ARDE Contra rebels in southern Nicaragua after he had split with the Sandinistas.

The U.S. had continued to give covert aid to the Contras, using funds that had been obtained through the illegal sale of arms to Iran. But after the Honduras incursion, Congress was again prepared to give open support to the Contras. The Sandinista response within Nicaragua was the curtailment of liberties. This included the closure of the opposition newspaper *La Prensa*, and the expulsion of the pro-Contra bishop, Pablo Antonio Vega.

When the news of the Iran-Contra scandal broke in Washington, DC, in November 1986, the Contra threat to Nicaragua, starved of funds, was already subsiding. Thereafter, the next phase of insurgency, from 1986 to 1990, consisted of negotiations between Nicaragua, the U.S., and other interested parties. The conflict seemed to be resolved in 1990, with the election as president of Violeta Barrios de Chamorro and the formal demobilization of the Contras under UN auspices.

However, with no jobs or land available for demobilized soldiers, land disputes resumed between former Contras and Sandinistas. Terrorism also continued. In August 1991, 16 civilians were killed when their truck drove over a Contra land mine. Contra commanders recruited veteran soldiers and the Sandinistas rearmed. In the first year of Chamorro's rule, more than 100 died in fighting. As one commentator noted: "Wars don't just end – especially in Third World countries."

Peter Calvert

SEE ALSO: REVOLUTIONARY TERRORISM; URBAN VERSUS RURAL TERRORISM; TERRORISM IN EL SALVADOR; NICARAGUAN GOVERNMENT'S RESPONSES TO TERRORISM.

FURTHER READING

- Kornbluh, Peter. *Nicaragua, The Price of Intervention: Reagan's Wars Against the Sandinistas.* Washington, DC: Institute for Policy Studies, 1987.
- Morley, Morris H. *Washington, Somoza, and the Sandinistas.* Cambridge and New York: Cambridge University Press, 1994.
- Rogers, Miranda. *The Civil War in Nicaragua: Inside the Sandinistas.* New Brunswick, NJ: Transaction Publishers, 1993.

TERRORISM IN PERU

Shining Path (Sendero Luminoso) is a left-wing revolutionary movement that began a guerrilla campaign in Peru in 1980. The movement has used terrorism in pursuit of its aim – to overthrow the American-backed government in Peru. Shining Path has a reputation for being the most brutal of the Latin American insurgencies and also for making the most effective use of terrorism as part of its strategy.

MARXIST-INSPIRED MOTIVATION

At the start of the 1970s, several lecturers at the National University of San Cristóbal de Huamanga in Ayacucho, a poor part of the southern Andes, founded what was to become a leading force in the communist revolution in Peru. Led by Abimael Guzmán Reynoso, the group based its ideology on Marxist theory. Shining Path believed that an armed struggle combined with the political education of Peru's peasantry and urban working class was the only way to achieve significant economic change in the country.

Guzmán and his like-minded colleagues – the intellectual nucleus of Shining Path – began operations by conducting a series of Marxist study groups at local universities. Guzmán believed that a transition to industrial capitalism in Peru could not involve an uprising of the capitalist class and its artisan and proletarian allies against the old regime, because they were too small and politically weak. However, its vast and land-hungry peasant class might join a revolution against the prevailing economic order. The challenge was how to meld these potentially revolutionary classes into a cohesive, progressive political force.

KEY FACTS

- From the outset of the terrorist campaign in May 1980 until June 1986, Shining Path activity was so intense that the group averaged between 30 and 40 operations a month.
- Shining Path insurgency has resulted in the death of around 25,000 people and the loss of more than $22 billion in damages and lost revenues.

REVOLUTION THROUGH EDUCATION

To facilitate a successful uprising, Shining Path activists concentrated on educating the local peasantry and the urban working class in Marxist theory and armed struggle. Political education was needed because the peasantry did not yet appreciate how their economic interests converged, and why the current economic order needed to be overthrown. Armed struggle was necessary, according to Shining Path, because Peru's landowning class, foreign investors, and government bureaucrats would never give up their wealth and political privileges without a bitter fight.

In 1979, Shining Path's national leadership established a school to train interested activists in guerrilla tactics and Marxist ideology. Some leaders dissented, arguing that guerrilla warfare would lead to repression and the movement's demise, and several of them were expelled by the advocates of military confrontation.

FIRST ARMED ACTION

On the eve of the 1980 presidential election, Shining Path carried out its first notable act of terrorism, although it was an inauspicious beginning to the violence that was to unfold over the following years. A few masked activists with malfunctioning pistols broke into an election office in the remote mountain town of Chuschi, then burned unmarked ballots and unused ballot boxes in a public plaza. The next day, the ballots were replaced and the election continued.

However, by the end of 1980, between 300 and 400 violent "actions" had been committed by Shining Path members, including the destruction of local tax records, the bombing of administration offices, and the sabotage of power lines.

In 1981, Shining Path guerrillas began to appear regularly in remote villages in the southern Andes and gained popular support, partly by enforcing village

Associated Press

Shining Path leaders: (standing, from left) Rosa Angelica Salas, Osman Morote, and Marta Huatay; (seated from left) Elena Iparaguirre, Abimael Guzmán, and Maria Pantoja.

laws and standards of behavior. The guerrillas caught and punished cattle rustlers, unfaithful husbands, and owners of small stores who were suspected of swindling costumers. They also stalked, verbally humiliated, whipped, and on occasion executed local government officials who were reputed to have abused their authority.

On the other hand, the guerrillas often antagonized villagers by imposing radical changes. Some guerrilla teams, for example, collectivized land, organized communal planting and harvesting, and prohibited peasants from selling produce at markets. Peasants seldom welcomed the revolutionaries' zealotry. Many peasants treasured their small, individualized plots, and many relied on cash crops to buy salt, matches, and other inexpensive comforts. Sometimes, if the guerrillas persisted in their attempts to reorder village life, peasants rebelled by stoning known guerrillas, turning them over to the police, or asking the police to build local stations.

GUERRILLA GATHERING RURAL SUPPORT

In 1982 and 1983, the guerrillas entered remote localities in Peru's southern tip and central mountains, where they established "People's Committees" (akin to democratic town meetings). The guerrillas organized popular land invasions, seized and redistributed cattle from haciendas, sabotaged machinery and pipelines, and ambushed police. In March 1982, around 150 guerrillas attacked a prison at Ayacucho, freeing 250 prisoners. Fourteen people died during the attack and a 30-day state of emergency for Ayacucho followed.

The government, having previously dismissed reports about Shining Path guerrillas as exaggerations about isolated criminals, dispatched a counterinsurgency force known as the "Sinchis." Indiscriminate violence by the Sinchis prompted outcries from human rights organizations. Shining Path argued that the government was committing genocide against destitute Indians, and the movement escalated its attacks

Hulton Getty Picture Collection

A Peruvian policeman steps over a dead soldier in the wake of a Shining Path guerrilla attack on an air force truck in Lima, on October 7, 1992.

on the police, soldiers, and politicians. In one confrontation on August 22, 1982, 200 guerrillas engaged security forces in a five-hour gun battle in Vilcashumán, 75 miles south of Ayacucho.

COMMUNITY CONTROL AND PROTECTION

During the 1980s, many hundreds of peasants were killed as a result of government or Shining Path violence. Each side denied responsibility for the majority of deaths. The police encouraged the peasants to form self-defense groups or *rondas*, and brutally punished them if they resisted this encouragement. These *rondas* brought about their own problems, stirring up old hatreds within the communities. Internal fights broke out, threatening the guerrillas' control of the villages.

In response, the guerrillas killed scores of villagers each year. For example, in 1983, the guerrillas attacked two villages in Ayacucho, axing and shooting to death around 80 so-called "traitor" peasants, who tried to defend themselves with stones. The following year, they attacked a number of towns in the Ayacucho region, killing 25 citizens. At the same time, Shining Path guerrillas protected the small farmers in the eastern jungles of Peru, who cultivated coco plants and sold the leaves to cocaine producers in Bolivia. Shining Path guerrillas fought Bolivian toughs, who tried to threaten farmers into selling coca leaves at below-market prices.

The Shining Path activists also provided an impressive array of public services. They organized vigilante committees to control prostitution and drinking, coordinated litter clean-ups, created local representative governments, and even supervised wedding ceremonies. In exchange, Shining Path took a share of the coca revenues to finance operations.

POWER BEHIND BARS

By the mid-1980s, the armed forces believed they had defeated Shining Path, but Guzmán had various other targets up his sleeve, including the election campaigns of 1985, won by Alan García of the American Popular Revolutionary Alliance Party (ARPA). Shining Path boycotted and sabotaged the elections wherever they had the power to do so, virtually obliterating them altogether in some areas, including Ayacucho. A wave of car-bombings, assassinations, and jail riots by Shining Path prisoners followed.

In 1985, Shining Path prisoners were granted special privileges and allowed to administer their own cell blocks. In October of that year, the Shining Path militants in Lurigancho jail set fire to their cell block, tying up and burning alive anyone who refused to participate in the riot. According to the prison authorities, around 30 inmates died, although no public investigation was carried out.

In 1986, Shining Path turned to Lima, bombing restaurants, shopping malls, government offices and banks in the capital, and assassinating the police. The group found an ally in a metropolitan labor newspaper, *El Diario*, which published favorable editorials about Shining Path. The guerrilla units in Lima also killed civilians, including the feminist and community organizer María Elena Moyano, who had urged less violent Shining Path members to end the terrorism.

MILITANT FORCE IN ACTION

While the group made its presence known in Lima, the power of Shining Path activists in Lurigancho, El Frontón, and Santa Bárbara prisons were making greater demands on the prison authorities, taking prison guards hostage until their demands were met. The armed forces, entrusted with the task of restoring order, conducted one of the biggest massacres in Peru. Around 120 prisoners were slaughtered, and hardly any of them were identified. The prison massacres immediately increased support for Shining Path.

As the 1980s drew to a close, Shining Path's capacity to take on the armed forces, not only in ambush but also in pitched battles, began to emerge. In July 1989, hundreds of guerrillas attacked the Madre Mía army barracks and, according to Shining Path, killed 39 soldiers. Also in 1989, the group used its militant force to devastate the municipal elections in many areas of the Andes. The guerrillas assassinated around 60 mayors and mayoral candidates in the run-up to the municipal elections, and around 500 municipal candidates resigned in fear. Almost 60 percent of registered voters either destroyed their ballot papers or were absent on election day. In Ayacucho alone, absenteeism was around 85 percent.

In the run-up to the 1990 general elections, Shining Path launched a campaign of car-bombings and industrial sabotage, assassinating several congressional candidates. The campaign had its impact: 35 percent of ballot papers were destroyed or left blank.

By 1991, between 3,000 and 5,000 armed Shining Path militants made up a sophisticated and highly organized network of support bases and battalions in the jungle areas along the east of the Andes, and in the valley of the Erne River. Shining Path guerrillas were the dominating political force in 40 percent of Peru.

Meanwhile, around 400 rebel captives were being held at the high security jail in Canto Grande, and once again the Shining Path inmates had complete control of their cell blocks, including the keys. In prison, they held Sunday parades, performed plays, organized lectures for visitors, and even sold souvenirs to raise funds for the movement.

A MISSION CRUSHED BY MASSACRE

Shining Path's guerrilla activity remained intensive in rural territory in the early 1990s. Another prime target for the group was the Cultivireni mission, the communal quarters of the Asháninkas. This Indian group – one of the largest remaining in the Peruvian Amazon – strongly resisted Shining Path's demands for recruits to their cause. In November 1989, 60 guerrillas armed with sub-machine guns and assault rifles pillaged and burned the mission, then shot three of the Indian mission leaders. One of them was the head school teacher, whom the guerrillas crucified, castrated, and disembowelled. Three months later in February 1990, Shining Path massacred 15 of the mission Indians in their camps. Although the Asháninkas retaliated with their own attacks, killing several Shining Path members, the guerrillas soon gained control over the mission and their attacks on the Indian community continued. In August 1993, in several villages outside Satipo, 185 miles east of Lima, the guerrillas massacred 55 people. Many victims were mutilated beyond recognition – 14 of them children whose ears had been cut off.

DEBATE OVER ABANDONING VIOLENCE

During the early 1990s, many Shining Path members argued over the continued use of violence against civilians. In 1992, the Peruvian president Alberto Fujimori declared himself a temporary dictator. The following year, security forces captured and imprisoned several Shining Path leaders, including Guzmán.

Fujimori boasted that his strong leadership had defeated Shining Path terrorists. Shortly afterward, a wave of car-bombings in Lima's wealthiest neighborhoods revealed that several guerrilla units remained intact. Pro-Shining Path banners in labor and neighborhood marches also indicated that some non-guerrilla cells were alive and well.

In 1993, from his prison cell, Guzmán urged Shining Path activists to abandon the armed struggle. Several subgroups ignored his instructions; others questioned more strongly than ever the wisdom of a guerrilla strategy. Nevertheless, the bombings and shootings have continued through the 1990s.

Bertrande Roberts

SEE ALSO: GUERRILLAS AND TERROR; REVOLUTIONARY TERRORISM; URBAN VERSUS RURAL TERRORISM; TERROR GROUP ORGANIZATION; TERRORIST FUNDRAISING; PERUVIAN GOVERNMENT'S RESPONSES TO TERRORISM.

FURTHER READING

- Koppel, Martin. *Peru's Shining Path: Autonomy of a Reactionary Sect.* New York: Pathfinder, 1993.
- McCormick, Gordon H. *The Shining Path and the Future of Peru.* Santa Monica, CA: Rand Corporation, 1990.
- Palmer, David Scott. *The Shining Path of Peru.* London: Hurst, 1992; New York: St. Martin's Press, 1994.
- Strong, Simon. *Shining Path: Terror and Revolution in Peru.* New York: Times Books, 1992.

TERRORISM IN URUGUAY

The National Liberation Movement – Tupamaros – operated in Uruguay from the early 1960s, specializing in kidnapping diplomats. Its aim was to achieve a fairer society and it became the blueprint for urban guerrilla movements in Latin America. In its early years, the Tupamaros grabbed the headlines with publicity stunts such as hijacking truck-loads of food on Christmas Eve, 1963, and distributing festive snacks in the slums of the capital Montevideo. In another public relations gesture, a terrorist paused to administer first aid to a bystander who fainted when caught up in a Tupamaros bank raid. But the Tupamaros's "Robin Hood" image faded as they found themselves with more and more blood on their hands.

ECONOMIC CRISIS

In a series of liberalizing reforms in the first half of the century in Uruguay, the ruling Colorado party had checked the powers of the military and set up a welfare state. The constitution was also restructured, initially to limit the powers of the executive presidency, and then in 1952 to replace it by a council of state. But by the 1960s, Uruguay was in economic decline. Lacking industrial or mineral resources, its economy was almost entirely based on the export of grain and beef. While the prices of its exports had been falling steadily, inflation within the country was rampant. The council of state seemed unable to make decisions while the declining economy created more and more difficulties in maintaining the welfare state.

By referendum, the executive presidency was restored in 1967, but the first president, the popular General Oscar Gestido, died soon afterward. He was followed by his vice-president, General Jorge Pacheco Areco, a former boxer with authoritarian tendencies. It was his government that had to deal with the first phase of the terrorist campaign.

SUMMARY

- The Tupamaros took their name from the Peruvian Inca chief Túpac Amaru. He led an unsuccessful revolt against the Spaniards in 1782 and was burned at the stake.
- The Tupamaros were a leftist urban guerrilla group intent on overthrowing the state and driving out foreign interests. They carried out a campaign of bank robberies, bombings, and kidnappings.
- Money seized from Tupamaros bank raids was distributed to the poor in Uruguay's cities.
- The terrorist campaign carried out by the Tupamaros is generally blamed for destroying democracy in Uruguay.

MARXIST BEGINNINGS

The Tupamaros were formed in Uruguay in 1962 as part of the continent-wide reaction to the Cuban revolution in 1959. Although they began operating in the countryside among impoverished cane-cutters in the rural north of Uruguay, the Tupamaros soon became an urban, middle-class movement. Their purpose was first to discredit and ultimately to overthrow the existing political order. The movement was led by Raúl Sendic Antonaccio, who had trained as a lawyer. Sendic began his political career acting as legal adviser to the cane-cutters he led in a march to Montevideo in 1962. The march was a decisive event since it marked his break with the Socialist party, which he considered guilty of inaction. The Tupamaros movement recruited former socialists as well as people with more radical beliefs.

Ideologically, the Tupamaros were fervently nationalist, arguing in their few public statements for the creation of an independent national community based on socialism. They sought to drive out foreign interests, since they felt that the Uruguayan economy was dominated by the U.S. and Brazil. Specific Tupamaros policies included the nationalization of banks and export houses, as well as a full land reform program.

The Tupamaros concluded that the only way to reform the system was through violence, in order to highlight the faults of the regime and to make the public conscious of the need for change. Many members found justification in Catholic liberation theology, that force could be used to redress the evils of society. Ironically, a large number of Tupamaros came from privileged positions, which gave them access to high-grade intelligence about government intentions. The information proved useful in organizing the daring mass jailbreaks that became one of the trademarks of the movement.

The Tupamaros had a well-deserved reputation for tight security and were organized in cells. Each cell had between five and ten members and was self-sufficient. By decentralizing operations, the Tupamaros sought to guarantee security against infiltration.

BEGINNINGS OF TERRORISM

The Tupamaros came to prominence in July 1963, with a raid on a gun club. The group then targeted U.S. and Brazilian diplomatic vehicles, and the homes of important politicians and businessmen, for bomb attacks and armed robberies. In January 1966, Sendic called the first national Tupamaros convention, in which he broke with the Latin American traditions of rural guerrila warfare established in Cuba. Instead, Sendic chose to concentrate Tupamaros operations in Uruguay's cities. In December 1966, the terrorists suffered their first casualties in shoot-outs, when police discovered a Tupamaros training center, a shooting range, and two safe houses. The Tupamaros were unable to carry out any attacks for a year.

A second phase began with the publication of its manifesto, "An open letter to the police," on December 7, 1967. The letter stated: "For these reasons, we have placed ourselves outside the law. This is the only honest action when the law is not equal for all; when the law exists to defend the spurious interests of a minority in detriment to the majority; when the law works against the country's progress; when even those who have created it place themselves outside it, with impunity, whenever it is convenient for them."

CLASHES WITH THE GOVERNMENT

In this second phase, between 1967 and 1970, the strategy was to concentrate on exposing the corrupt political and economic system and dramatizing the movement. Pacheco declared a state of siege in 1968 and sent in troops to break up strikes organized as a protest against the government's austerity measures.

Pacheco's actions alienated public opinion and the Tupamaros stepped up their action. In January 1968, after stealing over 1,000 pounds of explosives, Tupamaros terrorists conducted a campaign of bomb attacks throughout the year. They also carried out nine major bank raids. In three years, through the ingenuity of prominent members such as Jorge Amílcar Manera Lluveras, the Tupamaros movement had established itself as a powerful and impenetrable terrorist network.

There was a great deal of sympathy among ordinary citizens for the young rebels of the Tupamaros. Some of the episodes of this period had a decidedly prankish quality, such as publishing the president's income tax returns and circulating a photograph of him in the nude. His leading advisor was kidnapped but released unharmed after four days. In another notorious raid, Tupamaros members stole money from a casino and distributed it among the poor. They even advertised on radio stations they occupied for brief periods.

This phase of psychological warfare culminated in the temporary occupation of the town of Pando for a day in September 1969. On the way back to Montevideo, however, things went badly wrong. The participants, many of them students, were met by large forces of military and police. The security forces overreacted and killed three Tupamaros members. Hundreds more were arrested, beaten, and tortured.

A SPATE OF KIDNAPPINGS

The Tupamaros chose activities which could not be concealed from the press and so were certain to bring them attention. This led the Tupamaros to more overt acts of terrorism. The most striking was a spectacular sequence of kidnappings.

As with other Latin American terrorist groups at the time, victims were selected by occupation. Uruguayan hostages included a prominent banker, released after the payment of $60,000 to a Montevideo hospital, and the head of the National Energy Corporation.

The Tupamaros also targeted foreign nationals for kidnapping. U.S. citizen Dan Mitrione, an employee of the CIA, was kidnapped on July 31, 1970. He was an obvious target because he reputedly knew more than anyone else about the Tupamaros. He had also been instructing the police in methods of interrogation. At the time, the Tupamaros were outraged by the authorities' use of torture, including beatings, rape, submersion, suspension, and shocks with electric cattle-prods. Earlier that year, the Tupamaros assassinated

Associated Press

The Tupamaros kidnapped British ambassador Geoffrey Jackson and held him prisoner for eight months in 1971. His cell wall bears the star symbol of the movement.

one of the most notorious torturers, police inspector Héctor Morán Charquero, in broad daylight on the streets of the capital.

In return for Mitrione's release, the Tupamaros demanded the freedom of 150 jailed colleagues. They also stated that they had given Mitrione medical treatment as he had been wounded. Soon afterward, police arrested many of the Tupamaro leadership, including Sendic and the second-in-command, Raúl Bidegain Greissing. In response, the Tupamaros gave Mitrione a summary "trial" and shot him.

On August 8, the Tupamaros announced that they had shot Mitrione because the government had failed to meet their demands. They stated that a similar fate awaited Días Gomide and the U.S. agronomist Claude Fly, both of whom they had captured on the previous day. However, they released both men early in 1971. Días Gomide's wife had to pay a large ransom, and Fly was released in March, after he had suffered a mild heart attack. The Tupamaros targeted him merely because he was American and presumably of importance to the U.S. government.

PRIZE DIPLOMATIC TARGET

The British ambassador, Geoffrey Jackson, on the other hand, was a first-rate target. He had been under surveillance from the moment he arrived in the country, and was regarded as an especially valuable prize. The Tupamaros kidnapped him on January 8, 1971, and held him for eight months. Jackson, an experienced diplomat and devout Catholic, established a rapport with his captors. He made it clear that British policy was neither to make deals with terrorists nor pay ransoms. The extensive security operation to

Camera Press

Jorge Amílcar Manera Lluveras, a leading Tupamaros terrorist, was arrested by the Uruguayan authorities in 1970. He escaped in the mass breakout from Punta Carretas prison in 1971, but was recaptured on June 22, 1972.

find Jackson in his makeshift "people's prison" included a house-to-house search of Montevideo.

Meanwhile, the Tupamaros had organized some dramatic mass jailbreaks. Some 106 Tupamaros men, including Sendic and several of his key officers, broke out of jail or were freed by their colleagues in a spectacular mass escape from Punta Carretas prison. Soon afterward, 38 inmates escaped from the women's prison. These successes provided the Tupamaros with a convenient excuse to release Geoffrey Jackson.

The kidnappings of Jackson and Mitrione each had two purposes: to pressure the government and to secure publicity for the Tupamaros cause. The breach of the well-established principle of diplomatic inviolability increased the notoriety of the terrorists. But despite the emphasis in the movement on good organization and a commitment to securing the release of its jailed members to maintain support, the Tupamaros lost momentum when they suspended hostilities for the presidential elections in 1971.

THE COLLAPSE OF THE TUPAMAROS

The Tupamaros had achieved success as a secretive organization, but to achieve their ultimate objective of gaining power, they needed to cultivate a following among the masses. For the elections of November 1971, the Tupamaros gave their support to a new left-wing coalition, the Broad Front. However, in the elections, the Broad Front candidate, retired General Liber Seregni, got only 18 percent of the popular vote.

When the Tupamaros started their activities, they opposed a police force in a society which had been at peace for 60 years. Following the mass breakout from

Punta Carretas prison in 1971, President Pacheco placed the armed forces in charge of the counter-insurgency campaign. By this stage, the military were deploying death squads to hunt down Tupamaros members and other left-wing opposition. Moreover, on April 14, 1972, Pacheco was succeeded by the right-wing minister of agriculture, Juan María Bordaberry, who publicly proclaimed his sympathy with the dictatorial military regime in Brazil.

Consequently, the Tupamaros resumed operations with the simultaneous assassination of a number of government officials. These, according to the Tupamaros, were responsible for the death squads that were killing an increasing number of civilians. The new president immediately asked congress for and obtained a "state of internal war," and with this came the suspension of constitutional guarantees. The regime had time to regroup, and so the advantage shifted back to the government. At the beginning of 1972, Héctor Amodio Pérez, one of the Tupamaros movement's key figures, defected and gave the government a large quantity of information about the movement and its leaders.

In less than three months, the movement collapsed. After a series of successes, the security forces recaptured Sendic in September 1972, after a shoot-out in which he suffered serious facial wounds. He and eight other Tupamaros leaders were held hostage, and the military warned their organization that they would be killed if hostilities resumed. The Tupamaros were seriously weakened, but the movement did not abandon its commitment to violent struggle.

By December 1972, some 2,600 Tupamaros had been imprisoned and 42 killed. Police uncovered more than 200 safe houses and hideouts. Police also found an electronics laboratory, a weapons factory with a furnace, a laboratory for forging documents, and many other printing and information services. The Tupamaros also had a hospital complete with operating tables and x-ray equipment. When Sendic was recaptured in September 1972, the authorities discovered that he had undergone plastic surgery to avoid recognition.

MILITARY COUP

On June 27, 1973, a military coup supported by Brazil enabled President Bordaberry to eliminate rival centers of power. He closed congress, forbade the operation of political parties, banned trade unions and other organizations, and acted without constitutional restraints.

By this time, Sendic had been tried and condemned to death, a sentence later commuted to 45 years in prison. He was held captive, often in solitary confinement, until civilian government returned. The Broad Front party leader, General Seregni, was also arrested for a second time in 1976. He was deprived of his military rank and sentenced to 14 years in jail for "conspiring against the constitution."

The military state remained in place until a referendum brought about the restoration of constitutional government in 1985. A general amnesty was then offered to political prisoners. Among those pardoned in March 1985 were Sendic, who called on the Tupamaros to abandon the armed struggle for peaceful political action, and Seregni, whose military rank as general was restored at the same time.

By 1988, the Tupamaros had totally abandoned the armed struggle, preferring instead to re-enter democratic politics by means of the Broad Front party. The founder of the Tupamaros, Raúl Sendic Antonaccio, died in Paris on April 28, 1989, from injuries sustained during his torture by the Uruguayan authorities. One observer said of the Tupamaros that they "dug the grave of democracy and fell into it themselves."

Peter Calvert

SEE ALSO: GUERRILLAS AND TERROR; REVOLUTIONARY TERRORISM; URBAN VERSUS RURAL TERRORISM; HIJACKING AND KIDNAPPING; TERRORISM IN BRAZIL; BRAZILIAN GOVERNMENT'S RESPONSES TO TERRORISM; URUGUAYAN GOVERNMENT'S RESPONSES TO TERRORISM.

FURTHER READING

- Porzecanski, Arturo C. *Uruguay's Tupamaros: The Urban Guerrilla.* New York: Praeger, 1973.
- Rial, Juan. "Makers and Guardians of Fear: Controlled Terror in Uruguay," in *Fear at the Edge: State Terror and Resistance in Latin America*, edited by Juan Corradi, Patricia Fagen, and Manuel A. Garreton Merino. Berkeley: University of California Press, 1992.
- Sosnowski, Saul, and Louise B. Popkin. *Repression, Exile and Democracy: Uruguayan Culture.* Durham, NC: Duke University Press, 1993.
- Weinstein, Martin. *Uruguay: Democracy at the Crossroads.* Boulder, CO: Westview Press, 1988.

TERRORISM IN VENEZUELA

Terrorism occurred in Venezuela as part of a guerrilla campaign in the early 1960s. Left-wing militants formed the Armed National Liberation Forces (FALN) to wage a campaign of urban terrorism in order to prevent the presidential elections of 1963. When this failed, militants turned to a program of rural revolution, which also proved unsuccessful. By 1970, violent opposition of any significance had ceased.

In the early 1960s, Venezuela was regarded by many on the left as one of the most favorable areas in Latin America for successful armed struggle. It had been under dictatorship until a revolt in 1958 toppled the last dictator. The revolt originated among the armed forces, and gained strength from an alliance with a patriotic junta of left-wing elements led by a 29-year-old journalist, Fabricio Ojeda. A democratic government, led by Rómulo Betancourt, took office.

RURAL GUERRILLAS

Ojeda's Venezuelan Communist Party (PCV) opposed the new government and set up a militant wing to prepare for armed struggle. Led by Douglas Bravo, the PCV set up a *foco*, a small force of revolutionary guerrillas operating in the countryside. Meanwhile, a group called the Movement of the Revolutionary Left (MIR) had emerged in May 1960, after splitting from the ruling Democratic Action Party. The government moved speedily to arrest its leaders. As a result, there was fighting on the streets and at the university campus of Venezuela's capital, Caracas, from October to December 1960.

KEY FACTS

- Between 1962 and 1969, some 6,000 people were killed as a result of guerrilla insurgency.
- One of the first FALN terrorist acts, in February 1963, was an arson attack on the Sears Roebuck company offices in the capital, Caracas. It caused approximately $2.5 million in damage.

When the disturbances were suppressed, the MIR, with support from Cuba, also sought to establish guerrilla bases in the countryside. But before the MIR could begin operations, the army discovered a base in January 1962. As a result of this failure of security, the army began a series of small-scale ambushes in March. The ambushes were over such a wide area that many of the 20 groups set up were soon destroyed. The movement suffered excessive losses.

The guerrillas were inadequately trained and organization was poor. However, in isolated incidents during the same year, rebellions led by junior officers within the armed forces raised the scale of insurgencies. In one incident, on May 4, 1962, 450 marines seized the naval base at Puerto Cabello, 250 miles east of Caracas, and held it for 24 hours. Rebel forces took over the radio station and broadcast appeals for support against the government. But they surrendered when the air force bombed and strafed the radio tower and airport. Two rebels died and ten were injured.

Ojeda himself joined MIR in July, but he was captured on October 12, 1962. He was sentenced to 18 years' imprisonment, but he escaped in September 1963 with two companions to continue agitation underground. By that time, President Betancourt was taking a strong anti-communist line. Although he was from a Marxist background and initially had been sympathetic to the Cuban revolution, Cuba's support for insurrection in his country had alienated him. The anticommunist drive brought new recruits to the MIR.

FALN TERRORISM BEGINS

On February 24, 1963, members of the PCV and the MIR joined with rebels from the military to form the FALN in Caracas. Its first head was Captain Manuel Ponte Rodríguez, one of the leaders of the Puerto Cabello rebellion. On communist insistence, a political wing, the National Liberation Front (FLN), also was formed by the insurgents.

The FALN set out to attack U.S. interests. Terrorists sabotaged power stations and blew up pipelines owned

Popperfoto

In November 1963, Venezuelan security forces discovered a guerrilla arms cache, including this Belgian-made rifle, allegedly supplied by Cuba.

by U.S. companies. In February 1963, armed FALN stowaways captured the *Anzoategui*, a 3,000-ton ship on its way to New Orleans and took it to Brazil.

The FALN were intent on gaining publicity, and selected targets accordingly. In August 1963, guerrillas disguised as police officers abducted Argentine soccer superstar Alfredo di Stefano and held him for two days. In November, four terrorists seized a Venezuelan airliner with 17 people on board. After scattering communist leaflets over the city of Ciudad Bolívar, the hijackers demanded to go to Trinidad. On November 27, terrorists kidnapped U.S. army attaché Colonel James Chenault. They released him after the government freed several left-wing radicals. The same year, terrorists stole French paintings from an important exhibition, only to return them three days later.

THE ARMED STRUGGLE WANES

Raúl Leoni succeeded Betancourt as president in March 1964. He offered to lift the ban on the operation of the PCV on condition that the armed struggle was abandoned. The PCV accepted the offer and withdrew its support for guerrilla activity.

Douglas Bravo became leader of the FALN and issued a manifesto in March 1966. The FALN embarked on a campaign of urban terrorism in 1966, including the systematic assassination of police officers. This campaign alienated support in the cities, but the FALN remained popular in the countryside.

On March 1, 1967, FALN members abducted former director of social security, Dr. Julio Iribarren Borges, the foreign minister's brother. On March 2, his body was found with gunshot wounds and signs of torture. The terrorists also left the message: "For each member of the FALN killed, we kill three of our enemies." But by the end of 1967, the FALN was no longer a serious threat. Ojeda had died in police custody in July 1966 and the PCV had expelled Bravo.

The FALN continued to receive Cuban backing, however, until 1969, when the Christian Democrats took power in Venezuela. The Soviet Union, wishing to establish relations with the new government, pressured Cuba into withdrawing support for the guerrillas. The Christian Democrats offered an amnesty, which most of the guerrillas accepted, and FALN activity ceased. Bravo resisted and left the country. He returned in 1975 to help release his colleagues in a dramatic jailbreak. Finally, in 1979, after 18 years of militant opposition, Bravo accepted an amnesty.

Peter Calvert

SEE ALSO: GUERRILLAS AND TERROR; REVOLUTIONARY TERRORISM; URBAN VERSUS RURAL TERRORISM; VENEZUELAN GOVERNMENT'S RESPONSES TO TERRORISM.

FURTHER READING

- Hernandez, Tosca. "Extraordinary Police Operations in Venezuela," in *Vigilantism and the State in Modern Latin America, e*dited by Martha Kinsley Huggins. New York: Praeger, 1991.
- Hillman, Richard S. *Democracy for the Privileged: Crisis and Transition in Venezuela.* Boulder, CO: Lynne Rienner Publications, 1994.
- McCoy, Jennifer. *Venezuelan Democracy Under Stress.* Miami, FL: University of Miami North-South Center, 1995.

CHAPTER FOURTEEN

Nationalist Terrorism in Post-Colonial Asia and Africa

The post-colonial history of many states in Asia and Africa has been characterized by prolonged terrorist campaigns waged by separatist minority ethnic groups struggling for a measure of political recognition. Many of these conflicts became entangled in the Cold War between the United States and the Soviet Union, who frequently backed rivals in the struggle. They supplied the weapons and equipment used by the terrorists and their government opponents in their battles for power, and sometimes took direct action in support of their clients.

NATIONALIST TERRORISM IN POST-COLONIAL ASIA AND AFRICA: Introduction

The eviction of the European powers from their colonies after World War II was accompanied by acts of great brutality on all sides. Campaigns of terror involving massacres, assassinations, and the bombing of civilians were the norm rather than the exception. Victory for the independence movements did not, however, lead to peace in many of the newly free states. Sustained guerrilla and terrorist activity, invariably involving atrocities on a huge scale, have characterized the bloody history of post-colonial Asia and Africa.

Before their withdrawal, the colonial powers had generally maintained European-style legal systems and prevented large-scale outbreaks of ethnic conflict within the borders of their possessions. These borders were created by Europeans, who made no attempt to account for long-standing ethnic divisions. Often they sliced through traditional tribal areas, dividing communities into separate colonies.

Consequently, some post-colonial states contained substantial ethnic minorities, and these were usually excluded from the political process by the ruling majority, as remains the case with the Tamils in Sri Lanka. Other states, such as South Africa, were ruled by dominant minorities. Denied a voice, those excluded from power resorted to the gun and the bomb to press their claims. Their demands might be for a degree of power-sharing, the creation of their own independent nation, or union with a nearby state ruled by their own ethnic group.

Although the colonial powers may have given up direct control of their possessions, they continued to exert considerable influence over them. The new regimes were often economically and militarily dependent on their former masters for their survival. They often exploited their position by demanding favorable investment opportunities, or the right to set up military bases. These foreign installations and their personnel, reminders of colonial oppression, often became the targets of the minority group terrorists. In turn, the former colonial powers offered training, weapons, and sometimes troops to combat the terrorists.

Many of these post-colonial conflicts were also exploited by other external powers, both regional and global, for their own geopolitical ends. The Soviet Union, China, and the Western powers were keen to establish compliant client states during the Cold War. They were happy to prop up an existing regime or support those dedicated to its overthrow. The repressive regime of Ferdinand Marcos in the Philippines, for example, could count on U.S. support because of the state's strategic position in the Pacific. The Soviet Union offered military aid to the military regime in Ethiopia because of that country's strategic value at the entrance to the Red Sea and the Suez Canal.

The major players were generally unwilling to condemn terrorist acts committed by their proxies. Indeed, they were often the suppliers of the weapons used in acts of terrorism. However, they were very willing to score political points by highlighting outrages committed by guerrilla and terrorist groups supported by their rivals.

Struggles for political rights, particularly when the rivals are divided along ethnic lines, have always been vicious affairs. The norms of "civilized" behavior, the so-called rules of war, are frequently discarded. Deliberate mutilation, the burning of villages, and the poisoning of wells are seen as legitimate acts of war, not terrorist atrocities. Regarding opponents as somehow less than human destroys the moral restraints that are supposed to prevent such excesses. A cycle of escalating violence develops, as one side justifies committing an atrocity on the basis of a similar act carried out by an opponent. The use of terrorism gains legitimacy because the various warring factions condone and even encourage its use.

Some nationalist groups using terrorism have waged successful campaigns, often as part of a wider military and political effort. Their victories, however, have often hinged on two factors: the collapse of majority support for the existing regime or the withdrawal of its external backers. Some successes have been short-lived, when the victors themselves have later suffered internal schisms. ■

TERROR IN SOMALIA

Ethnic conflict between Somalia and Ethiopia escalated from terrorist insurgency into open war during the 1960s. The Western Somali Liberation Front (WSLF), a guerrilla movement, fought on behalf of Somali clans in eastern Ethiopia, but were defeated by 1980. Strife continued within Somalia between rival factions during the 1980s. Severe famine in the 1990s brought worldwide attention to Somalia, and with it a succession of multinational peacekeeping and famine-relief forces. Despite all efforts, the country is still riven by strife and starvation.

INDEPENDENCE AND ETHNIC UNREST

Previously colonized by Britain, France, and Italy in the nineteenth century, Somalia became independent in 1960. Nomadic Somalis in the Ogaden – an arid expanse of northeastern Ethiopia – agitated for inclusion in the Somali Republic, and in 1960, they came out in open revolt, looking to Somalia for aid. Successive Somali governments tried to liberate the Ogaden. In 1961, the new Somali republic helped to organize and arm a guerrilla force that, by the early 1970s, was known as the Western Somalia Liberation Front (WSLF). Between 1960 and 1964, there were violent clashes and terrorist attacks in the Ogaden between Ethiopian troops and Somali-backed guerrillas.

Meanwhile, a dispute had arisen in the Northern Frontier District (NFD) of northeastern Kenya, where nomadic Somali tribes were resentful of Kenyan rule. During the late 1950s and early 1960s, Somalis of the NFD waged a terrorist campaign in the region. From hide-outs in the desert, they attacked Kenyan police units. Although the NFD conflict escalated following Kenyan independence in 1963, the unrest was quelled the following year.

KEY FACTS

- Between May 1977 and March 1978, the Soviet Union supplied about $1.5 million in military aid to Ethiopia to help it regain the Ogaden region.
- By the time of its 1978 retreat from Harer, Somalia had lost 8,000 troops, three-quarters of its tank force, and about half its air force.
- Rival Somali factions have been locked in conflict ever since the close of the Ogaden war.

OPEN CONFLICT IN THE OGADEN

In May 1977, the guerrilla campaign for the Ogaden erupted into open war between the Ethiopian army and a 3,000-6,000-strong WSLF force. The WSLF aimed to regain for Somalia all the territory east of a line from Moyale on the Kenyan border to Lake Abbe, or roughly a third of Ethiopia. The WSLF had the initiative to attack without Somali approval. Faced with the reality of the attack, however, the Somali army rapidly joined in the fighting. Somali President Siad Barre had little choice but to permit his troops to "resign" and join the WSLF. The Somali troops and the WSLF easily overran the small Ethiopian garrisons in the Ogaden.

In July 1977, the WSLF cut off the Djibouti-Addis Ababa railroad, Ethiopia's only rail link to the sea. By September 12, 1977, Jijiga, the principal Ethiopian military headquarters in the Ogaden, had fallen to the WSLF. The Ethiopians only just managed to hold on to Harer and Dire Dawa, some 200 miles east of Addis Ababa. For their attack, the Somalis deployed some 35,000 regular troops and a substantial guerrilla force.

By the end of 1977, the WSLF and the Somali army had achieved a spectacular success: over 90 percent of the disputed region was in their hands and the Ethiopian army had mutinied and retreated. The morale of the Ethiopian army had not been helped by a series of bloody purges before the war. The Ethiopian Third Division retreated from the key defensive position in the Gara Marda Pass by Jijiga, abandoning their equipment to the WSLF and leaving open the road to Harer. As the theater of conflict expanded, the WSLF enlisted the support of other clans, including the Oromo, and an Oromo guerrilla force, called the Somali Abo Liberation Front (SALF), was formed. However, Barre was now critically short of arms and requested Soviet aid.

Rex Features

A guerrilla stands guard in Mogadishu, where rival ethnic Somali factions have clashed in the 1990s.

The Soviets had been supporting Somalia in opposition to Haile Selassie's U.S.-backed Ethiopian empire. In 1974, however, Selassie was ousted, and a revolutionary council – the Dergue – set about removing the U.S. presence in Ethiopia. The Soviets welcomed these developments, but their position was complicated by the Somali conflict and they were ultimately obliged to pick sides. In mid-1977, they withdrew support for Somalia in favor of Ethiopia. Accordingly, the Somalis ordered Soviet personnel from Somalia and renounced the Soviet-Somali treaty of friendship. These actions intensified Soviet support for the Ethopian Dergue.

Soviet support for Ethiopia gradually swung the balance of power away from Somalia, whose positions in the Ogaden were vulnerable. By August 1977, the Soviets halted military aid to Somalia. They began to supply arms to Ethiopia on a huge scale – far in excess of previous contributions to Somalia.

On February 3, 1978, the Ethiopians, now backed by Cubans and Soviets, were finally in a position to launch a counterattack. The Somalis officially committed army troops to the Ogaden on February 12, 1978, having previously claimed that all the fighting was being done by the WSLF. On March 4, the Ethiopians attacked Jijiga in the Gara Marda Pass. The town fell after two days' fighting, in which about 10,000 Cuban troops and 1,500 Soviet advisers were involved on the Ethiopians' side. The Soviets also used South Yemeni soldiers and some East German advisers. The Soviets airlifted a Cuban armored column with 60 to 70 tanks behind Jijiga, trapping the Somalis and forcing them into headlong retreat. Somali relief units were strafed by MiG fighters before they could even reach the front.

Somalia announced its withdrawal from the Ogaden on March 9, 1978. Despite this declaration, the WSLF and the Somali army persisted in their campaign, exploiting the distraction caused by the escalating war between Ethiopia and Eritrea to the north, but were finally routed in 1980. In the aftermath of Somalia's defeat, about 1.5 million refugees fled to Somalia.

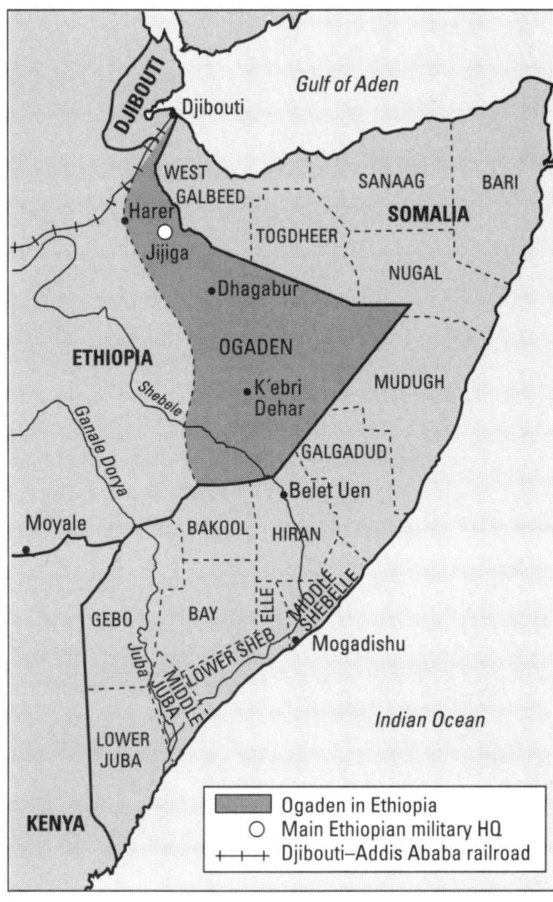

Armed conflict between Ethiopia and Somalia in the 1960s-70s centered on border disputes in the Ogaden.

After Somalia's defeat, Barre executed a number of Somali generals. Other officers staged a failed coup in April 1978. Somalis complained later that the U.S. had promised them aid if Barre ended his alliance with the Soviets, but had ultimately failed to support them.

CONTINUED CONFLICT

The conflict in the Ogaden continued after 1978, as the WSLF fought the Ethiopian government and their Cuban allies. In July 1982, clashes occurred near Belet Uen, involving the Somali Democratic Salvation Front (SDSF). This Ethiopian-backed guerrilla movement intended to overthrow Barre. Other guerrilla groups active at the time included the United Somali Congress (USC) and the Somali National Movement (SNM). Operating at first from bases in Ethiopia, the SNM waged a terrorist campaign against the Somali government. In 1988, it invaded northern Somalia and the conflict escalated into open war. By 1989, when government forces regained the upper hand, some 10,000 people had been killed in the civil war.

ANARCHY AND FAMINE

In 1991, the USC led a rebellion against Siad Barre and overthrew him. However, the USC was split by infighting, and the political climate remained unstable. At the same time, the effects of drought and famine were leading to mass starvation in Somalia. The scale of human suffering shocked the international community, and in December 1992, a U.S.-led United Task Force (UNITAF) intervened in Somalia to safeguard aid shipments to famine victims. In May 1993, the UN Operation in Somalia (UNOSOM) relieved UNITAF.

Tension rose between the UN forces and militant Somali factions, many of whom resented the intervention, and there were several skirmishes. When Somali guerrillas killed 24 UN troops in June, the UN diverted much of UNOSOM's resources toward hunting down the perpetrators. This prompted Somali citizens to accuse the UN of victimization and to switch their allegiance to rebel factions. When United States news networks showed a U.S. soldier being dragged through the streets of Mogadishu, President Clinton acknowledged changing opinion and ordered the withdrawal of U.S. troops from Somalia by March 1994. Although the UN intervention helped alleviate the famine, Somalia remains locked in bloody conflict to this day.

Matthew Hughes

SEE ALSO: NATIONALIST TERRORISM; TERROR IN ERITREA; INTERNATIONAL COOPERATION AGAINST TERRORISM; THE MEDIA AND INTERNATIONAL TERRORISM.

FURTHER READING

- Laitin, David D., and Said S. Samatar. *Somalia: Nation in Search of a State.* Boulder, CO: Westview, and London: Gower, 1987.
- Lewis, Ian M. *A Modern History of Somalia: Nation and State in the Horn of Africa.* London: Longman, 1980; Boulder, CO: Westview, 1988.
- Ricciuti, Edward R. *Somalia: A Crisis of Famine and War.* Brookfield, CT: Millbrook Press, 1993.

TERROR IN ERITREA

In May 1991, after 30 years of armed struggle, the Eritrean People's Liberation Front (EPLF) secured independence for Eritrea, finally defeating the Ethiopian army of occupation. A catalog of terrorist atrocities accompanied the bloody civil war.

Eritrea's 4 million people had long been subordinated to foreign-backed regimes in Ethiopia's capital, Addis Ababa. Eritrea was colonized by Italy in the late nineteenth century, subsequently becoming a British protectorate. The United Nations guaranteed a measure of Eritrean autonomy in 1952, but Haile Selassie, ruler of Ethiopia, annexed Eritrea in 1962. The Cold War era saw the U.S. lending its support to Haile Selassie while locating a strategically significant foreign base on Ethiopian soil. In response, the Soviet Union and Cuba armed and trained Eritrean rebels. By demanding full independence, however, against the grain of international relations, the EPLF was later denied support from abroad. Instead, it mounted a self-reliant campaign – based entirely within Eritrean territory and uniting all nine Eritrean ethnic groups – against a backdrop of a series of terrible famines.

THE FIGHT FOR INDEPENDENCE BEGINS

In late 1961, 11 Eritreans, formerly members of the Sudanese police, formed the Eritrean Liberation Front (ELF). Led by Idris Hamad Awate, they began harassing and attacking Ethiopian security forces. The ELF established strongholds in the mountainous western province of Barka. It waged a low-level terrorist campaign, extending its reach into much of Eritrea's rural territory. By 1968, it could claim to control as much as two-thirds of the countryside with just 2,000 guerrillas. ELF fighters were, however, unable to sustain conventional confrontations, although they fought almost 30 battles each year. In the cities, they ran a campaign of bombings and assassinations. In the provincial capital, Asmara, the ELF succeeded in keeping the army off the streets at night.

Ethiopian forces adopted a heavy-handed response to the successes of the ELF, setting up a network of controlled strategic hamlets. Villagers in areas thought to contain ELF bases were forcibly relocated into compounds in an attempt to deprive the ELF of practical support. When this failed to eliminate the ELF, villagers were simply dispersed into towns.

The failure of this policy led to a significant turn in the fight for independence. The Ethiopians resorted to increasingly crude methods targeted at civilians. In one instance, they executed a number of village elders. In another, they killed 100 villagers. Growing fear and hostility led to an exodus of some 25,000 Eritreans to Sudan. New recruits, many of them Christians from urban areas, swelled the ranks of the previously rural, and largely Muslim, membership of the ELF. Divisions over strategy and policy led to the formation of the breakaway Eritrean People's Liberation Front (EPLF) in 1970. The disparity of the two liberation movements was destined to arouse bitter and bloody conflict between them in the years to come.

KEY FACTS

- Colonel Mengistu ran a regime of terror in Ethiopia, executing any member of the revolutionary council who challenged his militarist policies.
- The Soviet Union provided Ethiopia with an estimated $12 billion in military and civilian aid.
- An estimated 350,000 casualties have resulted from the Ethiopia-Eritrea conflict.

THE END OF SELASSIE'S EMPIRE

The EPLF became one of the main factors in the fall of Haile Selassie in 1974. Frustrated by the war, the Ethiopian army grew demoralized. A series of successful small-scale mutinies over pay developed into a coup, with imperial authority dissolving into the hands of the army. The military regime declared itself to be revolutionary, promising to sweep away what was left of Haile Selassie's feudal order. However, Ethiopia's

The EPLF's struggle for Eritrean independence achieved unity among diverse ethnic groups.

new Dergue (revolutionary council) fell under the control of Colonel Mengistu Haile Mariam, who was more interested in power than in social reform. Rejecting calls for political negotiation, Mengistu continued the purely military approach toward Eritrea.

The Dergue strengthened its positions in Eritrea. It committed 50 percent of all regular troops to active duty – 25,000 in all – and called up more than 6,000 reservists. The Eritreans were attacked by mechanized divisions, led by a battalion of tanks and supported by helicopters and fighter-bombers. The use of heavy force against the EPLF/ELF, with continuing brutality against the civilian population, eroded any support for Ethiopia in Eritrea. EPLF strength continued to grow.

The political uncertainty that followed the military takeover in Ethiopia enabled the EPLF and ELF to shelve their differences and cooperate. By 1977, the EPLF's 40,000 fighters had made significant gains. Most of the countryside was under their control, the major port at Massawa was occupied, and the garrison at Asmara was under siege. Terrorists blew up five bridges along a vital rail link between Addis Ababa and the port of Djibouti in June. They attacked and damaged an oil supply depot at the town of Dire Dawa in July 1977. Ethiopian military presence on the ground in Eritrea appeared to be nearing the end.

THE SOVIETS STEM THE TIDE

At this critical point, the Soviets stepped in, prompted by the mid-1977 invasion of the Ethiopian Ogaden region by guerrillas and troops from neighboring Somalia. The Soviets had formerly supported Somalia and Eritrea against Selassie's U.S.-backed regime, but with the newly fledged, pro-Marxist Dergue now in power, the political situation presented new options. The Soviets proposed a communist federation of the three nations. When this was rejected, the Soviets withdrew support from Somalia and reinforced the Ethiopian army, enabling it to repel Somalia. The Dergue, with its wealth of new equipment and advisers, then turned its attention back to Eritrea.

Between 1978 and 1985, the Dergue launched six major offensives against the Eritreans and other opposition factions in Ethiopia. The ELF was driven back into Barka, while the EPLF withdrew into the highlands of the northern province of Sahel. The weakened ELF appeared to be willing to reach a settlement with Mengistu, which would include turning on the EPLF. In another episode of Eritrean civil war, the EPLF opted to launch a pre-emptive attack. The ELF was removed from Barka and played little further part in the independence movement. The majority of its remaining fighters, however, later joined the EPLF.

THE EPLF'S COUNTERATTACK

From its enhanced position in the north, the EPLF planned a new, and ultimately successful, strategy. For military purposes the Eritrean People's Liberation Army (EPLA) was founded. This was to become one of Africa's largest and best equipped military forces. The EPLA, in contrast to the conscript army of Ethiopia, was a volunteer force, reaching a peak strength of 100,000. EPLA members, who received a minimum of six months' training, constituted a disciplined military organization. Fighters, 35 percent of them women, also received an education, making the EPLA fully literate.

The EPLA adopted three basic tactics. First, it used positional warfare to defend the liberated areas and to attack Ethiopian bases for piecemeal territorial gains. Second, it practiced mobile warfare in the contested areas to reduce Ethiopian mobility and communications. And third, guerrilla activity in occupied Eritrea destroyed infrastructure and equipment. In the continuing absence of foreign support, the EPLF relied on the Ethiopian army itself for virtually all its military supplies. Its tactics depended entirely on the ability of the EPLA to capture equipment and on its own capacity to maintain it. The overall EPLF strategy was to drain the Ethiopians of resources and morale while gradually extending the liberated zone into Eritrea.

The EPLA advanced patiently, taking towns only to withdraw after securing supplies and/or inflicting damage on their enemy. In a single assault, one-third of the Ethiopian air force was grounded. Meticulous planning, and the dedication of its volunteers, gave the EPLA the advantage in battle. Its fighters were often outnumbered – by as many as eight to one – but suffered only about one-tenth the fatalities they inflicted on the Ethiopians. Behind the lines, EPLF supporters provided highly efficient intelligence from both military and administrative sources. Through this strategy the EPLA won the upper hand, and by 1983 it had acquired sufficient tanks to be able to defeat Ethiopian forces in open battle.

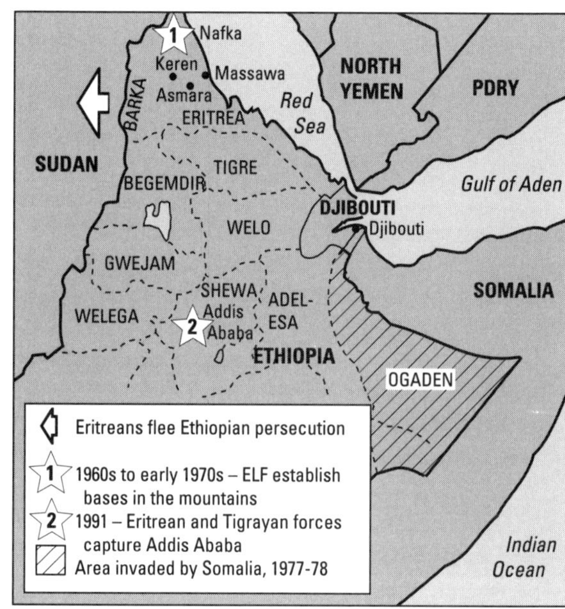

Eritrea successfully overthrew Ethiopian occupation and won independence in 1991.

BUILDING A NEW NATION

The EPLF existed primarily as a political organization, waging war only to enable the pursuit of political, social, and economic stability. The dissidents within the ELF had formed the EPLF because, in their view, the Arab-backed and largely Muslim base of the ELF encouraged a divide-and-rule approach, promoting competition between ethnic groups at the expense of the movement for Eritrea's independence. The EPLF, by contrast, evolved as a single organization dedicated to uniting Eritrea's nine ethnic groups, all of which were represented in the leadership.

This "nation-making" strategy also included widespread and progressive social reform. The EPLF, in its liberated zones, enacted popular land reform, guaranteeing land for the landless and ensuring local security. It established democratic village committees, giving local people responsibility for their own administration. The status of women improved and new marriage laws were introduced. The EPLF also promoted education, with the use of Eritrean languages through the media. To cope with more than 10,000 prisoners of war and the effects of famines, the Eritrean Relief Agency was established.

THE FINAL PHASE OF LIBERATION

Mengistu's regime began to show signs of increasing desperation. In its final offensive, in 1985, the Dergue used its crack troops and mechanized divisions to mount rapid air and ground attacks on EPLA positions. Despite the element of surprise, the EPLA absorbed this offensive as it had done earlier ones – and was able to inflict critical damage on Ethiopian forces. Losses of trained personnel and high-quality equipment were so extensive that Ethiopia was permanently deprived of offensive capabilities.

The Dergue reacted to its increasing military weakness with harsh measures against its own population. It reintroduced martial law and bolstered its army through drafting more than 100,000 men and boys as young as 14. Barely trained and poorly equipped, the conscripts were sent off to fight with no clear idea of who they were fighting or why. They found themselves raiding villages much like those from which they were taken. The army maintained discipline only by the

Rex Features

most brutal methods; it executed conscripts to keep troops fighting or to warn others against desertion. Soldiers rejected what was being demanded of them in Eritrea, and the last years of the Ethiopian regime were plagued with defections and mutinies. In one episode, Mengistu had 12 generals executed for their part in an attempted coup.

INDEPENDENCE AT LAST

The goal of Eritrean independence depended on the establishment of democracy in Addis Ababa, and with the renunciation of all Ethiopian territorial claims on Eritrea. Military victory would help this, but could not be an end in itself. Overall success, therefore, required cooperation with the Tigrayan People's Liberation Front (TPLF), which was spearheading Ethiopian resistance to Addis Ababa. Finally, in May 1991, the fate of the Mengistu regime was sealed when the TPLF-led coalition of opposition forces closed in on Addis Ababa. In Eritrea, on May 24, the war finally ended with the surrender of the capital, Asmara.

Overcoming past differences, the EPLF and TPLF reached an agreement on Eritrean independence. Economic ties remained strong, and Assab in southern

Rebels left destroyed convoys scattered over the harsh landscape of Eritrea.

Eritrea was declared a free port, granting Ethiopia access to the Red Sea. The EPLF reformed as the Eritrean Provisional Government (EPG). After 30 years of war, the Eritrean people now faced the daunting peacetime task of national reconstruction.

Nick Hostettler

SEE ALSO: TERROR IN COLONIAL CONQUESTS; NATIONAL LIBERATION WARS AND TERROR; TERROR IN SOMALIA.

FURTHER READING

- Prouty, Chris, and Eugene Rosenfield. *Historical Dictionary of Ethiopia and Eritrea.* 2nd ed. London and Metuchen, NJ: Scarecrow Press, 1993.
- Zegege, Abebe, and Siegfried Pansevang, eds. *Ethiopia in Change: Peasantry, Nationalism and Democracy.* London: British Academic Press, and New York: St. Martin's Press, 1994.

TERROR IN SOUTH AFRICA

Terrorism was used by opponents of racially segregated South Africa to achieve equal rights with the ruling white minority. The campaign for equality was spearheaded by the African National Congress (ANC).

The ANC was formed in South Africa in 1912 to further political reform and to protect the rights of blacks in South Africa. The founders advocated nonviolent political activity, but achieved little in early years to disturb white rule. At the time of the ANC's formation, the South African population was made up of various racial groups: the black majority, the "Cape coloreds" (the authorities' description for those of mixed race), Asian communities, and whites of British or Dutch descent. Those of Dutch descent, known as Boers or Afrikaners, could often trace their family's residence in South Africa back to the time when English settlers were arriving in North America. The Dutch established themselves in Cape Town in 1652, 30 years before English Quakers arrived in Philadelphia.

In 1948, the right-wing National party came to power. With its power base among the Afrikaners, the National party legislated a rigid system of racial segregation: *apartheid*. In response, the ANC issued the 1955 "Freedom Charter," calling for human rights for all people in South Africa. In spite of the ANC's continued policy of nonviolence, the National government arrested and prosecuted for treason much of the ANC leadership. Upset by the failure of the nonviolent policy, a splinter group led by Robert Sobukwe broke away in 1959, and formed a new radical organization known as the Pan-Africanist Congress. The Pan-Africanists objected to the multicultural nature of the ANC and its closeness to white liberals.

A confrontation between the new organization and the authorities was not long in coming. On March 21, 1960, the Pan-Africanists organized a demonstration against the identity cards – known as passes – that the black population was required to carry. The police opened fire, killing 67 blacks and wounding more than 200. Riots swept through the black townships and 30,000 blacks marched on Cape Town. The government declared a state of emergency and banned the Pan-Africanists and the ANC. The Pan-Africanists were suppressed, but the ANC weathered the government's response even though its leaders were arrested or forced into hiding. Besides, ANC Youth League leader Nelson Mandela had prepared for the ANC to continue as an underground organization.

KEY FACTS

- In 1961 the African National Congress (ANC) abandoned its 50-year-old policy of nonviolence and set up a militant wing.
- After political changes abroad, neighboring states provided training camps for ANC militants.
- The mid-1980s saw a dramatic escalation in terrorist incidents. In 1986, attacks increased by more than 300 percent compared to 1984-85.

BEGINNING THE ARMED STRUGGLE

The failure of the ANC policy of nonviolence caused a change in strategy, and in 1961 the organization opted for the selective use of violence – in other words, the use of terrorism. It was not easy to drop a 50-year tradition of nonviolent activity, and a faction of the ANC leadership argued strongly that terrorism would damage the international prestige of the movement. Nonetheless, the ANC leaders voted to form a military wing, Umkhonto we Sizwe (Spear of the Nation). Deciding upon armed struggle was relatively simple, but implementing it was much more difficult. There was no weaponry or competent military leadership available; the underground network was far from secure; and there were no sympathetic neighboring countries to provide bases or infiltration routes. Every state in southern Africa was governed by European colonial powers or entrenched white minorities.

Umkhonto's opening terrorist campaign consisted mainly of sabotage operations against utilities, communications networks, and government buildings.

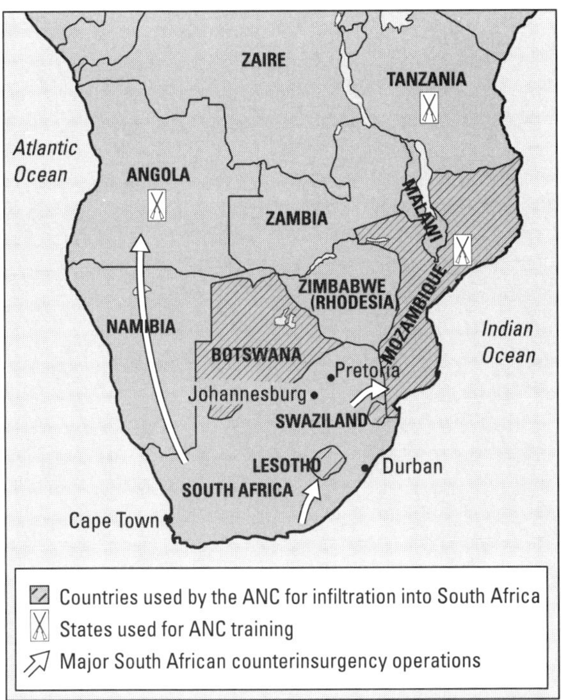

With the process of decolonization in southern Africa, South Africa's neighbors eventually supported opponents of the apartheid regime.

This achieved limited results: the government claimed that the 194 operations launched between June 1961 and July 1963 caused an average of only $125 damage per incident, with the highest event reaching $10,000. The insurgents also attacked police informants and similar nonwhite targets, but most of these were mere random acts of terror. No effort was made to explain Umkhonto's aims and methods, and the operations did not have grass-roots support. The government did not remain idle. Security police raided the Umkhonto headquarters in Johannesburg on July 11, 1963, capturing almost all the Umkhonto high command and valuable intelligence. A wave of arrests then jailed almost the entire ANC leadership, including Walter Sisulu, Govan Mbeki, and Nelson Mandela. The only leader to escape was Oliver Tambo, then living abroad.

REGROUPING AND REORGANIZING

Umkhonto's amateurish terrorist campaign had failed, and the arrests of the leadership transformed Tambo into the effective head of the ANC. He controlled a demoralized domestic organization with a discredited strategy. Umkhonto needed a secure domestic underground network and a safe base for training and infiltration routes into South Africa. The ANC accomplished the necessary regrouping during 14 years of comparative peace.

The complexion of South Africa's neighbors altered dramatically between 1963 and 1977. The Portuguese colonists left Angola and Mozambique in 1974, and the British colonies in the area had all gained independence in the 1960s. The only exception was the white renegade state of Rhodesia, which eventually came under black majority rule in 1980. As decolonization swept through Africa, sympathetic bases became available to the ANC in neighboring countries like Zambia. In 1967, Umkhonto tried to infiltrate guerrillas through Rhodesia (now Zimbabwe), aided by the Zimbabwe African People's Union and using bases in Zambia. But Rhodesian security forces tracked them down. For the rest of the 1960s, Umkhonto conducted no further acts of insurgency against the South African government.

Within South Africa, black resentment grew, and a new force arose in internal politics. Steve Biko's Black Consciousness movement intended to build self-reliance and pride within the black population – and Black Consciousness was resolutely nonviolent. Biko asserted: "We are not going into armed struggle. We'll leave it to the Pan-Africanists and ANC." However, the armed struggle came to them. On June 16, 1976, 20,000 schoolchildren marched into the black Johannesburg satellite township of Soweto. They were demonstrating against the introduction of compulsory Afrikaans (the language of the Afrikaners) courses into black schools. The demonstrators confronted large numbers of police. Scuffles broke out and by evening the township was ablaze. Within a week, 176 people had been killed. The violence spread across South Africa.

The death toll mounted and by the time the police regained control in 1977, as many as a thousand blacks were dead. The police beat and tortured Biko to death in September 1977. Black Consciousness could not control the rebellion and collapsed in its aftermath. Much of the township youth came to the conclusion that armed resistance was the only option left.

The failure of the Soweto uprising resulted in a large influx of recruits into the ANC training camps. Umkhonto launched a new guerrilla offensive beginning in the late 1970s to prove to the ANC domestic constituency that the armed struggle was feasible in

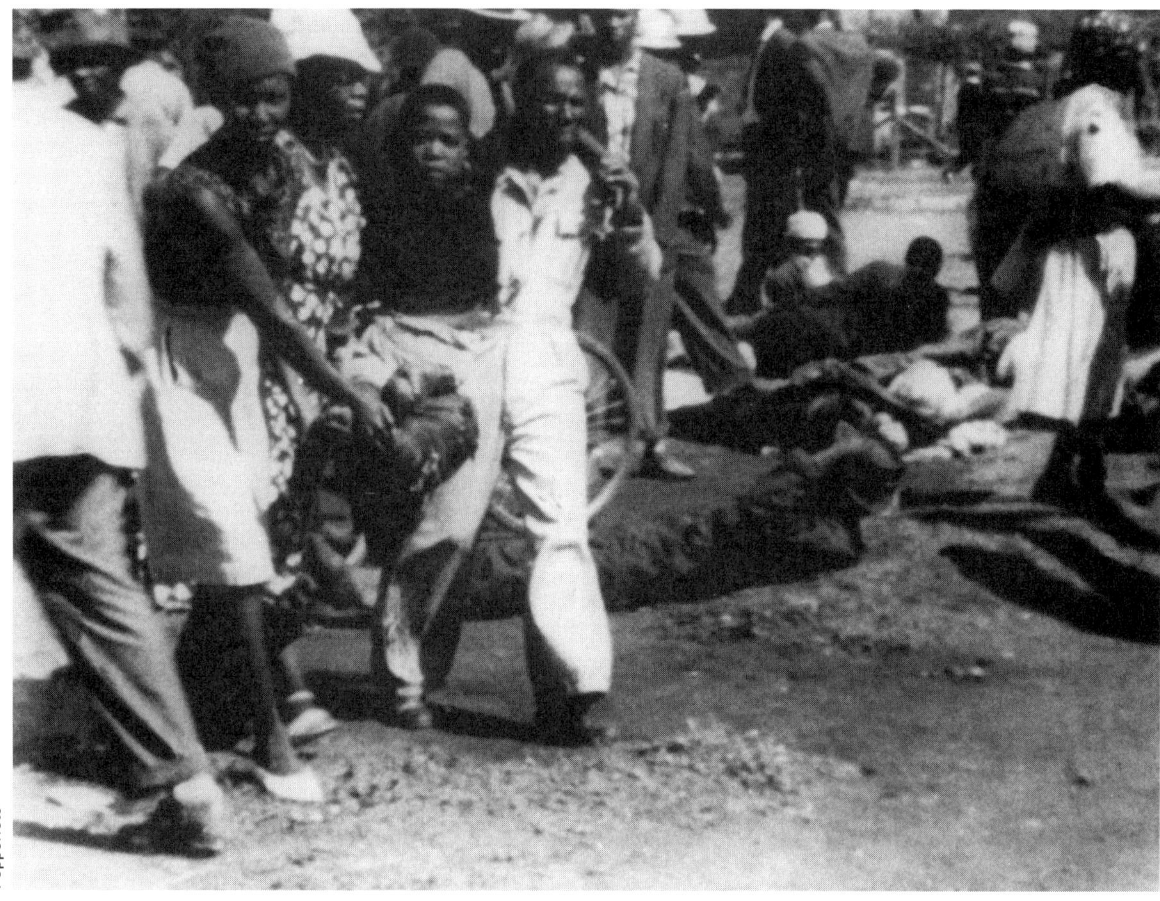

Popperfoto

Wounded Africans lie on the ground and a boy is carried to safety after the Sharpeville massacre on March 21, 1960.

South Africa. The Sasol oil-from-coal plant and South Africa's only nuclear power station were among the targets of several high-profile attacks. However, the South African army was ready to confront the challenge. South African leader P.W. Botha launched a deliberate policy of destabilization against neighboring states that were known to harbor ANC cadres. The South African army launched repeated commando raids against ANC targets within the "frontline states" (Angola, Zambia, Zimbabwe, Mozambique, and Tanzania), and invaded Angola. Attacks were launched as far north as the ANC headquarters in Lusaka, Zambia. A particularly violent attack on their offices in Lesotho in 1982 resulted in the deaths of 42 people. The Umkhonto campaign flagged once again in the face of the security forces' massive retaliatory capabilities. As a result, the ANC dropped guerrilla warfare and turned again to terrorist tactics.

THE 1984 REVOLT

In 1984, the ANC stepped up their campaign, but again with little success. In May, for example, terrorists fired grenades at a U.S. oil refinery in Durban. But the police chased the terrorists and, in a shootout, killed them along with some innocent black workers. In July, a bomb intended for a military convoy exploded after the trucks had passed, killing more blacks.

On October 3, 1984, riots broke out in the townships of the Vaal Triangle (an industrial area containing Johannesburg and Pretoria). Forty thousand mineworkers then went on strike. The police moved in and fighting between the police and residents became so fierce that the minister of law and order, Louis Le Grange, declared: "As far as we're concerned it is war, plain and simple." The violence spread across the

Transvaal, and Prime Minister Botha sent the army into the black townships. It was the first time the army had been used this way. On October 23, in Operation Palmiet, 7,000 police and troops poured into Sebokeng township, the heart of the revolt. After Palmiet, troops were regularly deployed in the townships, but could not quell the tide of disturbance. In 1985, the trouble spread into the Cape province. The police opened fire at a funeral procession in Uitenhage on March 21, 1985, the anniversary of the Sharpeville massacre, and 20 unarmed blacks died. On July 21, Botha declared a state of emergency, but this failed to halt the killing. By the end of 1985, 1,000 blacks had died and the authorities had detained more than 7,000 others, largely without trial. The state of emergency continued into 1986 and the military became increasingly aggressive.

Medical professionals cataloged the effects of state terror. A Port Elizabeth surgeon cited 153 cases where injuries to detainees could not have been inflicted lawfully. A doctor in Soweto noticed a change in the cases he treated: there was a decrease in whip and birdshot injuries and an increase in bullet wounds. It appeared also that the security forces had started to use high-velocity bullets. The same doctor explained: "A high-velocity bullet...is like a tornado – it just whips everything up inside you and you're finished. It's obviously a weapon designed to kill."

BOMBS IN GARBAGE CANS

The ANC was not slow in retaliating. Thirteen terrorist bombings in major downtown areas followed within 23 days of the declaration of a state of emergency. Sites for ANC attacks included a hamburger restaurant, the Anglo-American building, and the Holiday Inn in Johannesburg. In July 1986, an ANC grenade, thrown in through a window, injured a deputy cabinet minister of mixed race. But attacks went beyond establishment targets. The ANC also created an air of general terror with a series of bombs placed in garbage cans.

Other black African responses similarly became more violent. As well as the traditional methods of mass protest – strikes, boycotts, and demonstrations – militant black youths known as Comrades took the fight back to the security forces. Umkhonto guerrillas slipped into the townships to provide training. They dug trenches across roads to trap military vehicles and attacked the police and army with Molotov cocktails. Comrades obtained assault rifles. There was also much black-on-black violence, between Comrades and pro-government vigilantes. Journalist Allister Sparks described how the vigilantes made their captives "walk barefoot over hot coals, and had them flogged naked in a room flooded with soapy water until they floundered about like stranded fish in the slippery, bloodied grime." The Comrades responded by car-bombing vigilante leader Piet Ntuli and rampaging through the shanty towns. Extremist Comrades enforced discipline in the townships through beatings and intimidation. They "necklaced" some who broke consumer boycotts – burned them to death by hanging a gasoline-filled tire around the victim's neck – and forced others to eat all their purchases, including soap and drain cleaner.

The revolt petered out after a crackdown on the remaining leadership. By the end of the year, 23,000 people, including about 9,000 children, had been jailed. Although the authorities controlled the townships, the balance of confidence had changed. Black Africans believed the ultimate revolution could not be far away. That the final bloody confrontation did not occur is credited to two men. Botha's discredited leadership came under pressure from within the National party, and F. W. de Klerk maneuvered him out of office in 1989. De Klerk was aware that the situation as it stood could not continue. He released Mandela, removed the ban on the ANC, and dismantled *apartheid*. In the first multiracial elections, held in 1994, Mandela won the presidency with De Klerk as vice-president. The two formed a partnership that navigated through an extremely hazardous transition with great skill. But the legacy of the uses of terror in the struggle against apartheid is a high rate of violent crime.

M. Christopher Mann

SEE ALSO: TERROR IN ZIMBABWE (RHODESIA); TERROR IN NAMIBIA; TERROR CAMPAIGNS IN PORTUGUESE AFRICA; STATE VERSUS NON-STATE TERRORISM.

FURTHER READING

- Cock, Jacklyn, and Nathan Laurie. *War and Society: The Militarization of South Africa.* New York: St. Martin's Press, 1989.
- Davis, Stephen M. *Apartheid's Rebels.* New Haven: Yale University Press, 1987.
- Mandela, Nelson. *Long Walk to Freedom.* Boston: Little Brown, 1994; London: Abacus, 1995.

TERROR IN THE PHILIPPINES

Since World War II, more than 120,000 Filipinos have lost their lives in the course of three organized terrorist attempts to overthrow the Philippines government. These include the Huk rebellion in the early years after independence from the U.S. in 1946, a Communist rebellion that started in 1968, and a Muslim secessionist movement in the south of the country that began in the late 1970s.

THE HUK REBELLION

The Huk rebellion had its roots to a small communist organization – the Peasant Union – formed during the 1930s, which enjoyed widespread support from tenant farmers and landless peasants in central Luzon. It renamed itself the "Hukbalahap" in March 1942 – an acronym for *Hukbo ng Bayan Laban sa Hapon* (the People's Anti-Japanese Army) – transforming itself into a group of patriotic freedom-fighters opposed to the Japanese wartime occupation. The Huks achieved notable success, attacking Japanese convoys, troops, and supply lines, and by the end of the war it fielded 15,000 well-armed and trained soldiers.

The Hukbalahap, still essentially a peasant movement, participated in the 1946 elections and won several seats. President Manuel Roxas, however, prevented the party from taking its place in the assembly and effectively outlawed it. As a result, the Huks quickly commenced a guerrilla war against the regime. The government's military "iron fist" policy not only failed to suppress the revolt but directly contributed to its growth. The indiscriminate and brutal methods employed by government forces, against both innocent civilians and the guerrillas, ensured popular support for the insurgents. Huk guerrillas rapidly gained control of more territory. They attacked villages, kidnapped or killed dignitaries, and ambushed troops.

By 1950, Huk forces were poised to attack Manila when their leaders were arrested. Later that year, the tide turned against the insurgents. The government launched a counterinsurgency campaign combining economic and social reform with military operations, undermining peasant support for the Huks. Between 1950 and 1954, the army inflicted heavy casualties on the guerrillas, who were now without widespread popular support. In 1954, the Huk movement finally collapsed when its leader, Luis Taruc, surrendered.

KEY FACTS

- An estimated 50-100,000 Moros (Philippine Muslims) were killed during the MNLF insurgency.
- In the early 1980s, the New People's Army controlled 28 percent of the villages in the country.
- Between 1972 and 1981, the Philippine armed forces were dramatically increased from 60,000 to 200,000 to counter terrorist insurgency, placing a major burden on the economy.

THE COMMUNIST MOVEMENT

From the late 1960s, a combination of political corruption in President Ferdinand Marcos's government, economic crises, crumbling social structures, and human rights abuses bolstered support for the Communist Party of the Philippines and its military wing, the New People's Army (NPA).

In September 1972, Marcos declared martial law – ostensibly due to the communist threat, but in reality as a means of retaining power and a response to rising discontent throughout the population. The Philippines army dramatically increased in numbers, but it was plagued by corruption and underfunding. Nonetheless, a combination of martial law, the offer of an amnesty, political reforms, and slowly improving conditions in the army meant the insurgency movement lost its momentum. Internally, it was further weakened by arrests and dissent.

SOUTHERN PARTNERS

In 1977, the New People's Army linked up with the Moro New Liberation Front (MNLF). This Muslim secessionist movement, based in southern Mindanao, sought autonomy for the Philippines' 2.5 to 4 million

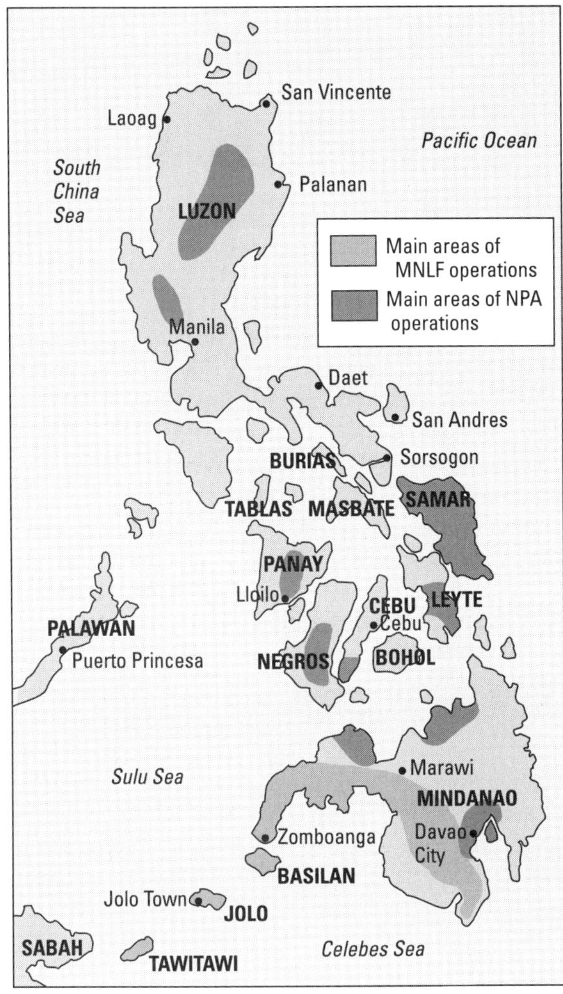

In the 1960s-70s, the New People's Army operated mainly out of Luzon, Mindanao, Samar, and Negros.

Muslims who were facing religious discrimination. Armed terrorist violence began in the 1970s, backed by Libya, Saudi Arabia, and Egypt.

After the declaration of martial law, the 30,000-50,000 guerrillas of the MNLF directly challenged the government, seizing extensive territory and badly damaging the army. It even captured the Philippines air force headquarters in Jolo Town in 1974. After mediation by the Libyans, a cease-fire was declared in December 1975, which collapsed early the next year.

The co-operation of these two disparate groups led to a revival of the New People's Army's fortunes. It regularly employed terror attacks to further its aims. For example, a grenade attack was carried out in the cathedral in Davao City in 1981, in which 13 were killed. After a few years suffering from internal dissent, the MNLF also returned to action in 1981, killing 119 troops on Pala island. In that year, an estimated 2,000 people were killing during the fighting.

During the early 1980s, the bankrupt Philippine economy provided a constant source of recruits for the insurgents. A new counterinsurgency program was initiated, combining small-unit operations by the military with a range of socio-economic development projects, but it failed to arrest communist progress.

After the fall of the Marcos regime in 1986, President Corazon Aquino initiated peace talks with the communists. The talks were followed by a 60-day truce, during which the communists and the New People's Army launched the New People's Party in an organized, legal bid for power. In 1987, however, the ceasefire collapsed and the reorganized New People's Army stepped up its guerrilla campaign. Unwisely, it adopted an aggressive military stance just as the Philippines army adopted a new policy of identifying and destroying the communist infrastructure. As a result, the communists suffered heavy losses. Forced on the defensive by the end of the 1980s, they resorted to targeting U.S. citizens in addition to their normal guerrilla activities.

Despite attempts to secure an agreement between the government and the MNLF, the secessionist war deteriorated into spasmodic fighting without a clear end in sight. The MNLF remained in existence during the 1990s, although the rebellion slowly subsided with only an estimated 2,000 insurgents active in Mindanao.

Tim Moreman

SEE ALSO: JAPANESE TERROR IN THE FAR EAST; JAPANESE TERRORIZATION OF PRISONERS.

FURTHER READING

- Kessler, Richard J. *Rebellion and Repression in the Philippines.* New Haven, CT: Yale University Press, 1989.
- Thompson, Mark R. *The Anti-Marcos Struggle: Personalistic Rule and Democratic Transition in the Philippines.* London and New Haven, CT: Yale University Press, 1995.

TAMIL TIGER TERROR IN SRI LANKA

The Tiger Movement of the island of Sri Lanka (formerly Ceylon), also known as the Liberation Tigers of Tamil Eelam (LTTE), is a formidable revolutionary organization. It is the only terrorist group to have assassinated two heads of government – Premier Rajiv Gandhi of India (1991) and President Ranasinghe Premadasa of Sri Lanka (1993) – as well as several prominent political and military figures. Today, the international security community rates the Tamil Tigers as the world's most ruthless terrorist group.

THE BEGINNINGS OF INSURGENCY

The Tamil Tigers are a by-product of Sri Lanka's ethnic conflict between the majority Sinhalese people and the ethnic Tamils, who constitute about 12 percent of the island's population. While the Sinhalese are chiefly Buddhists, the Tamils are Hindus or Christians.

Britain colonized Ceylon in the nineteenth century, and encouraged education among the Tamils but not the Sinhalese. After Sri Lanka gained independence in 1948, a succession of governments in the 1950s introduced Sinhala supremacy and repressed the Tamils, while forging policies that drove the country toward ruin. This led to high youth unemployment, social unrest, and bitter intercommunal recriminations.

SUMMARY

- The Tigers' bloody campaign for national self-determination has its roots in ethnic unrest between Tamil and Sinhala Sri Lankans.
- Some 100,000 people have been killed, and 20,000 maimed, since the Tiger insurgency began. The conflict has also created one million refugees in Sri Lanka and 500,000 Tamils overseas.
- The Tamil Tigers remain today one of the world's most indomitable terrorist groups.

The 1960s witnessed a series of bloody riots, and the Tamil youth sought a voice. This emerged in the form of the Liberation Tigers of Tamil Eelam (LTTE), which originated in 1972 along with other militant Tamil groups. The Tigers' charismatic leader and military commander, Velupillai Prabhakaran (also known as Karikalan), is a disciplined, dedicated leader, and a self-taught military genius.

The formative phase of terrorism in Sri Lanka was marked by the assassination of Tamils who were associated with the government. Branded as traitors, the targets were Tamil politicians, police officers, government officials, and suspected informants. To establish greater security, the Tigers and other Tamil militant groups realized the importance of creating an exclusively Tamil northern province, and began their campaign for the independence of Tamil Eelam, in the northeastern part of the island. To this day, nationalism remains the driving force behind the Tiger Movement.

Trained to perform only ceremonial functions, Sri Lankan troops were incapable of meeting the terrorist threat during the early years of the struggle. By the time the military had become more professional, the terrorists were already masters of rural and urban guerrilla warfare. Trained in farms and jungle hideouts in northern Sri Lanka, and later in the Middle East, the Tamil groups operated out of the island's northern jungles and from bases in India. They weakened the government's authority and restricted the movement of its troops by staging ambushes and mine attacks.

1983 – THE CONFLICT ESCALATES

The bloody ethnic riots of July 1983 polarized the two Sri Lankan communities and became a watershed in the history of the nation. The riots were a reaction by the majority Sinhala community to the death of 13 soldiers in a Tiger ambush. Several hundred thousand Tamils left the Sinhala south for the northeastern provinces; almost all the Sinhalese left the north. Many young Tamils felt

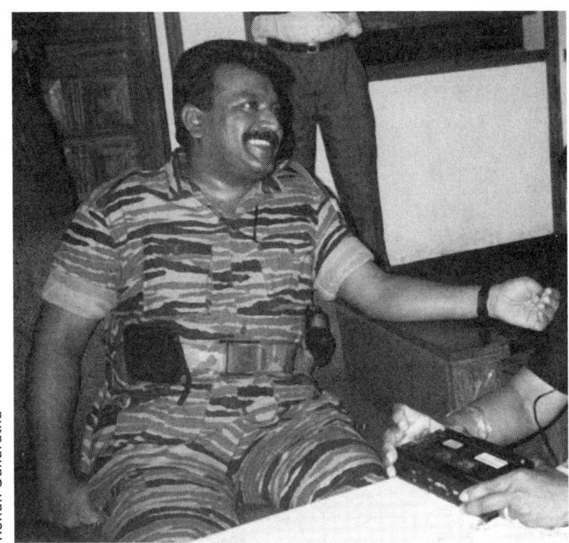

Velupillai Prabhakaran, the single-minded leader of the Liberation Tigers of Tamil Eelam.

that they had no future in an island dominated by Sinhala politicians. Within five years, the Tamil independence movements had recruited, trained and armed over 20,000 soldiers. About 500,000 Tamils left for India and the West, seeking asylum. They became the economic backbone of the terrorist campaign, and in the years that followed, the Tigers established offices and cells throughout the world, building a network unsurpassed by any other terrorist group.

INDIAN INTERVENTION

Between 1983 and 1987, the Tigers received clandestine support from India's premier intelligence agency, the Research and Analysis Wing. India, then politically friendly toward the Soviet Union, resented the Colombo government's pro-Western policy of supporting foreign intelligence personnel and mercenaries, and providing broadcasting and naval facilities to the U.S. India also resented Sri Lanka's friendship with China and Pakistan, two of its traditional foes.

Reinforced with Indian arms and explosives, the Tigers campaigned against vulnerable targets to pin down troops and undermine the government's search-and-destroy operations. They bombed Sri Lankan commercial aircraft, trains, and buses. They mowed down priests, nuns, pilgrims, and Muslims at worship, and frequently raided non-Tamil border villages and towns, massacring men, women, and children. They also ambushed military and police patrols. Reprisal killings and civilian deaths in crossfires merely empowered the terrorists, who targeted their recruitment at those families that had suffered at the hands of government forces. Gradually, the terrorist campaign evolved into full-blown insurgency. The authorities' ill-conceived counterinsurgency in May 1987, directed from 5,000 feet in the air with artillery to minimize military losses, resulted in heavy civilian casualties, and generated still greater support for the terrorists.

India became increasingly concerned that the Sri Lankan conflict was affecting its southern state of Tamil Nadu. A low percentage of the state's 60 million Tamils were supporting 22 small, but significant Indian Tamil political groups campaigning for Dravidasan, an independent Tamil state in India. The Indians were losing their grip on the terrorists; the civil war in Sri Lanka was escalating every day with consequences for Indian national security.

In July 1987, Indian Premier Rajiv Gandhi signed an Indo–Lanka Peace Accord with Sri Lankan President J.R. Jayewardene, ostensibly to give greater autonomy to the Tamils, but also to preserve India's political and strategic interests. India also deployed a force of 100,000 soldiers in Sri Lanka to maintain peace between government troops and Tamil terrorists. Only three months later, however, the Tigers declared war on the Indian peace-keeping force. During two years of fighting, the battle-hardened Tigers consistently outwitted a much larger and better equipped military.

The Sri Lankan government of R. Premadasa, elected in January 1989, renewed an offer of peace talks with the Tigers. At the same time, the Janatha Vimukthi Peramuna (People's Liberation Front), a powerful Sinhala nationalist group with strong anti-Indian sentiments and substantial support in the south, declared war on the state for collaborating with the Indian invader. In the ensuing violence, some 40,000 people, mostly young, were killed by state-sponsored death squads. Sri Lanka, up to that point a model democracy, proved incapable of fighting terrorism within the existing political structure. These atrocities and other human rights abuses deterred other nations from providing aid: the West still perceived the Tamil militants to be the underdogs in the conflict.

In a tactical move to relieve mounting Indian pressure, the Tigers agreed to talks with Colombo. And when Premadasa's call for the withdrawal of the Indian

Rohan Gunaratna

Tamil Tiger recruits in training in a jungle camp on the Jaffna peninsula, northern Sri Lanka.

peace-keeping force was refused by New Delhi, he sanctioned covert military assistance to the weakened Tigers. The Indians departed Sri Lanka in March 1990; although they left behind a heavily armed proxy force, this was decimated within a few weeks by the Tigers. Within three months, the Tigers declared war on the Colombo government, killing 400 Sinhala policemen.

Perhaps through fear that India – humiliated by its withdrawal and concerned at Tamil connections with Indian insurgent forces – would crack down on the Tigers, Prabhakaran took a dramatic and violent step. In May 1991, a Tiger suicide bomber killed Rajiv Gandhi. The event catapulted the terrorist movement into the global political arena.

GROWTH THROUGH ELIMINATION

The Tigers grew from a small force of 3,000 in 1986 to 16,000 in 1996. Through that decade, they systematically destroyed about 30 other Tamil terrorist groups. They also eliminated the alternative Tamil leadership, including Appapillai Amirthalingam, the leader of the Tamil United Liberation Front, the party that had dominated conservative Tamil politics for many years. After labeling rival Tamil groups as traitors to the cause of independence, the Tigers declared themselves the sole representatives of the Sri Lankan Tamil-speaking people. Through the use of suicide bombers, assassins, and mines, the Tigers also assassinated powerful Sinhala political and military leaders, including the United National Party (UNP) leader President Premadasa, the Minister of State for Defense, the former National Security Minister, the navy chief, and a number of northern and eastern military chiefs.

The assassinations created fear among political and military leaders, which restrained public condemnation of the atrocities. Furthermore, the Tigers never claimed responsibility for hitting the civilian targets. Instead, a Tiger front called Ellalan Force claimed responsibility for the strikes, and continues to do so.

The Tigers' ability to shift the theater of war to the capital Colombo proved highly destructive for the government. It gave a new dimension to the conflict,

Rohan Gunaratna

Tamil activists demonstrate in the center of London, England, to raise awareness for the Tamil Tigers.

up to that point confined to the northeast. The Tigers built a secure, sophisticated, and efficient intelligence network. They perfected the art of long-range reconnaissance and deep penetration operations; they mounted surveillance on almost all the targets earmarked for assassination, and even infiltrated the president's household. The politics of Colombo were no longer determined by ballot but, to a large extent, lay in the hands of the Tiger leader Prabhakaran.

TIGER CODE AND STRATEGY

The Tigers, unlike many other insurgent groups, have kept rigid control over their growth, steadily improving control through investing in training and discipline, using ideological indoctrination and psychological war conditioning. The Tiger code demands that its rank and file – who range in age from 14 to 40 – abstain from liquor, smoking, and extramarital sex. The penalty for violation is instant death. The commitment of the Tamil Tigers is demonstrated by the fact that each carries a potassium cyanide capsule strung around the neck. Faced with capture, the warrior is likely to choose instant martyrdom by biting into the deadly capsule. The Tigers eulogize and venerate such suicide victims as if they were Hindu gods and goddesses.

Although the Tigers have a central committee, this functions more as a forum for ideas. Nevertheless, all major decisions are taken by Prabhakaran, who is convinced that the success of the organization lies in his tight control and the excellent communication system that has been developed through the years.

The Tigers use bouts of peace to gain worldwide recognition, disseminate propaganda, generate funds, procure supplies, gather intelligence, regroup, retrain, and recruit. During conflict, the Tigers examine every success or failure to improve the next strike. They build life-size sand models and train on them, with the minutest details provided by intelligence operatives. With a capacity for innovation unequaled by any other terrorist group, the Tigers produce their own uniforms, antipersonnel and pressure mines, mortars, grenades, and other improvised explosive devices.

In battle, the Tigers do whatever is required to win. They fight like a professional military force when their strength is high, and less conventionally when their strength is low. When desperate, they hit vulnerable targets. Otherwise, they take on military targets. The Tigers' strikes, exploiting the element of surprise, have become increasingly audacious. In attack, the Tigers typically disorient the enemy, often by ramming fortified camps with vehicles full of explosives. By overrunning several military camps, the Tigers have amassed large stocks of weapons.

The Tigers constructed two airfields in northern Sri Lanka, and built a camp to train Air Tigers. However, the Sri Lankan air force bombed these bases in 1994. Suicide bombers, trained in France and Britain to fly miniature airplanes (which are invisible to radar), are adding a new dimension to the terrorist threat. The Tiger strategy is to use the explosive-laden airplanes to strike at military, political, and economic targets. The recent acquisition of gliders, gyrocopters, and mini-submarines suggest further innovation.

GLOBAL EXPANSION

The transnational character of the Tigers grew rapidly in the 1990s. The organization began to use the Internet for secure communications and the World

Wide Web for propaganda. It has established ties with terrorist groups within and outside southern Asia, and is able to exchange resources and share intelligence with several anti-Indian groups.

Today, the Tigers' international infrastructure includes 35 offices and cells. They use their state-of-the-art communication network to disseminate propaganda and raise – or, frequently, coerce – funds from half-a-million Sri Lankan Tamils overseas. The Tigers' income is estimated at $2 million per month, of which probably 60 percent originates abroad.

The worldwide network also aids the purchase of weapons from private dealers and governments. The Tigers have their international headquarters in London, as well as bases or front organizations elsewhere in the West. Offices in Australia, Canada, France, Germany, Italy, the Netherlands, Scandinavia, Switzerland, and, more recently, Japan, lobby against aid and assistance to Sri Lanka. In the United States, the Tigers have offices in Chicago, Boston, New Jersey, New York, and Washington, DC.

Uniquely among terrorist groups, the Tigers also own and operate a fleet of ocean-going vessels, which use sophisticated radar and satellites for communication. In mid-1990, the Tigers established a covert naval base in Twante, an island off Myanmar (Burma). To generate revenue, their ships smuggled weapons and narcotics from Myanmar to Europe, and legitimately transported fertilizer, timber, flour, sugar, cement, and other commercial goods. In 1994, the Tiger ship *M.V. Sweene* transported 50 tons of TNT and 10 tons of RDX (a plastic explosive), purchased from Nikolayev, a Black Sea port in the Ukraine. To save high registration costs, the ships received flags of convenience from Panama, Honduras, and Liberia. The Twante connection was exposed in 1995, and was subsequently closed down by Myanmar, but the Tigers continue to operate their fleet through other channels.

The Tigers invest in the money markets and real estate, including restaurants in Europe and Asia. Trading in gold and money laundering brings in substantial revenue. The terrorists have also played a role in providing identity papers, and engage in the smuggling of illegal immigrants.

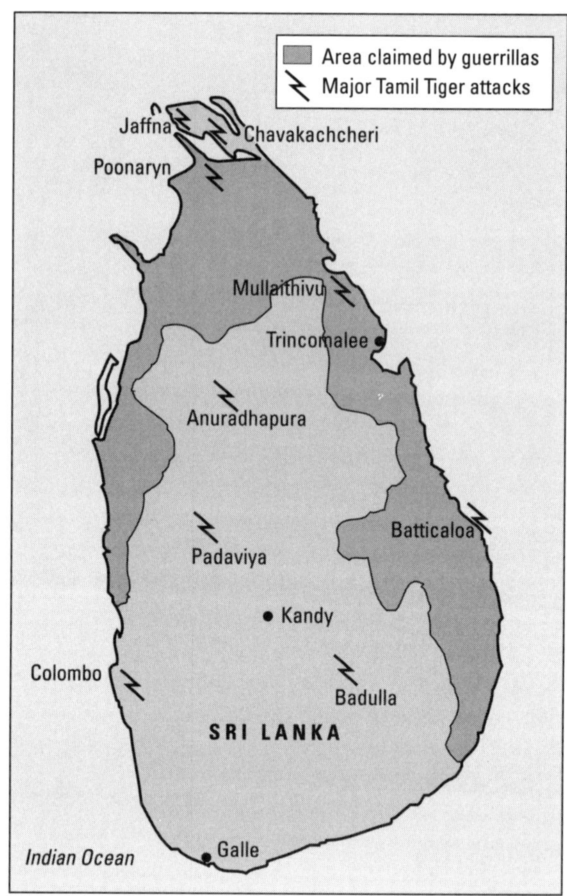

Despite the success of recent government offensives, northern Sri Lanka remains a Tiger stronghold.

TIGER TERRORIST ACTS IN THE 1990s

In a lightning, pre-dawn amphibious raid in November 1993, about 1,200 Tigers assaulted Poonaryn, the largest army-navy base in northern Sri Lanka, killing some 640 military personnel. The Tigers lost about 400 guerrillas but gained a mass of weapons, ammunition, and explosives, as well as naval vessels and two tanks. In 1995 (and again in 1996) Tigers destroyed military transport and fighter airplanes with Soviet-made, hand-held SAMs (surface-to-air missiles). The Tigers also used frogmen to mine naval vessels in Sri Lankan harbors. These tactics were intended to prevent the government from mobilizing troops and sending them into northeastern regions. Within the space of a year, Sri Lanka lost one-third of its air power and half of its naval power, including the loss of its largest seagoing vessel and her crew, as a result of Tiger efforts.

In November 1995, a Tiger suicide squad struck the heavily defended oil installations in Colombo in a further attempt to prevent troops from striking bases on the Jaffna peninsula, the heartland of the Tamil militants at the northernmost point of Sri Lanka. Ultimately, their tactics proved unsuccessful, as government troops managed to capture Jaffna town shortly afterward. However, the deployment of troops toward Jaffna weakened the Sri Lankan army's presence elsewhere, enabling the Tigers to regroup in the east and concentrate their resources in coastal regions around Batticaloa and Trincomalee.

Tiger bombing attacks continued into 1996. On January 31, a suicide bomber rammed a truck full of high explosives and shrapnel into the Central Bank in the heart of commercial Colombo, killing nearly 100 and injuring more than 1,600 civilians.

THE TERRORIST MOVEMENT TODAY

The globally televised bombing of the Central Bank helped the Tigers to cripple tourism, foreign and domestic investments, and economic growth in Sri Lanka, but it has also brought international condemnation. Many governments that previously tolerated seminars and demonstrations organized by Tamil citizens are now turning their backs; world opinion appears to be turning against the Tigers.

By mid-1996, with the exception of the government-held Jaffna peninsula, the Tigers controlled most of northern Sri Lanka. There, they ran an illegal, independent sub-government ruling an extensive Tamil area and operating like a multinational corporation. The Tigers established their own military, judiciary, postal, and economic systems, with departments ranging from medicine and engineering to reconnaissance and intelligence, education, and culture. By the fall of 1996, Sri Lankan forces were beginning to overrun Tiger strongholds, despite heavy opposition from the guerrillas.

The strengthening of the Tigers' infrastructure has prompted new international security arrangements. Tigers have assassinated opponents to the Tamil independence struggle not only in India, but also in France, Germany, Britain, and Canada. The Tigers have always been fearful of being branded a terrorist organization by the world community, as this would lead to the closure of their offices and deportation of supporters in the West. In 1995, however, the U.S. State Department branded the Tigers a "terrorist group." British politicians have also denounced the regime and its bombing campaigns, while commending the Sri Lankan government's attempts to achieve a peaceful solution.

President Chandrika Kumaratunga has been campaigning for the creation of a union of Sri Lankan regions. Through this, she will devolve power and offer a measure of autonomy to the Tamils, but will also maintain the national unity sought by the Sinhala majority. However, Sinhalese citizens remain distrustful of her intentions, and the UNP opposition party will not support her attempts for constitutional change until the Tamil militants have been suppressed.

But the Tigers won a spectacular victory in July 1996 at Mullaithivu, a Sri Lankan army base, killing or capturing some 1,400 army personnel. This Mullaithivu debâcle has been a massive setback for the government's peace plan, suggesting that, despite their losses at Jaffna, the Tigers remain a powerful military force.

After a quarter of a century of conflict, the Tigers remain at the cutting edge of insurgent technology, military adaptation and innovation. They have perfected the art of mobile warfare and suicide bombings. Their strategies continue to be lethal, despite the efforts of two strong opponents: the Indian military – the world's fourth largest army – and the highly trained Sri Lankan military. To date, all peace initiatives have failed.

Ultimately, the fortunes of the Tamil independence movement may lie with Prabhakaran and his single-minded nationalist policies. The Tiger leader may be forced to adapt his stance to changing world opinion and agree to negotiations for a political solution. He is, however, uncompromisingly ruthless, as illustrated by the recent decision to execute his long-time deputy and old friend Ajith Mahendrarajah. Furthermore, Prabhakaran has groomed an even more committed and equally uncompromising junior leadership to take over the Tigers, should he be captured or killed.

Rohan Gunaratna

SEE ALSO: TERROR GROUP ORGANIZATION; ASSASSINATION; TERRORIST FUNDRAISING; SUICIDE BOMBING.

FURTHER READING

- Austin, Dennis. *Democracy and Violence in India and Sri Lanka.* London: Pinter, 1994; New York: Council on Foreign Relations Press, 1995.
- Rubin, Barnett R. *Cycles of Violence: Human Rights in Sri Lanka.* Washington, DC: Asia Watch, 1987.

SIKH NATIONALIST TERRORISM IN INDIA

Religious and ethnic differences underlie militant Sikh nationalism in India. Since the early 1980s, Sikh extremists have used extortion, bombings, and hit squads to achieve their goal of an independent Sikh-controlled state. In the face of these terrorist attacks, the Indian government has responded severely, with torture and summary executions. In all, more than 20,000 people – civilians, terrorists, and police – have been killed. At the height of the violence, many ordinary citizens faced the terror of the Indian police by day and of the militants by night.

THE BIRTH OF SIKHISM

Sikhism originated in Punjab, in the northwest of India, with Guru Nanak (1469-1538). In 1526, Babur, a central Asian adventurer, conquered northern India and created the Mughal empire. Although the majority of the people in the north were Hindu or Sikh, the Mughal rulers established Islam as the dominant religion. To defend themselves against Mughal persecution, the Sikhs became a warrior community. In 1699, the tenth and final Guru, Gobind Singh, completed this transformation, establishing the *Khalsa*, which replaced caste distinctions with an ideal brotherhood. All Sikh men wore a steel bracelet, carried a knife, and took the name Singh, meaning "lion."

At the beginning of the nineteenth century, the Sikhs had established an independent state in Punjab, which lasted until conquest by the British in 1849. Many Sikhs joined the British military and police forces in Asia, and Sikhism waned. During the 1880s, however, the religion enjoyed a revival and by the 1920s had fostered a mass peasant movement. A Sikh political party, the Akali Dal, was established, which regained control of Sikh temples from non-Sikhs.

KEY FACTS

- Sikh terrorists have been behind the assassination of several major Indian political figures.
- Discrimination by predominantly Hindu governments is the reason militants cite for their terror campaign.
- In Punjab, Sikhs make up 63 percent of the population and Hindus 35 percent. But Sikhs make up only two percent of India's total population compared to 82 percent for Hindus.

INDEPENDENCE FOR INDIA

When India gained independence from Britain in 1947, a separate Muslim state of Pakistan was formed to the northwest of India. Punjab was split between the two new governments, and many Muslims from Indian Punjab moved to Pakistan. Over the next few years, the Akali Dal tried to win political control of Indian Punjab, but were frustrated by the Hindu majority and competition for Sikh votes from the Congress party. A militant, but nonviolent, Sikh campaign for self-rule followed and, in 1966, Punjab was split again to form a smaller, predominantly Sikh state within India.

When the Akali Dal came to power several times in the 1960s, their administrations were short-lived because of political maneuvers by the Congress party on one side and Sikh extremists on the other. Rapid social and economic change increased political frustration. The 1960s saw great advances in Indian agriculture, with small farms giving way to larger ones. The Sikh-controlled Punjab, a major farming area,

Indira Gandhi was a victim of Sikh terrorism. In October 1984 she was shot by two of her bodyguards, who were Sikhs.

embraced this "green revolution," and became India's leader in economic indicators such as per capita income, paved roads, and rural machinery.

BHINDRANWALE AND SIKH EXTREMISM

A new figure now emerged to lead the militant Sikhs in their demands for more autonomy. In 1978, Sant Jarnail Singh Bhindranwale rose from obscurity as the head of a religious seminary, to lead a movement that soon challenged both the Akali Dal and the Congress-led central government of India. With his thundering style, Bhindranwale urged Sikhs to return to orthodox practices, and called on them to defend themselves with violence against Hindu dominance.

Bhindranwale and his followers took control of the Golden Temple in Amritsar, the Sikhs' holy city. The Indian government, alarmed by Bhindranwale's repeated calls for violence, ordered the army to attack Bhindranwale's supporters in the temple in June 1984. The offensive was known as Operation Bluestar. During two days of fighting, more than 1,000 people were killed. Among them were Bhindranwale and two other important Sikh extremist leaders – Amrik Singh, who had provided recruits through his leadership of the All India Sikh Students Federation, and Shahbeg Singh, who supervised military training.

The operation, involving 70,000 army troops, became a symbol of Hindu repression for the Sikhs. Pictures of tanks destroying parts of the Golden Temple antagonized Sikhs worldwide.

ASSASSINATION OF INDIRA GANDHI

Following Operation Bluestar, militant Sikh activity increased. In October 1984, Indira Gandhi, prime minister of India, was gunned down by two of her Sikh bodyguards. The assassins then threw down their guns, proclaiming that the killing had been carried out in retaliation for the Golden Temple massacre. Other bodyguards arrested them and locked them up in a guardroom. The next morning, guards opened fire on the assassins when, it was claimed, they tried to grab some weapons. One was killed and the other paralyzed.

The assassination of Indira Gandhi triggered Hindu riots in cities across India, primarily New Delhi. The rioters killed more than 2,000 Sikhs and caused considerable damage to Sikh property. Large numbers of Sikhs began to question their Indian identity. Rajiv Gandhi, who succeeded his mother as prime minister, seemed to offer a "healing hand" to Sikhs, when he negotiated an accord with the Akali Dal leadership. After the death of Bhindranwale, the militants splintered and, for a while, prospects for reconciliation appeared good.

However, in May 1985, militants launched a bombing campaign in New Delhi to publicize the imminent anniversary of the Golden Temple incident. Most of the bombs were booby-trapped transistor radios, which exploded when turned on. The bombing campaign left 84 people dead and 100 injured. In a separate incident in Punjab, militants murdered Choudhury Balbir Singh, a prominent advocate of Hindu-Sikh brotherhood, on his farm. In October, extremists assassinated Akali Dal leader Harchand Singh Longowal at a political rally by Sikh extremists, who refused to accept any deal with the Hindus. During his address, four youths stood up and opened fire. One assassin, injured during the incident, later died from his wounds in police custody.

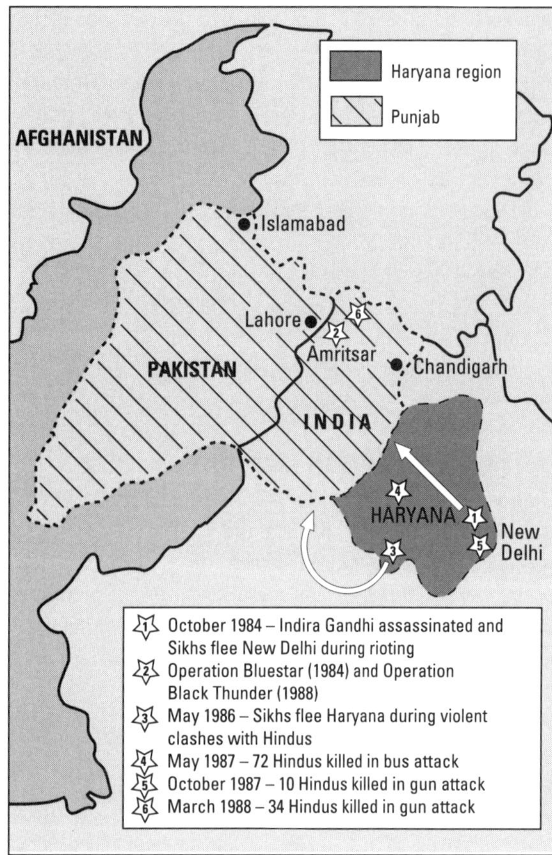

Major incidents in India in the 1980s arising from conflict between Sikhs and Hindus.

In 1985, the Akali Dal won a clear majority in state elections in Punjab. Rajiv Gandhi now proved unwilling to implement the accord, and, consequently, the Akali Dal began to lose support in Punjab. Terrorist acts continued and the situation deteriorated. In 1986, militant groups regained control of the Golden Temple in Amritsar, and a mass meeting declared the goal of an independent Sikh state. The following year the Akali Dal state administration fell, and the central Indian government imposed direct rule. The authorities suspended local government, and a demoralized police gave way to ever larger numbers of paramilitary forces.

GROWING SIKH TERROR

Four major groups dominated the Sikh terrorism at this time. Babbar Khalsa (BK), who were reputedly the most religiously zealous, specialized in bomb attacks. The Bhindranwale Tiger Force (BTF), Khalistan Liberation Force (KLF), and the Khalistan Commando Force (KCF) were the other major organizations. In turn, these four contained almost 150 subgroups. An additional 22 independent extremist movements made a total of 167 terrorist groups in operation. Their leaders had military titles like "General" or "Lieutenant General."

Innocent bus passengers were frequent victims of terrorist attacks. In Punjab in July 1987, seven Sikh gunmen forced Hindu passengers off a bus, then shot and killed 32 and wounded 38. A terrorist killed in the crossfire was carrying a letter saying he was a member of the Khalistan Commando Force. The next night terrorists boarded two buses and killed 36 passengers near the Punjab border.

Sikhs also used assassination against the Indian authorities. One of their more daring exploits was the killing of retired general A. S. Vaidya, who was commander-in-chief of the army when it stormed the Golden Temple in Amritsar. Four Sikhs drew up on motor scooters and ambushed him in his car. They shot him in the head and neck from point blank range.

There were about 600 killings in 1986 and more than 1,000 every succeeding year until 1993. Official figures recorded the number of killings in 1990, 1991, and 1992 as 3,787, 4,768, and 3,629 respectively. Increased firepower is probably the major reason for this escalation in the number of killings. In December 1987, Chinese-built AK-47 assault rifles flowed in large numbers from Afghanistan, through Pakistan, and into Punjab. They were followed by rocket launchers, grenades, bombs, plastic explosives, and mines. Various sources provided funding for these expensive weapons. Criminal activities included extortion, bank robberies, kidnappings, and drug and gun smuggling. Extortion alone is estimated to have raised more than $3 million between 1987 and 1992. Sikh communities in England and North America, and support from Pakistan, were also sources of funding.

Efforts at coordination between the Sikh militant groups led to the establishment of a Panthic (group of five) Committee in 1986, and an international body, the Council of Khalistan, in 1987. But competing Panthic Committees emerged, and control was difficult.

ARMY AND POLICE RESPONSE

Military responses to Sikh terrorism became more sophisticated. The surgical nature of Operation Black Thunder in May 1988 contrasted with the crude

Popperfoto

The remains of Chief Minister Beant Singh's car, blown up by a suicide bomber in August 1995.

Operation Bluestar in 1984. Militants were once again cleared from the Golden Temple, but this time with minimal force, and under the scrutiny of more than 100 journalists and television reporters. About 30 militants were killed and 200 surrendered. Most Sikhs recognized both the military's restraint and the desecration of the temple by the militants. As a result, Hindu-Sikh relations were not significantly harmed.

Civic action programs, reminiscent of US efforts to win the "hearts and minds" of villagers in Vietnam, were undertaken by the police and the army. They provided schools, teachers, bridges, footpaths, agriculture programs, sanitation, and even sports equipment and coaches for Sikh communities. Efforts to seal off with an elaborate fence the 75-mile border between Indian Punjab and Pakistan began in 1988.

A reorganized, well armed police force remained the core of the offensive against the terrorists. They used brutal methods, especially after police relatives became terrorist targets. Summary police executions of terrorist suspects were often preceded by prolonged torture. Both Indian and international human rights organizations such as Amnesty International and Asia Watch monitored the violence and documented police brutality against hundreds of innocent Sikhs.

Paramilitary security forces expanded. Two major units supporting the regular police and army were the Central Reserve Police Force and the Border Security Forces. More than 100,000 troops provided security for elections originally scheduled for June 1991 but eventually held in February 1992. They continued to assist with security long after this.

Improved security reduced terrorism, starting in 1992-3, and by 1995 terrorist numbers had dropped. State intelligence reported just 211 terrorists in operation. But small bands remained, and sporadic violence continued. On August 31, 1995, a suicide bomber killed the chief minister of Punjab, Beant Singh, as he approached his car outside the guarded government building in Chandigarh. The explosion killed 12 others and injured 30 more. Bombs also occasionally exploded in New Delhi, the national capital.

Restarting the political process also contributed significantly to the reduction in terrorist activities. One of India's leading newspapers, *The Times of India*, emphasized the importance of democracy in solving the situation in Punjab. "While security action can curb the terrorists temporarily," one editorial stated, "only the democratic process can destroy the roots of terrorism." Although most Sikhs boycotted the national elections in February 1992, resulting in a very low 21 percent participation, municipal elections in Punjab in September of the same year drew almost 70 percent of the electorate.

Participation remained high for rural local elections through the early 1990s and, gradually, the Akali Dal replaced the terrorist groups as the major vehicle for rural Sikh political expression. The Akali Dal replaced the Congress party as the dominant political party in Punjab as it swept the parliamentary elections in April 1996. Through a combination of severe police methods and effective politics, terrorism in Punjab began to be contained, although not eliminated.

Paul Wallace

SEE ALSO: TERROR IN COLONIAL INDIA 1900-1947; NATIONALIST TERRORISM; BOMBING OPERATIONS; ASSASSINATION, TERROR IN THE VIETNAM WAR.

FURTHER READING

- Biswakesh, Tripathy. *Terrorism and Insurgency in India, 1900-1985.* Lexington, MA: Pacific Press, 1986.
- Pettigrew, Joyce. *The Sikhs of the Punjab: Unheard Voices of State and Guerilla Violence.* Atlantic Highlands, NJ and London: Zed Books, 1995.
- Wallace, Paul "Political Violence and Terrorism in India," in *Terrorism in Context,* edited by M. Crenshaw. University Park: Pennsylvania State University Press, 1995.

TERROR BY THE HOLY WARRIORS OF KASHMIR

Away from the glare of the international media, a holy war in which terrorism plays an increasingly important part has raged in the 1990s in the beautiful Kashmir valley. This valley is part of the disputed territory of Jammu and Kashmir, incorporated into the state of India in 1957 and situated in the far northwest of that country. Jammu and Kashmir borders China and Pakistan, and is close to Afghanistan and the former Soviet Union.

In a campaign reminiscent of those waged in Vietnam or Afghanistan, 20,000 *mujahideen* ("holy warriors") face one of the largest fighting forces in the world, the 400,000 troops of the Indian military. The *mujahideen*, drawn from countries throughout the Middle East and elsewhere, have gained skills by fighting in conflicts in Afghanistan, Tajikistan, Chechnya, Algeria, and Bosnia. To counterbalance the disproportionate strength of the Indian army, the *mujahideen* employ guerrilla warfare and terrorism.

THE ORIGINS OF THE CONFLICT

When the British left India in 1947, the subcontinent was divided into a largely Hindu India and a largely Muslim Pakistan. A controversy arose over the fate of Jammu and Kashmir, a state ruled by a Hindu maharajah but with a population that was 80 percent Muslim. Indian troops occupied two-thirds and Pakistan one-third of the disputed territory. The United Nations proposed a plebiscite in which the Kashmiris were asked to opt for accession either to India or Pakistan. However, India repeatedly prevented this plebiscite from taking place, and in 1957 announced that Jammu and Kashmir was to be an integral part of the Indian Union. The part of Jammu and Kashmir that remained under Pakistan's control was known as Free Kashmir.

Both Pakistan and Free Kashmir have encouraged Kashmiri resistance to Indian rule, and India and Pakistan went to war over Kashmir in 1965, and again in 1971. India has consistently blamed Pakistan for supporting terrorism, while Pakistan has drawn attention to the shortcomings of the Indian government, notably in the manipulation of elections and failure to implement pledges to respect Muslim Kashmiri cultural identity.

In the 1970s and 1980s, the international environment, and in particular, the growth of fundamentalist politics, also favored the growth of insurgency in Kashmir. The Islamic revolution in Iran in 1979 boosted Kashmiri confidence in their ability to gain independence. Likewise, the neighboring Afghan campaign proved that a small, highly motivated force could could prevail against a large, highly trained conventional force.

KEY FACTS

- Terror and counterterror has claimed 20,000 lives ; unofficial figures placed the deaths at over 30,000. From October 1994, an average of 10 people have died each day in Kashmir.
- From 1993, Kashmiri *mujahideen* have used a vast array of sophisticated new munitions, including 107mm artillery shells, fin-stabilized 57mm rockets, 60mm mortars, high-velocity grenades for automatic launchers, disposable rocket launchers, and solar panels for charging wireless batteries.

FROM POLITICS TO TERRORISM

A group commited to revolutionary terrorism, the Jammu and Kashmir Liberation Front (JKLF), emerged in Jammu and Kashmir as early as 1966. The JKLF hijacked an aircraft from Kashmir to Pakistan, killed a police officer in Kashmir, and murdered an Indian diplomat in Britain. The group failed, however, to provoke a popular uprising. Traditionally, the

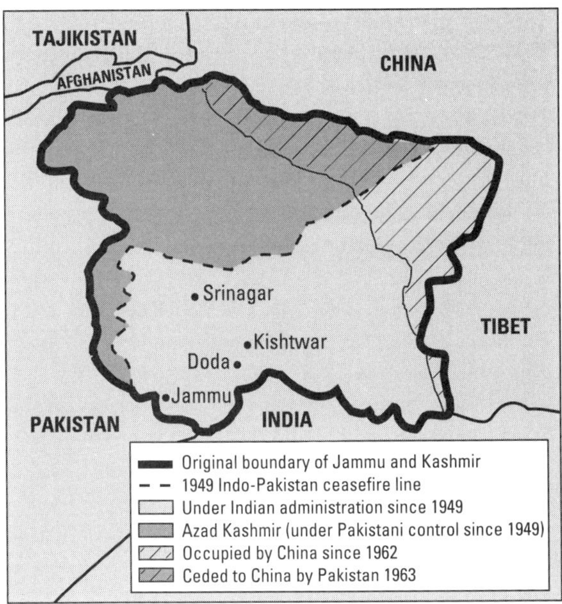

The disputed territory of Jammu and Kashmir in the frontier region of India and Pakistan.

Kashmiris were nonviolent, and agitation against Indian rule remained largely peaceful. However, there was no doubting popular sentiment. Kashmiris celebrated Pakistan Independence Day by raising green flags and denounced Indian Independence Day by raising black flags. Some Kashmiri political leaders exploited anti-Indian feelings to broaden their support. India's response, however, was frequently brutal. Security forces fired on nonviolent protest marches and rallies, and activists were imprisoned and beaten.

THE INFLUX OF *MUJAHIDEEN*

The transition from peaceful politics to violent resistance was accelerated by the massive influx of foreign *mujahideen* into Kashmir. After the Soviet withdrawal from Afghanistan in the late 1980s, many of the Pakistan-based war veterans drifted towards another conflict in the region. This movement accelerated in the 1990s when the Pakistani government, panicked by the growth of fundamentalist terrorism both within its borders and internationally, ordered the deportation of many of the 5,000 foreign veterans living in Pakistan.

As a consequence, there are *mujahideen* fighters of at least twenty nationalities and more than a hundred organizations currently active within Kashmir. The majority are Middle Eastern Arabs, but there are *mujahideen* from Afghanistan, Algeria, Azad Kashmir, Bangladesh, Bosnia, Kazakhstan, Nigeria, Pakistan, Somalia, and Sudan. The most powerful *mujahideen* organizations operating in the Kashmir include the Hizbal Mujahideen (Warriors of God), al-Jihad (Holy Warriors), Harakatul Ansar (Movement of Helpers), al-Umar (Warriors of Caliph al-Umar), Hizb'allah, and the Muslim Brotherhood. No political area has produced as many terrorist groups as Kashmir.

Most of the *mujahideen* fight out of the powerful conviction that Islam is in danger from "foreign" aggression, or to restore the Islamic character of the nation-state – ideas drawn from the teachings of the Iranian Ayatollah Khomeini. There is, however, disagreement over what should happen to Jammu and Kashmir. Almost all the fundamentalist religious groups favor accession to Pakistan, while a minority of JKLF-led Kashmiri nationalists favor independence. This division sometimes breaks out into violence. For example, in 1994, pro-Pakistan *mujahideen* abducted and killed Quazi Nissar Ahmed, a prominent religious leader who had accused some militant groups of "holding Kashmir to ransom, to hand it over to Pakistan on a plate."

IDEOLOGY AND STRATEGY

The Islamic fundamentalist groups take an ideological lead from the Organization of Islam, the equivalent of the Muslim Brotherhood in the Middle East. The leaders at the headquarters of the Organization of Islam, based in the Pakistani capital Lahore, play a critical role in almost all *jihad* (holy war) campaigns, from Bosnia in Europe to Mindanao in the Philippines.

The vast majority of *mujahideen* groups in Kashmir, and also the JKLF, are members of the All Parties Hurriyet Conference (APHC). The APHC was founded in 1993 to replace the Organization for the Freedom of Kashmir, which had previously coordinated activity. The APHC advocates neither accession to Pakistan nor independence, but calls for the right to self-determination. In accordance with UN resolutions, APHC calls for a plebiscite in Kashmir. APHC representatives in Indian-occupied Kashmir, Free Kashmir, and Pakistan organize political strategy. Its executive council of seven political parties representing *mujahideen* groups is responsible for policy making. Both India and Pakistan have negotiated with the APHC on political and security matters.

Hulton Getty Picture Collection/Reuters

Four Western hostages captured by the mujahideen *of the al-Faran group, Srinagar, Kashmir, in 1996.*

Military strategy is supposedly set by United Jihad Council (UJC), an alliance of six groups coordinating the war strategy – Operation Balakot, Hizbal Mujahideen, Muslim Janbaz Force, the Movement for the Islamic Jihad, al-Umar, and Hizb'allah. However, it has proved very difficult to establish a common strategy, and the various groups have usually been unwilling to accept central control. The importance of UJC has declined since its foundation in 1990, whereas the politcal direction of the APHC has been enhanced.

MUJAHIDEEN OPERATIONS

The *mujahideen* have been extremely careful to conceal the location of their training and sources of supplies. Although the Indian government accuses Pakistan's Inter-Services Intelligence (ISI) of training and arming Kashmiri insurgents, there was no strong evidence of ISI involvement until 1987. However, from 1989, evidence has emerged of batches of core groups being trained and sent across from Free Kashmir, with weapons ranging from the traditional bolt-action .303 rifle to fully automatic assault rifles. Most *mujahideen* are self-trained or are trained locally in Kashmir. To quote one *mujahideen* district commander: "We are a resistance movement. We are not fighting a planned war. It is an expression of hatred against India. People are fighting India and we cooperate with them. No training is required. I joined the national cadet corps while at school and learned how to operate a weapon."

On the whole, tactics employed by the *mujahideen* do not require formal training. The guerrillas make hit-and-run attacks against Indian army personnel or use sniper fire. By the time Indian forces retaliate, the *mujahideen* are out of sight and it is innocent civilians who bear the brunt of the counterinsurgency. Retaliatory strikes generate support for the *mijahideen* and have supplied fresh recruits. Initially, there were no fixed camps but only hideouts. To quote one *mujahid*, "We had no planned safe area. We exploited the negligence of the Indian patrols. It depended on opportunity. We survived by opportunity."

THE ESCALATION OF TERRORISM

Terrorism spread from the Kashmiri capital of Srinagar both to other urban centers and to rural areas. By 1991, insurgency had engulfed the rural area around Srinagar, while in 1992 and 1993, the insurgents were able to establish liberated zones in some built-up areas. Initially, Kashmiris were horrified by the violence, and were even critical of *mujahideen* action. But for every overreaction by the Indian forces, Kashmiri resistance to *mujahideen* violence waned. Violent incidents increased month after month.

The insurgency had so far been confined to the Kashmir valley, but in 1994, the *mujahideen* moved into Jammu. Here, the insurgents used new tactics, operating out of the sparsely populated mountain forests. This development marked a departure from the *mujahideen*'s usual practice of operating in heavily built-up, densely populated areas like the state capital Srinagar. It proved, however, just as effective and government forces were again unable to quell the insurgency. Schools, private and public buildings, and bridges were razed to the ground.

From 1992 to 1994, the *mujahideen* raided over 13 police stations, taking away more than 100 weapons, 12 radio sets, as well as other supplies. Government stores lost more than 5,000 detonators and 8,000 gelatin rods to the *mujahideen*. On January 26, 1995, India's Republic Day, the *mujahideen* detonated a bomb in the heavily guarded Maulana Azad Stadium in Jammu, killing nine and injuring more than 120 persons. However, a major target of this remote control-activated explosion, Governor General K.V. Krishna Rao, escaped injury.

NEW WEAPONRY

From mid-1993, increasingly more sophisticated weaponry entered the Kashmir valley, dramatically strengthening the *mujahideen*'s firepower and ability to carry out large-scale operations. The *mujahideen* used artillery shells as improvised explosive devices,

Hulton Getty Picture Collection/Reuters

Basharat Noori (center), local commander of the Jammu and Kashmir Liberation Front, gives order to militants. Noori claimed that India was behind the kidnapping of the four Western hostages in 1996.

and the 57mm rockets (designed to attack helicopters) were triggered with solar-powered improvised direction-giving devices. Other equipment included Japanese pen pistols, silencers for automatic rifles and pistols, and infrared telescopes for Soviet-made Dragnov sniper rifles. Some radio sets recovered had ranges up to 250 miles and possessed frequency-hopping, selective-broadcast, and digital-burst communication facilities. Large numbers of such radio sets were also distributed to sympathizers to provide warning of advancing troops.

The intensification of the insurgency is indicated by the increasing numbers of weapons recovered by the Indian authorities. In 1992, Indian troops seized 13 sniper rifles; in the following year, more than 60 were recovered. Troops recovered 1,474 AK-series assault rifles in 1988-90, but 3,775 in 1992 alone. In 1990, there were 36 *mujahideen* companies operating, but in 1993 there were 300.

Indian security forces found it difficult to match such well-equipped terrorists. Almost all service personnel, except elite troops, were armed with self-loading rifles – weapons inferior to the fully automatic AK types used by the *mujahideen*. Nor was the experience of counterterrorism gained in northeastern India, the Punjab, and Sri Lanka passed down to the troops on the ground in Kashmir.

The international community largely ignored the situation in Kashmir. In 1994, however, a *mujahideen* group called the Harakatul Ansar attempted to draw media attention by kidnapping two British tourists. The tourists were eventually released unhurt. The following year, another militant separatist group, al-Faran, took five Western tourists hostage, demanding the release of 21 imprisoned Kashmiri militants. When the Indian government refused, they severely tortured and then beheaded a Norwegian tourist. Despite attempts by, among others, U.S. President Clinton to put pressure on Pakistan to use its influence among the Kashmiri separatists groups, the remaining four tourists have not yet been released. It is not known whether they are dead or alive.

THE INDIAN ARMY RESPONSE

Indian Union Minister for Internal Security Rajesh Pilot had advocated a "soft line" in Kashmir since February 1993. And in mid-1993, when the Kashmir Governor Rao was reappointed, he told the press that the strategy was "to be soft on the public and hard on the militants." India has appointed human rights cells to monitor violations. But, in practice, it has been difficult for troops trained in conventional warfare to fight against a foe skilled in terrorism without inflicting heavy civilian casualties.

Rohan Gunaratna

SEE ALSO: COLLABORATION BETWEEN TERRORISTS; ROOTS OF FUNDAMENTALIST TERRORISM; TERRORISM AND REVOLUTION IN IRAN; IRANIAN SPONSORSHIP OF TERRORISM; SIKH NATIONALIST TERRORISM IN INDIA.

FURTHER READING

- Baker, William W. *Kashmir: Happy Valley, Valley of Death.* Las Vegas: Defenders Publications, 1994.
- Kadian, Rajesh. *The Kashmir Tangle: Issues and Options.* Boulder, CO: Westview Press, 1993.
- Newberg, Paula R. *Double Betrayal: Repression and Insurgency in Kashmir.* Washington, DC: Carnegie Endowment for International Peace, 1995.
- Rahman, Mustaqur. *Divided Kashmir: Old Problems, New Opportunities for India, Pakistan, and the Kashmiri People.* Boulder, CO: Lynne Rienner, 1996.
- Wirsing, Robert. *India, Pakistan and the Kashmir Dispute: On Regional Conflict and Its Resolution.* London: Macmillan, and New York: St. Martin's Press, 1994.

NATIONAL AND ETHNIC TERROR IN THE FORMER SOVIET UNION

The dissolution of the Soviet Union led inevitably to widespread terrorist activity resulting mainly from nationalist insurgency. Released from the tyranny of the state, ethnic enclaves sought self-identity and independence. When political solutions failed to materialize, extremists frequently turned to violence as a means to an end. Many such conflicts continue to this day.

STATE TERROR UNDER JOSEPH STALIN

Terror was not new to the former Soviet Union, having been used by the state to impose its political will on the people. The Soviet Union stretched from Eastern Europe across Asia to the Bering Straits west of Alaska. It comprised vastly different peoples with nothing in common other than formerly being part of the Russian empire. In a bid to stamp out national identity, whole peoples were forcibly relocated, many to the Soviet Far East, while others were brought in to take their place. Terrorist acts against the state occurred under Stalin, but were put down with the utmost ferocity. When Leningrad party boss Sergei Kirov was shot in December 1934 by dissident Leonid Nikolayev, Stalin ordered Nikolayev's execution, along with 13 other "plotters," while 66 "White Guard terrorists" were convicted and shot in Moscow. Stalin also relocated members of groups suspected of collaboration with the Nazis.

When the last Soviet leader, Mikhail Gorbachev, brought in *perestroika* (restructuring) in 1985, many ethnic groups began to demand more political control over their affairs. After the Soviet Union was dissolved in 1991, millions of displaced people sought to re-draw

SUMMARY

- National and ethnic identities were brutally suppressed during the 74-year existence of the Soviet Union.
- The dissolution of the Soviet Union in 1991 prompted claims for independence and a return of their former homelands by many ethnic groups.
- Terrorist campaigns have been part of a wider military strife by separatists during the early 1990s.

Hulton Getty Picture Collection/Reuters

Chechen rebels hold Russian-made anti-tank mines used in the war for independence from Russia.

Popperfoto

Abkhazian separatists leave the safety of a shelter during fighting with Georgian troops, June 6, 1993.

boundaries and recover their own territory, forcing out those who had been resettled there. Terror now became the weapon of the people.

TERROR IN THE TRANSCAUCASUS

In the late 1980s, as the government in Moscow lost control over the Soviet Union's smaller states, old enmities began to surface. Christian Armenians demanded the return of Nagorno-Karabakh, a landlocked Armenian enclave in neighboring Muslim Azerbaijan. They organized a riot in the Azeri city of Sumgait. Gorbachev responded by sending in the Red Army, but the fuse of ethnic conflict had been lit. A wave of nationalism swept through Azerbaijan, and Armenians bore the brunt of the violence. During a rally in the Azeri capital Baku in January 1990, Armenian homes were looted and set on fire, and hundreds were killed. Again, Soviet troops were sent in, killing 60 people as they smashed the uprising.

Terrorist acts were not confined within the borders of the warring states. In 1994, for example, Armenians murdered two Chechens in London for allegedly attempting to purchase arms for the Azeri government. But terrorism soon escalated into all-out civil war; although it was terminated by a cease-fire in 1994, the wrangling over Nagorno-Karabakh continues.

The state of Georgia was also convulsed by terrorism leading up to independence from the crumbling Soviet Union in 1991. Georgia was one of the few territories where the ethnic population remained largely intact. However, the small enclave of South Ossetia, of a different ethnic origin, declared itself a separate republic in 1990. The Georgian National Guard, made up of formerly illegal paramilitary troops, was mobilized to quell disturbances. It took the intervention of Soviet troops, and a ceasefire in 1992, to halt brutal reprisals.

Georgia's northwestern province of Abkhazia suffered a similar fate in 1992, when nationalists sought separation from Georgia and alliance with Russia. Although supported by Russian military intelligence and soldiers, the Abkhazis suffered the loss of 3,000 lives before the 1994 ceasefire ended hostilities.

CONFLICT IN CHECHNYA

Also involved in the Abkhazi uprising were some 8,000 north Caucasian volunteers, whose members came mostly from neighboring Chechnya. This state remained under the rule of Russia when the Soviet Union was dissolved, but separatist groups seeking

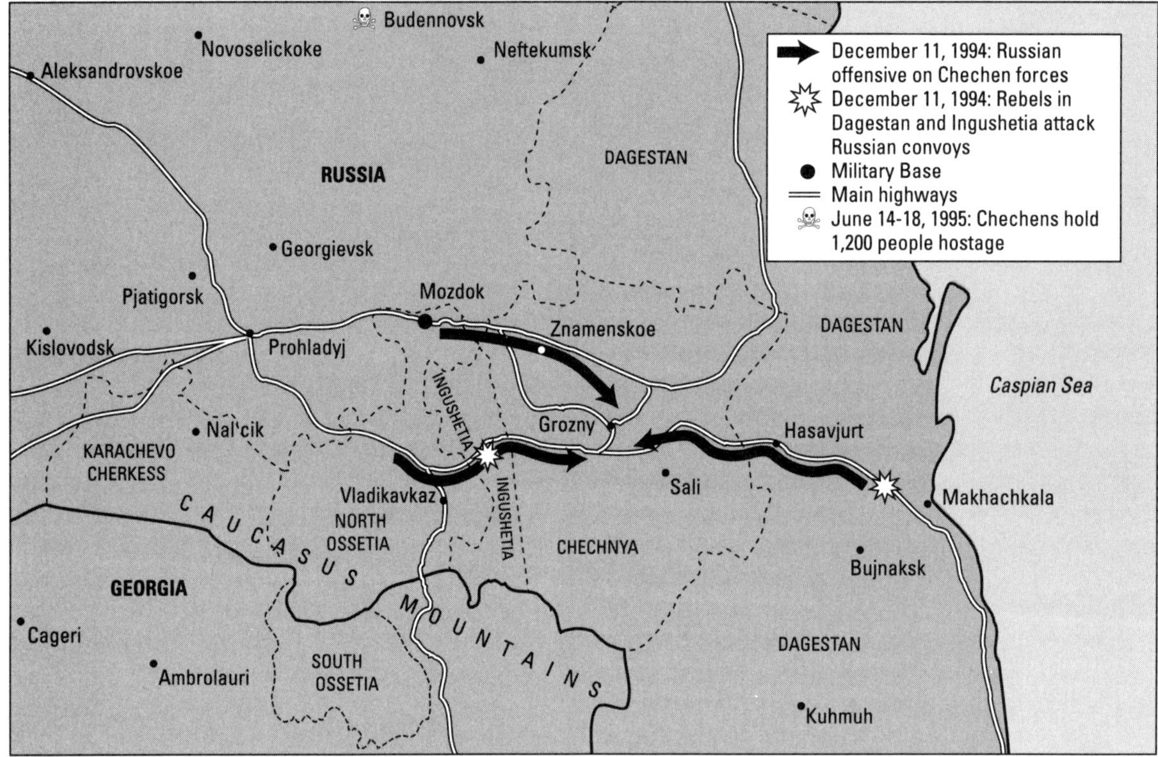

Principal incidents between Chechen rebels and Russian troops since the conflict began in 1991.

independence began a campaign of terrorism soon after, which included hostage-taking and attacks on Russian installations. The campaign spread to adjacent countries where large numbers of Chechens were settled. In January 1996, for example, Turkish Chechens hijacked a ship in the Black Sea to demonstrate solidarity with their compatriots.

The situation in Chechnya evolved into a show of military strength between Russian president Boris Yeltsin, determined to maintain Russian rule, and Chechen president and former Soviet air force general Dzhokar Dudayev. In response to Yeltsin's decision to send in the Russian army in December 1994, the Chechens launched terrorist operations, principally in the capital, Grozny. Snipers holed up in derelict buildings picked off Russian troops, while small teams disrupted military supply lines. Yeltsin denounced the Chechen separatists as terrorists and, indeed, a good proportion of their armed forces were rumored to be mercenaries from places as diverse as Azerbaijan, Ukraine, Lithuania, Egypt, Jordan, and Afghanistan.

The conflict developed into an extended war early in 1995, and over the next 18 months claimed the lives of up to 50,000 people – mostly civilians. In April 1996, Dudayev was killed by Russian forces. His successor Zelimkhan Yandarbiyev has indicated no change in the aim of complete and total independence.

TERRORIST THREAT TO RUSSIA

Prominent in perpetrating acts of terrorism in Russia were Chechen separatists. Prior to the Chechen war, there were numerous hijackings in the north Caucasus, frequently involving individuals demanding to be taken to Chechnya. For example, three hostage incidents in southern Russia between May and July 1994 involved bus hijackings by Chechens. From June 14 to 18, 1995, 100 fighters led by Shamil Basayev held 1,200 people hostage at a hospital in Budennovsk, 75 miles north of the Chechen border. The attack was an act of reprisal after Russian forces had taken Basayev's home town of Vedeno and killed his family. In response, the Russian government sent in crack troops, resulting in the deaths of more than a hundred people in Budennovsk. The Chechens also targeted

The Central Asian republics of the former Soviet Union. Many have experienced ethnic unrest and terrorism since 1991.

Russian civilians. In November 1995, they claimed that nuclear material had been hidden in a Moscow park and that they would contaminate the city if their demands were not met.

Russia itself has not been immune from terrorist factions. In 1992, government sources estimated that there were 15 groups with political aspirations in the Moscow region alone. These included Chechens, Azeris, and various northern Caucasian groups from Dagestan, Ossetia, Armenia, and Georgia.

Extremist groups in Russia represent further potential threats to central government. Many of these have openly developed paramilitary wings, are overtly fascist and anti-Semitic, and in some cases call for the overthrow of the state. Their public statements and documents often advocate terrorist actions, although they have perpetrated none so far. Strongholds of activity include St. Petersburg, Moscow, and Siberia. One such group, Russian National Unity, under former special forces officer Alexander Barkashov, is believed to have thousands of members, more than 350 regional branches, and a highly disciplined military arm. It has a Nazi-style agenda, seeking to keep Russia racially pure, and claims to have a surprise plan to take power.

Smaller and less focused groups led by ex-military officers include the Public Club Union of Officers, founded in 1991, which took part in the unsuccessful siege of the Russian parliament building in October 1993. The Congress of Russian Communities, who are committed to defending Russians in bordering states, has a paramilitary arm called the Russian Knights. They have been suspected of supporting Russian separatists in the Crimean part of the Ukraine.

ETHNIC CLASHES IN THE UKRAINE

Apart from a brief period after the end of World War I, the vast land of Ukraine – almost as large as Texas – had never been independent. In the twentieth century, Ukrainian nationalists have been responsible for a shocking catalog of terrorist atrocities.

As early as 1920, many thousands of Jews were massacred in a wave of anti-Semitism. And during World War II, Ukrainian nationalists assisted the Nazis in implementing the "Final Solution." Since the breakup of the Soviet Union, political parties have sprung up, such as the Union in Support of Ukrainian State Independence, whose aims include "ethnic cleansing." This xenophobia has been particularly directed against the Russian population, concentrated mainly in the Crimea in the south. This region is 70 percent Russian, and many would prefer to be ruled from Moscow than from Kiev, the capital of Ukraine.

A series of terrorist acts and assassinations in late 1993 and early 1994 preceded the Crimean presidential elections. Extremist groups, such as the Ukrainian People's Self Defense Force, were widely believed to be responsible for seeking to pervert the course of the election by terrorist means. Yuri Meshkov of the Republican Party of Crimea won the election on a platform advocating reunion with Russia.

Russian-Ukrainian antagonisms in Crimea have been further aggravated by the Muslims of Tatarstan. Since 1991, 250,000 Tatars have returned to their Crimean homeland. The majority are poor and have no vote, and so separatist groups, such as the All-Tatar Public Center under Marat Mulyukov, have threatened a terrorist campaign if their interests are ignored. They set up armed units in 1992, but these were banned after clashes with the Crimean authorities during October 1992. Several groups – the Majlis and Kurultai of the Crimean Tatar people, and the Crimean Tatars National Movement – have threatened violence against the Meshkov government.

ISLAMIC TENSIONS IN THE EAST

In the eastern regions of the former Soviet Union, religious as well as separatist aims have motivated many extremists to mount terrorist attacks on the ruling powers. The most serious conflict began in 1990 in Tajikistan, leaving over 50,000 people dead and half-a-million refugees. The communist government, led by Imamali Rakhmanov from 1992, controlled just one-third of the country, and then only with the help of 50,000 Russian troops. Against them were the Democratic Party aligned with the Islamic Renaissance Party, whose goals included power-sharing with democratic groups and bringing Islamic principles into government. There was also the more radical-nationalist Rastokhez Patriotic Movement, which allegedly had links to Iran. Driven from Tajikistan after Rakhmanov's rise to power, these parties continued to operate from refugee camps in Afghanistan. Cross-border incursions included attacks on Russian troops – for example, the killing of 20 border guards on July 20, 1993.

NO SCOPE FOR DISSENT

Not all former member states of the Soviet Union have experienced militant insurgency. In Belarus, there is almost no evidence of radical political groups, and in the states of Turkmenistan and Uzbekistan the governments have suppressed opposition. The Uzbek government banned all Islamic parties, and the Birlik (Unity) movement – the country's largest nationalist group – in 1993. However, Uzbekistan has seen bloodshed. In one incident, 100 people died in ethnic riots in June 1989. Kyrgyzstan, the most democratic state in former Soviet Central Asia, has also had its share of violence. Riots, sparked by Uzbek demands to be reunited with Uzbekistan, left 200 dead in June 1992.

Unstable conditions across the former Soviet Union threaten to create a generation of "proto-terrorists." If economic conditions and cultural identities are not respected, groups which already use institutionalized violence may turn to guerrilla warfare and terrorism to achieve their objectives. The proto-terrorists of today may turn into the full-fledged terrorists of tomorrow.

Elaine M. Holoboff

SEE ALSO: RUSSIAN ANARCHIST TERROR; THE ARMENIAN MASSACRES; STALIN'S GREAT TERROR; NATIONALIST TERRORISM.

FURTHER READING

- Berberoglu, Berch, ed. *The National Question: Ethnic Conflict and Self-Determination in the Twentieth Century.* Philadelphia: Temple University Press, 1995.
- Duncan, W. Raymond, and G. Paul Holman. *Ethnic Nationalism and Regional Conflict: The Former Soviet Union and Yugoslavia.* Boulder, CO: Westview Press, 1994.
- Kaiser, Robert J. *The Geography of Nationalism in Russia and the U.S.S.R.* Chichester and Princeton, NJ: Princeton University Press, 1994.
- Szporluk, Roman. *National Ethnicity and Identity in Russia and the New States of Eurasia.* Armonk, NY: M.E. Sharpe, 1994.

CHAPTER FIFTEEN

Terror in War and Civil War Since 1945

Civilians have been murdered in their millions in the years since the end of World War II. Deliberate campaigns of terror have been waged against them by their ethnic and ideological rivals, particularly during civil wars. Racial hatred of the enemy has allowed both regular soldiers and guerrillas to dehumanize their opponents, thereby making atrocities much more likely. Fear of the enemy and the absence of effective command have helped to create the conditions in which even trained troops have carried out terrorist acts.

TERROR IN WAR AND CIVIL WAR SINCE 1945: Introduction

The post-1945 world has been dominated by two types of conflict. First, the rival superpowers, the United States, the Soviet Union, and China, either directly or indirectly through their proxies, have fought to defend their spheres of influence. Examples include the Korean War, during which the North was backed by the Soviet Union and China, and the U.S supported the South. Second, there have been have been the numerous civil wars, often in former European colonies, usually involving ethnic or ideological rivals. Terror was a feature of both types of conflict and its victims were overwhelmingly civilians.

In both the Korean and Vietnam Wars, civilians were killed by indiscriminate fire and mass bombing. Others were assassinated because they actively supported the enemy or were believed to do so. In Vietnam, the North Vietnamese and Viet Cong targeted petty administrators for execution to undermine the South Vietnamese government's authority. The South responded by torturing and murdering villagers believed to be sympathetic to the North, or by razing their homes. Prisoners of war were frequently terrorized into providing intelligence or simply summararily shot.

Most of these wars and civil wars were fought in two ways. There was conventional fighting between trained regular troops, and counterinsurgency campaigns, usually involving state security troops and special forces. Terrorism was applied to undermine the enemy's effectiveness and, less justifiable, to deny him popular support. The creation of a state of fear by the threat of – or use of – assassination, beatings, and torture was the aim of the terror campaigns. Terror was never a publically stated policy of the conventional forces. However, both the U.S. in Vietnam and the Soviet Union in Afghanistan used terror to cow civilians. The creation of "free fire" zones in Vietnam, within which any individual was a "legitimate" target, and the bombing of villages suspected of harboring Afghan guerrillas, can both be regarded as acts of terror.

Trained soldiers, themselves terrrorized by the horrors of vicious booby traps, were often reduced to using their weapons indiscriminately. The massacre of South Vietnamese villagers at My Lai in 1968 was in part due to the indiscipline of the U.S. troops involved. Fear of the enemy had eroded the usual restraints instilled in soldiers by training and the authority of their commanders in the field.

Civil wars are regarded as potentially the bloodiest type of conflict. Nations where the inhabitants are divided along ethnic or political lines have been torn apart by vicious factional fighting. The deliberate use of terror has been a constant feature. Racial hatred has fueled some of the worst atrocities in the recent past. In former Yugoslavia, the collapse of strong central authority lead to the disintegration of the federation. Some of the individual states, all containing an ethnic minority, were rent apart by terror and guerrilla campaigns. The majority ethnic groups attempted to drive out the minorities, who turned to their own people in neighboring states for protection. Mass murder, the use of officially sanctioned rape and torture, and the creation of concentration camps were used to terrorize civilians into flight. Mortars and artillery were used to speed them on their way. These tactics of terror became known as "ethnic cleansing," a bland term that hardly reflected the scale and intensity of the violence.

Dehumanizing the enemy has allowed professional soldiers or civilians in uniform to commit the most barbarous acts. When the ethnic rivalries between the Hutus and Tutsis in Rwanda degenerated into virtual civil war, regular soldiers gave vent to their ethnic hatred through the mass murder of civilians. Many were hacked to death or mutilated; the frightened survivors fled to the relative safety of neighboring African states.

It is now widely accepted that civilian deaths are an inevitable part of modern conventional warfare involving regular forces. Most of the dead are not victims of a deliberate terror campaign, rather they are victims of weapons of mass destruction used legitimately. However, when these devices are in the hands of warring ethnic or ideological enemies, they are the weapons that allow terror campaigns to be waged. ■

TERROR IN THE KOREAN WAR

From 1910 to the end of World War II in 1945, Korea was a colony of Japan under a harsh military regime. The largest protests against Japanese rule took place on March 1, 1919, when more than a million Koreans demonstrated peacefully all over the country. In response, the Japanese executed more than 7,000 Koreans in order to terrorize the population into submission. An increasingly pervasive police force continued to practice state terror. By 1941, there was one security officer for every 400 people.

After the Japanese surrender in 1945, Koreans hoped that their country would achieve immediate independence. People's committees arose spontaneously, taking on the role of government throughout the peninsula. These committees included all political groups, except those that had collaborated with the Japanese. The groups tended to be dominated by the left, though not by the communists. The left had popular support because it had opposed the Japanese and sympathized with the desire of many rural Koreans for land reform.

All hopes of independence were thwarted, however, by the immediate arrival of Soviet forces in North Korea, and American forces in South Korea, with the occupation zones being divided at the 38th parallel.

The Soviet forces had made some preparations for the occupation. For example, they brought with them credible anti-Japanese Korean figures, including the communist former guerrilla leader Kim Il Sung. The Soviets initially worked through the people's committees, only gradually placing their own nominees in positions of power. In 1946, Kim became chairman of the North Korean Interim People's Committee and implemented the popular measure of land redistribution. The regime used intimidation against right-wing politicians, former collaborators, landowners, and Christians to force them off the land.

By contrast, the U.S. forces were not prepared for occupying Korea. They believed that the radical people's committees were communist fronts and refused to recognize them. They guaranteed a return to order in Korea by working through the existing Japanese government structure that most Koreans hated. In so doing, the U.S. occupation was forced to support politicians of the extreme right. These politicians offered the most reliable opposition to communism but represented only a narrow section of Korean society. Many who had collaborated with the Japanese occupiers were allowed to remain in their positions. For example, more than 75 percent of the senior police officers serving in November 1946 had previously worked with the Japanese colonial police.

SUMMARY

- Between 1945 and 1947, the communists in North Korea forced 800,000 of their opponents to flee to the South.
- Following a number of unsuccessful cross-border raids and terrorist attacks, North Korea finally invaded South Korea in June 1950.
- Reports from North Korea claim that the South Koreans killed 29,000 of their own people who they suspected of cooperating with the communists during the North Korean occupation.
- During the three-year war both sides used terror tactics both against each other and their own people.

THE UN BECOMES INVOLVED

Toward the end of 1947, the U.S. decided to remove its occupation force. It tried to involve the United Nations (UN) in order to strengthen the legitimacy of the government it left behind. In May 1948, a UN commission supervised and then endorsed elections. Seventy-five percent of voters participated, and southern leader Syngman Rhee and his supporters emerged as the largest group in the new National Assembly. As a result, the commission recognized Rhee's pro-Western Republic of Korea as the legitimate government of Korea in the southern zone.

Turkish UN troops search Chinese prisoners during the Korean War. China had entered the conflict in 1950 to repel the UN forces from North Korea.

The reality of the elections, however, was a long way from what might have been expected, given the endorsement of the UN commission and all that it implied. There was left-wing disruption and right-wing intimidation, and the polls were controlled by right-wing police auxiliaries, many of whom were still in their Japanese uniforms. During the 40 days of campaigning for the elections, nearly 600 people were killed in the widespread disturbances. The northern zone responded with its own elections. Little is known about how these elections were run. Much can be assumed, though, from the claimed 99.97 percent participation rate and the universal victory of the communist candidates of the North Korean Labor Party. The Democratic People's Republic of Korea was declared in the north in October 1948, and Soviet forces, their task complete, then withdrew.

From 1948 to 1950, the populations of these competing regimes were subject to widespread terrorism. In North Korea, resistance to the government seems to have been comparatively small, partly because of the popularity of measures such as land reform, and partly because many of the government's opponents had fled to the south.

In South Korea, by contrast, the communists continued to oppose the regime, gaining popular support because of the lack of social reforms instituted by Rhee's government. The government was also implicated in the assassination of politicians who refused to support it. In 1949, for example, an army lieutenant murdered Kim Ku, South Korea's leading moderate. The killer was sentenced to life imprisonment but released within months. Later, he was promoted to lieutenant colonel.

The largest uprising against Rhee's government came on the island of Cheju during 1948-49. The government responded with a program of state terror. The authorities destroyed all the villages in the interior of the island and massacred their inhabitants or moved them to refugee camps on the coast. About 30,000 people, or 10 percent of Cheju's population, were killed in the suppression of the revolt.

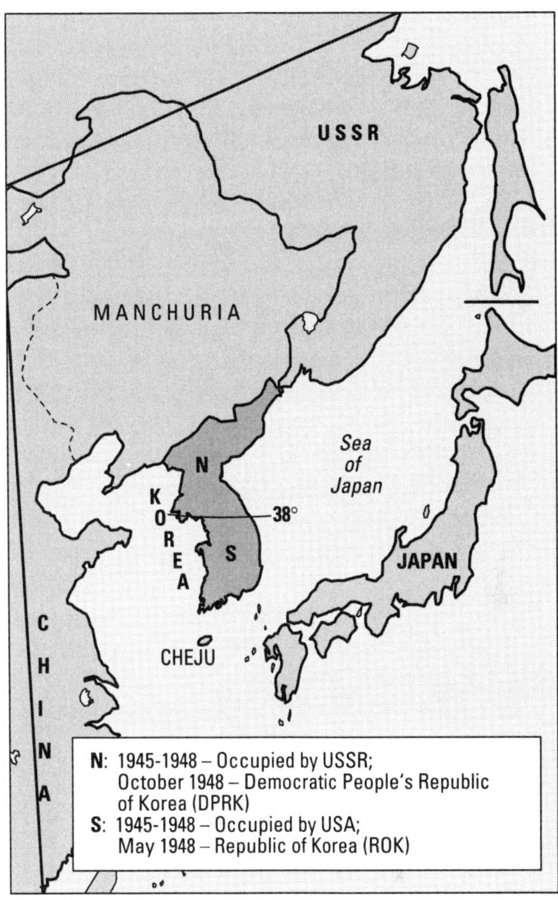

A map showing the 38th parallel, the line that divided the occupation zones during the Korean War.

TERROR IN THE SOUTH AND NORTH

In early 1949, North Korea launched a campaign of propaganda and cross-border raids aimed at weakening South Korean confidence in Syngman Rhee's government. However, by 1950, it was plain to the North Koreans that this campaign was not going to be enough to bring about the South Korean government's collapse. So, on June 25, 1950, North Korea launched an invasion across the 38th parallel. It is now clear that this attack was begun at North Korea's own instigation. The Soviet Union, however, gave the enterprise its blessing and provided the necessary equipment.

The North Koreans hoped that South Korea would fall before the intervention of the United States. In the event, the U.S. led a swift UN intervention. North Korea occupied 90 percent of the Republic of Korea during the summer of 1950 but was then forced back. The UN forces rapidly occupied 90 percent of North Korea between October and December 1950. At this point, the Chinese entered the war and forced the UN back. By the summer of 1951, the battle line was close to the 38th parallel, where it remained until the armistice of July 1953.

North Korea sought to legitimize its invasion by extending reforms in South Korea during the brief period of occupation. However, to demonstrate the price of opposition, it also conducted a purge of those who had collaborated with Rhee's government. Many target groups fled, but thousands of policemen, officials, landlords, and their families were executed without trial. Killings increased as the North Koreans retreated and tried to eliminate people who might collaborate with the UN forces. An estimated 20,000 to 23,000 people were executed during this period, including 300 U.S. prisoners of war.

In addition to this "red terror," there was a "white terror" enacted by South Korean security forces before the North Korean invasion. At the time of the invasion, up to 58,000 suspected communist sympathizers were

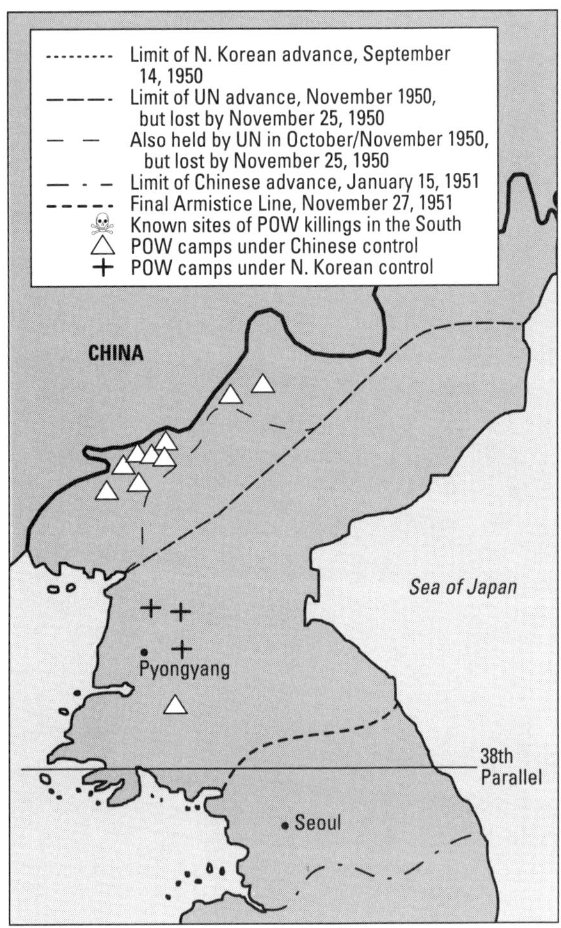

A map of Korea, showing advances made by the armies of North and South, and the many prisoner camps.

languishing in southern jails. When war broke out, many of these prisoners were executed – estimates are as high as 50,000 – because they were considered security risks. The chief of the South Korean police admitted to only 1,200 executions in the first three weeks of fighting. However, a French missionary witnessed the execution of 1,700 prisoners at Taejon early in the war. Before their execution, a British journalist saw 700 prisoners chained at Pusan, and gathered that this process had been "going on for months." A figure of 50,000 deaths is probably too high, but it is possible that as many died in this terror as in the communist occupation.

When Republic of Korea security forces reoccupied their country in October 1950, they unleashed terror on an even greater scale in their search for anyone suspected of having cooperated with the communists. Those defined as cooperating included people who had simply continued in their jobs during the occupation.

In his memoirs, U.S. diplomat Gregory Henderson claimed that "tens of thousands – probably over 100,000 – were killed without any trial whatsoever when [South Korean] soldiers…re-captured…areas of leftist repute." UN officials discounted the massacres publicly, but in private they were prepared to admit to the scale of the massacres.

The problem continued when UN forces entered North Korea in October 1950. The UN hoped that by taking responsibility for the occupation they might avoid the excesses that had taken place in the South. However, South Korean troops made up half the UN army, and all the American and British forces were required at the front. This meant that the occupation of North Korea was left in the very biased hands of the South Koreans. Needless to say, the fiercely anti-communist South Koreans were brutal in their methods. Their militia units were often under minimal central control. Additionally, All but one of the South Korean army's senior officers had previously served with the Japanese military, and many of the junior officers were from the dispossessed families of refugees from North Korea.

The South Koreans also had to cope with an extensive guerrilla campaign in areas occupied by the UN forces. This was waged by scattered bands of North Korean troops, who were ruthless in their exploitation of the civilian population, using children to carry ammunition and refugees to cover their assaults.

APPALLING TOLL ON CIVILIANS

The result of all this terror was that an enormous number of civilians died at the hands of South Korean forces. North Korea has claimed that the civilian death toll amounted to 170,000, with the majority killed when UN forces were forced to retreat after China's intervention in the war. The accuracy of this claim is impossible to verify. However, given the scale of killing undertaken by South Korean forces, it seems likely that tens of thousands were killed. Again, significant eyewitness evidence exists to indicate the extent of the brutality.

Other United Nations forces, which were overwhelmingly American, were not immune from the oppressive atmosphere created by this savage civil war, the stress of guerrilla warfare, and racial isolation.

Understandably, morale was lowest in retreat. Unable to tell friend from foe, many became suspicious of all Koreans and were ready to shoot at the slightest provocation. Suspicion, coupled with weak discipline in some U.S. units early in the war, led to many Korean civilian casualties. The situation improved dramatically from December 23, 1950, when American General Matthew Ridgway took command of the UN forces. He imposed the highest standards of discipline.

From the spring of 1951, the war became steadily less mobile, with the two Korean states maintaining control of their own territories. Both sides continued to use violence and arbitrary executions to suppress any elements of the population suspected of disloyalty. This was particularly the case after periods of enemy occupation, when allegiances became especially open to doubt. However, there are two other elements of terror associated with the latter part of the war: the treatment of prisoners of war and the air attacks.

TORTURE AND EXECUTION

Prisoners on both sides suffered terribly. In the communist camps South Korean prisoners were very badly treated, but 2,701 of the 7,140 U.S. personnel taken also died in captivity. Many died early in the war because of the primitive conditions in the camps, while others were executed. Those prisoners who would not cooperate in communist propaganda were tortured. The methods of torture included being forced to stand for long periods on tiptoe with a taut noose around the neck.

Prisoners in UN hands were guarded largely by South Korean troops. The troops were frequently left alone to physically abuse prisoners. British observers claimed that U.S. troops involved were often inclined to "regard the [prisoners] as cattle." As the war progressed, the prisoners polarized into pro- and anti-communist groups. UN and Chinese agents were placed among the prisoners in order to encourage the different factions. The leaders of both sides used terror to coerce prisoners to join their groups. This included beatings, mutilations, and executions. At one point, UN troops tried to screen the prisoners to see which of them wished to return to China and North Korea. Outraged, the pro-communist compounds rioted. In the ensuing battles, several UN troops and hundreds of prisoners were killed, some by their own comrades when they tried to surrender.

Further allegations of the use of terror emerged from UN air operations. Raids were restricted to defined military targets until the Chinese intervention. After this, the definition of a military target was broadened, in the words of Dean Acheson, the U.S. secretary of state, to include "every means of communication, installation, factory, city, and village in North Korea." North Korea accused the UN of terror bombing. The UN responded that only military targets were attacked, but this claim avoided the issue of the all-inclusiveness of such targets. Frustrated that the industries which supported the communist war effort were outside the country, the UN launched some raids simply to increase the strain of the war. British Prime Minister Winston Churchill wrote, with regard to the use of napalm against Korean cities, that he would take no responsibility "for the indiscriminate use of napalm not in warfare but to torture the civilian population." The final civilian casualty toll is uncertain, although estimates by U.S. High Command of two million killed or injured may be exaggerated.

Terror was a major aspect of policy during the Korean War. Ultimately, North Korea's population probably was terrorized to a greater degree than the South Korean population. However, in the post-conflict period, communist North Korea has conducted a terrorist campaign against a much stronger U.S.-aided South Korea that includes bombings and the assassination of prominent figures, such as President Park Chung Hee in 1979.

Stephen Prince

SEE ALSO: TERROR AGAINST THE FRENCH IN INDOCHINA; TERROR IN THE VIETNAM WAR; THE AMERICAN RESPONSE TO TERRORISM.

FURTHER READING

- Cumings, B. *The Origins of the Korean War, Vol. 2: The Roaring of the Cataract, 1947-1950.* Oxford and Princeton, NJ: Princeton University Press, 1990.
- Foot, R. *A Substitute for Victory: The Politics of Peacemaking at the Korean Armistice Talks.* Ithaca, NY: Cornell University Press, 1990.
- Knox, D. *The Korean War: An Oral History – Pusan to Chosin.* San Diego: Harcourt Brace, 1985.
- MacDonald, C. "So Terrible a Liberation: The UN Occupation of North Korea," in *Bulletin of Concerned Asian Scholars* 23, No. 2, 1991.

TERROR IN THE VIETNAM WAR

Of all the conflicts fought to contain communism during the Cold War, none has provoked so much debate as the Vietnam War. Commentators have questioned not only the validity of the U.S. forces' involvement, but also their methods of combat. Three major areas of terror were used by the various combatants. The first was the use of formal terrorism by the communist Vietcong; the second, the "search and destroy" missions of the U.S. ground forces; and the third was the extensive bombing campaigns carried out by the U.S. Air Force.

Vietnam was once a colony of the French empire. It gained its independence in 1954, after communist-led revolutionaries, the Vietminh, defeated the French Expeditionary Corps in a decisive battle at Dien Bien Phu in the north of the country. The resulting peace accord, signed in Geneva, partitioned Vietnam at the 17th parallel into two states, North and South Vietnam. The communists, headed by Ho Chi Minh, took over the administration of North Vietnam, with the capital at Hanoi. In South Vietnam, an American-backed regime was set up under premier Ngo Dinh Diem.

Both regimes immediately set about consolidating their power. The communist regime, the Democratic Republic of Vietnam (DRV), as North Vietnam became known, used methods that can only be described as state terror. As General Giap, creator of the Vietminh military organization that fought the French, has admitted: "We attacked on too large a front, and, seeing enemies everywhere, resorted to terror...disciplinary punishments, expulsions from the party, executions.... Worse still, torture came to be regarded as normal practice." Similarly, Diem's regime, the Government of (South) Vietnam (GVN), launched a drive against those Vietminh supporters who remained in South Vietnam. So called "security committees" tried and convicted many South Vietnamese, regularly using torture, execution, and incarceration in prison camps. Hence the people of Vietnam, both North and South, became used to living under conditions of oppression and terror.

SUMMARY

- Between 1959 and 1965, the Vietcong conducted a systematic terror campaign in South Vietnam, killing around 7,500 government officials.
- U.S. ground forces conducted "search and destroy" missions, for which officers who scored high body counts were rewarded.
- Between 1965 and 1971, the U.S. Air Force dropped 6.3 million tonnes of bombs on IndoChina – more than three times the amount dropped by the U.S. during World War II.

VIETCONG'S ASSASSINATION CAMPAIGN

Starting in 1959, North Vietnam encouraged and supported insurgency in their rival state, South Vietnam. This was designed to spread communist doctrine, reduce support for the government there and, ultimately, "liberate" South Vietnam. Using the guerrilla tactics pioneered by China's Mao Zedong, communist cadres – known collectively as the National Liberation Front, or Vietcong – began a program of armed revolt backed by political and logistical support from the North.

In indoctrination leaflets, the Vietcong's military organization claimed members of the Liberation Front would "perform armed propaganda, liquidate tyrants in the area, and subvert in all ways the enemy's hold on the people." Secret guerrilla and special activity cells, each one usually comprising three fighters, undertook this subversion.

Between 1959 and 1965, assassination teams drawn from the special activity cells killed thousands of village and district officials of the South Vietnamese Government. Many more were kidnapped or beaten. The purpose of this violence was to intimidate the general population. A 1962 Vietcong declaration specified this use of terror: "It is the duty of all to support

William Colby, who subsequently became director of the CIA, was in charge of the counterinsurgency organization Civil Operations and Revolutionary Development Support (CORDS) from 1969.

the Revolution. If you obey orders you will be forgiven by the people and the Liberation Army.... If you work for the enemy you will be punished according to the law." Assassination was not indiscriminate and great care was taken to make sure there were no unexplained killings. For example, leaflets were issued denouncing certain killings as being the work of bandits masquerading as Vietcong soldiers.

After 1965, the Liberation Front's assassination program tailed off. However, the terror continued in concerted attempts to undermine support for South Vietnam. The methods of terrorism were less discriminating than the assassination program. Dynamiting trains was commonplace. Despite warning leaflets stuck to train seats, many civilians were killed as a result of these attacks.

In urban areas, Vietcong death squads operated on a regular basis. Such was the terror that they instilled in people, that often, the mere threat of violence was enough for Vietcong subversion to be swiftly successful. Attacks against American personnel in Vietnam were not particularly widespread. The Hanoi leadership discouraged an all-out terror campaign against American forces as being tactically unjustified. The Vietcong terror campaigns were targeted mainly at the people of South Vietnam, to eliminate opposition forces and provoke an authoritarian response from South Vietnamese forces. However, the methods first used by the Vietcong against their own people were employed extensively in the ground war against the U.S. after 1965. Grenade traps, mines, trip wires, and spiked booby traps all contributed to the dangerous and terrifying conditions faced by American soldiers.

CONFLICT OF THEORY AND PRACTICE

In any fight against an enemy using guerrilla tactics, the main weapons in the arsenal of the defenders are psychological. Guerrillas use the civilian population to shield their operations. Their strength comes from their ability to melt into the countryside and disperse. A defense force must therefore isolate the guerrillas from the civilians, cutting them off from their source of protection. The defense must generate sympathy for the anti-guerrilla cause with the local inhabitants.

The Americans used this well-established principle in Vietnam. A card entitled "The Nine Rules" was given to every U.S. soldier in Vietnam. It began: "The Vietnamese have paid a heavy price in suffering for their long fight against the communists. We military men are in Vietnam because their government have asked us to help their soldiers and people in winning their struggle. The Vietcong will attempt to turn the Vietnamese against you. You can defeat them at every turn by the strength, understanding, and generosity you display with thc people."

It was counterproductive for the American forces in Vietnam to use any form of terror as a tactic against the population of South Vietnam. Hence, a pacification program was introduced to separate the population from the Vietcong. Military operations could then be undertaken without endangering civilians whose support was needed if the Vietcong were to be defeated. The villagers were to be moved to pacification camps where they would be safe from military actions. Such was the theory; the reality was different.

Hulton Getty Picture Collection

Vietnamese defense forces guard surrendered Vietcong prisoners and a cache of confiscated weapons in Saigon, February 1968.

Much of the civilian population remained outside the pacification camps. In August 1967, under Operation Benton, the camps became so full that the army was ordered not to drive any more civilians from their farms. As former chairman of the Joint Chiefs of Staff Admiral Thomas H. Sharp explained: "We should have fought in the north, where everyone was the enemy, where you didn't have to worry whether or not you were shooting friendly civilians. In the south, we had to cope with women concealing grenades in their brassieres, or in their baby's diapers."

To prevent such chaos, American troops were expected to operate under certain rules while on patrol. Any village could be bombed or shelled if American troops had received fire from within it. Any village known to be hostile could be bombed or shelled if its inhabitants were warned in advance by leaflet drop or loudspeaker from helicopter. Once the civilian population had been moved out, a "free fire" zone could be declared and the villages and surrounding countryside could be attacked at will. In practice, these restraining rules were flexibly applied or ignored completely. Warnings of impending bombardment by leaflet or loudspeaker were often useless to peasants who could not read or understand English.

"Free fire" zones were often designated in areas that were not fully "pacified." This resulted in the death of many civilians for whom there was no room in the overcrowded pacification camps. Many villagers had no control over, nor the ability to influence, the Vietcong cadres operating in their area. They were just as terrified of the punishments meted out by the Vietcong's special activity cells as they were of American firepower.

The Americans employed a "search and destroy" strategy that relied on killing as many of the enemy as possible. According to the commander of U.S. combat forces, General William Westmoreland, the aim was to "find, fix in place, fight, and destroy (or neutralize) enemy forces and their base areas and supply caches." The object was not to hold ground.

The emphasis in mission reports was on body counts. Officers were promoted and recreation passes granted to enlisted men for meeting body count quotas. As a result, at times, all pretense of following the "rules of engagement" was dropped. In some cases, because only body counts mattered, prisoners were in danger of on-the-spot execution. An unofficial history by "Cinncinnatus," a member of the U.S. army reserve, claims that some units' policy was to "kill them if they try to surrender – we need the body count."

Helicopter gunship pilot David Bressum testified that air cavalry units frequently followed unwritten rules. Individuals were often killed without proper clearance: "If we received clearance, we would report it as a kill. If we did not receive clearance, we would just forget about it. This happened all the time." This was, in part, a reaction to the hazardous nature of patrolling. Booby traps, snipers, and ambushes were the most frequent form of engagement and, with few clear targets except villages that might or might not be hostile, many American soldiers saw such an attitude as the only guarantee of survival.

While these factors do not add up to the use of terror as explicit policy, the real result was a population caught between punishment by the Vietcong for collaboration and attack by American or South Vietnamese ground and air forces. As in a situation of state-sponsored terrorism, villagers were killed for supporting either side or simply for being in the wrong place at the wrong time. As one soldier put it: "If a village is not VC [Vietcong] when we go into it, it's VC when we leave."

From 1968, U.S. Navy special forces and South Vietnamese forces undertook counterterror operations under the auspices of the Civil Operations and Rural Development Support (CORDS) – an organization that aimed to coordinate pacification. CORDS chief William Colby believed that the only possible path was to rebuild village society in South Vietnam, as a stronghold of pro-government influence.

At the core of pacification was the "Phoenix" operation, designed to smash the Vietcong cadres. According to Colby, Phoenix operatives were not authorized to engage in assassination or "other violations of the rules of land warfare." Evidence suggests, however, that between 1968 and 1971, some 28,000 Vietcong insurgents were captured and approximately 20,000 killed. U.S. Navy officer Mike Beamon reported that assassinations were devised to make it appear that the Vietcong had done the killing. North Vietnam claims that, in some provinces, 95 percent of communist cadres were neutralized by Phoenix.

Vietnam in 1954, showing the division of the country, and North Vietnam's supply route to the Vietcong.

AIR WAR

Between 1965 and 1973, at least eight million tons of munitions were dropped on Vietnam, Laos, and Cambodia. The intentions of strategic bombing under the so-called Rolling Thunder (1965-68) and Linebacker (1972-73) campaigns were roughly the same as those of the 1940s. The U.S. aimed to destroy the enemy's war-making capability and weaken morale, inflicting enough damage to persuade the leadership to sue for peace.

President Lyndon B. Johnson, explaining the objectives of Rolling Thunder in March 1967, claimed that bombing North Vietnam had three objectives. It aimed to deny the enemy a sanctuary, to exact a penalty against North Vietnam for violations of the Geneva Convention, and to limit the flow of materials and increase the cost of logistical support and infiltration from North to South Vietnam. The unstated objective, however, was to demonstrate the superiority of American technology and resources.

Civilian morale was not viewed as a primary target of the air campaign. In 1966, a paper by Assistant Secretary of Defense John McNaughton stated that "strikes at population targets are likely…to create a counterproductive wave of revulsion abroad and at home." The bombing was directed primarily at breaking the will of the Hanoi leadership to continue its support of the insurgency in South Vietnam.

As a measure of U.S. determination to minimize civilian casualties and deflect any accusations of terror bombing, geographical restrictions were placed on all bombing raids. The so-called "Hanoi Do-not," an area around Hanoi where much of the North Vietnamese population resided, was declared off-limits. The self-imposed restrictions left few legitimate military targets for the air force to hit. Lacking any heavy industry and arms factories, North Vietnam acted as a staging area for Soviet and Chinese material passing to the battlefields of the South. A CIA report of 1966 claimed that the geographical restriction meant that "almost 80

Women and children lie dead on a road outside the village of My Lai, following the massacre there in 1968. The revelation that U.S. servicemen had shot innocent villagers outraged the nation.

percent of North Vietnam's limited modern, industrial economy and 75 percent of the nation's population...have been effectively insulated from air attack." The Joint Chiefs of Staff argued in March 1968 that there were no real civilians left in the cities of Hanoi and Haiphong: "Air strikes in and around these cities endanger personnel primarily engaged, directly or indirectly, in support of the war effort." As a result, restricted areas were gradually reduced as militarily viable targets became harder to find.

The bombing campaigns, despite their intensity, did not achieve their objectives. Logistical support to the Vietcong transported down the Ho Chi Minh trail, a supply route through Laos to South Vietnam, continued to operate with increasing efficiency. The 1967 Jason Study (a U.S. Senate scientific investigation) reported that Operation Rolling Thunder had no measurable effect on North Vietnamese military support to the southern insurgents. Furthermore, they concluded that "the bombing clearly strengthened popular support of the regime by engendering patriotic and nationalistic enthusiasm to resist attacks."

It is clear that Rolling Thunder did not target civilians intentionally. However, numerous reports from foreign observers collected in 1971 maintained that a number of raids using antipersonnel weapons destroyed many schools, churches, and hospitals, resulting in significant civilian casualties. United States General Momyer claimed that many civilian casualties were self-inflicted by the North Vietnamese defense forces through indiscriminate firing of anti-aircraft rounds and surface-to-air missiles. "Never in the course of the war," he states, "was a target selected for any reason other than its military significance." However, in a report by General Westmoreland on the bombing campaign of 1966-68, over 10,000 objectives identified simply as "buildings" are listed as damaged or destroyed. It is inconceivable that these were all viable military targets, given that military installations are listed separately. A Defense Department study of 1966 calculated that 65 percent of the total tonnage of bombs and artillery rounds was expended against places where the enemy "might" have been. In other words, there was no reliable intelligence that the enemy was there.

Under the administration of President Richard M. Nixon, all geographical restrictions were lifted for the Linebacker Two campaign of 1972-73. With the objective of coercing the North Vietnamese into a ceasefire arrangement, 40,000 tons of bombs were dropped on the corridor between Hanoi and Haiphong. Although encouraged to exaggerate their statistics by American antiwar campaigners, the North Vietnamese set civilian deaths at approximately 1,600. These raids should be considered as terror bombing, because their aim was simply to "communicate" rather than destroy military capabilities. President Nixon himself described the action as an application of his "madman" theory. The intention was to convince North Vietnam that he would go to any lengths to reach a settlement, including massive urban air attacks and ultimately a nuclear strike.

DRAWING CONCLUSIONS

Throughout the war in Vietnam, the Vietcong employed terrorism as a specific tactic. It was designed to coerce the population of South Vietnam into supporting the insurgents. At the very least, the terrorism was intended to compel the South Vietnamese to stop supporting their government's efforts at controlling the insurgency. The explicit purpose of the assassination campaign was to wipe out any civilian opposition to the communist cadres operating in the villages. Similarly, the urban campaigns relied heavily on terror attacks. Assaults against American personnel cannot, however, be described as acts of terrorism. As combatants involved in or supporting the war effort, they should be considered legitimate military targets.

It was not the policy of American forces to engender a feeling of terror among the Vietnamese civilians. But the lax application of the rules of engagement created an atmosphere of terror, despite the fact that it ran counter to America's anti-guerrilla strategy. Indeed, the atmosphere of terror served only to legitimize the Vietcong's efforts. In addition, the strategy of attrition, which laid such emphasis on body counts, resulted in serious infringements of the self-imposed restrictions. Civilians were permanently at risk from attack by one side or the other.

On the other hand, the difficulties faced by American ground forces should not be underestimated. Vietcong tactics increased the terror faced by U.S. combat personnel and led to the indiscriminate methods used in some "search and destroy" missions.

The American bombing campaigns, especially Rolling Thunder, were not, as a matter of policy, terror attacks in the mold of the widespread bombing of civilian targets during World War II. President Johnson described Rolling Thunder as "the most careful, self-limiting air war in history." However, the gradual lifting of geographical restrictions as the conflict progressed and the sheer tonnage of munitions dropped on North Vietnam caused significant numbers of civilian deaths.

In the end, the temptation to strike at urban targets in an attempt to break the will of the North Vietnamese government led to Operation Linebacker Two. In terms of results, this could be described as a terror bombing campaign even though the civilian population was not a specific target of the raids.

During the Vietnam War, the citizens of both the North and the South suffered as a result of the strategies employed by both sides. The Vietcong created an atmosphere of terror as matter of policy. American forces contributed to this terror by default.

Gregory Simpson

SEE ALSO: NATIONAL LIBERATION WARS AND TERROR; TERROR AGAINST THE FRENCH IN INDOCHINA; NATIONALIST TERRORISM; BOMBING OPERATIONS; ASSASSINATION; ROCKETS, MORTARS, AND MISSILES; TERRORISTS' USE OF CHEMICAL WEAPONS; VICTIMS OF TERRORISM; TERROR IN THE KOREAN WAR; THE AMERICAN RESPONSE TO TERRORISM; STATE-SPONSORED TERRORISM.

FURTHER READING

- Gallucci, R. L. *Neither Peace nor Honor.* Baltimore: Johns Hopkins University Press, 1975.
- Gibson, J. W. *The Perfect War.* New York: Vintage, 1988.
- Walzer, M. *Just and Unjust Wars.* London: Penguin, 1980; New York: Basic Books, 1992.

TERROR IN AFGHANISTAN

Fears that Islamic fundamentalism would spread from Afghanistan to its own neighboring Muslim republics prompted the Soviet Union to invade Afghanistan in 1979. The Red Army withdrew in defeat after a decade of war, but the fighting continued. The intervention stirred up religious fervor among the Afghans, and the last few years have seen terrorist insurgency, political infighting, religious oppression, and civilian suffering on a horrific scale.

COUPS AND ASSASSINATIONS

The kingdom of Afghanistan experienced increasing political tension following the independence of India and Pakistan in 1947. Shortly after this period, the Soviets started to supply aid to Afghanistan. During the 1970s, rival Afghan factions conducted a series of coups and assassinations, and among the combatants were left-wing parties receiving Soviet aid. General Mohammed Daoud Khan proclaimed Afghanistan a republic after his coup in April 1973, but was himself toppled by the Soviet-backed People's Democratic Party of Afghanistan (PDPA) in a coup in April 1978.

However, the PDPA itself was riven by factions. The dominant Khalqs, led by Noor Mohammed Taraki, drew their support from the majority Pushtun ethnic group. Opposing the Khalqs were the Parchams, led by Babrak Karmal and supported by the Tajik ethnic group. After the 1978 coup, the Khalqs ruthlessly purged Parchams from the government and embarked on a communist program of reform. Their policies won little support among the mainly Islamic peasantry, who staged uprisings in the first six months of 1979. The government brutally crushed the insurgents, known as *mujahideen*, but law and order was not to prevail. In September, prime minister Hafizullah Amin overthrew Taraki and had him killed.

Despite massive Soviet military and economic assistance, Amin was unable to quell dissent, especially from terrorist groups based in neighboring Pakistan. By December, the Soviet leadership was alarmed. It feared that a surge of Islamic fundamentalism, in the wake of the Iranian Revolution one year earlier, would spread to Muslim-dominated Uzbekistan, Tajikistan, and Turkmenistan bordering Afghanistan. On December 24, Soviet airborne troops seized Kabul airport and armored columns entered the country. The Soviets shot Amin and his family, replacing him with Parcham leader Karmal. But Karmal, little more than a puppet figure, proved incapable of governing. Within a month, 80,000 Soviet troops were in Afghanistan.

KEY FACTS

- About 15,000 Red Army troops and 1-1.5 million Afghans were killed during the 10-year occupation.
- The Soviet-Afghan conflict resulted in more than 5 million Afghan refugees.
- Rival factions continue to fight for dominance in Afghanistan; more than 50,000 people have been killed since the Soviet withdrawal.

CLASHES WITH THE *MUJAHIDEEN*

The Soviets planned to use the Afghan army to seek out the *mujahideen*, and the Red Army to contain coordinated terrorist activity. However, the Afghan forces proved to be poorly trained and weak. The Soviet troops tried to drive the *mujahideen* from strongholds in the Hindu Kush mountains overshadowing Kabul, and along the borders with Iran and Pakistan. They cleared valleys and razed villages to deny the *mujahideen* food and shelter, but they could not deliver a knockout blow.

Mujahideen terror tactics against installations and troops included hit-and-run raids, assassination of officials and soldiers, and grenade attacks in public places. In April 1981, rebels killed the deputy head of the Afghan secret police and an army commander, attacked the homes of Soviet advisers, and firebombed the Sarobi power station, which supplied electricity to Kabul. Other terrorist acts included mass executions of suspected government traitors. In August 1981, *mujahideen* shot 70 officials in the provincial town of Gulbahar, and killed 60 in Herat in June 1982.

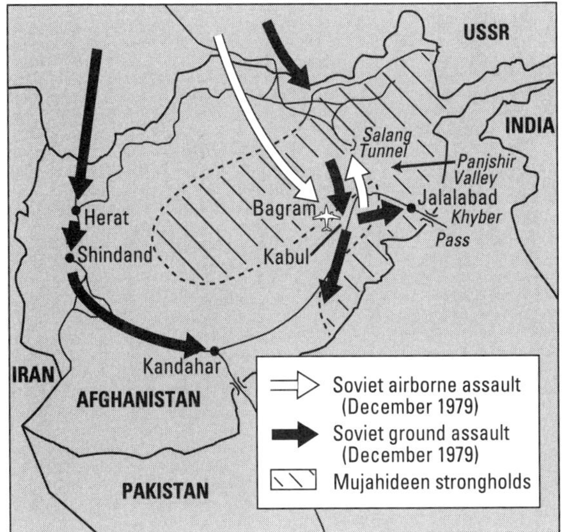

Afghanistan and neighboring countries, showing the main thrust of the Soviet attack in December 1979.

The government response was brutal. Troops rounded up suspects, torturing and murdering many of them. In September 1982, refugees from a village in Logar province related how Soviet troops set fire to gasoline poured down an underground irrigation tunnel, burning to death all 105 civilians hiding there. The Soviets attempted to seal Afghanistan's borders with Iran and Pakistan by laying millions of land mines, but these caused thousands of civilian casualties. Use of artillery, napalm, and rockets destroyed villages and their inhabitants, crops, and livestock.

SOVIET WITHDRAWAL

In the face of the Soviet military onslaught, the *mujahideen* continued their terrorist attacks. They planted a bomb at Kabul airport in the fall of 1984, killing about 30 people and injuring 200, and brought down a Soviet transport aircraft near Kabul using U.S.-supplied rockets. They also mounted military raids on Soviet troops. At first poorly equipped, the *mujahideen* were, by 1986, armed with sophisticated weapons such as Stinger surface-to-air missiles and rocket launchers. The fighting became locked in stalemate. In 1986, the Soviets replaced the ineffectual Karmal with Najibullah Ahmadzai, in the hope of winning popular support and achieving a political compromise. But this was to no avail. On April 7, 1988, Soviet President Mikhail Gorbachev agreed a timetable for Soviet withdrawal, which was completed on schedule on February 15, 1989.

TERRORISM CONTINUES

Fighting between the rebels and the new government continued. The *mujahideen* attacked Jalalabad in March 1989, laying siege for 15 weeks. On April 18, 1992, Najibullah was overthrown and replaced by Burhanuddin Rabbani. Radical groups, particularly the Iran-backed *Hizb-i-Islami* (Islamic Party) led by Gulbuddin Hekmatyar, continued to launch attacks on Kabul. A peace agreement between Hekmatyar and Rabbani signed on March 7, 1993, did not halt the war.

In 1994, the Talibans (Students of Islam), strict Islamic fundamentalists, moved in from Pakistan and took the provinces of Kandahar and Hefar. Within 12 months, the Talibans occupied half of Afghanistan. Since February 1995, they have been mounting repeated attacks on Kabul, pounding the capital with shells. In regions under their control, the Talibans conduct a regime of terror. Those who do not adhere strictly to Islamic law may be executed. Theft is punishable by death; women are forbidden education, and are beaten for not following the Islamic dress code. Women may also be executed if they are seen talking in public to an unrelated male.

In a bid to prevent anarchy, the Afghan government is meting out its own, equally harsh discipline, conducting public executions to intimidate the population. The rival Afghan factions appear unable to reach a peace settlement, and resolution appears unlikely in the near future.

Ian Westwell

SEE ALSO: MIDDLE EASTERN TERRORISM 1988-1996; ROOTS OF FUNDAMENTALIST TERRORISM; TERROR BY THE HOLY WARRIORS OF KASHMIR.

FURTHER READING

- Borovik, Arten. *The Hidden War: A Russian Journalist's Account of the Soviet War in Afghanistan.* New York: Atlantic Monthly Press, 1990; London: Faber, 1991.
- Galeotti, Mark. *Afghanistan: The Soviet Union's Last War.* London and Portland, OR: Frank Cass, 1995.
- Rais, Rasul Bux. *War Without Winners.* New York: Oxford University Press, 1994.

TERROR IN RWANDA

For three months in 1994, from April 6 to July 10, the interim government of Rwanda attempted to turn the entire population of that country into either killers or victims. It failed, yet hundreds of thousands of Rwandans died in one of history's most appalling reigns of terror.

Rwanda had no history of ethnic strife before or during the colonial period. The minority Tutsi tribe were interspersed among the majority Hutu. The process of decolonization began in 1959 as the Hutus asserted themselves against the Belgian colonial administration and against the economically stronger Tutsis. The early years of Hutu domination were marked by bouts of politically motivated violence. The Hutus drove Tutsi leaders out of the positions they had held under colonial rule. They killed thousands of Tutsis and forced many more to flee into exile.

An army of Tutsis exiled in Uganda, known by Hutus as the *inyenzi*, or cockroaches, invaded in 1963 in an attempt to take the capital, Kigali. The Rwandan army defeated them and took revenge on Tutsi civilians. About 10,000 died and still more went into exile.

In 1973, Major General Juvénal Habyarimana, a Hutu from northwestern Rwanda, staged a coup and established an army-backed, one-party regime. Habyarimana and his circle oversaw the development of a political machine for controlling every part of the state. This absolute control meant that the "Tutsi question" was not an issue during the 1970s and 1980s.

KEY FACTS

- Tutsis make up less than 10 percent of the population of Rwanda.
- On one day in April 1994, 250,000 Rwandans crossed the border to Tanzania in the largest movement of refugees ever witnessed by the UN.
- As part of their propaganda campaign, the Hutu extremists established a new radio station dedicated to broadcasting their message.

In the early 1990s, Habyarimana was forced to make a number of concessions to both Hutu opponents and Tutsi exiles. He responded to international pressure to introduce democratic reforms in exchange for desperately needed loans. The government began to lose its hold on power as new Hutu political parties emerged. Also, in 1990, a 20,000-strong army of the largely Tutsi Rwandan Patriotic Front (RPF) invaded from Uganda. The RPF forced the government to negotiate a settlement that would give them virtual control over the Rwandan army.

PREPARATIONS FOR GENOCIDE

Hutu extremists rejected all the concessions outright. Determined to hold onto power at any cost, they strengthened their organization. With vital French training and financial assistance, Habyarimana reinforced the Rwandan armed forces. The elite Presidential Guard grew to 1,500, while overall military strength rose from 5,000 to 35,000. The Presidential Guard then turned the youth wing of the National Revolutionary Movement for Development (MRND) into a new militia. Known as the Intrahamwe ("Those with a common goal"), this group by 1994 had nearly 2,000 fighters drawn from every part of the country. The Presidential Guard ran camps for these young men and prepared them for their central role in the coming genocide. The weapons needed for the killing were imported in huge quantities from South Africa and Egypt. They included small arms and ammunition, as well as vast numbers of machetes.

The extremists also developed a political ideology of Hutu supremacy to mobilize support. They exploited newspapers and even the state-run Radio Rwanda, calling on all Hutus to do their patriotic duty and defend so-called Hutu power. This required not only the extermination of the Tutsi, who, it was claimed, were all "RPF cockroaches," but also the elimination of their opponents among the Hutu themselves.

On April 6, President Habyarimana and the president of neighboring Burundi died when their plane crashed in suspicious circumstances near a Rwandan

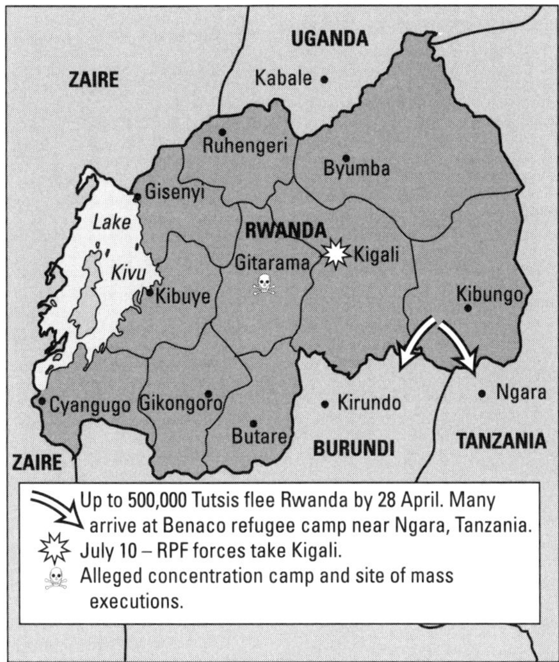

Rwanda and surrounding countries in 1994, showing principal incidents of the civil war and the refugee exodus into Burundi, Tanzania, and Zaire.

army base. The Presidential Guard took this as the signal to set their genocide machine in motion. The Hutu extremists had already drawn up lists of those who were to die at the hands of death squads, which included politicians, civil servants, and journalists. Prime Minister Agathe Uwilingiyimana, a moderate Hutu, was one of the first to die, and her family along with her. The Presidential Guard carried out a coup d'état, and two days later the new government, composed entirely of extremist Hutus, was announced.

TERROR INTENSIFIES

When the killing began, the Hutu radio and television station RTLMC called on Hutus to join with the Intrahamwe, asking publicly: "Who will fill up the half empty graves?" In towns and villages across the country, extremist *bourgmestres* (mayors) instructed the police to lead Intrahamwe groups in seeking out all those suspected of being Tutsi, especially the prosperous and educated. The killers went from house to house. They killed known Tutsis immediately, hacking them to death with machetes. They forced other Hutus to murder their Tutsi neighbors and join the Intrahamwe. Those who refused died along with the Tutsis. Hutu husbands were forced to kill their Tutsi wives and children. Tutsis were rounded up and held in churches, schools, and sports facilities, while elsewhere they gathered together of their own accord, hoping vainly that there would be safety in numbers. In either case, they were butchered in such great numbers that the community buildings became death camps. Tutsis and moderate Hutus formed defense committees to resist the Intrahamwe, only to be disarmed by the army and left to the mercy of ruthless killers. Faced with the prospect of brutal death by machete, many people paid their executioners to shoot them. Desperate mothers tried to hide their children in the piles of bodies. More than 500,000 fled the country.

As the killing intensified, however, the pro-Tutsi RPF military forces swept south, creating havens for hundreds of thousands of Tutsis. On July 10, the RPF took Kigali and, for Tutsis, the reign of terror ended. Many Hutus, however, feared for their own lives, believing that it was now they who faced genocide. Many fled to a zone in the west protected by the French. When the French withdrew, they moved on to camps in Goma, Zaire, where the Hutu extremists tried to retain what little power they had left. Sporadic violence by both sides has continued.

Nick Hostettler

SEE ALSO: TERROR IN COLONIAL CONQUESTS; THEORIES OF STATE TERROR; STATE VERSUS NON-STATE TERRORISM.

FURTHER READING

- Destexhe, Alain. *Rwanda and Genocide in the Twentieth Century.* London: Pluto, and New York: New York University Press, 1995.
- Dorsey, Learthen. *Historical Dictionary of Rwanda.* Metuchen, NJ: The Scarecrow Press, 1994.
- Malkki, Lisa H. *Purity and Exile: Violence, Memory, and National Cosmology Among Hutu Refugees in Tanzania.* Chicago: University of Chicago Press, 1995.
- Prunier, Gérard. *The Rwanda Crisis: History of a Genocide, 1959-1994.* London: Hurst, and New York: Columbia University Press, 1995.
- Vanderwerff, Corrine. *Kill Thy Neighbor.* Boise, ID: Pacific Press, 1996.

TERROR IN THE FORMER YUGOSLAVIA

In the summer of 1991, as communist Yugoslavia began to move toward democracy, the country dissolved into a bloody civil war. Families that had lived alongside each other for generations suddenly became bitter enemies, as ethnic group terrorized ethnic group. Between 1991 and 1995, hundreds of thousands of men, women, and children were victims of torture, rape, murder, and "ethnic cleansing." Not since the end of World War II, in 1945, had Europe witnessed such appalling atrocities.

THE FORMER YUGOSLAVIA

The former Yugoslavia was a complex mixture of six separate national groups: Serbs, Croats, Slav Muslims, Slovenes, Albanians, and Macedonians. Each group had its own history and culture, and each had a sense of its own national pride and identity.

From the Middle Ages until the nineteenth century, most of these groups had formed subject states of the powerful Muslim Ottoman empire. The Ottomans suppressed any kind of nationalism, and different ethnic groups often lived together in mixed communities. In the nineteenth century, as Ottoman power waned, nationalism grew, particularly among the Serbs.

In 1878, the Serbs gained their own nation state, Serbia. Almost immediately the new state attempted to expand its territory into Bosnia-Herzegovina, where there was a substantial Serb population. In June 1914, Serb nationalists assassinated Archduke Franz Ferdinand, heir to the throne of the Austro-Hungarian Empire, as he made a state visit to Sarajevo, the Bosnian capital. This event led directly led to World War I. After the war, the kingdom of Yugoslavia was established. The new kingdom included Serbia, Croatia, and Bosnia, and lasted until 1941, when Germany invaded during World War II.

When World War II came to an end in 1945, communists took over Yugoslavia and formed a federation of six republics: Serbia, Croatia, Slovenia, Macedonia, Bosnia-Herzegovina, and Montenegro. The new communist regime controlled the country from Belgrade, the Serbian capital.

Although the central government wielded considerable power, it regulated its citizens' everyday lives less than other communist countries. It granted a degree of self government to the individual republics; a secret police force operated, but there were few political prisoners; and, unlike other Eastern Europeans, Yugoslavs were allowed to travel freely abroad. In many ways, Yugoslavia seemed to be the model of a successful and comparatively prosperous communist state.

SUMMARY

- The civil war in the former Yugoslavia broke out as communist regimes throughout Eastern Europe were being toppled.
- In the first few months of the conflict in Bosnia-Herzegovina, 130,000 people were killed and 3 million were forced to leave their homes.
- By the end of 1995, almost 100 people were indicted of war crimes in the former Yugoslavia. Of these, two-thirds were Serbs.

GROWING ETHNIC UNREST

During the 1980s, however, tension mounted between Yugoslavia's ethnic groups. In 1981, the Serb-dominated Yugoslav Army suppressed demonstrations by Albanian students in Kosovo, a province of Serbia where Albanians were in the majority. Throughout the rest of the decade, Albanians living in Serbia were randomly arrested, beaten, and imprisoned. In 1989, the president of Serbia, Slobodan Milosevic, closed down all Albanian schools and dismissed 15,000 Albanian civil servants. In March, security forces shot dead Albanian protesters in Pristina, the Kosovo capital. Official figures claimed that only 24 people were killed, but eyewitnesses estimated that almost 200 lost their lives.

Frank Spooner Pictures

In August 1995, Croats shelled civilian refugees, in the belief that the groups included escaping Serb soldiers.

Ethnic unrest was growing in Croatia, too. In the spring of 1990, Franjo Tudjman, a nationalist Croat who had made clear his ambitions for a future independent Croatia, was elected the state's president. Serbs living in Croatia immediately carried out terrorist attacks on railway lines, public utilities, and private homes. In August 1990, several areas in Croatia with Serb majorities declared themselves autonomous.

In May 1991, Serb paramilitary troops ambushed 150 Croatian police in Eastern Slavonia, in northern Croatia. They killed and mutilated 12 policemen. In retaliation, the Croatian Ministry of Defense evicted Serbs living in ministry properties, and Croatian terrorists, backed by the Croatian government, bombed Serbian homes.

DECLARATIONS OF INDEPENDENCE

In June 1991, Croatia and nearby Slovenia declared themselves to be sovereign nation states, fully independent from the Yugoslav federation. The hard-line communists in Serbia were willing to concede independence to Slovenia but not to Croatia, where large numbers of Serbs lived. In the summer of 1991, war broke out between Serbian and Croatian forces as both sides fought for control of Croatian territory.

The principal feature of the war in Croatia was "ethnic cleansing." Ethnic cleansing means forcing out from an area all those of a different ethnic origin. It was practiced mainly by the Serbs. When the Serbian forces captured a town or village, the Croats were forced to leave the area and their homes were then given over to Serbs. Soon almost one-third of Croatia was under Serb control. In January 1992, however, the Serbs agreed to a ceasefire negotiated by envoys from the European Union and the United Nations, and 14,000 UN peacekeeping troops were sent to Croatia.

WAR IN BOSNIA-HERZEGOVINA

By this time, Bosnia-Herzegovina had also declared itself independent from Yugoslavia. The new Bosnian government, however, was unable to protect its territory. Its army was badly trained and had few weapons. In contrast, the Serbs living in Bosnia had organized and armed themselves with the help of the Yugoslav army in order to fight the Bosnian Muslim government.

Frank Spooner Pictures

These French soldiers were part of a UN peacekeeping force captured by the Serbs in May 1995.

In the spring of 1992, Bosnian Serb forces took over the northern, western, and eastern regions of Bosnia-Herzegovina where many Serbs lived. Meanwhile, Croatian forces advanced into the republic to protect Croats living there. Bosnian Muslims, Bosnian Serbs, and Croats were all soon caught up in ferocious fighting.

The Serbs again pursued a terroristic policy of ethnic cleansing in the areas that they occupied. Non-Serbs were forced to hand over all of their property before being allowed out of Serb-controlled areas. Sometimes, they were instructed to mark their homes by flying white sheets from the windows, ostensibly for protection. In reality, however, these homes then became targets of missile attacks from Serbian tanks.

Many non-Serb men, women, and children were imprisoned in concentration camps. The Bosnian Serbs had established a network of over 40 such camps as they seized control of eastern and northern Bosnia-Herzegovina. In the camps, prisoners were brutally terrorized, and beatings and rape were common. Prisoners were reportedly forced to bite off other prisoners' testicles, and in some cases individuals were dismembered alive. Hundreds of non-Serbs starved to death or were murdered in these camps.

By the winter of 1992, the Bosnian Serbs controlled and terrorized a large part of Bosnia-Herzegovina. They had surrounded many of the Bosnian Muslim areas and were holding them under siege. Sarajevo, for example, was completely cut off for most of the war. During this time, thousands of Bosnian Muslims died in the city. Many innocent civilians were killed as a result of continuous shelling from Serbian artillery and from sniper fire. Even more died from diseases caused by lack of food, water, fuel, and medical supplies.

Croatian and Bosnian Muslim forces also committed atrocities. Eyewitnesses claimed that Croatian units in central Bosnia-Herzegovina burned Muslim children alive. For their part, Bosnian Muslims were said to have murdered, raped, and driven Serbs out of villages in eastern Bosnia-Herzegovina. Both Croatians and Bosnians set up prisoner-of-war camps, in which torture and other acts of terror reportedly took place. These atrocities were, however, on a much smaller scale than those committed by the Bosnian Serbs.

Bosnia-Herzegovina, showing the territory under the control of the Bosnian Serbs in late August 1995.

The terror of Bosnian Serbs' ethnic cleansing had another, savage dimension. In an attempt to produce large numbers of children with Serbian blood, the Serbs systematically raped thousands of non-Serb women. For centuries, invading soldiers had raped their way through countries, but this was the first example of rape being used deliberately as an organized form of repopulation.

INTERNATIONAL RESPONSES

The terror in Bosnia-Herzegovina sent shock waves around the world. At first, however, the international community was reluctant to take direct military action. Instead, the United Nations and the European Union tried to negotiate a settlement. As the terror increased, however, the international community was forced to act. The UN imposed economic and political sanctions on Serbia and deployed a peace force, its largest ever, to deliver humanitarian aid to the cities under siege. It also established the International Criminal Tribunal for Former Yugoslavia (ICTY) to investigate allegations of war crimes.

In 1993, the UN went a step further and designated six "safe areas" in Bosnia-Herzegovina – Sarajevo, Bihac, Tuzla, Gorazde, Zepa, and Srebrenica – which were to be protected by UN troops. NATO also sent a force, its first ever active fighting force, to support the UN soldiers.

However, the Bosnian Serbs seemed to ignore all the UN and NATO measures, and they continued their terror unabated. Despite threats of NATO air strikes, the Serbs maintained their bombardment of Sarajevo. In May 1995, NATO bombers struck Bosnian Serb positions in the hills around Sarajevo. Large quantities of Serbian artillery were destroyed. Nonetheless, the Bosnian Serbs remained defiant. Their response to the air strikes was to capture more than a 100 UN soldiers, although they released them several days later.

THE TERROR IN SREBRENICA

In July 1995, the Bosnian Serbs' terror reached an unprecedented level when they attacked one of the UN "safe areas," Srebrenica. Although Dutch UN soldiers were stationed in Srebrenica, they were powerless to prevent the Bosnian Serbs overrunning the town. The Serbs expelled over 40,000 Bosnian Muslims – most of them already refugees from other areas – and murdered thousands more.

As the Serbian troops advanced, several thousand Bosnian Muslims fled. Around 15,000 headed for the nearby town of Tuzla, but the Serbs soon caught them. Only around one-third of the group managed to escape to Tuzla. The remainder were killed. A second group sought security in the Dutch UN compound. As the

A map of the former Yugoslavia, showing a breakdown of its many ethnic groups.

Hulton Getty Picture Collection

Serbs parade a group of blindfolded Muslims captured in central Bosnia-Herzegovina in October 1992.

Bosnian Serbs burned houses in the town, General Ratko Mladic, the Serbian military commander, assured the Muslims in the compound that they would not be harmed. He said that they would be safely transported by bus to Bosnian-controlled territory. However, as the Muslims boarded the buses on July 13, the Serbs separated the men from the women and children. The women and children were escorted to safety, but the men were all taken away and shot dead.

PEACE AT LAST

The massacre at Srebrenica was the most shocking atrocity of the four-year conflict in Bosnia-Herzegovina. The town's Bosnian Muslim population was almost entirely wiped out in an event described by ICTY as "unimaginable savagery…from hell, written on the darkest pages of human history." It caused widespread international outrage and prompted NATO to threaten further air strikes against the Bosnian Serbs. Faced with this threat, and under increasing pressure from Serbia, which was suffering under the UN sanctions, the Bosnian Serbs were finally forced to the negotiating table. In December 14, 1995, in Dayton, Ohio, a settlement was eventually reached which brought the conflict in Bosnia-Herzegovina to an end.

James Gow

SEE ALSO: WORLD WAR II RESISTANCE IN YUGOSLAVIA AND TERRORISM; NATIONALIST TERRORISM; RELIGIOUS EXTREMISM; ROCKETS, MORTARS, AND MISSILES; COLLABORATION BETWEEN TERRORISTS; VICTIMS OF TERRORISM.

FURTHER READING

- Cigar, Norman. *Genocide in Bosnia.* College Station: Texas A&M University Press, 1995.
- Gow, James. *Triumph of the Lack of Will: International Diplomacy and the Yugoslav War.* London: Hurst, and New York: Columbia University Press, 1997.
- Woodward, Susan L. *Balkan Tragedy: Chaos and Dissolution after the Cold War.* Washington, DC: Brookings Institute, 1995.

TERRORISM IN THE INDUSTRIALIZED WORLD

Hulton Getty Picture Collection

The 1973 ETA attack on Spanish Prime Minister Blanco's car. The blast sent the car over an eight-story building.

TERRORISM IN THE INDUSTRIALIZED WORLD: *Introduction*

Modern terrorism is by no means confined to the world's unstable regimes and regions split along ethnic or cultural lines. Many states, especially those in the industrialized world that are comparatively stable, mature democracries, have had to face the threats posed by both domestic and international terrorists. Domestic terrorism has been pursued by two types of organization. First, there are nationalists, such as the Irish Republican Army and the Corsican National Liberation Front, who are fighting for an independent homeland. They believe that they represent minority ethnic groups who have been denied an effective political voice by an oppressive state controlled by the majority. Second, there are social revolutionaries, who wish to bring down an existing regime and create a more equitable society. International terrorists strike at certain countries because they believe that they actively support the regimes they oppose.

Both types of domestic terrorist organization are essentially urban phenomena, and they target representatives or symbols of a state's authority. These include politicians, police officers, top military figures, bureaucrats, and government buildings. Funds are raised through hostage-taking, bank robberies, and collections among their own supporters. While the number of their members involved directly in terrorism is generally small for security purposes, they can draw on larger numbers of "helpers." These helpers provide safe houses, food, and intelligence while they lead a seemingly "normal" life that does not bring them to the attention of the state security forces.

The social revolutionaries believe that the governments of modern industrial states are basically repressive and that they use economic prosperity to hoodwink the general population. By using acts of terror to force regimes into tougher legislation, the terrorists argue that the authorities' "true" intentions can be revealed. Mass popular protest should then follow, leading to their downfall. West Germany did introduce certain restrictive measures in an effort to defeat the Baader-Meinhof Gang in the 1970s, but most civilians accepted the state's measures as an unavoidable necessity. This has proved the case in most mature democracies. The authorities have battled the terrorists with a considerable degree of success, and with little infringement of civil liberties for most of their populations.

Some of the social revolutionary groups have also attempted to find common cause with other terrorist groups, particularly those based in the Middle East. They have drawn parallels between the situation faced by the Palestinians and the disadvantaged sections of their own communites. As terrorism took on an international face in the early 1970s, a handful of joint operations were carried out, but the links were never strong. Some Western European terrorists trained in the Middle East, some were funded by Arab states on occasion, and many were provided with weapons from these governments. However, the Middle Eastern terrorists had little faith in the abilities of the social revolutionaries. They saw them as amateurish, ineffective, and lacking any deep understanding of the Middle East.

Homegrown terrorists in the industrialized world have generally failed to achieve their objectives. They may have highlighted unsatisfactory aspects of the way in which a society was run, but change for the better has usually been achieved through the democratic process, not through violence. ■

CHAPTER SIXTEEN

Terrorism in the United States

The U.S. has had to face a number of both left- and right-wing domestic terrorist campaigns since the middle of the nineteenth century. In the rural South and Midwest, reactionary groups have sought to preserve the status quo or to undermine the government. In the urban North, leftist radicals have sought to improve the lot of the poor and win rights for African-Americans. More recently, the U.S. has become the target of Islamic fundamentalist terrorists opposed to the country's dominant role in the politics of the Middle East.

TERRORISM IN THE UNITED STATES: Introduction

Before the 1990s, acts of terrorism faced by the U.S. authorities were overwhelmingly interracial and domestic, almost entirely lacking an international dimension. Violence was usually inflicted by reactionary sections of the white majority, usually in rural areas of the South, against the African-American minority, or other recently arrived white groups in the urban north. Random acts of terror – beatings, arson, and lynchings – were common. Organized campaigns became more prevalent with the creation of the white supremacist Ku Klux Klan in the immediate aftermath of the American Civil War.

The fortunes of the Klan and the scale of its terrorist activities have fluctuated since its debut in the mid-nineteenth century. It has gained some support during times of economic depression and lost it during periods of prosperity. Although the Klan is still active, frequent splits between rival factions, government crackdowns, and widespread revulsion at its activities have denied the movement a broad base of support. Since the 1960s, terror in the U.S. has been directed against the government by a number of homegrown lgroups, and, most recently, by foreign terrorists.

Left-wing terrorists have been based predominantly in northern urban areas; right-wing organizations have drawn support from the countryside. Both, although for very different reasons, believed that the U.S. authorities have failed the people. The Left claimed that governments were indifferent to the plight of the poor, and actively discriminated against ethnic minorities. The Right claimed that governments were corrupt, self-serving, and infringing civil liberties laid down in the Constitution. Both have proved willing to use the bomb and the bullet to make their poitical point. They believed that terrorist attacks would promote their cause and force administrations to introduce far-reaching political changes. In reality, both left- and right-wing groups have proved remarkably unsuccessful. Changes in political direction in the U.S. have come about through mass protest, such as the Civil Rights movement, and through the ballot box, rather than through violent acts.

Left-wing terror organizations grew out of the anti-Vietnam war protests and the Civil Rights movements of the 1960s. Groups like the Weathermen and the Black Panthers believed that the authorities were effectively ignoring the generally peaceful mass protests. They believed that only direct violent action would bring about change. Those in power would either accede to the terrorists' demands or introduce such repressive legislation to control them that they would lose the support of the electorate and collapse. However, left-wing terrorism invariably failed because the various groups were generally inept as terrorists or else they disintegrated into feuding cliques. The authorities also were unwilling to introduce legislation that the majority would view as infringing their constitutional liberties.

Reactionary groups, such as the rural-based Militias, have been more "successful" as terrorists, as the Oklahoma bombing of 1995 shows, but they have failed to undermine the government. Mass disgust at their activities and their own factionalism have seriously weakened their position. Potentially more successful are the anti-abortion activists, who have seized upon a sensitive issue that divides many Americans. However, it seems unlikely that bombing campaigns will serve their cause better than peaceful protest or political dialogue.

One potentially dangerous threat faced by the U.S. authoritities is that posed by Middle Eastern terrorists hitting targets on the U.S. mainland. This is a recent phenomenon and has developed from two factors. The U.S. has long been involved in the Middle East, but its role became even more dominant following the Gulf Crisis (1990-91) and as a result of its attempts to broker a peace between the Palestininans and Israel. Islamic fundamentalist terrorists, long opposed to a separate Jewish state, have taken the battle to the homeland of Israel's chief sponsor. The bombing of the World Trade Center in New York, on February 26, 1993, was the first indication that U.S. overseas installations and citizens were no longer the sole targets of Middle Eastern terrorists. This is likely to continue. ■

KU KLUX KLAN TERROR

Founded in Pulaski, Tennessee, in 1865, the Ku Klux Klan (KKK) began as a secret society for ex-Confederate officers, but soon became a widely feared terrorist organization. Although its membership and influence has experienced repeated rises and falls, the Klan survives to this day as one of the most extreme exponents of American racism.

THE FIRST WAVE OF TERRORISM

The term Ku Klux derives from the Greek *kyklos* – a drinking cup – suggesting that the Klan founders were both educated and intent on having a good time. But the post-Civil War South that spawned this secret club was populated by impoverished laborers and landless cotton planters. The Thirteenth Amendment, passed in 1865, abolished plentiful and cheap slave labor, and the freedmen, or ex-slaves, were to bear the brunt of white Southern recriminations.

The KKK took violent action against government officials and freedmen, who together threatened the supreme status of whites in the Southern states. Killings, beatings, lynchings, arson, and other terrorist attacks became common. By 1871, the KKK had attained considerable power in the South, attracting middle-class whites whom the Civil War had left poor and powerless. Riding at night, Klan members bedecked in white robes, masks, and hats intimidated juries, freed prisoners, and attacked officials who encouraged freedmen to vote.

> **KEY FACTS**
>
> - The KKK was formed to maintain white supremacy in 1865, at the end of the Civil War, and has been revived frequently for the same purpose.
> - Klan membership in the 1990s is thought to be between 9,000 and 20,000, and based principally in the Southern states.
> - Klan terrorist acts have included bombings, assassinations, arson, and lynchings.

The outrages compelled Congress to intervene. In 1870 and 1871, it passed a series of Force Acts, giving the president power to quash civil disturbances and to prosecute terrorist groups. Indictments under the Force Acts disrupted the formal KKK organization. After 1872, however, new legislation at the state level institutionalized Southern white supremacy. The KKK was quiet for the next 40 years, its aims satisfied.

In 1915, however, D.W. Griffith's epic motion picture *Birth of a Nation* was released. Glorifying the Old South and the Klan, it revived Southerners' fears of black equality, and aroused Northerners' anxieties over large-scale black migration northward. The film helped trigger a massive revival of the KKK.

After 1920, Klan membership soared as white Protestants reacted against the effects of Jewish and Catholic – especially Slavic – immigration. Economic factors played a part. The immigrants would work for lower wages, and wealthy factory owners such as Henry Ford eagerly hired the cheaper labor. The Klan became a legitimate pressure group with a peak membership of five million by 1925. Its appeal to the traditional values of patriotism, morality, and virtue brought it political success. The KKK helped elect 11 state governors and ten congressmen, and in 1924 it split the Democratic presidential convention, mainly because the Catholic Al Smith was a strong contender.

In addition to this legal activity, KKK terrorism continued in the Southern states. Klansmen tarred and feathered, tortured, and lynched blacks suspected of being involved with white women. Prosperous African-Americans and immigrants who jeopardized white economic power found their businesses burned and their possessions stolen. The KKK's administration tacitly supported such acts of vigilantism, maintaining that they embodied the popular will of the citizens.

This second period of KKK activity came to an abrupt end in 1925 with the imprisonment of Indiana Grand Dragon D.C. Stephenson, who was convicted of second degree murder. Revelations regarding the Klan's fostering of terrorism and corruption surfaced

Hulton Getty Picture Collection

A speaker denounces school desegregation at a Ku Klux Klan gathering in North Carolina, 1957.

during and after the trial. The nation was so appalled that this incarnation of the KKK was effectively finished as a political force by 1927.

The KKK experienced a renaissance after World War II, when African-Americans migrated to the North in search of work. Federal civil rights legislation, coupled with renewed fears of communist subversion, helped fuel white paranoia and hatred. In the 1960s, the Klan's popularity grew in response to efforts by the government, the Supreme Court, and civil rights workers to attack decades of legal segregation in the South. Many bombings and murders were attributed to the KKK during this period. Mississippi was the focus of renewed Klan violence as civil rights groups targeted the state in their voting rights drives of the mid-sixties. Between 1964 and 1969, led by Grand Wizard Samuel Holloway Bowers, the Mississippi KKK was allegedly responsible for nine murders, 75 bombings of black churches, and 300 beatings. The most infamous event in Mississippi occurred in 1964, when three student civil rights workers were murdered. Although the FBI investigated Klan activities, the collusion of the local police with the KKK hindered the Bureau's progress.

The KKK murder of Viola Luzzo, a white civil rights worker in Alabama in 1965, finally prompted a government crackdown. Investigations by Congress exposed gross misappropriation of KKK funds by Klan leaders. The revelations helped reduce the influence of the KKK leadership and, in concert with heightened FBI surveillance, its terrorist ability.

THE NEW EXTREMISTS

The KKK burst back onto the scene in the 1970s under the charismatic leadership of David Duke. However, the reborn KKK was factious, and by 1975, a new leader had emerged in the shape of Bill Wilkinson, the most influential KKK leader for the next decade. Adopting a policy of inflaming racial tensions wherever there was a spark of friction, Wilkinson pursued an increasingly militant stance by organizing KKK chapters in the American armed services and by recruiting retired ex-servicemen.

In North Carolina in November 1979, two carloads of white men ambushed a "Death to the Klan" march. They shot dead four demonstrators and wounded eight. Klan members were later arrested and charged, but were acquitted by a local all-white jury. Also acquitted was a Tennessee KKK member who shot and wounded four African-Americans in 1980.

In 1982, it was revealed that the KKK was operating a paramilitary camp in Texas. Vietnam War veterans and other retired servicemen were instructing Klansmen in guerrilla warfare and the use of explosives and sophisticated weapons. A judge closed the camp down after trainees threatened to turn their weapons on nearby immigrant communities. Other such camps, however, are known to exist.

By the late 1980s, the KKK had begun to work in earnest on its public image. It needed to garner public sympathy for its cause, and yet avoid surveillance by federal authorities. To evade prosecution, the KKK leadership now takes pains to deny involvement in terrorist activities. However, the rhetoric of its leaders remains violent and inflammatory. Furthermore, KKK members have been linked directly to a number of violent terrorist acts which, it is believed, could never have occurred without the approval of Klan leaders.

The KKK's membership dwindled to a few thousand during the early 1990s, and its violent acts became less frequent. Public condemnation and ubiquitous media coverage have made it difficult for extremist groups to sustain a national infrastructure. As an alternative, many Klan members have been drawn to the white supremacist Aryan Nation, to right-wing militias, and to neo-Nazi activists.

However, the outbreak of arson attacks on African-American churches in Southern states in 1996 has shown that the capacity of racist terrorists for violence is still as strong as ever. The FBI has failed to identify an organized conspiracy behind the recent attacks, with alleged culprits ranging from teenage deliquents to pyromaniacs. Nonetheless, it has attributed some of the attacks to Aryan Nation and to the Christian Knights, a KKK subgroup founded in 1985.

The challenge to the authorities may lie not so much in indicting the racist groups themselves, but in a more insidious threat. In the words of Jesse Jackson, "The Klan is the extreme expression of a deeper trend, of a white America that is targeting blacks as scapegoats..." Therefore, the Ku Klux Klan and other pro-white groups are still greatly feared and continue to be monitored by the government and by various civil rights groups.

Allison J. Gough

SEE ALSO: FAR-RIGHT EXTREMISM; VICTIMS OF TERRORISM; THE OKLAHOMA CITY BOMBING AND THE MILITIAS.

FURTHER READING

- Chalmers, David M. *Hooded Americanism: A History of the Ku Klux Klan.* 4th ed. Durham, NC: Duke University Press, 1994.
- Maclean, Nancy. *Behind the Mask of Chivalry: The Making of the Second Ku Klux Klan.* New York: Oxford University Press, 1994.
- Rice, Arnold S. *The Ku Klux Klan in American Politics.* Washington, DC: Public Affairs Press, 1962.
- Wade, Wyn Craig. *The Fiery Cross: The Ku Klux Klan in America.* London and New York: Simon and Schuster, 1987.

THE MOLLY MAGUIRES' TERRORIST CAMPAIGN

The Molly Maguires are best known in the United States as a terrorist organization that menaced the anthracite coal mining region of eastern Pennsylvania in the 1860s and 1870s. In fact, the group had their origin in Ireland, where the Molly Maguires formed the inner circle of the Ancient Order of Hibernians, a fraternal organization that opposed the abuses of English landlords. With the mass Irish Catholic emigration to the U.S. in the 1840s, the Molly Maguires found a new mission in the industrial workplaces of America. Contemporary accounts of Molly activities were invariably one-sided, portraying the Molly Maguires as the embodiment of evil. Since then, from Arthur Conan Doyle's thinly disguised vilification of the Molly Maguires in "The Valley of Fear" (1915), to the 1970 movie *The Molly Maguires*, the organization has entered the realms of folklore.

ORIGINS: POVERTY AND ETHNIC TENSION

Molly Maguire activity in the coalfields emerged as a response to both unfair labor practices and ethnic strife. The two were closely related. While the majority of the mineworkers were Irish Catholic, the coal bosses were largely old-stock Protestant Scotch-Irish and English immigrants. The mine superintendents and the brutal coal and iron police, on the other hand, drew their ranks from the Welsh Protestant community.

KEY FACTS

- In one county in Pennsylvania alone, in the first three months of 1865, the Molly Maguires were responsible for five murders, six assaults, and 27 robberies.
- McParlan's 1877 testimony resulted in the conviction of 20 Molly Maguires, 10 of whom were hanged, and the rest of whom were sentenced to jail terms ranging from two to seven years.

The first known instance of a terrorist act committed by the Molly Maguires occurred during disturbances surrounding the Union draft for the Civil War. During conscription protests on July 4, 1862, in Carbon County, Pennsylvania, a Molly Maguire allegedly murdered a mine foreman, F. W. Langdon. Although the incident grew out of the Copperhead (anti-war) sympathies of the miners, the murder points up the underlying motivations for much Molly Maguire violence in the coal towns. The murdered foreman was well known for his brutal exploitation of Irish Catholic workers. In 1863, opposition to the draft and violence spread throughout the coal field region. In the Audenreid mining region, the Molly Maguires murdered three mineowners and foremen known to be sympathetic to the draft and who were also known as hard taskmasters.

THE "LONG STRIKE"

The peak of Molly Maguire activity came in the 1870s. The catalyst for this violence was the savage depression of 1873. Unemployment and ruthless employer exploitation of workers precipitated a nationwide wave of demonstrations, protests, and riots. In Pennsylvania, the economy of the coal fields began to collapse. In November 1873, Franklin B. Gowen, owner of the Philadelphia and Reading Railroad Company, reduced workers' wages by 10 to 20 percent. Gowen's actions sparked a walkout in December 1874, and by the beginning of 1875, coal production had almost ceased.

The "Long Strike" lasted for four months. As the strike dragged on into the harsh winter of 1875, striking

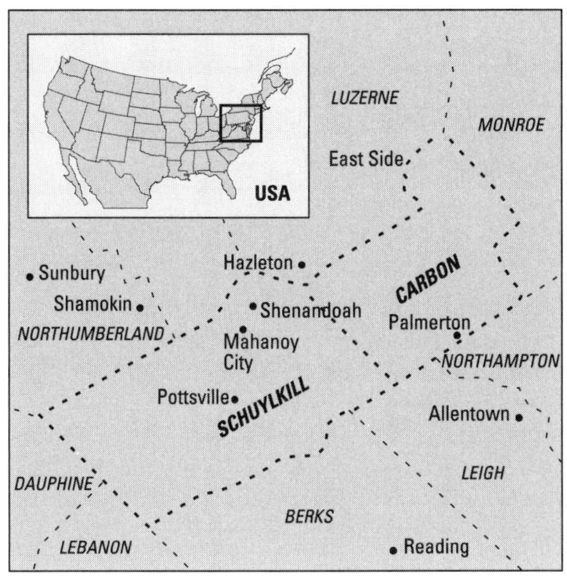

Molly Maguire attacks were concentrated in Schuylkill and Carbon counties, Pennsylvania.

mine communities reached starvation levels as company stores refused to extend to workers any more credit for provisions. As a result, the pace of violence increased. Much of the disorder was the work of the two most radical Molly Maguire lodges working out of Schuylkill and Carbon counties, led by John Kehoe and Alexander Campbell. Molly Maguires sabotaged as much coal production as they could. They uncoupled and derailed train cars, set engines on fire, and blew up rail lines and bridges to prevent strikebreakers from entering the coalfields. There were attempts, some successful, to burn company stores and offices, and even the headquarters of the Reading Railroad Company. Coal and iron police and pit bosses were beaten and sometimes slain. In particular, the murder of mine boss Thomas Sanger in the infamous Raven Run incident, on August 30, 1875, provoked a public outcry.

In all, the Molly Maguires probably assassinated at least 16 people, mostly mine bosses, and were responsible for countless acts of sabotage and robbery. If the group intended to intimidate the coal companies into improving wages and conditions for miners, then the policy failed. Coal mine owners refused to negotiate with the miner's union, and the Workingman's Benevolent Association (WBA); the miners, impoverished by months of idleness, returned to work in April 1875.

To complete his domination of the anthracite industry, Franklin B. Gowen aimed to destroy the WBA. Gowen realized that the way to break the back of the Union was to expose the Molly Maguires and link their violence and threats to the coalfield unions. In October 1873, Gowen had James McParlan, a Pinkerton detective, infiltrate the Molly Maguires. For two years, McParlan, operating under the alias James McKenna, worked inside the organization. In September 1876, McParlan's intelligence finally resulted in the arrest of three Molly Maguires, including Alexander Campbell, for the murder of mine foreman John P. Jones.

MOLLY MAGUIRES EXECUTED

On the strength of McParlan's testimony, Campbell and nine other Molly Maguires were convicted and then executed on June 21, 1877. McParlan's testimony failed to convict Kehoe, widely thought to be the major instigator of trouble in Schuylkill County, of anything other than conspiracy, for which Kehoe was sentenced to 14 years. However, in the climate of distrust that Gowen and McParlan had created, alleged witnesses to the murder of F. W. Langdon in 1862 came forward and accused Kehoe. In 1877, a court found Kehoe guilty of first degree murder, and he was executed in 1879. With the "King of the Mollies" dead, Gowen was able to move in and crush the WBA in the coalfields.

Later investigations have revealed that much of the violence of the 1870s had been instigated by Gowen to justify crushing the Molly Maguires and the union. In 1979, John Kehoe gained a posthumous pardon, and one year later a memorial plaque was placed on the wall at Schuylkill County Prison to commemorate the slain Molly Maguires as victims of a "campaign of repression directed against the fledgling mineworkers union of that historic period."

Allison J. Gough

SEE ALSO: SINGLE-ISSUE GROUP TERRORISM; ASSASSINATION; THE MINDSET OF THE TERRORIST.

FURTHER READING

- Broehl, Wayne G. *The Molly Maguires.* Cambridge, MA: Harvard University Press, 1964.
- Pinkerton, Allan. *The Mollie Maguires and the Detectives.* New York: Dover Publications, 1973; London: S. Low and Co., 1980.

BLACK PANTHERS AND TERROR

Two young black men, Huey P. Newton and Bobby Seale, founded the Black Panther Party in Oakland, California, in October 1966. Their ostensible aim was to protect the black community from police persecution, but by deliberately assuming an aggressive stance, their organization drifted into provocative and violent confrontation. At the height of its powers, the Black Panther Party became the leading black nationalist organization of the late 1960s. In the opinion of J. Edgar Hoover, head of the FBI, the Panthers were "the greatest threat to the internal security of the country."

IDEALS AND OBJECTIVES

Newton chose the group's name because "the panther never strikes first, but when backed into a corner, he will strike back viciously." However, the Panthers' initial ten-point program went far beyond the limited objective of communal defense. In addition to adequate education, housing, and standards of justice for the African-American community, they demanded black self-determination and the establishment of a black separatist state. To achieve these goals, the Black Panthers were willing to enlist the support of predominantly white groups, such as the communists. They also formed an alliance until 1969 with the radical student Weatherman organization.

KEY FACTS

- During its peak, the Black Panther Party had an estimated 1,500-2,000 members in more than 60 cities across 26 states.
- In disturbances during 1969, police arrested 749 Black Panther members and killed 27.
- Stokeley Carmichael, an activist and member of the Black Panther Party, had previously founded the Lowndes County Freedom Organization in Mississippi. This group was known locally as the Black Panthers.

Although the Panthers' eventual goal was political revolution, they did not embark on terrorist or guerrilla operations. They intended to stay within the bounds of legality until the conditions were right for revolution. However, their recruiting methods, rhetoric, and actions made confrontation inevitable. Dressed in black berets and black leather jackets, and openly carrying guns, Panther members presented an aggressive and appealing image to young African-Americans. They were not the first black group to take up firearms in "self-defense." In the 1950s and 1960s, armed blacks had banded together to protect themselves from the Ku Klux Klan and other white supremacists. However, most of the Panthers' recruits came from the street-gangs of the urban ghettos, and this created some problems for the group. Seale, the chairman, complained of "problems with a lot of people who came in and used the Party as a base for criminal activity which the Party never endorsed or had anything to do with."

The Panthers also employed highly inflammatory language. The party newspaper, *Black Panther*, was full of provocative statements and incitements to violence, for example: "America, you will be cleansed with fire, by blood, by death. We...will trample your...ashes beneath our naked black feet; we must step up our sniping – until the last pig is dead, shot to death with his own gun and the bullets in his guts that he had meant for the people." The Panthers' chief of staff, David Hilliard, attempted to justify such statements when brought to trial on charges of advocating the assassination of President Richard Nixon. He had said "We will kill Richard Nixon. We kill anyone...who stands in the way of our freedom." Hilliard maintained this was "political rhetoric. We can call it a metaphor. It is the language of the ghetto."

VIOLENT CONFRONTATION

The Black Panthers' policy of overtly "patrolling" the police out on the streets, while openly carrying guns, led to hazardous situations, which Newton described in his autobiography: "At times [the police] drew their

Associated Press/Topham Picturepoint

Bobby Seale took confrontation into his 1971 trial and was imprisoned for contempt of court.

Topham Picturepoint

By May 1971, Huey Newton had renounced violent struggle in favor of pursuing constitutional reform.

guns and we drew ours, until we reached a sort of stand-off.... I often felt that some day one of the police would go crazy and pull the trigger." Even though Newton, a university student, was well versed in the law – particularly in regard to freedom of speech – and was careful to stay within it, the atmosphere was dangerously confrontational.

From the beginning, the authorities watched the Panthers closely. Police infiltrated the organization, a task made considerably easier by the Panthers' haphazard recruiting methods. The inevitable crackdown began when local police and federal officials raided Panther offices. Violence also helped justify stronger measures to control the Panthers. In 1968, Newton was involved in a shoot-out with the police and was wounded in the stomach; a policeman was killed in the exchange of fire. Newton was accused of murder but was jailed for three years for voluntary manslaughter.

By 1969, all the Black Panthers' leadership had been imprisoned or – like Eldridge Cleaver, their Minister of Information – had fled the U.S. The most controversial case involved the death of two Chicago Panthers, Mark Clark and Fred Hampton, killed in a police raid on their apartment on December 4, 1969. A federal grand jury heard that the Panthers had been asleep, and in the incident, in which another seven Panthers were arrested, the police fired 83 shots into the apartment while only one shot was fired at the police.

In 1971, Seale was tried for inciting a riot in Chicago, and by mid-1971, the Black Panthers had effectively fallen apart. The party was split between the exiled Cleaver, who advocated bloody revolution and guerrilla warfare, and the increasingly law-abiding Newton. Newton later admitted his policy of confrontation with the police had been ill-conceived: "All we got was war and bloodshed." He said that the Panthers in the future would be ready "to operate within the system to see whether we can change it. It is wrong to say the system cannot give you anything because it is just not true."

M. Christopher Mann

SEE ALSO: KU KLUX KLAN TERROR; STUDENT TERROR: THE WEATHERMEN; URBAN TERROR: THE SYMBIONESE LIBERATION ARMY.

FURTHER READING

- Andrews, Lor B. *Black Power, White Blood.* New York: Pantheon Books, 1996.
- Foner, Philip S., ed. *Black Panthers Speak.* New York: Da Capo Press, 1995.
- Newton, Huey. *War Against the Panthers: A Study of Repression in America.* New York: Harlem River Press, 1996.

STUDENT TERROR: THE WEATHERMEN

The Weathermen – who later referred to themselves as Weather Underground – were an anarchic splinter group made up of various left-wing student factions in the late 1960s. They first declared their goal to be "the destruction of American imperialism and the achievement of a classless world." Through the 1970s, the Weathermen waged a campaign of bombings and other terrorist attacks, and included many high-profile institutions among their targets.

CAMPUS ORIGINS

One of the United States' most influential left-wing groups of the 1960s was Students for a Democratic Society (SDS), which aimed at revitalizing American democracy by shaking up existing institutions. By the late 1960s, however, the SDS was so frustrated with its lack of achievement that some of its members began waging a terrorist campaign.

In the spring of 1969, a number of SDS leaders in Chicago reformed into a national collective. They issued a manifesto entitled "You Don't Need a Weatherman to Tell You Which Way the Wind Blows." The manifesto spelled out the group's aims, which were essentially to subvert the government and bring about a mass revolution by the working proletariat.

The Weathermen formed collectives of between five and 25 members in a number of cities, all under the strict control of the so-called Chicago Weather Bureau. In these collectives, members gave up their possessions, their bank accounts, their privacy, and any monogamous relationships – all seen as undesirable sentimental ties. In effect, they had to surrender their individuality to serve the cause. Some of the Weathermens' first actions took place in the summer of 1969, when they carried out "jail breaks" in schools, taking over classrooms to deliver their revolutionary message to the pupils, and in the process sometimes became involved in violent scuffles with the police.

In the fall of 1969, the Weathermen began their so-called "Days of Rage" campaign. On October 8, the second anniversary of Che Guevara's death, 80 Weathermen marched into Lincoln Park in Chicago. Wearing black helmets and shouting slogans, they made speeches in front of a few hundred youths who had gathered there. The crowd of youths rushed out into the streets and rioted. Vastly outnumbered by the police, most of the rioters were beaten and arrested.

By the time the Weathermen conducted their National Council meeting in Flint, Michigan, in December 1969, the group was disillusioned – not only with the student left, but also with the working class. The Weathermen now saw themselves as the only revolutionary group in America, and were increasingly committed to violent insurgency.

KEY FACTS

- The Weathermen formed a loose alliance with the Black Panther Party in the late 1960s.
- By 1969, the Weathermen had become ardent admirers of Charles Manson, the hippie commune leader who was at the time on trial for murder.
- After the demise of Weather Underground, some of its members went on to found the left-wing May 19th Communist Coalition.

BOMBING CAMPAIGNS

Early on in 1970, about a hundred members of the Weathermen went underground to escape the law, and started a campaign of violence. Although it is difficult to establish the number of bombings they carried out, it is known that, between September 1969 and May 1970, various radicals were responsible for about 250 bombings, mainly against government buildings with Vietnam War connections such as draft board offices.

Associated Press

Weathermen founder Mark Rudd (in the plaid shirt) leading a riot at Columbia University in 1968.

Terrorists bombed a department at the University of Wisconsin where work on an army math research project was taking place, and killed a graduate student. Not only did the bombing campaign fail to achieve anything, it was also self-defeating: in March 1970, three members of the Weathermen blew themselves up while constructing a bomb in Greenwich Village.

Nevertheless, the Weathermen continued with their terrorist campaigns. In August 1970, they bombed the Bank of Brazil in New York; on September 13, they helped LSD guru Timothy Leary escape from prison; and on March 1, 1971, they bombed the U.S. Senate offices in the Capitol building in Washington, D.C.

THE BREAK UP OF THE GROUP

In 1971, the collective renamed itself Weather Underground, both to appease growing concern about feminist issues and to reflect the fugitive nature of its core command. It was about this time that the activists began to disagree over diverging aims and ideals. Although Weather Underground continued to commit terrorist acts, even bombing the Pentagon in 1975, the collective eventually broke up during 1976–77. Some of the more hard-line members went on to found new extremist groups. A number of founder members eventually surrendered to the authorities: Mark Rudd turned himself in in 1977, followed in 1981 by Bernadine Dohrn and William Ayers. The final fugitive from justice, Jeffrey Powell, gave himself up in January 1994.

John Finlayson

SEE ALSO: REVOLUTIONARY TERRORISM; BOMBING OPERATIONS; BLACK PANTHERS AND TERROR.

FURTHER READING

- Gitlin, Todd. *The Sixties: Years of Hope, Days of Rage.* New York: Bantam Books, 1987.
- Hoffman, Abbie. *Soon to Be a Major Motion Picture.* New York: Putnam, 1980.
- Zaroulis, Nancy, and Gerald Sullivan. *Who Spoke Up? American Protest Against the War in Vietnam.* New York: Doubleday, 1984.

URBAN TERROR: THE SYMBIONESE LIBERATION ARMY

The Symbionese Liberation Army (SLA), a leftover of 1960s radicalism, achieved notoriety in 1974 when its members kidnapped Patricia Hearst, grand-daughter of U.S. newspaper tycoon William Randolph Hearst. She in turn, the product of an affluent and conventional upbringing, achieved notoriety when she was pictured by security cameras taking part in a bank robbery carried out by the SLA.

The group originated in Berkeley at the end of 1972. Its founders included Berkeley graduate Nancy Ling, her partner Chris Thompson, and Willy Wolfe, a prison welfare visitor involved with the Black Cultural Association. Various others, most from comfortable middle-class backgrounds, gradually joined this circle.

One of the prisoners Wolfe visited was Donald DeFreeze, who led a group called Unisight. Although Unisight was ostensibly tackling African-American social issues, it was in fact preparing for an armed urban insurrection. When DeFreeze escaped from prison in March 1973, he went to Berkeley, and slowly this circle of friends consolidated into an active political group.

The SLA took its name from the concept of symbiosis – the mutual interdependence of organisms – because of its belief that the revolution would only come about through oppressed blacks and whites, and men and women, working together in a symbiotic relationship. Ideologically, the SLA were muddled, uneasily linking outlandish notions with orthodox socialist beliefs.

The SLA viewed people in terms of nationality and race rather than class, and wanted a system of sovereign nations of racial types. Declaring a revolutionary war against "the Fascist Capitalist Class," it offered its help to all liberation movements. However, only the Black Guerrilla Family – a splinter group of the Black Panthers – proved sympathetic, providing help when the SLA was later on the run.

KEY FACTS

- Founder SLA member Donald DeFreeze was strongly influenced by the methods of the Weathermen, the left-wing student terrorist group.
- On taking up the SLA cause, Patty Hearst adopted the nickname Tanya.
- The SLA adopted for its emblem the seven-headed cobra, an ancient Egyptian and Hindu symbol for indestructibility and unity in diversity.

MURDER AND KIDNAPPING

The SLA's first action was the murder of Oakland's African-American superintendent of schools, Dr. Marcus Foster, on November 6, 1973. The SLA chose him because of his controversial decision that pupils in local black schools should carry identity cards in the interests of their safety. As a number of black activists opposed this, the SLA thought the issue would provide a popular local cause to justify violent action. In fact, the terrorist act brough condemnation from all quarters, including Black Panther leader Huey Newton.

The next planned move was the kidnapping of Patricia Hearst. The SLA selected her because she was from a wealthy family and presented an easy target, as she was living unprotected in Berkeley. On February 4, 1974, three SLA members entered Hearst's apartment and forced her into the trunk of a car. Three days later, the SLA released a taped message in which it threatened to kill Hearst if any attempts were made to free her or if any action was taken against SLA elements. The next message demanded that a system of free food distribution to the poor be set up and funded by Hearst's father, Randolph Hearst. He agreed to the demand. A further

Associated Press/Topham Picturepoint

The authorities pounced on six SLA fugitives in Compton, Los Angeles, in May 1974. They fired 5,371 rounds, causing a lethal conflagration.

taped message, however, lent an unusual twist to the story. Patty Hearst insisted that it was the FBI who were trying to kill her, and that all the SLA wanted was to feed the people and get justice for two imprisoned members.

When Hearst's father promised $2 million at once and another $2 million in January 1975 for the food plan, the SLA promised to arrange her release. But to her parents' astonishment, Hearst decided to stay with the SLA. Following the bank raid in which Hearst took part, and during which she was caught on film, a warrant was issued for her arrest by the FBI.

FUGITIVES FROM JUSTICE

Now on the run, the SLA headed to Los Angeles. DeFreeze, Wolfe, and four others took refuge in an apartment in Compton. From previous incidents, the authorities knew the vehicles they were using. On May 17, 1974, 150 members of the Los Angeles Police Department, 11 FBI agents, and 100 Sheriff's Officers fired on the apartment, and the fugitives were killed.

Patty Hearst disappeared, but was finally captured on September 18. The court found her guilty of armed robbery and sentenced her to seven years, although the sentence was commuted and she walked free in February, 1979. To this day, Hearst still insists that she was brainwashed by the SLA.

For many, the SLA was merely a postscript to 1960s radicalism. But if the group left any legacy, it was in helping to reinforce the mistaken belief that terrorist acts in the U.S. would come only from the left.

John Finlayson

SEE ALSO: HOSTAGE NEGOTIATIONS; BLACK PANTHERS AND TERROR; STUDENT TERROR: THE WEATHERMEN.

FURTHER READING

- Hearst, Patricia. *Patty Hearst: Her Own Story.* New York: Avon Books, 1988.
- Kinney, Jean. *An American Journey: The Short Life of Willy Wolfe.* New York: Simon and Schuster, 1979.
- Weed, Steven, with Scott Stanton. *My Search for Patty Hearst.* London: Secker and Warburg, and New York: Crown Publishers, 1976.

TERROR BY PUERTO RICAN SEPARATISTS

The United States invaded the Caribbean island of Puerto Rico in 1898, during the Spanish-American war, and established a colony there. Since 1952, Puerto Rico has been an *associated free state* of the U.S. While many Puerto Ricans welcome the fact that their country is a possession of the U.S., there is a powerful movement for independent status. A minority engage in sporadic acts of terrorism, both on the island itself and on the U.S. mainland, in order to achieve their goal of independence.

"FREE PUERTO RICO"

There has always been a nationalist resistance to the U.S. presence in Puerto Rico, and occasionally this has exploded into violence. In 1954, the nationalists staged an uprising that was put down by troops, tanks, and aircraft. The town of Jayuya, held briefly by the nationalists, was bombed, and there were allegations of massacres in the streets of Utuando. At the same time, seeking to bring the plight of Puerto Rico to world attention, two Puerto Rican nationalists, Oscar Collazo and Giselio Torresola, attempted to assassinate President Truman. Torresola and a presidential guard were killed. Collazo was jailed for 29 years.

KEY FACTS

- During the 1930s, there were several armed clashes between Puerto Rican nationalists and U.S. security forces.
- During the 1970s and 1980s, there were four principal terrorist groups. The FALN alone committed over 100 terrorist acts on the U.S. mainland.
- In 1989, four members of Los Macheteros were convicted after a $7.1 million robbery of the Wells Fargo depot in West Hartford, Connecticut – it was the second largest cash haul in U.S. history.

Many nationalists saw the establishment of the associated free state in 1952 as a disguise for the continuing colonization of the island. In 1954, four Puerto Rican nationalists, shouting "Free Puerto Rico," sprayed bullets from the gallery of the U.S. House of Representatives, injuring five congressmen. Although no one was killed, Rafael Cancel Miranda, Andres Figueroa Cordero, and Irvin Flores received sentences totaling 75 years, while Lolita Lebron was sentenced to 50 years. All four were released in 1979.

A new wave of nationalist terrorism erupted during the late 1960s, with bombings aimed at U.S. businesses and military installations across the island. These were the work of a group called Armed Freedom Fighters, which was backed by Cuba. In 1975, two people were killed and 11 were injured when a bomb exploded in the town of Mayaguez, just minutes before the start of a socialist party rally. Two weeks later, terrorism spread to mainland America, when a bomb exploded at New York's historic Fraunce's Tavern. Four were killed and 45 were injured.

A new organization called the Armed Forces for National Liberation (FALN) claimed responsibility for this attack. Founded in 1974, the group was headed by Chicago-born Puerto Ricans William Morales and Luis Rosado Ayala. The group has claimed responsibility for more than 100 bombings, including 30 in New York and others in Chicago, San Francisco, and Washington, DC. These attacks have claimed the lives of six people, injured many more, and caused more than $3.5 million in damages.

In 1979, Morales lost an eye, one hand, and all but two of his fingers on the other, in an explosion at the FALN's bomb factory in Queens, in New York. He was imprisoned, but escaped while being treated in a hospital. Eleven other members of the FALN were indicted for bombings in Chicago, including the group's leader, Carlos Torres, who was on the FBI's "most wanted" list.

Frank Spooner Pictures

A Los Macheteros bomb attack on the Muñiz air base on Puerto Rico, on January 12, 1981, destroyed nine jet fighters and damaged two more.

Other groups, however, continued the struggle. In 1978, a nonviolent protester named Angel Rodríguez was murdered while serving time in a Federal prison in Tallahassee, Florida. The guards were suspected, but no one was arrested. In response, on December 9, 1979, a group calling themselves Los Macheteros (the cane cutters) attacked a navy bus, killing two sailors.

During the 1980 U.S. presidential elections, Puerto Rican nationalists seized the headquarters of the Carter and Bush campaigns in several U.S. cities, holding staff hostage. On December 21, 1980, a group calling itself the Puerto Rican Armed Resistance set off two pipe bombs in Penn Station, New York City. No one was injured.

On January 12, 1981, Los Macheteros blew up nine military jet fighters and damaged two more at the Muñiz air base on Puerto Rico. On November 28, they blew up a power station in the Puerto Rican capital, San Juan, blacking out part of the island. On May 16, 1982, terrorists attacked American sailors returning to the ship after a night of shore liberty in San Juan, killing one and badly injuring three others. The FALN, inactive for two years, set off a bomb on Wall Street on February 28, 1982.

On 16 September, 1983, Los Macheteros stole $7.2 million from the Wells Fargo terminal in Hartford, Connecticut. The raid, although a lucrative venture for Los Macheteros', gave the FBI enough evidence to arrest a number of the terrorist group's leaders. At the same time, in August 1985, the authorities also arrested several prominent members of the FALN, since when both groups have been relatively quiet.

There are currently moves within Congress to hold a referendum in Puerto Rico on its future status, whether as the United States' 51st state, or as a fully independent country. It remains to be seen whether the outcome of this referendum will finally put to rest the specter of terrorism that has haunted this island.

Nigel Cawthorne

SEE ALSO: NATIONALIST TERRORISM; ASSASSINATION.

FURTHER READING

- Fernandez, Ronald. *Puerto Rico: The Disenchanted Island*. 2nd ed. New York: Praeger, 1996.
- Jiménez de Wagenheim, Olga. *Puerto Rico's Revolt for Independence*. Boulder, CO: Westview Press, 1985.

THE WORLD TRADE CENTER BOMBING

On February 26, 1993, a truck laden with 1,200 pounds of dynamite exploded in the basement parking lot of one of the twin towers of the World Trade Center, in New York's downtown business district. The blast carved a 200-ft. crater in the parking lot, tore a hole in the ceiling, and poured rubble onto the subway station below. The explosion killed six people and injured more than a thousand. Fortunately, the structure of the 110-story tower remained unshaken, otherwise the death toll would have been enormous. In the aftermath of one of the United States' worst terrorist incidents to date, police and FBI agents set to work finding out who was responsible.

Just two hours after the explosion, a man named Mohammed Salameh entered a truck rental office in New Jersey. He claimed the truck he had rented had been stolen, and demanded the return of his $400 deposit. Five days later, FBI agents at the bomb site found the serial number of the van used in the attack. The FBI quickly traced the van to the truck rental company, and then arrested Salameh.

LINKS WITH ISLAMIC FUNDAMENTALISM

The FBI next exposed a network of Muslim fundamentalists, some with terrorist links, centered around Sheikh Omar Abdel-Rahman. He was the spiritual leader of the Islamic Group (al-Gamaa al-Islamiyya), a splinter group of the extreme al-Jihad ("Holy War") movement in Egypt. In 1981, Abdel-Rahman had been implicated in the assassination of Egyptian President Anwar Sadat. Eventually acquitted, Abdel-Rahman came to the United States in 1990. From a mosque in New Jersey, he broadcast his anti-Western sermons to militant Muslims in Egypt.

The presence of Islamic fundamentalists in the United States largely stemmed from the Soviet occupation of Afghanistan (1979-89). In the 1980s, the U.S. supported fundamentalists based in Pakistan, who fought alongside Afghan *mujahideen* (holy warriors) against the Soviets. Mahmud Abu-Halima, one of those implicated in the World Trade Center bombing, had fought in Afghanistan, and Sheikh Abdel-Rahman had visited the *mujahideen* bases in northern Pakistan. Initially, the CIA supported Abdel-Rahman. But with the Soviet withdrawal from Afghanistan in 1989, the U.S. was targeted by Islamic fundamentalists who were increasingly anti-American and anti-Western.

AN AUDACIOUS PLOT EXPOSED

Following investigations into the bombing, the FBI set a trap for their suspects. They sent into the group an undercover agent, who posed as a former Egyptian military officer with access to explosives. He drew in various fundamentalists – including Abdel Rahman – who were determined to avenge the arrests following the New York City explosion. During the course of meetings in May 1993, recorded secretly by the FBI, the fundamentalists hatched an extraordinary plot.

In a single day, the terrorists planned to assassinate UN Secretary-General Boutros Boutros-Ghali; to blow up the UN headquarters; and to destroy an office building with 10,000 workers, along with two New York City traffic tunnels under the Hudson River that allow access to the island of Manhattan from New Jersey. Had the plot succeeded, it would have brought immeasurable bloodshed and chaos to New York City – certainly more than the World Trade Center bombing.

In June 1993, FBI agents arrested the terrorists as they mixed explosives in a safe house in Jersey City. In August, Abdel-Rahman and three others were charged

KEY FACTS

- The twin World Trade Center towers attract 100,000 workers and visitors each day.
- The Islamic fundamentalists connected with the World Trade Center bombing had also planned to assassinate Egyptian President Hosni Mubarak.
- During the first 24 hours after the explosion, 19 different individuals or groups claimed responsibility for the terrorist act.

Popperfoto

The blast blew in the roof of the subway station below the twin towers, showering debris on commuters.

with participation in the World Trade Center bombing, and with the additional plots uncovered by the FBI. In March 1994, the four were found guilty on all charges and sentenced to life imprisonment. At a second ruling in October 1995, Abdel-Rahman and nine others were found guilty of planning a campaign of urban terrorism. Another suspect, Ramzi Ahmed Yousef, was extradited from Pakistan to New York in February 1995 to face charges of buying and mixing the explosives used in the 1993 bombing. He is also suspected in several other acts of terrorism.

WHO WAS RESPONSIBLE?

Although the terrorists were brought to justice, a query remains over the motives behind the bombing. The U.S. authorities are not convinced it was an isolated incident; they suspect it may represent part of a wider Islamic plot to destabilize the U.S. government and weaken its friendly ties with Israel and Egypt. Another theory is that Ramzi Yousef, an Iraqi, was an agent of Iraqi intelligence, but this has not been proven. Regardless of the tight security measures introduced in New York's financial district, it seems unlikely that the long sentences for the bombers will end the threat that terrorism poses to the United States.

Matthew Hughes

SEE ALSO: BOMBING OPERATIONS; TERROR IN AFGHANISTAN; THE OKLAHOMA CITY BOMBING AND THE MILITIAS.

FURTHER READING

- Jeffrey, Simon. *Terrorist Trap: America's Experience with Terrorism.* Bloomington: Indiana University Press, 1994.
- Nacos, Brigitte L. *Terrorism and the Media.* New York: Columbia University Press, 1995.
- Smith, Brent L. *Terrorism in America: Pipebombs and Pipedreams.* New York: State University of New York Press, 1994.

ANTI-ABORTION ACTIVISTS' TERROR CAMPAIGN

On December 30, 1994, John C. Salvi III walked into the Planned Parenthood clinic in Brookline, Massachusetts. He opened fire with a rifle, killing the receptionist and wounding three other people. Salvi then drove to the Preterm Health Services clinic, where he killed a second person and injured two more. The next day, he fired 23 shots at an abortion clinic in Norfolk, Virginia, before police apprehended him. Although Salvi's defense lawyers protested that their defendant was insane at the time of the killings, Salvi was sentenced to two consecutive life terms in prison.

Twenty years earlier, in the early 1970s, protests against abortion had been relatively peaceful events. Even when the landmark *Roe v. Wade* Supreme Court ruling of 1973 gave American women the constitutionally protected right to abortion, the reactions were initially mild. For example, two years after the ruling, The National Conference of Catholic Bishops merely issued a "pastoral plan for pro-life activities." And, it was not until 1979 that conservative lobbyists and fundraisers started working in earnest to defeat politicians who were known to support abortion rights. Although there were a few bomb and death threats, almost all anti-abortion activists were confident that the *Roe v. Wade* ruling could be reversed through the legitimate political process. By the late 1970s, however, this belief began to fade.

KEY FACTS

- Between 1993 and 1996, terrorists killed five people connected with abortion practices and wounded 11 others.
- Operation Rescue used children to blockade abortion clinics and stall arrests by police.
- Anti-abortionists have produced a number of publications that outline the various methods of direct action.

THE PATH TOWARD DIRECT ACTION

Groups such as the National Right to Life Committee (NRLC), which had formed after the 1973 ruling, were beginning to exert political pressure on the government. Some members, frustrated by the lack of progress in changing abortion law, formed more activist organizations. They used direct action tactics – picketing clinics and physicians' offices and homes, and filling the locks of clinic doors with glue. Another tactic was "sidewalk counseling," in which an activist would approach a woman entering a clinic and try to persuade her not to have an abortion.

In 1986, Randall Terry, together with Joseph Scheidler (founder of the Pro-Life Action League), formed Operation Rescue – a group which resorted to even more radical acts. Its members demonstrated outside clinics, and lay down in clinic doorways to prevent abortion patients from entering. When the police inevitably arrived to break up the human blockade, the activists simply relaxed their bodies so they had to be physically removed from the premises. In 1991, members of Operation Rescue staged a three-week blockade of local abortion clinics in Wichita, Kansas, where the police arrested 1,900 protesters.

ANTI-ABORTION TERRORIST ACTS

In addition to forming physical blockades, anti-abortionists have resorted to bombings, arsons, and shootings. According to the National Abortion Federation, activists committed 161 bombings and acts of arson against abortion clinics between 1977

Associated Press/Topham Picturepoint

Anti-abortionists demonstrate outside the U.S. Supreme Court in January 1989.

and 1992. In 1984, violence erupted in Pensacola, Florida, where activists bombed a women's clinic, and several other terrorist incidents followed. One group linked with the attacks in Pensacola is Rescue America, a militant organization that regularly advocates the use of violence. In March 1993, Michael Griffin – then a new recruit to Rescue America – shot and killed a doctor outside a Pensacola clinic. In July 1994, Paul Hill, a former church minister, shot dead a doctor and his bodyguard. Hill was executive director of Defensive Action, a militant anti-abortion group. The violence also spread over the border into Canada. In May 1992, a firebombing destroyed a clinic in Toronto. In November 1994, an activist shot and wounded an abortion doctor at his Vancouver home.

The U.S. authorities are increasingly concerned that some radical anti-abortionists may be linking up with right-wing militia groups. They fear anti-abortionists plan not only to use existing paramilitary training camps, but also to develop their own armed militia. Moreover, the Ku Klux Klan is taking a stance against abortion rights – for Caucasian women, if not for other races. In August 1994, the KKK demonstrated outside a Florida abortion clinic, protesting against the protection offered to clinics by federal marshals. The federal government is investigating anti-abortion groups to find out whether there is a mass conspiracy involved.

Most anti-abortion organizations in the U.S. have condemned extremist violence, pointing out that the bombers and arsonists are terrorist individuals on the fringes of the movement. However, not all such organizations are unequivocal in their condemnation. Some anti-abortionists blame bombings on the very existence of abortion clinics, while others defend the terrorist killings as justifiable homicide.

LEGISLATION AGAINST ACTIVISTS

The U.S. Congress has reacted to the escalation of violence among the more radical elements of the anti-abortion movement. In May 1994, President Clinton signed into law the Freedom of Access to Clinic Entrances Act (FACE), which restricts anti-abortion

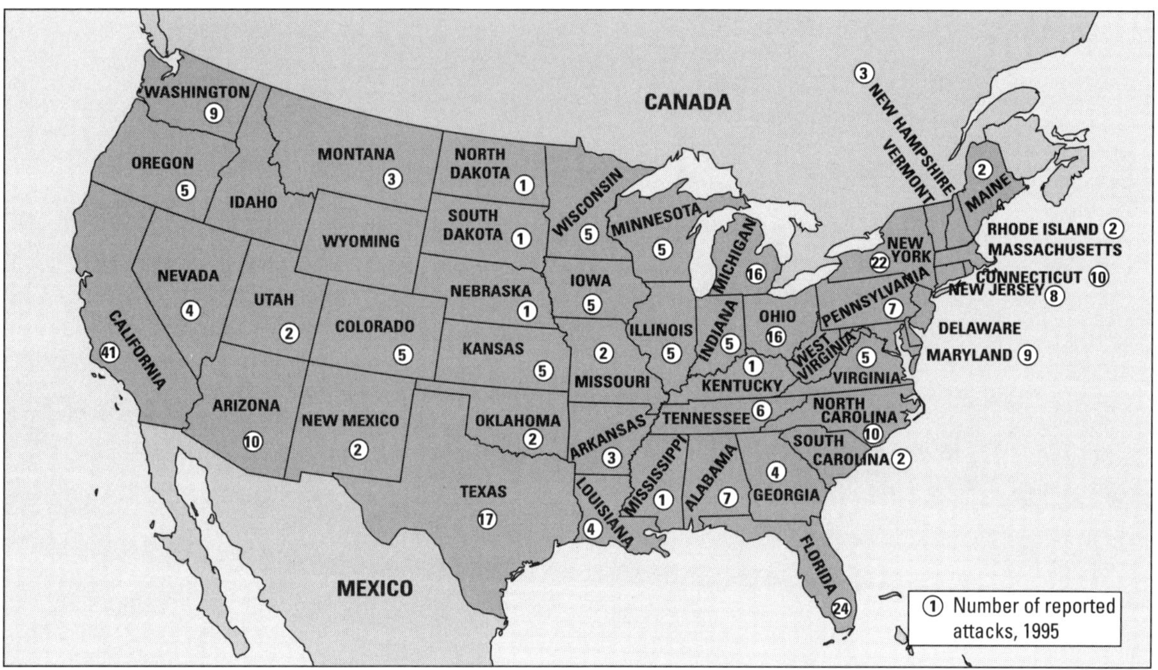

There were nearly 2,000 disruptive incidents reported at abortion clinics in 1995, including 295 violent attacks.

groups from interfering with or intimidating someone who is obtaining or providing any form of "reproductive health services." First-time offenders face fines of up to $100,000, with far stiffer fines and three-year prison sentences for subsequent offenses.

The government is also looking into the possibility of employing the Racketeer Influenced Corrupt Organizations Law (RICO) against some of the more radical anti-abortionists. Congress enacted RICO primarily to stop organized crime from taking over legitimate businesses, but federal courts have upheld broader applications of the law. On March 26, 1996, two anti-abortion activists were indicted on federal conspiracy and arson charges after an investigation into fires at two Virginia clinics.

In spite of the progress made in legislation, the tactics of the anti-abortion groups have been effective in making abortions more difficult to secure. Fear of harassment – or even death – is one reason for the decrease in the number of doctors seeking training or becoming approved abortion providers. Some landlords have refused to renew leases for abortion clinics through fear that their property might be damaged, and many insurance companies now place prohibitively expensive premiums on policies for abortion clinics.

There is no way of predicting the outcome of the confrontation between the anti-abortion and pro-choice forces. The commitment displayed by activists on both sides of the issue remains intense.

Gary R. Perlstein

SEE ALSO: SINGLE-ISSUE GROUP TERRORISM; BOMBING OPERATIONS; THE OKLAHOMA CITY BOMBING AND THE MILITIAS.

FURTHER READING

- Blanchard, Dallas A., and Terry J. Prewitt. *Religious Violence and Abortion.* Gainesville: University Press of Florida, 1993.
- McKeegan, Michele. *Abortion Politics: Mutiny in the Ranks of the Right.* New York: The Free Press, 1992.
- Staggenborg, Suzanne. *The Pro-Choice Movement.* New York and Oxford: Oxford University Press, 1994.
- Wilson, Michele, and John Lynxwiler. "Abortion Clinic Violence as Terrorism," in *Terrorism* 11, No. 4: 263-273.

THE OKLAHOMA CITY BOMBING AND THE MILITIAS

At 9:02 A.M. on April 19, 1995, a rented truck parked outside the Alfred P. Murrah federal building in Oklahoma City exploded with the force of 4,800 pounds of explosives. The blast ripped into the federal building, bringing down several floors and burying hundreds of victims beneath tons of rubble. Rescue workers spent days sifting through the debris in search of victims who may have been trapped. The bombing killed 169 people and injured more than 500. The horror grew worse when it was realized that many of the victims were children who had been in the day care center on the second floor. This incident was the deadliest terrorist attack to be perpetrated on U.S. soil, and the first such incident to occur in America's heartland. The nation was shocked and horrified.

Less than two hours after the explosion, a highway patrolman stopped a speeding 1977 Mercury near Perry, Oklahoma. The driver had a concealed weapon, and was taken into custody. Police were about to release him when an eyewitness description of the man who rented the truck used in the bombing reached the highway patrol station. The police discovered that they held the leading suspect in the Oklahoma City bombing. Contrary to immediate assumptions, the chief suspect was not an emissary of a Middle Eastern terrorist group but instead was an American citizen. His name was Timothy McVeigh, and the authorities later charged him with the bombing. They also charged Terry Nichols, a longtime friend of McVeigh's, with helping mix fertilizer with fuel oil to make the bomb. Michael Fortier, another of McVeigh's friends, has pleaded guilty to charges of transporting stolen guns, lying to the FBI, and failing to warn authorities about the bomb plot. Prosecutors planned to use his testimony against McVeigh.

Assuming McVeigh and Nichols are found guilty, their actions add to a lengthy, but often overlooked, tradition of American terrorism originating on its own shores. It has included the activities of the Molly Maguires in the 1870s, and the Black Panther Party, the Weathermen, and the Symbionese Liberation Army during the 1960s and 1970s.

SUMMARY

- On April 19, 1995, the United States was rocked by the worst terrorist outrage in its history. A massive fertilizer bomb wrecked the Murrah federal building in Oklahoma City, killing 169 people, many of them children.
- Timothy McVeigh, a Gulf War veteran, has been charged with committing the Oklahoma City atrocity.
- McVeigh is associated with the extremist right-wing militia movement. Some of the militias have advocated violent action in pursuit of their aims. These aims are diverse, but central to militia members' beliefs is the conviction that the U.S. government poses a threat to the constitutional rights of the American people.

THE MILITIA CONNECTION

When police arrested McVeigh, their investigation revealed him to be a 27-year-old drifter who had served in the army during Operation Desert Storm, and had earned a Bronze Star. However, as police accumulated more information about him, his friends, and associations, a different picture began to emerge. McVeigh was an individual who had been outraged by the federal government siege of the Branch Davidian compound at Waco, Texas, which ended on April 19, 1993. He believed this to be just one more example of U.S. government interference in the lives of its citizens. He also appeared to have an association with the Michigan Militia – an organization that has loose

Popperfoto

The Murrah federal building in Oklahoma City was devastated by a huge fertilizer bomb on the morning of April 19, 1995.

ties to other militias around the U.S., as well as other groups that can be placed in a category called the radical right wing.

THE PARANOID RIGHT

The militias have existed for more than 25 years, and have a heritage that goes back to the anti-immigrant or nativist movements of the middle of the nineteenth century, and the Populist party political campaigns of the 1880s and 1890s. The militias are just the most recent manifestation. The groups have various names like the Klan; Posse Comitatus (Latin for power of the county); the American Nazi Party; the Covenant, the Sword, the Arm of the Lord; the Aryan Nations; the Church of Jesus Christ Christian; the Minutemen; and the Order. The groups are not united, and members sometimes move from one organization to another. However, the groups usually share similar beliefs about religion and about a government conspiracy against the citizens of the United States.

The unifying religious force behind these paramilitary antigovernment groups is the Christian Identity Movement. Founded by Richard G. Butler in the 1970s, Christian Identity did not receive much attention until the 1980s, when representatives of several right-wing, extremist groups began having annual meetings at Hayden Lake, Idaho. Christian Identity is a mixture of anticommunism, anti-Semitism, and racism. These are combined with an eccentric school of thought known as British Israelism, which holds that Anglo-Saxons are God's true Chosen People. Members of Christian

Popperfoto

The suspected bomber, Timothy McVeigh, was a hero of the Gulf War, and was linked to an extreme right-wing militia movement that seeks to protect the right of individual Americans to bear arms.

Identity believe Jews are the children of Satan, that Jesus was not Jewish but an Aryan, and that the majority of true Israelites migrated from the Middle East to Western Europe in the sixth century BC. The United States, to members of Christian Identity, is the Promised Land.

There are many Christian Identity churches in various parts of the United States, but the most well-known is the Church of Jesus Christ Christian of the Aryan Nations located near Hayden Lake. The theology of Christian Identity also drives the political behavior of many right-wing groups.

Such organizations often believe in economic conspiracy theories. One example is that national and international forces, led by Jewish financiers, are responsible for the hardship and economic depression in rural America. Radical right-wingers also reject the policies and authority of the federal government. They refer to it as the Zionist Occupational Government, and see it as controlled by Jews, African-Americans, or the United Nations. Many right-wingers also emphasize survivalism, the idea of living self-sufficiently after some breakdown of society such as the aftermath of a nuclear war. This will ensure that they are prepared for the race war they expect to occur, and to protect them against the international conspiracy.

While it is true that many members of the militias and other members of radical right-wing organizations do not advocate the use of violence against the government, the 1980s witnessed several incidents where members of paramilitary groups had confrontations with federal law enforcement agencies.

VIOLENCE AND THE RADICAL RIGHT WING

The first incident concerned Gordon Kahl, a North Dakota farmer, who was a Christian Identity believer and a member of the Posse Comitatus movement. Posse Comitatus was founded in 1969 by Henry L. Beach, who in the 1930s was a member of a pro-Nazi movement. It held that the only legitimate government was at county level, and that the county sheriff should be the highest government official. Beach also proposed punishing any official who committed criminal acts or violated their oath of office with a public hanging at a busy intersection.

Posse Comitatus's main objection has always been to income tax and the Federal Reserve Bank. Its members have had many conflicts with the federal government over taxes and weapons. Kahl had stopped paying taxes in 1967, and later organized a Posse chapter. He was involved in setting up a shadow government composed of heavily armed men who would preserve order when the U.S. government collapsed. In 1983, federal marshals came to his home. He shot them dead and fled to Arkansas where, later that same year, FBI agents tracked him down. In the ensuing shootout, Kahl was killed.

The next incident also began in 1983, when Robert Mathews founded the organization most commonly referred to as the Order. The Order was formed to overthrow the so-called Zionist conspiracy in the United States. Members financed the Order through counterfeiting and armored car robberies during the 1980s. They also murdered Alan Berg, a Jewish radio talk show host known for his liberal politics and hostility to right-wing views, in Denver on June 18, 1984.

Hulton Getty Picture Collection/Reuters

Investigators clear rubble from the cinder block room at the Branch Davidian cult compound at Waco four days after the siege ended on April 19, 1993. McVeigh almost certainly considered the Oklahoma City bombing as an act of retribution for Waco.

With the help of informants, the FBI located Mathews on Whidbey Island, Washington, and killed him in the ensuing shootout on December 8, 1984. The authorities also arrested other members of the Order, convicting those who refused plea bargains. There is evidence that Mathews read and used information from the novel *The Turner Diaries*, written by William Pierce, using the pseudonym Andrew Macdonald, as a terrorist blueprint.

The last major confrontation of the 1980s occurred on April 20, 1985, when agents of the Bureau of Alcohol, Tobacco, and Firearms (ATF) raided the paramilitary compound of the Covenant, the Sword, the Arm of the Lord located in northern Arkansas. The members of this group believed that a race war was soon to come, and they had trained their members and other right-wingers in guerrilla warfare. After two days of negotiations, the Covenant, the Sword, the Arm of the Lord members surrendered to the federal authorities. Police arrested their leader, James Ellison, and secured his conviction for arson and the manufacture of automatic weapons.

RUBY RIDGE

Friends and associates of Timothy McVeigh have told reporters and government investigators that two confrontations between federal law enforcement agents and extremist paramilitaries, in 1992 and 1993, put him on the path to terrorism.

The first incident, in August 1992, happened when U.S. marshals attempted to serve a warrant on Randy Weaver for illegally trying to sell sawn-off shotguns to federal agents. Weaver and his family were followers of Christian Identity and lived at Ruby Ridge in rural Idaho. Since the federal marshals knew that Weaver was heavily armed, they arrived in force. A standoff developed, and during the first two days a deputy

Popperfoto

Michigan Militia commander Norman Olson (left) carries a teddy bear for one of the children under siege at the Clark ranch near Jordan, Montana. The ranch was the site of a lengthy standoff between federal authorities and a right-wing antigovernment group known as the Montana freemen.

federal marshal and Weaver's wife and son were killed. The standoff ended after 11 days when the FBI permitted former Green Beret Lieutenant-Colonel James "Bo" Gritz to mediate. Right-wingers respected Gritz because of his record during the Vietnam War. Weaver and a friend surrendered after Gritz's intervention. A federal case was brought against them for the murder of the federal marshals and the original firearms violation. The jury convicted them of the firearms count but acquitted them of murder.

Weaver's acquittal did not end the case. The Department of Justice and the Senate both investigated the FBI agents' tactics during the siege. The reports directed severe criticism at the behavior of the FBI Hostage Rescue Unit and the rules of engagement used by agents. Right-wingers saw the Weaver incident as another example of the continuing invasion of their private lives by the federal government.

THE WACO SIEGE

The second incident occurred on February 28, 1993, at Waco, Texas. ATF agents attempted to serve search and arrest warrants on the Davidian leader, David Koresh. The Davidians, forewarned of the raid, opened fire, killing four agents and wounding 20, while suffering seven casualties of their own, three fatal. The FBI took control of the situation on March 1 after the ATF requested their assistance. Negotiations that ensued during the 51-day standoff resulted in 35 people leaving the compound. But on April 19, 1993, the FBI decided that the siege should end and fired CS gas (a riot control agent) into the compound. It was the start of an assault that included tanks. The exploding gas canisters started a fire that destroyed the buildings and killed almost 80 people, including David Koresh and many children.

The violence of the Waco incident, and the fact that millions of people around the world saw film of it on television, led to two separate investigations into the handling of the confrontation. Both the Department of the Treasury and the Department of Justice issued reports. These, and various statements by the authorities about millenarian beliefs, do provide some understanding of what happened. Apparently, the authorities regarded the Branch Davidians as a cult holding hostages who needed rescuing. There is little evidence that they believed that Koresh and his followers genuinely thought themselves to be fighting against an evil regime.

While the Branch Davidians were not a Christian Identity group, right-wingers regarded the actions of federal law enforcement agencies as just another example of the government's tyrannical trampling over the liberties of American citizens. That the event took place on April 19, the date on which the American Revolution began in an exchange of fire between Redcoats and Minutemen in Lexington, Massachusetts, in 1775, gave it even greater significance in the minds of these extremists.

At some point after Waco, the planning of the Oklahoma City bombing began. McVeigh traveled to Kansas and Michigan, and also made a trip to the ruins of the Branch Davidian compound at Waco. On April 14, 1995, McVeigh checked in to a motel in Junction City, Kansas. On April 16, McVeigh called Terry Nichols from Oklahoma City, and asked him to pick him up. Nichols drove down from Herington, Kansas, and collected McVeigh. The next day, McVeigh rented a truck from a Ryder lot in Junction City. The last sighting of McVeigh before the bombing was at 4 A.M. on the morning of April 18, sitting in the Ryder truck.

CONSEQUENCES OF THE BOMBING

After the World Trade Center bombing in 1993, the Clinton administration proposed an Omnibus Counterterrorism bill. It was only after Oklahoma City that the bill started getting serious attention from legislators. The bill increased penalties for terrorist crimes, including a mandatory death penalty for terrorist murders. The FBI has kept a closer watch on militias and other right-wing groups, but there is disagreement about the guidelines under which the bureau must operate. Criticism of the FBI's harassment of civil rights groups during the 1960s and early 1970s has left the bureau cautious in its political surveillance.

One year after the bombing, McVeigh and Nichols still had not gone to trial. In March 1996, U.S. District Court Judge Richard Matsch moved their trial to Denver, ruling that constitutional rights of the defendants to a fair trial could not be observed in Oklahoma. Attorneys for both the government and the accused filed numerous motions, and these delayed the proceedings.

The far right did not go into hiding after Oklahoma City. A standoff between federal law enforcement agents and a group called the Freemen at a compound near the town of Jordan, Montana, began in March 1996. The Freemen, like other similar groups, believe that the federal government is illegal. The authorities have charged the group with writing fraudulent checks and money orders in a federal grand jury indictment. Law enforcement officials, mindful of the fateful consequences of the confrontations at Ruby Ridge and Waco, avoided an assault on the Freemen compound, which was occupied by heavily armed defenders.

Tension between right wingers and the federal government remains high. A statement from a pamphlet of the American Militia Organization is clear: "Political victory on a national scale can be considered a practical impossibility. There will be violence." Law enforcement agencies need to study and understand these groups if the threat they pose is to be contained.

Gary R. Perlstein

SEE ALSO: FAR-RIGHT EXTREMISM; RELIGIOUS EXTREMISM; BOMBING OPERATIONS; THE MINDSET OF THE TERRORIST; THE WORLD TRADE CENTER BOMBING.

FURTHER READING

- Aho, James A. *The Politics of Righteousness: Idaho Christian Patriotism.* Seattle: University of Washington Press, 1990.
- Barkun, Michael. "Millenarian Groups and Law Enforcement Agencies: The Lessons of Waco," in *Terrorism and Political Violence* 6, No. 1 (Spring 1994): 75-95.
- Corcoran, James. *Bitter Harvest: Gordon Kahl and the Posse Comitatus – Murder in the Heartland.* New York: Viking, 1990.
- Flynn, Kevin, and Gary Gerhardt. *The Silent Brotherhood: Inside America's Racist Underground.* London: Collier Macmillan, and New York: Free Press, 1989.

Social Revolutionary Terrorists

The Western world has been plagued by a number of left-wing terrorist groups whose ranks were filled with the educated, but discontented, children of the well-to-do middle classes. They mixed Marxist-Leninist beliefs with sympathy for the world's oppressed, and saw their own governments as reactionary. Postwar affluence, they argued, had made people politically immature. The social revolutionaries believed that their acts of terror would force governments into introducing repressive legislation, thereby revealing the state's true nature to the public, which would then clamor for change.

RED ARMY FACTION: THE BAADER-MEINHOF GANG

On October 18, 1980, three leaders of the West German terrorist group Red Army Faction (RAF) were found hanged in their cells in Stammheim high-security jail. Whether by murder or by suicide, the deaths were a watershed – both a dramatic conclusion to the wave of terrorism that had shaken a prosperous and complacent West Germany throughout the 1970s, and, for many, a final dashing of the hopes that had been born with the revolutionary idealism of 1968.

ON THE BRINK OF REVOLUTION

The origins of the RAF lay in the student movement of the late 1960s, when there was a revival of Marxist social and political theories in Western intellectual circles. West Germany, with a large student population, was no exception to this development. As in other Western countries, however, the emergence of the "New Left" was born out of a specific domestic context. In Germany, the attraction of the various brands of neo-Marxist theories was enhanced by a widespread dissatisfaction with the domestic political and social situation. Between 1966 and 1969, the country was governed by a so-called "Grand Coalition" of the conservative Christian Democrats and the Social Democrats, the two largest parties in German politics. For many younger Germans, the absence of a strong parliamentary opposition justified illegal methods. Moral concern about Germany's neglected Nazi past, the emergence of a neo-Nazi party, and concern over West German support for the regime of the shah of Iran also caused dissatisfaction. New ways of organizing political opposition soon came to dominate student thinking. Demonstrations and protest marches in the major university towns, under the slogan of "extra-parliamentary opposition," became a new phenomenon of German political life.

In June 1967, the student unrest erupted. During a visit of the shah of Iran to West Berlin, scuffles broke out between student protesters and the police, and a young theology student, Benno Ohnesorge, was shot dead. In response, violent protests erupted on almost every campus in West Germany. An unscrupulous tabloid press, 80 percent of which was owned by the right-wing media magnate Axel Springer, inflamed popular opinion against the students. During Easter 1968, apparently spurred on by the anti-student hysteria fanned by the tabloids, Josef Bachmann, a deranged 23-year-old student from Berlin, attempted to assassinate Rudi Dutschke, one of the student leaders. Rudi Dutschke was a leading light in the League of German Socialist Students (SDS), and one of the most vociferous advocates of "extraparliamentary opposition."

In the Western world at large, the summer of 1968 was the height of the student movement. In May, France seemed on the brink of revolution, when students and workers joined forces. The short-lived "Prague Spring" of 1968 raised hopes for "socialism

SUMMARY

- Formed in 1968, the Red Army Faction (or Baader-Meinhof Gang) and associated groups included 22 core members in the early 1970s.
- The leftist Red Army Faction targeted its terrorist activities on West German corporations and U.S. military installations in West Germany.
- Weakened by the collapse of communist East Germany, the group announced an end to its terrorist campaign in 1992.

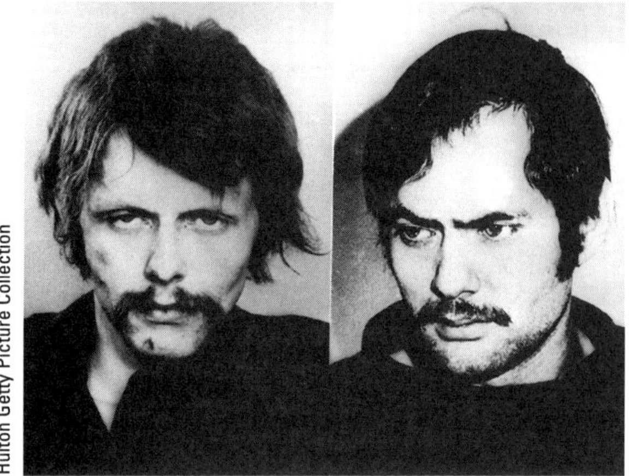

Four members of the Red Army Faction (RAF). Jan-Carl Raspe (far left) and Andreas Baader (center left) played key roles in RAF activities and strategy. Gerhard Müller (center right) and Irmgard Möller (far right) were found guilty of murdering a policeman in Hamburg in 1971.

with a human face," or a "Third Way" between Western capitalism and Soviet communism. However, the failure of the students in France, along with the Soviet invasion of Czechoslovakia, ended the utopian dream that had carried the student movement so far. But 1968 by no means marked the end of left-wing dissent. After 1968, leftist activities became more diverse, but also more isolated and secretive.

The response of the West German government to the events of 1968 was extreme. The West German parliament, the Bundestag, amended the country's constitution, the "Basic Law," in order to extend emergency powers of the government. Under the provisions of the new legislation, the government now had the ability, in the event of internal or external crises, to pass laws, draft citizens, use the police or the army, and take whatever measures it deemed necessary to secure order and the survival of the state. For many students, the new legislation was further proof of what they regarded as the oppressive character of the West German republic.

GRADUATION TO TERRORISM

The attempt on Dutschke's life in April 1968 and the enactment of the emergency legislation led to a split in the radical student movement. A small group began to distance itself from the idea of "extraparliamentary opposition." In the light of the apparent futility of street demonstrations and protest marches, this faction now moved toward terrorist measures. At the height of the protest season in the spring of 1968, two of the group's initial members, Andreas Baader, a high-school dropout, and Gudrun Ensslin, a teacher trainee, set fire to two Frankfurt department stores, fortunately without causing any casualties. Their action was inspired by an arson attack on a Brussels department store the previous year in which more than 250 people lost their lives. Baader and Ensslin were arrested shortly afterward. Both fled the country while on parole.

The arson attack was the first in a series of terrorist acts that came to haunt Germany in the 1970s. By setting fire to the department stores, Baader and Ensslin, and those who aided them, graduated from being members of the student protest movement to being terrorists.

Under false identities, Baader and Ensslin returned to Germany early in 1970. On June 5, 1970, they formally established the RAF, signaling the emergence of a new, hard core of left-wing radicalism. They called themselves a "faction" because they saw themselves as part of an international struggle of the oppressed. The gang rapidly developed into one of the most sophisticated and deadly effective terrorist organizations in Western Europe. Its leading members were Baader, Ensslin, and Ulrike Meinhof.

Like most of the other members of the RAF, Baader and Ensslin were well-educated and came from middle- or upper middle-class families. Most of them were born during the chaos and disruption of the war years of the 1940s. They have been called "Hitler's children," and it has been argued that the involvement of their parents' generation in the Third Reich was a powerful stimulant that led them to rebel against the post-1945 order.

Gudrun Ensslin, for example, was born in 1940, the daughter of a Lutheran vicar. The most crucial single event in her journey from student protester to hardened terrorist was the shooting of Benno Ohnesorge in June 1967. At the time, she noted in her diary: "They'll kill us all – you know what pigs we are up against – that is the generation of Auschwitz we've got against us – you can't argue with the people who made Auschwitz." After the formal establishment of the RAF, Ensslin became the group's leader, though it was popularly known as the "Baader-Meinhof Gang."

Ulrike Meinhof was the oldest member of the group. Born in 1934, she grew up in Jena, where her father was a museum director and her mother a junior lecturer at the university. From 1960, she served as editor-in-chief of the left-wing magazine *Konkret*, for which she wrote positive articles about Baader and Ensslin. In the later 1960s, she became involved with Baader and Ensslin. Together, the three formed the inner core of the RAF command.

"DON'T ARGUE, DESTROY"

The years between 1970 and 1972 saw the first phase of Baader-Meinhof terrorism. In the summer of 1970, the RAF made contact with Palestinian terrorist groups and flew to the Middle East for training. The Palestinians gave them weapons and instructed them on how to create a cell structure that the authorities would find difficult to penetrate. Their first raids were against property, and they undertook a series of bank robberies. During one such raid, the RAF killed a policeman. Meinhof commented: "We say the person in uniform is a pig – that is, not a human being – and thus we have to settle the matter with him. It is wrong to talk to those people at all, and shooting is a matter of course." One of the RAF's slogans was "Don't argue, destroy."

By 1972, there were six regional groups that were more or less part of the group, while in West Berlin the "Second of June" movement (June 2 was the date of Benno Ohnesorge's death) also carried out terrorist acts. In spring 1972, the RAF began striking at high-profile targets: U.S. bases at Frankfurt and Heidelberg, and at the Axel Springer press building in Hamburg, in the attack on which 38 people were injured.

The government's response was to move in the troops. In one typically melodramatic anti-terrorist operation in Frankfurt in 1972, armored cars and soldiers filled the streets. Fortunately for the authorities, the summer saw a respite in terrorist activity and the arrest of the original leaders. An informer led police to arrest Meinhof in a safe house; Baader was arrested after a shoot-out; and Ensslin was spotted while shopping in Hamburg. Eighteen other Baader-Meinhof members were taken in these incidents. The first wave of RAF terrorism was over.

THE SECOND WAVE OF TERRORISM

The terrorists were put into a high-security prison at Stammheim, in the outskirts of Stuttgart, and a long period of legal proceedings began. However, the publicity surrounding the trial, and the fact that there were other terrorists at large with support from the Middle East and with sympathizers within German society, meant that a new wave of incidents was soon breaking over West Germany.

Indeed, this new wave of terrorism posed a much more serious threat to West German democracy than the initial Red Army Faction group. Terrorist attacks began to increase again in 1974, after a two-year lull. Combating terrorism became one of the most important issues of West German domestic politics.

In late 1974, one of the terrorists arrested with Baader, Holger Meins, starved himself to death in prison. On the very next day, the Second of June movement murdered the president of the Berlin Supreme Court, Günter von Drenkmann. Shortly afterward, in early 1975, the group struck again in Berlin. They kidnapped the leader of the Berlin Christian Democrats, Peter Lorenz, which severely rattled the government in Bonn. Eventually the government gave in to the demands of the terrorists and set free five imprisoned RAF members. Though Peter Lorenz was released unharmed, the episode was a profound humiliation for the authorities.

Within weeks of the abduction of Lorenz, in April 1975, another terrorist group calling itself the Holger Meins carried out a rocket attack on the West German embassy in the Swedish capital, Stockholm. The group then occupied the embassy building and killed two members of staff, displaying one corpse in an embassy window for the benefit of the assembled media. Once again, they demanded the release of additional RAF terrorists imprisoned in West Germany. This time,

Pixfeatures

Hanns-Martin Schleyer pictured the day after his kidnapping by the Red Army Faction, September 5, 1977. The sign reads: "Prisoner of the R.A.F."

however, the government in Bonn rejected their demands, and, in response, the terrorists destroyed the embassy building. The explosion was inexpertly carried out, and two terrorists died in the blast. The remaining four were swiftly dispatched to West Germany for trail.

In this second wave of terrorism, the Middle East connection became very important for this new generation of terrorists, and they took part in a high-profile operation with Palestinian terrorists in December 1975. The oil ministers of the 11 Organization of Petroleum Exporting Countries (OPEC) states attending a meeting in Vienna were held hostage by a terrorist group. The group included one of the RAF terrorists released as part of the resolution of the Peter Lorenz kidnapping earlier that year.

In response to the increase in terrorist activities, the West German parliament tightened aspects of the criminal code and passed new anti-terrorist legislation in the first half of 1976. Arrested terrorist suspects were now no longer permitted to share a defense attorney in court; once convicted, they were not allowed to have further contact with each other in prison; and there were even provisions for their contacts with their defense lawyers to be broken. These laws were designed to prevent the Baader-Meinhof leaders from making contact with outside members and continuing to act as a focus for terrorist activity. It also reflected the government's strongly held belief that sympathy for the terrorists was widespread in German society, even among professional classes.

In May 1976, Ulrike Meinhof was found hanged in her cell, and in response, during the summer, terrorist pressure continued. Although it was officially announced that she had committed suicide, her lawyers claimed she had been murdered, and this claim found credence among supporters of the terrorists. Red Army Faction veterans continued to be involved in Palestinian terrorism: in July, they took part in the hijacking of an Air France airliner to Entebbe, Uganda, and two of them were killed when Israeli commandos rescued the passengers.

THE BLOODY CLIMAX

The year 1977 was one of major crisis for West German politics and the wave of terrorism reached its peak. In April, the RAF shot and killed general state prosecutor Siegfried Buback. Buback had been one of the chief advocates of stricter anti-terrorist measures and was thus a prime terrorist target.

Then, in July, the trial of Baader, Ensslin, and their colleague Raspe at the high-security complex at Stammheim finally came to an end. All three were sentenced to life imprisonment. In reaction, RAF members assassinated Jürgen Ponto, the chief of one of Germany's big commercial banks. One of the terrorists was Ponto's own goddaughter; she had convinced the bank's security guard to let her and her fellow RAF members into the building

In the autumn of 1977, the terror campaign came to a bloody climax. On September 5, RAF members abducted the president of the employers' association, Hanns-Martin Schleyer (who had held a high rank in Hitler's SS). Schleyer's four bodyguards were all killed during the action. The kidnappers demanded the release of Baader, Ensslin, and their henchmen from Stammheim prison. However, the government of Chancellor Helmut Schmidt remained unyielding.

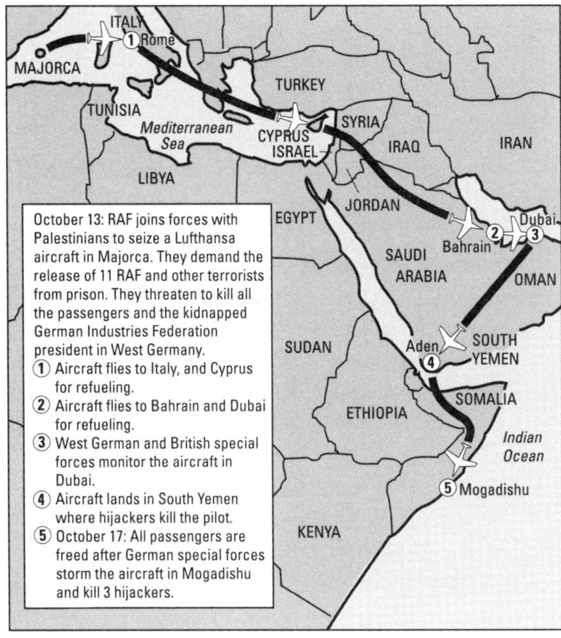

The Mogadishu hijacking of October 13, 1977. The Red Army Faction (RAF) demanded the release of 11 of its members from prison.

In response to the hard line of the authorities and to increase their pressure on the government, German and Palestinian terrorists hijacked a Lufthansa airliner on October 13, 1977. The airliner eventually landed in the Somalian capital, Mogadishu. The terrorists killed the pilot and threatened to kill passengers at regular intervals. Chancellor Schmidt sent, as special envoy to Mogadishu, Hans-Jürgen Wischnewski, whose ostensible purpose was to negotiate the release of the hostages. His true purpose, however, was to stall the terrorists while a special West German anti-terrorist unit (GSG-9), as well as members of the British SAS, were flown out to Somalia.

Having been kept busy by Wischnewski, the hijackers were unprepared for the GSG-9 attack. The GSG-9 freed all the passengers and either killed or captured the terrorists. The successful outcome of the government response to the hijacking undermined the RAF's blackmailing strategy. But it also sealed the fate of Schleyer, who was still being held by his captors. On October 19, Schleyer's body was found in the trunk of a car across the French border in Alsace. He had been strangled with a piano wire.

Schleyer's horrific murder nonetheless marked a turning point in the fight against terrorism. The West German government had demonstrated its ability to resist terrorist blackmail; from now on the authorities had the upper hand. The news of the storming of the airliner was too much for the imprisoned RAF leaders, and they committed suicide on October 18.

By 1980, the RAF's terrorism was at a low ebb. The groups of sympathizers dropped away, and the remaining terrorists were isolated. They still managed some more high-profile attacks, some in conjunction with the French terrorist group Action Directe. One of their final acts was the assassination of the director of Deutsche Bank, Alfred Herrhausen, in late 1989.

The year 1989 also saw the collapse of the Soviet Union and its satellites in Eastern Europe. This proved a mortal blow to social revolutionary terrorism in Germany, because it soon become known that East Germany had given refuge to a substantial number of former RAF terrorists.

During the major phase of RAF activity in the 1970s, 31 people were killed and there were 25 bombings and 30 bank robberies. While this may appear to be a relatively minor level of activity when compared to that elsewhere, the sometimes hysterical response of the West German government and of German society as a whole suggests the profound unease that the RAF provoked in a country at odds with its history and unsure of its identity.

Thomas G. Otte

SEE ALSO: HIJACKING AND KIDNAPPING; TERRORISTS' USE OF CHEMICAL WEAPONS; COLLABORATION BETWEEN TERRORISTS; ACTION DIRECTE; RED BRIGADES; JAPANESE TERRORISM.

FURTHER READING

- Becker, Jillian. *Hitler's Children: The Story of the Baader-Meinhof Gang.* 3rd ed. London: Pickwick, 1989.
- Horchem, Hans J. "European Terrorism: A German Perspective," in *Terrorism* 6, No.1 (1982): 141-63.
- Horchem, Hans J. "Terrorism in West Germany," in *Conflict Studies* 186 (April 1986): 1-20.
- Lee, Martin A. "Hitler's Offspring," in *The Progressive* (March 1993): 28-31.

ACTION DIRECTE

The French extreme-left terrorist group Action Directe (AD) was active between 1979 and 1987. Beginning as a loose collection of fringe activists, it quickly evolved into a full-fledged terrorist organization with connections in Europe and the Middle East. In a fast and furious campaign of bombing and assassination, AD targeted business leaders, government ministries responsible for immigrant workers, the real estate industry, the police, and the military. While AD's campaign was broadly anti-capitalist, anti-Zionist, and anti-American, the minority of the French left that might have supported violent direct action twenty years earlier no longer accepted it as a valid route to meaningful change by the 1980s. An early statement released by AD stressed the anarchism that underlay the group's activities: AD, it claimed, aimed "to wreck society through direct action by destroying its institutions and the men who serve it."

POLITICAL MAKE-UP

The group initially drew together an odd assortment of anarchists, Maoists, small-time hoodlums, Third World activists, and "fighters" trained in Palestinian camps. A number of AD leaders had also been involved in earlier extremist groups. For example, Jean-Marc Rouillan had previously belonged to International Revolutionary Action Groups, an anarchist organization that targeted the Franco regime in Spain during the 1970s. Régis Schleicher had been active in extreme-left groups that had existed in great numbers after the student uprising of May 1968. Another leader, Frédéric Oriach, was a founder of the Maoist group Armed Cells for Popular Autonomy, which in 1977 had assassinated Renault night-watchman Jean-Antoine Tramoni. Tramoni had murdered the left-wing activist Pierre Overney during a 1972 demonstration.

Throughout its brief history, AD was plagued by internal disagreements over objectives and methods, ultimately splitting into internationalist and nationalist factions. The internationalist faction, based in Paris, focused on material and human targets connected to European business and defense interests. The nationalist faction, based in the southern French city of Lyon, concentrated on domestic targets, but was much less discriminating in its choice of victims. Several passers-by together with clients and cleaning personnel in companies that it targeted were beaten, pistol-whipped, or occasionally, killed in cold blood.

KEY FACTS

- Action Directe carried out almost 80 terrorist bombings during its eight-year history, including 4 in 1981, 8 in 1982, 7 in 1983, 9 in 1984, 16 in 1985, and 13 in 1986. Five people died in these attacks, and another 58 were injured.
- Action Directe carried out 8 assassination attempts. Successful assassinations included the murder of French General René Audran (January 25, 1985) and Georges Besse, chairman of Renault (November 17, 1986).
- AD's financial needs were met by several bank robberies. In an October 14, 1983, hold-up, Ciro Rizatto, whom investigators linked to Italian terrorist organizations, was killed by police.

THREE PERIODS OF TERRORISM

AD's history can be divided into three periods, each characterized by shifts in ideology and varying levels of violence. During the first period (1979–81), the group's activities included vandalism, small-arms fire and bomb attacks on buildings, and arson. Leaders (and lovers) Rouillan and Nathalie Ménigon fired machine-gun rounds at the French Ministry of Cooperation on March 18, 1979.

However, the first attack for which the group claimed responsibility took place on May 1, 1979, when AD members peppered the headquarters of the French employers' association with machine-gun fire. In April 1980, the group launched a rocket attack on the Ministry of Transport, and in September of the same year, fired automatic weapons at the Military Academy. Fires were started at Philips Data Systems and at the University of Rennes.

Approximately 20 attacks occurred in this period but caused only material damage. On September 13, 1980, the French authorities arrested Rouillan and

Rex Features

An Action Directe (AD) bombing in Belgium. AD and the Belgian Communist Fighting Cells (CCC) jointly attacked targets on several occasions.

Ménigon in an ambush on the rue Pergolèse close to the Arc de Triomphe in Paris. The authorities were acting on information supplied by a former AD sympathizer, Lebanese painter Gabriel Chahine. Ménigon resisted arrest, shooting at a policeman and shouting, "I am Action Directe."

AD briefly suspended operations after François Mitterrand's election as French president in May 1981. Amnesties are traditionally granted after a new president takes office, and Rouillan, along with 25 other members of AD, was freed. Because she had resisted arrest, however, Ménigon was initially not included in the amnesty. She promptly went on hunger strike, and three weeks later won her release. If the government hoped that the amnesty would draw AD away from violence, it was to be gravely disappointed. The truce between the leftist president and the terrorists was soon over.

In the summer of 1982, AD issued a statement accusing the Mitterrand government of pandering to West German and American capitalism. It declared, moreover, an "anti-Zionist guerrilla" war. Accordingly, the violence that followed was directed against mainly Jewish and American targets. In 1982, AD machine-gunned the commercial mission of the Israeli Ministry of Defense, an Israeli diplomatic vehicle, and the Bank of America. Bombs were planted at the World Bank, the American School, and several Israeli and Jewish businesses in Paris. AD was also implicated in the two worst anti-Jewish atrocities of the period – the bombing of the Passy synagogue and the Chez Jo Goldenberg restaurant in the Marais, a district of Paris. While both attacks were almost certainly the work of Lebanese terrorist groups, it is likely that AD provided logistical assistance.

On August 18, 1982, the Mitterrand government declared war on the terrorists and banned AD. The terrorists responded by carrying out more bombings. AD spokesperson Oriach used the Arab-Israeli conflict as justification for the attacks, thereby underlining the close links that were developing between AD and

Palestinian terrorist groups. Meanwhile, AD settled an old score by murdering Gabriel Chahine, the painter who had betrayed the AD leaders in 1980.

Throughout 1983, AD carried out a number of minor political attacks, for example, setting off small explosive devices at the Socialist Party headquarters and the defense ministry in August. When cornered, the terrorists shot their way out. On May 31, 1983, five terrorists killed two police officers on the Avenue Trudaine, Paris, when caught off guard by a routine police patrol.

During the third period (1984-87), the internationalist faction consolidated its links with other European groups, as part of what it called its guerrilla war against the "Americanization of Europe." In January 1985, AD and the German Red Army Faction (RAF) issued a joint declaration, announcing the establishment of a pan-European politico-military network.

Throughout 1984 and 1985, the European terrorists worked together closely. AD had particularly close ties with the Belgian group Communist Fighting Cells (CCC). In June 1984, the CCC raided a quarry close to Brussels and carried away more than a ton of explosives used for rock blasting. In the following months, there was a spate of bombings throughout Europe using explosives from this supply. AD, for example, used the Belgian explosives in a bomb planted at the headquarters of the Western European Union.

In 1985, AD--RAF coordinated terrorism reached a peak. On January 25, 1985, AD assassinated General René Audran, director of foreign arms sales for the French Ministry of Defense. Just a few days later, the RAF murdered Ernest Zimmerman, a prominent figure in the West German aerospace industry.

In August 1985, in a joint RAF-AD operation, terrorists murdered an American serviceman and used his car to bomb a U.S. air force base near Frankfurt, West Germany. The blast killed two people and wounded another 16. It was at this point that the tide began to turn against the terrorists.

DEMISE OF ACTION DIRECTE

On November 17, 1986, Ménigon and Aubron, who called themselves the Pierre Overney–Action Directe Commando, murdered the president of Renault, Georges Besse, near his Paris apartment. Three weeks later, Schleicher and brothers Claude and Nicolas Halfen were charged with the 1983 Avenue Trudaine shootings. After Schleicher threatened the jury with violence, the trial moved to a court of professional magistrates. Schleicher was eventually convicted of murder and sentenced to life.

By now, police anti-terrorist action was bearing fruit. On March 28, 1986, when police arrested one of AD's founders, André Olivier, in Lyons, his car was packed with guns. Then, in February 1987, police carried out what was to be final body blow to AD. The government offered a reward worth $180,000 for information leading to the arrest of AD leaders. The temptation clearly proved too much. On February 21, police raided an isolated farmhouse near Orléans and arrested four of the five remaining leaders – Rouillan, Ménigon, Aubron, and Georges Cipriani. Police arrested Max Frérot, the last AD leader at large, after a shoot-out at a parking lot in Lyons in November 1987.

By then, however, both international and national wings of the group had lost virtually all of their support. While many of the early activists had supported direct-action techniques such as assistance to squatters and Turkish immigrant workers, and had even been prepared to accept bank raids as a way to achieve meaningful change, they were increasingly alienated by the extreme violence favored by the AD leaders. Despite their deep roots in French political history, AD's ideas lost their force as European communism entered the crisis that resulted in the collapse of the Eastern Bloc after 1989.

Michael Dartnell

SEE ALSO: FRENCH ANARCHIST TERROR; TERRORISM IN FRENCH ALGERIA; REVOLUTIONARY TERRORISM; COLLABORATION BETWEEN TERRORISTS; RED ARMY FACTION: THE BAADER-MEINHOF GANG; FRENCH RIGHT-WING TERRORISM; RED BRIGADES.

FURTHER READING

- Dartnell, Michael. "France's Action Directe: Terrorists in Search of a Revolution," in *Terrorism and Political Violence* 2, No 4 (Winter 1990): 457-88.
- Dartnell, Michael. *Action Directe: Ultra-left Terrorism in France, 1979-1987.* London and Portland, OR: Frank Cass, 1995.
- Francis, Samuel T. "Terrorist Renaissance: France, 1980-1983," in *World Affairs* 146, No. 1 (Summer 1983): 54-8.
- Moxon-Browne, Edward. "Terrorism in France," in *Contemporary Terrorism,* edited by William Gutteridge. New York: Facts on File, 1986.

FRENCH RIGHT-WING TERRORISM

During and after the Algerian war of 1954-62, which marked the end of French colonial power, Algerian nationalists and French activists carried out terrorist acts on the streets of France. In recent decades, however, French terrorist action has been limited. Right-wing terrorism has been instigated either by regional separatists, such as Breton and Corsican nationalists, or by relatively small groups of intellectuals and fascist romantics – such as Groupe Union Défense (GUD).

GUD was set up in 1969 within the Law Faculty of the University of Paris, at the rue d'Assas. It sprang up after the failed left-wing revolution of 1968, which had had extensive student support. GUD's founders, Alain Robert, Robert Allo, and Jack Marchal, had all belonged to an earlier right-wing group known as Occident. They set up GUD initially to represent anti-communist and nationalist opinion in intra-university council elections. GUD has survived for more than 25 years, and has continued to produce propaganda material over much of the period.

STREET VIOLENCE

With an ideological commitment to nationalism, anti-Semitism, and the glorification of masculine heroism, GUD has from the outset engaged in direct terrorist action. It typically harasses and attacks leftist students or members of ethnic minorities, using makeshift armaments such as metal batons and homemade tear-gas bombs. GUD incidents have traditionally centered on the Parisian university locations of Nanterre and the Sorbonne, and on the streets of the Latin Quarter.

In 1994, GUD claimed responsibility for disrupting two performances of *Tsahal*, a documentary on the Israeli army by Franco-Jewish movie-maker Claude Lanzmann. With a neo-Nazi hatred of both Marxism and capitalism, GUD has burned both American and Soviet flags during street demonstrations. Throughout the 1980s, it strove to persuade students to participate in a "Third Way": a nationalist new order independent of Washington and Moscow.

Extreme nationalism and a romantic attachment to war and sacrifice have led to some bizarre military adventures. GUD volunteers have fought alongside Palestinians in Lebanon, and helped the Croat nationalist army in the former Yugoslavia.

JOINING OTHER RIGHTISTS

In 1995, the University of Paris banned GUD as a student organization, withdrawing from the group all rights to meet at the rue d'Assas site and to display literature. New laws in France also prohibit the open sale and display of neo-Nazi literature.

Perhaps in response, GUD has developed links with the right-wing National Front (FN) party of Jean Marie Le Pen, but continues to campaign for a new European order. The GUD and FN have collaborated in commemorative street marches, and GUD cohorts have been recruited to police the FN's rallies.

Hugo Frey

SEE ALSO: TERRORISM IN FRENCH ALGERIA; FAR-RIGHT EXTREMISM; BASQUE NATIONALIST TERROR: ETA; THE FRENCH RESPONSE TO TERRORISM.

FURTHER READING

- Griffin, Roger. *Fascism.* Oxford and New York: Oxford University Press, 1995.
- Vaughan, Michalina. "The Extreme Right in France: 'Le Penisme' and the Politics of Fear," in *Neo-Fascism in Europe*, edited by Luciano Cheles, Ronnie Ferguson, and Michalina Vaughan. London and New York: Longman, 1992.

RED BRIGADES

From 1969 to 1984, Italy experienced an epidemic of terrorist violence. Extremists on both the political Left and Right killed or maimed more than 1,200 people during that period, and the most feared of the country's many left-wing terrorist organizations were the Red Brigades.

EARLY ACTIVITY

The Red Brigades began as a small Marxist-Leninist group, led by a former student radical agitator at the University of Trento, Renato Curcio. In 1969, Curcio moved with his wife, Margherita "Mara" Cagol, to Milan, where they met Alberto Franceschini. On September 8 of that year, the three helped launch the Metropolitan Political Collective, through which they hoped to radicalize students and workers. In October 1970, the Collective's journal announced the creation of the Red Brigades to spearhead the campaign. They declared their intention to overthrow capitalism by means of proletarian revolution. Acts of violence soon accompanied bellicose rhetoric. To destabilize the bourgeois state, the Red Brigades embarked on a terrorist program that included robbery, kidnapping, arson, retaliatory shootings, and assassination.

SUMMARY

- In October 1970, left-wing activists Curcio, Cagol, and Franceschini announced the creation of the Red Brigades.
- In 1977, the Red Brigades launched a campaign of kidnappings, robberies, kneecappings, and assassinations against people they regarded as capitalists.
- In March 1978, the Red Brigades kidnapped and killed Christian Democrat leader Aldo Moro.
- In 1980, the government introduced legislation, encouraging collaborators to speak out. Many Red Brigades terrorists were arrested or killed.
- On April 17, 1988, Professor Roberto Ruffilli, advisor to the Christian Democrats, became the final assassination victim of the Red Brigades.

The Red Brigades first targeted industries, and their physical attacks on the icons of capitalism soon emerged as the preferred technique. The terrorists torched directors' automobiles and company property, and abducted executives and right-wing trade union officials in brief symbolic kidnappings. The Red Brigades also committed robberies to fund their activities. In December 1973, they forced the Fiat company to reinstate 600 laid-off workers in return for the release of the kidnapped personnel director.

On April 18, 1974, the Red Brigades kidnapped Mario Sossi, a right-wing judge, in Genoa, and held him captive for 35 days. On May 23, the government agreed to a prisoner exchange. Following Sossi's release, however, the authorities went back on their word. The Red Brigades would later exact a terrible revenge for this broken promise.

MURDEROUS CAMPAIGNS

An ominous change of Red Brigades tactics emerged on June 17, 1974. The terrorist organization raided the headquarters of the neo-fascist Italian Social Movement party in Padua, then murdered two party officials who offered resistance.

With the capture of Curcio, Franceschini, and numerous other major Red Brigades figureheads by the police in the late summer and fall of 1974, the organization appeared to be decapitated. However, Mara Cagol proved to be an exceptionally able leader. She kept the organization going through its first crisis, and succeeded, on February 18, 1975, in rescuing Curcio from prison. By the late spring of 1975, terrorist incidents involving the Red Brigades were commonplace. On May 15, three Red Brigadists confronted Christian Democrat lawyer Massimo de Cairolis in his Milan office and shot him in the leg. This was the first of many trademark "kneecappings."

RETRIBUTION KILLINGS

On June 4, Cagol died in a gun battle with the Carabinieri (elite police). Then several key Red Brigades leaders, including Curcio, were arrested on January 18, 1976. While legal proceedings against these captives got underway in Turin in May, their

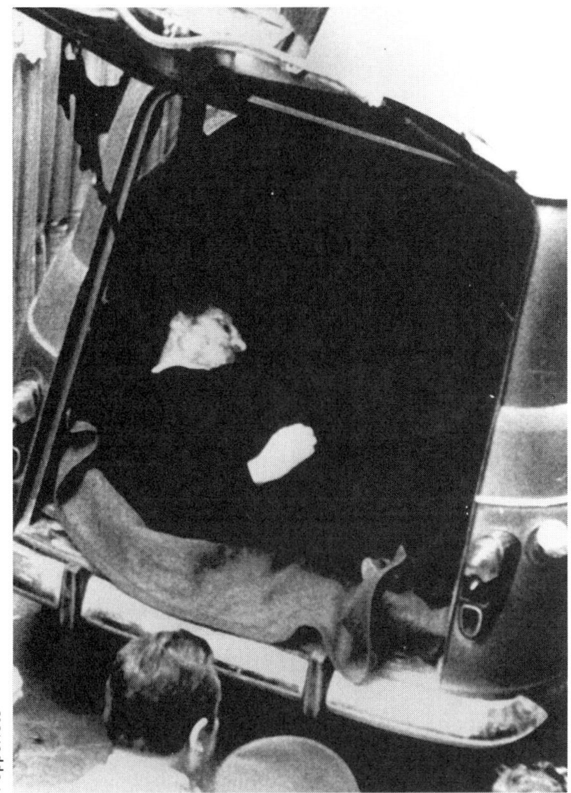

Popperfoto

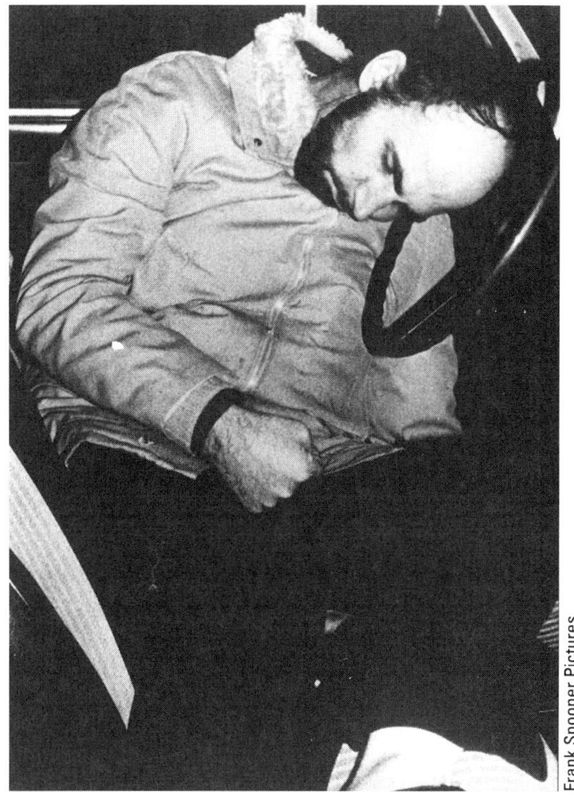

Frank Spooner Pictures

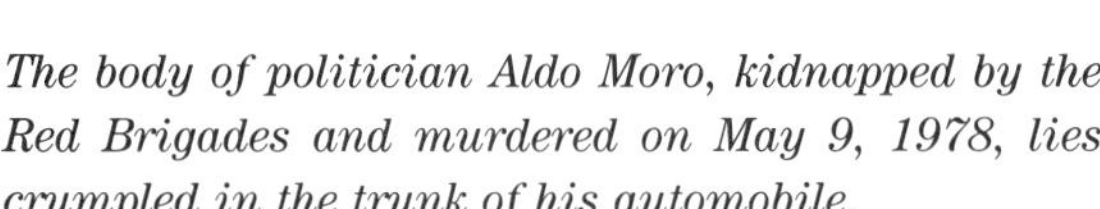

The body of politician Aldo Moro, kidnapped by the Red Brigades and murdered on May 9, 1978, lies crumpled in the trunk of his automobile.

The killing of Guido Rossa, a popular Italian Communist party activist, in January 1979, sparked off a wave of protests and strikes.

comrades on the outside continued to shed blood. On June 8, the Red Brigades killed Francesco Coco, the judge who had flouted the Red Brigades in the Sossi kidnapping, together with his bodyguard and driver. They also sought to sabotage the Turin trial by publicly issuing death threats against all lawyers who participated in the proceedings. On April 28, 1977, the terrorists killed Fulvio Croce, president of the Lawyers' Association and the selector of public defenders for indicted Red Brigadists. The murder of two policemen on May 2 brought the trial to a halt, as the court found it impossible to keep a sufficient number of judges impaneled.

During June 1977, the Red Brigades launched a campaign of systematic violence against their enemies in the media, kneecapping three conservative journalists whom they accused of spreading lies about the Brigades. On November 16, they shot and mortally wounded Carlo Casalegno, the vice-director of *La Stampa*, one of Italy's leading newspapers. In February 1978, the Red Brigades machine-gunned to death Riccardo Palma, the judge who had been in charge of organizing the country's penal system.

The following month, Turin commenced another Red Brigade trial, this time with unprecedented security measures: 8,000 armed men stood guard around the courthouse. On March 10, the Red Brigades murdered Turin's marshal of public security, and further terrorist actions of an overwhelming magnitude eclipsed the trial.

THE ALDO MORO AFFAIR

The most notorious of these terrorist actions occurred on March 16, when, led by Mario Moretti, a former factory worker, a group of Red Brigadists kidnapped Aldo Moro, the country's leading politician, and killed his five-man security team. The kidnapping of Moro in Rome shocked the nation and catapulted the Red Brigades into the international arena. Moro had dominated Italian politics since his appointment in 1959 as secretary of the Christian Democratic party, which had controlled the country since virtually the end of World War II. After 55 days of harrowing suspense over Moro's fate, his captors murdered him and left his corpse in the trunk of a car only a hundred yards from the Christian Democratic party headquarters in Rome.

It would require four trials and two parliamentary inquiries, conducted in the 1980s and 1990s, to plumb the depths of the Moro affair, and many feel that the bottom of it has still not been reached. Throughout the period of Moro's captivity, Prime Minister Giulio Andreotti refused to negotiate for his release, and the government conducted a dismayingly inept search for him. This prompted many critics, including Moro himself and his family, to accuse the government of not wanting to free him.

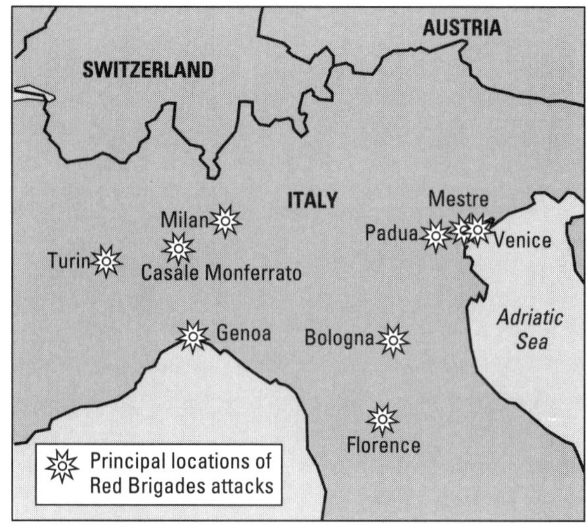

The major northern Italian cities bore the brunt of Red Brigades terrorist attacks.

STRUCTURE OF A TERRORIST GROUP

A detailed picture of the Red Brigades' organization, as well as its recruiting and training methods, came to light during the Moro murder trials. At the top stood the Strategic Direction, made up of representatives from "columns" based in Rome, Milan, Genoa, Turin, Naples, and other Italian cities. At the next level, the Executive Committee implemented the initiatives of the Strategic Direction. Diverse brigades, each with an independent command structure, made up the territorially based columns. Each brigade had in its ranks both "regulars" who had gone underground, and "irregulars" who had pursued ostensibly legitimate careers while working secretly for the Red Brigades.

Red Brigades recruits invariably came from radical left-wing factions and passed through a rigorous training period before joining the group. An unknown, but certainly large, number of revolutionary groups had taken hold in the schools and factories, and the individuals who belonged to them looked to the Red Brigades as their role models. Numbering only a few hundred active members at their peak, the Red Brigades remained small by choice. In this way, they could function as an elite revolutionary organization in the manner of their role models, the Bolsheviks, while drawing support from ideologically committed sympathizers whenever the need arose.

On August 11, 1978, the government gave General Carlo Alberto Dalla Chiesa virtually unlimited power as the nation's chief of anti-terrorist operations. A brilliant Carabinieri general, Dalla Chiesa had spent many years fighting the Mafia. Then, in the mid-1970s, he had been entrusted with the mission that had led to the arrest of Curcio.

As the authorities fought back against the Red Brigades, the violence escalated. Sensational Red Brigades kneecappings and murders of important national figures continued throughout the fall of 1978. In Genoa in 1979, the terrorists assassinated Guido Rossa, a communist worker who had actively supported party secretary Enrico Berlinguer's policies against the Red Brigades in the factories. The Red Brigades were almost as critical of the reformist Communist party as they were of the Christian Democrats. Spontaneous strikes and demonstrations in memory of Rossa erupted in all the major factories of Genoa. Anger over this terrorist act exceeded the public displays following Moro's death. It was arguably the greatest single public relations miscalculation in the Red Brigades' history.

SLAUGHTER AND SCHISMS

With more than 2,500 separate incidents, 1979 stood out as a record year for terrorist attacks in Italy. The Red Brigades' significant contribution to the carnage

Rex Features

In August 1978, with the nation demanding action against the Red Brigades, the Italian government appointed the highly qualified General Carlo Dalla Chiesa as chief of anti-terrorist operations.

established them as the pace-setters for other left-wing terrorist groups such as Front Line, the Fighting Communist Front, and many others.

However, schisms within the Red Brigades had already undermined the unity of the organization. Disunity began with the Moro murder, but it eventually involved the personalities of various leaders and a range of tactical issues. The Red Brigades splintered into three separate groups, and terrorist violence soared as they tried to outdo each other in revolutionary purity and intransigence.

SELLING SECRETS – THE *PENTITI*

With terrorist attacks at an all-time high, the government adopted unprecedented measures. It appointed a Carabinieri general to the post of prefect of Genoa, the first military man ever to hold this civilian office. The government also issued stop-and-search orders for terrorist suspects, who now could be detained by order of a magistrate and interrogated without the presence of a lawyer. Stiffer penalties for terrorism included an automatic life sentence for the murder of public officials.

The government also lightened penalties for individuals who came to be known as *pentiti* – terrorists who cooperated with the police. The special treatment of these informers ultimately proved decisive in the defeat of the Red Brigades. In February 1980, the police captured Patrizio Peci, a Red Brigades chief in Turin, who became the first major informer. While a furious terrorist campaign raged against the judiciary – three judges were killed in late March – Peci supplied information that resulted in the exposure of hideouts, the discovery of huge arms deposits, and the killing or arrest of dozens of terrorists.

Despite their losses, the Red Brigades continued to fight back. They kidnapped a judge in order to force the closure of a maximum-security jail, and killed General Enrico Galvaligi, one of Dalla Chiesa's key Carabinieri associates in the anti-terrorism campaign. Even the April 1981 arrest of Moretti, who organized the kidnapping of Aldo Moro, did not slow the pace of the terrorists' spring offensive, which included four kidnappings, two of them with fatal outcomes. One of these murder victims was Roberto Peci, the brother of the notorious informer. The Red Brigades tortured Peci, capturing the entire episode on film, before shooting him.

On December 17, the Red Brigades kidnapped General James Lee Dozier, a decorated Vietnam War veteran. They had recently issued theoretical statements denouncing NATO as the Cold War shield of international capitalism. At the time of his kidnapping in Verona, Dozier worked as the deputy chief of staff for logistics and administration at NATO's headquarters in Southern Europe.

THE BEGINNING OF THE END

While the Dozier kidnapping was in progress, the Red Brigades suffered a heavy blow when, on January 9, the police captured Giovanni Senzani in his Rome hideout. A respected professor of criminology at the University of Florence, Senzani had also been in residence at the University of California, Berkeley. Many informers identified him as the real leader of the

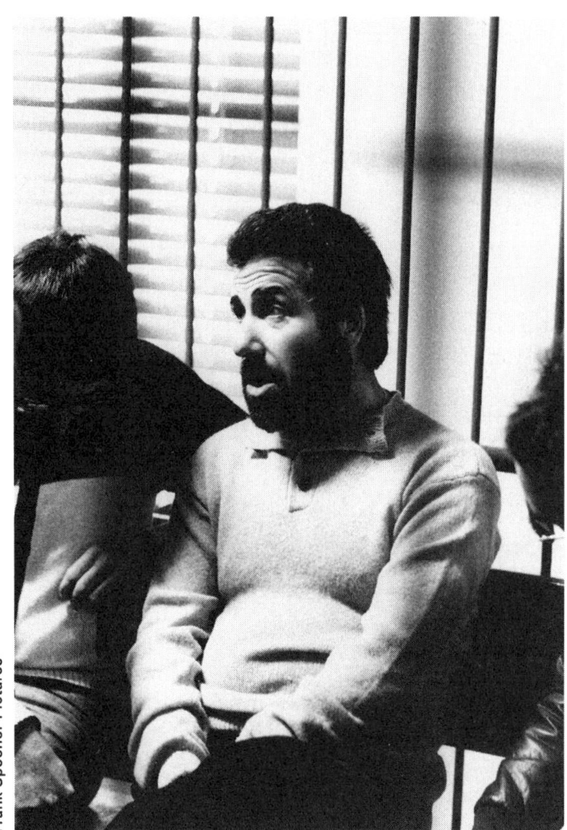

Renato Curcio, founder of the Red Brigades, was captured in January 1976 and imprisoned. He finally walked free in April 1993.

Red Brigades. His arrest interrupted plans for several ambitious terrorist attacks that had reached an advanced state of preparation.

Less than three weeks after Senzani's arrest, an informer gave police the address of the apartment where the Red Brigades were holding Dozier. In a tactically brilliant assault, an Italian anti-terrorist team rescued him and captured the kidnappers. In the aftermath of Dozier's rescue, informers came forward in greater numbers than ever, enabling more raids and arrests to take place.

The remnants of the Red Brigades continued to kill and maim in an effort to sustain their struggle. Nevertheless, they became increasingly marginalized on the radical Left and no longer commanded the following they had once enjoyed. After January 1982, the Red Brigades were hard-pressed to survive. Their terrorist acts, which included attacks on politicians, university professors, and military officers, became increasingly sporadic.

Though rapidly declining as a military force, the Red Brigades expanded their horizons as a revolutionary organization during the mid-1980s. The surviving members linked up with other European terrorist groups in promoting the Palestinian cause. To strike a blow at the Camp David Accords, the Red Brigades assassinated U.S. diplomat Leamon Hunt in Rome on February 15, 1984. Anti-Zionism in the Middle East became a supplementary campaign for the Red Brigades as they carried on with their traditional campaign to foment a Marxist-Leninist revolution at home. Both Red Brigades campaigns produced victims, though on a greatly reduced scale, during most of the 1980s. The last Red Brigades assassination – of Roberto Ruffilli, an advisor to the Christian Democrats – occurred on April 17, 1988.

The personal memoirs and courtroom testimony produced by Red Brigades terrorists make it clear that the group had tried to translate the revolutionary myths of communist ideology into political reality. They failed because of the increasingly obvious refusal of the Italian people to listen to their calls for revolution. By contrast, the defense of the Italian Republic against the most traumatic subversive challenge in its history stands out as the finest hour of Christian Democratic rule. The Red Brigades' total defeat at the hands of the state meant the virtual end of the revolutionary mystique in Italy.

Richard Drake

SEE ALSO: REVOLUTIONARY TERRORISM; TERROR GROUP ORGANIZATION; HIJACKING AND KIDNAPPING; ASSASSINATION; VICTIMS OF TERRORISM; HOSTAGE NEGOTIATIONS.

FURTHER READING

- Drake, Richard. *The Aldo Moro Murder Case.* Cambridge, MA: Harvard University Press, 1995.
- Drake, Richard. *The Revolutionary Mystique and Terrorism in Contemporary Italy.* Bloomington: Indiana University Press, 1989.
- Meade, Robert C. *The Red Brigades: The Story of Italian Terrorism.* New York: St. Martin's Press, and London: Macmillan, 1990.
- Weinberg, Leonard B., and William Lee Eubank. *The Rise and Fall of Italian Terrorism.* Boulder, CO: Westview Press, 1987.

MODERN GREEK TERRORISM

The Greek terrorist organization November 17 is probably the only such group in the world that has never had a single member arrested. The group takes its name from the date in 1973 when a student uprising in Athens against the military junta resulted in the death of at least 20 people. Although little is known about its membership, it is believed that November 17 consists of a hard-core unit and a secondary commando recruiting unit. The total number of members is unlikely to exceed 20 people.

IDEOLOGY – DOCTRINE – GOALS

November 17's ideology is Marxist-Leninist. It combines its long-term goals, however, with immediate reactions to domestic issues. On the one hand, November 17 advocates a violent shortcut to true socialism; on the other, it intervenes in everyday political and economic affairs such as the question of U.S. military bases and the Turkish occupation of northern Cyprus, as well as political and financial scandals. Consequently, its targets are mostly diplomatic or political. Its tactics include assassination and bombing, but never hostage-taking or kidnapping.

The political and social history of Greece since World War II is complicated. Civil war was followed by a period of conservative rule, initially by a monarchy, then by a junta. After becoming premier when civilian rule was restored, Constantinos Karamanlis put a democratic republic in place but failed to purge the old order. He was succeeded by Andreas Papandreou and his Panhellenic Socialist Movement (Pasok). To disillusioned leftists, whose aims had not been fulfilled by the democratic governments after the fall of the junta, terrorism seemed the only resort.

KEY FACTS

- Greeks call the terrorist group November 17 the "phantom" organization because no member has ever been identified.
- Its targets are mostly U.S. bases, their personnel, and prominent capitalists.
- Almost every assassination by November 17 has used the same weapon: a .45 Magnum.

TARGETS

November 17 directed its first phase of activities mainly against U.S. targets, focusing on the NATO military bases in Athens. Its first terrorist act, on December 23, 1975, was the murder of Richard Welch, whose identity as CIA station chief in Athens had been recently exposed in the anti-CIA publication *Counter Spy.* The second American victim was U.S. Navy Captain George Tsantes who, along with his Greek driver, was shot and killed on November 15, 1983.

In the second phase of terrorism, which occurred between 1983 and 1987 during Papandreou's Pasok government, the organization occasionally cooperated with other extremist groups, recruited new members, and almost exclusively targeted members of the Greek establishment. Nikos Momferatos, the publisher of the largest conservative Greek newspaper, *Apogevmatini*, and Demetrios Angelopoulos, a steel magnate and friend of Papandreou, were among its victims.

On November 26, 1985, the group began using explosives. They first attacked a police bus, killing one policeman. Amid political scandals clouding Pasok's (and mainly Papandreou's) public image in 1987, November 17 made two similar attacks, detonating car or roadside bombs, against military buses carrying mainly U.S. personnel. However, nobody was killed.

By 1988, two ideological forces were at work in the group. The traditional anti-imperialist radical wing focused on foreign, mainly American targets, assassinating among others U.S. Navy Captain and Defense Attaché William Nordeen. The second wing was a new hard-core unit, which advocated punishing those who they believed were exploiting the Greek people. This ideological power struggle has had a more significant influence on the group than any external factor. The

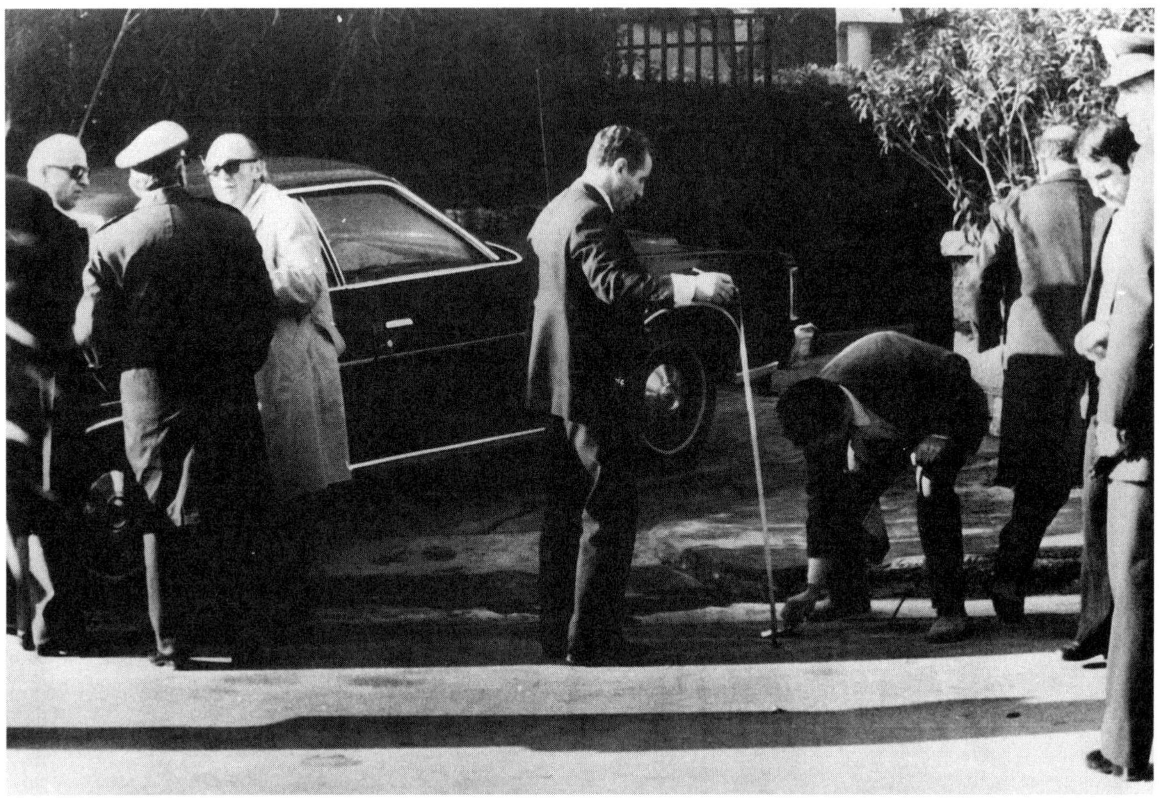

Hulton Getty Picture Collection

Police checking for clues around Richard Welch's car after he was murdered outside his home in Athens.

rise of this second unit led to conspiracy theories hinting at connections with the Greek establishment, particularly with Papandreou. The assassination of Pavlos Bakoyannis, son-in-law of Konstantinos Mitsotakis, then prime minister and head of the conservative party New Democracy, helped establish such scenarios in the public imagination.

After 1988, November 17 stepped up its activities by firing anti-tank rockets on targets that included the Athens office of British Petroleum in 1991 (as a protest against the U.S.-led war against Iraq), as well as European Community offices and embassies.

A WEAK ANTI-TERRORIST RESPONSE

November 17 has even operated in daylight. Terrorists once entered a police station, tied up the officers, and stole their weapons – all without firing a shot. Criticism of the government's response has focused on its lack of understanding of terrorism and on its exploitation of terrorist acts for its own political advantage. An official report, published in the newspaper *To Vima* in February 1996, highlighted the fact that November 17 has infiltrated the state system to such an extent that it receives first-hand information from the police.

Athena Gourdoumbas

SEE ALSO: NATIONALIST TERRORISM; TERRORISM IN GREECE; RED BRIGADES.

FURTHER READING

- Dobson, Christopher, and Ronald Payne. *The Never-Ending War: Terrorism in the Eighties.* New York: Facts on File, 1987.
- Kassimeris, George. "Greece: Twenty Years of Political Terrorism," in *Terrorism and Political Violence* 7, No. 2 (Summer 1995): 74-92.
- Yonah, Alexander, and Dennis Pluchinsky, eds. *European Terrorism Today and Tomorrow.* Washington: Brassey's, 1992.

JAPANESE TERRORISM

From the late 1960s to the mid-1970s, three closely linked Japanese terrorist groups – the Red Army Faction (RAF), the United Red Army, and the Japanese Red Army – conducted a campaign of hijacking, bombing, and hostage-taking as part of a struggle for a communist revolution. This took place against a background of unrest among Japanese left-wing students during the 1950s and 1960s. Determined to crush the unrest, the government passed a law in August 1969, to control the demonstrations. By this time, though, the left-wing movement had begun to lose momentum and had started to question its future.

THE RED ARMY FACTION

The Sekigun-ha, or Red Army Faction, was formed in September 1969 in response to this left-wing uncertainty. Established by dissident communists, it was far more militant than other radical groups. The RAF's ideology of worldwide communist revolution, of which a Japanese uprising would be just a part, called for the creation of a revolutionary army to wage war on the government. In fact, the group's initial activities were mere skirmishes. In one operation, the RAF attacked police stations with crude, home-made explosives.

Not surprisingly, these minor offensives had little impact, and the group soon realized that significant training would be required if they were ever to function as a real army. The RAF's leader, Takaya Shiomi, proposed establishing bases in communist countries, including North Korea and Albania, and in Western countries, including the United States and West Germany. RAF activists would receive military training there, and would then return to Japan with the aim of taking over the country. At the same time, the group sought alliances with sympathetic organizations throughout the world. It viewed the terrorist acts of other rebel forces, such as the Palestinians in the Middle East, as victories for the RAF. The group considered itself in the front line of a struggle for a global revolution. Defeats by the police at home mattered less if the struggle for the world was being won.

In November 1969, however, the RAF was dealt a severe blow when 53 of its members were arrested in mountains west of Tokyo. They had been training for an attack on the prime minister's residence, but after this setback, the RAF opted for small-scale guerrilla terrorism. Meanwhile, police activity against the group continued, and in March 1970, Shiomi was arrested.

Later that month, the RAF made the headlines when it carried out Japan's first ever airplane hijacking. Nine of its members, armed with swords and knives, captured a Japan Airlines jet on a domestic flight. They flew to North Korea, where they expected support from the communist leader, Kim Il Sung. However, the welcome was not forthcoming. The North Korean government immediately declared that the hijackers were "uninvited guests." Nevertheless, several of the hijackers remained in exile in the country for many years.

The absence from Japan of the group's leading members left a vacuum at the top of the RAF. Eventually, the group came under the control of Tsuneo Mori, a radical who concentrated the group's activities along more domestic lines. Between February and July, 1971, the group robbed eight banks in Japan, raising around $200,000. The group also announced "the age of bombs," and it began to use high explosives against the police.

Once again, the RAF sought cooperation with guerrillas in other countries. Its aim, as before, was to

KEY FACTS

- At present, there are about 30-40 active Japanese Red Army members, with about 100 sympathizers in Japan.
- Many criticized the Japanese government for its policy of cooperating with the Japanese Red Army. It claimed its principal concern was to protect innocent lives.
- Several terror group members remain in exile in North Korea, where they work as guides for Japanese tourists.

Hulton Getty Picture Collection

Kozo Okamoto, on trial after the Tel Aviv airport attack in 1972. He was sentenced to life imprisonment.

organize an army and prepare for a coup d'état, so the group's Central Committee established bases in the Middle East and the United States. In February 1971, Central Committee member Fusako Shigenobu was sent to Palestine to make contact with the Popular Front for the Liberation of Palestine (PFLP). The two groups quickly formed an alliance, and, in October 1971, a member of the Central Committee of the PFLP came to Japan to announce the joint Red Army Faction–PFLP "Declaration of World War."

THE UNITED RED ARMY

In January 1972, the RAF merged with the Keihin anpo kyoto (KAK). The KAK, also founded in 1969, was more nationalistic than the internationalist RAF, advocating a pro-Chinese, anti-American, one-country revolution. Despite the ideological differences between the RAF and the KAK, both groups believed in challenging political power with arms. Together, they established the United Red Army (URA), and formed a Central Committee of seven members.

Driven by police pressure, URA members fled to the mountains of central Japan to train to be what they termed "true revolutionaries." During the winter of 1972, 14 URA members were murdered in violent internal fighting and buried in shallow graves.

In February 1972, Mori and Yoko Nagata, another Central Committee member, were arrested as they returned to the group's hideout. In retaliation, five URA men took a woman hostage in a mountain cottage. Hundreds of police surrounded the cottage and, after the longest hostage incident in Japanese history, all five terrorists were arrested. The siege lasted nine days. It had cost the lives of two police officers and one civilian. It also virtually destroyed the URA. The organization had made no efforts to rally support for its campaign and, after the siege, it found itself alienated from the general public. It split into three major factions, amounting to about 100 members in all, but was no longer a serious terrorist threat.

A NEW FOREIGN RED ARMY

By this time, the RAF had established a group in the Middle East which started to act independently. After initially calling themselves the Arab Red Army, they took the name Japanese Red Army (JRA). In May 1972, three JRA members massacred 25 people and injured 76 in a gun and grenade attack at Lod Airport in Tel Aviv, Israel. It was a suicide mission, and two JRA activists, including Shigenobu's husband, were killed. The sole survivor of the operation, Kozo Okamoto, was arrested by Israeli police, tried, and sentenced to life imprisonment.

Following the ill-fated Tel Aviv operation, the JRA acquired international notoriety with a string of terrorist activities. In July 1973, one member of the JRA and four from the PFLP hijacked a Japanese jumbo jet en route from Amsterdam to Tokyo. The PFLP leader accidentally dropped a grenade and killed herself. Since only she knew what the group's demands were, the terrorists, unsure of what to do next, forced the aircraft to fly to Dubai in the United Arab Emirates, and then on to Benghazi, Libya. The terrorists released all the passengers, blew up the plane, and surrendered to the Libyan government. They were arrested but were released from jail within a year.

Hulton Getty Picture Collection

Police surround the French embassy at The Hague, where the JRA held nine people hostage in 1974.

In January 1974, two PFLP and two JRA terrorists attacked Shell Oil facilities in Singapore and subsequently seized a ferry and five hostages. The next month, five members of the PFLP took over the Japanese embassy in Kuwait. They captured the ambassador and 15 other hostages, and demanded a plane for the terrorists involved in the Singapore incident. The Japanese government sent a plane to pick up the terrorists and hostages in Singapore so they could join the others in Kuwait. They then flew to Aden, South Yemen, and surrendered to the authorities.

In September 1974, three members of the JRA seized the French embassy at The Hague in the Netherlands and held nine hostages, including the French ambassador. They demanded the release of Yoshiaki Yamada, who had been arrested in France in July. After he had been exchanged for the hostages, the terrorists flew to Damascus, Syria, and surrendered.

In August 1975, to coincide with the Japanese prime minister's visit to the United States, five members of the JRA seized the United States consulate and the Swedish embassy (in the same building) in Kuala Lumpur, Malaysia. They held more than 50 people hostage, including the U.S. consul general and a Swedish diplomat. They demanded the release of seven JRA members held in Japanese prisons. The Japanese government released five (two refused to leave) and flew them to Kuala Lumpur. After joining with the others, they flew to Tripoli, Libya, where they surrendered. In September 1977, five members of the JRA hijacked a Japanese airplane flying from Paris to Tokyo, and forced it to land in Dacca, Bangladesh. They took 151 hostages and demanded $6 million and the release of nine JRA members jailed in Japan. The Japanese government again caved in and released six (three refused to leave), and flew them to Dacca with the money. After joining the hijackers, they flew to Algeria and surrendered to the authorities.

A CHANGE OF DIRECTION

After a spectacular success at Dacca, the JRA paused to re-examine their tactics. Between December 1977 and June 1983, they published a small English-language newspaper in Beirut, Lebanon, called *Danketsu*, meaning "solidarity." In this paper, they appealed to so-called "New Left" groups in Japan for solidarity and called for the establishment of a "Japanese Revolutionary Congress."

In 1982, internal troubles in the Palestinian movement disrupted the JRA's activity, and they temporarily moved to Syria and southern Lebanon. In January 1984, JRA members returned to northern Lebanon to rebuild their headquarters. Between 1986 and 1988, several leading JRA members were arrested in Japan. In April 1988, another JRA member was arrested in New Jersey, while planning a bomb attack in New York City. This was, however, an isolated incident. The Red Army's campaign of violence had effectively ended.

Tadashi Kuramatsu

SEE ALSO: COLLABORATION BETWEEN TERRORISTS; THE POPULAR FRONT FOR THE LIBERATION OF PALESTINE; RED ARMY FACTION: THE BAADER-MEINHOF GANG.

FURTHER READING

- Farrell, William R. *Blood and Rage: the Story of the Japanese Red Army.* Lexington, MA: Lexington Books, 1990.
- Katzenstein, Peter J., and Yutaka Isujinaka. *Defending the Japanese State: Structure, Norms and Political Responses to Terrorism and Violent Social Protest in the 1970s and 1980s.* Ithaca, NY: Cornell University Press, 1991.
- Steinhoff, Patricia G. "Portrait of a Terrorist: An Interview with Kozo Okamoto," in *Asian Survey* 16, No. 9 (September 1976): 830-845.

CHAPTER EIGHTEEN

Nationalist Terrorists

Many countries contain significant ethnic minorities that claim a separate homeland, and these groups often turn to terrorism if their demands are ignored or frustrated by the authorities. They frequently target for assassination by bomb or bullet respresentatives of the regime they oppose, or else they attack symbols of its power. Alleged collaborators are also killed to control the very same minority whose aspirations the terrorists claim to represent.

BASQUE NATIONALIST TERROR: ETA

For 37 years, *Euzkadi ta Askatasuna* (ETA) – which means "Basque Homeland and Freedom" – has waged a terrorist campaign that has killed hundreds. Its aim is to create an independent Basque state in northern Spain. The Basques, ETA argues, are an independent people with a history that stretches back to Roman times. They are noticeably different in appearance from the other peoples of Western Europe and their language, Euskara, is unique.

Basques live around the western end of the Pyrenees; some 2 million on the Spanish side of the border, and 200,000 on the French side. However, the French Basques have largely assimilated, while in Spain their ancient language survives. In the nineteenth century, the independence of the Spanish Basques, guaranteed by an ancient written code called the *furores*, was threatened by the encroaching Spanish state. The Basques reacted by supporting the cause of Don Carlos, a pretender to the throne. When the Carlist rebellion failed, the central government punished the Basques by revoking the *furores*.

SUMMARY

- In 1959, students in Bilbao set up ETA as a revolutionary group bent on Basque independence. Its "revolutionary war" began in 1968. Some 700 people have died since.
- In December 1973, ETA had its greatest triumph when it blew up the Spanish prime minister, Admiral Luis Carrero Blanco, who had been designated the successor to General Franco.
- In 1995, ETA made a car-bomb attack on opposition leader José María Aznar. He survived and went on to become prime minister after his predecessor, socialist Felipe González, was implicated in a scandal over terrorist hit squads.

The Basques found their identify further threatened by an influx of non-Basque workers looking for jobs in the rapidly industrializing cities of Bilbao and San Sebastian. And in 1894, the Basque nationalist party, *Partido Nacionaliasta Vasco* (PNV), was set up. During the Spanish Civil War (1936–39), the Republican government allowed the Basques to set up an independent government in Bilbao. But in 1937, the Nationalists under General Franco responded with the brutal bombing of the ancient Basque city of Guernica carried out by the Condor Legion, the German air squadron sent by Hitler to help the fascist cause.

BASQUE TERRORISM UNDER FRANCO

With the establishment of the dictatorship of General Franco in 1939, Basque nationalism was ruthlessly suppressed, and Franco banned the use of the Basque language. Basque political leaders were either imprisoned or forced into exile. Usually they fled immediately across the border into the French Basque province, Pyrénées-Atlantiques. The PNV survived in exile in Paris, and Basque culture survived only in mountain-climbing and hiking clubs and other subterfuges. But in 1959, a small group of university students in Bilbao decided to take a more revolutionary approach and, on July 31, the feastday of the patron saint of the Basque country, St. Ignatius Loyola, they set up ETA as a terrorist organization.

For nearly a decade, ETA leaders debated their ideology. Some were purely nationalists, while others were communist revolutionaries as well. The communists believed that disenchanted non-Basque immigrants, who congregated in the region's cities, could be convinced of the economic benefits of an independent Basque state, and would join the struggle. Nationalists argued that this strategy was impractical as workers' organizations such as trade unions were outlawed by the Franco regime. The nationalists said

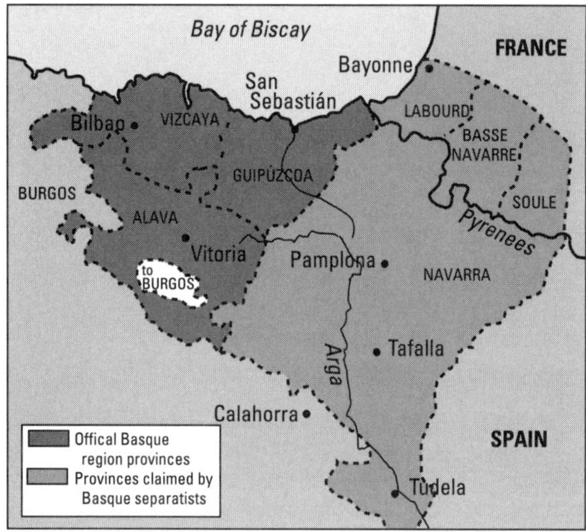

Spain only recognizes three provinces as an autonomous Basque region, but ETA claims other provinces of Spain and France as their homeland.

that only ethnic Basques should be recruited and argued instead for a spiral-of-violence strategy. They planned to attack the most oppressive symbols of the Spanish state – the police, the Civil Guard, and the military. Given Franco's record of brutal repression, ETA's leaders expected that their terrorist acts would provoke violent and indiscriminate countermeasures by government forces. This, they believed, would lead to a civil war, which would force the Spanish to give up on their costly occupation of the Basque "colony."

AN ARMED STRUGGLE WITH POLICE

ETA's "*lucha armada*" (armed struggle) and "*guerra revolucionaria*" (revolutionary war) began in 1968 when the police killed a respected ETA leader in Guipúzcoa in a shoot-out at a roadblock. ETA responded by murdering the police chief of San Sebastian. As ETA activists predicted, the Franco government's response was immediate and indiscriminate. It involved the imprisonment, torture, and exile of thousands of Basques.

Sixteen ETA leaders were arrested and tried in Burgos in 1970. Six were sentenced to death. But in December that year, ETA kidnapped Eugene Beihl, the West German honorary consul in San Sebastian. Franco was forced to commute the death sentences in exchange for his release.

The group barely survived this period of government repression. However, a charismatic leader named Eustatus Mendizabel, and an unexpected influx of new members from disillusioned members of the youth wing of the PNV revitalized the organization. In 1972, ETA kidnapped a Spanish industrialist whose employees were on strike and, in return for his release, demanded he comply with the strikers' demands. The following year, ETA terrorists kidnapped another industrialist, this time to obtain a ransom.

A DRAMATIC ASSASSINATION

ETA's most audacious act took place in December 1973, when they assassinated the Spanish prime minister, Admiral Luis Carrero Blanco, who was the designated successor to the aged and ailing General Franco. Four amateur assassins dug a tunnel under the road which Carrero drove along each day on his way to church. They packed it full of explosives and detonated them just as the admiral's car passed over it. The resulting explosion was enormous, throwing the car over an eight-story apartment building. It lodged on a balcony two stories up on the other side.

Such a bold terrorist strike kept ETA on the political map. At the same time, it sparked a new debate within the organization. A moderate faction challenged the militants' strategy of employing such risky terrorist acts, which not only precipitated a violent government response but also alienated supporters. They proposed to abandon the armed struggle and resurrect the strategy of joining forces with broad-based workers' organizations. The two factions split formally in 1974 after a bomb attack on a Madrid café. The resulting groups became known as ETA-*militar* (ETA-M – the militants who favored violent action) and ETA-*político-militar* (ETA-PM – the moderates who wanted to build up a political base first).

TERRORISM IN THE POST-FRANCO ERA

After the death of Franco in 1975, and the rapid institution of democracy in Spain that followed, ETA found that it had lost international sympathy. It was no longer seen as a group of freedom fighters opposing a detested fascist regime, but a bona fide terrorist group attacking a fledgling democratic state. ETA's response was to accelerate its efforts to provoke a violent reaction from the Spanish military police and the Civil Guard by assassinating their members – and sometimes their wives and children. During the first

Hulton Getty Picture Collection

Lieutenant General Guillerme Quintana Laccai, minutes after his assassination, on January 1, 1984, by ETA terrorists as part of their campaign against the military police and Civil Guard.

year of Spain's democracy, 19 people were killed. In 1977, 30 people were murdered; in 1978, 66; and in 1979, 130. By 1980, the total had reached 275 – but the expected retaliation never came.

Democratic institutions and processes quickly took hold throughout Spain. The government gradually released political prisoners, and many Basque exiles, including ETA veterans, were permitted to return home. Moreover, the central government supported the gradual evolution of a more federal relationship with the Basque country and other Spanish regions such as Catalonia. The conciliatory attitude of the new government exposed splits within ETA. The leader of ETA-PM Moreno Bergareche, who had tried to combine communist theory with Basque nationalism, was murdered by unsympathetic colleagues in 1976. And in 1978, Miguel Beñaran Ordeñana, one of the ETA-M leaders who had participated in the assassination of Admiral Carrero, was himself assassinated in France on the fifth anniversary of the event.

With violence spreading across the border, the French government banished ETA militants from the Basque Pyrénées-Atlantiques province. The militants moved to Paris, then to Brussels, where they were taken in by the Belgian communists. From there, they moved to Algiers, where the Algerian government gave them weapons and training. Meanwhile, the Spanish government proposed a new constitution – the Statute of Guernica – which set up a Basque regional parliament with considerable powers. The majority of the Basque people were satisfied with the arrangement – only four percent voted against the statute when it was put to a referendum in the Basque country in 1979.

By the early 1980s, many from ETA-PM had negotiated an amnesty agreement with the Spanish government for its imprisoned and exiled members. In return, ETA-PM disbanded, with supporters joining various Basque socialist parties and coalitions.

THE CONTINUING TERROR CAMPAIGN

Even ETA-M softened its hard line. As early as 1978, it had dropped its strategy of continuing its campaign of violence until full independence was achieved. Terrorism, it conceded, would now only be employed to ensure that, first, the Spanish government agreed to six key demands and, second, to ensure that these were properly implemented. Some of their demands included a general amnesty for all Basque prisoners; substitution of Basque police for Spanish police in Basque regions; Basque government control of the Spanish army in the Basque country; and the right to self-determination of the Basque people.

Nevertheless, terrorist action continued. On February 6, 1986, ETA assassinated Vice-Admiral Cristobal Colón (a descendant of Christopher Columbus). In July of the same year, there was a flurry of attacks. A bomb on a Madrid bus killed ten members of the Civil Guard. A rocket attack on the Ministry of Defense building a week later wounded nine people. At the end of the month, a nine-year-old boy was injured in a bomb explosion in the tourist town of Marbella.

THE FRENCH CRACKDOWN

Beginning in the mid-1980s, the French Socialist government led by President François Mitterrand finally took decisive action against ETA, in part because of its own fear of growing terrorism in French cities and the onset of a French Basque nationalist movement. The French police made several key arrests that struck at the core of ETA's decision-making structure, when its main military and political leaders were detained along with a major weapons expert. Virtually an entire generation of ETA leaders were imprisoned as a result of the joint French-Spanish operations. Some 500 ETA members, including most of its leaders, were then held in Spanish and French prisons. In 1988, the frequency of ETA's attacks dropped back to the lower levels of the mid-1970s, but the campaign continued. In 1995, the car bombing of an air force van killed six servicepeople. By 1996, ETA attacks had claimed a total of approximately 700 lives.

Hulton Getty Picture Collection

The car of Spanish opposition leader José Maria Aznar, and another parked behind, were wrecked by an ETA car-bomb attack on April 19, 1995. Aznar escaped with only slight injuries thanks to the car's armor plating.

ETA has a political front called *Herri Batasuna* (HB) or "One People." The HB continues to insist on full independence for the Basque state, but it has never managed to win more than 20 percent of the votes in an election. However, at the height of its popularity, HB did win a seat in the European Parliament.

The HB has refused to oppose terrorism in all circumstances, but has condemned specific ETA acts, such as the 1994 bombing of a store in a working-class area of Barcelona, which killed 21 people. This attack was admitted to be a mistake by the terrorists, whose warning to evacuate had not been effective. The result was a substantial drop in electoral support for the HB. Soon after, it lost its seat in the European Parliament.

ETA TODAY

ETA's most spectacular recent action was the attempted car-bombing of the opposition leader José María Aznar in 1995. Though he emerged with only minor injuries, the message was clear: major politicians, let alone local and regional officials in the Basque region, remain terrorist targets. This message was repeated to lethal effect during the 1996 national election campaign when, in February, terrorists shot dead the Basque regional leader of the Socialist Party. Shortly afterwards, a former president of Spain's highest court, the Constitutional Court, was murdered.

Spain's Congress of Deputies elected Aznar prime minister in May 1996, after he formed a majority coalition with several regional parties. Under this arrangement, it was unlikely that Aznar would attempt to reverse the decentralization policies of the previous four González administrations.

An important factor in Aznar's electoral success was the link between former Prime Minister González and the secret government Anti-terrorist Liberation Group (GAL). The group's death squads had been implicated in the killing of 27 ETA members between 1983 and 1987. Given the continued popular fury against the GAL and its illegal counterterrorist activities, it is unlikely that the Aznar government would resort to a similar strategy.

ETA remains a viable organization that is clearly capable of being murderously effective in targeting high-profile politicians and police officials. Its durability is impressive, given that it has lost its strategic sanctuary in neighboring France, where, for most of its existence, the key leadership and operational structures had been based.

Estimates of ETA's core membership suggest that it has declined considerably since the early 1990s. On several occasions, the González government and ETA representatives engaged in informal negotiations. Even though their talks were unsuccessful, they did reinforce the idea that non-violent tactics might still advance the cause of Basque nationalism. In addition, the new generation of political ETA recruits, despite the crackdown between 1984-87, have not been motivated by the crude totalitarian tactics of the Franco regime. Instead, they have lived in Basque provinces that are governed by moderate Basque nationalist politicians who openly acknowledge the importance of Basque culture. The public disgrace of the GAL was followed by the successful prosecution and sentencing of government and police officials to long terms in prison. This is further evidence that, in a multi-party democracy, nonviolent methods can ensure the continued existence of a Basque nation, even though it is not a fully independent state.

It seems extremely unlikely that any Spanish government would ever negotiate the dismemberment of Spain, even though there seems to be a general acceptance that regional parliaments do not threaten national integrity. However, moderate Basque nationalist parties and voters now feel they control their own destinies, both within Spain and the European Union. Nevertheless, ETA continues to represent the pure concept of Basque nationalism. Throughout its history, several attempts have been made to curtail its use of violence to gain an independent Basque homeland. All have failed. Each time a new militant faction has formed, which has continued to wage a murderous terrorist campaign.

Raymond R. Corrado

SEE ALSO: NATIONALIST TERRORISM; BOMBING OPERATIONS; ASSASSINATION; COLLABORATION BETWEEN TERRORISTS; INTERNATIONAL COOPERATION AGAINST TERRORISM.

FURTHER READING

- Sullivan, John. *ETA and Basque Nationalism: The Fight for Euskadi, 1890-1986.* London and New York: Routledge, 1988.
- Waldmann, Peter. "From the Vindication of Honour to Blackmail: The Impact of the Changing Role of ETA on Society and Politics in the Basque Region of Spain," in *Tolerating Terrorism in the West,* edited by Noemi Gal-Or. London and New York: Routledge, 1991.
- Zirakzadeh, Cyrus Ernesto. *A Rebellious People: Basques, Protests, and Politics.* Reno: University of Nevada Press, 1991.

IRA: ORIGINS AND TERROR TO 1976

The origins of the Irish Republican Army (IRA) in the struggles of Irish partisans seeking independence have for some acquired a romantic glamor. Today, however, the Provisional IRA is one of the world's deadliest and most efficient terrorist organizations, involved in a whole gamut of gangster-style activities, from racketeering to "kneecapping." Its campaign to force the British government to withdraw its forces from Northern Ireland, and to bring about a united Ireland, has been prolonged and bloody. Since 1969, when the recent "Troubles" began, over 3,000 people have died in Northern Ireland, almost two-thirds of these murdered by the IRA. Although the IRA announced a cease-fire in August 1994, it resumed its bombing campaign in February 1996, amid recriminations from all sides about the lack of a real commitment to the peace talks.

THE IRISH PROBLEM

Britain has ruled Ireland since the twelfth century. The vast majority of the Irish has never accepted the union with England. Since the English Reformation, resistance to control from London has been colored by the fact that while the English embraced Protestantism, the Irish remained Catholic. Moreover, in the sixteenth and seventeenth centuries, successive English monarchs settled the northern provinces of Ireland with Protestant immigrants from England and Scotland, thereby fomenting religious conflict within the country itself.

There has been a long tradition of armed rebellion against British rule in Ireland, and of brutal repression by the British authorities. In the 1640s, for example, there was a massive Catholic revolt in Ireland, which was eventually crushed by the troops of Oliver Cromwell. In 1801, a complete political union between Ireland and Britain was enacted.

In 1858, a group of Irish emigrants living in New York formed the Fenians, a revolutionary society whose aim was to win Irish independence from Britain. At first, the Fenians struck at Britain by making raids from the U.S. into Canada – at that time a British colony. The Fenian movement spread to Ireland itself and to England, where, during the 1880s, it carried out a bombing campaign that included an attack on the Houses of Parliament in London. In 1885, the Fenians announced ominously that "this dynamite work will go on till Ireland is free, or till London is laid in ashes."

At the beginning of the twentieth century, the question of Ireland could no longer be ignored. While the British Parliament debated Home Rule (partial independence), Irish extremists demanded full independence. At Easter in 1916, there were violent uprisings in Dublin, the largest city in Ireland. In the general elections of 1918, the pro-independence party Sinn Féin won a slight majority of the Irish vote. The following year, Irish activists, led by Michael Collins, formed the Irish Republican Army (IRA), which began a guerrilla war against the British.

In 1921, the British offered the nationalists a treaty. Under this, an Irish Free State would be created in the predominantly Catholic south, while six counties of an area in the north (which formed the bulk of the traditional province of Ulster) would remain under British control. In these provinces, the Protestant loyalist majority wished to remain in the United Kingdom.

KEY FACTS

- The Irish Republican Army (IRA) has antecedents that stretch back to the eighteenth century. In 1798, for example, a secret movement called the Society of United Irishmen was formed with the intention of launching an uprising against the British.
- The worst year of violence was 1972, with 474 deaths in Northern Ireland. Of these, 255 were killed by the IRA, 103 by Protestant terrorists, and 74 by the security forces. The remainder could not be firmly attributed to a specific group.

Popperfoto

Propaganda posters in the Catholic Falls Road area of Belfast, in September 1969. The "B-Men" or "B-Specials" were a Protestant military police often used against Catholic demonstrators and rioters.

Ulster was to have its own parliament at Stormont Castle, near Belfast, the north's largest city, and would maintain a certain amount of autonomy. While the moderate nationalists accepted the settlement, the IRA, led by Eamon de Valéra, vehemently opposed it. The treaty was signed in London on December 6, 1921. However, the split in the nationalist movement provoked a bitter civil war, during which the Irish Free State crushed the dissident IRA. Over 12,000 IRA members were imprisoned and 77 were executed. By the time a cease-fire was called in May 1923, the IRA had been decimated.

In the late 1920s, de Valéra led the majority of the IRA in renouncing violence and entering Irish democratic politics as the Fianna Fail party. A splinter group under the leadership of Sean Russell, however, continued the armed struggle against the partition. In 1939, Russell developed a strategy for an audacious, but indiscriminate, bombing campaign on mainland Britain. During World War II, six people were killed in more than 250 attacks. The Irish government, to avert a possible British invasion, vigorously pursued IRA suspects. Internment, or imprisonment of suspects without trial, was introduced, and some 2,000 IRA activists were incarcerated for the duration of the war. Unable to function in Ireland or on the mainland, the IRA's campaign and organization fell apart.

After the release of the detainees at the end of the war, the IRA regrouped and pursued a new strategy of attacking British targets in Northern Ireland. A number of raids

Popperfoto

British troops search suspects during "Bloody Sunday." The events of January 30, 1972, hold a key place in nationalist mythology.

in Ireland and Britain helped build up supplies of weapons, but all attacks from the what had now become the Irish Republic into Northern Ireland (the so-called "Border War") failed. In 1957, the Republic reintroduced internment, and the campaign collapsed. In 1962, the IRA called a cease-fire. A debate followed within the organization concerning the direction it should take. Under the leadership of Cahal Goulding in the 1960s, the IRA moved away from violence and associated itself with the growing civil rights movement. The Catholics of Northern Ireland were beginning to agitate for political and social rights. The Northern Ireland Civil Rights Association campaigned for an end to discrimination in employment and to voting abuses that kept Protestants in power on local councils.

"PROVISIONALS" AND "OFFICIALS"

In July 1969, Protestant paramilitary police (known as the "B-Specials") brutally broke up a peaceful civil rights demonstration in Derry, and anti-Catholic violence spread through Northern Ireland. In August, the British government sent in troops, initially to defend Catholic communities from Protestant mobs. The Catholics defended themselves, establishing "No Go" areas in the Catholic sections of both Derry (known as the Bogside) and Belfast. The Catholics erected barricades and prevented the British forces from crossing them.

The IRA, meanwhile, was stirred into action by the events of 1969. Economic recession, in which Catholics tended to be the hardest hit, helped to ensure that hundreds of new recruits were attracted into the movement. Almost simultaneously, however, the organization split. Goulding and the so-called "Official" IRA continued to espouse civil rights, while Sean MacStiofain, a member of the leadership, formed the "Provisional Army Council," which soon became the militant Provisional IRA – sometimes known as the "Provisionals." By the 1970s, the "Official" IRA had drastically declined in importance, and the Provisionals were often simply known as the IRA.

In 1970, the Provisionals were divided into three main brigades, based in Derry, Belfast, and the border counties of Tyrone and Armagh. The Belfast Brigade alone, first under the command of Billy McKee and then Joe Cahill, comprised over 1,000 active members by 1971.

Despite a shortage of both funds and weapons, both Provisionals and Officials were prepared to use terrorism as a means of achieving their political ends. The Provisonals frequently took on Protestant groups in gun battles, particularly in Belfast, and in 1970, they started a campaign of bombing aimed principally at economic targets. In 1971, terrorists targeted British security forces for the first time. For the first time, too, the Provisionals began using a devastating new weapon – the car bomb.

"BLOODY SUNDAY" – "BLOODY FRIDAY"

The British government responded to the violence by flooding the province with troops. The army tore down the barricades and entered the "No Go" areas. Internment of terrorist suspects was reintroduced. Unfortunately, this highhanded response alienated the Catholic community. The violence reached a climax on January 30, 1972, when, in what became known as "Bloody Sunday," British paratroopers fired on Catholic civilians rioting in Derry, killing 13. The deaths unleashed a wave of Catholic violence. In one of the earliest IRA attacks on the British mainland, the Officials killed five cleaning women, an army chaplain, and a gardener in a bomb blast at the Parachute Regiment's headquarters in Aldershot, southern England. In 1972, deaths in the violence in Northern Ireland peaked at 474, of whom 255 were killed at the hands of the IRA.

In July 1972, there was a brief cease-fire. The British government held secret talks in London with the Provisional IRA. The Provisionals' delegation included Martin McGuinness of the Derry brigade and Gerry Adams. The talks, however, proved fruitless, and the Provisionals returned to violence. Only by an escalation of terror, they believed, would they achieve their objective. On July 21, 1972, in what was quickly dubbed "Bloody Friday," the Provisional IRA unleashed an unprecedented series of atrocities against civilians in Northern Ireland. Twenty-two bombs exploded in Belfast city center, killing nine people and causing widespread panic among shoppers.

TERROR ON THE MAINLAND

After "Bloody Sunday," IRA terrorism entered a new phase. Under increasing threats from the security forces in the province, the Provisionals saw the mainland as a tempting, and relatively easy, means to strike at the heart of British resolve. In March 1973, a series of attacks that was to last until 1975 began on the mainland. The Provisionals attacked prestige and tourist targets in London, including the Tower of London. In 1973, a bomb exploded in a pub in Birmingham, central England, killing 21 and injuring 164, and in 1974, a pub in Guildford, a small town in the southeast of England, was targeted, killing five and injuring 54. The pub bombings caused widespread outrage in Britain.

One of the most successful Provisional IRA units was the "Balcombe Street gang" that operated on the British mainland from 1974 to 1975. It carried out a series of bomb and gun attacks on hotels and restaurants, and attempted to assassinate the former British prime minister, Edward Heath. The gang was eventually caught in December 1975, after attempting a drive-by shooting into a restaurant. Police trapped the gang in an apartment in Balcombe Street, central London, where it took an elderly couple hostage for six days before surrendering. At their trial the gang members were charged with 10 murders and 20 bombings, and each received 30 years' imprisonment.

A result of the 1973-74 London bombings, the British government revived contacts with the Provisionals. Secret negotiations began at the end of 1974, and, in February 1975, the Provisional IRA agreed to an indefinite cease-fire, which lasted until the spring of 1976. After the collapse of the cease-fire in spring 1976, the Provisionals would radically change their organization and tactics, and a new phase in the terrorist war in Northern Ireland would begin.

Bertrande Roberts

SEE ALSO: TERROR IN IRELAND 1916-1923; NATIONALIST TERROR IN NORTHERN IRELAND 1976-1996; LOYALIST TERROR IN NORTHERN IRELAND; BRITISH COUNTERTERROR METHODS AFTER DECOLONIZATION.

FURTHER READING

- Davis, Richard. *Mirror Hate: The Convergent Ideology of Northern Ireland Paramilitaries, 1966-1992.* Aldershot, Hants, England and Brookfield, VT: Dartmouth, 1994.
- Dunn, Seamus, ed. *Facets of the Conflict in Northern Ireland.* New York: St. Martin's Press, 1995.
- O'Day, Alan, ed. *Dimensions of Irish Terrorism.* Aldershot: Dartmouth, 1993; New York: G.K. Hall, 1994.

NATIONALIST TERROR IN NORTHERN IRELAND 1976-1996

Terrorism in Northern Ireland since 1976 has had various aspects. The most important, however, has been the continued campaign of the Provisional Irish Republican Army (IRA). Since 1976, the Provisional IRA (sometimes known as the "Provisionals," but usually just as the IRA) has been the most important terrorist organization fighting the nationalist cause – that is, challenging Britain's control over a part of Ireland. Support for the Provisionals comes from parts of the Catholic community in Northern Ireland and also from people living in southern Ireland (the Republic of Ireland), which is an independent state.

THE IRISH NATIONALIST LIBERATION ARMY

The structure that has made the Provisionals such an effective terrorist force was set up in the mid-1970s. In February 1975, the Provisionals agreed to a cease-fire with the security forces, and this lasted until the spring of 1976. During the cease-fire, the various nationalist groups tore themselves apart. The "Official" IRA, the parent body from which the Provisionals had split in 1970, and which had ceased to be a real force two years earlier, effectively broke up. Some of its members formed the Irish Nationalist Liberation Army (INLA). The INLA itself, adopting an avowedly socialist philosophy, carried out many terrorist atrocities over the next two decades. The most notorious of these was the murder of Airey Neave, British Conservative party spokesman on Northern Ireland affairs. INLA members placed a bomb underneath his car in the House of Commons parking lot, in March 1979. In 1994, members also carried out many attacks on Protestant organizations, including the murder of three members of the Protestant paramilitary group, the Ulster Volunteer Force. The INLA has never achieved the importance of the Provisional IRA, partly because it has been riven with internal feuds, often over obscure matters of political doctrine. From December 1986 to March 1987, for example, 12 INLA terrorists died during one such feud. In the mid-1990s, there was further internal strife in which two rival chiefs of staff died: Gino Gallagher in January 1996 and Hugh Torney in August 1996.

SUMMARY

- The Provisional IRA adopted a new structure of cells and active service units in the mid-1970s.
- The Provisional IRA has combined assassination and terror in Northern Ireland with spectacular attacks on British mainland targets.
- From 1994 to 1996, there was a cease-fire, during which peace talks took place. When negotiations failed, an IRA bombing in London brought the cease-fire to a dramatic end.

THE IRA RESTRUCTURES

Meanwhile, the Provisional IRA was reorganizing. The IRA's structure had remained unchanged since the 1920s. Each active IRA unit sent delegates to an Army Convention. The Convention appointed a 12-person Army Executive Committee, from which was elected a seven-person Army Council. The council then appointed one of its members as chief of staff with complete operational command.

In the mid-1970s, the Army Council disbanded the old companies and battalions in favor of smaller, cell-like structures known as "active service units" (ASUs).

TRH/Pacemaker Press International

The wreckage of the vehicle carrying members of the Second Battalion, The Parachute Regiment, at Warrenpoint in County Down, Northern Ireland, on August 27, 1979. Eighteen people died in the blast.

These contained between 6 and 12 active members, and were grouped under geographic "brigades," such as the Belfast, Derry, and East Tyrone brigades. Recruits were from predominantly working-class backgrounds. Numbers were deliberately limited because of the danger of infiltration by the security forces, with brigades normally having no more than 60 members. Active Service Units in Britain usually reported to the chief of staff or the Army Council. In the autumn of 1976, however, after the end of the cease-fire, the Army Council approved the establishment of a semi-independent Northern Command. This decision gave the much more aggressive units who were active in Northern Ireland a much greater degree of autonomy.

The Provisionals simultaneously took up a more aggressive stance with regard to controlling (or what they described as "policing") the Catholic population. In 1977, 126 "kneecappings" occurred. This gruesome punishment for such antisocial behaviour as drug-trafficking involved breaking knees by dropping concrete blocks on them or by shooting through the kneecap. In one incident alone, 23 youths were assaulted in a street that was soon nicknamed "Kneecap Alley."

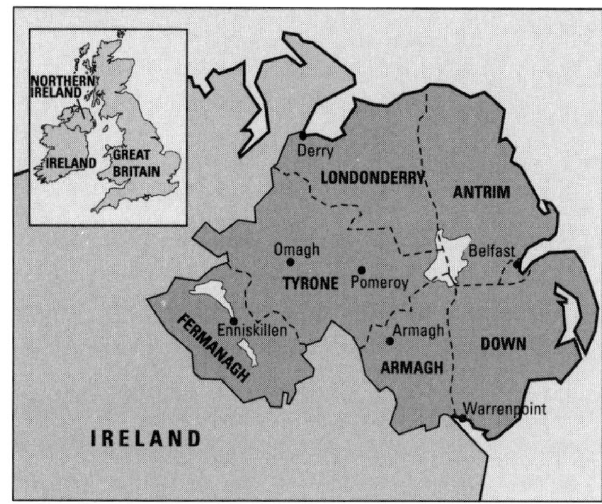

The six counties of Northern Ireland, set up by the 1922 treaty between nationalists and the British government.

HUNGER STRIKES

During the late 1970s, the Provisionals attacked the security forces and Protestant paramilitary groups in Northern Ireland. There was also a half-hearted attempt to attack economic targets by assassinating businessmen, but this was short-lived. There were some high-profile incidents: in August 1979, Earl Mountbatten, a prominent former admiral and politician, and the last British viceroy of India, was murdered by a bomb while sailing on a lake in the Irish Republic. On the same day, 18 British soldiers died in an ambush involving two bombs at Warrenpoint, County Down, the single biggest loss suffered by the British army in Northern Ireland.

More significant in the long term, however, were events that took place in the prisons of Northern Ireland. Until 1976, IRA activists in jail had effectively enjoyed prisoner-of-war status. In that year, however, the British government decided they should be treated as common criminals. The IRA prisoners protested. From the fall of 1976, they refused to wear prison uniforms and the so-called dirty protest began, in which prisoners wore only blankets and smeared their cells with excrement. By the summer of 1978, almost 300 republican prisoners had joined the "dirty protest."

By 1980, the fourth year of protest, the prisoners turned to hunger strikes to keep up the pressure on the British government. Prime Minister Margaret Thatcher took a tough stance and refused to give in to the hunger strikers' demands. Rioting returned to the streets of Belfast and Derry on a scale not seen since the early 1970s. One of the hunger strikers, Bobby Sands, ran as a candidate in a parliamentary election, and won. As a prisoner, however, he was unable to take his seat in the House of Commons. On May 5, 1981, Sands died. More than 100,000 people attended his funeral. Nine more hunger strikers died before the protest was called off in October 1981.

At the beginning of the 1980s, the pattern of violence in Northern Ireland was also changing. Since 1976, the British Army had scaled down its presence, acting mainly as support for the police, known as the Royal Ulster Constabulary (RUC), in the province's cities. Consequently, the Provisional IRA took its campaign to the countryside, assassinating Protestants in rural areas where army presence was minimal and intelligence gathering was weak. The IRA also targeted off-duty policemen and army reservists. In 1981, the total number of security force members murdered reached 44.

From this peak, however, the number of killings dropped sharply. The security forces appeared to have changed their tactics. In 1982, following the shooting of two IRA activists by the Special Air Service, many believed that the army and the RUC were pursuing an assassination policy against Provisional IRA suspects. Under increasing pressure from the security forces in Northern Ireland, the Provisionals again shifted their campaign to mainland Britain.

SPECTACULAR TARGETS

The new mainland campaign included a series of attacks on military and prestige targets. On July 20, 1982, eight soldiers were killed and 41 civilians were

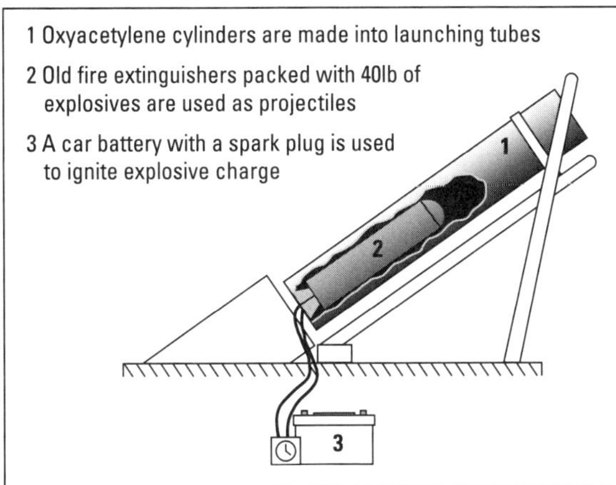

A home-made mortar was used to attack the official residence of the British prime minister, 10 Downing Street, London, England, in February 1991.

injured when bombs exploded in Hyde Park and Regent's Park in London. Three more people later died of their injuries. On December 17, 1983, a bomb exploded outside the famous London department store, Harrods. In October 1984, the IRA mounted its most spectacular attack when it almost managed to assassinate Margaret Thatcher by planting a bomb at the Brighton hotel in which she was staying. She was visiting the south coast of England, attending the Conservative party's annual convention. When the bomb went off during the night, Thatcher was herself unhurt, but her room was badly damaged. Five people were killed, including one MP and the wife of a cabinet minister. Another 30 people were injured.

BALLOTS AND BOMBS

Because of the clandestine nature of the IRA, it is difficult to make accurate estimates of the size of its membership. However, unlike terrorist groups elsewhere in the world, the Provisional IRA's level of support can be tested through democratic politics. By the early 1980s, Sinn Féin had long been recognized as the political wing of the Provisional IRA, despite repeated denials from the party.

Sinn Féin leaders Martin McGuiness and Gerry Adams have publicly distanced themselves from the IRA. Sinn Féin's peak of 102,000 votes in the 1983 election in Northern Ireland, or 13.4 percent of the nationalist vote, demonstrated the level of support for the Provisional IRA in the province. Electoral success enabled Sinn Féin to distance itself from the IRA's military campaign against the British in Ireland.

Financially, the organization was growing, too. For many years it had resorted to robbery and extortion for much of its finances, but in the 1980s this changed. Legitimate businesses, such as real estate and restaurants, both in Northern Ireland and among the Irish community on the British mainland, also appeared to account for a significant proportion of the IRA's income. At the same time, money flowed in from the Irish Northern Aid Committee (Noraid), which had been set up in the United States by Irish emigrants. On the face of it, Noraid was a charitable organization raising funds for the poor and needy in Ireland. The FBI, however, believed that the contributions were being used to purchase arms, and several members of the committee were convicted for refusing to reveal how funds were distributed. With the Provisional IRA's increased wealth, weapons were acquired in gun-running operations and were also supplied by countries such as Libya and Iran.

During the mid-1980s, the Provisionals suffered setbacks. In November 1985, for example, Britain and the Irish Republic signed the "Anglo-Irish Agreement," which led to increased security cooperation between the two governments. And although Provisional IRA assassinations continued in the province, with regular attacks on police stations in rural border areas, a considerable number of terrorists died during operations. In the 1987 general election, Sinn Féin's vote dropped to 11.3 percent. Further atrocities drew condemnation from all sides. On Remembrance Sunday (Veterans' Day) in 1987, a bomb attack in Enniskillen, a town in Northern Ireland, killed 11 and injured 63, almost all of them civilians. In Dublin, thousands marched to protest against the atrocity.

A RETURN TO THE BRITISH MAINLAND

The groundswell of opinion against the Provisional IRA in Northern Ireland encouraged the group to turn its attention to the British mainland. The first damaging attack of the new campaign came in September 1989, when the Provisional IRA detonated a bomb at a military base at Deal, on the south coast of England. Ten bandmembers of the Royal Marines School of Music died in the blast. Then, in July 1990, Ian Gow, a Conservative member of parliament was murdered. In February 1991, the Provisionals again came very close to killing a British

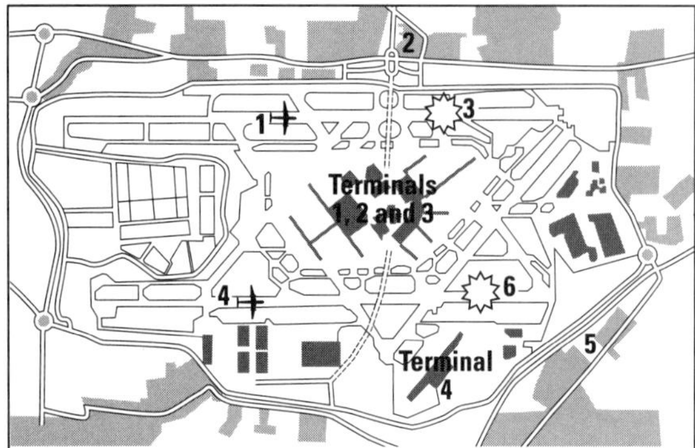

1 March 10: Passenger aircraft begins takeoff run one minute before mortar attack.

2 Four mortars are launched from a vehicle parked in the Excelsior Hotel parking lot.

3 Mortars land around runway but fail to explode.

4 An aircraft carrying members of the British Royal Family lands despite security warnings.

5 March 11: Four mortars are launched from a concealed launch pad.

6 Mortars land near aircraft and runway but fail to explode.

Mortar attacks on Heathrow Airport, London, took place on March 10 and 11, 1994. The attacks caused severe disruption but no one was injured.

prime minister. Provisional IRA members launched a mortar attack on John Major's official London residence, 10 Downing Street, from a street nearby, just missing the entire British cabinet. The Provisional IRA had shown that it could penetrate the tightest security.

During 1991, the organization returned to its policy of hitting economic targets, aware perhaps of the precarious state of the British economy at that time. In Northern Ireland, there had been a shift toward a traditional war against the army and the RUC, but by the start of the 1990s it was apparent that the security forces were not going to be defeated over the long term. In this context, it was natural for the Provisional IRA to resort to economic pressure. In late 1991, four large bombs were detonated in Belfast city center. The Provisional IRA knew the economic cost that such bombs imposed: from 1970s until the early 1990s, the British government had paid out over $1 billion to repair damage caused by almost 10,000 explosions. The Provisional IRA campaign against commercial property reached a new level in April 1992, when a device hidden in a van exploded outside the Baltic Exchange in London's financial district, killing three. In April 1993, a explosion devastated the Bishopsgate area of London. The cost of the damage from this one bomb alone was estimated at $1 billion. On March 20, 1993, two children died after two bombs exploded in succession in Warrington, in northern England.

THE DOWNING STREET DECLARATION

In December 1993, the prime ministers of Britain and Ireland, John Major and Albert Reynolds, agreed to an initiative called the "Downing Street Declaration." This opened the door to negotiations with the Provisional IRA. Renunciation of violence was difficult for the Provisionals, but the evidence of opinion polls was that the nationalist community at large wanted them to take such a step. If they rejected the Downing Street Declaration, they risked a loss of grass-roots support. At the end of August 1994, the IRA announced a "complete cessation of hostilities."

The violence stopped almost immediately. Protestant terrorist groups also announced cease-fires, and security measures in Northern Ireland were relaxed. However, disputes over the decommissioning (handing over) of IRA weapons caused delays in the peace talks, and little progress was made. The IRA cease-fire lasted only until February 1996, when a huge device exploded in Docklands, a business district of London. In June 1996, the IRA announced that a new cease-fire was "unlikely" in the near future, and that the armed campaign would now continue.

Bertrande Roberts

SEE ALSO: TERROR IN IRELAND 1916-1923; IRA: ORIGINS AND TERROR TO 1976; LOYALIST TERROR IN NORTHERN IRELAND.

FURTHER READING

- Doumitt, Donald P. *Conflict in Northern Ireland: The History, the Problem, and the Challenge.* New York: Lang, 1985.
- Lee, Alfred McClung. *Terrorism in Northern Ireland.* New York: G. K. Hall, 1983.
- O'Leary, Brendan, and John McGarry. *The Politics of Antagonism: Understanding Northern Ireland.* 2nd ed. London and Atlantic Highlands, NJ: Athlone Press, 1996.

LOYALIST TERROR IN NORTHERN IRELAND

Although the best-known form of terrorist violence in Northern Ireland has been the campaign carried out by such groups as the Provisional Irish Republican Army (IRA), there is another set of terrorists at work in this troubled part of the world. These terrorists are the Loyalists, who are fighting to keep Northern Ireland as an integral part of the United Kingdom, as opposed to the nationalists, or republicans, who are fighting for a united Ireland.

While nationalist terrorists rely on support from the Catholic minority of Northern Ireland, the Loyalist terrorists are from the majority Protestant community. Within Ireland as a whole, the majority of the population was always Catholic. In the seventeenth century, however, the English encouraged Protestants from Scotland to settle in the north of Ireland, in the province known as Ulster. During the period just before World War I, when independence for all Ireland seemed likely, Ulster Protestants formed the formidable Ulster Volunteer Force, which threatened open revolt if a Catholic-dominated government was given control over them. In the settlement of 1922, six northern counties of Ireland became Northern Ireland, a constituent part of the United Kingdom. Within Northern Ireland, Protestants formed a majority, and there were attempts to minimize Catholic political influence, partly by gerrymandering but also by intimidation. In 1966, Protestant activists formed a new Ulster Volunteer Force (UVF), which received covert support from the British army. The UVF murdered two Catholics before being outlawed.

KEY FACTS

- The Protestant community makes up roughly two-thirds of the population of Northern Ireland.
- Despite their use of terrorism, Protestant militia groups enjoy massive support in the Protestant community.
- In May 1974, bombs went off in Dublin and in the southern Irish town of Monaghan, killing 30 and injuring 151. The Red Hand Commandos were the likely perpetrators.

ANTI-CATHOLIC VIOLENCE

In the late 1960s, the Northern Ireland Civil Rights Association (NICRA) began organizing demonstrations to protest against the effective disenfranchisement of many Catholics and received support from the British government of the time. Protestants responded once again with violence directed against the Catholic community. In particular, a Protestant-dominated auxiliary police force, the B-Specials, used brute force to break up civil rights marches.

The British government disbanded the B-Specials in 1972. Even before then, however, Protestants were turning to other paramilitary forces. The Ulster Defence Association (UDA) was formed in 1971, and the Ulster Vanguard Movement in 1972. These were groups that paraded in public in military style, and were connected to mainstream political parties. Nevertheless, members from both organizations participated in sectarian killings. The first bomb attack on Catholics took place in December 1971, when the well-known McGurk's bar was destroyed, killing 15. In 1972, UDA men set up "No-Go" areas from which they excluded the British Army, and from March to July 1972, some 40 Catholics were killed. UDA leader Andy Tyrie defended his organization's use of terror: "We're a counterterrorist organization. The only way we'll get peace here is to terrorize the terrorists." Groups such as the Ulster Freedom Fighters (UFF) and the Red Hand Commandos claimed responsibility for the killing

Hulton Getty Picture Collection/Reuters

Loyalist terrorist prisoners, one carrying a rifle and another wearing a prison official's cap, on the roof of the Maze prison in Northern Ireland, March 14, 1996.

of Catholics during the 1970s. These groups, however, were almost certainly not independent organizations but occasional combinations of UDA members.

There have been numerous assassination campaigns directed against prominent nationalists. In June 1980, UDA members shot and killed John Turnley, a nationalist member of the British parliament. In March 1984, the UFF attempted to assassinate Sinn Féin president Gerry Adams as he was being driven through Belfast. In February 1989, UFF terrorists broke into the home of a prominent Catholic lawyer and murdered him in front of his family.

LINKS WITH THE SECURITY FORCES

There was strong Catholic concern about the pro-Protestant stance of the British security forces. Until 1973, no member of any Protestant paramilitary organization had been interned (imprisoned without trial) by the security forces, although there had been large-scale internment of Catholics and nationalist sympathizers since 1971. Such suspicions seemed to be confirmed when, in 1970, the British government formed the Ulster Defence Regiment (UDR). This was an official military body of part-time soldiers, designed to back up the army and the police force of Northern Ireland – the Royal Ulster Constabulary (RUC). There was widespread belief among Catholics that members of the mainly Protestant UDR took part in killings, and, in March 1979, the RUC publicly admitted that UDR members had been involved in at least 30 known cases of murder.

By the 1980s, the Protestant terrorist groups had become a permanent part of the Northern Irish scene. The groups established their own political front organizations, and, like the IRA, used protection rackets and gangsterism to provide funds. Some of their activities were astonishingly brutal: the "Shankhill Butchers" murdered at least 12 Catholics, torturing their victims before they killed them. Protestant terrorist activities were mainly confined to Northern Ireland, although in 1974 bombs exploded in the Irish Republic that were almost certainly the work of Protestant terrorists. Again, like Republican terrorists, the Protestant terrorists had their internal feuds: two leaders of the UDA, Tommy Heron and Ernie Elliott, were killed for "going soft" on republicanism.

Protestant terrorists took part in the cease-fire of 1994, and have kept to it, despite the strains of the protracted 1996 peace talks.

Ashley Brown

SEE ALSO: IRA: ORIGINS AND TERROR TO 1976; NATIONALIST TERROR IN NORTHERN IRELAND 1976-1996.

FURTHER READING

- Bruce, Steve. "The Problem of Pro-State Terrorism: Loyalist Paramilitaries in Northern Ireland," in *Terrorism and Political Violence* 14, No. 1 (Spring 1992): 67-88
- Davis, Richard. *Mirror Hate: The Convergent Ideology of Northern Ireland Paramilitaries, 1966-1992.* Aldershot, Hants, England and Brookfield, VT: Dartmouth, 1994.
- Dunn, Seamus, ed. *Facets of the Conflict in Northern Ireland.* New York: St. Martin's Press, 1995.

TERROR BY QUEBEC SEPARATISTS

The Quebec Liberation Front (FLQ) was a violent separatist movement active from approximately 1963 to 1971. It championed the independence of the French-speaking (or francophone) majority in the Canadian province of Quebec from the rest of English-speaking (or anglophone) Canada. Using publicity, demonstrations, bombings, and kidnappings, it attempted to undermine anglophone domination of Quebec's economy as well as the province's identity as part of the rest of Canada.

THE FLQ MEMBERSHIP

The organization of the FLQ made it difficult for the authorities to identify its membership. It comprised small cells of two to four people, and only one person in a cell might know the identity of people in other cells. The FLQ did not have a rigid hierarchical structure, nor did it present any particular member as its leader – although Pierre Vallières was often portrayed in the news media as the ideological leader of the FLQ. In 1967, Vallières published his book, *Les Nègres blancs d'Amérique* (The White Niggers of America), which compared the plight of the Québécois (the francophone Canadians living in Quebec) to people in the developing world. The same year, Vallières was arrested in New York for protesting in front of the United Nations. Even though Quebec was an industrialized society, many FLQ terrorists drew inspiration from the insurgent movements in the developing world, particularly in Algeria, where one of the early FLQ bombers fled to avoid arrest. The FLQ also showed great admiration for the Cuban revolution and made many references to it in their political statements.

Many of the original members of the FLQ were young. In the mid-1960s, there was an abundance of discontented and politically conscious francophone youth in Quebec. The eldest of the more prominent FLQ members, Belgian-born Georges Schoeters, who had often traveled between Europe and Cuba, was only 33 when the organization began action. His wife Jeanne was 23. Another leading figure, Gabriel Hudon, was 21, and bombers Yves Labonté and Richard Bizier were only 18.

KEY FACTS

- In the early 1960s, the minority anglophone population in Montreal was more affluent than the francophone majority.
- The Front for the Liberation of Quebec (FLQ) was organized as small cells, which made it harder for the authorities to investigate the group.
- In 1980, Quebec voted down the first referendum on secession.

MAIL-BOMBS AND MANIFESTOS

The activities of the FLQ can be divided into three main phases. Beginning in 1963, the first phase was characterized by the bombing of mailboxes and public institutions in Montreal, Quebec's largest city. The bombers concentrated on downtown Montreal and Westmount, an affluent anglophone residential neighborhood. The terrorists killed a security guard during an attack on an army recruiting center in Montreal in April. A month later, a bomb-disposal expert was injured while handling an FLQ bomb in a mailbox in Westmount. However, the police experienced little trouble arresting most of the perpetrators.

During their bombing campaign, the FLQ published a manifesto demanding the end to what they termed "English colonialism" in Quebec. The manifesto, submitted to various newspapers, included the image of an 1837 *Patriote* (Patriot). The Patriots had rebelled against Britain's colonial administration in Quebec before Canada achieved federal self-government in

Hulton Getty Picture Collection

Pierre Laporte, labor minister for the Quebec government, was kidnapped and killed by the FLQ in 1970.

1867. The FLQ used this symbol to emphasize the ethnic divide, and to appeal to the perennial concern of the Quebec citizens for their cultural survival in a chiefly anglophone country. The provincial government attempted to respond to this concern by nationalizing certain key industries, such as hydroelectricity. This government policy came to be known as the *Révolution tranquille* (Quiet Revolution). Its aim was to make the francophone majority *maîtres chez nous* ("masters in our own home"). But the supporters of the FLQ demanded more radical action.

SELECTIVE VIOLENCE

The FLQ displayed greater professionalism in the second phase of its activity, and selected its targets more precisely. The organization broadened its leftist political stance by publicly supporting labor union activity (even the Montreal policemen's union) and other revolutionary movements outside Canada. It also became bolder and more international, sending some of its members out to train in guerrilla warfare with Palestinian terrorist groups in the Middle East.

In 1968, FLQ terrorists set off more powerful bombs, one of which injured 27 people at the Montreal Stock Exchange. The same year, FLQ members and supporters clashed with Montreal police during a riot in which pro-separatist demonstrators confronted Prime Minister Pierre Trudeau during the St. Jean Baptiste Day celebration. Two men arrested at the time, Paul Rose and Jacques Lanctôt, headed the two cells that dominated the next phase of action.

THE OCTOBER CRISIS

The third and final phase led to two sensational acts of terrorism known together as the October Crisis. On October 5, 1970, Jacques Lanctôt's FLQ cell kidnapped James Cross, the British trade commissioner in Canada. The kidnappers demanded the release of prisoners, the publication of their political manifesto, and the payment of $500,000 in gold.

Five days later, while the government was negotiating his release, the Chenier cell under Paul Rose kidnapped Pierre Laporte, the labor minister in the Quebec government, because the demands made by the kidnappers of James Cross had not been met. The attention attracted by these two kidnappings, and the subsequent murder of Laporte, proved to be the climax of FLQ terror. On October 15, 1970, the provincial government of Quebec asked the federal government for relief from what was termed an "apprehended insurrection." In addition to sending in military personnel to guard official buildings in Montreal, Quebec City, and Ottawa, the federal government took the extreme step of invoking the War Measures Act. This allowed the police to arrest suspects without warrant or cause and hold them for up to 90 days without charge. The Act was in force for six months. Almost 500 people were detained, yet most were released without charge.

Local, provincial, and federal law enforcement agencies were all involved in anti-terrorist measures. The City of Montreal and the Sureté de Québec (the provincial police force) set up anti-terrorist squads, which cracked a number of FLQ cells even before they had started criminal activities. Certain civil liberties violations at this time were looked into by the Keable Commission on police operations in Quebec. The federal police force, the Royal Canadian Mounted Police (RCMP), also investigated subversive groups

Popperfoto

James Cross, British trade commissioner for Quebec, was kidnapped by the FLQ in 1970.

such as the FLQ. Although the War Measures Act lapsed in 1971, limiting the ability of city and provincial police to detain subjects without charging them, the RCMP retained additional investigative powers. This was of great concern to civil liberties organizations.

The FLQ released Cross on December 4, 1970. The police eventually found his kidnappers, but had to negotiate safe passage for the abductors to Cuba. From there, in 1974, most of this cell went on to France. Later, many of Cross's kidnappers returned from exile and were given short prison sentences. The Laporte abductors were apprehended by the end of 1970, and were tried and sentenced to life imprisonment in 1971. After years of exile and imprisonment, they have been released, and some – such as Paul Rose – have since gone on to become involved in legitimate political activity, such as the campaign for the referendum on Quebec sovereignty in October 1995.

The conduct of the RCMP during and after the October Crisis led to an inquiry in 1977, by the McDonald Commission on Certain Activities of the RCMP, which reported in 1981. Among its recommendations was the creation of a separate organization to investigate terrorist and other subversive activity. An Act of Parliament in 1984 created the Canadian Security Intelligence Service (CSIS), which is accountable to Parliament. Like the RCMP, though, the CSIS has been criticized for investigating and infiltrating legitimate dissident movements, such as labor unions and pacifist organizations.

After the October Crisis, FLQ activity ceased. The emergency measures used by the government effectively destroyed the group. There were claims that bank robberies committed after 1970 were FLQ-financing operations, but they may just as easily have been acts of criminal opportunism. Violent dissent in Quebec now generally surfaces in acts of vandalism, such as the defacing of English and bilingual street signs. Since the 1970s, the francophone community has become more affluent, partly because some anglophone businesses and individuals have moved away. Rather than through terrorism, most separatist sentiment is expressed through legitimate political movements. One such movement, the provincial Parti Québécois, was created by René Lévesque in 1968 and became the provincial government in 1976. Along with this party, the federal Bloc Québécois promises to make Quebec sovereign without resorting to violence.

Christopher W. Cook

SEE ALSO: NATIONALIST TERRORISM; TERROR GROUP ORGANIZATION; BOMBING OPERATIONS; HIJACKING AND KIDNAPPING; COLLABORATION BETWEEN TERRORISTS; HOSTAGE NEGOTIATIONS.

FURTHER READING

- Borque, Gilles. "Quebec Nationalism and the Struggle for Sovereignty in French Canada," in *The National Question, Nationalism, Ethnic Conflict and Self-Determination in the Twentieth Century*, edited by Berch Berberoglu. Philadelphia: Temple University Press, 1995.
- Ignatieff, Michael. *Blood and Belonging: Journeys into the New Nationalism*. London: Vintage, 1994; New York: Noonday Press, 1995.
- Wainstein, Eleanor Sullivan. *The Cross and Laporte Kidnappings, Montreal, October 1970*. Santa Monica, CA: Rand Corporation, 1980.

TERRORISM IN TURKEY

Terrorism has been a fact of life in Turkey since the late 1960s. The present-day Turkish state was established amidst the chaos at the end of World War I and is the heir to a multitude of problems that arose then. There are religious and ethnic divisions within the population; conflicts between secularizers and religious fundamentalists; and a three-way political split between those who favor a liberal democracy, those who favor an authoritarian state, and those who seek a radical socialist solution. All three areas have sparked terrorism.

ARMENIAN TERROR

The main religious divide in Turkey is between the majority Muslim population and the Christian Armenians. The Armenian people inhabit a region split between Turkey and the former Soviet Union, of which Armenia was a constituent republic. During World War I, the Armenians in Turkey were attacked by Turks and Kurds in what amounted to an attempt at genocide. The resentment caused by these "Armenian massacres," and the desire to liberate Armenian-populated areas from Muslim rule, provoked some Armenians into starting a terror campaign in the 1970s.

The Armenian Secret Army for the Liberation of Armenia (ASALA) was officially founded in 1975. It carried out a series of bombings and assassinations over the next 15 years, concentrating on targets such as Turkish government officials and buildings, and tourist and airline offices. It is believed that over 200 attacks were undertaken by this group. There were bombings in France and Switzerland after these nations arrested ASALA agents travelling with false passports. The Marxist ASALA is thought to have been aided by the communist bloc and also to have had contacts with radical Palestinians, possibly including the Abu Nidal Organization. Because of these links, ASALA transferred its base to Beirut, Lebanon, in the late 1970s and suffered during the Israeli invasion of 1982. ASALA became less active in the late 1980s, partly because it split into two groups.

Another Armenian terrorist organization, the Justice Commandos of the Armenian Genocide (JCAG), set up in the 1970s, was not Marxist and received most of its funding from Armenian communities worldwide. This group may have evolved into the Armenian Revolutionary Army in the early 1980s – at any rate, JCAG activities stopped at that time. Yet another Armenian nationalist terrorist group, the Armenian Liberation Army, carried out some attacks on Turkish targets in Western Europe in the 1970s. After the Soviet Union's collapse in 1991, Armenians worldwide focused their attention on the former Soviet Armenian republic and on its struggle with Azerbaijan for the enclave of Nagorno-Karabakh. Terrorist activity against Turkey itself then declined still further.

KEY FACTS

- In 1895, 1909, and 1915, the Turks massacred more than a million Armenians. After others had fled or been deported, only 100,000 were left in Turkey.
- The foundation of a Kurdish state was included in the treaty between Ottoman Turkey and the Allied powers in 1920, but was omitted from the treaty that the new Turkish republic signed with the League of Nations in 1923.
- From 1968 to 1980, the Turkish People's Liberation Army was responsible for around 2,300 deaths.

LEFT-WING POLITICAL TERRORISM

There have been three major Marxist terrorist groups operating within Turkey: two of them, the Turkish People's Liberation Army (TPLA) and the Turkish People's Liberation Front (TPLF), were most active during the early 1970s, when they had connections with Palestinian revolutionary groups, notably Yasser Arafat's organization, Fatah. They also received support from the Soviet Union. They assassinated government officials, robbed banks, and kidnapped servicemen at NATO bases in Turkey. When the main

The Turkish army, like the Iraqi army, has attacked Kurdish terrorist camps.

TPLF leader was killed by police in 1972, his widow, Mahir Çayan, formed the third terrorist group, the Marxist-Leninist Armed Propaganda Unit, which carried out murders of NATO personnel in Turkey and attacked Israeli targets in Turkey.

By the late 1970s, left-wing terrorists were engaged in a struggle not only with the official security forces, but also with right-wing terrorist groups that they believed had been infiltrated by members of the security forces. After a military coup in 1980, there was a ruthless crackdown on leftist terrorists. Although former members of the TPLA managed to keep a terrorist group going (and were able to resume some of their activities in the late 1980s), the main strand of Turkish political terrorism was now right-wing terror against leftist and liberal groups, with some Muslim fundamentalists also attacking liberals.

KURDISH TERRORISTS

The Kurds are a people inhabiting a region that is divided principally between the present-day states of Turkey, Iraq, and Iran (there are also small Kurdish groups in Syria and the former Soviet Union). Of the 20 million Kurds, about half live within Turkish territory. Perhaps surprisingly, given Kurdish involvement in the Armenian massacres earlier in this century, the ASALA had also forged a link with a Kurdish terrorist group: the Kurdistan Workers' Party (PKK). This group joined forces with the ASALA because of their common hostility to the Turkish state, and also because the two groups shared a Marxist philosophy.

The PKK, which was set up in 1978, tried to establish a Kurd-controlled zone in southeast Turkey and northern Iraq. They attacked Turkish villages and killed the inhabitants, but their terrorism was much less international in scope than the ASALA's attacks on Turkish government institutions worldwide. It is estimated that in 1988, over 300 people died as a result of PKK attacks.

The PKK was aided by Syria and probably by the Soviet Union, and PKK offices were established in Beirut, Lebanon. The PKK was funded partly from Kurdish workers in Europe, and to a certain extent by trading in narcotics. In countering PKK activity, the Turkish army used heavy-handed methods that alienated much of the Kurdish population.

However, the PKK themselves alienated some of their natural supporters. As a group believing in a Marxist ideology, they could have expected support from Turkish Marxist organizations. However, their attacks on Turkish villagers meant that they lost any such potential support.

Ashley Brown

SEE ALSO: THE ARMENIAN MASSACRES; NATIONALIST TERRORISM; TERRORIST FUNDRAISING; ABU NIDAL; TERROR IN LEBANON 1980-1987; KURDISH NATIONALIST TERRORISM.

FURTHER READING

- Bulloch, John, and Harvey Morris. *No Friends but the Mountains: The Tragic History of the Kurds.* London: Penguin, and New York: Oxford University Press, 1992.
- Fay, James R. "Terrorism in Turkey: Threat to NATO's Troubled Ally," in *Military Review* 61, No. 4 (1981): 16-26.
- Gunter, Michael. "Cycles of Terrorism," in *Journal of Political Science* 14, Nos. 1-2 (1986): 58-73.
- McDowall, David. *A Modern History of the Kurds.* London: Tauris, and New York: St. Martin's Press, 1996.

CORSICAN NATIONALISTS' TERRORIST STRUGGLE AGAINST FRANCE

The small Mediterranean island of Corsica has been the setting for a campaign of nationalist terrorism since 1976. The most significant terrorist group is the Corsican National Liberation Front (FLNC). Small and lightly armed, this organization has bombed public buildings and tourist complexes. In 1990, the FLNC formally rejected violence, although a splinter group continues with armed struggle.

A CHANGING CORSICA

Corsica has been part of the French state since 1768. After World War II, the expansion of France's economy, along with that of the rest of Western Europe, had a considerable impact on Corsica's traditional social and economic life. Between 1957 and 1975, over a quarter of its native population left the island for the new employment and educational opportunities offered by France. The loss of younger people has particularly affected traditional ways of farming.

KEY FACTS

- Between 1957 and 1975, more than one in four of the 160,000 native Corsicans left the island to work or study in France.
- In the late 1970s, Corsica had the highest number of police in France, 2,400 for just 240,000 inhabitants.
- During the 1990s, vendetta killings more than doubled and bomb attacks rose to around 400.

The French government has promoted tourism on the island in the hope that it would solve Corsica's employment problems. Nationalists have rejected this solution, arguing that tourism is owned by French and Italians who do not care that it damages the local culture. They earlier expressed alarm at the wave of refugees who arrived from France's former North African colonies to start businesses and take jobs in the new economic areas. All these immigrants were French speakers and, by 1975, they accounted for nearly half the population. Nationalists, fearing that their native Italian dialect faced extinction, campaigned for Corsican to be taught in the local schools and demanded the reopening of the university.

POLITICAL RESPONSES

Nationalist groups singled out the French administration, the tourist industry, and settler farms as targets for attacks. In August 1975, a group demanding greater Corsican autonomy occupied a settler's farm at Aléria, a town on the east coast, in a public protest. Gendarmes were killed and injured when a heavy-handed police response provoked an exchange of shots. The leaders of the protests were arrested and sentenced to several years in jail. The FLNC was founded shortly after the Aléria incident. Learning from its outcome, the FLNC decided to avoid such public confrontations with the police and armed forces and chose instead to bomb public buildings and tourist settlements. A series of attacks on police and military stations included a spectacular raid on the radar station at Solenzara in 1978. The FLNC also attacked

Hulton Getty Picture Collection

French gendarmes attack a vineyard at Aléria held by armed farmers demanding Corsican autonomy.

targets on the mainland: motorcycle-launched rockets were fired at public buildings in Marseille; and the finance ministry in Paris was damaged by a bomb. Corsican tourist complexes were a favored target. FLNC groups would take over an area, clear any people from the site, then mine and destroy all the villas. Such raids were the commonest form of action during the 1980s.

A MEASURE OF AUTONOMY

The initial strategy had some success in forcing the French government to reconsider its relationship with Corsica. In the late 1970s, the French government increased the subsidies it paid to the Corsican economy and improved transportation and communications. It also heavily reinforced the police. Political reforms introduced after 1981, part of the Socialist party administration's strategy for strengthening local government, gave Corsica a more powerful regional assembly. Government agencies were placed under local control. The combination of political reforms and bigger subsidies has proved effective. No more than ten percent of the Corsicans now want independence.

The FLNC allowed its political strategy to stagnate during the 1980s. It made few gains for the status of the island, and there was also a rise in the level of attacks on rival national groups. As many as 20 deaths per year were linked to political infighting, although all killings were denied by the FLNC. The difficulty it faced was that its methods became increasingly associated with the island's criminal violence.

By the early 1980s, the police had made considerable progress in their investigations of violent organizations and discovered significant amounts of arms and explosives. However, it became clear that 80 to 90 percent of incidents were criminal rather than political. The FLNC announced a so-called revolutionary tax in 1982. It seemed little different from extortion to the local inhabitants when bands of armed men, difficult to distinguish from criminal gangs, would arrive at their village demanding money. This pattern persisted throughout the 1980s and into the 1990s. Mafia-style gangs, rather than the smaller nationalist groups, became the focus of police priorities.

The FLNC came to regard the flourishing mafia-style gangs as a major problem and recognized that their association, both direct and indirect, with rising levels of criminal violence was alienating public support. In 1990, the official wing declared an end to the use of violence for political ends and began to campaign for the eradication of the violent criminal groups. During the 1990s, confusion over what is political violence and what is purely criminal violence has continued. However, despite difficulties caused by the unwillingness of witnesses to give evidence, police believe only a few killings can be related to the nationalists and that most are either criminal or acts of individual revenge.

Nick Hostettler

SEE ALSO: NATIONALIST TERRORISM; BOMBING OPERATIONS; THE FRENCH RESPONSE TO TERRORISM.

FURTHER READING

- Francis, Samuel T. "Terrorist Renaissance: France, 1980-1983," in *World Affairs 146*, No. 1 (Summer 1983): 54-58.
- Savigear, Peter. "Corsica," in *Contemporary Minority Nationalism*, edited by Michael Watson. New York and London: Routledge, 1990.
- Wieviorka, Michel. "France Faced with Terrorism," in *Terrorism 14*, No. 3 (1991): 157-70.

RESPONSES TO TERRORISM

Hulton Getty Picture Collection

An FBI hostage-rescue team carries out training exercises.

RESPONSES TO TERRORISM: *Introduction*

There have been two dominant strands in the response of governments to terror campaigns in the twentieth century. Responses have been conditioned to a large extent by the nature of the government in question. First, authorities have used conventional military formations, state security forces, and specialist anti-terrorist units to defeat the terrorists. This has been a policy pursued by governments of all political persuasions against both domestic and international terrorist organizations. The second strand has been the use of state-sponsored terror to destroy internal opposition groups and their supporters. This phenomena has not usually taken place in mature democracies, but has been commonplace in many right-wing military dictatorships in Latin America and many former European colonies. Many of these regimes have undermined or abolished the rule of law and abandoned any pretext of ruling by popular consent. They rely on their military forces, state-backed death squads, and networks of paid informers to deal with any threats to their position. Any individuals who express discontent, however mild, can face kidnapping, torture, and summary execution. The victims' bodies are then buried in secret graves or abandoned in public places to intimidate other civilians.

Legitimate acts to combat terrorism, ones undertaken with the consent of the people, focus on two key areas. Governments attempt either to prevent terrorist acts or to minimize their impact when they take place. The key to the first is excellent intelligence, usually provided by organizations such as the FBI or Britain's MI5, whose operatives run networks of informers and deploy all forms of modern intelligence-gathering technology. Through these means, they can build up an accurate picture of a terrorist group's membership, its strategies, and its potential targets. Minimizing the effects of a terrorist campaign can be achieved through good planning and denying the terrorists the targets they wish to attack. The so-called "Ring of Steel" (a cordon of police checkpoints backed by video surveillance) around London's financial center, for example, has effectively stopped the Provisional Irish Republican Army from targeting a previously vulnerable area.

No government can entirely prevent a terrorist strike, however, and most countries can now call on a number of specialists to deal with terrorist incidents. These include armed units trained to launch hostage-rescue missions, bomb-disposal teams, psychologists, and expert negotiators. With certain exceptions, states equipped with such forces have proved remarkably successful in defeating terrorists who have been discovered in the process of carrying out a mission.

Intelligence-gathering and having the specialists available to neutralize a threat are, however, probably insufficient to eradicate a group of dedicated terrorists. Some will always succeeed in carrying out attacks and, because most terrorists are highly motivated and dedicated to their cause, they are unlikely to give up the fight, no matter how many setbacks they have to face. Some commentators believe that to defeat terrorism, governments may be best served in the long run by addressing those grievances that have led normally law-abiding individuals to use violence to achieve their political ends. ■

CHAPTER NINETEEN

Responses to Terrorism

Legitimate governments have adopted a two-pronged approach to neutralizing the threat posed by terrorist groups. First, they employ conventional forces or elite counterterrorist units to deal with any incidents. Second, they attempt to deny the terrorists the means to wage their campaigns of assassination, kidnapping, and bombing. The gathering of intelligence on the terrorists and their intentions is an essential part of government counterterror strategy.

COUNTERTERROR IN THE BRITISH EMPIRE BEFORE 1945

The British empire reached its greatest territorial extent after World War I. New acquisitions meant that the empire encompassed an area of 13 million square miles across the globe, with over 450 million people of different races, religions, and languages. Even before World War I, however, there had been outbreaks of rebellion in support of independence in several colonies. In the period after 1918, the British political and civil authorities were faced with nationalist opposition to imperial rule – opposition that was prepared to use terrorism.

RETURN TO IMPERIAL POLICING DUTIES

British forces became engaged in military operations in Ireland, Egypt, and Iraq almost immediately after the war, while they were deployed to quell further disturbances in Cyprus and Palestine in the two decades leading up to the outbreak of World War II in 1939. The army in India, comprising British and Indian troops, faced similar problems during the Moplah Rebellion on the Malabar coast of southern India in 1921 and in the Burma Rebellion of 1930-32. In two of these campaigns – Ireland and Palestine – the British authorities were confronted with a full-blown terrorist campaign that required a combined political, social, and economic response in addition to conventional military operations. Imperial troops were also frequently called out to maintain internal security within India. They acted in support of the civil authorities to suppress ethnic, communal, and political riots (as at Peshawar and Cawnpore in 1930) and to deal with a resurgent terrorist campaign in Bengal.

These operations ranged in scale from minor skirmishes to major campaigns involving tens of thousands of troops. The enemy were invariably mobile terrorists, often hard to identify within the general population (among whom they had support), and who employed hit-and-run guerrilla tactics.

The British Army had always adopted a pragmatic, highly flexible approach to the conduct of colonial warfare during the nineteenth and early twentieth centuries. "Imperial policing" within the British empire was no exception. It had evolved a distinctly British approach to maintaining internal security, based on the three broad principles of minimum force, civil-military cooperation, and tactical flexibility.

KEY FACTS

- British anti-terrorist techniques between 1919 and 1939 initially depended chiefly on superior military might, as in Ireland and India in 1919.
- The Royal Air Force was widely used in internal security and frontier campaigns during the inter-war period in the Middle East, Sudan, and India.
- A coherent counterinsurgency doctrine did not come into existence until after 1945.

ATROCITIES AND REPRISALS

In the colonial campaigns fought during the nineteenth century, imperial troops had exercised little restraint regarding the use of violence when conquering new colonies and maintaining order. The most extreme examples of this occurred in the aftermath of the Indian Mutiny of 1857, when in response to events such as the massacre of surrendered troops and women and children at Cawnpore, troops killed tens of thousands of Indians using grotesque cruelty. After World War I, however, attitudes changed. The atrocities and reprisals carried out during the Irish troubles of 1919-21 (most notoriously by the "Black and Tans" and the Auxiliary Division of Royal Irish Constabulary) aroused widespread criticism in the press in England, Ireland, India, and the U.S. So, too, did Britain's failure to appreciate the need for building up good relations

Hulton Getty Picture Collection

In the aftermath of the Indian Mutiny of 1857, the British imperial authorities met bloody uprisings with brutal reprisals.

with the local population. There was equal condemnation of the massacre of 379 unarmed civilians by British troops in India on April 13, 1919. The troops had been ordered to break up an unlawful assembly in Amritsar in the Punjab.

Amritsar cast a long shadow on the British Army's approach to dealing with civil disturbances. When called to "aid the civil power" in subsequent colonial campaigns, troops employed the minimum force necessary to restore order, and strictly on the orders of the civil authorities. Military chiefs also increasingly recognized the need to maintain good relations with the local population in areas of unrest.

CIVIL-MILITARY COOPERATION

It was soon understood that a common strategy had to be devised by civilians and the military to deal with unrest. In this strategy, the deployment of armed force went hand-in-hand with economic and political developments to alleviate underlying causes of discontent. A unified command structure and central coordination of civil and military power were essential to get all branches of the imperial authorities to act together to quell disturbances. It often proved difficult to prevent friction between civil and military authorities, but on the whole the principle generally worked as long as a conflict was of small size and limited duration. When acting in aid of the civil power, military officers came under the direction of the local judiciary (in the form of magistrates), but they were solely responsible for the deployment of troops and any decision to open fire. Meanwhile, magistrates, district officers, and the local police provided troops with useful criminal and political intelligence. It was recognized, for example, that the campaign in Ireland had been hindered by poor local intelligence.

The British Army also learned to dispense with conventional military tactics during imperial policing operations, and to adopt methods more appropriate to dealing with terrorists. Flexibility was essential, and was achieved by deploying troops in small, mobile units. Battalions and companies were broken up into smaller components to find and engage terrorists on equal terms. During the initial stages of the Moplah campaign of 1921, for example, the Indian army initially deployed massed lines of troops, but then switched to using small patrols.

NO TRAINING MANUALS

The British Army's approach to the conduct of colonial warfare and imperial policing traditionally emphasized the importance of practical experience over theory. The army produced little training literature after World War I, relying instead on a work published in 1896, called *Small Wars: Their Principles and Practice*, for guidance in conducting such operations. Its author, Colonel Charles Callwell, has been hailed by historians as the "father of modern counterinsurgency." Some of the lessons learned after 1919 were compiled by the British War Office in 1934. These *Notes on Imperial Policing* pointed out that "the enemy, although possibly well armed, has usually no open and recognized military organization, and acts largely by subterranean methods, offering no opportunity of locating and defeating his forces by the ordinary methods of war." This manual acknowledged that situations might arise in which disturbances could "no longer be dealt with by a series of isolated actions in aid of the civil power and that their suppression demands a concerted military plan of operations."

CONTAINING THE ARAB REVOLT

The Palestine campaign of the 1930s was the closest the British Army came to actually conducting a campaign on the lines of a modern operation, employing a mixture of the principles of colonial policing and modern counterinsurgency techniques. In 1936, Arab resentment of the influx of Jewish refugees into the country erupted into outbreaks of anti-British rioting in several cities. Organized Arab opposition to Jewish immigration took the form of terrorist attacks on road, rail and telephone communications, and oil pipelines.

The British Army and local police were caught off-guard. At first, the British sought a military solution, sending troops into action against Arab guerrillas in Samaria, in northern Palestine. Villages were searched and control reestablished, but intelligence was poor, and troops found it difficult to distinguish the terrorists from the law-abiding population. This caused local resentment, which made the situation worse.

After the failure of a Royal Commission to find an acceptable settlement, there was a resurgence of Arab violence and renewed attacks on Jewish settlers. This time, the British immediately banned the Arab terrorist organization, the Arab High Committee, arrested its leaders, tightened press censorship, and called out the local garrison to maintain order. High Commissioner Sir Harold MacMichael acted as overall coordinator: he laid down a definite political aim and directed a military campaign against the terrorists to isolate them from rural supporters. MacMichael placed the police under military control, and used the Jewish Settlement Police to supplement troops in Jewish areas. British-led patrols of Jewish police – known as Special Night Squads – raided terrorist camps and amassed valuable intelligence. Next, physical barriers were constructed between villages, restricting the movement of terrorists. The result was a dramatic fall in terrorist attacks. Meanwhile, the imposition of identity cards, checkpoints, and night curfews severely curtailed the movement of the Arabs. Imperial authorities firmly reestablished military control and curbed dissent in the area until the end of World War II.

The British experience of countering terrorism before 1945 gave later British security forces a valuable head start. However, it was not until the campaign in Malaya (1948-60) that a more formal doctrine for countering terrorism was actually laid down.

Tim Moreman

SEE ALSO: TERROR IN COLONIAL CONQUESTS; TERROR IN IRELAND 1916-1923; THE AMRITSAR MASSACRE; TERROR IN COLONIAL INDIA 1900-1947; BRITISH COUNTERTERROR IN THE ERA OF DECOLONIZATION; BRITISH COUNTERTERROR METHODS AFTER DECOLONIZATION.

FURTHER READING

- Killingray, David, and David Anderson, eds. *Policing Empire: Government, Authority, and Control, 1830-1940.* Manchester: Manchester University Press, and New York: St. Martin's Press, 1991.
- Mockaitis, T. R. *British Counterinsurgency, 1919-1960.* London: Macmillan, and New York: St Martin's Press, 1990.
- Omissi, David. *Air Power and Colonial Control: The Royal Air Force, 1919-1939.* Manchester: Manchester University Press, and New York: St. Martin's Press, 1990.

BRITISH COUNTERTERROR IN THE ERA OF DECOLONIZATION

The British enjoy a reputation for success in what is known as "counterinsurgency" (COIN), a form of warfare in which terrorism has played a major part. After the end of World War II, as the empire dwindled, British political and military authorities faced widespread armed opposition, much of it under the guise of insurgency. Their COIN methods – while not always successful – contained valid responses, particularly when compared with those used by other Western powers. Most terrorism since 1945 has been in the context of nationalist and Marxist insurgencies, so the British experience is critical in the West's response to terrorism.

The British Army defines insurgency as "the actions of a minority group within the state, intent on forcing political change by means of a mixture of subversion, propaganda and military pressure, aiming to persuade or intimidate the broad mass of the people to support such change." Here, "military pressure" is taken to include both guerrilla warfare and terrorism, the latter being seen as an integral part of insurgency and not a separate phenomenon. Once this is accepted, a broad definition of counterinsurgency is relatively straightforward: "The actions of an existing government and its security forces to combat insurgency and prevent its resurgence." Two interrelated points are worth noting. First, there is a recognition that insurgency is essentially a political problem, and, second, there can be no such thing as a purely military solution.

KEY FACTS

- The British view is that terrorism as a part of insurgency is a political problem that demands a political solution.
- Sir Robert Thompson summarized his principles of counterinsurgency in *Defeating Communist Insurgency,* which was published in 1966.
- The British authorities deduced that a critical measure is to win the backing of the mass of the people – the "middle ground."

A RANGE OF TERRORIST CAMPAIGNS

The period after 1945 saw the British involved in a long round of counterinsurgency campaigns. When World War II ended, there was already trouble in Palestine, where Jewish nationalist groups were intent on ousting the British from the mandate of the League of Nations established in 1920. That campaign ended in British withdrawal and the creation of an independent state of Israel in May 1948.

Less than a month later, a State of Emergency was declared in Malaya, where communist terrorists, following the pattern of revolt advocated by Mao Zedong in China, tried to overthrow colonial rule. The Malayan Emergency ended in British-Malayan victory in 1960. The British waged campaigns in Kenya against the Mau Mau, 1952-60, and in Cyprus against EOKA, 1955-59. The former may be termed a success, in that the Mau Mau failed to gain political power when Britain granted independence to the country in the early 1960s. The latter ended in compromise: EOKA failed to achieve its aim of union with Greece, while the British failed to retain political control of the island, which received its independence in late 1959.

Meanwhile, an Irish Republican Army (IRA) campaign had been going on in Northern Ireland since 1956, characterized by armed raids on military establishments and attacks on Royal Ulster Constabulary

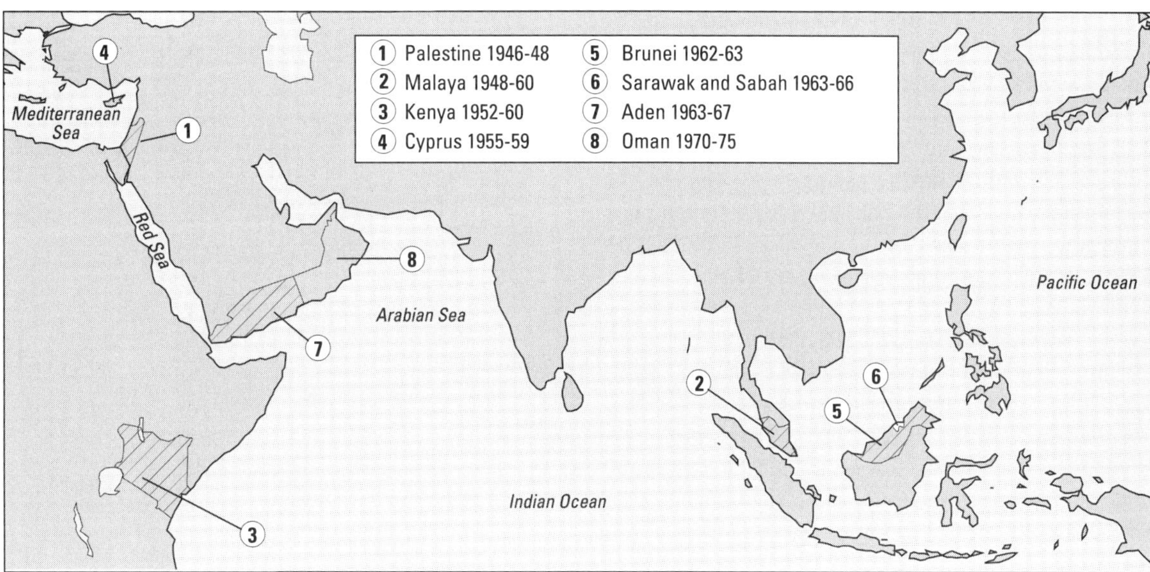

The British Army formulated responses to terrorism during postwar counterinsurgency campaigns.

(RUC) bases in the province. By 1963, the IRA campaign had lost all momentum and come to a halt. By then, however, British forces had become involved in Brunei, where they put down a revolt against the sultan. In neighboring Borneo, the British faced Indonesian-backed rebels (and later regular Indonesian troops) in operations that, although not strictly counterinsurgency, incorporated and refined many of its techniques. The Borneo Confrontation concluded in an Indonesian backing down in 1966, by which time further revolts against British rule had broken out in Aden in the Middle East. The Aden campaign ended in a British withdrawal in late 1967, after which Marxist insurgents seized power in what was to become the People's Democratic Republic of Yemen (PDRY).

THE THOMPSON PRINCIPLES

Of all the specified campaigns, that in Malaya between 1948 and 1960 seems to offer the best example of British success – at least until the 1970s – and much of what we now know as British counterinsurgency had its origins there. The relevant "lessons" of the campaign were summarized by Sir Robert Thompson, a colonial administrator who had served in Malaya throughout the Emergency. Thompson drew five "principles" from his experiences in Malaya: that the government must have a clear political aim; that the government and its security forces must function in accordance with the law; that the government, its agencies, and forces, must have an overall plan; that the government must give priority to defeating political subversion, not guerrilla action; and that the government must make sure it secures its own base areas first, before moving into the insurgent-affected locations.

1. A CLEAR POLITICAL AIM

That the government needs a clear political aim seems to be an obvious principle to lay down. Thompson defined this aim, when describing the situation in Malaya, as "to establish and maintain a free, independent and united country which is politically and economically stable and viable." The British have always viewed insurgency essentially as a political process, designed to "force political change," and so any counterinsurgency campaign must also be essentially political in nature.

But the government must also ensure the political aim is realistic and attainable. In this respect, the British in Malaya adopted a sensible approach by promising independence to the country by 1957 and ensured that this was carried out, regardless of the persistence of insurgency. If the other aspects of counterinsurgency had not worked effectively by 1957, the offer would probably have been withdrawn. As it was, the offer acted as a powerful incentive to the ordinary people to accept government authority; having attracted this support from the middle ground, the British policy left the insurgents isolated.

Elsewhere, the viability of such a straightforward political aim could not be assumed. No one on the British side was prepared, for example, to contemplate full withdrawal from Cyprus because of the island's key strategic importance in the eastern Mediterranean.

2. KEEPING WITHIN THE LAW

The government and its security forces have an obligation to uphold the authority they represent in the face of rebellion from those who wish to overturn it. This "minority group within the state" is, by definition, opposing the rule of law, and if the government or its agencies go beyond that law themselves, they are no better than the rebels they are confronting. Of course, the government can change the law to suit the circumstances of the campaign. During colonial policing activities before 1939, for example, it was normal for British authorities to declare local versions of martial law, introducing packages of emergency legislation that were, in retrospect, repressive. However, soldiers and policemen have always remained subject to the law of the land since 1945. As long as such a democratic system prevails, the middle ground should not be alienated by government actions, although it must be admitted that the dividing line between acceptability and alienation can be extremely thin.

3. AN OVERALL PLAN

The principle that the government, its agencies and forces, must have an overall plan ties in closely with the first principle of a clear political aim. If such an aim is laid down, it is only sensible to ensure that all government agencies and forces are aware of it, and are prepared to work toward it in a unified manner. If this does not happen, energies will be wasted and gaps in government policy will be created that may be exploited by the insurgents.

In Malaya, Thompson helped to set up a unifying structure based on committees at various levels within society, so that policy made at the top by the high commissioner filtered down the "pyramid" to state, district, and even village locations. This meant that once an overall plan, incorporating political and military efforts, had been created, there was no excuse for anyone to deviate from it. And as that plan was essentially political in nature, designed to gain the loyalty of the middle ground by offering independence on government terms, there was less chance of military action getting out of hand.

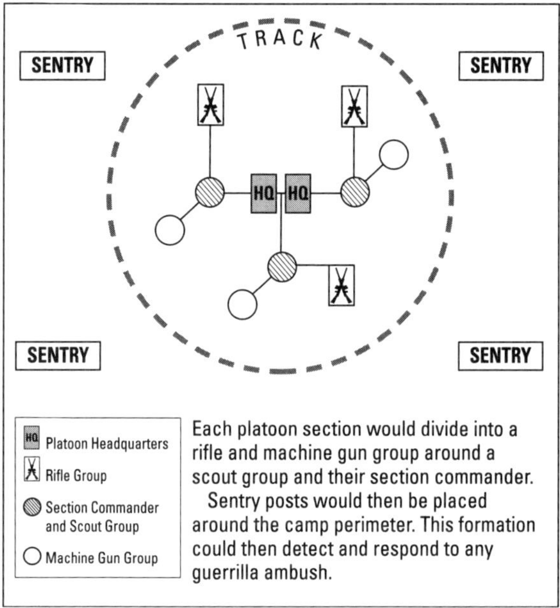

During the Malaya campaign, the British Army set up jungle bases in guerrilla-infested terrain.

4. THE DEFEAT OF POLITICAL SUBVERSION

Thompson's fourth principle, that the government must give priority to defeating political subversion, was based very much on a British interpretation of Maoist-style insurgency. Once it had been recognized that guerrilla action was only a method of obtaining political change, the focus of counterinsurgency could be directed toward ensuring the loyalty of the middle ground to the prevailing regime, thereby denying rebel groups popular support.

This did not mean anti-terrorist action was ignored, but it was seen as only a part of the overall threat. If a government ordered its security forces merely to seek out and destroy guerrillas, not only would this be intensely difficult, but it would also stand a good chance of alienating the ordinary people. By its very nature, guerrilla warfare is secretive and clandestine, with activists hiding among the people. If the government does not prepare the way politically, but sends its security forces among civilians to flush out insurgents, they run a very high risk of killing innocent people and losing support for using strong-arm tactics. In Malaya, that had been the case during the early years, leading to counterproductive incidents. Once the nature of the problem became clear, however, and attempts were made specifically to counter political subversion, security forces focused on guerrillas who were finding it difficult to retain support. This principle represented a key feature of the British view of insurgency.

5. PROTECTING THE BASE AREAS

The final principle put forward by Thompson represents the closest he came to acknowledging the role of the security forces. This was to protect areas loyal to the government from terrorist attack or infiltration first, before moving into insurgent-affected areas. Clearly, it would be foolish for a government affected by insurgency to devote all its efforts to confronting the activists in areas they control, while leaving its own base unprotected. In such circumstances, the guerrillas would merely bypass the main government effort and infiltrate that base, undermining what remained of government control.

Again, Thompson was aware of the importance of this principle from his experience in Malaya. Some areas were obviously under close communist control, temporarily outside the influence of the colonial government, while others were in the process of being subverted. However, quite substantial areas were not yet involved, and they represented the government's "safe base," within which it was essential to ensure continued loyalty. If the British had concentrated all available forces and policies in the communist-controlled areas after 1952, they would have left the unaffected areas vulnerable to infiltration. Instead, they ensured that security forces were available to protect the "safe bases," while regular army troops fought campaigns elsewhere.

An important aspect was to separate the terrorists from the population they were trying to subvert. Tangible action to split the active insurgent from his supporters sometimes took the simple, but nonetheless effective, form of creating physical barriers to movement. For example, in Kenya, security forces constructed a huge ditch along the border of the forests, leading into an area of cleared ground, so that any Mau Mau who ventured out had difficult and exposed terrain to cross in order to reach the people. The aim was to make movement into populated areas difficult for the terrorists. This policy was followed elsewhere in British counterinsurgency campaigns. It depended on the ability of security forces to recognize and target guerrilla-affected areas. If this could be done, the policy went a long way to undermining terrorist strategy.

Every one of Thompson's five principles is sound and, taken together, the five provide a valuable insight into British counterinsurgency methods. However, they are not perfect. For example, the principles are not complete. Two vitally important factors are not specified. These are the need to gather information and turn it into usable tactical intelligence, and the use of the policy of "hearts and minds" – winning over the loyalty of the ordinary people. Fortunately, other theorists filled in the gaps. Sir Frank Kitson, a British Army officer of wide counterinsurgency experience advocated a closer emphasis on low-level intelligence. British campaigns since 1966, when Thompson published his principles, clearly employed the hearts and minds approach.

No two insurgencies are ever the same, so responses always have to be adapted to suit the circumstances. The British enjoyed proven counterinsurgency success, implying that the principles they adopted and refined contained some measure of relevance, applicable across the board. However, neither the Thompson nor Kitson principles provided the British Army with a comprehensive strategy for counterterrorism. It was not until the 1980s that a set of principles was codified into an army order that could be followed in all campaigns.

John Pimlott

SEE ALSO: TERRORISM IN CYPRUS; TERRORISM IN MALAYA; TERRORISM IN KENYA; NATIONALIST TERRORISM.

FURTHER READING

- Carruthers, Susan L. *Winning Hearts and Minds: British Governments, the Media and Colonial Counter-Insurgency.* Leicester: Leicester University Press, 1995.
- Lawrence, James. *Imperial Rearguard: Wars of Empire, 1919-1985.* Elmsford, NY: Pergamon Press, and London: Brassey's, 1988.
- Pimlott, John. *British Military Operations, 1945-1984.* London: Hamlyn, and New York: Military Press, 1984.

BRITISH COUNTERTERROR METHODS AFTER DECOLONIZATION

British forces have been actively engaged in warfare in all but one year – 1968 – since 1945. In most of these years they have been engaged in campaigns in which terrorism played a greater or lesser role. The year 1968 marks something of a watershed, however. Before 1968, British forces were chiefly engaged in campaigns of decolonization, while after it, the campaigns they engaged in were more varied.

The British Army examined its counterinsurgency campaigns since 1945 and identified several common denominators. From these, it outlined six principles designed to provide an analysis of counterinsurgency success. The six principles were as follows: (1) political primacy and political aim; (2) coordination of government machinery; (3) obtaining intelligence and information; (4) separating the insurgent from his support by means of propaganda, a "hearts and minds" campaign, and physical barriers; (5) neutralizing the insurgent; and (6) long-term post-insurgency planning. These principles were refined in the early 1990s.

THE CAMPAIGN IN DHOFAR

The codification of the army's principles largely grew out of the counterinsurgency campaign in Dhofar, southeastern Arabia. Between 1970 and 1975, British soldiers and administrators helped the Sultan of Oman to gain victory against Marxist rebels in his western province of Dhofar.

In Dhofar, the first two principles – of a political aim and a coordination of government machinery – were established as soon as Sultan Qaboos bin Said seized power in July 1970, and were strictly adhered to afterward. There was, for example, an overall plan to prepare the province for "civil development" that would appeal to the mass of the populace. There was also an effective flow of intelligence and information set up, partly by offering generous bounties to members of the insurgent groups who crossed to the government side.

The separation of the insurgents from their popular support was an area in which British troops played a key role, putting the government message across to the people and letting them know the terms and conditions of any change. In Dhofar, the 22nd Special Air Service (SAS) Regiment took charge of government propaganda in late 1970, dropping leaflets over the rebel-affected areas to inform the people that the new Sultan was intent on modernization that would benefit those who remained loyal to his rule.

At the same time, Radio Dhofar was set up to beam out pro-government information in direct opposition to the communist-controlled Radio Aden. In an effort to ensure that people listened to Radio Dhofar, the SAS purchased cheap transistor radios, fixed the dials so they were permanently tuned to Radio Dhofar, and gave them away to people in the affected areas when they came down to the markets. Unfortunately, the rebels realized the danger and destroyed any radios they found – a loss that had little impact as the people did not value radios that were free. Once they realized this, the SAS

KEY FACTS

- In the wake of its post-war campaigns, the British Army listed six key principles to serve as a blueprint for counterterrorist procedure.
- The principles were not successfully applied in Northern Ireland, but the Army has used the experience to develop its counterterrorist skills.

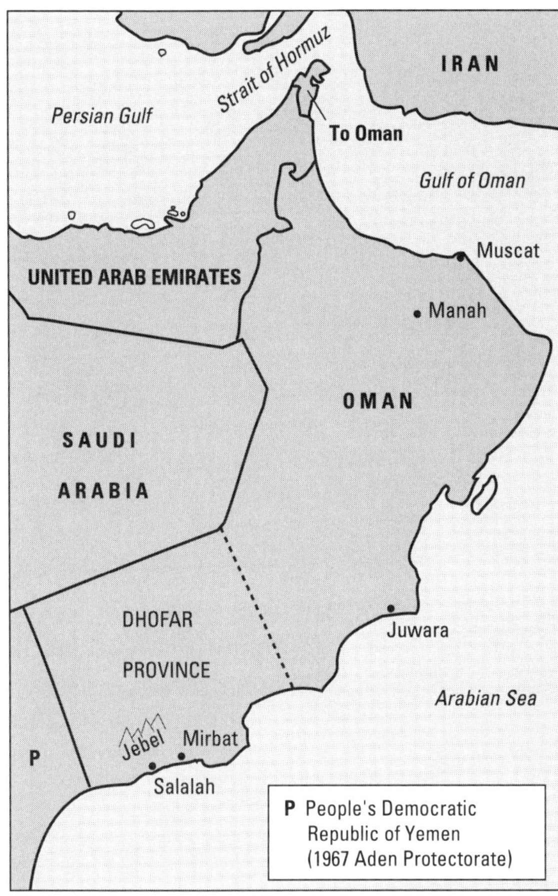

The Dhofar campaign of the early 1970s provided a blueprint for British Army counterterrorist strategy.

then began to *sell* the radios, so that when the sets were destroyed, people resented the loss. In time, people began to listen in regularly to Radio Dhofar.

A second method of splitting insurgents from their supporters involved a "hearts and minds" policy. In Dhofar, Sultan Qaboos's promises of civil development always had the potential to attract support, but he needed to be seen as carrying them out. This was done by means of Civil Action Teams comprising engineers, teachers, and medical personnel, and set up under military protection from 1972 onward. The teams would, for instance, dig a well in the mountains, attracting essentially nomadic people with the prospect of running water even during the dry period. Then they would set up a clinic and school to keep the people in one place, away from rebel influence.

Finally, physical barriers – large-scale defended lines – were built to keep the insurgents in set areas. Then, the fifth principle, that of neutralizing the insurgents, could come into play. At this level, with the previous principles having been established, the relative strength of government firepower quickly overpowered the rebels. Finally, the long-term planning for a more modern nation ensured that once defeated, the insurgency did not come back.

TERRORISM IN NORTHERN IRELAND

Just as the Dhofar insurgency was beginning, a further, much more long-term and intractable problem was arising for the British Army. In 1969, British troops were sent to Northern Ireland: civil protest by the Roman Catholic minority had provoked a violent reaction. Intervention was at first intended to protect the ordinary Catholic population from reprisals by Protestant extremists and the infamous, and now disbanded, "B-Specials" division of the Royal Ulster Constabulary. However, the conflict evolved into a war against nationalist factions in which Protestant Loyalist terrorists were also involved. These troubles presented the British with a new problem: that of operating under the full glare of publicity in the home islands.

In Northern Ireland, it was difficult for the British Army to implement a set of principles along the lines of those used in Dhofar. For a start, there was no political solution that would satisfy the terrorists or their supporters. Independence for Northern Ireland was not a realistic option because the Protestant majority did not wish it. The move would also have broken up the United Kingdom – an unthinkable solution in British eyes. Whatever is proposed as a likely "end-state" is virtually guaranteed to alienate someone. The negotiations of the mid-1990s, aimed at involving all sides in moves toward compromise, represented a logical approach, but their slow progress meant the campaign could not be ended overnight.

The second principle, of coordinated government machinery, has also been absent at important points in Northern Ireland's recent history. Sometimes this has just been because of too many agencies competing, but it has mainly been due to a fundamental lack of political aim. In 1972, when the British government set up direct rule from Westminster, it provoked anger within the Protestant community. In 1974, encouraged by Protestant politicians, Protestant workers went on strike and destroyed a British government initiative that would have led to so-called "power sharing." Effectively, the British government and the political representatives of the majority Protestant community are often at odds. There is, therefore, no coordinated response to terrorism.

INTELLIGENCE IN NORTHERN IRELAND

Given the failure to achieve at the highest levels, the security forces on the ground have always struggled, managing to contain violence but failing to strike decisive blows against terrorists. Intelligence and information is the third principle British Army theorists have identified, and in this respect, there were some successes, but also some signal failures. Initially, there were various government agencies involved, including the secret services MI5 and MI6, and the special branch of the Royal Ulster Constabulary. A Military Reconnaissance Force (MRF) was also established.

The interrogation methods used by security forces in the early 1970s included "deep interrogation" using sensory deprivation. The techniques included making suspects wear hoods for hours at a time, exposing them to continuous monotonous noise, depriving them of sleep and food, and forcing them to stand at walls for 20-30 hours. In 1978, the European Court of Human Rights decided the British government had inflicted "inhuman and degrading treatments," while agreeing there had been no torture. Undercover agents were frequently employed by the British: in one noteworthy incident in 1977, Captain Robert Nairac posed as a Catholic in a bar in South Armagh, but aroused the suspicions of the local Provisional Irish Republican Army (IRA). Nairac was seized, tortured, and shot.

The most effective intelligence was provided by so-called "supergrasses" – members of terrorist organizations who gave the security forces information in return for large sums of money, a pardon, and a safe identity away from Ireland if the terrorists suspected them. During the 1980s, a committee known as "The Department" effectively coordinated much of the intelligence gained through the various channels.

INTERNMENT AND CATHOLIC RESENTMENT

However, even with this improved intelligence, the security forces have been unable to achieve the fourth principle: separating the terrorists from their support. Republicanism – in Northern Ireland, self-government without British involvement – remains popular among the Catholic population of Northern Ireland. Strong support for the Provisional IRA among some of the population of the Republic of Ireland has prevented the security forces from stemming the flow of recruits and sympathizers that is the real strength of the terrorists. In 1981, 100,000 supporters of Republicanism attended the funeral of Bobby Sands, the Provisional IRA hunger striker, making plain their political allegiance.

Far from leading to a "hearts and minds" campaign, many actions of the security forces and government have fueled the resentment of Catholics through the years. In August 1971, for example, in a period when various political solutions might have been possible, the British government alienated the Catholic population by introducing internment (imprisonment without trial) and interning only Catholics. The result was predictable: while there had been 13 security force deaths in the seven months to August of 1971, in the remaining five months there were 46 as Catholic anger spilled over. Then, on January 30, 1972, "Bloody Sunday," British paratroopers shot dead 13 Catholics after a march against internment in the city of Derry. In

Pacemaker Press International

Bomb disposal experts deploy a "wheelbarrow" – a remote machine for handling suspect devices.

Popperfoto

The Gibraltar Navy Hospital, under armed guard, held the bodies of three suspected Provisional IRA terrorists shot dead by the SAS in 1988.

1996, cross-party talks were under way and peace seemed achievable, but Catholic sensibilities were again offended when, after a decision to ban a Protestant march through a Catholic area, the march was allowed to proceed, following a confrontation between marchers and police. It looked to many Catholics as though Protestant pressure had led to the reversal of the decision by security forces sympathetic to Protestant activists. The result was days of rioting.

BRITISH TECHNICAL EXPERTISE

It is hardly surprising that the British security forces have been unable to achieve principle five: neutralizing the terrorists in Northern Ireland. However, they have had individual successes, and have made themselves experts in many aspects of counterterrorism.

One such area of success is in bomb detection and disposal. The Royal Logistic Corps controls a number of Ammunition Technical Officers who are frequently at the "sharp end" of bomb disposal, and who constantly update their techniques and technology. Allied to this experience in bomb disposal is the use of specially trained dogs and sophisticated X-ray equipment. British security forces also lead the world in the computerization of records and the instant relaying of such records to troops on the ground, so that ownership and history of vehicles, for example, is instantly available. The detailed and long-term tracking of individuals has also become an important modern counterterrorist tool.

For the public, perhaps the most celebrated aspect of counterterrorism growing out of the experience in Northern Ireland has been the role of special forces. The SAS has been prominent in various incidents connected with terrorism in Northern Ireland, sometimes because its members were accused of operating an assassination policy towards members of the Provisional IRA. For example, the killing by the SAS of three unarmed terrorists in Gibraltar in 1988 excited much controversy and comment.

The most stunning single exploit of the SAS was their storming of the Iranian Embassy at Princes Gate in London in 1981. By the speed and efficiency of their action against terrorists from the Iranian province of Arabistan, the SAS introduced a new element into hostage taking: the fact that in such situations, properly trained security forces might actually strike more quickly than terrorists could react. The SAS and other British counterterrorist units are now involved in training other such units worldwide. Ironically enough, the long war in Ireland has probably benefited Western anti-terrorist forces.

Ashley Brown

SEE ALSO: NATIONALIST TERROR IN NORTHERN IRELAND 1976-1996; LOYALIST TERROR IN NORTHERN IRELAND; BRITISH COUNTERTERROR IN THE ERA OF DECOLONIZATION.

FURTHER READING

- Beckett, Ian F. W., and John Pimlott. "The British Army: The Dhofar Campaign, 1970-1975," in *Armed Forces and Modern Counter-Insurgency.* London: Croom Helm, and New York: St. Martin's Press, 1985.
- Pimlott, John, ed. *War in Peace.* New York: Marshall Cavendish, 1987.
- Urban, Mark. *Big Boys' Rules: The Secret Struggle Against the IRA.* London and Boston: Faber and Faber, 1993.

TERRORISM IN THE CITY OF LONDON

The City of London, a semi-autonomous square mile in the heart of the capital, is Britain's main financial center. Home of the largest number of financial institutions and foreign banks in Europe, the City was a target for the Provisional Irish Republican Army (IRA) during its mainland bombing campaign in the 1990s. The City responded with the most extraordinary security measures ever seen in Britain, with the exception of Northern Ireland itself.

Although the City had been hit in earlier campaigns, such as the bombing of the Stock Exchange and the Old Bailey Courts in 1973, the nature of the campaign in the late 1980s-90s revealed a shift to economic targeting. This was substantiated by a bombing in the City in April 1992, which killed three people and injured 91. Only attacks against leading politicians were thereafter seen to be as valuable in undermining the will of the British government.

How far this was true was revealed two years later, in April 1994, when a massive bomb devastated Bishopsgate in the City, killing one person. Politically, it was not clear that Provisional IRA tactics were paying off, at least in the short term. Economically, however, a possible crisis of confidence among foreign banks and institutions, which might seek to relocate to alternative centers such as Frankfurt, Germany, now loomed. Insurance premiums were escalating and estimates of damage caused by the bomb exceeded $1 billion. Policy-makers in the City's governing body, the Corporation, felt they had to react.

The City was by no means the most frequently attacked part of London, but it was the size of the bombs (homemade devices mounted in commercial vehicles) used against the City, rather than their frequency, which gave rise to concerns. Furthermore, it was not the ruined buildings that mattered so much, but the activities conducted inside them – notably foreign exchange trading. The challenge for the City was to prevent another major explosion, and to ensure its disaster recovery systems minimized the dislocation of business activity if its defenses were breached. The problem for the City's planners was that the greater the effort to prevent another attack, the more attractive the challenge for the Provisional IRA to breach any security measures.

KEY FACTS

- The Bishopsgate bomb of April 25, 1994, was the largest ever detonated in Britain's capital during peacetime.
- Police blocks set up in the aftermath of the explosion restricted vehicular entry to the City to just eight routes.
- One security measure was the removal of more than 1,000 garbage cans from the City's streets.

NEW SECURITY MEASURES

In mid-1993, the City ratified a series of measures to reassure residents and prevent another bomb attack. A Traffic Management Scheme (plan) monitored all traffic entering the square mile. Officially designed to meet traffic and environmental needs, the plan dramatically reduced the number of entry points into the City by sealing off streets and establishing police checkpoints. All vehicles entering the City passed police cordons where random searches took place, mainly of larger commercial vehicles. Closed-circuit TV cameras were placed at strategic sites around the City. Private companies were encouraged to join a Camera Watch plan, whereby existing security cameras were positioned to cover the streets. Backing up the static security measures were mobile, armed City of London police units, which established checkpoints at random, checking vehicles and occasionally pedestrians.

Hulton Getty Picture Collection

Police cordoned off the City's financial district in the wake of the 1994 Bishopsgate bombing.

Disaster recovery measures were taken at all levels. The Corporation introduced a pager alert system to keep businesses informed about potential and actual threats. It encouraged companies to develop disaster recovery plans, establishing back-up facilities where, for example, foreign exchange trading rooms could be relocated. By 1994, the majority of all firms operating in the City had some form of contingency plan.

There were objections to the traffic management plan from nearby boroughs and motoring organizations, which feared an increase in traffic and pollution – and even terrorism – in their districts. Politicians expressed concern that the measures gave a propaganda victory to the Provisional IRA, encouraging it to target the City. Such concerns were not without force. In July 1993, a Provisional IRA operative was arrested at a bus stop; he had a bag of explosives, and may have been traveling to the City. For the Corporation, however, the plan proved effective: no major bombings struck the City following its implementation. When the Provisional IRA broke its cease-fire, in February 1996, with a 1,000-pound bomb, it targeted London's Docklands, a satellite business district.

In implementing its security measures, the City benefited from a number of unique circumstances that set it apart from other London districts. Perhaps most significantly, it possessed its own police force, the City of London Police. Furthermore, the unusual structure of the Corporation, which included representatives from the business community, allowed for rapid consensus on developments. Public support increased when it emerged that the security measures greatly reduced the level of crime in the City. Public approval had been aided by the low resident population of the City (only 5,000, swelling to 280,000 during a working day). Commuting workers and large businesses were found to be less likely to object to tight security, on civil liberty grounds, than would residents of the district.

SECURITY: THE WAY FORWARD

Given the City's unique circumstances, the extent to which lessons can be drawn from its experience is questionable. Clearly, the threat of bomb attacks remains, but the danger of large, vehicle-borne devices was much reduced. The major problem in implementing the security measures was the drain of police manpower away from other duties, and the long-term sustainability of such a plan remained in doubt. However, in terms of disaster contingency planning, the City pointed the way forward for modern business districts – and specifically financial centers – where the dislocation of business needs to be counted in hours, not days, before the costs become prohibitive. Only through coordinated planning between public and private authorities could contingencies be effectively met and beaten. The experience of Provisional IRA terrorism gave the City greater confidence in its security capabilities, and no significant relocation of foreign institutions from London occurred.

John Gearson

SEE ALSO: NATIONALIST TERRORISM; BOMBING OPERATIONS; VICTIMS OF TERRORISM; IRA: ORIGINS AND TERROR TO 1976.

FURTHER READING

- Jeffries, Francis M. *Terrorism and Multinational Business Operations.* Poolesville, MD: Jeffries and Associates, 1989.
- Roukis, George S., Hugh Conway, and Bruce H. Charnow, eds. *Global Corporate Intelligence: Opportunities, Technologies and Threats in the 1990s.* New York: Quorum Books, 1990.

THE FRENCH RESPONSE TO TERRORISM

The French armed forces formed their own particular response to terrorism and guerrilla warfare during the 1950s. This had significant importance for later anti-terrorist campaigns, because it emphasized that terrorists were likely to form part of an international communist conspiracy, and accepted that unpopular measures might be necessary to defeat them. However, French theories contributed to illegal attempts by France's armed forces to intervene in politics in the late 1950s and early 1960s.

French theories of counterterrorism were born in Indochina, where France fought Vietminh rebels from 1946 to 1954. The conflict was treated as a traditional colonial revolt, requiring only military forces to put down. Once defeated at Dien Bien Phu in 1954, the French were forced to accept the loss of Indochina.

The soldiers captured at Dien Bien Phu spent about a year in Vietminh hands, during which time they were subjected to communist propaganda. A number of the more astute officers grasped this opportunity to learn all they could about the nature of the enemy who had defeated them. They began to form their own opinions about revolutionary warfare based on the teachings of Mao Zedong. The French officers came to two interrelated conclusions. First, that the conflict in Indochina was part of a global communist conspiracy; and, second, that the Vietminh was a professional, dedicated revolutionary movement, with a political and military strategy.

Hulton Getty Picture Collection

Wounded French soldiers are airlifted from Dien Bien Phu in 1954. Many other French troops were captured and subjected to communist propaganda.

KEY FACTS

- French attitudes toward counterterrorism were greatly influenced by experiences in Indochina.
- French theorists of counterterrorism were given free rein during the successful campaign against terrorism in Algiers in 1957.
- The belief of army theorists in the inflexible implementation of counterterrorist ideas led the French army to intervene in domestic politics from 1958 to 1962.

COUNTERING MAO'S STRATEGY

It was this strategy that was important, for if it could be fully understood, it could be countered stage by stage. Officers such as Colonels Roger Trinquier and Charles Lacheroy produced a "model" of Maoist revolution, identifying certain key phases, starting with the infiltration of the population by communist cadres. They also noted factors such as popular support, international backing, and the demoralization of government forces by means of terrorist attacks. But the strategy, so the

French argued, did have inherent weaknesses in its early stages when the communists had logistic difficulties and were outnumbered by government forces.

The first stage in countering revolutionary war depended on intelligence, for if the government kept a close eye on its subjects, it would be able to monitor the first signs of subversion and nip revolution in the bud. Simultaneously, the government had to be prepared to introduce reforms, backed by firm military action, to ensure that most of the population remained loyal. However, if the government ended up facing a full-blown insurgency, it should not hesitate to take decisive action at once. This should involve splitting insurgents from their supporters among the people by forcibly moving populations away from affected areas.

The French theorists also insisted that once an insurgency had begun, countermeasures had to be put into immediate effect. If the army was committed, it had to be sure of full political backing. In short, the French military theorists of the mid-1950s were advocating a coordinated politico-military response to a political and military threat, with guarantees that the governments of the West would display a dedicated resolve. This was expecting a lot from liberal democracies and, in the end, allowed no room for political compromise.

THE ALGERIAN CRISIS

Much of this analysis took place as the French were facing a terrorist campaign in Algeria that began in 1954. Important theorists such as Trinquier and Lacheroy served in Algeria and refined their thinking through first-hand experience. However, in important respects, this insurgency did not fit their model. The main insurgent group – the Front de Libération Nationale (FLN) – was not communist-inspired and was certainly not part of a global conspiracy orchestrated from Moscow; rather, the insurgency was an Arab nationalist attempt to gain political independence. The situation was complicated by additional factors, notably the fact that Algeria contained a large population of European settlers for whom any compromise with Arab aspirations was unthinkable. In such circumstances, the political backing required by the new theorists was soon undermined by the sheer complexity of the conflict.

A critical episode was the so-called "Battle of Algiers." Late in 1956, terrorist bombings and assassinations in Algiers threatened a full-scale breakdown in authority. In early 1957, General Jacques Massu's 10th Colonial Parachute Division was deployed to Algiers. Massu's orders were to destroy the FLN without political interference. But the theorists – many serving under Massu – saw their chance to experiment. What resulted was a ruthlessly successful military campaign. By mid-1957, Algiers had effectively been cleared of the FLN.

Once the details of army torture and executions emerged, however, the army suddenly found it had lost the backing of many people in France. Regardless of the success of counterinsurgency measures, politicians in Paris hesitated in their support. To the believers in the new theories, this was potentially fatal. Disgust with the politicians quickly grew into a belief that, if the existing leaders lacked the necessary resolve, then it was the task of the army to replace them. The result was four years of disastrous military intervention in French politics, from 1958 to 1962. It was an object lesson in the need for political considerations to prevail in all forms of counterterrorism.

These disasters of the early 1960s have colored the French response to terrorism ever since. French governments have shown themselves very flexible in responding to terrorist activity, whether in the Middle East or on French soil, and have always tried to grasp the nature of the terrorism. For example, French governments in the early 1980s were prepared to release convicted Action Directe terrorists. The gesture was part of a general amnesty announced by incoming President François Mitterrand. However, other Western governments have accused the French of being too willing to negotiate deals with Middle Eastern terrorists.

John Pimlott

SEE ALSO: TERRORISM IN FRENCH ALGERIA; TERROR AGAINST THE FRENCH IN INDOCHINA; NATIONALIST TERRORISM.

FURTHER READING

- Guillane, Gilbert. "France and the Fight Against Terrorism," in *Terrorism and Political Violence* 4, No. 4, 131-135.
- Trinquier, Roger. *Modern Warfare: A French View of the Counterinsurgency.* New York: Praeger, and London: Pall Mall Press, 1964.
- Wieviorka, W. "French Politics and Strategy on Terrorism," in *The Politics of Counter-Terrorism: The Ordeal of Democratic States.* Washington, DC: The Johns Hopkins Foreign Policy Institute, 1990.

THE ISRAELI RESPONSE TO TERRORISM

Since its foundation in 1948, Israel has experienced four full-blown wars with its Arab neighbors, and, in the 1980s, Israel itself undertook a large-scale invasion of Lebanon. Even when not actually at war, Israel has been the target of continuous terrorism. These more recent experiences have only added to a Jewish history in which persecution goes back centuries, a persecution that culminated in the deaths of six million Jews under the Nazis during World War II.

For Israelis, the protection of their country is the single most important issue, and they are uncompromising in their responses to terrorism or any other threat to national security. The threat of possible annihilation by its neighboring states haunts Israel.

The Israeli response to terrorism has been founded on the principles of deterrence, preemption, prevention, and reprisals. The response began to take shape even before the foundation of the state of Israel in May 1948. From the early 1930s, Jewish organizations had been faced with hostility and terrorist attacks from Palestinian Arabs. The most important of these organizations was Haganah, which developed into the present-day Israeli Defense Forces (IDF).

SUMMARY

- In the 1950s and 1960s, the Palestinians began a campaign of cross-border raids on Israel, mainly from the neighboring states of Egypt and Jordan.
- After its victory in the Six-Day War of 1967, Israel began its occupation of the West Bank and Gaza Strip.
- Since 1987, Israel has faced terrorist attacks from Palestinian fundamentalist groups inflamed by Israel's continuing presence in the West Bank and Gaza Strip.

Israel employs three major agencies in its fight against terrorists. First, the IDF, the military arm of the state; second, the Israeli National Police, particularly the Border Police; and third, the Israeli intelligence community. The Israeli intelligence community includes three organizations that respond tactically to terrorism. They are the Military Intelligence arm of the IDF; the General Security Services, usually known as Shin Bet after its Hebrew initials, and which resembles the FBI in terms of duties and scope; and the Central Institute for Intelligence and Security, known as Mossad. Mossad runs teams of agents at home and abroad. Its operations include securing Israeli dignitaries and embassies, spying, hostage rescue, and, on occasion, assassination.

PALESTINIAN HOSTILITIES ESCALATE

Palestinian terrorism against Israel began in the mid-1950s, with cross-border attacks launched from neighboring states, particularly Egypt and Jordan, which were known as the sanctuary states. Palestinian *fedayeen* (fighters) crossed the Israeli border and attacked Israeli civilians and targets of strategic importance such as irrigation systems, electric supplies, agricultural equipment, and buses.

In response, the IDF set ambushes across the border, launched attacks on training facilities and camps, and carried out raids against a range of targets. These operations were intended to destroy the infrastructure of the Palestinian *fedayeen* and inflict collateral damage on the armed forces of host countries.

ISRAEL AND COUNTERTERROR

Some Israeli raids were against Egyptian army bases such as those at Khan Yunis and Sabha. But most were against villages. The largest early attack was on the village of Qalqiliya in the West Bank in October 1955. During this period, Israel also enhanced its borders by defensive means: barbed wire, border patrols, guard

Hulton Getty Picture Collection

Israeli commandos wipe out a Palestinian guerrilla base in a raid on the port of Sidon, Lebanon, in 1971.

dogs, watch towers, and army ambushes on the Israeli side of the border line.

Israeli retaliation produced results. Jordan and Lebanon, for example, showed themselves unwilling to be used as bases for terrorism against Israel, and when Yasser Arafat's Fatah group began launching attacks from Jordanian territory in 1964, the Jordanian authorities clamped down on the group.

Fatah claimed over 70 attacks into Israel up to the Six-Day War in 1967. In response, Israel raided villages along the borders, destroying houses suspected of providing shelter, food, and information to terrorists. In November 1966, Israeli paratroopers raided the village of Samua on the West Bank south of Hebron. They destroyed several targets, including houses used by Palestinian marauders. They also set an ambush, which caused more than 50 Jordanian army casualties.

The destruction of the air forces and the defeat of the armies of Egypt, Syria, and Jordan by the Israelis in the 1967 war led to the Israeli occupation of the West Bank and the Gaza Strip. Israel now had control of a large Palestinian population. It also faced the threat of terrorist attacks from Jordan, Syria, and, most importantly, Lebanon. Terrorists associated with the Palestine Liberation Organization (PLO) became the predominant organizers of terror.

The efficiency of Israeli counterror measures during this period had the effect of considerably reducing terrorist activity in the occupied territories of the West Bank and Gaza Strip (although there were, for example, grenade attacks on Israeli forces in Gaza in the period around 1970). Three security forces – the IDF, the Border Police, and Shin Bet – operated in the occupied territories, cooperating and coordinating their operation. The

IDF and Border Police were mainly engaged in overt operations, while Shin Bet was involved in covert activities. The overt operations included searching suspects; making arrests; demolishing houses; setting up road blocks and check points; patrolling villages, checking identification cards, work licenses and travel permits; profiling the Palestinian laborers who came to work in Israel proper; and handling prosecutions and administrative detentions.

After the 1967 war, the PLO attempted to set up an effective organization in the West Bank and Gaza Strip. To eradicate the new terrorist cells, General Ariel Sharon, commander of Southern Command, initiated a sweeping military operation. The IDF surrounded the refugee camps, divided them into a grid-like system, and allocated units to monitor each sector.

Working on Shin Bet intelligence, IDF units searched houses and demolished the homes of suspected terrorists or of anyone found to be involved in insurgency activities. When demonstrations occurred, the IDF or the Border Police imposed curfews and enforced closure of various parts of the camps, including schools. Such crackdowns succeeded in controlling violence for most of the 1970s and 1980s.

THE PLO AND LEBANON

In the immediate aftermath of the 1967 war, PLO terrorists launched attacks from Jordanian territory. However, strong Israeli retaliation persuaded Jordan to discourage such raids.

In 1970, tension between the Jordanian authorities and the Palestinians reached boiling point. Jordan cracked down viciously, killing thousands of Palestinians. In September of that year, the PLO was forced to move its headquarters to Lebanon, an event marked by the Palestinians as "Black September."

The first line of defense against incursions from Lebanon was enhanced border security. If this did not work, then a combination of the IDF, the police, and Shin Bet was employed. A case in point was the incident known as the Bus Number 300 case, in April 1984. All three security forces were involved. The police bargained and negotiated with the Palestinian hijackers; the IDF stormed the bus; and Shin Bet interrogated the two captured terrorists.

The PLO virtually controlled much of southern Lebanon during the 1970s. Israel retaliated to raids with artillery and air strikes on terrorist bases. Since these bases were often situated within refugee camps, civilian casualties were inevitable. Such attacks were not necessarily made in response to a specific terrorist incident. In October 1972, Israeli aircraft struck at targets in Lebanon and Syria, carrying out a policy that an Israeli spokesman explained as follows: "...we are no longer waiting for them to hit first. This is the operative phase of our pledge to hit the terrorists wherever they are..." This policy certainly had some effect. Syria, for example, a sponsor of various terrorist groups, was extremely wary of letting Palestinian terrorists operate against Israel from its soil, after being hit by severe air attacks in the 1972-73 period. However, the policy of bombarding areas that were known to harbor both terrorists and large civilian populations made for adverse worldwide publicity.

OPERATION "PEACE FOR GALILEE"

In March 1978, a 20,000-strong Israeli force drove into southern Lebanon. The Israelis forced the Palestinian fighters north. They then set up a Christian militia force that controlled a strip of Lebanon from Naqoura on the coast to the Syrian border southeast of Marjayoun.

A full-scale Israeli invasion of Lebanon took place on June 6, 1982. Operation "Peace for Galilee" was ostensibly a retaliation for increased terrorist activity, including an attempted assassination of the Israeli ambassador to London. However, it seems likely that the intentions behind it were to root out the PLO from Lebanon for good. During the confused fighting that followed, the PLO was forced to abandon Lebanon and move its headquarters to Tunisia. Unfortunately for Israel, another result of the invasion was the rise to prominence of Hizb'allah, a Shiite fundamentalist group that used the tactic of suicide bombings to great effect.

When Israel eventually abandoned Lebanon (although it still maintained a buffer zone in the south), Hizb'allah and another fundamentalist group, known as Islamic Jihad, moved into confrontation with the Israelis. Although the sheer number of terrorist incursions was less than during the mid-1970s, the emergence of Hizb'allah, meant that Israel still had the problem of terrorists on its northern border. As a result, Hizb'allah rocket attacks followed by Israeli retaliation continued into the mid-1990s.

INTERNATIONAL TERRORISM

PLO activity in Lebanon in the 1970s was seen by Israel as complementary to the international terror that Palestinians directed against Israel. This consisted of attacks on targets such as embassies, diplomatic staff, Jewish cultural centers, and aircraft belonging to the Israeli national airline, El Al. The methods of attack could be car-bombs, mail-bombs, or personal assassination attempts. At the Munich Olympic Games in 1972, Palestinian terrorists of the Black September Organization killed two Israeli athletes and held hostage nine others, all of whom later died.

The first level of defense against this form of terrorism was heightened security at various Israeli and Jewish institutions around the world. Israeli diplomatic and trade missions drew on the experience of Mossad and other security forces to increase their security apparatus. From the late 1960s, El Al adopted a ferocious security program that made it a most unattractive target for terrorists.

The next level of defense was to create small teams of specialists who could deal with hostage situations. In May 1972, three Black September terrorists hijacked a Belgian Sabena airliner to Tel Aviv and demanded the release of 317 Palestinians held by the Israelis. While negotiations were taking place, an elite Israeli counterterrorist unit, the Sayaret Matkal, stormed the plane, killing the two male hijackers and capturing the female. Four years later, in 1976, members of the Popular Front for the Liberation of Palestine (PFLP), aided by members of the West German Baader-Meinhof Gang, hijacked an Air France airliner and descended on Entebbe airport, Uganda. They demanded the release of 53 terrorists held in prisons around the world. In a plan known as Operation Thunderball, Israeli commandos descended on Entebbe to rescue the hostages. All but one were saved, while all the terrorists were killed.

Mossad has been the main source of intelligence used to predict terrorist attacks on Israeli institutions and individuals outside Israel. Controversially, Mossad also strikes at Israel's enemies abroad. During the 1970s, there was a policy of hunting down Palestinian terrorists in Europe, as well as in the Middle East. The most important victim was Mohammed Boudia, the European organizer for the PFLP, who was killed in Paris by an enormous car-bomb in June 1973.

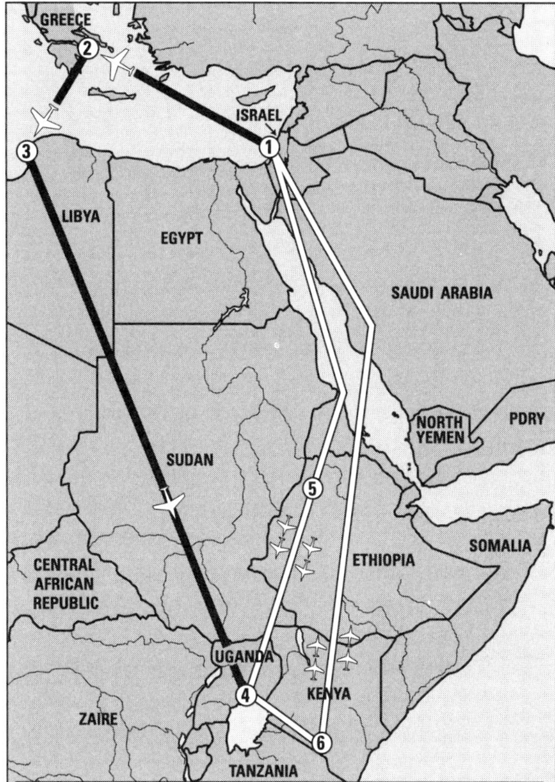

① June 27, 1976: Air France Tel Aviv to Paris flight via Greece leaves Israel.
② Baader-Meinhof and PFLP terrorists board the flight in Athens and seize the aircraft after takeoff.
③ Aircraft flies to Benghazi, Libya, for refueling and departs for Entebbe, Uganda.
④ June 28: Hostages are transferred to an airport terminal at Entebbe. The next day the non-Jewish and non-Israeli passengers are freed and terrorists demand the release of 53 terrorists from prison. A large group of hostages arrive in Paris on June 30.
⑤ July 3: Israeli assault team flies to Entebbe and rescues the remaining 103 passengers.
⑥ July 4: Rescue mission refuels in Nairobi, Kenya, and then departs for Israel.

PFLP and West German Baader-Meinhof Gang terrorists hijacked an Air France flight from Tel Aviv, on June 27, 1976, diverting it to Entebbe airport, Uganda.

THE INTIFADA

A new threat to Israel came in 1987: the uprising of Palestinian Arabs in Gaza and on the West Bank, known as the Intifada. Much of the Intifada did not involve terrorism. Teenagers held noisy demonstrations, hurled stones, and occasionally used knives against Israeli soldiers. However, the Intifada also targeted Israeli civilian settlers living on the West Bank and the Gaza Strip. Almost 300 Israeli civilians have died in attacks in various parts of the West Bank and Gaza Strip.

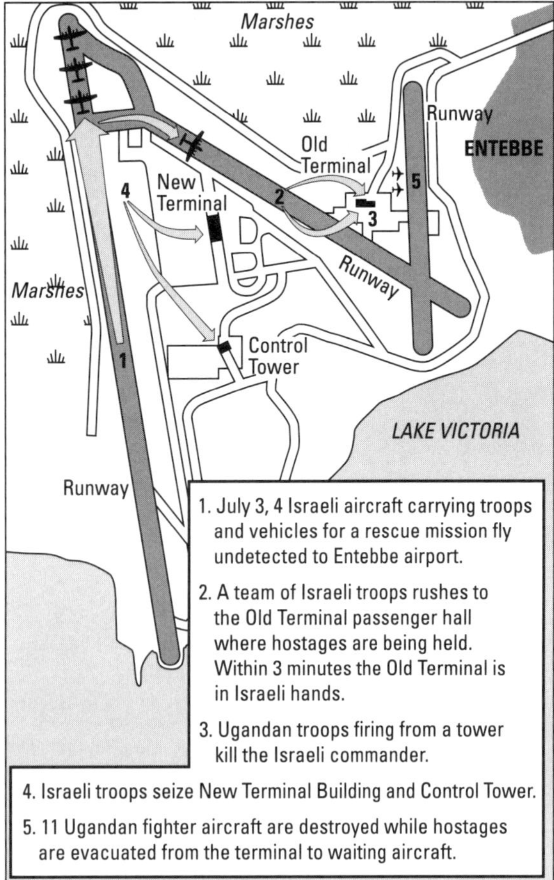

In Operation Thunderball, on July 4, 1976, Israeli commandos rescued 103 hostages from Entebbe.

The security forces imposed long-term curfews, closed businesses, sealed homes, and deported Palestinian leaders. They also closed schools and universities, cut electricity and telephone services to villages, stopped exports of agricultural goods, and imposed monetary controls. Those believed responsible for insurgent or terrorist attacks were arrested, sometimes tortured, and brought before military courts. To identify leaders, Shin Bet used coercive methods, including interrogations and beatings, to elicit vital information as quickly as possible.

Special secret Israeli military units carried out covert operations in the territories. Members of these units dressed like Palestinians and mixed with the general Arab population. Once disturbances occurred, they would identify the leaders and point them out to the IDF. At times they engaged in assassination. Other methods used by Shin Bet included kidnapping, and the use of informers and collaborators.

After the agreement to set up a Palestinian National Authority in parts of the West Bank and Gaza Strip in 1993, the large-scale demonstrations ended. However, fundamentalist groups such as Hizb'allah and Islamic Jihad rejected any agreement with Israel, and carried on their own terrorist campaign, with suicide bombing a favorite tactic. The initial response was to pressure the Palestinian authorities into apprehending those responsible. Later, Israel resorted to methods it had used in the Intifada, including the careful checking of all Palestinians crossing into Israel, the use of informers, and selective attacks.

THE BOTTOM LINE

While Israeli counterterrorism has certainly hampered terrorism, it has not put an end to it. Meanwhile, Palestinian determination has not weakened, and many of the problems of territory and nationality have worsened. The years of violence, counterviolence, and repression have only served to harden attitudes on both sides.

What is undeniable, however, is that terrorism has not become a serious threat to Israel's national security. Quite apart from tactical responses, the best answer to terrorism for Israel has been to persuade its neighbors that they should not support terrorists.

R. Reuben Miller

SEE ALSO: THE BIRTH OF THE PLO AND THE 1967 WAR; THE BLACK SEPTEMBER ORGANIZATION; THE POPULAR FRONT FOR THE LIBERATION OF PALESTINE; THE PLO AND THE ARAB STATES; ENTEBBE; ISRAELI RAIDS ON THE PLO; THE PALESTINIAN INTIFADA.

FURTHER READING

- Alon, Hanan. *Countering Palestinian Terrorism in Israel: Toward a Policy Analysis of Countermeasure.* Santa Monica, CA: The Rand Corporation, 1980.
- Black, Ian. *Israel's Secret Wars: The Untold History of Israeli Intelligence.* London: Hamish Hamilton, and New York: Viking Penguin, 1991.
- O'Brien, William V. *Law and Morality in Israel's War with the PLO.* New York: Routledge, 1991.

THE AMERICAN RESPONSE TO TERRORISM

Like other modern industrialized nations, the United States has been forced in the latter part of the twentieth century to confront terrorist threats with a combination of tactics. These include a legal framework defining terrorism, as well as diplomacy, intelligence gathering, intensified security measures, and the use of force.

An estimated two-thirds of all victims of terrorist actions worldwide are Americans, and most of them are attacked outside the U.S. According to the State Department, 162 lethal attacks occurred abroad between 1973 and 1986, claiming 440 American lives.

During the Cold War, the U.S. preoccupation with international terrorism focused primarily on radical, left-wing insurgent groups that sought to overthrow anti-communist regimes friendly to the U.S. Beginning with the Kennedy administration in 1961, the U.S. developed counterinsurgency policies to combat communist or communist-inspired guerrillas. However, the U.S. interest in the terrorist aspect of such campaigns was limited. In Vietnam, for example, successive U.S. administrations expected the South Vietnamese government to undertake police actions to deal with terrorist incidents.

The same was true in Latin America, where U.S. support for friendly regimes in the 1960s and 1970s involved help and training. The U.S. forces themselves were rarely involved in specific anti-terrorist activity.

SUMMARY

- Late 1960s: widespread terrorist activities in Europe and the Middle East force the U.S. to recognize that terrorism is an international threat to all democracies.
- 1972: the Nixon Administration sets up an anti-terrorist committee under the Secretary of State after the murder of Israeli athletes at the Munich Olympics.
- 1977: in an era of hijackings, the Pentagon authorizes the creation of the Delta Force, an unconventional military body with a hostage-rescue capability.
- 1980s: terrorists target U.S. diplomatic and military personnel, particularly in the Middle East. The State Department sets up the Bureau of Diplomatic Security.
- 1990s: terrorists, both foreign and domestic, set off major bombs within the U.S., with great loss of life.

NEW TERROR GROUPS

The U.S. perception of a terrorist threat as distinct from an insurgency threat began to emerge in the late 1960s. A major background factor was the worldwide spate of anti-Vietnam War demonstrations, and the emergence of anti-capitalist terrorist organizations such as the Baader-Meinhof Gang. At about the same time, radical Palestinian groups began to undertake terrorist activities.

The violent tactics of these militant groups differed from guerrilla and insurgency tactics mainly in that they had no military or paramilitary objectives. Their aim was purely psychological – to intimidate governing authorities and their constituencies through the use of terror. The U.S. was faced with what it defined as non-military political violence that was international in scope, radical in ideology, and carried out by groups organized in small cells. The U.S. had to develop its anti-terrorist methods almost from scratch.

In this period, numerous terrorist incidents did occur within the United States. The anti-establishment Weathermen (later known as Weather Underground), founded in 1969, carried out some 30 bombings. Nationalist groups such as the Armed Forces of Puerto Rican National Liberation (FALN) and the anti-Castro

TRH Pictures

Training exercise of the crack Delta Force. The organization drew its inspiration from the British Special Air Service (SAS) regiment.

Cuban group, Omega-7, were still bombing and murdering on U.S. soil in the 1980s. These attacks, however, were generally not viewed as terrorism, but instead as straightforward criminal behavior, which U.S. federal, state, and local law enforcement agencies had the primary responsibility for tackling. As a result, the prevalent view in the U.S. was that terrorism as such was an international, not a domestic threat.

In contrast, most other countries were primarily concerned about terrorism as a domestic problem, rather than as an international one, regardless of the nationality of the victim. An attack on American citizens in a third country, for example, while considered an international incident in the United States, would be considered an internal problem in the country in which it occurred. This difference of perspective constituted the greatest challenge to U.S. diplomacy in seeking a multinational, cooperative approach to countering international terrorism.

FACING UP TO THE PROBLEM

The creation of modern U.S. counterterrorism policy stemmed neither from the Cold War nor even from an incident involving Americans or American property. Instead, it was a result of the kidnapping and massacre of Israeli athletes at the Munich Olympics by Palestinian terrorists in September 1972. The terrorists were members of the Black September Organization, the paramilitary wing of Yasser Arafat's Fatah organization. The West Germans badly bungled the rescue operations, and as the entire world watched in horror on television, nine Israelis were killed, another two having been killed earlier.

The incident not only left the world in shock – a major triumph from the terrorists' point of view – but it caused the major world powers to review their capabilities and the organizational structures available

Popperfoto

U.S. airplanes bombed Tripoli, Libya, in April 1986, after a reportedly Libyan- and Syrian-backed terrorist bombing at a Berlin disco killed a U.S. soldier.

to cope with similar situations. Following the attack, President Nixon established a cabinet-level committee chaired by the Secretary of State to coordinate U.S. efforts in countering terrorism. The president delegated responsibility for coordinating responses to incidents occurring within the United States to the FBI. Responsibility for incidents aboard aircraft over which the United States exercised jurisdiction was assigned to the Federal Aviation Authority (FAA).

One of the greatest impediments to an effective counterterrorism policy is interagency rivalry. For the politician, terrorism is primarily a political problem. From a law enforcement viewpoint, it is a matter of criminal justice. From a military point of view, it is at the lowest end of the scale of low-intensity conflict. From security and intelligence points of view, it is a matter of keeping one step ahead of adversaries through accurate intelligence and perpetual vigilance. All these viewpoints are reflected in U.S. policy.

POLITICAL ANALYSIS

The U.S. approach to counterterrorism gives the highest priority to the political aspects of terrorism. Deciding who is or is not a terrorist, and how to respond to terrorist acts, are essentially political decisions. The political nature of terrorism is expressed in that often-heard expression, "the only difference between terrorists and freedom fighters is what side they are on." This is not mere cynicism. No country, including the U.S., would be willing to base its response to terrorism merely on a set of definitions.

The U.S. government's list of state supporters of terrorism is a good case in point. As of June 1996, the list included Libya, Sudan, North Korea, Cuba, and Syria. Although the State Department testified to Congress in June 1995 that there had been no evidence of direct Syrian involvement in terrorism since 1986, Syria remains on the list, presumably until peace terms are worked out between it and Israel.

By contrast, Serbia, which in the early 1990s did support large-scale acts of terrorism by Bosnian Serbs against Bosnian Muslims, was never placed on the list. Nor were the terrorist acts committed by both sides in

Bosnia generally included in the State Department's annual report of incidents. Presumably it was thought that to have done so would make the task of working out a peaceful settlement in Bosnia more difficult.

The vigor with which the United States pursues counterterrorist policies abroad has always reflected broader U.S. foreign policy priorities. Energetic diplomatic efforts against terrorism in the 1980s were spurred on, in part, by the U.S. global confrontation with the Soviet Union, and in part because much Middle Eastern terrorism was aimed not merely at the United States, but also at its close ally, Israel. Renewed U.S. emphasis on Iraq and particularly on Iran as state supporters of terrorism in the 1990s was also motivated to a great degree by broader political considerations than terrorism.

The political dimension aside, U.S. concern over terrorism is also a response to specific attacks on American citizens and property. The major focus of the U.S. diplomacy in countering terrorism, therefore, has been multinational. The United States realizes that attacks against Americans abroad cannot be stopped without international cooperation. The U.S. diplomatic message is that terrorism is everybody's problem.

SECURITY: FIGHTING THE HIJACKERS

In September 1970, the Popular Front for the Liberation of Palestine (PFLP) carried out a spectacular multi-aircraft hijacking to Dawson's Field in Jordan, involving more than 300 hostages. In the aftermath of this event, President Nixon appointed a director of aviation security to coordinate anti-hijacking measures. Eventually, some 1,500 Customs Security Officers were recruited to travel alongside passengers. Also, in 1973, passenger searches became compulsory. The searches proved to be valuable: in 1973 and 1974 alone, security staff discovered 4,400 firearms and thousands of pounds of high explosives.

In recent years, American officials have often been singled out as terrorist targets. Between 1979 and 1993, there were 460 attacks on U.S. diplomatic personnel, buildings, and vehicles. Twenty-five diplomats were killed and 55 were wounded. Military personnel have also been targeted, including the suicide bomb attack by Hizb'allah at the Marine Barracks in Beirut, Lebanon, on October 23, 1983, which killed 241 U.S. Marines and 58 French soldiers.

In 1986, the State Department moved to enhance physical security abroad by creating the Bureau of Diplomatic Security (DS). In addition to protecting U.S. personnel and missions abroad, the DS is responsible for investigative work and collecting intelligence. The DS also works closely with private U.S. firms and non-governmental organizations in foreign countries through its Overseas Security and Advisory Council. This body maintains an electronic bulletin board for exchanging security-related and terrorist information abroad. The State Department, as a matter of public policy, also regularly issues warnings to citizens traveling to countries considered dangerous because of terrorist threats.

The rule of law is a basic tenet of U.S. constitutionalism, and it is a major goal of U.S. foreign policy. In legislative terms, the rule of law is all the more accentuated by the large number of lawyers in Congress who tend naturally to look for legal solutions to what are often essentially political problems – such as terrorism. There is also a practical element involved. The more highly politicized terrorism is, the more difficult it is for the U.S. government to reach an international consensus on concerted action. It is a major strategy of the United States, therefore, to "depoliticize" terrorism as much as possible, and to justify collective counterterrorism measures in terms of simply bringing criminals to justice.

Despite the absence of an acceptable legal definition of terrorism, virtually all terrorist activity is criminal in nature, not only in the United States but in most countries. Within U.S. borders, the Justice Department and the FBI have the primary responsibility for terrorist incidents. Cooperation against terrorism with national law enforcement agencies abroad, as well as with international organizations such as Interpol, is a major policy goal. FBI agents and State Department Regional Security Officers abroad maintain close liaison with law enforcement agencies in host countries, sharing intelligence and cooperating on investigations.

LEARNING TO SHARE

Institutionally, U.S. law enforcement has had to adjust to a new environment as it assumed its responsibilities in counterterrorism policy. For example, the FBI had never before had to share its mission to any great degree with other U.S. agencies, particularly at the state and local levels. An example of how counterterrorist law enforcement has broken new ground was shown in the creation of a joint FBI–Los Angeles

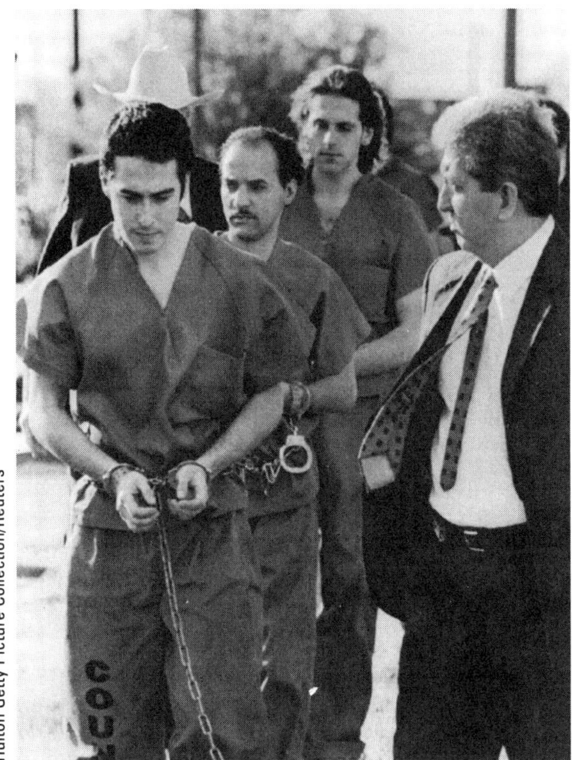

Hulton Getty Picture Collection/Reuters

Survivors of the Branch Davidian cult are led away after the fire at the cult's Waco, Texas, compound in April 1993. The inept handling of the 51-day siege by federal agents is believed to have provided a motive for the Oklahoma City bombing the following year.

Police Department anti-terrorism task force to provide security for the 1984 Los Angeles Olympics. Since then, similar joint task forces have been created in major cities throughout the country.

The FBI has had an even greater adjustment abroad. By law, its jurisdiction ended at the water's edge, just as the CIA could not operate inside the U.S. Moreover, crimes such as murder were subject to state law but not federal law in the U.S. When Americans were killed in terrorist attacks at Rome and Vienna airports in 1985, the FBI could not intervene. Therefore, Congress passed legislation designating various criminal acts, including murder committed in a terrorist context abroad, as federal crimes, empowering the FBI to investigate. Even then, however, the FBI had no legal jurisdiction in a foreign country and could proceed only with the permission of the host governments.

International law is another area of emphasis in U.S. counterterrorism policy. The United States has extradition treaties with most countries, but generally insists on a political exclusion clause exempting the extradition of those wanted for "political crimes." Where terrorism is involved, the problem is not always clear-cut. On the one hand, the U.S. opposes political trials as contrary to the rule of law. On the other hand, preventing exploitation of this position can be difficult. Terrorists from Northern Ireland for years regularly fled to the U.S., claiming the crimes for which they were wanted by the British were political in nature, and thus exempted under a political exclusion clause of the Anglo-American extradition treaty. To close this loophole, the British and Americans negotiated a supplementary extradition treaty in the 1980s, which stated political exclusion clauses should not impede extradition for violent crimes to democratic countries that respect due process of law and provide a fair trial.

INTERNATIONAL TREATIES ON TERRORISM

Gaining support for multinational treaties to combat terrorism has long been a major goal of U.S. policy. There is no single convention or treaty proscribing terrorism. Instead, over the years, specific categories such as airline and maritime sabotage, hijackings, hostage-taking, protection of diplomats and of nuclear materials have been singled out for treaties. By mid-1995, there were 11 major international treaties and conventions against various forms of terrorist acts.

Gathering intelligence on the structure, organization, tactics, and plans of terrorist groups is one of the most important components of counterterrorism policy, but Americans have historically had a strong aversion to "spying" in peacetime. In 1929, Secretary of State Henry Stimson, who believed that "gentlemen do not read other gentlemen's mail," closed the State Department's "Black Chamber," where codes were broken, and banned the reading of other nations' coded messages.

With the advent of the Cold War, intelligence operations came to be considered a necessary evil. Such operations have continued to have strong domestic critics, however, which in some respects has reduced efficiency. The Amended Freedom of Information Act was one of a series of restrictions placed on the intelligence-gathering activities of the CIA and the FBI in the 1970s, following a public reaction to overzealous

Rex Features

Relatives of a child killed in the 1995 Oklahoma City bombing hold up her photograph. The incident presented U.S. citizens with a brutal introduction to domestic terrorism.

surveillance and other tactics. For a while, these restrictions hampered cooperation between the CIA and intelligence organizations in Israel and Europe. However, with the end of the Cold War, U.S. intelligence agencies have had to restructure their priorities. Nevertheless, terrorism has remained a major threat to the U.S., and as such an important information collection target – one reason why counterterrorism policies have been relatively successful in recent years.

Nowadays, the electronic revolution has sharpened the surveillance capacities of intelligence agencies. There is no longer such a thing as a private telephone conversation. In addition, coded information can be transmitted between agencies and countries at high speed, encouraging national governments to collaborate in antiterrorist operations.

COERCIVE FORCE

Just as diplomatic and law enforcement perceptions of terrorism differ, military perceptions differ again. From a military point of view, armed conflict can be placed on a linear scale from global nuclear war to localized low-intensity conflict. The latter includes insurgencies and guerrilla warfare, with terrorism at the lowest end of the scale. Because most terrorism involves civilians, and because the most suitable responses to it could be through law enforcement or diplomatic means rather than the use of military force, terrorism cannot be placed wholly within the concept of warfare. Nevertheless, the fact that it is a form of low-intensity conflict means that, in certain circumstances, the use of force is the preferred response.

The highest priority military response to terrorism is hostage rescue. The U.S. was not the first country to develop a covert military force with a hostage rescue capability. Following the rescue of a hijacked Lufthansa jet by German special operations forces in Mogadishu, Somalia, in 1977, the Pentagon authorized the creation of such a specialized force. The so-called Delta Force was originally led by Colonel Charlie Beckwith, who for years had advocated the creation of a unit similar to the British Special Air Service (SAS).

Despite its superb training and capabilities, the Delta Force is best known for its failure to rescue the American hostages in Tehran in 1980. The operation turned out to be far too complicated for the margin of error built into it, and was aborted at the last minute. Nevertheless, as an integral component of U.S. counterterrorism policy, Delta Force fulfills a vital role.

The Delta Force and its maritime equivalent, SEAL Team Six, eventually came under the Special Operations Command, with unconventional combat responsibilities far beyond hostage rescue. The Special Operations Command's capabilities fall into the dim category where terrorism, insurgencies, and guerrilla warfare overlap. In a hostage crisis situation, an Emergency Support Team lead by a State Department officer is generally sent to the country where the incident is taking place. Composed of intelligence, special operations, and communications specialists, as well as a senior diplomat, the team serves in an advisory role with the U.S. ambassador, as well as with the host country. It is in constant communication with crisis managers in Washington.

Since the end of the Cold War, regional and local conflicts have replaced global confrontation as the major cause of terrorism. The Iranian revolution in 1978-79 demonstrated that religious fundamentalism was far more appealing as a justification for terrorist tactics than was an ideology such as communism.

With small-scale conflicts posing only marginal threats to U.S. strategic interests, the United States is now far more reluctant to become involved abroad than it was during the Cold War, even when U.S. lives and property are at stake. As before, however, broader foreign policy considerations continue to shape U.S. counterterrorist priorities.

NEW THREATS AT HOME AND ABROAD

In the Middle East, where the Arab-Israeli peace process is a foreign policy priority, the United States now considers militant Islamic terrorism as a major threat, particularly from those groups opposed to the Arab-Israeli peace process, such as Hamas and Hizb'allah. Nevertheless, the United States has repeatedly stressed that the enemy is terrorism, not Islam.

The greatest change in attitudes toward terrorism in the 1990s, however, has been on the home front. The New York World Trade Center bombing in February 1993 and the Oklahoma City bombing in April 1995 have added a new dimension to U.S. perceptions of the terrorist threat. The New York attack shattered the myth of U.S. domestic immunity to terrorist attacks. The Oklahoma City bombing further refuted the perception that no American groups or individuals would ever carry out a large-scale terrorist attack.

The two attacks have not lessened U.S. preoccupation with international terrorism, but they have boosted efforts to upgrade local counterterrorism measures, particularly in law enforcement and intelligence gathering. Security measures were put in effect for the 1996 Summer Olympics when it was announced they would be held in Atlanta. However, this did not prevent the detonation of a bomb in Centennial Park on July 27.

The U.S. approach to terrorism is not likely to change greatly in the near future. The government will probably continue to focus primarily on international terrorism, while evolving a greater sensitivity to the threat of domestic terrorism. The main focus at home and abroad is likely to continue to be on targeting the criminal nature of terrorism and disassociating it from legitimate political activity.

David E. Long

SEE ALSO: KU KLUX KLAN TERROR; THE MOLLY MAGUIRES' TERRORIST CAMPAIGN; BLACK PANTHERS AND TERROR; STUDENT TERROR: THE WEATHERMEN; URBAN TERROR: THE SYMBIONESE LIBERATION ARMY; THE WORLD TRADE CENTER BOMBING; THE OKLAHOMA CITY BOMBING AND THE MILITIAS.

FURTHER READING

- Adams, James. *Secret Armies: Inside the American, Soviet and European Special Forces.* London: Hutchinson, and New York: The Atlantic Monthly Press, 1987.
- Long, David E. *The Anatomy of Terrorism.* New York: The Free Press, 1990.
- Martin, David C., and John Walcott. *Best Laid Plans: The Inside Story of America's War Against Terrorism.* New York: Harper and Row, 1988.
- Sterling, Claire. *The Terrorist Network: The Secret War of International Terrorism.* New York: Holt, Reinhart and Winston, 1981.
- United States Department of State. *Patterns in Global Terrorism.* Washington, DC: Government Printing Office, April 1996.

Responses to Terrorism in Latin America

Most governments in Latin America have had to deal with the threat from guerrillas and terrorists attempting to overthrow the established order. These typically right-wing regimes have employed conventional anti-terrorist techniques, but have themselves also resorted to terrorism to defeat their opponents. Against a background of state repression of the people, security forces have assassinated, tortured, and kidnapped those suspected of supporting the insurgents. In many cases, civilians have been simply picked up in the dead of night by government-sponsored death squads and executed on the flimsiest of pretexts.

RESPONSES TO TERRORISM IN LATIN AMERICA: Introduction

Terrorism has been practiced by many right-wing dictatorships in Latin America to stifle internal dissent. These regimes have frequently gained power through military-led coups and have maintained their grip on the people through repressive measures. The suspension of the rule of law, the denial of the freedom of political expression, and the curtailment of individual liberties were used to prevent people's legitimate expression of grievances. Many of these countries' internal security organizations and armed forces have also waged terror campaigns to strangle opposition groups. The violation of human rights by government agencies has taken place on a persistant and massive scale. Tens of thousands have died at the hands of state death squads.

Many governments have faced popular unrest at various times. Many of their people live in acute poverty and have often taken part in mass demonstrations to highlight the governments' indifference to their plight. The authorities believed that the urban poor were likely to support their opponents and acted to intimidate them into remaining neutral. Individual suspects were beaten to frighten others or to gather intelligence. Torture was used routinely by state security forces against people who had expressed only the slightest opposition to a regime or its policies.

Death squads picked up suspects, tortured them for information, and then carried out summary executions. Their bodies were either buried secretly or dumped in a public place as a warning. Many of the squads consisted of extreme right-wing members of the state security forces and they operated with the knowledge of the authorities. Others were reactionary extremists. The Guatemalan *Mano Blanca* (White Hand) death squad was fairly typical in its choice of targets: labor organizers, the left-wing intelligentsia, and students. These it claimed were "traitors to the homeland." A visit by the squad was preceded by intimidation; a white hand inside a red circle was daubed on their target's home. If the individual persisted in "subversive activities," he or she was "disappeared" by the *Mano Blanca* or another death squad.

While the death squads and internal security forces were most active among the shanty towns of the urban poor, the armed forces carried out terrorist acts in the countryside. It was in these often remote areas that left-wing guerrillas had their bases. They could also count on receiving aid, such as food and shelter, from the landless peasants. Consequently, rural areas became the scene for many of the governments' most brutal and protracted terror campaigns.

The armed forces targeted villages or individuals believed to be harboring or in some small way supporting the guerrillas. Whole villages were razed to the ground by army units or attacked with napalm from the air. The attacks were indiscriminate and took place without warning, and the vast majority of the dead were innocent civilians. In May 1980, for example, members of the Salvadoran military destroyed a village suspected of revolutionary sympathies on the Honduran border. The Catholic Church estimated that 1,400 people, mostly peasants, died in the countryside during that month.

Generally, these terror campaigns against the rural and urban poor have not aided the cause of the dictatorships. They have tended to strengthen opposition to the regimes and fueled support for the left-wing guerrillas. In the case of Nicaragua, for example, the government's assassination of Pedro Chamorra, a moderate news editor, in early 1978, helped to unite the previously divided opposition. Strikes and mass demonstrations against the right-wing regime followed the murder, and the Catholic Church called for the resignation of the regime's leader.

Despite the occasional overthrow of a right-wing dictatorship in Latin America, most regimes have proved resilient. This is in part due to the massive backing some of them receive from the United States. This economic and military support, coupled with the regimes' widespread use of terror, has ensured their survival. Where they have fallen, they have been ousted by coups backed by rival elements in the armed forces. Some others have moderated their excesses due to international pressure for reform. ■

ARGENTINE GOVERNMENT'S RESPONSES TO TERRORISM

The Argentine government instituted a program of exterminating political opponents to counter terrorism in the 1970s. Violations of human rights and due process of law were extensive. The security forces became notorious throughout the world for the staggering number of "disappearances" – people suspected of being terrorists or sympathizing with them in any way were taken prisoner and never seen again.

The Argentine military regimes of 1966-73 initially saw insurgency as a police problem. It was only with the escalation of violence in 1969 that the national security doctrine came to the fore. The doctrine began with the premise that the armed forces were the custodians of the state and were not merely entitled but were actually required to use all their resources to defend it. The armed forces' objective must then be to combat subversion within the country. The definition of subversion steadily widened to include all forms of opposition to military rule.

Following the 1959 Cuban revolution, U.S. President John F. Kennedy set up a program to create greater stability in Latin America and to prevent the spread of communism there. As part of this program, U.S. military instructors, both in the United States and in military academies throughout Latin America, taught the national security doctrine and trained military officers in counterinsurgency measures. This training was complemented by humanitarian programs. By 1976, when the worst of the armed forces' campaign of terror began, much of Argentina's military elite had attended U.S. training programs.

KEY FACTS

- During the years of "the Process," security forces unofficially arrested, tortured, and killed an estimated 15,000 people. Another 20,000 were officially jailed and tortured.
- More than 1,000 people had direct involvement in the interrogation, torture, and murder of suspects between 1976 and 1979.

RISE OF MILITANCY

An upsurge in violent opposition began in the industrial city of Córdoba in May 1969. Students and auto workers rioted in the streets for two days in protest against the government's austerity measures. The *cordobazo*, as the uprising became known, led to a resurgence of revolutionary militancy, partly because of its impact and partly in reaction to the authoritarian responses of the military regime.

The military's tactics against the threat were conventional, deploying police in the cities and infantry and armored patrols in the countryside. However, there was a growing emphasis on intelligence-gathering. As the government enhanced its surveillance abilities, each branch of the armed forces was also developing its own intelligence unit.

After his victory in the presidential elections of 1973, Juan Domingo Perón was reasonably tolerant of left-wing insurgency. However, he was already a sick man, and as his strength waned, the militants were jockeying for position. A new paramilitary organization, the Argentine Anticommunist Alliance (AAA) supplemented the efforts of the police and armed forces to root out leftist subversion. Founded by the minister of social welfare, José López Rega, the AAA's goal was to carry out an "ideological cleansing" of the Peronist

Popperfoto

The Mothers of the Plaza de Mayo demonstrating in 1985 for the punishment of those responsible for state terror. This organization held public protests during the worst years of the terror, despite the threat of violence and death.

movement in particular and of the country in general. Its targets included left-wing intellectuals and politicians, as well as revolutionary activists.

Perón died on July 1, 1974. That November, a state of emergency was declared, giving the military a free hand in its "dirty war" against the guerrillas. It was in this period that the notorious disappearances began, although as yet on a small scale. After a coup on March 24, 1976, power passed into the hands of a junta, made up of the commanders of the army, navy, and air force.

"THE PROCESS"

The new military junta appointed General Jorge Rafael Videla as president and launched the Process of National Reorganization, commonly referred to as "the Process." Based on an extreme form of the national security doctrine and sanctioned by an extremely conservative religious hierarchy, the Process soon became a euphemism for state terror directed against any form of opposition. The meticulous planning of the Process began in 1975, around six months before the junta took power. In essence, the Process was designed as a mass purging of all people deemed to be opposed in any way to the regime.

The armed forces competed with one another and within each service to root out subversives. Quotas were established for commanders to fill. They accomplished this by mass arrests, not only of known and identified suspects, but of political activists, students, and anyone else who incurred suspicion on the most trivial grounds. Relatives of people who already had been arrested were themselves liable to come under suspicion. This was not accidental. As one army commander, General Luciano Menéndez, openly admitted: "We are going to have to kill 50,000 people: 25,000 subversives, 20,000 sympathizers, and we will make 5,000 mistakes."

Such ferocity was what distinguished this crackdown on subversives – the authorities had no intention of releasing those arrested; anyone taken in by the army could expect almost certain death. Most arrests took place at night, under cover of darkness. Police ransacked houses and often took away entire families, bundling people, handcuffed and blindfolded, into the trunks of cars. If relatives or friends sought information, they were told either nothing at all or else lies. The families of the "disappeared," as these unfortunates were called, lived with the fear that if they pursued their investigations too rigorously, they too would be arrested. Friends, neighbors, lawyers, and public officials were also reluctant to offer any support, fearful of reprisals.

Security forces subjected prisoners to systematic, barbarous torture in special centers throughout the country. The most notorious was the Naval Engineering School (ESMA) in Buenos Aires. As the commission investigating the disappearances stated afterward: "ESMA not only was a clandestine detention center where torture was applied, but one which functioned as the driving axle of a complex organization that, being enclosed, tried as far as possible to hide by the extermination of its victims the crimes that were committed."

Methods of torture included beating, rape and sexual harassment, submersion, suspension by limbs, and the use of the electric cattle-prod. Many people died under torture. If they managed to survive, their stay of execution did not last long. While shooting was the most common form of murdering prisoners, some victims were taken on "doorless flights" and dropped out of aircraft over the countryside or the ocean. Otherwise, burial was in unmarked graves in cemeteries throughout Argentina. Independent investigations have shown that more than 15,000 people either died under torture or were later "disappeared."

MOTHERS OF THE PLAZA DE MAYO

The military government's human rights violations began to attract international attention as early as 1977. The Mothers of the Plaza de Mayo, an organization of the relatives of the "disappeared," can take much of the credit for this. Despite the threat of death over anybody who spoke against the military government, they held their first demonstration in April 1977. Despite violent responses from the authorities, they continued to hold public meetings nearly once a week until the end of military rule. In the early days of the organization, many of the leaders were "disappeared." Police also arrested foreign journalists attending the demonstrations, but released them after a few hours.

The military regime remained in power until 1983, having been weakened by the conflict with Britain over the Falkland Islands in the previous year. It was only after the return to civilian rule, when bodies were being unearthed by the score, that Argentina began to understand and confront the truth.

COUNTING THE LOSS

In the last days of its rule, in September 1983, the military government tried to pardon itself of its crimes during the Process. In 1984, a presidential commission released a report of its investigation into the Process, which contained more than 50,000 pages of eyewitness statements. It estimated that a minimum of 8,960 people died in at least 340 illegal jails.

In February 1995, a former naval officer, Adolfo Francisco Scilingo, admitted publicly that thousands of victims of the military government had been drugged and thrown from aircraft over the South Atlantic. Their bodies have never been recovered. Under a decree from President Carlos Saúl Menem, Scilingo was then stripped of his rank on the pretext of a previous conviction for fraud in 1991. In an effort to win military support, Menem had praised the army for its war against "subversives," and has pardoned some of those accused of human rights violations.

Peter Calvert

SEE ALSO: STATE VERSUS NON-STATE TERRORISM; URBAN VERSUS RURAL TERRORISM; TERRORISM IN ARGENTINA; CHILEAN GOVERNMENT'S RESPONSES TO TERRORISM.

FURTHER READING

- Anderson, Martin Edwin. *Dossier Secreto: Argentina's Desaperecidos and the Myth of "Dirty War."* Boulder, CO: Westview Press, 1993.
- Guest, Ian. *Behind the Disappearances: Argentina's Dirty War against Human Rights and the United Nations.* Philadelphia: University of Pennsylvania Press, 1990.
- Hodges, Donald Clark. *Argentina, 1943-1987: The National Revolution and Resistance.* Albuquerque: University of New Mexico Press, 1988.

BRAZILIAN GOVERNMENT'S RESPONSES TO TERRORISM

Before the upsurge of guerrilla insurgencies in Brazil during the mid-1960s, the country's military regime had been primarily engaged in restoring economic stability. However, extremists within the army capitalized on the wave of violence and turned the moderate military regime into a repressive dictatorship. Since the regime was unchecked by constitutional restraints, it had no need to compromise with rebels. On the other hand, the regime was able to make strategic concessions to terrorists that would have cost a civilian government its support. Moreover, the regime was able to blunt through censorship the effect of the more spectacular incidents.

Historically, the military have regarded themselves as performing a corrective role in Brazil to keep the power of civilian governments in check. Such was the case in 1964, when General Humberto Castelo Branco staged a military coup to reverse the reforms of President João Goulart, which were destabilizing the economy. Castelo Branco had intended to return power to civilian rule as soon as the military had rescued the economy. However, hard-line elements within the army took advantage of the rise in terrorism and left-wing political violence to suspend the constitution in 1968.

KEY FACTS

- Death squads first appeared in 1958 as a police response to criminal violence. They were resurrected ten years later to carry out political killings.
- In April 1970, counterterrorist forces discovered the training camp of the Revolutionary People's Vanguard. They arrested about 100 militants, effectively destroying the organization.

In the first phase of the 1960s insurgency, marked by unsuccessful attempts to set up rural guerrilla movements, government action proved very effective. All the rural insurgent groups were crushed, and the surviving members regrouped as "urban guerrillas."

SUPPRESSION OF ALL OPPONENTS

The second phase of insurgency was marked by the beginning of the urban guerrilla campaign carried out by the Action for National Liberation (ALN) in 1968. Police intensified operations and started sending out death squads composed of off-duty officers. As rebel attacks continued, the government tightened its control in December 1968 by suspending basic legal rights, limiting the powers of judges, imposing strict censorship, and giving full presidential powers to the ruling general, Artur Costa e Silva. When Costa e Silva suffered a stroke in August 1969, an electoral college of 107 generals shunted aside his civilian vice-president and chose General Emilio Garrastazu Médici, head of the military intelligence service (SNI), as his successor.

The SNI directed a massive counterterrorist operation throughout the country. Suspects were imprisoned and clandestinely subjected to torture. The information gained hastened the destruction of the remaining insurgency groups. Thousands, including many civilian politicians, were arrested. Some were imprisoned and others deprived of their civil rights. A number of offenses, including the publication of material considered hostile to the regime, were subject to the death penalty.

Brazilian counterterrorists had their biggest success in November 1969, when they located and killed Carlos Marighella, leader of the ALN, in a shoot-out. The ALN never found a suitable replacement. Joaquim Camara Ferreira briefly took charge, but he was arrested in January 1970 and died in prison that October.

Hulton Getty Picture Collection

In 1964, General Castelo Branco followed the Brazilian military tradition of overthrowing a reform-minded civilian government.

As the authorities redoubled their efforts in the pursuit of terrorists, stories of systematic, intensive torture began to circulate, despite censorship. As reports of atrocities spread, the minister of justice, on December 2, 1969, twice denied any knowledge of torture, but promised to punish the guilty if any were discovered. It was not long, however, before the government was forced to admit that torture had taken place.

As a result of the publicity, President Garrastazu Médici demanded the termination of death squad activity and ordered the federal police to ensure that this was done. A substantial number of arrests and trials followed, and by the end of 1973 it was clear that death squad activity had come to an end.

CONCESSIONS TO TERRORISTS

Where the Brazilian government did not take a hard line was in response to the terrorist kidnappings that plagued Brazil from 1969. The first abduction took place on September 3, 1969, when four armed men seized U.S. Ambassador C. Burke Elbrick on the streets of Rio de Janeiro. The government acceded almost at once to the ALN's two main demands. They permitted the publication of the terrorists' manifesto, and released the 15 political prisoners named by the ALN.

In March 1970, the Japanese consul-general in São Paulo was kidnapped. The government agreed to free five prisoners in exchange for his release. On June 11, 1970, eight ALN members kidnapped the West German ambassador, Ehrenfried von Holleben. The West German government stated that it expected Brazil to comply with the kidnappers' demands. Consequently, on June 14, the Brazilian government agreed to the publication of a new ALN manifesto and the release of 40 prisoners. The ambassador was released unharmed.

In December 1970, Swiss ambassador Giovanni Enrico Bucher was kidnapped. This time, the terrorists demanded the publication of a series of manifestos and the release of 70 prisoners. The government ignored the demand for publicity, but agreed to negotiate on a list of prisoners. Two days after the prisoners were freed, the ambassador was released unharmed.

From 1974 onwards, a gradual relaxation of military rule took place. In 1979, an amnesty freed all members of guerrilla groups in prison and enabled those in exile to return to Brazil. The lesson of Brazil's failed urban guerrilla movement was stark: the strategy of the rural guerrilla could not simply be transplanted to the urban environment. Government strategies of counterterrorism were more effective in the city, where the authorities could exercise greater control.

Peter Calvert

SEE ALSO: REVOLUTIONARY TERRORISM; URBAN VERSUS RURAL TERRORISM; TERRORISM IN BRAZIL; URUGUAYAN GOVERNMENT'S RESPONSES TO TERRORISM.

FURTHER READING

- Alves, Maria Helen Moreira. *State and Opposition in Military Brazil.* Austin: University of Texas Press, 1985.
- Bacchus, Wilfred A. *Mission in Mufti: Brazil's Military Regimes, 1964-1985.* New York: Greenwood Press, 1990.
- Skidmore, Thomas E. *The Politics of Military Rule in Brazil, 1964-1985.* New York: Oxford University Press, 1988.

CHILEAN GOVERNMENT'S RESPONSES TO TERRORISM

Chile was little affected by the wave of Latin American insurgency that followed the 1959 Cuban revolution. However, by 1967, the Movement of the Revolutionary Left (MIR) had begun operations in Chile and the group was sufficiently vociferous to be included in party talks in 1970 by the left-wing Marxist president, Salvador Allende Gossens. The MIR tried to accelerate Allende's land reform program by direct action, and set about organizing peasants into militias to carry out land seizures. In response, landowners also took the law into their own hands and hired their own private armies to protect their land. Finally on September 11, 1973, military and naval officers staged a coup, claiming that civil unrest would escalate into a communist insurrection.

The new regime set about quelling opposition with ruthless brutality. Military patrols rounded up members of Allende's coalition government. Leading figures were spared torture and death, apparently because of their international standing, but known or suspected civilian supporters were not so fortunate. Seven thousand were herded into the National Stadium in Santiago. Many were tortured and abused, more were detained in barracks or on prison ships in even worse conditions, and at least 200 were shot out of hand. In the countryside, those who had seized land were targeted by landowners and their armed guards. The real death toll remains unknown.

KEY FACTS

- Pinochet's government officially recognized that 30,000 Chileans had fled the military regime by 1979. The real figure was more like 200,000.
- The Chilean police's methods of torture included beatings, rape, application of electrodes to the head and genitals, submersion in sewage, suspension from a pole, exposure to bright lights or loud noises, and burning with cigarettes.

THE MYSTERIOUS "PLAN Z"

The fury of the first wave of military repression was fueled by the story of "Plan Z" – a plot supposedly hatched by communists to attack the armed forces. Troops were ordered to uncover the plot and eliminate suspects. Officers who showed insufficient zeal in carrying out these orders were demoted, imprisoned, or dismissed. As a result, atrocities went unpunished and violence was justified as a necessary measure to defeat the hard-line leftists. The military took the failure of Plan Z to be put into action as proof of the efficiency of counterinsurgency tactics. However, the only evidence that Plan Z ever existed lies in a "White Book" prepared by the CIA, giving rise to suspicions that it was a conjured-up pretext for suppression.

Once firmly in power, the military junta created the National Directorate of Intelligence (DINA) in June 1974 to eradicate terrorist "subversion." The junta appointed General Augusto Pinochet Ugarte as Supreme Chief of the Nation on June 27. He quickly established a network of spies throughout Chile, operating without legal restraints. Agents in unmarked cars arrested suspects, took them to detention centers in military barracks, abandoned convents, and colonial villas, where they were tortured. Prisoners' families were also tortured to extract "confessions."

The Chilean system of state terror was more centralized than its counterparts in Argentina or Brazil, and more ruthless in its attempts to pursue its victims. In

Popperfoto

In 1973, Santiago police used tear gas to disperse students opposed to Allende's educational reforms.

September 1974, for example, General Carlos Prats González, who had acted as Allende's deputy, was assassinated in Buenos Aires, Argentina, and former foreign minister Orlando Letelier was killed by a car bomb in Washington, DC, in September 1976. Between 1973 and 1977, excluding those executed after some semblance of a trial, some 670 Chileans "disappeared."

Pinochet dissolved the agency in 1977 and set up the National Information Center (CNI). Psychological torture replaced physical abuse, and "disappearances" almost ceased. But when left-wing terrorists assassinated army intelligence officer Roger Vergara in July 1980, repression was again stepped up. All news media were censored and agents were sent into schools and colleges. Military patrols regularly raided working-class districts where dissent was thought to be rife.

In 1988, Pinochet decided to hold a referendum in order that he could legitimize his presidency until 1997. To his surprise, Pinochet lost the vote and he reluctantly handed over power to civilian rule in 1989. Pinochet stayed in command of the army and the new government found it prudent to offer an amnesty to all who committed crimes during the military regime.

Peter Calvert

SEE ALSO: REVOLUTIONARY TERRORISM; TERRORISM IN CHILE; ARGENTINE GOVERNMENT'S RESPONSES TO TERRORISM; BRAZILIAN GOVERNMENT'S RESPONSES TO TERRORISM.

FURTHER READING

- Brown, Cynthia. *Chile Since the Coup: Ten Years of Repression.* New York: Americas Watch Committee, 1983.
- Constable, Pamela, and Arturo Valenzuela. *A Nation of Enemies: Chile under Pinochet.* London and New York: Norton, 1991.
- Spooner, Mary Helen. *Soldiers in a Narrow Land: The Pinochet Regime in Chile.* Berkeley: University of California Press, 1994.

COLOMBIAN GOVERNMENT'S RESPONSES TO TERRORISM

State terror, guerrilla insurgency, and state counterterror in Colombia have escalated into a cycle of violence that has no parallel elsewhere in Latin America. The toll of violent deaths is now counted in the hundreds of thousands. The ceaseless bloodshed originated as a product of, and as a reaction to, the repressive acts committed over decades by the Colombian state and armed forces.

In 1964, for example, the Revolutionary Armed Forces of Colombia (FARC) was created after the Colombian army bombarded a group of peasant farmer families in the south of the country who were demanding land rights. The disproportionate army crackdown effectively triggered a guerrilla response which remains active to this day.

In the early years, most guerrilla groups espoused revolutionary ideologies. In the last two decades their motives for violence have become increasingly mercenary, with the rapid and widespread development of the Colombian cocaine industry. The government has come to concentrate its counterterrorist activities on combating drug-related violence. However, the huge financial stakes in the illegal drug industry have spawned a number of state and paramilitary factions that are kidnapping, assassinating, and bombing in pursuit of protection or a piece of the profits.

KEY FACTS

- In 1995, more than 35,000 people met a violent death in Colombia, giving the country the world's highest number of homicides *per capita*.
- Between 1978 and 1992, an estimated 1,500 Colombians "disappeared" after state detention.
- Crackdowns on the Medellín cartel during the 1980s caused the drug barons to expand their operations into Mexico and Europe.
- Drug baron Pablo Escobar conducted 60 car-bombings in 1993 in an attempt to persuade the government not to bring him to trial.

DEFENSE GROUPS AND DEATH SQUADS

Traditional Colombian exports, such as coffee and cocoa, and industries such as cattle-ranching, have in many areas yielded to cocoa cultivation, and today, Colombia produces about 80 percent of the cocaine consumed worldwide. In the 1970s, as guerrilla forces expanded their territories and influence, they began to kidnap landowners to extort money. In defense, many of the landowners allied themselves with the army and with the infamous Medellín drug cartel. In 1981, they formed the first paramilitary group, known as Death to Kidnappers (MAS). Very rapidly, MAS assumed an offensive stance, targeting civilians whom it suspected of guerrilla activity. Hundreds of other paramilitary groups, including death squads, sprang up in MAS's wake. By 1988, there were some 140 active death squads and at least 300 paramilitary groups.

THE EXTRADITION TREATY

One of the key anti-terrorist initiatives of the state was the bilateral Colombia-U.S. extradition treaty, signed in 1979 to come into effect 1982. This was to enable the government to enforce the extradition of known drug-traffickers to the U.S. to stand trial. The treaty provoked a strong reaction from the drug barons. In November 1985, the Medellín cartel paid guerrillas a reported $5 million to take over the Palace of Justice

Rex Features

The U.S. dispatched military aid in the 1980s and 1990s to help Colombia crush drug operations.

and kill most of the judges who were in the process of debating the constitutionality of the treaty. In 1986, the Supreme Court unilaterally annulled the treaty. During the mid-1980s, a number of key cartel leaders were arrested, but through a combination of threats and the murders of legal officials, together with rigged trials, they managed to walk free again. Nevertheless, increased efforts by the Colombian government, in combination with U.S. support, have reaped rewards. Today, the leaders of the Medellín cartel, and its successor, the Cali cartel, are either dead or serving long prison sentences. Much of Colombia's drug-trafficking is now administered by guerrillas.

In the process of combating drug barons and guerrilla groups, the Colombian government has itself created a terror regime. Some 20,000 Colombians died in political violence between 1986 and 1993. In 1992, it was estimated that 20 percent of politically motivated killings were carried out by guerrillas, while about 70 percent were attributed to the security forces and paramilitary groups. Until the state offers the peasants of Colombia a viable alternative crop to cocaine, the drugs war will continue. And for as long as the security forces continue to abuse human rights, a political solution to Colombia's misery remains out of sight.

Jorge Ramírez

SEE ALSO: TERROR GROUP ORGANIZATION; BOMBING OPERATIONS; ASSASSINATION; TERRORISM IN COLOMBIA.

FURTHER READING

- Bergquist, Charles, Ricardo Peñarada, and Gonzalo Sánchez, eds. *Violence in Colombia: The Contemporary Crisis in Historical Perspective.* Wilmington, DE: SR Books, 1992.
- Dix, Robert H. *The Politics of Colombia.* New York: Praeger, 1987.
- Oquist, Paul. *Violence, Conflict, and Politics in Colombia.* New York: Academic Press, 1980.

SALVADORAN GOVERNMENT'S RESPONSES TO TERRORISM

In El Salvador, it was the government's security forces and not the rebel guerrillas who first employed terrorist tactics. A small number of wealthy landowners in the country, who were politically and economically dominant, used the military as their private army to quell unrest. As the power of the armed forces increased, they deployed death squads to wipe out any opposition to the regime.

In the early twentieth century, El Salvador was almost a feudal society. A small ruling elite, known as the "14 families," ruled over the peasants, who toiled to produce coffee, the country's main source of income. Any dissent was quickly dealt with. In 1932, for example, some 30,000 peasants were massacred after a failed uprising. For decades, the regime used violence to maintain the social and political order.

From the 1960s, as the number of landless peasants rose, so did the pressure for reform. In 1961, approximately 12 percent of the peasantry had no land. By the 1980s, the figure was over 50 percent. There was also a growing urban working class, mainly in the capital, San Salvador. During the 1960s, the Christian Democrats, led by José Napoleón Duarte, and other reformist parties made impressive gains in elections. One of the opposition Right's first moves in response to the reform movements was to form the paramilitary Democratic Nationalist Organization (ORDEN), which enforced landowners' authority in the countryside by using terror and violence against the peasantry.

In 1972, a coalition of reformist left-wing parties won the general election. However, when the result was declared, military leaders seized control of the country and prevented the coalition from forming a government.

KEY FACTS

- Government death squads gave themselves names such as the Squadron of Death and the White Warriors Union.
- Death squads and other military units killed more than 1,000 people in 1980 alone.
- It is estimated that between 30,000 and 50,000 people were killed during the civil war. Around 75 percent of these were victims of government forces.

RIGHT-WING DEATH SQUADS

Once in power, the army stepped up its violence. Under Colonel Arturo Molina, and then General Humberto Romero, army death squads were widely active, selectively killing opponents of the regime. They made a special assault on the Catholic church since many priests advocated social reform.

Meanwhile, armed opposition to the regime was growing. Assassinations of prominent politicians were commonplace. Rebels kidnapped and ransomed foreigners to provide funds. The army responded to guerrilla activity with public demonstrations of the death squads' power. In one incident, death squads dumped the headless bodies of four young men in the capital's main streets, along with leaflets proclaiming "Long live the massacre of 1932!"

In October 1979, open warfare broke out after a second military coup. Junior officers, wishing to undertake a program of land reform, overthrew General Romero. They declared an end to the "state of anarchy" and called on the Left and the Right to begin the democratic process. However, neither the revolutionaries nor the right-wing extremists believed that democracy would serve their purposes.

Rex Features

Archbishop Oscar Romero was an outspoken critic of the military regime. He was murdered in March 1980.

By this time, the death squads were almost out of control and were becoming ever more ruthless in their attempts to silence opposition. In 1980, there were four particular outrages. First, in January, security forces massacred unarmed demonstrators marching in protest through San Salvador. Second, Archbishop Oscar Romero, who had urged the U.S. to stop aid to the Salvadoran government, was assassinated while he celebrated mass in March of that year. Third, in November 1980, during a press conference given by members of an opposition coalition, 20 heavily armed men in plain clothes dragged off five individuals. Their bodies, bearing evidence of torture, were later discovered on the shore of Lake Ilopango. Finally, in December, three American nuns and a woman missionary were raped and murdered. Although six National Guard members were later arrested, because of pressure from army leaders their cases never reached court. Faced with the deadly might of the death squads, many members of the opposition resorted to terrorism, including a series of bomb attacks in the capital.

ARMY CRACKDOWN

As popular armed opposition took over large areas of the countryside, the government's response was direct. Using large quantities of U.S. equipment, forces trained by the Americans attacked key guerrilla areas. Once again, there were widespread reports of military atrocities, and more than 70,000 peasants fled their homes. Many became refugees in neighboring countries. Although the army succeeded in its primary objective, to prevent a rebel takeover of the country, it failed to eradicate the guerrillas.

In 1983, a peacemaking program called Operation Well Being was introduced. However, the army's death squads continued to function. The recognized leader of the squads, Major Roberto "Bob" D'Aubuisson, who was believed to be responsible for the murder of Archbishop Romero, was also the right-wing Arena Party's candidate in the 1984 presidential election. The election resulted in victory for the Christian Democrat Napoleón Duarte. He immediately offered peace to the guerrillas, and negotiations took place between the rebels and the new government. The talks continued for the rest of the 1980s, despite frequent death squad murders and the threat of further military coups. By 1992, however, peace had been restored to El Salvador.

Peter Calvert

SEE ALSO: STATE VERSUS NON-STATE TERRORISM; URBAN VERSUS RURAL TERRORISM; TERRORISM IN EL SALVADOR.

FURTHER READING

- Americas Watch. *El Salvador's Decade of Terror: Human Rights Since the Assassination of Archbishop Romero.* New Haven, CT: Yale University Press, 1991.
- Fish, Joe. *El Salvador: Testament of Terror.* London: Zed Books, and New York: Olive Branch Press, 1988.
- Landau, Saul. *The Guerrilla Wars of Central America: Nicaragua, El Salvador, and Guatemala.* London: Weidenfeld and Nicolson, and New York, St. Martin's Press, 1993.

GUATEMALAN GOVERNMENT'S RESPONSES TO TERRORISM

The insurgency campaigns of communist and peasant opposition groups such as the Guerrilla Army of the Poor (EGP) against a succession of right-wing military juntas have lasted more than 35 years. This is proof enough of the failure of the Guatemalan authorities' counterinsurgency strategies. Not only did such strategies fail to stem civil unrest; in fact, the scale of the repression broadened support for the terrorists and, in 1982, resulted in the development of a mass peasant movement.

The first organized counterinsurgency campaign, from 1966 to 1969, was guided by U.S. military advisers. On the model of U.S. tactics in Vietnam, it involved intensive search-and-destroy operations, including air strikes and the use of napalm against suspected terrorist hideouts. The rural civilian population in the rebel strongholds of the northeast was also resettled to try to eradicate support for guerrillas of the Rebel Armed Forces and the Revolutionary November 13th Movement. U.S. aid, channeled into civic action programs such as small construction projects, was carried out in collaboration with the local municipal leaders. These were often members of the opposition National Liberation Movement (MLN), a right-wing party with close ties to the armed forces.

Intellectual dissent was counteracted more harshly. For the first time in Latin America, death squads were used to slaughter a whole generation of left-wing student leaders, academics, and lawyers. Bodies were found daily bearing the marks of two vigilante groups, White Hand (Mano Blanca) and An Eye for an Eye (Ojo por Ojo), whose members were junior officers in the armed forces and civilians in the MLN. The violence was only checked when White Hand kidnapped the archbishop of Guatemala in March 1968. Finally, Guatemala's military leaders cracked down and forced White Hand officers, including leader Colonel Carlos Arana Osorio, into exile.

KEY FACTS

- Between 1960 and 1996, more than 100,000 people were officially reportedly dead and 50,000 more "disappeared" as a result of government counterinsurgency campaigns.
- Following his election in 1970, Colonel Arana's death squads carried out 700 political murders in four months. In four years, his security forces were believed to have killed 15,000 people.
- In 1981, the armed forces began systematic attacks on civilians, wiping out whole communities.

STATE OF SIEGE

The army, however, ensured that Colonel Arana was quickly able to return to Guatemala, and, in 1970, engineered his election as president. Arana immediately revived his old tactics and dispatched death squads on a ruthless mission to wipe out opposition to his government. This had the desired effect of neutralizing the communist terrorist threat. In the first three years of his presidency, there was a massive increase in the numbers of people who "disappeared."

Two events in 1976 brought matters to crisis level. An earthquake in February that year gave rise to government reconstruction programs that strengthened peasant communities. At the same time, the creation of a development zone for oil and mineral exploration in the north allowed army officers to annex large tracts of land. This prompted the peasants

TRH Pictures

A tiny percentage of terrorist weapons, posters, and flags captured by Guatemalan armed forces during 36 years of conflict.

to protest and led to the Panzós massacre on May 29, 1978, in which troops killed over 100 Kekchi Indians. The counterinsurgency campaign then became an undisciplined rampage. Villages were raided, looted, and razed, and local landowners or military commanders seized more land. The armed forces worked in conjunction with death squads, dealing out murder with such ferocity that the terrorist groups gained massive support from terrified, defenseless peasants.

In 1981, the armed forces launched a new offensive. For the first time they targeted civilians to destroy the terrorists' support base. On April 9, troops used machetes to kill 24 people in the village of Chuabajto, near Chimaltenango in the southwest, while on April 15, and again two weeks later, the town of San Mateo Ixtatán was attacked with the combined loss of 100 lives, mostly of peasant Indian farm workers.

CIVILIAN ATROCITIES

Over the next year, atrocities became commonplace. Troops regularly marched into villages – many in the region of El Quiché, a stronghold of the Guerrilla Army of the Poor – and butchered the inhabitants. Between April 3 and April 5, 1982, for instance, soldiers attacked the villages of Chel, Juá, and Amachel, beheaded the men, raped the women, and hurled the children onto the rocks in the river nearby. Ten days later, soldiers killed more than 100 children and 73 women in Río Negro and left their bodies hanging in the trees. Despite these atrocities, the government received military supplies and financial aid from many countries, including the U.S.

After a coup in 1982 brought new president Efrain Ríos Montt to power, government counterinsurgency strategy changed from outright repression of the peasants to subduing them through inducements. In return for creating militia forces to combat the rebel guerrillas, peasant communities were rewarded.

After another coup in 1983, signs of stability began to emerge, and by 1985 the economy was beginning to recover. In 1986, the civilian leader of the Christian Democrats, Vinicio Cerezo Arévalo, was elected president and, on October 25, the Guatemalan National Revolutionary Unity (URNG), the umbrella organization of the three main peasant groups, made the first formal peace overture in 25 years of conflict.

Nevertheless, ten years passed before both sides finally agreed to a cease-fire under United Nations mediation. In the interim, initiatives such as the 1986 "Arias Plan," devised by Costa Rican president Oscar Arias for peace in Central America, and peace agreements in 1990 and 1994 did not stop terrorist attacks and brutal government reprisals. In 1991, even as peace talks were continuing, official human rights sources reported 228 "extrajudicial executions" and 45 "disappearances" at the hands of the military, the civil patrols, and the police. Moreover, while members of the armed services were charged with human rights violations for the first time, no action followed.

Peter Calvert

SEE ALSO: STATE VERSUS NON-STATE TERRORISM; URBAN VERSUS RURAL TERRORISM; TERRORISM IN GUATEMALA; TERROR IN THE VIETNAM WAR.

FURTHER READING

- Carmack, Robert M. *Harvest of Violence: The Maya Indians and the Guatemalan Crisis.* London and Norman: University of Oklahoma Press, 1992.
- Falla, Ricardo. *Massacres in the Jungle: Ixcán Guatemala, 1975-1982.* Boulder, CO: Westview Press, 1994.
- Landau, Saul. *The Guerrilla Wars of Central America: Nicaragua, El Salvador, and Guatemala.* London: Weidenfeld and Nicolson, and New York: St. Martin's Press, 1993.

NICARAGUAN GOVERNMENT'S RESPONSES TO TERRORISM

Nicaragua provides an example of a country which has experienced terrorism from both left-wing and right-wing guerrillas. After seizing power in 1936, the U.S.-backed dictatorships of the Somoza family ruthlessly clamped down on any left-wing opposition. Then, the left-wing Sandinista regime, which overthrew the last Somoza dictator in 1979, responded to U.S.-backed guerrilla troops in two different ways. On the one hand, the Sandinistas suppressed civil liberties in order to neutralize terrorist activity. On the other, they instituted reforms to retain the loyalty of the people whom they needed to mobilize against the rebels' superior arms.

Until 1933, the U.S. had pursued a policy of intervention in Nicaragua. In the 1920s, U.S. marines began training the Nicaraguan National Guard to replace them as a military police force. In 1926, Nicaraguan patriot Augusto Sandino launched a guerrilla war against the occupying forces which lasted until they left the country in 1933. As he attended a "truce" dinner in 1934, he was assassinated by the National Guard. By 1936, the National Guard had assumed power under the leadership of Anastasio Somoza García.

KEY FACTS

- In a failed insurrection in 1978, fewer than 1,500 Sandinista guerrillas fought 14,000 National Guardsmen. Some 5,000 people were killed, and more than 15,000 injured, mostly civilians.
- A commission originally set up to chart human rights abuses under Somoza's regime counted the disappearance of 785 people arrested by Sandinista authorities between July 1979 and September 1980.

During the rule of the Somoza family, which continued through Anastasio's two sons, Luis and Anastasio, opposition was put down with the utmost ferocity. For example, after the seizure of the U.S. embassy in 1974, the younger Anastasio Somoza declared a national "state of siege," and imposed martial law. At least 400 people "disappeared" in the aftermath.

The Sandinista movement (FSLN), which formed in 1961, was the main perpetrator of terrorist attacks, including the embassy siege, during the Somoza regimes. Internal rivalry hampered the movement, but in October 1977, the Sandinistas launched a new offensive. Somoza stepped up repression, calling for and getting substantial help from the U.S. However, massive repression and extensive breaches of human rights by Somoza's National Guard alienated moderate opinion. In January 1978, Pedro Joaquín Chamorro, the popular editor of the newspaper *La Prensa* and outspoken critic of Somoza, was assassinated. Most Nicaraguans assumed Somoza was responsible.

In September 1978, the Sandinistas called for a general rebellion. After heavy fighting, the uprising was suppressed. But in 1979, strengthened by a greater unity among opposition groups and increased military forces, the Sandinistas led a second rebellion. As the Sandinista forces fought their way into Managua, Somoza ordered his air force to bomb his own capital.

ENTER THE SANDINISTAS

The resultant civil war ended with the flight of Somoza in July 1979. The Sandinistas had already proclaimed a provisional government-in-exile from Costa Rica and took power under Daniel Ortega Saavedra. The National Guard had effectively been Somoza's private army, so Ortega saw nothing wrong in restructuring the

Popperfoto

National Guard troops move in to end a five-day student occupation of Matagalpa in January 1978.

police to enforce party rule. Sandinista Defense Committees, with Cuban and Soviet advisers, were set up to collect information about opposition groups.

Over the next year, the Sandinistas shared power with non-Marxist groups, but as Marxist hardliners consolidated control, toleration of other groups ended. In 1980, state-controlled mobs attacked a rally organized by Nicaraguan Democratic Movement leader Alfonso Robelo. In a speech, Ortega threatened to unleash these *turbas divinas* (divine mobs) on any opponent. Mobs attacked the homes and businesses of Sandinista opponents, often beating the victims as well. During March 1981, mobs painted insults on the house of Violeta Chamorro, widow of editor Pedro Chamorro. Mobs also destroyed the home of Robelo.

Although Ortega cultivated support by introducing reforms and measures such as free health care, terrorists still managed to destabilize the country. The U.S. established and sponsored a guerrilla force. Initially, the Nicaraguan Democratic Force (FDN), or "Contras," were not much of a threat. But when the Contras bombed two bridges in March 1982, Ortega declared a state of emergency the next day. It was not lifted until 1988. Contra attacks escalated and included the mining of harbors in 1984. Ortega responded by taking his case to the World Court and, in 1986, the U.S. was found guilty of training, arming, equipping, and financing the Contras.

In response to U.S. accusations that they lacked the support of the people, the Sandinistas held an election in November 1984. Following his victory, Ortega offered a general amnesty, but refused to negotiate with the Contras, whose terrorist attacks continued. When his forces shot down two U.S. helicopters entering Nicaragua from Honduras, Ortega claimed it was the U.S. and not Nicaragua that was supporting terrorism.

PAN-CENTRAL AMERICAN PEACE PLAN

A plan drawn up in 1986 by Costa Rican President Oscar Arias called for an immediate cease-fire in all civil wars in Central America, cessation of aid to guerrilla groups, a general amnesty, and negotiations among all parties. It also imposed a series of deadlines. By the first of these, November 7, 1987, much of the plan had already been achieved.

Nevertheless, the Contras launched a spring offensive in 1988. Attacks on civilian targets alienated opinion at home and abroad. Sandinista troops repelled the attacks, and Contra leaders accepted the offer of negotiation as stipulated in the Arias plan.

Ortega's concessions included the reopening of the opposition newspaper *La Prensa* and the Catholic radio station, along with promises of free elections in 1990. However, the war against the Contras had been a great strain on an already troubled economy, and on February 25, 1990, voters rejected Ortega in favor of Violeta Chamorro. She responded to the Contras' presence by engaging the archbishop of Managua as peace mediator. The final demobilization of the Contra forces took place on June 27, when 19,197 troops surrendered under the auspices of the United Nations.

Peter Calvert

SEE ALSO: STATE VERSUS NON-STATE TERRORISM; URBAN VERSUS RURAL TERRORISM; TERRORISM IN NICARAGUA.

FURTHER READING

- Morley, Morris H. *Washington, Somoza, and the Sandinistas.* Cambridge and New York: Cambridge University Press, 1994.
- Pastor, Robert A. *Condemned to Repetition: The United States and Nicaragua.* Princeton, NJ: Princeton University Press, 1987.
- Thomas, W. Walter. *Reagan Versus the Sandinistas: The Undeclared War.* Boulder, CO: Westview Press, 1987.

PERUVIAN GOVERNMENT'S RESPONSES TO TERRORISM

Before 1980, terrorist factions in Peru were loosely organized and the security forces had little trouble in destroying them. Guerrilla activity in the 1960s was rapidly and ruthlessly put down. In 1980, however, after ten years of meticulous planning, Abimael Guzmán Reynoso unleashed his terrifying Shining Path (Sendero Luminoso) movement on an unsuspecting country.

MILITARY COUP

Although terrorist opposition of the 1960s had little success, it was obvious that the movements easily gained popular support. The bulk of the population, mainly native Indians, were desperately poor with negligible basic services, such as education and health care. General Juan Velazco Alvarado, who came to power after a left-wing military coup in 1968, recognized their plight. He introduced land reform and made efforts to improve social welfare. If these policies had been developed, Shining Path would have gained less support. However, opposition from the wealthy landowners, combined with inflation at a time of world recession, meant that Velazco achieved little.

KEY FACTS

- According to UN reports, in each year between 1987 and 1990, more people in Peru were detained by security forces and consequently "disappeared" than in any other country.
- The use of torture by the police and army was commonplace to extract prisoners' confessions. Methods include burning with cigarettes, electric shocks to the genitals, stabbing, and tying prisoners to sheets of metal to roast in the sun.

In 1980, the military organized elections in order to hand over power to a civilian government. At the same time, Shining Path emerged as a terrorist organization. Based chiefly in the province of Ayacucho, to the southeast of the capital Lima, Shining Path gained support among the Indians, whose social deprivation had worsened in the late 1970s. Guzmán deliberately timed the beginning of Shining Path's terrorist operations to coincide with elections in 1980, in an effort to undermine the new democracy. Peruvian intelligence failed to recognize the scale of the unrest and the action took the government completely by surprise.

Since most Shining Path terrorist attacks were confined initially to the Ayacucho province, responses were left to local police. The police were notoriously corrupt and hugely unpopular. Many Indians and peasants looked to Shining Path for protection, particularly in areas where coca production was beginning to attract drug traffickers and their brand of terrorism.

COMBATING THE TERRORISTS

During the early 1980s, DIRCOTE (the Directorate of Counter Terrorism) was set up to gather intelligence. Some army commanders copied Shining Path tactics by using Indian languages to appeal directly to the people. General Adrián Huamán, a Quechua-speaking Indian, used this strategy in Ayacucho in 1984. However, this was the exception rather than the rule.

As Shining Path activities increased, Fernando Belaúnde, who had been elected president in 1980, allowed the military to operate in "Emergency Zones." There, they used ruthless methods against the local populace, whether terrorist sympathizers or not. For example, in November 1983, 31 people were massacred at a wedding on the day of the municipal elections in the village of Soccos, 20 miles east of Ayacucho. The

Popperfoto

Abimael Guzmán, Shining Path leader, caged like an animal after being captured on September 12, 1992.

police alleged guerrillas had been responsible for the slaughter, but in February of the following year, a judge in Ayacucho ordered the arrest of 27 members of the civil guards on charges of murder. Stories of massacres and of suspects "disappearing" while in army detention only served to increase popular support for the terrorists.

NEW GOVERNMENT, OLD POLICIES

President Alan García inherited this situation when he was elected in 1985. There were hopes of reform, but the government soon found its policies frustrated by landowners and by the failing economy. Social welfare reform was too expensive to implement, thus denying the government a political weapon to combat terrorist subversion. A military solution seemed the only option. In May 1988, a military unit attacked the village of Cayara, in Ayacucho province, in apparent retaliation for a Shining Path ambush. Most of the civilian population was massacred. At the same time, U.S. agencies became involved, providing training and equipment in an anti-drugs initiative throughout Latin America. The resultant destruction of coca plantations spelled ruin for the local peasants, who turned increasingly to Shining Path.

In 1986, over 200 rebel prisoners were killed after they had organized mutinies in three separate prisons. Eventually Lima came under attack. A favorite Shining Path ploy was to blow up power lines, plunging the city into chaos. García declared a state of emergency, which allowed security forces to detain suspects and intensify repression. In June 1990, police raided six Shining Path safe houses in Lima, arresting 35 alleged guerrillas and seizing the plans for past and future missions and the identity cards of 176 rebels.

FUJIMORI'S "NEW DEMOCRACY"

Congress was alarmed by Alberto Fujimori's election as president in 1990 and blocked his reforms. Fujimori responded by suspending Congress and by assuming special powers. He introduced counterinsurgency measures that included a penal code making it easier to convict terrorists. His "Repentance Law" allowed active insurgents to become government witnesses without fear of prosecution, which helped bring about the capture of Guzmán.

In September 1992, following an intelligence breakthrough, DIRCOTE forces raided a Shining Path safe house in the suburbs of Lima. They captured Guzmán with most of his command staff, as well as Shining Path archive material. Masked security forces exhibited Guzmán in a cage before he was prosecuted, found guilty of treason, and sentenced to life imprisonment.

Peru's response to the terrorist threat has been uncoordinated, however. The security forces have gained a reputation for brutality, while counterinsurgency has become inextricably linked with the fight against drugs. If Shining Path is similar to other terrorist movements, Guzmán's capture may actually result in the emergence of a stronger organization.

John Pimlott

SEE ALSO: REVOLUTIONARY TERRORISM; STATE VERSUS NON-STATE TERRORISM; TERRORISM IN PERU.

FURTHER READING

- Bland, Gary, and Joseph S. Tulchin, eds. *Peru in Crisis: Dictatorship or Democracy?* Boulder, CO: Lynne Rienner Publications, 1994.
- Gorman, Stephen M., ed. *Post-Revolutionary Peru: The Politics of Transformation.* Boulder, CO: Westview Press, 1982.
- McCormick, Gordon. *The Shining Path and the Future of Peru.* Santa Monica, CA: Rand Corporation, 1990.

URUGUAYAN GOVERNMENT'S RESPONSES TO TERRORISM

From 1966, the Uruguayan government's harsh reaction to strikes, together with the decline of the economy, paved the way for the Tupamaros terrorist group. The ensuing campaign of terror destabilized Uruguay to the extent that the democratic civilian government was replaced by military rule in 1973. The primary aim of the military regime was to put an end to the demoralizing terrorist campaign.

POLICE HYSTERIA

Until the end of the 1960s, the government's campaign against the Tupamaros was unsuccessful, and the potential for crisis was never far from the surface. After their peaceful, day-long occupation of the town of Pando in September 1969, Tupamaros activists on their way back to the capital, Montevideo, were ambushed by security forces. In the ensuing confrontation, three activists were killed and hundreds more were arrested and imprisoned. Survivors described how the police, in a state of hysteria, kicked and beat them into prison vans.

KEY FACTS

- Following a security breakthrough in May 1972, Uruguayan police penetrated the Tupamaros network and discovered more than 200 safe houses and enough weapons and supplies to maintain an army of at least 2,000.
- From May to November 1972, 2,600 alleged Tupamaros supporters were jailed and 42 killed.
- By 1980, there was a higher proportion of political prisoners per head of population in Uruguay than in any other South American country.

This was a defining event for both sides. From then on, operations by the Tupamaros became more circumspect. The government issued a decree banning all positive references in the media to the Tupamaros, in order to deprive them of publicity. The effect was the reverse of what was intended. In the absence of hard information, wild rumors circulated about the achievements of the Tupamaros.

ESCALATION OF VIOLENCE

From 1970 to 1972, as the Tupamaros turned to kidnapping and armed confrontation, the government used its power of detention more freely, and torture became commonplace. In June 1970, a commission of inquiry concluded unanimously that psychological and physical torture was "normal, frequent, and habitual."

In August 1970, police captured most of the Tupamaros leaders. This seemed to have no effect on the movement and the leaders later escaped in a mass jailbreak of 109 Tupamaros from Punta Carretas prison. On September 9, 1971, following the escape, President Pacheco Areco placed the armed forces in charge of the counterinsurgency campaign. After a series of assassinations of government officials, the military admitted they were dealing with "organized groups that are seeking to take power." Congress agreed to proclaim a state of "internal war," initially for 30 days, suspending constitutional guarantees.

The armed forces responded with a substantial escalation of violence. They used torture and drugs to break down suspects arrested in mass sweeps. In May 1972, the security forces located the movement's "people's prison" and freed two members of the former government who had been imprisoned there. By June, more than 1,200 people had been arrested without

Hulton Getty Picture Collection

Security forces carried out an extensive search of vehicles and houses following the kidnapping of British diplomat Geoffrey Jackson in 1971.

significant response from the Tupamaros. With the capture of Tupamaros leader, Raúl Sendic Antonaccio, in September 1972, the armed forces made it clear to the insurgents that he and other senior Tupamaros in detention would be shot if the violence did not stop.

MILITARY COUP

Meanwhile, in its Law of State Security, the government instituted new penalties for terrorist offenses and gave military courts the right to try them. The law effectively made it illegal to criticize the armed forces and gave the president power to prohibit public meetings. The military leaders, however, were still not satisfied that they had rooted out subversion. They gave an ultimatum to the president, Juan María Bordaberry, which forced him to accept the creation of a military-led National Security Council to direct antiterrorist operations. Congress, however, would not agree to a law that would effectively turn Uruguay into a police state by allowing the indefinite detention of any citizen on any pretext. It also voted to investigate charges of torture against the armed forces.

In the meantime, the military government in neighboring Brazil believed that the relative freedom of Uruguay was a threat to its own national security and exerted pressure on Uruguay's armed forces to take control. Consequently, Bordaberry, acting on behalf of the army, decreed the closure of Congress and assumed dictatorial powers on June 27, 1973.

Following this coup, the Uruguayan armed forces established a military dictatorship. Bordaberry set about the task of eradicating the roots of revolution from Uruguayan society, in imitation of the strategy in Brazil. For this purpose, the entire population was classified into three categories. Category A, those

Popperfoto

General Liber Seregni was arrested in 1976 and sentenced to 14 years in prison. He accepted the general amnesty in March 1985.

known not only to be acceptable but also well disposed towards the regime, were given all important and governmental jobs. Category B, those acceptable to the regime but not active in its support, were excluded from the best jobs. Category C, those who came under any suspicion whatever or proved politically unreliable, were excluded from all jobs, subjected to petty harassment, and could be arrested on suspicion at any time and detained without trial. Many of the democratic politicians active before 1973 came into Category C, including General Liber Seregni, who had stood for the left-wing coalition party in the 1971 democratic elections. Seregni was arrested in 1976 and stripped of his military rank. The measures were extreme and conditions for the detainees were appalling, but the military achieved their primary aim by destroying the organization of the Tupamaros.

Military rule continued with civilian figurehead presidents throughout the 1970s. In 1976, Bordaberry was overthrown when he proposed a fascist-style regime, with himself at its head. After a succession of problems finding acceptable civilian leaders, military leader General Gregorio Alvarez Armellino assumed the presidency himself in 1981.

THE END OF MILITARY RULE

Over the next four years, he tried to gain popular consensus by referendum on constitutional amendments that would safeguard the power of the military. However, the Uruguayan people, despite ominous warnings from the armed forces, twice refused to ratify the constitutional changes. The government was thus forced to make further concessions. In the latter part of 1983, massive spontaneous demonstrations began to take place. Contrary to expectation, the government did not respond with massive repression, and as a result the demonstrations remained peaceful.

In the end, the armed forces proved unwilling or unable to withstand pressure for the restoration of democratic government. Instead, the military was finally able to negotiate a path to elections in November 1984 that was acceptable to the main political parties. Uruguay returned to civilian government in 1985, and its political prisoners received a general amnesty.

Peter Calvert

SEE ALSO: REVOLUTIONARY TERRORISM; STATE VERSUS NON-STATE TERRORISM; URBAN VERSUS RURAL TERRORISM; TERRORISM IN BRAZIL; TERRORISM IN URUGUAY; BRAZILIAN GOVERNMENT'S RESPONSES TO TERRORISM.

FURTHER READING

- Kaufman, Edy. *Uruguay in Transition: From Civilian to Military Rule.* New Brunswick, NJ: Transaction Press, 1979.
- Rial, Juan. "Makers and Guardians of Fear: Controlled Terror in Uruguay," in *Fear at the Edge: State Terror and Resistance in Latin America*, edited by Juan Corradi, Patricia Fagen, and Manuel A. Garreton Merino. Berkeley: University of California Press, 1992.
- Sosnowski, Saul, and Louise B. Popkin, eds. *Repression, Exile, and Democracy: Uruguayan Culture.* Durham, NC: Duke University Press, 1993.
- Weinstein, Martin. *Uruguay: The Politics of Failure.* Westport, CT: Greenwood Press, 1975.

VENEZUELAN GOVERNMENT'S RESPONSES TO TERRORISM

In the 1960s, democracy was a fragile flower in Venezuela. Rómulo Betancourt, the country's first democratically elected president, had led a long underground campaign against the dictatorship of Peréz Jiménez, who was ousted in 1958. Betancourt was elected in 1959. However, although a Marxist in his youth, Betancourt found himself facing opposition groups who felt that he was simply not left-wing enough. Castro's communist revolution in Cuba in 1959 had inspired uprisings in Latin America. Many Venezuelans also wanted a communist revolution in their country and felt that terrorism was the only way to make it happen.

The principal groups opposing the government were the Moscow-leaning Venezuelan Communist party (PCV) and the radical Movement of the Revolutionary Left (MIR). Both sought to instigate a mass uprising of the country's workers. On August 4, 1959, Betancourt ended the Emergency Plan, set up the year before to ease unemployment in Caracas during the transition to democracy. Serious rioting followed. The government responded with a temporary suspension of the constitutional right to public assembly. Liberal economic measures were implemented to quell opposition.

The government came under fire from other quarters, with unsuccessful right-wing military insurrections in San Cristóbal in April 1960 and in the Venezuelan city of Barcelona in June 1961. Left-wing opposition also began to harden, following the withdrawal of the remaining leftist elements from the government. During a series of strikes in October–December 1960, the MIR had unsuccessfully called for the resignation of the government. But MIR opposition leader Domingo Alberto Rangel later admitted that these moves came too late. The government had already established a broad base of support through realistic social reforms. This helped government security forces remain loyal.

Betancourt's personal standing had already been elevated when he survived an assassination attempt on June 24, 1960. And at a mass rally at El Silencio on December 1, 1960, Betancourt successfully defended his decision to deploy troops to secure the capital. A lull followed. However, at the beginning of 1962, the MIR began a rural guerrilla war, urged on by Che Guevara in Cuba. This plan also failed. The guerrillas made basic mistakes, and routine searches easily uncovered many of their camps. Also, the terrorists' campaign of bombings and attacks on the police proved unpopular and only succeeded in consolidating support for the government.

KEY FACTS

- Venezuela's first democratically elected president Rómulo Betancourt, survived terrorist assassination attempts in June 1960 and June 1963.
- Since the 1960s terrorist campaign, Venezuela has enjoyed over three decades of democracy.

THOUSANDS OF CASUALTIES

Meanwhile, the government was again threatened by the military. There was a revolt of naval and marine officers at Carupano in May 1962. A second mutiny in Puerto Cabello the following month took days to suppress, at the cost of several thousand casualties. These revolts were inspired by the Left and were openly supported by the PCV and the MIR. The government again responded with the suspension of constitutional guarantees. It also ended the parliamentary immunity of two deputies implicated in the risings.

Popperfoto

Armed government troops attempt to quell rioting by communist-led students in December 1959.

The high-water mark of the insurgency campaign came with the creation of the Armed Forces of National Liberation (FALN; unrelated to the Puerto Rican group of the same name) in 1961, and its sister organization, the communist-dominated National Liberation Front (FLN), in 1963. Both attempted to assassinate Betancourt on June 13, 1963. In response, Betancourt ordered the arrest of all known communists. In October, Congress again lifted parliamentary immunity so that suspected sympathizers could be detained.

DEMOCRACY SURVIVES

The insurgents then tried a variety of terrorist methods to disrupt the presidential elections of December 1963. Their failure to achieve this was a blow to their credibility. The PCV accepted the amnesty offered to them by the new president, Raúl Leoni. This ended the possibility of mass insurrection. Although substantial elements of the FALN remained in the field through 1967, they did not pose a significant threat to the fledgling democracy.

The terrorists were neutralized largely by the government's political strategy. Both Betancourt and his successor showed themselves ready to act against the insurgent threat without trying to create a dictatorship. They were helped both by the mistakes of the insurgents, especially in the unpopular use of terrorism in the cities, and by Venezuela's growing economic strength, which they used to reward their supporters and so isolate the guerrillas. Deprived of popular support, the terrorist movements were unable to survive.

Peter Calvert

SEE ALSO: GUERRILLAS AND TERROR; REVOLUTIONARY TERRORISM; URBAN VERSUS RURAL TERRORISM; TERRORISM IN VENEZUELA.

FURTHER READING

- Blank, David Eugene. *Venezuela: Politics in a Petroleum Republic.* New York: Praeger, 1984.
- Ellner, Steve. *Venezuela's Movimiento al Socialismo: From Guerrilla Defeat to Innovative Politics.* Durham, NC: Duke University Press, 1988.
- Lombardi, John V. *Venezuela: The Search for Order, the Dream of Progress.* New York: Oxford University Press, 1982.

CHAPTER TWENTY-ONE

State Terrorism

Authoritarian regimes, particularly those states that are ruled by nonelected dictators, continue to use terrorism to control their populations. Violence is usually directed against separatist ethnic minorities or ideological enemies. The state's security and military forces, often backed by a network of informers, use murder, torture, and imprisonment without trial to destroy these opposition groups. Potential rivals for power within the regime itself are also subject to sudden arrest and execution on the flimsiest of evidence.

STATE-SPONSORED TERRORISM

In the period since 1945, there have been many examples of states using terror as an element of policy against their own citizens, or against the citizens of other states. The methods used have been diverse. For example, the notorious "Tonton Macoutes" – François "Papa Doc" Duvalier's secret police in Haiti – used voodoo as one means of scaring their victims. On a different level, the Chinese army used tanks to crush student protests in Tienanmen Square in 1989. States have also been involved in various forms of covert action that are similar to the attacks of avowedly terrorist groups. For example, in 1983, the South Korean cabinet was blown up in Rangoon by a North Korean commando unit, and, in 1985, French secret agents bombed the Greenpeace ship *Rainbow Warrior* in New Zealand.

However, the most common, and most insidious, form of state involvement with terrorism is state sponsorship of terrorist groups in order to further foreign policy aims. The sponsoring state benefits by distancing itself from the terrorist activity, since it can easily deny any involvement. This form of terrorism has received increased attention since the mid-1970s when U.S. analysts first classed it as "surrogate warfare," and suggested that such sponsorship was a coherent program undertaken by various communist bloc and Arab states.

SUMMARY

- States sponsor terrorist groups in order to direct violence against their enemies while being able to deny that they are responsible.
- State sponsorship of terrorism has been most common is the Middle East, where Iran, Syria, Libya, Iraq, and Israel have aided terrorists.
- During the Cold War communist bloc countries helped terrorist groups, and the U.S. also aided forces that employed terrorism in Afghanistan and Nicaragua.
- Sponsoring states have provided terrorists with everything from military training and funding to safe havens and support in the media.

Support and sponsorship can take many forms, ranging from encouragement by a state's media to the integration of the terrorist group into a state's intelligence services. For governments and states targeted by this type of terrorism, it can often be difficult to find the "smoking gun" that links terrorists to their sponsors, and thus to bring the sponsoring state to be held responsible.

State-sponsored terrorism has a long history. In the late nineteenth century, for instance, Russia provided support to revolutionary groups in the Balkans trying to set up Slavic states. During World War I, Germany supplied arms to the Irish nationalists fighting British rule. In the late twentieth century, numerous states have backed terrorist groups. Weaker countries have found the technique a useful method to strike out at opponents who outgun them in terms of conventional military strength.

The main sponsors of terrorism have been radical Middle Eastern states (primarily Iran, Syria, Libya, and Iraq), the Soviet Union and other communist states (including the Eastern bloc, North Korea, and Cuba), and South Africa, the U.S., and Israel.

IRAN: WORLDWIDE ISLAMIC REVOLUTION

While Iran under the shah used terror against its own citizens, the Islamic Republic took terrorism to the heart of its foreign policy. Some of the terrorist acts linked to Iran are assassinations by Iranian intelligence agents, such as the killing of a number of political exiles in Europe. An example was the assassination of former Iranian prime minister Shahpur Bakhtiar in Paris in 1991. A bitter covert war has also been under-

Hulton Getty Picture Collection

On July 10, 1985, French secret service agents mined the Greenpeace ship Rainbow Warrior *and sank it in Auckland harbor, New Zealand, killing a Portuguese photographer. The* Rainbow Warrior *was intending to sail to Muroroa atoll to protest against French underground nuclear testing there.*

way since the early 1980s between the Iranian regime and the opposition People's Fighters, a paramilitary force based in Iraq. This group carries out terrorist attacks inside Iran, and the Iranian intelligence often assassinate its members and raid its bases.

In line with its claim to be the vanguard of a worldwide Islamic revolution, Iran has also become a major sponsor of international terrorism. Iran encourages many revolutionary movements, and has hosted conferences bringing together radical Muslim and Palestinian groups. More concretely, the Iranian state has forged close ties with groups such as al Da'awa and the Supreme Council for the Islamic Revolution in Iraq, Hizb'allah in Lebanon, Islamic Jihad in Palestine, and a variety of tribal militias in Afghanistan.

Of these groups, Hizb'allah is the best known in the West. It was set up in the 1980s by radical Lebanese Shiites, with assistance from Iran's Revolutionary Guard Corps. The movement received extensive military, financial, and diplomatic support from Iran during the 1980s confrontation in Lebanon with America and its allies. Groups linked to Hizb'allah bombed Western embassies and a U.S. Marine barracks, kidnapped dozens of Westerners, and carried out attacks on Israeli targets based on raids into southern Lebanon.

The anti-Iraqi groups al Da'awa and the Supreme Council, which carry out terrorist attacks inside Iraq, are based in Iran. In the 1980s, Iran additionally sponsored a number of Shiite groups that carried out terrorist attacks in Arab states along the Gulf.

ARAB AID TO TERRORISTS

Syria, whose military dictatorship does not hesitate to use terror to keep its citizens in line, has made extensive use of terrorism abroad since the 1960s. Although it sometimes does use its own agents, Syria has frequently used proxy groups to deflect attention from

Popperfoto

The bomb attack on "La Belle" discotheque in West Berlin, West Germany, on April 5, 1986, killed two people, including one U.S. serviceman. Both the Syrian and Libyan governments were implicated in the atrocity.

its role. Early in the 1960s, Syrian military intelligence sponsored Yasser Arafat's Fatah, the dominant group in the Palestinian Liberation Organization (PLO). The group was provided with arms, training, intelligence, trained personnel, and operational direction to help it launch attacks inside Israel. Since then, Syria has used a variety of groups to further its objectives.

Saiqa is ostensibly an independent Palestinian group based in Syria. Since the early 1970s, however, it has been little more than a branch of the Syrian armed forces. Similarly, the Popular Front for the Liberation of Palestine – General Command (PFLP-GC) is effectively an arm of Syrian intelligence. Both groups have carried out terrorist attacks against Israel. In the mid-1980s, Syria hosted the Abu Nidal Organization (ANO), encouraging it to assassinate those Palestinian leaders who adopted a moderate stance towards Israel. Syria has also supported the Kurdistan Workers' Party (PKK), which attacks Turkish targets. Syria wants to apply pressure to Turkey, which is threatening to deprive Syria of its water resources by damming the Tigris and Euphrates rivers.

Under Muammar al-Qaddafi, Libya has become a notorious sponsor of international terrorism. He has used Libya's oil wealth to lavish support on a bewildering variety of groups. Unlike President Assad of Syria, Qaddafi openly proclaims his support for revolutionary movements and frequently praises acts of "anti-imperialist" violence. Libya's support includes provision of training camps and supplies of arms and funds. Libya has supported a wide variety of groups, including the Polisario Liberation Front in the former Spanish Sahara and the Moro National Liberation Front in the Philippines. Abu Nidal was based in Libya for many years,while the Provisional Irish Republican Army (IRA) received arms supplies from Libya.

Other groups that have received Libyan support include the Turkish PKK, the Peruvian Tupac Amaru Revolutionary Movement (MRTA), and the Palestine Liberation Front (PLF). In 1991, British and French courts accused Libyan intelligence agents of being behind the 1988 bombing of Pan Am flight 103 over Lockerbie, Scotland, in which 270 people died.

Iraq is another dictatorship that uses terror to repress internal dissent. Saddam Hussein has also made extensive use of terrorism as part of his foreign policy. In the 1970s, Iraq sponsored a variety of Palestinian terrorist groups whom it encouraged to mount attacks on Syria, and it hosts the anti-Iranian People's Fighters, which it encourages to carry out attacks inside Iran. Over the years, the targets of Iraqi-sponsored terrorism have included Palestinian leaders, Syrians, Israelis, Iranians, and Americans. In 1991, Iraq sponsored a number of attacks against American targets in response to the U.S. conventional military incursion in Desert Storm, but most were frustrated by tight security. Iraq continues to maintain contact with groups such as the ANO and the PLF.

COMMUNIST SPONSORSHIP OF TERRORISTS

The former Soviet Union and its client states in Eastern Europe supported a variety of revolutionaries during the Cold War. The extent of such support was a topic of much debate at the time. Some Western analysts alleged that the Soviet Union gave extensive aid to terrorist groups in Europe, the Middle East, and Latin America in order to destabilize pro-Western governments. The Soviet authorities, though admitting they supported revolutionary groups, condemned acts of terrorism. However, the release of communist East German secret police (Stasi) documents, after the reunification of Germany in 1990, provided evidence of the aid that the East German intelligence services (presumably with the full knowledge of the Soviets) had given to terrorist groups operating in West Germany, notably the Baader-Meinhof Gang. This aid involved providing training and information, as well as safe havens. After the reunification of Germany, former members of the Baader-Meinhof Gang were found living in East Germany.

Communist North Korea has often used terrorism against South Korean targets, though it has normally used its own agents rather than proxy groups. It has, however, sponsored the Philippines-based New People's Army (NPA). In 1991, a reconciliation agreement was reached with South Korea in which North Korea agreed to end paramilitary attacks on the south. North Korean agents have nevertheless continued to operate in the south.

Cuba has reduced its support for leftist revolutionary groups in Latin America in recent years, but in the past it gave aid to revolutionary groups who sometimes used terrorism: these included the Chilean Manuel Rodriguez Patriotic Front (MRPF), and the El Salvadoran Farabundo Martí Liberation Front (FMLN).

WESTERN SPONSORS OF TERRORISM

The U.S., like most other sponsors of terrorism, claims to have clean hands. Senate hearings in the 1970s, however, discovered that the Central Intelligence Agency (CIA) had organized several plots to assassinate foreign political leaders, notably Fidel Castro. In addition, the U.S. has provided aid to insurgent groups that have practiced terrorism. The leading examples in the 1980s were the Nicaraguan Contras fighting the Sandinista government and the Afghan guerrillas fighting the Soviets. Both groups used terrorism and assassinations as tactics in their struggles. The CIA provided both groups with shipments of arms, financial aid, and military training.

Israel has been involved in sponsoring terrorist groups in Lebanon. In its struggle against Palestinian and Shiite terrorists, Israel generally relied on assassinations carried out by its special forces or on military reprisals, but also provided arms, training, and military assistance to local militias such as the right-wing Phalange. Like other militias involved in Lebanon's civil war, the Phalange carried out numerous terrorist attacks. The most notorious was the massacre of Palestinian civilians at the Sabra and Chatila refugee camps near Beirut in 1982.

Numerous other states have sponsored terrorism abroad in conjunction with their foreign policy goals, though it has often been hard to establish a direct link. India, for example, has accused Pakistan of sponsoring Kashmiri rebels who use terrorism in addition to guerrilla warfare as part of their campaign. The association of South Africa (during the Apartheid era) with terrorist movements in such neighboring states as Mozambique. The RENAMO organization, in particular, was a South African-backed group that carried out large-scale atrocities in Mozambique in an attempt to destabilize the Marxist government there.

THE MECHANICS OF SUPPORT

Sponsorship of terrorism can be graded from limited support to full sponsorship or even control. A state can, for example, support a terrorist group by using its media to encourage and applaud particular operations. Another form of limited support is to refuse to extradite an accused terrorist. At the other extreme, a sponsoring state may be closely involved in planning and controlling specific terrorist acts. A common middle ground is for sympathetic states to give military assistance to insurgent groups whom they know also engage in terrorism.

The specific types of support that may be given to terrorists include intelligence support, training (basic military as well as specialized terrorist), and use of the state's diplomatic network. Material support may include the provision of high technology, weapons and explosives, logistic assets, and transportation. A state may also permit the use of its own territory. Some of the main sponsors of terrorism in recent years – Syria, Iraq, Libya, and Iran – have given what amounts to across-the-board support to terrorist groups or individual agents. These countries have allowed terrorists to operate paramilitary training camps, political offices, and social institutions on their territories.

Some sponsoring states have also allowed access to their diplomatic networks overseas. In many cases, a diplomatic pouch has been used to smuggle arms that

Soviet rocket-launcher supplied to the Provisional IRA by the Libyan regime of Colonel Qaddafi.

are then passed onto terrorists working on behalf of the sponsor. Some terrorists have been issued with diplomatic passports, while others have been given false ones by their host country. By these means terrorists have been able to travel freely worldwide. At times terrorists have turned to a friendly embassy when in trouble. For instance, in 1986, a Syrian agent fled to the the Syrian embassy in London when his attempt to plant a bomb on an El Al aircraft at Heathrow airport was discovered.

Technical experts of the sponsoring state are often involved in aspects of terrorist operations. Reports indicate that the massive truck bombs that devastated U.S. facilities in Lebanon in the 1980s were prepared with assistance from Syrian explosives experts. Sponsoring states have also been useful sources of weapons and explosives, even though terrorist groups can obtain many weapons on the black market. In 1985 and 1986, the Provisional IRA received some 120 tons of arms and explosives from Libya.

TRAINING ASSISTANCE

The training of professional terrorists is often hard to distinguish from that of guerrillas. When states assist in such training, often the most useful step is in providing basic and advanced military training for recruits. Sometimes, if the sponsored group is virtually part of the state's armed forces, as is the case with the People's Fighters in Iraq, then the group's military training is carried out alongside that of army troops. For example, until the late 1980s, Palestinians attended regular military courses in the Soviet Union.

More specific instruction has also been provided to sponsored groups. After the reunification of Germany in 1990, evidence emerged that Arab and leftist terrorists had received extensive training in East German camps. In these facilities, recruits were trained in the use of small arms and explosives, in intelligence-gathering, surveillance, and mission-planning techniques. Cuba issued a handbook to Latin American revolutionaries giving instructions on sabotage techniques against vehicles, telephone and electrical systems, and gasoline supplies. The CIA issued similar instructions to the Nicaraguan Contras in its own handbook on covert warfare. In addition it gave instructions on how best to "neutralize" representatives of the ruling establishment.

In a world increasingly dominated by a single superpower, some smaller states outside the Western mainstream will continue to give covert support to terrorist groups in a bid to influence international affairs. In this climate, international cooperation in the fight against terrorism will be vital to the future.

Andrew Rathmell

SEE ALSO: DOMESTIC VERSUS INTERNATIONAL TERRORISM; TERROR IN LEBANON 1980-1987; LIBYAN SPONSORSHIP OF TERRORISM; IRAQI SPONSORSHIP OF TERRORISM; IRANIAN SPONSORSHIP OF TERRORISM; TERROR IN AFGHANISTAN; RED ARMY FACTION: THE BAADER-MEINHOF GANG.

FURTHER READING

- George, Alexander, ed. *Western State Terrorism.* Cambridge: Polity Press, and New York: Routledge, Chapman, and Hall, 1991.
- Kidder, Rushworth. "State-Sponsored Terrorism," in *The Christian Science Monitor* (May 14, 1986): 11-24.
- Murphy, John Francis. *State Support for International Terrorism.* Boulder, CO: Westview Press, and London: Mansell, 1989.
- Stohl, Michael, and George A. Lopez, eds. *Terrible Beyond Endurance? The Foreign Policy of State Terrorism.* London and New York: Greenwood Press, 1988.

SADDAM HUSSEIN'S TERROR IN KURDISTAN

The state terrorism of Saddam Hussein's regime, in power in Iraq since 1979, has been most brutally demonstrated in its treatment of the Iraqi Kurds. In 1987, the regime launched a campaign of terror involving massacres and mass deportations of civilians, which human rights groups have labeled a policy of attempted genocide. The campaign was the regime's attempt to achieve a "final solution" to the problem posed by the Kurdish population's desire for independence which has destabilized Iraq since its foundation after World War I.

THE KURDS

There are more than 20 million Kurds living in the mountainous areas covering northern Iraq, northeastern Syria, northwestern Iran, and southeastern Turkey. They enjoyed autonomy under the Ottoman empire until the late nineteenth century. In the 1920 Treaty of Sèvres, signed during the Paris Peace Conference after World War I, the Western allies promised the Kurds an independent state.

The territorial ambitions of Turkey, Iraq, and Syria, however, ended these hopes. Ever since, Kurds in all of these countries have been denied their national rights and, to a greater or lesser extent, have been repressed by each of these governments. Kurdish nationalism has been strongest in Iraq, and since the 1930s, Kurdish guerrillas (*peshmerga*) have frequently clashed with the Iraqi army. In the late 1960s, widespread fighting occurred. Despite a peace treaty with Baghdad, the Kurds, encouraged by Iran and the United States, rose up again in the 1970s, and the fighting intensified. In 1975, Iran and the U.S. withdrew their support. The Iraqi army was able to crush the Kurds, and up to 250,000 Kurds were forcibly resettled by the Iraqi government. During the Iran–Iraq War (1980-88), Kurdish groups, with Iranian help, took the offensive and seized control over areas of northern Iraq. In July 1987, rival Kurdish groups formed the Iraqi Kurdistan Front (IKF) and launched successful offensives against the Iraqi army.

KEY FACTS

- More than 20 million Kurds live in Kurdistan, a region in the Middle East comprising parts of Syria, Iran, Turkey, and Iraq.
- The Iraqis first used chemical weapons against the Kurds in an air attack on settlements in the Suleimanieh region on April 15, 1987.
- On April 5, 1991, the UN Security Council passed Resolution 688 condemning Iraq's violations of Kurdish human rights.

SADDAM'S REPRESSION

Saddam Hussein responded to the Kurdish threat by implementing in 1988 a campaign, known by the Arabic codename *al-Anfal* ("spoils of battle"), which was more intense even than his previous policies of mass terror. By 1983, the regime had already been responsible for the disappearance of 8,000 members of the leading Kurdish Barzani clan. Between 1987 and 1989, the Iraqi army deported hundreds of thousands of civilians from northern Iraq and razed some 4,000 Kurdish villages. Whole areas of northern Iraq were declared free-fire zones, and their inhabitants were considered legitimate targets. Artillery bombardments, massacres, and attacks with chemical weapons were all used against Kurdish civilians. The most notorious incident occurred on March 16 and 17, 1988. The Iraqis bombed the Kurdish border town of Halabja with chemical weapons, and more than 6,000 civilians died.

It is estimated that around 180,000 Kurds were killed in total during the Anfal campaign. However, the numbers will never be established definitively, since

Popperfoto

Fighters of the pro-Baghdad KDP guard a checkpoint outside Irbil on September 15, 1996, from which they had earlier driven out their PUK rivals.

many individuals remain unaccounted for. The Iraqi offensive also forced hundreds of thousands of Kurdish refugees to flee to Iran and Turkey.

In March 1991, after coalition forces had driven the Iraqi army out of Kuwait and ended their occupation of that country, Kurdish guerrillas rose up against the Iraqi government and liberated much of Iraqi Kurdistan. Within two weeks, they controlled most of northern Iraq. However, the Iraqi army swiftly counter-attacked, forcing hundreds of thousands of Kurds to seek refuge in Turkey and more than 1.2 million to flee to Iran. In response to the suffering of the Kurds, the United States, Britain, and France together guaranteed them a "safe haven" in Iraqi Kurdistan. These countries mounted aerial patrols for their protection and began relief operations.

KDP VERSUS PUK

Despite this help from the Western coalition, Kurdish leaders were unable to transform this self-governing area into an independent state, in part because of disagreement between different Kurdish factions. Internal fighting between the main Kurdish groups, the Kurdistan Democratic Party (KDP) and Patriotic Union of Kurdistan (PUK), has claimed hundreds of lives since 1994.

At different times, successive Iraqi governments have either negotiated with the Kurds or fought them. Saddam Hussein has been no different, and he has often sought to exploit divisions between Kurdish leaders by alternately offering them concessions and then threatening violence. His unique contribution to the Kurdish condition has been an unparalleled use of repressive state terror. This has dual aims: to terrorize the Kurds into submission, and also to destroy the Kurdish communities of northern Iraq so that they can no longer form a cohesive national society opposed to his regime. In this, he has had a measure of success: the massacres and deportations that took place during the Anfal campaign changed the ethnic balance in Iraqi Kurdistan, since many deported Kurds were replaced by Arab families from other parts of Iraq.

Nonetheless, Saddam's terror did not succeed in obliterating the Kurdish determination to preserve their national culture and autonomy. It was evident, though, that without the Western military protection that began in 1991, Iraq's Kurds would be unable to resist effectively the force of the Iraqi army. In August 1996, an Iraqi force entered the Kurdish city of Irbil at the request of Massoud Barzani, the KDP leader, to help him defeat the rival PUK. Although the Iraqi troops have supposedly withdrawn, Saddam Hussein, with Barzani now his client, has increased his influence in the Kurdish enclave.

Andrew Rathmell

SEE ALSO: NATIONALIST TERRORISM; STATE VERSUS NON-STATE TERRORISM; KURDISH NATIONALIST TERRORISM.

FURTHER READING

- Black, George, Jemera Rone, and Joost Hiltermann. *Middle East Watch. Genocide in Iraq: The Anfal Campaign Against the Kurds.* New York: Human Rights Watch, 1993.
- Bulloch, John, and Harvey Morris. *No Friends but the Mountains: The Tragic History of the Kurds.* New York: Oxford University Press, and London: Viking, 1992.
- McDowall, David. *A Modern History of the Kurds.* London: Tauris, and New York: St. Martin's Press, 1996.

INDONESIAN TERROR IN EAST TIMOR

East Timor occupies the eastern half of a large island in the Indonesian archipelago. Since 1975, it has been the victim of one of the most brutal terror campaigns perpetrated by one state against the people of another. For centuries, East Timor was a poor and neglected Portuguese colony. In 1974, the Portuguese Armed Forces Movement overthrew the Caetano regime in Portugal, and began to withdraw from its colonies. Political parties were organized in East Timor, resulting in a coalition of the two main parties – the East Timorese Democratic Union (UDT) and the Revolutionary Front for East Timorese Liberation and Independence (FRETILIN) – to prepare for independence. The Indonesian government tried to destabilize this coalition, and sponsored a coup attempt in August 1975 by a UDT faction. During this, the Portuguese withdrew, leaving FRETILIN in *de facto* control after its defeat of UDT forces.

INDONESIA INVADES EAST TIMOR

Unwilling to tolerate the presence of a potential independent state within its sphere of influence, Indonesia invaded East Timor and set up a puppet regime. FRETILIN forces withdrew into the mountainous region in the center of the island, where they organized the Timorese resistance. Indonesia, frustrated by its inability to achieve a lasting victory over the guerrillas, began its reign of terror over the people of East Timor.

The brutality of the occupation was evident from the start. Paratroops shot people dead in the streets of East Timor's capital, Dili, while many Timorese were rounded up and executed. The Indonesians razed villages and sometimes used chemical weapons. In March 1978, Lopez Cruz, vice-chairman of the East Timor puppet government, admitted that 60,000 people had been killed in the months following the invasion.

In September 1977, the Indonesian military adopted a new approach to suppressing nationalist resistance. The army launched attacks against guerrilla-held areas in the western, central, and southern areas of East Timor. Inhabited areas were subjected to saturation bombing accompanied by the defoliation of trees and plants. People were pushed into increasingly confined areas. Deprived of food, they were forced down to the lower reaches of the mountainous interior, where Indonesian troops awaited them.

Throughout 1978, many massacres were reported. Those who escaped death were placed in newly created resettlement camps. Internees were prevented from traveling beyond camp boundaries. As a result, they could neither cultivate nor harvest crops and thus became dependent on the Indonesians for food and also for medical supplies. The Timorese received little of either, and starvation became widespread.

The FRETILIN guerrillas, however, persisted with their struggle against the occupiers. The Indonesian army adopted a new tactic of using noncombatants to flush out resistance groups. Operation Final Cleansing involved taking men between the ages of 16 and 60 from villages, organizing them into small groups, and forcing them to walk in front of soldiers searching the countryside for guerrillas. The latter had to choose between surrendering or firing on their own people. This tactic continued to be used into the mid-1990s.

KEY FACTS

- Relief workers estimated that 100,000 people were killed between 1975 and 1979.
- By 1979, Indonesian forces had placed some 300,000 people in resettlement camps.
- Bishop Carlos Ximenes Belo and José Ramos-Horta (East Timor's external representative) were awarded the 1996 Nobel Peace Prize.

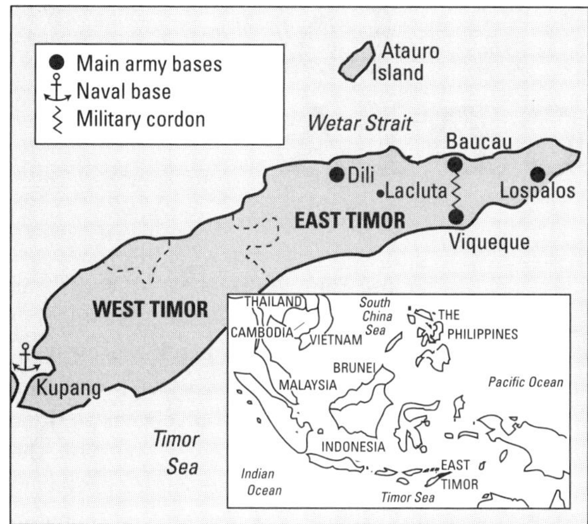

Indonesia's massive military presence in East Timor included army and naval bases, and a cordon to prevent the free movement of guerrillas and civilians.

The Indonesian government also created and perpetuated a climate of terror and intimidation in the areas it controlled, notably in the two main towns, Dili and Baucau. People would be arbitrarily detained on the streets or in their homes at night. They were then interrogated at the local subdistrict military command, for days, weeks, or even months. Some suspects were then released, but others simply disappeared without trace. During the early years, the military focused on supporters of the nationalists and on educated people – academics, doctors, and engineers among them. Particular sites were designated as killing grounds, where people would be murdered in groups.

The use of intimidation and torture is further evidence of the military's aim of terrorizing the population into submission. Imprisonment has been both arbitrary and indeterminate. There have been cases of imprisonment for refusal to give troops food, or for straying too far from a resettlement village. Reports indicate that at any time during detention, prisoners could be taken out of their cells by troops and killed. Prisoners were often used as labor on military projects, and many were forced to become servants to officers.

The Indonesian authorities officially sanctioned the use of torture throughout East Timor. Army guidelines issued in July 1982 outlined a four-step program of procedures: preliminary interrogation, classification of suspects, main interrogation, and decision to execute, imprison, or release. Torture was systematic and extreme. Beginning with beatings, burning with cigarettes, and sexual abuse, the army and police progressed through electric-shock treatment, to systematic cutting of the skin, and even crucifixion with nails.

In 1991, East Timor began to experience *ninja* death squads. These men, dressed in black, masked, and armed with knives, attacked people on the street at night, stoned livestock, and burned houses. Although the military deny any involvement with these gangs, many of the Dili population saw them as linked to Indonesian special forces units. Most of the victims of these gangs have been either pro-independence activists, or relatives of known activists.

RESISTANCE TO TERROR

The people of East Timor resisted Indonesia's terror policies in a number of ways. In the early years of the occupation, their main effort was to provide food, shelter, and cover to the guerrillas. Additionally, the Catholic church in East Timor has played an increasingly important role.

Priests have recorded human rights abuses, protected people from military intimidation and arrest, and mediated in tense confrontations between youths and soldiers. Through its bishop, Carlos Ximenes Belo, the church in East Timor publicized abuses and, together with East Timorese refugees, worked hard to keep the cause of East Timor in the world's headlines and on the diplomatic agenda. As a result, the United States, the United Nations, and Portugal have actively pursued discussions with the Indonesian government to find a solution to end Indonesia's brutal occupation.

John G. Taylor

SEE ALSO: TERROR CAMPAIGNS IN PORTUGUESE AFRICA; STATE-SPONSORED TERRORISM.

FURTHER READING

- Carey, Peter, and G. Carter-Bentley. *East Timor at the Crossroads: The Forging of a Nation.* London: Cassell, 1995.
- Taylor, John G. *Indonesia's Forgotten War: The Hidden History of East Timor.* London and Atlantic Highlands, NJ: Zed Books, 1991.

TERROR IN CAMBODIA

More than 1.7 million people died in the killing fields of Cambodia between 1975 and 1978. The country had already been destabilized by the Vietnam War, and extensively damaged by U.S. bombing, when the fanatical Pol Pot seized power and began a murderous experiment to turn Cambodia back to "Year Zero." Under his reign of terror, summary execution, starvation, and disease consumed more than one-fifth of the country's 8 million people.

During the 1940s, Pol Pot, whose real name is Saloth Sar, joined the anti-French resistance in colonial Indochina led by Ho Chi Minh. Then, in 1946, he joined the Cambodian Communist Party (CPK). During the French colonial war in Indochina (1946–54), the CPK, backed by Vietnamese communist military support, infiltrated the Cambodian nationalist movement. However, the communist ascendancy in Cambodia was halted by the signing of the Geneva Accords in 1954, which ended the war.

The communist movement was repressed by the Kingdom of Cambodia's hereditary ruler, Prince Norodom Sihanouk, who contemptuously dismissed the CPK as the "Khmer Rouge" – or Red Khmer (the Khmers are the indigenous people of Cambodia). Meanwhile, the party was purged from within. Then, in 1962, CPK leader Tou Samoth disappeared on his way back from a trip to Hanoi, and Pol Pot seized control of the party. In March 1970, while Sihanouk was away on vacation in France, Marshal Lon Nol seized power. Lon Nol was backed by the U.S., which urged him to drive the North Vietnamese army (NVA) out of the Cambodian strongholds they were using to prosecute the war in South Vietnam. However, the NVA counterattacked and by the late summer of 1970, it controlled half the country.

KEY FACTS

- Some 21 percent of the population of Cambodia was wiped out by summary execution, disease, and starvation under Pol Pot's murderous regime.
- Over 75 percent of the Cambodian communist party's original membership was slaughtered in recurrent purges.
- Half of the country's ethnic Chinese and third of the Islamic Cham perished.
- A quarter of the Khmer evacuated from the cities died, along with 15 percent of the peasantry.

BEHIND VIETNAMESE LINES

Remaining covert, the CPK expanded its control behind Vietnamese lines. It also dominated the exiled Sihanouk's united front against Lon Nol's nationalist Khmer Republic. By 1973, Pol Pot felt strong enough to strike out on his own with an intensification of the "class struggle." Those who opposed the formation of agricultural cooperatives in CPK-controlled areas were branded "feudalists" or "capitalists" and killed. Cambodian communists trained in Vietnam were dubbed "Vietnamese lackeys," and they, too, were arrested and killed. Chinese, Islamic Cham (people of Malay extract), and other ethnic minorities were excluded from power, and the Khmer peasantry, known as "base people," were elevated.

Lon Nol's ill-trained and corrupt army was no match for the youthful fanatics of the CPK, but the communists were held at bay by U.S. air power, which turned its full force on Cambodia in January 1973, after the signing of the Paris Peace Accords ended the bombing of Vietnam and Laos. However, when the U.S. bombing was halted at the beginning of 1974, the CPK were in shelling range of Cambodia's capital, Phnom Penh, and a prolonged siege of the city began.

Despite his U.S. backing and an army that outnumbered the enemy, Lon Nol fled on April 1, 1975. Fifteen days later the fighting was over and, on the morning of April 17, Pol Pot's army of teenage guerrillas marched into Phnom Penh. Pol Pot had promised that only a handful of "supertraitors" would be killed. Instead, he

Popperfoto

The skulls of victims of the Cambodian Communist party (CPK) found in mass graves near Phnom Penh, Cambodia.

secretly exterminated all former Khmer Republic civil servants and military personnel. When they took over Phnom Penh, the CPK began a lethal ideological experiment. Cambodia, renamed Kampuchea, was to return to Year Zero and to be rebuilt from scratch.

The population of Phnom Penh – swelled by refugees to four times its prewar number – was marched out of the city. Those people who refused to go were killed. For the aged and the sick, this evacuation amounted to a death march. Those who survived had to "reeducate" themselves through back-breaking labor. "Base people" killed any of these so-called "new people" who faltered or complained.

Religion was outlawed and Cham Muslims were massacred, while Marxists and middle-ranking communist cadres who opposed Pol Pot "disappeared." Pol Pot was left with a free hand to intensify his collectivization policies. The result was starvation, epidemics, and the murder of more "new people," both Chinese and Cham.

In early 1977, Pol Pot ordered the systematic extermination of all CPK members who had a middle-class or educated background. A secret security apparatus – S-21 – tortured fellow party members into confessing that they were CIA agents. Peasant leaders were summarily put to death after "confessing" to being agents of the Vietnamese.

CADRES FLEE

In 1978, the purges culminated in a series of massacres in Cambodia's Eastern Zone, one of the seven major administrative areas set up by Pol Pot and one of Cambodia's most prosperous regions. Pol Pot had long feared that opposition might coalesce around the zone chief there, Sao Pheum, and an army was sent to surround Pheum's headquarters. Pheum committed suicide, and Pol Pot slaughtered the local population – more than 100,000 people were butchered. He also ordered military incursions into Vietnam, bordering the Eastern Zone, and thousands of Vietnamese peasants were murdered. To maintain control, Pol Pot set the zone chiefs against each other, favoring Ta Mok, leader of the Southwest Zone and the country's most efficient killer. Nevertheless, by late 1978, Ta Mok's cadres were also marked for extermination. No one was safe.

Former CPK commissar Heng Samrin organized the Kampuchean National United Front for National Salvation in exile. Some 20,000 United Front troops invaded, along with 100,000 Vietnamese. On January 7, 1979, Samrin declared the People's Republic of Kampuchea, supplanting the CPK's Democratic Kampuchea. Pol Pot took to the jungles where, with the backing of the U.S., Chinese, and British governments, he and his cohorts have exercised considerable political influence ever since. However, in early 1996, there were rumors that Pol Pot was dead.

Nigel Cawthorne

SEE ALSO: TERROR AGAINST THE FRENCH IN INDOCHINA; STATE VERSUS NON-STATE TERRORISM; TERROR IN THE VIETNAM WAR.

FURTHER READING

- Chandler, David P. *Brother Number One: A Political Biography of Pol Pot.* Boulder: Westview, 1992.
- Kiernan, Ben. *The Pol Pot Regime: Race, Power and Genocide in Cambodia Under the Khmer Rouge.* New Haven: Yale University Press, 1996.
- Yathay, Pin. *Stay Alive My Son.* London: Bloomsbury, and New York: Free Press, 1987.

TERROR IN IDI AMIN'S UGANDA

General Idi Amin Dada's bloody reign of terror in Uganda began in 1971 and lasted eight years. Only a few years earlier, in 1962, the country had gained its independence after 62 years of British rule. Although exact numbers are hard to verify, it has been estimated that more than 300,000 Ugandans were killed during Amin's dictatorship. Most were victims of terror. People were imprisoned, tortured, and murdered, often on the personal orders of Amin himself. He used the army as an instrument of terror to intimidate his own people, especially those who belonged to tribes other than his own. Tribal warfare has characterized the recent history of many African states – Zimbabwe, the Central African Republic, and Rwanda, for example – but Amin's regime stands out for the sheer scale of its brutality.

AMIN COMES TO POWER

Major-General Idi Amin Dada, commander-in-chief of the Ugandan army, and once a sergeant in the British army's King's African Rifles, overthrew President Milton Obote on January 25, 1971, while Obote was out of the country. The former army boxing champion accused Obote of corruption, tribalism, and of lining the pockets of his favorites at the expense of the largely poor population. Amin promised free elections, an end to Obote's martial law, and the release of political prisoners jailed on trumped-up or flimsy charges.

Unsurprisingly, Amin's coup was popular with many Ugandans. Fewer than 100 casualties were reported during sporadic fighting in the capital, Kampala. The coup was equally popular with many Western nations suspicious of Obote's recent left-wing economic reforms. Amin, a member of the small Muslim Kakwa tribal group of northern Uganda, swiftly moved to guarantee the future of his regime. Pro-Obote officers, mostly from the Lango and Acholi tribes, were purged. An estimated 1,000 soldiers, many badly beaten, were seen being transported to Kampala's notorious Luzira prison. Less than a month later, Amin promoted himself to general, proclaimed himself president, and put off the promised elections for five years until the country was "calm." He then drafted into the army supporters on whose loyalty he could rely, particularly Sudanese, Palestinians, and Nubians. Amin then tripled the strength of his army by forcing the poor to enlist.

KEY FACTS

- Amin set up two secret police bodies: the State Research Bureau and the Public Safety Unit. Agents had the power to detain, torture, and murder.
- Amin reigned as heavyweight boxing champion of Uganda during his dictatorship. Fighters who challenged him in the ring invariably disappeared.

250,000 DEAD IN THREE YEARS

Although Amin released 55 political prisoners on coming to power, hundreds of thousands met a grisly death instead – 250,000 by June 1974. Many were members of rival tribes. The Asian minority also came in for persecution, although they escaped with their lives, if not much else. Accusing the 50,000 prosperous Ugandan Asians of "sabotaging the economy," Amin expelled them all to Britain in the fall of 1972. Soldiers assaulted them and confiscated their possessions even as they mounted the aircraft steps.

Initially, Amin curried favor with several Western or pro-Western powers to equip his forces. Weapons worth several million dollars were imported from Britain and Israel, following a visit to both countries by Amin in July 1971. The international community tended to regard Amin as something of a buffoon. Stunts such as launching a "Save Britain" fund in 1973, to help Britain out of an economic crisis, persuaded some governments that he posed no threat.

However, Amin was forging links with anti-Western groups, such as the Palestinian Liberation Organization (PLO). Then, as relations with the West deteriorated during 1973-75, Amin turned to the Soviet Union for arms. Amin's pro-Palestinian stance led terrorists from the

Hulton Getty Picture Collection

General Idi Amin's genial manner concealed an insane brutality. Under his rule, between 250,000 and 350,000 people were killed.

extremist Popular Front for the Liberation of Palestine (PFLP), aided by the German Baader-Meinhof Gang, to land a hijacked El Al Airbus at Kampala's Entebbe airport on June 29, 1976. When Israeli commandos flew in to free the hostages on July 4, Amin deployed his troops to defend the terrorists. In response to the Israeli action, Amin's troops murdered one of the hostages, Dora Bloch, in an Entebbe hospital.

Meanwhile, Amin's grip on Uganda was strengthened by the formation of the State Research Bureau and the Public Safety Unit. These outfits used intimidation, torture, and murder to cow the population and liquidate opponents. Informers throughout the society reported to their superiors, who acted with extreme ruthlessness on the least evidence. Bodies of victims were found almost daily dumped in Lake Victoria or in the Namanve Forest.

Amin also replaced the independent judiciary with military tribunals, which sat in judgment on all major violations of the law. Policing was dominated by army officers, who controlled day-to-day police activities. By controlling the army, destroying the independence of the courts, and creating a brutal apparatus of internal state security, Amin limited organized dissent. He also took economic measures, such as nationalizing over 40 foreign-owned businesses, ostensibly to gain the support of the people. In reality, the "reforms" were just a smoke-screen behind which Amin and his supporters were able to line their pockets. Embezzlement and inefficiency crippled the Ugandan economy: the output of raw materials, principally copper, fell dramatically, and inflation rocketed.

THE TIDE TURNS

By 1977, the economy went into free fall and what little popular support Amin enjoyed evaporated. There was also discontent within the armed forces. A group of noncommissioned officers protested at all positions of power being held by members of Amin's Kakwa tribe. Retribution was swift. Bodies of dissenters were soon seen floating down the Malaba River on the border with Kenya. About 130 people were massacred, and the period of unrest led to the notorious political murder of Kampala's Anglican bishop, Janana Luwum, on February 16, 1977.

Amin's regime came to an end in April, 1979, following a failed attempt to invade neighboring Tanzania. The Tanzanian armed forces, supported by exiles of the Uganda Liberation Front counterattacked. Amin's troops deserted or surrendered in droves, despite last-minute support from 2,000 Libyan troops.

Amin pursued no ideological goals and supported no known cause during his reign of terror. Neither was he called to account for his crimes. On fleeing Uganda, he was sheltered by sympathetic countries, and he now resides in Saudi Arabia.

Ian Westwell

SEE ALSO: TERROR IN ZIMBABWE (RHODESIA); TERROR IN RWANDA; RED ARMY FACTION: THE BAADER-MEINHOF GANG; SADDAM HUSSEIN'S TERROR IN KURDISTAN.

FURTHER READING

- Avirgan, Tony, and Martha Honey. *War in Uganda, the Legacy of Idi Amin.* Westport, CT: Lawrence Hill, 1982.
- Kyemba, Henry. *State of Blood: The Inside Story of Idi Amin.* London: Corgi, and New York: Ace Books, 1977.
- Pirouet, Louise M. *Historical Dictionary of Uganda.* Metuchen, NY: Scarecrow Press, 1995.

CHAPTER TWENTY-TWO

International Cooperation Against Terrorism

The nature and substance of the collective international response to terrorism is far from well defined, although domestic intelligence organizations are in regular contact. The dissemination of valuable information on the terrorists does occur and, on a more obviously practical level, anti-terrorist units have combined to deal with a specific terrorist act. However, because certain countries either harbor or sponsor terrorist groups, it remains extremely difficult to present a united worldwide front to deal with terrorism.

INTERNATIONAL COOPERATION AGAINST TERRORISM

The fight against international terrorism requires international cooperation. There have been innumerable transnational conventions to try to formalize strategies at the government level, but governments remain too hamstrung by self-interest to cooperate effectively. The most effective anti-terrorist collaborations are the informal, everyday links between police forces and intelligence services.

In an era of globalization and increasing interdependence, almost every significant terrorist campaign has an international dimension, even when it is mounting a challenge to a specific government within its own territory. For example, the Provisional Irish Republican Army (IRA), which is struggling to force the British government out of Northern Ireland, uses the Republic of Ireland as a safe haven, as an organizational base, and as a source of recruits. The Provisional IRA raises funds in the United States, and it buys weapons on the international arms market. It supplements its armory with weapons it receives as gifts from sympathetic states such as Libya.

SUMMARY

- In 1937, the League of Nations proscribed international terrorism, and tried to set up an International Criminal Court.
- In 1976, the European Economic Union (EEC; later the European Union) set up the TREVI structure to coordinate the efforts of European states against terrorism.
- In 1977, the Council of Europe Convention on the Suppression of Terrorism attempted to clarify the rules of extradition, defining terrorist acts as common crimes.
- In 1992, French and Spanish police arrested over 200 Basque terrorists, the culmination of 13 years' collaboration.
- In 1996, ministers of the G7 group of major industrial countries held a summit in France to refocus strategies on the upsurge of terrorism. International cooperation, however, has yet to prove itself effective in the effort to quell terrorism.

THINKING GLOBALLY

There were attempts to deal with terrorism on a global basis as early as the 1930s. In 1937, the League of Nations, forerunner of the United Nations (UN), drafted two conventions. The first proscribed acts of terrorism, which included attempts on the life of heads of state or their spouses and other government representatives. The first convention also prohibited acts of international terrorism involving injury to persons or damage to property committed by citizens of one state against citizens of another. The other convention set up an International Criminal Court, with jurisdiction over terrorist crimes. These bold measures, however, never came into effect – only 13 states had ratified the conventions before World War II broke out in 1939.

The UN was able to build on the work of the League of Nations in the 1940s and 1950s. The UN's Universal Declaration of Human Rights, in addition to guaranteeing the right to life, liberty, and the security of the person, also states that "no one shall be subjected to torture or to cruel, inhuman, or degrading treatment or punishment." The right to enjoy "freedom from fear" is stressed in the preambles of both the International Covenant on Economic, Social, and Cultural Rights, and the International Covenant on Civil and Political Rights. The UN Convention on the Prevention and

Hulton Getty Picture Collection

A memorial service to the Israeli athletes who died in the Munich Olympics massacre of 1972. The worldwide outrage at the massacre fueled calls for international cooperation against terrorism.

Punishment of the Crime of Genocide forbids the targeting of members of a national, racial, ethnic, or religious group, killing them, or causing them serious bodily harm or severe mental distress. This amounts to an explicit prohibition of terrorist violence, whether committed by states, factions, or individuals. In addition, the UN Declaration on Principles of International Law, calls upon states to refrain from "organizing, assisting, or participating in acts of civil strife or terrorist acts in another State."

However, there is a fatal ambivalence in the UN's treatment of the whole question of politically motivated violence. The Declaration on Principles of International Law spells out that all states have a "duty to promote...realization of the principle [of self-determination]...in order to bring a speedy end to colonialism..." and that "every state has the duty to refrain from any forcible action which deprives peoples...of their right to self-determination." The declaration continues: "In their actions against, and resistance to, such forcible action in pursuit of their right to self-determination, such peoples are entitled to seek and to receive support."

A MATTER OF INTERPRETATION

Many take these clauses to mean not only that the UN legitimizes any struggle undertaken in the name of the principle of national liberation, but also that it condones international support for such struggles. This can place the UN in an awkward, if not untenable, position. Israel, for example, as a UN member state, is accorded full "sovereign equality" and protection of that sovereignty. Simultaneously, other member states of the UN can claim that they are fully entitled to arm and support movements dedicated to the liquidation of Israel, on the ground that they are merely supporting a legitimate national liberation struggle.

This ambiguity is clearly reflected in the UN's faltering attempts to deal with terrorism. After the Munich Olympics massacre in 1972, UN Secretary General Kurt Waldheim requested that the UN deal with the menace of international terrorism. Subsequent discussion revealed a clear split between those states wishing the UN to condemn and act against factional terrorism, and those states wanting to legalize such terrorism as a justifiable means of struggle. In December 1973, the UN

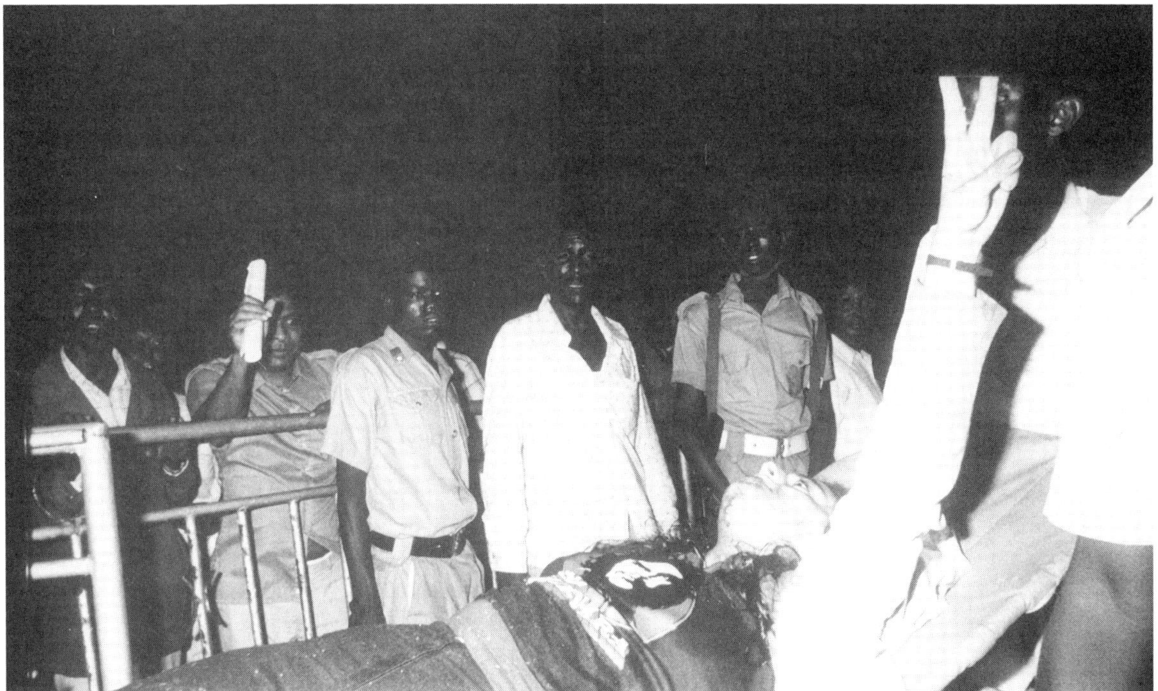

Frank Spooner Pictures

The Mogadishu hijacking, October 13, 1977. The successful outcome of the counterterrorist operation, which resulted in the freeing of the passengers, was in part due to close cooperation between members of the British SAS and the West German GSG-9.

General Assembly did, however, agree to adopt a Convention on the Prevention and Punishment of Crimes against Internationally Protected Persons, including Diplomatic Agents, and this has now acquired sufficient ratifications by member states to come into force. There was also progress in the area of hijackings of aircraft. The 1970 Hague Convention requires signatories either to extradite apprehended hijackers to their country of origin, or to prosecute them under the judicial code of their native state. The Montreal Convention of 1971 extended the scope of international law to encompass sabotage and attacks on airports and grounded aircraft.

Substantial progress has been made in the field of international cooperation in Western Europe, where there are high levels of terrorist attacks. The European Union (EU) ministers of the interior, and the police forces and intelligence services of the member states, have since 1976 developed a machinery for discussion and practical multilateral cooperation. However, the most ambitious attempt at European cooperation on terrorism at the judicial level occured in 1977. The Council of Europe, a body of 23 European countries, was set up in 1949 to achieve greater mutual unity, to facilitate social and economic progress, and to maintain human rights and basic fundamental freedoms. The Council of Europe's Convention on the Suppression of Terrorism, was signed by 17 of its member countries in January 1977. Ratifying states agreed to exclude the whole range of major terrorist offenses (such as assassination, hostage-taking, and hijacking) from the political offense exception clauses that had been previously used to justify a state's refusal to extradite terrorists.

GOOD NEIGHBORS

One of the most effective methods of cooperation against terrorism takes the form of bilateral agreements between neighboring states. A notable instance of this occurred in the U.S.-Cuba Hijack Pact of February 1973, in which both governments agreed to return hijacked aircraft, crews, passengers, and hijackers. Cuba did insist on a caveat enabling it to refuse to return terrorists affiliated with a national liberation movement recognized by Cuba.

An even more unlikely example of partnership was the cooperation in 1977 between Somalia and West Germany in the operation to rescue the Lufthansa hostages held at Mogadishu. Somalia, after all, was a Marxist regime that had previously been used as a base by terrorists organizing the Entebbe hijacking, which involved the West German Baader-Meinhof Gang. Yet, encouraged by the prospect of economic assistance, Somalia rendered a valuable service by allowing the German rescue squad GSG-9 and the British SAS to operate on its territory.

In Europe, there is some encouraging recent evidence that bilateral security cooperation is being developed in areas particularly hard hit by terrorist violence over the past decade. The joint effort of France and Spain to combat Basque nationalist terrorism is an example in which counterterrorist collaboration has been highly effective.

French border country had long been regarded as a valuable sanctuary and launchpad for Basque nationalist (ETA) terrorism. The French authorities began to warm to the notion of cooperation when terrorism began to spill over to their side of the border. Most worrying of all was the fact that an extreme right-wing death squad calling itself the Anti-Terrorist Liberation Group (GAL) was stepping up its assassination attacks against Basque targets on French territory. The French strengthened their controls on the frontier and began to deport and extradite ETA activists to Spain. In January 1979, France abolished refugee status for Spanish nationals in France, on the grounds that Spain, as a democracy, no longer had political refugees. Almost simultaneously, 13 Spanish Basques living near the Spanish border were banished to a remote area in eastern France.

This cooperation has led to the dismantling of ETA's network in France. In 1991, 40 ETA members, both Spanish and French, were arrested in France, and the following year the French and Spanish police arrested three terrorist leaders and 199 terrorists and collaborators, thereby totally disrupting ETA's financial and logistical support.

Extradition is where one state surrenders an alleged criminal to another. Extradition proceedings succeed in the cases of only a small minority of terrorist suspects. Instead, many states use deportation as a form of disguised extradition. Because deportation is a civil rather than a criminal proceeding, it merely shifts the problem to another country, and does not ensure that a suspected terrorist is brought to justice. A far more desirable course is for states to attempt to standardize their criminal codes and procedures.

PROFESSIONALS COOPERATE

Far and away the most important advances in international cooperation against terrorism among the democratic countries have taken place at police and intelligence service levels. In 1976, the EU established TREVI (International Terrorism, Radicalism, Extremism, and Violence), a valuable structure for exchanging intelligence and coordinating EU efforts against crime and terrorism. It provides an ideal mechanism for developing informal collaboration and exchanges of information between national police and intelligence officials.

Police and intelligence cooperation is generally most effective at the bilateral level, when there is a considerable degree of personal trust between the officials involved. As a means of fostering a culture of international cooperation, the encouraging of police officers and officials to work with friendly countries has proved most effective in building up a network of informal international links.

Among EU member states, the need for enhanced cooperation on security issues, including terrorism, was given added urgency with the Single European Act of 1986, which aimed at the establishment of a European internal market. In preparation for this, the governments of Germany, France, Belgium, the Netherlands, and Luxembourg signed the Schengen Agreement (which came into effect in 1994), committing them to dismantling controls on their common borders. Their plan was to enable free movement of persons, goods, and services across their mutual borders, while simultaneously strengthening their external borders. This created concerns over controlling trans-European terrorist activity. During the 1970s, collaboration between terrorist groups such as the Baader-Meinhof Gang and the Italian Red Brigades had worked to deadly effect. The establishment of a satisfactory computer link between national police forces, and arrangements for the hot pursuit of criminals and terrorists should help prevent such problems from arising again.

DON'T CALL INTERPOL

International police and intelligence cooperation on terrorism and related matters outside Europe remains fairly limited in scope. Some observers point to Interpol (International Criminal Police Organization),

Frank Spooner Pictures

In 1988, the case of Patrick Ryan, a former Catholic priest suspected of acting as the Provisional IRA's quartermaster on the European continent, pointed up the difficulties of extradition. Both Belgium, where Ryan was originally arrested, and the Republic of Ireland, where he was subsequently held, refused Britain's repeated requests for extradition.

which pools the expertise of more than 100 national police forces, as a possible mechanism for enhancing police cooperation. However, under Article 3 of its constitution, Interpol is explicitly barred from investigating political matters. Consequently, Interpol plays a relatively minor role in combating terrorism. Another reason for this is thc fact that the countries engaged in sponsoring terrorism actually belong to Interpol, and other member nations are therefore reluctant to allow highly sensitive information into the Interpol network.

In the 1990s, there has been a growth in transnational terrorist activity by groups motivated by religious fanaticism, and by groups involved in transnational organized crime, such as the Russian mafias. Terrorist successes included the severe disruption of the Middle East peace process by a series of Hamas suicide bombings in February and March 1996.

By the summer of 1996, it had become apparent that the degree and quality of international cooperation against terrorism was lagging far behind what was required. The urgent need for improvement is demonstrated by the increase in terrorist attacks – and their deadly nature – during 1995-96. The Rand-St. Andrews Database statistics on international terrorism for 1994 showed that no less than 27 percent of attacks led to one or more fatality, the highest level of killing since the late 1960s.

A recurring problem in the evolution of international cooperation against terrorism is called "the politics of the latest outrage." For example, in the wake of a major atrocity, such as the terrorist bombing of Pan Am Flight 103 over Lockerbie, Scotland, in December 1988, public outrage is reflected in promises of major governmental and international action to ensure that it never happens again. However, once the memory of the atrocity begins to fade, the public begins to lose interest in measures against terrorism, and governments fail to fully implement preventive measures.

SHORT MEMORIES

In the 1990s, there have been several clear illustrations of just how fragile the international consensus against terrorism can be. For example, in 1996, the Saudi

Arabian authorities failed to provide adequate assistance and access to U.S. investigators pursuing those responsible for the Dharhan bombing of U.S. servicepeople. The continuing problems in moving beyond mere government rhetoric to effectively implement international cooperation against terrorism may at first seem surprising. After all, over half the world's nations experience some form of international terrorist attack every year. The Group of Seven (or G7 – the group of the world's most economically influential states, including the U.S., Britain, France, Germany, and Japan) have every reason to favor stronger international measures.

In 1995, a flurry of multilateral cooperation appeared promising. At the meeting of the G7 states and Russia at Halifax, Nova Scotia, in Canada, in June 1995, the political leaders called for a special counterterrorism conference of ministers. The conference was held in Ottawa in December. One of its most important pledges was to pursue measures to prevent terrorists' use of nuclear, chemical, or biological weapons. This was in part a response to the nerve-gas attack by the Shinri-kyu cult on the Tokyo subway system on March 20, 1995.

There were also vital new initiatives regarding the protection of aviation, maritime, and other forms of transportation, and measures to prevent the falsification of documents. Moreover, the conference pledged to work toward universal adherence to international treaties and conventions on terrorism by the year 2000.

The assassination of Israeli Prime Minister Yitzhak Rabin by a Jewish extremist in November 1995, and the Hamas suicide bombings against Israel in 1996, provided the catalyst for further summits on strengthening international cooperation. The theme was at the top of the agenda of the 1996 G7 meeting in Lyon, France, where President Clinton presented 40 U.S. initiatives for enhancing counterterrorism. The G7 summit agreed to hold an unprecedented three-day ministerial meeting on countering terrorism in Paris in July 1996.

At the Paris meeting, the security ministers of the G7 states and Russia agreed to back 25 measures. Some of the counterterrorism steps agreed to, such as improved intelligence sharing, and facilitating the extradition of suspect terrorists, have been the subject of many previous agreements.

Some, however, were quite new. For example, ministers agreed to clamp down on the use of charitable organizations as fronts for terrorist fundraising, and on the use of the Internet by terrorists. Another fresh measure was an agreement to establish a directory of counterterrorist skills.

Hulton Getty Picture Collection/Reuters

Rafael Caride Simon, a suspected member of the Basque terrorist group ETA, leaves court in the southern French town of Bayonne, on February 21, 1993. France and Spain have collaborated over many years to combat the ETA threat.

LOOKING AFTER NUMBER ONE

Although there is ample evidence of growing concern about international terrorism on the part of the U.S. and the other G7 states, many other countries afflicted by severe terrorist campaigns (such as India, Pakistan, Turkey, Peru, Algeria, Egypt, Sri Lanka, and the Philippines) focus primarily, if not exclusively, on domestic counterterrorism measures. Their main interest in international cooperation is understandably directed at cross-border security relations with their immediate neighbors. Often these relations are extremely hostile, as between India and Pakistan.

In cases of severe terrorist insurgency, effective bilateral cooperation with neighboring states really counts, especially for those sharing a land frontier.

Frank Spooner Pictures

A 1996 anti-terrorist conference at Sharm el-Sheikh, Egypt, involving Middle Eastern leaders and UN Security Council leaders.

High-sounding multilateral declarations and agreements are not seen as having much practical value. The state of Israel, plagued by terrorism almost continuously throughout its history, has placed little reliance on international cooperation, but has followed a determined and often ruthless policy of self-help. Counterterrorist measures have included military intervention in neighboring states and retaliatory actions, sometimes against innocent Palestinian civilians.

The prolonged and bitter Arab-Israeli conflict is a powerful reminder that the ethnic and religious struggles, which have spawned a high proportion of late twentieth-century terrorist violence, have deeply divided the international community. It is obvious that it is going to be impossible to achieve a common international security policy against terrorism when there is fundamental disagreement over the legitimacy of those who use violence to pursue their aims.

There is a huge gulf between the rhetoric and reality of international cooperation against terrorism. There is no agreement to install an international sovereign authority. As a result, there are no clearly defined and universally accepted binding international laws.

In what is essentially an anarchical international system, there is no universal agreement about what constitutes the illegitimate use of violence, or the legitimate suppression of revolt by the state. Each national government inevitably places the pursuit of its own national interest above all other considerations, including even general international declarations about common responsibilities to combat terrorism.

Paul Wilkinson

SEE ALSO: DOMESTIC VERSUS INTERNATIONAL TERRORISM; COLLABORATION BETWEEN TERRORISTS; STATE-SPONSORED TERRORISM; THE MEDIA AND INTERNATIONAL TERRORISM; THE CHANGING FACE OF TERRORISM.

FURTHER READING

- Bell, John Bowyer. *A Time of Terror: How Democratic Societies Respond to Revolutionary Violence.* New York: Basic Books, 1978.
- Guelke, Adrian. *The Age of Terrorism and the International Political System.* London and New York: Tauris Academic Studies, 1995.
- Rubin, Barry, ed. *The Politics of Counterterrorism: The Ordeal of Democratic States.* Washington, DC: Johns Hopkins Foreign Policy Institute, 1990.

CHAPTER TWENTY-THREE

The Media and International Terrorism

The media has a legitimate right to report and comment on acts of terrorism, but must remain vigilant to make sure it is not being manipulated by terrorist organizations. Standards of impartiality have to be maintained, and it is critical that reporters are aware of the fact that terrorists require publicity to air their demands. Terrorists also know that their "spectacular" operations, such as those against key installations or prominent individuals, will be reported widely by news agencies as they engage in a battle for ratings.

THE MEDIA AND INTERNATIONAL TERRORISM

Terrorism and the media are uneasy bedfellows. Their relationship is one of mutual distrust and mutual need. Terrorists need publicity, and the media need audience ratings.

Terrorism, by its very nature, is a weapon that depends on the communication of a threat to the public at large. Fortunately, use of the media has proved remarkably ineffective as a weapon for toppling governments and capturing political power. Unfortunately, the media has proved a remarkably successful means of publicizing political causes and relaying threats to a wider audience, particularly in the open and pluralistic countries of the West. This is, in essence, why terrorism and the media enjoy a close relationship.

The free media clearly do not represent terrorist values. Instead, they generally represent the underlying values of the democratic society in which they operate. But media in an open society compete fiercely for the attention of their audiences and are constantly under pressure to be the first with news, and to provide information, excitement, and entertainment. As a result, terrorist acts are almost bound to be seen as dramatic news. Of course, this does not mean that the media support the terrorists. However, it does mean that terrorists continually attempt to manipulate and exploit the free media for their own ends. It also means that responsible media professionals and the public need to be constantly on their guard against such manipulation.

SUMMARY

- The Munich Olympics massacre of 1972 was witnessed by a TV audience of 500 million.
- In the first three weeks of the 1979 Tehran hostage crisis, the major U.S. TV network ratings went up 18 percent.
- In 1980, the Italian Red Brigades negotiated for the life of kidnapped judge Giovanni D'Urso via newspapers, TV, and radio, and won a massive propaganda victory.
- In 1984, the Spanish government put a gag on media coverage of terrorist events.
- During the 17-day hijacking of TWA Flight 847 in 1985, American TV saturation coverage ensured that the hijackers' demands were met. The Israelis released 756 Shiite prisoners in exchange for the 39 American passengers.

THE GLOBAL VILLAGE

The term mass media includes newspapers, radio, and television, but also other important forms of communication such as books, films, music, theater, and the visual arts. The late twentieth century has seen the globalization of the mass media, but it should not be overlooked that throughout history, informal means of communication such as word of mouth have been the standard method of transmitting information. The modern terrorist has access to graffiti and street posters, as well as the latest multimedia technology.

THE SPREAD OF TERROR

When terrorist groups want to spread terror among a large target group, they inevitably resort to a method of transmitting information, however informal. The Assassin sect of Shia Islam, which attempted to spread terror in the Muslim world in the Middle Ages, relied on word of mouth in the mosques and marketplaces to relay news of their attacks. Similar methods of transmitting fear were employed by Russian and Balkan terrorists in the nineteenth century. Such historical examples disprove the theory that the twentieth-century development of mass media is the prime cause for the existence and spread of terrorism.

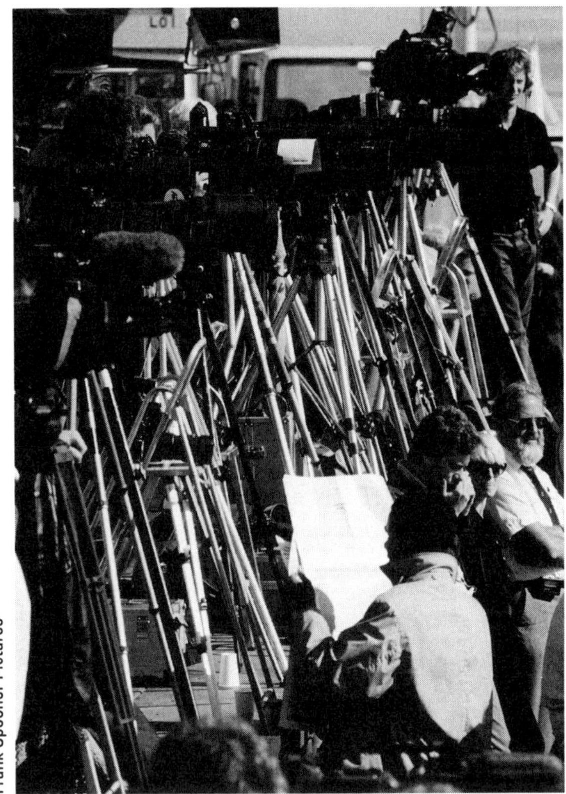

Frank Spooner Pictures

The release of the Beirut hostage Jackie Mann in September 1991. The tremendous scale of attention that the media are able to focus on "sensational" events relating to terrorism often helps publicize terrorists' aims.

Terrorists communicate on two very different levels. The mass media provide a means of getting the terrorists' message across to the population at large, but rarely replace the terrorists' own press releases, communiqués, pamphlets, and magazines. The terrorists' own methods of propaganda generally have a very limited circulation. However, such publications are a vital means of maintaining ideological fervor among rank-and-file members and sympathizers, and of spreading creeds, philosophies, and news of developments to other potential supporters.

It is significant that when terrorist leaders set up supporting infrastructures for their terrorist activities overseas, the production of newspapers and magazines is seen as a key element. There is no denying, however, that modern media technology, communications satellites, the rapid spread of television, and the growth of publicly accessible computer networks have all had an effect on the terrorists' publicity potential.

TERROR ON SCREEN

A dramatic early illustration of the usefulness of the media to terrorist organizations was provided by the 1972 Munich Olympics incident in which the Black September Organization took hostage and massacred Israeli athletes. It is estimated that these events were watched in horrified fascination by a worldwide TV audience of over 500 million people.

For as long as the mass media exist, terrorists will hunger for what former British Prime Minister Margaret Thatcher notably described as the "oxygen of publicity." In addition, for as long as terrorists commit acts of violence, the mass media will continue to rush to cover them in order to satisfy the desire of their audiences for dramatic news stories.

Most terrorists view the mass media in a free society in entirely cynical and opportunistic terms, and have nothing but contempt for their values and attitudes. For example, terrorists view the media's concern for human life as nothing but hypocrisy and sentimentality. However, terrorists have powerful reasons for wishing to appear on prime-time TV and on the front pages of the popular press. They may obtain not only massive or even worldwide publicity, but also an air of legitimacy in the eyes of their own followers. By bombing an installation, or by taking hostages for several days, terrorists achieve what is for them invaluable status.

Apart from general publicity for their cause, terrorist organizations often have specific requirements when using the mass media. First, they are anxious to ensure that the maximum number of people find out about the actions they have taken. This has the desirable effect, from the terrorists' point of view, of creating fear among their target audience. Second, they want to mobilize wider support for their cause among the general population, at home and abroad, by emphasizing the righteousness of their cause. Third, terrorists aim to disrupt the security forces – publicity for a successful terrorist attack helps prove the ineptitude of the security forces. Finally, terrorists use publicity to boost their actual and potential supporters, to increase recruitment, to raise more funds, and to inspire further terrorist initiatives.

The relative importance of any of these objectives varies according to the terrorist group involved. For example, Palestinian aircraft hijackers of the early

Popperfoto

David Jacobsen, a former U.S. hostage in Beirut, launched a media campaign in 1987 for the release of fellow hostages still held captive. He wore prayer bracelets bearing the names of other hostages who at that time were still held captive in Lebanon.

1970s wanted to gain publicity for their cause in the West. Red Brigades revolutionaries in Italy during the 1970s wanted to expose what they saw as a repressive state. Palestinian fundamentalist suicide bombers of the 1990s wanted to show both Israelis and fundamentalist sympathizers in the Middle East what Islamic fundamentalists could achieve. Some terrorists have very specific demands, particularly in hijacking and kidnapping situations where the terrorists have something to trade. Usually, such demands are for the release of other terrorists held in prison, and for large money payments to finance their movements.

SUCCESSFUL MEDIA MANIPULATION

In December 1980, the Italian Red Brigades terrorist group kidnapped Judge Giovanni D'Urso and embarked on an extraordinary, media-based campaign to focus public attention on the Italian prison system. D'Urso was the senior official in the Ministry of Justice, and was responsible for the allocation of prisoners to special prisons. Using a well-tried technique, the terrorists left written communiqués in hiding places and telephoned the whereabouts of these to newspapers. Their first demand, for the closure of a special island prison off Sardinia, was met almost immediately.

Initially, about half of the media imposed a voluntary blackout on coverage of the kidnapping. The TV channel controlled by the ruling Christian Democrat party also imposed a blackout, but the news-hungry public merely switched over to the Socialist channel, which was covering the kidnapping. On January 10, the Red Brigades announced that D'Urso had been "tried" and sentenced to death and that the sentence would be carried out in 48 hours unless the major newspapers and broadcasting media transmitted the text of documents written by a number of prisoners. These included Red Brigades members who had formed groups called "Action Committees of Prisoners Accused of Terrorism" in certain high-security prisons.

Most newspapers ignored the ultimatum, but *Avanti*, the official Socialist party paper, published the prisoners' documents, while the Radical party gave them publicity in both radio and TV programs. The prisoners announced that they were satisfied with this response, and D'Urso was freed on January 15, 1981. By manipulating the media, the terrorists had succeeded in closing a prison and securing a massive propaganda victory.

In June 1985, Shiite Islamic Jihad terrorists hijacked TWA Flight 847, which was on its way from Athens to Rome, forcing it to fly to Beirut. Most of the passengers were American citizens. The terrorists had many demands, including the release of 776 Shiites held in Israel. The hostages were released in batches in the course of a 17-day ordeal, during which one American was shot dead. Ultimately, the Israelis released 756 Shiite prisoners.

The NBC news channel devoted no less than two-thirds of its total news time to the hostage crisis throughout the 17 days of the hijacking. Significantly, the hostages received about ten times the attention given to the terrorists in the overall news coverage. In their intense competition for audience share, all the major TV networks gave huge exposure to the hostages. Opinion polls showed that 89 percent of the American public applauded the media's intense coverage. Yet it has been claimed, not without reason, that the media effectively assisted the terrorists in achieving their aims.

The media-hype of terrorist acts was no accidental miscalculation. The major TV networks all compete fiercely for an increased market share of the audience,

Frank Spooner Pictures

Former hostage Judge Giovanni D'Urso speaks at a press conference following his release by the Italian Red Brigades in January 1981.

and for the increased advertising revenue they can get by exploiting the public's interest in events that generate powerful emotions. For example, in the first three weeks of the Tehran hostage crisis in 1979, the major TV networks achieved an 18 percent increase in audience ratings. It was estimated that, in 1979, the networks secured an annual revenue increase of $30 million for each percentage point of audience ratings increase.

Coverage of such events may also have an effect on domestic politics. In the case of the Tehran hostage situation, the TV networks' constant emphasis on the fate of the hostages, and their portrayal of an administration apparently powerless to obtain their release, helped undermine Jimmy Carter's presidency and may well have cleared the way for the election of Ronald Reagan in 1980.

THE MEDIA AND THE LAW

The other side of the coin is the relationship between the media and the law enforcement agencies dealing with terrorism. In cases of hijackings and hostage-takings, for example, their aims seem totally at odds with each other. The prime concern of the mass media is to "scoop" their rivals with news stories that will grip and sustain the public's attention. The police and other security organizations, however, are only concerned with bringing the siege or hijacking to a safe conclusion. Publicity, at least of the intrusive kind, can only hinder this.

There have been many examples in which the efforts of the security forces have been directly threatened by the behavior of certain sections of the media. For example, during the 1980 Iranian embassy siege at Princes Gate, London, the Metropolitan Police wanted to ensure total secrecy so that the rescue bid by the British Special Air Service (SAS) would succeed. However, one ITN film crew defied police instructions, and filmed the rescuers as they were abseiling down the embassy walls. If the pictures had been transmitted live, they could have jeopardized the entire rescue.

Another striking example of media irresponsibility occurred during the hijacking of a Kuwaiti airliner by Hizb'allah terrorists in 1988. While the airliner was on

Frank Spooner Pictures

Members of the National Front for the Liberation of Corsica (FLNC) deliberately adopting the terrorist image that the media likes to present.

the ground at Larnaca, Cyprus, there might have been an opportunity to mount a hostage rescue operation with an elite commando group. A major obstacle to such an operation was the intrusiveness of the international media, which surrounded the aircraft with infrared equipment. Even at night it would have been impossible to launch a rescue operation without its being given away.

In an open society, it is impossible to guarantee that anti-terrorist actions will not be disrupted by irresponsible media activity. However, a great deal can be achieved by ensuring that expert press liaison and news management are an intrinsic part of the police response to terrorist activity. In a democratic society, a sound and effective public information policy, harnessing the power of the mass media, is a vital element in a successful anti-terrorist campaign.

UNDERESTIMATING THE MEDIA

One crucial flaw in the terrorists' publicity strategy is their contemptuous dismissal of the power of press and the government to mobilize public opinion. Terrorists often assume that the target group they seek to coerce will always give in to threatened or actual violence. This is a naïve assumption that often leads to a hardening of society's resistance.

THE ROLE OF A RESPONSIBLE MEDIA

There are a number of important ways in which responsible media in a democracy can frustrate terrorists' aims. Terrorists go to great lengths to present themselves as Robin Hood-type popular heroes, or champions of the oppressed and the downtrodden. The media can help shatter this myth by showing the savage cruelty of terrorist violence, and the ways in which terrorists violate the rights of the innocent. It is easy to show, with plain photographic and video evidence, how terrorists have failed to observe humanitarian rules of war, and how they have murdered without compunction women, children, the old, and the sick. Ultimately, in terrorist terms, no one is innocent or neutral. All are potentially expendable in reaching the all-important end result of the terrorists' cause.

Many terrorist leaders are well aware that their cause can be damaged by unfavorable publicity. For this reason, the more established and sophisticated terrorist movements have political "front" organizations, such as the IRA's Sinn Féin. Such bodies invest considerable time, money and effort in waging a propaganda war directed at both domestic and international audiences. The media can also provide positive, practical help in the fight against terrorism. Responsible and accurate reporting of incidents can create a heightened vigilance in the public, for example, when looking for unusual packages and suspicious persons or behavior.

At a practical level, the media can deliver police warnings to the public, with instructions on how people should react in an emergency. Frequently, international media coverage can provide valuable data and leads concerning foreign movements, links between different terrorist personalities and organizations, new types of weaponry, and possible future threats, such as the planning of an international terrorist act or the warning signs of a new threat.

THE MEDIA AS TARGETS

Where the media take a stand against terrorism, they may themselves become targets of terrorist actions. This has often been the case in areas of severe conflict such as in Italy and Turkey in the 1970s, and in Lebanon in the 1970s and 1980s. Journalists and editors have been attacked for offending terrorist sensibilities. In 1976, the Italian Red Brigades kneecapped three conservative journalists whom they accused of spreading lies about the group. The following year, they shot and mortally wounded the assistant director of the Italian newspaper *La Stampa*.

However, such attacks on sections of the media do not signify that the relationship between media and terrorists is suddenly no longer useful. Both the terrorists and the media still need each other. It is an awkward partnership, with the partners holding one another at arm's length, but with neither relinquishing their grip.

Finally, the media also provide an indispensable forum for informed discussion concerning the social and political implications of terrorism, and for the development of adequate policies and countermeasures. And media that place a high value on democratic freedoms will, rightly and necessarily, continually remind the authorities of their broader responsibilities to ensure that the response to terrorism is consistent with the rule of law, with respect for basic rights, and with the demands of social justice.

To be of assistance in frustrating terrorist aims, though, the media must be responsible. The media need for immediate and simple stories can always backfire, even when the aim is specifically anti-terrorist. There is always the tendency in some parts of the media to demonize terrorists, or to rush in with publicity where restraint is more valuable to the authorities.

In one example of this type of media irresponsibility, an Irish court refused to extradite Father Patrick Ryan for trial in England, even though he was suspected of being involved in IRA terrorism in Europe in 1989. The Irish court felt that reports about Ryan in the British media had hopelessly prejudiced his case and that, in consequence, he could not be guaranteed a fair trial.

CENSORSHIP

The policy of noninterference concerning media coverage, however serious the violence or threat of violence, has obvious dangers. Media-wise terrorists may exploit the tremendous power of the mass media to enhance their ability to create a climate of fear and disruption, to publicize their cause, and to force concessions. Media censorship or statutory regulation has sometimes appealed to hard-pressed governments during severe terrorist campaigns. British Prime Minister Margaret Thatcher put a ban on broadcasting the actual voices of terrorist spokespersons, although this ban has since been rescinded. In another example, in 1984, the Spanish government introduced a law that made it a criminal offense to publish material that described terrorist activities.

It is important to avoid manipulation of the mass media by terrorist groups. However, most countries that are plagued by terrorism are reluctant to go down the dangerous path of media-suppression and censorship. Most countries recognize that if the freedom of the mass media is sacrificed trying to combat terrorism, then society will have allowed terrorist groups to destroy one of the key foundations of democratic society. Censorship, in whatever form it takes, only plays into the eager hands of the enemies of a democratic society.

The option most favored by the more responsible mass-media organizations is voluntary self-restraint. Many media groups have adopted guidelines for their

Frank Spooner Pictures

Arab leaders, including Yasser Arafat, joined the U.S., Russia, Japan, and the European states to condemn all forms of terrorism at a summit in Egypt on March 13, 1996. The summit was extensively covered in the media and gave leaders an opportunity to be seen to be taking a positive stance against terrorism.

staff, with the aim of avoiding the most obvious pitfalls. For example, CBS News' guidelines commit the organization to "thoughtful, conscientious care and restraint" in its coverage of terrorism, to avoid giving "an excessive platform for the terrorist/kidnapper... ." Yet there still remain many media workers unaware of the existence of or need for guidelines on terrorism in news coverage. It is some governments' frustration over the apparent inadequacy of media self-restraints that leads them to advocate statutory regulation.

THE FIGHT CONTINUES

The contributions made by the mass media in the fight against terrorism are so valuable that they outweigh the undoubted risks of damage caused by irresponsible journalists and broadcasters. The positive work of the mass media has often been underestimated or ignored by their critics. Politicians, who are themselves so exposed to media scrutiny, may be quick to attack the media as fair game. Nevertheless, a more considered assessment suggests that the media can also be used as a major tool to defeat terrorism.

Paul Wilkinson

SEE ALSO: TERRORIST FUNDRAISING; THE MINDSET OF THE TERRORIST; HOSTAGE NEGOTIATION; THE BLACK SEPTEMBER ORGANIZATION; RED BRIGADES.

FURTHER READING

- Jamieson, Alison. *The Heart Attacked – Terrorism and Conflict in the Italian State.* London and New York: Marion Boyars, 1989.
- Nacos, Brigette L. *Terrorism in the Media.* New York: Columbia University Press, 1994.
- Schmid, Alex. "Terrorism and the Media: The Ethics of Publicity," in *Terrorism and Political Violence* 1, No. 4 (October 1989): 539-65.

CHAPTER TWENTY-FOUR

The Changing Face of Terrorism

It is unlikely that terrorism will be eradicated in the foreseeable future because the causes of political violence – ethnic rivalries, ideological conflict, and state repression – are unlikely to disappear. Perhaps the best that can be hoped for is that terrorism will be contained and reduced to a level that politicians and the people they represent will find "acceptable." Such containment will not, however, address the causes of terrorism. Prolonged negotiation, sustained even in the face of terrorist attacks, by thoughtful representatives of all the parties involved may offer a better solution in the long term.

THE CHANGING FACE OF TERRORISM

Terrorism – the use of indiscriminate violence for political ends – is now a fact of life in most parts of the world. A hijacking, assassination, or kidnapping is invariably reported by news networks with global links, while the increase in international travel allows terrorists to project their grievances beyond their own geographical area. Access to sophisticated weapons and technology means most terrorists can continue to surprise their opponents in state organizations, exploiting gaps in security to attack key targets. Each incident, in which usually the innocent suffer, spreads fear among the vast majority in a threatened society and undermines confidence in the government to protect its citizens. If part of that government's response to the threat is to sanction counterterror or to support terrorist groups against rival states, the suffering of the innocents, the "middle ground," is that much worse.

What motivates individuals to suspend their sense of morality and engage in terrorist acts is simply frustration, triggered by the difficulty of achieving the desired ends through existing political and legal channels. Within the main areas of frustration in the world today, terrorism can still find a fertile soil.

High on the list of frustrations that lead to terrorism is nationalism, a motivation that has always been difficult to counter. If a minority within a state feels that its identity is being threatened or that it is not gaining the political recognition it deserves, often it will resort to violence. This is both to attract attention to its cause and to try to force the government under which it suffers to grant concessions. Currently, the world population is divided politically into 189 states. As this division does not cover every national subgroup, nationalist activity is guaranteed and unlikely to diminish. Groups such as the Kurds or the Basques have realized that the present lineup of states is unlikely to satisfy their aspirations, so they turn to violence in an effort to force the issue. Commentators are particularly apprehensive about what may happen in the former Soviet Union.

SUMMARY

- Minority groups, frustrated by their inability to be "heard," may resort to terrorist violence.
- Certain countries will give invaluable support to terrorist groups to further their own political ends.
- The end of the Cold War between communism and democracy has simply shifted the focus of terror to areas such as the Middle East.

IDEOLOGICAL MOTIVATION

Political ideology is just as significant as nationalism as a reason for terrorism. Like nationalism, it permits no compromise on the part of its adherents and it encourages them to be ruthless. If a group believes firmly that its ideals in pursuit of a Utopian society are the only ones to be followed, its members will readily die for the cause, and they will insist that any opponents should be swept away. Such beliefs may, of course, affect entire states, drawing them into conflicts in which no holds are barred. The clashes in the twentieth century between democracy and fascism, fascism and communism, and democracy and communism have all produced bloody conflicts. Some commentators therefore find little to distinguish between the methods employed by such ideological states and those used more recently by minority terrorist groups. In all cases, it is those people occupying the middle ground who are targeted and whose fears are exploited for political ends.

Ideology is perhaps less of a potential motivator now that the Cold War has ended, for the threat of a steady spread of Marxist beliefs seems to have receded

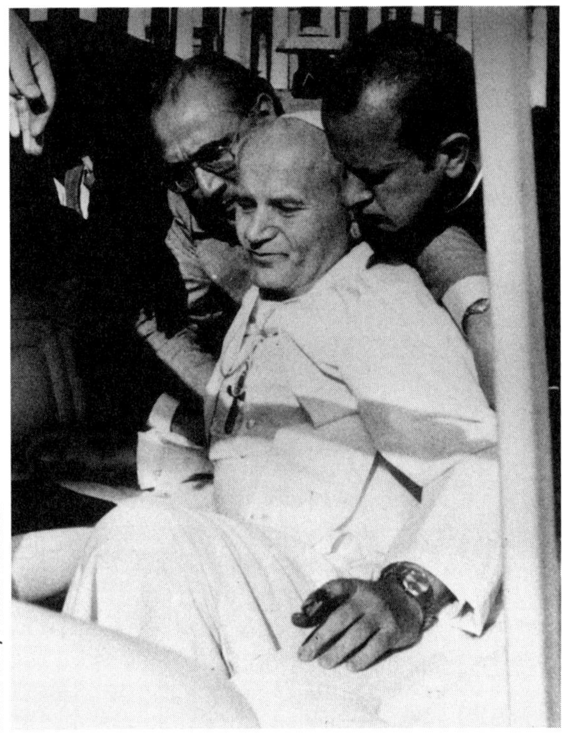

Hulton Getty Picture Collection

Pope John Paul II was wounded when a Turkish terrorist, Mehmet Ali Agça, tried to assassinate him in St. Peter's Square on May 13, 1981.

with the collapse of the Soviet Union. But the influence of ideology should not be underestimated. More than a quarter of the world's population still lives under communist regimes, which, especially in China, North Korea, and Cuba, may feel sufficiently threatened to lash out. In addition, new ideologies may well emerge from the ashes of communism, appealing to those people caught in the aftermath of social and political disruption. Extreme ideas thrive among desperate, dispossessed, and disenchanted people, and there are plenty of such people around in the world today.

In liberal democracies, the frustration which leads to terrorism may arise when ideologically committed groups – invariably a minority of the population – cannot get their voices heard through the electoral process. Furthermore, if the aims of such a group appear to be at odds with the social and political norms of the state, the group may be deliberately blocked from all means of publicizing its cause and exerting legitimate pressure, leaving its members unable to see how they can get their message across without recourse to violence. Groups such as West Germany's Baader-Meinhof Gang certainly followed this path in the late 1960s and early 1970s. They came to believe that the only way to change society so that it reflected their often Utopian ideals was to destroy the existing political and legal establishment, thus opening the way to reform. The aims of the Baader-Meinhof Gang were, as Ulrike Meinhof observed enigmatically in 1972, "to recreate the Hollywood of the 1930s by blowing everything up." This general opposition to the state is also reflected in groups such as the anti-government militia in the U.S.

RELIGIOUS BELIEFS AS MOTIVATION

Closely allied to ideology is religion. It too deals with human souls rather than territory or class structures, but it has an added ingredient in that true believers are often more than willing to sacrifice their own lives in obedience to the word of their particular god. Muslim fundamentalism, based on the Koran's strict law, appeals to many people throughout the world, who see it as their duty to ensure that others share their ideals or perish if they do not. Based in Iran, where the Ayatollah Khomeini came to power in 1979, fundamentalism has spread into those areas of the Muslim world where poverty and political persecution thrive. These conditions trigger responses from the authorities that merely persuade the true believer that these same authorities should be entirely swept away. Lacking the means to do this by conventional means, the fundamentalists turn to terror, directing it not just at the rival state but also at that state's supporters worldwide.

Terrorist acts can be used to show how feeble even the most powerful state is at protecting its own people, who start to fear that to oppose fundamentalism is to court disaster. Terrorist methods have been used in a number of areas with substantial Muslim populations. In Sudan, a civil war between Christian and Muslim has been going on for decades, and the same religions clash in both Lebanon and the former Yugoslavia. So long as people have beliefs that close their minds to the possibility of alternatives, violence will persist. Terrorism offers the cheapest and often the most effective means of perpetrating such violence.

INTERNAL SPLITS CAUSE VIOLENCE

Terrorism is, however, not limited to a few specific groups with strongly held beliefs. Terrorist groups often split, causing internal violence that spills over into the

Popperfoto

An IRA honor guard accompanies the coffin of the IRA hunger striker Bobby Sands on May 7, 1981. The pall bearers were senior Sinn Féin members, including Gerry Adams (front right).

ordinary population. Splits may be caused by rival views about the best way to achieve political ends. The split in the IRA in the early 1970s, for example, arose from the desire by some of the more traditional activists to pursue power through the democratic process, alienating those who felt that the only thing "the Brits" understood was violence. A similar split occurred among the Palestinians a few years later, when Yasser Arafat decided to seek international recognition. In such cases, the rival subgroups will invariably turn their terrorist methods against their erstwhile colleagues.

Terrorist groups may also split because of corruption within their ranks when some members realize that material profits, gained by the disruption to state law and order, are more attractive than the cause they had originally embraced. The spread of narco-terrorism, arising from the enormous profits to be made from the sale of drugs, which has occurred in both the Far East and Latin America, has destroyed the ideological roots of existing terrorist groups and led to internal violence between the traditionalists and the entrepreneurs. Again, as in Burma, Peru, and Colombia, it is the ordinary people who are caught in the crossfire as the rival factions slug it out using terrorist methods.

All this may be exacerbated by the ease with which terrorist actions are reported. Not only do terrorists themselves seize upon tactics that appear to have been successfully used by other groups, but also disturbed or inadequate individuals often perpetrate terroristic acts merely because of the publicity they gain – it is a desperate way of achieving immortality and fame. These incidents often occur in the aftermath of the assassination of a celebrity, whether a president or a pop-star, and lead to a widespread fear among people of a similar status that they too will become targets. The general atmosphere of fear can thus disrupt society.

THE INTERNATIONAL DIMENSION

Finally, terrorism today is complicated by international politics. The old adage that "my enemy's enemy is my friend" applies just as much to relations between recognized states and terrorist groups as it does between recognized states themselves, ensuring that even the smallest terrorist organization can gain much-needed support. This can take the form of training bases, military equipment, safe havens, and political support in the corridors of international politics. It is not only the enemies of the Western powers who provide support to terrorist groups in this way. Many countries whose leaders would be among the first to condemn acts of terror perpetrated on their soil, or that of their allies, will support groups that use terror as a weapon if they see a political advantage in doing so. U.S. support of the Contras in Central America in the 1980s, to counter what was perceived as the spread of communism into Nicaragua, is an obvious example, although this was merely the latest in a series of similar policies throughout Latin America after Castro assumed power in Cuba in 1959. Colonel Qaddafi of Libya has traditionally supported any terrorist group that attacks the West, and the Iranians are often accused of doing the same.

TERROR IN THE FUTURE

Terrorism has not declined as a political weapon, nor is it likely to do so in the foreseeable future. It remains an effective way for a minority or oppressed group to get its message across to the rest of the world, and some are better at it than others.

Palestinian splinter groups such as the Popular Front for the Liberation of Palestine (PFLP) and PFLP-General Command (PFLP-GC) are past masters at global publicity, with the IRA and ETA not far behind. But even the smallest or least-organized group can be sure of gaining the world's attention and can expect to get state sponsorship through its actions. In the end, terrorism is a simple tactic. Once a man or woman is prepared to ignore the accepted morality and to use violence against other human beings, he or she will find ample opportunities to cause indiscriminate mayhem.

Nevertheless, terrorists rarely, if ever, achieve their aims through violence alone. Most people, once they have recovered from the shock of an indiscriminate attack, will usually shrug their shoulders and accept the countermeasures adopted by their governments, even if those countermeasures prove to be repressive. The best that a terrorist group is likely to achieve is a militarization of the society it is attacking – which can clearly be counterproductive. This happened in Uruguay in the early 1970s, and led to the virtual destruction of the Tupamaros. Some commentators believe it has happened more recently in Peru, where President Fujimori's "New Democracy" has led to the arrest of Shining Path's leader, Abimael Guzmán Reynoso. Some terrorist theorists would argue such militarization is a step in the right direction, alienating the people to such a extent that revolution will result, but this has yet to happen. The only terrorist groups that succeed are those which, having attracted attention to their cause, alter course and shift emphasis to the political arena, while sustaining the threat of violence to ensure that they are taken seriously. This has happened in the case of Palestinian nationalists like Yasser Arafat, who are now key players in the Middle East peace process. If terrorism is seen as a means to an end rather than as an end in itself, it may, to this extent, serve its purpose, but any attempt to shatter the resolve of a state by using indiscriminate violence alone seems, from the record of history, to be doomed to failure.

Hulton Getty Picture Collection/Reuters

Israeli soldiers arrest an Arab demonstrator during clashes at Nablus on the West Bank, in November 1995.

COUNTERING THE THREAT

For most governments, the key question is how to counter terrorism. At one level, this can be treated as a problem to be solved by security forces. Over the past few decades, government and security forces

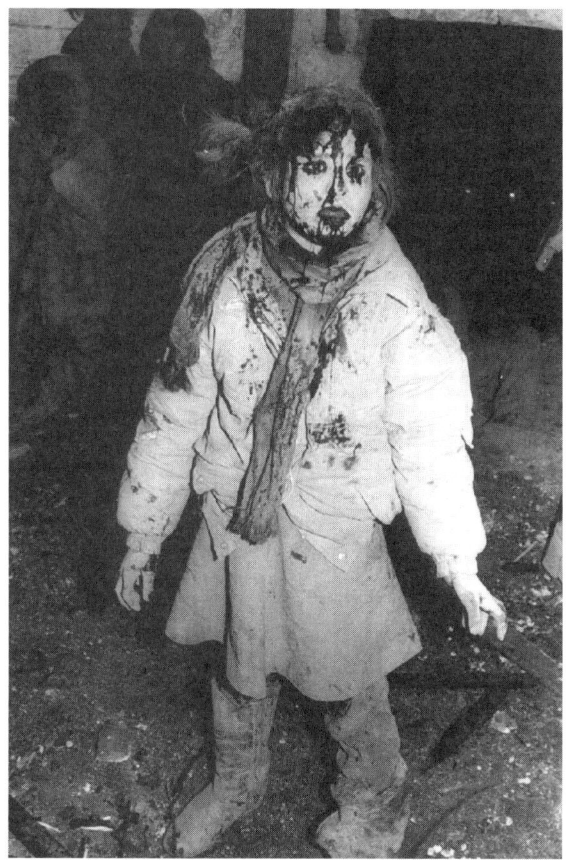

Popperfoto

In Grozny, Chechnya, a Chechen girl stands covered in blood and dust after narrowly escaping death in a building hit by a tank shell, January 1995.

have become more sophisticated in their response to terrorist threats. The war between terrorist and counterterrorist is constant in many societies, with both sides searching for an advantage. Sometimes terrorists manage to find deadly new weapons – such as the car-bombs used by the IRA in the 1970s, the suicide bombers Hamas recruited in the 1990s, or the nerve gas used in the Tokyo subway in the 1990s. Sometimes the security forces can gain an advantage, as happened when elite squads mobilized by the governments of Israel, Germany, and Britain showed that sheer expertise could wrest the initiative from terrorists in hostage-taking incidents or hijackings.

However, such tactical victories rarely win campaigns, although it would be dangerous to claim that they never have done so or never will do so. Only by convincing terrorists that terror is not the way to achieve their aims will they be made to stop. The most important element in accomplishing this is to ensure that the terrorists get no support from outside – whether that support be concrete (arms, money, and training) or moral (favorable propaganda and encouragement). Terrorist groups that operate without outside support rarely cause as much damage to society as those that receive outside help. The world is perhaps less ideologically fragmented since the end of the Cold War in 1989, but there are still countries actively aiding terrorists. Unfortunately, theoretical discussions on how to deal with them soon get bogged down in the messy relativism of regional politics in the real world. How, for example, can the West resolve its dilemmas in the Middle East, where the key economic interest of oil is locked together with allies that regularly deny basic human rights to their citizens, and religious fundamentalist terrorism with a genuinely popular basis?

Ultimately, however, terrorist acts are committed by individuals who feel that their aims are so important that they will use any means to achieve them. Few, if any, will achieve what they desire, but they will continue to try, if only for the thrill of using violence and attracting publicity. Government agencies and security forces, which are now more accustomed to dealing with the problem, will be able to score successes, but care will always have to be taken to avoid militarization and repression. It is a delicate balance, the fulcrum of which is, as always, the ordinary citizen.

John Pimlott

SEE ALSO: NATIONALIST TERRORISM; REVOLUTIONARY TERRORISM; FAR-RIGHT EXTREMISM; RELIGIOUS EXTREMISM; THE MINDSET OF THE TERRORIST; STATE-SPONSORED TERRORISM.

FURTHER READING

- Giddens, Anthony. *Beyond Left and Right: The Future of Radical Politics.* Cambridge: Polity Press, and Stanford, CT: Stanford University Press, 1994.
- Rubin, Barry. *The Future of Terrorism.* Washington, DC: Johns Hopkins Foreign Policy Institute, 1992.
- Weiman, Gabriel. *The Theater of Terror: Mass Media and International Terrorism.* New York: Longman, 1994.

CHRONOLOGY OF TERRORIST EVENTS SINCE 1945

1945

October 31 With the end of World War II, the three leading Jewish activist groups in Palestine – Irgun, Haganah, and the Stern Gang – form an alliance to fight against British rule. Their campaign begins with a number of bomb attacks on police vehicles, railroad sites, and an oil refinery, in which four people die.

November 27 Eight British soldiers die in a bomb attack by Jewish Irgun terrorists on a police station in Jerusalem, Palestine.

1946

January 7 Three American civilian officials die when Nazi Werewolf terrorists burn down their house in Passau, Germany.

March 11 Iranian Islamic fundamentalists begin a 10-year assassination campaign by killing Ahmed Kasravi, a leading intelectual, in Tehran, Iran.

July 22 Jewish Irgun terrorists kill 91 people and injure 45 after placing a bomb in the King David Hotel, which houses British government and military offices in Jerusalem, Palestine. The terrorists hold workers at pistol point while they plant the explosives in the basement of the hotel.

September 30 U.S. soldiers are ambushed by local communist terrorists at Fort McKinley, Philippines.

1947

July 12 Jewish Irgun terrorists kidnap, and later hang, two British Army sergeants, in an unsuccessful attempt to secure the release of three Irgun members sentenced to death by the British authorities in Palestine.

September 29 Jewish Irgun terrorists bomb a police station in Haifa, Palestine, killing four British and four Arab policemen and two Arab civilians, and injuring 46.

December 3 A train is derailed near Arras, France, by French communist terrorists, killing 20 and injuring 40.

December 12 Twenty Arabs, five Jews, and two British soldiers are killed and 30 people wounded in bomb attacks by Jewish terrorists on buses in Haifa and Ramleh, Palestine.

December 29 Jewish Irgun terrorists throw grenades from a passing taxi into a café near the Damascus Gate, Jerusalem, Palestine, killing 11 Arabs and two British policemen.

1948

January 30 Indian independence leader and statesman Mahatma Gandhi is shot dead in Delhi, India, by Nathuram Godse, a Hindu extremist.

March 7 Two American diplomats are murdered by Vietminh terrorists in Saigon, Indochina.

March 11 The headquarters of the Jewish Agency, Jerusalem, Palestine, is destroyed by an Arab car bomb which kills 13 people and injures 84.

April 9 Jewish Irgun and Stern Gang terrorists attack the village of Deir Yassin, Palestine, murdering 254 Arab men, women, and children captured in the remains of the village. As a result, many Arabs subsequently flee the state of Israel (formally proclaimed May 14).

April 9 A bomb explodes near the U.S. embassy in Bogotá, Colombia, during a conference of the Organization of American States.

April 13 Palestinian Arabs attack a convoy of mainly Jewish doctors and nurses near Mount Scopus, Palestine, killing 77.

May 8 American CBS correspondent George Polk is murdered by three communists in Salonika, Greece, after being lured to a meeting on a boat in the city's harbor. His body is dumped in the sea.

July 22 Peace activist Stephen J. Supina drops a home-made dynamite bomb on the United Nations headquarters in New York. No damage is caused and Supina later surrenders to the authorities.

September 17 United Nations mediator for Palestine, Swedish Count Folke Bernadotte, is murdered in Jerusalem by a Jewish Stern Gang terrorist who fires at point-blank range through the window of his car.

1949

December 3 British governor of Sibu, Sarawak, Duncan George Stewart, is stabbed to death by anti-British Malayans in North Borneo.

1950

November 1 Puerto Rican nationalists attack Blair House in Washington, DC, in an unsuccessful attempt to assassinate U.S. President Harry S. Truman. One U.S. Secret Service agent and one terrorist are killed.

1951

July 20 King Abdullah of Jordan is assassinated by an Arab extremist in the Jordanian-controlled Old City of

Jerusalem, while entering the al-Aqsa Mosque to pray. The assassin and four accomplices are hanged.

September 11 Pakistani Prime Minister Liaquat Ali Khan is shot dead by an Afghan fanatic while addressing a meeting in Rawalpindi, Pakistan.

October 6 Sir Henry Gurney, British high commissioner in Malaya, is killed together with 13 British soldiers when his motorcade is attacked by communist guerrillas. This leads to a major shake-up of British counterinsurgency operations against the communists.

1953

October 14 Israeli soldiers enter the village of Qibya, Jordan, and kill 66 Arab men, women, and children.

1954

March 1 Five U.S. congressmen are wounded when four Puerto Rican nationalists open fire in the Capitol, Washington, DC. The terrorists are arrested after firing 25 rounds.

March 17 Eleven bus passengers are machine-gunned to death when Palestinian terrorists ambush the vehicle in the Negev desert, Israel.

1955

April 1 A Greek Cypriot group, the National Organization of Cypriot Fighters (EOKA), begins a campaign for independence for British-controlled Cyprus with a series of bomb explosions around the island.

August 20 Several dozen French civilians are killed by National Liberation Front (FLN) guerrillas in the Philippeville area of Algiers, Algeria. French security forces stage retaliatory attacks on Algerian civilians and raze entire villages.

October 17 Five French soldiers and eight civilians are killed in attacks by Arab nationalist guerrillas in Algeria.

1956

February 29 A new Greek Cypriot bombing campaign begins against British rule in Cyprus. Conducted by the National Organization of Cypriot Fighters (EOKA), it includes the destruction of two British aircraft at Nicosia airport on March 3 and April 27. Violence continues for four years until Cyprus is granted independence by Britain in 1960.

October 3 The wife of a British soldier is shot in Cyprus while shopping by Greek Cypriot terrorists belonging to the National Organization of Cypriot Fighters (EOKA) .

1957

September 27 Political prisoners being flown from Santa Cruz to La Paz, Bolivia, take over the aircraft and force it to fly to Argentina, where they gain political asylum.

December 12 Irish Republican Army (IRA) terrorists attack a British Army barracks at Armagh, Northern Ireland, but are repulsed after a gun battle with guards.

1958

February 24 Former world champion motor racing driver Juan Manuel Fangio of Argentina is kidnapped in Havana, Cuba, by Castro's July 26 Movement. Their intention is to embarrass the Cuban government by preventing him taking part in a race there.

June 27 Thirty U.S. Marines are kidnapped by communist guerrillas in Cuba, near the U.S. naval base at Guantanamo Bay. All are eventually released unharmed.

November 1 In the first-ever airplane hijacking incident, a Cuban airliner is hijacked by Castro's July 26 Movement and forced to attempt a night landing at a remote airfield in Cuba. It crashes, killing 17 of the 20 people on board.

1960

March 4 One hundred are killed and 200 are injured when anti-Castro rebels blow up a French freighter in Havana harbor, Cuba.

March 20 South African police kill 69 protesters at a civil rights demonstration (the Sharpeville massacre). In reply the African National Congress (ANC) abandons its policy of nonviolence.

April 9 South African Prime Minister Henrik Verwoerd is shot in the face at a fair in Johannesburg, South Africa, by an anti-apartheid white farmer of English extraction.

August 29 The Jordanian prime minister and 11 others are killed by a bomb in the foreign ministry building, Amman, Jordan. Two of the bombers flee to safety, but 11 others are sentenced to death for the attack.

1961

January 22 The cruise liner *Santa Maria* is hijacked by Portuguese rebels, who take more than 550 passengers hostage. U.S. and Brazilian warships subsequently intercept the ship and force the hijackers to surrender to the Brazilian authorities.

May 1 The first-ever hijacking of a U.S. aircraft, when Puerto Rican-born Antulio Ramírez Ortiz forces a National Airlines airliner to fly at gunpoint to Havana, Cuba, where he is given asylum.When he returns to Miami in 1975, he is jailed for 20 years.

September 9 Secret Army Organization (OAS) terrorists, opposed to moves to give independence to Algeria, attempt to blow up French President Charles de Gaulle in Aube, France, but their roadside bomb fails to explode.

December 16 The African National Congress (ANC) launches a bombing campaign that damages government buildings throughout South Africa. This first ANC terror campaign lasts 18 months and involves some 200 attacks.

1962

January 22 One person is killed and 13 are injured when Secret Army Organization (OAS) terrorists bomb the French foreign ministry building at Quai d'Orsay, Paris, France.

August 22 Secret Army Organization (OAS) terrorists stage a machine-gun attack in a Paris suburb on a car carrying French President Charles de Gaulle. He escapes the attack unhurt, and the former French soldiers responsible are all later arrested. Further unsuccessful attempts to assassinate de Gaulle are made by the OAS on March 1 and 15, 1963. Five more attempts fail in 1964, and three in 1965.

1965

February 21 Malcolm X, a former Black Muslim leader and founder of the Organization for Afro-American Unity, is shot dead during a public meeting in Harlem, New York.

May 25 Three Israeli civilians are killed in a Fatah Palestinian terrorist attack on a Jewish settlement at Ramat Hakovash, Israel.

September 1 The British speaker of the Aden state council is murdered by Arab nationalists as he drives to a tennis club in Aden City, Western Aden Protectorate, south Arabia. Two weeks later, seven British children are injured when a grenade is exploded at the airport terminal in Aden.

1966

August 4 One American and two Colombians are killed by a bomb planted by left-wing rebels in Bogotá, Colombia.

September 26 Argentine El Condor nationalists hijack an Argentine aircraft from Buenos Aires to the British-occupied Falkland Islands, in a bid to attract attention to Argentina's claim to the islands. They eventually surrender their hostages and are returned to Argentina by the British authorities.

November 22 A DC-3 aircraft blows up in mid air near Aden, Western Aden Protectorate, south Arabia, killing all 28 people on board. Investigation reveals that a bomb was placed in the baggage area of the aircraft.

1967

March 23 Six government soldiers are killed in Bolivia by communist guerrillas led by Che Guevara. Seven months later, his group is tracked down by government troops and Guevara is killed.

June 30 An aircraft carrying Katangan rebel leader Moise Tshombe is hijacked en route to Ibiza, Spain, and forced to land in Algeria, in a bid to extradite him to his native Congo. The Algerians keep him under house arrest until he dies two years later.

October 12 A British European Airways Comet airliner is destroyed by a bomb that detonates in the passenger cabin over Rhodes, Greece. All 66 on board are killed.

1968

February 21 A Delta Airlines DC-8 is forced to fly to Havana, Cuba, in the first successful hijacking of a U.S. commercial airliner since 1961. The hijacker is granted political asylum.

March 18 A school bus hits a land mine in the Negev desert, Israel, killing two adults and injuring 28 children. The Israelis stage a major retaliatory raid into Jordan to hunt down the Palestinian Fatah terrorists responsible.

June 5 American presidential candidate Robert Kennedy is murdered by Jordanian terrorist Sirhan Bishara Sirhan in Los Angeles. More terrorist attacks follow when Arab terrorist groups demand Sirhan's release.

July 22 The Popular Front for the Liberation of Palestine (PFLP) carries out its first aircraft hijacking, seizing an Israeli El Al Boeing 707 in Rome, Italy, and diverting it to Algeria. Thirty-two Jewish passengers are held hostage for five weeks.

August 28 John Gordon Meir, U.S. ambassador to Guatemala, becomes the first U.S. ambassador to be assassinated by terrorists when his car is attacked by a rebel faction.

September 4 Three bombs in central Tel Aviv, Israel, kill one Israeli and wound 71 others.

October 12 A U.S. Army officer serving as an advisor to the Brazilian army is gunned down in his home in São Paulo, Brazil, by left-wing guerrillas who claim he is a "war criminal" because of U.S. actions in Vietnam.

November 22 Mahaneh Yehuda market, Israel, is bombed by Palestinian Fatah terrorists, killing 12 civilians and injuring 52 others.

December 26 One Israeli is killed in a machine-gun attack by the Popular Front for the Liberation of Palestine (PFLP) on an Israeli El Al aircraft at Athens airport, Greece. Two terrorists are captured but later released after a Greek aircraft is hijacked to Beirut. Three days after the Athens attack, Israeli commandos raid Beirut airport, Lebanon, and blow up 13 Arab airliners worth $43 million.

1969

February 18 Palestinian terrorists attack an Israeli El Al Boeing 707 on the runway at Zurich airport, Switzerland, killing the pilot and three passengers. An Israeli skymarshal returns fire, killing one of the terrorists and driving off the others.

February 21 Palestinian terrorists explode a bomb in a crowded supermarket in Jerusalem, Israel, killing two people and injuring 20.

August 29 A TWA airliner is hijacked after taking off from Rome, Italy, by Popular Front for the Liberation of Palestine (PFLP) terrorists led by Leila Khaled, and forced to fly to Damascus, Syria. All the passengers and crew are released unharmed by the terrorists, despite a bomb being exploded in the cockpit of the aircraft.

September 4 American ambassador Charles Elbrick is kidnapped in Rio de Janeiro, Brazil, by left-wing terrorists – the first-ever diplomatic kidnapping. He is freed after 15 terrorists are released from jail.

October 22 Four civilians are killed and 20 are wounded by Palestinian bombs in Haifa, Israeli.

December 12 Left-wing anarchist terrorists kill 16 people and wound 90 when they blow up a bank in Milan, Italy. In July 1970, the same group derails a train near Rome, Italy, killing six and injuring 100.

1970

February 10 Three Arab terrorists try to hijack an Israeli El Al Boeing 707 at Munich airport, West Germany, but are thwarted by the pilot who grapples with a terrorist in a terminal lounge. One person is killed and 11 wounded.

February 21 The Popular Front for the Liberation of Palestine (PFLP) blows up a Swiss airliner just after it has taken off from Zurich, Switzerland, killing all 47 people on board.

May 14 German left-wing terrorist leader Andreas Baader is freed from a West Berlin jail, in a rescue raid led by fellow terrorist Ulrike Meinhof. The two become notorious as leaders of the Baader-Meinhof Gang.

September 6 "Skyjack Sunday": three aircraft are hijacked, with more than 400 hostages, by the Popular Front for the Liberation of Palestine (PFLP). Two of the aircraft are taken to Jordan, where the hostages are taken off and the aircraft blown up, the third is blown up in Egypt. Another team tries to hijack an El Al Boeing over London but fails. One of the hijackers, Leila Khaled, is captured alive. On September 9, another airliner is hijacked to Jordan. German, Swiss, and British governments all agree to the PFLP's demands and release a number of terrorists, including Khaled.

October 10 Quebec separatists kidnap state government minister Pierre LaPorte and later murder him. The same group kidnaps British trade commissioner James Cross but releases him unharmed.

1971

January 8 The British ambassador to Uruguay, Sir Geoffrey Jackson, is taken and held for nine months by Tupamaros terrorists demanding the release of political prisoners.

May 17 Turkish radicals assassinate the Israeli consul general in Istanbul, Turkey, in a joint operation with Palestinian terrorists.

August 8 Black Panther leader George Jackson is killed in a gun battle inside California State Prison, San Quentin, California.

November 28 Jordanian Prime Minister Wasfi Tal is shot and killed by Palestinian Black September terrorists at the Sheraton Hotel in Cairo, Egypt. A month later the Jordanian ambassador in London, England, is shot and wounded by a Black September squad.

December 4 Protestant Ulster Volunteer Force (UVF) terrorists explode a bomb in a Catholic area of Belfast, Northern Ireland, killing 15 civilians.

1972

January 30 "Bloody Sunday": British troops open fire on Catholic civil rights protesters in Derry, Northern Ireland, killing 13.

February 22 The Irish Republican Army (IRA) carry out a bomb attack on the British Parachute Regiment Officers Mess (club) in Aldershot, England, killing seven people.

March 4 Two people die and 131 are injured when Protestant terrorists bomb the Abercorn restaurant in Belfast, Northern Ireland.

May 5 Italian terrorist and publisher Giangiancomo Feltrinelli accidentally blows himself up while planting a bomb on an electricity pylon near Florence, Italy.

May 8 Israeli commandos storm a hijacked Belgian Sabena airliner at Lod airport, Israel, killing three Palestinian Black September terrorists and freeing the hostages. Five Israeli soldiers and one passenger are killed.

May 11 The U.S. Army headquarters in Frankfurt, West Germany, are attacked by a Red Army Faction car bomb, killing one American officer and injuring 13 people. Three more U.S. servicemen are injured in another Red Army Faction car-bomb attack on the U.S. Army headquarters at Heidelberg, West Germany, later in the month.

May 30 Japanese Red Army members, acting on behalf of the Popular Front for the Liberation of Palestine (PFLP), open fire in the passenger terminal of Lod airport, Israel, killing 26 civilians and wounding 78 others. Japanese terrorist Kozo Okamoto survives and is captured by the Israelis.

July 21 "Bloody Friday" in Belfast, Northern Ireland: Irish Republican Army (IRA) bomb attacks kill 11 people and injure 130. Ten days later, three IRA car bomb attacks in the village of Claudy leave six dead.

September 5 Eight Palestinian Black September terrorists kill two Israeli athletes and take nine hostage in the Olympic Village in Munich, West Germany. In a bungled rescue attempt, all nine hostages, one police officer, and five terrorists are killed.

September 9 A member of the Israeli embassy staff in London, England, is killed by a Palestinian letter bomb.

1973

February 4 The Irish Republican Army (IRA) explodes a bomb on a coach full of British soldiers on the M62 highway in northern England, killing 12 people.

March 12 Palestinian Black September terrorists murder an Israeli businessman in Cyprus.

August 5 A Black September suicide squad attacks passenger terminals at Athens airport, Greece, killing three civilians and injuring 55.

August 8 Twelve people die and 48 are injured when neo-fascists explode a bomb on a train approaching Bologna, Italy. In May another right-wing bomb in Brescia, Italy, kills eight people.

September 5 Five Palestinian terrorists from a Black September splinter group seize the Saudi Arabian embassy in Paris, France. They are flown to Kuwait, and their hostages are released when the terrorists surrender three days later.

September 28 Two Palestinian terrorists from the Syrian-backed Saiqa group seize a train in Vienna and take three Russian Jews hostage. They are released when Austrian Chancellor Bruno Kreisky promises to shut down a transit camp in Austria for Jews emigrating to Israel.

December 17 Palestinian terrorists bomb a Pan Am office at Fiumicino airport, Rome, Italy, killing 32 and injuring 50. The terrorists then take seven Italian police officers hostage and hijack an aircraft to Athens, Greece. After killing one hostage, they fly on to Kuwait, where they surrender.

December 20 A Basque Fatherland and Liberty (ETA) bomb kills Spanish Prime Minister Admiral Luis Carrero Blanco in Madrid, Spain.

1974

January 31 Two Popular Front for the Liberation of Palestine (PFLP) and two Japanese Red Army terrorists seize a boat and five hostages after attacking oil installations in Singapore. A week later, five more terrorists attack the Japanese embassy in Kuwait, demanding safe passage for their colleagues. All nine terrorists are flown to safety in South Yemen.

February 4 American heiress Patty Hearst is kidnapped by Symbionese Liberation Army terrorists. She later joins the group, participating in a raid on the Hibernia Bank in San Francisco.

March 1 The Saudi Arabian embassy in Khartoum, Sudan, is seized by Black September terrorists, and a number of diplomats from Arab and Western countries are taken hostage. The terrorists murder one Belgian and two American diplomats.

April 11 Terrorists of the Popular Front for the Liberation of Palestine-General Command (PFLP-GC) seize part of the Kiryat Shmona settlement in northern Israel. Eighteen Israelis die when the terrorists detonate explosives during a rescue attempt.

May 15 Ninety children are held hostage by Popular Democratic Front for the Liberation of Palestine terrorists in a school at Ma'alot, Israel. During the bungled rescue attempt by Israeli special forces, 21 people are killed and 65 are wounded.

May 17 Car bombs planted by Protestant terrorists kill 22 people in Dublin, in the Irish Republic.

June 13 The Shamir kibbutz in Israel is raided by the Popular Front for the Liberation of Palestine (PFLP). All four terrorists and several Israelis are killed in the ensuing gun battle.

June 26 Palestinian Fatah terrorists land by boat near Nahariya, Israel, and attempt to take civilians hostage. Three Israelis and all the terrorists are killed in a firefight.

August 19 Cypriot nationalist terrorists belonging to the revived National Organization of Cypriot Fighters (EOKA-B) attack the U.S. embassy in Nicosia, Cyprus, and kill ambassador Rodger P. Davies in revenge for U.S. support of Turkey.

November 21 The Irish Republican Army (IRA) sets off bombs in bars in Birmingham, England, killing 21 civilians, as part of a major bombing campaign on the British mainland.

November 23 A British DC-10 airliner is hijacked at Dubai, United Arab Emirates, by Palestinian Rejectionist Front terrorists and flown to Tunisia where a German passenger is killed.

1975

January 19 Arab terrorists attack Orly airport, Paris, France, seizing ten hostages in a terminal washroom. Eventually, the French authorities provide the terrorists with a plane to fly them to safety in Baghdad, Iraq.

January 21 Indian railroad minister Narayan Mishra is blown up in Bihar, India, by Ananda Marg terrorists.

January 24 Puerto Rican nationalist FALN terrorists bomb Fraunces Tavern on Wall Street, New York, killing four and injuring 60.

January 27 Politician Peter Lorenz is kidnapped in West Berlin, West Germany, by terrorists of the June 2 Movement. Four days later, the West German government gives in to their conditions for his release and five jailed terrorists are allowed to fly to freedom in South Yemen.

January 29 Weather Underground terrorists bomb the U.S. State Department in Washington, DC, causing considerable damage.

April 13 Christian militia members massacre 25 Palestinians in Zgharta, Lebanon. Muslim retaliation follows, triggering civil war.

April 24 German left-wing terrorists seize the West German embassy in Stockholm, Sweden, and take 12 staff hostage to force the release of Baader-Meinhof Gang terrorists. Two hostages are murdered, and a terrorist is killed when explosives are detonated by accident.

August 4 Ten Japanese Red Army terrorists seize the U.S. consulate and the Swedish embassy in Kuala Lumpur, Malaysia, and secure the release of seven Japanese Red Army prisoners. Two prisoners refuse to leave.

October 3 Irish Republican Army (IRA) terrorists kidnap Dutch industrialist Teide Herrema in Dublin, in the Irish Republic. After a month-long hunt, the Irish police surround the terrorists' hideout, forcing his release.

October 4 Members of the Spanish left-wing group GRAPO (Antifascist Resistance Group of the First of October) murder four Spanish police officers, after five members of the group in custody are executed.

November 27 British publisher Ross McWhirter is shot by Irish Republican Army (IRA) terrorists at his home in London, England, after offering a reward for information leading to the arrest of terrorist bombers.

December 2 South Moluccan terrorists seize a train at Beilen, Netherlands, for 12 days. Three hostages are shot before the terrorists surrender.

December 4 Seven South Moluccan terrorists seize the Indonesian embassy in Amsterdam, Netherlands, beginning a two-week siege. One of the 36 hostages dies jumping from a window to escape the terrorists.

December 6 Four Irish Republican Army (IRA) terrorists seize two hostages in Balcombe Street, London, England. After six days, they surrender to police, releasing their hostages unharmed.

December 21 International terrorist "Carlos the Jackal" holds 11 oil ministers and 59 civilians hostage during a meeting of the Organization of Petroleum Exporting Countries (OPEC) in Vienna, Austria. After flying to Algeria and receiving several hundred million dollars in ransom money, Carlos and his Popular Front for the Liberation of Palestine (PFLP) terrorists escape.

December 23 Greek left-wing terrorists of the November 17 movement kill Richard Welch, CIA station chief in Athens, Greece, as the beginning of a campaign opposing Greek membership of NATO.

1976

June 27 An Air France airliner is hijacked by a joint German Baader-Meinhof/Popular Front for the Liberation of Palestine terrorist group and is forced to fly to Entebbe airport in Uganda. Some 258 passengers and crew are held hostage, but all non-Israeli and non-Jewish passengers are eventually released. The Ugandan authorities assist the terrorists. On July 3, Israeli commandos fly to Uganda and rescue the remaining hostages. All the terrorists and three passengers are killed in the rescue.

July 21 British ambassador to the Irish Republic Christopher Ewart-Biggs is killed when an Irish Republican Army (IRA) landmine destroys his car near Dublin, in the Irish Republic.

August 11 Terrorists from both the Popular Front for the Liberation of Palestine (PFLP) and the Japanese Red Army attack a passenger terminal at Istanbul airport, Turkey, killing four civilians and injuring 20.

September 10 A TWA airliner flying from New York to Chicago, is hijacked by Croatian terrorists, seizing 93 hostages, and flown to Paris, France, where the terrorists surrender and release their hostages. A New York police officer is killed by a bomb left by the terrorists in a locker in Grand Central Station.

September 21 Chilean exile Orlando Letelier is murdered by a car bomb in the center of Washington, DC, by Chilean secret service agents.

October 10 Seventy-three people are killed when Cuban exiles of the Miami-based El Condor group explode a bomb aboard a Cuban Airlines jet as it takes off from Barbados.

1977

January 10 Ten civilians die when their mini-bus is ambushed by the Irish Republican Army (IRA) at Kingsmills, Northern Ireland.

May 23 Thirteen South Moluccan terrorists seize 85 hostages on a train at Assen, Netherlands. Two hostages and all the terrorists are killed when Dutch Marines storm the train to end a 19-day siege.

September 5 West German business leader Hanns-Martin Schleyer is kidnapped by the Baader-Meinhof Gang. He is later murdered.

October 13 Four Palestinian terrorists hijack a West German Lufthansa Boeing 737 and order it to fly to a number of Middle Eastern destinations over four days. After the plane's pilot is killed by the terrorists, it is stormed by German counterterrorist troops, assisted by two British Army Special Air Service (SAS) soldiers, when it puts down at Mogadishu, Somalia. All 91 hostages are rescued and three terrorists are killed.

1978

February 17 An Irish Republican Army (IRA) bomb kills 12 civilians at the La Mon House restaurant, Comber, Northern Ireland.

February 19 An airliner is hijacked at Larnaca airport, Cyprus, by two Arab terrorists who have just murdered a leading Egyptian publisher at a nearby hotel. After being refused permission to land at various Arab capitals, the hijackers return to Larnaca. Egyptian commandos land and try to storm the plane but end up in a gun battle with Cypriot troops. Fifteen Egyptian troops, seven Cypriot soldiers, and a West German cameraman are killed.

March 11 A nine-strong Palestinian Fatah seaborne raiding party lands in Israeli and hijacks a bus, killing 26 civilians and wounding 70. All the terrorists are killed by Israeli security forces. The Israelis retaliate by invading southern Lebanon, under code name Operation Litani.

March 16 Former Italian Prime Minister Aldo Moro is kidnapped by Red Brigade terrorists and later murdered after 55 days in captivity.

May 16 One person is injured in a package bomb explosion at Northwestern University, Illinois. This is later accepted as the first attack by the Unabomber.

August 20 An Israeli El Al air steward is killed when a crew bus is ambushed by Popular Front for the Liberation of Palestine (PFLP) terrorists outside the Europa Hotel, London, England.

September 7 Exiled Bulgarian journalist Georgi Markov is killed by Bulgarian secret service agents who inject him with poison using a specially modified umbrella on a street in London, England.

1979

March 30 British politician Airey Neave is killed when a bomb planted under his car by the Irish National Liberation Army (INLA) explodes in the parking garage of the House of Commons, London, England.

May 9 One person is injured in a bomb explosion at Northwestern University, Illinois, which is blamed on the Unabomber.

June 18 NATO's Supreme Allied Commander Europe General Alexander Haig escapes death when a terrorist bomb explodes under a bridge just after his motorcade has passed over it. The German Red Army Faction is blamed by intelligence sources.

August 27 Eighteen British Parachute Regiment soldiers die in two bomb attacks on a patrol operating near Warrenpoint, Northern Ireland. The Irish Republican Army (IRA) detonate the bombs by remote control from across the border in the Irish Republic. On the same day, Earl Mountbatten of Burma is murdered by an IRA bomb which destroys his boat during a fishing trip off the coast of the Irish Republic.

November 4 Iranian radicals seize the U.S. embassy in Tehran, taking 66 American diplomats hostage. A U.S. rescue effort, led by the Delta Force counterterrorist unit, fails on April 25, 1980, when a Marine Corps CH-53 helicopter crashes into a U.S. Air Force C-130 transport aircraft at a forward refueling site in central Iran, killing eight Americans and injuring five. The crisis continues until January 20, 1981, when the hostages are released by diplomatic means.

November 15 Twelve people are injured in a bomb explosion on an American Airlines flight. The blast is blamed on the Unabomber.

November 20 Two hundred Islamic terrorists seize the Grand Mosque in Mecca, Saudi Arabia, taking hundreds of pilgrims hostage. Saudi and French security forces retake the Islamic world's most holy shrine after an intense battle, in which some 250 people are killed and 600 wounded.

1980

February 1 Six Spanish police officers die in an ambush by Basque terrorists near Bilbao, Spain.

February 27 Fifty-four hostages are seized in the Dominican Republic embassy in Bogotá, Colombia, by Colombian terrorists demanding the release of 311 prisoners. Eventually, after they release their hostages, the terrorists are given sanctuary in Cuba.

March 24 Archbishop Oscar Romero is killed by a right-wing death squad while saying mass in his cathedral in San Salvador, El Salvador.

April 30 Six Iraqi-backed Iranians storm the Iranian embassy in Princes Gate, London, taking 26 hostages. Six days later, British Special Air Service (SAS) counterterrorist troops recapture the embassy, killing five of the terrorists and freeing the remaining hostages. Two hostages are killed by the terrorists and two more are wounded.

May 2 A British Special Air Service (SAS) officer is killed in Belfast, Northern Ireland, in a gun battle with an Irish Republican Army (IRA) active service unit armed with an M60 heavy machine gun.

June 1 The African National Congress (ANC) bombs strategic oil-from-coal plants in South Africa, causing $7 million worth of damage.

July 17 Two people die in a failed Iranian attempt to assassinate the shah's last prime minister, Shahpour

Bakhtiar, in Paris, France. Five terrorists are captured by the police.

July 21 Christian militiamen shoot down a Palestinian terrorist team attempting an attack on Israel from Lebanon in a hot air balloon.

August 1 Bologna rail station in Italy is devastated by a massive bomb, believed planted by right-wing terrorists linked to rogue elements in the country's intelligence services. The blast kills 75 people and injures 300.

August 13 An Air Florida flight from Key West to Miami is hijacked by seven Cubans and flown to Cuba, where the hijackers release their hostages and are then taken into custody. Six more U.S. airliners are hijacked to Cuba over the next month. All the passengers are freed without harm, but three passengers are killed when anti-Castro Cubans hijack an aircraft in Peru and demand to be flown to the United States.

October 3 Four Jews are killed and 12 are injured in a Palestinian bomb attack on a synagogue in Paris, France.

October 6 The president of United Airlines is injured in a bomb attack in Chicago attributed to the Unabomber.

October 13 Four Iranian hijackers are killed when Turkish security forces storm a hijacked Turkish Airlines aircraft after it lands in eastern Turkey. One hostage is killed by the terrorists.

October 26 A neo-Nazi bomb attack on the October beer festival in Munich, West Germany, leaves 13 people dead and 72 injured.

December 4 Three U.S. Catholic nuns and one U.S. Catholic lay missionary are found murdered outside San Salvador, the capital of El Salvador. They are believed to have been assassinated by one of the right-wing government's death squads.

1981

January 21 Sir Norman Stronge, former speaker of the Northern Irish, Parliament, and his son are shot and killed by the Irish Republican Army (IRA) during an attack on their home in Northern Ireland.

March 3 Swedish Prime Minister Olaf Palme, unaccompanied by bodyguards, is shot dead by a lone gunman as he leaves a movie theater in Stockholm, Sweden. Swedish police never succeed in making an arrest for the crime.

April 16 Palestinian terrorists attempt an attack on Israel from Lebanon in a hot air balloon. Israeli air defenses shoot down the balloon, killing all the crew.

May 13 Pope John Paul II is seriously wounded in an assassination attempt in Vatican City by Turkish terrorist Mehmet Ali Ağça. Formerly of the Turkish Grey Wolves, Ağça has been trained by a number of Middle Eastern terrorist groups and has links to Warsaw Pact intelligence services.

August 31 A large bomb explodes in a parking lot at a U.S. Air Force base at Ramstein, West Germany, injuring 20 people. The Red Army Faction claims responsibility.

September 15 Red Army Faction terrorists make an unsuccessful rocket attack on the car of U.S. Army commander in West Germany, General Fred Kroesen.

October 6 Egyptian President Anwar Sadat is shot dead by rebel troops who machine-gun the reviewing stand at a military parade in Cairo, Egypt. Seven others are killed and 28 wounded. The assassins are later executed.

October 8 An unexploded bomb is found and defused at the University of Utah, Salt Lake City. The so-called Unabomber is linked to the attack.

October 10 An Irish Republican Army (IRA) bomb kills two civilians and injures 40 others outside an army barracks in Chelsea, London. Seven days later another bomb injures Lieutenant-General Sir Stuart Pringle, a senior Royal Marines officer, outside his home in London.

December 17 U.S. Army Brigadier-General James Dozier is kidnapped from his home in Verona, Italy, by Italian Red Brigade terrorists. He is held for 45 days until Italian special forces rescue him on January 26, 1982.

1982

February 2 Syrian President Hafez Assad orders the destruction of the Syrian town of Hama, after its occupation by Muslim Brotherhood forces attempting to overthrow the regime. Estimates of fatalities range from 10,000 to 25,000.

April 3 The Lebanese Armed Revolutionary Faction (FARL) kills an Israeli diplomat in Paris, France.

June 3 The Israeli ambassador in London, England, Shlomo Argov, is shot and seriously injured by terrorists from the Abu Nidal Organization. The attack is used to justify the Israeli invasion of Lebanon that begins immediately after the attack.

July 2 A professor is injured in a bomb attack at the University of California, Berkeley, attributed to the Unabomber.

July 20 Four Household Cavalry soldiers and seven horses are killed when the Irish Republican Army (IRA) explodes a bomb in Hyde Park, London, England. Two hours later, another bomb explodes under a bandstand in Regent's Park, killing seven additional soldiers. Fifty-one people are injured by the two bombs.

August 22 Six civilians are killed in an attack on a restaurant in Paris, France, by the Action Directe group.

September 14 Lebanese President Bashir Gemayel is assassinated by a massive car bomb at the Beirut headquarters of his Phalange political party. Scores of civilians are injured in the blast. Two days later, Phalange Christian militiamen occupy the Sabra/Chatila Palestinian refugee camps in Beirut, Lebanon, and start to massacre civilians in revenge for the death of Gemayel. Some 460 men, women, and children are killed in the attack while Israeli troops watch nearby.

November 11 The Israeli military headquarters in Tyre, Lebanon, is destroyed by an Islamic suicide bomber, killing 75 Israeli soldiers and 15 Lebanese and Palestinian prisoners.

December 6 Seventeen people are killed and 60 are injured by an Irish Republican Army (IRA) bomb in a bar at Ballykelly, Northern Ireland.

December 12 An anti-nuclear protester holds eight tourists hostage in the Washington Monument, Washington, DC. He is later shot dead by a police sniper.

1983

April 18 Sixty-three people, including the CIA's Middle East director, are killed and 120 are injured in a 400-pound suicide truck-bomb attack on the U.S. embassy in Beirut, Lebanon. Islamic Jihad claim responsibility.

July 23 Eight people are killed and 55 injured when a suitcase bomb explodes near a check-in desk at Orly airport, Paris, France. Armenian terrorists are later arrested by French security forces for the attack.

July 27 Armenian terrorists seize the Turkish embassy in Lisbon, Portugal, taking the staff hostage. Five terrorists, a Portuguese policeman, and Turkish women are killed when a terrorist bomb explodes prematurely.

October 9 The Martyr's Mausoleum bombing in Rangoon, Burma, leaves five South Korean cabinet ministers and 15 other people dead. South Korea's President Chun survives the attack which is blamed on North Korean intelligence agents.

October 23 Italian right-wing terrorists explode a bomb on a train, killing 15 people and injuring 115.

October 23 Simultaneous suicide truck-bomb attacks are made on American and French compounds in Beirut, Lebanon. A 12,000-pound bomb destroys a U.S. Marine Corps base, killing 241 Americans, while 58 French troops are killed when a 400-pound device destroys a French base. Islamic Jihad claims responsibility. U.S. and French aircraft strike suspected terrorist bases in retaliation.

November 4 Twenty-eight Israeli soldiers, along with 30 Palestinian and Lebanese civilians, are killed in another suicide truck-bomb attack on the Israeli military headquarters in Tyre, southern Lebanon.

November 6 A U.S. Senate cloakroom is bombed by the Armed Resistance Unit terrorist group in protest against the U.S invasion of Grenada.

November 15 A U.S. Navy officer is shot by the November 17 terrorist group in Athens, Greece, while his car is stopped at a traffic light.

December 12 The U.S. embassy in Kuwait is targeted by an Iranian-backed Iraqi Shia terrorist who attempts to destroy the building with a truck bomb. The attack is foiled by guards and the device explodes in the embassy forecourt, killing five people.

December 17 The climax of an Irish Republican Army (IRA) Christmas bombing campaign in London, England, sees two policemen and three civilians killed in a car-bomb attack on Harrods department store.

1984

March 8 A car bomb in Beirut, Lebanon, kills 80 and wounds more than 200 civilians, in what is believed to have been an American CIA-backed attempt to kill the leader of the Hizb'allah terrorist group.

March 16 The CIA station chief in Beirut, Lebanon, William Buckley, is kidnapped by the Iranian-backed Islamic Jihad. He is tortured and then executed.

April 12 Eighteen U.S. servicemen are killed and 83 people are injured in a bomb attack on a restaurant near a U.S. Air Force base in Torrejón, Spain. Responsibility is claimed by Hizb'allah as revenge for the bombing incident in Beirut in March.

April 17 British security forces, including Special Air Service (SAS) counterterrorist troops, lay siege to the Libyan People's Bureau (embassy) in London after a British woman police officer is killed by small-arms fire originating from inside the building.

April 22 Four Palestinian terrorists hijack a bus carrying Israelis in Gaza. Israeli special forces storm the bus and kill two of the terrorists after they have been captured.

June 5 Sikh terrorists seize the Golden Temple in Amritsar, India; 100 people die when the holy shrine is retaken by Indian security forces.

August 2 Tamil Tiger terrorists blow up an airport terminal at Madras, India, killing 30 people and injuring 24 more. The bomb's intended target was a Sri Lankan airliner.

September 20 A suicide bomb attack on the U.S. embassy in East Beirut kills 23 people and injures 21 others. The U.S. and British ambassadors are slightly injured in the explosion, which is attributed to the Iranian-backed Hizb'allah group.

October 12 British Prime Minister Margaret Thatcher and her cabinet escape death in an Irish Republican Army (IRA) bomb attack on the Grand Hotel, Brighton, England, during the Conservative Party Congress. Five people are killed and 30 injured in the attack, which destroys the front of the hotel.

October 31 Indian Prime Minister Indira Gandhi is gunned down by her own Sikh bodyguards in Delhi, India. Almost 3,000 people die in the riots that follow her assassination.

December 4 A Kuwaiti airliner is hijacked en route to Pakistan from Dubai by Iranian-backed Iraqi Shia terrorists. The aircraft is forced to land in the Iranian capital, Tehran, after two Americans have been killed. The terrorists surrender to the Iranian authorities and are later released.

1985

January 15 General René Audan, head of French international arms sales, is shot dead at his home in Paris, France, by terrorists from the Action Directe-Red Army Faction, a pan-European radical group. Two weeks later, industrialist Ernest Zimmerman and his wife are murdered in their home in Munich, West Germany, by Red Army Faction terrorists.

February 28 Nine Royal Ulster Constabulary officers are killed and 57 people are wounded in a mortar attack by the Irish Republican Army (IRA) on Newry police station, Northern Ireland.

March 8 A car bomb explodes outside Hizb'allah's headquarters in Beirut, Lebanon, killing 80 people.

March 16 U.S. journalist Terry Anderson is kidnapped in Beirut, Lebanon, by Iranian-backed Islamic radicals. He is finally released in December 1991.

May 15 One person is injured in a bomb explosion in a computer room at the University of California, Berkeley, attributed to the Unabomber.

May 20 The African National Congress (ANC) bombs the South African air force headquarters in Pretoria, South Africa, killing 19 civilians and injuring over 200 people.

June 6 A Red Army Faction bomb explodes at Frankfurt airport, West Germany, killing three people.

June 9 U.S. academic Thomas Sutherland is kidnapped by Islamic terrorists at the American University in Beirut, Lebanon, and held until November 18, 1991.

June 14 A TWA Boeing 727 is hijacked en route to Rome, Italy, from Athens, Greece, by two Lebanese Hizb'allah terrorists and forced to fly to Beirut, Lebanon. The eight crew and 145 passengers are then held for 17 days, during which one American hostage is murdered. After being flown twice to Algiers, the hostages are released on the aircraft's return to Beirut, after the U.S. government pressure the Israelis to release 435 Lebanese and Palestinian prisoners.

June 23 An Air India Boeing 747 is destroyed by a bomb over the Atlantic, killing all 329 people aboard. Both Sikh and Kashmiri terrorists are blamed for the attack, which remains the worst single terrorist incident to date. Two cargo handlers are killed at Tokyo airport, Japan, when another Sikh bomb explodes in an Air Canada aircraft en route to India.

July 9 Industrialist Karl-Heinz Beckurte is killed in car bomb attack in Munich, West Germany. The Red Army Faction claims responsibility.

July 10 French secret service agents plant a bomb on the *Rainbow Warrior*, flagship of the Greenpeace ecological protest group, in Auckland harbor, New Zealand. Greepeace are engaged in protesting against French nuclear testing in the Pacific Ocean. The bomb sink the vessel and kills one member of Greenpeace.

July 13 The Unabomber is believed responsible for an explosive device mailed to the Boeing aircraft company headquarters in Auburn, Washington.

August 8 Three U.S. servicemen are killed and 17 are injured in a Red Army Faction bomb and gun attack on a Rhein-Main airbase, West Germany.

September 25 A Palestine Liberation Organization (PLO) Force 17 commando squad kills three Israeli tourists aboard a yacht in Larnaca marina, Cyprus. The three-strong squad, including Briton Ian Davison, are imprisoned by the Cypriots.

September 30 Four Soviet diplomats are kidnapped in Beirut, Lebanon, by the Islamic Liberation Organization, thought to be a front for the Iranian-backed Hizb'allah. One of the Russians is killed, but the others are released unharmed after a relative of the terrorist group's leaders is kidnapped and killed by the Soviet KGB.

October 1 Israeli aircraft bomb the Palestine Liberation Organization (PLO) headquarters in Tunisia in retaliation for the murder of three Israeli tourists in Larnaca on September 25.

October 7 Four Palestinian Liberation Front terrorists seize the Italian liner, *Achille Lauro*, during a cruise in the eastern Mediterranean, taking more than 700 people hostage. One U.S. passenger is murdered before the Egyptian government offers the terrorists safe haven in return for the hostages' freedom. U.S. Navy fighters intercept the Egyptian aircraft flying the terrorists to safety in Tunis and force it to land at a NATO airbase in Italy, where the terrorists are arrested. The Italian authorities, however, let two of the terrorist leaders escape using diplomatic passports.

October 11 The Jewish Defense League bombs an Arab-American lobbying office in Los Angeles, killing its director, Alex Odeh.

November 10 A senior government official, Gerold von Braunmuhl, is shot at his home in Bonn, West Germany, by Red Army Faction terrorists.

November 11 Two are hurt in an alleged Unabomber attack on the University of Michigan. A month later, a computer store owner is killed in another possible Unabomber attack in Sacramento, California.

November 13 The Palace of Justice in Bogotá, Colombia, is seized by left-wing M-19 terrorists and 100 hostages are taken, including a number of judges. All the terrorists and most of the hostages are killed when the Colombian army storms the building.

November 23 Ninety-eight passengers and crew of an Egyptair aircraft are held hostage by Palestinian terrorists at Luqa, Malta. Five passengers are shot by the terrorists and two killed. An ill-fated assault by Egyptian Force 777 commandos results in some 57 passengers being killed when the terrorists set off explosives.

December 23 A bomb planted by the African National Congress (ANC) explodes in a shopping area in Durban, South Africa, killing five people and injuring 48.

December 27 Suicide grenade and gun attacks against passenger terminals at Rome, Italy, and Vienna, Austria, airports by the Abu Nidal terrorist group result in 16 people being killed and more than 100 injured.

1986

February 6 Basque Fatherland and Liberty (ETA) terrorists assassinate Spanish Admiral Cristobal Colón in Madrid, Spain.

April 5 Two U.S. soldiers are killed and 79 American servicemen are injured in a Libyan bomb attack on a night club in West Berlin, West Germany. Ten days later, U.S. Air Force and Navy jets bomb Libya in reprisal, hitting targets in Tripoli and Benghazi. One U.S. Air Force F-111 is shot down in the raids, killing its two crew. Some 93 Libyan civilians are killed in the raids. Three British hostages held by Islamic groups in the Lebanon are killed in response.

April 17 British television journalist John McCarthy is seized in Beirut by Iranian-backed terrorists and held hostage with a large group of other Westerners until August 8, 1991.

May 1 Cargese holiday camp, on the French island of Corsica, is seized by separatist rebels, who kill two hostages and injure three.

June 26 Communist revolutionary Shining Path guerrillas bomb a train in Peru, killing eight people.

September 5 A Pan American Boeing 747 is seized by Arab terrorists in Pakistan. They kill 17 hostages and wound another 127, after panicking and thinking they are under attack. Pakistani security forces then storm the aircraft and free the hostages.

September 12 U.S. academic Joseph Cicippio is seized at the American University in Beirut, Lebanon, by

Iranian-backed Islamic terrorists. He is not released until December 1, 1991.

September 17 A 10-month series of bombings in Paris, France, attributed to Lebanese, Armenian, and Iranian terrorists, culminates in a bomb that kills five people and injures 52.

October 21 American businessman Edward Tracy is kidnapped in Lebanon by Islamic terrorists and held for almost five years, until August 11, 1991.

November 7 The president of the French automobile company Renault is killed by the Action Directe group in Paris, France.

1987

January 10 British church envoy Terry Waite disappears in Beirut, Lebanon, while on a mission to secure the release of other Western hostages held in the city by Iranian-backed groups. He is eventually released on November 18, 1991.

January 24 American citizens Jesse Turner and Alan Steen are seized in Beirut, Lebanon, by Islamic terrorists. Turner is held until October 22, 1991, and Steen until December 3, 1991.

February 20 One person is injured in an alleged Unabomber bomb attack on a computer store in Salt Lake City, Utah.

May 8 An Irish Republican Army (IRA) team moving to attack Loughall police station, Northern Ireland, is ambushed by British Army Special Air Service (SAS) commandos. All eight terrorists are killed and a civilian is injured in the shoot-out.

November 11 An Irish Republican Army (IRA) bomb eplodes during a Remembrance Sunday (Veterans' Day) ceremony at Enniskillen, Northern Ireland, killing 11 civilians and injuring 60 others.

November 25 Two hang gliders are used by Palestinian terrorists to cross into Israel from Lebanon. They attack an army camp, killing six Israeli soldiers and wounding eight others.

December 9 Palestinian protests against an Israeli motorist, who has killed Palestinian pedestrians in the Gaza Strip, turn into riots. This marks the beginning of the Intifada uprising.

1988

February 17 U.S. Marine Corps Lieutenant-Colonel W. Higgins is kidnapped and murdered by the Iranian-backed Hizb'allah group while serving with the United Nations Truce Supervisory Organization in southern Lebanon.

March 6 Three Irish Republican Army (IRA) terrorists preparing to explode a bomb in the British colony of Gibraltar are ambushed and killed by British Special Air Service (SAS) soldiers.

March 16 During the funeral in Belfast, Northern Ireland, of the three Irish terrorists killed in Gibraltar, Ulster Protestant Michael Stone throws hand grenades and opens fire on mourners, killing three and wounding 50. Four days later, two British soldiers are dragged from a car in Belfast during an Irish Republican Army (IRA) funeral procession, beaten, and then shot dead.

March 16 Four thousand Kurdish civilians are killed during an Iraqi nerve gas attack against Halabja in northern Iraq after the Iraqi President Saddam Hussein orders this weapon to be used to put down a Kurdish revolt.

April 5 Iranian-backed Shia terrorists hold 122 people hostage when they hijack a Kuwaiti Boeing 747 and divert it to Mashad, Iran, before flying on to Cyprus. The Kuwait government rejects their demand for the release of 17 convicted terrorists. After 15 days, Algeria grants the hijackers asylum. The hostages are released unharmed.

April 14 The car-bombing of a U.S. Navy club in Naples, Italy, kills five people. The attack is carried out by Japanese Red Army terrorists with Libyan backing, on the second anniversary of the U.S. raid on Libya.

May 1 Three British servicemen are killed by the Irish Republican Army (IRA) in two shooting and bombing incidents in Holland.

June 15 Six British Army soldiers are killed by an Irish Republican Army (IRA) car bomb during a charity sports event in Lisburn, Northern Ireland.

June 8 A U.S. Naval attaché is killed by the left-wing November 17 group in Athens, Greece. The group's actions against U.S. armed forces personnel in Greece also include attempts to bomb U.S. military shuttle buses in April and August of the same year.

August 1 The Mill Hill British Army base in London, England, is bombed by the Irish Republican Army (IRA).

August 8 Pakistan President Zia al-Haq and the U.S. ambassador are killed, along with 37 other people, when a bomb explodes on a C-130 Hercules aircraft just after takeoff from Bahawalpur, Pakistan.

August 20 Eight British soldiers are killed and 27 are injured when the Irish Republican Army (IRA) blows up the bus carrying them to their barracks in Tyrone, Northern Ireland.

November 15 An independent Palestinian state is declared in the West Bank and Gaza Strip. In return, the Palestinian Liberation Organization (PLO) acknowledges Israel's right to exist within its pre-1967 borders.

December 21 A Pan Am Boeing 747 is blown up over Lockerbie, Scotland, by a bomb believed to have been placed on the aircraft at Frankfurt airport, West Germany. All 259 people on the aircraft are killed by the blast, which is attributed to a number of Middle Eastern terrorist groups. As yet, no one has been tried or claimed responsibility for the incident.

1989

February 14 Iranian religious leader Ayatollah Khomeini issues a *fatwa* against British author Salman Rushdie for his book *The Satanic Verses*. The *fatwa* declares Rushdie an enemy of Islam and urges any true believer to kill him. Rushdie goes into hiding.

May 12 British World War II veteran Jackie Mann is seized by Iranian-backed terrorists in Beirut, Lebanon, and held until September 23, 1991. Four days later, German aid workers Heinrich Struebig and Thomas Kemptner are also kidnapped in Lebanon by Islamic terrorists and held until June 1992 – the last of some 80 Westerners taken hostage in Lebanon to be released.

July 31 U.S Marine Lieutenant-Colonel William R. Higgins, kidnapped while serving in the Lebanon in February 1988, is killed by the pro-Iranian Hizb'allah group that are holding him captive.

September 19 One hundred and seventy people are killed when a French airliner explodes in mid air over the African state of Niger. The French government issues warrants for the arrest of four Libyans.

September 22 A British Army barracks at Deal, England, is attacked by the Irish Republican Army (IRA), killing 11 British Army band members.

September 26 Greek politician Pavlos Bakoyannis is assassinated by November 17 terrorists.

1990

February 25 Nicaraguan President and Sandinista leader Daniel Ortega is defeated in elections. The U.S.-backed, anti-Sandinista Contras demobilize.

April 10 An Irish Republican Army (IRA) bomb at the Baltic Exchange in the City of London financial district, England, kills three civilians and injures 91.

May 30 An seaborne attack on Tel Aviv, Israel, by the Palestine Liberation Front is thwarted by Israeli forces. The Palestine Liberation Organization (PLO) fails to condemn the attack, and as a result the U.S. government halts talks with PLO representatives.

July 30 British Conservative Party politician Ian Gow is killed by an Irish Republican Army (IRA) bomb at his home in England.

August 1 Iraqi troops invade Kuwait and subsequently seize 10,000 civilians living in Iraq and Kuwait as "human shield" hostages, in response to U.S. and allied military preparations for recapturing Kuwait. All hostages are released by the end of the year.

October 7 Israeli police open fire on Palestinian worshippers at al-Aqsa Mosque, Jerusalem, in the Israeli-occupied West Bank, killing 17 and wounding nearly 150.

1991

February 7 The Irish Republican Army (IRA) fires a mortar at the Downing Street residence of British Prime Minister John Major in London, England. No one is injured and the terrorists escape.

April 1 Red Army Faction terrorists kill German industrial chief Detlev Rohwedder at his home in Dusseldorf, Germany.

May 21 Like his mother before him, Indian Prime Minister Rajiv Gandhi is assassinated – in his case by a Tamil Tiger suicide bomber in Madras, India.

June 4 Three Irish Republican Army (IRA) terrorists attempting to kill local Protestant civilians are killed in a gun battle with British Special Air Service (SAS) troops in Coagh, Northern Ireland.

August 6 Shapur Bakhtiyar, the last Iranian prime minister before the fundamentalist revolution, is assassinated by Iranian agents in Paris.

December 5 Terry Anderson, the last and longest-held U.S. hostage, is released in Lebanon. Six U.S. hostages and several other Westerners, including Terry Waite, have been released in the space of four months.

1992

February 5 Five Catholic civilians are killed by Protestant terrorists in a betting shop in Belfast, Northern Ireland.

February 16 Four Irish Republican Army (IRA) terrorists are killed by British Special Air Service (SAS) troops during an abortive IRA attack on a police station in Tyrone, Northern Ireland.

March 17 A bomb at the Israeli embassy in Buenos Aires, Argentina, kills 20 and injures scores more. Islamic terrorists are suspected.

May 2 One tourist is killed by Islamic Jihad terrorists who attack the Israeli Red Sea resort of Eilat. Two terrorists are killed and one is captured during the follow-up operation by the Israeli Defense Forces.

June 29 Algerian Armed Islamic Movement (GIA) terrorists assassinate Algerian president Muhammad Boudiaf.

July 16 Shining Path terrorists plant two massive car bombs, killing 18 and wounding 140 in Lima, Peru, to show defiance of the rule of newly elected president Alberto Fujimori.

October 21 A female tourist is shot during an Islamic terrorist attack on a tourist group in Beirut, Lebanon.

1993

January 8 Islamic terrorists attempt to bomb a bus carrying German tourists in Egypt, but cause no casualties. A day earlier, Japanese tourists have been fired upon by terrorists in southern Egypt.

February 26 The World Trade Center in New York City is badly damaged by a massive bomb placed by Islamic terrorists. The car bomb, planted in a basement parking lot, leaves six people dead and more than 1,000 injured.

February 28 Members of the Branch Davidians cult barricade themselves into their compound at Waco, Texas, after an abortive Bureau of Alcohol Tobacco and Firearms raid leaves four federal agents and six cult members dead. The cult leader, David Koresh, and 85 cult members die when their compound burns down during an assault by federal agents on April 19.

March 20 The Irish Republican Army (IRA) bombs a shopping area in Warrington, England, killing two children and injuring 56 civilians.

April 14 The Iraqi intelligence service attempts to assassinate former U.S. President George Bush during a visit to Kuwait. Two months later, the U.S. launches a cruise missile attack on the Iraqi capital Baghdad in retaliation.

April 24 Part of the City of London financial district, England, is devastated by an IRA bomb, killing one civilian and causing $1.5 billion in damage.

May 1 The president of Sri Lanka, Ranasinghe Premadasa, is blown up by a Tamil Tiger suicide bomber.

June 22 A geneticist at the University of California, San Francisco, is injured in a bomb attack attributed to the so-called Unabomber.

June 24 A computer scientist at Yale University, New Haven, is injured in another alleged Unabomber attack.

June 27 A German antiterrorist commando is killed in a shoot-out with Red Army Faction terrorists at Bad Kleinen, Germany. One terrorist is killed and another is captured.

September 8 Nineteen people are killed and 22 injured in Johannesburg, South Africa, by pro-Zulu terrorists.

September 12 Dr. Abimael Guzmán, leader of the Shining Path guerrilla group, is captured by the Peruvian security forces. It is believed he still leads the group's terrorist campaign from his jail cell.

September 13 An Israeli-Palestinian peace agreement is signed in Washington, DC, by Israeli Prime Minister Yitzhak Rabin and Palestine Liberation Organization (PLO) leader Yasser Arafat. Palestinian terrorist groups, such as Hamas, and Israeli ultra-nationalists try to use terror to destroy the accord.

October 23 The Irish Republican Army (IRA) bombs a shop in Shankill Road, Belfast, Northern Ireland, killing ten. A week later, seven civilians are shot dead by Protestant terrorists in a bar in Greysteel, Northern Ireland, in retaliation for the Shankill bombing.

December 2 Colombian drug cartel chief Pablo Escobar is killed in a gun battle with security forces in Medellín, Colombia. It is estimated that he has been responsible for the deaths of 1,000 civilians and 500 police officers.

1994

February 25 Jewish right-wing extremist Baruch Goldstein machine-guns Moslem worshippers at a mosque in Hebron, Palestine, killing 29 and wounding about 150. Israeli security forces are later criticized for not intervening more quickly to halt the killing.

April 6 Rwandan President Juvenel Habyarimana is killed when his aircraft is shot down by a surface-to-air missile while approaching Kigali airport, Rwanda, on his return from a regional government leaders meeting. The incident sparks a massive outbreak of ethnic violence that results in more than a million people being killed.

April 24 African National Congress (ANC) offices in Johannesburg, South Africa, are devastated by a 200-pound bomb, killing nine civilians and injuring 92. Right-wing extremists trying to disrupt the country's first democratic election are blamed. Three days later, another right-wing bomb attack wounds 20 at Jan Smuts airport, Johannesburg.

June 14 Chechen rebels take 1,000 hostages at Budennovsk, Russia. About 150 are killed during an abortive rescue attempt by the Russian Army. The Chechens are later allowed to escape by the Russian government in return for the freedom of the remaining hostages.

June 20 Six civilians are gunned down in a bar at Loughinisland, Northern Ireland, by Irish Republican Army (IRA) terrorists.

June 20 A bomb explosion in Mashhad, Iran, kills 25 civilians. Opposition groups fighting to overthrow the country's Islamic regime are blamed for the attack.

July 18 Forty civilians are killed in a bomb attack on a Jewish social center in Buenos Aires, Argentina. Iranian diplomats in the city are expelled on suspicion of being connected with the incident.

July 26 Khmer Rouge terrorists kidnap Australian, British, and French tourists in Cambodia. Along with two other Western tourists, they are all killed later in the year.

August 15 The French Interior Ministry announces that "Carlos the Jackal" has been arrested in Sudan by French agents.

September 19 Terrorists of the November 17 organization explode a bomb on a bus in Greece, killing one policeman and injuring 13 others.

October 19 A Hamas suicide bomber kills 22 civilians and injures 47 on a bus in the center of Tel Aviv, Israel.

October 23 Two Spanish nuns are murdered by Armed Islamic Group (GIA) terrorists in Algeria.

December 12 An advertising executive is killed in a bomb attack in North Caldwell, New Jersey. He is the second fatality linked to the Unabomber.

December 24 Algerian Islamic terrorists seize an Air France Airbus and force it to fly to Marseilles airport, France. All the terrorists are killed when French counterterrorist troops storm the aircraft and rescue the 170 passengers and crew, 16 of whom suffer minor injuries.

1995

March 20 Twelve civilians are killed and 5,700 are injured in a Sarin nerve gas attack on a crowded subway station in the center of Tokyo, Japan. A similar attack occurs in the Yokohama subway system. The Aum Shinri-kyu cult is blamed for the attacks. A major police clampdown on the cult follows the incidents. Cult leader Shoko Asahara is arrested two months later.

April 19 A federal building in Oklahoma City is totally destroyed by a massive car bomb, killing 169 people and injuring hundreds more. The bombing occurs on the second anniversary of the climax of the Waco siege in 1993. Right-wing extremists Timothy McVeigh, a Gulf War veteran, and Terry Nichols are subsequently arrested for the largest terrorist attack in modern American history.

April 24 The Unabomber's third and final victim, a lumber lobbyist, is killed in Sacramento, California.

May 5 Five foreign oil workers are killed by Armed Islamic Group (GIA) terrorists in Algeria, as the group steps up its campaign against the Algerian military regime.

May 26 More than 360 United Nations peacekeepers are held hostage by the Bosnian Serb army as "human shields" after NATO air strikes on the Bosnian Serb capital, Pale. The UN personnel are tied to key military targets for several days until being released during June.

June 19 A bomb planted by Basque Fatherland and Liberty (ETA) terrorists kills a police officer in Madrid, Spain.

June 26 Islamic radicals attempt to assassinate Egyptian President Hosni Mubarak in Addis Ababa, Ethiopia, by ambushing his motorcade.

July 7 Five American, British, and German tourists are kidnapped by rebels in the north of the disputed Kashmir province of India. One is found beheaded in October, the other four remain unaccounted for until May 1996, when it emerges that they have been shot and buried as their captors try to escape from pursuing Indian security forces.

July 25 Algerian Armed Islamic Group (GIA) terrorists explode a bomb in a subway station in Paris, France, killing seven people and injuring 84.

October 20 Eight civilians die when a mosque is bombed in Riyadh, Saudi Arabia.

November 4 Israeli Prime Minister Yitzhak Rabin is assassinated by right-wing Jewish radical Yigal Amir after a peace rally in Tel Aviv, Israel.

November 13 Seven foreigners, including a number of US servicemen, are killed in a bomb attack on a National Guard training center at Riyadh, Saudi Arabia.

November 19 Islamic radicals plant a bomb in the Egyptian embassy in Pakistan, killing 17 people.

December 11 A large bomb planted by Basque Fatherland and Liberty (ETA) terrorists kills six sailors and injures 18 civilians in Madrid, Spain. A major anti-ETA demonstration in the city follows.

December 11 Car-bombings in Algiers by Algerian Armed Islamic Group (GIA) terrorists kill 15 civilians and leave hundreds more injured.

December 25 Six hundred Zulu Inkatha party supporters seize a Shobashobane village in South Africa, killing 19 African National Congress (ANC) supporters.

1996

January 9 Nine Chechen rebels seize 3,000 civilian hostages in Kizlyar, Dagestan, in protest at the continued Russian occupation of their homeland. Russian troops try to rescue the hostages but the operation turns into a bloody battle, with the security forces using artillery and attack helicopters to kill the rebels. Hundreds are killed and most of the Chechens escape.

January 9 Three civilians are killed in a gun attack on a bus in Turkey by Dev Sol left-wing terrorists.

January 16 Chechen rebels seize a ferry in Turkey, taking 118 Russians and four Turks hostage before they surrender to the Turkish authorities.

January 31 Tamil Tiger suicide bombers set off a massive car bomb in the center of the business district of Colombo, Sri Lanka, killing eight and injuring 1,400 civilians. Security forces intercept other suicide bombers and prevent further carnage.

February 11 Algerian Armed Islamic Group (GIA) terrorists explode a car bomb in Algiers, killing 17. In March, two more are killed by another GIA bomb and 10 are killed in a train ambush in western Algeria.

February 16 The Irish Republican Army (IRA) breaks its 18-month-old ceasefire by exploding a massive bomb in the Docklands office district of London, England. Two civilians are killed and scores injured. Two days later an IRA member is killed when a bomb he is carrying explodes prematurely on a London bus. Several other passengers are seriously injured.

February 24 Two Cuban MiG fighters shoot down a light aircraft flown over the Gulf of Mexico by four Cuban exiles belonging to the Brothers to the Rescue organization. The Cuban exiles die as a result.

February 25 A Hamas suicide bomber kills 26 Israeli civilians on a bus in the Palestinian town of Hebron. An hour later, one Israeli is killed and 35 injured in Ashkelon, Israel, by another Hamas bomb. The following day, a Palestinian motorist rams a bus queue in Tel Aviv, Israel, killing one person and injuring 23 others.

March 3 Eighteen people are killed and 10 wounded in a Hamas suicide bomb attack on a bus in Jerusalem. The following day, 13 civilians are killed and scores are wounded when another Hamas suicide bomber attacks a shopping mall in Dizengoff Street, Tel Aviv, Israel.

March 25 The so-called Montana Freemen begin a confrontation with U.S. federal authorities in Montana. Some 25 members of the group hold out until surrendering in June 1996.

April 4 Theodore J. Kaczynski is finally arrested by the FBI under suspicion of being the Unabomber. In total, three people have been killed and 23 wounded in the 16 bombings attributed to the Unabomber since 1978.

April 19 Eighteen Greek tourists are shot near the historic pyramids in Egypt by Islamic terrorists seeking to destroy the country's tourist industry.

April 25 An Irish Republican Army (IRA) bomb in London – the biggest ever placed in Britain – fails to explode.

May 20 A bomb in Córdoba, Spain, presumed to have been planted by Basque Fatherland and Liberty (ETA), kills a Spanish army sergeant and wounds three people. A further bomb explodes on June 19.

June 14 Basque Fatherland and Liberty (ETA) release a Spanish businessman held for a year. A ransom of $780,000 is believed to have been been paid.

June 15 The Irish Republican Army (IRA) detonate a large bomb in the center of Manchester, England, injuring several hundred people and causing $450 million in damage.

June 25 A massive truck bomb devastates a U.S. Air Force housing compound in Khobar, near Dhahran airbase, Saudi Arabia, killing 19 U.S. servicemen and wounding almost 400 other people, mostly Americans.

July 17 A TWA Boeing 747 jet explodes shortly after takeoff from Kennedy Airport, killing all 230 passengers and crew when it plunges into the Atlantic Ocean off Long Island, New York.

July 20 Basque Fatherland and Liberty (ETA) begin a major bombing campaign aimed at damaging Spain's tourist trade. One bomb injures 35 people, mostly British tourists, while another injures 33.

July 27 A bomb detonates in the Centennial Olympic Park, Atlanta, Georgia, killing one woman and injuring 110 other people. A man also dies of a heart attack.

August 26 Six Iraqi dissidents hijack a Sudan Airways airliner flying from Sudan to Jordan, and divert it to Stansted, England. After eight hours, the hijackers surrender and release all 193 passengers and crew unharmed.

September 23 A major bombing campaign by the Irish Republican Army (IRA) is thwarted when police raid a house in London, England. One IRA member is shot dead in the raid and five are arrested.

October 7 Two Irish Republican Army (IRA) car bombs explode at the British Army headquarters at Lisburn, Northern Ireland. One soldier is killed and 30 people injured.

A-Z DIRECTORY OF TERRORIST ORGANIZATIONS AND INDIVIDUALS

Directory entries are under the most common English-language usage – whether an English-language name (Palestine Liberation Organization), a foreign-language name (Hizb'allah), an abbreviated name (Dev Sol), or an acronym (EOKA). Cross-references within the glossary link foreign- and English-language versions of a name, if both are common. The key below shows how to find a main entry from a group's initials. Naturally, the initials used by foreign-language groups usually follow the word sequence in their own language. For example, the Italian group Armed Revolutionary Nucleus calls itself NAR, because its Italian name is Nuclei Armati Rivoluzionari.

Glossary of initials and acronyms

AAA (Argentina): Argentine Anti-Communist Alliance
AAA (Spain): Apostolic Anti-Communist Alliance
ALF: Arab Liberation Front
ALN: Action for National Liberation
ANC: African National Congress
ANS: Action Front of National Socialists
ARC: Caribbean Revolutionary Alliance
ARENA: *under* ARENA *in Directory*
ASALA: *under* ASALA *in Directory*
CCC: Communist Fighting Cells
CERF: Clara Elizabeth Ramírez Front
CIA: Central Intelligence Agency
CSA: (the) Covenant, the Sword, and the Arm of the Lord
DFLP: Democratic Front for the Liberation of Palestine
EGP: Guerrilla Army of the Poor
ELA: Revolutionary Popular Struggle
ELF: Eritrean Liberation Front
ELN (Bolivia; Colombia): National Liberation Army
EOKA: *under* EOKA *in Directory*
EOKA-B: *under* EOKA-B *in Directory*
EPL: Popular Liberation Army
EPLF: Eritrean People's Liberation Front
ERP (Argentina; El Salvador): People's Revolutionary Army
ESA: Secret Anti-Communist Army
ETA: *under* ETA *in Directory*
FALN (Puerto Rico; Venezuela): Armed National Liberation Forces
FANE: Federation for National European Action
FARC: Revolutionary Armed Forces of Colombia
FARL: Lebanese Armed Revolutionary Faction
FARN: Armed Forces of National Resistance
FIS: Islamic Salvation Front
FLB: Breton Liberation Front
FLN: National Liberation Front
FLNC (Corsica): Corsican National Liberation Front
FLNC (Cuba): Cuban National Liberation Front
FLNKS: Kanak Socialist National Liberation Front
FLQ: Quebec Liberation Front
FMLN: Farabundo Martí National Liberation Front
FNE: European National Fascists
FNLA: National Front for the Liberation of Angola
FPL: Farabundo Martí Popular Liberation Army
FRELIMO: *under* FRELIMO *in Directory*
FRETILIN: *under* FRETILIN *in Directory*
FSLN: Sandinista National Liberation Front
GAL: *under* GAL *in Directory*
GIA: Armed Islamic Group
GRAPO: *under* GRAPO *in Directory*
IMRO: Internal Macedonian Revolutionary Organization
INLA: Irish National Liberation Army
IRA: Irish Republican Army
KKK: Ku Klux Klan
M-19: April 19 Movement
MAS: *under* MAS *in Directory*
MIR (Chile; Venezuela): Movement of the Revolutionary Left
MJL: Lautaro Youth Movement
MNLF: Moro National Liberation Front
MPLA: Popular Movement for the Liberation of Angola
MPLC: Cinchoneros Popular Liberation Movement
MRTA: Tupac Amaru Revolutionary Movement
NAFF: New Afrikan Freedom Fighters
NAR: Armed Revolutionary Nuclei
NORAID: *under* NORAID *in Directory*
OAS: Secret Army Organization
ORDEN: *under* ORDEN *in Directory*
PAIGC: African Party for Independence for Guinea and Cape Verde
PFLO: Popular Front for the Liberation of Oman
PFLP: Popular Front for the Liberation of Palestine
PFLP-GC: Popular Front for the Liberation of Palestine – General Command
PIRA: Provisional IRA
PKK: Kurdish Workers Party
PL: Prima Linea
PLF: Palestine Liberation Front
PLO: Palestine Liberation Organization
POLISARIO: *under* POLISARIO *in Directory*
PRTC: Revolutionary Party of Central American Workers
RATF: Revolutionary Armed Task Force
RENAMO: *under* RENAMO *in Directory*
RZ: Revolutionary Cells
SLA: Symbionese Liberation Army
SPLA: Sudanese People's Liberation Army
SSNP: Syrian Social Nationalist Party
SWAPO: *under* SWAPO *in Directory*
TPLA: Turkish People's Liberation Army
TPLF: Tigre (or Tigray) People's Liberation Front
UDA: Ulster Defence Association
UFF: Ulster Freedom Fighters
UNITA: *under* UNITA *in Directory*
URNG: Guatemalan National Revolutionary Unity
UVF: Ulster Volunteer Force
VZJ: Free South Moluccan Youth Organization
ZANU: *under* ZANU *in Directory*
ZAPU: *under* ZAPU *in Directory*

Abu Iyad (Salah Khalaf), deputy to Palestine Liberation Organization (PLO) Chairman Yasser Arafat. He established the Black September Organization in 1970 and led the attack on Israeli athletes at the 1972 Olympic Games in Munich. After Black September suspended operations in 1974, Abu Iyad continued to hold his position in the PLO. He was killed by Abu Nidal group members posing as bodyguards in January 1991.

Abu Jihad (Khalil Wazir), deputy to Palestine Liberation Organization (PLO) chairman Yasser Arafat, he played a leading role in directing the Intifada. He was assassinated by an Israeli Mossad hit squad in April 1988.

Abu Nidal (Sabri Khalil al Banna), leader of the Fatah Revolutionary Council (also known as the Abu Nidal Organization), based in Damascus, Syria, from 1983 to 1987, and in Libya since then. In June 1982, Abu Nidal attempted to assassinate Israeli ambassador to the UK, Shlomo Argov. The group was active in France for several years. In December 1985, it carried out simultaneous attacks at Rome and Vienna airports in which 20 people were killed by gunmen trained in Lebanon. Nidal, a leading member of the Palestine Liberation Organization (PLO) until 1974, was condemned to death by the PLO in 1985. He is an extreme radical who rejects any negotiations with Israel. Members of his group were implicated in the killing of PLO leader Abu Iyad in January 1991, and Abu Nidal has reportedly attempted to assassinate Yasser Arafat on several occasions.

Abul Abbas, leader of the Palestine Liberation Front (PLF) whose Palestinian guerrillas hijacked the Italian cruise liner *Achille Lauro* in October 1985.

Ação Libertadora Nacional, *see* Action for National Liberation

Action Directe, a group of extreme left-wing terrorists active in French cities in the 1980s. Their targets were symbols of capitalism and the state as well as computer equipment; they also opposed French colonialism. In 1980, two leaders, Jean-Marc Rouillan and Nathalie Menignon, were arrested but soon released under an amnesty by French President Mitterrand. Bombing activity resumed and the group was, at different times, linked to the Basque separatist movement ETA, pro-Palestinian militant organizations, and the German Red Army Faction.

Action for National Liberation (ALN), a revolutionary movement formed in Brazil in 1967. It engaged in urban guerrilla activity and bank robberies, and in 1969 abducted U.S. Ambassador Charles Burke Eldbrick, released (as were the West German and Swiss ambassadors later) in return for the release of ALN prisoners held by the authorities. One of the movement's leaders was Carlos Marighella and it declined following his death in 1969.

Action Front of National Socialists (ANS), a West German neo-Nazi group, founded in 1977 and engaged in violent attacks on Jews, immigrants, and socialists. Its founder, Michael Kühner, died in 1991 having established a network of neo-Nazi groups and exploited popular resentment against guest workers and immigrants.

African National Congress (ANC), formed in South Africa in 1912. At first appealing to libertarian middle-class professionals who believed in multiracism and nonviolence, the ANC broadened its appeal in the 1940s and shifted leftward. A Youth League, led by Nelson Mandela and Oliver Tambo, was formed in 1943. The ANC campaigned vigorously against the policy of apartheid and white supremacy. It abandoned nonviolence after the 1960 Sharpeville massacre, and was banned in that year and forced into exile in 1964. An armed wing, Umkhonto we Sizwe (Spear of the Nation), was led from outside South Africa by Joe Slovo. The ANC was increasingly active in the 1970s. During the 1980s, ANC terrorists attacked economic targets. The ban was lifted in 1990 and the ANC officially abandoned its armed struggle. In 1994, it won the most seats in the first free election in South Africa.

African Party for the Independence of Guinea and Cape Verde (PAIGC), an armed group formed in Guinea Bissau by Amilcar Cabral in 1956 to fight Portuguese colonial rule. Trained in the former Soviet Union and Cuba, and supplied with Soviet arms, the PAIGC established a rural guerrilla army, carrying out sabotage, and killing Portuguese soldiers. Cabral was murdered in 1973 by dissidents within his organization. PAIGC became the first governing party of independent Guinea Bissau in 1974.

Agça, Mehmet Ali, pro-Soviet Turkish terrorist, supported by Bulgarian agents, who attempted to assassinate Pope John Paul II in the Vatican in 1981.

Aktiongemeinschaft Nationaler Sozialisten, *see* Action Front of National Socialists

Alfaro Vive Caruzo Organization, a left-wing group active 1983-87 against foreign interests in Ecuador. Its actions included bombing of the U.S. embassy compound, seizure of the Costa Rican and Mexican embassies, bombing of a police station, seizure of a radio station, and kidnapping.

Alianza Anticomunista Argentina, *see* Argentine Anti-Communist Alliance

Alianza Apostólica Anticomunista, *see* Apostolic Anti-Communist Alliance

Alianza Republicana Nacional, *see* ARENA

Alliance Révolutionnaire Caraibe, *see* Caribbean Revolutionary Alliance

Amal (Lebanese Resistance Detachment), a Shiite milita group formed in 1975 by an Iranian cleric after the outbreak of civil war in Lebanon. From 1982, it was increasingly pro-Syrian, and at its peak had about 30,000 under arms. Its terrorist activities included a major bombing, a hijacking, and several kidnappings, but in general it acted as an armed defense force rather than as a terrorist group. In 1991, its residual members were integrated into the Lebanese army.

Amin (Dada), Idi, Ugandan head of state, 1971-79, and a notable exponent of state terror. A career soldier, he overthrew elected President Milton Obote in 1971. He crushed opposition ruthlessly and expelled non-African nationals including Uganda's Asians. In 1979, Amin was deposed and fled into exile.

Ananda Marg (Path of Eternal Bliss), a Hindu sect with many followers in America, Europe, and Australia which undertook terrorism 1975-78 to try to force the release of its leader from prison. It attacked Indian officials at home and abroad, killing India's railroad minister in January 1975, and bombing a conference of Asian and Pacific heads of state in February 1978.

Angry Brigade, a British student anarchist group active 1968-71. It carried out a number of bank robberies and planted 27 bombs. The British minister for employment's home was twice targeted, but the Angry Brigade's aims were generally symbolic and no deaths resulted. Several leading members of the group were arrested in London in August 1971, after which its activities ceased.

Animal Liberation Front, a U.K. pressure group that opposes scientific experiments involving live animals and vivisection. A loose alliance of various animal rights campaigners, it has targeted laboratories, cigarette and drug companies, cosmetics manufacturers, and stores that sell garments made from animal fur and skins. More recently, actions have aimed at halting the live export of sheep and cattle for slaughter in continental Europe. Animal rights supporters have been accused of sending letter bombs to prominent U.K. politicians.

Apostolic Anti-Communist Alliance (AAA), a Spanish group, originally state-sponsored, active in the 1970s against socialism and regional separatism. It killed four leftist lawyers in Madrid in 1977.

April 19 Movement (M-19), a revolutionary group formed in 1973 in Colombia to reform society. Led by Carlos Toledo Plata and Jaime Bateman Cayon, the movement was named for election day April 19, 1970, when militant dissidents split with the National Popular Alliance party (ANAPO). Bateman studied in the Soviet Union and Czechoslovakia, and claimed to be inspired by the Tupamaros in Uruguay. Rural guerrilla activity led to kidnappings and murder, and to attacks on economic targets, especially U.S.-owned businesses. The group's actions continued into the 1980s.

Arab Liberation Front (ALF), an Iraqi-sponsored Palestininan guerrilla faction, founded in 1969, and opposed to peace with Israel. It has carried out raids into Israel and terrorist acts in Western Europe, but is now inactive.

Arafat, Yasser, chairman of the Palestine Liberation Organization (PLO) since 1968. He helped to found Fatah in 1958 with the aim of establishing a Palestinian state. Following peace talks in the Middle East, Arafat became head of the Palestine National Authority in 1994. He is now regarded as a moderate and is frequently challenged by more extreme groups.

ARENA (Alianza Republicana Nacional), a right-wing Salvadoran political party which played a major role in the government from 1982 and won the presidency in 1989. In the 1980s it was heavily involved in death squad activities against political rivals.

Argentine Anti-Communist Alliance (AAA), a right-wing death squad of police officers and security personnel, 1973-76. It was succeeded by the state-backed right-wing terror of 1976-83.

Armed Islamic Group (GIA), an Algerian Islamic fundamentalist group, involved in numerous assassinations and terrorist incidents since 1992. It is the most active organization in the Islamic Salvation Army, which forms the armed wing of Algeria's outlawed Islamic Salvation Front (FIS).

Armed National Liberation Forces (FALN) (Puerto Rico), a Puerto-Rican separatist group active in the U.S. in the 1970s. Dedicated to full independence from what it saw as U.S. colonial rule, it bombed a target in New York City in 1975, killing four people, and later launched incendiary and bomb attacks against the FBI and multinational businesses. Toward the end of the 1970s, it started to attack targets within Puerto Rico and these attacks continued into the 1980s.

Armed National Liberation Forces (FALN) (Venezuela), a left-wing guerrilla movement formed in 1961 in Venezuela to attack foreign, especially American, individuals and businesses. Primary targets were power stations and pipelines; kidnappings and assassinations followed. The FALN's effectiveness diminished when the Venezuelan Communist party was granted official status and withdrew its backing. A prominent leader, Douglas Bravo, was granted an official pardon in 1979.

Armed National Resistance Forces (FARN), a Salvadoran terrorist group that split from the People's Revolutionary Army (ERP) in 1975. It derived most of its support from radical students and, with the aim of building a guerrilla army, attacked the military and kidnapped leading foreign business figures. FARN's campaign of terror continued into the 1980s. In 1982, it joined the Farabundo Martí National Liberation Front.

Armed Revolutionary Nucleus (NAR), an Italian neo-fascist group, founded 1977 or earlier, seeking to overthrow the constitutional democracy. It targeted public buildings and offices, 1977-81. In 1980, it assassinated a judge and bombed a railroad station killing 85 people and injuring 194. In 1985, 53 of its members were jailed.

Armenian Secret Army for the Liberation of Armenia, *see* ASALA

Aryan Nations, U.S. umbrella organization linked to a theology known as Christian Identity and seeking a whites-only homeland in Washington, Wyoming, Montana, and Idaho. It has not engaged in violence, but its membership includes terror groups such as The Order and Ku Klux Klan.

Asahara, Shoko, leader of the Aum Shinri-kyu cult in Japan. After nerve gas attacks in the subway systems of Tokyo and Yokohama, Asahara was arrested in May 1995. The hijacker of an All Nippon Airways airliner in June 1995, unsuccessfully demanded the release of Asahara, who later confessed to ordering the gas attacks.

ASALA (Armenian Secret Army for the Liberation of Armenia), a left-wing group founded in Beirut in 1975 to win Armenian independence from Turkey, and known mainly for attacks on Turkish diplomats abroad. By 1982, it had carried out 100 bomb attacks and killed 24 Turkish officials. Since the mid-1980s, it has been less active due to power struggles between competing factions within the group.

Aum Shinro-kyu (Aum Supreme Truth), a Japanese cult group led by Shoko Asahara. It came to international attention in 1995, when the organization was accused of ordering nerve gas attacks in the Tokyo and Yokohama subway systems, and of the hijacking of a Japanese airliner. In October 1996, Asahara confessed to the cult's involvement in these events.

Baader, Andreas, an early leader, with Ulrike Meinhof, of the Red Army Faction, also known as the Baader-Meinhof Gang, in West Germany. As a student radical, he took part in an arson attack on a department store in Frankfurt in 1968. Arrested in 1970, Baader was set free by Meinhof and Horst Mahler but re-arrested in 1972. He had links with Palestinian terrorist organizations and his release was demanded by the hostage-takers at the 1972 Munich Olympic Games and at the Lufthansa hijacking to Mogadishu in 1977. Sentenced to life imprisonment, Baader committed suicide.

Baader-Meinhof Gang, *see* Red Army Faction

Babbar Khalsa, a shadowy Sikh group seeking an independent Sikh homeland (Khalistan). Some terrorist acts in India, Germany, and Canada have been claimed in its name.

Bandera Roja, *see* Red Flag

Basque Armed Revolutionary Workers' Organization, *see* Iraultza

Basque Fatherland and Liberty, *see* ETA

Begin, Menachem Wolfovitch, prime minister of Israel from 1977-83. He became leader of the Betar Zionist movement in Poland in 1931 and was sent to British-ruled Palestine in 1942. In 1943, he became commander-in-chief of the Irgun Zvai Leumi resistance movement, which carried out terrorist attacks on British officials and Arabs in Palestine. Begin founded the Herut Freedom Movement in 1948. He attended a peace conference with Egyptian President Sadat at Camp David in 1978, and shared the Nobel Peace prize with Sadat.

Black Brigades, a shadowy Kuwaiti Shiite group backed by Iran and active against the Kuwaiti establishment mainly in the period 1985-88.

Black June (Munadamat Huzairan al-Aswad), a terrorist group formed in Lebanon by Abu Nidal in 1976. It took its name from June 1976, when Phalangist troops massacred Palestinians in a refugee camp. Backed by Iraq, it fought against Syrian forces in the Lebanese civil war. Black June opposed the Palestine Liberation Organization's conciliatory policy and assassinated several PLO members. In the early 1980s, it made terrorist attacks in Europe.

Black Liberation Army, an African-American group in the 1960s and early 1970s, mainly targeting police officers. Remnants merged with the Weather Underground to form the Revolutionary Armed Task Force.

Black Order (Ordine Nero), an Italian neo-fascist group, successor to the New Order party banned in 1973. In 1974, two of its bombs killed 20 and injured 143, but subsequently Armed Revolutionary Nucleus became the main Italian right-wing terror group.

Black Panther Party (BPP), a militant political organization formed by Huey Newton and Bobby Seale in the United States in 1966 to fight for black rights and promote black nationalism. Inspired by Fidel Castro, Frantz Fanon, Malcolm X, and, later, Eldridge Cleaver, the BPP was involved in armed confrontations with the police and was accused of bomb attacks. Many members had criminal records but the organization did not generally promote violent urban activity.

Black September (Munadamat Aylul al-Aswad), a terrorist group set up by Abu Iyad, deputy leader of the Palestine Liberation Organization (PLO) and Hassan Salameh in 1970, following Jordan's expulsion of PLO guerrillas in the "Black September" of 1970. In 1971, Black September murdered the Jordanian prime minister in Cairo, and in 1972 it took Israeli athletes hostage at the Munich Olympic Games and 11 athletes were killed as a result. The hijacking of a Lufthansa airliner secured the release of jailed Black September terrorists from Germany. The name is now used by the Fatah Revolutionary Council.

Breton Liberation Front (FLB), a separatist movement in Brittany, western France, active in the 1970s. Its campaign included the bombing of government buildings and other targets in Breton towns. The FLB was briefly linked to Basque, Scottish, and Welsh separatist organizations.

Brigate Rosse, *see* Red Brigades

Caribbean Revolutionary Alliance (ARC), a left-wing group seeking independence for Guadeloupe from France and responsible for many bomb and arson attacks.

"Carlos the Jackal" (Illich Ramírez Sánchez), Venezuelan terrorist and guerrilla leader, believed responsible for various attacks mostly in Europe and the Middle East. He led the 1973 kidnapping of OPEC ministers in Vienna. Arrested in Sudan in 1994, Carlos was taken to France, tried, and sentenced to life imprisonment.

Castro, Fidel, president of Cuba since 1976. He led opposition to President Batista in 1959 and established a communist regime after the latter's overthrow. Castro, with his deputy Che Guevara, then sought to encourage guerrilla movements and terrorist groups in various Latin American countries. In turn, the CIA and various Cuban exile groups sought to undermine Castro's regime.

Cellules Communistes Combattantes, *see* Communist Fighting Cells

Central Intelligence Agency (CIA), a federal agency established in the United States in 1947 to coordinate government intelligence services. During the Cold War period, its scope of activity spread overseas, where it was involved in the Cuban Bay of Pigs incident (1961) and the overthrow of Chilean President Allende (1973). The CIA is believed to have engaged in covert operations in several countries including Nicaragua, where it backed the Contras against the Sandinistas.

Chukaku-Ha, the largest militant group in Japan, Marxist and set up in 1960. It opposes the corporate state and all links with the U.S. Its terrorist cell, the Kansai Revolutionary Army, has used bombs, mortars, and rockets against offices, construction sites, the rail network, embassies, and the Imperial Palace in Tokyo. In an attack on an international economic summit in May 1986, their five rockets flew over two miles and came within 1,800ft of the target. The group often use public demonstrations to divert attention from their targets. Assassinations mainly have been of rival radicals.

Cinchoneros Popular Liberation Movement (MPLC), a left-wing group in Honduras, founded 1978, the armed wing of the Revolutionary People's Union (URP). It opposes the government and U.S. interests, and has carried out bomb attacks, hijackings, and hostage taking. In 1989, it killed the ex-head of the Honduran army.

Clara Elizabeth Ramírez Front (CERF), a small well-trained urban group in El Salvador, which in 1983-85 wounded the deputy commander of the U.S. military mission and killed the chief spokesman of the Salvadoran military, the security supervisor of the U.S. embassy, and the founder of the right-wing terror group ORDEN. CERF was almost destroyed by counterterrorist operations in 1985.

Communist Fighting Cells (CCC), a small communist group, founded by a former member of Action Directe, and responsible for anti-NATO bombings and killings in Belgium in the mid-1980s.

Communist Party of Malaya, a Chinese political organization founded in Malaya (now Malaysia) in 1930. Defeated by government forces in the 1950s, it resumed guerrilla activities and used extortion under the leadership of Chin Peng from the 1960s to the 1980s.

Contras, a U.S.-backed guerrilla force that undertook operations in Nicaragua against the left-wing Sandinista government between 1979 and 1990. It was officially disbanded following the electoral defeat of the Sandinistas in 1990.

Corsican National Liberation Front (FLNC), a terrorist movement set up in 1976 in Corsica to fight for independence from French rule. Led by Jean Paul Roesch until his arrest in 1979, the FLNC carried out bomb attacks in Corsica and later in Paris, where banks and other financial institutions were targeted. Although the movement declared a truce in 1981, sporadic activity was continued by dissident members.

(the) Covenant, the Sword, and the Arm of the Lord (CSA), a U.S. white right-wing group linked to Aryan Nations. In 1983-84, it firebombed a church and a Jewish center and murdered two men, one an African-American police officer. Its associated commune in Arkansas was raided by the authorities in 1985.

Croatian National Resistance, a U.S. group, active 1976-82, seeking Croatia's independence from then-communist Yugoslavia. It hijacked a TWA Boeing 727 in September 1976, at the same time placing a bomb in Grand Central Station, in New York City, which killed a police officer. It also carried out five other bombings, 1980-82, without causing injury.

Cuban National Liberation Front (FLNC), one of the main anti-Castro exile groups in the U.S. in the late 1960s and early 1970s. It engaged in attacks on individuals and organizations deemed too tolerant of Castro.

Dal Khalsa, a Sikh organization, founded 1979, seeking an independent Sikh homeland (Khalistan) in the Indian Punjab. It grew out of sectarian conflicts between different Sikh groups. Dal Khalsa hijacked an Indian Airways airliner to Pakistan in September 1981, and played a major part in instigating anti-Hindu violence in Punjab from 1981 on. In 1982-93, followers of the Sikh religious leader Bhindranwale, probably including Dal Khalsa, were responsible for two attempted hijackings, an attempt to kill the chief minister of Punjab, and the assassination of the Punjab deputy chief of police. In June 1984, in Operation Blue Star, the Indian army overran the Golden Temple of Amritsar, where Bhindranwale was living in sanctuary; 700 troops and 5,000 civilians died in the incident. Thereafter, Sikh extremists targeted moderate Sikhs as well as government officials. In August 1986, Dal Khalsa claimed responsibility for the assassination of the Indian general who had been chief of staff at the time of Operation Blue Star. Dal Khalsa may have had Pakistan state backing.

Dashmesh Regiment (Tenth Regiment), a shadowy Sikh group which has claimed responsibility for several assassinations, including a Hindu member of the Indian parliament, and for the attempted assassination of Indian Prime Minister Rajiv Gandhi in October 1986. Outside India, it has claimed two actions also claimed by the Kashmir Liberation Army: the explosion of a bomb at Tokyo airport (intended for an Air India plane), and the blowing up of an Air Indian Boeing 747 on June 23, 1985, killing 329 people. The name may be a cover for Dal Khalsa or another group.

Dawa (Islamic Call Party), an Iraqi Shiite political party formed in 1969 and given Iranian backing from 1979. It tried to assassinate the Iraqi deputy prime minister in 1980 and President Saddam Hussein in 1987, and acted as a sabotage and assassination group during the Iran-Iraq war.

Debray, Regis, French Marxist writer and theorist, closely associated with Che Guevara in the 1960s. Captured in Bolivia and sentenced to 30 years' imprisonment in 1967, Debray was released in 1970 and became adviser to French President Mitterrand.

Democratic Front for the Liberation of Palestine (DFLP), a guerrilla movement founded in 1969 by dissident members of the Popular Front for the Liberation of Palestine (PFLP) and led by Naif Hawarmeh. It identified closely with liberation struggles in Africa, Asia, and Latin America, and received support from South Yemen and Libya. Its terrorist activities were confined to within Israeli borders. The DFLP was allied to the Popular Front for the Liberation of Oman (PFLO).

Democratic Revolutionary Front for the Liberation of Arabistan, an Iraqi-backed group claiming to seek independence for the Arab-populated Khuzistan province of Iran. Its only significant action was the seizure of the Iranian embassy in London on April 30, 1980, which resulted in the deaths of two of the 26 hostages and five of the six terrorists.

Dev Sol (Devrimci Sol), a Turkish left-wing group aiming at a socialist revolution, which killed right-wing Turks, 1975-80, conducted bombing, hostage taking, and hijacking from 1980 to 1981, and has re-emerged since 1990 to attack Turkish officials and Western businessmen and servicemen.

Ejército de Liberacíon Nacional, *see* National Liberation Army (Bolivia; Colombia)

Ejército Guerrillero de los Pobres, *see* Guerrilla Army of the Poor

Ejército Popular de Liberación, *see* Popular Liberation Army

Ejército Revolucionario de Pueblo, *see* People's Revolutionary Army (Argentina; El Salvador)

Ejército Secreto Anticomunista, *see* Anti-Communist Secret Army

EOKA (Ethniki Organosis Kyprion Agoniston), a Cypriot political organization led by George Grivas that opposed British rule in Cyprus and campaigned for union with Greece. It conducted a guerrilla war between 1955 and 1959, targeting government offices and buildings. EOKA effectively ceased to exist when Cyprus became independent in 1960.

EOKA-B, a guerrilla force in Cyprus that conducted a terror campaign in the 1970s. George Grivas had returned to Cyprus from Greece and opposed Makarios's presidency. EOKA-B resorted to bombings and kidnappings and briefly ousted Makarios in 1974. Grivas died in 1974 and EOKA-B ceased activity in 1978.

Eritrean Liberation Front (ELF), a separatist and nationalist guerrilla organization founded in Cairo in 1958 to fight for Eritrean autonomy from Ethiopia. By the 1970s, with support from Iraq, Libya, Syria, and the Palestinian Fatah movement, it was conducting a guerrilla campaign from a base in the Sudan. After Haile Selassie was overthrown in 1974, the ELF struggled against Mengistu Haile Mariam's Soviet-backed government. It also conducted a prolonged power struggle with the breakaway EPLF. Eritrea became self-governing in 1991 and fully independent in 1993.

Eritrean People's Liberation Front (EPLF), a group in Ethiopia that broke away from the ELF in 1970. After a prolonged power struggle, the EPLF emerged as the principal Eritrean guerrilla movement throughout the 1980s. Operating in both urban and rural areas, it carried out kidnappings, assassinations, and bombings.

ETA (Euskadi ta Askatasuna), a Basque separatist movement founded in Spain in 1959. It conducted a terrorist campaign with the aim of creating an independent Basque state, receiving support from Basques living across the border in France. ETA has frequently split into rival factions. Initially unsuccessful, its early leaders fled to France. Its killings and kidnappings increased in the late 1970s and the 1980s, with prominent military and business figures targeted. ETA activists murdered Spanish Prime Minister Carrero Blanco in 1973. Links were established with Latin American revolutionary groups in exile and training was provided by Palestinian guerrilla groups in Yemen. ETA has become less active, though it is still held responsible for sporadic killings and bombings in Spain, including several in tourist locations in 1996.

European National Fascists (FNE), a French fascist group founded in 1980 as successor to the Federation for National European Action. It has been claimed that up to a third of its members are police officers.

Extraditables, a terror organ of the Medallín drug cartel, aimed at forcing the Colombian government to halt its anti-drug campaign. Set up in 1989, it carried out 200 bombings in that year, including blowing up an airliner. The death of Medellín boss Pablo Escobar in December 1993 ended its activities.

Faisceaux Nationaux Européens, *see* European National Fascists

Fanon, Frantz, revolutionary theorist in Algeria during French colonial rule and the liberation struggle fought by the FLN. He advocated violence as a unifying force that would restore their self-respect to oppressed peoples. His best-known work is *The Wretched of the Earth.*

Farabundo Marti National Liberation Front (FMLN), an alliance of Marxist guerrilla groups in El Salvador formed in 1980 and deriving support from the rural peasantry. It fielded about 5,000 trained troops, but also carried out economic sabotage, assassinations, and kidnappings, especially when unsuccessful on the battlefield.

Farabundo Martí Popular Liberation Army (FPL), a militant group established in El Salvador by Salvador Cayetano Carpio in 1972. Named for the former leader of the El Salvador communist party, the FPL took Cuba as its role model and supported the Sandinistas in Nicaragua. Its attacks, including bombings, sabotage, kidnappings, and murder, often targeted U.S. individuals and property, including the U.S. embassy in the capital San Salvador.

Fatah (Palestine National Liberation Movement), a Palestinian political and military organization co-founded in 1956 by Yasser Arafat. Its aim was the establishment of a Palestinian state. Fatah has dominated the Palestine Liberation Organization (PLO), though it is frequently challenged by more extremist groups.

Fatah Revolutionary Council (Abu Nidal Organization), a breakaway faction founded in 1975 by Abu Nidal after his expulsion from Fatah. It has been credited with more than 90 major terrorist incidents and with killing or injuring more than 900 people, claiming responsibility under a variety of names, including Black June, Arab Revolutionary Brigades, and the Revolutionary Movement of Socialist Muslims. It now resembles a crime syndicate rather than an ideological terrorist group. A major internal purge in 1988 has reduced its activities.

Federation for National European Action (FANE), a French fascist group founded in 1966 which used arson and violence against Jews, North Africans, and black Africans. Its campaign peaked in 1980, after which it was banned, but reemerged under the title European National Fascists.

Force 17, Yassar Arafat's personal bodyguard, sometimes used for terrorist acts, including the attack on a yacht in Larnaca marina, Cyprus, on September 25, 1985.

Free South Moluccan Youth Organization (VZJ), a group campaigning in Holland in the 1960s and 1970s for independence for Moluccans in Indonesia following the end of Dutch colonial rule. In 1975, it attempted unsuccessfully to kidnap Queen Juliana and Prime Minister Andreas van Agt. Between 1975 and 1978, many hostages were held by this group and deaths resulted.

Free Wales Army, an intermittently active organization that carried out arson attacks on English-owned homes in Wales in the early 1980s.

FRELIMO (Frente du Libertação de Moçambique), a nationalist political party founded in 1962 in Mozambique to fight for independence from Portuguese colonial rule. Its leader, Eduardo Mondlane, was murdered in 1969 as were other faction leaders at various times. FRELIMO engaged in widespread guerrilla activity. Samora Machel rose to prominence in the organization and became the first president of independent Mozambique in 1975.

Frente de Liberación Nacional Cubana, *see* Cuban National Liberation Front

Frente Nacional da Libertação de Angola, *see* Angolan National Liberation Front

Frente Sandinista de Liberación Nacional, *see* Sandinista National Liberation Front

FRETILIN (Frente Revolucionária Timorense de Libertação e Independência), a left-wing liberationist political movement formed to free East Timor from Portuguese colonial rule. Indonesia intervened when East Timor declared itself independent in 1975 and made the territory a province of Indonesia. FRETILIN's guerrilla activities were then directed against the Indonesian forces, which crushed them ruthlessly using napalm, defoliants, and heavy bombing. It is estimated that between 100,000 and 250,000 people were killed. Since 1982, the organization has been gradually rebuilding itself.

Front de la Libération Nationale de la Corse, *see* Corsican National Liberation Front

Front de Libération de la Bretagne, *see* Breton Liberation Front

Front de Libération du Québec, *see* Quebec Liberation Front

Front de Libération Nationale, *see* National Liberation Front (Algeria)

Front de Libération Nationale Kanake Socialiste, *see* Kanak Socialist National Liberation Front

Front Line, *see* Prima Linea

Fuerzas Armadas de Liberación Nacional, *see* Armed National Liberation Forces (Puerto Rico and Venezuela)

Fuerzas Armadas de Resistancia Nacional, *see* Armed Forces of National Resistance

Fuerzas Armadas Revolucionarias de Colombia, *see* Revolutionary Armed Forces of Colombia

Fuerzas Populares de Liberación Farabundo Martí, *see* Farabundo Marti Popular Liberation Army

GAL (Grupos Anti-terroristas de Liberacíon), a Spanish government-backed group, mainly recruited from police officers, which in the 1980s killed ETA members and other Basques in both Spain and France.

George Jackson Brigade, a small U.S. African-American group, claiming to be pursuing militant left-wing goals, which committed various small robberies and bombings in Oregon and Washington states in the mid-1970s.

Giap, Vo Nguyen, a Vietnamese military leader who directed wars in which terrorism played an important part against the French, the U.S., and the government of South Vietnam. He was vice-premier and defense minister of North Vietnam when U.S. troops withdrew from Vietnam in 1973. Giap is author of *People's War, People's Army* (1961), an influential book among revolutionaries.

GRAPO (Grupo de Resistencia Antifascista, Primero de Octubre), a Spanish Maoist group set up in 1975, the armed wing of the Reconstituted Spanish Communist party. As well as financing itself from ransom, extortion, and bank robbery, it carried out about 25 bombings, mostly of U.S. and French-owned targets, as well as armed attacks. Many of its activists have now been arrested.

Grey Wolves, a far-right Turkish terror group and wing of the National Action party. It killed perhaps 700 people in the period 1976-80. Mehmet Ali Agça, who tried to kill Pope John Paul II in 1981, was once a member.

Grivas, George Theodore, a Greek Cypriot who advocated union with Greece and led the EOKA guerrilla campaign against British rule in the 1950s. After Cyprus became independent in 1959, Grivas returned and organized EOKA-B's opposition to President Makarios.

Grupos Antiterroristas de Liberación, *see* GAL

Guatemala National Revolutionary Unity (URNG), an alliance of left-wing guerrilla groups in Guatemala, formed in 1982.

Guerrilla Army of the Poor (EGP), a Guatemalan terrorist organization founded in 1975 by César Montes and supported by Cuba. It campaigned against the exploitation of the poor, particularly by industrialists and landowners. EGP carried out arson attacks on sugar plantations and a number of bombings and kidnappings, including that of the Salvadoran and Nicaraguan ambassadors and the Guatemalan army chief of staff.

Guevara, "Che" (Ernesto Guevara de la Serna), Argentine revolutionary and guerrilla leader. A significant contributor to the Cuban revolution, he served in Fidel Castro's government in the early 1960s. He was captured and shot in 1967 while training guerrillas for an uprising against the Bolivian government. He remains influential both as an icon – the romanticized image of the dedicated revolutionary – and for his book, *Guerrilla Warfare.*

Guzmán (Reynoso), Abimael, Peruvian guerrilla fighter, first leader of the Shining Path organization. He eluded the Peruvian authorities until 1992, when he was captured and imprisoned. Some say that he still manages to direct the group's operations from his prison cell.

Habash, George, founder in 1968 of the Popular Front for the Liberation of Palestine. A convinced Marxist who rejected any involvement with religion, he enjoyed great prestige among Palestinians. He demanded a large ransom for the release of the kidnapped OPEC ministers in Vienna in 1973. More militant than his former colleague Yasser Arafat, Habash favored terrorism as a legitimate weapon for a short time in the 1970s as part of a strategy of rejecting all compromise.

Haddad, Wadi, a leader of the Popular Front for the Liberation of Palestine who tried to move it to more widespread use of terror against the wishes of George Habash. In 1975, with "Carlos the Jackal," he directed the siege in Vienna against a meeting of the Organization of Petroleum Exporting Countries, at which 70 hostages were taken. Haddad founded the PFLP-SOG, and died in 1978.

Haganah, a secret Jewish defense organization founded in Palestine before World War II. Acting separately from Irgun and the Stern Gang, it attacked British and Arab targets in the 1940s. After the establishment of the state of Israel in 1948, many members of Haganah were recruited into the Israeli army.

Hamas, a Palestinian Islamic fundamentalist movement, a wing of the Jordanian Muslim Brotherhood. More militant than the PLO, Hamas targets Israeli nationals and property in the occupied territories, opposes peace with Israel, and is believed to operate cells on American soil. Its military wing, the Islamic Resistance Movement, has continued to launch suicide attacks against Israeli targets.

Hindawi, Nezar, Jordanian journalist and mercenary. With Syrian backing, he attempted to blow up an El Al airliner in April 1986 by planting a bomb on his unsuspecting pregnant girlfriend. He was sentenced to 45 years in jail in October 1986.

Hizb'allah (Party of God), a militant Lebanese Shiite organization led by Sheikh Abdul Karim Obeid. When Obeid was seized by Israeli commandos in 1989, American nationals were held hostage for his release. Among these were William Higgins, Joseph Cicippio, and Terry Anderson. Hizb'allah, with close ties to Iran, hijacked a TWA airliner at Beirut airport in 1985. It is believed to operate cells on American soil.

Hizb'allah of the Hijaz, an Iranian-backed Shiite group based in Lebanon and seeking an Islamic revolution in Saudi Arabia. It claimed responsibility for the killing of Saudi diplomats in Turkey and Thailand, 1988-89. In fact it is probably identical with Hizb'allah. Iran has also used Mecca pilgrims to attempt arson and bomb attacks in Saudi Arabia.

Ho Chi Minh (Nguyen That Thanh), president of North Vietnam, 1954-69. He fought for independence from French colonial rule and in 1930 founded the Indo-Chinese Communist party. He led guerrilla activity against Japanese forces during World War II. Following the defeat of the French and the division of Vietnam, Ho Chi Minh's struggle to reunite his country escalated into the Vietnam War.

Hoffmann Military Sports Group, a West German neo-Nazi group, most active 1976-81. In September 1980, one of its bombs exploded (probably accidentally) at the Munich October Festival, killing 13 and injuring 217. In December 1980, it assassinated a Jewish publisher. Some of the group's members were trained at PLO camps in Lebanon, though these were arrested on their return to Germany. After the arrest of its leader in 1981, his followers set up many similar cells in different parts of the country.

Holy War, *see* Jihad

Hukbalahap (Huks), a left-wing guerrilla group on the island of Luzon in the Philippines. Formed to fight the occupying Japanese in World War II, in 1947-50 the Huks led a peasant uprising against the government.

Hussein, Saddam, president of Iraq since 1979. In 1968, he was a leader of the coup which brought the Ba'ath Socialist Party to power. In 1980-88, Iraq fought a prolonged and indecisive war with neighboring Iran. In 1990, his troops invaded Kuwait, which was liberated by U.S. and allied forces in the Gulf War of 1991. Internal dissent is ruthlessly crushed by Hussein, who has attacked Kurdish rebels in the north and Marsh Arabs in the south.

Internal Macedonian Revolutionary Organization (IMRO), an early 20th-century group seeking an independent Macedonian homeland. In 1901, it held a U.S. citizen (a female Congregationalist missionary) hostage for ransom, one of the first times this was ever done for political ends. The proceeds of $66,000 were used for an abortive rising against the Turks. Later, IMRO undertook contract assassinations for various regimes.

Intifada, the Palestinian popular uprising against Israel in the Gaza Strip and West Bank, 1987-93, initially spontaneous but later coordinated by various Palestinian activist groups.

Iraultza (Basque Armed Revolutionary Workers' Organization), a Basque separatist group that uses very small bombs set to explode at night to avoid injury to people. In 1982-87, it targeted many U.S. and French businesses in the Basque region.

Irgun, a right-wing Zionist organization founded in Palestine in 1931 to fight for the establishment of a Jewish state. It carried out a series of terrorist attacks on Arab and British targets between 1937 and 1948, but was disbanded when the state of Israel was created. From 1945, its leader was Menachem Begin, the future prime minister of Israel.

Irish National Liberation Army (INLA), a paramilitary organization active in the UK and fighting for union between Northern Ireland and the Republic of Ireland. It was formed in the 1970s as an offshoot of the Provisional IRA.

Irish Republican Army (IRA), the military wing of the Irish nationalist movement, Sinn Féin. Originally set up during the struggle for independence from Britain, 1916-21, the IRA later campaigned for an independent state encompassing all 32 counties of the island. In 1969, it split into the Official and the Provisional IRA. The Official IRA had become inactive, but the Provisionals established a campaign of violence against military and civilian targets in Northern Ireland, Britain, and Europe. The Provisional IRA declared a ceasefire in 1994, but in 1996 it again began bombings in Britain and Northern Ireland.

Islamic Amal, a Lebanese radical Shiite group founded in 1982 to fight Israeli occupation of that country and calling for an Islamic revolution throughout the Middle East.

Islamic Front for the Liberation of Bahrain, an Iraqi-backed group, set up in 1979 and seeking an Islamic revolution in the Persian Gulf state of Bahrain. In 1981, it plotted to topple the Bahrain government by assassination and sabotage, but the security police arrested 73 people on charges that included illegal possession of firearms and explosives.

Islamic Jihad (Lebanon), a label used since 1983 for some activities linked to the pro-Iranian fundamentalist terrorist group also known as Hizb'allah. This is probably to allow the leaders of Hizb'allah, and their Iranian sponsors, to deny responsibility for actions such as suicide bombings, randomly destructive vehicle-bombs, and kidnappings of foreigners – all acts that many Muslims would regard as violations of Islamic law.

Islamic Jihad (Palestine), a group founded in 1981 that claimed a major role in the Intifada. It opposes the Israeli-PLO accord and continues to attack Israeli targets.

Islamic Liberation Organization, a Sunni group that in September 1985 took four Soviet diplomats hostage in Beirut, Lebanon, hoping to force the USSR to put pressure on Syria, whose forces were then besieging another Sunni group in Tripoli. One hostage was killed by the group after being wounded and developing gangrene; the rest were released after a month.

Islamic Revolutionary Guards Corps, a major organization in post-1979 Iran, growing from a political militia to a regular military force in the Iran-Iraq war. It is an instrument of state terror against the population, and also runs the training camps in Iran for foreign Islamic activists and in the Lebanon for Hizb'allah.

Islamic Revolutionary Organization, one of the names used by Iranian-backed groups in the Lebanon when acting against Saudi Arabia.

Islamic Salvation Front (FIS), an Algerian fundamentalist political party. The Armed Islamic Movement, which killed the Algerian president in June 1992, is believed to be linked to it. FIS has also been responsible for attacks on officials, on unveiled women, and on foreign residents. In turn, 7,000 FIS members were arrested in Algeria in 1992 and 270 killed.

Islamic Tendency Movement (Nahdha), a group supported by Sudan and Iran that aims to achieve an Islamic revolution in Tunisia. It is believed responsible for bomb attacks on hotels in August 1987. In May 1991, 300 of its members were arrested and accused of plotting a military coup.

Jammu Kashmir Liberation Front, a militant separatist group based in England and with support in several countries, which campaigns for independence for the state of Jammu and Kashmir, in northern India, together with the part of Kashmir that is in Pakistan. It operates opportunistically and has seized Western hostages.

Japanese Red Army (Sekigun), a militant left-wing organization formed in Japan in 1969 with the aim of creating a revolutionary army using urban guerrilla tactics. In 1970, it hijacked a Japanese airliner and later carried out bombings and bank robberies to finance its activities. With support from North Korea, and links to the Popular Front for the Liberation of Palestine (PFLP), Japanese Red Army gunmen killed 25 travelers at Lod airport in central Israel in 1972. In 1975, it seized hostages at the U.S. consulate in the Malaysian capital, Kuala Lumpur, later releasing them in exchange for the freedom of Red Army prisoners. The group's last known action was the hijacking of a Japanese airliner in September 1977, after which it became inactive.

Jewish Defense League, a militant pro-Israeli Jewish organization founded in New York by Meir Kahane in 1968. It was set up to protect Jews from attack and to campaign for the release of Jews held in the former Soviet Union. Many of its targets were Soviet-owned; it also attacked blacks whom it suspected of anti-Semitic activities. Some of its members have been jailed for bombing offenses.

Jihad (Holy War), a fundamentalist Egyptian group dedicated to changing society and the power structure by using violence. Five of its members were executed for the 1981 assassination of Egyptian President Anwar Sadat.

June 2 Movement, a small left-wing group set up in West Berlin in 1973. It committed bombings, bank robberies, and abductions. Most of its members were arrested in the late 1970s, others joined the Red Army Faction.

Justice Commandos of the Armenian Genocide, a right-wing group fighting for Armenian independence, responsible for attacks in the United States and elsewhere.

Kahane, Meir, a New York rabbi, founder of the Jewish Defense League in 1968.

Kanak Socialist National Liberation Front (FLNKS), a political coalition in New Caledonia seeking to represent the indigenous Kanaks against French rule. It has killed local police officers and set off bombs in Paris.

Karen National Liberation Army, a militant armed group struggling for independence for the state of Karen in southeast Burma (now Myanmar). Led by Bo Mya, the movement supported British troops against the Japanese in World War II. It aimed to restore autonomy to Karen, lost under reorganization in 1974. The KNLA's last outpost was reported to have fallen in February 1995.

Kenyatta, Jomo, president of Kenya, 1964-78. He was imprisoned by the British authorities from 1953-61, suspected of being implicated in the Mau Mau terrorist uprising. Kenyatta led his country to independence in 1963 when he became prime minister. He later became Kenya's first president.

Khaled, Leila, a member of the Popular Front for the Liberation of Palestine, who tried unsuccessfully to hijack an El Al airliner flying from Tel Aviv to New York in September 1970. Her fellow hijacker Patrick Arguello was killed. The plane landed in London where Khaled was arrested. To secure her release, a British airliner was forced down in Jordan and its passengers were taken hostage.

Khmer Rouge, a communist guerrilla organization that fought against the government of Kampuchea (now Cambodia) in the 1960s and 1970s. In 1975, it seized power under Pol Pot and embarked on a campaign of terror, expulsion, and murder during which thousands of Cambodians were killed in what came to be called "the killing fields." The Khmer Rouge was overthrown in 1979, when Vietnam invaded Cambodia, but has continued to wage guerrilla warfare principally from bases in Thailand and despite UN attempts to promote peace.

Khomenei, Ruhollah (Ayatollah Khomenei), Iranian Shiite Muslim leader. He spent 16 years in exile before returning to Iran and leading the Islamic revolution that deposed the last shah. Khomenei supported the seizing of the U.S. embassy in Tehran in 1979 and conducted the 1980-88 war with Iraq. He famously described the U.S. government as the "Great Satan." Khomenei's apocalyptic belief that a catastrophe threatened the Muslim world was influential in justifying Muslim fundamentalist terrorism.

Ku Klux Klan (KKK), an extreme racist organization based in the southern United States and formed after the American Civil War to resist the granting of rights to African-Americans. It used violence and intimidation against them and those supporting their cause. Disbanded in 1949, the KKK became active again in the 1950s and 1960s.

Kurdish Workers Party (PKK), the most radical Kurdish group in Turkey, set up in 1974 to pursue the goal of an independent Kurdish state in Kurdish areas of Turkey, Iraq, and Iran. It has killed many Turkish civilians, but since 1988 has focused on military and official targets. It has bases in northern Iraq, and aims to create a "liberated zone" in eastern Turkey.

Lautaro Youth Movement (MJL), a left-wing or anarchist group in Chile since 1989. It has attacked police and bombed police stations in protest at the failure to investigate the state terror that had occurred pre-1989.

Lebanese Armed Revolutionary Faction (FARL), a group set up by a single family, initially as a splinter group of the Popular Front for the Liberation of Palestine. It killed U.S. and Israeli officials in Europe and Israel in the early 1980s, and was thought responsible with ASALA for a wave of bombings in France, 1985-86.

Lebanese Resistance Detachment, *see* Amal

Lehi, *see* Stern Gang

Lorenzo Zelaya Popular Revolutionary Forces, a left-wing group in Honduras, 1980-87. It attacked several embassies and offices associated with the U.S., and hijacked an airliner in 1982. Some of its members were trained in Nicaragua and Cuba. Its leaders were arrested in 1983 and 1987.

McVeigh, Timothy J., American ex-soldier indicted, with Terry L. Nichols, in the April 1995 Oklahoma City bombing of a federal building in which more than 100 people died.

Machel, Samora Moises, Marxist president of Mozambique, 1975-86. He led resistance to Portuguese colonial rule and became commander-in-chief of FRELIMO (1966-70). As first president of independent Mozambique, Machel fostered good relations with Western governments and with South Africa.

Macheteros (Machete Wielders, or Boricua Popular Army), a small but well-organized Puerto Rican separatist group, established 1978 and mainly targeting U.S. military facilities and personnel on the island. In one raid in January 1981, it destroyed eight U.S. jet fighters, causing damage in excess of $45 million. On the U.S. mainland in 1983, it stole over $7 million from a Wells Fargo truck in Connecticut. Several leaders were arrested in 1985.

Malcolm X (Malcolm Little), African-American nationalist leader who served a prison sentence (1946-53) for burglary and on release converted to the Black Muslim movement led by Elijah Muhammad. He pressed for separation from white American society and for the use of violence in self-defense. Malcolm X founded the Organization of Afro-American Unity in 1964. He was assassinated by Black Muslim opponents at a rally in Harlem.

Manuel Rodriguez Revolutionary Front, also known as the Manuel Rodriguez Patriotic Front, a guerrilla group founded in 1983, possibly the armed wing of the Chilean Communist Party. It has a fighting strength of 1,000 to 2,000 and has been supplied with arms from Soviet and Cuban sources. Originally set up to oppose the Pinochet regime and the U.S. presence in Chile, it has carried out kidnappings, assassinations, bombings, and economic sabotage.

Mao Zedong (Mao Tse-tung), chairman of the Chinese Communist party, 1949-76. He was a founder of the party in 1921 and became its leader following the Long March (1934-35). His forces defeated the occupying Japanese and the Kuomintang nationalists, and the People's Republic of China was established with Mao as head of state in 1949. His theories of guerrilla warfare were enormously influential in the period after 1945.

Marighella, Carlos, Brazilian revolutionary philosopher and ideologue, who was expelled from the Brazilian Communist party in 1967 for his advocacy of armed struggle. He advocated urban guerrilla activity as the most effective weapon against imperialism and capitalism. Inspired by the militant ALN, he received support from Cuba. He was the author of *The Minimanual of the Urban Guerrilla* (1969) published in the year in which he was shot dead by the Brazilian police.

Marxist-Leninist Armed Propaganda Unit, a left-wing Turkish death squad founded in 1973 in Paris, trained in the Middle East, and mainly targeting U.S. servicemen. It was violently suppressed, along with other groups, following the Turkish military coup of September 1980.

MAS (Muerte a Secuestradores), a prominent Colombian death squad set up in 1981 by drug traffickers. Aimed originally at countering kidnappings by guerrilla groups, it soon became used to attack anti-drug authorities and left-wingers, and then to act as an umbrella organization for right-wing death squads. Police officers and soldiers are said to be members.

Mau Mau, a secret resistance organization that developed from the Kikuyu Association founded in the 1920s to expel European settlers from Kenya and bring an end to British rule there. Mau Mau was most active in the period 1952-56. Initially it favored intimidation rather than guerrilla warfare, destroying crops and slaughtering cattle. But later it became more violent and carried out a large number of murders. Jomo Kenyatta was imprisoned from 1953 to 1961 under suspicion of being linked to Mau Mau. The organization was damaged by the capture and defection of a leadin member in 1954, and broken by the capture and execution of a second key member in 1956. Kenya gained independence in 1963.

May 1, a small Greek left-wing group working with the November 17 group and the People's Revolutionary Struggle (ELA).

May 15, an obscure splinter group of the Popular Front for the Liberation of Palestine – Special Operations Group, active 1978-86. It bombed a variety of targets, ranging from a London hotel to a Pan Am airliner flying from Tokyo to Honolulu.

Meinhof, Ulrike, leader with Andreas Baader of the Red Army Faction (Baader-Meinhof Gang) in West Germany. With Horst Mahler, she engineered Baader's escape from custody in 1970. In 1974, Meinhof was sentenced to eight years' imprisonment, and later committed suicide.

Montoneros, a left-wing political force founded in Argentina in the

1960s and led by Mario Firmenich. Although supporters of Juan Peron, they were opposed to the right wing of the Peronist movement. Their activities included kidnappings and murder, with victims including U.S. Consul John Egan in 1975. They also used arson and sabotage. Contributions were made to support the Sandinistas in Nicaragua. Denounced by Peron, the Montoneros were in decline by the early 1980s.

Morazanist Patriotic Front, a small left-wing Honduran guerrilla group, founded 1979, mainly targeting U.S. service personnel. It has received support from Cuba and Nicaragua.

Moro National Liberation Front (MNLF), a left-wing Muslim political organization established in the Philippines in the early 1970s. A formidable military force, it occupied large parts of the south of the country and received funds and arms from Libya. Following a ceasefire in 1976, sporadic terrorist activity continued, including the kidnapping and murder of foreign nationals. Internal dissension led to the MNLF's decline in the 1980s.

Mossad, the principal Israeli secret intelligence agency, founded in 1951. During the prolonged and continuing struggle with Palestinian and other forces hostile to Israel, Mossad has frequently been implicated in violent attacks and assassinations.

Movement for the Liberation of Bahrain, an Iranian-backed group for promoting an Islamic revolution in Bahrain – successor to the Islamic Front for the Liberation of Bahrain, but placing greater emphasis on recruiting within the country.

Movement of the Revolutionary Left (MIR) (Chile), an extreme left-wing revolutionary movement founded in Chile in the 1960s. Trained in Cuba, its members engaged in a campaign of murder and intimidation. It enjoyed an amnesty during the rule of Chilean President Salvador Allende, 1970-73. Following the coup which toppled and assassinated Allende and brought Augusto Pinochet to power, MIR made sporadic terrorist attacks through the 1970s and 1980s, and attempted to link with the ERP in Argentina. Its leaders included Miguel Enriquez, killed in 1974, and Andres Pascal Allende, nephew of the former president.

Movement of the Revolutionary Left (MIR) (Venezuela), a Marxist political movement founded in 1960. Originally part of FALN, it broke away in 1967, and in 1972 took part in the kidnap of a millionaire businessman for whom a large ransom was paid. MIR was legalized in 1973 and entered the mainstream political process.

Movimiento 19 Abril, *see* April 19 Movement

Movimiento Popular de Libertação de Angola, *see* Angolan Popular Liberation Movement

Mozambique National Resistance Organization, *see* RENAMO

Mugabe, Robert Gabriel, first prime minister and president of Zimbabwe. He escaped from detention to found the Zimbabwe African People's Union (ZAPU) with Ndabaningi Sithole. After ten more years in detention, 1964-74, Mugabe based himself and ZAPU in Mozambique. After independence, ZAPU and Joshua Nkomo's Zimbabwe African National Union (ZANU) merged under Mugabe's leadership.

Mujahideen, Islamic fundamentalist guerrilla groups active in several countries including Afghanistan. In Iran the People's Mujahideen conducted an armed insurrection against the shah in the 1970s and was responsible for deaths including those of U.S. military personnel.

Mukti Bahini, a guerrilla army that fought for independence for East Pakistan (now Bangladesh) in 1971. It used conventional warfare as well as guerrilla tactics.

Muslim Brotherhood (Majallar al-Ikhwan al-Musalamin), a fundamentalist religious Muslim organization originally founded by Hassan al-Banna in 1928 and active in Egypt in the 1940s and 1950s. Through acts of violence, including murder, it aimed to revitalize Islam and resist secularization. The brotherhood was implicated in the overthrow of the last Egyptian king Farouk in 1952, and in an attempt to assassinate Egyptian President Nasser. Its activities spread to other African and Arab states.

Narodnaya Volya (People's Will), a Russian revolutionary group of the nineteenth century. It assassinated the governor-general of St. Petersburg, the head of the internal security police, and, in March 1881, Tsar Alexander II.

National Front for the Liberation of Angola (FNLA), an organization formed in 1962 from the merging of the União das Populacoês de Angola (UPA) and the Partido Democratico de Angola (PDA) to fight for independence from Portuguese colonial rule. Under the leadership of Holden Roberto, the FNLA had its base in neighboring Zaire. Following Angolan independence in 1975, the organization was in prolonged conflict with the MPLA and UNITA.

National Liberation Army (ELN) (Bolivia), a shadowy umbrella organization, covering the Nestor Paz Zamora Commando and other groups, and possibly sponsored by the Tupac Amaru Revolutionary Movement of Peru. The same name was earlier used by the pro-Cuban guerrilla force led by Che Guevara, 1966-67, and destroyed by the Bolivian army.

National Liberation Army (ELN) (Colombia), a rural guerrilla force, established 1964, and most active 1969-73 and since 1980. It conducted a major bombing campaign in 1983, and refused to join the post-1984 national reconciliation movement. It is now the most active terrorist force in Colombia, with units in several regions, some of them effectively independent factions. As well as targeting offices and individuals, the group has committed extensive economic sabotage, mainly of oil production and export.

National Liberation Front (FLN), a revolutionary political party that supported the Algerian independence struggle between 1954 and 1962. With support from Egypt, Morocco, and Tunisia, it conducted an urban guerrilla campaign that was crushed by the authorities. With more success in rural areas, the FLN set up a nationalist government in exile in Tunis that was officially recognized by a number of African and Arab states and by the Soviet Union and China. A military campaign was led by Houari Boumedienne. When Algeria won independence in 1962, the FLN formed the only legitimate political party.

National Organization of Cypriot Fighters, *see* EOKA

National Socialist Liberation Front, a U.S. neo-Nazi group, founded 1969, and probably responsible for bomb attacks on left-wing groups in California in the 1970s.

Naxalites, an extreme left-wing revolutionary group that broke away from the Indian Communist party in the 1950s to spread communism throughout India. Advocates of armed struggle, the organization has carried out a number of assassinations.

Nechayev, Sergei, Russian author of *Catechism of the Revolutionist* (1869). This portrayed an idealized political terrorism that inspired many later terrorist ideas and actions.

Nestor Paz Zamora Commando, a pro-Cuban group in Bolivia, active since 1990 and sponsored by the Peruvian Tupac Amaru Revolutionary Movement. In October 1990, it bombed the U.S. embassy Marine guards' residence in La Paz.

New Afrikan Freedom Fighters, a militant leftist group based in New York and seeking an independent African-American homeland in the U.S. It has been involved in robberies and some terrorist actions.

New People's Army, the armed wing of the Philippines Communist party, formed in 1969. With Chinese support, later withdrawn, it fought a rural guerrilla campaign. Internal dissension hastened its decline.

New World Liberation Front, a U.S. left-wing group active in the 1970s and responsible, according to the FBI, for about 100 bombings in the San Francisco area, 1974-78. Banks, corporations, and police stations were the chief targets. The group's activities ceased in 1979, after one of its founders killed the other and was arrested for his murder.

Nkomo, Joshua Mqabuko Nyongolo, president of the Zimbabwe African People's Union (ZAPU), 1961-82. In 1976, he formed the Patriotic Front with Robert Mugabe to press for black majority rule in then Southern Rhodesia. Nkomo lost his post in Mugabe's government in 1982.

NORAID (Irish Northern Aid Committee), a U.S.-based fundraising organization, supporting nationalist elements in the conflict in Northern Ireland. Chiefly active in New York and Boston, it supplies the IRA and other groups despite official opposition from the American, British, and Irish governments.

November 17, a Greek left-wing guerrilla group that claimed the assassination of Athens CIA chief Richard Welch in December 1975. It later admitted killing two high-ranking Greek police officers in 1976 and 1980.

Nuclei Armati Rivoluzionari, *see* Armed Revolutionary Nucleus

Omega 7, an anti-Castro Cuban group in the U.S., targeting Cuban diplomats and those seen as too conciliatory to the Castro regime. In September 1980, it assassinated a Cuban diplomat to the United Nations. Omega 7 collapsed after its founder was exposed as an FBI informant in 1983.

ORDEN (Organización Democrática Nacional), an organization of up to 50,000 members set up by the Salvadoran army in 1968 to act as a rural civil militia. It gave rise in turn to the Salvadoran death squads.

Order, a small U.S. west-coast white supremacist group, mainly active 1983-84. It killed a Jewish radio talk-show host, bombed a movie theater and a synagogue, and conducted robbery and counterfeiting to finance its activities.

Ordine Nero, *see* Black Order

Organisation de l'Armée Secrète, *see* Secret Army Organization

Organization for the Armed Arab Struggle, a small group run by "Carlos the Jackal" that claimed a number of bombings on French targets, 1983-84. The group probably also undertook contract terrorism on behalf of other Arab clients.

Organization of Volunteers for the Puerto Rican Revolution, a Puerto Rican group linked to the Macheteros and joining them in various attacks since 1979.

Ortega (Saavedra), Daniel, president of Nicaragua, 1985-90. He became leader of one faction of the Sandinista National Liberation Front in 1966, and used a strategy of propaganda actions to encourage urban uprisings. In 1979, these brought about the overthrow of the existing dictatorship of Somoza. Ortega led a provisional socialist government from 1979 to 1984.

Palestine Liberation Army, the military wing of the Palestine Liberation Organization (PLO), formed in 1964 to fight for the liberation of Palestine and the destruction of the state of Israel. Its fighters were trained in Egypt and support came from Jordan and Syria.

Palestine Liberation Front (PLF), a group supported by Iraq and Libya which split from the PFLP-GC in 1977 over the latter's links with Syria and the Lebanon. It is a member of the Rejectionist Front.

Palestine Liberation Organization (PLO), a political and military organization founded in 1964 to fight for a Palestinian state and the destruction of the state of Israel. Though supporting these aims, Arab governments attempted to distance themselves from the PLO and from Yasser Arafat, leader of its most militant and dominant faction Fatah (the Palestine National Liberation Movement) and chairman of the organization. A split into factions followed Israel's victory in the 1967 Six Day War and the expansion of Israeli territory. Apart from Fatah, another major faction was the Popular Front for the Liberation of Palestine (PFLP) led by George Habash. After more than ten years of guerrilla and other military activity, and terrorist attacks in many parts of the world, the PLO declared the establishment of a Palestinian state in the West Bank and Gaza, and the U.S. government lifted its ban on negotiating with the PLO. The organization supported Iraq in the 1992 Gulf War but signed a peace accord with Israel in Washington DC in September 1993.

Palestine National Liberation Movement, *see* Fatah

Party of God, *see* Hizb'allah

Party of the Poor (Partido de los Pobres), a left-wing fighting group founded by Lucio Cabanas in Mexico in 1967 to nationalize private property through armed struggle. Active during the 1970s, it kidnapped and killed a number of landowners, attacked government troops, and bombed a hotel. With the death of Cabanas in 1974, the party declined.

People's Revolutionary Army (ERP) (Argentina), an armed wing of the Argentinian Workers' Revolutionary Party, set up in 1969 and led by Roberto Santucho. It had ties with Cuba and took much of its inspiration from the writings of Che Guevara. The ERP aimed to promote revolution and the working-class struggle against poverty and exploitation. It targeted foreign-owned businesses and the military, American business leaders being singled out in its main period of activity from 1973 to 1977.

People's Revolutionary Army (ERP) (El Salvador), a revolutionary movement formed in 1971 and led by Joaquin Villalobos. Opposed to what it saw as U.S. imperialism, it targeted government and business premises. The ERP split in 1975, with one branch becoming FARN. It supported the Sandinistas in Nicaragua's civil war and was in decline by the 1980s.

Phalange, a Lebanese Christian far-right party founded in the 1930s and its militia. The Phalange massacre of a busload of Palestinians on April 13, 1975, triggered civil war in Lebanon.

Pol Pot (Saloth Sar), prime minister of Kampuchea (now Cambodia), 1976-79. Active in the resistance to French colonial rule led by Ho Chi Minh, he joined the Communist party in 1964. He became leader of the Khmer Rouge guerrillas and overthrew the Lon Nol government in 1976. His totalitarian administration brought imprisonment, exile, and death to millions of Cambodians. Pol Pot was ousted when Vietnam invaded Cambodia in 1979, but he continued to lead the Khmer Rouge forces. He was reported to have died of malaria in May 1996.

POLISARIO (Popular Front for the Liberation of Saguiat al Hamra and Rio de Oro), a guerrilla movement founded in Mauritania in 1973 to undermine Spanish colonial rule in the Sahara and later to fight against joint rule of the territory by Morocco and Mauritania. Supported with training and weapons by Algeria, POLISARIO undertook guerrilla action principally against economic targets in Mauritania, and in 1976 declared the independent Sahara Arab Democratic Republic which was recognized by several countries. In 1979, Morocco gained complete control of the former Spanish Sahara, but POLISARIO resistance continued for some time.

Popular Forces of April 25, a Portuguese left-wing revolutionary group formed in 1980. The name refers to the successful anti-fascist coup of April 25, 1975. The group carried out mortar and antitank rocket attacks, bombings, assassinations, and robberies, including two attacks on the U.S. embassy in 1984 and one in 1986. After 1986 it probably continued as the Armed Revolutionary Organization.

Popular Front for the Liberation of Oman (PFLO), founded in 1971 as the Popular Front for the Liberation of Oman and the Arabian Gulf. Based in Aden and with support from South Yemen, this movement fought to subvert traditional Arab rulers in the Gulf states, especially the sultan of Oman. Guerrilla fighters were supplied by the Soviet Union. The rulers fought back with support from Britain and Iran. In 1974, the name was changed to PFLO. The group maintained links with the Popular Front for the Liberation of Palestine (PFLP).

Popular Front for the Liberation of Palestine (PFLP), a militant group within the Palestine Liberation Organization (PLO), set up in 1967 by George Habash following Israel's victory in the Six Day War. With support from Algeria, Libya, and South Yemen, the PFLP was violently anti-West and dedicated to destroying Israel. In the 1960s and 1970s, several aircraft were hijacked and some blown up. The PFLP organized the massacre by the Japanese Red Army at Lod airport, Israel, in May 1972, in which 26 civilians were killed.

Popular Front for the Liberation of Palestine – General Command (PFLP-GC), a Palestinian terrorist group created in 1968 by Ahmad Jibril, former leader of the Palestine Liberation Front. With support from Libya and Syria, it pursued ruthless terrorist activities including suicide attacks on Israeli villages.

Popular Front for the Liberation of Palestine – Special Command, an Iraqi-based group set up in the mid-1970s after the PFLP-GC renounced the use of terrorism.

Popular Front for the Liberation of Palestine – Special Operations Group, an Iraqi-based splinter group, set up in 1975 and led by Wadi Haddad till his death in 1978. It claimed responsibilty for hijacking a West German airliner in 1977 and for an attack on an Israeli El Al airline bus in London in 1978.

Popular Liberation Army (EPL) (Colombia), a Maoist rural guerrilla force established in 1967 by the Communist party of Colombia, Marxist-Leninist. Between the late 1970s and mid 1980s, its membership rose to about 750, while it conducted a campaign of kidnappings, sabotage, bombings, armed attacks, and bank robberies. It frequently clashed with a pro-Moscow group, the Revolutionary Armed Forces of Colombia. It has also maintained support groups in several Colombian cities.

Popular Movement for the Liberation of Angola (MPLA), a Marxist organization founded in the 1950s to resist Portuguese colonial rule. Its most prominent leader was Agostinho Neto, who was its president for 17 years. The MPLA came to power after independence in 1975. With Soviet and Cuban backing, it was engaged in prolonged power struggles with UNITA and the FNLA.

Popular Resistance Front, an Argentinian group of former members of the People's Revolutionary Army and chiefly known for an attack in January 1989 on an army base near Buenos Aires, which ended in the deaths of 28 terrorists, nine soldiers, and two policemen.

Popular Struggle Front, a Syrian-backed group that split from the Palestine Liberation Organization in 1974 and opposed any negotiations with Israel. It kidnapped a U.S. Army colonel in 1975, and has carried out several guerrilla attacks within Israel. In 1991, it rejoined the PLO.

Posse Comitatus, a U.S. anti-tax group founded in 1969 and initially peaceful, advising its members on legal and other bookkeeping methods of avoiding tax. Its name is Latin for "power of the county." After an IRS crackdown in 1980, some violent incidents occurred, including an attempted bombing of a Federal judge. A splinter group, the Arizona Patriots, was accused in 1986 on charges of plotting to bomb IRS and other offices, including Jewish organizations.

Prima Linea (PL), an Italian left-wing group, active 1976-81 and carrying out assassinations, kneecappings, and attacks on buildings. Founded by a Red Brigade member, it differed from the latter by maintaining contact with the nonviolent left.

Provisional IRA (PIRA) is an independent offshoot of the original Irish Republican Army. Set up in 1969, the Provisional IRA engages in terrorist activity against British targets and aims for union between Northern Ireland and the Republic of Ireland.

Qaddafi (or Gaddafi), Muammar Muhammad al, president of Libya since 1977. He led the coup that deposed King Idris in 1969 and became chairman of the revolutionary council. He established the Libyan Arab Republic and appointed himself head of state in 1970. He has been accused of supporting international terrorism and has often been in conflict with Western nations as well as with Arab and African neighbors.

Quebec Liberation Front (FLQ), a French-Canadian terrorist organization founded in 1963 to campaign for secession from predominantly English-speaking Canada. A bombing campaign targeted the police and the military, as well as English language (including U.S.-owned) businesses. There were links in the 1960s with the Black Power movement in the U.S. The FLQ declined in importance when the Parti Québecois won electoral support, thereby carrying on the separatist campaign through legitimate political channels.

Qutb, Sayyid, an Egyptian Islamic theologian and writer, and a leader of the Muslim Brotherhood. He greatly influenced the development of Islamic fundamentalism, both in its theory and its practice. In particular, his interpretation of *jihad* (holy war) has been used to justify terrorist actions against secular and non-fundamentalist Muslim leaders and Western countries. Qutb was twice implicated in attempts to kill Egyptian President Nasser and was executed in 1965.

Rahman, Sheikh Omar Abdel, an Egyptian Islamic cleric who lives in the U.S. He and his accomplices were convicted in October 1995, of conspiring to commit terrorists acts in New York City. His organization had been implicated in an assassination plot against Egyptian President Mubarak in 1993.

Red Army Faction (Rote Armee Fraktion), a left-wing terrorist group active in West Germany, 1972 to the present. Its roots lay in the 1968 student revolt and its first protest was in that year – the bombing of a department store in Frankfurt in protest against the Vietnam war. The RAF, named for an extremist Japanese group of the same name, was led by Andreas Baader and Ulrike Meinhof (and was popularly known as the Baader-Meinhof Gang). Other targets included Israeli property. The RAF derived its finances from bank robberies. In 1972, there was a series of bomb explosions in Hamburg in which one American official died. The RAF had links with revolutionary groups in other European countries. It was implicated in several killings and hijackings, and by 1981 was attacking military targets in Germany. By this time, both Baader and Meinhof had committed suicide.

Red Army for the Liberation of Catalonia, a small offshoot of Terra Lliure. During 1987, it bombed several U.S. targets in Barcelona.

Red Brigades (Brigate Rosse), an extreme left-wing terrorist organization founded in Italy in 1970 and active 1974-88. Its aim was to free Italy from the tyranny of multinational industrial power. It was founded by Renato Curcio and Margherita Cagol and operated a structure of small "cells." Initially idealistic, it nevertheless derived funding from kidnappings and bank robberies, and became increasingly violent under new leadership in the late 1970s. In 1978, it kidnapped and murdered former Prime Minister Aldo Moro, and in 1981 held hostage U.S. Brigadier-General Dozier. The Red Brigades became increasingly less active in the 1980s. Some members probably joined groups overseas.

Red Flag (Bandera Roja), a left-wing revolutionary Venezuelan group, whose acts include kidnappings for ransom, hijackings of domestic flights, and sporadic attacks on military convoys and small towns.

Red Guerrilla Resistance, a U.S. left-wing group active in New York City in the mid 1980s and opposed to U.S., Israeli, and South African policies and to U.S. police racism. It bombed several targets, including the South African consulate in 1984 and U.S. Police Benevolent Association offices in 1985.

Red Hand Commandos, an Ulster Protestant militia set up in 1972 and responsible for killing Catholics in Belfast and probably for bombings in the Irish Republic. Its original leader, John McKeague, was killed in 1982 by the Irish National Liberation Army.

Rejectionist Front, an Iraqi-backed alliance of Palestinian groups opposed to political settlement with Israel.

RENAMO (Resisténcia Nacional Moçambicana), a right-wing force set up by white Rhodesians and subsequently backed by South Africa. In the 1980s it numbered up to 20,000, and fought a guerrilla war against the left-wing FRELIMO government of Mozambique.

Revolutionary Armed Forces of Colombia (FARC), initially an independent guerrilla group, FARC emerged in 1966 as the armed wing of the Colombian Communist party. It was led by Manuel Marulanda Velez, an experienced guerrilla fighter. Active in rural areas, the organization was anti-imperialist and pro-Soviet; it was undermined by counter-insurgency measures that had U.S. backing. In 1975, FARC kidnapped the Dutch consul in Cali.

Revolutionary Armed Task Force (RATF), a U.S. left-wing terrorist group formed in 1979 from remnants of the Black Liberation Army and the Weather Underground. It financed itself from robbery, taking about $1 million in 1979-81. The group targeted offices of the U.S. federal government and of businesses trading with South Africa. It bombed IBM and South African Airways offices in 1981, a U.S. Senate washroom in 1982, and the New York FBI offices in 1984. The group was broken by the arrest of key members in 1985-86.

Revolutionary Cells (Revolutionare Zellen), a group dedicated to promoting revolution, its cells operated in West Germany in the

1970s, targeting U.S. and NATO military bases. A guerrilla campaign had petered out by the early 1980s.

Revolutionary Party of Central American Workers (PRTC), one of the armed left-wing "political-military organizations" in El Salvador.

Revolutionary Popular Struggle (ELA), a Greek revolutionary terrorist organization active in the late 1970s and early 1980s. Its bombing campaign targeted U.S.-owned businesses and official buildings, including the U.S. ambassador's residence in 1982.

Ricardo Franco Front, a small Colombian Marxist guerrilla group formerly linked to FARC and violently anti-American. In a purge in late 1985 it killed many of its own members: a mass grave of 164 corpses was found. Other leftist groups broke links with the group as a result.

Roberto, Holden, leader from 1962 of the Revolutionary Government of Angola in Exile, which had its base in Leopoldville (now Kinshasa), capital of the Congo (now Zaire), and later of the FNLA, which fought for independence from Portuguese colonial rule and had U.S. and Chinese support. His leadership of the FNLA ended in 1981.

Roderigo Franco Command, a right-wing Peruvian death squad linked to the American Popular Revolutionary Alliance party (APRA).

Rote Armee Fraktion, *see* Red Army Faction

Saiqa, a Palestinian commando force founded in 1967, and under the control of the Syrian defense ministry from 1970. It recruits from the Palestinian refugee camps in Syria, and has rejected the 1993 Israeli-PLO accord.

Sandinista National Liberation Front (FSLN), a left-wing political movement set up by Carlos Fonseca Amador in Nicaragua in 1961. Named after national hero Augusto César Sandino, who fought against U.S. forces in the late 1920s and died a martyr in 1934, the FSLN took its inspiration from Fidel Castro's Cuban revolution and had support and safe havens in Costa Rica. It opposed and sought to undermine the dictatorship of Anastasio Somoza Debayle through urban guerrilla activity, including kidnappings and aircraft hijackings. Fonseca was killed in 1976 and the organization split into factions, one led by Daniel Ortega and his brother. Eden Pastora Gómez became military commander in 1978 but later turned against the Sandinistas. Somoza was deposed in 1979 and the FSLN formed the government with Ortega as leader. He became president in 1984. As Ortega took his party leftwards, U.S. antagonism grew and it sponsored the opposing Contras. The Sandinistas suffered electoral defeat in 1990.

Savimbi, Jonas, founder in 1966 of UNITA. He studied medicine in Lisbon, 1957-60, and joined the revolutionary government of Angola in exile. With South African and Chinese support, he competed for power in Angola with the FNLA and Soviet-backed MPLA.

Secret Anti-Communist Army (ESA), a right-wing guerrilla group formed by César Montes in Guatemala in 1977. It aligned itself with other extreme groups to defend capitalism. Its main targets were student activists and left-wing politicians and it carried out a number of murders.

Secret Army Organization (OAS), an organization formed by French settlers in Algeria who opposed France's negotiations with the National Liberation Front (FLN) over independence for Algeria. A terror campaign in the 1960s targeted Algerian nationalist institutions and selected targets in France.

Sekigun, *see* Japanese Red Army

Shining Path (Sendero Luminoso), a Maoist terrorist organization founded in Peru in 1970 and led by Abimael Guzmán until 1992. In the 1980s, it launched terrorist attacks on Peruvian cities and towns.

Sithole, Ndabaningi, president of the Zimbabwe African National Union (ZANU), and advocate of violent resistance by black African nationalists to white minority rule in Southern Rhodesia (now Zimbabwe). He was imprisoned in the 1960s and later formed a political alliance with moderate African National Congress leader Abel Muzorewa.

Slovo, Joe, South African lawyer, the first white to be elected to the executive council of the African National Congress (ANC). He joined the South African Communist party in the 1940s and after 1963 worked for the party and for the ANC from outside South Africa. He was chief of staff of Umkhonto we Sizwe, the armed wing of the ANC. Slovo returned to South Africa in 1990 and worked closely with Nelson Mandela. He died in 1996.

Stern Gang (Lehi), a splinter group of Irgun, founded in 1940 by Abraham Stern. Like Irgun it sought to expel British forces and Arab people from Palestine, but unlike Irgun refused to observe a truce during the war with Germany. It also targeted moderate Jews. In 1944, Lehi assassinated Lord Moyne, British minister for Middle Eastern affairs. It was largely broken up by the British in 1945, but in 1948 group members killed the two United Nations mediators to Palestine. A Lehi leader, Yitzhak Shamir, eventually became prime minister of Israel.

Sudanese People's Liberation Army (SPLA), a guerrilla force set up in 1983 which became the main fighting force of the southern Christian Sudanese in their civil war against the northern Islamic government.

SWAPO (South West Africa People's Organization), a militant nationalist organization founded in Namibia in 1964 to fight against South Africa's illegal rule. SWAPO conducted a guerrilla campaign from neighboring Angola. It won elections to power in independent Namibia in 1990.

Symbionese Liberation Army (SLA), a dissident group formed in 1973 in San Francisco, California, by Donald DeFreeze. Claiming to speak and fight for oppressed minorities everywhere, the SLA killed a school caretaker in 1973. In 1974, the group kidnapped Patty Hearst, of the wealthy U.S. publishing family, and she later took part in an SLA bank raid in San Francisco, bringing the group huge publicity. DeFreeze was killed in a gun battle with police later in the same year, after which the SLA fell apart.

Syrian Social Nationalist Party (SSNP), a Syrian-backed Lebanese militia, responsible for many terrorist attacks including the bombing of the Phalangists' headquarters in Beirut in September 1982 that killed President-elect Bashir Gemayel. It specializes in suicide car bombings, often using young Arab women who have become pregnant outside marriage.

Tamil Tigers, a name used by a large number of different guerrilla and terrorist groups formed in Sri Lanka since 1972, often clashing among themselves, but with the common goal of creating a separate Tamil state in the northeast of the island. The largest of these groups is the Liberation Tigers of Tamil Eelam. Based in Jaffna, and with safe havens in the Indian state of Tamil Nadu, the movement has waged war since 1983 on the majority Sinhalese community and has also assassinated moderate Tamil politicians. Bombs have been planted in Sri Lanka and India.

Tanton Macoutes (National Security Volunteers), a state-backed militia in Haiti, set up in 1957 by dictator "Papa Doc" Duvalier. Originally a bodyguard, it grew to 15,000 members and was used to intimidate and eliminate opposition to his regime. It was officially disbanded in 1985, but has in fact remained a major force in Haiti.

Terra Lliure (Free Land), a leftist Spanish group set up in 1980, seeking an independent Catalan homeland. Among many small attacks, it bombed the U.S. consulate general offices in Barcelona in 1987. It reportedly renounced terrorism in 1991.

Tigre (or Tigray) People's Liberation Front (TPLF), a separatist organization founded in the Province of Tigre after Ethiopian emperor Haile Selassie was overthrown in 1974. Initially pro-Western, it moved leftward and linked with the Eritrean People's Liberation Front (EPLF). The TPLF's main guerrilla campaign was fought 1975 to 1991, when the region was ravaged by drought and famine.

Tupac Amaru Revolutionary Movement (MRTA), a Peruvian Marxist terrorist group set up in 1984. Its 200-300 members were mostly students. An attempt in 1987 to launch a "rural column" was rapidly suppressed by the Peruvian army.

Tupamaros (Movimiento de Liberación Nacional), an urban guerrilla organization founded by Raul Sendic Antonaccio in 1963 in Uruguay. Its name derives from the eighteenth century Inca ruler Tupac Amaru. Dedicated to fighting corruption and reforming society, the movement carried out bombings and bank robberies, and targeted U.S. diplomats and multinational businesses. With Cuban support, it later concentrated on attacking the capital Montevideo. Often the proceeds from its raids were distributed among the poor. In 1970, the Tupamaros seized and killed U.S. aid worker Dan Mitrione, and in 1971 held British Ambassador Geoffrey Jackson for 8 months. Crushed by 1972, the organization had maintained links with the ERP in Argentina and MIR in Chile.

Turkish People's Liberation Army (TPLA), a left-wing group set up in about 1968 and involved in bombings, murders, and abductions prior to the military clampdown in 1980. By 1977, it had killed 260 people. A splinter faction, Dev Yol, gave rise to current terrorist group, Dev Sol.

Ulster Defense Association (UDA), a militant Protestant paramilitary organization formed in 1971. First led by Charles Harding Smith, the UDA later became more active under Jim Anderson. It set up Protestant barricades in Northern Ireland in 1972 and challenged the British Army. At its most active in the mid-1970s, it placed bombs in the Republic of Ireland.

Ulster Freedom Fighters (UFF), a militant Protestant paramilitary organization that split from the Ulster Defense Association in 1973. Active until the early 1980s, the UFF carried out several assassinations.

Ulster Volunteer Force (UVF), a militant Protestant loyalist organization that was active in Northern Ireland in the 1970s. It was set up by Augustus Spence (later imprisoned) in 1966 and was banned by the Northern Ireland government. Financed by protection rackets, it carried out petrol bomb attacks and declared war on the Irish Republican Army. The UVF had a long feud with the Ulster Freedom Fighters.

Unabomber, a lone American who eluded the FBI from the 1970s and whose "manifesto" was published by the *Washington Post* in September 1995. Believed to have carried out sixteen bomb attacks, the Unabomber claimed to belong to an anarchist group targeting leading figures in technological fields deemed hostile to the environment. A suspect, Theodore Kaczynski, was arrested in April 1996.

UNITA (União Nacional para a Independência Total de Angola), Angolan nationalist movement founded by Jonas Savimbi in 1966 to fight for independence from Portuguese colonial rule. Most effective in rural areas, UNITA won support from South Africa in its struggle for power with the MPLA after Angolan independence in 1975.

United Freedom Front (UFF), a U.S. left-wing group, successor to the Sam Melville-Jonathon Jackson Unit, based in New York. It opposed U.S. policy on Central America and South Africa, targeting military and defense industry sites. In 1986, eight members were charged with ten bank robberies, 19 bomb attacks, and three murders.

Weathermen, a pro-communist faction that split from the Revolutionary Youth Movement in the U.S. in 1969. Led by Bernardine Dohrn and Mark Rudd, the movement advocated Third World rather than Soviet-style communism and preached armed struggle against the forces of law and order. Claiming inspiration from African-American dissident groups, the Weathermen claimed credit for 17 bombings and its leading members were charged and imprisoned. From 1971, the movement was renamed the Weather Underground. It was ineffective by the mid 1970s.

ZANU (Zimbabwe African National Union), a guerrilla force founded in Southern Rhodesia (now Zimbabwe) to oppose white minority rule. Based on the Shona tribe in the north and east of the coutry, with support from China and Tanzania and bases in Mozambique and Zambia, ZANU conducted a violent guerrilla struggle and was outlawed in 1964. After independence in 1980, with its leader Robert Mugabe becoming Zimbabwe's first head of state, ZANU was clearly the dominant political force in the country, and finally merged with ZAPU to form ZANU-PF.

ZAPU (Zimbabwe African People's Union), a guerrilla force formed in 1961 to oppose white rule in Southern Rhodesia. Based on the Matabele tribe and led by Joshua Nkomo with Soviet support, it was instrumental with ZANU in achieving independence.

SELECT BIBLIOGRAPHY

GENERAL

Adams, James. *The Financing of Terror.* New York: Simon and Schuster, 1980.

Agger, Inger and Soren Buus Jensen. *Trauma and Healing under State Terrorism.* London and Atlantic Highlands, NJ: Zed Books, 1996.

Alexander, Yonah, Yuval Neeman, and Ely J. Tavin. *Terrorism: Future Trends.* Washington, DC: Global Affairs, 1991.

Allison, Graham. *Avoiding Nuclear Anarchy.* Cambridge, MA: MIT Press, 1996.

Antokol, Norman. *No One a Neutral: Political Hostage-Taking in the Modern World.* Medina, OH: Alpha, 1990.

Barry, Rubin, ed. *The Politics of Terrorism: Terror as a State and Revolutionary Strategy.* London: University Press of America, 1989; New York: St. Martin's Press, 1991.

Bjorgo, Tore, ed. *Terror from the Extreme Right.* London and Portland, OR: Frank Cass, 1995.

Bradbury, Jim. *The Medieval Siege.* Rochester, NY: Boydell and Brewer, 1992.

Bushnell, P.T., ed. *State Organized Terror: the Case of Violent Internal Repression.* Boulder, CO: Westview Press, 1991.

Charters, David, ed. *Democratic Responses to International Terrorism.* Ardsley-on-Hudson, New York: Transnational Publishers, 1991.

Chomsky, Noam. *Pirates and Emperors: International Terrorism in the Real World.* New York: Black Rose Books, 1991.

Ellis, John. *From the Barrel of a Gun: A History of Revolutionary and Counter Insurgency Warfare.* London: Greenhill Books, 1995.

Gallis, Paul E. *Combating State-Supported Terrorism: Differing US and Western European Perspectives.* Washington, DC: Congressional Research Service, Library of Congress, 1988.

Giddens, Anthony. *Beyond Left and Right: The Future of Radical Politics.* Cambridge: Polity Press, and Stanford, CA: Stanford University Press, 1994.

Gilbert, Paul. *Terrorism, Security and Nationality.* London and New York: Routledge, 1994.

Guelke, Adrian. *The Age of Terrorism and the International Political System.* London: Tauris, and New York: St. Martin's Press, 1995.

Haffey, Neil. *The United Nations and International Efforts to Deal with Terrorism.* Washington, DC: Pew Charitable Trusts, 1988.

Harris, Nigel. *National Liberation.* London: Penguin, 1992; Reno: University of Nevada Press, 1993.

Howard, Lawrence, ed. *Terrorism: Roots, Impact, Response.* London and New York: Praeger, 1992.

Jeffries, Francis M. *Terrorism and Multinational Business Operations.* Poolesville, MD: Jeffries and Associates, 1989.

Kegley, Charles W., ed. *International Terrorism: Characteristics, Courses, Controls.* London: Macmillan, and New York: St. Martin's Press, 1990.

Kennedy, Paul. *Preparing for the Twenty-First Century.* London: Fontana, and New York: Vintage Books, 1994.

Killingray, David, and David Anderson, eds. *Policing Empire: Government, Authority and Control, 1830-1940.* Manchester: Manchester

University Press, and New York: St. Martin's Press, 1991.

Livingston, Marius, ed. *International Terrorism in the Contemporary World.* Westport, CT: Greenwood, 1978.

McKnight, Gerald. *The Terrorist Mind.* London: Michael Joseph, and Indianapolis, IN: Bobbs-Merrill, 1974.

Mainwaring, Max G., and William T. Olson, eds. *Managing Contemporary Conflict: Pillars of Success.* Boulder, CO: Westview Press, 1996.

Murphy, John Francis. *State Support for International Terrorism.* London: Mansell, and Boulder, CO: Westview Press, 1989.

Nacos, Brigitte. *Terrorism and the Media: From the Iran Hostages to the World Trade Center Bombing.* New York: Columbia University Press, 1995.

Netanyahu, Benjamin. *Fighting Terrorism: How Democracies Can Defeat Domestic and International Terrorists.* New York: Farrar Straus Giroux, 1995.

Norton, Augustus R., and Martin H. Greenberg, eds. *Studies in Nuclear Terrorism.* Boston: G. K. Hall, 1979.

O'Brien, Conor Cruise. *Passion and Cunning: Essays on Nationalism, Terrorism and Revolution.* London: Weidenfeld and Nicolson, 1988; New York: Simon and Schuster, 1989.

Olson, James E., et al., eds. *Historical Dictionary of the British Empire.* Westport, CT: Greenwood, 1996.

Omissi, David. *Air Power and Colonial Control: The Royal Air Force, 1919-1939.* Manchester: Manchester University Press, and New York: St. Martin's Press, 1990.

Porter, A. N. *European Imperialism.* London: Macmillan, 1994.

Purnell, S. W. *How International Businesses Cope with Terrorism.* Santa Monica, CA: Rand Corporation, 1986.

Roukis, George S., Hugh Conway, and Bruce H. Charnow, eds. *Global Corporate Intelligence: Opportunities, Technologies and Threats in the 1990s.* New York: Quorum Books, 1990.

Rubenstein, Richard E. *Alchemist of Revolution: Terrorism in the Modern World.* London: Tauris, and New York: Basic Books, 1987.

Rubin, Barry. *The Future of Terrorism.* Washington, DC: Johns Hopkins Foreign Policy Institute, 1992.

Seymour, William. *Great Sieges of History.* Washington and London: Brassey's, 1991.

Smith, Woodruff D. *European Imperialism in the Nineteenth and Twentieth Centuries.* Chicago: Nelson-Hall, 1982.

Spiers, Edward M. *Chemical and Biological Weapons.* London: Macmillan, and New York: St. Martin's Press, 1994.

Spiers, Edward M. *Chemical Weaponry.* London: Macmillan, and New York: St. Martin's Press, 1989.

Stohl, Michael, and George A. Lopez. *Terrible Beyond Endurance: The Foreign Policy of State Terrorism.* London and New York: Greenwood, 1988.

Streissguth, Thomas. *International Terrorists.* Minneapolis, MN: Oliver, 1993.

Taylor, Maxwell. *The Fanatics.* London and Washington: Brassey's, 1991.

Taylor, Maxwell, and Ethan Quayle. *Terrorist Lives.* London: Brassey's, and Washington, DC: Macmillan, 1994.

Watson, Bruce. *Sieges: A Comparative Study.* Westport, CT: Praeger, 1993.

Weimann, Gabriel. *The Theater of Terror: Mass Media and International Terrorism.* New York: Longman, 1994.

Zulaika, Joseba, and William A. Douglas. *Terror and Taboo: The Follies, Fables and Faces of Terrorism.* New York: Routledge, 1996.

NORTH AMERICA

Andrews, Lor B. *Black Power, White Blood.* New York: Pantheon Books, 1996.

Blanchard, Dallas A. *Religious Violence and Abortion.* Gainesville: University Press of Florida, 1993.

Bodansky, Yossef, and Duncan Hunter. *Terror! Inside the Terrorist Conspiracy in America.* New York: SPI Books, 1994.

Borque, Gilles. "Quebec Nationalism and the Struggle for Sovereignty in French Canada," in *The National Question, Nationalism, Ethnic Conflict and Self-Determination in the Twentieth Century,* ed. Berch Berberoglu. Philadelphia, PA: Temple University Press, 1995.

Braungart, Richard G., and Margaret M. Braungart. "From Protest to Terrorism: The Case of the SDS and the Weathermen," in *Social Movements and Violence: Participation in Underground Organisations,* ed. Donatella Della Porta. Greenwich, CT: JAI Press, 1992.

Broehl, Wayne G. *The Molly Maguires.* Cambridge, MA: Harvard University Press, 1965.

Cable, Larry. *Conflict of Myths: The Development of American Counter-Insurgency Doctrine and the Vietnam War.* New York: New York University Press, 1986.

Campbell, Patrick. *A Molly Maguire Story.* Jersey City, NJ: Templecrone Press, 1992.

Clark, Charles S. *Abortion Clinic Protests: Is Violence Changing the Abortion Debate?* Washington, DC: Congressional Quarterly Inc., 1995.

Corcoran, James. *Bitter Harvest: The Birth of Paramilitary Terrorism in the Heartland.* New York: Penguin, 1995.

Dwyer, Jim, and David Kocieniewski. *Two Seconds Under the World: Terror Comes to America.* New York: Ballantine Books, 1995.

Ginsberg, Faye. "Saving America's Souls: Operation Rescue's Crusade Against Abortion," in *Fundamentalisms and the State,* ed. Martin E. Marty, and F. Scott Appleby. Chicago: University of Chicago Press, 1993.

Goldstein, Leslie. *Contemporary Cases in Women's Rights.* Madison: University of Wisconsin Press, 1994.

Grathwohl, Larry. *Bringing Down America: An FBI Informer with the Weathermen.* New Rochelle, NY: Arlington House, 1976.

Griswold, Terry. *Delta: America's Elite Counter-Terrorist Force.* Osceola, WI: Motorbooks International, 1992.

Haggart, Ron. *Rumors of War.* Chicago: Follet, 1971.

Hearst, Patricia. *Patty Hearst: Her Own Story.* New York: Avon Books, 1988.

Hillard, David. *This Side of Glory: The Autobiography of David Hillard and Story of the Black Panther Party.* Newport, CA: Backbay Books, 1993.

Ignatieff, Michael. *Blood and Belonging: Journeys into the New Nationalism.* London: Vintage, 1994; New York: Noonday Press, 1995.

Kennedy, Stetson. *The Klan Unmasked.* Boca Raton, FL: Florida Atlantic University Press, 1990.

Kinney, Jean Brown. *An American Journey: The Short Life of Willy Wolfe.* New York: Simon and Schuster, 1979.

Lens, Sidney. *The Labor Wars, From the Molly Maguires to the Sitdowns.* Garden City, NY: Anchor Press, 1974.

McClintock, Michael. *Instruments of State Craft: US Guerrilla Warfare, Counter-Insurgency and Counter-Terrorism, 1940-1990.* New York: Pantheon, 1992.

MacLean, Nancy. *Behind the Mask of Chivalry: The Making of the Ku Klux Klan.* New York: Oxford University Press, 1994.

McLellan, Vin. *The Voices of the Guns.* New York: Putnam, 1977.

The Maldon Institute. *Again the Terrorist.* Washington, DC: The Maldon Institute, 1993.

Marks, Rick. *America Under Attack.* New York: Carlyle Communications, 1995.

Newton, Huey. *War Against the Panthers: A Study of Repression in America.* New York: Harlem River Press, 1996.

Novick, Michael. *The Klu Klux Klan in US History.* Burbank, CA: PART, 1993.

Ross, Jim, and Myers Ross. *We Will Never Forget: Eyewitness Accounts of the Bombing of Oklahoma City.* Austin, TX: Eakin Press, 1996.

Stern, Susan. *With the Weathermen.* New York: Doubleday, 1975.

Stickney, Brandon H. *"All-American Monster": The Unauthorized Biography of Timothy McVeigh.* Amherst, NY: Prometheus Books, 1996.

Tucker, Richard K. *The Dragon and the Cross: The Rise and Fall of Ku Klux Klan in Middle America.* Hamden, CT: Archon Books, 1991.

Utley, Robert. M. *The Indian Frontier of the American West, 1846-1890.* Albuquerque: University of New Mexico, 1984.

Wainstein, Eleanor Sullivan. *The Cross and Laporte Kidnappings, Montreal, October 1970.* Santa Monica, CA: Rand Corporation, 1980.

Waldman, Carl. *Encyclopedia of Native American Tribes.* New York: Facts on File Publications, 1988.

Washburn, Wilcomb E. *Handbook of North American Indians.* Vol. 3, *History of Indian-White Relations.* Washington, DC: Smithsonian Institution Press, 1988.

Weinberg, Maye. *Racism in Contemporary America.* Westport, CT: Greenwood, 1996.

Wolfe, Tom. *The Electric Kool-Aid Acid Test.* London: Black Swan, 1989; New York: Quality Paperback Books, 1990.

SOUTH AMERICA

Alves, Maria Helen Moreira. *State and Opposition in Military Brazil.* Austin: University of Texas Press, 1985.

Americas Watch. *El Salvador's Decade of Terror: Human Rights Since the Assassination of Archbishop Romero.* New Haven, CT: Yale University Press, 1991.

Anderson, Martin Edwin. *Dossier Secreto: Argentina's Desparecidos and the Myth of "Dirty War."* Boulder, CO: Westview Press, 1993.

Arriagada Herrera, Genaro. *Pinochet: The Politics of Power.* Boulder, CO: Westview, 1991.

Bacchus, Wilfred A. *Mission in Mufti: Brazil's Military Regimes, 1964-1985.* New York: Greenwood, 1990.

Bergquist, Charles, Ricardo Peñarada, and Gonzalo Sánchez, eds. *Violence in Colombia: The Contemporary Crisis in Historical Perspective.* Wilmington, DE: SR Books, 1992.

Bland, Gary, and Joseph S. Tulchin, eds. *Peru in Crisis: Dictatorship or Democracy?* Boulder, CO: Lynne Rienner Publishers, 1994.

Blank, David Eugene. *Venezuela: Politics in a Petroleum Republic.* New York: Praeger, 1984.

Brown, Cynthia. *Chile since the Coup: Ten Years of Repression.* New York: Americas Watch Committee, 1983.

Browning, Christopher. *Ordinary Men.* New York: Harper Perennial, 1993.

Calvert, Peter. *Latin America in the Twentieth Century.* 2nd. ed. London: Macmillan, and New York: St. Martin's Press, 1993.

Carmack, Robert M. *Harvest of Violence: The Maya Indians and the Guatemalan Crisis.* London and Norman: University of Oklahoma Press, 1992.

Carrigan, Ana. *The Palace of Justice: A Colombian Tragedy.* New York: Four Walls Eight Windows, 1993.

Chevigny, Paul. *Edge of a Knife: Police Violence in the Americas.* New York: New Press, 1995.

Constable, Pamela. *A Nation of Enemies: Chile under Pinochet.* New York and London: Norton, 1991.

Dix, Robert H. *The Politics of Colombia.* New York: Praeger, 1987.

Doggett, Martha. *Death Foretold: The Jesuit Murders in El Salvador.* Washington, DC: Georgetown University Press, 1993.

Drake, Paul W., and Iván Jaksic, eds. *The Struggle for Democracy in Chile.* Lincoln, NE: University of Nebraska Press, 1995.

Dulles, John W. F. *Unrest in Brazil: Political–Military Crisis, 1955-1964.* Austin: University of Texas Press, 1970.

Falla, Ricardo. *Massacres in the Jungle, Ixcán, Guatemala, 1975-1982.* Boulder, CO: Westview Press, 1994.

Fish, Joe. *El Salvador: Testament of Terror.* London: Zed Books, and New York: Olive Branch Press, 1988.

Garvin, Glenn. *Everybody Had His Own Gringo: The CIA and the Contras.* Washington, DC: Brassey's, 1992.

Gillespie, Richard. *Soldiers of Peron: Argentina's Montoneros.* New York: Oxford University Press, and Oxford: Clarendon, 1982.

Giraldo, Javier. *Colombia: The Genocidal Democracy.* Monroe, ME: Common Courage Press, 1996.

Gorman, Stephen M, ed. *Post-Revolutionary Peru: The Politics of Transformation.* Boulder, CO: Westview Press, 1982.

Gude, Edward W. *Political Violence in Venezuela, 1958-1964.* Washington, DC: American Political Science Association, 1967.

Guest, Iain. *Behind the Disappearances: Argentina's Dirty War Against Human Rights and the United Nations.* Philadelphia: University of Pennsylvania, 1990.

Hernadez, Tosca. "'Extraordinary' Police Operations in Venezuela," in *Vigilantism and the State in Modern Latin America*, ed. Martha Kinsley Huggins. New York: Praeger, 1991.

Hillman, Richard S. *Democracy for the Privileged: Crisis and Transition in Venezuela.* Boulder, CO: Lynne Rienner Publications, 1994.

Hodges, Donald Clark. *Argentina, 1943-1987: The National Revolution and Resistance.* Albuquerque: University of New Mexico Press, 1988.

Huggins, Martha Kinsley, ed. *Vigilantism and the State in Modern Latin America.* New York: Praeger, 1991.

Hunter, Wendy. *Eroding Military Influence in Brazil: Politicians Against Soldiers.* Chapel Hill: University of North Carolina Press, 1997.

Johns, Christa Jacqueline. *The Origins of Violence in Mexican Society.* Westport, CT: Praeger, 1995.

Kaufman, Edy. *Uruguay in Transition: From Civilian to Military Rule.* New Brunswick, NJ: Transaction Press, 1979.

Koppel, Martin. *Peru's Shining Path: Autonomy of a Reactionary Sect.* New York: Pathfinder, 1993.

Lake, Anthony. *Somoza Falling: A Case Study of Washington at Work.* Amherst: University of Massachusetts Press, 1990.

Landau, Saul. *The Guerrilla Wars of Central America: Nicaragua, El Salvador and Guatemala.* London: Weidenfeld and Nicolson, and New York: St. Martin's Press, 1993.

Lara, Patricia. *The M-19: Sow the Wind and Reap the Whirlwind.* 4th ed. Washington, DC: The Foreign Broadcast Information Service, 1983.

Leacock, Ruth. *Requiem for Revolution: The United States and Brazil, 1961-1969.* Kent, OH: Kent State University Press, 1990.

Levenson-Estrada, Deborah. *Trade Unionists Against Terror: Guatemala City, 1954-1985.* Chapel Hill: University of North Carolina Press, 1994.

Lombardi, John V. *Venezuela: The Search for Order, the Dream of Progress.* New York: Oxford University Press, 1982.

McClintock, Michael. *State Terror and Popular Resistance in Guatemala.* London and Atlantic Highlands, NJ: Zed Books, 1987.

McCormick, Gordon H. *From the Sierra to the Cities: The Urban Campaign of the Shining Path.* Santa Monica, CA: Rand Corporation, 1992.

McCoy, Jennifer. *Venezuelan Democracy Under Stress.* Miami: University of Miami North-South Center, 1995.

Masterson, Daniel M. *Militarism and Politics in Latin America: Peru from Sáchoz Cerro to Sendero Luminoso.* New York: Greenwood, 1991.

Mélendez, Edgardo. *Puerto Rico's Statehood Movement.* New York: Greenwood, 1988.

Mendez, Juan E. *Political Murder and Reform in Colombia: The Violence Continues.* New York: Americas Watch, 1992.

Menzel, Sewall, H. *Bullets Versus Ballots: Political Violence and Revolutionary War in El Salvador.* New Brunswick, NJ: Transaction Publishers, 1994.

Miranda, Roger. *The Civil War in Nicaragua: Inside the Sandinistas.* New Brunswick, NJ: Transaction Publishers, 1993.

Mogano, Maria Jose. *Argentina's Lost Patrol: Armed Struggle: 1969-1979.* New Haven, CT: Yale University Press, 1995.

Morley, Morris H. *Washington, Somoza and the Sandinistas.* Cambridge and New York: Cambridge University Press, 1994.

Movimiento de Liberacion Nacional Puertorriquero. *Program and Ideology of the MLM.* Chicago: MLM, 1987.

Oquist, Paul. *Violence, Conflict and Politics in Colombia.* New York: Academic Press, 1980.

Palmer, David Scott. *The Shining Path of Peru.* London: Hurst, and New York: St. Martin's Press, 1994.

Politzer, Patricia. *Fear in Chile: Lives Under Pinochet.* New York: Pantheon Books, 1989.

Porzecanski, Arturo C. *Uruguay's Tupamaros: The Urban Guerrilla.* New York: Praeger, 1973.

Potash, Robert A. *The Army and Politics in Argentina, 1945-1965, Perón to Frondizi.* London: Athlone, and Stanford, CA: Stanford University Press, 1980.

Rial, Juan. "Makers and Guardians of Fear: Controlled Terror in Uruguay," in *Fear at the Edge: State Terror and Resistance in Latin America,* ed. Juan Corradi, Patricia Fagen, and Manuel A. Garreton Merino. Berkeley: University of California Press, 1992.

Sater, William. *Puerto Rican Terrorists: A Possible Threat to U.S. Energy Installations?* Santa Monica, CA: Rand Corporation, 1981.

Skidmore, Thomas E. *The Politics of Military Rule in Brazil, 1964-1985.* New York: Oxford University Press, 1988.

Sosnowski, Saul, and Popkin, Louise B., eds. *Repression, Exile and Democracy: Uruguayan Culture.* Durham, NC: Duke University Press, 1993.

Spooner, Mary Helen. *Soldiers in a Narrow Land: The Pinochet Regime in Chile.* Berkeley: University of California Press, 1994.

Stanley, William Deane. *The Protection Racket State: Military Extortion and Civil War in El Salvador.* Philadelphia: Temple University Press, 1996.

Strong, Simon. *Shining Path: Terror and Revolution in Peru.* New York: Times Books, 1992; London: Fontana, 1993.

Taylor, Diana. *Disappearing Acts: Spectacles of Gender and Nationalism in Argentina's "Dirty War."* Durham, NC: Duke University Press, 1997.

Thomas, W. Walter, ed. *Reagan Versus the Sandinistas: The Undeclared War.* Boulder, CO: Westview Press, 1987.

Trudeau, Robert H. *Guatemalan Politics: The Popular Struggle for Democracy.* Boulder, CO: Lynne Rienner Publications, 1993.

Tutino, John. *From Insurrection to Revolution in Mexico.* Princeton, NJ: Princeton University Press, 1986.

Uekert, Brenda K. *Rivers of Blood: A Comparative Study of Government Massacres.* Westport, CT: Praeger, 1995.

Valenzuela, J. Samuel, and Arturo Valenzuela, eds. *Military Rule in Chile: Dictatorship and Opposition.* Baltimore, MD: Johns Hopkins University Press, 1986.

Weinstein, Martin. *Uruguay: Democracy at the Crossroads.* Boulder, CO: Westview Press, 1988.

Wilson, Carlos. *The Tupamaros: The Unmentionables.* Boston: Branden Press, 1974.

EUROPE

Alexander, Edward. *Crime of Vengeance: An Armenian Struggle for Justice.* New York: Free Press, 1991.

Avrich, Paul. *Anarchist Portraits.* Princeton, NJ: Princeton University Press, 1988.

Avrich, Paul. *The Russian Anarchists.* London: Thames and Hudson, 1973; Westport, CT: Greenwood, 1980.

Axworthy, Mark, Cornel Scafes, and Cristian Craciunoiu. *Third Axis, Fourth Ally.* London: Arms and Armour, and New York: Sterling, 1995.

Becker, Jillian. *Hitler's Children.* London and New York: Panther, 1978.

Beckett, I. F. W., and John Pimlott. *Armed Forces and Modern Counter-Insurgency.* London: Croom Helm, and New York: St. Martin's Press, 1985.

Berberoglu, Berch, ed. *The National Question, Ethnic Conflict and Self-Determination in the Twentieth Century.* Philadelphia: Temple University Press, 1995.

Bowyer Bell, John. *The Gun in Politics: An Analysis of Irish Violence.* New Brunswick, NJ: Transaction Publishers, 1991.

Bowyer Bell, John. *The Secret Army: The IRA.* 3rd ed. New Brunswick, NJ: Transaction Publishers, 1997.

Brubaker, Roger. *Citizenship and Nationhood in France and Germany.* London and Cambridge, MA: Harvard University Press, 1994.

Bunson, Matthew. *Encyclopedia of the Roman Empire.* New York: Facts on File Publications, 1994.

Butnaru, I. C. *The Silent Holocaust: Romania and its Jews.* New York: Greenwood, 1992.

Carruthers, Susan L. *Winning Hearts and Minds: British Governments, the Media and Colonial Counter-Insurgency.* New York and London: Leicester Universtiy Press, 1995.

Catanzaro, Raimondo. *The Red Brigades and Left-Wing Terrorism in Italy.* London: Pinter, and New York: St. Martin's Press, 1991.

Chamberlain, William H. *The Russian Revolution.* Vol. II, *1918-1921: From the Civil War to the Consolidation of Power.* Princeton, NJ: Princeton University Press, 1987.

Christiansen, Rupert. *Paris Babylon: The Story of the Paris Commune.* London: Minerva, and New York: Penguin, 1995.

Clark, Robert P. *The Basque Insurgents: ETA, 1952-1980.* Madison: University of Wisconsin Press, 1984.

Conquest, Robert. *The Great Terror: A Reassessment.* London: Hutchinson, and New York: Oxford University Press, 1990.

Coogan, Tim Pat. *The IRA: A History.* Niwot, CO: Roberts Rinehart Publishers, 1994.

Cull, Nicholas J. *Selling War: The British Propaganda Campaign Against American Neutrality in World War I.* New York: Oxford University Press, 1995.

Dadran, Vahakn N. *The History of the Armenian Genocide: Ethnic Conflict from the Balkans to Anatolia to the Caucasus.* 3rd ed. Providence, RI: Berghahn Books, 1997.

Dallin, Alexander. *German Rule in Russia, 1941-1945.* London: Macmillan, and Boulder, CO: Westview Press, 1981.

Dallin, Alexander. *Odessa, 1941-1944.* Santa Monica, CA: Rand Corporation, 1957.

Dartnell, Michael York. *Action Directe: Ultra Left Terrorism in France, 1979-1987.* London and Portland, OR: Frank Cass, 1995.

Doyle, William. *The Oxford History of the French Revolution.* New York and Oxford: Oxford University Press, 1989.

Duncan, W. Raymond, and Paul G. Holman. *Ethnic Nationalism and Regional Conflict: The Former Soviet Union and Yugoslavia.* Boulder, CO: Westview Press, 1994.

Dunnigan, John P. *Deep-Rooted Conflict and the IRA Cease-Fire.* Lanham, MD: University Press of America, 1995.

Falk, Richard A., Gabriel Kolko, and Robert J. Lifton. *Crimes of War.* New York: Vintage Books, 1971.

Felix, David. *Walther Rathenau and the Weimar Republic: The Politics of Reparations.* Baltimore, MD: Johns Hopkins University Press, 1971.

Finley, M. I. *Politics in the Ancient World.* Cambridge and New York: Cambridge University Press, 1983.

Foster, Roy. F. *Modern Ireland, 1600-1972.* London and New York: Penguin, 1989.

Gibson, W. *Paris During the Commune.* London: Whittaker, 1972; New York: Haskell House, 1974.

Gilbert, Martin. *Atlas of World War I.* 2nd ed. London: Routledge, 1994; New York: Oxford University Press, 1995.

Gilbert, Martin. *The First World War: A Complete History.* London: Routledge, and New York: Henry Holt, 1994.

Grant, Michael. *The Fall of the Roman Empire.* London: Weidenfeld and Nicolson, 1996.

Grant, Michael. *Myths of the Greeks and Romans.* Rev. ed. London: Phoenix, 1994; New York: Meridian, 1995.

Griess, Thomas, ed. *Atlas for the Wars of Napoleon.* Wayne, NJ: Avery Publishing Group, 1986.

Hamalainen, Pekka K. *In Time of Storm: Revolution, Civil War, and the Ethnographic Issue in Finland.* Albany, NY: SUNY Press, 1979.

Harrison, Michael M. "France and International Terrorism: Problem and Response," in *The Deadly Sin of Terrorism,* ed. David Charters. Westport, CT: Greenwood, 1994.

Hayes, Paul M. *Quisling: The Career and Political Ideas of Vidkun Quisling, 1887-1945.* Newton Abbot: David and Charles, 1971; Bloomington: Indiana University Press, 1972.

Hoffman, Bruce. *Right-Wing Terrorism in West Germany.* Santa Monica, CA: Rand Corporation, 1986.

Hovannisian, Richard G., ed. *The Armenian Genocide.* London: Macmillan, and New York: St. Martin's Press, 1992.

Jelavich, Charles, and Barbara Jelavich. *The Establishment of the Balkan National States, 1804-1920.* Seattle: University of Washington Press, 1986.

Johnson, Amanda. *Norway: Her Invasion and Occupation.* Decatur, GA: Bowen Press, 1948.

Joll, James. *The Anarchists.* London: Methuen, 1979; Cambridge, MA: Harvard University Press, 1980.

Joll, James. *Origins of the First World War.* London and New York: Longman, 1992.

Jordan, David. *The Revolutionary Career of Maximilien Robespierre.* New York: Free Press, 1985.

Joyce, C. Patrick. *Sarajevo Shots: Studies in the Immediate Origin of World War I.* Brooklyn, NY: Revisionist Press, 1978.

Judt, Tony. *Marxism and the French Left: Studies in Labor and Politics in France, 1830-1981.* Oxford: Clarendon, and New York: Oxford University Press, 1989.

Kedward, H.R. *In Search of the Maquis.* Oxford: Clarendon,

and New York: Oxford University Press, 1993.

Kellen, Konrad. *The Impact of Terrorism on the Federal Republic of Germany, 1968-1982.* Santa Monica, CA: Rand Corporation, 1987.

Khazanov, A. M. *Ethnicity, Nationalism and Inter-Ethnic Relations in the Former Soviet Union.* Washington, DC: National Council for Soviet and Eastern European Research, 1993.

Killingray, David, and David Anderson, eds. *Policing Empire: Government, Authority and Control, 1830-1940.* Manchester: Manchester University Press, and New York: St. Martin's Press, 1991.

Kraut, Richard, ed. *The Cambridge Companion to Plato.* London and New York: Cambridge University Press, 1992.

Lawrence, James. *Imperial Rearguard: Wars of Empire, 1919-1985.* Elmsford, NY: Pergamon Press, and London: Brassey's, 1988.

Linz, S. J., ed. *The Impact of World War II on the Soviet Union.* Totowa, NJ: Rowman and Allanheld, 1985.

Lukas, R. C. *Forgotten Holocaust: The Poles under German Occupation, 1939-1944.* 2nd ed. New York: Hippocrene Books, 1997.

Mandelstam, Nadezhda. *Hope Against Hope: A Memoir.* New York: Atheneum, 1987; London: Collins-Harvill, 1989.

Marshall, S. L. A. *The American Heritage History of World War I.* Boston: Houghton Mifflin, 1987.

Mawdsley, Evan. *The Russian Civil War.* Boston: Unwin Hyman, 1989.

Meade, Robert C. *The Red Brigades: The Story of Italian Terrorism.* London: Macmillan, and New York: St. Martin's Press, 1990.

Meier, Christian. *Caesar: A Biography.* New York and London: HarperCollins, 1995.

Mirskii, G. I. *On Ruins of Empire: Ethnicity and Nationalism in the Former Soviet Union.* London and Westport, CT: Greenwood, 1996.

Morris, Allan. *Collaboration and Resistance Reviewed.* New York: St. Martin's Press, 1992.

Moss, David. *The Politics of Left-Wing Violence in Italy, 1969-1985.* London: Macmillan, and New York: St. Martin's Press, 1989.

Moxon-Browne, Edward. *European Terrorism.* Aldershot: Dartmouth, 1993; New York: G. K. Hall, 1994.

Nicholls, A. J. *Weimar and the Rise of Hitler.* 3rd ed. London: Macmillan, and New York: St. Martin's Press, 1991.

Nordstrom, Byron J. *Dictionary of Scandinavian History.* Westport, CT: Greenwood, 1986.

Novick, Peter. *The Resistance Versus Vichy.* London: Chatto and Windus, and New York: Columbia University Press, 1968.

O'Ballance, Edgar. *The Greek Civil War, 1944-1949.* London: Faber, and New York: Praeger, 1966.

Omissi, David. *Air Power and Colonial Control: The Royal Air Force, 1919-1939.* Manchester: Manchester University Press, and New York: St. Martin's Press, 1990.

Perry, Duncan. *The Politics of Terror: The Macedonian Revolutionary Movements, 1893-1903.* Durham, NC: Duke University Press, 1988.

Petrow, Richard. *The Bitter Years: The Invasion and Occupation of Denmark and Norway, April 1940-May 1945.* London: Hodder and Stoughton, 1975; New York: Morrow Quill, 1979.

Peukert, Detlev J. *Weimar Republic.* London: Penguin, and New York: Hill and Wang, 1993.

Pimlott, John. *British Military Operations, 1945-1984.* London: Hamlyn, and New York: Military Press, 1984.

Pimlott, John, ed. *War in Peace.* New York: Marshall Cavendish, 1987.

Pribichevich, Stoyan. *Macedonia: Its People and History.*

University Park: Pennsylvania State University Press, 1982.

Ramsay, Robert. *The Corsican Time-Bomb.* Manchester and Dover, NH: University of Manchester Press, 1983.

Roy, Jules. "Twilight of the Gods" (French Foreign Legion in Vietnam), in *True Stories of the Elite Forces*, ed. Jon E. Lewis. London: Robinson, and New York: Carroll and Graf Publishers, 1993.

Ryan, Mark. *War and Peace in Ireland.* London and Boulder, CO: Pluto Press, 1994.

Sauigear, Peter. "Corsica," in *Contemporary Minority Nationalism*, ed. Michael Watson. London and New York: Routledge, 1990.

Scarre, Chris. *Chronicle of the Roman Emperors: The Reign-by-Reign Record of the Rulers of Imperial Rome.* London and New York: Thames & Hudson, 1995.

Schama, Simon. *Citizens: A Chronicle of the French Revolution.* New York: Knopf, 1991.

Sciascia, Leonardo. *The Moro Affair.* New York: Carcanet, 1987.

Scriven, Michael, and Peter Wagstaff. *War and Society in Twentieth Century France.* New York: St. Martin's Press, 1991.

Sereny, Gita. *Into that Darkness.* New York: Vintage Books, 1983; London: Deutsch, 1991.

Shirer, William L. *The Rise and Fall of the Third Reich.* London: Mandarin, 1991; New York: Crescent Books, 1994.

Singleton, Fred. *A Short History of Finland.* Cambridge and New York: Cambridge University Press, 1989.

Sonn, Richard D. *Anarchism.* New York: Twayne Macmillan, 1992.

Stavrakis, Peter J. *Moscow and Greek Communism, 1944-1949.* Ithaca, NY: Cornell University Press, 1989.

Stead, Philip. *The Police in France.* New York: Macmillan, 1983.

Stein, George H. *The Waffen SS: Hitler's Elite Guard at War, 1939-1945.* Itaca, NY: Cornell University Press, 1966.

Sternhell, Zeen. *Neither Right Nor Left: Fascist Ideology in France.* Chichester and Princeton, NJ: Princeton University Press, 1996.

Stewart, Ian, and Susan L. Carruthers, eds. *War, Culture and the Media: Representation of the Military in Twentieth Century Britain.* Madison, NJ: Farleigh Dickinson University Press, 1996.

Sullivan, John. *ETA and Basque Nationalism: The Fight for Euskadi, 1890-1986.* London and New York: Routledge, 1988.

Taylor, Telford. *The Anatomy of the Nuremberg Trials.* New York: Knopf, 1993.

Tombs, Robert. *The War Against Paris, 1871.* Cambridge and New York: Cambridge University Press, 1981.

Toolis, Kevin. *Journeys within the IRA's Soul.* London: Picador, and New York: St. Martin's Press, 1996.

Tucker, Robert C. *Stalin in Power: The Revolution from Above, 1928-1941.* New York: Norton, 1990.

Urban, Mark. *Big Boys' Rules: The Secret Struggle Against the IRA.* London and Boston: Faber and Faber, 1993.

Vague, Tom. *Televisionaries: The Red Army Faction Story, 1963-1993.* Edinburgh and San Francisco, CA: AK Press, 1994.

Vaughan, Michalina. "The Extreme Right in France: 'Le Penisme' and the Politics of Fear," in *Neo-Fascism in Europe*, ed. Luiciano Cheles, Ronnie Ferguson, and Michalina Vaughan. London and New York: Longman, 1992.

Volkogonov, Dmitri. *Trotsky: The Eternal Revolutionary.* London: HarperCollins, and New York: Free Press, 1996.

Waldmann, Peter. "From the Vindication of Honour to Blackmail: The Impact of the Changing Role of ETA on Society and Politics in the Basque Region of Spain," in *Tolerating Terrorism in the West*, ed. Noemi Gal-Or. London and New York: Routledge, 1991.

Ward, Alan J. *The Easter Rising.* Arlington Heights, IL: Harlan Davidson, 1980.

Williamson, Samuel R., Jr. *Austria-Hungary and the Origins of the First World War.* London: Macmillan, and New York: St. Martin's Press, 1991.

Windebank, Janice. *Violence and Conflict in the Politics and Society of Modern France.* Lewiston, NY: E. Mellen Press, 1995.

Wright, Joanne. *Terrorist Propaganda: The Red Army Faction and the Provisional IRA, 1968-1986.* London: Macmillan, and New York: St. Martin's Press, 1991.

Zirakzadeh, Cyrus Ernesto. *A Rebellious People: Basques, Protests and Politics.* Reno: University of Nevada Press, 1991.

THE MIDDLE EAST

Abraham, A. J. *The Warriors of God: Jihad and the Fundamentalists of Islam.* Bristol, IN: Wyndham Hall Press, 1989.

Abu Amr, Zigad. *Islamic Fundamentalism in the West Bank and Gaza: Muslim Brotherhood and Islamic Jihad.* Bloomington: Indiana University Press, 1994.

Alexander, Y, ed. *Middle East Terrorism: Current Threats and Future Prospects.* Aldershot: Dartmouth, and New York: G. K. Hall, 1994.

Alexander, Y, ed. *Middle East Terrorism: Selected Group Profiles.* Washington, DC: The Jewish Institute for National Security Affairs, 1994.

Alon, Hanan. *Countering Palestinian Terrorism in Israel.* Santa Monica, CA: Rand Corporation, 1980.

Barsky, Yehudit. *The Struggle Is Now Worldwide: Hizballah and Iranian-Sponsored Terrorism.* New York: Anti-Defamation League, 1995.

Benvenisti, Meron. *Intimate Enemies: Jews and Arabs in a Shared Land.* Berkeley: University of California Press, 1995.

Black, Ian. *Israel's Secret Wars: The Untold History of Israeli Intelligence.* London: Hanish Hamilton, and New York: Viking Penguin, 1991.

Black, Ian, and B. Morris. *Israel's Secret Wars: A History of Israel's Intelligence Services.* London: Futura, and New York: Grove Weidenfeld, 1992.

Blechman, Barry M. "The Impact of Israel's Reprisals on Behaviour of the Bordering Arab Nations Directed at Israel," in *Journal of Conflict Resolution* 16, No. 2 (June 1972): 155.

Blundy, David. *Qaddafi and the Libyan Revolution.* London: Weidenfeld and Nicolson, and Boston: Little, Brown, 1987.

Cleveland, William L. *A History of the Modern Middle East.* Boulder, CO: Westview Press, 1994.

Cobban, Helena. *The Palestinian Liberation Organisation: People, Power, Politics.* Cambridge and New York: Cambridge University Press, 1984.

Department of State, United States. *Patterns of Global Terrorism.* Washington, DC: Department of State, annual.

Finklestone, Joseph. *Anwar Sadat: Visionary Who Dared.* London and Portland, OR: Frank Cass, 1996.

Freedman, Robert Owen, ed. *The Intifada: Its Impact on Israel, the Arab World and the Superpowers.* Miami: Florida International University Press, 1991.

Fuller, Graham E. *Algeria: The Next Fundamentalist State?* Santa Monica, CA: Rand Corporation, 1996.

Guenena, Nemat. *The Jihad: An Islamic Alternative in Egypt.* New York: American University Press, 1986.

Hadawi, Sami. *Bitter Harvest: A Modern History of Palestine.* 4th ed. New York: Olive Branch Press, 1991.

Harris, William W. *Faces of Lebanon: Sects, Wars and Global*

Extensions. Princeton, NJ: Markus Wiener Publishers, 1997.

Hodgson, Marshall G. *The Order of the Assassins.* New York: AMS Press, 1980.

Human Rights Watch. *Iraq's Crime of Genocide: The Anfal Campaign Against the Kurds.* London and New Haven, CT: Yale University Press, 1995.

Inbar, Efraim. *Regional Security Regimes: Israel and Its Neighbors.* Albany: State University of New York Press, 1995.

Inbari, Pinhas. *The Palestinians Between Terrorism and Statehood.* Brighton: Sussex Academic Press, 1996.

Izz al-Din, Ahmad Jalal. *Terrorism and Political Violence: An Egyptian Perspective.* Chicago: University of Illinois at Chicago, 1987.

Jabbur, Nabil. *The Rumbling Volcano: Islamic Fundamentalism in Egypt.* Pasadena, CA: Mandate Press, 1993.

Kazhdan, Alexander P., ed. *The Oxford Dictionary of Byzantium,* 3 vols. Oxford and New York: Oxford University Press, 1991.

Kedourie, Elie, and Sylvia Kedourie. *Zionism and Arabism in Palestine and Israel.* London and Totowa, NJ: Frank Cass, 1982.

Laizer, S. J. *Martyrs, Traitors and Patriots: Kurdistan After the Gulf War.* London and Atlantic Highlands, NJ: Zed Books, 1996.

Lawson, Don. *America Held Hostage: The Iran Hostage Crisis and the Iran-Contra Affair.* New York: Franklin Watts, 1991.

Lederman, Jim. *Battle Lines: The American Media and the Intifada.* Boulder, CO: Westview Press, 1993.

Lewis, Bernard. *The Assassins: A Radical Sect in Islam.* London: Zed Books, 1985; New York: Oxford University Press, 1987.

McDowell, M. *A Modern History of the Kurds.* London: Tauris, and New York: St. Martin's Press, 1996.

Malley, Robert. *The Call from Algeria: Third Worldism, Revolution and the Turn to Islam.* Berkeley: University of California Press, 1996.

Mansfield, Peter. *The Arab World: A Comprehensive History.* 3rd ed. New York and London: Penguin, 1992.

Miller, R. "Responding to Terrorism's Challenge: The Case of Israeli Reprisals," in *Virginia Social Science Journal* 25 (Winter 1990): 109.

Mishal, S. *The PLO Under Arafat – Between Gun and Olive Branch.* New Haven, CT: Yale University Press, 1986.

Nicol, Donald. *The Last Centuries of Byzantium, 1261-1453.* 2nd ed. Cambridge and New York: Cambridge University Press, 1996.

Norwich, John Julius. *Byzantium: The Apogee.* London: Penguin, and New York: Knopf, 1991.

O'Brien, Conor Cruise. *The Siege: The Story of Israel and Zionism.* New York: Simon and Schuster, 1987; London: Weidenfeld and Nicolson, 1988.

O'Brien, William. *Law and Morality in Israel's War with the PLO.* New York: Routledge, 1991.

Oren, Michael. *Hamas: Terror in the Service of God.* New York: American Jewish Committee, 1992.

Ranstorp, Magnus. *Hizb'allah in Lebanon.* New York: St. Martin's Press, 1997.

Reich, Bernard, and Gershon Kieval. *Israeli National Security Policy: Political Actors and Perspectives.* New York: Greenwood, 1988.

Ridley, F. A. *The Assassins: A Study of the Cult of the Assassins in Persia and Islam.* New York: Gordon Press, 1980.

Salem, Elie Adib. *Violence and Diplomacy in Lebanon.* London: Tauris, and New York: St. Martin's Press, 1995.

Sykes, Christopher. *Crossroads to Israel: Palestine from Balfour to Bevin.* Bloomington: Indiana University Press, 1973.

Winslow, Charles. *Lebanon: War and Politics in a Fragmented Society.* London and New York: Routledge, 1996.

Wooten, James P. *Hamas: The Organization, Goals and Tactics of a Militant Palestinian Organization.* Washington, DC: Congressional Research Service, Library of Congress, 1993.

Wright, Robin B. *Sacred Rage: The Wrath of Militant Islam.* London: Deutsch, and New York: Touchstone, 1986.

Yapp, Malcolm E. *The Near East Since the First World War.* 2nd ed. London and New York: Longman, 1996.

SOUTHERN AND EASTERN ASIA AND THE PACIFIC

Andrade, D. *Ashes to Ashes: The Phoenix Program and the Vietnam War.* Lexington, MA: Lexington Books, 1990.

Austin, Dennis. *Democracy and Violence in India and Sri Lanka.* London: Pinter, 1994; New York: Council on Foreign Relations Press, 1995.

Baker, William W. *Kashmir: Happy Valley, Valley of Death.* Las Vegas: Defenders Publications, 1994.

Borovik, Arten. *The Hidden War: A Russian Journalist's Account of the Soviet War in Afghanistan.* New York: Atlantic Monthly Press, 1990; London: Faber, 1991.

Brackett, D. W. *Holy Terror: Armageddon in Tokyo.* New York: Weather Hill, 1996.

Brown, Judith M. *Gandhi: Prisoner of Hope.* London and New Haven, CT: Yale University Press, 1991.

Chambers, James. *The Devil's Horsemen.* New York: Atheneum, 1985; London: Cassell, 1988.

Co-ordinator of Counter Terrorism, U.S. Department of State. *The Japanese Red Army.* Washington, DC: The Office of the Secretary of State.

Cox, Steve. *Generations of Resistance.* London and New York: Cassell, 1995.

Farrell, William Regis. *Blood and Rage: The Story of the Japanese Red Army.* Lexington, MA: Lexington Books, 1990.

Fein, Helen. *Imperial Crime and Punishment at Jallianwalla Bagh and British Judgment.* Honolulu: University of Hawaii Press, 1977.

Galeotti, Mark. *Afghanistan: The Soviet Union's Last War.* London and Portland, OR: Frank Cass, 1995.

Jackson, Karl D. *Cambodia, 1975-1978: Rendezvous with Death.* Princeton, NJ: Princeton University Press, 1989.

Jardine, Matthew. *East Timor: Genocide in Paradise.* Tucson, AZ: Odonian Press, 1995.

Kadian, Rajesh. *The Kashmir Tangle: Issues and Options.* Boulder, CO: Westview Press, 1993.

Katzenstein, Peter S. "Coping with Terrorism, Norms and Internal Security in Germany and Japan," in *Ideas and Foreign Policy: Beliefs, Institutions and Political Change,* ed. Judith Goldstein, and Roberto Keohane. Ithaca, NY: Cornell University Press, 1993.

Katzenstein, Peter S., and Yutaka Tsujinaka. *Defending the Japanese State.* Ithaca, NY: East Asia Program, Cornell University, 1991.

Kessler, Richard J. *Rebellion and Repression in the Philippines.* New Haven, CT: Yale University Press, 1991.

Kiernan, Ben. *Genocide and Democracy in Cambodia: The Khmer Rouge, the United Nations and the International Community.* New Haven, CT: Yale University, South East Asia Studies, 1993.

Kiernan, Ben. *The Pol Pot Regime: Race, Power and Genocide in Cambodia under the Khmer Rouge, 1975-1979.* New Haven, CT: Yale University Press, 1996.

Knox, D. *The Korean War: An Oral History – Pusan to*

Chosin. San Diego: Harcourt, Brace, 1985

MacDonald, C. "So Terrible a Liberation: The UN Occupation of North Korea," in *Bulletin of Concerned Asian Scholars* 23, No 2, 1991.

Maclear, Michael. *The Ten Thousand Day War.* London: Thames Methuen, and New York: St. Martin's Press, 1981.

Minear, Richard H. *Victors' Justice: The Tokyo War Crimes Trial.* Princeton, NJ: Princeton University Press, 1971.

Morgan, David. *The Mongols.* Oxford and Cambridge, MA: Blackwell Publishers, 1990.

Moses, Larry, and Stephen A. Halkovic, Jr. *Introduction to Mongolian History and Culture.* Bloomington: Research Institute for Inner Asia Studies, Indiana University, 1985.

Nalty, Bernard. *The Vietnam War: The History of America's Conflict in South East Asia.* London: Salamander Books, and New York: Smithmark, 1996.

Newberg, Paula R. *Double Betrayal: Repression and Insurgency in Kashmir.* Washington, DC: Carnegie Endowment for International Peace, 1995.

Newell, N. P., and R. S. Newell. *The Struggle of Afghanistan.* Ithaca, NY: Cornell University Press, 1982.

Pandey, B. N. *The Break-Up of British India.* London: Macmillan, and New York: St. Martin's Press, 1969.

Pettigrew, J. *The Sikhs and the Punjab: Unheard Voices of State and Guerrilla Violence.* London and Atlantic Highlands, NJ: Zed Books, 1995.

Rahman, Mustaqur. *Divided Kashmir: Old Problems, New Opportunities for India, Pakistan and the Kashmiri People.* Boulder, CO: Lynne Rienner Publishers, 1996.

Rais, Rasul Bux. *War Without Winners.* New York: Oxford University Press, 1994.

Rubin, Barnett R. *Cycles of Violence: Human Rights in Sri Lanka.* Washington, DC: Asia Watch, 1987.

Sarkar, Sumit. *Modern India, 1885-1947.* London: Macmillan, and New York: St. Martin's Press, 1989.

Seagrave, Stirling. *The Marcos Dynasty.* London: Macmillan, 1989; New York: Ballantine Books, 1990.

Sonal, Ashish. *Terrorism and Insurgency in India.* London and Hartford, WI: Spantech and Lancer, 1994.

Taylor, John G. *Indonesia's Hidden War: The Hidden History of East Timor.* London and Atlantic Highlands, NJ: Zed Books, 1991.

Thompson, Mark R. *The Anti-Marcos Struggle: Personalistic Rule and Democratic Transition in the Philippines.* London and New Haven, CT: Yale University Press, 1995.

Wallace, P. "Political Violence and Terrorism in India," in *Terrorism in Context*, ed. Martha Crenshaw. University Park: Pennsylvania State University, 1995.

Walzer, M. *Just and Unjust Wars.* London: Allen Lane, 1978; New York: Basic Books, 1992.

Wolpert, Stanley. *A New History of India.* 5th ed. New York: Oxford University Press, 1997.

SUB-SAHARAN AFRICA

Adibe, Clement. *Managing Arms in Peace Processes: Somalia.* New York: United Nations Press, 1996.

Beckett, I. F. W. *The Roots of Counter-Insurgency: Armies and Guerrilla Warfare, 1900-1945.* London: Blandford, and New York: Sterling Publishing, 1988.

Bruce, Neil. *The Last Empire.* Newton Abbot, Devon, and North Pomfret, VT: David and Charles, 1975.

Charlton, Michael. *The Last Colony in Africa.* Oxford and Cambridge, MA: Blackwell, 1990.

Cilliers, J. K. *Counter-Insurgency in Rhodesia.* London and Dover, NH: Croom Helm, 1985.

Clayton, Anthony, and Killingray, David. *Khaki and Blue: Military and Police in British Colonial Africa.* Athens: Ohio University Center for International Studies, 1989.

De Waal, Alexander. *Evil Days: Thirty Years of War and Famine in Ethiopia.* New York: Human Rights Watch, 1991.

Destexhe, Alain. *Rwanda and Genocide in the Twentieth Century.* London: Pluto, and New York: New York University Press, 1995.

Egerton, Robert B. *Mau Mau: An African Crucible.* London: Tauris, 1990; New York: Ballantine Books, 1991.

Godwin, Peter, and Ian Hancock. *"Rhodesians Never Die."* Oxford and New York: Oxford University Press, 1993.

Henriksen, Thomas H. *Revolution and Counter-Revolution: Mozambique's War of Independence, 1964-1974.* Westport, CT: Greenwood, 1983.

Henze, Paul B. *Ethiopia: The Collapse of Communism, the Transition to Democracy and Adjustment to Eritrean Independence.* Santa Monica, CA: Rand Corporation, 1995.

Herbstein, Denis, and John A. Everson. *The Devils Are Among Us: The War for Namibia.* London and Atlantic Highlands, NJ: Zed Books, 1989.

Hirsch, John L. *Somalia and Operation Restore Hope.* Washington, DC: U.S. Institute of Peace Press, 1995.

Iyob, Ruth. *The Eritrean Struggle for Independence.* Cambridge and New York: Cambridge University Press, 1995.

Kapferer, Bruce. "Remythologizations of Power and Identity: Nationalism and Violence in South Africa," in *The Culture of Violence*, ed. Kumar Rupe Singhr and Macial Rubin Correa. New York: United Nations University Press, 1994.

Leys, Colin. *Namibia's Liberation Struggle: The Two-Edged Sword.* London: J. Curry, and Columbus: Ohio University Press, 1995.

Prendergast, John. *The Gun Talks Louder than the Voice: Somalia's Continuing Cycle of Violence.* Washington, DC: Center of Concern, 1994.

Prunier, Gerald. *The Rwanda Crisis: History of Genocide.* London: Hurst, and New York: Columbia University Press, 1995.

Ricciuti, Edward R. *Somalia: A Crisis of Famine and War.* Brookfield, CT: Millbrook Press, 1993.

Vanderwerff, Corrine. *Kill Thy Neighbor.* Boise, ID: Pacific Press, 1996.

Zegeye, Abebe, and Siegfried Pansevang, eds. *Ethiopia in Change: Peasantry, Nationalism and Democracy.* London: British Academic Press, and New York: St. Martin's Press, 1994.

ABOUT THE CONTRIBUTORS

Robert P. Anderson is an Irish freelance journalist and author working in Britain, who has written widely on Middle Eastern affairs and has traveled extensively in Iran.

Dr. R. Scott Appleby is an associate professor of history and senior fellow of the Joan B. Kroc Institute for International Peace Studies, University of Notre Dame.

Trevor Barker is an associate lecturer at the École Nationale des Ponts et Chaussées, Paris, and also writes on Franco-Algerian relations.

Chris Baxter is a MacArthur research fellow at King's College, University of London. He specializes in Pacific military history and security.

Ian Beckett is professor of modern history at the University of Luton. He has written extensively on terrorism and counterinsurgency.

Dr. John Bowyer Bell is president of the International Analysis Center, Inc., New York. He has written widely on political violence, especially with reference to Northern Ireland.

Dr. Tore Bjorgo is a research fellow at the Norwegian Institute of International Affairs. He is an authority on far-right activity in Europe.

W. B. Brabiner is a freelance writer on modern military history working in Britain.

Michael Brewer is an American author working in Britain, who has written extensively on political and defense issues.

Ashley Brown is a London-based publisher specializing in historical and military reference works. As an author he is a recognized authority on modern international affairs and security issues.

Stephen Brumwell teaches in the School of History at the University of Leeds. He is researching into the British Army in North America during the eighteenth century.

Peter Calvert is professor of comparative and international politics at the University of Southampton. He has written widely on terrorism and counter-insurgency.

Gavin Cameron is a doctoral student in the Department of International Relations at the University of St. Andrews, where he is researching nuclear terrorism.

Nigel Cawthorne is a freelance journalist specializing in modern political affairs who is working in Britain.

John Collis is a freelance journalist and has written widely on current affairs for the British press.

Christopher Cook is a doctoral student at the Department of War Studies, King's College, University of London. He specializes in European politics and international relations.

John Cooley is Middle Eastern correspondent for ABC News in Nicosia, Cyprus.

Raymond R. Corrado is a professor in the School of Criminology at Simon Fraser University in Vancouver. He has written widely on terrorism.

Dr. Gregor Dallas is a freelance writer on modern historical subjects based in the United States.

Dr. Michael Dartnell is a lecturer in European government at the Department of Political Science at Concordia University, Montreal. He is a specialist on left-wing terrorism in France.

Toby Dodge is a doctoral student at the School of Oriental and African Studies, University of London, researching Middle Eastern affairs.

Dr. Richard Drake teaches modern European history at the University of Montana. He specializes in politics and terrorism in contemporary Italy.

Professor John Erickson is director of the Center for Defense Studies at the University of Edinburgh. He has written widely on Soviet military history, organization, and operations.

John Finlayson is at the School of History, University of Leeds. He is researching British colonial policy in the postwar period.

Dr. Chris Flood is a senior lecturer in European studies at the University of Surrey. He has written widely on French political thought.

Hugo Frey is a doctoral student at the University of Surrey, specializing in modern France.

Dr. Noemi Gal-Or is at Kwanten University College, British Columbia. She is the author of a number of works on terrorism.

Dr. John Gearson is a visiting fellow in the Department of War Studies, King's College, University of London.

Allison Gough teaches at Ohio State University, Columbus. She is currently researching aspects of modern American social history.

Athena Gourdoumbas is researching contemporary Mediterranean affairs and history at the London School of Economics.

Dr. James Gow teaches in the Department of War Studies at King's College, University of London. He has written on Yugoslav politico-military affairs and was adviser to the Office of the Prosecutor at the International Criminal Tribunal for the former Yugoslavia.

Rohan Gunaratna is a Hesburgh Scholar at the University of Notre Dame, and was previously a foreign policy fellow at the University of Maryland. He is currently researching Asian security issues at the University of St. Andrew's.

Dr. Nadine Gurr is a researcher at the Council for Arms Control at the Center for Defense Studies, King's College, University of London.

Russell Hart is a part-time lecturer in modern history at Ohio State University. He is currently researching operational and strategic aspects of World War II.

Dr. Stephen Hart is a senior lecturer at the Department of War Studies at the Royal Military Academy, Sandhurst. He specializes in World War II and contemporary European defense issues.

Dr. Bruce Hoffman is an authority on terrorism at the University of St. Andrews. He has written widely on contemporary political violence.

Dr. Elaine Holoboff teaches in the Department of War Studies, King's College, University of London. She specializes in security and military affairs of the Soviet successor states.

Nick Hostettler is a doctoral student at the University of London's School of Oriental and African Studies, researching into contemporary African affairs.

Dr. Matthew Hughes lectures in modern history at Nene College, Northampton. He specializes in the Middle Eastern theater during World War I.

Colin Jones is a professor of history at the University of Warwick. He specializes in the French Revolutionary period.

Tadashi Kuramatsu is a doctoral student in modern political history at the London School of Economics.

Dr. David E. Long is a former U.S. diplomat and is an international consultant on Middle Eastern and antiterrorism issues.

Henry Longstreet is a British freelance consultant who has written widely on politico-military matters.

Chris Mann lectures at the Department of International Studies at the University of Surrey. He is researching Anglo-Norwegian relations during World War II.

Chris Marshall is a British freelance writer, specializing in twentieth century history.

Dr. Evan Mawdsley is reader in modern history at the University of Glasgow. He has written on Russian Revolutionary and Civil War history.

Dr. Reuben Miller is an independent research analyst specializing in terrorism and Middle Eastern affairs. He lectures at the University of Colorado, Denver.

Dr. Tim Moreman lectures in war studies at King's College, University of London. He is researching Indian history and counterinsurgency.

Dr. David Morgan is a reader in the history of the Middle East at the School of Oriental and African Studies, University of London.

Dr. P. Morris is at the University of Exeter. He specializes in Russian and Middle Eastern history.

Dr. Thomas G. Otte is a part-time lecturer at the University of Birmingham. He has written widely on nineteenth-century diplomatic history and strategic thought.

Neil Partrick is a researcher for the British House of Commons foreign affairs committee. He specializes in Middle Eastern political and security issues.

Gary R. Perlstein is professor and chair of the Department of Administration of Justice, Portland State University, Oregon. His recent work has included research into the American far right.

Dr. John Pimlott is head of the Department of War Studies, Royal Military Academy, Sandhurst. He has written widely on military history and strategic issues.

Stephen Prince is a doctoral student at the University of Warwick, researching the Korean War. He holds an MA in war studies from King's College, University of London.

Dr. Martyn Rady is senior lecturer in Central European history at the University of London's School of Slavonic and East European Studies. He is a specialist in Balkan history.

Jorge Ramírez is a Colombian journalist based in Britain, writing on Latin American affairs.

Dr. Magnus Ranstorp is a specialist in Middle Eastern terrorism and Senior Research Associate of the Center for the Study of Terrorism and Political at the University of St. Andrews.

Dr. Andrew Rathmell teaches in the Department of War Studies at King's College, University of London.

Bertrande Roberts is a U.S.-based freelance writer who has written widely on politics and history.

Professor Alex P. Schmid is a professor of conflict resoultion at the Erasmus University, Rotterdam. He is currently an adviser on crime and justice to the United Nations. He has written extensively on political violence, with special reference to the media and Western responses to terrorism.

Dr. Theo Schulte is a senior lecturer in European history at Anglia Polytechnic University.

Antony B. Shaw works for a British publisher of military and historical reference works. He holds a degree in war studies from King's College, University of London. He specializes in modern military history and international relations.

Gregory Simpson is a postgraduate student at the Department of War Studies, King's College, University of London. He is currently researching U.S. foreign policy and Pacific security issues.

Donald Sommerville has an MA in war studies from King's College, University of London. He has written on aspects of military and naval history.

Andrew Stewart is a doctoral student at the Department of War Studies, King's College, University of London. His PhD thesis concerns the British Dominions in World War II.

Paul Szuscikiewicz studied ancient history at the University of Southampton. He has written widely on military history and international affairs.

John G. Taylor is professor of politics at South Bank University, London. He has written several books and articles on East Timor and its history.

Dr. Heinz Tittmar is a reader in psychology at the School of Behavioral and Communication Sciences at the University of Belfast.

Dr. Paul Wallace is Middlebush Professor of Political Science at the University of Missouri, Columbia. He is the author of several works on political violence in India.

Dr. Steve Weiss is a visiting research fellow at King's College, University of London. He specializes in Anglo-American relations in World War II and was attached to the French Resistance during part of his war service.

Ian Westwell is a freelance writer based in Britain, specializing in modern colonial conflicts.

Paul Wilkinson is a professor of international relations at the University of St. Andrews. He is editor of the academic journal *Terrorism and Political Violence.*

GENERAL INDEX

The entry for an organization is usually under its full name, not its initials. Entries under initials (e.g. PLO) simply guide you to the main entry (Palestine Liberation Organization). The main exceptions are those organization usually referred to by an acronym (a set of initals used as a word, such as POLISARIO); in these cases, the main entry is under the acronym. The only other exceptions are a very few organizations that are almost always referred to in English by their initials, such as the SS in Germany and the NKVD in the Soviet Union.

Notes. Page numbers in *italics* refer to photographs, maps, or diagrams, or their captions. Arabic names beginning with "al" are listed according to the next word. The index covers the main text and Chronology (pp 687-99). See the A-Z Directory (pp 700-15) for further entries on many organizations and individuals.

INDEX OF NAMES

Notes. Page references in *italics* refer to photographs, maps, or diagrams, or their captions. Arabic names beginning with "al" or "el" are listed according to the next word.

The index covers the main text and the Chronology (pp 687-99). See the A-Z Directory (pp 700-15). for further entries on many individuals.

A

B

Z

GEOGRAPHICAL INDEX

Notes. 1) Page references in *italics* refer to photographs, maps, or diagrams, or their captions. 2) Arabic names beginning with "al" or "el" are listed according to the next word. 3) The index covers the main text and Chronology (pp 687-699). Additional entries for certain individuals and organizations are given in the A-Z Directory (pp 700-15).